CW00662482

The Dublin Penny Journal

Philip Dixon Hardy

My great great Granfather
G.C. DRAPER

Nabu Public Domain Reprints:

You are holding a reproduction of an original work published before 1923 that is in the public domain in the United States of America, and possibly other countries. You may freely copy and distribute this work as no entity (individual or corporate) has a copyright on the body of the work. This book may contain prior copyright references, and library stamps (as most of these works were scanned from library copies). These have been scanned and retained as part of the historical artifact.

This book may have occasional imperfections such as missing or blurred pages, poor pictures, errant marks, etc. that were either part of the original artifact, or were introduced by the scanning process. We believe this work is culturally important, and despite the imperfections, have elected to bring it back into print as part of our continuing commitment to the preservation of printed works worldwide. We appreciate your understanding of the imperfections in the preservation process, and hope you enjoy this valuable book.

THE

DUBLIN PENNY JOURNAL.

1834—5.

CONDUCTED BY PHILIP DIXON HARDY, M. R. I. A.

AUTHOR OF "THE NORTHERN TOURIST," "PICTURE OF DUBLIN," &c. &c. &c.

DRAWN BY H. NELSON.

R. CLAYTON. S.

Once the harp through the valleys of Erin resounded :
    Erin ma vourneen, Erin go bragh !
The shamrock and laurel luxuriantly crowned it :
    Eriu ma vourneen, Erin go bragh !

Sweet was its tone, when pensively mourning ;
As bold and as warm, when with gratitude burning,
It thrilled for the heroes from battle returning ;
    Erin ma vourneen, Erin go bragh !

BODLEIANA · BIBLIOTHECA · BODLEIANA

DUBLIN:

PHILIP DIXON HARDY, 3, CECILIA STREET,

SOLD ALSO WHOLESALE BY

W. F. WAKEMAN, AND W. CURRY, JUN. & CO.; IN LONDON BY RICHARD GROOMBRIDGE; WILLMER AND SMITH
LIVERPOOL; AMBERY, MANCHESTER; GUEST, 91, STEEL-HOUSE LANE, BIRMINGHAM; N. BOWACK, EDINBURG
J. M'LEOD, GLASGOW; GALIGNANI, PARIS; AND JACKSON, PHILADELPHIA.

Price 5s. in Twelve Monthly Parts, and 6s. 6d. bound in Cloth.

PREFACE.

In presenting our readers with the concluding number of a Third Volume, we are sure it will afford them pleasure to be informed, that our little work not only holds its ground, but is really still on the advance; and that from the encouragement experienced during the past year, we have resolved on carrying forward our Fourth Volume with still greater spirit, and a more determined effort to render the publication deserving of universal patronage. Already we have had drawings made of the various public Statues and Monuments throughout the City, and have one or two new hands at work making sketches of the finest scenery in the country; and having ordered a new Machine from the respectable house of Girdwood and Co. of Glasgow, we trust we shall be able to do greater justice to our wood engravings than has heretofore been the case.

That we should have succeeded, situated as Ireland is at the present moment, in establishing here a publication altogether free from party, politics, and personalities, is, we are aware, a matter of surprise to many; and we candidly confess, that it has rather surprised ourselves. It is indeed a circumstance on which we again reflect with satisfaction, that in glancing over the volumes we have published, there is scarcely a single line which we would now wish to expunge, or a sentiment which we would desire to alter. While our object has been to instruct and amuse, we have never wittingly permitted a paragraph to appear which could injure the morals, or hurt the minds or feelings of any of those various classes for whose reading the Journal is designed. In any incidental observations we may have made relative to men and manners, or to the existing state of things, we can conscientiously affirm, that the good of the lower orders of the people was constantly kept in view; and would appeal with confidence to the entire volume, to testify that we have steadily adhered to the promise originally made in our prospectus, not to admit the discussion of subjects connected with party or politics to form any portion of the present work.

Of the difficulties of conducting a Journal like ours at the present moment, especially in Ireland, some idea may be formed from the opinion expressed by Lord Chancellor Brougham, with respect to similar publications in England. Where there is a much wider field for them. Before the Select Committee of the House of Commons on the Law of Libel, in June, 1834, he stated, " as a member of the Society of Useful Knowledge," that " although the Penny Magazine had been enabled to be sold so cheap, in consequence of its immense numbers, and still increasing sale, that that was a price *which could not be afforded by any private individual;* a society can afford it; and a sale of tens and hundreds of thousands can afford it." Here, then, we have had a task to perform which has been declared impossible for a private individual, by a late Lord High Chancellor of England—and we have performed it. Although we cannot boast of hundreds, we certainly can of tens of thousands; and we still look with confidence, not only for continued, but increased public support. Indeed, had we no other ground on which to claim public patronage than the constant employment which the Journal gives to a number of persons, engaged in the various departments of wood engraving, printing, stereotyping, folding, boarding, &c. the claim would be a valid one, in a country like ours, where encouragement in every branch of the arts and manufactures is so requisite at the present moment. But we have other, and stronger claims—the information the work affords, and the extent to which it serves to make known our country among the different nations of the world. The work is a national one. It is received as such in every direction. Already it has made its way to some of the more distant regions of the earth; and we are at this moment preparing stereotype plates to expedite its more extensive diffusion throughout America, where it is to be reprinted. We shall, however, leave the publication to speak for itself; and again say, that we only claim for it public support while it continues to merit it, by a strict adherence to its avowed principles, and a steady effort to retain the patronage bestowed upon it.

June, 1835.

TABLE OF CONTENTS.

1834–35.

CONTENTS.

LIST OF ENGRAVINGS TO VOLUME THIRD.

VIEWS IN DUBLIN,

BEING A

Double Supplement

TO THE THIRD VOLUME OF

THE DUBLIN PENNY JOURNAL.

Robert Clayton, sc.

Drawn by A. Duncan.

VIEW OF THE IRISH PARLIAMENT HOUSE,

From an original Drawing made by Henry A. Baker, Esq. Architect to the Dublin Society, in the year 1767, (forty eight years ago) before the alterations took place.

VIEWS IN DUBLIN.

Dublin, the metropolis of Ireland, in population and extent the second city of the British empire, and supposed to be the sixth or seventh in Europe, is situated on the eastern coast of the island, in latitude 53° 21' N. and long. 6° 15' W. It is traversed from west to east, and divided into nearly two equal parts, by the Anna Liffey, a river of considerable magnitude.

In the reign of James I. stone or brick began to be commonly used in the construction of private habitations, and from that period the city has continued progressively to increase both in extent and beauty. In 1610, the entire circuit of its walls, which were wholly confined to the south side, did not exceed a mile. At present the length of the city from east to west is little short of three miles, and its breadth almost the same. It contains above 800 streets, squares, lanes, alleys, courts, &c. more than 22,000 houses, and above 200,000 inhabitants.

To the eastward, on both sides of the river, streets and squares of the most spacious, airy, and elegant description, have been erected within the last fifty years. Fitzwilliam-square, together with several elegant streets, have recently been formed towards the south-east. Most of the streets are well paved, being Macadamized in the centre for carriages; while on either side, generally speaking, and with the exception of that part of the city denominated the Liberty, there is a well-flagged foot-path. The city is lighted with gas, and the inhabitants enjoy a plentiful supply of excellent water from the Grand and Royal Canals, conveyed by pipes from large reservoirs, or basins, constructed at the north and south sides of the river. The city is encompassed by a circular-road, about nine miles in length, and nearly on three sides by the Grand and Royal Canals, which terminate in docks communicating with the Liffey near its mouth.

Previous to the Union, Dublin was the constant or occasional residence of two hundred and seventy-one temporal and spiritual Peers, and three hundred members of the House of Commons. At present, about half a dozen Peers, and some fifteen or twenty members of the House of Commons have a settled dwelling within its precincts. Other persons of this exalted class of society, whom business or amusement may draw to the capital occasionally, take up their residence at one of the hotels, of which there are a great number in the city. The resident gentry of Dublin now amount to about two thousand families, including clergymen and physicians, besides nearly an equal number of lawyers and attornies, who occasionally reside there. The families engaged in trade and commerce are calculated at about five thousand, and the whole may yield a population of sixty or seventy thousand in the higher and middle ranks of society.

A material change is observable in the manners of the populace of Dublin; their ancient amusements of bull-baiting, hurling, cudgel-playing, and wrestling, are almost wholly laid aside. They are still, however, careful to observe memorable days, particularly the festival of St. Patrick, which is distinguished by the shamrock being almost universally worn; and copious libations of the native beverage are poured out to the patron saint. A grand ball and supper is given on that night in the Castle. Formerly there were seven theatres well supported; at present the only one which remains is frequently very thinly attended. Club-houses and gaming-houses are nearly deserted; and even among the lower classes, open vice and profligacy have visibly diminished. The King's Birth-day is observed with much ceremony in Dublin. It commences with a grand review of the troops in the Phœnix Park, by the Lord Lieutenant, which is succeeded by a levee at the Castle, to which the Lord Mayor, Aldermen, and Sheriffs proceed in state; and the mail-coaches, splendidly equipped, move through the principal streets.

The following sketch of the Irish metropolis, by "*An American Tourist*," who travelled through the country about thirty years since, will not, perhaps, be out of place; unfortunately the descriptions, although a little too highly coloured, are in many instances but too just, as the stranger travelling through this beautiful island has seldom much fault to find with the house or demesne of a gentle-

man; but all his sympathies are called forth by seeing the miserably wretched condition of the Irish cottager. As far as the eye can reach, tracts of ground are in the possession of these poor people, who, having nothing to lay out upon them but the sweat of their limbs, extort by reiterated toil what will barely keep their families from starvation, and pay their rents, but have not a shilling left with which to make any improvement.

"This city," says the Tourist, "presents the most extraordinary contrast of poverty and magnificence to be met with in Europe. As you approach it, you find the suburbs composed of hovels, the sides of which are partly stone and partly earth, the roofs of turf, the whole dimensions of each not exceeding twelve or fourteen feet square. These miserable caves may or may not have a hole for a window, and an aperture on the top, to let out the smoke, if the luxury of fire can be afforded. Around the door the dirty children are huddled—not one half of them are decently clad; some of them still evince notions of civilization by slinking into a house, or turning their bare parts against a wall. I saw hundreds whose whole dress, consisting of a mass of rags, of all colours and all sorts of fabrics, will not furnish one piece of cloth eight inches square—and these tatters seemed to be sewed together only to prevent them deserting each other. Having passed the suburbs, the dwellings improve; and, on reaching Sackville-street, you imagine yourself in one of the most elegant cities in Europe. In walking over the city, the late Parliament House, (now the Bank,) the Exchange, the quay along the Liffey, and several of the public squares, excite the stranger's admiration. There is no part of London which can compare with the centre of Dublin in beauty and magnificence. But, in turning the eye from the architectural splendour which surrounds him, upon the crowds which flow along the streets, the stranger will be struck with the motley nature of the throng. Here is a lass almost buoyant with satin and feathers; there is a trembling girl of eighteen, purple from cold, shrinking from shame, and drawing around her the poor rags which, with all her care, scarce cover her body; here is an *exquisite*, perfuming the air as he passes, with rings on his fingers, diamonds on his brooch, and a gemmed quizzing-glass at his side; there is an honest fellow who cannot afford a hat, whose feet, summer or winter, know not the luxury of shoe or stocking, and whose whole wardrobe consists of two articles, viz. a tattered jacket, and about half a pair of small-clothes; and, not to multiply pictures, while the Lord Lieutenant dashes by in a coach and four, the stranger gazes at the gallant and costly pageant, while he empties his pocket to satisfy the throng of beggars who pray him, in the name of God, to give them a penny."

Happily for the citizens and the traveller, the last remark does not now apply, as beggars are not allowed on the streets; the Mendicity Society providing what is at least sufficient to keep them from starvation. Should the American Tourist again have occasion to visit the metropolis, he would find the state of things much improved; although it must be admitted that in many parts of the interior of the country his descriptions would be found to be but too faithful delineations of what still really exists, but, at least for a considerable distance around the city, the squalid wretchedness and the miserable dwellings he describes, are not now to be met with.

CARLISLE BRIDGE.

Carlisle-bridge, which connects Sackville-street, the greatest leading street in the City, with Westmoreland-street, is a point from which several views present themselves, unequalled in grandeur, beauty, and extent, by any which could be obtained from any one given point in any other city of Europe. The long continued line of quays extending right through the centre of the city from Kingsend Point to the Military-road, a distance of nearly three miles. In the direction of the Bay, the Custom House, rising at a little distance in all the beauty of classical architecture, and surrounded by ships and other vessels of considerable size, which approach quite close to the bridge; to the west, (the opposite direction,) the bridges, crowded with busy mortals passing and repassing; in the distant perspective, the Four Courts, and different Churches, whose lofty domes and rising spires are seen towering above the intervening buildings. In front (to the north,) Sackville-street, one of the most splendid streets in Europe, having in its centre the noble Pillar erected to commemorate the achievements of the immortal Nelson; on the left, the New Post Office, a specimen of elegant and chaste architecture—the view being terminated by the Rotunda and Rutland-square: while on the south side, at the extremity of Westmoreland-street, (a modern and splendid pile of building,) stands Trinity College to the left, and to the right the eastern portico and wing of the Bank of Ireland, and College-green.*

The Custom-House, which stands on Eden-quay, on the north bank of the Liffey, a short distance from Carlisle-bridge, is a magnificent structure. It is 375 feet in length, and 205 in depth, and exhibits four decorated fronts, answering almost directly to the four cardinal points of the compass—the south being the principal front. In the interior are two courts, divided from each other by the centre pile, which is 100 feet broad, and runs from north to south the whole depth of the building. The south, or sea front, is composed of pavilions at each end, joined by arcades, and united to the centre. It is finished in the Doric order, with an entablature, and bold projecting cornice. A superb dome, one hundred and twenty feet in height, surmounts the whole, on the top of which is a statue of hope resting on her anchor, sixteen feet high. The north front has a portico of four pillars in the centre, but no pediment. The south front is entirely of Portland stone; the other three of mountain granite. This great edifice is jointly the House of Customs and Excise. The Long-room is the only apartment worthy the visitor's notice. On the east of the Custom-house is a wet dock, capable of containing forty sail of vessels; and along the quay that bounds it on the east and north is a range of capacious and commodious houses.

It is a curious circumstance, that about two hundred years since, nearly the entire space that the eye can command from right to left, in this position, including the ground on which stands the Custom House, the houses on the Bachelor's-walk, the two Ormond-quays, Inns-quay, &c. was entirely covered with ouse, and overflowed by the tides, to within about eighty yards of Trinity College on the south.

THE BANK OF IRELAND, FORMERLY THE PARLIAMENT HOUSE,

Is situated in College-green, and stands nearly at right angles with the west front of the College, giving a grandeur of scene to that fine area, which can scarcely be surpassed. This noble edifice, built entirely of Portland stone, while appropriated to its original purpose, was considered the finest senate-house in Europe. The grand portico in College-green, which extends 147 feet, is of the Ionic order, and though destitute of the usual architectural decorations, derives all its beauty from a simple impulse of the art, and is one of the few instances of form only, expressing true symmetry. It was commenced in 1729, under the administration of Lord Carteret, and completed in ten years, at an expense of nearly £40,000. In 1785, it being deemed necessary to give a distinct entrance to the House of Lords, a noble portico of six Corinthian columns, covered by a handsome pediment, was erected. This, though evidently an architectural incongruity, (the columns of the principal front being Ionic,) has a very fine effect when viewed from College-street, as represented in one of the accompanying drawings. The front view which we give, is an exact representation of the building before the alterations or improvements in Westmoreland-street were made. An entrance was afterwards made on the western

side, and completed in 1794. The expense of these additions was upwards of £50,000.

Since the purchase of this fine building for its present use, many alterations have taken place to accommodate it to the purposes required. The exterior has been much improved. A complete connection was effected between the east and west ends and the centre, by circular screen-walls, ornamented with Ionic columns, between which are niches for statues, the whole producing a fine effect. The tympanum of the pediment in front has in the centre the royal arms, and on its apex a figure of Hibernia, with Commerce on her left hand, and Fidelity on her right. The pediment over the east front is also ornamented with statues of Fortitude, Justice, and Liberty. The interior of this superb edifice fully corresponds with the majesty of its external appearance. While used as a senate-house, the middle door under the portico led directly to the House of Commons, passing through a great hall called the Court of Requests. The Commons-room formed a circle, 55 feet in diameter, inscribed in a square. The seats were disposed around the room in concentric circles, rising above each other. A rich hemispherical dome, supported by sixteen Corinthian columns, crowned the whole. Between the pillars a narrow gallery was handsomely fitted up for the convenience of the public. A beautiful corridore communicated by three doors with the committee-rooms, coffee rooms, &c. The House of Lords, to the right of the Commons, is also a noble apartment, ornamented at each end with Corinthian columns. An entablature goes round the room, covered with a rich trunk ceiling, and in a circular recess at the upper end was placed the throne of the Viceroy, under a rich canopy of crimson velvet. This room remains unaltered; it is now designated the Court of Proprietors. It is 73 feet long by 30 broad, and the walls are ornamented with two large pieces of tapestry, representing the battle of the Boyne and the siege of Londonderry, in a state of excellent preservation. At the upper end stands a statue of his late Majesty in his parliamentary robes, admirably executed in white marble, by J. Bacon, jun. of London, at the expense of £2000. The pedestal on which it stands is ornamented with figures of Religion and Justice. Elegant corridores lead to the different offices, which are lighted from the roof or the interior courts.

On the 27th of February, 1792, between the hours of five and six in the evening, while the members were sitting, a fire broke out in the Commons-house, and entirely consumed that noble apartment, but did little other damage. It is conjectured to have taken place by the breaking of one of the flues, which run through the walls to warm the house, and so communicated fire to the timber in the building. Its present construction very nearly resembles the old: it is circular; the other was octangular.

In 1804, this beautiful edifice was again threatened with destruction, a fire having broken out under the portico, which did considerable damage before it could be extinguished. Several of the columns were so much injured, that pieces had to be inserted in them in different places.

The Union between Great Britain and Ireland having rendered a Parliament House in Dublin altogether unnecessary, this noble building was purchased from Government by the Bank of Ireland, for the sum of £40,000, subject to a ground-rent of £240 per annum. The interior was then fitted up in the most elegant and convenient manner, from the plans of Francis Johnston, Esq. The Cash-office stands nearly on the site of the Court of Requests, to the right of the hall; the length of this fine room is 70 feet, the breadth 53, and the height 50, and it contains 550 square feet more than the Cash-office of the Bank of England. The walls are pannelled with Bath stone, and ornamented with twenty-four fluted Ionic columns of Portland stone supporting a rich entablature. The doors, desks, &c. are mahogany, and the office is well lighted by an elegant lantern in the ceiling, which is coved, and richly ornamented. There is besides, under the entablature, a range of twenty-four windows, seven of which being glazed with looking-glass, produce an admirable effect. In this office lodgments are made, notes issued and exchanged, and drafts examined, marked,

---

* This spot was formerly the place of public execution. In the year 1328, Adam Duff O'Toole was burned here, having been convicted of blasphemy, in denying the incarnation of Christ and the Trinity in Unity; and for affirming that the Virgin Mary was a harlot; that there was no resurrection; that the Scriptures were a mere fable; and that the Apostolical See was an imposture and usurpation. Roger Outlaw, the prior of Kilmainham, was accused of heresy at the same time, but he was honourably acquitted.

Horatio Nelson, del.   Robert Clayton, sc.

UPPER CASTLE YARD.

CARLISLE BRIDGE.

THE LYING-IN HOSPITAL AND ROTUNDA.

Horatio Nelson, del.

Horatio Nelson, del.

R. Clayton, sc

EAST FRONT OF THE BANK OF IRELAND, FROM COLLEGE STREET.

and paid; it is opened from ten to three o'clock each day. In the western front is a room called the Library, 86 feet by 34, with presses for books, papers, &c. In another room is to be seen a fine model of this superb edifice. It will give a more correct idea of the professional talents of the architect than a view of even the building itself. Every precaution is adopted to guard against fire and external violence. There are two large tanks in the yards, and one on the roof, well supplied with water, and several fire engines. The whole of the building, including courtyards, covers one acre, two roods, and thirteen and a half perches of ground; and on the roof, which is for the most part flat, a regiment of soldiers might be drawn up in time of danger. In Foster's-place, on the west side, a handsome guard-room has been erected, to accommodate fifty men. Here is also the printing-office, an object well deserving the attention of the curious in mechanics. It is situated in the rere of the building, and is under the immediate superintendence and control of Mr. Oldham, a very ingenious artist. The notes are printed by machines worked by steam, on a construction altogether new, being Mr. Oldham's own invention. To prevent forgeries, a machine has been adopted, which produces fac-similes of the various copper plates; and to render the imitation still more difficult, and at the same time to prevent the workmen employed from appropriating any copies to themselves, there is another machine, which numbers the notes consecutively as far as one hundred thousand, without being subject to the control of the operator; to this a small box, glazed in the top, is attached, in which a duplicate impression appears of each number, as worked off by the printer.

To increase the means of security, the clerks and officers of the Bank are formed into a corps of yeomanry; and a neat armoury, containing a sufficient quantity of arms and accoutrements, are kept in perfect order within the Bank. By an application to the Secretary, or by an introduction to any of the clerks, the whole of the interior may be viewed at any time.

This establishment was first incorporated in the year 1783, and is under the superintendence of a Governor, Deputy Governor, and fifteen Directors, who are annually chosen, the first week in April, five new Directors, at least, being elected every year. The qualification necessary for a Governor is to be in the actual possession of £5,000 in stock; for a Deputy Governor £3,000, and for the Directors £2,000 each. The profits of the Bank arise from their traffic in bullion, and the discounting of bills of exchange.

DUBLIN CASTLE

Is situated on the highest ground, and nearly in the centre of the city. It is divided into two courts, the upper and the lower. The upper court, which contains the apartments of his Excellency the Lord Lieutenant, is a quadrangle, two hundred and eighty feet long by one hundred and thirty feet broad, with uniform buildings on every side. Over the principal entrance from Cork-hill, is an elegant statue of Justice, and over the other gate a statue of Fortitude. The Viceroy's apartments occupy the whole of the south side, and part of the east end: the remainder of the court being occupied by the apartments and offices of the Chief Secretary and various officers of the household.

The grand approach to the viceregal apartments is a colonnade, at the termination of which is a handsome flight of steps, which leads to the yeomen's hall, and from thence to the presence-chamber, which is furnished with a throne and canopy, covered with crimson velvet, and richly ornamented with gold lace and carved-work, gilt. The object which attracts the greatest attention is the ball-room, or St. Patrick's hall, so called since the institution of the Order of Knights of St. Patrick. This noble room, which is eighty-two feet long, forty-one feet broad, and thirty-eight high, is decorated with some fine paintings, particularly the ceiling, the flat of which is divided into three compartments, an oblong rectangle at each end, and a circle in the middle. In one of the rectangles, St. Patrick is represented converting the Irish to Christianity; and in the other, Henry II. seated under a canopy, receives

the submission of the Irish chieftains. In the circle, his late Majesty King George III. is seen, supported by Liberty and Justice, while various allegorical representations allude to the happy effects resulting to this country from his auspicious reign. The cornice of the room is also richly painted. At either end is a gallery for the musicians and spectators.

The lower court, though larger, (being two hundred and fifty feet by two hundred and twenty,) is more irregular in form, and very inferior in appearance. On the north side are the Treasury, the Hanaper, Register, and Auditor-General's Offices. The Ordnance Office, which is a modern brick building, stands at the east end, where is also the arsenal, and an armoury, containing arms for forty thousand men, with some cannon and mortars, besides guard-houses, riding-houses, stables, &c. There is a small lawn, adorned with trees and shrubs, called the Castle-garden, with which the viceregal apartments communicate by a large flight of steps from the terrace before the garden front.

This building was first intended to be a fortress or citadel to secure the English interest in Ireland, and was deemed a place of considerable strength. The entrance from the city on the north side was by a draw-bridge, placed between two strong round towers from Castle-street, the westward of which subsisted till the year 1776. A portcullis, armed with iron, between these towers, served as a second defence in case the bridge should be surprised by an enemy. A high curtain extended from the western tower to Cork-tower, so called after the great Earl of Cork, who in 1624 expended a considerable sum in the rebuilding of it. The wall was then continued of equal height until it joined Bermingham tower, the strongest and highest of the whole. This tower, which was afterwards used as a prison for state criminals, was taken down in 1775, and the present building erected on the site, for preserving part of the ancient records of the kingdom. From this another high curtain extended to the Wardrobe-tower, which served as a repository for the royal robe, the cap of maintenance, and the other furniture of state. From this tower the wall was carried to the North or Store-house tower (now demolished,) near Dame's-gate, and from thence it was continued to the eastern gate-way tower, at the entrance of the Castle. This fortress was originally encompassed with a broad and deep moat, which has been long since filled up. There were two sally-ports in the walls, one towards Sheep (now Ship) street, which was closed up in 1663, by the Duke of Ormond, after the discovery of Jephson and Blood's conspiracy. The other, which afforded a passage to the back-yard and out-offices north of the Wardrobe-tower, remained till the curtain on that side was taken down to make room for a new pile of buildings, where the Council-chamber and a new range of offices for the secretaries stand.

The Castle of Dublin is generally supposed to have been commenced in 1205 by Meyler Fitzhenry, Lord Justice, natural son to king Henry II. and finished in 1220 by Henry de Loundres, Archbishop of Dublin, but did not become the royal seat of government until the reign of Queen Elizabeth. Previous to that period, the Chief Governors sometimes held their court in the Archbishop's Palace at St. Sepulchre's, sometimes at Thomas-court, but more frequently at the Castle of Kilmainham. A tempest having damaged this house in 1559, Queen Elizabeth issued her mandate for preparing the Castle of Dublin for the reception of the Chief Governors; and the work was completed by Sir Henry Sidney in 1567, and from that period it has continued to be the town residence of the viceroy. The custody of the Castle was formerly entrusted to a constable, gentleman-porter, and a body of warders, consisting, previous to the invention of gunpowder, of archers and pikemen.

A guard of horse and foot, with regimental music, mounts at the Castle every morning, at 11 o'clock, in the same manner as at the Horse Guards in London.

Numerous interesting narratives might be collected relative to transactions which occurred from time to time within the precincts of the Castle of Dublin, of individuals who, as state prisoners, were confined in its strong holds. There can be no doubt that sufficient materials exist for a work, fully as interesting as any of those published by Sir Walter Scott, in reference to the olden times of the sister kingdom, which have been perused by thousands with such interest and pleasure.

The following is an account of a judicial combat, being an appeal at arms to support the justice of a cause, which was decided in the presence of the Lords Justices in the inner court of the Castle, at so comparatively recent a date as the 16th century :—

In the year 1583, Connor Mac Cormack O'Connor impeached Teig Mac Gilpatrick O'Connor, before the Lords Justices (Adam Loftus, Archbishop of Dublin, and Sir Henry Wallop) and Council, for killing his men under protection. Teig, the defendant, pleaded that the appellant's men had, since they had taken protection, confederated with the rebel Cahir O'Connor, and, therefore, were also rebels, and that he was ready to maintain his plea by combat. The challenge being accepted by the appellant, all things were prepared to try the issue, and time and place appointed, according to precedents drawn from the laws of England in such cases. The weapons, being sword and target, were chosen by the defendant, and the next day appointed for the combat. The Lords Justices, the Judges, and Councillors, attended in places set apart for them, every man according to his rank, and most of the military officers, for the greater solemnity of the trial, were present. The combatants were seated on two stools, one at each end of the inner court of the Castle. The Court being called, the appellant was led forward from his stool within the lists, stripped to his shirt, and searched by the Secretary of State, having no arms but his sword and target ; and taking a corporal oath, that his quarrel was just, he made his reverence to the Lords Justices and the Court, and then was conducted back to his stool. The same ceremony was observed as to the defendant. Then the pleadings were openly read, and the appellant was demanded, whether he would aver his appeal. Which he answering in the affirmative, the defendant was also asked, whether he would confess the action, or abide the trial of the same. He also answered, that he would aver his plea by the sword. The signal being given by the sound of trumpet, they began the combat with great resolution. The appellant received two wounds in his leg, and one in his eye, and thereupon attempted to close the defendant, who, being too strong for him, pummelled him till he loosened his murrion, and then with his own sword cut off his head, and on the point thereof presented it to the Lords Justices, and so his acquittal was recorded.'

THE LYING-IN HOSPITAL AND ROTUNDA.

These magnificent buildings form a very distinguishing feature in the city. The principal front is to Great Britain-street. Its centre, decorated with four Doric columns on a rustic basement, and supporting a beautiful entablature and pediment, the whole crowned with a domed steeple, has a very elegant effect. Ornamental colonnades communicate with the wings—which have also Doric columns, and vases at top—that to the east serving as an entrance to the Rotunda, a noble circular room erected in the year 1757, and the other buildings connected with the Hospital, which run parallel with Cavendish-row.

The inside of the Rotunda has a very pleasing appearance. It is eighty feet in diameter, and forty feet in height, without any middle support. It is decorated around with pilasters of the Corinthian order, eighteen in number, and twenty-five feet high, standing on pedestals; above which, between the pilasters, are enriched windows, which appear on the outside. The ceiling is flat, with large and bold compartments. The ornaments of the whole are now somewhat antiquated, but it has, nevertheless, a grand effect when illumined on public nights.

The other rooms consist of two principal apartments, one over the other; the lower is the ball, thirty-six feet long by forty broad ; There is a smaller ball-other the supper and tea room. also serves as a room for the ground floor, which refreshments when the larger is occupied.

The Rotunda Gardens were to out by Dr. Bartholomew Mosse, fully planned and laid viding a fund, to arise out of their purpose of providing the maintenance of the noble hospital exhibition, for erection he

contemplated. He had previously opened an asylum for poor pregnant women in George's-lane, (the first attempted in the empire,) but finding it much too small for the reception of the numerous applicants, conceived the idea of the princely Lying-in Hospital of Dublin. The benevolent man had already risked his whole fortune in the completion of the garden; but, undeterred by this obstacle, he raised money for his favourite purpose by lottery-schemes, and on his own credit; and commenced the building in 1751. The entire failure of one of his schemes in 1754, alone induced him to petition Parliament in behalf of his laudable undertaking, when the sum of £12,000 was liberally granted him to finish the edifice, with the addition of £2,000 as a personal remuneration. In 1756, the doctor obtained the charter of incorporation ; in 1757, the structure was opened for the reception of patients ; and, after the lapse of two years only, having much impaired his health by too unremitting attention to his grand object, the philanthropic founder was no more. His bust in the interior surmounts a pedestal, on which appears the following pithy and expressive inscription :

Bart. Mosse, M. D.
Miseris Solamen
Instituit.
MDCCLVII.

The gardens are open as a promenade on several evenings of the week during the summer season, with the attractions of a band of music and illuminations. Admittance is obtained at the small charge of a six-pence.

Besides the levees and the assemblies occasionally held at the Castle, balls and concerts are frequently given at the Rotunda for charitable purposes, which are generally well attended.

AQUEDUCT, PHIBSBOROUGH.

This handsome structure, which crosses the great north-western exit from the city, connects the Royal Canal, by a branch of one mile and a half, with its spacious docks in the immediate vicinity of the Custom House. It is an object well worthy the attention of those who may not before have had an opportunity of examining similar specimens of human contrivance. The engraving will afford a better idea of the structure, than any verbal description we could give, in the space allotted to the subject.

KING'S-BRIDGE.

This useful and ornamental building crosses the Liffey a little way from the south-east entrance to the Phœnix Park. The foundation stone was laid on the 12th December, 1827, by the Marquis Wellesley, at that time the Lord Lieutenant of Ireland. It forms one great arch one hundred feet in diameter, composed entirely of cast metal —the butments are of handsomely cut mountain granite. It is called King's Bridge from the circumstance of the amount paid for its erection, £13,000, having been collected for the purpose of raising a national monument to commemorate the interesting event of his Majesty George the Fourth's visit to Ireland in 1821. Several plans and measures were proposed, and a considerable delay took place in appropriating the fund collected; at length a bridge across the Liffey on the present site was agreed upon, and the idea sanctioned by his Majesty. The original intention was to place a triumphal arch over the centre, surmounted by an equestrian statue of his Majesty; but whether or not this will now be done is doubtful.

The buildings seen in the distance are the Royal Barracks, which are not to be surpassed in Europe, for extent and grandeur of architecture. These barracks, erected by government in the year 1706, possess a commanding view both of the city and adjacent country, with the Wicklow mountains in the distance. They consist of four squares, of which the Royal Square is the principal, and the most embellished. Altogether they can accommodate five thousand men.

⁎ It is right, perhaps, to say, that the foregoing descriptions have principally been taken from "*The Picture of Dublin,*" a work (though published anonymously) prepared by ourselves, for Messrs. W. Curry, Jun. and Co. of Sackville-street, and to which we would refer those of our readers who may be anxious for further information relative to the history of the City, its buildings, and inhabitants.

Horatio Nelson, del.

KING'S BRIDGE, MILITARY ROAD

Horatio Nelson, del.   Robert Clayton, sc.

AQUEDUCT, PHIBSBOROUGH.

THE
DUBLIN PENNY JOURNAL

CONDUCTED BY P. DIXON HARDY, M.R.I.A.

Vol. III.	JULY 5, 1834.	No. 105.

STRANCALLY CASTLE.

Strancally Castle, the subject of the above sketch, and residence of John Kelly, Esq , is beautifully situated on the river Blackwater, about five miles from the town of Tallow, and seven from Youghal. It is a modern structure, built in the Gothic style, from the design of Mr. G R. Payne, of Cork. From the porch front, which is high, and tastily executed, may be seen the termination of the navigable river Bride. It affords a pleasing and never ending scene of countless market-boats, passing and repassing between the above mentioned towns: underneath the castle there is both shelter and anchorage for ships of a heavy burthen, and from the conservatory side may be seen the river, as far as Old Strancally Castle, whose once massive walls have, by the hand of time, been humbled and cemented with its rocky base, and forms beneath the water's surface a most extraordinary and impenetrable mass, although presenting at present little more than the traces of its former site. Leaving the " Old Castle," and passing up the several windings of the river, no place can boast of more variety, or be more truly picturesque than the irregular embrasure towers and other ornamental parts of

the new edifice, crowning the foliage of an apparently endless forest, while on the other side a still more varied scene of wild landscape, terminates with the park and mansion of H. V. Stuart, Esq., opposite which is Camphier House, in the cottage style, and a little further on the town of Cappoquin. E. H.

" *Outlines of Humbug ; or Thoughts on the 19th Century—a fragment.*"—Dublin, p.p. 92.

Here, good reader, is a work which we can fairly recommend to your notice, as containing within itself one of the best *practical* demonstrations of the theory which it propounds, that we have ever met with. It is, moreover, printed on thick post paper, with an embossed cover and gilded edges ; and within the limit of ninety-two tiny pages contains no fewer than *seven* chapters, treating upon no less than *seventy* different subjects, arranged under as many different heads in an elaborate table of contents.— Its title is certainly no misnomer ; from beginning to end the " Outlines of Humbug" may be plainly traced—in the very wood-cuts this is apparent, being miserable imitations from designs in " The Boy's own Book."

REMINISCENCES OF A ROCKITE.

THE DEBUT.

It has often puzzled me to find out what qualification my good old father could possibly have seen in me to induce him to educate me for the church. Indeed the only way I can solve the riddle is by giving him credit for the possession of much of that absurd opposition to nature which regulates the conduct of many parents towards their children. He was an honest farmer, of means, which although moderate in the days he lived, would, by proper management, now, most undoubtedly, entitle their possessor to the universal rank of esquire, and perhaps to a seat on the bench. As I was his only child, on expressing my dislike to the profession for which he intended me, he at once renounced his resolution, and I was allowed to remain as I was, spending the morning of my existence in idleness and dissipation. He died, and I consequently became the possessor of the farm and all his other worldly property—still I was unhappy. The attainments which I had laboured to acquire, and on which I founded my expectations of an entry into genteel society, were apparently despised or thought valueless by those of my neighbours, who looked upon themselves as entitled to the rank of gentlemen—to me low society and drinking were the consequence.

On a cold September morning I had gone out shooting, and having traversed much bog, was both cold and hungry by the time I reached a poteen distillery, where I had been once before in company with some of my usual associates, and to which that circumstance gave me a facility of entrance. The occurrences of that evening are easily described: I was soon drunk—reason left me first, and I have an indistinct recollection of doing and saying many foolish things, with the clearest possible conception of their absurdity. On my waking next morning, the owner of the house, after the usual congratulations, accosted me with,

"An', faith, your honour took it mighty stout.'

"Aye, that reminds me,' said I, pulling out my purse; "how much did I take?'

"Oh! sure it isn't the liquor I mane, much good may do you with it, but the other thing—it'll be a feather in your cap while you live."

A little doubtful of that, and puzzled by his manner, I asked him—but there's no use in detailing the conversation: in my drunken fit I had taken the Rockite oath, and he was the bearer of a summons to me to join the body at an appointed place on the following evening; and now for my—Debut.

With a nondescript mixture of sensations, and a firm intention to make the most of my new situation, I left home, as if for night shooting, and set off for the rendezvous: it was in the mountainy country, in the opposite direction from the bog where my servants conceived me to be engaged, and a part, too, where my acquaintances were very few, (that is my old acquaintances,) and my friends easily counted. I had never seen the leader who was now master of my destinies; but report, which spoke much of his skill, his valour, and his extraordinary power over his followers, said little of his mercy, and less of his disposition. He had been, for many years previously, an outlaw, and all the wild characters who managed to get themselves into a similar predicament, sought his retreat, and shared his fortunes; so that at the time I mention, he had no less than a score followers who never parted him, and whose retreat never could be discovered by the government: independent of those, half the country owned him the leader of their political combinations; and the strict discipline that he enforced—the strict obedience that he exacted, and the certain, and often horrible punishment with which he followed up a breach of either, rendered him at once the terror of government, and the master of those over whom his authority extended. These considerations began to have some weight with me: the idea of returning presented itself, but was soon banished, since I had no particular desire to form an example to any of those who were engaged in the mad schemes of such a desperado; I proceeded, and was already close to the spot appointed: the night was utterly dark, yet I was near enough to perceive that I was alone, and likely to be so; the possibility of my being humbugged by my friend of the stile occurred, and was welcomed. I had turned to retrace my steps, intent only on how I should resent the trick, when "Who goes there?" "A friend." "What friend?' followed in quick succession. I gave my name, and close by my side a stranger sprung over a low hedge, which had concealed him from my view. He grasped my hand in a provokingly familiar style, as I thought, and set out with a long string of compliments on my punctuality, spirit, &c.

We proceeded up the valley, and as we went, I ventured to ask him some questions relative to the captain, not telling much for my idea of his amiability, and was answered by an, "I am he," that made me pause, and I ventured to stammer out a description of excuse, which he cut short, by assuring me, in rather a bitter tone, that none was necessary; that my ready acceptance of the oath, and strict adherence to his command, proved I could not be guilty of any disrespect. I was in a precious pickle: he relieved me, however, by a strong whistle. There was a heavy sound on all sides; a rush, and a clamour, and in less than a minute we stood in the midst of two hundred armed men. Long ere I had recovered my astonishment, and, perhaps, my fright, I was marching by his side, followed in stealth and silence by the whole body. We had scarcely passed the populous district, when the moon rose, and I had an opportunity of beholding my extraordinary comrade. He was a large, strong man; partly grey, with a cast of features and demeanour which left me in doubt whether I should set him down for a gentleman turned ruffian, or a ruffian turned gentleman. The results of the march certainly helped me to a conclusion which, however far from the truth, I most implicitly believed, until circumstances, and a knowledge of his history, led me to form one more charitable, and more merited. After a march of nearly an hour, we stood on the skirts of a wood, which formed part of the demesne of Major *****, a magistrate who, on some occasions, had been rather troublesome to my new friend. The whistle was repeated, and answered; and a peasant, armed, as he would say himself, emerged from the shade, and, with a low obeisance, stood before the captain.

"Well, Coghlan, any thing since?" inquired the leader.

"Nothing, your honour, since last night."

"Perhaps you made a mistake,' said the captain.

"Bedad," replied the new-comer, "may be I did, your honour; but, anyhow, twasn't for nothin'that he was with the major all yesterday working in the garden—mauryiagh: but can't your honour send for him, and see him yourself; he's up, an' writing, for I peeped into his cabin, as I passed by; the colleen an' her mother is both with him; so maybe you'd find one o' the strangers, and get him here quietly, and thin sure we'll see."

The captain turned round, and having selected a man from the ranks, directed him to go for Flood, the person alluded to in the above conversation, and tell him he was wanted for parade; adding, that if possible he should have the paper he was writing, brought, without alarming him or his companions.

After an interval of about twenty minutes, spent by all in the deepest silence, by me in the deepest anxiety, the messenger arrived, accompanied by the countryman, Flood, for whom he had been sent. The silence was first broken by the latter making his reverence to the captain, and adding, ' that he didn't know the boys were to be out to night, or sure he'd be wid them; but, anyhow, he didn't keep his honour long waiting; for it was lucky he was up making out his account agin the major."—"Humph!" was the only answer, and mounting a style that led into the wood, he gave the command, "follow, boys;" and in a very short time we were in its farthest recesses. The silence was still unbroken, save by the suppressed whisper among the party, or some remark of careless gaiety, delivered by the unsuspecting new-comer, in rather a louder key, and left unnoticed. He was evidently strictly watched, and his conversation as strictly shunned. I was still beside the leader—and although in the deep darkness I could not recognize more than his figure; his emotion was evident by his restless gait, and even by his breathing. After a little time we reached a part of the wood, where was about a rood of land clear of any timber, except here and there a stunted thorn or holly; and there the word "halt," was given, in a whisper that thrilled to the farthest rank, and of itself half told of some horrible intention in the mind of him that pronounced it; in the same tone he directed them to light a fire; and having seated himself on a bank, motioned me to sit beside him. Alas! the honours of this world are hard to bear. I'd as soon have sat on a kish of pike-heads. However, I conquered my repugnance, and obeyed him. His head sank upon his hand, and he remained in that position until the blaze, rising higher and higher from the crackling and sapless branches that had been gathered and lit at his command, gave to its immediate precincts the full light of noon-day, and with its highest flickerings, half defining the trunks of the distant trees, made our really formidable number appear as if surrounded and defended by one still more formidable. Its effect on my companions was singularly wild and uncouth, as thrown in lazy groups on the elastic brushwood, or standing beside the blaze, which in its different gradations of light, according to their different distances, varied the expression of their countenances, and glanced upon their savage weapons—they afforded such a strikingly romantic, I might almost say classical appearance, that it half reconciled me to their lawless society. The outlaw again raised his head, and the usual stern calmness of his countenance was the only expression that my scrutiny could discover there; and when he called out to Flood to come forward, there was not a tone in his voice that betrayed him.— The wretch presented himself with the same carelessness as before, and which, whether real or affected, excited my strongest pity for his dangerous situation; but standing, as he did, between me and the fire, it was utterly impossible to distinguish any thing but the darkness of his figure, contrasted with its almost dazzling brightness.

"Flood," proceeded the captain, "you were up when I sent for you; what were you doing?"

A dawn of the truth seemed to burst upon his mind, but recovering himself quickly, he answered,

"Sure I tould your honour I was making out an account of the day's work agin the major, had luck to him I'm a poor boy, your honour, depending on my day's work, and I'd like to have every thing fair and straight."

"Indeed!" answered the outlaw; "an' I'll be bound an industrious, quiet boy like you has a long balance in your favour. Would you let me look at that account now?"

"I—I—haven't it about me, your honour," replied he.

"You lie you have;" responded a voice from the crowd—"didn't you put it in your pocket when I opened the door?"

"Eh—in my pocket," stammered the detected ruffian, and thrusting his hand in, the crackling of paper was distinctly heard, "not it at all, your honour," he proceeded, "only a bit of an ould copy that I was trying the pens on, no use at all;" and drawing it out, he made an effort to throw it into the flames, but his nerveless arm refused its office—the paper fell within a foot of the blaze, and was handed to the captain before the terrified wretch recovered his surprise. Every eye started into eager watchfulness; and the agonized breathings of Flood were all that could be heard, until the captain, after glancing his eye over the paper, exclaimed,

"Why, Flood, I believe you were going to ask me to make a serjeant of you, you have taken such a correct list of us. What was the major to give you for this?"

Every demonstration of despair that he had so long laboured to control burst out with double violence. His head sunk upon his breast, and his knees tottered so, that the arm of an infant might have hurled him to the ground. His guilt was but too evident.

"Well, Sir," said the captain, turning round to me, and placing his arm on my shoulder in such a manner that his fingers fell on my breast, and could perceive every beat of my heart; "what, think you, should be the fate of an informer?"

My voice was choked, but he could read my feelings too well from my heart.

"You are young, Sir," he said bitterly, and after a short pause, thundered out to Flood, "Villain, if you know a prayer, say it, for your time is short."

"Mercy! mercy!" shrieked the victim; and "mercy! mercy!" repeated a young female, rushing from her covert in the brushwood, immediately behind us, and throwing herself on her knees before the captain, ere an arm could arrest her progress.

"Ha!" shouted he, "who the deuce is this!"

"His sweet heart, your honour," answered Coghlan; "she followed us, I suppose, and that's what brought her here."

The poor girl clung to his knees, still shrieking for mercy; but with one vigorous effort he unloosed her grasp, and gave her into the unwilling charge of Coghlan, who stood next to him. She still struggled with her detainer, until at one time she caught a view of his face, and recognised him: to him her prayers were then directed. She knelt to him—she shrieked—she almost dragged his herculean frame from his place, when the report of a dozen muskets cut short her entreaties. She turned round, and saw the dying blaze light up the convulsed features of the informer, and then fell powerless into the arms of Coghlan.

"Dead, is he?" asked our leader, of one of those who had gone up to examine him.

"Nothing surer, your honour," was the answer.

He then rose from his seat, as if to depart, but was stopped and whispered by Coghlan.

"Indeed," said he, "then there's more to be done."

But whatever that more was, he seemed to have but little relish for it, as after a short pause he continued,

"No, no, we've done enough—try what you can do now," and handing him a pistol from his belt, departed, attended by his followers. Seeing me accompanying him, he desired me make for home as quick as I could, for I had a far way to go, a command which was, undoubtedly, the only pleasing one to my ears that he uttered since I had the pleasure of his acquaintance. I obeyed him, and just as I was on the road, heard a shot fired in the wood, which I supposed was by accident, or some signal. However I hastened home, and arrived just at day-dawn, unperceived by any one. The first news I heard next day was that a man and his sweetheart had been found shot in Major *****'s wood, by the shepherd. An investigation was held by the magistrates, and immense rewards were offered for the slightest information, but in vain.

(Continued in our next Number.)

INDIAN ZOOLOGY.

While it shall at all times be our study to give to the Dublin Penny Journal as national a character as possible, it is our intention from time to time to lay before our readers such articles on various subjects as we may deem calculated to amuse, inform, and instruct, although altogether unconnected with, and even far removed from our native land; feeling satisfied that by so doing we shall not by any means be departing from the original design of our publication. In pursuance of this design, we now give the following article on Indian Zoology:

An Indian forest scene is the most picturesque that can be imagined; the trees seem perfectly animated; the fantastic monkies give life to the stronger branches; and the weaker sprays wave over your head, charged with vocal and various-plumed inhabitants. It is an error to suppose that nature hath denied melody to the birds of hot climates, and formed them only to please the eye with their gaudy plumage. Ceylon abounds with birds equal in song to those of Europe, which warble among trees, grotesque and even picturesque in their appearance, and often laden with the most delicious and salubrious fruit. Birds of the richest colours cross the glades, and troops of peacocks complete the charms of the scene, spreading their plumes to a sun that has ample powers to do them justice. The landscape, in many parts of India, corresponds with the beauties of the animated creation: the mountains are lofty steep, and broken, but clothed with forests, enlivened with cataracts of a grandeur and figure unknown to this part of the globe.

But to give a reverse of this enchanting prospect, which it is impossible to enjoy with a suitable tranquillity; you are harassed in one season with a burning heat, or in the other with deluges of rain : you are tormented with clouds of noxious insects; you dread the spring of the tiger, or the mortal bite of the naja.

During the summer season, in many places in some of the higher latitudes, the inhabitants undergo the most intense heats, arising to the 114th, nay even to the 120th degree of Fahrenheit's thermometer; so that men are scarcely able to breathe, plunge into water up to the chin, and ascend the higher trees that they may inhale a somewhat cooler breeze; whilst they whose occupations oblige them to endure the hot air abroad, not unfrequently fall suddenly dead. The birds too are often killed by the heat, while flying, or sitting on trees, and fall to the ground.

Then, as the flat country is inundated, about the solstice, by the swoln waters of the Ganges, which returning into their channel, leave many stagnant pools, the exhalations raised by the sun's heat form a body of intensely hot vapour, extremely noxious, so as to occasion putrid fevers of the highest malignity, which frequently prove fatal within three hours.

THE LITTLE HORNED OWL.

This elegant species of the owl is found in Ceylon. Indeed it can scarcely be called a species. In the engraving it is represented of its natural size. The irides are scarlet; the horns take their origin from the base of the bill, and point to the sides of the head : on their inner side they are dusky, on their exterior, white. The bill is dusky surrounded with long bristles : the circle of feathers round the eyes is of a very pale ash colour : the external circle of a yellowish brown. The head of a deep ash-colour : the back dusky ; coverts of the wings grey. marked with narrow lines of black, pointing downwards ; the quill-feathers regularly barred with black and white ; the breast buff-colored, marked with small sagittal black spots ; the legs feathered half way down ; the naked part of a reddish yellow.

The plant on which it is represented as standing, is one of the most beautiful of the Indies ; but at the same time its roots are the most venemous. It is found in Ceylon and Malabar, and, on account of its charming appearance, is called by Linnæus, *Gloriosa Superba.* By the natives it is styled *Najajala* and *Nyaghala,* possibly from its being possessed of a poison as potent as that of the serpent *Naja,* or *Cobra de Capello,* whose bite is the most fatal of any yet known.

THE LONG-TAILED SQUIRREL.—(*SCIURUS MACROURUS.*)

This species is found in Ceylon and Malabar. In the Cingalese tongue it is called *Dandoelana ;* and, from the noise it makes, *Roekea.* It is about three times the size of the European squirrel. The ears are tufted with black hairs ; the end of the nose is pink-colored ; the cheeks, legs, and belly are of a dull yellow ; between the ears is a yellow spot ; the crown of the head, and the back, are black : from each ear is a bifurcated line of the same colour, pointing down the cheeks ; the upper part of the feet is covered with black hairs ; the lower part naked and red The tail is near twice the length of the body, of a light ash colour, and extremely bushy. The part next the body quite surrounded with hairs ; on the remainder the hairs are separated, and lie flat.

The tree is the *Eugenia Malaccensis.* It is the most excellent of the Indian fruits, delicious in taste, grateful in smell, pleasing to the eye, and salubrious in its effects. Its native place is Malacca ; and is only cultivated in Goa and Amboina, on account of its fine qualities, its roseate scent and color, and its happy faculty of allaying the rage of thirst in the burning fevers of the torrid zone.

That India, whence the animals which we have described are taken, is called East India ; there is, however, much variation as to the countries to which this name is proper and peculiar. In the first place it is maintained, that India is only wherever the Hindu nation inhabits, or the country called by the Persians, Hindostan, which is comprehended between the rivers Sind and Ganges, closed to the north by the ridge of Imaus or Caucasus ; and on the south surrounded by the ocean ; so that the whole peninsula on this side the Ganges, belongs to Hindostan.— But in a more extended sense, the peninsula beyond the Ganges also is a part of India ; and its limits are much more extensive, if under this second signification of India are reckoned all the islands of the Indian sea, from the east and north of Madagascar, as far as New Holland, and thence eastward to the Phillippine islands, together with New Guinea ; and it is principally with this meaning that the English and Dutch sailors use the word India, and Mr. Pennant seems to have adopted it in his account of the animals of India It must be evident that a disquisition concerning the climate, soil, and seas of India, thus largely understood, would be a matter of much difficulty. It is our intention, in a future number, with some other interesting illustrations of birds and animals, to enter more at length into the soil and climate of those distant portions of our globe.

POPULAR LECTURES ON THE PHYSIOLOGY OF
ANIMALS,
IN COURSE OF DELIVERY BY DR HENRY.

*The following is an abstract of Dr. Henry's first
Lecture :*

LECTURE I—ON THE SCARF-SKIN, HORNS, HOOFS, NAILS,
AND HAIR.—The skin is a most important and interesting
part of the body in many respects, but particularly in being the organ wherein the sense of *touch* is seated. It
consists of three layers: first, the *scarf-skin*, or cuticle;
secondly, the mucous *network*; and thirdly, the *true skin*

The *scarf*, or *external skin*, is that which we touch
when we lay our hands on the skin. It is devoid of all
feeling, and is quite inert; it is so closely joined and
adapted to every little irregularity of the body, as to form
an exact mould of the parts underneath. It is naturally,
and even before the parts are used, thicker on those parts
which are intended to bear most pressure; thus it is naturally thicker on the palms of the hands and the soles of
the feet, than on the backs of the hands and feet, and
thicker on the outside of the hands and arms than on the
inside. It is produced in proportion to the occasion there
is for it, and is therefore found on parts much exposed to
pressure. Scarf-skin is produced by the true skin underneath, and is at first soft and nearly fluid, as it is seen
when a blistered surface is healing; afterwards it becomes
hard by exposure to the air. Its uses are to protect the
sensitive and delicate parts underneath, for which it is admirably fitted, and by its own insensibility, to prevent the
poration of the fluids of the body, while it permits the
passage of the perspiration; this power of preventing evaporation is particularly observable in cases where the
scarf-skin has been removed before death, either by scald,
burn, or the application of blistering plaster; the parts
from which the scarf-skin has been so removed, becoming
in the dissecting-room as hard as leather or paste-board,
while the parts covered with it remain supple and soft.—
It serves also to protect the subjacent parts from sudden
vicissitudes of temperature, being an exceedingly bad conductor of heat. It enjoys this property in common with
hair, wool, feathers, and horn; being nearly identical
with those substances in its chemical composition, and
serving the same purposes, that is, of keeping the parts underneath at an even temperature. The scarf-skin likewise
prevents the absorption of poisonous substances by the
skin; hence sores can be handled by the physician with
impunity, which he dare not touch if the scarf-skin were
removed from his fingers. Were it not for this protection,
no poisonous substances could be handled either by the
physician or mechanic, and thus many articles commonly
employed in the arts, would be rendered useless, not so
much by the pain they would occasion to the part they
touched, as by the poisonous effects produced on the system by their absorption into the blood, the necessary
consequence of their coming in contact with the true
skin denuded of the scarf-skin.

The *Nails* are of the same nature as the scarf-skin.—
Like it, constantly growing and wearing away—like it, being a delicate intermediate agent of touch, although themselves insensible—like it, protecting the very delicate
parts underneath from injury; and like it, so firmly attached to the skin underneath as not to be separable without violence sufficient to tear and injure both the nail
and subjacent parts. This firm attachment of the nail to
the skin underneath (for the part underneath is nothing
but the true skin, and the nail covers it as the scarf-skin
covers the other parts of the true skin) is effected by
longitudinal projections of the skin, which are received
into corresponding depressions on the lower surface of
the nail. The hoof of hoofed quadrupeds corresponds to
the nail of man; its mode of attachment is the same; and
so firmly does it adhere to the subjacent bone, called in
the horse, the *coffin bone*, that the hoof or nail is able to
bear the violent exertions of the animal, whether in leaping or galloping, or in heavy draughts up hills. The strength
of the connexion between these parts will appear more
evident, when it is considered that the horse does not
tread on the sole of the foot, but only on the anterior

edge of the hoof. The nails in the human subject, beside
serving the purposes abovementioned, are a very great ornament, and strongly distinguish man from the inferior
animals, in which the nail is an instrument of offence or defence, and not an agent of delicate touch.

Horn is of the same nature as scarf-skin and nails; it
always grows over bone. The horny scales of the tortoise
grow upon a shell of solid bone, as does also the horn of
the ox, sheep, and goat. In the last mentioned animals,
the horn forms a sheath for the bone, like the finger of a
glove. Between the horn and bone is a very sensible,
tender substance, which is of the nature of skin, and produces the horn in the same way that the skin produces
the scarf-skin. As fast as the horn wears away on the
outside, this sensible skin or *quick* is producing it on the
inside, just as is the case in the hoof and the nail. Deers
horns are *called* horn from analogy, but there is nothing
horny in their composition; they are real bone, and are
shed annually. In horned cattle the *horns* are bones covered with horn and are never shed.

Hair is of the same nature as horn, scarf-skin, hoofs,
and nails. Imbedded in the substance of the skin, (not the
scarf-skin, but the true skin,) are a number of little bags
or *follicles*, extremely minute, and very little larger than
is sufficient to contain the end of a hair. The hair is produced in the interior of the bag, and its end always remains inclosed in the bag. As long as the bag remains,
the hair grows; when the bag is destroyed, the hair falls
out, and never can be reproduced. In this consists true
baldness, for which no remedy is known, as there is no
mode known of reproducing the follicle, without which
the hair cannot be produced. The growth of hair is promoted by whatever is beneficial to the skin, and invigorates
the system. The use of the warm bath, of oil, and the
frequent cutting of the hair, are found to stimulate the
follicle to the production of new hair. The growth of
hair is diminished by every thing that diminishes the circulation in the skin. Want of exercise; anxiety of mind,
which has so wonderful an effect on the circulation of
the skin; want of due care in oiling, washing, and cutting
it, tend to prevent its growth. Age produces baldness by its effect on the follicles, which are absorbed
in old age. No satisfactory reason has ever yet been assigned why females are so much less apt to grow bald
than men. It is a common opinion that hairs are hollow,
and have a tube in the interior. The accurate observations of Hook showed that this was a mistake, and
later observers have confirmed the truth of Hook's opinion. The tube of the hair is very short, and scarcely
enters beyond the level of the skin. While the opinion
prevailed that hairs were hollow tubes, it was supposed
that the tube was colourless, and that the colour resided in
the pith; and it was said that grey hairs were owing to
the decay of the pith leaving the colourless tube empty.
I suppose the true explanation, as we must now seek one
elsewhere, to be this; the colouring matter is embodied
in the very substance of the hair; a change takes place
in the follicle, which becomes no longer able to produce
coloured horn, but produces *transparent horn* only, and
the effect is grey hairs. That this is the true explanation
of the mode in which hairs become grey, is shown by the
circumstance of hairs always growing grey at the root first;
so that as the hairs grow grey you have the part of the
hair furthest from the skin retaining its natural colour,
while the part near the root alone is grey. The stories
which are told of hairs growing grey in one night contradict this explanation; but I suspect that in those stories
there is some exaggeration. I have mentioned that one
of the uses of the scarf-skin is to keep the skin moist and
warm—this is preeminently the use of hair: so warm and
comfortable a covering does it make for other animals,
that we strip them of it to put it on ourselves, who are
less bountifully provided with it by nature, having been
intended by nature to cloth ourselves artificially. The
hair best fitted for our covering, is the soft hair, known
by the distinguishing name of wool.

The *feathers* of birds correspond exactly to hair, and
also grow from a follicle. The part inserted into the
skin, or the barrel, while the feather is growing, contains
blood-vessels which, when the feather is perfectly dried

up, forms the dry pith which we find in the barrels of quills. The projecting *processes* at the further end from the barrel, have on their edge other smaller processes. By means of these the parts lock into each other, so as to make a surface impermeable to the air, even during the most violent action of the bird's wing. The effects of this structure in preserving the skin of birds from rain, and that of waterfowl from the action of the water, is also evident. In order to render the protection thus afforded more secure, the bird is provided with a gland, which produces oil; this is placed over the extremity of the back bone of the bird, who, pressing it with his bill, extracts the oil, and smears his feathers with it. By this double protection the skin of the cormorant and seagull, and of the swan and duck, is kept as dry while they are swimming on the water as while they are walking on the land. It is well known that the plumage of the males is more beautiful than that of the female birds. When the female becomes so old as no longer to lay eggs, she not unfrequently assumes the plumage of the male. This is a change analogous to the growth of the beard in the female of the human species after the middle period of life.

THE CORSAIR CHIEF—A FRAGMENT.

The crew of a well-oared boat were seen hastening towards shore; in the stern sat a large figure wrapped in a loose cloak; his head rested upon his hand in a pondering attitude, and he seemed to take no part with the others in the boat. The lofty plume in his cap partly concealed his features; but the broadsword which was fastened to his side, and four large pistols which hung from his belt, plainly indicated his profession.

It was a fine moonlight night; the storm was completely hushed; the face of the heavens unclouded and serene; the waters, which a short time before dashed their white spray to the sky, were now peacefully dancing in the light of the moonbeams, and all was silent and serene.

The chieftain ordering his men to remain silent until they heard the signal, first sprung on the beach, and ordered his faithful Hugo to follow: he did so, and they proceeded. They had not gone far when the attendant looking around, suddenly stopped, and exclaimed,

"We proceed no farther."

"Why?" said Alberto, in astonishment.

"Because we dare not," answered the ruffian. "Soldiers advance, and Alberto is your prisoner."

"Treacherous villain," said the corsair, "be this thy reward," and he made a desperate lounge at him; but the other quickly springing aside, evaded the blow.

"Tear that bugle from him," said he to the soldiers, who now advanced, "or he will yet be rescued."

But it was now too late; already had it sounded an animated war-note, and as the last strains were dying o'er the waters, was answered as loudly from the boat, and immediately the splashing of oars was heard at a distance.

"Distraction!" said Hugo, "we will yet be lost; surround him quickly."

The glittering broadsword of the corsair flashed bright in the light of the moon-beam, but not so bright as the blaze from his indignant eye: three of his antagonists had already fallen beneath his powerful arm, when a faint scream was heard. Alberto turning round, beheld Victoria endeavouring to rush to the scene of slaughter, withheld by two of the soldiers. Maddened at the sight, he furiously attacked his remaining assailants, and tried to burst a passage through them to reach the object of his love: the cowardly assassins poured around him in numbers; Alberto gave a wistful look towards the sea, and beheld his faithful band pressing towards him. Their bright falchions blazed over their heads, and with a loud shout they sprung upon the beach.

"They came—'twas but to add to slaughter,
His heart's best blood was on the water."

* * * * * *

On the following morning a dreadful scene was presented to the eye—the entire band of pirates had been either slain or taken prisoners, but ere they had been overpowered, their chieftain's death was avenged, for Hugo was found a stiffened corpse among the heaps of the slain.   MACÆNAS.

THE FUGITIVE LOVERS.

In 1774 an officer arrived at Portpatrick from Ireland with a young lady who had eloped with him from her parents. As they were stepping into a chaise for Ayr, her father and a friend of his came up to them, stopped the chaise, and brought them both into the inn, where the father offered to accommodate matters, by giving the officer his daughter in marriage, with one thousand pounds fortune. The lover, however, refused to marry the lady, which so enraged her cousin, that he instantly knocked him down; upon which a challenge ensued. The military gentleman fired, and missed; his antagonist's pistol also missed fire, on which they attacked each other with swords, but were parted by the spectators, and disarmed. The officer, however, had a short hanger under his coat, wherewith he attempted to stab the cousin: being observed by one of the lookers-on, he sprang in upon him, wrenched the hanger out of his hand, and carried him back into the inn as a prisoner. The fair cause of the fray observing her lover in this plight, produced a pair of pocket pistols, which she offered to shoot her father and cousin with. They, however, carried her back captive; and her gallant, a few hours after, hired another vessel, wherein he set out for Ireland after them; but meanwhile measures were taken to prevent any further communication between him and his runaway.

ORIGIN OF CROPPED HAIR.

Cropped hair first came into fashion in Ireland at the period of the French revolution. The wearing of hair powder was also discontinued at this time: the appearance of the fair sex was much improved by this change as they did not always confine themselves to the use of white hair powder, but occasionally wore brown, pink and yellow, which falling on their skins, disfigured the fairest belles. Crops were considered a mark of republican sentiments, yet the first French Crop was a royal one, and one of her most distinguished monarchs, Francis the First. The martial manners of his age characterised every diversion; and the king, with a small band of gentlemen, attacked with snow-balls, and weapons of that nature, the house of the Count de St. Pol, who defended it with another party. A torch from the hand of one of the defendants unfortunately struck Francis on the head, and wounded him severely. His life was long despaired of; and during the course of the wound, as it became necessary to cut off his hair, he never would suffer it to grow again, but introduced the fashion of wearing it short.— Even on this occasion the magnanimity of his mind was conspicuously displayed; nor would he ever permit any attempt to be made to discover the person who had wounded him.

HIGHWAYMEN.

In September, 1774, about three o'clock in the morning, the Stamford fly was attempted to be robbed near Stukely, in Huntingdonshire, by a single highwayman, who desired the coachman to stop, but the guard who travelled with the coach, ordered him to keep off or he would shoot him. The highwayman persisting in his intention to rob the coach, the guard fired a blunderbuss, and lodged two slugs in his forehead. He was immediately put into the basket of the coach, where he lived but a few minutes. His corpse was carried to Huntingdon, where it appeared that he was a horsekeeper belonging to the Cross Keys inn at that place. . He had no fire-arms about him, but made use of a candlestick instead of a pistol; he had robbed the Peterborough stage about a fortnight before he was shot in his attempt on the Stamford fly. About the same time a coach going to Lincoln, was stopped a few miles from London by a single highwayman, who was shot dead by the guard. He was muffled up to the eyes in a great coat, to prevent his being known; but he proved to be one of the hostlers of an inn, and it is supposed that he had robbed that coach several times. It appears that as soon as he saw the coach set off, he had a saddle ready in a bag, and went to an adjacent place where a horse was ready for him. He had been often missing from the inn, but was not suspected of going upon such business.

A TRAVELLER'S TRICK—A FACT.

During a period of a very active opposition between the rival coach proprietors on the Wexford road, the down coach stopped at Rathnew, in the county of Wicklow, to breakfast ; this repast, so indispensable to a traveller among the Wicklow mountains, was delayed, under various pretences, till the coachman's horn announced the moment of departure : in vain the passengers remonstrated against this precipitancy ;—he must drive to time, and could not delay. When at length he had succeeded in getting his grumbling company together, one gentleman was found wanting ; and on " mine host" opening the door of the breakfast-room, he found him quietly seated at the deserted table.

" The coach will be off," exclaimed the landlord.

" And so would I too, could I have got a spoon to eat my egg," replied the guest.

" A spoon, Sir."

" Yes, Sir, a spoon."

" Why, why, where are my spoons. Stop, stop coach ;

Jack, Patt, Joe, run every one of you ; stop the horses—stop the coach till I get my spoons," vociferated the landlord ; while struck with consternation, each passenger looked to his neighbour for an explanation of the scene. In a few minutes a crowd had collected around the carriage, to whom the robbery of the spoons was detailed, with the resolution of the host, that all the passengers should be searched, with the assistance of his party. He was about commencing his operation, when out walked the dilatory passenger from the breakfast-table, who immediately demanded what was the matter.

" Matter !" roared out the landlord ; " have I not been robbed of a dozen of silver spoons by some of your rascally company—and your blackguard coachman is preventing me searching ?"

" Then drive on, Paddy—all's right ;" exclaimed the wag, and turning to the exasperated host, he said, " look into the tea-pot for your spoons, and for the future make more haste with your breakfast."

C. H. W.

Wexford.

CURIOUS AMERICAN STEAM VESSEL.

NO. 1—PLAN.

NO. 2—ELEVATION.

NO. 3—CYLINDER.

The above wood cut is from a copy of a drawing made at New York, of a novel and very curious steam-vessel, built for the navigation of the great river Hudson. The design of this vessel is by a man who, by his industry, and by some ingenious inventions, has raised himself from the station of " a common workman" to that of a master.—Its construction is altogether so original and extraordinary, that we think a brief description of it may not be uninteresting.

Two hollow bodies, or buoys, " shaped like cigars," eight feet diameter in the centre, and three hundred feet in length, placed about sixteen feet apart,* and connected by light frame-works, support the deck. These buoys are formed of white pine staves, precisely like a hogshead, without caulking, or external hoops, but are rendered perfectly water-tight, and the staves can be drawn together with any degree of force, by means of iron rods passing from the staves through holes in the circumference of hoops, placed at suitable distances within the buoys, which rods are drawn close to the centres of the hoops by screws extending outwards. The circumference

at the centre was diminished three inches by these screws. The deck (a, fig. 1) is ninety feet long, and in the middle is an enormous paddle-wheel, (c) thirty feet in diameter, with paddles fourteen feet wide. The cylinder (b) is of ten feet stroke, and the steam engine is provided with three boilers, like the locomotive engines.

The advantage of this construction is the very great buoyancy of the vessel : no load can sink the buoys more than two feet and a half—nor is she effected by the wind or tide. Her average speed is twenty-five miles, but at times she has been propelled at the rate of thirty miles an hour. The distance from New York to Albany, 145 miles, on the Hudson, is performed in about six hours. Her appearance is said to be very beautiful ; and the captains of some American vessels described her to Dr. Lardner, as seeming " to skait along the water, without noise or swell, as if by magic." Vessels of such a form would not answer for sea navigation, but are admirably adapted for the broad and rapid rivers of America, and might be introduced with advantage on a smaller scale, upon some of the rivers and canals of Europe. C. E. C.

---

* In Dr. Lardner's lectures on the steam-engine, delivered a few months since at the Mechanics' Institution of Manchester, they are said to be thirty-two feet apart. The account we have given is taken chiefly from a letter from New York.

DUBLIN:
Printed and published by P. D. Hardy, 3, Cecilia-street ; to whom all communications are to be addressed.
Sold by all Booksellers in Ireland.
In London, by Richard Groombridge, 6, Panyer-alley, Paternoster-row ; in Liverpool, by Wilmer and Smith ; in Manchester, by Ambery, in Birmingham, by Drake ; in Glasgow, by W. R. M'Phun ; and in Edinburgh, by N. Bowack.

THE
DUBLIN PENNY JOURNAL

CONDUCTED BY P. DIXON HARDY, M.R.I.A.

| Vol. III. | JULY, 12, 1834. | No. 106. |

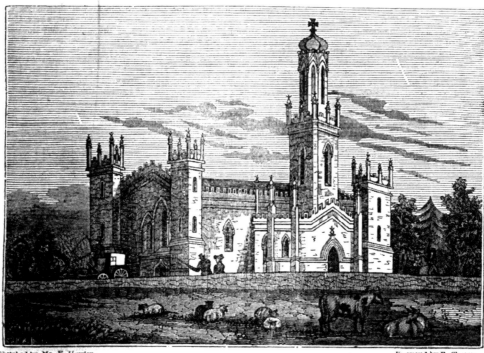

Sketched by Mr. E. Heyden. Engraved by R. Clayton.

MONKSTOWN CHURCH.

The parish of Monkstown at present occupies rather a conspicuous position, owing to the smart little town which has sprung up within the course of a few years, in consequence of the elegant and extensive harbour recently erected there.

The ruins of the old Church of Monkstown stand between the new Church and the Castle, in a neat churchyard, and form rather a picturesque object.

It is difficult to fix on the order of architecture of the present gorgeous edifice, it is *sui generis;* outside it looks somewhat of a *mule* between the Gothic and Saracenic: the steeple is surmounted by a cross, but the minarets have something of the crescent, though on the whole it has not an unpleasing effect. The interior is of the oddest *fancy,* we will not call it *taste.*— It is of plaster made to represent immense blocks of granite, and even *the galleries ! !* are of the same character, *to keep the congregation in awe,* we suppose. Immense blocks are represented ready to tumble on their heads, and crush them to atoms. Were they really granite, no earthly power could prevent the attraction of gravity from pulling them from their places. Perhaps the architect, as the whole inside is in the Arabesque style, wished, by the position of these ponderous blocks, to give the idea of the Prophet's tomb suspended in the air. Altogether, we never saw a greater perversion of judgment and taste, than is displayed throughout the entire building. Many other equally preposterous defects will at once strike an attentive observer—there is not a spot in the church where the eye can rest without pain. From the cross-lights behind the pulpit, *where there should be no light,* is a large window of three divisions, so that it is impossible

to see the preacher; and under, and in the recess of the same window, the space is occupied by a curious sort of falling roof, *somewhat like the top of a cow-shed, with battlements* in the front !

Scattered over the manor of Dalkey, are many old buildings, *entitled castles,* which certainly partook of that character, but, at the same time, were merely so many defensive depots for the merchandize of the city of Dublin in former times, which was embarked in Dalky Sound, where the vessels lay, in consequence of the shallowness and difficulty of the navigation of the Liffey. There are many entries on the Pipe Rolls, of the embarkation of wine and provisions at Dalkey, to be sent to the army of Edward the First in Scotland.

The walls and towers of the little fortified town of Bullock still remain, an interesting exhibition of the puny efforts of former times.

TO THE EDITOR OF THE DUBLIN PENNY JOURNAL.

Sir—The rule for finding the length of the day is by doubling the sunsetting; and the length of the night by doubling the sunrising, and add both together, which, if right, make exactly twenty-four hours. Now the first day of February, by the above rule, amounts to twenty-four hours fifty-six minutes, being an excess of fifty-six minutes. Look into any almanack published prior to 1831, and you find that in no case whatsoever do they exceed twenty-four hours. As your Journal will be read by many scientific men, I hope some of them will be able to elucidate this strange phenomenon, if I may call it so.

Millford. J. A.

REMINISCENCES OF A ROCKITE.

[Continued from our last.]

FIRST BLOOD.

As the associates of my drunken jollity were for the most part to be the partners of the more honourable career that had now opened before me, it seemed unnecessary, that in our military character, we should change the haunts we had used as bacchanalians. The poteen-house was therefore still the head-quarters and rendezvous, and never did the moonshine glitter on a temple better suited for the two-fold rite; a priest and priestess more punctual in the presidency, or a set of more zealous votaries altogether than our cabin, our landlord, and ourselves presented. Accordingly, for almost every night during the first week or fortnight after the occurrence mentioned, we wooed the sister spirits of mischief and poteen.

On the last of those nights a circumstance occurred to me, which made such a powerful impression on my mind, and wakened so many of its wildest emotions, that I doubt if I shall ever forget it. Before I launch into the account, I shall briefly describe the situation of the house and its environs, and thus save myself much circumlocution and confusion when I come to the localities of my scenery.— It was a large comfortable cabin, of the old style, with a floor nearly three feet below the earth outside, whether from that unaccountable desire of the peasantry to have low floors, or as an additional concealment, I cannot tell; behind were some rude out-houses, standing at right angles with the mansion, in one of which, almost inaccessible to any unfriendly visitor, the dear destructive beverage was manufactured. The immediate position of the premises was among a cluster of rocky swellings, where the grey limestone, scantily covered by the niggard and sun-burnt verdure, and in many parts utterly bare, by the similarity of its appearance to the rude built walls and roofing of the distillery, rendered discovery from a distant point impossible, or from a near one improbable. A wide extent of bog, whose other border was lost in the horizon, stretched almost to the scrubby point I have described, and afforded it, with but little trouble, and as short carriage as possible, the indispensable requisites of turf and water, a fine clear stream being the only division. Beyond it, on the other side from the bog, the country partook of the same uncultivated, savage character, until it was lost amid the general sterility of that mountainy tract, wherein was the concealed residence of our lawless captain and his followers. In fact, it was so situated that even a friend might wander through scrub and moor, and over rock and hillock for a long summer's day, and yet fail to discover the object of his search, were it not for a large, old ush, which towered on an adjacent eminence, to the view of the whole surrounding country.

As the night referred to had been fixed upon to finish off the chief stock for the ensuing winter, a larger number than ordinary were met to celebrate the joyful occasion. The song and story were put in alternate requisition, and at the close of each, the cruiskeen was sent on its maddening circuit, until one simultaneous roar of drunken merriment drowned all the efforts of the ambitious artists. A loud rapping at the door checked it more suddenly than if the priest himself had come in; fear and doubt were the unanimous features of the whole gathering, until the ragged colleen that attended us went to the door, and on receiving some private signal from without, opened it for the entrance of a small, middle aged man, muscular and wiry, with a bushy beard, and hair that would defy the exertions of the most skilful frizeur in Dublin. On his back was slung a wallet, that betokened his calling, and the few rags that screened him from the winds of heaven, seemed to say but little for his profits. However, with all that easy confidence so peculiar to his caste, as well as other vagabonds, he came forward into the full glare of the blaze from the burning deal, that served us for candles, and with its lurid and awful light gave rather an unprepossessing appearance to our orgies and ourselves, and to the new-comer in particular

"Why, then, boys," said he, looking round, "ye are putting in a night of it; couldn't ye give a body welcome?"

"Shemus! Shemus!" was echoed from all quarters; and then half a dozen sprung from their seats to grasp the rough hand he offered; while "Shemus, avich, here," and "no but here," and "Shemus, agrah, with me you know," and every form of uncouth invitation that such poor courtesy could bestow, was lavished on the happy individual; and one of my herculean neighbours, through his eagerness for the close company of that important personage, shoved me half off the best chair, where I had been ensconced as the lion of the night, before the coming of my more fortunate rival. At last he was seated and I began to recognise him as a fellow that used frequently to call for small jobs at my house, though the little respect then and there paid him, almost made me doubt he could be the much honoured being before me. He was in reality the general agent of the disaffected in all parts of the country, and had served to extend the influence of our redoubted leader perhaps more than any other individual in existence. He now commenced a tirade upon our recent horrible performances—and cursed all informers in a manner very amusing to his listeners.

"Bedad, boys, ye have the shine of the country now to yeerselves; the Glin lads are beat down intirely; they only kilt one, but ye finished two. Oh! ye're the darlints; an' who's this we have here?" continued the ruffian looking over towards me. "Ah, I'm mighty proud to see you in sich honest company, avich," at length exclaimed he, after recognising me, and at the same time offering his hand with the most provoking air of patronage imaginable. Not considering it very safe to insult such a popular gentleman, I accepted it with as much appearance of humility as I could command, which seemed to soothe him a little, as patting me on the head he went on, "a fine, likely gossoon, heaven bless him; an' on the straight road to glory. Well, avich, an' did ye shoot ere a policeman yet?"

I was actually struck dumb with the fellow's impudence; and the bewildered stare with which alone I answered the question, excited such loud merriment, that I had a little time to recover myself; by that time he was expressing some loud encomiums on our captain, but was interrupted by one of those most familiar with him inquiring,

"Arrah, Shemus, tell us who was he afore he turned out; for some how or other he doesn't look like one of ourselves, at all at all."

"Give us the cruiskeen, then, an' I will," answered he, and after a long draught, that would have inspired eloquence in a bog-stick, thus proceeded:

"Why, then, indeed, it's thrue for you, he's not like one of ourselves; an' myself seen the time when he'd be hard set afore he'd keep company with the likes of uz, until the blow came on him, and then sure he was glad enough to do it. Ye see I can't tell ye his raal name, bekase I'm sworn not; but anyhow his father was a great gintleman of the ould stock; an' he had the ould house, an' a bit of lund about it that kept him equal, ye see, to the upstarts; an' they got angry at that, an' one o' them, a black villian, took advantage o' the law on him, and dhruv him out of house and lund, a beggar, all as one, on the world. Well, my dear, the ould gintleman an' his gossoon, him that's captain now, were tbrated mighty dacint by all the honest people about the country; everybody offered to keep them, but he was too spirited for that, an' used to work his day's work, though in throth 'twas a poor hand he made of it; but anyhow it satisfied his pride, an' every now and then a present 'id come to him by post of a pound or two from some one that pitied him, for no one dare offer it open; but still it fretted him greatly, to think himself, an' his poor innocent gossoon, should live an' die the way that none of their people afore them ever did; so at last he took courage, an' wrote a letter to a relation, that lived beyant in Spain, or Amerikey, or some where thereabouts, axing him to take them over, an' make a soger or something o' the boy, an' he'd be contint with any thing for himself. But still, with all the hope of the good living before him, he couldn't bear the thought o spending his days away from Ireland, and never see the ould friends and ould sights again; so his poor heart broke within him afore an answer could come back, or the boy's fate be settled; and he had his wish at last, for he died in his own country, and was buried with his own people. Well, boys, a mighty dacent wake and berrin he had; an' just when 'twas over, a bit o' comfort came to the orphan in the shape of a letter, from the relation, consinting to take him, and having the travelling money inside, an' away he went, for he hadn't many good byes to say, or much to settle; and though he wasn't much more nor a gossoon, still he was mighty cute, an' understood well what killed his poor father; an' by raison of that, whin he was going away, he swore black vingeance on king an' country, an' more especially the ould villian that was in his father's place, an' all his kith, kin, and generation. Well, after staying a few years with the relation, he become a great pet, an' there was talk of his leaving him all his goold, for he had no child of his own, until an unlucky split kem between them, by raison of his wanting him to marry a great rich lady in them parts, and, bedad, the captain didn't like her; and more be token, he was mindful of a promise he made one Kathleen Carroll, a little girl that was kind to him somehow or other, afore he went; so he renounced them intirely, and came home with little weight enough in his purse, but plenty on his heart; an' more the pity, for as I tould ye afore, he was the raal ould breed. To make a long story short, boys, he married Kathleen, an' with what little he had, bought out an' out a little farm that was jist then to be sould, outside his own right estate, an was getting on right well, an had raison, as you'd think, to be happy; for the wife was handsome and genteel, an' brought him one little girl, the only one he'd ever seem to make free with. Well, my jewel, what I'm after telling ye, I had mostly from hearsay; but now I'm going to tell ye what I saw with my own two eyes, an' a quare story it is, as ye'll say yerselves when ye hear it. One time that myself an 'my father, the heavens be his bed, was rambling thereabouts doing a little job now and thin when we could get it, we came to his house at the fall of one of the long winter nights, and settled to stay there till morning; we got the failta, to be sure, as every one did, but the sorra a word more, for he was mighty dark and proud, and sat in front of the fire with his little Aileen dhu on his lap; that's her that's in the mountains with him now, an' a fine, likely girl she's grown up, an' the living image o' the mother that was the beauty of the world intirely. But, murther boys, I was running away with the story. I must tell yees, the ould rascal that put his father out was dead, and left a son behind him, that was the darlint of the whole country; kept horses and hounds, and gave parties to the quality, and lived half his time in Dublin, and was, altogether the raal sort of a boy. Well, to turn back to the captain, he sat with us the way I mentioned for a good half hour, with the little crathur on his knee, playing an' cooxing him, but all to no use, till at last a neighbour came in, an' afther, 'good look to all here,' an all that, he asked where was Kathleen. 'I don't know,' says the captain sulkily; 'but I know where she ought to be.' 'Sure enough, you're just right,' says the other, 'she's where she oughtn't to be, for one that's come from the big house this minute, saw her come out o' one of the plantations with the master, an' she's gone in with him.' My jewel, he flung the child out of his arms into mine, like a clod, and leaped into the middle of the flure, eyeing the man like a wild beast. At last says he, half choked, 'my Kathleen in company with one of that cursed breed—that's a lie, Martin.' 'Sorra a lie in it,' says the other, 'an', more betoken, it's not her first time neither, though nobody liked to tell you of it.' When he heard that, he gave a groan, as if his heart was bursting, and ran out of the house, without hat or any thing. We all followed, but 'twas no use—we couldn't come up to him at all, at all; but we saw 'twas towards the ould place he ran.—Whatever he saw or heard there, no one ever knew from him; but, at any rate, the sarvints tould us after, that the coach was ordered to be ready in the dawn of the morning, to take the couple off to Dublin in all secrecy; an' I suppose he found that out too; for before you'd think he

was there, he was back again, and tould us all to follow him. We knew well what was in his mind, but not a word he said until he gother a number of the boys; an' them were the boys that were afraid of nothing. 'Deed ye're good, likely boys yeerselves; and I wouldn't like to make little of ye—ye're good, brave boys, and showed yeer pluck right well the other night; but now ye're no more to them boys—no, no more than they were to Fann M'Coul, as I'll show ye if ye have patience. Well, as I said, he gothered the boys, and tould them what happened, in a long, grand speech, for all the world like a counsellor; and he asked wouldn't they revenge him; and they all said they would; so without more delay he led the way to the big house. One had a gun, another a bayonet on a pole, another a soord, another a stave, all had something or other but myself, for I was only a spalpeen, and besides had the child in my arms, for I didn't like to leave her behind, and no one to take care of her, though the father didn't seem to notice her at all, even when she cried with the cowld, as she did once or twice afore we got there. Well, when we came to the big house it was all bolted and barred, and we made so much noise breaking in, that the chap within guessed what we were at, and ran with Kathleen, that was shouting and roaring, into the parlour, bekase the door of it was the strongest in the house, so that when we came to it, we found all we could do wouldn't break it in. 'That won't do,' says the captain, laughing, 'he shan't foil us this way.' So he got furniture, and barred up the door with it on the outside, and sent a parcel round under the window, that was a good way from the ground; and then, after sending out the sarvints prisoners, he went into a room under the parlour, and made a bonfire of tables and chairs, and boxes, and every thing he could lay his hands on, and came out, and locked the door behind him.—Well, we all knew rightly what he was at, and the blood run cowld in us, but not a word was spoke until the ceiling above began to take fire, and then we heard them opening the door, and trying to get out, but that was impossible, by raison of all the furniture against it. The captain burst out laughing, as if it was the pleasantest job he ever done in his life; and the next minute the shutters were unbarred and opened, and all without was as clear as the noon-day, for the fire was beginning to take head inside; then he laughed louder than ever, 'till at last the unfortunate wretch ran, with Kathleen in his arms in a dead faint, and stood on the window-stool, to escape the fire behind. The first that noticed them rightly was the child in my arms, and she began to cry out, 'mammy, mammy,' so that you'd pity her, and to stretch out her little hands to get to her; then every body saw them, and gave a loud shout, except the captain, for, with all his laughing, the child's call cut him to the heart, and his head sunk down on his hand, and myself thought he was going to fall. Well, as soon as the shout was over, the chap above began to beg and pray that they'd save him, and he'd give up house and land, and never throuble any one about it. 'Yis to be sure,' says the captain, and taking a gun from one of the boys, he fired up at him quietly, and man and woman tumbled headlong back into the fire. He just looked for a moment in at the window below, and then ordered us all to march the sarvints down to the gate-house, and leave the place to the fire. Bedad the stoutest man there trembled at his voice and obeyed him, so he locked the sarvints up in the gate-house, and commanded them, on pain of death, not to attempt to stir out until morning. A little after they all scattered, and nobody was with him but the father and myself, and the man that brought the bad news; so we went home with him, and there, my dear, he cried like a child for a good long hour, and took poor Aileen from me, and almost swallowed her with kisses. He then went into his room, and made a bundle of whatever he thought valuable, and with it on his back, and the child in his arms, went off to the mountain, where he's living ever since, and that's all I know more nor yeerselves about the captain."

Amid the confused and stammered applauses of his rude auditory, the story-teller proceeded to light his pipe, and whiffing it away, with his eyes thrown round his companions, in evident self-gratulation, and his caubeen placed side ways on his bewildered-looking head, he formed, for the moment, the most perfect picture of complacency and rakish pride that ever fell to my lot to laugh at. His enjoyments were, however, soon interrupted by the renewed inquiry—

" But, Shemus, agrah, you didn't tell us what happened the boys afther. How did they got off, avich ?"

" Why, then," answered he, " they got off as all bould men in the world get off; for good courage always brings good luck along with it, as yeerselves 'ill find out yit, never fear. Not one more nor six of them, besides the captain, was ever swore against, an' they managed to make off to him, where they're all safe to this blessed day, barrin' two of them that was shot, and one o' them dhrowned a year or two ago. But, saints above, what's this ?" exclaimed he, springing from his seat in utter dismay, followed by the whole assembly, as a ragged little boy rushed in, and by the contortions of his body and countenance seemed to warn us of some dreadful danger, for which his tongue could not find utterance.

" Aw, aw, aw !" gasped the terrified creature, convulsed with his exertions, as the tinker rushed forward to seize him, and was checked by his sister, the servant of the house, throwing herself in his way, with,

" Oh ! sure you wouldn't hurt the poor afflicted crathur, that's that way from the cradle ; he stutters, Sir, he stutters. What is it, Paudh, avich ; take time and tell us."

The appearance of the whole group was highly ludicrous, eagerly and vainly watching for the tidings which the boy found it utterly impossible to articulate. At last the tinker roared out,

" Sing it you brat ;" and the boy availing himself of that well-known specific to his impediment, chanted forth in admirable style,

" The gauger is coming."

The effect was electric. In a moment the whole house was full of the half naked workmen ; each questioning the little informant as to the number, &c., of the enemy, which on discovering to be smaller than is usually sent out on such expeditions, they determined to face, and if possible compel them to retreat. The safety of all depended on this movement, which, however, could be only managed by stratagem, as almost the only weapon of worth amongst us was my gun, on which they did not seem much to rely, and which, at any rate, could be of but little avail against our well-armed opponents. We at once proceeded out on the side the enemy approached. A rude sort of ditch lay in their advance, and in the cover of that we were all drawn up, and the necessary directions given. The moon was pretty bright, and we could see them stealthily approaching, ignorant of our discovery of their intentions ; their number was so small as almost to invite more decisive operations ; for a moment that counsel was entertained, but, to my ineffable satisfaction, was abandoned, and the original one adhered to, in time enough to save some of our number from the gallows, and more from the bayonet. They were already within a few yards of the ditch, utterly unsuspecting its hostile contents, when a wild yell of defiance running along our line arrested their further progress, and was answered by a harmless volley over our heads from the whole detachment ; and then they wavered, and fulfilled my wishes at least, by a speedy retreat. At length, after seeing them, as we thought, fairly out of the neighbourhood, we ventured from our concealment ; and having enjoyed some hearty laughs at the expense of the disappointed excisemen, were about to return, when the quick eye of the tinker caught an object moving rather suspiciously in our direction. A hasty examination followed, and then the universally expressed opinion, that the soldiers had returned to the attack, most probably with such a reinforcement as it would be in vain to contend with. Retreat was the only measure proposed, and was acceded to by all but the distiller, who opposed it with prayers and entreaties, that we shouldn't leave him to the mercy of the soldiers, after his decent treatment, and suggesting the possibility of " Mr. ——— shooting the straggler beyant, bad fortune to him !"

Had he proposed to me to blow out my own brains I could not have been more astounded, and my too evident reluctance made him instantly change his ground.

" Oh, Shemus, agrah ! take the gun you, and shoot, for the boy is timid you see."

" Me shoot," shrieked the tinker ; " what do I know about yeer guns an' things, or any but this ; an' by this an' by that, I'll drive it into the coward's skull if he doesn't ; so shoot this minit, or"—at the same time brandishing his hammer over my head, ready to perform his horrid resolution if I persisted in my disobedience. The full misery of my situation presented itself to my awakened senses ; now for the first time the consequences of what I had looked on as a frolic began to assume a serious character, and the alternative of dying or murdering seemed inevitable. I looked round for assistance—there was none ; all gave a tacit consent to the motion, or shunned interference. Habitually indifferent whether I lived or died, I looked up almost for mercy to the tinker, and his grim eye glared on me full of decision, and the murderous hammer was poised ready for the descent. I grasped the gun nervously, and presented it. Had I attempted an aim I had most assuredly failed, such was my trepidation ; but the random shot succeeded. I did not, I could not see my success, for I fell back half senseless on the ditch ; but the unearthly groan that followed, and the glad shout of my comrades told me that I had saved my life, and was now—a murderer. They all rushed simultaneously forward to take advantage of the panic which they supposed one death would strike in the hearts of their opponents, and I was alone. I cannot exactly understand now, why the mere act of charitably sending a fellow creature out of this dirty world, should excite such misery in any man's mind : but that may be the effect of habit ; for nothing is more certain, than that in that moment of loneliness I underwent pangs which it would be madness to attempt describing. All bodily sense left me ; confused recollections of the comparative innocence and respectability of my past life, were placed in horrible contrast with the present and the future ; and all these were heightened by the loud laugh of joy that echoed in my ears from my savage companions when they had reached their murdered victim. It awakened me to a deeper sense of my guilt, and the cup was full when that laugh subsided from exhaustion, and the wild cries of the tinker broke on my ear, that but too well recognised them. Gracious heaven ! thought I, have I done a deed that even that wretch can mourn—this was too much : I reloaded my gun, and was about to finish my wretchedness, when the return of some of the party prevented me. The laugh was renewed, and they seemed very devils.

" You did it, Sir, you did it !" exclaimed one fellow, amid the convulsions of laughter. " You dhr v the ball through an' through him."

" Who ! who !" I shrieked, recovering the power of speech with an almost herculean effort, and the laugh rose louder than ever as I was answered,

" Shemus the tinker's jack ass."

CONTENT—A PASTORAL.

O'er moorlands and mountains, rude, barren, and bare,
　　As wilder'd and wearied I roam ;
A gentle young shepherdess sees my despair,
　　And leads me o'er lawns to her home.
Yellow sheaves from rich Ceres her cottage had crown'd ;
　　Green rushes were strew'd on her floor ;
Her casement sweet woodbines crept wantonly round,
　　And decked the sod-seats at her door.

We sat ourselves down to a cooling repast—
　　Fresh fruits ! and she cull'd me the best ;
Whilst thrown from my guard, by some glances she cast,
　　Love slily stole into my breast.
I told my soft wishes : she sweetly replied,
　　(Ye virgins, her voice was divine !)
I've rich ones rejected, and great ones denied,
　　Yet take me fond shepherd—I'm thine.

Her air was so modest, her aspect so meek,
　　So simple—yet sweet were her charms !

I kissed the ripe roses that glow'd on her cheek,
  And lock'd the lov'd maid in my arms.
Now jocund together, we tend a few sheep,
  And if, on the banks by the stream,
Reclined on her bosom I sink into sleep,
  Her image still softens my dream.

Together we range o'er the slow-rising hills,
  Delighted with pastoral views ;
Or rest on the rock whence the streamlet distils,
  And mark out new themes for my muse.
To pomp or proud title she ne'er did aspire,
  The damsel's of humble descent ;
The Cottager, Peace, is well known for her sire,
  And shepherds have named her Content.

M. H.

THE COMMON SEAL OR SEA-CALF.

(PHOCA VITULINA.)

The seal is often seen on our shores, and frequents the
estuaries of rivers. When full grown it commonly varies
in size from five to six feet in length, and is found with
some variety in every quarter of the globe. It is covered
with a short glossy fur, of a dark brown colour, sometimes
spotted. Formerly their skins were kept in houses as pre-
ventatives against the effects of thunder and lightning.

The fore legs of this animal are very short in proportion to the size of the body, and the front parts have a
considerable resemblance to those of land animals, but
the hinder part narrows off like a fish. The hind legs are
nearly united to the body, and lie backwards, like fins, on
each side of the tail. The feet are webbed, and on each
foot are five toes furnished with sharp claws, which enable the animal to climb the rocks, on which it is often
seen to bask. On those occasions the seals have always a
sentinel awake for fear of surprise. If alarmed, they swim
with great strength and swiftness.

Lively and gentle in its manner, it is easily tamed, it
seems even to feel affection, and is fond of the society of
men. Of its attachment several remarkable instances are
recorded, perhaps none of these more striking than the
following, which occurred in the neighbourhood of Porta-
ferry, county of Down, in the spring of 1822.

One fine morning, a farmer walking along the shore,
near the bay of Strangford, observed a young seal lying
in a grass plot. It was soon secured, as it made no effort
to get away, and he carried it home, put it into a barn,
and fed it on new milk. During the day it appeared
quite contented, but at night it expressed its uneasiness
by frightful screams.

The humane farmer, anxious to restore the animal to
its natural element and friends, took a boat and carried it
out to that part of the bay where seals were known to resort, about one mile from the place where it had been
taken ; and on putting it into the water, it immediately
disappeared. Early on the following morning the same
seal was observed within a few yards of the barn where it
had been lodged. It again suffered itself to be taken and
conducted to its former quarters, apparently well pleased
with the attentions of its host. It now seemed more contented than on its former visit, as it was less noisy at

night—it was again supplied with its former food—new
milk.

The farmer not relishing the visits of such a strange
pet, after a few days gave it away to a gentleman in Porta-
ferry, who kept it alternately in a house and garden. It
became familiar and followed him like a dog, and made
its way through the dust with evident difficulty from the
shortness of its legs. It died suddenly at the end of a few
weeks.

Belfast. W. W.

ON SOME OF THE WATER BIRDS FRE-QUENTING BELFAST LOUGH.

BY JAMES D. MARSHALL, ESQ., M. D.

The number of water birds which either constantly
reside on the shores of our extensive bay, or resort to it
at certain seasons of the year, is probably as large as in
any other harbour in Great Britain or Ireland. Of one
hundred and forty-three species mentioned as having
been found at any period, in any part of the British islands, there are eighty-three species which have been
found in our harbour. Many of these are residenters, but
the greater number are met with at the periods of their
respective migrations northward and southward. Our
harbour is not only extensive, but well sheltered ; and on
its shores, and the long ranges of banks which at low water are exposed, the *Grallatores*, or waders, find an ample supply of their respective foods ; while in the deep
waters the *Natatores*, or swimmers, are never at a loss
for small fish of various descriptions, which constitute
their principal mode of subsistence.

In the autumnal months our lough is annually visited
by immense flocks of wild geese. Brent geese, wigeon, and
others of the Natatores, which having completed the process of incubation in the Arctic regions, seek a milder climate for spending the winter. Directed by their instinctive knowledge, they leave their summer haunts, and in
innumerable crowds seek a southern residence. Arriving
at the northern coast of our island, they separate into
smaller flocks ; and some pursue their way into Larne,
Belfast, and Strangford loughs, while others go further
south, and find in the bays of Killough, Carlingford,
Dublin, Cork, &c., situations equally desirable, where they
remain till March or April, when they again desert our
shores for the wild, uninhabited districts near the pole.

Among the Grallatores, or waders, which are met with
in Belfast lough, the

COMMON HERON—*(Ardea Cinerea,)*

may be mentioned, as one of the most conspicuous. To
enter into any description of its plumage would be quite
superfluous, as it is a bird almost universally well known.
By the lower orders it is most frequently denominated
crane, although the latter is a totally different species
now extinct in Britain.

There is no bird better entitled " to claim the protection of the admirers of nature and picturesque scenery, from the striking effects its presence can produce in the solitary haunts in which it delights, and where it is most commonly found." When seen, it is usually standing immoveable in the shallows of rivers, on a stone on the edge of a pond, or on the bank recently deserted by the ebbing tide, its neck bent and drawn in between its shoulders, watching attentively the motions of its finny prey, upon which, when once within its reach, it darts with unerring aim, transfixing it by a single stroke of its sharp bill. So motionless does the heron remain when watching for its prey, (its eye intently fixed on the water below, eagerly seeking for the slightest ripple on the surface, or other indication of the vicinity of its victim,) that it is not unfrequently taken for the stump or root of an old tree. So wary is it when fishing, that it is seldom or never seen with its back towards the sun, by which a shadow would be thrown on the water, and affright the fish —but on the contrary, always places itself, when possible, in such an attitude that it resembles rather something inanimate.

Its food consists principally of fish, but it will eagerly devour frogs and other reptiles, and occasionally young water-rats and mice, &c. In the Magazine of Natural History, a case is mentioned of one of these birds, which had been run down by a boy in a marsh, and when opened, was found to have in its stomach a very large male water-rat. It had been lately swallowed, occupying, even to distension, (with portions of partially digested fish) the ventriculus of the heron. The only injury apparent to the rat, was a puncture, made by the beak of the heron, in the frontal part of the skull, by which life was destroyed. No evident cause of the easy capture of the bird existed, but the probable one of repletion.

In some countries this bird is migratory; but in Britain and Ireland it remains throughout the year. During winter they assemble in very small flocks on the shores of our rivers and bays, where they may be almost constantly seen during the day, retiring, for the most part, at night to the highest trees in the neighbourhood; although in moonlight nights the heron may not unfrequently be seen as eagerly watching its prey as during the clearer hours of the day. About the beginning of March they congregate in considerable numbers at their breeding stations, or heronries, where, from year to year, they resort for the purposes of incubation. These heronries are usually situated in some retired domain, where there are very lofty trees on which they can form their nests. The only two heronries with which I am acquainted in the vicinity of Belfast, are those at Sir Robert Bateson's and the Marquis of Downshire's : the former is situated on some very lofty poplars, at no great distance from the river which flows through the domain : that at Lord Downshire's is fixed on some trees in an island in one of the ponds ; a very suitable situation, where they may rear their young in safety, and where they are furnished with an abundant supply of necessary food. I visited that at Sir Robert Bateson's in the middle of March ; the birds were collecting in pairs on the trees, repairing old nests, or building new ones when necessary. Some were sitting in dull, listless attitudes, while others were busily engaged examining the future habitation of their young. They were much tamer than they usually are— allowing us to approach very near to them, without exhibiting those symptoms of alarm which at other periods of the year, and in other situations they invariably do. No bird, perhaps, possesses greater wariness than the heron ; and it is consequently a very difficult matter to approach within gun-shot. In our lough they always keep far beyond range of the gun from the shore, and if approached in a boat, they seem equally well aware of our hostile intention, and direct their motions accordingly. They are, however, occasionally surprized by the gunner ; and generally fall an easy victim, from the extent of surface presented to his view, and the slowness of their flight. When thus taken by surprise, they rise in the greatest alarm, uttering their peculiarly harsh cry ; a cry, when once heard by the sportsman, can never be forgotten. A few years ago, when fishing on one of the small rivers in the county of Antrim, I was rather alarmed by one of

these birds. The day was remarkably fine, and at the time I speak of, scarcely a cloud was to be seen ; I was standing on the bank of the stream, shaded from the sun by a small planting, and was intent on the capture of my flies by the wary trout. While my eyes were directed to the water, a dark, swift-moving shadow passed over that part of the river near which I stood. Startled, I looked up, and the moment I lifted my head, a loud, wild scream was uttered by a heron then passing over me It was within about four yards of me, and its flight had been so easy, and it so silent, that I was perfectly unconscious of its vicinity till I heard the scream it gave.— On being so unexpectedly disturbed in its flight, it raised itself as quickly as possible to a considerable height in the air, and pursued its journey towards the shores of Larne lough, whither it had been bound.

Towards high water some of these birds leave the shore and proceed up the rivers in their respective neighbourhoods, where frogs, with trout and other fish may be had, and where they remain till the tide begins to ebb, leaving the bank again uncovered, to which they regularly resort, till the returning flood drives them again inland.

The quantity of fish destroyed by the heron is very great. Willoughby has found no less than seventeen carp in the stomach of one ; and he has taken a fish nine inches and a half long from the stomach of another bird. It has been ascertained that one of these birds will devour, on an average, from forty to fifty small fish, such as roach or dace, in one day, and on such a calculation, about fifteen thousand a year. This, however, is the number calculated to be taken by a heron in a state of domestication, when plenty of food was always placed at its command. In its wild state, in fine weather, it can always procure a plentiful supply ; but in cold or stormy seasons its prey is no longer within its reach ; the fish now shunning the shallows, and keeping in deep water, finding it the warmer situation. Even frogs seldom leave their lurking places, and the poor heron is thus not unfrequently obliged to subsist on very scanty fare, and to have its patience severely tried.

However the Count de Buffon may be admired for the beauty of his writings, no one will hesitate to say, that in many cases the descriptions he has given of the state of animals is both distorted and exaggerated. He pourtrays the state of feelings in an animal, not as they really are to the animal, but as he himself would find them to be, were he in a similar situation. Now this mode of viewing the subject is totally incorrect. If to him an animal may have appeared to be placed in a situation of wretchedness instead of ease, he should have borne in mind that the Almighty Creator had endowed it with powers and feelings suitable to its situation ; and that in consequence one animal may partake of as much enjoyment as another, provided they both stand equally high in the scale of animated beings. Buffon, in speaking of the heron, describes it " as exhibiting the picture of wretchedness, anxiety, and indigence, condemned to struggle perpetually with misery and want, and sickened by the restless cravings of a famished appetite," &c.

To any person accustomed to view the different natural objects everywhere presented to him as so many indications of the goodness and wisdom of his Creator, the appearance of the heron would convey a very different idea. He would view it as a fine example of the adaptation of the instinct of animals to their respective modes of life.— Were the heron of a restless disposition—in constant motion from place to place—it would very frequently be totally deprived of the necessary supply of food ; but formed as it is, it will stand rooted to a spot for a very long time, apparently lifeless, though in fact it is in momentary expectation of its prey. Why should we imagine that it does not enjoy as much pleasure in such a situation as any other bird ; surely its Creator could render it as capable of enjoying as high a degree of pride and satisfaction in capturing its prey, however insignificant, as that experienced by the eagle or falcon in pursuing nobler game ! Each must feel happy in the situation allotted to it, and that man exhibits but little confidence in the wisdom and goodness of God, who can view in many of the various tribes of animals, only so many instances of defective formation, while their lives to him exhibit, from the moment of their birth, one uninterrupted chain of wretchedness and misery.

A PEEP AT DAYS GONE BY.

THREE ODD FELLOWS.

Dublin, January 20, 1749, " died in the Earl of Meath's Liberty, John Collier, aged 137 years."

" Dublin, January 16, 1754, " died of a violent match of *Funking*, Thomas Eclin, remarkable for his vivacity and drollery, and for eating of *living cats*, leaping into the river in frosty weather, and performing many shocking and unnatural tricks to please and excite wonder."

Dublin, February 17, 1761, " there is at present at New-Row in the Poddle, one Henry Golding, who has entered in the 20th year of his age, and measures only 27 inches in height."

STORMS IN DUBLIN AND CORK.

" Dublin, August 7, 1710—On Saturday we had the greatest fall of rain that has been known for many years, which continued all night, attended with a violent storm. The rain was so heavy that upwards of forty sparrows, who went to take shelter, were found in St. Mary's Church-yard, most of them dead, and in Mount Town one hundred and forty-three were found dead under some trees.

" Dublin, September 7, 1762—Last night and this morning we had a violent storm. In the College Park fourteen large trees were levelled to the ground, some of which were torn up by the roots, and others broken in the middle and carried to a considerable distance by the wind."

" Cork, January 30, 1749—The tide here on Sunday and last night swelled to so prodigious a height, that the whole city was under water. In the houses in Duncombs-marsh the water was four feet deep, and three in the middle of the city."

IRISH LEGEND.

In the church-yard of Erigle Truagh, in the barony of Truagh, county of Monaghan, there is said to be a spirit which appears to persons whose families are there interred. Its appearance, which is generally made in the following manner, is uniformly fatal, being an omen of death to those who are so unhappy as to meet with it. When a funeral takes place, it is said to watch the person who remains last in the grave-yard, over whom it possesses a fascinating influence. If the person be a young man, it takes the shape of a beautiful female, inspires him with a charmed passion, and exacts a promise that he will meet her in the church-yard on a month from that day ; this promise is sealed by a kiss, that communicates a deadly taint to the individual who complies. It then disappears, and no sooner does the individual from whom it received the promise and the kiss pass the boundary of the church-yard, than he remembers the history of the spectre—which is well known in the parish—sinks into despair and insanity, dies, and is buried in the place of appointment on the day when the promise was to have been fulfilled. If, on the contrary, it appears to a female, it assumes the form of a young man of exceeding elegance and beauty.

I was shown the grave of a young person about eighteen years of age, who was said about four months before to have fallen a victim to it: and it is not more than ten months since a man in the same parish declared that he gave the promise and the fatal kiss, and consequently looked upon himself as lost. He took a fever, died, and was buried on the day appointed for the meeting, which was exactly a month from that of the interview. Incredible as it may appear, the friends of these two persons solemnly declared—at least, those of the young man did to myself—that the particulars of the meeting were detailed repeatedly by the two persons, without the slightest variation. There are several cases of the same kind mentioned, but the two now alluded to are the only ones that came within my personal knowledge. It appears, however, that the spectre does not confine its operations to the church-yard only, as there have been instances

mentioned of its appearance at weddings and dances, where it never failed to secure its victims by dancing them into pleuritic fevers.

I am unable to say whether this is a strictly local superstition, or whether it is considered to be peculiar to other church-yards in Ireland, or elsewhere In its female shape it somewhat resembles the Elle maids of Scandinavia ; but I am acquainted with no account of fairies or apparitions in which the sex is said to be changed, except in that of the devil himself. The country people say it is death.

SIR TURLOUGH, OR THE CHURCH-YARD BRIDE.

The bride she bound her golden hair—
    Killeevy, O Killeevy !*
And her step was light as the breezy air
When it bends the morning flowers so fair,
    By the bonnie green woods of Killeevy.

And oh, but her eyes they danc'd so bright,
As she longed for the dawn of to-morrow's light,
Her bridal vows of love to plight,
    By the bonnie green woods of Killeevy.

The bridegroom is come with youthful brow,
To receive from his Eva her virgin vow ;
" Why tarries the bride of my bosom now?"
    By the bonnie green woods of Killeevy.

A cry ! a cry !—'twas her maidens spoke,
" Your bride is asleep—she has not awoke,
And the sleep she sleeps will never be broke,"
    By the bonnie green woods of Killeevy.

Sir Turlough sank down with a heavy moan,
And his cheek became like the marble stone—
" Oh, the pulse of my heart is for ever gone !"
    By the bonnie green woods of Killeevy.

The keen† is loud, it comes again,
And rises sad from the funeral train,
As in sorrow it winds along the plain,
    By the bonnie green woods of Killeevy.

And oh, but the plumes of white were fair,
When they flutter'd all mournful in the air,
As rose the hymn of the requiem prayer,‡
    By the bonnie green woods of Killeevy.

---

* In the original poem this line is repeated at each verse.
† The Irish cry, or wailing for the dead. Speaking of this practice, which still prevails in many parts of Ireland the Rev. A. Ross, rector of Dungiven, in his statistical survey of that parish, observes that " however it may offend the judgment or shock our present refinement, its affecting cadences will continue to find admirers wherever what is truly sad and plaintive can be relished or understood." It is also thus noticed by the author of " Traits and Stories of the Irish Peasantry :"

" I have often, indeed always, felt that there is something exceedingly touching in the Irish cry ; in fact, that it breathes the very spirit of wild and natural sorrow. The Irish peasantry, whenever a death takes place, are exceedingly happy in seizing upon any contingent circumstances that may occur, and making them subservient to the excitement of grief for the departed, or the exaltation and praise of his character and virtues. My entrance was a proof of this ; for I had scarcely advanced to the middle of the floor. when my intimacy with the deceased, our boyish sports, and even our quarrels, were adverted to with a natural eloquence and pathos, that, in spite of my firmness, occasioned me to feel the prevailing sorrow. They spoke, or chanted mournfully, in Irish ; but the substance of what they said was as follows :—' Oh, avourneen ! you're lying low this mornin' of sorrow ! lying low are you, and does not know who it is (alluding to me) that is standin' over you, weepin' for the days you spent together in your youth ! It's yourself, *acushla agus asthore machree*, (the pulse and beloved of my heart) that would stretch out the right hand warmly to welcome him to the place of his birth. where you had both been so often happy about the green hills and valleys with each other !' They then passed on to an enumeration of his virtues as a father, a husband, son, and brother—specified his worth as he stood related to society in general, and his kindness as a neighbour and a friend."

‡ It is usual in the North of Ireland to celebrate mass for the dead in some green field between the house in which the

There is a voice that but one can hear,
And it softly pours, from behind the bier,
Its note of death on Sir Turlough's ear,
 By the bonnie green woods of Killeevy.

The keen is loud, but that voice is low,
And it sings its song of sorrow slow,
And names young Turlough's name with woe,
 By the bonnie green woods of Killeevy.

Now the grave is closed, and the mass is said,
And the bride she sleeps in her lonely bed,
The fairest corpse among the dead*,
 By the bonnie green woods of Killeevy.

The wreaths of virgin-white are laid,
By virgin hands, o'er the spotless maid ;
And the flowers are strewn, but they soon will fade,†
 By the bonnie green woods of Killeevy.

" Oh go not yet—not yet away,
Let us feel that *life* is near our clay,"
The long-departed seem to say,
 By the bonnie green woods of Killeevy.

But the tramp and the voices of *life* are gone,
And beneath each cold forgotten stone,
The mouldering dead sleep all alone,
 By the bonnie green woods of Killeevy.

But who is he who lingereth yet?
The fresh green sod with his tears is wet,
And his heart in the bridal grave is set,
 By the bonnie green woods of Killeevy.

Oh, who but Sir Turlough, the young and brave,
Should bend him o'er that bridal grave,
And to his death-bound Eva reave,
 By the bonnie green woods of Killeevy.

" Weep not—weep not," said a lady fair,
" Should youth and valour thus despair,
And pour their vows to the empty air ?"
 By the bonnie green woods of Killeevy.

There's charmed music upon her tongue,
Such beauty—bright and warm and young—
Was never seen the maids among.
 By the bonnie green woods of Killeevy.

A laughing light, a tender grace,
Sparkled in beauty around her face,
That grief from mortal heart might chace,
 By the bonnie green woods of Killeevy.

The charm is strong upon Turlough's eye,
His faithless tears are already dry,
And his yielding heart has ceased to sigh,
 By the bonnie green woods of Killeevy.

" The maid for whom thy salt tears fall,
Thy grief or love can ne'er recall ;
She rests beneath that grassy pall,
 By the bonnie green woods of Killeevy.

" My heart it strangely cleaves to thee
And now that thy plighted love is free,
Give its unbroken pledge to me,
 By the bonnie green woods of Killeevy."

" To thee," the charmed chief replied,
" I pledge that love o'er my buried bride ;
Oh ! come, and in Turlough's hall abide,"
 By the bonnie green woods of Killeevy.

Again the funeral voice came o'er
The passing breeze, as it wailed before,

And streams of mournfu music bore,
 By the bonnie green woods of Killeevy.

" If I to thy youthful heart am dear,
One month from hence thou wilt meet me here,
Where lay thy bridal, Eva's bier,"
 By the bonnie green woods of Killeevy.

He pressed her lips as the words were spoken,
And his *banshee's** wail—now far and broken—
Murmur'd " Death," as he gave the token,
 By the bonnie green woods of Killeevy ;

" Adieu ! adieu !" said this lady bright,
And she slowly passed like a thing of light,
Or a morning cloud, from Sir Turlough's sight,
 By the bonnie green woods of Killeevy.

Now Sir Turlough has death in every vein,
And there's fear and grief o'er his wide domain,
And gold for those who will calm his brain,
 By the bonnie green woods of Killeevy.

" Come, haste thee, leech, right swiftly ride,
Sir Turlough the brave, Green Truagh's pride,
Has pledged his love to the church-yard bride,"
 By the bonnie green woods of Killeevy.

The leech groaned loud, " come tell me this,
By all thy hopes of weal and bliss,
Has Sir Turlough given the fatal kiss ?"
 By the bonnie green woods of Killeevy.

" The banshee's cry is loud and long,
At eve she weeps her funeral song,
And it floats on the twilight breeze along,"
 By the bonnie green woods of Killeevy.

" Then the fatal kiss is given ;—the last
Of Turlough's race and name is past,
His doom is seal'd, his die is cast,"
 By the bonnie green woods of Killeevy

" Leech, say not that thy skill is vain ;
Oh, calm the power of his frenzied brain,
And half his lands thou shalt retain,"
 By the bonnie green woods of Killeevy.

The leech has failed, and the hoary priest
With pious shrift his soul releas'd,
And the smoke is high of his funeral feast,
 By the bonnie green woods of Killeevy.

The shanachies† now are assembled all,
And the songs of praise, in Sir Turlough's hall,
To the sorrowing harp's dark music fall,
 By the bonnie green woods of Killeevy.

And there is trophy, banner, and plume,
And the pomp of death, with its darkest gloom,
O'ershadow's the Irish chieftain's tomb,
 By the bonnie green woods of Killeevy.

The month is clos'd, and Green Truagh's pride,
Is married to death—and side by side,
He slumbers now with his church-yard bride,
 By the bonnie green woods of Killeevy.

---

* Treating of the superstitions of the Irish, Miss Balfour says, " What rank the *banshee* holds in the scale of spiritual beings, it is not easy to determine ; but her favourite occupation seems to be that of foretelling the death of the different branches of the families over which she presided, by the most plaintive cries. Many stories to this purpose are related by the lower Irish ; and even Christianity has not been able to destroy those superstitious ideas." Every family had formerly its banshee, but the belief in her existence is now fast fading away, and in a few more years she will only be remembered in the storied records of her marvellous doings in days long since gone by."
† The shanachies were those who recorded the exploits of great men, and recounted their deeds previous to their interment.

---

deceased lived and the grave-yard. For this the shelter of a grove is usually selected, and the appearance of the ceremony is highly picturesque and solemn, exhibiting that melancholy beauty for which this rite of the Church of Rome is so remarkable.
* Another expression peculiarly Irish, 'What a purty corpse !'—' How well she becomes death !' ' You wouldn't meet a purtier corpse of a summer's day !' ' She bears the change well !' are all phrases quite common in cases of death among the peasantry.
† These ceremonies are not peculiar to Ireland ; except the wreaths of white paper, which are more frequent here than in the sister kingdom.

DUBLIN:
Printed and Published by P. D. HARDY. 3, Cecilia-street ; to whom all communications are to be addressed.
Sold by all Booksellers in Ireland.
In London, by Richard Groombridge, 6, Panyer-alley, Paternoster-row ; in Liverpool, by Willmer and Smith ; in Manchester, by Ambery, in Birmingham, by Drake ; in Glasgow, by W. R. M'Phun ; and in Edinburgh, by N. Bowack.

THE
DUBLIN PENNY JOURNAL

CONDUCTED BY P. DIXON HARDY, M.R.I.A.

| Vol. III. | JULY 19, 1834. | No. 107. |

Sketched by A. Nicholl, Esq.

NARROW WATER CASTLE.

The scenery along the shores of Rostrevor and Carlingford Bay is of the most varied and delightful description. To the 4th and 96th Numbers of our former Journals we must refer the reader for a minute description of some of the more prominent objects along this line of our northern coast. The Castle of Narrow Water, of which the above presents a faithful view, is only interesting as adding much to the effective beauty of the scenery with which it is surrounded. It is situated within about 2½ miles of Newry, on the Narrow Water river. It was some years ago converted into a salt work, and more recently (since the duty was taken off English salt) into a kennel for a pack of hounds. To the right, in the distance, are the Carlingford mountains; towards the opening of the bay appears the picturesque village of Rostrevor, and to the left the mountains of Mourne. The castle itself is an insignificant building, originally erected to defend the passage across the river, which narrows very much at this particular point.

THE BATTLE OF THE FROGS.

DEAR SIR—The following particulars relative to a more extraordinary occurrence than I have read or heard of in the *natural* world, I published a few years ago in one of the Dublin papers, in the hope of eliciting some remarks as to the cause of so singular a proceeding among animals I had always, till then, considered as the "meekest and mildest" of the animal creation; but not having succeeded in my wish in getting the subject taken up, I am induced to state the case to you, in order, if you should consider the matter worthy of investigation, that for the information of the *unlearned* in this kind of *ology*, you will give it insertion in your entertaining periodical.

Early in the month of April, 1821, during an evening's walk in the neighbourhood of Hitchin, in Hertfordshire, in company with a friend, our attention was arrested by an unusually loud croaking of frogs, which proceeded from a piece of stagnant water, a little distance from the path. The first impulse of our astonishment was communicated by an idea of the vast number which must exist to produce a noise so loud and discordant; but on our proceeding to the spot, our amazement was increased beyond the power of expression, by observing that, in every direction, at the bottom of an extensive pond, were to be seen many hundreds of the little animals dying, or dead; some swollen to a size three or four times their original bulk; and several with a part of their intestines appearing through their perforated bodies. Many hundreds had been killed outright, but by far the greater number were still gasping for life, apparently in the greatest torment. In the midst of this extraordinary scene, we observed numerous masses, coagulated, as it were, into lumps, some of which we drew to land, and with difficulty separated with our walking sticks, and found them to contain, as a common centre, one of their own species, bloated to an inconceivable size, (which, had I not seen, I would not have believed to be possible,) either dead or in a dying state. An evident contention of the most determined and destructive nature had prevailed among these, and lesser masses, as they floated about over the expanse of death and destruction that lay around and beneath them. My friend having suggested the idea of the possibility of its being a contest between frogs and toads, we at once satisfied ourselves on the point ; but on examining most carefully the belligerents, we found them so completely to correspond both in shape and colour, that no doubt could be admitted of their all belonging to the same species. The battle so celebrated by the immortal Homer, was, in fact, a "trifle light as air" to this contest : his was but the creation of an exuberant fancy—here was flesh and blood in reality.

Hoping, Sir, that the occurrence may meet the eye of some naturalist who will be able to enter more at length into the merits of the case, I remain yours, faithfully,

A. De B.

Cottage Terrace, June, 1834.

POPULAR LECTURES ON THE PHYSIOLOGY OF ANIMALS,

The following is an abstract of Dr. Henry's second Lecture :

The scarf, or *outside* skin, which is that we touch by laying the hand on our body, is, excepting on the palms and soles, nearly transparent ; the true skin under it is red, being full of minute blood-vessels carrying red blood. How, then, are we to account for the different colours in the human race ; white, black, tawney, red, copper, yellow,-&c ? There is an intermediate substance between the scarf or outer, and true skin, called the mucous network, of very delicate texture, and carrying in its meshes a coloured pigment or paint. In the negro this network is very much developed ; and the coloring matter contained in its interstices is of a deep black, which being seen through the nearly transparent outer skin, gives the black colour to the negro. On the palms and soles of the Negro, the outer skin is so thick as scarcely to allow this pigment to be seen through it, and therefore these parts of his body have the dirty white colour of the scarf-skin, rendered a little darker only by the pigment being seen very indistinctly through it. In the white man this network is much thinner, and more delicate, and has a slightly grey tinge : the color of the white is the result of the combined colors of the nearly transparent outer skin and net-work, with the red color of the true skin seen dimly through them. The use of the coloring matter is to protect the sensitive and delicate parts underneath from the influence of light, as that of the outer, or scarf-skin, is to protect the same parts from the effects of friction and pressure ; we, therefore, find it, like the scarf-skin, produced according to the occasion for it. The skin becomes first freckled, then tanned, and then swarthy by exposure to the light, and reverts to its original state again when the light is excluded. An argument has been drawn against the truth of that history, which refers all mankind to one common stock, from the extreme difference of colour between the European and Negro : but this argument is founded on an imperfect consideration of the subject. It is true, indeed, that the Negro child is of a very dark colour in the womb, and becomes black soon after birth ; but this does not prove that there must always have been a black race of men, for that colour might have been gradually acquired in the course of many generations, until at last it became hereditary ; or what is more probable, the black, or at least a dark colour, may have been the colour of the original stock, and his may, on the one hand, have degenerated into white, and on the other hand have become developed under accidental circumstances of climate and clothing, until it became in some races quite black.* The true skin varies in thickness, being strong where strength is required, and thin on those parts not much exposed to friction. As the true skin contains a multitude of blood-vessels, carrying red blood, it contributes much to the colour of the face, especially of the cheeks, in those races where the pigment

---

* In confirmation of this opinion it may be further observed, that the division of the human race into black and white is not correct, the colour varying from white to black through an infinite variety of intermediate shades, yellow, brown, red, tawny, &c., &c., and these shades again running into each other by insensible gradations.

---

is almost imperceptible, as in the white man. Under excitement of mind, or exercise of body, the blood flows in increased quantities to the skin, producing the flushed face ; while, under depressing passions, as fear, and under fatigue, the vessels of the skin become less full, and paleness is the result. The paleness is extreme in fainting, during which the blood-vessels become nearly as empty as in death. These changes of colour are much less perceptible in the dark-colored races, because in them the pigment interposes a veil between the eye and the blood-vessels. In some animals the changes of color are very remarkable ; as in the Chameleon, the tubercles of whose skin being yellow, when the animal is seen in a quiescent state, it appears of that colour, but when irritated, the blood flows in great quantities to the skin, and being seen through the transparent yellow tubercles, the purple colour of the blood united to the yellow of the tubercles gives the animal a green colour.

The use of the skin is to protect the internal parts ; this appears more obviously in those animals who have thicker hides than it does in man. We make garments of the hides of other animals. The skin is not only a protecting organ, but also a secreting or producing one. It produces those bulbs in the skin from which hair grows, the pigment that protects the internal parts from light, the outer skin, and also an oily substance which causes the water of a bath to gather in drops on the skin, as it does upon an oiled table. Some persons, who abound much in this secretion, come nearly dry out of a bath : it is most abundant, where there is hair, as on the scalp ; and its use is to soften the hair, to render it pliant, and prevent it from cracking or chapping It is produced by little follicles, crypts or bags embedded in the skin, which in some situations, as about the lips and nose, are so distinct that the fatty matter, when concreted in them, can be squeezed out in the form of little worms.—Sometimes these follicles become so distended as to inflame, and thus disfigure the countenance greatly. This oily secretion renders the use of soap, in washing the body, necessary ; and it is so abundant in woolly animals, as sheep, that much trouble is required to cleanse it, and fit it for manufacture. The large gland, which birds have for the production of oil, has been already mentioned. Another important use of the skin is the production of perspiration, which in health is always going on from the surface of the body, generally in a state of vapour, and not sensibly, but when increased in quantity, this vapour, especially in cold weather, becomes condensed, and is visible in the form of water called *sweat.*

This subject will be continued in the next.

ON MUSIC.

There is a language in the tone,
   Which breathes from music's string ;
It speaks of years for ever flown,
   Of youth's hesperient spring !
There is a language in the peal—
   The cadence of its wire ;
Then memory's cup doth fondly deal
   Its spirit-soothing fire !

I've felt, I've own'd its charm divine,
   As sorrow damp'd my brow ;
When friendship coo'd at friendship's shrine—
   When cross'd its deepest vow !
How soothing when at pensive calm
   Of eve's ambrosial hour,
It oft flings round my soul a balm
   Of sympathetic power !

What spot of earth, say, shall we find
   Without its magic spell ?
Its voice is in the varying wind—
   It breathes in Ocean's swell ;
Its voice is in the warbling rill,
   In marble cave 'twill sigh ;
In grove, in glen, its language still
   Echoes from earth to sky !

                        AMOLINA.

IRISH SUPERSTITIONS.

Sir,—As the following superstitious practices, which were very prevalent some short time since in this part of our island, are now flitting fast away in the march of intellect, it may not be uninteresting to some of your readers to know that such things were at one time looked upon as matters of great importance :

Never to stand at the door of a house while a funeral is passing.

If your friend is going on a journey, not to neglect throwing your slipper after him, as he will then have success.

If the fire burns at one side of the grate, and not at the other, some one will soon leave the house.

If a coal or cinder flies out of the fire towards any particular person, that person will get a purse soon if it is round and hollow, and a coffin, if it is long and hollow.

Never relate a story in the day-time, or whistle at night.

Never attempt to churn milk without putting three pinches of salt into the churn, mentioning, at the same time, the three Persons of the Trinity.

Should you find it difficult to churn butter, go to a boundary river, that is, a river which separates one parish from another, and get a mouth full of the water, and put it on the ground under the churn, and, without doubt, your butter will soon gather ; or put the churn behind the door, or put the poker in the fire, or make the sign of the cross with the staff.

When you hear a person speak in his sleep, put his hand into a basin of warm water, and he'll tell you all his secrets.

If a nail should enter your foot, prevent it if possible from getting rusty, or the foot will mortify.

Go to a tree full of leaves nine mornings, fasting, and tell it a dream, and at the termination of that time, there will not be a single leaf on the tree—it will be quite withered and faded.

Never tell a dream fasting to any living person.

If you walk backwards, or look into a looking-glass at night, you will certainly see Old Nick.

To see one magpye is sorrow, and two is mirth ; Three is a wedding, and four is a birth.

When a dog howls opposite a house at midnight, some one in that house will soon die.

If a raven hovers over a house and croaks, some one in that house will soon die.

If an infant, before it is christened, is fed out of a raven's scull, it will ever after be able to understand what ravens say, or the raven's language.

If a child, whose parents are unknown, is fed with a raven's scull, when it comes to maturity it will be acquainted with every thing concerning them.

If you find a pod, with nine peas in it, and put it behind the door, the first person that comes in, will be the name of your husband or wife.

When you perceive the new moon on the first night, turn what money you may have in your pocket, saying three times, " God bless the new moon," and spitting on the money.

If you keep water in a house after washing your feet, the fairies will be washing in it all night.

A crowing hen, and a whistling woman, are not fit to be kept about a house.

When moving into a new house, let the first things you bring into it be a little coal and salt.

MITES.

Mites are those very small creatures generally found in great abundance in decayed cheese. To the naked eye they appear like moving particles of dust ; but the microscope discovers them to be animals perfect in all their members—as perfect as creatures that exceed them many millions of times in bulk.

They are usually transparent. Their principal parts are head, neck, and body. The head is small in proportion to the body, with a sharp snout, and a mouth that opens like a mole's. They have two little eyes, and are extremely quick-sighted. If you touch them but once with a pin or needle, you will perceive how readily they avoid a second touch. Some have six legs, and others eight, which proves that there are different sorts, though in every other respect they appear alike. Each leg has six joints, surrounded with hairs, and two little claws at the extremity thereof, which can easily take up any thing. The hinder part of the body is plump and bulky, and ends in an oval form, with a few exceedingly long hairs growing therefrom. Other parts of the body and head are thinly set with hairs.

The female mite lays eggs so small, that ninety-one millions and one hundred thousand of them would not be larger than a common pigeon's egg. The young ones come out of the shell with all their members perfect ; and though they cast their skins several times before they are full-grown, yet they do not alter in shape. Their eggs, in warm weather, hatch in twelve or fourteen days ; but in winter, or cold weather, not under several weeks.

Mites are voracious animals, and will devour not only cheese, but fish, flesh, fruit, grain of all sorts, and almost every thing that is moist, without being over wet ; nay, they may, sometimes be seen preying on one another.

It must be remembered that there are several kinds of mites, differing in some things, though in general nature and appearance the same. For instance, mites in malt-dust and oatmeal are nimbler than cheese-mites. The mites among figs have two feelers at the snout, and two very long horns over them, with three legs on each side, and are more sluggish than those in malt.

PRESSURE OF FLUIDS.

In any fluid the particles that are below bear the weight of those that are above, and there is therefore a pressure among them increasing in exact proportion to the perpendicular depth, and not influenced by the size, or shape, or position of the containing vessel.

The atoms of matter having gravity, it is evident that the upper layer of any mass of fluid must be supported by the second, and this, with its load, by the third, and the third, with its double load, by the fourth, and so on.

A tube, of which the area is an inch square, holds, in two feet of its length, nearly a pound of water ; hence, the general truth, well worth recollecting, that the pressure of water at any depth, whether on the side of a vessel or on its bottom, or any body immersed, is nearly one pound on the square inch for every two feet of depth. The striking effects from the increase of pressure in a fluid, at great depths, are of course most commonly exhibited at sea. The following instances will illustrate them :

If a strong, square glass bottle, empty and firmly corked, be sunk in water, its sides are generally crushed inwards by the pressure before it reaches a depth of ten fathoms. A chamber of air, similarly let down, with a man in it, would soon allow him to be drowned by the water bursting in upon him, as really happened to an ignorant projector.

When a ship founders in shallow water, the wreck, on breaking to pieces, generally comes to the surface, and is cast upon the beach ; but when the accident happens in deep water, the great pressure at the bottom forces water into the pores of the wood, and makes it so heavy that no part can ever rise again to reveal her fate.—*Arnot's Physics.*

Captain Scoresby, in the course of his experiments on the impregnation of wood with sea-water, let down a strong oblong vessel of copper to a depth of 5040 feet, and allowed it to remain an hour and a half, but the enormous pressure to which it was subjected, being about 50 tons, (a ton per square inch), crushed the vessel, though every part was an arch, into an irregular flat form, and tore the copper in four different places.

CONJUGAL AFFECTION.

FROM THE GERMAN OF GELLERT.

The tender-hearted Araminta loved her husband sincerely, for they had been but two months married ; he constituted her sole felicity—their desires and aversions were the same. It was Araminta's study, by diligent attention, to anticipate her husband's wishes. " Such a wife," says my male reader, who entertains thoughts of matrimony, "such a wife would I desire"—and such a wife may'st thou possess. Araminta's husband fell sick of a very dangerous malady. "No hope," said the physician, and shook his awful wig. Bitterly wept Araminta. "Oh, Death! might I prefer a petition? Spare, oh spare my husband, and let me be the victim in his stead!"

Death, to her astonishment, straight appeared. "And what," cried the grim tyrant, "is thy request?" "There," said Araminta, trembling with fear and amazement, "there he lies, pierced with intolerable agony; he implores thy speedy relief—put him instantly out of his misery."

Engraved by Clayton.   Sketched by A. Nichol, Esq.

RUINS OF BALLAGH CHURCH.

The above interesting ruin lies at the foot of the Mourne mountains, near Newcastle. It is another of those picturesque objects of which we spoke in a former Number, in describing the bold and magnificent line of coast from Rostrevor to Tullymore Park, and to which we shall have occasion again to allude in some future article.

LOVER'S LEGENDS AND STORIES.

Well had it been for Mr. Samuel Lover's fair fame had he rested satisfied with the success of his *first volume* of Legends and Stories. His *Second Series*, the work now before us, we pronounce a decided failure. The stories which Mr. Lover picked up through the country, and by the *viva voce* recitation of which he was in the habit of enlivening the social circle, there can be no question he has in his first volume transferred to *print* in an admirable manner. The stories in the present volume are altogether of another character or description, and, with a single exception, are any thing but good. In truth, Mr. Lover appears incapable of writing an original story: the Spanish Boar and the Irish Bull, an attempt at originality, is one of the most miserable things we have ever seen in print. The "Fairy Finder" is little more than another version of the "Leprawhaun," which appeared in the 91st Number of our Journal. Barny O'Reardon is certainly the best in the volume, and yet this, besides having appeared in the University Magazine, the curious reader will find (the perfect skeleton of it at least) in the last edition of "Joe Miller." "The Legend of the White Horse of the Peppers" is the second best, and from the extract we give of it, our readers may form their own opinion of the merits of the work.

In speaking of "Irish Story Tellers," we have more than once heard individuals institute a comparison relative to the merits of Carleton and Lover. It has ever been our decided and avowed opinion, an opinion which we consider fully borne out by the present volume and a volume just published by Carleton, that in this consists the difference between the "Traits and Stories of the Irish Peasantry" by the latter, and the "Legends and Stories" of the former, that Carleton is no mere retailer of stories he has heard—he sketches from life, with the boldness and vigour of an original artist; while Lover can re-tell a story he himself has heard, but at the same time appears altogether deficient of the prime ingredient in an Irish story-teller—there is nothing whatever of originality in any of his sketches; wherever he has attempted this, the failure is at once apparent. Why he should have brought out the present volume unaccompanied by illustrations similar to those which carried off so many of his former series, we cannot imagine. The wood-cuts are excellent in their way, they are, however, but poor substitutes for the spirited outline sketches on copper with which the first volume was illustrated. In reference to remarks which we have observed in some Irish periodicals relative to the work being published in England, we think it only fair to state that it is within the compass of our own knowledge, that Mr. Lover was offered for the second series, by the Dublin publisher who purchased his first series, a sum much beyond what we feel quite convinced the book will ever produce; and while there can be no blame to Mr. Lover for making the most of his writings, we think it scarcely fair to blame the Irish publishers for not giving more for the copy-right than they might consider its real value.

THE WHITE HORSE OF THE PEPPERS.

A LEGEND OF THE BOYNE.

"A horse! a horse! my kingdom for a horse!"

It was the night of the 2d of July, in the year 1690, that a small remnant of a discomfited army was forming its position, in no very good order, on the slope of a wild hill on the borders of the county of Dublin. In front of a small square tower, a sentinel was pacing up and down, darkly brooding over the disastrous fight of the preceding day, and his measured tread was sometimes broken by the fierce stamp of his foot upon the earth, as some bitter thought and muttered curse arose, when the feelings of the man overcame the habit of the soldier. The hum of the arrival of a small squadron of horse came from the vale below, borne up the hill on the faint breeze that sometimes freshens a summer's night, but the laugh, or the song, that so often enliven a military post, mingled not with the sound. The very trumpet seemed to have lost the inspiring tingle of its tone, and its blast sounded heavily on the ear of the sentinel.

"There come more of our retreating comrades," thought he, as he stalked before the low portal it was his duty to guard.—"Retreating—curse the word!—shall we never do any thing but fall back and back before this Dutchman and his followers? And yesterday, too, with so fine an opportunity of cutting the rascals to pieces,—and all thrown away, and so much hard fighting to go for nothing. Oh, if Sarsefield had led us! we'd have another tale to tell." And here he struck the heavy heel of his war boot into the ground, and hurried up and down.—But he was roused from his angry musing by the sound of a horse's tramp that indicated a rapid approach to the tower, and he soon perceived, through the gloom, a horseman approaching at a gallop. The sentinel challenged the cavalier, who returned the countersign, and was then permitted to ride up to the door of the tower. He was mounted on a superb charger, whose silky coat of milk white was much travel-stained, and the heaviness of whose breathing told of recent hard riding. The horseman alighted: his dress was of a mixed character, implying that war was not his profession, though the troubled nature of the times had engaged him in it. His head had no defensive covering, he wore the slouched hat of a civilian common to the time, but his body was defended by the cuirass of a trooper, and a heavy sword, suspended by a broad cross belt, was at his side—these alone bespoke the soldier, for the large and massively mounted pistols that protruded from the holsters at his saddle-bow, were no more than any gentleman, at the time, might have been provided with.

"Will you hold the rein of my horse," said he to the sentry, "while I remain in the castle?"

"I am a sentinel, Sir," answered the soldier, "and cannot."

"I will not remain more than a few minutes."

"I dare not, Sir, while I'm on duty—but I suppose you will find some one in the castle that will take charge of your horse."

The stranger now knocked at the door of the tower, and after some questions and answers in token of amity had passed between him and those inside, it was opened.

"Let some one take charge of my horse," said he, "I do not want him to be stabled, as I shall not remain here long, but I have ridden him hard, and he is warm, so let him be walked up and down until I am ready to get into the saddle again." He then entered the tower, and was ushered into a small and rude apartment, where a man of between fifty and sixty years of age, seated on a broken chair, though habited in a rich *robe de chambre*, was engaged in conversation with a general officer, a man of fewer years, whose finger was indicating certain points upon a map, which, with many other papers, lay on a rude table before them. Extreme dejection was the prevailing expression that overspread the countenance of the elder, while there mingled with the sadness that marked the noble features of the other, a tinge of subdued anger, as certain suggestions he offered, when he laid his finger, from time to time, on the map, were received with coldness, if not with refusal.

"Here at least we can make a bold stand," said the general, and his eye flashed, and his brow knit as he spoke.

"I fear not, Sarsefield," said the king, for it was the unfortunate James the Second who spoke.

Sarsefield withdrew his hand suddenly from the map, and folding his arms, became silent.

"May it please you, my liege," said the horseman, whose entry had not been noticed by either Sarsefield or his sovereign. "I hope I have not intruded on your majesty."

"Who speaks?" said the king, as he shaded his eyes from the light that burned on the table, and looked into the gloom where the other was standing.

"Your enemies, my liege," said Sarsefield, with some bitterness, "would not be so slow to discover a tried friend of your majesty—'tis the White Horseman;" and Sarsefield, as he spoke, gave a look full of welcome and joyous recognition towards him.

The horseman felt, with the pride of a gallant spirit, all that the general's look and manner conveyed, and he bowed his head, respectfully, to the leader, whose boldness and judgment he so often had admired.

"Ha! my faithful White Horseman," said the king.

"Your majesty's poor and faithful subject, Gerald Pepper," was the answer.

"You have won the name of the White Horseman," said Sarsefield, "and you deserve to wear it."

The horseman bowed.

"The general is right," said the king. "I shall never remember you under any other name. You and your white horse have done good service."

"Would that they could have done more, my liege," was the laconic and modest reply.

"Would that every one," laying some stress on the word, "had been as true to the cause *yesterday!*" said Sarsefield.

"And what has brought you here?" said the king, anxious perhaps to escape from the thought that his general's last words had suggested.

"I came, my liege, to ask permission to bid your majesty farewell, and beg the privilege to kiss your royal hand."

"Farewell?" echoed the king, startled at the word.—"Are *you*, too, going?—every one deserts me!" There was intense anguish in the tone of his voice, for, as he spoke, his eye fell upon a ring he wore, which encircled the portrait of his favourite daughter, Anne, and the remembrance that she, *his own child*, had excited the same remark from the lips of her father—that bitter remembrance came across his soul and smote him to the heart. He was suddenly silent—his brow contracted—he closed his eyes in anguish, and *one* bitter tear sprang from under either lid at the thought. He passed his hand across his face, and wiped away the womanish evidence of his weakness.

"Do not say I desert you, my liege," said Gerald

Pepper. " I leave you, 'tis true, for the present, but I do not leave you until I can see no way in which I can be longer useful. While in my own immediate district, there were many ways in which my poor services might be made available ; my knowledge of the county, of its people and its resources, its passes and its weak points, were of service. But here, or farther southward, where your majesty is going, I can no longer do any thing which might win the distinction that your majesty and General Sarsefield are pleased to honour me with."

" You have still a stout heart, a clear head, a bold arm, and a noble horse," said Sarsefield.

" I have also a weak woman and helpless children, general," said Gerald Pepper.

The appeal was irresistible—Sarsefield was silent.

" But though I cannot longer aid with my arm—my wishes and my prayers shall follow your majesty—and whenever I may be thought an agent to be made useful, my king has but to command the willing services of his subject."

" Faithfully promised," said the king.

" The promise shall be as faithfully kept," said his follower ; " but before I leave, may I beg the favour of a moment's private conversation with your majesty ?"

" Speak any thing you have to communicate before Sarsefield," said the king.

Gerald Pepper hesitated for a moment ; he was struggling between his sovereign's command and his own delicacy of feeling ; but overcoming the latter, in deference to the former, he said—

" Your majesty's difficulties with respect to money supplies."

" I know, I know," said the king, somewhat impatiently, " I owe you five hundred pieces."

" Oh ! my liege," said the devoted subject, dropping on his knee before him, " deem me not so unworthy as to seek to remind your majesty of the trifle you did me honour to allow me to lay at your disposal ; I only regret I had not the means of contributing more. It is not that ; but I have brought here another hundred pieces, it is all I can raise at present, and if your majesty will further honour me by the acceptance of so poor a pittance, when the immediate necessities of your army may render every trifle a matter of importance, I shall leave you with a more contented spirit, conscious that I have done all within my power for my king." And, as he spoke, he laid on a table a purse containing the gold.

" I cannot deny that we are sorely straitened," said the king, " but I do not like."

" Pray do not refuse it, my liege," said Gerald, still kneeling—" do not refuse the last poor service your subject may ever have it in his power to do in your cause."

" Well," said the king, " I accept it—but I would not do so if I were not sure of having, one day, the means of rewarding your loyalty and generosity." And thus allowing himself to be the dupe of his own fallacious hopes, he took from poor Gerald Pepper the last hundred guineas he had in his possession, with that happy facility that kings have always exhibited in accepting sacrifices from enthusiastic and self-devoted followers.

" My mission here is ended now," said Gerald. " May I be permitted to kiss my sovereign's hand ?"

" Would that all my subjects were as faithful," said James, as he held out his hand to Gerald Pepper, who kissed it respectfully, and then arose.

" What do you purpose doing when you leave me ?" said the king.

" To return to my home as soon as I may, my liege."

" If it be my fate to be driven from my kingdom by my unnatural son-in-law, I hope he may be merciful to my people, and that none may suffer from their adherence to the cause of their rightful sovereign."

" I wish, my liege," said Gerald, " that he may have half the consideration for his Irish subjects that your majesty had for your English ones ;" and he shook

his head doubtfully as he spoke, and his countenance suddenly fell.

A hard-drawn sigh escaped from Sarsefield, and then, biting his lip, and with knitted brow, he exchanged a look of bitter meaning with Gerald Pepper.

" Adieu, then," said the king, " since you will go. See our good friend to his saddle, Sarsefield. Once more, good night ; King James will not forget the White Horseman." So saying, he waved his hand in adieu.—Gerald Pepper bowed low to his sovereign, and Sarsefield followed him from the chamber. They were both silent till they arrived at the portal of the tower, and when the door was opened, Sarsefield crossed the threshold with the visitor, and stepped into the fresh air, which he inhaled audibly three or four times, as if it were a relief to him.

" Good night, General Sarsefield," said Gerald.

" Good night, my gallant friend," said Sarsefield, in a voice that expressed much vexation of spirit.

" Don't be too much cast down, general," said Gerald, " better days may come, and fairer fields be fought."

" Never, never !" said Sarsefield. " Never was a fairer field than that of yesterday, never was a surer game if it had been rightly played. But there is a fate, my friend, hangs over our cause, and I fear that destiny throws against us."

" Speak not thus, general,—think not thus."

" Would that I could think otherwise—but I fear I speak prophetically."

" Do you then give up the cause ?' said Gerald in surprise.

" No ;" said Sarsefield, firmly, almost fiercely. " Never —I may die in the cause, but I will never desert it, as long as I have a troop to follow me—but I must not loiter here. Farewell ! Where is your horse ?"

" I left him in the care of one of the attendants."

" I hope you are well mounted ?'

" Yes ; here comes my charger."

" What !" said Sarsefield, " the white horse !"

" Yes ; surely," said Gerald ; " you never saw me back any other."

" But after the tremendous fatigue of yesterday," said Sarsefield in surprise, " is it possible he is still fresh ?"

" Fresh enough to serve my turn for to-night," said Gerald, as he mounted into the saddle. The white horse gave a loud neigh of seeming satisfaction as his master resumed his seat.

" Noble brute !" said Sarsefield, as he patted the horse on the neck, which was arched into the proud bend of a bold steed who knows a bold rider is on his back.

" And now farewell, general," said Gerald, extending his hand.

" Farewell, my friend. Fate is unkind to deny the charm of a victorious cause to so gallant a spirit."

" There is more gallantry in remaining unshaken under defeat ; and you, general, are a bright example of the fact."

" Good night ; good night," said Sarsefield, anxious to escape from hearing his own praise, and wringing the hand that was presented to him with much warmth : he turned towards the portal of the tower, but before he entered, Gerald again addressed him.

" Pray tell me, general, is your regiment here ? before I go, I would wish to take leave of the officers of that gallant corps, in whose ranks I have had the honour to draw a sword."

" They are not yet arrived. They are on the road, perhaps, by this time ; but I ordered they should be the last to leave Dublin, for as, yesterday, they suffered the disgrace of being led the first out of the battle*, I took care they should have the honor of being the last in the rear to-night, to cover our retreat."

" Then remember me to them," said Gerald.

" They can never forget the White Horseman," said Sarsefield ; " and they shall hear you left the kind word of remembrance for them. Once more, good night."

---

* At the battle of the Boyne, when the Irish were driving the enemy with great slaughter before them, James was heard often to exclaim, " Oh ! spare my English subjects,"

* Sarsefield's regiment, after having repeatedly repulsed the enemy, was obliged to leave the field in order to protect the person of the king, who chose to fly unnecessarily soon

'Good night, general; God's blessing be upon you!"
" Amen !" said Sarsefield : " and with you."

They then wrung each other's hand in silence. Sarsefield re-entered the tower, and Gerald Pepper giving the rein to his stead. the white horse left the spot as rapidly as he had approached it.

[Pepper having remained some time in Dublin to find out what was going forward, on discovering that his property is forfeited, sets off for home, in order to save as many moveables as possible. On the way he meets his foster brother, Rory Oge, who being informed of what was about to occur, takes means to delay the progress of the trooper to whom the property had been granted—the many manœuvres to accomplish this are drawn out to such a length as to prevent our giving more than an outline. The story, we should have observed, is divided into three chapters—the Legend of the White Horse, if " *legend*" it can be called, is nearly complete in the first and last, the intermediate chapter being almost altogether occupied with " The Little Weaver of Duleek Gate," another legend, introduced by way of episode, to entertain the trooper. In the third chapter Mr. Lover continues :]

Let the division I have made in my chapters serve, in the mind of the reader, as an imaginary boundary between the past day and the ensuing morning. Let him, in his own fancy, also, settle how the soldier watched, slept, dreamt, or waked through this interval. Rory did not make his appearance, however; he had left the public on the preceding evening, having made every necessary arrangement for carrying on the affair he had taken in hand; so that the Englishman, on enquiry, found that Rory had departed, being " obliged to lave the place early on his own business, but sure his honour could have any accommodation in life that he wanted, in the regard of a guide, or the like o' that."

" Now, for this, Rory had provided also, having arranged with the keepers of the public, to whom he confided every thing connected with the affair, that in case the trooper should ask for a guide, they should recommend him a certain young imp, the son of Rory's cousin, the blacksmith, and one of the most mischievous, knowing, and daring young vagabonds in the parish.

To such guidance, therefore, did the Englishman commit himself on this, the third day of his search after the lands of the Peppers, which still remained a *Terra Incognita* to him; and the boy, being previously tutored upon the duties he was to perform in his new capacity, was not one likely to enlighten him upon the subject.—The system of the preceding day was acted upon, except the carting of the horse's shoe; but by-roads and crooked lanes were put in requisition, and every avenue, but the one really leading to his object, the trooper was made to traverse.

The boy affected simplicity or ignorance, as best suited his purposes, to escape any inconvenient interrogatory or investigation on the part of the stranger, and at last, the young guide turned up a small rugged lane, down whose gentle slope some water was slowly trickling amongst stones and mud. On arriving at its extremity, he proceeded to throw down some sods, and pull away some brambles, that seemed to be placed there as an artificial barrier to an extensive field that lay beyond the lane.

" What are you doing there?" said the soldier.
" Makin' a convenience for your honour to get through the gap," said the boy.
" There is no road there," said the other.
" Oh, no, plaze your ho our," said the young rascal, looking up in his face with an affectation of simplicity that might have deceived Machiavel himself.—" It s not a road, Sir, but a short cut."
" Cut it as short then as you can, my boy," said the soldier (the only good thing he ever said in his life) " for your short cuts in this country are the longest I ever knew— I'd rather go a round."
" So we must go round, by the bottom o' this field, Sir, and then, over the hill beyant there, we come out an the road."
" Then there *is* a road beyond the hill."
" A fine road, Sir," said the boy, who, having cleared a

passage for the horseman, proceeded before him at a smart run, and led him down the slope of the hill to a small valley, intersected by a sluggish stream that lay at its foot. When the boy arrived at this valley, he ran briskly across it, though the water splashed up about his feet at every bound he gave, and dashing on through the stream, he arrived at the other side by the time the trooper had reached the nearer one. Here the latter was obliged to pull up, for his horse, at the first step, sunk so deep, that the animal instinctively withdrew his foot from the treacherous morass.

The trooper called after his guide, who was proceeding up the opposite acclivity, and the boy turned round.
" I can't pass this, boy," said the soldier.

The boy faced the hill again, without any reply, and recommenced his ascent at a rapid pace.
" Come back, you young scoundrel, or I'll shoot you," said the soldier, drawing his pistol from his holster. The boy still continued his flight, and the trooper fired, but ineffectually, upon which the boy stopped, and after making a contemptuous action at the Englishman, rushed up the acclivity and was soon beyond the reach of small arms, and shortly after out of sight, having passed the summit of the hill.

The Englishman's vexation was excessive, at finding himself thus left in such a helpless situation. For a long time he endeavoured to find a spot in the marsh he might make his crossing good upon, but in vain,—and after nearly an hour spent in this useless endeavour, he was forced to turn back and strive to unravel the maze of twisting and twining through which he had been led, for the purpose of getting on some high way, where a chance passenger might direct him in finding his road.

This he failed to accomplish, and darkness at length overtook him, in a wild country to which he was an utter stranger. He still continued, however, cautiously to progress along the road on which he was benighted, and at length the twinkling of a distant light raised some hope of succour in his heart.

Keeping this beacon in view, the benighted traveller made his way, as well as he might, until, by favor of the glimmer he so opportunely discovered, he at last found himself in front of the house whence the light proceeded. He knocked at the door, which, after two or three loud summonses, was opened to him, and then briefly stating the distressing circumstances in which he was placed, he requested shelter for the night.

The domestic who opened the door retired to deliver the stranger's message to the owner of the house, who immediately afterwards made his appearance, and, with a reserved courtesy, invited the stranger to enter.
" Allow me first to see my horse stabled," said the soldier.
" He shall be cared for," said the other.
" Excuse me, Sir," returned the blunt Englishman, " if I wish to see him in his stall. It has been a hard day for the poor brute, and I fear one of his hoofs is much injured; how far I am anxious to see."
" As you please, Sir," said the gentleman, who ordered a menial to conduct the stranger to the stable.

There, by the light of a lantern, the soldier examined the extent of injury his charger had sustained, and had good reason to fear that the next day would find him totally unserviceable. After venting many a hearty curse on Irish roads and Irish guides, he was retiring from the stable, when his attention was attracted by a superb white horse, and much as he was engrossed by his present annoyance, the noble proportions of the animal were too striking to be overlooked; after admiring all his points, he said to the attendant, " what a beautiful creature this is !"
" Throth, you may say that," was the answer.
" What a charger he would make !"
" Sure enough."
" He must be very fleet."
" As the win'."
" And leaps."
" Whoo!—over the moon, if you axed him."
" That horse must trot at least ten miles the hour."
" Tin !—faix it wouldn't be convaynient to him to trot

undher fourteen," and with this assurance on the part of the groom, they left the stable.

On being led into the dwelling-house, the stranger found the table spread for supper, and the owner of the mansion, pointing to a chair, invited him to partake of the evening meal.

The reader need scarcely be told that the invitation came from Gerald Pepper, for, I suppose, the white horse in the stable has already explained whose house chance had directed the trooper to, though all his endeavours to find it had proved unavailing.

Gerald still maintained the bearing which characterized his first meeting with the Englishman on his threshold—it was that of reserved courtesy. Magdalene, his gentle wife, was seated near the table, with an infant child sleeping upon her lap; her sweet features were strikingly expressive of sadness; and as the stranger entered the apartment, her eye was raised in one timorous glance upon the man whose terrible mission she was too well aware of, and the long lashes sank downwards again upon the pale cheek that recent sorrows had robbed of its bloom.

"Come, Sir," said Gerald, "after such a day of fatigue as yours has been, some refreshment will be welcome;" and the Englishman, presently, by deeds, not words, commenced giving ample evidence of the truth of the observation. As the meal proceeded, he recounted some of the mishaps that had befallen him, all of which Gerald knew before, through Rory Oge, who was in the house at that very moment, though, for obvious reasons he did not make his appearance; and, at last, the stranger put the question to his host, if he knew any one in that neighbourhood called Gerald Pepper.

Magdalene felt her blood run cold, but Gerald quietly replied, there was a person of that name thereabouts.

"Is his property a good one?" said the trooper.

"Very much reduced of late," said Gerald.

"Ballygarth they call it," said the soldier; "is that far from here?"

"It would puzzle me to tell you how to go to it from this place," was the answer.

"It is very provoking," said the trooper; "I have been looking for it these three days and cannot find it, and nobody seems to know where it is."

Magdalene, at these words, felt a momentary relief, yet still she scarcely dared to breathe.

"The truth is," continued the soldier, "that I am entitled, under the king's last commission, to that property, for all Pepper's possessions have been forfeited."

The baby, as it slept in its mother's lap, smiled as its legalised despoiler uttered these last words, and poor Magdalene, smote to the heart by the incident, melted into tears; but, by a powerful effort, she repressed any audible evidence of grief, and, shading her eyes with her hand, her tears dropped in silence over her sleeping child.

Gerald observed her emotion, and found it difficult to master his own feelings.

"Now it is rather hard," continued the soldier, "that I have been hunting up and down the country for this confounded place, and can't find it. I thought it a fine thing, but I suppose it's nothing to talk of, or somebody would know of it; and more provoking still, we soldiers have yet our hands so full of work, that I only got four days' leave, and to-morrow night I am bound to return to Dublin, or I shall be guilty of a breach of duty; and how I am to return, with my horse in the disabled state that this detestable country has left him, I cannot conceive."

"You will be hard run to accomplish it," said Gerald.

"Now will you make a bargain with me?" said the soldier.

"Of what nature?" said Gerald.

"There"—said the soldier, throwing down on the table a piece of folded parchment,—"there is the debenture entitling the holder thereof to the property I have named. Now, I must give up looking for it, for the present, and I am tired of hunting after it, into the bargain; besides, God knows when I may be able to come here again. You are on the spot, and may make use of this instrument, which empowers you to take full possession of the property whatever it may be; to you it may be

valuable. At a word then, if I give you this debenture, will you give me the white horse that is standing in your stable?"

Next to his wife and children, Gerald Pepper loved his white horse; and the favourite animal so suddenly and unexpectedly named startled him, and, strange as it may appear, he paused for a moment; but Magdalene, unseen by the soldier, behind whom she was seated, clasped her outstretched hands in the action of supplication to her husband, and met his eye with an imploring look that, at once, produced his answer.

"Agreed!" said Gerald.

"'Tis a bargain," said the soldier; and he tossed the debenture across the table as the property of the man whom it was intended to leave destitute.

Having thus put the man into possession of his own property, the soldier commenced spending the night pleasantly, and it need not be added that Gerald Pepper was in excellent humour to help him.

As for poor Magdalene, when the bargain was completed, her heart was too full to permit her to remain longer, and hurrying to the apartment where the elder children were sleeping, she kissed them passionately, and, throwing herself on her knees between their little beds, wept profusely, as she offered the fervent outpourings of a grateful heart to heaven, for the ruin so wonderfully averted from their innocent heads.

The next morning the English soldier was in his saddle at an early hour, and he seemed to entertain all the satisfaction of an habitual horseman, in feeling the stately tread of the bold steed beneath him. The white horse champed his bit, and, by his occasional curvettings, evinced a consciousness that his accustomed rider was not on his back; but the firm seat and masterly hand of the soldier shortly reduced such slight marks of rebellion into obedience, and he soon bade Gerald Pepper farewell.

The parting was rather brief and silent; for to have been other, would not have accorded with the habits of the one, nor suited the immediate humour of the other. In answer to the spur of the soldier, the white horse galloped down the avenue of his former master's domain, and left behind him the fields in which he had been bred. Gerald Pepper looked after his noble steed while he remained within sight, and thought no one was witness to the tear he dashed from his eye when he turned to re-enter his house.

FORMER TIMES.

Light is intended by our Maker for action, and darkness for rest. In the fourteenth century the shops in Paris were opened at four in the morning. The king of France dined at eight in the morning, and retired to his bedchamber at the same hour in the evening. During the reign of Henry the Eighth fashionable people in England breakfasted at seven in the morning, and dined at ten in the forenoon. In Elizabeth's time, the nobility, gentry, and students dined at eleven forenoon, and supped between five and six afternoon. In the reign of Charles the Second, four in the afternoon was the appointed hour for acting plays. The diversions of the day were tournament, tennis, hunting, racing, and such active exercises. Formerly active exercises prevailed among a robust and plain people—the milder pleasures of society prevail as manners refine.

At Dutch Guiana, or Surinam, grows an herbaceous plant called Troolies: its leaves lie on the ground, and sometimes are thirty feet in length and three in breadth; it serves as a general covering for houses, and will last several years without any repair.

DUBLIN:
Printed and Published by P. D. Hardy, 3, Cecilia-street; to whom all communications are to be addressed.
Sold by all Booksellers in Ireland.
In London, by Richard Groombridge, 6, Panyer-alley, Paternoster-row; in Liverpool, by Willmer and Smith; in Manchester, by Ambery; in Birmingham, by Drake; in Glasgow, by W. R. M'Phun; and in Edinburgh, by N. Bowack.

THE
DUBLIN PENNY JOURNAL

CONDUCTED BY P. DIXON HARDY, M.R.I.A.

Vol. III.   JULY 26, 1834.   No. 108.

KANTURK CASTLE.

Kanturk, anciently called Ceann-tuirc—i. e. a boar's head, from one of these animals having been slain there, after a long chase, by one of the Irish chieftains—is a fair and market town, in the county of Cork, about twenty-four miles north-west of the city : it belonged to a branch of the M'Carthys, called M'Donough, who forfeited his estate in 1641. In the reign of Elizabeth they erected a most magnificent pile near this place, the walls of which remain entire. It was a parallelogram, one hundred and twenty feet in length by eighty in breadth, flanked with four square buildings; but being represented to the Council as a place which might be made dangerous to government, the building was put a stop to, though far from being capable of being rendered subservient to that purpose. All the window-frames, quoins, beltings, and battlements were of hewn stone ; and the whole made a most grand and regular appearance. This castle, with the town and manor of Kanturk, gave title of Viscount to the Egmont family, under whose patronage it is now considerably improved and extended. Fairs are held in May, July, November, and December. As, in the Emerald Isle, there is scarcely a town or village, streamlet or castle, that is not associated with some romantic or characteristic tale, the following description of that wit and humour so strongly abounding in the Irish character, may not be undeserving of record :

BASTABLE AND HOLY FOWKS.

Beneath the walls of M'Donough's Folly, a name given to the old ruined castle of Kanturk, from the vast extent of preparation and want of adequate means in the original projector, M'Donough, to complete the work, runs or rather glides the Brogeen, or Blue Pool, as it is called, from a load of coloured glass which upset and shattered in crossing the ford, and which was destined to adorn the windows of the rising court, but which, according to an old prophecy in the neighbourhood, was fated never to be finished. This interesting stream, after supplying the valuable bolting-mill of Mr. Barry, disembogues into the Alla, a river whence the extensive barony of Duhallow derives its name.

By the aborigines and seanachists of the country, the old court, built about the year 1564, is called, *Cuirt carrig na Seaghan saor*, from the builders employed being all of the name of John, or as some more knowing ones must have it, because the master, in his lordly and feudal pride, pressed not only his neighbours but every passing stranger to work at the building gratis, or, in case of refusal, his life was the forfeit, and his blood was cast, as an additional cement, into the mortar ; and sure, gentle reader, it is no great wonder that a heavy curse should hang for ever on such an undertaking. But it was not from the dark overshadowing of even such a castle, nor from the broken and glittering crystal embedded in its pebbly bottom, that the Brogeen acquired notoriety, but from the following circumstance, which, for a long time, kept the adjacent country in a roar, and filled the wide hearths of Duhallow with merriment and gratitude, at the happy and comic termination of what threatened to be a tragedy indeed.

In the Autumn of 17—, lived a gentleman of ancient and respectable family, named Fowks, in the town of Kanturk : his wit and drollery were so proverbial, that he was a universal favourite with all classes, high or low, in the surrounding neighbourhood. A feast, wedding, or christening, for fifty miles round, was not worth a traneen without him; and a patron, or gala day was splendourless and gloomy, unless, like the quivering sunbeam, Holy Fowks, as he was sirnamed, was there to cheer and gladden the scene.

By one of those strange accidents of life, which sometimes yokes the lion and the lamb, or brings fire and water into contact, our hero became the intimate acquaintance of Mr. Bastable, a gentleman residing within a few miles of the town : their dispositions were wide as the poles asunder; for while the one possessed all the native elasticity and genuine humour of the Irish character—the other, of Scottish origin, seemed to inherit all the gloom and reservedness of his ancestors, without the many redeeming qualities which often distinguish them : he was a bodach —dark, sullen, credulous and irritable ; fond of " tales of days gone by," and a great admirer of the miraculous and astonishing. Between such a pair the best understanding existed for some time, till one day, returning from hunting, the discourse happened to turn on the natural curiosities of the country, and the wonderful though well authenticated properties attributed to certain raths, caves, or tobars in the vicinity. The evening was about to close, and the faint twilight, that still rendered visible the beauties of the nether world, seemed to invite the genius of superstition to walk forth, and claiming as her own the peculiar hour, assert her awful and uncontrolled dominion over the minds of her votaries.

" Hold !" cried Fowks, suddenly starting, and filled, as if by unearthly inspiration, he grasped the arm of his startled companion ; " seek not in remote districts—travel not into other lands for evidence of that which lies at our own doors. Look there at the Brogeen—see the peculiar aspect of the old cursed and unfinished court that darkles and froans over it like the evil genius of the spot. See the strange curl of its rippling waters, and listen for a moment to the shrill whistle of the breeze that floats along its surface."

Bastable, struck with the emphasis of the words, and prone, from his childhood, to listen to every well told story, eagerly asked what was told of the stream—all his old fairy reminiscenses were uppermost in his thoughts, and at the moment the fearful melody of the banshee, or the chirping of the leprawhaun sounded in his imagination.

" The thing," said Fowks, " is not very generally known ; but alight, and let us judge for ourselves. Step across to the opposite bank—call me as loud as you can, and all the powers on earth could not make me hear you."

Bastable did as he was desired—he called long and loud, but in vain ; for though he roared loud as Tim Connor's bull, or the cascade of O Sullivan, still Holy Fowks would not pretend to hear him. The astonished Bastable returned back.

" Well, Mr. Fowks, 'tis strange I never heard of this before, though so long in the neighbourhood; but, to be doubly sure, do you cross over now and cry out, to try if I could hear you. '

Fowks crossed, and opening his mouth, with various contortions, he seemed to call out most violently, pretending to do all in his power to make himself heard, yet at the same time, like one of Virgil's Tartarean shadows, not a single syllable or the slightest sound ever escaped his lips.

Bastable, deeply impressed with the marvellous, and struck with the magic properties of the Brogeen, soon after parted from his companion, and returned home to muse on what he had not heard, but seen.

At a select meeting of convivial friends, on that very night, Holy Fowks related the joke, with many circumstances of aggravation—it soon spread like wild-fire through the country. Bastable and the Brogeen associated together, and badgered about without mercy, became a bye word of ridicule, and the unfortunate wight was pointed at, even by the little gorsoons and cailinogs, as the greatest omadhawn in the parish. This was more than human nature could bear. Bastable became outrageous, and nothing but the blood of the aggressor could atone for the insult. A challenge ensued, the day of combat was named, and it was arranged that they should fight, ' secundem morem,' with swords, and on horseback. It was a holiday ; and as an affair of such importance could not be a secret in the barony, a living stream issued forth from every dale and valley, or rushed, at break of morn, like a torrent, from each of the surrounding hills. Men, women, and children ran with eagerness to see the sport ; and though cold-blooded, preconcerted duels were held in utter abhorrence, as they should be, by the good people of Kanturk, yet, on this occasion, tragedy was instinctively forgotten, and all looked forward to something strange and frolicsome wherever Fowks was an interested party. The eventful day was come ; and oh, Mr. Editor ! could you but figure to yourself such a day —so replete with sunshine and bustle, with ætherial glory, and earthly anticipation.

Jack M'Carthy, from Newmarket, on his one-eyed Rozinante, led in a numerous tribe of his fellow-townsmen : his handsome bit of a doe-skin breeches and leather gaiters just peered out, to astonish the vulgar, from beneath his big frieze cotamor, made to keep out the summer's heat as well as the winter's cold ; his blooming daughter, Mary, was pillioned in state behind him, and ever and anon, as he passed Teigue Leary's little public-house, where a swinging sign proclaimed that ample accommodation was to be found for man and horse, he tickled his jaded steed with his one spur, and cracked his loaded whip in token of his gallantry and independence. Here the nucleus of the assembly was to be seen ; and while the neighbours from Mill-street and Mushra, Kilcorney and Clonmeen were regaling themselves with a drop of drink, Owen Beecher, the *speaker* of the seven parishes, was telling the history of all the girls of the district, every one of whose names and dowries he had deeply noted in his oaken staff, to a select pack of dulheens, who encircled him in the extreme corner of the tap-room.

" This," said he, in answer to a chuckling querist, and pointing to a deep cut in his wooden tablet, is " Maire bhan, who rides so nately to-day behind her honest father, Jack Carty ; and shure a dacenter man never peeled a pratee. He has fifty acres for half nothin' ; five featherbeds and a fine bawn of cows ; and, beyant all, 'tis he that is good and charitable to the stranger and bocach ; and Maire herself was three seasons with her aunt in Cork, and, barring that she is a taste purblind, she is the natest and best cailin in the parish." But here the garrulity of Owen was suddenly interrupted by a loud shout from without, announcing the arrival of one of the combatants. 'Twas Holy Fowks, wrapped in a large travelling cloak, and mounted on his little chesnut mare, that pranced with unusual agility, as if conscious of the important part she and her master were destined to perform. Loud and hearty were the huzzas which greeted his approach, and the cead mile failte, that met him at every turn, showed that he was the people's favourite. The welkin scarcely ceased to ring, when a buz from the opposite direction gave notice of Bastable's proximity, armed, ' en chevalier' cap a pee.

" A bright sword in his hand, and such fire in his eye,
Determined in battle to conquer or die."

A few of his associates, unable to dissuade him from setting his life on a venture, and still loath to abandon him in the hour of trial, accompanied him, rather reluctantly, to the sod. They felt that, after all, 'twas but a joke, and trembled at the headlong violence and reckless anger of their friend ; but, no, Bastable considered his honour deeply wounded, and eager to repair it in his adversary's blood, he drew his sword, and flung down the gauntlet of defiance. Fowks, cool and determined, am-b'ed forward, with an arch smile on his countenance, to meet him, still enveloped in his cloak. "Ca bhuil a chloidheamh," mut'ered the astonished crowd, when they saw him, apparently unarmed, going to meet the fatal stroke of his enraged antagonist.

"N i bi he'gal ort," replied Jemmie, the fool, who, with an old soldier's cap and a scarlet jacket, marched up and down the course as a sentinel, shouldering the felled branch of a lime tree, with all the pomp and pride imaginable, " na bac leish a vourneen—'tis he that will pull the sword out," "go luath, my darlins, 'tis he will cut the world afore him."

The words were scarcely uttered when Fowks, who was now arrived within a short distance of his opponent, by a sudden jerk flung the cloak from his shoulders, and exhibited, to the wonder of all, not a flaming scimitar, not a pointed lance or a Cossack spear, but what the sequel shewed was a better, though a bloodless weapon, a long pole, at the top of which was fastened a blown bladder containing some dried pease ; this he pointed at his enemy, and rushing forward with a mighty shout, be shook the bladder close at the head of Bastable's mettlesome charger. The noble animal, unaccustomed to so strange a salute, suddenly took to the right about, and, notwithstanding the rage and exertions of his maddened and outwitted master, he bore him fairly off the field, flying, as if old Nick was at his heels, still pursued by Holy Fowks, shaking his undoubted weapon, and calling out in the most ludicrous and earnest tone,

"Oh, Mr. Bastable—oh, you coward, won't you wait to fight me ?"

But no—poor Bastable was carried off, nolens volens, through brambles and ditches, bogs and quagmires, to his home, tired, vexed and disappointed ; and that which he thought would crown him with immortal honour, heaped disgrace and ridicule a thousand fold on his devoted head. Fowks was carried off in triumph. The incomparable tale was told, aye, and even to this day is told over many a sparkling bowl, or at the winter's fire side. Fowks, who was really good-natured and desirous of a reconciliation, made several advances to effect it afterwards, but in vain ; and though he tendered an ample apology, as a salvo for the wounded spirit, and employed many intercessors to make up the breach, all would not do. The dart had pierced into his very soul—he pined beneath the weight of his fancied misery ; and poor Bastable, a burden to himself, and secluded from the world, died an old bachelor.

Cork. O. F.

POPULAR LECTURES ON THE PHYSIOLOGY OF ANIMALS.

The following is an abstract of Dr. Henry's third Lecture :

(The Skin continued.)

It had been long supposed that the skin absorbed foreign substances readily, and carried them into the circulation, but accurate and recent experiments show that the skin does not absorb, or absorbs very sparingly, unless the outer skin be removed or wounded, (as in the case of inoculation), or the substance be made to penetrate by much rubbing, as in the application of mercurial ointments. Hence it is impossible, in cases of impeded deglutition, to maintain life by immersing the patient in baths of milk or broth. The skin is an organ capable of receiving and transmitting impressions of various kinds. We proceed to consider the effects of different agents on it. When cold is applied in a moderate degree with some permanency to the skin, it diminishes—first, the vascularity ; secondly, the sensibility ; thirdly, the perspiration of the part : these effects are accompanied by very uncomfortable sensations, both bodily and mental. On removing the cooling cause, what is called *reaction* takes place ; the part becomes redder and warmer, the sensibility and perspiration increase, the feelings become more agreeable, and a certain degree of lightness and invigoration of spirits is experienced. The reaction is proportioned to

the cold applied. If the cold has been but of momentary application, as in the shower-bath, the reaction is immediate, of short duration, and moderate in degree. The shower-bath may, therefore, be used by very delicate persons who have small powers of reaction. The reaction being always proportioned to the depression and the depression being proportioned to the length of time for which the cold is applied, persons with small power of reaction cannot endure the long continued cold of the common bath. In such persons there is not sufficient power of reaction, and the depressing effects of the cold continue after the bath, the individual remaining chilly, with face, and hands, and feet white or blue, the vessels being emptied, or the blood stagnating in them. In such cases, when at last reaction does commence, it is excessive in proportion to the excess of the preceding depression—there is head-ache—sometimes inflammation of an internal organ—not unfrequently actual fever. From this principle useful rules may be drawn respecting the cold bath. 1.—The time for which the individual stays in the water must be proportioned to his powers of reaction. 2—The cold bath should never be used immediately after a meal, because the powers of life are called to the stomach, and the skin is in a less energetic state, and less fit for reaction. 3.—We should never bathe while chilly, but rather when warm, or gently perspiring, otherwise there is no shock. If in good health, an individual, provided he does not remain long in the water, may bathe with safety, even when perspiring copiously. This is the common practice of the Russians. Above all things never go into the cold bath when fatigued, for during fatigue the powers of life are less capable of reaction: a violation of this rule nearly cost Alexander the Great his life, when he bathed in the Cydnus after a fatiguing day's march. The cold air-bath is seldom taken in this country, notwithstanding the recommendation and example of Dr. Franklin. The air-bath is particularly useful at night, when the skin is hot, and the mind nervous and agitated, and sleep banished from the pillow. You should on such occasions rise, and walk about the room in your night dress for five or ten minutes—wash your face and hands in cold water, swallow a mouthful or two of cold water, and return to bed, composure and sleep will almost invariably follow. When cold is long continued and severe, particularly when persons are at the same time undergoing fatigue, as in struggling against a snow storm, torpor, and sleep terminating in death, are produced. In many cases, where this termination does not take place, some parts of the body, as the nose, fingers, and toes, die from excess of cold. If the danger is discovered before the part is actually killed by the cold, a new danger arises, that of reaction : the reaction, if excessive, will produce the death of the part. Hence it is necessary, instead of applying warmth, to endeavour to bring back the circulation by rubbing with snow first, and then with cold water. The object of the warm bath is quite different from that of the cold ; its use is to increase the quantity of blood in the part, to soothe the sentient surface of the skin, and to promote the perspiration. By the warm bath these objects are obtained without reaction ; it is therefore suited for those from whom reaction could not be expected, and in cases where reaction would be injurious. It may be taken soon after meals, and was much used by the ancient Romans to counteract the ill effects of repletion. It may also be employed in cases of extreme fatigue, but never at a temperature exceeding 98°, or for a longer time than twenty minutes. From the circumstance that baths were formerly used at too high a temperature, and that such a use of them was sometimes followed by a bad consequence, has arisen the popular prejudice, that the warm bath debilitates and exposes to the danger of catching cold ; these effects are never produced unless the bath has been taken at too *high* a temperature, or has been remained in for too long a time. Tepid bathing is practised on the continent much more than in these countries. At Leuk, in the Vallais, the bathers spend whole days in the baths. The baths are very spacious, and the bathers, both ladies and gentlemen, spend whole days in them—the former perusing novels or working at their needle, while the latter read the newspaper or smoke cigars. Each bath having a little passing bowl or table, holding, according to the taste of the individual, a book, a snuff-box, a newspaper, or a piece of needle-work, &c. The same mode of passing the time while in the water was formerly practised by the bathers at Bath, and has been humorously described by Defoe.

DISTANT VIEW OF CARLOW TO THE NORTH.

This town is seated on the east bank of the river Barrow, thirty-nine miles from Dublin; its ancient name was Catherlough, i. e. The City on the Lake, from its proximity to a large lake or pond which formerly existed here.

It is not my intention to trace this town from its origin, through its gradual rise and progress, nor even those various epochs and events which are entwined with and enliven its local history, but merely to present a slight notice or abstract of its present statistics.

The town of Carlow is the emporium of the trade and business of this and the adjoining counties, chiefly on account of its advantageous and rapid water communication with the sea-port towns of Ross and Waterford, and also with Dublin, a passage which occupies but two or three days.

Carlow cannot be said to possess any particular staple trade or manufacture. The inhabitants are engaged in the ordinary routine of town business, in the various branches of industrious occupation; but the corn and butter trades are very extensively carried on—the county of Carlow being richly productive of these articles, which always find here a ready market.

But I wish particularly to mention its butter trade—the quality of which is of the finest description—superior to any in Ireland, and giving precedence to the Dutch butter alone in the London market. The average of the delivery is about thirty thousand casks annually.

The Barrow, to which this town is indebted for its origin and increase, was anciently called Berva—in Irish, Bearbha ; though some suppose its present name derived from the word Barragh, or boundary river, it being for some centuries the boundary between the English pale and the Irish septs.

This river, to which Denman wished that his style of writing would be assimilated, thus,

" Though deep, yet clear—though gentle, yet not dull ;
Strong without rage—without o'erflowing, full,
rises in the Slieve-Bloom mountains, in the Queen's

county, and, passing several small towns, arrives at Carlow, to which, as before-mentioned, it contributes life prosperity, and increasing commercial importance. It then pursues its winding and placid course, until it mingles its waters with its sister river, the Nore, near New Ross. It is navigable from Ross to Athy, where it meets the canal, which continues on to Dublin : reckoning from its source, it runs in its whole course a distance of about one hundred and twenty miles.

Carlow is rapidly progressing of late years—it is extending its limits on all sides—new streets being added, one in particular, now laying out for the erection of private houses, will, if finished according to the plan at present intended, be one of its greatest ornaments. The public buildings are in number suitable to the size of the town : amongst them the new cathedral for Roman Catholic worship claims preeminence, for the beauty of its style and architecture, a new court-house, a new jail, a lunatic asylum, also a modern building, laid out on an extensive scale, for the reception of about one hundred and twenty patients, from the counties of Carlow, Kilkenny, Wexford, and Kildare, the college, of which there is a view given in your 14th Number, a fine Protestant church, also one house of worship for Presbyterians, one for Methodists, and another for Quakers ; a large horse-barrack, infirmary, dispensary, &c. ; three public free schools, and in Graige (which might be said to be part of the town, although in a different county, being connected by Wellington-bridge,) there is a handsome Protestant church, a Roman Catholic chapel, and a public school, built by the donations of the parishioners, and conducted on the Lancasterian system. But in mentioning the modern buildings of Carlow, let us not pass unnoticed and neglected the dilapidated remains of " the days of other years." The old castle then, " nobly picturesque of former greatness," claims our attention, and deserves a place in your Journal among the antiquities of Ireland.— But, indeed, with the exception of this castle, this town does not possess any thing worthy the eye of the anti-quary—no monastic ruin—no monument of bye-gone times.

There was a fine abbey founded here in the seventh century, a trace of which no longer remains.

The population of Carlow at present is about eleven thousand persons, and contains thirty streets and lanes, and above twelve hundred houses; though in the recollection of a person, not long since deceased, the town was not more than one fourth its present extent. Carlow returned two members to the Irish parliament, and sends one now to the British legislature. There were three charters granted to Carlow—one by James the First, one by Charles the Second, and a third by James the Second.

A poem entitled Mount Leinster, &c., has the following lines relative to this town :

" Where Carlow's undulating fields extend,
Whose varied shades in sweet disorder blend ;
'Mid which the raptured eye delights to stray,
And dwells, though oft reviewed, " with fond delay."
On wood, on tillage, or on pasture green,
Or seeks the Barrow through the lengthened scene :
Fair stream ! whose placid waters glide
In winding course, a gentle tide ;
As through thy own green vales they stray,
And flow, untired, their ceaseless way ;
Still, as the parent main they join,
Drawn from thy streams new rills combine ;
Thence nature's course unerring keep,
Thy source the clouds, thy home the deep !"
                                                    H.

CARLOW CASTLE.

This lofty and massive building, which rears its high head in solemn grandeur, and seems to look down with fostering protection and watchful guardianship on the town beneath it, was built by Hugh de Lacy, about the year 1180, in the reign of John. Though some difference of opinion exists on this point—some referring it as the work of Eva, daughter of Dermot M'Murrough, and others attributing it to Isabel, daughter of Strongbow, and others, to King John, &c. ; but concurrent, circumstantial, and historical evidence, fix on de Lacy as the founder." It was built after the Anglo-Norman style of architecture, i. e. a square area strongly enclosed with walls, fortified and strengthened at each corner with a round tower of large dimensions.* The whole building was amply provided with loop-holes, and with arched and mullioned windows, &c., from which to pour, if necessary, on their assailants the sweeping shot of artillery and musketry, or the less destructive missile.

The prefixed view is intended to convey a notion of its present ruinous condition—the mere isolated wreck of

what it once was—which is attributable, not to the all prostrating hand of time, nor even to the generally still more destructive hand of man, although it had been exposed for centuries to the influence of the one, and to the repeated, and often long-continued attacks of the other—but to the pseudo improvement, and unskilful alterations of its then occupier, Dr. Middleton, who in 1814 effected its almost total overthrow, by disturbing and undermining its foundations. It fell with a dreadful crash, that alarmed those towns-people who were not aware of the coming event, and it fortunately happened on a Sunday morning, while the people were engaged about their religious duties, otherwise it might possibly have been the destruction of many, for it was at that time a place of general resort for purposes of pleasure and amusement.

This castle is situated on a sloping height which overlooks the town on the west side, close to Wellington-bridge, which crosses the Barrow here, and unites the county of Carlow with the Queen's county.

During a troubled period of Irish history, that is, almost from the time of its erection to the year 1650, when it felt the effect of Ireton's cannon, this castle experienced many a reverse of fortune ; one time in the hands of the Irish, and the next in those of their enemies ; now affording its protection to the besieged rebels, and again the English soldiers hurl, from its battlemented walls, missiles, and other implements of defence on the "Irish enemy" below ; now proposed to the government to be granted, with " its lands and appurtenances," to some young adventurers from England, to induce them to carry on an exterminating warfare, an unholy crusade against the inhabitants of the neighbouring districts ; and at another time given by the English possessors of the soil to some " Irish military agent, who (in the exaction of their tributes) might employ the law of the land or the sword, as circumstances would require."

And often have the walls of its lofty towers rung and re-echoed with the wild convulsive shriek, and expiring groan of its butchering inhabitants, when the "fortune of war" favoured the sanguinary besiegers of either party.— In fine, there is many a wild traditionary story connected with it, and many a tale of blood, which in a great measure clouds the " glory of its history."

The castle was once walled, and the space inclosed was very considerable : it may be inferred from part of the walls, lately found in throwing down a house, that they surrounded the castle entirely to the east, and terminated at the Barrow, that river forming its boundary to the west.

A spiral stone stairs led to the summit of one of the towers, which has fallen, from which there was gained an extended and beautifully varied prospect. Seated on this lofty eminence, the lover of nature might gratify his fondest wish ; for there presented itself to him a landscape which was truly beautiful, interspersed with every variety of mountain and lowland scenery. On one side, the thickly wooded mountains of Clogreman, which in a long continued chain of hills bounded the ruin to the west, rose before him, teeming with cultivation to their very summit, swelling out of, and crowning the rich and verdant fields and vallies which lie extended at its base, with the Barrow, whose serpentine course could be traced for miles, flowing through them. Towards the east the Wicklow mountains, with the beautiful intermediate country, engage the attention ; then turning towards the south, in the blue distance might be recognised the dim and weary outline of Mount Leinster.

" Lord of the landscape, lofty Leinster, hail !
From whose high crown we view the distant sail,
As on the horizon's misty verge it flies,
Where distant ocean mingles with the skies ;
With thy majestic beauties varying wide,
As from the base we mount the rocky side ;
On an extensive tract the eye first dwells,
Where Erne's shore the rolling surge repels."

The height of the walls yet remaining is about sixty-five feet, which seems to have been the original altitude of the structure ; the length of the side from the extremity of one tower to that of the other is 105 feet, and as the building was square, or nearly so, an idea can be formed of its former great extent. The thickness of the walls of the fortification, at least if we may judge from

* The walls of the tower are of the amazing thickness of seven feet two inches ; the inner diameter of the same, ten feet, and the exterior circumference is seventy-seven feet.

the one which still remains, and there is no reason to think there was any difference, was eight feet.

The chimney-like structure which tops the castle is tottering to its fall, as it seems to stand pinnacled upon a single stone, some of those which formed its basement on the tower having disappeared, but for what purpose it was intended I cannot tell: as there are no traces of fire-place, or funnel, it could not have been a chimney.

H.

ARCHY CONWAY.

On a fine day, late in the lovely month of May, such a day as has been sung by poets, but which the temperature of our Emerald Isle does not often cheer us with, the roads of a certain parish, in a certain county and province of this gem of the ocean, were thronged by groups of people young and old, male and female, hurrying to one common centre—an annual fair held in a field, which was anxiously looked forward to for half the year, and by which the memoranda of the good wives were dated: ask one the age of her child—the answer will be, "so old agin the fair iv Kill;" and among the men it was, "wid the help iv goodness I'll pay ye afther the fair iv Kill;" so that this fair was, as it were, a finger-post to the memories of the neighbourhood. Hither had the crowds been congregating since early dawn; some on one intent, some on another—but all agreeing in the desire of enjoying the pleasures of the fair.

"An' any way, thanks be to goodness, its a fine day," said an elderly female, in the centre of a group of others, who were trotting along barefooted, with petticoats tucked up, and shoes in hand.

"Sorra finer ever cum out iv the sky," replied another; " un' Onny acushla, d'ye mind fwhat a sore day it was this time twel'month: teems iv rain, tundher an' lightnin', an' great big hard snow balls fallin' thick, an' all the sport spiled."

"Nera loss that was, any way, Katty," replied Onny, "only fur it the green id be runnin' wid blood."

"D'ye think they'll strike era stroke the day," asked another woman.

"Iv yeere in the fair afther dinner time, maybe ye'd see that," said Onny.

"Fwhat news ye tell us," retorted the other, " any way they're ruffens iv both sides, an' it's well for them that has no call to the scrub."

"Sorra great things yersel' is," cried Onny, " that ye speak in disparagement iv any body; there's them iv both parties, though I don't love or like one side, that's the full iv a masther to any one ever ye had belongin' t'ye, Biddy Moran."

"I didn't know, Onny, ye wor any thing to either party," said a girl.

"Hooh!" that's a wondher dear; was'nt my mother's aunt's husband's cousin marrid to Tom Bruin's aunt's third cousin—fwhy would'nt I be for the Bruins?—an' any way, that they may win."

"I b'lieve that gridge is long betune them," said one.

"Nigh hand two score years," replied Onny.

"An' fwhat was it put betune them at first?" was another query.

"Sorra much, dear," answered Onny; " a hen that was scrapin' oats was kilt be a boy iv the Bruins. A woman iv the Fellins, who owned the hen, fell to beatin' him; his mother cum to save him—the women boxed; iv coorse the men tuk their parts—an' from that day to this there's a gridge betune them."[*]

"No great things to make sich a rout about," said a woman; " it'd be more fitter for them that day to be mindin' their wheels, nor fightin' an' drawin' sich a gridge betune the men."

Honor, or Onny, as she was called—a woman of masculine figure and disposition, was on the point of justifying the persons of her own clan, who had been the aggressors in this feud, which was, as she affirmed, of near forty years standing; but a party of young men overtaking them, a scene of bantering and coquetry ensued, which put the women in good humour: when the men passed on there was no further recrimination.

"Well, there's nera cleaner boy in the four walls iv the world nor Archy Conway," remarked Onny, " an' always has the pleasant word for the girls."

"D'ye think, Onny, he'll be marret to Nancy Sweeny?" asked one.

"As lek as not," was the reply.

"He'll be for the Fellins, iv there's strokes the day," said a girl.

"Sorra a blow ever he'll strik for them," answered Onny; " isn't his mother a friend iv Thady Bruin's—oh, yis, indeed, fwhat a fool he is."

They now drew near to the field in which the fair was held, and a general scene of dressing took place: shoes and stockings were put on—petticoats and gowns released from confinement—hair sleeked up and down—shawls, cloaks, and handkerchiefs heaped on each other before they could enter this scene of rustic amusement.

Archy Conway was the son of a widow—a fine-looking young man, who possessed an unbounded flow of spirits which, when among his companions, led him into sundry scrimmages, as he termed them; in fact, when he was induced to drink more than usual, he was apt to be exceedingly frolicsome. He was foster-brother to a young gentleman in the neighbourhood, who was much attached to him.

Archy's mother, aware of his frailty, endeavoured to keep him as much as possible away from public places, and above all dreaded the annual fair of Kill; knowing all she could urge against his going there would not avail, she went to her foster-child, to request his interference, to keep, if possible, Archy from the fair. For this purpose, on the day previous to the fair, Archy was summoned to the residence of his master; having some idea of the cause, as it was by no means the first time this authority had been resorted to, he went rather unwillingly, and a shade of gloom darkened his handsome features, as he was ushered into the presence of his young master.

"Sit down, Archy," said the gentleman, pointing to a chair—"I wish to speak with you."

"Yis, Sir," replied Archy, placing himself on the corner of a seat, and in rather a pettish way twirling his hat in one hand.

"Have you got your potatoes finished during this fine weather?" said the young master.

"Not all out, Sir. Shure, Masther Henery, they're down since betune the two Mays—time enough to finish them yet."

"I have frequently endeavoured to convince you, Archy, that your habit of procrastinating is extremely wrong."

"Fwhat's that, Masther Henery?"

"Putting off until to-morrow, what might better be done to-day."

"I'll not be passin' two hours away, Sir; an' sorra sup I'll take, barrin' one glass—won't that do, Sir?"

"I had much rather you did not go at all. What business have you to transact there?"

"Ah then, Masther Henery, ye're goin' very tight on me entirely; but I promised to—" and, blushing deeply, Archy more vehemently twirled the hat, and sent it spinning to the other end of the apartment; after picking it up, he went on: "I promised to meet somebody there, Sir."

Henry smiled while replying, "there would be no use in my saying, Archy, don't go, as you are determined to disobey; but I will say, avoid bad company, and be home early."

Archy promised to do all his master wished; joyfully made his bow, and was hastening off when called back, and enjoined, above all things, to beware of fighting. "It is probable," continued Henry, " the Bruins may be defying their adversaries; I desire you will not take part with them."

"Never dread, Sir."

Archy lost no time in arraying himself in "all his best" and hurrying to the fair. The stipulated two hours so passed over, and he thought not of returning; after a further stay he thought it would be soon enough to be goin' till dinner time; sorra bit iv fun he seen yet.— Dinner time went by, and a couple of hours after Onny, with another female, were standing at the outside of a tent. She appeared, amid the babel of confusion that reigned within and without, to be hearkening to some conversation that was carried on in the tent; and to ascertain if she was right as to the speakers, with a piece of stick she perforated a hole in the slight covering sufficient to see through, and putting one eye to it, remained for some time in close espial; then silently touching her companion on the shoulder, motioned her to look through the aperture, and whispered,

"Now, Mary a hagur, if them leaves the tent afore I cum back, mind an' tell me fwhere they go to."

So saying, Onny set off at full speed, muttering as she went. "Maybe, Tim Casey, ye thought no one was listenin' to yer villany; but I'll be up t'ye an' yer faction. Oh, wirra! isn t it a wondher fwhere's Archy Conway; it can't be he went home." She rushed in and out of the tents like a person deranged, many saying as she drove by them, "that woman's early drunk."

In the mean while the object of her search was enjoying the society of the being he loved best on earth. The pretty Nancy Sweeny had long been admired by Archy, and admiration became love of the most ardent kind; and he had the delight of knowing that his passion was returned. But when did the course of true love run smoothly? The parents of Nancy had a match in contemplation, which they thought better; therefore Archy Conway's suit was discouraged by them. Nancy was to have a good fortune, both in money and cattle, consequently she was an object of interest to the youths of the neighbourhood. However, knowing his interest in the damsel's heart, he determined to carry off the prize if he could not obtain her on any other terms; and for the purpose of gaining her consent to this plan, he had drawn her apart from the crowd, and they were in earnest conversation at the rere of a large pedlar's standing, while Onny was in search of him. He had brought forward every argument the eloquence of love prompted, to induce her to run away with him, but in vain.

"Then ye don't care for me," he exclaimed in a tone of passion.

"Archy," replied she, "ye know well I care for ye above the world: an' that I'd thravel Ireland with a bag on my back along with ye."

"It's easy to talk," interrupted Conway, "but fwhy won't ye agree to cum with me, an' sorra bag ye need put on—I've plenty, thanks be to goodness."

"The Lord increase yer store," she answered: "now listen to me, Archy, avourneen—I'll never bring throuble on my father an' mother by goin' away wid any one; but iv they kill me for it, no man, barrin' yersel', will ever put a ring on my finger."

Before he could reply two young men joined them, and Nancy instantly walked away; almost at the same moment Onny arrived, her face flushed, and out of breath.

"Faix I thought the ground opened and swalled ye," she exclaimed in broken accents; "I'm afther killin' myself huntin' for ye through the fair."

She took him aside, and with vehement gestures told him something in a low tone. The effect was electric— his face became inflamed with passion, and, flourishing an oak stick over his head, he leaped up, exclaiming, 'who dare say a word to a Bruin,' and 'huzza for the Bruins,' responded the young men, also cutting the usual caper preparatory to a fight. They then rushed into the fair, sounding the alarm, and in an incredibly short time a number of persons joined them. An instantaneous attack was made on the tent, which soon exhibited but the bare poles without, and within the utmost confusion; Archy all the time calling,

"Come out, Tim Casey—come out ye villan—shew me the Fellin dar shew his head—the Bruins for ever!"

After the first surprise was over, Casey and his party lost no time in escaping, for it would have been madness to contend with the others, who were much more numerous. Archy's party then set out in procession through the fair, leaping, flourishing hats and sticks, and yelling with might and main—

"Down with the Fellins—the Bruins for ever."

On their return in the same order, Archy was, ere he could ward it off, struck with violence by Tim Casey, who had collected a party; Conway soon recovered, and a general battle ensued, to the no small annoyance of the fair, in which the Bruins were victorious, driving their adversaries triumphantly out of the green.

By this time evening was far advanced, and Archy having remained so much longer at the fair than he had promised, set out on his return, but was induced by some companions to step into a shebeen-house on their way, and there they sat drinking a long time. Another party soon afterwards came in, among whom was Tim Casey. Archy rushed at, and would have struck him, did not the landlord and some others prevent him.

"I'll pay ye, ye villan," he exclaimed with fury, while the men were dragging him off, "ye struck me lek a coward."

"Didn't ye first, wid yer party, smash the tent; was I doin' any thing t'ye, only sittin' wid my friends," replied Casey.

"Yes, ye wor match-makin' for a girl that hates ye; I tell ye, Tim Casey, ye'll never put a ring on Billy Sweeny's daughter—never, never," roared Archy.

"That's more nor ye can tell," said Tim.

"I say it, an I'll maintain it till death," cried Conway.

"Whisht, boys, whisht," interposed the landlord, "its a great shame to hear sich an alligation betune dacent boys."

"Dead or alive I ll be revenged iv ye, Tim Casey," said Archy.

The two rivals were separated, and Tim Casey left the house alone, and proceeded on his way home. Archy followed some time after.

On the day after the fair Archy Conway arose late; he walked into the fields, and throwing himself listlessly on a sunny bank, lay for a considerable time so immersed, not in thought, but in a want of thought, that he heard not a sound, until a smart tap on the shoulder with a switch, and the words—

"What Archy! are you asleep?" aroused him; and starting up with a countenance crimsoned over, he replied, not well knowing what to say,

"Ye freckoned me, Masther Henery."

"I believe so," was the young gentleman's answer; "but how comes it, Archy, you are not at work this fine day."

I—I—I—I'm not very well, Sir; there's a pain in my head," stammered Archy.

"I thought you were not to have drank more than one glass yesterday, and to return in two hours."

With a little more confidence, Archy replied, "Shure, Masther Henery its not so asy for a body to get out iv a fair as to go into it; so many friends meets one every minit, an' it's onpossible not to drink a little wid them, and that ye know well, Sir."

"I hear there was an engagement between the factions yesterday—I suppose you took a part."

"Sorra haporth there was, Sir, barrin' a bit iv a scrimmage, nothin' worth relatin'."

"But trifling as it was you were a participator."

"Nera much part I had in it, Sir, only you know I couldn't see my frinds—"

His further comments were cut short by the arrival of two policemen; they touched their caps to Mr. Henry, and laying hold on Archy, arrested him on a charge of murder.

"There must be some mistake," said Henry, after a moment's silent surprise.

"None, Sir," replied one of the police respectfully; if you will take the trouble of walking about a mile with us you will meet your father and the jury, when all can be explained to you."

On coming to the place mentioned by the police, they found a great concourse: the coroner, with such a jury as he could muster, and around them men, women, and children; some talking, some standing with uplifted hands, and some bitterly weeping. The crowd made way for Henry, who went up to his father, asking what all this meant.

"It is, indeed, a dreadful business, my dear," replied the Coroner. "A man was this morning found barbarously murdered, and suspicion, nay more, strong circumstances tend to criminate Archy Conway."

By the time Henry had arrived, the witnesses were examined, and the jury had given in their verdict of wilful murder against Archy. The amazed young man was led within the circle where the murdered remains lay, the face was so dreadfully beaten in by stones that it was impossible to identify it, except by the clothes, which were positively sworn to. A woman was seated on the ground, with the head of the corpse in her lap, who, when she saw Archy, screaming and clapping her hands, exclaimed,

"Look at yer work, ye murdherin' ruffen—look at my fine boy there that ye kilt, an' he'll never spoke to me. Och, Tim Casey, avourneen machree, did yer poor ould mother ever think to see the day ye'd be stretched a disfigured corp; och hone, och hone, fwhat'll I do at all."

The surprise of being immediately brought in contact with a dead body—the screams and words of the afflicted woman, and the charge against himself affected Archy powerfully; he frequently changed colour, and gasped for breath; he once or twice attempted to speak, but his voice was mute, emotion overpowered him.

"Unfortunate young man," said the coroner, "behold the fatal effects of faction, of passion, and drunkenness."

"I wasn't drunk, Sir—I never kilt him nor no other one," sobbed Archy.

The coroner then recapitulated the evidence that had been given, to which Archy replied, "I never kilt him, Sir."

"What became of the deceased after he left the house, and that you followed?" asked the coroner

"A then fwhat would I know, Sir—shure I didn't see him good or bad," was the reply.

"Very well—I don't ask you to say any thing that might criminate yourself," said the coroner, and then directed the prisoner to be removed to the magistrate's.

"An' am I to go to jail for fwhat I never dun, nor even cum into my mind. Oh, wirra, wirra, but that's a poor law. Och, Masther Henery, dear, speak to yer father not to kill me this away," and the poor young man wept bitterly, wringing his hands in the agony of despair.

Henry, also much affected, took Archy's hand, and tried to comfort him; explaining that his father could not act otherwise · and he accompanied him to the house of the magistrate, and waited until Archy, more dead than alive, was taken off to prison.

His friends were not prevented seeing him on the appointed days. On one of the days that Henry came to the prison he was accompanied by a female, closely muffled, who Archy conceived to be his mother; and when Henry left them together, saying he would soon return, Archy began—

"Mother, dear, ye oughtn't to be comin' so often this long road; it'll wear ye out entirely."

The female spoke not, but uncovering her head, Archy gave a cry of joy, for it was Nancy Sweeny who stood before him, blushing deeply at her own temerity. Long and fervent was the embrace with which he folded her in his arms; and only in broken accents could he give utterance to his rapture: tears alike of delight and shame chained his tongue.

"I never thought, asthore machree,[*] ye'd see me in this place," he murmured, pressing her more closely to his breast.

"The will iv God be dun," she replied, gently disengaging herself, "the will iv God be dun, Archy, ahashki,[†] I don't b'leeve ye ever dun any harm; ye're the same to me as ever; it can't be the judge 'll heed fwhat they say agin ye."

"Never dread, Nancy; there's no law in the world to hang the innocent; an', God know's, I'm as innocent as the child that's not born.'

"1 b'leeve ye Archy; I never misdoubted a word ye sid yet; but och, och, every one won't be so;" and she

* Beloved of my heart.
† A term of endearment.

took up the corner of her apron to dry the tears that were dimming the lustre of her eyes.

"Nancy," he said, while a deep shade of sadness clouded his brow, "Nancy, iv they hang me," and a convulsive shudder ran through his frame, "iv they hang me, don't grieve, avourneen; forget Archy Conway, that loves ye above the world, aye an' thinks iv ye (God forgive me!) more nor iv heaven; forget me asthore, an be—" he could not utter ' happy,' but, bursting into a passion of tears, sobbed long and loudly. · Nancy, though suffering as much agitation, endeavoured to comfort him, and gave him the most solemn protestations of never-ceasing affection. But for a length of time she spoke to the winds; at last she threw herself on her knees at his feet, saying,

"Hear me, Archy—iv I didn't think more iv ye than all the world, would I come here, unknownst to father or mother—an' now I declare I'll never be the wife iv any man iv I'm not Archy Conway's."

Archy raised her up, but the entrance of Henry put a period to the interview.

The awful day of trial at last came round, and Archy's friends hurried to the court-house with a feverish impatience, though there was not a human probability of his acquittal. Henry stood by the dock, and occasionally the poor prisoner's hand was locked in his. When Archy was called on to plead, he answered with a tolerably steady voice, ' not guilty, my Lord, not guilty—och, God forbid.' But the evidence was most circumstantial; judge, counsel, and jury seemed of the unanimous opinion that a verdict of guilty must be the result.

During the latter part of the trial a slight bustle was heard in court, which the police soon quelled; one of whom put a paper into Henry's hand. When the case on the part of the crown closed, the prisoner, as a matter of course, (for he was generally deemed guilty), was called on for his defence. Henry then whispered something to him; he seemed confounded; the blood rushed suddenly to his face, and as suddenly retreated. Henry again said, ' speak;' and, to the amazement of all, he called loudly, ' Tim Casey;' the man for whose supposed murder he was on trial. To the increased wonder of the hushed spectators, Tim Casey, alive and well, came forward.

When the universal exclamation of surprise and pleasure (for Archy was greatly commiserated) had subsided, Tim Casey proceeded to solve the enigma.

On leaving the public-house the night of the fair, he was warned that the police were in search of him, for some whiteboy offence; he therefore fled without acquainting any of his family; and the man who had been murdered, being dressed exactly as he was on that day, was easily mistaken for him by his family; as, in consequence of the face being disfigured, he was identified merely by his dress.

The case thus made plain, proved the prisoner innocent. The judge told the jury it were needless to charge them. A verdict of not guilty was handed down, and Archy restored to his expecting friends, among whom none experienced more real pleasure and gratitude to the all wise disposer of events than Henry.

The appearance of Tim Casey at this critical moment remains to be briefly accounted for. Onny, in some of her gossipings, got a hint of the matter from a person who had seen Casey in a distant county, but not clear enough to warrant its being made public. She informed Nancy Sweeny, and they both set out in search of him; after many disappointments they were at length successful, and Tim Casey nobly consented to accompany them, careless of consequences, for the purpose of justifying his rival, and they only arrived in the court-house a few moments before the trial ended.

This escape was a useful warning to Archy Conway—he gave up idle meetings and faction quarrels—married Nancy Sweeny, and became industrious and respected by all his neighbours. W.

DUBLIN:
Printed and Published by P. D. Hardy, 3, Cecilia-street; to whom all communications are to be addressed.
Sold by all Booksellers in Ireland.
In London, by Richard Groombridge, 6, Panyer-alley, Paternoster-row; in Liverpool, by Willmer and Smith, in Manchester, by Ambery, in Birmingham, by Drake; in Glasgow, by W. R M'Phun, and in Edinburgh, by N. Bowack.

THE

DUBLIN PENNY JOURNAL

CONDUCTED BY P. DIXON HARDY, M.R.I.A.

| Vol. III. | AUGUST 2, 1834. | No. 109. |

QUIN ABBEY.

Quin, called also Quint or Quinchy, is situated in the barony of Bunratty, about five miles east of Ennis. An abbey was founded here at an early period, which was consumed by fire, A. D. 1278.

In 1402, Mac Cam Dall Macnamara, lord of Glancoilean, erected the present monastery, being a beautiful strong building of black marble; his tomb is still remaining. This monastery, with all the manors, advowsons, &c. of Daveunwall, Ichanee, Downagour, and divers others, with the site of all the hereditaments thereof, was granted to Sir Turlough O Brien, of Innishdyman (Innistymon) in fee, December 14, 1583.

The monastery was repaired in 1604. Bishop Pococke thus describes its present state : " Quin is one of the finest and most entire monasteries that I have seen in Ireland ; it is situated on a fine stream, with an ascent of several steps to the church : at the entrance one is surprised with the view of the high altar entire, and of an altar on each side of the arch of the chancel. To the south is a chapel, with three or four altars in it, and a very gothic figure in relief of some saint; on the north side of the chancel is a fine monument of the family of the Macnamaras of Rance, erected by the founder ; on a stone by the high altar the name of Kennedye appears in large letters ; in the middle, between the body and the chancel, is a fine tower built on the gable ends. The cloister is in the usual form, with couplets of pillars, but is particular in having buttresses round it by way of ornament ; there are apartments on three sides of it, the refectory,

the dormitory, and another grand room to the north of the chancel, with a vaulted room under them all ; to the north of the large room is a closet, which leads through a private way to a very strong round tower, the walls of which are near ten feet thick. In the front of the monastery is a building, which seems to have been an apartment for strangers, and to the south-west are two other buildings."

Dutton, in his Statistical Survey of the county of Clare, published in 1808, observes, that it remains nearly in the same state as when the bishop wrote, but greatly disfigured by the superstitious custom of burying within the walls of churches. The south end, built by one of the family of Macnamara, is much superior in neatness of workmanship to the adjoining parts. There are the remains of a curious representation of a crucifixion in stucco on the wall near the high altar, that have escaped, I believe, the observation of all travellers.

ACCOUNT OF HIGHLAND ROBBERS.

There is not an instance of any country having made so sudden a change in its morals, as the Hebrides. Security and civilization possesses every part ; yet not many years have elapsed since the whole was a den of thieves, of the most extraordinary kind. They conducted their plundering excursions with the utmost policy, and reduced the whole art of theft into a regular system. From habit it lost all the appearance of criminality : they considered it as labouring in their vocation; and when a party was formed for any expedition against their neighbours' prosperity, they and their friends prayed as earnestly to heaven for success, as if they were engaged in the most laudable design. The constant petition at grace of the old Highland chieftains, was delivered with great fervour in these terms: "Lord! turn the world upside down, that Christians may make bread out of it." The plain English of this pious request was, that the world might become, for their benefit, a scene of rapine and confusion. They paid a sacred regard to their oath; but as superstition, among a set of banditti, infallibly supersedes piety, each (like the distinct casts of Indians) had his particular object of veneration; one would swear upon his dirk, and dread the penalty of perjury, yet made no scruple to forswear himself upon the bible: a second would pay the same respect to the name of his chieftain: a third again would be most religiously bound by the sacred book: and a fourth regard none of the three, and be credited only if he swore by his crucifix. It was also necessary to discover the inclination of the person, before you put him to the test; if the object of his veneration was mistaken, the oath was of no signification. The greatest robbers were used to preserve hospitality to those that came to their houses; and, like the wild Arabs, observed the strictest honour towards their guests, or those who put implicit confidence in them. The Kennedies, two common thieves, took the young Pretender under protection, and kept him with faith inviolate, notwithstanding they knew an immense reward was offered for his head. They often robbed for his support; and to supply him with linen, they once surprised the baggage horses of one of our general officers. They often went in disguise to Inverness, to buy provisions for him. At length, a very considerable time after, one of these poor fellows, who had virtue to resist the temptation of thirty thousand pounds, was hanged for stealing a cow, value thirty shillings. The greatest crime among these fellows, was that of infidelity among themselves: the criminal underwent a summary trial, and, if convicted, never missed of a capital punishment. The chieftain had his officers, and different departments of governments: he had his judge, to whom he entrusted the decision of all civil disputes; but in criminal cases, the chief, assisted perhaps by some favourites, always undertook the process. The principal men of his family, or his officers, formed his council, where every thing was debated respecting their expeditions. Eloquence was held in great esteem among them, for by that they could sometimes so work on their chieftain as to change his opinion; for notwithstanding he always kept the form of a council, he always reserved the decisive vote in himself. When one man had a claim upon another, but wanted power to make it good, it was held lawful for him to steal from his debtor as many cattle as would satisfy his demand, provided he sent notice (as soon as he got out of the reach of pursuit, that he had them, and would return them, provided satisfaction was made on a certain day agreed on.

When a creach, or great expedition had been made against distant herds, the owners, as soon as discovery was made, rose in arms; and with all their friends made instant pursuit, tracing the cattle by their track, for, perhaps, scores of miles. Their nicety in distinguishing that of their cattle from those that were only casually wandering, or driven, was amazingly sagacious. As soon as they arrived on an estate where the track was lost, they immediately attacked the proprietor, and would oblige him to recover the track from his land forwards, or make good the loss they had sustained. This custom had the force of law, which gave to the Highlanders this surprising skill in the art of tracking. It has been observed before, that to steal, rob, and plunder with dexterity, was esteemed as the highest act of heroism. The feuds between the great families was one great cause. There was not a chieftain but kept in some remote valley in the depth of woods and rocks, whole tribes of thieves in readiness to let loose against his neighbours, when (from some public or private reason) he did not judge it expedient to resent openly any real or imaginary affront.— From this motive, the greatest chieftain robbers always supported the lesser, and encouraged no sort of improvement on their estates but what promoted rapine. The greatest of the heroes in the sixteenth century, was Sir Ewin Cameron: he long resisted the power of Cromwell, but at length was forced to submit. He lived in the neighbourhood of the garrison, fixed by the usurper at Inverlochy. His vassals persisted in their thefts, till Cromwell sent orders to the commanding officer, that on the next robbery he should seize on the chieftain, and execute him in twenty-four hours, in case the thief was not delivered to justice. An act of rapine soon happened: Sir Ewen received the message; but, instead of giving himself the trouble of looking out for the offender, he laid hold of the first fellow he met with, and sent him bound to Inverlochy, where he was instantly hanged.— Cromwell, by this severity, put a stop to these excesses till the time of the restoration, when they were renewed with double violence till the year 1745. Rob Roy Macgregor was another distinguished hero in the latter end of the 16th, and the beginning of the 17th century.— He contributed greatly towards forming his profession into a science, and established the police above mentioned. The Duke of Montrose unfortunately was his neighbour. Rob Roy had frequently saved his Grace the trouble of collecting his rents; he used to extort them from the tenants, and at the same time give them formal discharges. But it was neither in the power of the Duke, or any of the gentlemen he plundered, to bring him to justice; so strongly protected was he by several great men to whom he was useful. Roy had his good qualities: he spent his revenge generously; and, strange to say, was a true friend to the widow and orphan. Every period of time gives new improvement to the arts. A son of Sir Ewen Cameron refined on those of Rob Roy; and, instead of dissipating his gains, accumulated wealth. He, like Jonathan Wild, the Great, never stole with his own hands, but conducted his commerce with an address and to an extent unknown before. He employed several companies, and set the more adroit knaves at their head; and never suffered merit to go unrewarded. He never openly received their plunder, but employed agents to purchase from them their cattle. He acquired considerable property, which he was forced to leave behind, after the battle of Culloden gave the fatal blow to all their greatness. The last of any eminence was the celebrated Barrisdale, who carried these arts to the highest pitch of perfection. Besides exalting all the common practices, he improved that article of commerce called the 'Black Meal,' to a degree beyond what was ever known to his predecessors. This was a forced levy, so called from its being commonly paid in meal, which was raised, far and wide, on the estate of every nobleman and gentleman, in order that their cattle might be secured from the lesser thieves, over whom he secretly presided and protected. He raised an income of five hundred a year by these taxes; and behaved with genuine honour in restoring, on proper consideration, the stolen cattle of his friends. In this he bore some resemblance to our Jonathan; but he differed in observing a strict fidelity towards his own gang; yet he was indefatigable in bringing to justice any rogues that interfered with his own. He was a man of polished behaviour, fine address, and a fine person—and considered himself in a very high light, as a bene actor to the public and preserver of general tranquillity.

THE COCKNEY.

The cockney lives in a go-cart of local prejudices and positive allusions; and when he is turned out of it, he hardly knows how to stand or move. He ventures through Hyde Park Corner as a cat crosses a gutter. The trees pass by the coach very oddly. The country has a strange blank appearance. It is not lined with houses all the way like London. He comes to places he never saw or heard of. He finds the world bigger than he thought it. He might have dropped from the moon, for any thing he knows of the matter. He is mightily disposed to laugh, but is half afraid of making some blunder. Between sheepishness and conceit, he is in a very ludicrous situation.— He finds that the people walk on two legs, and wonders to hear them talk a dialect so different from his own. He perceives London fashions have got down into the country before him, and that some of the better sort are dressed as well as he is. A drove of pigs or cattle stopping the road is a very troublesome interruption. A crow in the field, a magpie in the hedge, are to him very odd animals—he can't tell what to make of them, or how they live. He does not like the accommodations at the inns—it is not what he has been used to. He begins to be communicative—says he was "born within the sound of Bow bells," and attempts some jokes at which nobody laughs. He asks the coachman a question, to which he receives no answer. All this is to him very unaccountable and unexpected. He arrives at his journey's end, and instead of being the great man he anticipated among his friends and country relations, finds they are barely civil to him, or make a butt of him; have topics of their own which he is as completely ignorant of, as they are indifferent to what he says, so that he is glad to get back to London again; where he meets with his favorite indulgences and associates, and fancies the whole world is occupied with what he hears and sees.

It is curious to see to what a degree persons brought up in certain occupations in a great city, are shut out from a knowledge of the world, and carry their simplicity to a pitch of unheard of extravagance. London is the only place in which the child grows completely up into the man.

POPULAR LECTURES ON THE PHYSIOLOGY OF ANIMALS.

The following is an abstract of Dr. Henry's fourth Lecture :

SENSE OF TOUCH.

I have mentioned three kinds of sensibility as possessed by the skin. I come now to treat of that sort of sensibility of the skin, which conveys to the mind knowledge of impressions made on it by external objects. Whatever makes an impression on the skin, so as to produce a considerable change in it, must, more or less, through its medium, make an impression on the mind. Of such impressions I have spoken at length in the preceding lectures. but numerous impressions may be made on the skin without producing any sensible change in it, and yet operate perceptibly on the mind through its intervention ; all these impressions are comprehended under the term, *impressions of touch*. The sense of touch resides in the external papillary surface of the true skin. When any object comes in contact with an external part of the body, the individual is rendered sensible of its presence and contact, by means of the nerves, which terminating at one extremity in the papillary surface of the true skin, communicate by their other extremity with the brain.— This is the simplest form of the sense of touch. In this, its simplest form, the sense of touch does little more than convey to the mind an intimation of the presence and contact of external objects. It is obviously necessary that all the external surface of the body should possess this property, in order to secure it from injuries which might be inflicted upon it if the skin were destitute of this power ; injuries which the individual might be able to avert, if only he were warned of their approach. The skin may, therefore, be considered as a sentinel, or warder, which gives notice to the individual of the contact of external substances. The sense of touch in this, its simplest form, is generally diffused through the whole animal kingdom. The possession of this sense enters into our very idea of an animal. It is plain that an animal without this sense would not only be exposed defenceless to the aggressions of other animals, but would be unable to seek its food, or even to perform any regulated movement, or, in other words, would be reduced to the rank of a vegetable. Although the whole surface of the skin possesses the sense of touch, yet all parts are not equally endowed with it. Those parts in which the papillæ are most developed, possess this sense in the greatest perfection. The papillæ are most developed at the extremities of the body, particularly at the points of the fingers and toes. First.—Because the extremities are most likely, from their position, to come into contact with other bodies. Secondly—Because the extremities are the instruments by which the whole body is moved ; and thirdly, because from the great mobility of these parts they are adapted for voluntary application to other bodies, for the purpose of exploring their characters, viz :—their shape, size, consistence, temperature, &c. For these reasons the extreme projecting parts of animal bodies have the most delicate sense of touch. In man the great instrument of touch is the hand. By means of this instrument he is enabled to seize and hold the object—to explore it in all directions—to make pressure on it—to move and shift it about, so as to expose it to the scrutiny of his other senses. No other animal has an organ of touch at all to be compared with the human hand. Many animals have the extremities shut up in hard, solid, horny hoofs. Although through the hoof the presence of objects can be ascertained, yet it is quite evident that no other, or very little other knowledge can be obtained through the medium of this organ. The extremities of hoofed animals are also unfit for reacting upon objects, their motions being necessarily confined to striking or propelling. They are utterly incapable of seizing, turning, holding, or examining an object, and even if capable, could not be spared for such purposes, being constantly employed in supporting the weight of the trunk. The claws of the *cat* tribe are admirably adapted for seizing, holding, and tearing soft substances, like the bodies of other animals, into which their sharp points can sink, but are incapable of holding hard or flat objects. These animals are compelled, for want of thumbs, to hold objects between the paw and the ground. They are also incapable of using tools, or of holding, or examining minute objects. First, for want of broad tips of fingers ; the tips of their fingers being narrow and pointed, and in many instances incased in horny claws. Secondly—for want of a free, separate motion of the fingers. Thirdly—for want of a thumb, so placed that the object can be held between it and the tips of the other fingers. Fourthly—the extremities of these animals are encumbered with hair, nor can they be spared for any considerable length of time from the necessary office of supporting the body ; for which reason the common cat, when she plays with an object, lies down on the ground, in order to obtain the free use of her paws. Even in the ape kind, the paws, or hands as they are sometimes called, are quite inferior to the human hand. Although the ape has a thumb, yet it is small and weak, and not proportioned to the length of his fingers —in the Ouran Outang, and Chimpanzee, reaching only to the metacarpo-nedigital joint. For this reason the ape cannot hold objects as they are held by the human hand, between the fingers and thumb ; although he is enabled by means of his long fingers and short thumbs, to surround and grasp the branches of trees ; and accordingly we find the thumb very constantly on the hind extremities of apes, the thumb serving the same office to the ape, as the hind toe to the bird. It has been much disputed whether the ape is intended to go on all-fours, or to walk erect, like man, on his hinder extremities. The truth is, the ape is not intended for either of these modes of progression, but for living amongst trees, and moving about or swinging from branch to branch. For similar reasons the feet of birds are adapted for grasping the branches of trees, for which purpose the toe at the back of the foot is useful. The toes of birds are adapted also for scraping, seizing, and tearing, but not for the performance of those acts which are performed with such ease by the human hand. The hands and feet of *fishes*, being enveloped in membrane, so as to form fins, are obviously quite unfit for any other purpose than that of propelling the animal through the water. The so-much-famed elephant's trunk is an instrument of touch and prehension, given to the animal as a compensation for his enormous bulk and unwieldiness. It serves partly as an instrument of offence and defence, but principally to supply him with food and drink. Suppose the elephant without his trunk—on account of his height and bulk he could not bring his mouth to the ground, to obtain food and drink like other animals, nor could he seize or hold his food with his paws, which have enough to do to support his body. By means of the trunk he breaks off branches of trees, and tears up succulent plants out of the ground, and puts them into his mouth, as a man would with his hand. In the same manner his drink is taken up by the trunk and conveyed into his mouth. Although the trunk is so strong, so flexible, and so admirably adapted for its purpose, yet it is quite inferior as an instrument of sensation and action. First, because it is single; and secondly, because its extremity is not divided, so as to be capable of embracing an object on all sides at the same time, and consequently is quite unfit for holding tools. It follows, therefore, that although the intellectual faculties of the elephant were much greater than they really are, yet the animal must ever remain ignorant and incapable of performing any work of art.

From this comparison of the human hand with the corresponding parts of other animals, (for the anterior extremities of man, and all animals which have a skeleton, are made on one plan,) you will perceive the great excellence of this organ in man. When you consider the freedom of motion at the shoulder joint—the curious structure of the anterior part of the arm, consisting of two bones, the one turning freely on the other—the flexibility of the wrist—the thumb like a second hand, inasmuch as by the joint action of the thumb and fingers of one hand a variety of acts may be performed, which would otherwise require two hands—the breadth of the tips of the fingers, so peculiar to the human race—the admirable support given to the skin at the points of the fingers by the nail behind—the strength of the hand, and the wonderful sensibility of the points of the fingers themselves, by which the slightest object can be felt and distinguished, you no longer wonder at the works which the hand of man is able to execute—the instrument is equal to the work.— Inferior to many other animals in quickness of smell, sight and hearing, and not much, if at all, superior in the sense of taste, man is raised to an infinite pre-eminence above all other animals by the hand alone. His superior intellectual endowments would not by themselves be sufficient to raise him to this preeminence ; for intellectual power must, of necessity, be useless without knowledge to afford it food, and without an agent by means of which to re-act in consequence of that knowledge. The sense of touch, or the hand, in which this sense mainly resides, is, as we shall see as we proceed with the history of the senses, the main source of all human knowledge, and the principal agent of all human power.

THE OLD CHURCH AT SELSKER, WEXFORD.

The annexed sketch represents the remains of the once celebrated priory of St. Peter and St. Paul, usually styled Selsker, situate near the west gate of Wexford. It was founded about the year 1190 for Regular Canons, of the order of St. Augustine, by the Roches, lords of Fermoy, though it was not an original foundation, but like most of the ecclesiastical buildings in this county, a re-erection on the site of an old church dedicated to the same apostles. The square tower or castle, formerly attached to the priory, is in a high state of preservation, adjoining to which there has been lately built a church, under the inspection of Mr. Semple, architect to the Commissioners for First Fruits. The interest we feel in inspecting these ruins is considerably increased by the recollection that the first treaty ever signed in this kingdom with the English was on this spot, in the year 1169, when the town of Wexford surrendered to Dermod M'Murrough and his allies.

This church, with six others, were demolished by order of Oliver Cromwell, when in possession of the town in 1649. The churches so destroyed were St. Patrick's, St. Mary's, St. Bride's, St. John's, St. Peter's, and St. Maud's, commonly called Maudlin Town. Not satisfied with levelling these various places of worship, together with the plate belonging to the priory of Selsker, he took possession of a very fine ring of bells, which he shipped for Chester, but which, being of a superior description, were removed a few years afterwards to the Old Church, near River-street, in Liverpool, where they remain to this day.

A very melancholy circumstance took place in this churchyard a few years since. A mate of a Welch vessel, then lying at the quay, was taken violently ill at night and after a few hours' illness, having apparently died, a contagious fever then raging in the town, the fear of spreading the infection caused his speedy interment. A few hours after the funeral had taken place, some children playing in the church ground declared that they heard a strange noise in the grave. On this story spreading through the town, it induced several persons to attend, when the grave being re-opened, and the coffin examined, it was found that the poor man had actually turned himself round on his face; and from the quantity of blood appearing about the corpse, it was concluded he must have made a most violent struggle, and had the grave, on the first alarm, been opened, there is little doubt but the life of the individual would have been saved. Several persons now living in this town were at the opening of the seaman's grave. C. H. W.

Wexford, June, 1831.

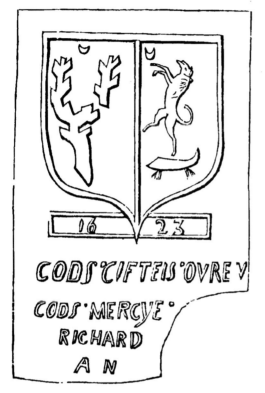

Sir,—The above are correct copies of two flags at present among the ruins of St. Peter's and Paul's abbey, commonly called Selsker, in the town of Wexford. The first is evidently to represent a shield, bearing on the right side a lion rampant over a crocodile, and on the opposite, a tree, both surmounted by crescents : it bears the date 1623, but as to the inscription, I am perfectly at a loss to conjecture what the object of it was. The second is in old English, and I have transcribed it, as it is no easy matter to read.

" God who raised us to build and buy
  For life and death posterity
  Grant do our life to the grace death crowned
  And do our posterity gain the same renown
  That this thy grace in us begun descend
  He them increasing to the world's end
  That each confess God's gifts is our possession
  And ever sing God's mercies our protection."

In the transcription I have not adhered in the spelling to the original.
Wexford. C. D.

⁂ We are much obliged by such communications as these ; they are not only curious and interesting but often throw light on bygone times, and sometimes settle difficult points of national history.

No. 1, is a sepulchral flag, which, no doubt, covered the grave of Richard Stafford, of Wexford, and Anstace, his wife, who was the daughter of Leonard Sutton, of Ballykeroge in the county of Wexford : they died in the year 1622, and were buried in the abbey of St. Peter and Paul.

The Staffords were descended from John Stafford, a third son of a Buckinghamshire family, who acquired the estate of Ballymachrane, in the county of Wexford, about the reign of King Henry the Seventh ; and from him descended the families of Ballyconnor ; George Stafford, who built the castle and hall of Wexford ; Richard Stafford, above-mentioned, who was descended from a second brother of Ballyconnor ; and two other branches who possessed considerable property in Wexford in the reign of James I. and Charles I.

The family of Sutton were also of very ancient residence and respectability in Wexford and the adjoining counties : they possessed Old Court, as well as Ballykerogmore, and were of the same original stock as the Suttons of Tipper, in Kildare.

The arms on the stone are empaled, baron and femme.— 1—Argent, three staffs of oak, ragulee, two and one *for Stafford.* 2—Or a lion rampant gules, treading on a lizard, vert, *for Sutton.* The lower of the staves is joined with the first in the stone, but that is but a clumsy error of the stone cutter. The name, *Richard,* was probably followed by *Stafford* on the broken part of the flags, as was A N with Sutton.

The other flag probably stood in the wall of the abbey under a mural epitaph. W. B. U.

THE BANSHEE.

Any person however partially acquainted with the wild superstitions prevalent amongst the peasantry of Ireland, must h -e heard of the banshee. To those who are unacquainted with the terrible and more than eastern wildness and magnificence with which the people of Ireland clothe their legend of unearthly beings, and the depth of imagination that characterizes every belief associated with their world of spirits, some short explanation may be necessary. The banshee is believed to be an unearthly attendant on certain ancient families in this country, and it is only seen or heard previous to the decease of some of its members. It is usually represented as a small though beautiful female, dressed in the fashion of the early ages, and who, with a particularly mournful and melancholy cry, bewails the misfortune about to fall upon the family she loves. I have read[*] it somewhere given, that some of those fair forerunners of sorrow are actuated by a feeling inimical to the line which they lament.— This, however, is not the opinion of the people among whom the superstition is entertained, and even cherished. Their belief is, that the spirit is the friend of the family it follows ; that it at one period enjoyed life, and walked the earth in the light and shadow of loveliness and mortality. This, I think, is the more natural turn for such things to take in the human mind, however rude ; and the very fact of its always crying its sweet dirge bears me out, for if otherwise than a friend why not rejoice ? It is also said to be very shy of encountering a mortal eye ; and the slightest sound wafted on the breeze of evening drives it from the sight like a thing of mist. Now for my tale.

On the borders of the small and ruinous village of Ballintobber,[†] in the county of Roscommon, there lived a small farmer, named James Moran, or as he was stiled by the country folk, in their own peculiar manner *Cooleen bawn*[‡], alias *Shemus Gal*.[§] He was married but a short time to the servant of a gentleman in the neighbourhood, in whose family she had lived for a good many years, and being of careful habits, she brought to *Shemus* the better part of her earnings. One fine evening in the month of April, when the grey gloaming is beginning to extend itself, dim and shadowy, into the long nights, giving promise, at intervals, of the glory and beauty of the approaching summer, Madgy (Marcella) sat alone in her cottage, plying her household affairs with a happy heart, and expecting her husband to his evening repast after the toils of the day. Night came, and the hour that should have brought her husband to his home, passed away without his coming. She began to grow anxious and uneasy, and setting his supper by the fire, to keep it warm, she closed her door, and sat down beside her spinning-wheel with a sigh. Another hour passed away, and sad thoughts began to rise in her mind. All the wonderful and fearful stories she had heard about ghosts and fairies, and all the goblins that haunted the castle of the O'Connors, and all the blood that was spilt around it, crowded upon her imagination ; and as the blaze of the sprightly fire cast flickering shadows about the house, the agitated and imaginative Madgy would start, and look around her with frightened glances. "I'll sing a song," said she to herself ; " it will relieve my mind and prevent such idle thoughts from disturbing me, besides making the time pass quickly until *Shemus* comes home ;" and she began singing in her native Irish a wild legend, still in connexion with the subject that haunted her imagination, and which being translated might run pretty much like the following :

---

[*] I think by no less a personage than Mr. Crofton Croker, but I do not give this as fact, that is, I am not certain, but I believe it.

[†] *Ballintobber*, situated in the barony of the same name, county of Roscommon ; here are the ruins of the ancient residence of the O'Connors, kings of Connaught ; it was at one time surrounded by deep woods, which have all disappeared. The extensive ruins stand in an angle where the road divides, and are very picturesque.

[‡] Fair hair.

[§] James of the fair hair, or fair James.

BALLAD.

Fair Eveleen sat in her tower high,
 On a calm and a silent night ;
And she gazed on the twinkling lamps of the sky,
 Than her own blue eyes less bright.

And the silver moonbeams bathed her brow,
 But her cheek was as cold and pale ;
" Darmuid's fleet foot is lagging now,
 Ah ! what means that dreadful wail !"

For wofully sad was the thrilling strain,
 Now borne upon the breeze ;
And it fell on her brain like an icy chain,
 And her heart's blood began to freeze.

And still as the dying pauses swept,
 In their wailing sounds of fear ;
The sobs and the plaints of one that wept,
 Rose sadly upon her ear.

It was the banshee ! and she came to tell
 A tale of sorrow and death ;
For Darmuid that night 'neath a rival fell,
 Upon *Moin-more's*[*] dreary heath.

" Such unearthly sounds !" poor Eveleen well
 Their meaning could discover ;
For the morning sun-beams fairly fell
 On her corse, beside her lover !

The wild song was scarcely concluded when Moran entered. He was much agitated, and looked about him with a haggard glance. Madgy started in alarm at his bewildered air, and tenderly enquired what was the matter with him.

" Oh, sit down, Madgy, *aroon*, sit down, and give me my supper, for I'm scarcely able to faint, then I'll tell you all about it—ochone, ochone !"

While Madgy was preparing the humble repast, he became more composed, but still the thoughts of something terrible seemed to linger about him.

" Now, *Shemus, asthore*, tell me what in the world frikened you out of your life."

" Arrah hould your whisht, Madgy, 'tall I gather up the bit ov gumption that I had afore this night, Och, *wurra sthrue*."

" Were you murthered or kilt, *Shemus*, jewel—or what came across you at all at all ?"

" Och, thin, it's yourself that's the foolish woman antirely ; don't you see I'm neither cut or bleedin', an' how can I be murthered ? an' iv I was kilt, itself, sure it's nothin' to what came over me this blessed night !"

" Arrah, then, maybe it's somethin' that happened the mare, or the heifer, or the pig, or the—"

" Ochone, ochone ! thin I b'lieve it's yourself that's mad, or ravin', or murthered in arnest, for one woman like you, that couldn't let a misforthenate man alone for a while ; will you just sit down, an' say nothin' an' show that you didn't lose your seven senses as well as myself."

This was too much for the fond Madgy. She thought some unheard of misfortune, too terrible for her even to conceive, had befallen her husband ; for murdering or killing was only a trifling injury ; the next in the scale of evil would be any damage done to the mare, or the cow, or the sow ; any thing beyond that should be something out of the common line of calamity : so, unable to restrain her emotions, she threw herself on a seat in a paroxysm of grief, and began the Irish cry, in all its tones and variations, from the wild burst of lamentation, rising into a shriek, to the low, sorrowful moaning of smothered anguish.

" Och, och, ochone, *gra ma chree ma cuishleen baun* ;[†] is it yourself that's come to the black misforthen unknownst to the world, an' your own Madgy, that used to be your *Colleen asthore*,[‡] och, ochone !"

---

[*] The great bog.

[†] The love of my heart—my fair darling.

[‡] Dear girl.

This touching appeal was too much for the feelings of the tender-hearted *Shemus*. * He started up, clasped his arms about her neck, and joined in the thrilling chorus to this particularly sad and melancholy wail. After exhausting the fountains of their tears, and in some degree easing their hearts, for tears bring relief, they sat down quite composed at the fire.

"Och, Shemus, *a vick sa goltha**," began the anxious wife, "what, in the name of all the saints and angels came over you?—do tell your own Madgy."

"Oh! then, just listen now Madgy, an' I'll tell you all about it; an' don't say a word to stop me or stay me till I have done."

Madgy did not answer, but bent herself forward with eagerness to hear the tale.

"Well, you know Miss Norah at the big house," began *Shemus*; "she's sick with a head-ache these two days."

"Aye, Shemus—I hope the crather's betther anyhow."

"She'll die as sure as a gun, Madgy—I know it all."

"Ah, don't say that now, Shemus; sure the Lord wouldn't take the masther's one daughther from him that way."

"She's a dead and gone corpse, I tell you, Madgy; didn't I see the banshee, and hear her too, this very evenin', comin' through the grove at the ind ov the garden, as I crossed the stile. I thought I heard somethin' at first cryin' and keenin' down by the sthream, and every hair on my head stood up as stiff as a hackle, an' I thought my *caubeen* would have run away off my head, so I stood where I was, an' didn't say a word; then the screeching came nearer and nearer, an' the sorra such a murtherin' screech did I ever hear afore, for I thought it was comin' up out ov the wather all along; at last up come the banshee to the very turn of the sthrame, where the big sally three (sallow willow) hangs over it, an' there she sat down, an' roared as iv her heart was bruck in two; rockin' herself backward and forward, and meltin' herself down into the wather wid the *parfid* (perfect) grief; an' then she stood up, an' I was afeerd she was goin' to come to myself, so took to my heels, and never cried crack till I was inside the door with you."

"Och, *wirra sthrue*, an' did she look at you my darlint?"

"All the saints in the calendhar forbid—no she didn't; for iv she did I'd have dhropt as dead as mutton."

"But didn't you tell the masther and the misthress ov all this, *Shemus*?"

"Arrah no I didn't—ketch me at it: Oh, no, faix, I'm not such a fool as that, an' have to come back an' face a banshee."

"An' you wouldn't go an' warn the good family ov their misery. I'll go this very minit."

"Is it you, Madgy, *ma gragal*;† and will you go over the sthrame this night, after all that came across me?"

"I don't care, *Shemus*—come what will I'll go to the big house this mortual night."

"The blessed Vargin purtect us—it's myself that wouldn't let you go alone. Come, Madgy, we'll go together; and both stood up to depart. Madgy put on her warm cloak, and pinned her kerchief tightly over her cap, and under her chin, and together they jogged towards the mansion of her former master. Silent and tremblingly did they pass over the stile that led by a short cut to the rear of the house. Cautiously and slowly did they approach the haunted stream, and with hasty steps did they glide by the shadowy *Sally* tree, and up to the door. They rushed in about the apartment, like people pursued by some dreadful spectre, and gazed about with wild and haggard looks, while the servants thronged around them with anxious and curious enquiries.

"How is Miss Norah?" were the first words uttered by the affectionate Madgy.

"Why she is purty well, I thank you," replied one of the servants.

"Where is she, let me see her?" said Madgy, doubtingly.

---

* Son of my neighbour.
† My white love.

"Did yous hear nothin', said *Shemus*."

"Yes—we heard that the poor widow Conry was dead; and Miss Norah went down to bring up poor little Aylee, her daughter."

"Thank heaven!" said Madgy in a relieved tone of voice.

"Oh, then, it was for her the banshee was cryin' as sure as I'm alive,' said *Shemus*.

"Banshee!" said one. "Banshee!" echoed another; and all took the alarm.

"Ah, thin, did you see the banshee, *Shemus*?' was ventured as a question by a third.

"Did I ever hear father Con ov a Sunday, do you think?" said *Shemus* with an air of consequence; "did I ever hear the banshee! Ah, thin, it's myself that did; an' its she that cried herself sick aither poor *Shuawn*, (Julia, alias Judy) Conry, below at the three, at the turn ov the sthrame."

"What sort was she?" "How did she look?" "How was she dhressed?" "What did she say?" was asked by all the listeners in a breath.

"Iv yous want the knowledge," said *Shemus*, "go down an' take a peep at her yourselves, an' I'll be bound that she'll *insince* yous into the ins and outs ov id in a hurry."

"No but *Shemus*, what did she say to you?"

"Why then I ll tell yous—sorra resave the word at all, nor I to her; but I ran away an' left her there."

Here Miss Norah entered with a girl of about fifteen years of age, all in tears, and the whole circumstance of the banshee was explained. The widow's poor daughter had broken away in the excess of her grief, and wandered by the lonely stream side to indulge in and give vent to her sorrows and miseries alone; and, as *Shemus* expressed it, was "near frikenin' the life out ov him, an' sure she might as well kill him out and out at once." So he lost his consequence in the country as the wonderful man who had seen a banshee. Miss Norah was pleased with the affection evinced for her by Madgy, and blamed *Shemus* for giving way to such absurd superstitions; wondering how people could give up their reason to the chimeras of their own heated imaginations, and allow themselves to become the fools of every passing shadow or idle sound. This was received with doubtful and uneasy looks by the auditory, and one old man who was almost a silent listener to all that passed before, now broke in upon the wondering audience.

"Then maybe, Miss Norah, I was never tellin' you," said he, "about the banshee ov the O'Connors ov the Castle, in the ould ancient times."

"No Malachi," replied Miss Norah; "but won't you tell us now, for though I don t believe all I hear, still I like to hear the old stories of other times."

"Indeed an' I will, Miss Norah," said the old man; "and may you never meet with such a cross either before or aither your marriage, for it's yourself that's good, and kind, and purty, may heaven bless you;" and the whole crowd collected round the old man, who related his legend of other days in nearly the following words:

"Well you must know in the ould times ov all, when the kings and princes were as plinty about the counthry as jackstones on the shores of *Lough Ree*,* the O'Connors lived below there, at their grand palace ov Ballintobber, in the middle of the deep woods that are now all cut away. The O'Connors were the ould kings ov Connaught; an' a mighty grand sort ov high kind of people they were antirely, an' as wicked as murdher. Well, there was one ould king that they used to call *Phaudhereen Grumagh*,† and he had but one son, and a fine young joutleman he was, by all accounts. He was out huntin' one day, not very far from his own place, and at that time there was plenty ov deers and other wild bastes about the counthry, and the right sort ov fine

---

* *Lough Ree*, or "the King of Lakes," situated between Ros-common and Westmeath, is a very extensive and beautiful lake, formed by the Shannon: it has several wooded islands, in one of which are some very romantic ruins. On the banks of this lake stood the celebrated convent of Bethlehem.
† Patrick, the stern, or severe, or churlish.

sport they used to have ov it. Well, you see, the stag took down by the little river, near *Toemonia*,* and the young king, being a rale mad cap, was the first in with him, as he turned at the rock by the end ov the pool; an' by my conscience, 'twould be betther for him to be a hundred miles off, for the stag made a dash ov a burst on him, and, afore he could cry 'the Lord have mercy on me,' he was whipt off his horse, and soused, all tore to pieces, into the middle of the pool, 'ithout a word in his cheek. Then up come all the noblemen and jontlemen, powdherin' on their horses like fire, and they fished him out of the pool, and carried him to the house ov a dacent man nigh hand, a farmer or a cottier, or somethin' ov the kind, where he was put to bed, an' docthered about, for he was in a ragin' fever for three weeks.

"'Och, murder *in eelish*, where am I at all,' sez he one evenin' after comin' to his senses.

"'Your with friends,' my Lord, sez a purty, rosy-cheeked *colleen* that was sittin' at the foot ov the bed watchin'him.

"'An' who brought me here,' sez he, ' or what ails me?'

"'Why, my lord,' sez the purty girl, ' you were kilt, an' dhrownded there beyant, near Toemonia, by a big baste ov a stag, bad win' to him, and all the jontlemen carried you here; an' faix, my lord, I'm glad to see you gettin' betther.'

"'An' have I no one to watch or nurse-tindher me but you, *avourneen,*' sez he.

"'Oh, yes, my lord,' sez she, ' the docther 'ill be here immegently, an' sure I thought no one could take so much care ov you as myself.'

He began to grow well from that day out; and the little *Noneen* used to take care ov him and bring him his whay and his tay, an' whatever kind of dhrinks the docther used to ordher him; an' the sorra the least hurry ne was in to lay (leave) the house, for they were deep in love with one another; an' who can help such things.— At last the wars broke out, an he was forced to go, but afore he went he come to take his leave ol *Nona*.

"'I'm goin' away from you, my darlint, sez he, ' in the coorse of a week to the fightin', achorra; an maybe I'd never see your purty face agin;' and then she began to cry as iv her heart id break antirely. 'But hould up your head, *Nona*,' sez he again, 'I'm just come to marry you afore I go. I've a frind, a priest, here beyant at the abbey, an' he's just at hand, an' 'ill do the job for us out ov the face;' an' then he kissed her, an' she cried more an' more. At any rate they got married, an' in the coorse of a week he went to the wars They had fine fun murdherin' an shootin' one another, till it was all over; and then they come home, and the ould king sez to his son one day,

"'Come here, Phelim, my own *boucheleen,*' sez he.

"'Well, your honour, what is it you want?' sez the young prince quite polite.

"'I want to get you a wife,' sez the ould *grumagh*, mighty grand.

"'Oh, then you may spare yourself the throuble,' sez Phelim, 'for I don't intend to have done with myself that way for a couple of summers longer.'

"'What would you think ov the King of Munsther's daughther,' sez the ould king.

"'I don't think she's half so purty as the people say she is,' sez the prince.

"'But you know, I suppose, that I past my word on the matther when I was makin' the pace,' sez his father.

"'More shame for you, iv you did, 'ithout axin' me,' sez the prince, very stout ; for you see he had the right sort iv blood in him—' more shame for you, afther I gettin' myself all smashed to pieces fightin' for you.'

"'*Bathershin*,† sez the ould chap; but it's done, you know now, an' there's no back doors, so you must marry her.'

"'Why, then, an' that's more than I can do,' sez the prince.

"'How so?' sez the *Grumagh*.

"'Bekase I'm marred already,' sez the prince, ' an' there's no man can have two wives accordin' to the laws ov God an' man,' for he was mighty well larned.

"Then the king got into a murdherin' big passion, an' swearin' a great oath, sez he, ' iv I had another son, I'd knock your head off you spalpeen, an' then you might go look for a kingdom where you liked. But who are you marred to?' sez he, somethin' cool agin. So the prince ups and tells him the whole of the affair from beginnin' to end ; an' the king sed nothin' but shook his head. Well, that very night, a party of sodgers, with their guns and bagnets, surrounded the house where *Nona* lived, and took her away, body an' bones, an' no one could tell what become ov her.

"The prince was like a mad man for the loss of his wife : he sarched the kingdom from one end to the other, but he couldn't hear a word about her, no more than iv the ground opened and swallowed her; an' a whole year passed away, an' the prince's grief was dyin', an' the ould king again proposed to get him marred, and he was so tormented about it, that at last he sez,

"'Sorra may care,' sez he ; ' my heart is a'most bruck in two, an' I don't care what yous do with me.' So the day was fixed, and the king of Munsther and his daughter, and all their noblemen came to Ballintobber ; an' there was fun there you may be sure. Bullocks and sheep were roasted, an' whiskey an' wine galore was goin' about 'ithout end. Such doin's were never seen in the counthry since or before. Well they were all in the chapel, and the ould bishop was marryin' the young couple, and just as he was takin' the first kiss o' the bride, a terrible big screech was heard, and the people were all started ; an' who should run up to the very althar, but Nona herself. Well she looked about her, first at the bishop, next at the king's daughther, and then at the prince. ' My husband,' sez she, quite easy, and her head fell upon her bosom, and before any one could stretch out a hand, she dhropt dead on the stone steps. Well the young prince lifted her up, and kissed her, and cried over her. The bishop sed the marriage was no use, and the King ov Munsther and his daughther went home ashamed ov themselves. The prince never went near his father afther, nor never marred, but its said that the night he died, little *Nona* was heard cryin' at his window, an' that he knew her voice. And when he went, another branch of the family came in for the crown, but there was none of the family that ever died but Nona comes to cry them. Didn't I see her myself the time the last young masther died in Jarmany at the wars cryin' round the ould towers, and in through the arches ; and when the misthress got the account ov her son's death, wasn't that the very night he died."

The most breathless attention was paid to the story of old Malachi until he finished. All expressed their pity for the innocent and unfortunate *Nona*, and their wonder at the concluding part. "But," said Miss Norah, "where was she, Malachi, during the year that they were looking for her ?"

"Tundher an turf," Miss Norah, "didn't I tell you that she was confined in one ov the dungeons of the very castle of Ballintobber; an' the night ov the weddin', when all the sarvints got dhrunk, she made her escape, and come to the chapel, where her heart broke."

"You did not, indeed, tell me that before," said Miss Norah.

"Well, then, if I didn't, I ought, *alanna*," said old Malachi.

Such is the legend of the banshee of the O'Connors.

J. L. L.

---

* In Irish, *Touathmona*, was formerly a place of some consideration ; for there was a large monastery for Dominican friars founded here by the O'Connors : here are also the remains of a very ancient castle belonging to the same family, but there are no other restiges of its former inhabitants. It is near Tulsk, county of Roscommon.

† Perhaps—maybe so.

DUBLIN:
Printed and Published by P. D HARDY, 3, Cecilia-street ; to whom all communications are to be addressed.
Sold by all Booksellers in Ireland.
In London, by Richard Groombridge, 6, Panyer-alley, Paternoster-row, in Liverpool, by Willmer and Smith ; in Manchester, by Ambery; in Birmingham, by Drake ; in Glasgow, by W. R. M'Phun ; and in Edinburgh, by N. Bowack.

THE

DUBLIN PENNY JOURNAL

CONDUCTED BY P. DIXON HARDY, M.R.I.A.

| Vol. III. | AUGUST 19, 1834. | No. 110. |

MENAI STRAIT AND BRIDGE.

TOURIFICATIONS OF BARNY O'TRUE AND THRO.

Lunnun.

Mister Edithur and Sir—This here note comes hopping your honour will excuse the liberty I takes in forwarding you the hinclosed bundle of letthers, picked up to'ther day in the Strand. Seeing how it is, though I be so long out of ould Hireland, as to be now a riglar bred and born Hinglashman, still you see the froth o' my quart, and the beard of my naggin, is iver warm and wilcome to a countryman; and you understand, by the here *goodness* of the writein', for my masther in the Timple says *ould Nick* himself *couldn't read* it. I guessed it must be something mighty larned and good intirely, and must, by coorse, have come out of Connaught, Munster, or those parts : at any rate out of some place in ould Hireland.—For, afther all,' from where but the hiland of saints could any morthal pin cum able to puzzle his Black Majesty, God between us and harm ! So, Sir, your honour, wishing, as I said before, a countryman to sarve a countryman, or, mayhap, anent all the world, a coleen bawn ; and, thirfore, to have these litthers reech their owner, and knowing that your honour was like the sun in a fog through all Hireland, *universally red*, I thought the only sure way to gain my ind was to sind thim to your honour for printein' ; for says I, to myself, as thin every mother

VOL. III.—NO. 6.

sowl, from Cape Clear to the Giant's Causeway will see thim, they must come to the person intinded. This I now do Misther Edithur,

Remaining ever to command,

Your honor's obedient sarvant,

Terry O'Rourke.

P. S.—If writein' an answer, please to direct to me, *Esquire*, for I am my masther's own gentleman, and haven't cleaned a boot, or brushed a coat those seven years.

London.

Dear Sir—I arrived here yesterday evening, and only yesterday evening, all sound in wind and limb, last by " the Red Rover." My first start on English ground was in " The Wonder," and sure enough it was a wonder it had me to start with. We embarked at Kingstown in " The Dragon" at nine o'clock on Friday the 7th, and had a very short and pleasant passage. I was never less sick, and stood on Irish and Welsh soil within six hours and a quarter. This too, and the animal as she " walked the waters," certainly in much need of a *doctor ;* for she growled and grumbled, was *ricketty* as a' " changeling" from the fairies, and *shook* in the ribs, until there seemed no other remedy for staunching her own, while she smothered ours, but a somerset some hundred feet under water, and a " safe delivery" of us, one and all, into the kindly keeping of the sharks! "Her keepers" should certainly be blown up for their neglect or carelessness of her wants and ailments. And here I may mention, for the information of any of your friends who may be coming to the great city, that such is the opposition from the Head to London, that I have little doubt whoever makes a "hard bargain" ensures his seat up for a pound, or at the utmost a guinea, outside; and from thirty to five and thirty shillings in. Without being once asked the question, the contending parties offered to book me as a "cabin passenger" for two pounds; and *agreed* to take me "on deck," or rather among the "rigging" for one pound five!

The opponents are the "Wonder" and "Nimrod" coaches. The first a four, the latter a twohorsed vehicle. I preferred the former, but am much inclined to think my patronage misplaced. However, before we reached shore, the vessel was regularly boarded by "the rival candidates for our support and interest." My companions de voyage gave a preference. I thought they must know best about the matter, so followed in their "tail"—gave my "vote" for the flash machine—sat at the coachman's back, and was whirled through the "royal arch" to "Spencer's hotel." No harper here as of old: only another gentleman and myself dined—a most fortunate circumstance; were it otherwise we must have eaten the plates. "Our dinner?" A shoulder of mutton, yea verily of Welsh mutton; three chickens; four cold potatoes, mashed; one head of brockley, large as an apple of ten a penny size; a pint of undrinkable ale—by the bye, a rarity in Wales; two ounces of stale bread; and what would cover a smooth sixpence of cheese—price, 3s. 6d.: waiter, 6d.—Total 4s. each! Mem.—we eat the whole shoulder, "barrin' the bone," and two chickens to boot!

Mastication performed—"coach ready, Sir," jingling in my ears—"all right," (and no de capo expected every moment. I dashed into the office—threw two sovereigns upon the counter—paid my fare—without counting pocketted my change—took my old seat—and recommenced my journey. As you know the road to Bangor, nothing I can tell you of it could give wings to an heavy hour. In truth were it otherwise, and were you as unacquainted with the country and people as with the primitive parish and flock of poor Cochrane's father-in-law in Kamschatka, I would find it exceedingly difficult to weave an interesting page for you out of the twenty-five or twenty-six miles. A colder soil, or more chilling and repulsive trip, though through a thickly inhabited district, than that across "The Head" and Anglesea, is not easily to be met with, the last couple of miles, on your approach to Menai Bridge, excepted.

When alluding to the "Royal Arch" I should have mentioned that the Welsh, following our example, would raise something to commemorate the visit of George the Fourth—that, therefore, on landing, what first meets your eye is a—you know not what. A "*dacentish* sort" of entrance for a barrack of "horse marines." Neither Ionic, Doric, Gothic, Composite, or any other order of architecture, from the tower of Babylon to Wellington's milestone—his monument I mean, could match this loyal gateway. As you approach from Ireland, or on the *Irish* side of the lump of granite thrown over your head, is an *English*, rigmarole inscription. On the Welsh side a *Welsh* one. A hard hit that, to a true Milesian of the "jim of the say." Still I hold Pat has the best of this contest for *stamping* with *glory* the foot-marks of sceptred wisdom, virtue, and valour! First, *his* pillar of remembrance is chaste in design, and pleasing to look at; and second, the waggish memento is to mark the *departure*, not the arrival of royalty.

You are aware that the piece of land known by "The Head," or "Holy-head," though apparently a peninsula, is, in reality, an island, separated by a salt pool, rather than an inlet of the sea, from the adjoining island of Anglesea. The length or width of either separately, I cannot tell you exactly. From where you land at "The Head," across both, to Menai Bridge, by a post-boy's reckoning, would be at least twenty-four English miles. Both are now connected by a wall, similar to that from Ring'send to the Pigeon-house. It has a large covered

gully in the centre, to allow the water a passage from side to side, is about half an English mile in length, has been either built or rebuilt within a few years back, and sitting on the coach top, the spray dashing some dozen yards over my head, I began to think such a drive not altogether the most agreeable in the world during a stormy day.

As you approach this causeway, on the left, is the seat of a Sir somebody Stanley. The house is a castellated building, and in a different situation, would engender very different ideas. Where it stands, the tower-head—the lofty battlement, is but a pompous arm, pointing out, bringing before us, in bolder relief, the surrounding nakedness and poverty of the land.

Crouch your head into your shoulders—draw your nose under your comfortable, and gather your cloak around you from "The Stanley turnpike gate," until you come within a quarter of an hour's drive of "The Bridge." Then sit once more erect. If it be day-light, from this to Bangor is a series of views, each following more magnificent than that before; if moonlight, nothing is lost by the change to my taste, the view from the bridge gains considerably. Where then you are to revive your faculties, there is a monument to the Marquis of Anglesea, or his lost leg, I forget which. It was a darkened moon when I passed, and though having seen this little pillar to chivalry before, I cannot now call to recollection any thing more particular concerning it. May it be long, however, until we see a monument over old Bayard, or what *remains* of his *understanding*. "But the Menai Bridge?" Not one word descriptive of it—first, because you have already seen it—secondly, because if you have not, you ought—thirdly, because a proper description would require a moderate sized volume—fourthly, because the best description would be useless without a plate*—fifthly, lastly, and for the best

---

* Our kind friend and correspondent, will, we are sure, excuse our spoiling the point of his paragraph, by heading his article with a correct engraving of the bridge, to which he refers, and of which the following brief description, may not prove unacceptable to the reader:

Menai Strait, is a strait about half a mile across, between the island of Anglesey and the coast of Wales, which has become of considerable importance, in modern times, as a point of communication between Great Britain and Ireland.

In the year 1811, several plans of Bridges were proposed for effecting a regular and unobstructed passage in the place of the Bangor ferry. All the bridges proposed were to be of cast iron, and of sufficient width of span, and height of elevation not to obstruct the navigation. Among those approved by the committee of the House of Commons, after due investigation, was one of a single arch, of cast iron, of 500 feet span, and 100 feet above the level of high-water in the middle of the arch, projected by Mr. Telford. Although the least expensive of any cast iron bridge of those dimensions, the estimated cost of the bridge was upwards of £127,000. But the construction of such a bridge presented a difficulty in the fixing of proper centering, which could not be accomplished by ordinary means from below, owing to the rocky bottom of the channel, and the depth and rapidity of the tide way. Mr. Telford was, however, led to devise a new mode of suspending the centering from above, and furnished a design of this kind.

The report of the commissioners being made to parliament, and the necessary funds being granted, in July, 1818, directions were given for the commencement of the work, at Ynysy-moch, on the Anglesey shore. It consists of one opening of 560 feet between the points of suspension, and 100 feet in height between the high-water line and the lower side of the road-way; and, the road-way being horizontal, this height uninterrupted for the whole 560 feet, except where the natural rock, which forms the western abutment, interposes. In addition to these 560 feet, there are four arches on the western, and three on the eastern side of the main opening, each 50 feet in span, that is, making in all, 850 feet of opening. The road-way consists of two carriage-ways, each twelve feet in breadth, with a foot-path of four feet between them; and the whole suspended from four lines of strong iron cables by perpendicular iron rods, placed five feet apart. The suspending power calculated at 2016 tons, and the weight suspended, exclusive of the cables, at 342 tons, leaving a disposable power of 1674 tons. The expense was £70,000.

reason of all, the Mayor's reason, not having the bells, for not ringing them, because not having the powers of description, I must leave it undescribed. The lamps were lighted in the lofty arches above our heads, as we rumbled through between the massy chains, metal wicker-work, and pallisading of this stupendous triumphal arch of human handicraft. The moon was abroad, but clouded. The waters, as it were in a distant world, on another earth beneath us, leaped up and down, catching the stray beams, like children in a summer's sun. Have you ever marked them ? With how light a heart have I joined in the amusement. Three or four small vessels, and one of a large size, rode quietly at anchor below, and we riding yards upon yards above their highest mast's-head. The fires glistened upon the decks, and over one blazing grate was busied a brawny sailor, I suppose the swarthy cook of the hardy crew. The lights in houses too, here and there, along the shore, winding off in the arch of a circle to Beaumaris on the left, together with those skirting the waters on the right, round to Bangor, added greatly to the scene. Here in truth was discernable the pencil of the Mighty One ; and here, before me, suspended with all the paripharnalia of a coach and horses, between earth and heaven, was displayed such a picture of real, living, animated life as I shall not quickly forget. Believe me your sincere and affectionate friend,

BARNY O'TRUE AND THRO.

March 11, 1834.

DEAR ——, You complain of the abrupt termination of my last letter. Want of space, not of matter, " cut short the thread of my discourse." If it can be avoided hereafter it shall ; if not, you must take the will for the deed.

It is two miles and a quarter from Menai Bridge to Bangor, and another quarter at least to "The Penrhyn Arms,' one of the most commodious and best hotels in England. Were there a *moderate* and *comfortable* one adjoining " the bridge," it would be a great convenience, and as a speculation I think must succeed. Perhaps the goodness of the road and beauty of the distant bay, or of the hanging hills, the cliffs, and crags, between the straits and the present establishment may compensate for the intervening distance. But for myself, whether in Killarney or Wicklow, Bangor or Langellen, I dislike excessively to live by the mere use of my eyes. I blush to confess myself so little romantic, as at certain times to prefer the use of my knife and fork, and, therefore, I would wish much to see a second " Penrhyn" roasting and boiling, brewing and baking on the *banks* of the ferry.

You must not expect from a pen flying on four horses the history of Bangor. The surrounding scenery is beautiful, as it must ever be. The town itself is narrow and ill-built, but of great antiquity. Here is a cathedral containing some good modern monuments : and if I recollect rightly, the monastery established here in the early days of Christianity, gave birth to the Pelagian heresy, before the coming of St. Patrick into Ireland, for Pelagius was one of the Bangor brotherhood. Indeed I have no doubt it was to preach against this heresy in Ireland, where it had made great advances, and not to convert us from Paganism, that the saint was sent thither from Rome.

Afterwards, when the Saxons drove all traces of Christian worship into the mountains, or out of the kingdoms of England and Wales, the Bangor establishment was received amongst us with open arms. Its members were presented with a grant of land in the county of Down, on the borders of Belfast Lough. There they re-established their " order," and there the name of the place, " Bangor," commemorates their residence to this day.

We, pair of unfortunates, who, as I told you in my last letter, paid our 4s. each for getting "the cold shoulder" at " The Head," of course took no dinner at " the Penrhyn," but we saw that given our fellow-travellers ; heard them descant upon its merits, while our teeth watered at the general commendation, and indulged ourselves with tea and coffee ; muffins and toast. Dinner here, 5s. ; wine, very good, 6d. a bottle. Tea, coffee, &c., 2s. ; bed, 2s. ; waiter, 6d. ; boots, do ; *housemaid*, do. Total for dinner, minus wine, tea, bed, and servants, 8s. 6d. Memoranda,

not a single *shilling* housemaid from Dublin to London— all fac similes of *withered* apples.

The situation of the " Penrhyn" is beautiful. It stands on the rise of a hill, and from its neat grass garden, into which a glass door opens from " the Travellers' room," is a fine view across the straits, along the opposite shore to Beaumaris, and out to sea. This house was built by a Mr. Tenant, the great landholder of " those parts"—the greatest slate quarry owner in the kingdom, perhaps in Europe, and given, I believe, by him to the proprietor at a nominal rent until it became established. As usual with hotel keepers in England, the owner of the house is also one of the coach company. On going to bed, I discovered that the book-keeper at " the Head" " did me out of 5s." He agreed to have myself and luggage taken to London for £1 5s., but when changing the two sovereigns deducted £1 10s. out of them ; cheap enough, in all conscience for two hundred and sixty miles : still it was a shabby trick, for " a bargain is a bargain." So, on the following morning, I called for the proprietor of " the Penrhyn," but found a widow proprietress ; however, her man of all work appeared. I told him my story. He agreed " it was *werry* unfair."—so did I ; but he had learned when once money got into his pocket to keep it there, and I have learned to count my change.

At eight o'clock we remounted, and started for breakfast and Capel Curig-carrig, fourteen miles off. The morning was dry, but dark and threatening. On our left four-fifths of the mansions worth looking at the entire way are on the left—on our left, almost at the starting post, in the centre of extensive and thriving improvements is the castle of Mr. Tenant. As modernised, it is as yet unfinished, but will be a splendid thing when complete ; and any one stopping at our last night's quarters can have a ticket to see both the exterior and interior of the building. Immediately after passing Mr. T's very elegant entrance, and massive, cast, square-looped, metal-gate, you meet his rail-road, and waggons descending from the quarries to the water's edge. Three or four miles further on you come to the quarries themselves. Of what immense service can one man be to his fellowmen ! To how many thousands of human beings does a single individual give comparative comfort in this secluded district. The quarries are immense mountains of wealth, higher than Douce-jouce, in the county of Wicklow. Many of them as perpendicular as the Waterfall ; some more overhanging than the eagle's nest at Killarney. They appear an inexhaustible treasury. From the ceaseless mists that roll over their brown-glazed fronts, they seem as if ever, and everywhere dripping water ; while here and there birch, and mountain ash-tree, and shrub, grown from crack and crevice, polish and re-polish the " cloud-capped" cliffs as the branches bend to the blasts of the mountain gorge.

The practicability of doing good extensively among mankind without spreading a proportionate share of evil, has been often a matter of speculation to my mind. As if to puzzle me the more, and show how closely one effect, if not allied to, treads upon the steps of the other— here, separated from the world, in one small village of between forty and fifty cottages, are *four houses of worship* and sixteen gin-shops !

Shortly after we passed this extraordinary mixture, the day commenced blowing tremendously, and drizzling thickly. I had no objection to the change. The remainder of the road to Capel Curig is through that brown, blake, grand mountain scenery for which Wales is chiefly celebrated. In the valleys of such scenery I cannot fancy a brilliant sun any great addition. To wildness nature gave the cloak of mist and staff of storm—on wildness I like no other dress so well. It may be want of taste—it may be prejudice—what you will. But would that we clambered together from " Lagduff" through " Glenmalure" into the mountains beyond, and if, even there, I could not shew you more wild, magnificently wild, scenery than any in Wales, may I meet the fate and honors of a Welsh sheep—be starved while living, and fed on as a dainty when dead.

I could not, it is true, point to any one mountain as lofty

as the highest in Wales, but as to every other particular, na-boc-lish.

Capel Curig forms an excellent centre for a pedestrian tourist for two or three days. He has of course made the same delay at least in Bangor, and, while there, explored to mid-way between that and this "station." Here he can do the same half way to "Carnidge;" and if he return from the Chapel of the Rock—Capel Curig—not having visited, with all due reverence, the *white-headed* patriarch of Welsh mountains—Snowden—let him never speak, in the presence of a Welshman, of having seen the country. I would not, however, recommend a drink of the half-way waters, a sparkling well on the side of the mountain. It "bloats" on the walk, without quenching the thirst, and the brandy-bottle is a bad counteractor. Notwithstanding, a visit to the hoary-headed monarch of the hills, overtopping the top of "Glyden Bach" should not be neglected; and if the traveller rejoice in a passion for that laziest of lazy-time-killers, fishing, of all the land of Glendower this is the spot to meet with amusement. Yet, whoever "played a salmon" on the banks of the Blackwater, from Mallow to Youghal, "tied a hackle," or "cast a line" in Loughs "Bray," "Luggalaw," or "Lough-Dan" will deny to poor Paddy's streams fish as *good*, and as *plenty* as ever were caught.

When we arrived, there were few amongst us either unable or unwilling to take "the goods the gods provided," and were our meal the reverse of what it was—a very good one—I fancy there would have been still fewer complaints, at all events until it was too late to complain. A blazing fire, in a good room, romantically placed in the bosom of the mountains, and peeping through a hedge of ever-greens, over the surface of a lake, with tea, coffee, bread, butter, muffins, toast, eggs, three or four sorts of meat, and *trout leaping up* on the gridiron, *considering* lent times, gave neither an unwelcome or uninviting reception after the morning's drive. Cost of our comfort two shillings.

It would appear experience of those *watery* regions has taught the inhabitants sympathy towards their fellows immersed in distress; for while busied at 'the board,' our cloaks and comfortables were completely dried. So, comfortably dry without, and comfortably wet within, I drew my muffler round my neck, gathered my cloak close to the shoulders, had some fresh straw for my feet, and in another minute the remnants of beef, ham, trout, and chops were out of sight, far in the distance. Where you must leave, for the present, your sincere friend,

BARNY O'TRUE AND THRO.

POPULAR LECTURES ON THE PHYSIOLOGY OF ANIMALS.

The following is an abstract of Dr. Henry's fifth Lecture:

THE TONGUE.

The tongue is the organ of taste. The sense of taste is so commonly supposed to be seated in the palate, that we use the term palate as equivalent to the sense of taste; but in correct language, the palate signifies the roof of the mouth, and the tongue, not the palate, is the organ of taste. The palate, indeed, as well as the inside of the cheeks, and a considerable part of the intestinal canal, possesses considerable sensibility to impressions, particularly to those which are made by very pungent substances, as mustard, pepper, salt, &c.; but as the tongue alone is supplied by the gustatory nerve, so the tongue alone perceives the impressions of sapid bodies. There is an analogy to be observed here between the nose and mouth, viz :—that although the whole of the interior of the nostrils is lined by the pituitary membrane, yet the upper part only of that membrane, or that part which receives the olfactory nerves, actually smells: so although the whole of the interior of the mouth is lined by a membrane of considerable delicacy and sensibility, yet the tongue alone tastes. The gustatory nerve is not, like the olfactory, auditory, and optic nerves, a separate nerve coming directly from the brain, and going to supply the organ of sense; but it is a branch of another nerve, commonly

called the *fifth pair*, which supplies a great many other parts of the head, giving to them the power of common, feeling only. whilst that branch of it which goes to the tongue gives to that organ the sense of taste. The tongue although apparently single, being placed on the central line, is yet in reality a double organ, and is divided along the middle by a line, very evident in some persons, into two similar and equal halves. This division of the tongue into two similar halves is much more evident in some other animals than in man; many quadrupeds having the extremity notched, and in the serpent tribe the extremity being bifid, so as to give the tongue the appearance of being double. As the nostrils are subservient alike to the function of respiration and the sense of smell, so the tongue performs several important offices besides serving as an organ of taste. First—In man it serves for the articulation of sounds, which is one of its principal uses. Secondly—For moving the food in the process of mastication, and in the first part of the act of swallowing. Thirdly—Some animals, as the dog, cat, &c., lap fluids with the tongue. Fourthly—Some, as reptiles, catch their prey by means of this organ. Of this there is a well known instance in the chameleon, the extremity of whose tongue is formed like a hollow cup, and besmeared with a glutinous substance. This animal darts the tongue with great precision at the insect on which it preys; the insect becomes entangled in the viscid mucus, and is drawn into the animal's mouth. The tongue is probably much less susceptible of the impressions of sapid bodies in most other animals than in man. This is shown—First by the well observed fact, that animals judge of the qualities of their food principally by their smell, and cannot, without the greatest difficulty, be brought to taste any substance which they have once examined by the smell and decided against. This is very observable in the horse, who can not be brought to eat hay which he has once *blown upon.* On the other hand, animals seldom reject food as disagreeable when they have once taken it into the mouth. Secondly—By observation of the structure of the tongue, which is in most animals ill adapted for the perception of savours, except in a limited portion; whilst in others the tongue seems, from its structure, to be quite unfit for perceiving savours at all. Thus, in the ruminating animals, the tongue is covered by a thick, horny coat, particularly towards the back part, which must greatly interfere with its power of taste. There are numerous sharp-pointed papillæ on this coat, all pointed backwards, which are of material service to these animals in enabling them to direct their food, whether of grass, or corn, or hay, towards the gullet, and in preventing its being pushed forward by its elasticity, and its sharp points, while the animal is endeavouring to force it towards the back part of the throat. In birds, with some exceptions, (as the parrot tribe,) the tongue is horny, and unfit to serve as an organ of taste. They have, beside, no teeth by which the food could be bruised and the juice expressed. In those of them particularly which live on grain, an organ of taste would be useless, as the grain is swallowed whole, and with great rapidity lodged in the crop. In fishes also the tongue has evidently little power of taste, and in many animals of this class there is only a rudiment of a tongue. In some it is studded with teeth, which are also to be found on the palate, and in the throat of some species.— These teeth being sharp, and having their points turned towards the throat, serve to prevent the egress of the small fishes, on which the larger ones live, and which enter the stomach of the latter living and whole.

INDIAN ZOOLOGY.

The greater islands of the Indian sea are all mountainous, and full of burning or extinguished volcanoes. The parts neglected by human culture are full of woods, which abound with the most beautiful and singular birds, especially parrots, peacocks, pigeons, and others infinitely diversified with the gayest and most varied plumage; together with herds of antelopes, tribes of monkeys, and numbers of lions and tigers. The elephant and rhinoceros also inhabit these forests, which scarcely ever lose

.heir leaves, but are always verdant, and perpetually loaded with fruits of one kind or another.

Here, however, the brute creation are more at enmity with one another than in other climates, and the birds are obliged to exert unusual artifice in placing their little broods out of the reach of an invader. Each aims at the same end, though by different means. Some form their pensile nest in shape of a purse, deep, and open at the top, others with a hole in the side; and others, still more cautious, with an entrance at the very bottom, forming their lodge near the summit.

THE TAILOR BIRD—*(Motacilla Sutoria.)*

The little species we describe, seems to have greater diffidence than any of the others; it will not trust its nest even to the extremity of a slender twig, but makes one more advance to safety by fixing it to the leaf itself. It picks up a dead leaf, and sews it to the side of a living one, its slender bill being its needle, and its thread some fine fibres; the lining, feathers, gossamer, and down. Its eggs are white. The color of the bird light yellow: its length three inches, its weight only three-sixteenths of an ounce, so that the materials of the nest, and its own size, are not likely to draw down a habitation that depends on so slight a tenure.

Had Providence left the feathered tribe unendowed with any particular instinct, the birds of the torrid zone would have built their nests in the same unguarded manner as those of Europe; but there the lesser species, conscious of inhabiting a climate replete with enemies to them and their young—with snakes that twine up the bodies of the trees, and apes that are perpetually in search of prey—taught by instinct, elude the gliding of the one, and the activity of the other.

THE WHITE-HEADED IBIS—*(Tantalus Leucocephalus.)*

In size it is much superior to our largest curlews. The bill is yellow, very long, and thick at the base, and a little incurvated: the nostrils very narrow, and placed near the head: all the fore part of the head is covered with a bare yellow, and seems a continuance of the bill, and the eyes are, in a very singular manner, placed very near its base. The rest of the head, the neck, back, belly, and secondary feathers are of a pure white; a transverse broad band of black crosses the breast; the quill-feathers, and coverts of the wings are black: the coverts of the tail are very long, and of a fine pink color; they hang over and conceal the tail. The legs and thighs are very long, and of a dull flesh color; the feet semi-palmated, or connected by webs as far as the first joint. This bird makes a snapping noise with its bill like a stork; and, what is remarkable, its fine rosy feathers lose their color during a rainy season.

IMPROMPTU,

On a lady's asking a gentleman which of all the views in the county of Wicklow was the *sweetest* :—

You bid me name the sweetest view
In Wicklow's lovely county,
Where nature sports with beauties new,
And charms us with her bounty:

Avoca's vallies seem supreme,
The Dargle's views are neatest;
But men of *taste* will all exclaim,
The *Sugar Loaf's* the *sweetest.*　　**W. J.**

FOX AND CAT HUNTING—OR CHRISTMAS IN THE OLDEN TIMES.

In good old times, when the festivities of Christmas were generally kept up in every respectable house in Ireland, the county of Longford was one of the foremost to maintain the national character for hospitality. Among the numerous mansions of the then resident nobility and gentry of that county was Tenelick, the noble seat of the late John, Lord Annaly, Chief Justice of the Court of King's Bench. He was a nobleman of large estate, whose hand and heart were ever in unison in promoting the comforts of the poorer of his fellow creatures; and he took much pleasure in assembling his friends around him at that season, which long established custom had consecrated to cheerfulness and festivity. His house was constructed on a very extensive scale; and, exclusive of the usual reception rooms, and the apartments necessary for his family, contained thirty chambers, which, on those occasions, were filled with gentlemen from different parts, the Viceroy not unfrequently making one of the number; and each and all of whom his lordship could supply with a hunter of generous breed and in good condition, as he always kept thirty of the first rate in his stud: he also maintained two packs of hounds, with the necessary huntsmen, whippers-in, and other attendants. There was a smith at all times in attendance at the chace, with his budget of horse-shoes, &c., strapped before him. All these, dressed in scarlet and splendidly mounted, made a most imposing appearance in the field. But, Mr. Editor, *tempora mutantur*, not a vestige of that noble mansion now remains to mark the place on which it stood—of the ornamented parks, the woods, the lawns, once the seats of elegance and splendor, even the memory has almost passed away; the very name of its venerable and noble owner is never mentioned but by a few ancient and withered cottiers, when they contrast those days of noble and generous hospitality and plenty, with the present times of penury and want; and the condescension and kindness of the landlords, who then resided in the midst of their tenantry, with the overbearing insolence and griping avarice of the subalterns to whom they are now delivered over, bound hand and foot, by their selfish and heartless absentees. The remains of that much lamented nobleman are deposited in the family vault in Taughshinney churchyard, about a mile from Tenelick; over which tomb a pillar is erected, having on its pinnacle an urn entwined with serpents, emblematic of his lordship's wisdom. On the entablatures of this pillar is the following inscription:

" John, Lord Annaly, moved by the grateful remembrance of the honour conferred on him by his king and country, and by the pleasing recollection of the happiness which he enjoyed with his friends, in these delightful fields here adjoining, ordered, by his last will and testament, this column to be erected, as the tribute of a grateful mind. 'I know that my Redeemer liveth.' Terra hospita, vale.'

Some years since, when riding through the townland of Cloncullen, in the vicinity of which Lord Annaly's mansion rose, my horse dropped a shoe; I hastened to a smithy in that neighbourhood, and on entering it perceived the vulcan of this rustic Lemnos, ycleped Paddy Gordon, exercising himself in repairing an axe for an old carpenter, named Larry Burke; a person who, from his conversation, appeared to have a very extensive knowledge of the surrounding country and its inhabitants of every class. Finding this man at once intelligent and communicative, I asked him several questions respecting the habits and pursuits of the neighbouring gentlemen— who were sportsmen?—who kept hounds? &c.

" Ah, Sir," said he, " the good ould times are gone by, when every gintleman had his deer-park, and his pack of hounds; but now there is neither one or the other to be seen, nor scarce a gintleman, let alone hounds and the like."

He then recounted the names of a number of places that had once been the residence of persons celebrated for their love of field sports; " but, above all, Sir," said he, " what brings tears into my ould eyes is the destruc-

tion iv the fine house and grand park iv Tenelick, that belonged to my Lord Annaly. There is not a glimpse of the house to be seen, and the park is let to freeholders, and, between you and I, Sir, I believe it is a raal deer (*dear*) park to them. Oh but, Sir," continued he, " if you but knew that same Lord Annaly as well as I did, your heart would ache to look at the place, especially as you are a sportsman. I was always a little inclined that way myself, when young, and kept a brace of as good terriers as any in the county, and, I may say, it was them brought me acquainted with Lord Annaly. If yer honor 'ill be plazed, I'll tell you how I came to the knowledge of his lordship. Well, Sir, it happened one Christmas that the Lord Lieutenant, the Lord Chancellor, and other great lords come down to visit Lord Annaly, as they often did afore. Well, sure, the first divarsion they took to was hunting, and off they all set from the county of Longford to Skea-hill, in the county of Westmeath, to look for a fox; for they say it is the greatest place at all for foxes. The day was fine, and, after drawing many covers, and striving for half the day to find one, Lord A. got wonderfully annoyed, and calls out to a crowd of men and gossoons that was standing by, and siz, ' is there any man among yez there that could find a fox to entertain my friends, and I'm the man that will reward him well?' On which a farrier iv the name iv Micky Farrell stept up and tould his lordship, with submission, that he knew iv but two men in the three counties that could bate the world out for finding a fox. One iv them was Darby Lee, the rabbit-catcher; and the other was Larry Burke, the carpenter, who was at Mr. Fitzgerald's, at Churchtown, six miles off, mending some ould cars : (be the same token Farrell tould a lie, for I'm a cabinet-maker by thrade, and was at that time making a chest iv drawers, and can do more nor any man iv the thrade iver could do afore me, by complatin' the work without any tool in the world, barrin' my hatchet, and with that same I can put on the locks and brasses in as good stile as ever Eagleson did, and a great man at the business he is : they say he is livin' in Dublin too; no doubt, Sir, you hard iv him.— But, to make a long story short, when Lord Annaly hard there was a man that could find a fox, ' Arrah,' siz his lordship, ' Micky, my good fellow, which is the rabbit catcher or Mr. Burke the most convanient?' Upon which Farrell ups and tells him that myself was the nearthest, and, what was betther nor that, that I was the raal boy for the sport : on which his lordship ordered an English groom to set off to Churchtown, like a Will-o'-the-wisp, ' and bring Mr. Burke,' as he was plazed to call me, ' without delay;' and it isn't that I say it, that oughtn't to say it, I ought to have a little more respect than another iv my sort. I was at that time, a dapper, purty-like man, wore a tie-wig, doe-skin small-clothes, and a buff belt, and active withal, as I could leap one and twenty feet, backward and forward on the surface iv the level earth. But what will you have of it, Sir? When the groom kem to Mr. Fitzgerald, he inquired for Larawence Burgoo, as he was plazed to call me, and so he ups and he tells me Lord Annaly's commands, axing me at the same time had I any convaniency about me for catching a fox.

" ' That's what I am never without, Sir,' siz I ; ' look at them lads there,' (showing him a brace of good terriers lying under the bench where I was working ; one of them was called Proudfoot and the other Rookaun), ' and, from what you tell me, his lordship must be in a hurry; so that I may be there the speedier, if you'll plaze to give me the horse you ride, I'll make no delay.'

" ' It's well done,' siz he, and with that same he gives me the horse. Up I mounts and away with me, and never cried stop till I was furnent his lordship, among all the rest iv the great lords, with my two dogs at my heels. Well, Sir, you must know his lordship was a little short in the sight; and before I had time to let him know who I was,

" ' Pray, young man,' siz he, ' where did you get that horse ; I am purty sure he is one iv mine ?'

" ' Your lordship never was out yet,' siz I, takin' off my hat, and makin' a genteel bow; ''tis your lordship's horse and nobody else's. It was your groom gev him to me, to be with you the speedier, to help your lordship to find a fox.'

"'Is your name Burke?' siz he.

"'Yes, my lord,' siz I: 'one of the old Balydoogan stock.'

With that he tuck off his glove and shuck hands with me. It is azy to know where the gintleman is: an upstart musheroon wouldn't do that. with the likes iv me, you know, Sir. And when I found he made so free with me, I swore by the bones of St. Patrick, that if there was a fox over or under Irish ground, I'd put him on foot before his lordship and all his noble company. With that same I turned round, and went over to some badgerholes that was nigh hand where we were all standing, and soon discovered that there was a fox in the earth, but that he was very deep down.

"'The fellow that you're all day lookin' for is here, my lord,' siz I; but he is farther down in the earth than I ever know'd a fox to be before.'

"'That's bad news,' siz his lordship.

"'Don't be afeard, my lord, siz I, 'for, if he was as deep down as Lough Drumon, (which all the world knows has no bottom,) I'll have him up.'

"While I was saying the word I pops in Proudfoot, and clapt my ear to the mouth iv the hole. I listened awhile, and knew, by the noise below, that he had the boy by the scruff of the neck : well I hard great hustling betwixt thim both, so I begun to think it would be a good way to send down both; so in I puts Rookawn to get hoult of Proudfoot of course. Well I waited a considerable time, and when I thought they were all stayin' too long, in I goes myself and gets hoult iv Rookawn by the tail. Lord Annaly, thinkin' that we all staid too long, comes in afthur us, and takes hoult iv myself by the feet ; but to make a long story short, in comes the one half the present company in search of the other half; and sure enough it was their hands that was well tore with the grand spurs my Lord Annaly had on; so that's the way they were all draggin' one another, like a chain, till at last they all landed safe upon the surface of the level earth. And, sure enough, the shout that was set up by the min and gossoons, when they seen ourselves once more in the face iv the day, bet the world hollow ; and, by the same token, (added he, laying his hand on the right side of his head,) I have never had the right use iv my hearin' in this ear from that good day to this. But his lordship was as good as his word with regard to rewardin' me well, for he gave me a ten-guinea note on the spot, and ordered me to attend him on all sporting days in future, which I was happy to do while he lived, and, ferrier gure, (to my grief), that he's not alive to-day, and I wouldn't be the man that you see me, Sir, all as one as a stack iv rags." And as he said these words, he uttered a deep drawn sigh, and dropped a tear to the memory of his noble and generous patron.

At the conclusion of this narrative, to which, notwithstanding its whimsicality, I listened with deep attention, Gordon, the smith, laughed heartily, and said,

"Well, Larry, you have the impudence of ould Nick to call yourself a cabinet maker ; tell the thruth, man : you know, at best, you was never betthur nor a hedge carpenter, and no great shakes either iv that. This is like the straddle you made for Mr. Nugent's two year ould mule. Don't you remember when you laid it on the ground, and said, 'Oh, Larry, jewel, who will you lay your hands to?' and at the same time it wid fit the Lord of Newcastle's big bull that was forty cwt.; and I think, after that, Sir, you may believe as much of his story as you plaze. But if you want to hear about huntin' and the likes, it's I that'll tell you the raal thrue story, and if you'll be plazed to hear it, it's little air (car) you'll give to Larry Burke and his lies ; aye, and it's to his face I say it, there's not a bigger liar from the sea to the Shannon. But, no matthur, Sir, I'll tell you the story.

"You must know my grandfather was a blacksmith as well as myself, and I often heard the neighbours say that there never was a lie hard out iv his mouth from the hour he came into the world; and though you may think the story sthrange, yit, comin' down from him, it must be thrue. It happened that every Saturday he used

to go to Athlone to sell locks and keys, and, one Friday night, my father, that was then a slip iv a gosson, was sittin' at the fire with his two little brothers ; knowin' that the ould man would go to the market next day, they axed him to take their measure for three pair of brogues, as their feet was all cracked with the frost, the weather being very hard ; so he did take it very exact with a bit of a kippeen, (stick), and afther so doin', all iv a sudden a lump of a cat that was lyin' in the ash-hole, jumpt up on the hob, and cocked his tail over his back, and every hair on him was standin' up like a hedge-hog, and his eyes like two blazing coals iv fire in his head. Well, in throth, they all wondhered what haled (ailed) him at all, whin he attacked spakin' Irish for the bare life, and said to my grandfather,

"'Arrah, then, good look to yer honor, and take my measure for a pair of pumps.'

"At this the poor ould man and the gossoons was frightenout iv their wits, and began to thrimble like any thing, and when my grandfather began to get over his fright a little,

"'Oh, Sir!' siz he to the cat, (for he was afeard not to spake civil to him), 'I'll obey your orders, but I wouldn't know how to go about takin' your measure.'

"'Haven't you plenty of oatenmeal in the house?' siz the cat.

"'Sure enough I have, Sir, goodness be praised,' siz the ould man.

"'Then make a lump of dough, and I'll lave the print iv my fut in it, and put it on the hob, and it'll be dhry in the mornin'.

"Well, so he did, and went to his bed, not knowin' what to make iv the cat; but, instead of sleepin', he tuck his bades and fell to prayin' as hard as he could lick, and never stopt till day-break in the mornin', when he set off for Athlone ; and who should he meet in the way but Mr. Handcock's huntsman, and he ups and tells him the whole story, and the fright he was in.

"'Wat," siz he, (for that was my grandfather's name,) if you'll bring me that cat in a bag on Saturday, I'll engage you I'll make him throw off his oatenmale pattens; for I've a pack iv hounds that'll chase him out of them, if he was ould Nick himself.'

"'Och, avich, siz my grandfather, how could I get him into the sack?'

"'Tell him,' siz the huntsman, 'that the brogue-maker couldn't make the brogues without seein' himself. Won't that do?'

"'Sorra betther,' siz the ould man, and off he goes, and standin' the market all day, he came home at night, wary enough, but the ne'r a pump he brought the gossoons, becaze he hadn't a pair for the cat. 'Gud luck to yez all together,' siz he, as he came to the cabin-door. 'Don't be angry, any iv yez. The brogue-maker sez yez must all come into Athlone nixt Sathurday, and get your measure taken right.'

"'And how am I to thravel?' siz the cat.

"'Sir,' siz he, 'I'll put you in the mouth iv the sack, wid a wad iv straw about you, to keep you dhry and clane ; and the gossoons will come wid us for company'

"'Ah,' siz the cat, lookin' mighty knowin' at my grandfather, 'I'm afeard you'r playin' tricks on me.'

("And I think, Sir," observed Gordon, "he suspected all was not right.")

"'I want to know is Mr. Handcock at home, or is his lady at home, or is the huntsman at home, or any iv the family,' continued the cat.

"'I never axed a word about a mother's sowl iv them,' says the ould man, 'or went that way at all at all.'

"'Well, afther all, I believe your an honest ould buck,' siz the cat, and that I can depind on you.'

"'You may depind your life on me,' siz my grandfather.

"But for all the civil talk iv the cat, the poor ould man was sweatin' like a bull, in favour to ye,) and shakin' like an aspin lafe, and thought that the nixt week was a year, till he'd get him out iv the house. Well, this all happened well and good, and the cat never spoke a word from that day out until Saturday kem, when, at the first peep in the mornin', what should my grandfather see but ma bouchal, sittin abow (above) on the collar-beam, washing his face with his paws, to look sleek and purty for the journey. Well, the gossoons got ready iv coorse, and my poor grandfather put the locks and keys into the sack, and a wad iv sthraw on the top iv them for the cat; so he walked into the mouth iv the sack without the laste throuble in life, and the ould man tied it up courmagh and snug, and set off. Whin the cat felt him goin'—

"'Now,' siz he, 'if I find you goin' the road to Wellbrook, (Mr. Handcock's residence) I'll never forgive you, dead or alive.'

"'Never fare, Sir,' siz Wat, 'I never bethrayed any man yit, nor never will—you may thrust your life to me.'

"At the same time the ould fellow, cute enough, took the straight road to Wellbrook, where the huntsman promised to meet him. Well, though the cat could spake well enough, he couldn't see through the bag what road they wor goin', so he never felt himself till afther two miles thravellin' they heard the yelp iv a hound: they stopt short, and the cat began to grow unazy in the sack, and, without more ado, he stuck his nails in my poor grandfather's back, and roared out as loud as was in his head.

"'Wassa Watha (for your life Wat.)'

"'What ails you avich?' says Wat, lettin' on that he didn't know.

"Wid that up comes the huntsman wid the whole pack iv hounds yelpin' and snarlin' about. The chap in the bag began to twist and to turn like a dhaudeel (a reptile like a leech,) and stuck his claws iuto the ould man's back as far as ever he could.

"'Hard fortune to you and all your sort,' siz my grandfather, takin' courage, and flingin' the sack in the road.

"No sooner said nor done; for the weight iv the locks, d ye see, Sir, burst the ould sack, and out hopt the cat, and maybe he didn't take to his heels, and the hounds afther him as hard as they could leg. Well, sich a day's sport wasn't seen in the country from that blessed hour to this. Away they scampered acrass the counthry down to Kilkenny, from that to Clotherstown, and from that to Sunday's Well, near Ballymore; and when the hounds pressed close upon him, he dashed straight ahead into the loch. One Hanly, a fisherman, the heavens be his bed, was there in his boat the same day, and when he seen the cat divin' like an otthur, he looked down to see what become iv him, an' sure enough, (for he was a man that wudn't tell no lie about it,) he seen him go down one iv the chimlies in the loch, (iv coorse, Sir, you've heard how the town iv Ballymore was dhrowned in the loch more nor a hundred years ago; and iv a clear day you can see the tops iv the houses.)"

I expressed my ignorance of the circumstance.

"Oh, dear, Sir, exclaimed Gordon in amazement, I thought all the world heerd iv the dhrownin' of Ballymore."

Then resuming his narrative in his usual tone, he said,

"But, as I was tellin' you, Sir, the cat run down one iv the chimlies as nimble as if he had a rat afore him, and tale or tidin's never was heerd iv him since."

Thus ended the tale of Mr. Paddy Gordon, the worthy and veracious rival of the equally worthy and veracious Mr. Larry Burke, of cabinet-making, fox-finding, and straddle-making fame. What their respective merits, as annalists of the events of the olden times may be, I cannot presume to judge. Perhaps some future historian, when searching out materials for the history of those days of hunting and hospitality, may derive benefit and information from your pages, should you think proper to give this a place in them; and I remain, Sir, your obedient servant,
W. C. L.

———

Baby, the dwarf that lived with Stanislaus, the exiled King of Poland, was so diminutive that he was presented on a plate to be baptized, and for a long time lay in a slipper: at two years he was able to walk alone, and was then fitted with shoes that were about an inch and a half long: at the age of sixteen he was twenty-nine inches tall, and very beautiful, and from this period began to decline in health, and died in the twenty-second year of his age.

TRESPAN-ROCK, COUNTY OF WEXFORD.

On the road leading to the barony of Forth from Wexford, there lies a range of rocks, forming in themselves a very picturesque object, extending about a mile in length and half a mile in breadth; that part nearest the town is called Trespan rock, a subject worthy the study of the geologist. The formation is the kind of rock commonly called trapstone; the rock is upwards of sixty feet in height from the field in which it stands, and near the centre there is a chasm, or cut, about fifteen feet wide, dividing the rock from the summit to the base; and so perfect is the fracture, that wherever there is a projection on the one side, on the reverse is the cavity corresponding thereto; what is singular, the smaller part, or half of the rock, has actually sunk upwards of ten feet from the natural level. Besides the singularity in the formation of the rock, it is allied to one of the most memorable periods of Irish history, when this town sustained a siege, and was gallantly defended by Colonel David Synnot against the Parliamentarian army, under the command of Oliver Cromwell, in the month of October, 1648. Cromwell formed his camp on the rocks alluded to, part of which still retains his name. There is a tradition here, that when Captain Stafford, the governor, treacherously surrendered the castle to him, he marched his troops through the fissure in the rock, but whether that be the fact or not, so late as the summer of 1829 there could be traced the breast-work of a battery for four guns, erected by him on the top of Trespan rock; this has been effaced by the working of a quarry, from whence most of the stone now used in Wexford is drawn. A constant reader, C. H. W.

Wexford, 1834.

WRITTEN ON A TOMBSTONE, WHERE IS LAID THE SKULL OF A WOMAN.

Blush not ye fair, to own me, but be wise,
Nor turn from sad Mortality your eyes.
Fame says, and Fame alone can tell how true,
I once was lovely and beloved like you.
Where are my vot'ries—where my flatt'rers now?
Gone with the subject of each lover's vow.
Adieu the roses red and lillies white,
Adieu those eyes, which made the darkness light.
No more, alas! that coral lip is seen,
No longer breathes the fragrant gales between;
Turn from your mirror and behold in me,
At once what thousands can't or dare not see.
Unvarnished I the real truth impart,
Nor here am plac'd but to direct the heart.
Survey me well, ye fair ones, and believe
The grave may terrify—but can't deceive.
On beauty's fragile base no more depend,
Here youth and pleasure, age and sorrow end;
Here drops the mask—here shuts the final scene,
Nor differs grave threescore from gay fifteen.
All press alike to that same goal, the tomb,
Where wrinkled Chloe smiles at Laura's bloom.
When coxcombs flatter, and when fools adore,
Learn here the lesson to be vain no more.
Yet Virtue still against decay can arm,
And even lend Mortality a charm.

DUBLIN:
Printed and Published by P. D. Hardy, 3, Cecilia-street; to whom all communications are to be addressed.

THE

DUBLIN PENNY JOURNAL

CONDUCTED BY P. DIXON HARDY, M.R.I.A.

Vol. III. | AUGUST 16, 1834. | No. 111.

BALLINACARRIG CASTLE.

RIDES THROUGH THE COUNTY OF CORK.

Ballinacarrig or "The Hamlet of the Rock," is situated in the barony of the east division of East Carbery, in the county of Cork. In a former number we promised our readers a description of this edifice; we now redeem our promise. The castle is a tall, square pile, ninety-six feet in height, built, as its name imports, on a rocky ledge which overhangs a lake of moderate extent. The hall is rudely vaulted, and occupies nearly the entire extent of the castle. The thickness of the walls is very great, and intimates the great necessity for strength which existed in the troublesome times when the castle was founded. A narrow spiral stair-case ascends to the top of the building, leading, in the course of its ascent, to three small apartments, and at top to a large room, which was probably the principal apartment in the days when the castle was inhabited, as it possesses two large windows, one looking over the lake, and the other commanding a dreary view of the great bog of Moneneurig, and the low, furzy hills which form its northern boundary.—These windows are extremely curious. They exhibit the round Saxon arch, and the stones which form their castings are rudely adorned with various devices. On the southern window appears the Virgin and Child. On the northern window is the date 1585, with the initials R. M. C. C., which tradition explains as implying the names of Randal M'Carthy, and his wife, Catherine Collins, the founders of the castle. On this window are also the forms of a ladder, a cock, a hand, a heart pierced with transverse swords, and some masonic emblems, roughly

cut in the stones which compose the arch. A long, low stone seat extends the whole length of the apartment.—Immediately under the rock on which the castle is built, flows a rapid, brawling stream, fed by the neighbouring lake, which is here constrained into temporary tranquillity by the mill-dam of Mr. John Neagle, whose snug cottage, mills, and garden form a very pleasing feature in the scene. On Sundays and holidays the neighbouring peasants exhibit their agility by walking round the summit of the castle; an exploit which requires no common share of nerve, and steadiness of head; as in addition to the height of the building itself, the rock at its base falls almost perpendicularly down to the stream, to the depth of thirty or forty feet. In front of the castle stands a small, circular watch tower, completely isolated. It formerly guarded an angle of the wall, which enclosed the court of the building, and of which few vestiges now remain. This little tower is overgrown with ivy, ferns, and briony—like the castle, it is roofless. Up to 1815, (when the chapel of Ballinacarrig was built,) divine service was performed for a series of years in the hall of the castle.

It is said that the erection of Ballinacarrig was attended with the following singular circumstance. Randal M'Carthy, the founder, until then a poor peasant, dreamed that a man clad in grave-clothes, (a strangely inauspicious costume, one would think,) desired him to go to Thomond-bridge, in Limerick, and there await the appearance of the first soldier who should pass. The nocturnal visitant added, that great wealth would reward the dreamer's compliance with this recommendation. Accordingly Randal set off at the first peep of dawn, and after a few days journey arrived in Limerick, where, in obedience to his shadowy instructor, he posted himself upon the bridge.—Many minutes had not passed when a soldier appeared, who asked every one he met where a certain place, called "Croise-na-Eirigh" was to be found. No one could inform him, and at length he applied for information to our friend, Randal.

"Why do you ask?" demanded Randal.

"Because," replied the soldier, "I dreamed last week there was a large store of gold buried at the root of a whitethorn there. I have asked a thousand people since, and nobody seems to know any thing about it; and now frankly tell you that my guide shall have half the treasure."

"I never heard of such a place," answered Randal, and the soldier passed on.

Now, as it happened, the place called "Croise na-Eirigh," was within a stone's throw of Randal's cabin, as Randal knew right well; and Randal and the whitethorn were ancient friends, for it was beneath its boughs that he had wooed and won the bright-eyed and rosy cheeked Cathleen Colins. Homewards, therefore, he sped, with all possible haste; and at the dead hour of night he proceeded with his pick and shovel to disturb the sturdy roots of the old thorn. He dug well, and found the gold; and with his newly discovered wealth (the mode of acquiring which, he long kept secret) he built the Castle of Ballinacarrig, and also the smaller Castles of Ballyward and Derry, which still are to be found in the neighbouring parishes of Kilmeen and Desertserges. It will gratify the lovers of "auld lang syne" to learn that the progress of decay in the subject of our sketch, will soon be substantially arrested by Mr Townshend, the present proprietor, who is now quarrying stones in the neighbourhood, with a view to repair it as a shooting residence.

Before we close our notice of this wild neighbourhood, we cannot avoid mentioning a characteristic legendary tale, which we learned in the course of our rambles from an aged peasant, concerning a former proprietor of K——, (which domain is distant a mile and a quarter from Ballinacarrig). It is now considerably more than a century since the family of D—— first came to reside at K——. It is said that the first proprietor of that name was a dashing, jovial bachelor, who, at the time of his arrival at his new abode, was in search of that "honey-drop" in life's mixed cup—a loving wife. There stood at that period in the upper part of the domain, the ruins of a small old priory or convent, whose walls were surrounded with the undistinguished graves of monks and peasants. A crumbling gable of the building was shadowed with the branches of a gnarled oak tree, one side of which was scathed by lightning, while the other still sent forth a rich green canopy of foliage.

One sweet summer's evening, D—— bent his steps in an idle, sauntering mood to the low, broken enclosure of the ruined priory, and on entering its precincts, he beheld a female form, kneeling on a new made grave beneath the tree, apparently engaged in some office of devotion for the weal of the deceased. Unwilling to disturb the mourner, he took his seat upon a moss grown stone, and attentively regarding her, he felt much struck with the exquisite beauty of her face and form. She was clad in the ordinary dress of the female peasantry, but her clothes were arranged with a scrupulous attention to neatness.—The gazer was enamoured—"That's the lass for me," he exclaimed to himself; and when the girl had arisen from her prayers he approached her, and asked her name.

"Maureen M'Carthy," was the answer.

"And whose is the grave over which you have been praying?"

"It is my father's, Sir," replied Maureen; while the tears rose afresh to her eyes.

Her lover, for so we must now term him, could not refuse the natural sympathy of sorrow to so lovely a being.

"Your father?" he repeated. "and where did he live?"

"In the cottage at the end of the wood," replied Maureen; "my nurse and I are alone there now. My mother died two years ago—my brother Daniel has gone off to the west, and left us to do for ourselves: they say he's married to a blacksmith's daughter. I'm expecting him this many a day to come back to the cottage, but I believe I may as well give him up."

The smitten swain accompanied Maureen to her lonely dwelling, through a wood of tall shady oaks, which have long since felt the axe. He learned from Maureen that humble as her class of life was now, the M'Carthys, from whom she was descended, had once possessed, not only the lands of Kilcascan, but a large tract of country extending to the west for several miles on both sides of the river. They had lost it all by confiscations in the days of Elizabeth and James.

"It's little matter now, at any rate," said Maureen in Irish, "maybe if we were richer we would not be better nor happier."

When they reached the cottage, D—— felt surprised at the extreme old age of Maureen's nurse. Such was her very great decrepitude and feebleness that he could not imagine the relationship of nurse and foster-child between the youthful girl and this very antique-looking personage. Maureen seemed eighteen or nineteen years of age; her nurse appeared to have fully completed a century.—Weeks passed away, during which the lover became a constant visitor at the cottage. He felt some occasional twitches of internal pride, which forbade him to form an alliance with a peasant; but the beauty and innocence of Maureen and, more than all, the affection she evidently felt for him, bore down all obstacles before them.

Ere the summer closed—we believe it was in the year 1713 or 14—he poured forth his vows of eternal love to Maureen, at her father's grave, where he had learned to sit and to weep with her; and where, in return, he had taught her to mingle her sorrow for the dead with the fond and soothing feelings of affection for the living. The scathed oak tree was above their heads—around them were scattered the touching mementos of mortality—the long, rank, grave yard grass glistened in the slanting sunbeams of evening; and there, alone, in this solemn and melancholy scene, did the two youthful lovers blend their lips, and plight their troth to each other for their future life. A day was appointed for the bridal.

We must mention, that behind the old oak wood, of which we have already spoken, was a field, containing some three or four acres, surrounded with a strong dry stone wall, nine feet high. The chimney gable of Maureen's cottage formed part of this wall. Mr D——t had turned some milch-cows into the field to graze, and, after they had remained a few weeks there, his steward informed him that the quantity of milk they gave was very much diminished. "I thought, at first," said he, "that somebody milked them in the field at night, but I watched for several nights, and could not see anybody."

The great diminution in the milk excited much surprize, as it seemed impossible to discover the thief. Mr. D——t set half a dozen men, successively, to watch the field by night, but in vain—the thief was still impervious to their watchfulness and sagacity. At length, an omadhawn, or half-witted lad, belonging to the place, volunteered his services as sentinel; his offer was accepted, and the following night he took his station in the field. At the grey dawn, while the cattle were still lying down, dispersed through the field, the omadhawn, wiser than his betters, discerned a hare sucking the teats of one of the cows, and then proceeding, in turn, to all the rest. Immediately he went to his master's kennel, and unleashed a couple of strong greyhounds, which he brought to the gate of the field, and cautiously admitted into its precincts, knowing that the hare would probably make a rush to escape at the gate, as the wall which surrounded the field seemed so high as to defy her agility. The instant the greyhounds were admitted, and the gate closed behind them, a brisk pursuit of puss commenced; she showed great game, and was making an effort to double, when one of the dogs snapped at her haunch, and carried off a large piece of flesh between his teeth. The hare, thus closely pressed, made an unexpected bound, and jumped up on the gable of Maureen's house, (which, as we have said, formed part of the wall round the field.) The lad, who was watching, had foreseen this possibility, and was already stationed on the top of the wall, in order to descry the hare's destination, but she suddenly became invisible; on which, concluding she had jumped down the chimney, he unceremoniously entered the cottage, where he found its aged owner up, dressed, and seated on a stool at the hearth: Maureen was fast asleep in her bed.

"Did a hare jump down the chimney?" he demanded. The old woman affected to be deaf, and made no answer. The lad searched every corner of the cottage, but no hare was to be found; and, knowing that this animal, when very hardly pressed, will take refuge with the human species, he renewed his inquiries of the aged woman. Again she pretended deafness. "Perhaps she's hid under your gown?" said the crafty omadhawn: and, suddenly raising up her clothes, he beheld—not the hare —but the mark of the greyhound's teeth in the woman's hip, the fresh wound still bleeding, where the dog had bitten out the piece of flesh!

"Bedad," cried the lad, "you're no woman, but a colliaheen*!" and, seizing a broomstick, which lay in a corner, he ran off with it, saying, "you sha'n't have this to ride away on, any way."

He then proceeded to his master, to whom he narrated his singular adventure, adding, "I hope, Sir, your honour won't marry a witch's foster child."

Notwithstanding the ardour of the lover's attachment, and notwithstanding that the following day had been fixed for the nuptials, it is said that he felt some repugnance to fulfil his matrimonial engagement; love, however, ultimately triumphed.

On proceeding to the cottage, the old woman was found lying dead upon the hearth; Maureen was still asleep, in happy unconsciousness of the strange and fantastic vagaries which had recently been played. The corpse was removed, and interred with all possible haste, the assistants fearing that the devil might whisk it away from among them, before it was deposited beneath the lap of mother earth.

"What a wild, foolish, fanciful legend!" we observed to the old peasant who narrated this strange tale.

"Foolish enough, Sir, to be sure," he replied, "but when people get together, by a winter's fire-side, on holiday nights, they must always keep ould stories of this sort going to amuse them."

"And, pray, my old friend," we continued, "do you believe this story?"

"Why, plase your honour, I've my doubts about the part of it where the ould hag took the form of a hare to suck cows—I'd never believe that any ould won an could do the like of that—but it's as true, and as true as true can be, that the beautiful Maureen was married to the young squire the day her ould nurse died, and she never knew one word about her death until after the wedding, they managed it so cute. And it's their childher's childher, in the sixth jinneration, has the place at this day: and M'Carthy, the blacksmith, in the parish of Cagheragh, west of Skibbereen, is great grandson to Dan, Maureen's brother; and M'Carthy has got the length of a fishing-rod of fine ould parchment title deeds of his ancesthor, M'Carthy More's, property † More's the pity that he should be working at the forge and bellows this blessed day!"

"And, pray," we demanded, "is there any trace of Maureen's cottage standing?"

"Not a stone of it left, Sir—her husband threw it down, and also the wall round the field, the year he was married. And it's she that made him the good, loving wife; twenty years they lived together, and at last she died in child-birth, and he didn't long survive her. They were both buried without any funeral, (barring the family and tinants,) under the ould blasted oak, by the ruins of the priory—the very spot, your honour, where he first laid eyes on her, and where he proposed for her! ullagone!"

"Is the priory standing still?" we asked.

"No, Sir; it's fifty years since the ould gable walls were taken down, and the graves all levelled in. There's a tall grove of sycamose and elms growing now on the spot, taking root in the corpses of the dead. You'd never know there was a grave in the place, to look at it."

"Would the present possessor of K———," we continued, "be displeased at having the story of his ancestor's marriage with Maureen M'Carthy spoken of?"

"Oh, no, Sir!" cried the old peasant, warmly; "heaven bless his honour's true Irish heart! he'd feel ten times prouder of being come from the ould Milesian stock, if they only were peasants, than if he was sprung from a hundred Sassenagh kings and queens! He's Irish to the core of the heart he loves the green sod as he loves his own life! And, besides them M'Carthys, he's come from the O'Neills, O'Connors, the Hagarties, and Feigheries, and a score of ould Irish families besides."

We were shown, by an old parish priest, a miniature picture of Maureen; it is strikingly beautiful, and said to resemble some of her female descendants of the present day.   J. F. W.

In the year 1663, an old dame, named Julian Cox, was convicted of witchcraft, chiefly on the evidence of a huntsman, who declared on his oath that he laid his greyhounds on a hare, and coming up to the spot where he saw them mouth her, there he found on the other side of the bush Julian Cox, lying panting and breathless, in such a manner as to convince him that she had been the creature which afforded him the course. The unhappy woman was accordingly executed.

ON PLANTING.

The shopkeeper turns his capital once in a week or a month. The farmer turns his money once in a year, but the forest planter must discard the commercial maxim "a small profit and *quick return*" for he can scarcely turn his capital once in his lifetime. Still, however, nothing can pay better than the planting of waste lands with forest trees. Oaks, pines, and willows, will give more profit than ferns, heath, and rushes, and a practical man with four labourers under him could superintend 500 acres. A man cannot amass a large property for his children by a small outlay so surely as by planting.

POPULAR POISON.

When pure ardent spirits are taken into the stomach, they cause irritation, which is evinced by warmth and pain experienced in that organ; and next, inflammation of the delicate coats of this part and sometimes gangrene. They act in the same manner as poisons. Besides the local injury they produce, they act on the nerves of the stomach which run to the brain, and if taken in large quantities, cause insensibility, stupor, irregular convulsive action, difficult breathing, profound sleep, and often sudden death. The habitual use of ardent spirits causes a slow inflammation of the stomach and liver, which proceeds steadily, but is often undiscovered till too late for relief.—*London Medical and Surgical Journal.*

AN ANTIQUARY

Is one that has his being in this age, but his life and conversation are in the days of old. He despises the present age as an innovation, and slights the future; but has a great value for that which is past and gone; like the madman that fell in love with Cleopatra. He is an old frippery philosopher, that has so strange a natural affection to worm-eaten speculation, that it is apparent he has a worm in his skull. He honours his forefathers and foremothers, but contemns his parents as too modern, and no better than upstarts. He neglects himself, because he was born in his own time, and so far off antiquity, which he so much admires; and repines like a younger brother, because he came so late into the world. He spends the one half of his time in collecting old insignificant trifles; and the other in strewing them, which he takes singular delight in; because the oftener he does it, the further they are from being new to him. All his curiosities take place one of another, according to their seniority, and he values them not by their abilities, but their standing. He has a great veneration for words that are stricken in years, and are grown so aged, that they have outlived their employments. These he uses with a respect agreeable to their antiquity, and the good services they have done. He throws away his time in inquiring after that which is past and gone so many ages since, like one that shoots away an arrow to find out another that

---

* Witch.

† This is really true—the parchments are in perfect preservation, and are extremely curious.

was lost before. He fetches things out of dust and ruins, like the fable of the chymical plant raised out of its own ashes. He values one old invention that is lost and never to be recovered, before all the new ones in the world, though ever so useful. As every man has but one father, but two grandfathers, and a world of ancestors, so he has a proportional value for things that are ancient, and the further off the greater.

He is a great time-saver but it is out of time out of mind, to which he conforms exactly, but is wholly retired from the present. His days were spent and gone long before he came into the world, and since this his only business is to collect what he can out of the ruins of them. He has so strong a natural affection to any thing that is old, that he may truly "say to dust and worms, you are my father, and to rottenness, thou art my mother." He has no providence nor foresight, for all his contempla-tions look backward on the days of old, and his brains are turned with them, as if he walked backwards. He had ra-ther interpret one obscure word, in any old senseless discourse, than be the author of the most ingenious new one. He devours an old manuscript with greater relish than worms and moths do; and, though there be nothing in it, values it above any thing printed, which he accounts but a novelty. When he happens to cure a small botch in an old author, he is as proud of it, as if he had got the philosopher's stone, and could cure all the diseases of mankind. He values things wrongfully upon their anti-quity, forgetting that the most modern are really the most ancient of all things in the world, like those that reckon their pounds before their shillings and pence, of which they are made up. He esteems no customs but such as have outlived themselves, and are long since out of use.

KILKEA CASTLE.

Kilkea Castle, situated in the southern part of the county of Kildare, about thirty-one miles from the me-tropolis, and one and a half from the town of Castleder-mot, is an extensive though irregular pile of castellated building. A castle on this site was first erected by Hugh de Lacy the younger, Earl of Ulster, who obtained the barony of Kilkea by a marriage with Emmelina, daughter of the Lord de Riddlesford. The property afterwards passed into the Kildare family, by whom the castle has been re-edified at different times. This fortified residence was a place of some distinction in the fourteenth century. Sir Thomas Rokeby. Lord Justice of Ireland, died here, in the year 1356. The buildings were much enlarged and improved by John, sixth Earl of Kildare, who died in 1427. Considerable alterations and repairs have taken place at subsequent periods; the most recent of which were effected by the late Daniel Caulfield, of Levitstown, Esq., who obtained a lease of these premises from the Duke of Leinster.

The interior presents, in many parts, curious examples of ancient arrangement: and from several of the win-dows are obtained fine views, embracing, among other ob-jects, the demesne of Lord Aldborough, the banks of the river Greece, and the mountains of the Queen's County.

The staircase is composed of massy oak. Connected with the chimney-piece in the great drawing-room are some ancient basso-relievos, of much curiosity. On the right side of the fire-place is represented an ape, the crest of the Fitzgeralds, beneath which is the following inscrip-tion:

Si Dieu plet.

Crom—aboo.

MDLXXIII.

On the left side is an eagle with expanded wings, resting on a perch. This, as we are informed by the MSS. of the Chev. de Montmorency, is the crest of Mabel, second daughter of Sir Anthony Brown, master of the horse to King Edward VI. sister to Anthony Viscount Montacute, and wife of Gerald, eleventh Earl of Kildare.

Inserted in the gate-house of this castle is a stone, sculptured in a singular and grotesque manner. The sculpture represents a monster, having the head of a fox, the claws of a dragon, and the legs of a man. The mon-ster is prostrate, and over it is a female figure, nurturing at the breast an eagle. The monster presses her to him with his claws, and a dog behind appears to hold, or to bite her.—Near the castle is a large conical mount, in re-cent years covered with trees.

WILLIAM HUNTER, THE PARRICIDE.

Of all the seasons in the year give me spring—pure, clear, and beautiful spring : summer may be prized for its genial glow of heat—winter for its bracing cold—autumn for its calm and gentle breezes—but the joyous, the bright, and the laughing spring, with its fresh green buds and its fragrant breathings, is to me infinitely dearer than any. Are not the spring flowers more beautiful than the gaudy minions of summer ? Is not the spring rain more dewy, more gentle, and more refreshing ? Is not the spring sunshine more replete with purity and softness ?—and is not the spring—but, psha ! where's the use in talking ? Will any one attempt to tell me that spring is not the most decidedly delightful of all the seasons ?

It was one of those evenings when, as a poet would say, the glorious sun was burning with redoubled lustre, and his head would droop as if to seek its ocean pillow ; but as poets are sometimes unintelligible, I must say that this means it was the time of sunset, when a yellow flood of light overspread the western heaven, and covered every tree, every leaf, and every flower with a golden and beautiful tinting : everything looked happy and peaceful ; the fields, with their new livery of green, the budding shoots of the low hawthorn, and the little trout-brook that bubbled merrily along, seeming to chant forth its hymn of gladness. But, alas ! in this world too often are looks deceitful, and very often doth a smile, that brightens the cheek and eye, conceal an anguished and breaking heart. That sun looked down on a narrow glen or valley, situated between two of the mountains bordering on the little village called Step-aside, and shone upon the white-washed walls of its few scattered cabins, and on the bright yellow blossoms of the mountain furze, giving them a cheerful appearance, as if content and peace held there a constant dwelling.

One of those cabins was situated entirely apart from the rest, in the middle of a patch of green verdure that seemed as if worked with much labour from the very mountain side, as all round it was barren rock, mingled with tall and thick heath. Its walls were dirty and decayed-looking ; a bunch of rags was stuffed into the small orifice that formerly contained a window, and not a single wreath of blue smoke issued from the hole in the roof originally constructed for its escape. The little piece of ground surrounding it, though it had evidently once been tilled and well cared, bore now a neglected, wild appearance : the furrows of the past year were yet marked out, and a heap of rank weeds sprang up where formerly the stalks of green oats used to uprear their well-laden heads ; in fact, one might discern at a glance that it was the abode of poverty, and perhaps of misery ; and yet, notwithstanding all this, that half ruined cabin, lit up with the departing gleams of sunlight, was a picturesque feature in the general landscape. The door was open, and against its side was leaning, in thoughtful attitude, a tall, squalid-looking figure ; his head, with its tangled masses of grey and black hair, drooped upon his breast ; his sunken eyes looked intently on the earth, and one hand was thrust into his bosom, while the other hung listlessly at his side. He did not always remain in that fixed attitude, for he sometimes started, as if the spirit within suddenly moved and urged him, and would clasp his hands with a phrenzied, despairing action, and knit his brows till they completely shaded his dark and gloomy eyes.— There was in his features an appearance of youth, but yet his cheeks were thin, and his brow wrinkled ; he had evidently once been handsome, but now there was an uneasy look—a wild glare in his eye, and a twitching at the corners of his compressed lips that spoke fearfully of want, and misery, and wretchedness—wretchedness that urged on almost to crime.

The wailing of an infant was heard within, accompanied with the weak, though sweet tones of a female voice, striving to hush its little cries ; and on his name being called by the latter, the man who was standing at the door started suddenly from his reverie, and entered the cabin. Its interior was destitute of almost every article of common country furniture : a low, ricketty table, one stool, and a

small bed seemed its only contents. On this latter lay a miserable-looking female figure, covered with a blanket, and holding a little child to her bosom, whose smothered sobs she tried in vain to hush. Her face was thin and worn ; her blue eyes dull and leaden ; and her long and once beautiful golden hair lay in thick clotted folds on her poor, wan neck. He advanced to the bed-side, and half sitting, half kneeling, bent down, and taking her worn hand, exclaimed in broken tones, and with a distracted, though fond and tender air—

" Did you call me, my heart's love ?"

" Yis, William, darlin', I did," was the meek and quiet answer—evidently forced, for her face was convulsed with suffering ; I'm wake wid the dhruth, an' want you to hand me that cup ov wather. The poor, weeny one here is cryin', an' I can't stop him ; bud, William, you can't blame him, fur ye know he's hungry."

A feverish flush flew rapidly over his face as she concluded, and his lip shook with emotion as he handed her the liquid. While she was raising it to her lips, her hand trembled so violently that a part of its contents fell upon the child, who roused by this, looked up, and on seeing its father, in low, almost incoherent accents, it sobbed forth a request for some food—food that he had not to give ! He sprang up with despair and distraction written in legible characters upon his brow, and striding to the table, where there were three or four cold potatoes, he seized one, and giving it to the child, muttered—

" There—take that : it's the last almost we have—an' God only knows what 'ill become ov us whin they are gone."

" William !" said the female ; but he was too full of agony to hear her. " William !" said she a second time— " dear William, he whose name you've mentioned is grate an' good, an' 'ill look down on us yet, an' give us relief from our throubles. You know iv I could only get over this sickness an' be able to go about, we might remove an' do somethin' : so don't be so despairin', love ; we'll hope fur the best."

" Hope fur the best," he bitterly repeated ; " what have we to hope fur ? Desarted be all our friends—turned off be our relations, athout one to own us or help us—poor, an'starvin', an miserable—Father of Mercies, it's a cruel prospect !"

" Id brakes me heart intirely to hear you talkin' so, William, jewel ; fur I know I'm the cause ov all this. Iv you hadn't married me agin the wishes ov yerfather, an' provoked his anger, you'd be livin' now, snugan' comfortable, insted ov bein' as you are, in this hovel, full ov misery an' want—'

" Me father !" he wildly interrupted ; " don't call him father, fur he never acted as one : he was as hardened to me as the very stranger that owns this cabin, an' this ground—who wouldn't let me pull a bit of hathe to make a few brooms, though it's growin' in oceans, an' is made no use ov, simply fur fare ov my spilin' his shootin' an' his sport."

" Iv you war to thry him onst more, William, darlin'," exclaimed she in a tone of deep though repressed intreaty, " iv you wor to take yer little son in yer arms, an' stand afore him in his well-filled house, an' tell him you are starvin', an' your wife is dyin' fur the want ov a bit ov comfortable food. Iv he was to see you now, he couldn't, I'm sure he couldn't refuse, or if he does his heart is steel."

He hesitated for a moment, and looked anxiously into the sufferer's face, and saw too plainly that she told the truth.

" Yis, my poor Mary," he exclaimed, stooping down and touching his lip to her cheek, " I will go to him onst more, an' beg an' inthrate ov him to help me ; bud I won't bring the child, fur its clothes are too—too ragged—an' it 'ill be company fur you while I'm away. May the great God soften his hard heart !"

So saying, he kissed the child, and having arranged some little necessaries, such as a drink of water beside the bed, with one long look of unabated love on its altered occupant, he went forth and closed the cabin door.

The moment he disappeared the tears, which had been

pent up; to bring no addition to his grief, burst forth in an uncontrollable flood, and fell, hot and scalding, on the cheeks of her child, who had then a second time fallen into a short, calm slumber. On perceiving this she strove also to repress them, but could not, while her thick, heavy sobs betokened the extreme suffering of her mind.

Gentle reader! have you ever seen a beautiful white and yellow butterfly disporting all day amongst the summer flowers?—living on in light and joy, with its fragile wings bearing it from one sweet to another, untouched by grief and unsated with pleasure—like such was Mary Law when she first met with the being whom her heart soon elected as its lord. She was the only surviving daughter of a cottier or working man, in the employment of Phil Hunter, an opulent farmer, whose land extended every year to a greater length; for he was prudent and industrious, and besides that had "the book larnin'," and "wasn't like thim poor crathurs that didn't know B from a bull's fut!"— Mary was universally allowed to be 'the prettiest of all the girls round about, and as such was generally elected to be queen of May, and was the first in all such rural sports. Her temperament was lively in the extreme. She thought not of grief, but laughed and sported from morning till night; and her bright, cloudless eye, and her merry, shrill, laughing voice had irresistible fascination, "fur all de bits o' boys;" but Mary was too sensible to be caught completely with their professions, and so amused herself in dismissing them one by one as they tendered their hands and hearts for her acceptance. When she was about eighteen, William Hunter, the son of her father's employer, returned home from visiting a relative in the south, where he had been since he was a boy. At a rural wedding they first met, and danced together—sat together— chatted together—and fell in love. His warmth of manner, bursts of delight, and long and earnest gazings on her rich face and golden hair, revealing the secret to *her*; and her embarrassment, trembling hand, and blushing cheek, making *his* heart bound to his very lip at the idea of her not being indifferent to him.

Though he was infinitely above her in circumstances, having ascertained the state of her affections, he ventured to propose her to his father as his future bride, thinking he might meet with a little opposition, but never even dreaming of the flat refusal he encountered.— But the fact was, old Hunter was growing rich, and consequently was not only desirous of more, but was proud into the bargain; and expected his son to marry some comfortable farmer's daughter, not the child of one of his workmen, who had only a pretty face to recommend her. Accompanied with the refusal, was an order not to see her any more; which was of course disobeyed, as opposition inflamed William's excited passions doubly, and he resolved to have her whether his father would or not.— "Marry in haste and repent at leisure," is an old proverb, and a good one; they married in haste, quite sure that when this final step was taken they would be easily forgiven; and then, when the first transports of joy was over, he found himself an inmate in Law's cabin, and an outcast from his father's house, with a curse upon his head if he ever again dared to cross its threshold.

The first blow of any weight the young couple had to endure was the death of Mary's father, who was long declining, and at last sunk to his everlasting sleep, pillowed in the arms of his beloved child. They then were left the possessors of his little cabin, without a shilling to begin the world, and both unused to great exertion or labour. Upon this William went to his father, bringing his wife with him, and prayed for his forgiveness; but the stern old man, who had lately got married a second time, was involved in new cares, and urged by his wife, dismissed them with menace and contumely. After this their affairs gradually declined, and poverty stared them in the face. However, they struggled on for some time, till the increasing stagnation of affairs involved them also in its miseries, and they fell into actual want. It was a touching thing to see her light elastic form grow thin, and spare, and weak, while she still strove to smile, lest *he* should be unhappy; and to see him labouring with untiring nerve for her support, and yet not able to ensure even *that.*

In the midst of all this Mary caught cold, and, for the want of some little restoratives, continued severely ill, and unable to rise; and such was the situation precisely of their affairs on the evening I first have introduced them to the reader. I will now follow his footsteps as he proceeds towards his father's house. It stood at the base of the mountain, and was shaded by the wide branches of some tall trees that grew in front, while its rear was extended considerably with barns and outhouses, some old, and some of recent structure. A neat, green paling enclosed the garden before the door; and there the monthly roses were in full bloom, while the green kale, and other more useful plants had also their places. A cheerful burst of thick smoke proceeded from the chimney, and ascended into the unruffled atmosphere, while the sounds of laughter and mirth were heard within.— When, after an hour's walking, William stood outside the slight paling, the last faint light of even had declined, and the night had gradually set in, so that the clear blaze of fire light, that gleamed through the window, shone with a more ruddy effulgence. He did not hesitate a moment, for he had nerved himself beyond that, and so at once pushed open the little wicket, and advanced to the house. After knocking twice, the door was opened by his stepmother, who, with well feigned ignorance, stared at him as if he were a stranger: and then, on his addressing her as her son, told him that her husband was in Dublin, and that she could not admit *beggars* into the house at such an hour. His proud spirit, that had been crushed by misfortune, at this taunt, swelled within him, and he retorted bitterly; but this line of conduct, in such a case, is not the wisest that can be pursued, for she had the power in her hands, which he had not, and exerted it by slamming the door in "the intherloper's face" without further ceremony. He raised his hands to heaven, and a malediction, deep and fierce, against the author of his being actually mounted to his lip; but a swelling sob, that even in the tumult of passion he could not restrain, smothered it ere it burst forth into words, and pressing his face in his hands he strode gloomily away, his mind filled to the very utmost with bitterness and gall. As he proceeded slowly along, his thoughts were in one wild and mingled chaos of dreams of revenge. He brooded fiercely over his repulsion : he thought of his wife's sickness and starving state : he felt the rags that covered his own emaciated limbs, and he asked himself why should this be, when a remedy yet presented itself? He dreamed, as all do when crushed by any deep blow, that the world was leagued against him, and why not he against the world? In a word, he was in that humour when the nature of man seems to have undergone a change, and he is in the vein for deeds of desperation. Suddenly, as he came upon the highway, in a part of the road where a rough path, that in winter was a torrent, led to the mountain top, a solitary traveller emerged from the shade of a high wall that stood at the opposite side, and proceeded on towards the place he had just quitted. That fiend, who is ever on the watch for a new victim, whispered into his ear the words of temptation. Imagination brought before him his child crying for food and his wife lying in agony on her bed of straw, and then showed him the stranger's gold, and how easily it might be procured; and in one moment of deep, desolate despair, the principles of years were uprooted, and all worn and feeble as he was, he rushed upon the unwary man who was advancing, and seizing him with the grasp of a giant demanded his money

The stranger, who was somewhat advanced in years, trembled violently, but did not answer; while the half maniac, for such he was, shook him wildly, and again exclaimed, in tones of forced calmness, that were infinitely more appalling than his former unbridled fury,

"I'm a desperate man—I'm driven on to despair, an' even madness; so don't make me frantic wid delay; give me yer money this instant, I command you—" then a suddenness of better feeling allaying the bad spirit, he continued, "bud, no—stranger, no—I don't conim and—I beg, I inthrate, I pray you to keep me from starvin'— God 'ill reward you; do, stranger, do—only a few shillin's an' the Almighty 'ill bless you!"

"Relase me this instant—*robber*, relase me!" cried the traveller in a fierce passion, unmoved by his fervent prayers; and at this foul epithet, which his heart told him *he* hardly deserved, all that good, that generous humanity with which his soul was a moment before imbued, vanished as if by magic, and he tightened his gripe of the stranger's throat to suffocation, and the veins of his forehead filled to bursting, and his quivering lip grew livid, and a furious torrent of bitter curses proceeded from those very sources from whence so lately had flowed words of deep supplication and intreaty: his trembling fingers, swayed by that mad will which scarcely knew why it so urged them, twisted and twined in the neck-cloth of the old man, and his loud and choking gasps grew less and less distinct, till at length they entirely ceased; and then flinging him rudely from him, the changed William shrieked—

"Now will you call *me robber?*"

A low sigh proceeded from the figure, which in consequence of the darkness of the night could be but indistinctly seen, and it tottered and fell; and at this sight the first tinglings of remorse shot like a bolt of living fire through the heart of the furious Hunter. He stood for a second or two irresolutely watching the dark body before him, when suddenly the clear, pale, silver moon appeared like a crescent surmounting the edge of a dark cloud that had hitherto concealed her, and brightly illuminated the face of the entire earth. At this William's gaze became fixed; his eyes turned not, stirred not, did not wink—his hair slowly began to rise off his temples, and his cheek, lately red with fury, became blanched as snow. His knees tottered, he moved slowly towards the yet insensible victim of his passion, and kneeling at his side fearfully lifted up his head, and looked at his wrinkled features. Then, the wild spasm of agony that twisted up his shaking lip, the fearful working of the maddened spirit that shook his entire frame, as in a voice louder than thunder, he shrieked—

"Gracious heaven! I have murdhered me own father!"

His hands then relaxed their hold of the old man's head, and it fell heavily with the face against the earth; upon which William leaned down, and subduing, or trying to subdue his agony and dread, in a tone of the bitterest and deepest supplication cried—

"Oh, Almighty Ruler of heaven! dar I look up to you fur forgiveness of my crime!—dar I hope fur his yet recove in' —father, dear father! look on your agonised son; only sigh, only brathe an' I'll bless you—bless you—bless you."

Then a second time his agitated and trembling hands raised up the old man's head; but a dark stream of clotting gore now flowed from a wound in the forehead, received in the last violent fall, and grew thick as it passed down the deep furrows of his aged cheek. On seeing this he grew mad, and with his fingers crimsoned with a father's blood, tore his hair in handfulls from his head, and distractedly flinging his arms towards heaven, cursed and blasphemed himself, the world, and all created things. This violent paroxysm did not last, for again the hyena within grew tame, and he lay down on the cold earth beside the dead body, and, like an idiot, laughed fiercely and unmeaningly, as he rubbed down the white hair of his victim, some of which already adhered together, as the thick blood from his temple penetrated its long folds.

He remained thus for some time, alternately cursing in a frightful manner, and giving way to the most appalling and withering bursts of maniac laughter, when suddenly, in the pause occurring between the two, the noise of footsteps approaching struck on his ear. At the first impulse which stirred within, he bounded up, and without casting another glance on the murdered body, fled up the mountain with the rapidity of a stricken deer, unconscious why he did so, but striving as it were, in the violence of exertion, to banish those agonizing thoughts that seared and tortured the very inmost recesses of his soul.

The silver moonbeams shone on the white walls of Hunter's cabin, as distracted with agony and remorse he a second time madly hastened towards it. The fields round about looked fresh and green as the drops of living dew descended from heaven to refresh the mountain flowers, and the bubbling stream shone like a molten mass of silver, as it quietly glided through the deep-worn course, singing,

> "A merry and a sprightly song,
> As it leaped from stone to stone along."

The door was left unfastened, and he pushed it back, and, gloomily entering, flung himself on a rude seat, and covering his face with his hands did not, could not speak."

"William!" said the faint but sweet tones of his wife's voice, "William, is that you? Oh! I have been so very ill sence, an' I wanted you so badly, an'—bud, William, what's the matther—why don't you spake? It was your thread I shurely hard—husband won't you spake?"

"It was me, Mary," he harshly uttered; "I'm tired—I can't be humourin' you now; don't be annoyin' me wid yer questions."

Even as he finished this sentence, which came from a sore, sore tried heart—that heart smote him for his cruelty; and when he heard her sob with grief, though she did not answer, he sprang to the bed-side, and continued,

"Bud no, no Mary—don't mind what I say—spake what you like; I'm distracted; oh, heavens! mad to blame *you*—you, me furst love an' me last—my own darlin' Mary!"

"I fear, William, there is somethin' wid you not right. I never heard your voice so hollow afore; I can see yer eyes like lumps ov blazin' coal, an' yer manners entirely althered. Tell me, fur God's sake tell me, what has happened: William, don't turn away, bud tell me!"

"No—nothin'—nothin' I say has happened. Why should you think there has? Mary, do you think I could rob, or murdher, that you ask me this? I tell you nothin' has happened!"

The frightful tone with which this was uttered froze the blood in her very veins, and she raised herself up and strained her burning eyes to look in his face as she exclaimed,

"William Hunter, I did not spake of robbin', nor ov murdher, an' why do you bring thim down. Oh! I feel a cold dhread witherin' up me very sowl. *Husband, what have you done?*"

"Nothin'," he eagerly answered, with a sudden and superhuman effort, calming his voice, and swallowing, as it were, his agony.

"Then God Almighty bless you fur that word," fervently prayed the poor deluded one, now nearly convinced by the returned and forced calmness of his manner, "fur yer voice an' yer groans frightened me to death. Now, William darlin', tell me did *he* listen to you, an' forgive you, or did he spurn you from him, an' behave cruel an' unfeelin'?"

The same hollow, unearthly calmness pervaded every tone of his voice as he answered; and she again became alarmed at its strange monotony, but kept her fears within her own bosom, and did not, even by a single expression or sigh, give him to understand the deep dread that was seated, like a lump of cold iron, in her soul.— Her question he at first evaded; but, on its being a second time repeated with more earnestness, he exclaimed,

"I did go, an' I saw him, an' asked him, an' begged of him, and prayed—bud he refused, an reviled me, an—I— I left him *never to revile again!*"

"Oh, William," she exclaimed, "there is a fearful meanin' in yer last words; a dhreadful hollowness in yer manner ov uttherin' thim: answer me, fur the sake ov the mother that bore you, do I think wrongfully ov you?"

Her hand was laid on his as she thus spoke, and when he felt the light touch of her wasted fingers, he snatched it away, as if an adder stung him, and no longer able to control the feelings which his powerful efforts had for some moments kept in check, he absolutely roared,

"Mary—wife—woman! don't touch that hand; don't place a finger near id—it is covered wid the blood of a *father!*"

The low pallet whereon she lay absolutely shook with the terrible spasms that agitated her worn frame at this confirmation of her very worst suspicions; but a moment after, when she thought of his nature, so soft and so gentle, she refused to let her heart believe that it could be so, and rising to her knees, clasped her hands together, and prayed, while the big, round, scalding tears ran down her cheeks.

"Oh, William, William, dear William, say that it is not so; let me bless you as my own guiltless husband afore I die; let me pray for you as the lover I once knew, who was innocent as the lamb, an' not as the blood-stained murdherer ov his own father. Oh, William! oh, my young heart's furst choice, listen to me, an' conthradict yer cruel, cruel words: say id—whisper id—brathe id—an' I'll bless that God who looks down on us, an' sees that I'll not live long in happiness or misery!"

He stood for a second without motion, and then essayed to answer, but a single word uttered would have choked him; and a noise being heard outside—'twas but the wind sighing through the trees—(but the heart of the guilty is always fearful) he gasped forth a sob that, more than words, confirmed all she had imagined; and straining his sleeping child to his bosom, laid it again beside his paralyzed mother, and rushed from the cabin with a haste and fury as if legions of enemies were at his heels. On his sudden departure Mary did not shriek or cry, but without seeming power to uphold her weak frame, fell on her face on the bed, and twined her arms round the crying child, shivering and sobbing with the deepest agony of mind.

The following morning the whole neighbourhood was in consternation. The body of old Hunter was found where his son had left it, for the footsteps which scared him away were passing in an opposite direction; and on the suspicions of the neighbours being aroused, in consequence of William's stepmother giving an account of his phrenzied manner the night previous, they went in a body to his cabin on the mountain.

The sight which there presented itself was fearful, and affecting in the extreme. Mary, the once beautiful and laughing Mary, was a cold, stiff corse. During the night she had died; for the agonies she endured were too much for her already worn and exhausted frame, and her eyes were open, but glazed, and her lank thin jaw dropped, and both hands clasped tightly on her shrunk bosom. Her child was playing with the long masses of her once lovely golden hair, and calling on her in tones of infantine endearment to awake. Tears filled the eyes of all present.

'Tis needless to dwell too long on scenes of agony such as these, but yet there is a lesson to be gained in all; for, alas! the harshness of parents too often drives their children to crime and misery, that they otherwise never would have encountered, and vice is inculcated, and even infamy takes root in hearts that before but knew of their existence, as dangers to be shunned, and quicksands to be avoided. Parents reflect on this, and recollect that human nature is frail, and do not dare to elect yourselves as judges over faults to which all mankind are naturally prone and inclined.

Mary was interred in the village burial ground, and her father-in-law was laid by her side, while some compassionate neighbour took charge of the child, who died before he could prove his gratitude. William for a long time evaded pursuit, but at length, not being able to endure the pangs of remorse, he gave himself up, confessed the murder, and was executed.

DENIS O'DONOHO.

ASTHMATIC MIXTURE.

Ether tincture of bladder-podded lobelia half an ounce, camphorated julep six ounces. Mix.—Two tablespoonfulls to be taken two or three times a day for chronic difficulty of breathing, and spasmodic asthma.

For spasmodic asthma, particularly when attended with flatulence, oppression of the chest, and increased susceptibility of the nervous system, this is a most valuable mixture, the first dose generally affording immediate relief.

He is more fool than wit who will offend,
For sake of jest, the man who was his friend;
In such a case we by experience know,
To lose a friend is to create a foe.   TABO.

STANZAS.

" All that's bright must fade."

As gladly I woke from my morning dreams,
With pleasure I gazed on the sun's warm beams,
While light on the world beneath him threw,
As he smiled from his palace of azure hue.

But evening came with its misty shade,
And I marked the sun in his glory fade;
With pleasure I gazed at meridian hour,
On the glowing tints of the rosy flower.

Its blossoms, like joy, looked happy and gay,
And its leaves, like hope, smiled verdantly;
But evening came with its dusky shade,
And I marked the floweret's beauty fade.

I saw the poet's raptured eye,
And I thought that its light could never die;
I saw the youthful maiden's bloom,
And I thought not of the withering tomb.

But the fire of the bard and the bloom of the maid,
Like the sun and the floweret grew cold and decayed
And they who prize each earthly thing,
Like me will find them withering.

The hearts round which you cling to-day,
Ere morning's noon will turn to clay;
This world and all on earth were made
To perish, sink, decay, and fade.

THE RETURNING EXILE'S SONG.

Once more, dear land, I see thee
In evening's silent hour,
And a feeling cometh o'er me,
As with a magic power;
For I think since last I saw thee,
When I left thee for the wave,
How many who have loved me
Are cold within the grave.

Thy sons are still as mighty,
Thy children still as brave,
And the thunder of thy high ones
Still peals along the wave;
But the blackening pall of sorrow
Hath o'er our hearts been spread,
And from every tone we borrow
Some relic of the dead.

Thy fields are still the same,
Thy shore is still as bright,
And the terror of thy name
Hath still its wonted might;
But ah! how lorn and cheerless
Our sad and gloomy lot—
The loved—the young—the fearless,
Are not!—alas!—are not.

Yet, though the valued faces,
The eyes of beaming light,
Have left their vacant places,
And are gone from mortal sight;
Yet every fairy woodland,
And every old oak tree,
And every smiling hedge-row,
Hath charms for memory.

Still graceful are thy daughters,
In innocence and youth,
And still is all untarnish'd,
The glory of thy truth;
And tho' remembrance weepeth,
Yet still I can but smile,
When I think on all thy virtues,
My own—my own green isle.

DUBLIN:
Printed and published by P. D. Hardy, 3, Cecilia-street; to whom all communications are to be addressed.

Sold by all Booksellers in Ireland.

In London, by Richard Groombridge, 6, Panyer-alley, Paternoster-row; in Liverpool, by Wilmer and Smith; in Manchester, by Ambery. in Birmingham, by Drake; in Glasgow, by W. R. M'Phun; and in Edinburgh, by N. Bowack.

THE
DUBLIN PENNY JOURNAL

CONDUCTED BY P. DIXON HARDY, M.R.I.A.

| Vol. III. | AUGUST 23, 1834. | No. 112. |

DOON POINT, ISLAND OF RATHLIN.

THE WIDOW'S WEDDING

Some half dozen miles from the coast of the County Antrim, and opposite to the bay of *Ballycastle*, rises, from the stormy ocean of the north, the island of *Rahery*.* It is seldom visited now, in consequence of the wild turbulence of its rough shores, exposed on all sides to a rude surf, and the very irregular tides which ebb and flow around it. It is the *Ricinia* of Ptolemy, and Pliny calls it *Ricnia*. It is supposed by some to be the island mentioned by Antonius by the name of *Reduna*, but the Irish annalists and historians call it *Racam*. Buchanan calls it *Raclinda*, and Mackenzie mentions it by the name of *Rachri*, while Ware calls it *Ragh*, or Rathlin ; but by the natives, and people of the coast of Antrim, it is universally called *Rahery*. It commands a wide extent of coast, and is the first land seen by vessels coming to our northern shores; and, in consequence, Mr. Hamilton thinks its *etymon* must be *Ragh*, or Rath-erin, the fort of Erin, or fortress of Ireland : and, as far as my little knowledge of the Irish language leads me to think, I agree with him, as most of the antient names were taken from the particular situation or feature of the place. The

* In our Guide to the Giant's Causeway, published as a Supplement to our Second Volume, will be found a brief description of this interesting spot. The pillars are similar to those forming the Causeway, although by many esteemed much more curious, from the variety in the positions which they have assumed, of which the above engraving affords a very correct idea—some standing perpendicular, others lying on their sides, while the greater proportion of those on the top are bent or curved downwards.

inhabitants are a poor simple race of people, and their island is not very productive. Rahery was a long time the resting place of the Scots in their expeditions, and their place of refuge in danger : it was also the place of assembly for the great northern chieftains, before making their descents on the Scotch or English coast. There are the ruins of a very old castle here, called Bruce's castle, from its being the retreat of the famous hero, Robert Bruce, during the disturbances in Scotland at the time of Baliol. About the middle of the sixth century, the patron saint of the north, Columbus, otherwise Colum-kille, founded a religious establishment on the island of Rahery, which was destroyed by the Danes. In the year 973 they also plundered this island, and barbarously murdered St. Feradach, the abbot. The Scots held possession of it in 1558, but were attacked and driven out, with great slaughter, by the Lord Deputy, Sussex. The people of the coast and the island are all expert seamen, and at one time were famous smugglers, very much given to superstitious customs and observances. The Irish cobles of wicker-work, covered with a tarred and pitched horse-hide, were much in use here of old, and even still are sometimes seen skimming along, with their one or two conductors, in fine weather. And though I have said that the island is seldom visited, I did not wish to be understood as saying that there was not a constant communication between its inhabitants and the main shore ; there is a kind of friendly intercourse subsists between them, and even in the most tempestuous weather, boats to and fro, are seen passing, despite of danger and difficulty.

In the island of Rahery there resided a farmer, named M'Cahan. He was one of the most wealthy men in the little district, being possessed of a very large farm and two fishing boats. He had one daughter, the flower of the island, and the pride of her parents. Many suitors came to gain young Mary from her father's house, as she had the largest portion of any maiden in Rahery. Her father and mother were anxious that she should choose one from among the young men of her little native isle, or the surrounding coast, but she continually declined entering into any engagement with any of them. Neither was it from coldness or caprice that she refused to comply with the wishes of her parents—her heart had been smitten by the manly form and pleasing address of Kennedy O'Neil, the son of a widow who resided on the mainland, near the cliff of Ballycastle. She was in the habit, during summer weather, in company with a number of the young women and men of the island, to visit the opposite shores, and join in the dance with the villagers; in this way she first became acquainted with Kennedy, *mock na buinthee*, or, the widow's son. His frank, obliging, and manly manners won upon the unsophisticated heart of the simple, yet tender and faithful islander. Kennedy was fondly attached to Mary, and the dance on Sunday without her, appeared the most monotonous and pleasureless spot in the world.

The mother of Kennedy was one of those beings which are to be found in many parts of the country, even in this enlightened era—a believer in, and a practiser of, spells and charms, or, what is commonly called, a fairy woman She professed the curing of all unaccountable and uncommon diseases, and which are attributed to the waywardness or malignity of that imaginary class of spiritual beings called fairies. Cattle suddenly taken ill, and children in a decline, or with pains or swellings, were taken to her, from a great distance, to "thry her skill on," but whether she was successful in all her operations or not is more than can be said at present. She was feared and respected in the neighbourhood, and, at the same time, was considered one of the most useful personages within many miles of Ballycastle. She perceived, with delight, her son's attachment to Mary M'Cahan, and encouraged it with all her soul; and being, as she boasted, of the "rale ould anshint race," and having a small farm in her possession, she had, she imagined, every hope that Kennedy's suit would be successful with the father of the fair Mary. Ensured of Mary's affection, and incited by his mother's approbation and wish on the subject, he took an opportunity of waiting on the farmer, and claiming her as his bride; but met with a decided and insulting refusal. This was a shock which his young and ardent nature was not prepared to meet, and which the proud heart and revengeful disposition of his mother could but ill brook. Mary was equally unprepared to meet it, for she had cherished hopes which were suddenly blighted; and her lover had pictured such warm scenes of domestic felicity, in the anticipated enjoyment of their homely fireside pleasures, that a second paradise of happiness had been opened to her young soul. Still hope, and promises of mutual affection, to be fairly and firmly kept "for ever and a day," helped to reconcile them to what they considered the hardships of their situation.

Months glided by, and M'Cahan was anxious to have his daughter married to some of the very respectable young men who proposed for her, but Mary modestly, yet firmly, resisted every effort made to induce her to forego her promise to the *mock na buinthee*.

"Where are you goin' the day, dear?" said the widow O'Neil to her son, as she perceived him fitting his tackle for the water one fine Sunday.

"Just over right to the island," replied Kennedy.

"Say at home, Kennedy, dear, then, this day,' said the mother.

" D'dnt I send word over to Mary M'Cahan that I'd be over to the sport this evenin'?—throth did I," said Kennedy.

"There's a storm to the nor-west this evenin', then," said the mother; "an' though fine the sun shines above us just now, God help the sail it ketches atween Rahery and the cliffs this evenin', when he looks his last over the wathers, with the black clouds afore his face."

"Why, it looks a little grey and misty, to be sure, an that where it ought to be brightest, too, the foot ov the win'; but, then, it's goin' round it is, an' not coming for'ad—it s a shittin' freshner, you see, and that's all nother."

His little bark was soon in trim and at sea, and soon the cliffs of Rahery, with all their bleak and wave-washed caverns, frowned upon his skiff, as it flew, like the dark-sided gull, silently and swiftly along. The day was passed in a round of pleasure, for Kennedy was a general favourite, and the young men of the island endeavoured to entertain him in the best possible manner; and, as evening was closing, he had the happiness to " meet wi' and greet wi " his true and faithful Mary. Therefore, it was late before he thought of returning, and the sun was setting in the ocean before he stepped into his little "skimmer of the waves." The forebodings of the storm pointed by his mother, were now increased into actual threatenings, of the very worst description. The wind had veered, and was sounding over the ocean, in the distance, like the meanings of a coming spirit, on an errand of misery and sorrow to mankind, while the ocean heaved and swelled, and the waves rolled heavily and forcibly to the shore, giving certain indications of the fury of the storm that was raging in the distance. Notwithstanding all these terrible omens, he launched his boat, and turned its tiny prow to the rising billows, and steered for the cliff of Ballycastle. The wind was partly against, and the tide, in its usual rapid manner, was rushing to mid-ocean; still Kennedy set his sail, and, taking a sweeping tack, stood away from the point of Rahery. Though appearances were very disheartening while in the shelter of the shore, yet as he stood far out, before the breeze, he trembled for the consequences of his rashness, and was sorry that he did not take the advice of his companions, and not have ventured out to sea that evening. But his pride would not allow him to think of returning, for as he had the name of being the best sailor round the shore, it would fix itself as a stain on his character, should he fly to the land, after having put out to sea against their wishes. In the mean time the gale increased, and the waves became too fierce and high to leave almost a hope that his light frail bark could ever reach the shore; still he held on, keeping her head to the foaming billows, upon which it rose like the *wild bird*, who dwells amid the storms.

The winds now bellowed like the voices of many spirits, and the agitated deep, roused by their calls, answered by tossing its many crested waves to the clouds, and roared its responses to the furious element in tones of destruction and power. Kennedy, in taking in his small sail, lest his little bark should be overturned even by its breadth of canvass, was cast out, by one tremendous gust, into the howling waters; but, with the steadiness, firmness, and presence of mind, of a man used to meet danger and to combat it, he soon grasped the side of his dancing boat, but, in attempting to regain his position, her side was turned to the coming wave, which cast her over, and there she lay, in the trough of the sea, with her keel upwards. Even here Kennedy's native courage and hardihood did not forsake him; he dived, and rose again just beside his upset and shivering vessel, upon which he seized with that desperate force which the fear of death supplies to the man in jeopardy. He clung to the keel with the tenacious grasp which one should lay upon their last hold of life, determined, while strength remained, to use every effort to preserve his existence. It was now dark night, and as his wreck would rise high upon the back of the yelling billows, he could discern the lights on shore, faint and dim in the distance, fainter and more dim than ever he had remarked them before—and the dreadful thought came across his mind, that the boat was driving out to sea, and that, if not swallowed up by the devouring waves during the storm, he would be left to perish, through weakness and excess of toil, far out in the ocean. Yet even still he determined to hold on, and trust in the goodness of that Almighty Being who caused the winds to blow, and the stormy waves to rage around him.

Towards morning the wind abated, and the waves subsided by degrees, though now and then fierce gusts and mountain billows came, like the bursts of passion which break abruptly from the bosom of the angry, after their violent fit has poured the full rage of its wrath. The morning dawned, and when the harassed and terror-stricken Kennedy looked around him, the land was in no place visible. He was alone, riding on the back of his upturned bark, a solitary living being amid the waste of waters. Despair filled his bosom; and, after having outlived the terrors of the night-storm, he was about casting himself headlong into the deep, sooner than die a death of lingering and protracted agony; but hope, the ever-dweller in the human heart, came again to his aid, and the thought of meeting some vessel coming from, or going to Belfast, or any of the northern ports made him resolve to preserve his life as long as possible. Nor was he disappointed, for towards evening a distant sail appeared coming in the direction in which he lay. Various hopes and fears now thronged heavy and quick upon his mind—she might be going in a contrary direction—he might not, even if coming any way near her, be able to make himself observed. He took off his coarse blue jacket, and stripped off his shirt and red neck cloth, both of which he held as high as his hand would allow over his head; and when one hand would tire, he would hold it in the other. On she came, and at length he was perceived, and a boat lowered, into which he was taken, exhausted and gasping. The ship belonged to a merchant in Belfast, and was taking a large cargo of fine linens and other goods to the West Indies. They were some leagues away even from the sight of land, and Kennedy had no other alternative but to make the voyage with them—a thing the master appeared to be very proud of, as he found, after leaving Belfast, that his complement of hands were too few to work the vessel.

In the morning the mother of Kennedy despatched a person to the island to inquire for her son; but no other account could be given, but that he had put to sea at night-fall, just as the storm was beginning. All round the bay of Ballycastle was explored, even for his corse, but not the slightest vestiges of him or his boat could be discovered. He was given up as lost, and the unfortunate mother was wild and loud in her grief and lamentations; nor were the sorrows of the faithful Mary less, though not so noisy; deep in the inmost recesses of her heart she deplored the loss of Kennedy, and the big tear rolling down her cheek, while pursuing even her household affairs, told plainly of—

"The secret grief was at her heart."

She pined, and the rose fled from her cheeks. She shunned the usual amusements in which she delighted, and gave herself up to melancholy. Her father and mother became anxious about her health, and wished, when it was too late, that they had given her to Kennedy O'Neil. They did every thing to rouse her, in which, after some months, they succeeded; and she became more resigned and composed. Again they urged her to marry a very wealthy young man from the opposite shore, who had proposed for her hand, even before the supposed death of Kennedy. She gave a passive consent, and after some time they were married. She was any thing but happy; she did her best to please and make her husband as happy as she could, but still there was a coldness and apathy in her manners which she could not banish; and though she did her best to be cheerful, yet still, in the midst of her efforts to appear gay, a chill would creep over her, and the thoughts of Kennedy *Mock na Bointhee*, and how he lost his life in coming to see her, would mar with sadness every attempt she made to please others, or appear happy herself. Four months after her marriage were scarcely elapsed, when her husband, who had been out fishing, quarrelled with one of his companions as they were returning, and commenced fighting, even in the narrow boat. The other two men endeavoured to separate them, but without effect; and while the confusion reigned, the boat struck against a sunken rock, and the four men were ejected into the ocean, at the same time that the husband of Mary received a violent blow on the head with a boat-hook. The boat heeled with the shock, and imme-

diately filled with water, and settled down beneath the wave as three men rose to the surface—but the husband of Mary never rose; stunned by the blow, he was unable to struggle when precipitated beneath the waves, and became the victim of his own rash and quarrelsome habits.

Mary was now alone in the world, and possessed of, comparatively, a comfortable independence, and she determined never to marry again. Several proposals were made, but all rejected, with a firmness that told the solicitor that it would be useless to apply a second time. She remained in this state for nearly six months; and one evening in the month of October, as the shortening autumn day was closing, a sailor, with a short stick in his hand, and a bundle slung on the end of it over his shoulder, made his appearance at the door, and addressing the servant-maid, who was preparing the supper, requested a drink, and liberty to light his pipe.

"Walk in, Sir," said Mary, who was employed at the other end of the house, with her back to the door.

The sailor started, and drawing back a few steps, surveyed the house from roof tree to foundation, and from end to end.

"Won't you come in, Sir?" said the servant girl.

"No, no," said he, "I thank you—I want nothing from you now;" and his tone was hurried and agitated, and he turned away from the door, and ran like a man who had beheld some frightful, devouring monster, and from which he was trying to escape.

It was Kennedy O'Neil, *Mock na Bointhee*, who, after a variety of adventures during ten months, had returned to his native land with some little money, and high in the hope that he would find his Mary faithful, and ready to reward all his sufferings by becoming his wife.

"It is her," said he to himself, after turning from her door, and when he had gained a sufficient composure to arrange his thoughts. "It is her—I could not be mistaken in her voice or form—but I could not bear to look on her: and did she so soon forget me? not a twelvemonth gone, yet she is married, dear knows how long.— What's the use in my coming home? I may as well turn back this moment, and go to the Indies again:" and he stopt, as if to return on his path: "but I must see my poor mother, and give her what I have gathered after my hardship and danger. Yes, she deserves it better from me than the false-hearted and the forgetful—the breaker of promises, and the betrayer. And is it of Mary M'Cahan that I'm obliged to say all these shameful things? Well, it's no matter: 'man proposes, but God disposes;' if she's happy maybe it's better for both her and me, for surely a stronger arm than poor mortyual man's separated us in the beginnin'; and there's a fate in marriage: but after all—all that passed between us!—all that she promised me, and all that I promised her; and all the vows and *hand an' words* that she give me.' However—'what is to be, will be;' and there's no contending against a body's luck: but Mary M'Cahan, if I never knew you it would be better for me—that I know to my cost, anyhow."

In such soliloquies and reflections was his mind occupied until he reached the cottage of his mother. It was dark and chilly; and mournfully the breeze blew from the sea with a wailing sound, and the booming of the distant ocean, intermingled with the hoarse and dashing noise of the breakers on the shore, served to add a gloom of an additional shade to his melancholy.

His mother was sitting alone by her now desolate hearth —the last embers of the dying turf-fire were flickering faintly from between two "sods of turf," which were placed over them to inspire a renovated life into them, in order to preserve them for 'the morrow.' She also held communion with her heart. "It was a curious dream," she said, thinking alone; "and why should he come in that way to me, as if there was a joy to visit my old and withered heart, after the dark waves concealed him for ever from my sight. The dead can come no more to give gladness to the living; nor can the fallen tree ever be set upright amongst its companions in the thick wood, to bear green leaves and young branches; and why should he

* In contracting or plighting their troths among the peasantry, the affair of pledging a hand and word is considered even more binding on the parties than the most solemn oath.

come to me in the disguise of joy, even in my dreams.—He was not fond of tormenting or crossing me, and I know he would not wish to break my heart *now* entirely." Here a rap of a particular kind at the outside made her start from her reverie. "Ha! my God! that rap! Oh, if it's a warnin' for me it's welcome—I hope I am prepared to go; but maybe it's some of the good people who want *to catch me* noddin'—let them knock again;' * and she listened with impatience, strongly mingled with superstitious fear, and again the knock was repeated more markedly than before, and again she became pained and agitated.

"I never in my life heard any thing so like; but it's only to desave me the betther; so the sorra a latch I'll rise, or a boult I'll dhraw till it raps again, anyhow;" and again the rap was repeated with a certain degree of impatience, and she then approached the door with a cautious, stealthy step, and demanded who was there?

"Friend," was the laconic reply; to which was added—"isn't it a shame for you not to let a poor man in this hour of the night."

"Oh, gracious, it is his very voice. Speak—who are you?" she exclaimed, "for the love of goodness speak, and tell me who you are?"

"Who am I? Well, but that's a queer question to ask a man at his own mother's door—who he is?"

She uttered a loud scream, and endeavoured to spring to the door; but her emotions overpowered her, and her limbs refused to do their office, and down she fell upon the floor. Kennedy hearing the cry, burst open the door, and made every exertion in his power to reanimate the corpse-like figure of his mother, which he after some time effected. The meeting of the mother with the son, whom she now found, after believing him buried deep within the secret depths of the sea, was truly affecting.—It is impossible to describe a scene of this kind; but a man will feel the pleasure which such a sight must impart to the benevolent heart. The mother cried in frantic joy, and hung upon his neck, and wept over him. After the first paroxysm had abated, he described to her his wonderful and miraculous escape; and she thanked heaven for restoring to her her only child.

"But, mother," said he, "there's a great many changes have taken place since I left this."

"It's yourself that may say that, dear," said the old woman, "and not one of them for the better."

"It's you I believe, mother," said he; "I have not seen any improvement since I left it."

"No, dear; there's the miners tearing up the earth at the ould head to look for coals; and there's the polish (police) placed all round for fear we'd get a pinsworth from the say (sea), and there's the ould castle there going to be levelled with the rock, for fear it id hide a bale, or a cask, and—"

"There's Mary M'Cahan marred, mother," said he convulsively.

"Yes, *agra*," replied the mother; "there's no depending upon any one, or upon any thing in this deceiving world."

"Well, mother, I'm only come just to see you, and bring you a litttle money to help to keep you comfortable, and then to bid you good bye, and then to go to seek my fortune again,"

"And are you going to leave me afther all, when I thought that God had pursarved you just to be the comfort of my old days?"

"I could not live here now mother; every thing is strange, and cold, and changed, and every thing looks worse than ever I saw it before—even you, mother, are sadly worn since I left you."

"And am I to lose you again? Why did you ever come to me, when my mind was settling after your loss, and God was making me reconciled to your death?"

"But Mary M'Cahan, mother, to forget me so soon; not one year till she got marred to another;—would I do so? No, never.'"

"Yes, an' its little comfort she had; for she did not long enjoy him; she was but four months marred till he was killed."

"And is she a widow now, mother?—ah, God help her! and who killed her husband?'"

"I did," replied the mother. "Could I bear to see another where my son should be? No. I went to the sthream three nights, and I made a float of the *flaggers*.*—I took from its grave, in the middle of the night, the skull and left hand of a child that never was christened. I dressed it up, and christened it by his name. I then put it into the float, with the hand tied to the ruddher, and sent it down the sthream, under the quiet moon and all the stars; 'twas racked (wrecked) at the fall of the rocks—'twas I done it —afore that day month he was murdhered.*

The son shuddered as the mother concluded her horrifying recital, but he said nothing; he was accustomed to hear such things, and he firmly believed in their efficacy and power.

However, his thoughts had undergone a material change since he heard that Mary was a widow. He promised to remain with his mother, for a while at least, and they retired for the night.

Nothing could exceed the surprise and astonishment of the neighbourhood when the news was spread abroad the next morning, that Kennedy O'Neil was returned, and some would not believe but that it was his mother who had redeemed him from fairy-land. All his old acquaintances flocked to see him, and hear his wonderful story, and every one had some news or another to tell him about Mary M'Cahan. Week after week passed away, and he never made an attempt to see her, nor she to see him. At last, one evening as he was returning from the dance in the neighbouring village, a little warmed with the exercise, and heated with liquor, some strange sailors, belonging to a vessel that took shelter in the bay, for the purpose of refitting, had joined in the amusements, and had left the scene of gaiety some time before him. As he walked on with a rapid step, he thought he heard cries at a distance before him on the road. The voice was that of a woman, and he hurried on, and soon came up to two ruffians in the garb of sailors, who were pulling a female between them, and whose piercing screams excited pity in his heart. He came up, and before they were aware of his approach, he felled one of the villains to the earth. The other immediately let go his hold, and grappled with Kennedy, and being a powerful man, the struggle was desperate; and O'Neil felt, that though few in the country were his equals in the athletic exercises, that here at least he had met with his match. So, with surprising presence of mind, he seemed to yield by degrees before his antagonist, until the other, being almost sure of the victory, was thrown off his guard, when Kennedy, collecting all his strength for the effort, and stringing every nerve for the one push, placed his foot behind him, and flinging himself forward upon him, hurled him with irresistible force to the earth. The other, who was a small and light man, was recovering from the effects of the first blow, and preparing to attack him behind, when Kennedy, untired from the strife, turned on him with the fierce fury of an enraged tiger, and a second time felled him, senseless and bleeding, to the ground; and twisting an ash bough from a stunted tree that grew by the road side, he again prepared for the attack of the larger man, whom he knocked down three times in succession. At last they begged for mercy, and were permitted to depart. But what can be imagined as the surprise and astonishment of Kennedy on lifting the female, who had fainted, to find that it was his Mary. He laid his hand on her heart—it beat with life. He lifted her in his arms, and as her cottage was but at a short distance, he carried her home. On entering the cottage she came to her senses, and gazed about wildly until her eye rested upon Kennedy.

"It's you then, Kennedy," she said "that saved my life though I did not deserve the smallest kindness at your hand. Well, God is good, and brings every thing round, for his own wise purposes."

Kennedy gazed upon her. She was no longer the

---

* There is a superstition among the country people, that when a knock is heard at the door at night, it should never be opened until repeated three times.

* The green flag-leaved annual that grows in marshy soils, and by the side of streams.

healthy, bright-eyed, and rosy girl, with the smile upon her lip, and gaiety and good humour in her bright blue eye. Her cheek was now pale, and her eye had lost its lustre, and Kennedy pitied the beautiful wreck—for she was still young and beautiful. They were alone ; the conversation naturally verged towards old times ; an explanation ensued, a reconciliation followed, and promises and vows were again reuewed with double the fervour and truth of former years.

Kennedy told his mother of the circumstance ; and she advised him, to prevent a recurrence of any accident or misfortune, to urge a speedy marriage. She wished to keep her son at home, for she feared he had acquired a taste for rambling during the time he had been away; besides, the idea of Mary's comfortable farm, and the happy home her son would be master of, made her bosom dance with joy. Kennedy was but too anxious to follow her advice, and accordingly urged Mary to make him happy, pointing out the consequences that ensued from their first delay—how he had been driven away ; how she was married ; and how near she was being murdered, only that heaven sent him to her assistance. She consented, and the following Sunday was appointed for the ceremony to take place.

The sailors who had been discomfited in their attempt, made their case known to their comrades on board, and a confederacy was entered into by them to attack the house of Mary on the night of her marriage, while the guests were engaged with their mirth and revelry ; and as they were to sail with the tide of that night, they might take their revenge in safety to themselves.

The mother of Kennedy could not be induced by any means to be present at the wedding ; and when her son came to know the reason, and to endeavour to induce her, she merely replied—

Never mind me, Kennedy, dear ; you know that there is no one prouder to see you happy than your mother ; but there is something over me this evening, and you know I never do any thing without having good reason ; so never mind me, Kennedy, dear, I'll see you early in the morning."

Kennedy, who knew the eccentric turn of his mother, did not press her ; and the festivities of the night were at their height : the rustic jest and the simple song passed round, and the whiskey flowed in brimmers, and all were merry and happy, when the mother of Kennedy, out of breath, and pale and panting with fatigue and terror, rushed in.

"For the sake of heaven, if you be men, stand and defend yourselves. The strange sailors have left the vessel, and are coming in a body to murder all before them. I ran over by the short cut, and roused the boys as I came along—but the sailors are not many perches from the door. The women began to scream, and the men to look about them, not knowing which side to turn.

"Hold your screaming throats," she said to the women, "and you stir about, and bar the door and windows, iv you have the spirit of men within yez ;" and she dragged a large oak table against the door. Kennedy leapt to his feet to assist her, and in a few minutes every portable article of furniture in the house was piled against the door and windows.

"Now put out the lights," said she, "and leave us in darkness."

The noise of the feet of many men advancing rapidly fell upon their ears, and in a few minutes a rap at the door announced their arrival.

"Don't one of you speak a word," said she.

A second rap, louder, echoed through the house, but no one stirred inside. The men were heard to whisper for a while, and then to try if the doors and windows were any way accessible. They succeeded in breaking in some glass at the top of the window, to which one of them was elevated.

"Here, Kennedy," said the mother, handing him the large kitchen tongs, "don't let him tell what he s seen when they take him back."

Kennedy mounted upon a chair near the window, and as the man put in his head through the broken part, Kennedy struck him a terrible blow on the forehead, and he dropt back senseless into the arms of his companions.

"Now shout," said the mother ; and the men joined in one loud and simultaneous shout, which was answered by cries of revenge from the men outside, and a terrible rush was made against the door, which, however, defied all their efforts. The attack was renewed and redoubled with equal success, and cries were heard of 'set fire to the house,' when the shouts and bustle of men coming along at a distance, made them pause. The men inside shouted, and they were answered by the villagers coming to their assistance.

"Now, boys," said Kennedy, "take the things from the door, and let us be ready to rush out upon them."

But the sailors had anticipated their movement, and fled towards the shore, leaving the wounded man behind them. He was not killed ; they took him into the house, and bathed his wound, and the farrier of the village bled him with his phleme. The rest of the night was spent in mirth and festivity.

Kennedy and Mary lived happy together, and their wedding night was the most troublesome of the days and nights of their long and prosperous lives ; and Kennedy often remarked, that it is happy for the man whose misfortunes come before marriage, and not after.   J. L. L.

POPULAR LECTURES ON THE PHYSIOLOGY OF ANIMALS.

The following is an abstract of Dr. Henry's seventh Lecture :

THE EAR.

The essential part of the ear, or organ of hearing, is contained in the side of the skull, and makes a projection into the interior of the cavity containing the brain.—Hence it happens that inflammation of the ear is readily communicated to the brain, and produces death, the only symptom of the disease at first being an intense pain in the ear. The impressions from without enter by a passage into which they are collected or directed by the external ear, (as this gristly appendage is called,) just in the same manner as they are collected by the wide part of the ear-trumpet, and directed into the tube ; the ear-trumpet being only a contrivance which deaf people use to enlarge that part of the ear which collects sounds. The external ear is then simply a mechanical instrument for collecting sounds, and directing them into the passage which leads to the *drum*, as it is called. The *drum* is a cell or cavity interposed between the external passage and the true auditory or sentient part of the ear : no communication exists in the natural state between the external passage and this hollow cavity or *drum*. A thin membrane, called the membrane of the drum, is spread across the bottom of the external passage, and cuts off all communication between it and the drum, so that the fear which many entertain of insects, or foreign substances insinuating themselves from the external passage into the drum is quite groundless. In some persons, when the ear is placed in a favourable light, the membrane of the drum can be seen at the bottom of the external passage : it can at all times be touched by a probe introduced into the ear. The cavity of the drum contains air, and communicates with the external atmosphere by a tube opening into the back part of the mouth ; by means of this communication, some individuals are enabled to force tobacco-smoke from their mouth out of their ears. In such cases the smoke passes from the back part of the mouth into the tube ; from thence into the cavity of the drum, and thence (through some opening in the membrane of the drum, made either by ulceration or accident, or, perhaps, existing there as an original malformation) into the external passage, and so to the exterior of the head. In the interior of the drum are found three minute bones, articulated with each other, so as to form a chain or series of bones, which stretches across the cavity of the drum, from the membrane of the drum, on the one side, to the internal part of the ear, or the labyrinth, on the other. These bones are called, from their forms, the hammer, the anvil, and the stirrup. The hammer is attached to the inner side of the membrane of the drum ; the stirrup, by its flat side, fills up an opening which leads from the drum into the labyrinth. The head of the hammer rests on the anvil, and the other end of the anvil is attached to the arch of the stirrup. Impressions of sound received by the membrane of the drum are conveyed by this chain of bones across the drum to the labyrinth. The bones are supplied with muscles, by which they can be moved within certain limits. The internal or sentient part of the ear is on the farther side of the drum; it is called the labyrinth from its complicated structure. It consists of three parts, called the vestibule, snail-shell, and semicircular canals : these parts are all hollowed out of the solid bone. The vestibule contains a very thin membranous bag, which spreads offsets or branches into the semicircular canals ; the interior of this bag, and of the offsets, contains a liquid which is entirely shut up in this membranous bag with its offsets, and has no communication with any thing outside : again the space between this bag, and the bony shell by which it is contained, is filled by a meshwork of exceedingly delicate fibres, and the interstices of these fibres are filled with liquid, so that commencing from the outside you have,

1st. The bony exterior or case.

2dly. A space filled with a transparent liquid, contained in a net-work so delicate that the liquid seems quite at large.

3dly. The membranous bag, having very nearly the shape of the vestibule and semicircular canals.

Lastly. On the interior of the bag, and washed by the liquid which it contains, is spread the auditory nerve coming from the brain, and penetrating, first the bone, and afterwards the membranous bag contained in the bone. From this description you will understand that any sonorous impression from without, before it can be perceived by the mind, is first collected by the external trumpet of the ear, and directed into the external passage ; then received by the membrane of the drum, and communicated from thence by the bones of the drum to the labyrinth, where it sets in vibration the liquid outside the membranous bag, then the bag itself, then its liquid contents, and last of all the expansion of the auditory nerve. While the parts constituting the essential organ of hearing contained in the labyrinth are of such extreme delicacy and tenuity as scarcely to be capable of examination by our instruments of sense, the bony case in which they are situated consists of the firmest and hardest bone in the body, so as to be technically called the petrous or rocky portion of the temple bone.

As it is of more use to be able to hear sounds coming from before than from behind, the external ear is formed for catching sounds coming from before, by its concavity having a slight direction forward. In the same degree as this structure is favorable for catching sounds coming from before, it is unfavourable for catching sounds coming from behind ; but the inclination in the human ear is so inconsiderable, and the opening so patulous, that we can distinctly hear sounds in whatever direction they may come. In quadrupeds the external ear is more in the form of a tube than it is in man, and, therefore, does not so readily catch sounds coming in any other direction than that of the open mouth of the tube. To counteract this defect, animals have a considerable power of moving the external ear so as to turn the open mouth of the tube towards that quarter from which the sounds come. Birds are without an external ear, similar to that possessed by man and quadrupeds, but sometimes the feathers are arranged so as to form a very perfect apparatus for carrying sounds into the external passage ; this may be seen in the owl. Birds have the drum and membrane of the drum, but their labyrinth is less perfect than the labyrinth of the higher classes of animals.

Rory Oge M'Quillan, of Dunluce Castle, could trace his family from their departure from Babylon, three thousand years ago, whence they came to Scotland, and being called Chaldeans, gave origin to the corruption of the word Caledonians: the M'Quillans afterwards removed to Ireland.

As trees with submission bow down to the blast,
So we when we sigh must remember the past.

THE HAPPY SHEPHERD—A SONG.

Yes, Phillis, we'll trip o'er the meads,
  And hasten away to the plain ;
Where shepherds attend with their reeds,
  To welcome my love and her swain :
The lark is exalted in air,
  The linnet sings perch'd on the spray ;
Our lambs stand in need of our care,
  Then let us not lengthen delay.

The pleasure I feel with my dear,
  While gamesome young lambs are at sport,
Exceeds the delight of a peer,
  That shines with such grandeur at court :
While Colin and Strephon go by,
  They form a disguise for awhile ;
They see how I'm blessed with a sigh,
  But envy forbids them to smile.

Let great folks of liberty prate,
  T'enjoy it take infinite pains ;
But liberty's primitive state
  Is only enjoyed on the plains.
With Phillis I rove to and fro—
  With her my gay minutes are spent ;
'Twas Phillis first taught me to know,
  That happiness flows from content.   M. H.

LINES WRITTEN BY THE SEA SIDE.

One evening, as the sun went down
Gilding the mountains bare and brown,
  I wandered on the shore ;
And such a blaze o'er ocean spread,
And beauty on the meek earth shed,
  I never saw before.

I was not lonely : dwellings fair
Were scattered round and shining there !
  Gay groups were on the green
Of children, wild with reckless glee,
And parents that could child-like be,
  With them and in that scene.

And on the sea, that looked of gold,
Each toy-like skiff and vessel bold
  Glided, and yet seemed still ;
While sounds rose on the quiet air,
That mingling made sweet music there,
  Surpassing minstrel's skill.

The breezy murmur from the shore,
Joy's laugh re-echoed o'er and o'er
  Alike by sire and child ;
The whistle-shrill, the broken song,
The far-off flute-notes lingering long,
  The lark's strain rich and wild.

'Twas sunset in the world around,
And, looking inwards, so I found
  'Twas sun-set in the soul ;
Nor grief, nor mirth were burning there,
But musings sweet, and visions fair,
  In placid beauty stole.

But moods like these the human mind,
Though seeking oft, may seldom find,
  Nor, finding, force to stay ;
As dews upon the drooping flower,
That, having shone their little hour,
  Dry up, or fall away.

But though all pleasures take their flight,
Yet some will leave memorials bright
  For many an after year ;
The sun-set that dull night will shade
These visions, which must quickly fade,
  Will half-immortal memory braid,
For me, when far from here.

PETIT SESSIONS SKETCH.

CASE OF ASSAULT AND BATTERY.

At the sessions of ————, a short time ago, Timothy, or Tim Reilly, (his grandfather had doffed the O,) appeared before the sitting magistrates, to prefer a charge of assault and battery against the pigs of his near neighbour, the widow Delany. The case, from its peculiarity, excited considerable interest among the "*neighbours*;" and the little court-house, adjoining the chief constable's house, was crowded to excess. Several of those important personages, familiarly designated "*peelers*," helped to fill it; and, in a corner, between a couple of them, Mr. Tim Reilly had placed himself.

The case being called on, Tim boldly stepped forward, and, in his best style, made his obeisance to the bench. It would require the pen of a Cervantes or a Scott to do justice to the description of Tim's person. He was fully six feet two in height, with arms, were they stretched, that would reach much below his knees; the latter, while he stood, appeared to commune with each other in the most friendly manner, but when he walked, they must have been at open war; his head was a little inclined to the right, as if the fall of some heavy matter upon it had given it a *friendly* twist; his nose was a caricature of the aquiline; and his mouth, extending from ear to ear, now made a terrible grimace, as seconding some violent motion of his arm, again relaxed into a condescending smile as he "*grinned complaisance*." On the whole, a figure so extraordinary was seldom beheld; and it was evident it required the greatest possible exertion, on the part of the magistrates, to keep their countenance during his appeal.

Magistrate—" Where's the defendant ?"

" Mrs. Delany," exclaimed a policeman.

" Mrs. Delany," roared Tim, with a stentorian bawl.

Mrs. Delany was echoed by fifty voices without, and, in a few minutes, Mrs. Delany herself appeared, bustling through the crowd that thronged the hall, and presently placed herself by the side of our hero.

Magistrate—" What's your complaint, Reilly ?"

Tim—" And, plase your honor, this woman's pigs that assaulted me, an' near kilt me."

" Oh, don't mind a word he says, your worship," interrupted the widow, " for——"

Magistrate—" Silence, woman, you will be heard in your turn."

" Yes, silence, Mrs. Delany," exclaimed Tim, " you will be hard in your turn."

The serious and theatrical manner in which Tim gave utterance to this mandate was too much for the gravity of the spectators, already a little shook by his *outre* appearance, and a roar of laughter, in which the bench heartily joined, followed his words.

" Now, then," said Tim, " it would be much better for them there *peelers* to be minding their goats, than to be laughing at an honest man—it's ugly enough they are already without making themselves more so; troth, they ought to sell themselves for tobaccy signs, half of them."

Magistrate—" Proceed with your complaint, Sir, at once."

Tim—" I will, your honor. You must know, your worships, that I farm a taste of arable land outside the town here, and this woman is my right hand neighbour. Well, your worships, whin I used to come into the market here, to sell one little thing or another—and, maybe, to buy something, too—whin I'd go home, the crathurs of chilthers would up and tell me how Mrs. Delany's three pigs would be rootin' my little grain of piatees; and whin I'd go out to the field, your worships, I'd find that the sorra a lie was there in the chilther's mouths, for sure enough my piatees would be all rooted, but the sorra a pig could I lay my clutch upon. Well, your worships, I'd go in thin to Mrs. Delany, and I'd up and tell her how her pigs had mis-behaved."

" Oh, no, Mr. Reilly," interrupted the defendant, " you never tould me but once."

" Tin times, Mrs. Delany, begging your pardon. And Mrs. Delany, says I, your pigs is badly edicated— they know as much about larnin', Mrs. Delany, says I as a dancin' master does about navigation. (Here the court was convulsed with laughter.) Well, your worships, it's how I was remarkin' that Mrs. Delany's pigs was badly larned; and, as I tould her one mornin', if she didn't know how to tache her chilther better nor her pigs, they'll be a cryin' disgrace to her."

Magistrate—" What has that to do with the case."

Tim—" I'll tell you, your worship. Last Tuesday mornin', whin I was tying some straw to cover a turf reek, the chilther come cryin' to me, that the pigs was at their ould work, rootin' my piatees—up I leaps, and straight I runs to the field, and, sure enough, your worships, there they were, and their noses in clover. Hurish, hurish, muck, muck, says I; well, wid that, as soon as ever they hard me, straight they galloped towards me, and, before I could get out of the way, the biggest of them, bad manners to him, leaps up and hot me right here"— suiting the action to the word, Tim stretched forth his gigantic arms, and made his enormous hands meet on his breast in full force.

It would be impossible to describe the state of the court during the delivery of Tim's *eloquent* harangue, several shed tears from the laughter.

" Oh, your worships," exclaimed Mrs. Delany, " he has ma-lined my pigs, for betther behaved bastes never lay upon straw; I tould my little gesha of a daughter to keep them out of his pratees from the first mornin' he spoke to me, and as for striking him, your worships, the poor animals knew no betther, for they were makin home, and he stood in the gap."

Magistrate—" You must compensate Reilly for the damage your pigs have done his potatoes."

Tim—" Oh, plase your worship, I'm not lookin' for compensation, but in regard of their bad behavor, and their strikin' me, that I complain; and, Mrs. Delany," he added, turning to the widow, " if you promise to keep them out of my arable land, and tache them betther manners in future, I'll not prosecute them no farther."

This being faithfully promised, and Tim, having made another bow to the bench, and begged their " honors' pardon," for the trouble he had given them, retired amidst the laughter of the spectators, he himself, however, filled with the importance of the part he had performed, and giving sundry frowns at those gentlemen he denominated " *peelerers*." R. T.

Balbruggan.

OPTICAL ILLUSIONS.

THE FATA MORGANA.

In the immediate neighbourhood of the Giant's Causeway, a very extraordinary optical illusion, something similar to the phenomenon known by the name of the " Fata Morgana" in the straits of Reggio, between the Isle of Sicily and the coast of Calabria, is frequently observed. It is thus described by a talented writer who some time since visited the Causeway coast :—

Portrush point, which a few moments before presented a very unmeaning appearance, and was certainly the least interesting object on the coast, now assumed a most commanding aspect. A lofty mountain arose, instead of a long flat—a conical peak like Croagh Patrick, rugged rocks, with their serrated points, pierced the clouds; and instantly all this vanished, and a beautiful softly swelling wooded hill presented itself, a lofty embattled castle, a broad belt of full-grown wood, green lawns, and all the decorations of a nobleman's domain. You might conceive yourself at once transported to Plymouth harbour, and that you saw Mount Edgecombe before you; and again, as by talismanic touch, all this disappeared, and on a plain, two embattled armies seemed to oppose one another, and dense masses of troops, horse and foot, stood motionless, as if in suspense for the battle signal; and now they rushed together, and the opposing battalions closed on each other, and a loose shapeless cloud rose up, as if it were the mingled dust and smoke ascending from the conflict; and all at once the whole vision dissolved away, and the next moment nothing was seen but the low, uninteresting peninsula of Portrush.

Menasi supposes that the objects seen in the *Fata Morgana* in the Straits of *Reggio* to which we have alluded, are representations of objects seen on the coast. He accounts for the appearance by the supposed inclination of the surface of the sea, and its subdivisions into different planes by the contrary eddies. He explains the Aerial Morgana, by referring it to the reflective and refractive powers of effluvia suspended in the air.

When the rising sun shines from that point whence its incident rays form an angle of 45° on the sea of Reggio, and the bright surface of the water is not disturbed either by the wind or the currents, the spectator being placed on an eminence of the city, with his back to the sun, and his face to the sea, on a sudden there appear on the water, as in a catoptric theatre, various multiplied objects, viz.—numberless series of pilasters, arches, castles—well delineated; regular columns, lofty towers, superb palaces, with balconies and windows, extended alleys of trees, delightful plains, with herds and flocks, armies of men on foot and horseback, and many other strange figures, in their natural colours and proper actions, passing rapidly in succession along the surface of the sea—during the whole of the short period of time while the above-mentioned causes remain.

Wilson, in his travels, mentions a singular optical illusion which he observed in Egypt:—"I perceived the turrets and sycamore trees of Rosetta, at which time I found myself greatly exhausted from oppressive heat and fatigue; and, like other travellers, was deceived by the mist and apparitional lake so celebrated under the name of the *Mirage* or *Al Serah*, the illusory lake of the desert, which, even at a very short distance, had the most perfect resemblance to a vast sheet of water, with trees planted in it at certain distances, and reflecting every surrounding object as a mirror. We fancied this watery wilderness to be an insurmountable barrier to our reaching Rosetta, and that our guide had mistaken the proper track through the desert; but as we advanced, the supposed lake and its objects vanished: so powerful was the optical delusion. This prospect is at first sight cheering, but ultimately is most delusive. The traveller quickens his steps to reach the place where he hopes to quench his thirst, and feels the bitterness of disappointment; in truth, an *ignis fatuus* is not more tantalising. Even swallows in great numbers skim over these imaginary pools. This singular phenomenon is in all probability that which is alluded to by one of the prophets, and psalmist; and it may serve to point out how false the objects pursued by men of the world are, and how like these streams of the desert; besides it reminds us of that 'mist' which 'went up from the earth, and watered the whole face of the ground,' when 'God formed man out of the dust of the ground.'"

VILLAGE OF WARRENSPOINT.

About five miles from the town of Newry, and commanding a fine view of the Rostrevor and Carlingford mountains, stands the handsome village of Warrenspoint. In one direction the houses form a little square, and in another, stretch along the edge of the shore, where there is a convenient quay, at which there are in general several sailing and steam vessels. It is esteemed one of the best and most frequented bathing-places in the North of Ireland. In 1827 a neat small church was erected here; and immediately adjoining the town there is a Presbyterian meeting-house, and also a Roman Catholic chapel. Although, but a few years since, this was a very inconsiderable village, it at present contains from eight hundred to one thousand inhabitants. A large windmill stands nearly in its centre, and adds considerably to the picturesque and pleasing appearance which the village presents at a distance. There was formerly a very extensive rabbit-warren here, from which circumstance the place derives its name. From this point there is a most delightful view of the scenery of Rostrevor.

DUBLIN:

Printed and Published by P. D. Hardy, 3, Cecilia-street; to whom all communications are to be addressed.

Sold by all Booksellers in Ireland.

In London, by Richard Groombridge, 6, Panyer-alley, Paternoster-row; in Liverpool, by Willmer and Smith; in Manchester, by Ambery; in Birmingham, by Drake; in Glasgow, by W. R. M'Phun; and in Edinburgh, by N. Bowack.

THE
DUBLIN PENNY JOURNAL
CONDUCTED BY P. DIXON HARDY, M.R.I.A.

| Vol. III. | AUGUST 30, 1834. | No. 113. |

Engraved by Clayton.   Sketched by A. Nicholl, Esq.

THE RAILWAY FROM THE ROAD AT LORD CLONCURRY'S, LOOKING TOWARDS KINGSTOWN.

THE DUBLIN AND KINGSTOWN RAILWAY.

In the last number but one of our second volume, with two or three engravings suited to the subject, we took the opportunity of pointing out the great importance of establishing railroads in various directions throughout this country—we described the construction, and stated the expense of several of those at present used in England ; and now proceed, according to our promise in that number, to lay before our readers some particulars relative to the new line which is nearly completed between our city and Kingstown ; a work, which we have no hesitation in saying, reflects the highest credit on all the parties engaged in its construction—on those with whom the idea originated—on those who had the public spirit to embark their capital in such a concern—on the engineer who planned the work and carried the design into execution—as well on the various individuals who in subordinate situations, have lent their varied talents and their energies to its completion. Were it not that under present circumstances it might appear a work of supererogation, we should have felt disposed to notice some of the many calumnies which we have from time to time heard poured forth on the promoters and designers of this important national undertaking. We forbear, however, under the impression that the authors of such calumnies have seen

VOL. III.—NO. 9.

their errors, and that they will hereafter judge of the railway by its own merits. At the same time, it would be unjust if the deserved meed of praise were not given to the spirited and liberal minded body of Directors, who have weathered the storm, and who have thus successfully introduced into Ireland the best promoter of internal peace—rapidity, facility, and economy of communication. But we now proceed to the railway itself.

The Entrance Station is on the east side of Westland Row. The design is sufficiently characteristic of a public building without any attempt at embellishment. The chief points worthy of attention are the beautiful granite door-cases, and cornices, from the rocks near Seapoint cliffs, and the light elegant iron roof over the passengers' station. The details of the internal arrangements for the reception and distribution of passengers can only be explained by inspection, or by an examination of the plans and drawings ; but it appears evident that the public accommodation has been studied in every respect. Indeed nothing but system and simplicity could effect the arrival and departure of trains of carriages every quarter of an hour without danger or confusion.

To preserve the ordinary traffic of the public thoroughfares, the railway starts at an elevation of about twenty feet from the surface, and spans in succession over each street by flat elliptical arches. For the more important streets, smaller arches for the foot-ways have been made on each side of the principal openings.*

The intervals between the streets consist of high retaining walls of limestone, obtained from the Donnybrook quarries, the space between which has been filled with sand, gravel, dry rubbish, and similar materials ; the cartage gave employment during the whole of the last autumn, winter, and spring, to hundreds of the humble proprietors of carts and cars.

The breadth of the railway from Westland Row to Barrow-street, beyond the Grand Canal docks, is nearly sixty feet between the parapets, and is calculated to receive four lines of rails : the two central roads for the going and returning passenger trains, and the two exterior ones for the coal, granite, timber, and general merchandize-waggons, which will load and unload with great facility at the sides, and without the slightest interruption to the continual stream of the passenger traffic.

The railway is carried across the quays, and a part of the Grand Canal docks, by a granite bridge of three oblique arches of peculiar workmanship, which, though well known in England, is now introduced for the first time in Ireland, and has drawn the attention and admiration of all the operative mechanics. One arch is intended for a future street, marked out, to pass parallel to the docks : a second is for the business of the quays—the third is to pass the boats of the trade, and is provided with a towing-path, ranging with the general line of the dock wall. This bridge will form one of the most remarkable features of the works.

Some difficulties appear to have occurred in getting the railway past the distillery near the docks, at which it ought to be mentioned that a large station or depot is provided for the accommodation of trade. Over Barrow-street the arch is built with what is technically called *knee'd or elbow quoins* ; the stones being cut so as to form an oblique or skew bed on the face of the ring, and to return to a square bed within : these quoins are of granite—the rest of the arch stones are of the usual limestone. At this place also the rail-road contracts to a breadth of thirty feet, being adapted for two lines only for the remainder of the distance, the breadth between each of the lines of railway track, being as much, however, as eight feet.— The bridge over the Circular road is square, but across the Irishtown road the angle of intersection is only fifty-three degrees; and a granite elliptical arch, built on the oblique principal, has been introduced with good effect. The intervals between the bridges are still sustained by retaining walls, which, however, diminish in height, and the crossing at Haig's distillery is the first accessible point to the railway from Dublin. This being but little frequented, the roadway has been raised by gentle approaches, and passes on the level of the rail-road. A neat lodge is built, and, according to the act of parliament, gates will be placed across the railway, and a vigilant watch kept. We next come to a handsome bridge of three arches, across the river Dodder, with a side opening for foot passengers. The railroad here approaches the surface of the country, A little further forward, and on the north side, are erecting the buildings for the repairs and construction of the locomotive engines, coaches, waggons, &c. ; and the other necessary shops and conveniences for the company.

At Serpentine avenue the railroad crosses on the present level of the road, with gates, lodge, &c., as before.— All appearance of masonry now ceases : a green sod bank marks the boundary on each side, with a double row of quick-set plants on the top, which, in a few years, will form a fine hedge. Externally, the mound is formed like a slight field fortification, with a berm or set off, on which another hedge-row is planted. A very wide and deep trench forms an effectual fence against cattle and trespassers ; and thus the line runs on through Simmonscourt-fields, crossing Sandymount-lane and Sydney Parade, which will be protected, like the other roads, with gates, lodges and watchmen. At Merrion the Strand road is crossed close to the old baths, with similar protection,

but on account of the liability of intrusion, the railway from Merrion-hall on to the strand is guarded by high stone fence-walls. From Old Merrion to the place where stood the bathing places at Black Rock, the railroad is elevated across the strand, and at high water appears like a long mole stretching into the sea. A smile will be raised at the recollection of the many good-natured predictions of the direful and destructive effect the winter-storms were to produce upon this attempt to force nature ; and observing the facility and rapidity with which this embankment was completed, as well as that the effect of the storms has been to accumulate a protecting bank at the footings of the outer slope : not the slightest apprehension can be entertained of any future danger from the severest eastwardly gales, when the stone facing next the sea is finished all along, as it has been completed in parts. To afford additional stability and protection, an increased breadth is given to the banks seaward, which will form a delightful promenade on fine summer evenings. A cross embankment is made from opposite Booterstown-lane to the railway, to give an access to passengers ; and it is the intention of the noble lord of the manor to cultivate the land thus redeemed by the railway operations, which will, therefore, in the course of a few months, present the appearance of a luxuriant garden, where lately was only a barren sandy beach. The quantity of land to be brought into useful occupation is about fifty English acres. At Williamstown, the railway nearly touches the shore by Seafort Parade, and another access is afforded : while ample culverts allow the water to flow in as usual to the bathing places all along the coast, which now, that the construction of the sea embankment is nearly finished, will be as pure as ever, with the additional advantage of being always smooth and still.

At Black Rock, the company are constructing bathing accommodation for both sexes, on the outer sides of the railway embankment, to which approach will be had by a handsome foot-bridge from the high ground. These baths, will be, as nearly as practicable, on their former sites.— Access will also be had by a second cross embankment from the railway to Merrion avenue, and handsome lodges with waiting-rooms for passengers, will be constructed at this station, as also at the cross bank from Booterstown.

From Black Rock to Kingstown, the character of the work changes continually—high walling on the land side, and open to the sea ; then passing under Lord Cloncurry's demesne, among the beautiful granite pavilions erecting for his lordship ; next, below the noble archway or tunnel ; and beyond, through a deep, rocky excavation, upwards of forty feet in depth ; and below, the bridge connecting the severed portions of the elegant lawn of Sir Harcourt Lees ; emerging from whence, the eye catches the noble sea-view, with the distant harbour. The road will now pass close under Seapoint boarding-house, which has been accommodated with a bridge over the railroad, descending to neat baths, and to a boat pier, and other conveniences. Again occurs a portion of deep cutting, through granite rocks, with a handsome bridge of granite, to the Martello tower at Seapoint, from whence to Salthill the railroad runs at the bottom of Monkstown cliffs, with an ample promenade on the sea side, and divided from the new foot-path by a neat iron railing. All the rugged cliffs have been levelled down, and formed into pleasing slopes, which the taste of the owner of the adjacent cottages will soon cover with flowers and shrubs.— The house at Salthill is now converting, with vast additions, into a splendid tavern, which will rival its celebrated namesake in the vicinity of Eton college in all, it is to be hoped, except its extravagant charges ; and the hill itself will be cut into beautiful terraces and slants, and planted in an ornamental manner. To this extent, terminating on the western pier of the old harbour of Dunleary, the works of the company are completed, and nearly ready for opening ; but the last portion, on which a commencement is now making, yet remains to be described. Four acts or scenes have been passed over, viz :—

1. The city, or mural portion, from Westland-row to Serpentine avenue.

2. The country or rural district, from that station to Old Merrion.

3. The isolated sea embankments, as far as Black rock, and,

4. The coast road portion under the cliffs, and among the rocks, with the boating and bathing accommodations seaward, as far as Salthill. What follows, though less beautiful, is not less useful, and may be styled the 5th or commercial district.

It commences by striking a chord line across a segment of the old harbour of Dunleary, which segment will be filled up, and, ere long, probably covered with bonded warehouses and yards. With the accommodation of an ample wharf, sufficient cranage and other conveniences—the cargoes of colliers, steamers, and all trading vessels may be quickly and economically transported to the railway waggons, and by these brought into Dublin at a very low rate.

The old harbour traversed, the railway will pass between the Martello tower and the battery opposite Crofton terrace. It will here be in deep cutting, and a granite bridge will preserve the communication with the old pier and landing place, with a considerable improvement in the approaches. Between the battery and the admiralty stores, the railroad will closely border on the harbour, and a convenient bonding-yard for timber may be formed with ready communication with the railway, whereby a great convenience would be afforded to the Canada and Baltic merchants. The road then goes at the back of the admiralty stores, and close to the boat harbour and landing place of the Royal harbour, and thence runs to a termination on the large open space opposite the Commissioners'-yard and what is termed the Forty-foot road, being immediately connected with the magnificent quay and landing-place, now in course of construction by government, for the accommodation of the Post Office and other steamers, and when the works are completed, passengers may step from the railway coaches to the steamers, and again, on arriving will, with the mail bags, be conveyed in a quarter of an hour from the Royal Harbour of George the Fourth to the centre of the Irish metropolis.

Stations will be erected at this end of the railway : and for the protection of the public, an iron railing will be placed between the railway and the common road, for the whole length of the harbour, from Dunleary to the Forty-foot road, and such communications will be made across as the harbour commissioners may direct.

In addition to the tavern at Salthill, a new hotel near Seapoint Martello Tower, is spoken of. It is understood also that the company are about to erect splendid baths on a scale of accommodation hitherto unknown in this country ; and in every point of view, the taste, the wants, and the wishes of the public will be studied and provided for; an excellent policy, which will be well compensated by the additional intercourse of passengers upon the railway.

The preceding outline will convey to the distant reader, who may be familiar with the country between Dublin and Kingstown, some idea of the works, and of their general character ; but to those who have not seen the beauties of Dublin bay and its vicinity, it will be difficult to convey an accurate impression of the effect the railway will present. Hurried by the invisible, but stupendous agency of steam, the astonished passenger will now glide, like Asmodeus, over the summits of the houses and streets of a great city—presently be transported through green-fields and tufts of trees—then skim across the surface of the sea, and taking shelter under the cliffs, coast among the marine villas, and through rocky excavations, until he finds himself in the centre of a vast port, which unites in pleasing confusion the bustle of a commercial town with the amusements of a fashionable watering place. Of the manner in which the work has been executed, it is sufficient to observe that the utmost solidity and severest simplicity mark the entire. The formation of the railway bed consists of layers of gravel and concrete, with longitudinal and numerous cross drains. Immense blocks of granite, at intervals of three feet, support the iron rails, by means of supports called chairs; at every fifteen feet a larger block extends across and unites the two rails together, and the appearance of firmness and solidity is very remarkable in the course of construction,

though at the parts which are quite finished off, nothing is to be seen except four parallel lines of iron bars, laid with almost geometrical precision. To those who may interest themselves in the details which combine, it is believed, all the most recent improvements, it may be satisfactory to know, that at the offices of the company every facility is afforded for the inspection of the working, as well as the embellished drawings, and that a morning will be satisfactorily employed in examining these as well as the various models.

Six locomotive engines have been built for the Dublin and Kingstown railway : three of these are from the manufactory of Messrs. George Forrester, and Co., of Liverpool; and three from the house of Messrs. Sharp, Roberts, and Co., of Manchester. The greatest mechanical perfection has been attained in these machines ; and the useful and honorable rivalry between two such eminent houses, cannot but result in advantage to the present company as well as to the public, by combining superiority of workmanship with the most improved adaptation of principles. A great and interesting experiment is also conducting at the same time, inasmuch as the working parts of the engines is totally different by each house. Messrs. Forrester have horizontal cylinders, fore and hind wheels of unequal diameter, elastic pistons working with improved valves, a small number of tubes in the boiler, &c. Messrs. Sharp Roberts and Co. have introduced vertical cylinders, the whole of the wheels alike; bell-crank motion, solid pistons, patent valves without friction ; numerous tubes, &c. Both have put unequalled workmanship —both have adopted wrought iron frames, and straight axles, and it is believed have avoided all the errors and weaknesses observed in the locomotive engines hitherto produced.

The carriages for the accommodation of passengers are of three classes : most of these have been made in Dublin by Mr. Dawson, of Capel-street ; and by Messrs. Courteney and Stephens, of Blackhall-place. A few only were made in Manchester. The wheels, axles, &c. were necessarily constructed in England. Trucks are also provided for conveying gentlemen's carriages, &c.

The railway coaches of the first and second class may be almost called elegant ; the third class carriages are superior to those in use on the English railways, and all are covered. The fares will be on a very low scale.

It is impossible to describe all the details connected with the railway establishment, and indeed they would scarcely be interesting to the general reader. To form an accurate judgment, the work itself should be seen ; and as it is now opened, public curiosity and individual enquiry will be fully gratified.

The character of the works, the variety of the different constructions, and the costly expenditure upon the Dublin and Kingstown railway, form a remarkable contrast to the appearance of flatness which the country presents to the eye of a casual observer, which glancing over the level ground, between the south side of Dublin and the shores of the bay, prompts the not unnatural remark, of the cheapness and facility with which a railway might have been constructed. But many causes have concurred in requiring a continual change in the transverse section of the railway, which have, certainly, greatly added to the novelty and interest of the work, though, at the same time, difficulties have been increased, and expenses augmented far beyond what has ever yet been required to force a level passage through the most difficult districts where railways have been introduced.

Among those causes may be enumerated the expediency of penetrating deeply into the centre of the metropolis ; the attention requisite to be paid to public safety, and to vested and incorporated rights ; the great value of the property, whether as building or suburban grounds ; the interposition of secluded demesnes ; the preservation of the bathing, boating, and other accommodations of individuals, and of the public along the coast ; the necessity of making the course of the road as direct as possible, and of connecting the several changes of direction by easy curves, and the caution to be exercised in tracing a complete and isolated route, for the peculiar machines to be employed, through the rich and populous district in the vicinity of a large commercial city, to a termination on the quays of the finest artificial harbour in the world; where the smallest nautical conveniences had to be preserved from interference, or to be amply compensated for and replaced; and close to the streets of a rising and populous borough, the conveniences and even the apprehensions of whose inhabitants had to be consulted.

The original intention was to have commenced the railway at the rere of the college buildings, and to have skirted the college park, parallel to Great Brunswick-street. This would have made the starting point about the Clarendon stables, and within a very short distance of the very centre of Dublin business. Vague fears, misrepresentations, and other causes created an outcry against such a proposition, which it is hoped at a future and not distant period may still be realized.

Indeed it is fondly anticipated that this measure may be the means of introducing the railway system generally into Ireland, and, independent of all other considerations, this is the light in which it becomes most interesting to every well-wisher for the happiness and prosperity of our country. Capital, intelligence, and enterprize exist abundantly in Ireland; and nothing is wanting to render it the most flourishing part of the empire but confidence, and the diffusion of information.—What can more readily bring these than railroads, whereby the English landlord and the traveller may visit the remotest parts of Ireland with the same rapidity and safety with which he now posts down from London to Brighton. When the landed proprietor can have the means of visiting his estates frequently and expeditiously, he will perceive that to the want of employment and education are to be attributed the whole of the evils of Ireland.

VIEW OF THE RAILWAY FROM BLACK ROCK.

There is nothing exhibits so much the overgrown amount of the population in Ireland, when brought into comparison with its capital and property, as the lowness of wages. In many parts of Ireland, labour is not higher than it was when Arthur Young wrote his travels; fifty years ago his report of the wages of the labouring poor, shows the rate to have been nearly, if not altogether, as high as it is now; and while all kinds of agricultural produce have nearly doubled in price, the labourer must still put up with six-pence or eight-pence per day; and moreover, happy is that poor peasant, who is sure of constant employment even at that rate. Let railways be introduced in various directions throughout the country, and this will not long be the case. Give the landlord an opportunity of adding to his rent-roll, or even of improving his estate, by transporting the produce of his grounds from the interior of the country, at nearly the same rate of charge as those now living on the coast, and even were there no higher motive than self-interest, he will soon give employment to numbers of those who are now dragging out a miserable existence in poverty and wretchedness. But we must also remark, that to enable the people to benefit by the advantages which railways will offer, they must be educated. The great deficiency of the Irish is in the quantum of educated labour that is amongst them; and therefore it is, that though the market is overstocked with gross, untrained, shall we say, brute labour, yet there is a lamentable deficiency in those minds and hands that are requisite to carry into effect the nicer operations of art, or agriculture, or manufacture. It is, therefore, essential that our people should be educated : educated up to trustworthiness—educated so as to be capable of productive labour—educated so as to have a respect for themselves—educated so as to acquire a religious restraint over their hitherto uncurbed passions—educated so as to acquire a dislike for secret association, and a respect for the law—educated as becomes Christian freemen, and Ireland will yet be the finest and fairest portion of the British empire.

The evils that counteract the great natural blessings which Providence has showered down on this country, are of long standing—they have existed before history had a record—they have exercised their baneful influence on the character of the people for centuries; and it cannot be the work of a day to remove what is wrong and replace it with what is right : still let us hope that the introduction of steam navigation, and the construction of railroads throughout the land, will prove one great step towards abating the evil.

KINGSTOWN HARBOUR.

'Tis noon! The sky is clear—the sunny deep
Is still, save where the rippling breezes sweep
Wooing, and whispering along, to sleep.
Each stately ship reposed at anchor rides—
By it the sportive ripple, as it glides,
Laughs in the sun-beams, and uncertain plays
On the dark vessel with reflected rays.
Now o'er the lulling waters flit awhile,
Broken reflections of the floating pile;
Th' inconstant breeze each trembling charm enhancing,
As beauty's eye most fascinates in glancing,
Or as the glimpse *our* parting clouds bestow
Of heav'ns blue ether, gladdens more the view
Than in those realms of sultry solstice glow,
    Their one unchang'd expanse of azure hue.
Hush'd every sound of man, of toil, of care,
The wanton pennons dally in mid-air,

All silent though not still. For ev'n the bark
That fleets as rapid as electric-spark
O'er the blue surface—mystic motion giv'n—
Seems by a silent secret impulse driv'n;
Unheard the music of the plashing oar,
    That brightly sparkles on the raptur'd sight
Though lost its sound—so distant from the shore—
    It gleams in measur'd harmony of light!
Gliding, like pleasure's form, o'er floweret's bright
Of aerial fairy tread—no sound awaking,
It seems to move " in light of its own making."
Soothing the scene! Haply those realms of bliss
May prove a haven, typified in this—
A calm eternity of peaceful light,
Where wearied souls may rest them from their flight,
And happy spirits, like those fleet barks, move
Ever in radiant harmony above!

A VIEW FROM THE RERE OF SEAPOINT HOUSE.

A CITIZEN'S RELAXATIONS—A TRIP TO KILLINEY.

I do not know any city in the British empire, whose environs afford more various and attractive scenery, than the metropolis of Ireland. Thus, while the Londoner may actually pass out of life, without having cast one admiring look at a mountain prospect, with all its peaks and ridges, lakes, waterfalls, and glens, and while he may have no idea of the sea, but what the turbid tide-waters of the Thames present—a Dublin citizen—yes, even its poorest artisan—can, in an hour or two, either wander among the sea-cliffs of Bray or Bullock, or climb the Wicklow hills, and fill his admiring mind with all the grand images connected with mountain phenomena.—Nay more—he can, when tired of this—if a man, a city-circumscribed man, can be tired of such things—ramble up the banks of the lovely and lively Liffey; he may direct his jaunting-car along the lower road that leads to

Lucan—admire, perhaps, the finest river landscape in the world—observe cultivation carried forward with the greatest accuracy, and in keeping with the greatest beauty. He may spend his day at the Salmon Leap at Leixlip, or proceeding farther, admire the thousand and one acres in the centre of which Ireland's only Duke resides. Or, if it should better please him, he can go northward, and exercise his antiquarian propensities and recollections, while admiring the venerable remains of Fingallian grandeur, as exhibited in the old parliament-house of Swords —its round tower—or the still more beautiful one at Lusk. He may venture to Holm-Patrick, and see not only the church built by St. Patrick, but also his very footprints, as, with a hop-skip-and-jump, he popped from island to island, until he reached mainland. He may thence return home, and on his way observe the ancient stone roof and crypt of St. Doulough, only inferior in antiquity to Cormac's chapel, on the Rock of Cashel. Thus the vicinity of Dublin presents her varied attractions for the excursionist and tourist; and foul befall the character of the Dublin *literati*, that there has not been yet found *one* who has adequately, with pen or pencil, described and brought into notice the environs of the metropolis of Ireland.

Mr. Editor, one would think I was a native of the county or city of Dublin, from my anxiety to trumpet forth their praises. But, indeed, it is no such thing; I am a stranger—mercantile business has but given me *here* a local habitation; and were it not that a good old uncle in India had lately left me some few thousands, you would have never received this, or heard of " the destiny obscure" of a pains-taking rider to a Manchester firm. It is to me a riddle, how it was it came to the ears of Alderman Fitzburgh, a very respectable Dublin dealer in soft goods, that I had acquired those Indian rupees: but so it happened; and with all due respect to my good address, mercantile responsibility, and prepossessing *personnel*, I do indeed, with becoming modesty, attribute to this oriental ore, an invitation I received from the worthy alderman, to spend the next Sunday with him, and his family at Mermount, a villa of his worship's near the road to the far-famed village of Kingstown.

I confess I had often wished to see the interior of a rich Dublin citizen's villa—perhaps, also, I had no objection to be a partaker at his hospitable board—for no one on earth, if report speaks truly, has such facilities for good eating and drinking, or knows better how to enjoy the rich capabilities of a Dublin market or cellar.

I accordingly accepted the invitation; and on the following sabbath arose early, and saluted the blessed sun, as he shone cheerily in at my window, and assured me that he would gladden the hearts of thousands by walking his cloudless course on this fine autumnal day. Proceeding with all due despatch, about ten o'clock, through that narrow, busy, bustling place, half lane, half street, which leads from Stephen's-green to Baggot-street, I was saluted by the Jehu of one of those elegant vehicles, called jaunting cars—" Goin' out, Sir?—get up, yer honour—here's a seat; I'm just off—only waitin' for two like yerself.— Tim Dunn, ye'd betther lend me the two gemmen you've got on yer car. Come, masther, get up—I'm off in a giffy."

After tarrying half an hour, during which patience was exhausted in hearing the drivers cursing, swearing, lying, trucking with each other for passengers, and exhibiting what degraded, audacious, and profligate knaves, these jinglemen are, we at length, with infinite manœuvring, had six mounted on our fragile vehicle, and so started; and proceeded with great rapidity along the Rock-road: and oh, the dust! The Nubian desert could scarcely send its simoon cloud of impalpable sand with more oppressive density, than did the south-easterly wind on that breezy morn. I certainly was attired in a very *recherché* manner: my cravat tied scientifically—my waistcoat of the newest Parisian pattern—my hat elegant—coat exquisite—trowsers inexpressibly contrived, so as to cover and yet reveal proportions I was not a little proud of.— But, oh, what a figure I was before I got to Ball's-bridge! If ever there was a marvellously well-dressed man marred, I was one—changed from top to toe—a snow-heap, thawing away in the midst of a populous street, its virgin purity defiled, its heavenly whiteness polluted with mud and ashes, and every stain most filthy and unsuitable, was not worse off than I was before I got to Williamstown. There I found the road blocked up by a long string of coaches, headed by a hearse, which " blackened all the way." As we passed by, I could perceive that the whole procession had now made a full stop at a public-house, and that the mourners in the coaches were washing down their sorrow and the sad dust, by plentiful libations of porter and whiskey. One fat lady in particular, who rode in the mourning-coach next the hearse, and who, from the redness of her cheeks and eyes, seemed to be in the full flush of sorrow—some near and much-loved friend—could it be the bereaved relict of the dear departed husband? She was lifting her little finger over her forehead, in draining to the last dregs the glass of cordial with which she sought to alleviate her sorrow— " Poor soul!" said I, internally, " thou dost right to moisten thy clay, which might otherwise lose all radical moisture, by thy excessive weeping. Whiskey is indeed

a cordial for care—see how it ' tempers the wind to the shorn lamb.' "

With these expressions of tender sympathy I found myself arrived at the Black Rock; and here, considering myself within a mile of my destination, I brushed off, as well as I could, the powdery taint, which mildewed, as it were, all my freshness, and proceeded up one of those numerous avenues that verge off in so many directions from that very ugly village. With the elastic foot of one who was inured to country exercise, but latterly " in populous city pent," I soon arrived at my hospitable inviter's villa. How different from a London citizen's retreat! which usually is on the outskirts of some village within sound of the Bow-bell, the smell of the lamps, and the breathing of the road-dust—which rejoices in a small court or flower-garden, with yew-trees and bay-trees separating it from the king's high way; or enjoys a little lawn before it, just large enough to graze a donkey or whip a cat. On the contrary, our Dublin alderman had quite a PLACE; a large screened-in lawn, a swelling green sward, with flower-plats interspersed; sunk fences, to keep out cattle; invisible palings, to mark off pleasure-grounds from the wider extent of the farm. Behind the house, I could observe lofty walls, long ranges of graperies, hot-houses, and conservatories. But more of this by and by. Having knocked at the hall-door, and announced my name to the servant, I was ushered into the morning sitting-room, where I was introduced by my friend the alderman, to Mrs. and the Misses Selina and Cordelia Fitzburgh, who were certainly comely for their respective ages, and not behind hand in the graces that Providence has lavished on the softer sex. Neither were they backward in those additions that fashion, in her caprice, chooses to add to the attractiveness of ladies. The statue " that enchants the world," represents the perfect woman as having falling shoulders, neither broad nor high. The beauties who stood before me, had shoulders broader than the Farnese Hercules; instead of wings, under which Cupids might disport and shelter, they wore big bladdery excrescences, more fit for swimming than for flying—more adapted to keep them over water, than to exalt them up to heaven —more fit to prove they were true witches, than to satisfy they were very angels; besides, their waists were intolerably small—so that they seemed like spiders, ready to come out of their webs, to catch and claw men; or like the continent of America, with its northern and southern divisions swelling out large and rich—not forgetting that the ends are at Capes Turnabout or Horn—while the middle, at Porto-bello and Darien, is contracted to the thickness of a span. Well, I am, for a Manchester-rider, a very discursive dealer in *piece*-goods. To return to my narrative: after making my bows to the ladies, I was informed they were about to proceed to church—which I might have known from the accompaniments of the party; for each fair one had a sort of ecclesiastical portative library (bible, prayer-book, week's preparation, and hymn-book, cased up together) in the one hand—while the *ridicule* (I spell as things are pronounced) hung gracefully from the other arm. So, handing the ladies, in my best travelled *savoir comme il faut*, into the landau, we proceeded towards church. I have not time, Mr. Editor, to enlarge on how the service was performed; suffice it to say, the moment it was over, even at the church-doo . Fitzburgh, very politely, and perhaps to exemplify how little she was affected by what she had heard, said—

" I hope, Mr. Bobbinbottom, you will have no objection to join my daughters and me in a drive to Killiney! We mean to go through Kingstown, and join there some of our neighbours: with them we mean to spend an hour or so at Malpas' Obelisk, and they are good enough to say they will then return home with us to dinner; and I do assure you, Mr. Bobbinbottom, that we go not empty—I speak to the apprehension of an Englishman, who I know, loves not a long fast—that our landau conveys creature comforts—sandwiches, and sundry bottles of Guinness's porter."

" Careful soul," thought I, as I bowingly accepted the invitation—" thou art a wife worthy of any Gilpin whether he belong to famous Dublin or London town.

I wish, Mr. Editor, I had wit, or you had space, for me

to describe all that was said and seen during our drive to Kingstown. Let no man tell me that room for observation, and scope for adventure, are not to be found from Newtown Avenue to Kingstown. The different physiognomies, the various characters and groupings of all who pass along in coach, chaise, landau, dennet, gig, jaunting-car, or jingle, would be sufficient to answer any man's purpose who was resolute to write, even suppose it were on a broomstick. But, indeed, I do not mean to trespass on your or the reader's patience; suffice it to say, that we arrived at Kingstown, and at this instant, a Swiss carriage, a jaunting-car, and cabriolet drove up, containing Mr. Flounce, a respectable common-council man, from Grafton-street, with his family; Mr. Brittlebowl (and wife) a fashionable china dealer, and a man, as Mrs. Fitzburgh described him, who knew how to enjoy the *delassemens* of the Sunday elegantly; and Mr. Figgins, an eminent grocer. So, after a sufficiency of bows, greetings, compliments, &c., we " all precious souls, and all agog," started for the summits of Killiney. The drive is not handsome from Kingstown to the hills, which were the object of our excursion; the country, ugly, rocky, and swampy; large boulder stones of granite rolled and rounded under the operation of the primeval flood, interspersed through wet and rushy fields; here and there a new villa or a cottage in the process of building; recent walls; infant plantations—the whole picture of the neighbourhood reminded you of a young township in America; and only there were no wooden houses, no zig-zag palings, no profusion of felled or growing timber, and no forest in the back ground, with straight-stemmed and blazed pines, you might suppose you were in the States; but, no matter, whether here or there, you were satisfied that a country while being improved, though it may be interesting, is not handsome. After a drive of about three miles, we came to the foot of the central hill, on which the obelisk is built, and observing, that though the road was good the ascent was steep, I requested permission to alight, and stretch my legs by walking to the top of the hill. In this desire I was joined by the Misses Selina and Cordelia, and, offering an arm to each, which they modestly but complacently refused, we ascended the eminence, directly under the residence of some foolish, tasteless, city Goth, who has contrived to make a burlesque upon castellation, by affixing certain indentures to the top of his house, like the toothed deed by which he himself was bound out to be an attorney or dealer; and with the accompaniments of slashes in the walls, and things like mustard-pots, and pepper-castors at the corners, has turned a good, old, plain country mansion into a Babel building, where all art is confounded, taste abused, and there it stands like a fool upon a cock-horse—nonsense set upon a hill. I am now, as I was then, obliged to the man for the contrivance of this extravaganza; for, while descanting with Miss Selina, who, by the way, every now and then smiled most complacently at my observations on affairs general and particular, we were insensibly led to the crest of the hill, and while I was showing, with no little lore, what were the characteristics of the true Anglo-Norman Gothic castle—

" Stop, Mr. Bobbinbottom !" cries Miss Selina—" if you are not a Saxon, or Dane, or Goth, look about you *now*, and you shall see what you shall see !" and so, taking my eyes from out of myself, I looked north and I looked south, and truly I *was* astonished.

Mr. Editor, I have been a rider for some years, and have cast not a listless eye over, not only the British Isles, but over much that is beautiful and grand on the European and American Continents; I have not only passed over the spines and ridges of the Alps and Pyranees, and listened with delight to the Shepherd's pipe, at evening's close, rising from the vine covered hills of Auvergne and the Bourbonnais, but I have heard the downright dash of Niagara, and seen where the Potowmac and Shenandoah burst their united waters, through the pine-covered ridge of the Allegany mountains—but, after all, I know not any landscape that ever came under my eye, so rich, so various, so comprehensive as the view from Killiney-hill. The whole valley of the Liffey, with the rich and wooded plains of the county of Dublin under my feet —the Mourne mountains, in the far northern distance,

rising in serrated peaks—the hills of Kildare in the far west—and just as it were beneath, the mighty city, covered with its wreathed smoke.

The peculiarity of the spot on which I stood was, that turning round on your heel, your eye opened on almost as different a prospect as if you were transplanted into a different clime ; or, as if looking into a showman's box, the rapid and voluble man had, with a turn of a pin, discarded one picture and substituted another; so, here, by looking to the south, you have a different sea, shore, valley, hills, mountains ; nay, even the character of the air and sky, and clouds seem changed ; and, as before, you had the counties of Dublin, Kildare, and Meath before you, with the grand city, landlocked bay, and the pier of Kingstown; and Howth and Lambay, reposing on the waters like couchant, sentinel sea-monsters ; so now you have the silvery shore of Killiney, bending its graceful crescent line, until it terminates in one of the finest of all Irish promontories —Bray Head ; and then, the narrow, quiet vale, and the mountains, pile on pile, above it, and the Sugar-loaf, piercing its white silicious head over all. Mr. Figgins, the grocer, who had alighted out of his cabriolet, and had joined us here, could not restrain his admiration.

" Oh, Sir, is that yonder the great county of Wicklow Sugar-loaf ? Well, then, is it not barbarous big, all out ? What, if Killiney-bay was a bowl of *tay*, and the Sugar-loaf thrown in to sweeten the cup, would it not make a mighty pretty breakfast for Fin M'Coul, provided, as how he had Bray Head yonder for a manchet ?"

" Ha, ha, ha ! always for eating, Mr. Figgins," said Mr. Flounce, who had just come up. " You gentlemen of the Corporation are always for *that* entertainment. Your ideas all seem to rise out of your stomach, like fogs out of a bog."

To this rather pert remark of the man of mode, I saw Mr. Figgins in the act of engendering some repartee, when one of the young ladies cried—" Oh, dear me, I am afraid something has happened to beloved mamma ; there is a crowd round the landau. Selina, dear, let us run on ; and so, like Camilla and Atalanta, these young ladies started forward, and I, to show my gallantry, like young Hippomenes, was not far behind ; and sure enough, when we arrived at the carriage, an ugly accident had occurred to dear, good Mrs. Fitzburgh. She, careful soul, had, as was hinted at before, stowed in the front of the open landau, a basket of prog, consisting of sandwiches and bottles of porter. Now, one of these bottles lying under the influence of the sunbeams, and agitated by the jolting of the carriage, had taken it into its head to explode, and the neck of the flask taking the direction of Mrs. Fitzburgh's left cheek, had not only covered the dear woman with all its froth, but the glass had inflicted a wound on the lobe of her ear, and truly, she was a sad spectacle when we came up. It was altogether a tragic scene, such as no pen of mine could adequately describe—the daughters fainting on the road-side—the worthy Alderman endeavouring to wipe away the streaming brown-stout, and staunch the blood that flowed profusely—for she was plethoric and full of the sanguineous fluid. Here it was that fortune was greatly on my side. In early life, before I had taken to mercantile matters, I had done some business in a barber surgeon's shop, and had learned not only how to breathe a vein, but also how to apply styptics, plasters, and bandages ; and I ever since have carried my case of instruments, with lint, sticking plasters, &c. &c. about me ; so here I fell to work in Esculapian style—soon found that a little blood makes a great show—the earring orifice was only a little enlarged—the soft and silky lobe was, in some measure, lacerated ; but, by the help of a few strips of sticking-plaster, and the bandaging influence of a silk pocket handkerchief, all was soon set to rights ; but, alas ! the whole spirit of the excursion was spoiled. The young ladies, though revived with a little cold water, had lost the zest for enjoyment.

The alderman himself felt even his masculine nerves shaken ; and " poor mamma," though in a measure set to rights, was but a sorry sight to exhibit to all the loungers and city tourists who were grouped around the hill ; for the disaster had disclosed a mystery that ought never to have passed the precincts of the boudoir. Mrs. Fitzburgh, when setting out in the morning, in all the richness of attire and fullness of *en bon point*, fat, fair, and but little more than forty, sat between her two delicate and slender daughters, as the full moon between two sparkling planets, or a plump partridge flanked by two quails; and she had such a good complexion!—neck, nose, and forehead, as fair as alabaster; cheeks " *à coleur de rose*" no broken veins, no faded swarthiness betraying the cruel fact, that the sear and autumnal tints were evidencing how time had frost-bitten her beauty.

You may suppose that our horses' heads were soon directed down the hill; and as fast as we could drive we wended our way to Mermount; the particulars of our entertainment there, with its accompanying casualties, shall, perhaps, form the subject of a future epistle.

MATTHEW BORRINBOTTOM.

POPULAR LECTURES ON THE PHYSIOLOGY OF ANIMALS.

An abstract of Dr. Henry's sixth Lecture.
THE NOSE.

The apparatus belonging to the sense of smell consists simply of a nerve expanded upon a delicate membrane lining the interior of the upper part of the nose. The odorous particles enter with the air, and make an impression on the sentient extremities of the nerve, by means of which the impression is conveyed to the brain. In order that you may better comprehend how this is effected, you will recollect, First, that there is a free passage through the nose to the back part of the mouth or throat. Secondly, that every time we inspire, the external air rushes through this passage and enters the lungs, and that every time we expire, the air passes from our lungs through the nose to the external atmosphere. Thirdly, that there is also another passage from the back part of the throat—I mean through the mouth—by which the air passes and repasses from the lungs at the same time as it passes through the nose, and that, therefore, it passes with greater force, and in greater quantity through the nose than if the mouth be shut. Accordingly, when we wish to smell any object or to snuff up any odour, we shut the mouth and inspire freely through the nose, so that a greater quantity of the effluvia may pass through the nose, and come more readily into contact with the olfactory nerves, which are seated high up in the nose. As there are two eyes and two ears, so there are, properly speaking, two organs of smell, or two nostrils; but these two nostrils being placed close beside each other, have the appearance of being only one organ, and this organ is called the nose. The two nostrils are perfectly distinct, having no communication with each other, and each being supplied with a separate olfactory nerve. The membrane lining the nostrils and having the sentient extremities of the olfactory nerve in its substance, must be moist, in order that the impression of odours may be perfectly received by the nerve; and, accordingly, we find it smeared with a peculiarly tenacious fluid, which performs the two offices of keeping the membrane moist, and of entangling the odorous particles, so as to render their contact with the sentient extremities of the nerve more permanent. When this fluid is increased, as in a common cold, it constitutes what was formerly called a rheum, or defluxion from the head; because, before the nature of the secretion was understood, it was supposed that this discharge came from the brain: even at this day there are some persons to be met with who retain this notion. The nostrils are moistened not only by this secretion of their own lining membrane, but by the tears or moisture of the eyes, which is carried off from the eyes and discharged into the lower part of the nostrils by means of the nasal ducts, to be described when we come to speak of the eye. To these two sources of moisture we may add a third, the expired air, which is always charged with moisture acquired in the lungs. If the expired air were dry, like the inspired air, the natural moisture of the air passages would be quite insufficient to keep them in a moist state. They would speedily be dried up by the dry air passing through them, and would become unfit for their offices. The extreme distress arising from a dry state of the air-passages, i.e., of the mouth and nostrils, is well known to those who have suffered typhus fever, or witnessed the sufferings of others in that disease. Those parts of the pituitary or lining membrane

of the nostrils which are nearest to the external atmosphere or the tip of the nose, do not perceive scents; the power of perceiving scents being confined to the upper parts of the membrane, which receive the branches of the olfactory nerves; hence the snuffing of animals when they trace objects by the scent. The other parts of the membrane are, however, not useless. They serve to break the too sudden and violent approach of the air to the olfactory part of the membrane, and to give notice to the individual of the entrance of foreign substances, as insects, dust, motes, &c., into the nostrils, and so to stop the access of such bodies both to the windpipe and to the olfactory portion of the membrane, which should be always kept clean from foreign substances, and which should, moreover, in order to the perfect exercise of its function, be a little removed out of the way so as to be occasionally only, not constantly, acted upon by external impressions. The extremity of the nostrils, just where the internal membrane merges into the common skin, has the most delicate sense of touch, and is furnished with hairs, which serve the purpose of feelers, while at the same time they close up the passage against foreign bodies. This is less necessary in man who has such an excellent protection in his hand, and who is besides less liable to the attacks of insects, but in other animals this defence to the opening of the nostril is absolutely necessary. An additional protection is afforded by the power which man and some other animals possess of expelling extraneous bodies from the nostrils by the act of sneezing.

The elephant is remarkable for his delicate sense of smell. His trunk is the continuation of the nose or nostrils. It is so flexible, and at the same time so well supplied with muscles, as to constitute an exquisite organ of touch or prehension, as well as an organ of smell. There is a sudden turn in the tubes of the proboscis, at some distance from the tip, which prevents liquids drawn into them from passing further, and thus enables the animal to hold water in them, which he can afterwards discharge into his mouth or into the air at pleasure. In the whale tribe the existence of an olfactory nerve, and consequently of the sense of smell, is still disputed by physiologists. In these animals the blowing hole serves the double purpose of respiration and of rejecting the water which is taken in along with their food. In birds, the structure of the organ of smell is similar to that which is found in man and quadrupeds.—There are as great differences in this respect among birds as among quadrupeds. The grallæ, or waders, and the anseres, or swimming birds, have the keenest powers of smell. Scapa relates that in making experiments on the relative powers of smelling in birds, he gave a piece of scented bread to a duck: the duck snatched the food eagerly, but perceiving the extraordinary odour, dropped it suddenly, then, as it were, recollecting itself, took it up again, carried it to a pool of water, dipped it in it several times until it was well washed, and then swallowed it. In the osseous fishes there are two openings on the upper part of the snout, one on each side; at the bottom of each of these cavities there is a membrane disposed in folds radiating from a centre: on this membrane the olfactory nerve is distributed. As fishes live in water, and do not breathe through nostrils, as land animals do, the odorous particles are not drawn into the nose by respiration, but being involved in the water, the water is admitted into these openings, and thus the odorous particles brought into contact with the olfactory membrane. These membranes are thickly smeared with a glutinous substance, in order to protect them from the injurious influence of the water. The opening of each of these cavities is furnished with a sort of a lid or valve, which the animal moves at will by means of a muscle, and can thus admit, exclude, or retain the water in the cavity, and so, if not perfectly, at least to some extent, regulate the sense of smell. It is said that the sense of smell fishes is so acute, that by merely scattering odoriferous substances about the mouth of a cavern containing water in which there are fishes, they can be enticed to the mouth of the cavern so as to become the ready prey of the fisherman.

DUBLIN:

Printed and published by P. D. Hardy, 3, Cecilia-street; to whom all communications are to be addressed.

THE

DUBLIN PENNY JOURNAL

CONDUCTED BY P. DIXON HARDY, M.R.I.A.

| Vol. III. | SEPTEMBER 6, 1834. | No. 114. |

BRICKEEN BRIDGE—LAKES OF KILLARNEY.*

A GUIDE TO KILLARNEY AND GLENGARIFF.

Good Reader! mistake not our title—though in our
second volume, recently published, we performed the
part of a friendly guide through some of the most interesting portions of the county of Wicklow, and acted as Ci-
cerone to the caverns of the Causeway : at present our
only intention is to bring before your notice a little work
just published in our city, bearing the title which we have
taken, and which, as "a Tourist" by profession, we can
professionally recommend to tourists and travellers in
search of the picturesque and the pleasing, as these are to
be discovered among the wilds, the woods, and the waters
of Killarney and for fifty miles along the coast in that
direction of our Island—aye, gentle Reader! even for
fifty miles, for as we are informed in the preface to the
work before us—"If a traveller look westward from Cape
Clear, he may obtain an unimpeded prospect, for fifty
miles along a steep and ironbound range of coast, equally

imposing for its bold promontories, and for the deep and
landlocked bays which stretch far within their mountainous and craggy ranges. The splendid mountain and sea
views—the picturesque glens and vallies—the objects of
historical or legendary interest—are numerous, beyond the scope of the ordinary tourist. These particulars will present themselves variously to the traveller
according to his time, and emerge into distinct notice as
the country grows familiar. In a few seasons the O'Sullivans, aboriginal lords of Bear and Bantry, may become
as renowned in the tourist's tale as their traditionary
brethern of Killarney;—the geologist's hammer will have
echoed from the argillaceous schistus of every valley,
and struck sparks from the flint of every summit. In
the mean time, the characteristic features of the district
—the splendid sterility of the mountain side—the rude
cultivation of the vale—the earthbuilt hovel—the real
Kerry cow, which (by a peculiarly appropriate Iricism, is
only to be found in the mountains of Cork—and the flock
of goats, forming no mean feature of the upland scene—
will have told their own tale to the most careless eye."

"The town of Killarney is but forty-five miles and one
furlong from Cork, and as the coach starts at so early an
hour, the journey is made totally in daylight. The intervening country does not possess many attractions of a

---

* This bridge unites the extremity of the promontory of
Mucruss with Brickeen Island ; it consists of one Gothic arch,
whose altitude is seventeen feet, and span twenty-seven, and
was built by the late Colonel Herbert.

picturesque description, but acquires much interest from its vicinity to the splendid scenery of Lough Lein; at every step, some remarkable remnant of the strength, or ancient splendour of the feudal castles, and many a venerable monastic pile, excite attention and awaken curiosity."

But we have said it is not our intention just now to furnish a regular guide to Killarney; perchance ere our present volume arrive at its close it may come into our cranium to take a trip in that direction; and our readers may rest satisfied it shall not be without their knowledge or without having their amusement and entertainment in view. With several of the more attractive scenes which present themselves in the "Upper, Middle, and Lower lakes," the readers of our former volumes must be already well acquainted; but if spared health and strength till the opening of another season, we promise ourselves the pleasure of procuring with them not only an appetite for dinner in passing over Hungry Mountain, but of assuming our thirst at the Devil's Punch-bowl, after having invaded the territories of Turk mountain and Mangerton, and visited the Hermit of the Lakes in his abbey of Mucruss. For the present, however, we shall merely proceed as far as the pass of Cooleagh, and most willingly do we go back for fifty miles to join the learned and pleasant traveller from whom our guide has quoted, and from whose remarks, oral and written, we have more than once before derived pleasure and improvement.* Proceeding from Skull in the direction of Bantry, he observes—"On my way, I passed the dark and lofty Mount Gabriel to the left, and took my dreary way over a most comfortless tract of country, the peninsula of Ivaugh, the ancient territory of O'Mahony Fune; a prince this O'Mahony was of bogs and rocks enough; and here the tribe of the O'Mahonys have contrived to increase and multiply, and have replenished those wastes with Paddies, pigs, and potatoes. Let no one say, after looking at these moors, studded over with cabins, and these cabins crowded with children, pigs, goats, cocks and hens, that a poor Irishman is not an industrious creature. No; look at that string of men, women, boys, and girls, toiling up the mountain-side with sea weed and sea-sand, in baskets on their backs. See them reclaiming, from amidst rocks and bogs, patches of ground on which to cultivate their only food, the potato; and no one witnessing this struggle of human industry against nature, but must acknowledge that the Irish can be industrious."

PANORAMIC VIEW OF BANTRY BAY.

"The road from Dunmanus Bay brings you over another parallel mountain ridge; and after a tedious ascent you crown the summit, and at once see the whole panorama of Bantry Bay under your feet; I challenge the British Empire to show such a harbour, or such fine land and sea scenery. Nothing I have as yet seen in Wales, or England, or Ireland, is at all comparable to it; perhaps Lough Swilly comes near it—but it must yield the palm. It is inferior in climate, mountain outline, and expanse of harbour. Besides, Bantry Bay holds that beautiful gem, Glengariff, within the setting of its wide and gorgeous ring.

"As I stood on the southern ridge of mountain, and looked across on a fine clear March day—to the east, in the far blue distance, rose Mangerton, in dark and lofty massiveness: to the left of it, M'Gillicuddy's Reeks, their points piercing the 'cumulo stratus' of the clouds, and leaving you to guess at their mysterious altitudes; nearer still to the north-west, Hungry Mountain rising like an embattled wall before you, and down its mural descent, as relieved from its black ground, fell the cataract of Adrigoll, in a perpendicular silver column of 800 feet! nearer still, facing the north, the Sugarloaf mountain, almost as white in its silicious quartzose formation, as if it were chrystalized sugar; directly under my feet was the inner harbour of Bantry, protected and divided from the outer bay by the green island of Whiddy; and up and down on that placid water were studded isles and islets, one crested with an ancient castle, another crowned with

* Sketches in the North and South by C. O., a work that ought to be in the hands of every traveller in Ireland.

a modern battery—here a Martello tower, and there the ruins of a fishing palace; and to finish the setting of this rich jewel, the trees, woods, hills, and fine mansion-house of Lord Bantry, his green and highly dressed lawn, sweeping down in easy undulations to the very water's edge. I cannot say how much I was struck with this delightful tout ensemble. And certainly, as was exemplified here, any thing that is admirable is made much more so by contrast. I had for miles travelled over a dull and dreary way—bare, desolate, unsatisfactory—rocky elevations, or gloomy moors, crowded with miserable huts, a population evidently and fearfully increasing, amidst difficulties and privations altogether insufficient to check its monstrous progress; and I had read Malthus's convincing but gloomy book; and war, pestilence, and famine, ' terribiles visu formæ,' rose up in necessary association, as summoned to feast on and make prey in future of this teeming population. It therefore was a pleasant relief, coming down from this district, to rest on the sweet green shores of Bantry Bay, to feast my eyes on the wooded hills, with all their herds and deer, of Lord Bantry's park, hanging as it does in umbrageous verdure over the noble sheet of water; and to add to the full keeping of this fine landscape, a large West Indiaman rode in all the quiet repose of the secure and land-locked anchorage."

But we again join our Guide, who thus describes the Harbour of Bantry Bay:

"This capacious harbour is twenty six miles in length, and in breadth from six to eight—its depth varies from ten to forty fathoms. Its entrance lies between Sheep-head point and the mountains of Beerhaven. It contains several islands, of which the principal are Bear Island and Whiddy. Whiddy is nearest to the town; it presents a surface of gentle inequalities, covered by a highly fertile soil. It is about three miles in length, and from one to a quarter of a mile in breadth, and maintains about four hundred and fifty inhabitants. Besides some excellent springs, it has two considerable lakes, one of fresh and the other of salt water, the latter of which abounds with large eels. On this island are three batteries, erected subsequent to the attempted invasion of the French in 1796. It contains the remains of an ancient castle of the O Sullivans, to whom the whole of this district once belonged. The present proprietor is the Earl of Bantry.

"Near the entrance of the harbour, Bear Island lifts its rude wild cliffs against the south-western storms, affording a shelter, which is not likely to be undervalued by any one who has witnessed the inconceivable fury and mountain volume with which the waves of the Atlantic rush against these rocky barriers. This island is about six miles long, and one in distance from the western shore, forming an interval which is called Beerhaven harbour, on the mainland side of which is the little town of Beerhaven. Beerhaven was formerly defended by a strong castle. It was a place of no small importance in the fifteenth and sixteenth centuries, when the Irish chiefs maintained a frequent intercourse with Spain.— The other islands which lie near the town are, Chapel, Horse, Hog, and Rabbit Islands.

"In exploring this Bay, the informed tourist will find its interest heightened by many traditionary and historical recollections. He will hear or recollect, with a smile, the antiquarian dreams of the venerable visionary Keating, according to whom the antediluvian Beth landed here, and first took possession of the green Island, with three men and fifty women. Here, on a small island, his attention will be directed to the site of a fortress belonging to that consummate statesman and leader, Carew, Lord President of Munster in the days of Elizabeth.— Here also he will recollect the descent of a French fleet in 1789, under the command of Monsieur Perrault, which was only saved from the English fleet under Herbert by the unfavourable state of the wind, which did not permit more than a partial attack. And here also, last not least, he will recal the more formidable event of 1789, when this island was providentially rescued, by a hurricane of unparalleled fury, from the most formidable fleet that ever left the shores of France, bearing a force which there was no preparation to repel."

So far we have travelled in close company with our

Guide; but we now turn again to the interesting travel-ler to whom he before introduced us, who we find at

THE PASS OF COOLEAGH.

"I now proceeded on my road towards Inchigeela, in an eastern direction. I rolled rapidly along a capital road, and coasting the river Ouvane, by its northern bank, I came within the gorges of the hills, which now closed me in on every side, and still ascending along the banks of the noisy and sparkling stream, I entered a pretty moun-tain valley, wherein was a slated cottage, and a pleasant little meadow, the whole surrounded by mountains; and at length

' The ascending vale
Long straightened by the mountain here was closed.'

"The road seemed to have got into what the French call a Cul de sac, and you seem at a dead stop unless you can say some such talismanic words to the mountain as "open Sesame." But all of a sudden you turn a jutting rock, and enter the singular and stupendous pass of Coo-leagh. I have been through the pass of the Scalp near Dublin. I have never been at the pass of Bearnosmore in the county of Donegal; but the scalp at any rate bears no comparison to this chasm, which nature has cut for two miles through these mountains.

"Reader, have you ever read Southey's poem of Rode-rick, the last of the Goths? and if so, don't you recol-lect his awful description of the vale of Covadonga, in the Asturias. By the bye, fine as it is, and good as is the story of the destruction of the Moors there, I believe he has ta-ken his outline from Hofer's overthrow of a French army in one of the passes of the Tyrol. At all events, good reader, read if you can get it, Southey's poem of Rode-rick, and if this little tour in no other respect pleases you, you will owe it thanks for directing you to one of the most delightful Poems of modern times. What Southey says of Covadonga may be well applied to the pass of Cooleagh—

' Here amidst heaps
Of mountain wrecks, on either side thrown high,
The wide spread traces of its watery night
The tortuous channel wound '

' No fields of waving corn were here,
Vineyard, nor bowering fig, nor fruitful vine,
Only the rocky vale. The mountain stream,
Incumbent crags, and hills that over hills
Arose on either hand. Here hung the yew—
Here the rich heath that o'er some smooth ascent
Its purple glory spread—or golden gorse—
Bare here, and striated with many a hue
Scored by the wintry rain, by torrents here,
And with o'erhanging rocks abrupt.
Here crags loose hanging o'er the narrow pass
Impended.

"This deep and extraordinary chasm, which nature has excavated through these mountains, and which, within these last ten years, has been taken advantage of, in or-der to make an excellent road between Macroom and Bantry, is really one of the most picturesque things in Ireland. It is well worth a journey to see its rocks and precipices: its cliffs clothed with ivy, and here and there interspersed through the masses of rock, old holly and yew trees, and occasionally an arbutus:—And then its strange and sudden windings. You look back, and you cannot find out how you got in—before you, and you cannot imagine how you are to get forward. You might imagine that the spirit of the mountain had got you into his strong hold, and that you were impounded here by everlasting enchantment. Then the surpassing loveliness of the place—

' I never
So deeply felt the force of solitude.
High over head the eagle soared serene,
And the grey lizard on the rocks below
Basked in the sun.'

"And now I had arrived at one part of the Pass where an immense square castellated rock, a keep of na-ture's own construction, seemed to stop up the road for ever. The sides of this natural fortress were clothed and garnished with ivy, maiden hair, feathery ferns, and Lon-don pride; and on the very top of the crag, as if a war-der on the battlements, on the very extreme beetling point, a goat, a high horned shaggy fellow stood—and how he stood I could not explain, or scarcely imagine—but there he was in all bearded solemnity. Salvator Rosa would have painted for a month gratis, to be indulged with an opportunity of fixing such a scene and such an accompaniment on his canvass. My companion in the gig in which I travelled, was an orderly, well-conducted servant; he had journeyed with me over many a hill, and along many a coast, and yet so imperturbable and so un-susceptible was he, that hitherto in all my journeyings he had never ventured to make a remark on scenes so sub-lime or so beautiful, that they used to make me wild with delight and noisy admiration. But here the soul of the man could not contain itself, and he cried out—'Oh, dear Sir, what a mighty grand place;—this flogs all we have seen yet. But then, master, take care you don't stay too long here looking at it, for sure enough Munster has no readier place for cutting a throat.' 'I declare, George, you are quite right as to the grandeur of this wondrous spot, and you are not wrong in saying, that it is a close convenient place for cutting throats.' This brought to my mind that this very spot was, not long ago, a scene of blood and battle. It was the strong hold of the poor misguided Rockites, in the winter of the year 1822, when instigated by incendiaries, and deluded by dark and cur-tained men. Hither the deluded peasantry retired, as to a strong hold, where they imagined

' That nature for the free and brave prepared
A sanctuary, where no oppressor's power—
No might of human tyranny could pierce.'

SINGULAR EXPLOITS OF LORD BANTRY AND CAPTAIN ROCK.

"From hence, as from an insurrectionary centre, they made incursions in search of arms towards Bantry, Mac-room, and Dunmanway. After an incursion of this kind, and an attack on a gentleman's house near Bantry, Lord B——y, and his brother, Captain W——e, of Glengariff, at-tended by about forty mounted gentlemen, and a party of the 39th foot, commanded by an officer, pursued the in-surgents, who retreated before them, and sought the re-cesses of the mountains that surround the Pass. On coming at the jaws of the defile, the pursuers halted and held council; the hills were not accessible to horsemen, and the officer commanding the military declared, that unless the heights were scoured by a large body of troops, he would not enter such a man-trap as the glen. Where-upon Lord B——y and his brother, urged on by their contempt of the rebels, and reckless of unascertained danger, persisted in pushing forward, and dashed into the straits, while the cautious officer persisted that his small detachment could only serve to keep the gates of the mountain open, and cover their retreat. The grey of a winter's morning was just opening as the horsemen burst into the pass, and on they pricked at full gallop, as it was his lordship's desire to proceed onward towards some vil-lages situated on the lakes of Inchigeela, where he hoped to apprehend some notorious characters, the leaders and promoters of the present insurrection. About half way in the Glen a scout of Captain Rock lay on a bed of fern, under a cliff, wrapped in that loose frize coat which Spencer, two hundred years ago, so graphically described as a fit house for an outlaw, and a meet bed for a rebel. This man started up from his lair, pike in hand, and join-ed the horsemen, supposing that they were some of the Boys, that had returned from a marauding expedition.— The poor creature, while huzzaing for Captain Rock, was cut down, and left there for dead, and the troop got through the pass. But other scouts were more on the alert, and the leader of the insurgents was soon informed that there was a party of the military stationed at the western mouth of the pass, and that a large body of horse-men was passing through it. He who personated on this day the ubiquitarian Captain Rock, was not calculated to throw discredit on his "nom de guerre." He was not one to overlook or forego the advantages his enemy pre-sented him with. He felt that his foes were within his grasp, for he stood secure that they must repass the de-

file : and he counted on their capture as much as if he
had them within the clenching of his fist.   No one could
tell who this young man was, his bearing, address, attire,
accent, bespoke him much above the common sort, and as
not a native of Cork. Be he whom he might, no one
presumed to question his power—all were on oath bound
to obey, and with a blast of his bugle he summoned in
his forces, and called to his side his generals of division, Lieu-
tenants Pat Peep-o-day, and Sylvester Starlight, and then
in a speech, not so round and set as Livy or Tacitus would
record, but in that abrupt, joyous, presumptuous tone, fast
and fiery, like a Milesian Irishman, addressed his followers—
' Only, boys, look this day to your cause and your oaths—
mind my bidding; be steady but for this one morning, and the
whole west country is your own ; and I promise you all, boys,
the tap of Lord B——y's cellar.   Peep-o-day, off with
you westward—take sixty of the smartest boys in the
whole mountain, and run round the red coats—watch
them well—keep them at play as you would a ball on the
hoop of your hurl—never come to close quarter—keep
behind the rocks and turf-clamps—never fire till sure of
your man.   Run away as they advance—coax them if you
can into the hills—teaze them until you see they quit the
pass, and follow you into the mountain—amuse them as a
plover would a spaniel on a moor, and when we have
houghed all the horsemen, I will come to you and ham-
string all the soldiers.

" ' Starlight, take you fifty of the stoutest men on our roll
—each man must carry a spade along with his gun or
pike. Go to the Red Deer's Rock—that big stone which
overhangs the pass, and from which the Fairy Buck
bounded and cleared the Glen when Fin M'Coul hunted
him for a summer's day, with his good dog Brun. The
stone, big as it is, is loose already ; I almost shook it the
other evening with my shoulder.   Twenty men, in ten minutes, will undermine and leave it so, that at command
you can kick it down like a foot-ball.   Off, Starlight, lose
no time; dig away as if you were digging by night for
dreamt-of gold.   Work for the Virgin and St. Patrick,
and when the rock is ready to rattle down, clap your
Kerry cow's horn to your mouth, and blow me the old
Whiteboy's blast, and then wait quietly until you hear
three distinct flourishes of my bugle, and then, in the
name of all the saints, down with the rock.   It will plug
up the pass, as this cork stops my dram bottle ; and then,
my brave boys, these Orange oppressors, these pityless
men, who rode rough shod over the country, are in our
power.   The foxes of Bantry and Glengariff are bagged—
we who have been hunted and hallooed at—our blood
spilt like water—our necks broken on the gallows—our
heads rolling on their scaffolds.   We who have borne
a century of suffering and of shame ; now, now our time
is come ; we have all the vermin of the country in our
power—fox, and badger, marten, weasel, and pole-cats—
come, boys, we shall have rare sport ; we shall all be in at
the death, and every man can choose his game.'

" Thus spoke Captain Rock ; and forward marched Lieu-
tenants Peep-o-day and Star-light to their respective positions ; Captain Rock disposed his own main body on either side of the eastern end of the defile, each man effectually secreted and covered by his own gray rock ; so that
were any traveller to bend his way at that hour through
the pass, he would have felt awe-struck as he went along
at the loneliness of his wayfaring. But not so at the western end of the glen.   There Peep-o day, the moment he
arrived, began his tactics ; some of the fleetest and most
enterprising of the *Boys* crept along the brow of the pass,
and under shelter of the rocks and heath, came within
shot of the military party—fired a volley, and then fled
towards the hills.   The officer, a cool veteran, whose experience taught him self-possession, who was well seasoned
in Guerilla practice during the Peninsular war, saw the
hazard of dispersing his small detachment amongst the
mountains, and ordered his men to stand to their post and
not attempt pursuit. Again Peep-o-day tried his practice, and
some of his men came so near as to taunt and scold the red-
coats from behind the rocks and here a few of the soldiers,
irritated by the insolent forwardness of the whiteboys
started forward in pursuit, and ascended the mountain,
but they had not gone very far when from amongst the

hills and bog-holes, up started the enemy on every side
and a bloody, and hand to hand contest ensued. Luckily
all effected their escape except one light infantry man,
who more forward than the rest, fell, pierced with a hundred pike wounds.

" In the mean time Lord B——y returned from a fruitless search through the villages along the lakes of Inchigeela. He found every house deserted, and water thrown
on every hearth, and it was high time to turn homewards,
disappointed and weary,—with horses blown and jaded,
and many lame from want of shoes. They entered slowly,
in long and loose array, the eastern opening of the defile.
Captain Rock, with head and neck protruded from behind
the shelter of a cliff, and still protected from observation
by an old yew, that waved its palmated foliage around
him, hung in deep suspense, watching the entrance of the
last Bantry man into the pass—he seemed to fear lest he
should lose one of them—he counted them as a rat-
catcher would count the vermin that he was enticing into
his cage ; and now he crossed himself—he heard the beat-
ings of his own heart like the tick of a death-watch, as he
counted the seconds, expecting every moment to hear
Starlight's horn announcing that the rock was uprooted.

" The Bantry men had about a mile to pass on, before
they came to the point over which the loosening rock impended.   At the rate they were proceeding, about ten minutes would have brought them to it.   Rock's hopes, or
dashed or realised, hung in suspense these ten minutes ;
and still onward the horsemen wound their toilsome
march, through the silence of the defile.   At this instant
an old man of the Mahony's looked down from his covert,
and saw Lord B——y and his brother just passing under
him.   This poor fellow had once two sons, the pride of
his name and the consolation of his descending years—
active, honest, industrious ; but, alas ! seduced into the
Rock system, their house near Gougane Barra was searched under the provisions of the Insurrection Act, and arms
and ammunition being found concealed, they were tried
at Bantry, and sentenced to be transported, which sentence was instantly put into execution, and their aged
parents were left desolate and destitute ; the mother wept
her life away, and her grey hairs descended in sorrow to
the grave ; and the old man joined the rising, and cared
not how he died.   This bereaved old man saw now, as he
thought, the very man in his power who robbed him of
all the props of his existence, and in an agony of passion
that brooked no restraint, he started up on the gray rock
that hitherto concealed him, and holding high in his withered arms a ponderous stone,

> His loose coat floated on the wind
>   His hoary hair
> Streamed like a meteor in the troubled air ;

And muttering the curse of him that was made childless,
he cast the stone with wonderful energy down on Lord
B——.   The stone missed his Lordship, but wounded severely his horse, and immediately Captain W—— drew
forth his pistol, and with accurate aim, fired at the old assailant, who stood over head, still foaming forth wrath and
curses.   The bullet, true to its mark, passed through the
streaming hair of the poor impassioned wretch, and closed
for ever his sorrows and sufferings. Down he came,
tumbling from rock to rock, until he lay along the road, a
mortal ruin, grey and blasted and bloody. The sight was
too much for Irishmen to bear; all the prudential commands of Captain Rock were forgotten ; and setting up
one universal yell, each man started forth from behind his
rock, and the whole glen bristled with pikes and muskets.
Move ;—march—away, cried Captain W—— ; a gallop or
a grave.—Lord B—— y, keep a head ; I will bring up the
rear.—Spur, spur for your lives ;—keep moving and they
cannot mark us. Never was advice better given, or more
carefully taken. Lame and jaded, the spur's rowel and
the sword's point goaded the horses on, and forward the
whole party rushed ; and just as Lieutenant Starlight had
loosened his rock ; just as it was tottering to its fall ; just
as the horn sounded; the last loyalist passed beneath it
and turned the point ; and then down it came, a smoking

ruin, closing up the pass effectually, too late to bar retreat, but just in time to preclude the enemies' pursuit.

"Thus the whole well contrived military speculation of young Rock was defeated. The destinies of Providence dashed his enterprize, and dissolved it like a mist upon the mountain. The Bantry men soon got through the defile; they joined the detachment of the king's troops at the Glen's mouth, and they all retreated unmolested to Bantry.

"Some time after, a large body of troops surrounded and scoured the mountains, but no Captain Rock; he had retreated in hopelessness into the fastnesses of Slievelogher and it cost the sappers and miners of the King's army, many a blast, and many a pound of powder, before they broke up the rock with which Lieutenant Starlight, a minute too late, closed up the pass of Coolengh."

GIANT'S RING.

About four miles from Belfast, in the parish of Drumbo, there is a very extraordinary monument of antiquity, called the Giant's Ring. It consists of an enormous circle, perfectly level, about five hundred and eighty feet in diameter, or nearly one third of an Irish mile in circumference. This vast ring is enclosed by an immense mound or parapet of earth, upwards of eighty feet in breadth at the base; and though it is probable, in the lapse of nearly two thousand years, the height of this bank must have much decreased, it is still so great as to hide the surrounding country, except the tops of the mountains, entirely from the view; and in its original state there is not a doubt but that they were also invisible.

Near the centre of the circle stands the *cromlech*, or rude altar of stone; and whether the proofs that such monuments were used in the idolatrous adoration of the sun, be or be not satisfactory, it is a circumstance that deserves to be remembered, that the Giant's Ring would exclude from the gaze of a mistaken multitude every object but the glorious luminary himself, whose beams they worshipped. It is a place which is calculated to inspire an uninformed druid with additional superstition, or with the necessity of increased mortification; and they who formed it had a just conception of those human feelings which are extensive in their influence, powerful in their operation, and most deeply to be moved by external nature. The sloping stone of the altar is almost circular, being seven feet in one direction, six and

a half in the other, and upwards of a foot in thickness at the edges, but in the centre considerably more. This *cromlech* is either very erroneously described by Mr. Harris, or its appearance has greatly altered since the year 1744. We are informed in the History of the County of Down, that "two ranges of pillars, each consisting of seven, support this monstrous rock, beside which there are several other stones fixed upright in the ground, at the distance of about four feet. Of these latter there remains but one; the upper stone at present rests upon four, and not upon fourteen supporters; the entire number which compose the altar is only ten—and though it is probable that several may have fallen down, or in some manner changed their position, it is inconceivable how so great a disproportion as the two accounts present could ever be reconciled."*

HERCULANEUM AND POMPEII.

Sir—The following particulars of the destruction of Herculaneum and Pompeii—the former laid under a leaden covering of lava, and the latter immersed in an ashy grave of pulverized matter, may not be uninteresting or useless to *some* of your readers.—Those sepulchred remains of Roman splendour which give us a knowledge of a true Roman city, with its temples, palaces, and baths—

---

* Stat. Acc. pp. 256—278.

theatres and amphitheatres—its splendid forum—its triumphal arches—its Doric, Corinthian, and Ionic columns—its pilastered halls and peristytes—its frescoed walls and friezes.

Pompeii and Herculaneum are situated very near the burning Vesuvius[*]—the former five miles distant from it—the latter much nearer, and it is owing to its approximation, that Herculaneum suffered so severely and received the worst effects of this fearful visitation, the full force of its destructive wrath—being completely enveloped in an impenetrable mass of lava—while Pompeii was by its greater distance and its elevated situation buried *only* beneath clouds of ashes and showers of molten stones, (called lapille) and cinders, but these fell in such vast volumes that they obscured the light of day—and it may be attributed to this circumstance that Pompeii is much easier of excavation than Herculaneum, yet it takes about a year to disinter one house, for the vapouring steam which proceeded from the crater of the volcanic Vesuvius, " descending in torrents of rain united with the ashes suspended in the air, washed them after they had fallen into places where it could not well have penetrated in a dry state," filled up every cranny and left perfect casts of whatever substances it enveloped.

" There it found
The myriad fantasies of hearts and brains,
Young lovers, and hopes, and pleasures, all abroad,
Spreading their painted wings, and wantoning
In life's glad summer breeze, from flow'r to flow'r,
And, with the fatal spell of one dread glance,
Blighted them all!"

The air was still at the time of the first indications of an eruption, a cloud of smoke mounted up straight from Vesuvius, and spread itself about : which Pliny the younger, who was an eye witness, compared to the trunk and branches of an enormous pine tree, but some clearer indications of the coming storm was soon given.—dreadful murky clouds saturated with " igneous serpentine vapour," rose about them—and parted at the same time with lightning-like trains of fire ; "the vital air was changed into a sulphurous vapour, charged with burning dust,' and the heat which accompanied the showers of volcanic scoriæ, was "sufficient to char wood, and volatilize the more subtle part of the ashes"—add to this, the darkness which overspread the city, "not," says Pliny, "like a cloudy night, or when there is no moon, but of a room when it is shut up and all the lights extinct." Nothing then was to be heard but the shrieks of women, the screams of children, and the cries of men ; some calling for their children, others for their parents, others for their husbands, and only distinguishing each other by their voices ; one lamenting his own fate, another that of his family ; some wishing to die for the very fear of dying ; some lifting up their hands to the gods ; but the greater part imagining that the last and eternal night was come, which was to destroy the gods and the world together.

Pompeii was evacuated in all the hurry of a precipitate retreat—what a scene ! Every person and thing thrown into the utmost confusion ; darkness surrounding them—the prisoners in the jails craving to be released. That such a frightful scene did take place, is evident from the state in which the town is found on excavation. Human skeletons and household utensils in the greatest disorder presented themselves to the eyes of the miners. The bones of a sentinel were discovered outside the gate of the city in a niche in the wall, still on his post, and grasping even in death his spear. But the most affecting and melancholy instance of it is, the shin bones of the inmates of the prisons still in the iron shackles that bound them at the time of the evacuation of the city, after having endured an incarceration of 1676 years. Another striking instance of the shortness of the notice this ill-fated people received, is exhibited " in the forum, opposite to the temple of Jupiter ; a new altar of white marble, exquisitely beautiful, and apparently just out of the hands of the sculptor, had been erected there—an enclosure

was building all round ; the mortar just dashed against the side of the wall, was but half spread out ; you saw the long sliding stroke of the trowel about to return and obliterate its own tracks—but it never did return ! the hand of the workman was suddenly arrested, and, after the lapse of 1800 years, the whole looks so fresh and new, that you would almost swear the mason was only gone to his dinner and about to come back immediately to smooth the roughness."[*] How feelingly does this remind us of the confusion that reigned in the city ; the noise is heard, and the people shout that Vesuvius is pouring on them its red hot cinders—the sound is re-echoed from street to street, the mechanic catches the alarm, casts away his trowel, and flies. To such an extent did fell destruction operate on Pompeii, that where it stood was a mystery, its site was unknown for ages, till chance brought it again to light. The first indications of ruins were observed in 1689 ; but the excavations did not commence till 1755. It thus lay from the year A. D. 79 sealed up. It, however, on this account escaped the ravages and plunder of the barbarian hordes who from time to time swept over Italy, and annihilated every work of art that their destroying hands could reach. It now appears to us, as it was 1800 years ago—the pictures still against the walls, exhibiting all their original freshness of tint ; the domestic furniture, pots and pans scattered about in the hurry of use.

The area of Pompeii is about 161 acres, the excavated part is about one fourth of the city, yet that portion has occupied 83 years. When it is entirely cleared, (if we may hope that such will ever be the case,) our knowledge of Roman customs, architecture, habits and literature, &c., &c., will be much increased.

How awfully sudden was its transformation ! now the " busy hum of men" and the rattling of different vehicles is heard through the streets, and re-echoed through its lofty temples, domes, and porticoes, all the noise and bustle of civic pride and pomp resounds——

" But louder rose the terrible voice of ruin,
Over their mirth, ' be still,' and all was hushed,
Save the short shuddering cries that rose unheard,
The upturn'd glances from a thousand homes
Thro' the red closing surge ! the awful groan
Of agitated nature—and beneath,
Ten thousand victims turn'd to die—above,
Bright sunbeams lit the plain—a nameless tomb."

Yes, in a moment all was still and hushed for ever ; the oblivious voice of destruction closed above its unhappy inmates, and shut them at the same time from the light of day and life. All were involved in a common grave.

H.

THE IRISH HERCULANEUM.

I chanced the other day to light on a MS. headed "The Irish Herculaneum," and recollecting that there was a description of the town of Bannow in your Journal, I referred to it for the purpose of ascertaining, whether this was a transcript, or an extract from that, for at first sight I supposed it to be either, but perceived that the MS. account was entirely different, and that it treated, though briefly, rather of the appearance of the country around—that it was just an opening description to the town itself. I think, however, that it must be interesting, as every circumstance connected with such a remarkable phenomenon is worth attention.

A town in Ireland swallowed up by a devouring sand ! and, like its illustrious prototypes, Pompeii and Herculaneum, converted in a short time, from a flourishing, beautiful, busy town, with its inhabitants engaged about their various affairs, (though not by the agency of melting lava or red hot cinders, but by a substance which completed its work as effectually,) into a noiseless dreary waste of moving sand, like an African desert scene, where its whirling, sandy drifts are agitated by a gale of wind, and looks like a troubled sea, undulating to every passing breeze, and making all that comes within its reach one universal scene of wide-spread desolation. I will now add the description given in the MS.

---

[*] The crater of Vesuvius is still supposed by the superstitious to be the road to the infernal regions.

[*] Library of Entertaining Knowledge.

"Between the harbours of Wexford and Waterford is a tract of fertile land containing about 60 square miles, called the baronies of *Forth* and *Bargie*. The appellations are significant—*Bar* is fruitful, *Forth* is plenty, and *Gis* the sea—the names therefore indicate exactly the character of the place, a fertile and plentiful tract on the sea coast. Behind it runs a ridge of mountains and before it is the sea, so that it is in some measure insulated, and retains much of the primeval and original character of a place cut off from free intercourse with the rest of the country. It moreover lies directly opposite Cardiganshire in Wales, and certain promontories projecting to the east, approach so near to the contiguous coast as to invite the inhabitants of the other side to come over and visit it. From the earliest periods therefore, long before the Anglo-Norman invasion, a free intercourse had taken place between the two principalities, and many Irish families settled in Wales, and many Welsh in Ireland. The latter are so numerous that a large district in the county of Wexford is called *Scarla* (Welsh), and there is a long tract of Highland in the neighbouring county of Kilkenny, called the Welsh mountains, from the number of families of this name and nation which occupied them, where at this day they form a clan or sept; and as the colonization was gradually effected by free consent, and friendly intercourse, the name of Welsh is held in more esteem by the peasantry." Here it seems to be cut short. I suppose the writer intended to go on and speak of the town of Bannow situate in this fertile spot; but as its interesting history is already so accurately, and so fully discussed in your Journal, the loss is of little consequence.

In my opinion, the name " Irish Pompeii" would be better applied to this place, than Irish Herculaneum, as there was a greater similarity in their awful extinction. It may be presumed, however, that the inhabitants of Bannow were not, like those of Pompeii, involved in the common fate and ruin of their town, as they must have had warning and time enough to escape.

But what a spectacle does it now present! calculated to excite the most unpleasant and gloomy sensations, as we cast our eye on the infertile hillocks and ridges of shifting sand surrounded by hills of the same; the sea rolling on the beach close to it, still casting up its mite of sand to add to the mass—and every thing about it bespeaking nothing but wild, untamed, uncultivated nature, as if it was just emerging from its primitive chaotic rudeness. Bannow is now a dull, monotonous wilderness, nothing to relieve the eye, the only *Oasis* an old steeple peering up which still asserts its supremacy, and lifts its old head high above its former companions, who lie deeply buried beneath. And as its surface is, as mentioned before, continually agitated by every breeze that blows, no expectation need be indulged, of its being ever reclaimed from its present confused mixture of wind, and sand, and wave.   H.

THE SANDS OF ROSAPENNA.

On the Donegal Coast, in the vicinity of Horn Head, lie the Sands of Rosapenna, a scene that almost realized in Ireland the sandy desert of Arabia; a line of coast and country extending from the sea deep into the land, until it almost meets the mountain on which we stood, and exhibiting one wide waste of red sand; for miles not a blade of grass, not a particle of verdure—hills and dales, and undulating swells, smooth, solitary, desolate, reflecting the sun from their polished surface of one uniform and fleshlike hue. Fifty years ago this line of coast was as highly improved in its way as Ards, on the opposite side of the bay, now is: it was the much ornamented demesne, and contained the comfortable mansion, of Lord Boyne, an old-fashioned manorial house and gardens, planted and laid out in the taste of that time, with avenues, terraces, hedges, and statues, surrounded by walled parks, and altogether a first rate residence of a nobleman—the country around a green sheep-walk. Now not a vestige of this to be seen; one common waste of sand—one undistinguished ruin covers all. Where is the house?—under the sand—where the trees, the walks, the terraces, the green parks, and sheep-walks? all under the sand.— Lately the top of the house was visible, and the country

people used to descend by the roof into some of the apartments that were not filled up; but now nothing is to be seen. The Spirit of the Western Ocean has risen in his wrath, and realised here the description Bruce gives of the moving pillars of sand in the deserts of Sennaar; or it recals to memory the grand description which Darwin gives of the destruction of the army of Cambyses in the Nubian desert. Nothing, indeed, can exceed the wintry horrors of the north-westerly storm, when it sets in on this coast—and its force has been for the last half century increasing. The Atlantic bursting in, mountain-high, along the cliffs—the spray flying over the barrier mountain we were standing upon, and falling miles inland, the sand sleeting thicker and more intolerable than any hailstorm, filling the eyes, mouths, and ears of the inhabitants—levelling ditches, overtopping walls, and threatening to lay not only Rosapenna, but the whole line of coast, at some not very distant period, in one common waste and ruin.

I have been informed by a friend resident in the neighbourhood of Rosapenna, that the blowing of the sand to its present extent may be attributed to the introduction of rabbits, that were permitted to encrease, and their burrowing disturbing the bent grass which kept the sand down; the tremulous west and north-west winds on this coast began, and have continued to operate with increasing mischief. At Rutland, in that district of Donegal called the Rosses, there was expended, about forty years ago, the sum of £30,000, which expenditure was defrayed partly by Government and partly by the landlord, the Marquis of Conyngham, in order to create a town and fishing establishment on a coast that teemed with herrings. It is a curious fact, that the year after these buildings were erected and all the expense incurred, the herrings deserted the coast; and what is equally surprising—the sands began to blow, and now large ranges of lofty buildings, three or four stories high, are covered on the sea side with sand; you can walk up to the ridge-poles of the roof.

POPULAR LECTURES ON THE PHYSIOLOGY OF ANIMALS.
An abstract of Dr. Henry's Eighth Lecture:
THE EYE.

The eye is entitled to our attention on account of its unrivalled beauty—of its curious and delicate structure—of its uses, so varied, and so constantly occurring, that it may be considered, in the present state of society, and, especially, since the invention of printing, the great inlet of all human knowledge. By means of this organ, objects—whether near or remote—whether large or small—whether in the firmament or on the earth—are brought, as it were, into the actual presence of the understanding.

As the shape of the skull is modified, in order to afford a convenient situation for the ear, so it undergoes a still greater modification in order to afford a convenient situation for the eyes. They are lodged in two large excavations, called orbits, under the forepart of the brain. It was convenient that the eye should be placed near the brain, in order that the communication between the eye and brain should be less liable to interruption; it was necessary that the eye should be placed in a commanding situation, in order that it might have the greater extent of view; it was desirable that it should be in a sunk situation, in order that it might be safe from injury. For these reasons we find the eyes placed in the highest part of the body, very near to the brain, and, at the same time, sunk in their receptacles or cavities, and protected above by the forehead and eyebrows, at one side by the nose, and at the other by the temples. The only quarter in which the eye is exposed to injury is the forepart, which must necessarily be open in order to admit the light: but even in this quarter there are defences provided, of which we shall have occasion to speak by and bye. The eyeball is so called from its figure, which is that of a sphere, though not a perfect one. The inverting membranes, or coats of the eye, as they are commonly called, are, as we proceed from the inside outwards, 1st. the retina. On this membrane, which is perfectly transparent, the rays of light, proceeding from external objects, are collected to a focus in such a manner, that, if the retina were opaque, Images of all objects presented to the eye would be formed on it, as they are formed on the receiver of a camera obscura. From the retina these impressions are conveyed, by the optic nerve, to the brain, where the mind takes notice of them. 2dly. The middle coat of the eye, external to the retina, and concentric with it. This coat contains the principal parts of the blood destined for the nutrition of the eye. It is of a dark colour, and is rendered still darker by a pigment with which it is loaded. This coat, loaded with its pigment, is seen through the transparent retina, when we look from the interior of the eye. 3dly. The external coat, which invests the two preceding, and is concentric with them. This coat gives support to the more delicate parts within, and, at the same time, protects them from external injury. This external coat forms four-fifths of the exterior envelope of the ball, the remaining one-fifth being formed by the sight of the eye, which is that transparent part which is in the centre of the *white*, as the visible part of the exterior coat is commonly called.

The quantity of light admitted through the sight to the interior of the eye is regulated by a curtain placed behind the sight, and having, in its centre, a circular aperture, called the pupil. This curtain is called the iris : it is variously coloured in different persons; and, according to its color, the eyes are denominated black, or blue, or hazel, or grey, &c. In a weak light the curtain is drawn in on every side, until it is reduced to a mere ring, leaving the pupil very large, so as to admit as many rays as possible to the interior of the eye. On the contrary, when the light is strong, the curtain falls on every side, until the papillary aperture is contracted almost to a point, and thus the retina is effectually protected from the glare of light.

In order that objects presented to the eye should be perceived by the mind, it is necessary that the rays of light, emanating from the objects, should be brought to a focus at the retina. This is effected by the *humors*, which are situated in the interior of the ball, and are so placed that the rays of light must pass through them, in their course from the sight to the retina. The principal of these is the crystalline humor, so styled from its beautiful transparency. By anatomists it is generally called "the lens," because it exactly resembles, in shape, a convex glass lens. When this "lens," which should be crystalline and transparent, becomes opake, it constitutes the disease called cataract ; the rays of light are no longer able to reach the retina, and blindness, more or less perfect, according to the greater or less capacity of the lens, is the result. This disease is cured by extracting from the eye the opake lens. The deficiency occasioned by the absence of the lens is supplied by means of spectacles, with very convex glasses ; these glasses enable the individual who had been rendered blind by the cataract, to enjoy a very useful degree of vision.

In young persons the powers of the humours are apt to be too great, and the rays of light are brought to a focus before they arrive at the retina. In this consists shortsightedness. It is remedied by the use of concave glasses, which giving a greater divergence to the rays, before they enter the eye, the great powers of the humours barely suffice to bring the very divergent rays to a focus at the retina, and thus perfect vision is acquired.

In old age, on the contrary, the powers of the humors are not sufficient to bring the rays to a focus at the retina ; convex glasses are, therefore, necessary to assist the humors. By means of this kind of glasses old persons have their failing sight restored, and are enabled to see accurately many years after the decay of the powers of the humors.

From this explanation you will understand why the eye of young persons require concave, and those of old persons convex, glasses.

[To be continued.]

Who are they who most easily gain and lose friends? Four sorts of people ; the rich, the young, the powerful, and the favourites of the rich and powerful : but when the rich become poor, the young old, the powerful reduced to privacy, and the favourite disgraced, they are left like a whale on the shore.

MOVABLE MELON BEDS.

In the valley of Cashmeer there are movable beds of melons, which, in some degree, may be considered in the light of islands. The ingenious people of that valley spread a thick mat on the surface of their lake, and sprinkle it over with soil : it soon acquires a consistency, from the grass growing upon it. On the following year they sow melons and cucumbers, and reap the harvest from a boat : and thus turn to account the very surface of the lake in their rich country.

Montserrat had Irish colonists for its early settlers, and the Negroes to this day have the Connaught brogue curiously and ludicrously engrafted on the African jargon. It is said that a Connaughtman, on arriving at Montserrat, was, to his astonishment, hailed in vernacular Irish by a negro from one of the first boats that came alongside—" Thunder and turf," exclaimed Pat, " how long have you been here ?"—" Three months," answered Quashy—" Three months ! and so black already ! ! *Honum a diaoul*," says Pat, thinking Quashy a ci-devant countryman, " I'll not stay among ye"; and in a few hours the Connaughtman was on his return,. with a white skin, to the emerald isle."

LINES
WRITTEN ON FINDING A ROSE LYING WITHERED ON A WALK IN THE GARDEN OF A FRIEND NEAR DUBLIN.

Sweet rose, what hand could blight thee,
　And crush thy blooming pride ;
Sweet rose, what hand could slight thee,
　And throw thee thus aside ?

Sweet rose, who could bereave thee,
　Of all thy freshness gay ;
And then, sweet rose, could leave thee,
　To wither here away ?

The dew in glittering splendour,
　Still clusters o'er thy breast ;
The breeze still sweet and tender,
　Doth woo thee to thy rest.

For it is evening hour,
　And all nature seeks repose ;
And each sweetly breathing flower,
　Doth its tinted petals close.

But no more shall dewy morning,
　With its beams of purple hue,
All thy native charms adorning
　Catch an answering smile from you.

Nor where the sun's descending,
　At the balmy hour of eve,
Wilt thou fondly towards him bending,
　His last golden light receive.

But tho' thou canst not flourish
　Or bloom in pride again,
I will not let thee perish
　And wither where thou'st lain.

Then thus, sweet rose, I leave thee,
　Beneath thy parent tree,
Its shade will fond receive thee,
　Its tears will fall on thee.

And when the smiling bowers,
　Now breathing fragrance round,
Shall lose their sunny flowers,
　Whose leaves shall strew the ground.

That stem from which they tore thee,
　Tho' now so full of bloom,
Will shed its flowrets o'er thee,
　To form thy simple tomb.

　　　　　　　　　　　　JULIAN.

DUBLIN :
Printed and Published by P. D. HARDY,.3, Cecilia-street ; to whom all communications are to be addressed.
Sold by all Booksellers in Ireland.
In London, by Richard Groombridge, 6, Panyer-alley, Paternoster-row ; in Liverpool, by Willmer and Smith ; in Manchester, by Ambery, in Birmingham, by Drake ; in Glasgow, by W. R. M'Phun ; and in Edinburgh, by N. Bowack.

THE
DUBLIN PENNY JOURNAL

CONDUCTED BY P. DIXON HARDY, M.R.I.A.

| Vol. III. | SEPTEMBER 13, 1834. | No. 115. |

DUBLIN AND KINGSTOWN RAILWAY.

THE TUNNEL OR ARCHWAY THROUGH LORD CLONCURRY'S GROUNDS.

PUBLIC WORKS IN IRELAND.

Having in our last described the line of Railway from the entrance station in Westland row to the Pier at Kingstown, we now take the opportunity, while presenting our readers with two other views of the road, of inserting an article which, since our last publication went to press, has appeared in *The Sun* newspaper, relative to the carrying on of Public Works in Ireland. Our readers will perceive that its general bearing is in perfect accordance with the opinions we have more than once before expressed, when speaking on the subject of railways. We have already stated our reasons for giving a preference to railways over other modes of conveyance; but we fully agree in opinion with the writer of the article to which we refer, that no greater benefit could be conferred upon Ireland than the introduction of a cheap and expeditious means of conveying her agricultural produce from the heart of the country to the extremities—whether this be by canals or railways is a matter to be decided by the locality of those districts through which the lines of road may pass.

"We do not often derive so much pleasure from the perusal of a public document as we have from a careful inspection of the plans, and consideration of the suggestions, contained in the Second Report of the Commissioners of Public Works in Ireland, just printed by order of the House of Commons. Notwithstanding the low ebb at which the tide of Ireland's prosperity stands at present, we predict, from the great improvements that are now being carried on, in clearing harbours, opening canals, and making roads along the eastern, southern, and northern coasts, that the day is not very long distant when Ireland will, from being a bye-word among the nations of Europe, become equal to some of its proudest states in industry, wealth, intelligence, and love of order. The worst crimes of Ireland are the results of the poverty and despair, rather than of the evil disposition of her population. Public works, besides giving employment to thousands of her labouring poor, whom want has rendered almost desperate, will be the means of inducing capitalists to establish factories where facilities are afforded for carrying on an extensive trade; and will enable agriculturists to raise produce wherever a line of good road, a cheap water carriage, or convenient shipping, supplies them with a sure market for the fruits of their industry. During the last eighteen months the sum of one hundred and twenty-nine thousand, six hundred and thirty-three pounds were expended in the improvement of Kingstown and Dunmore harbours, the making of roads on the Antrim coast, and the building of bridges, and other improvements in different parts of Ireland. The consequences of these works are already beginning to be manifested in the improved condition of the inhabitants in their vicinity, and the altered aspect of the immediately adjoining face of the country. The commissioners themselves say that, 'Wherever a new road is constructed, flourishing farms at once spring up, and the carts of the countrymen press on the heels of the road-makers as the work advances.' And in a p eceding paragraph the following most important information is given:—'In traversing a country covered with farms, and in a high state of cultivation, showing every sign of a good soil and of amply remunerating produce, it becomes difficult to credit the fact that, ten or twelve years since, *the whole was a barren waste, the asylum of a miserable and lawless peasantry,* who were calculated to be a burden rather than a benefit to the nation; and that this improvement may *entirely* be attributed to the expenditure of a few thousands of pounds, in carrying a good road of communication through the district.'

"What Ireland stands most in need of at the present moment is, a cheap and expeditious means of having her agricultural produce conveyed from the heart of the country to the extremities. Now, in our judgment, the best way of effecting this would be by canals, of which she stands in the greatest need. The first of these should be a canal from Dublin to Galway, which would cut the whole island across, from east to west, uniting St. George's channel with the Atlantic ocean. This line of communication between the capital of Ireland and a great commercial town on the extreme coast, would be of immense importance to the inhabitants of both, but of still more so to the whole population of Connaught, among whom it would be the direct means of introducing manufacturing industry, and a taste for the arts, enjoyments, and elegancies of civilized life. The distance between Dublin and Galway is about one hundred and four miles, through which a direct line of canal has already been carried for forty-two miles—namely, from Dublin to Philipstown; so that in point of fact the work is already begun, and only wants the aid of government, and the assistance of the landed proprietors in King's County, Roscommon, and Galway, the value of whose estates would be trebled by it, to effect its entire completion. The next line of canal should be from Ballyshannon Harbour to Dundalk, by Enniskillen, by which the greatest facilities would be given to agriculture and manufacturing improvements in the counties of Donegal, Fermanagh, and Leitrim; and more especially to the trade of Ballyshannon and Dun-

dalk, which, though capable of being made emporiums of provincial industry and wealth, are now little better than marts for the fish caught along their coasts. However, great praise is due to Colonel Conolly, the member for Donegal, who has advanced a thousand pounds, and given security for four thousand more, for repairing the harbour of Ballyshannon, which, when finished, will be of great benefit to the people of the town, and the inhabitants along the western coast, from Sligo to Killybegs. The last line of communication which we would suggest to the government, besides the navigation of the Shannon, which is sufficiently dwelt upon in the reports of the select committee on that subject, is a canal from Waterford to Sligo, intersecting the canal from Dublin to Galway, somewhere about Philipstown. This, with such a line of communication from Dublin to Belfast, would unite all Ireland; and in a very few years would render the country as prosperous, as rich, and as contented as any in Europe. The intercourse which those canals would give rise to between the people in every part of the provinces, would extinguish that spirit of religious animosity which now divides and destroys them. Bring men only together, and they will soon remove the prejudices of each other. The people of Ireland are at present as much removed from each other at the distance of fifty miles apart, as if the whole Indian ocean rolled between them. Hence, the jealousies, and hatreds, and cherished recollections of feudal wrongs, so common in almost every district of Munster and Connaught. But let once manufacturing industry prevail in these districts —let the voice of the mechanic be heard in the villages— and we will pledge ourselves that the people of Ireland, with all their alleged love of mischief, will find other employment than that of parading nightly in a Captain Rock uniform, or recording vows of vengeance against Sassenachs and collectors of king's taxes."

THE MOTHER'S HOPE.

(FROM THE "CASKET OF AMERICAN AND EUROPEAN GEMS,"

JUST PUBLISHED.)

She was my idol. Night and day to scan
The fine expansion of her form, and mark
The unfolding mind, like vernal rose-buds, start
To sudden beauty, was my chief delight.
To find her fairy footsteps following me—
Her hand upon my garments—or her lip
Long sealed to mine—and in the watch of night
The quiet breath of innocence to feel
Soft on my cheek—was such a full content
Of happiness, as none but mothers know.
Her voice was like some tiny harp that yields
To the slight-finger'd breeze—and as it held
Long converse with her doll, or kindly soothed
Her moaning kitten, or with patient care
Conn'd o'er her alphabet—but most of all
Its tender cadence in her evening prayer,
Thrill'd on the ear like some ethereal tone,
Heard in sweet dreams.
                    —But now I sit alone,
Musing of her—and dew with mournful tears
The little robes that once with woman's pride
I wrought, as if there was a need to deck
What God had made so beautiful. I start,
Half fancying from her empty crib there comes
A restless sound—and breathe accustom'd words,
"Hush, hush, Louisa, dearest."—Then I weep,
As though it were a sin to speak to one
Whose home is with the angels.
                    Gone to God!
And yet I wish I had not seen the pang
That wrung her features, nor the ghastly white
Settling around her lips. I would that heaven
Had taken its own like some transplanted flower,
Blooming in all its freshness.
                    Gone to God!
Be still, my heart!—what could a mother's prayer,
In all its wildest ecstacy of hope,
Ask for its darling like the bliss of heaven?

EXTRAORDINARY CAVERN.

A remarkable stalactitical cavern has been discovered at Erpfingen, in the bailiwick of Reutlingen. The entrance is between two rocks, and was closed with three large stones, carefully fitted together. The cavern itself is 515 feet long, and contains in one suite six chambers, which are nearly of equal length, from 24 to 32 feet in height, and from 54 to 48 feet in breadth ; but they are all separated from each other by irregularities of the ground. Besides this principal cavern, there are several smaller ones on the left and right : the most remarkable of the latter is near the entrance, and forms a kind of gallery, thirty feet long, from five to nine feet high, and ten feet broad. The other lateral caves are generally small and low. Though shut up, probably, for centuries, it must have formerly been inhabited, or at least served as a place of refuge, as not only pieces of pottery, but also two combs and some rings have been found , everywhere, but especially in some of the lateral caves, there are numerous human bones of extraordinary size, also vitrified and petrified bones of large animals, and teeth belonging to animals not known to the sportsmen of the present day. The cavern is dry, the temperature very mild. It is situated in the forest, on the Höhlenberg, or Höllenberg, three leagues and a half from Reutlingen, half a league from Erpfingen, and one league from Lichtenstein.

FASHIONS.

In part of Tartary the widows of rank are distinguished by wearing a full blown ox bladder slung round their necks. The Tschutki beaux think that their dress is complete when they have a tail of the feathers of birds ; their wings, or the tail of some animal. In the reign of Charles the Sixth of France, Queen Isabel, of Bavaria, young and beautiful, displayed a luxury unknown to former times ; no queen had ever before appeared so richly dressed. She first introduced the fashion of naked shoulders and neck ; heart-shaped bonnets were then in vogue ; the two uppermost extremities of this heart were gradually lengthened, till, at last, they formed a kind of horns. Juvenal des Ursins says, on this subject, " the women ran into great excesses in dress, and wore horns of wonderful length and size, having on either side, ears of such monstrous dimensions that it was impossible for them to pass through a door with them on. About this time the Carmelite, Cenare, a celebrated preacher, exercised his talents against these horns. The size of the horns continued increasing, and, to accommodate the fair wearers, the door-ways were widened and heightened.

POPULAR LECTURES ON THE PHYSIOLOGY OF ANIMALS.

An abstract of Dr. Henry's Ninth and Last Lecture :

THE EYE CONTINUED.

It is not enough that the eye should be capable of receiving the impressions of external objects—it should also have a power of moving, in order to choose at pleasure the objects which are to be presented to the mind. The eye is, indeed, moved about by the head as the head moves ; but this motion, if it had no independent motion of its own, would be quite insufficient for perfect vision. Where considerable extent of motion is required, the large wide movements of the head answer sufficiently well ; but it would be very awkward if it were necessary to move the head whenever you wished to change your view from minute object to minute object—as in reading, or writing, or drawing, or in conversation. If the head were to be moved for each minute change in the view required on such occasions, our heads would be always shaking, like those of the figures of Chinese Mandarines, carried about our streets by the showmen.

The muscles of the two eyes are associated together in such a manner, that when the one eye moves towards the nose the other moves from it, and vice versa. By means of this association the two eyes move harmoniously.— This association is so perfect, that when you shut one eye, and move the other about in different directions, if you place your finger on the lid over the closed eye you will feel the ball moving in unison with the open eye. When this harmony of the two eyes is disturbed by any cause, so that both eyes are directed towards the nose at the same time, or both from the nose at the same time, great deformity of countenance is produced, and this discordant movement of the two eyes is called a squint.

In order to facilitate the motion of the eye, there is a considerable portion of fat placed at the back of the ball, between it and the bone. This serves the triple purpose of allowing free motion to the ball— of protecting the optic and other nerves on their passage to it, and of affording to the ball itself a yielding cushion, by means of which blows on the eye-ball have their force broken—the ball sinking into the fat instead of being pressed against the bone.

As it is necessary that the eye should have a perfect protection against too strong or too long continued light, and as the Iris (the curtain already described) can only regulate the quantity of light, not exclude it altogether the eye is provided with lids, which the individual is enabled to open and shut at pleasure by means of appropriate muscles. The upper lid, being the larger, hangs like a curtain over the upper and fore-part of the ball, and thus affords protection to the eye from the direct rays of the sun and the strong light of the sky. In this climate, where the sky is so constantly clouded, we are less sensible of the advantage of this arrangement ; but those who have been in more southern climates know how great is the distress which arises from the direct light of the sun ; such climates could scarcely be inhabited by man were it not for the superior size and the drooping of the upper lid.— Besides this advantage, arising from the greater size of the upper lid, the vision of objects below the level of the eye (and it is upon such objects that the eye is almost always employed) is much less interfered with than it would have been had the lower lid been the larger. Three other advantages arise from this apparently trivial circumstance of the upper lid being larger than the lower :

First—A disagreeable uniformity in the appearance of the lids is avoided.

Secondly—The eye is exposed more fully to the view of the observer—a circumstance of great consequence, as connected with the expression of the countenance. And,

Thirdly—The closing of the eye—an act which requires to be performed speedily, frequently, and with as little exertion as possible, is facilitated by the upper lid being so large that it drops over the ball, requiring scarcely any muscular effort to bring it to meet the lower. In order to render still more complete the protection which the lids afford to the ball not only against light, but against foreign substances—as mites, insects, drops of perspiration from the forehead, &c., their edges are studded with several rows of fine hairs, called the eye-lashes. These hairs, in order that they may not mat or entangle each other when the lids meet, are turned in different directions—those of the upper lip being arched upwards, and those of the lower lid downwards.

In order that vision may be perfect, the *sight* of the eye must be kept clear and moist, and free from dust or motes. This is effected by means of the *tears*. The tears are secreted by the lacrymal gland, and are poured out on the upper and anterior part of the ball through very minute pores. The tears not only keep the eye-ball moist and bright—a condition indispensable for vision, but facilitate the motions both of the ball and the lids, and these motions in their turn spread the tears uniformly over both. As vision would be imperfect without a constant supply of tears, to keep the eye clear and moist, and to wash away motes, so on the contrary would it be impeded by the tears collecting on the ball and between the lids. There is, therefore, an apparatus expressly for the purpose of disposing of them ; an apparatus by which they are not only disposed of, but rendered a second time useful in the economy of the animal. In each eye-lid, at the inner part next the nose, there are two minute tubes, (of diameter not much more than sufficient to admit a bristle) opening on the edges of the lids by two round orifices, which any one can distinguish in his own person, by means of a common looking-glass. At their further extremities these tubes open into a little bag, placed at the very angle of the eye next the nose, and the lower part of this bag communicates with the nostrils. The tears having been secreted by the lacrymal gland, and having been spread over the ball by the action of winking, are directed towards the inner angle of the eye, where they are sucked up by the gaping orifices of the tubes, conveyed into the little bag at the corner of the eye, and from thence into the nostrils, which they moisten, and thus serve the purpose of assisting the secretion of the nostrils to counteract the drying effect of the air constantly passing through them in the act of respiration.— When, from any stimulus, the quantity of tears is much increased, as from a strong light suddenly admitted to the eye, or from an irritating substance, as dust or smoke coming in contact with the ball, or from a lively emotion of the mind, whether of grief or joy, the orifices of the tubes are unable to suck up the moisture with sufficient rapidity ; it accumulates between the lids, and runs down the check, constituting what is called a shower or flood of tears. This increased flow of tears, if it come from a mote on the ball, is intended to wash away the offending substance ; if it is produced by an emotion of the mind, it serves the purpose of manifesting the emotion, whilst, at the same time, the copious secretion relieves the brain and powerfully contributes to restore the mind to its wonted equanimity.

. In the preceding sketches of Dr. Henry's lectures we have been compelled, by the narrowness of our limits, to be very concise ; to omit a considerable part of each lecture, and greatly to condense the remainder. While we have employed our own language, we have taken the utmost care to adhere strictly to the meaning of the lecturer, and to give his facts and principles faithfully. We have been obliged to use description in those instances in which Dr. Henry, by means of anatomical specimens, pointed out the objects themselves as they exist in nature.

DUBLIN AND KINGSTOWN RAILWAY.

Geometrical Section of the First, Second, Third, and Fourth Class Carriages, with the Engine and Tender, passing Merrion, on their way to Kingstown.

The Railway will be opened on the 18th of the present month. His Excellency the Lord Lieutenant, several Noblemen, Members of Parliament, and a number of scientific men, have signified their intention of being present on the occasion. We have heard that there will be on the road *fifty* carriages, and six locomotive engines, such as those shown in the engraving, which will convey one thousand persons, who have been particularly invited for the occasion.

THE POTEEN STILL.

A TALE FOUNDED ON FACT.

The Irish peasantry practice the distillation of that illicit spirituous liquor, so well known by the name of *poteen whiskey*, with a most unaccountable infatuation. I do not think that it would be altogether fair to say that this is from the mere love of ardent spirits, as the *article* distilled according to law is now so very cheap, that a single shilling will purchase a sufficient quantity to satisfy even a drunkard: nor can it be from the hope of gain, as the profits arising must be very inconsiderable, and not in any manner such as could tempt any reflecting mind to risk the severe penalties inflicted by the law in case of detection. Notwithstanding, in almost every part of the country where a facility of secrecy, or a means offer, the practice is persevered in despite the dreaded punishment. On the rude brow of the heathy mountain, in the nearly inaccessible bog, in the lonely island of the lough, in the dark cave of other days, and the desolate and neglected ruins of the ancient abbey or mouldering castle, night after night, arises the smoke of the *poteen kettle*. Informers, (the most detested name in Ireland,) are sometimes found, from either a spirit of malice or revenge, to betray the secret to the revenue officer; and then follows the destruction of what may be called all the peasant's harvest and hope. His kettle is destroyed; all the vessels used in the process are broken: his malt is scattered, and his liquor spilled; and imprisonment and fine, and consequently the utter ruin of himself and his unfortunate family, winds up the catastrophe. But the informer, if known, or ever discovered, is made to suffer all the penalties of outlawry. His property is destroyed in every shape —his house is burned—and his neighbours shun his presence as they would a pestilence. In vain he flies the district: he is watched and hunted—his character, and the curse of the betrayer follow hot upon his footsteps; and not unfrequently his life pays the forfeit of his deceit.

Near *Castleconnell*,[*] in the county of Limerick, there resided some years ago a small farmer of the name of Dunne. His wife was the daughter of a neighbouring farmer—an affectionate, warm-hearted, simple woman— the faithful partner of her husband's toils. They had no children—yet they did not murmur at their lonely lot, but—

"Kept the even tenor of their way,"

undisturbed by unseemly broils or dissatisfied repinings. Their means, though small, were more than sufficient for their humble wants; and being sober, careful, and industrious, they were considered as comfortable a couple as any within the bounds of the barony of *Clanwilliam*.[†] Nicholas Dunne was an early riser: and one morning, in the autumn of the year 1805, as he was proceeding with some reapers to cut down the ripened produce of his fruitful fields, after crossing the stile that led from his little garden into an adjoining meadow, where there was a well of clear spring-water, his ears caught the faint sounds of an infant's cries. His house was in a particularly lonely situation: the lark had scarcely risen

from her dewy bed—and what could bring, at such an hour, an infant in such a place, surprised Nicholas Dunne. He turned in the direction from which the sound proceeded, and, by the side of the solitary spring, he discovered an infant, wrapped warmly in an old coarse blue mantle, such as is usually worn by the poorer sort of country people, and without any other dress. The men searched about on all sides, but could discover no traces whatever of any person being near the place. Nicholas considering that the infant was purposely left there, and deserted by its unnatural mother, and that it must die of cold or hunger if immediate care was not taken of it, he rolled his great coat round it and returned to his house. He placed it in the arms of the kind-hearted Nelly, who looked at it with astonishment, and then turned an enquiring and searching, yet anxious glance upon her husband. He met her looks with a smile. "There's a present for you this mornin', why, *a heager*," said Nicholas. "It's welcome, then, as the flowers ov May," said Nelly, and the big tear stood large and sparkling in her eye. "I found it down by the side of *Tubber na boo*,[*] said Nicholas, wishing to remove the suspicion that appeared to move Nelly, "and sure Jem and Paddy heerd it afore myself, why."

"An' you don't know who owns it, then?" enquired the somewhat relieved Nelly.

"*Yerra* the sorra know then, why;" responded Nicholas, and Nelly was satisfied.

They agreed to keep and take care of the young deserted one, until claimed by those who might prove their natural right to it; and as heaven had withheld the blessing of children from them, it perhaps placed this one in their hands to recompense and bless them.

It was a boy; and upon further examination it was discovered that its legs were crooked, and its feet twisted into a hoof-like shape, and a small slip of paper, with the words "not christened yet," writ in a twisted and an awkward hand pinned upon the blue cloak that enwrapped it. The kind Nelly set about tending and nursing it with a new pleasure awakened in her heart; and Nicholas, notwithstanding the satire and jeers of his neighbours, looked on with a heart-felt satisfaction.

Nicholas Dunne had the boy christened on the following Sunday evening.

"What name do you intend to give him, Nick," said the priest.

"Why, you see, Father James," replied Nicholas, "the little weeny crether has been sent asthray very early in the beginning of his days, and as your reverence is about to put your holy hand over him, I was just sayin' to Nelly that we ought to call him *James Sthray*,[†] your reverence."

"Its just a good name, Nicholas," said the priest; and the little foundling was forthwith baptized by the original cognomen of James Stray.

Master Stray, despite his distorted legs and feet, grew and flourished like a young tree planted by the side of living waters, and Nelly was proud of her success as a nurse. In the due course of time he was placed under the tuition of the village teacher, along with some eighty or ninety of the country youngsters, where he obtained the nick-name of *Crubeen*, or *Comrellickeen*[‡] Dunne. In person he was small and misshapen; his skull was uncommonly large, and projected in an unusual manner over his keen small eyes, which twinkled in their cavities like small torches from the recess of a beetling cave. His legs were without flesh or muscle, and curved out in op-

---

[*] On the east side of the river Shannon, about seven and a half miles from Limerick. The castle was a very ancient building, being the residence of the O'Briens kings of Munster. The celebrated Brien Boroimhe lived here for some time, and his grandson was basely and treacherously slain in the north tower by the prince of Thomond. When the English took possession of this part of Ireland, Castleconnell was granted to the Red de Burgo; and William de Burgo, in the reign of Elizabeth, was created the first baron of Castleconnell. The de Burgos were afterwards attainted, but the estates were restored on the accession of James. In 1688 they were again attainted, and the castle taken by the Prince of Hesse, under the command of Ginkle, who ordered it to be blown up. This castle was very large, and situated on a height. There is an excellent spa here, famous for curing ulcers and sores, and for destroying worms in children.

[†] The name of the barony in which Castleconnell is situated is Clanwilliam.

[*] The well or spring of the cow.

[†] This story is really founded on fact, and this is the name which was actually given to the little foundling. The after circumstances are only a fair narrative of facts which came under the writer's own observation.

[‡] These words are nearly synonymous, and it would be impossible to find any one word in the English language to express the complicated meaning which they convey. They are applied to persons who have crooked or deformed feet; the latter word in particular is generally used for this purpose. The former word is more properly the term given to the feet of pigs and cows, and also applied, as in the case of the latter word, but not so generally.

posite directions; and his feet appeared like clumsy knobs appended to their extremities; but his arms were long, strong, and muscular; and his body was large and strong; his chest expanded and full, promising uncommon strength, as if nature wished to make up what was wanting in the other parts by doubly fortifying this. His temper was warm, and even playful, unless when insult, or injury, or any remark upon his decrepitude, roused him, and then revenge alone seemed to be the master passion of his soul; and often did his young school-fellows, who thought to mock and taunt the poor cripple with impunity, feel that his blow and his courage were much above the sum of their calculation.

Being made acquainted at an early age with his unfortunate and dependant situation, he strove to evince by his gratitude to his protectors that their time and attention were not thrown away upon an unworthy object. He watched over their concerns with a diligent and careful eye; he strove to anticipate their wishes, and always met their reproofs with humility.

At length his good mother, the tender Nelly, died; and the affectionate Nicholas soon followed her, leaving the poor deserted foundling, now about eighteen years of age, the sole inheritor of his little property.

Crubeen, being both intelligent and industrious above his neighbours, during the time he could spare from his farm, commenced a trade in cattle; and so prosperous was he in his dealings, that in a short time he was said to have amassed a considerable sum of money, besides improving and adding to his farm; and the farmers around him, who had daughters to dispose of in marriage with some little dower, began to look on the once despised Crubeen Stray, the child of destitution, and, perhaps, of shame, as the most eligible match in the country.

Nor was the warm-hearted Crubeen unsusceptible of the softer emotions of the soul. He became enamoured of a young woman, the daughter of a farmer who lived some miles distant, and whom he beheld several times at prayers. He was not long in finding an opportunity of being introduced, but, to his infinite mortification, he found he had a favoured, and consequently a powerful rival to contend with, when comparing a fine, well-formed, handsome young fellow, with his own crippled and ill-formed appearance. Still, being of a lively and warm temperament, he did not despair, but pushed his suit with much vigour.

Crubeen had one enemy in the world—a young man in his own immediate vicinity, and nearly of his own age.— He was called Jeremiah O'Sullivan; and since they were children he seemed to be actuated by the most malicious feelings towards the orphan, Crubeen. At school they had fought several desperate battles, in the most of which the superior address and strength of arm of the cripple brought him off the conqueror. They were usually class-fellows, and here the quickness and attention of the boc-*caugh*[*] rendered him the superior; and thus, by degrees, the shame of defeat, and the feeling of contempt with which he regarded Crubeen, rendered O'Sullivan, even from his boyhood, the fixed and determined enemy of the decrepid foundling, which enmity his future success in life only served to confirm. O'Sullivan turned out a drunkard and idler, and neglected his business and wasted his means. His constant resort was to the ale-house or the dance-house. He left his sowing or mowing for the funeral, the fair, and the pattern, where no business could lead him, and where his presence was not required. In this way he was fast running to ruin, when an unfortunate spirit of confederacy found its way among the peasantry, and O'Sullivan was the first to join in their nocturnal deliberations. His hatred to Crubeen led him several times to propose injuring him in person or property, but this was constantly rejected by his companions, to whom the boccaugh had endeared himself by his kindness and humanity.

"No"—said they, "Crubeen Dunne is the best master in the country, and the best employer, and the best friend to the poor, and no one shall hurt the hair of his head while we can prevent it."

Such was the state of affairs near Castleconnell when "Misther Dunne," as the deserted child of Tubber na boo was now called, was induced at a time, when, as the people expressed it, "there was worse than no price for corn," to try the speculation of distilling the produce of his farm into *poteen* whiskey, as he imagined it might bring something of a profit, which he could not hope for if he brought it to market. Accordingly he sent a special messenger to the most famous person in the country for making the "right sort," and appointing to meet him at a fair to be held some few miles distant on the following week. The distiller was universally known by the name of *Sthawka*;[*] a rambling, houseless, homeless being, who had no family or fixed residence, and who wandered from place to place, wherever his services were required. His only trade was making *poteen*—his highest gratification was in drinking it—and his whole delight was in fighting at markets or fairs.

The fair day came, and Crubeen having finished his business, at an early hour, proceeded to search among the town of tents, which was erected on one side of the fair-green for the *Sthawka*. It was about the mid-hour—and what was a very uncommon circumstance, there was as yet no sign of riot or disturbance, when Crubeen observed Sthawka issuing in a zig-zag from one of the tents. He had a tough ash sapling in his dexter hand, which he twirled about with inimitable dexterity. He gazed up and down with an eager glance, round about, right and left—all was quiet. Men, horses, cows and sheep passed and repassed in mingled confusion and discord; lowings, and bleatings, cries and curses were heard all around, but still no positive signs of a "ruction" were apparent. Obstinate pigs held long and angry discussions with their drivers, but still no distant "hurroo" gave the well-known signal for attack. No cheering shout met his ear. No stick flourished on high above the moving mass. No tent demolished of its wattles met his eye. He looked up at the sun, and perceived it was past the usual hour.

"Och, thundher and turf," shouted he, capering among a crowd of men collected round a large lot of sheep, and flourishing his *alpine* high over his head—

"Boys, jewel, it's past twelve, and the divil a blow struck yet. Och, Jimmety Hagerty, where are you why? Is there no one to make a beginnin'?" and he stared about fiercely and wildly upon the faces around him. The men took no notice of this sudden burst of pugnacity, most of them were acquainted with the person and character of the *Sthawka*, and no one wished to give an opportunity to begin the *sport*. He was astonished to find his summons unattended to, and throwing off his great coat, and taking it by one of the sleeves, he dragged it after him on the ground to where a sensible looking man was surveying the lot of sheep.

"Will you be pleased just to stand on[†] the tail ov my coat, if you please, Sir?" said the *Sthawka*, with the most undesigning air.

"No, no, *Sthawka*," said the man, with a good humoured smile. "I'm your friend—but I'd like to see the man that 'id be asther doin' it, faix, I'd shew him a ha'p'ny why."

At this instant Jerry O'Sullivan, seeing the *Sthawka* with his coat on the trail, inspired by some dozen glasses of the native, and urged by his mischievous disposition, leaped, with a sudden bound, upon the coat, at the same time, contrary to the rules to be observed on such occasions, laid the poor *Sthawka* prostrate, with a tremendous blow on the back of the head. "Foul play." "Foul play," "He took him false," were repeated by sundry voices, yet no one dared to oppose the ruffian, until the

---

* Cripple, literally.

* The idler—the stalker—the lounger.

† This was really the custom when two factions were gathered at a fair; if there was any seeming unwillingness in one of the parties to begin the sport, the champion of the other was frequently known to drag his coat after him through them, as a tacit challenge; and it was considered an acknowledgment of their defeat if no man was found who would tread on it, and fairly face the challenger. The custom is still used where any remains of the old clanships are found.

boccaugh, hobbling up on his misshapen stumps, faced O'Sullivan, with eyes flashing angry and determined indignation from beneath his far p̄——ing and heavy brows. "Coward!" he exclaimed, in accents of bitter contempt, "you struck a man with his back turned to you, and without giving him notice of your challenge—turn now an' face a poor cripple, iv you dare."

O'Sullivan turned his face towards the hobbling *Crubeen* Dunne, but so struck was he by the animated and ireful expression of his strongly marked countenance, that his heart became appalled; but the shame of retiring before so contemptible an antagonist in appearance, after the act he was just after perpetrating, prevented him from actually turning to fly.

"He's afraid of the poor *boccaugh*," said a bystander, observing the change in his countenance and the hesitation of his manner.

"Och, sure it's only Jerry O'Soolivan," exclaimed another, in accents of contempt, "that's always quarrellin' and never fightin', and that no one thinks it worth their while to fight for or agin why!"

"What's id all about?" asked a stranger, coming up; "is id the Malownys and the O'Flahertys that's goin' to kick up the stir when all's quietness?"

"Augh, no, then, it's only Jerry O'Soolivan, that's always first in the fight and first to run away; an' he kem false upon poor *Sthawka* and kilt him, an' now he's afeerd to face *Crubeen* Dhunne," was the reply.

O'Sullivan, during the moment the above remarks were passing around him, felt all their force, and the estimation in which he was held galled and fired him. He had never met "the outcast of his parents," in personal combat, since they were boys before. He conceived a hope, from the appearance of the cripple, striving, as it seemed, to support his athletic body upon his weak and bending limbs, and, without replying, he levelled a desperate blow at the head of *Crubeen*, which the *boccaugh*, hobbling a step or two on one side, avoided, and driven by the force of the blow, and the disappointed nerve, which not finding its object at the point to which its might was levelled, impelled the striker forward some yards. *Crubeen*, with an agility unexpected, seized O'Sullivan, with his left hand, by the poll, as he bent forward, and wheeling him round him, with uncontrollable force, struck him across the legs, and brought him prostrate to the earth. A shout of triumph rung round on all sides, mingled with execrations of shame and reproach upon O'Sullivan, who, after some time, recovering the use of his limbs, sneaked away.

The *Sthawka*, who had arisen from the earth as his foe was levelled to it, now came up to his defender, and, extending his hand, cried out—

"Give us your hand, *Misther* Dunne, you're the ' right sort,' let you be what you will, and you did for me to-day what one good man only does for another; but it's no matther, I'll go home with you to-night."

Crubeen, and his friend the *Sthawka*, retired to a tent where the *boccaugh* expected to meet the idol of his soul, Kathleen O'Brien, whose father had appointed this day for arranging and settling all things connected with his future happiness or deciding his fate in a contrary way. They met O'Brien and his daughter according to appointment, and the excited heart of *Crubeen* expanded into joy and love under the bright eyes of the blooming Kathleen, and he felt how happy his lot would be if blessed with such a partner for life. The moments flew as lightsome and quick as butterflies on the summer wind; Kathleen seldom joined in the conversation, and when obliged to answer, did so in monosyllables, and in a distressed and constrained tone of voice. They had not been long together, when a young man, whom *Crubeen* knew as the lover of Kathleen, entered the tent; he looked at the daughter first, then at the father, and lastly, with a scowl of contempt, fixed his flashing eyes upon the cripple, and, flinging himself carelessly into a seat on one side, called for some liquor, and sat, without touching it, seemingly absorbed in bitter reflection. Kathleen started and blushed as he entered, but suddenly turned ghastly pale, and appeared ready to faint. *Crubeen* watched all her motions with the eye of a lynx, and the deductions which he drew were certainly not of the most

pleasing nature, for he, too, looked confused, and bit his lip until the blood started. Shortly after the *boccaugh's* evil genius, Jerry O'Sullivan, with three desperate looking ruffians, pooked in his head at the opening, and, spying *Crubeen*, he whispered his companions, and they stalked in; and as they passed, O'Sullivan fixed his stare, with a malicious expression of mingled hate and revenge, upon the cripple, and pushed his way to a seat within earshot of what was passing at the bench where the cripple sat, and near to where the lover of Kathleen sat, silent and alone. Liquor being brought to them, and the health of each individual having passed in succession—"Mushn, then, Christy Kilday," said one of them, "did you listen to the song on 'the sportin' ould gray mare' to-day, why?"

"No," replied Christy, "I was busy all the day selling the *bonnives*,* why, then."

"What was it all about, why?" said another.

"Why, it's all about the *Dews*† and Boneypark, and St. Pathrick and the Scripthers, and the Peelers," said Christy.

"Did id say a gradle about the Scripthers, then?" asked Jerry O'Sullivan.

"Augh, thin, sure it did, a power antirely, but the sorra word ov id myself remimbers," replied Christy.

"Did it advise a body to shun those that God puts his bad mark upon?" asked O'Sullivan, glancing spitefully at *Crubeen*.

"Why, then, I dunna," replied Christy; "but what's the manin' ov the same, why?"

"Why, you must know," said Jerry, in a loud voice, "the construction ov the manin' ov all that is, that any body born wid a blind eye, or a hump on his back, or wid crooked legs, or *comrellickeen* feet, is n't lucky, and we're ordhered to shun them as a body would a sarpint, for God has put his own bad mark on them."

Crubeen heard all this—so did O'Brien and his daughter Kathleen—they looked alternately on each other, but the expression of the *boccaugh's* face struck them with astonishment: a glow of burning indignation had bespread his usually pallid features, his brow hung fearfully over his fiery eyes, and the muscles worked beneath the skin in a variety of contortions. He appeared a few moments deprived, by his wrath, of the power of speech; at length his words found way. Kathleen glanced at her lover, blushed, and hung her head, and her father bit his lip in inquietude and anger, as the cripple gave vent to his feelings.

"Listen to me, then, Jerry Soolivan," exclaimed *Crubeen*; "who is crippled in the heart—who is crucked inside—and who is blind to every thing but badness—who is black within and white without—these are the people that God has set his mark upon: the false-hearted, the coward, the rogue, and the liar. It's you I mane, Jerry Soolivan, the man with the white liver and the desavin' sneer—you are the man that every good and honest man should shun!" and the withering glance and the deep tones which accompanied these expressions seemed to sink into the very soul of O'Sullivan.

But he quickly recovered himself, and leaping to his feet—"Come, boys," he shouted, "let's smash the ugly *boccaugh*, that hasn't the face or the tongue ov a Christhen," and he made a rush towards where the cripple stood, ready to meet him, but the lover of Kathleen crossed him, and, with one well-aimed blow, sent his stick, shivered in pieces, to the other end of the tent. The *Sthawka*, at the same time, brandished his *alpine*, and sent forth the shriek of defiance in the joy of his heart. The ruffian was astounded, so were his companions who accompanied him, in the hope of having but a decrepid, lame object, and a drunken "*shoughraan*"‡ to contend with. "Stand back," said the young man, the lover of Kathleen—"Stand back this blessed minit; the first man that offers to strike a stroke here in this tint this day, 'ill have the sorest head he ever had in his life. I know

---

* *Bonnives*—small sucking pigs.

† *Dews*—Jews—the usual mode of pronouncing the word by the peasantry.

‡ *Shoughraan*; an unfortunate outcast and rake.

some ov you, boys, and yous know me. As for you," turning to O'Sullivan, "you are a coward and a bad hearted man. I watched your words, and I saw your mind: never come across me agin in a fair or patthern iv you have a regard for your own self."

O'Sullivan and his companions sneaked out of the tent. *Crubeen* invited the young man to sit down, with which he was about to comply, when, catching the bright eye of Kathleen fixed on him, he turned away. "No," said he, "I'm much obleeged to you, but it's growin' late, an' I must be goin'," and he walked slowly out of the tent.

It was wearing late in the afternoon, and *Crubeen*, who had watched every thing that passed, and who knew the young man to be the lover of Kathleen, felt that it would be useless for him to pursue a suit which could never end in his happiness, and making some trivial excuse for going, he stood up, and wished the parties a good evening, appointing the following Sunday to meet them at the little chapel, and departed with his friend the *Sthawka*.

Next day *Crubeen* and his friend set to work in constructing their still house. The farm bordered upon a deep arm of the Shannon, that stretched like a minor creek far into a hollow between two hills. The banks were, in most places, broken and precipitous, and it was in one of those chasms that the *Sthawka* hollowed out for himself a shelter and a house. The malt had been steeped the regular time. The kettle and worm, the stand and keeve were all in their proper places, and the work progressed with what *Sthawka* termed "wondherful success." But the plans best laid are those which oftenest are frustrated, and so it was with *Crubeen's* distillation. O'Sullivan, who watched with the assiduity of unwearied malice, beheld with delight the work in which his foe was engaged, and allowed it to go on until the last moment, when his triumph and revenge would be most complete. The last stage of the process had commenced, and *Sthawka* pronounced it the master work of the art—" Such a sup wasn't in the County of Limerick that blessed night." A bottle was sent up to the *Crubeen*, for his gratification, and expectation and hope was at its height, when a little boy rushed into the still house, and exclaimed, in hurried accents—" Run then, why, *Sthawka* jewel, for here's the gauger and the *sidewry sollogh*[*] comin' a top ov ye as fast as they can."

"You're a liar now," said the *Sthawka*, casting an anxious and alarmed look at his work, " an' you want only to friken me, the way I'll give you a *cruiskeen*."[†]

"No, no, pon my sowkens, then," exclaimed the boy; " an' more be token, Jerry O'Sullivan just left them at the turn ov the *boreheen*."[‡]

"Augh, then, bad cess to the dirty negur," exclaimed *Sthawka*, " it's all up with us why," and he seized on two or three kegs which he had drawn off, and cast them into the water, and leaving the rest to their fate, he rushed out. The gauger and the soldiers came up and surrounded the hut. The gauger was the first to enter, and looking about, he exclaimed—" Walk in, gentlemen; the nest is here, but the bird is gone." They then commenced breaking up the vessels and spilling the liquor about the place; and when the work of destruction was complete, a party proceeded to the *Crubeen's*, and taking his horse out of the stable, they harnessed it to his car, and loaded it with the still and other utensils belonging to the apparatus.

"It's the first and the last," exclaimed *Crubeen*, as he saw his property disappearing beneath the moonlight down the road towards the town—" It's the first time I ever engaged in such a business, and it's the last time I will ever meddle with the like; but, thank God, they have no prisoners along with them."

As soon as the gauger and the soldiers were gone, *Sthawka* made his appearance, with a countenance expressive of the deepest calamity.

"All's gone, *avick*," said he; " but then iv that villain,

O'Sullivan, doesn't pay for peeping in that way, may I never have a hand in a dhrop as long as I live."

"*Sthawka*," said *Crubeen*, " it's my wish that you never mention this affair, or the name of Jerry Soolivan again."

"Ha, ha!" laughed the *Sthawka*, " do you think I could live in the same counthry with a blaguard informer why. I couldn't earn a bit or a sup where the likes ov him id be then."

The appointed Sunday came, and the *Crubeen* repaired to hear prayers, and to keep his appointment with old O'Brien and his daughter. On the day previous, he had sent word to the young man who stood up in his defence at the tent, and who he since learned was a distant relation of his self-adopted parent, Nicholas Dunne, desiring that he might meet him at the little chapel. When prayers were over they retired to the little public house opposite, and *Crubeen* introduced his friend, much to the surprise of Kathleen and her father. After some preliminary conversation, the generous cripple opened the wishes of his heart in the following words :—

"Jemmy O'Brien," said he, " I liked your daughther from the first hour I saw a sight ov her face, and every time I saw her afther I liked her betther ; but at that time I didn't think there was another that was more fittin' for her than me, and one that she loved before I ever spoke a word on the matther to man or mortual. Here's a dacent boy, and one of an ould stock of honest people, and he likes Kathleen, and if I am not greatly mistaken, Kathleen isn't behind hand in that way. The father of Kathleen looked serious and fidgetty at this part of *Crubeen's* address. " I know he is not so well off in the world," continued *Crubeen*, " as you'd wish the husband of your daughter should be—Aye, but don't turn away your head till you hear me out—I know he's not to your likin' in the way of the world, but still he's not so bad. He has a snug spot of land, if the little arrears were paid, and it stocked and put in heart for him. I know what you have to give Kathleen, and as he's the relation of an ould friend of mine, here, now, give him your daughter, and I'll give him as much as you will give her, with, maybe, a few pounds more in the bargain."

O'Brien stared at *Crubeen*; he couldn't conceive how any one could be so mad as to give away their hard earned wealth to a stranger, but perceiving the cripple to be serious, he muttered forth something like an acquiescence; and the precise amount of Kathleen's fortune being stated, the *boccaugh* produced a long chequer bag, and told out, in the presence of the landlord, an equal sum, which he handed to the young man. "And here," said he, " is a full receipt for all arrears due by you, which I got from the agent last week, as I was paying my own rent." He stood up. " Now I must go," he added ; " May God bless you, and may you, Kathleen, be as happy as I wish you," and he departed. The marriage ceremony was solemnized the following Sunday. *Crubeen* was invited to the wedding, but he was ill and could not attend.

Sthawka promulgated the tale of O'Sullivan's treachery through the country. The society to which he belonged, and who long suspected his fidelity, became alarmed for their own general safety, and resolved on his destruction. He was taken on a fishing excursion one night down the Shannon, but he never returned. Search was made, but he never was found. *Crubeen* never married ; he lived to a good old age, the general benefactor of all around him. Careful, industrious, and intelligent, he became wealthy ; and, being naturally generous, humane, and benevolent, he was the benefactor of the poor, and the idol of the needy.

J. L. L.

---

* Sidewry sollogh—the dirty soldiers.

† Cruiskeen, a tin measure for drinking out of ; hence the old song of " Ma cruiskeen lawn," or my fair cruiskeen.

‡ Boreheen ; a small, narrow bridle road.

DUBLIN :

Printed and Published by P. D. HARDY, 3, Cecilia Street ; to whom all communications are to be addressed.

Sold by all Booksellers in Ireland.

In London, by Richard Groombridge, 6, Panyer-alley, Paternoster-row ; in Liverpool, by Wilmer and Smith ; in Manchester, by Ambery ; in Birmingham, by Drake ; in Glasgow, by W. R. M'Phun ; and in Edinburgh, by N. Bowack.

THE

DUBLIN PENNY JOURNAL

CONDUCTED BY P. DIXON HARDY, M.R.J.A.

| Vol. III. | SEPTEMBER 20, 1834. | No. 116. |

Sketched by A. Nicholl, Esq.   R. Clayton, Sc.

RUINS OF DUNGIVEN CASTLE.

The ruins of this ancient building stand at the head of the town of Dungiven; it is evidently a bawn built in the time of James I. The house, which is one hundred and fifty feet long and twenty feet wide, is seated on a gentle slope and fronting the south-west, and having a fosse and mounds for a defence in front, and at either end of the building round towers projecting a little, and furnished with loop-holes for musquetry. On the north-east are two courts, each fifty yards in length and forty in breadth, through which is the principal entrance; the outer court is surrounded by a low wall, having a reservoir of water within it; the inner court, which is rectangular, is defended by a wall twenty feet high, with embrasures, &c. and at each angle are square towers as flankers : on the inside this wall is strengthened by an arched rampart, and runs round three sides of the rectangle. The situation is commanding, and the views around it are truly admirable.

Though the O'Cahans had a castle at Dungiven, yet the principal residence of the chief was at Limavady, (Lim an madadh, the dog's leap,) a delightful spot on the banks of the Roe, about four miles below Dungiven, where the river has sought out a narrow way between lofty and approaching rocks; the situation was happily chosen, and affords no mean proof of the taste of these early chieftains. Nature has there so assembled and disposed of her choicest features of wood, and rock, and water, that they could derive or acquire but little aid from art, to heighten the charms of the scene. The last considerable chief of the O'Cahans, being implicated in treasonable practices with O'Nial and O'Donnel, early in

the reign of James I. was seized, and his estates forfeited in the year 1607. There is a melancholy little anecdote respecting a member of this fallen family, which is well known and attested here, and is given at length in the County Survey. In substance, it is this :—The Duchess of Buckingham on her way by Limavady, in the time of Charles I. was induced by curiosity to visit the wife of O'Cahan, whose castle was demolished, and himself banished. The situation of this venerable matron was characteristic of her fortunes : she was discovered amid the ruins of her once splendid residence; the broken casements stuffed with straw, and a miserable fire of a few branches before her. 'Thus lodged the aged wife of O'Cahan. She was found by her noble visitant sitting on her bent hams in the smoke, and wrapt in a blanket.' Such are the only facts which could be collected concerning the former chiefs of this country.

There is not, perhaps, in any part even of the South, a more truly primitive race than that which is to be found in the mountains of Dungiven, who, although surrounded on all sides by the Scotch and English settlers, still retain, in their manners and customs, the unvarying stamp of antiquity. This will be seen by the subjoined extract from the writer in the Survey to whom we have alluded.

"The inhabitants of the parish are divided into two races of men, as totally distinct as if they belonged to different countries and regions, and may be distinguished by the usual names of Scotch and Irish—the former including the descendants of all the Scotch and English colonists, who have emigrated since the time of James I.

and the latter comprehending the native and original inhabitants of the country. The Scotch are remarkable for their comfortable houses and appearance, regular conduct, prudence and perseverance in business, and their being almost entirely manufacturers : the Irish, on the other hand, are more negligent in their habitations, less regular and guarded in their conduct, and have a total indisposition to manufacture : both are industrious, but the industry of the Scotch is steady, patient, and directed with great foresight ; while that of the Irish is rash, adventurous, and variable : both are extremely frugal and simple in their ordinary food ; but the advantage arising from this is often lost to the Irish, by their extravagance at fairs, wakes, and merry-makings, an indiscretion of which the Scotch are seldom guilty. It is a matter of fact also, that the state or condition of the Scotch is gradually progressive, while that of the native Irish is in general stationary and unchanged. This inferiority of the native inhabitants is not to be ascribed either to their religion or to the effect of restraining laws ; but it may with more justice be attributed to the remains of barbarous tastes and habits derived from their ancestors, which all the arts of civilization has not been able entirely to remedy or overcome. The natural genius of the inhabitants of this part of the country may be divided by the same line as their occupations and languages ; but as in the former case the superiority of the Scotch was manifest, so in this the advantages are altogether on the side of the native Irish. The inhabitants of the lowlands are in general an educated people—that is, they can almost all read and write, and understand a little of arithmetic ; but it is very rare to meet among them any traces of remarkable talent, either for writing or conversation. Among these, prudence and good sense predominate, rather than literary taste or lively fancy : but in the mountains, where education does not so generally prevail, the few who receive any kind of instruction, surmount by ardent zeal and persevering talent every obstacle to knowledge, and often arrive at attainments in literature, of which their wealthier and more favoured neighbours never dream. They have more peculiarly a taste for and facility in acquiring languages, which is very remarkable ; every one who converses with a mountaineer, acquainted with the English language, must be struck with the singular precision and eloquence of his expressions, which have rather the air of a written than of a colloquial style : there is, too, a natural politeness and urbanity in their manner of address, which forms an agreeable contrast to the rough and ungracious salutation but too common among the descendants of the Scotch. Even in the wildest districts, it is not unusual to meet with good classical scholars ; and there are several young mountaineers of the writer's acquaintance, whose knowledge and taste in the Latin poets might put to the blush many who have all the advantages of established schools and regular instruction. Nothing is more surprising than the similarity of manners which exists among the native inhabitants in every part of Ireland. The same customs which prevail in the most unmixed district of the South are also to be found in this remote part of the North. The poems attributed to Ossian, and other bardic remains, are still repeated here by the old Senachies (as they are called) with visible exultation. They have been handed down, from time immemorial, by tradition alone ; nor is it apparent that they ever existed here in manuscript. The usual hospitality and attention to strangers are observable among the Irish here—their attachment to their several families and clans, and their readiness to revenge any insult offered to their name or connections, also prevail. The absurd custom of showing respect to the dead by mirth and merriment has not in the least subsided in the mountains. Whenever a person of any respectability dies, two wake-houses are laid out, in one of which is placed the deceased, surrounded by aged persons and near relatives ; in the other are assembled all the young people of the neighbourhood, who entertain themselves with every species of frolic and amusement which their invention can devise. It would be difficult, perhaps, to give a better representation of the value they place on this strange token of respect, than by the following actual conversation, concerning a person not much esteemed in the country. It was repeated to me *verbatim*, with true Irish vivacity, by a mountaineer, from whom I was making some inquiries on the subject. 'Barney, you won't go to Billy ——'s wake, sure ?' 'Is it to Billy's ! Oh, set him up with mirth at his wake, indeed ; let them make mirth. at it that think much of him. For my part, let him lie there—the less noise about him the better.' 'Ay, ay, neighbour, the less noise about some people the better ; I'll warrant it will be but a poor gatherin'.' 'Gatherin' ! it will be no gatherin' at all. O, the deil send jokes to such wakes for me ! If there be a bit of decency or fun about it worth stepping over the threshold for, my name 's not Barney Kane.' It would be to no purpose to argue against a custom which thus gratifies at once the vanity of men and their love of pleasure. The Irish cry has not yet been banished from the funerals ; and however it may offend the judgment, or shock our present refinement, its affecting cadences will still continue to find admirers, wherever what is truly sad and plaintive can be relished or understood."

Mr. M'Skimmin, in his History of Carrickfergus, gives the following account of the superstitions of the people inhabiting the line of coast from that town in the direction of the Causeway :

"They are, generally speaking, very superstitious, believing in the existence of brownies, fairies and witches, of whose exploits they tell many extraordinary stories. The received opinion of witches is, that they are old wrinkled hags, who sold themselves to the devil, to obtain a part of his occult art, such as the power of taking the milk or butter from their neighbour's cows, or riding through the air upon a broomstick ! A belief yet prevails of the existence of fairies, and their non-appearance at present is alleged to arise from the general circulation of the Scriptures. Fairies are described as little spirits who were always clad in green, and who inhabited the green mounts, called *forths*. Numerous stories are told of their being seen at these places, ' dancing on the circling wind,' to the music of the common bag-pipe. The large hawthorns growing singly in fields are deemed sacred to fairies, and are hence called *gentle thorns*. Some fields east of this town were formerly called ' the fairy fields.' Brownies, now alleged to be extinct, were another class of the same family. They are described as large, rough, hairy sprites, who lay about the fires after the people went to bed. A warning spirit, in the likeness of an old woman, called *Ouna*, or the *Banshee*, is said to have been anciently heard wailing shortly before the death of any person belonging to certain families. At present this spirit is almost forgotten. Wraiths are still talked of as being seen. These are described as the shadowy likeness of a person, appearing a short time before the decease of the real person. Other warnings or appearances are also believed to exist as death-warnings— such as strange noises, the shadowy likeness of a waving napkin, &c. It is believed that the *luck* of a cow or any other animal may be taken away by a look or glance of the eye of certain people, some of whom are said to be unconscious of their eye having this effect. It is called ' the blink of an evil eye,' and the charm is believed in some instances to extend to children. When this is alleged to occur, the persons are said to be ' overlooked or overseen,' and it is supposed that the person will not recover, unless some charm is used to counteract its effects. There is an opinion that certain people are able to take milk from a cow without touching her, or the butter from the milk, letting the milk remain. When churning or making cheese, fire is never suffered to be taken out of the house during the operation. The first time that a cow is milked after calving, it is common to put a piece of silver in the bottom of the pail, and to milk upon it. Salt is in daily use with some, in a similar way, to prevent witchcraft. Horse-shoes are nailed on the bottom of the churn for a like purpose ; and old nails from horse-shoes are sometimes driven in churn-staffs. Certain days are deemed unlucky : few persons will remove from or to a house or service on Saturday, or the day of the week on which Christmas was held that year. On New Year's-day, and May-day, fire is rarely permitted to be taken out of the houses, lest they lose their *luck*. Persons going on a journey have sometimes a man's old shoe thrown after them, that they may come speed in the object of their pursuit. Crickets coming to a house are held to bode some change to the family, but are commonly deemed a good omen. A stray dog or cat coming and remaining in a house, is deemed a token of good fortune.

"The people who follow the fishing business retain a different class of superstitions, but are not communicative to others on this head. The following have been observed : Meeting certain persons in the morning, especially women when barefooted, is deemed an omen of ill fortune for that day. To name a dog, cat, rat, or pig, while baiting their hook, is surmised to forebode ill luck in that day's fishing. They always spit on the first and last hook they bait, and in the mouth of the first fish taken off the hook or line.

"On the death of a person, the nearest neighbours cease working until the corpse is interred. Within the house where the deceased is, the dishes, and all other kitchen utensils, are removed from the shelves or dressers ; looking glasses are covered or taken down, clocks are stopped, and their dial-plates covered. Except in cases deemed very infectious, the corpse is always kept one night, and sometimes two. This sitting with the corpse is called the wake, from *Like-wake*, (Scottish) the meeting of the friends of the deceased before the funeral. Those meetings are generally conducted with great decorum ; portions of the Scriptures are read, and frequently a prayer is pronounced and a psalm given out fitting for the solemn occasion. Pipes and tobacco are always laid out on a table, and spirits or other refreshments are distributed during the night. If a dog or cat passes over the dead body, it is immediately killed, as it is believed that the first person it would pass over afterwards, would take the *falling-sickness.* A plate with salt is frequently set on the breast of the corpse, which is said to keep the same from swelling. Salt was originally used in this way, as ' an emblem of the immortal spirit.' "—pp. 257—263.

THE FISHERMAN'S HUT.

She listens—tis the wind, she cries :
  The moon that rose so full and bright,
Is now o'ercast—she looks, she sighs—
  She fears 'twill be a stormy night.

Not long was Anna wed—her mate,
  A fisherman, was out at sea—
The night is dark—the morn is late—
  The wind is high, and where is he?

Oh who would love, oh who would wed
  A wandering fisherman—to be
A wretched lonely wife, and dread
  Each breath that blows when he's at sea.

Not long was Anna wed, one pledge
  Of tender love her bosom bore—
The storm comes down, the billows rage,
  Its father is not yet on shore.

Oh who would think her portion blest,
  A wandering seaman's wife to be,
To press the infant to her breast
  Whose father's on the stormy sea.

The storm now bursts, the lightning falls,
  The casement rattles with the rain ;
And as the gusty tempest brawls,
  The little cottage quakes again.

She does not speak, she does not sigh—
  She gazes on her infant dear,
A smile lights up the cherub's eye
  Which dims the mother's with a tear.

Oh who would be a seaman's wife,
  Oh who would bear a seaman's child—
To tremble for her husband's life
  To weep because her infant smiled ?

Ne'er hadst thou borne a seaman's boy,
  Ne'er hadst thy husband left the shore—
Thou ne'er hadst felt the frantic joy
  To see thy Robin at the door.

To press his weather-beaten cheek,
  To kiss it dry and warm again ;
To weep the joy thou canst not speak—
  Such pleasure is the debt of pain.

Thy cheerful fire, thy plain repast,
  Thy little couch of love I ween,
Blazed ten times sweeter than the last,
  And not a cloud that night was seen.

Oh happy pair ! the pains ye know,
  Still hand in hand with pleasures come,
For often does the tempest blow,
  And Robin still is safe at home.

H. N.

NEW YORK IN 1834.

AMUSEMENTS AND PLACES OF RECREATION.

From the New York Evening Star.

There are few places in the world, not even London, Paris, or Rome, that possess as many attractions as our own city—some of them are such as no other town, perhaps, can boast of. Upon the scenic beauties of our bay, it is needless to descant, for they are unrivalled in all that is picturesque and admirable. It seems as if Providence, and the taste of man, had purposely so designed and arranged these objects, and thrown them together in such harmonious diversity and combination of hill, island, fortress, villa, and mountain, that it were vain to attempt to improve them by any alteration, as much so as to hope—

  "To gild refined gold,
    Or add another perfume to the violet."

With the geographical position of New York, in respect to internavigable communications, and its extraordinary facilities and advantages for commerce, all the world are familiar. Nor are there but few towns where the stranger may find more resources for his pleasure and instruction, as well as for business, than a residence in this city. The variety is so great, that it is difficult to choose. The gourmand, the bon vivant, and the epicure, may find in our spacious hotels and markets all that the most fastidious *gastronome* can desire, from the turtle and pine apple of the tropics, to the sheep's head, the canvass back, the trout and venison of our own streams and forests. The man of taste, and letters, and science, may not unprofitably pass his leisure hours in our various museums, theatres, and operas, from the boa constrictor at Peale's, and the necromancy of Professor Saubert, to the Widow Wadman of Hughes, the cartoons of Raffaelle, or the lecture rooms of our colleges and institutes. The pious worshipper of the religion of God has here also nearly two hundred temples, of every denomination, some of them almost daily opened to his devotions. The poet and the sentimentalist may find exhaustless food for contemplation upon our unrivalled Battery, the terrace of Castle Garden, and even in the Park, which, though within the city, is now tastily ornamented, and become a most beautiful lounge. Or, if his desires are not so bounded as those of a London cockney, he can extend his excursions to the numerous lovely retreats in our immediate neighbourhood. A few minutes' walk carries him to the admired heights of Brooklyn, and the rural scenery on the retired and picturesque shore of Long Island, in the direction of Guanus and Utrecht, which, though seldom visited, are among the most agreeable rambles upon the circuit of our bay.—Or, if he choose a more romantic stroll, the bosques of Hoboken, and the classic precipices of Weehawken, which, indeed of a sabbath, judging by the thousands who resort there, are the most favored of all. Perhaps he would prefer to snuff up the sea breezes, and obtain a coup d'œil view of the entire scenery of our harbor and city. The elevated summits of the Pavilion and Howard Place, on Staten Island, furnish him with the most sublime prospect that can be imagined, and there, while he beholds the stately and " rich argosies" of our merchants wafted in from sea, he can, if mineralogically inclined, study, as at Hoboken also, the peculiar geology of those regions, abounding in steatite, serpentine, hematite, and basalt, and also, what is more curious, offering in

some places specimens of native magnesia. If his imagination is fired with a still warmer enthusiasm, what can
more abundantly gratify it than a trip to the Highlands,
the military school of West Point, or the Mountain House
on the snow-clad peaks of the Catskill—all of which he
may reach in a few hours, on board of one of our floating
palaces. And when the summer heats make a jaunt to
the country still more coveted, he may extend his journey a half day farther, and join the gay throng at the watering places of Saratoga, Lebanon, and Ballston—where,
like other travellers, as "increase of appetite grows by
what it feeds on," his ambition may carry him in the wake
of our enterprising tourists, in a few days' pleasant travelling on the canal and lakes, to the frowning battlements
of Quebec, the shores of Ontario, and Niagara's wondrous
cataract; and a few hundred miles still further, and
without fatigue, to the pictured rocks of Lake Huron, the
Indian tribes at our outposts of Michilimakinack and
Prairie du Chien, or even to Captain Back's arctic solitary hut on the banks of the frozen Capermine. But our

sober old citizens, who do not like to ramble quite so far,
and who are not much given to these exploring expeditions, however delightful and easy in accomplishing, prefer shorter trips nearer by. Among them we need scarcely
mention the attractions of the scenery upon our own island, now almost forgotten, and among them Aarlaem
and Yorkville. Then the passage through Hell Gate, and
the quiet, Quaker-town of Flushing, with Prince's superb
Botanical Garden, worth travelling one hundred miles to
see. Then, perchance, he is among the number of our
sportsmen. There is all Long Island for him—its snipe-
shooting, and plover, and grouse, and the deer, that noble
game of the forests of Suffolk, and the thousand nooks,
and creeks, and brooks, which the lover of bass and trout
is wont to frequent. Add also the trotting matches in
Queens—the Marine Pavilion at Rockaway—the cities
and towns upon the Sound—New Haven, and its college
—beautiful Newport—Montang—Nantucket, and so on
to Boston, Nahant, &c.

CASCADE AT BRYANSFORD, NEAR NEWCASTLE, COUNTY OF DOWN.

Those who have visited Newcastle, that beautifully
situated little bathing-place on the Mourne shore, in the
county of Down, must have felt their attention attracted
to the wild grandeur of the scenery, which presents itself to the eye a little way beyond the southern extremity of the village. To the right, rise the mountains of
Mourne, at the foot of which lie an immense number of
large blocks of granite, thrown together in such confusion, and in such quantities, that a fanciful person might
suppose they had been collected for the purpose of building another link to the chain of mountains, but which

nature (being too busy with the more animated portion
of her works,) had never found time to begin to. Here,
far away from the haunts of man, and surrounded by
wildness and desolation, " the bitch-fox hides her helpless brood," rears them in safety, and steals out, in the
darkness of night, to plunder the neighbouring hen-roosts
or rabbit-warrens; while, higher up, among the cliffs of
the mountains, amid the silence and solitude of nature,
which is never broken, save by the bark of her neighbour
the fox, or by her own wild scream, the eagle builds her
eyrie, reigns undisturbed, and produces her royal birds

securely; while, to the left of the road, stretches out the broad expanse of St. George's Channel, where, as far as the eye can reach, until the sight is bounded by the horizon, extends one livid plain of dark blue waters, the monotonous appearance of which is only broken by the reflection of the sun upon the sails of some distant vessel, as she glides across the bay: or by the white top of some distant billow, as it curls into foam, and sparkles in the light, when descending from its momentary elevation to join its kindred waters. Such is the scene which presents itself, after leaving Newcastle, now a thriving village, but which not very long since, with the exception of the castle which gives name to it, consisted of a few fishermen's huts, scattered at random along the beach, wherever the convenience or fancy of the owner suggested. At this place, the shore, which has hitherto been a beautiful level sandy beach, several miles in length, rises perpendicularly up to the height of more than a hundred feet, in the shape of a rocky precipice, in whose rugged fall are several natural caves or excavations, one of which is said by the fishermen to run far under the mountains, and to stop directly under the highest point of Slieve Donard, and is therefore called "Donard's cave;" but the one which we have more immediately to do with, and which is represented in the subjoined engraving, is a perpendicular gap, about thirty feet wide, and running from thirty to forty feet deep into the fall of the rock, thereby forming a chasm, into the basin of which the tide beats with a roar sufficient to deaden the sense of hearing in any person who is hardy enough to approach the brink of the precipice, a task requiring both a stout heart and a steady head. It is said to have derived its name of Armer's hole from the following story of guilt and terror, which we are informed by our correspondent appeared some few years since in "The Northern Whig," but which we feel assured will prove no less acceptable to our readers, as connected with an interesting and romantic portion of our island, to which we have had occasion more than once before to refer with feelings of gratification and pleasure.

ARMER'S HOLE.

EDWARD ARMER, THE PARRICIDE.

More than a century ago, the father of Edward Armer resided in the Barony of Mourne, and was an extensive grazier; held a good farm, with a long lease, and a cheap rent, and was considered wealthy. His wife had been long dead, and his only child Edward was to be the inheritor of all his father's possessions. But Edward's conduct had often cost his father many a sleepless night, and many a fruitless sigh; for though he had been for some years arrived at man's estate, yet his conduct was wild, and extravagant, and self-willed, and exhibited none of the steadiness of purpose, or integrity of principle, which was to be expected from his years: he was the strongest man, and the most expert gambler in the whole country; and few ever encountered him in either ways, who did not leave him convinced of his superiority. These practices, therefore, raised in the heart of his father a kind of prophetic fear, that the course of life he was pursuing would yet bring *his* grey hairs in sorrow to the grave. He had been often urged, by his father, to quit his wild way of life, and to get married; but he either returned no answer, or else a sullen and decided negative to all his entreaties. Yet he was not insensible to the charms of beauty; and though he gave his father no satisfaction on the subject, he had "woo'd and won" the heart of one of the fairest maids in a county famous for the beauty of its women. When the County Down is mentioned for this quality, it is not done unwarrantedly, or without due consideration; it is done on the strength, not only of personal experience, but on the faith of an old distich, which puts

> " The County Fermanagh for men and horses,
> And the County Down for bonny lasses,"

in competition with any other counties in Ireland, in their respective excellencies. Mary O'Hagan, the daughter of a farmer, was the maid whose beauty had, like the eyes of the rattle-snake, fascinated and tamed down the wild and roving heart of Edward Armer. He had first seen her at a fair, where he had gone to buy cattle, and, though it was at a considerable distance from his own neighbourhood, he found no difficulty in introducing himself, as, in the sphere of life in which he moved, the cold and formal etiquette of polished society was unknown. From that period he had visited her regularly and often, and soon gained the love of her young and susceptible heart; for though she had heard of his character, yet his handsome manly form had made such an impression on her mind, as to cover all its deformities. He was the idol of her heart; she felt her fate bound indissolubly with his; and as they roved together along the banks of the wild and romantic Bann, her lips echoed the sentiments of her soul—

"I but know that I love thee, *whatever* thou art."

Matters were in this state, when the circumstance which forms the principal feature of this story took place. Edward had had a long run of ill luck, and, by this means, had become very considerably in debt to his gaming companions; he had, therefore, nothing for it, but, as usual, to apply to his father, who had hitherto, in the hope of being able to *wean* him from his vices, never refused him;—but "hope deferred maketh the heart sick;" and his father, wearied with long expectation, not only lectured him severely on the mode of life he was pursuing, but also absolutely refused to supply his extravagance any longer. Stung to the quick by this refusal, and by the attempt to control him, his bad passions rose in his soul, triumphed over his reason and his duty, and—he formed the horrid resolution to take away his father's life, that he might thereby at once enjoy the property, in the way of which he stood! In pursuance of this impious plan, he went, a few evenings after, to his father, and, with well-dissembled penitence, told him that he had been considering what he had said to him; that he acknowledged the justice of it; that he was determined to amend his life; and, as the first step towards the accomplishment of this end, had come to get his consent to be married. He then told him of his acquaintance with Mary, and that he had no doubt of getting her parents' consent to their union, and that, if he pleased, they would set out the next day for that purpose to her father's house; and at the same time he requested him not to mention it to any one, as he feared the ridicule of his former companions, and that, to lull suspicion, his father should set off first, and that he himself would follow in some time after. The old man, overjoyed to find such a change, consented at once, and immediately went about making preparations for that purpose. Accordingly, each, the next day, mounted on horseback, departed at different hours from that home, where both were doomed never to return. Edward rode quick, and soon overtook his victim, whom he purposely delayed on the road, until it began to draw towards the close of an October evening, that he might thereby have both time and place for the tragedy he was about to act. Into the hole or gap already described, did the unfortunate Armer resolve on consigning the parent to whom he owed such a debt of gratitude and love. It has been stated, that he purposely delayed upon the road, contriving that it should be nightfall ere they reached the place which has been attempted to be described; he also found means, as they neared the fatal spot, to raise his father's anger, so that he gave him some abusive language, upon which, stretching across the horse, he seized the old man by the collar, and, throwing himself off, pulled him to the ground also, and began dragging him towards the mouth of the hole, which lies but a few paces from the road. At first, the old man did not perceive his intentions; but as he approached the precipice, the dreadful conviction flashed upon him—the horrid death that awaited him stared him in the face. Despair seized upon him; and, clasping the villain round the knees, he implored him, by the sacred name of God, by all the ties which he had broken, and by his own hopes of forgiveness from the Father of All, to spare a hoary head, which must soon, in the natural course of events, descend to the grave, without the assistance of violence. But no—the ruffian was inexorable; his flinty heart was proof against the tender appeal for mercy, although urged by the lips of a parent pleading for his own life; and he continued dragging him towards the mouth of the pit, when the old man, seeing there was no hope from his pity, grew desperate, seized him by the limbs, and threw him down. Dreadful was then the struggle, despair giving the old man strength, the young one assisted by his evil passions—the ground beneath them giving evidence of the struggle which was going on, being trampled and torn, and stained with the mingled blood of father and son, till at length the old man's strength failing, the other, by a sudden movement, got uppermost, and seizing him by the throat, beat his head several times violently against the ground, until he rendered him almost senseless; he then trailed him forward to the brink, and endeavoured to push him over, but found himself fastened to him by a grip, the strength and tenacity of which can only be estimated, when it is reflected that it was all that held its possessor to life. After several vain attempts on the part of Edward to loosen the hold, he tore the piece madly away, and hurled his victim from the rock, followed with his eyes, until, in his descent, he saw him strike against the side of the precipice, then turned shuddering away: a wild shriek followed his striking the rock—a heavy splash—and then all was still. For a few minutes, a faint stupor came over the murderer; a chilly sweat broke out on him; he closed his eyes convulsively and covered them with his hand, as if to shut out the sight of his guilt; but the "mind's eye" was still open, and conscience, "the worm which dieth not," gnawed him again into recollection of the deed he had done. When he awoke from his dream of forgetfulness, the scene which presented itself was not much calculated to soothe him. He was still sitting on the brink of the precipice: the night was beginning to deepen around him, and gave a murkier hue to the already sombre mountains; dark and ominous looking clouds scudded, fugitive like, along their tops; the wind whistled, with a melancholy sound, through the long dry grass and heather by his side, and seemed to be wailing for the deed that had been done; the sea-bird, startled from its nest in the rocks by the old man's fall, flew hurriedly around, adding, by its wild cry, to the terror of the scene. Large drops of rain began to fall at intervals, and one of which, falling on his face, awakened him from the lethargy into which he had fallen; he looked around him, and listened;—nothing was to be heard but the heavy roar of the sea, as it dashed against the rocks beneath: yet once he thought he heard a sound come out of the abyss by his side;—the bare idea was enough to freeze his blood; to wait for certainty on the subject was too much for him; so, darting forward, he laid hold of the horses, and throwing himself on one of them, galloped away wherever they chose to carry him. Such is the story connected with "Armer's hole," the name which this place has ever since borne.

The sounds which he heard from beneath, and which his fears attributed to something supernatural, arose from some fishermen who were waiting in their boat, under shelter of the rocks, for the signal to land goods from a smuggling vessel in the bay, and who left their hiding-place on hearing the shriek, and which being followed by the galloping of horses, convinced them that there had been some foul work a doing. They, therefore, immediately set about searching, and after some time, succeeded, with a boat-hook, in bringing up the body, which they had immediately conveyed on shore, and a party despatched in pursuit of the murderer. He was traced, in the course of the next day, to a public-house in a distant part of the country, where he was found coolly enjoying himself, and was in the act of selling the horse from which he had torn his unfortunate parent. Upon seeing his pursuers, he attempted to escape by leaping through a window, but was prevented ; and, after very considerable resistance, during which, those who attempted his capture suffered severely, he was secured, and conveyed to Down jail. When there, he denied all knowledge of the deed, and became so outrageous, that it was found necessary to iron him ; but these he treated as if they had been ropes of straw, twisting them in pieces the moment they were put on ; and such was his strength, that the strongest irons in the jail were found insufficient to secure him. The jailor was, therefore, under the necessity of having manacles of treble strength, and particular formation, forged especially for his use : these, which are still preserved, and which it is seldom found necessary to put in requisition, are shown to the stranger who visits Down jail, as " Armer's bolts ;" with these, therefore, he was secured until his trial, which came on shortly after ; and, though there was no direct evidence against him, yet the circumstances were so strong that he was found guilty, and ordered for execution.

The sequel of the tale is soon told. Poor Mary, whose very existence was entwined with his, never smiled again : the story of his guilt struck with the effect of lightning upon her heart, and blighted the tender plant for ever. She visited him in the prison ; and he, in whom every other tender emotion seemed dead, or rather never to have had existence ; he, to whose stony heart the tender voice of pity spoke in vain ; he, steeped as he was in infamy and guilt, whom even the grey hairs of a parent could not move to mercy—yet even he was not proof against the force of powerful love. The poor girl's altered appearance, and dejected look, struck him the moment she entered his cell ; and hiding his face with his hands, tears, scalding tears, the first he had shed since childhood, fell in torrents o'er his haggard cheeks, at beholding the ruin he had wrought upon one so lovely, and the only being for whom he had ever felt the slightest affection. Their interview was long and tender ; and when the rules of the jail would admit of no longer delay, she left him ; but she never returned to bless, with her presence, that home she had hitherto made so happy ; her reason sunk under the weight of misery which oppressed it ; and she wandered through the country, for a few months, a broken-hearted maniac, until death relieved her from a miserable existence. In a short time after his condemnation, the unhappy parricide paid the debt due to the offended laws of his country and of humanity, sinking early into an ignominious grave, without the tribute of a single sigh, and leaving, like Byron's Corsair,

'A name o other times,
Linked with one virtue and a thousand crimes.''

INTERESTING AND IMPORTANT TO PERSONS INTENDING TO EMIGRATE TO BRITISH AMERICA.

To the kindness of an unknown correspondent at the other side the Atlantic, we are indebted for a copy of the *Montreal Herald*, of a very recent date, containing some excellent observations on the subject of Emigration. The subjoined judicious statement, relative to the comparative value of labour in Lower and Upper Canada, we would recommend to the notice of those who may have it in contemplation to try their fortune in what may, to many persons leaving the British Islands, be literally termed a " New World."

We have likewise, by the kindness of a friend, been put in possession of several numbers of the Montreal *Weekly Advertiser*, containing several articles on the same subject, of the information in which we purpose availing ourselves on some future occasion. It is gratifying to us to find, that the observations which we have offered, from time to time, in the Penny Journal, on the important subject of Emigration, have so far attracted the attention of our Transatlantic friends, as to induce them to send us Journals, containing articles on a similar subject.

" A paper contest has been for some time carrying on between the *Daily Advertiser* and the *Quebec Gazette*, regarding the rate of wages in Lower Canada. A writer under the signature of A. B. C. in the *Quebec Gazette*, asserts, that the condition of labourers in Great Britain and Ireland is fully equal, if not superior, to what it is in Lower Canada ; this has been denied by the *Quebec Mercury* and *Daily Advertiser*, and we are of opinion that they have the best side of the question. It is, however, beyond doubt, that interested individuals represent this country in by far too favourable terms—so much so, that a majority of the emigrants who arrive on our shores are disappointed, and would return to the land of their birth if they had the means. It cannot be too strongly impressed on the minds of intending emigrants, that this is not a *Canaan*—that it is not a land flowing with milk and honey —that, emphatically, it is on the sweat of his brow man must depend for a livelihood ; but, at the same time, he has the *certain* prospect, *if he is industrious and sober*, but not otherwise, of raising himself in society, and leaving to his children a property they can call their own. It is in this particular, more than in any other, that the peculiar advantage of this colony, over the mother country, exists, and no man who arrives in this country, with moderate ideas and a determination to " press forward to the mark" of independence, need be afraid of the result.—The following are the official tables of the average rates of labour in Upper and Lower Canada in 1831 and 1832, to which there has been no alteration since ; indeed, throughout the country generally, labour is in greater demand than at those periods. From these tables it will be perceived, that wages are higher than at home ; but, as a counterbalance, comforts are fewer, and clothing much dearer.

The average rate of labour in Lower Canada, in 1831 and 1832, taken from the answers to the official circular forwarded by the Civil Secretary, to about 200 persons in various parts of the province, show :—

1st. Agricultural labourers capable of managing a farm, average, throughout the year, 2s. 6d. per day, or from £30 to £50 per annum, without board or lodging.

2d. Common labourers, 2s. 2½d. per day, average, throughout the year, without food or lodging.

3d. Mechanics of peculiar qualifications, 8s. a day.

4th and 5th. 2d and 3d rate do., from 3s. 9d. to 5s. 6d. scarce.

6th and 7th. Carpenters, 4s. to 5s. average, scarce.

8th. Working Blacksmiths, 5s. 6d. average, scarce.

PUBLIC WORKS.

Rates of wages paid for labour, at public works in Lower Canada in 1831 and 1832 :—

For labour at Cape Diamond, under the Royal Engineer Department, 2s. to 2s. 6d. the year round.

At the Chambly Canal and other works, 2s. 6d., 2s. 9d. and 3s., without food.

IN THE TIMBER TRADE.

At the Coves about Quebec, and on board ships for about six months ; labourers on shore, 3s. to 4s. without food ; on board ship, 3s. 6d. to 4s. 6d. with food, and a large allowance of rum.

Broad-axe men, 4s. to 7s. 6d. per day.

Narrow-axe men, 4s. to 5s.   do.

Boom-men, 4s. to 5s.   do.

Sawyers, 5s. to 6s.   do.

Rate of porterage or labour at the wharves and warehouses, by the job or piece, generally from 6d. to 7½d. or 8d. per hour, or from 2s. 6d. to 4s. a day in summer.

UPPER CANADA.

From official returns in 1831 and 1832.

Agricultural labour, average throughout the province, 2s. 11d., 3s. 2d. per day, or lowest rate, 2s., highest, 4s., without food. Wages per month, and found, by the year, lowest 9 dollars, highest 14 dollars.

Blacksmiths and Millwrights, 5s. to 8s. per day.

Masons, 4s. to 7s. 6d.

Carpenters, 3s. 6d. to 7s. 6d.

Female servants, 15s. to 30s. per month, and found.

" A few days ago we transferred to our columns, from the *Settler*, an article on the superior advantages, in a commercial and agricultural point of view, of Lower over Upper Canada—advantages which have been long overlooked, not so much from their not being known as from the impossibility of possessing them. Now, however, that the British American Land Company has commenced operations, the fine section of the Eastern Townships will be a manifest object for intending settlers, and will hasten the downfall of that " baneful domination"—the Clique—which has so long been an incubus on the energies and resources of this otherwise happy country. Yesterday's *Settler* contains a continuation of the article we formerly copied ; and as it is written in a clear and comprehensive style, it deserves universal circulation.

In resuming the thread of our remarks on the comparative advantages of the two Canadas, we beg to congratulate the Eastern Townships on the establishment of a temperate and constitutional journal at Sherbrooke, which, we trust, will labour steadily in the useful and honourable task of drawing public attention to a country so unaccountably neglected in spite of its fertility and its beauty. The *Stanstead Colonist* and the *St. Francis Courier*, which, we believe, have both died very natural deaths, were filled with revolutionary politics, to the almost entire exclusion of local news, and the utter neglect of local interests, and, but for the dates, might have been supposed to be created at Berthier or Rawdon, at Hobart Town or Swan River. How differently are the journals of Upper Canada conducted. From Cornwall to London a choir editorial—made up, in a good measure, of pretty bad singers—chants one universal hymn of patriotic vanity. " Home, sweet home, there is no place like home" is the weekly theme of some thirty or forty wits and sages.

Not a cottage rears its head unsung ; every tree is made to rival the sacred oaks of Dodona in speaking of its own lofty praises ; there is not a river, not a lake, that has not had more ink than it could contain, expended on its many and matchless virtues ; the Rideau Canal, if it has any feelings of modesty, must soon blush itself into beautiful claret or fine old port, and thus secure a striking superiority over the St. Lawrence, in the eyes and palates of sensible travellers.

But although many journals of the Upper Province do frequently overstep the bounds of modesty and truth, yet a certain degree of partiality is not only excusable but praiseworthy ; and total silence as to local advantages, though not absolutely ridiculous, is far more pernicious to the country than extravagant praise. The *Farmer's Advocate*, however, may say much in praise of the Eastern Townships, without verging either on flattery or on folly. Descend we now from this poetical digression to sober matters of fact.

In drawing a comparison between the two provinces for the practical guidance of the agricultural emigrant, we may consider the eastern townships as constituting the whole of Lower Canada, for many circumstances, moral as well as physical, must recommend them to intelligent settlers in preference to the French seigniories or the unproductive townships of the north. We proceed then to show, that, in a pecuniary point of view, the eastern townships are more favourably situated than almost any portion of Upper Canada. The farmer gets more for what he has to sell, and pays less for what he must buy in the townships than in Upper Canada—a double advantage which must go far to overbalance the real or supposed inferiority of soil. As most of the surplus of both districts finds its way to Montreal or Quebec, it is manifest that the Upper Canadians, who have not only to pay the more expensive conveyance but to lose the profit of several intermediate dealers, come into a very disadvantageous and unprofitable competition with the Eastern Townships. But, in truth, the prices in the townships are often so high as to prevent the necessity of bringing produce to Montreal, and we can state positively that in one village

in Missiskoui wheat averaged last year about a dollar a bushel, and that in another village of the same county salted pork brings at present sevenpence halfpenny a pound, or fourteen dollars a cwt. Our personal knowledge is limited to these two villages ; but we have no reason to believe that the cases quoted are extreme ones. Can such prices be got in any part of Upper Canada?

It may, however, be doubted whether produce can be brought to Montreal more cheaply from the townships than from the head of Lake Ontario, on the very plausible ground, that water-carriage, more particularly if accomplished by steam, is cheaper than the labour of men and horses, and the wear and tear of vehicles on a bad road. To this it may be answered that neither is freight by steam cheap, nor do the townships send their surplus produce to market over a bad road. Freight by steam has been almost always high in this country, sometimes from the want of competition, and sometimes from the coalition of tried competitors. The freight of a quarter of wheat from Niagara to Quebec is fully four times as much as that of the same quantity for about the same distance from Aberdeen to London, and we know one instance, in which a vessel, that was unable to deliver goods in Montreal according to contract in London by reason of the lateness of the season, paid more than the whole of its freight for the transporting of the goods by steam from Quebec to Montreal. On the other hand the road from the townships is one of the best and most economical in the world. At the proper season it is beautifully macadamized with snow —not the whitey-black, foggy, slushy substance dignified with the name of snow in England and parts of Upper Canada, but with real snow, white as innocence or superfine flower, hard as iron and dry as fire. Every path, if properly treated, is as smooth and level as a railroad, and every piece of water, stagnant or running, obligingly joins its opposite banks with a peculiar kind of ice-cream. The whole country is a road. One may ride a steeple-chase without a scratch, or a tumble, or a ducking.

The economy of transporting produce by such a road is more considerable from the circumstance that in the winter the labour of men and horses can hardly be turned to account in any other way. Their absence from home is less felt, than it must necessarily be in a milder climate even in winter.

" Although the aggregate number of persons who left the shores of Great Britain, and landed upon those of Canada, was greater in the year 1832 than in this, or in any preceding year, yet a great proportion of those emigrants were avowedly destined for the United States, and these, before they parted from their fellow passengers, after landing upon our wharves, generally succeed in persuading a number of those who had started from home without any fixed plan or prospect, to accompany them to their point of destination. Canada was thus, in many instances, the mere stepping-stone to an ulterior object ; and we believe we are quite correct in stating, that however great may have been the former emigration from the British European dominions, it is in 1834 that immigration, with a fixed purpose of remaining in the Canadas, has commenced upon an extended scale. The rising institutions, in this colony, for the purpose of fixing a point of attraction, and of smoothing the way of the immigrant and his family to that point, were calculated to produce the effect, already so perceptible. In the Upper Province the number of actual settlers has, this year, far exceeded that of former years ; and it may fairly be anticipated, that the lands which the Government has so judiciously transferred to the Land Company, in Lower Canada, will next year attract a body of actual settlers, which in point both of numbers and respectability, will far exceed any thing that this Province ever yet saw, or even contemplated.

" Number of Emigrants arrived at Quebec, to noon

7th July this year 20,478

Same period last year 11,912

Difference in favour of 1834........................ 8,566."

Printed by P. D. Hardy, 3, Cecilia-street.

THE

DUBLIN PENNY JOURNAL

CONDUCTED BY P. DIXON HARDY, M.R.I.A.

| VOL. III. | SEPTEMBER 27, 1834. | No. 117. |

THE TURKEY—Meleagris gallopavo.—*Linnæus.*

ORNITHOLOGY.

In some former numbers of our Journal we took occasion to notice the preceding volumes of the work, from which we copy the above engraving.* The present, "Vol. III—Ornithology," is devoted to the "Natural History of the Gallinaceous Birds"—an order which includes all the game birds and all our domestic poultry, to which is prefixed an interesting memoir of the father of natural science, Aristotle, by the Rev. Andrew Crichton.

Whether regarded in a scientific, a moral, or a commercial point of view, Ornithology is a department of natural history which deserves particular attention; and from the very pleasing manner in which it is brought forward in such works as the one before us, there can be no question it will become a greater favourite with students than it has heretofore been. Formerly the science was so involved in technicalities, and in general treated of in so dry and uninteresting a way, that but few were induced to take it up for the purpose of recreation or pleasure. Such is not the case at present. To scientific information is added such interesting details relative to the instincts and habits of the animals or birds of which engravings are given, as must render the study pleasing to all tastes and disposi-

tions. With the natural history of the Turkey our young readers, we have no doubt, will be much amused and gratified; and as they occasionally observe them strutting through the poultry yard, will bring to mind from whence they were originally brought, and will thus have an instance furnished, that to the exertions of travellers and navigators we are indebted not only for a great proportion of the luxuries, but even what may now be termed the necessaries of life.

"Although the turkey is one of the most important of the feathered race in the luxury and domestic economy of man, the exact period of its introduction into Europe and to Great Britain has been lost sight of, and by the older naturalists attempting to recognise in it some of the poultry of the ancients, it was conjectured to have come originally from India and Africa, and the knowledge of its native country was, even for a considerable time, placed in uncertainty.

"The wild turkey should have been the emblem of North America, and so thought Benjamin Franklin. The turkey is the national bird, truly indigenous, and not found beyond the limits of that continent: he is the herald of the morning, and around the log-house of the squatter, must convey associations similar to those produced by the crowing of the cock around the cottage of the European farmer. 'I was awakened,' says Bartram, 'in the morning early, by the cheering converse of the wild turkey cocks saluting each other from the sun-brightened tops of the lofty cypress and magnolia. They begin at early dawn, and continue till sunrise. The high forests ring with the noise of these social sentinels, the

* The Naturalist's Library, by Sir William Jardine, Bart., F. R. S. E., F. L. S., &c. &c. Edinburgh: W. H. Lizars, and Stirling and Kenney; Longman, Rees, Orme, Browne, Green, and Longman, London; and W. Curry, jun. and Co., Dublin.

watchword being caught and repeated, from one to another, for hundreds of miles around, insomuch that the whole country is, for an hour or more, in an universal shout; or, in the poetry of Southey,

—————— on the top
Of yon magnolia, the loud turkey's voice
Is heralding the dawn; from tree to tree
Extends the wakening watch-notes, far and wide,
Till the whole woodlands echo with the cry.'

"There can be little doubt that we are indebted to the Spaniards for the introduction of the turkey to Europe, and that it would be brought from Mexico upon the discovery of the New World. From Spain a bird of such value, and so easily domesticated, would easily find its way to Britain; and although we cannot trace its introduction, we may confidently assert that it was not before 1525, and most probably between that and the year 1530.

"A person who has seen the turkey only in the poultry-yards of this country, can have no idea of the splendour of a fine cock in his full plumage, previous to the breeding season. His plumage gleams with the brightest golden-bronze, tinged, according to the position, with blue, violet, and green, and beautifully broken by the deep black bands which terminate each feather, and which also have a metallic lustre. The length of the male figured by Mr. Audubon was four feet and an inch; the expanse of the wings five feet eight inches. This is beyond the average size and the bird was a remarkably fine specimen.— The extraordinary accounts of the great weight and size of the wild turkey have been only the licensed tales of travellers, heightened by the idea, that a New World must produce every thing on a scale proportioned to its extent. Mr. Audubon says, that from 15lb. to 18lb. may be a fair estimate of their average weight; and he only once saw one in the Louisville market which weighed 36lb.: the tuft of hair on the breast of this bird measured upwards of a foot. Bonaparte confirms this account, but says that birds of 30lb. are not rare, and had ascertained the existence of some which weighed 40lb. The male turkey may be said to be adult at the third year, though it increases in both beauty and weight for some seasons afterwards. Upon the approach of the first winter, the bunch of hair upon the breast begins to appear: at the commencement of the second, it is from three to four inches in length, and the caruncles about the head and neck have become large, and have assumed their deep and livid hue: by the third winter, all these marks of maturity have nearly reached their greatest development.

"We shall now introduce the account of their manners from the Prince of Musignano's continuation.

"'The males, usually termed *gobblers*, associate in parties, numbering from ten to a hundred, and seek their food apart from the females; whilst the latter either move about singly with their young, then nearly two-thirds grown, or, in company with other females and their families, form troops, sometimes consisting of seventy or eighty individuals, all of which are intent on avoiding the old males, who, whenever opportunity offers, attack and destroy the young, by repeated blows on the skull. All parties, however, travel in the same direction, and on foot, unless they are compelled to seek their individual safety by flying from the hunter's dog, or their march is impeded by a large river. When about to cross a river, they select the highest eminences, that their flight may be the more certain; and here they sometimes remain for a day or more, as if for the purpose of consultation, or to be duly prepared for so hazardous a voyage. During this time the males *gobble* obstreperously, and strut with extraordinary importance, as if they would animate their companions, and inspire them with the utmost degree of hardihood; the females and young also assume much of the pompous air of the males, the former spreading their tails, and moving silently around. At length the assembled multitude mount to the tops of the highest trees, whence, at a signal note from a leader, the whole together wing their way to the opposite shore. All the old and fat ones cross without difficulty, even when the river exceeds a mile in width; but the young, meagre, and weak, frequently fall short of the desired landing, and are

forced to swim for their lives; this they do dexterously enough, spreading their tails for a support, closing their wings to the body, stretching the neck forwards, and striking out quickly and forcibly with their legs. If, in thus endeavouring to regain the land, they approach an elevated or inaccessible bank, their exertions are remitted, they resign themselves to the stream for a short time, in order to gain strength, and then, with one violent effort escape from the water. But in this attempt all are not successful; some of the weaker, as they cannot rise sufficiently high in the air to clear the bank, fall again and again into the water, and thus miserably perish. Immediately after these birds have succeeded in crossing a river, they for some time ramble about without any apparent unanimity of purpose, and a great many are destroyed by the hunters, although they are then least valuable.

"'When the turkeys have arrived in their land of abundance, they disperse in small flocks, composed of individuals of all sexes and ages intermingled, who devour all the mast as they advance; this occurs about the middle of November. It has been observed, that, after these long journeys, the turkeys become so familiar as to venture on the plantations, and even approach so near the farm-houses as to enter the stables and corn-cribs in search of food; in this way they pass the autumn, and part of the winter. During this season great numbers are killed by the inhabitants, who preserve them in a frozen state, in order to transport them to a distant market.

"'Early in March they begin to pair; and, for a short time previous, the females separate from, and shun their mates, though the latter pertinaciously follow them, uttering their gobbling note. The sexes roost apart, but at no great distance, so that, when the female utters a call, every male within hearing responds, rolling note after note, in the most rapid succession; not as when spreading the tail and strutting near the hen, but in a voice resembling that of the tame turkey, when he hears any unusual or frequently repeated noise. Where the turkeys are numerous, the woods, from one end to the other, sometimes for hundreds of miles, resound with this remarkable voice of their wooing, uttered responsively from their roosting places. This is continued for about an hour; and, on the rising of the sun, they silently descend from their perches, and the males begin to strut, for the purpose of winning the admiration of their mates.

"'If the call be given from the ground, the males in the vicinity fly towards the individual, and, whether they perceive her or not, erect and spread their tails, throw the head backwards, distend the comb and wattles, strut pompously, and rustle their wings and body-feathers, at the same moment ejecting a puff of air from the lungs.— Whilst thus occupied, they occasionally halt to look out for the female, and then resume their strutting and puffing, moving with as much rapidity as the nature of their gait will admit. During this ceremonious approach, the males often encounter each other, and desperate battles ensue, when the conflict is only terminated by the flight or death of the vanquished.'

"The conqueror now selects the objects of his gallantry, and one or more females thus associated follow their favourite, and roost in his immediate neighbourhood, if not upon the same tree, until they begin to lay, when they change their mode of life, in order to save their eggs, which the male uniformly breaks, if in his power. After the love season, the sexes again separate, the males cease entirely to gobble, and 'retire and conceal themselves by prostrate trees, in secluded parts of the forest, or in the almost impenetrable privacy of a cane-brake. Rather than leave their hiding-places, they suffer themselves to be approached within a short distance, when they seek safety in their speed of foot; at this season, however, they are of no value to the hunter, being meagre and covered with ticks. By thus retiring, using very little exercise, and feeding on peculiar grasses, they recover their flesh and strength, when they again congregate, and recommence their rambles.

"'About the middle of April, when the weather is dry, the female selects a proper place in which to deposit her eggs, secured from the encroachment of water, and, as far as possible, concealed from the watchful eye of the crow:

this crafty bird espies the hen going to her nest, and having discovered the precious deposit, waits for the absence of the parent, and removes every one of the eggs from the spot, that he may devour them at leisure. The nest is placed on the ground, either on a dry ridge, in the fallen top of a dead leafy tree, under a thicket of sumach or briars, or by the side of a log; it is of a very simple structure, being composed of a few dried leaves. In this receptacle the eggs are deposited, sometimes to the number of twenty, but more usually from nine to fifteen; they are whitish, spotted with reddish brown, like those of the domestic bird. Their manner of building, number of eggs, period of incubation, &c. appear to correspond throughout the Union, as I have received exactly similar accounts from the northern limits of the turkey range, to the most southern regions of Florida, Louisiana, and the western wilds of Missouri.

"'The female always approaches her nest with great caution, varying her course so as rarely to reach it twice by the same route; and, on leaving her charge, she is very careful to cover the whole with dry leaves, with which she conceals it so artfully, as to make it extremely difficult, even for one who has watched her movements, to indicate the exact spot; hence few nests are found, and these are generally discovered by fortuitously starting the female from them, or by the appearance of broken shells, scattered around by some cunning lynx, fox, or crow. When laying or sitting, the turkey hen is not readily driven from her post by the approach of apparent danger; but, if an enemy appears, she crouches as low as possible, and suffers it to pass. A circumstance related by Mr. Audubon will show how much intelligence they display on such occasions; having discovered a sitting hen, he remarked that, by assuming a careless air, whistling, or talking to himself, he was permitted to pass within five or six feet of her; but, if he advanced cautiously, she would not suffer him to come within twenty paces, but ran off twenty or thirty yards with her tail expanded, when, assuming a stately gait, she paused on every step, occasionally uttering a chuck. They seldom abandon their nests on account of being discovered by man; but should a snake, or any other animal, suck one of the eggs, the parent leaves them altogether. If the eggs be removed, she again seeks the male, and recommences laying, though otherwise she lays but one nest of eggs during the season. Several turkey hens sometimes associate, perhaps for mutual safety, deposit their eggs in the same nest, and rear their broods together. Mr. Audubon once found three females sitting on forty-two eggs. In such cases the nest is constantly guarded by one of the parties, so that no crow, raven, nor even pole-cat dares approach it.

"'The mother will not forsake her eggs, when near hatching, while life remains; she will suffer an enclosure to be made around and imprison her, rather than abandon her charge. Mr. Audubon witnessed the hatching of a brood, while thus endeavouring to secure the young and mother. 'I have lain flat,' says he, 'within a very few feet, and seen her gently rise from the eggs, look anxiously towards them, chuck with a sound peculiar to the mother on such an occasion, remove carefully each half empty shell, and with her bill caress and dry the younglings, that already stand tottering and attempting to force their way out of the nest.'

"'When the process of incubation is ended, and the mother is about to retire from the nest with her young brood, she shakes herself violently, picks and adjusts the feathers about the belly, and assumes a different aspect; her eyes are alternately inclined obliquely upwards and sideways; she stretches forth her neck in every direction, to discover birds of prey or other enemies; her wings are partially spread, and she softly clucks to keep her tender offspring close to her side. They proceed slowly, and, as the hatching generally occurs in the afternoon, they sometimes return to pass the night in the nest. While very young, the mother leads them to elevated dry places, as if aware that humidity, during the first few days of their life, would be very dangerous to them, they having then no other protection than a delicate, soft, hairy down. In very rainy seasons wild turkeys are scarce, because, when completely wetted, the young rarely survive.

"'At the expiration of about two weeks, the young leave the ground on which they had previously reposed at night under the female, and follow her to some low, large branch of a tree, where they nestle under the broadly curved wings of their vigilant and fostering parent. The time then approaches in which they seek the open ground or prairie land during the day, in search of strawberries, and subsequently of dewberries, blackberries, and grasshoppers; thus securing a plentiful food, and enjoying the influence of the genial sun. They frequently dust themselves in shallow cavities of the soil, or on ant-hills, in order to clean off the loose skin of their growing feathers, and rid themselves of ticks and other vermin.

"'The young turkeys now grow rapidly, and in the month of August, when several broods flock together, and are led by their mothers to the forest, they are stout and quite able to secure themselves from the unexpected attacks of wolves, foxes, lynxes, and even cougars, by rising quickly from the ground, aided by their strong legs, and reaching with ease the upper limbs of the tallest tree.— Amongst the numerous enemies of the wild turkey, the most dreaded are the large diurnal and nocturnal birds of prey, and the lynx (*Felis rufa,*) who sucks their eggs, and is extremely expert at seizing both parent and young; he follows them for some distance, in order to ascertain their course, and then, making a rapid circular movement, places himself in ambush before them, and waits until, by a single bound, he can fasten on his victim.

"'The following circumstance is related by Bartram: 'Having seen a flock of turkeys at some distance, I approached them with great caution, when, singling out a large cock, and being just on the point of firing, I observed that several young cocks were affrighted, and in their language warned the rest to be on their guard against an enemy, who I plainly perceived was industriously making his subtle approaches towards them, behind the fallen trunk of a tree, about twenty yards from me. This cunning fellow-hunter was a large fat wild cat or lynx; he saw me, and at times seemed to watch my motions, as if determined to seize the delicious prey before me; upon which I changed my object, and levelled my piece at him. At that instant my companion, at a distance, also discharged his piece, the report of which alarmed the flock of turkeys, and my fellow-hunter, the cat, sprang over the log, and trotted off.'

"'These birds are guardians of each other, and the first who sees a hawk or eagle, gives a note of alarm, on which all within hearing lie close to the ground. As they usually roost in flocks, perched on the naked branches of trees, they are easily discovered by the large owls, and, when attacked by these prowling birds, often escape by a somewhat remarkable manœuvre. The owl sails around the spot to select his prey; but, notwithstanding the almost inaudible action of his pinions, the quick ear of one of the slumberers perceives the danger, which is immediately announced to the whole party by a *chuck*; thus alarmed, they rise on their legs, and watch the motions of the owl, who, darting like an arrow, would inevitably secure the individual at which he aimed, did not the latter suddenly drop his head, squat, and spread his tail over his back; the owl then glances over without inflicting any injury, at the very instant that the turkey suffers himself to fall headlong towards the earth, where he is secure from his dreaded enemy.

"'On hearing the slightest noise, wild turkeys conceal themselves in the grass, or among shrubs, and thus frequently escape the hunter, or the sharp-sighted birds of prey. The sportsman is unable to find them during the day, unless he has a dog trained for the purpose; it is necessary to shoot them at a very short distance, since, when only wounded, they quickly disappear, and, accelerating their motion by a sort of half flight, run with so much speed, that the swiftest hunter cannot overtake them. The traveller, driving rapidly down the declivity of one of the Alleghanies, may sometimes see several of them before him, that evince no urgent desire to get out of the road; but on alighting, in hopes of shooting them, he soon finds that all pursuit is in vain.

"'In the spring, when the males are much emaciated by their attendance on the females, it may sometimes happen that in cleared countries, they can be overtaken by a swift cur-dog, when they will squat, and suffer themselves to be caught by the dog or hunter, who follows on horseback. But from the knowledge we have gained of this bird, we do not hesitate to affirm, that the manner of running down turkeys, like hares or foxes, so much talked of, is a mere fable, as such a sport would be attended with very trifling success. A turkey hound will sometimes lead his master several miles, before he can a second time *flush* the same individual from his concealment; and even on a fleet horse, after following one for hours, it is often found impossible to *put it up*. During a fall of melting snow, turkeys will travel extraordinary distances, and are often pursued in vain by any description of hunters; they have then a long straddling manner of running, very easy to themselves, but which few animals can equal. This disposition for running, during rains or humid weather, is common to all gallinaceous birds.

" ' The males are frequently decoyed within gun-shot, in the breeding season, by forcibly drawing the air through one of the wing bones, producing a sound very similar to the voice of the female; but the performer on this simple instrument must commit no error, for turkeys are quick of hearing, and, when frequently alarmed, are wary and cunning. Some of these will answer to the call without advancing a step, and thus defeat the speculations of the hunter, who must avoid making any movement, inasmuch as a single glance of a turkey may defeat his hopes of decoying them. By imitating the cry of the barred owl (*Strix nebulosa*), the hunter discovers many on their roosts, as they will reply by a gobble to every repetition of this sound, and can thus be approached with certainty about daylight, and easily killed.

" ' Wild turkeys are very tenacious of their feeding grounds, as well as of the trees on which they have once roosted. Flocks have been known to resort to one spot for a succession of years, and to return after a distant migration in search of food. Their roosting place is mostly on a point of land, jutting into a river, where there are large trees. When they have collected at the signal of a repeated gobbling, they silently proceed towards their nocturnal abodes, and perch near each other: from the number sometimes congregated in one place, it would seem to be the common rendezvous of the whole neighbourhood. But no position, however secluded or difficult of access, can secure them from the attacks of the artful and vigilant hunter, who, when they are all quietly perched for the night, takes a stand previously chosen by daylight, and, when the rising moon enables him to take sure aim, shoots them down at leisure, and by carefully singling out those on the lower branches first, he may secure nearly the whole flock, neither the presence of the hunter, nor the report of his gun, intimidating the turkeys, although the appearance of a single owl would be sufficient to alarm the whole troop: the dropping of their companions from their sides excites nothing but a buzzing noise, which seems more expressive of surprise than fright. This fancied security or heedlessness of danger, while at roost, is characteristic of all the gallinaceous birds of North America.

" ' The more common mode of taking turkeys is by means of *pens*, constructed with logs, covered in at top, and with a passage in the earth under one side of it, just large enough to admit an individual when stooping. The ground chosen for this purpose is generally sloping, and the passage is cut on the lower side, widening outwards. These preparations being completed, Indian corn is strewed for some distance around the pen, to entice the flock, which, picking up the grain, is gradually led towards the passage, and thence into the enclosure, where a sufficient quantity of corn is spread to occupy the leader until the greater part of the turkeys have entered. When they raise their heads and discover that they are prisoners, all their exertions to escape are directed upwards and against the sides of the pen, not having sagacity enough to stoop sufficiently low to pass out by the way they entered, and thus they become an easy prey, not only to the experienced hunter, but even to the boys on the frontier settlements.

" ' The Indians make much use of their tails as fans;

the women weave their feathers with much art on a loose web made of the rind of the birch-tree, arranging them so as to keep the down on the inside, and exhibit the brilliant surface to the eye. A specimen of this cloth is in the Philadelphia Museum; it was found enveloping the body of an Indian female, in the great Saltpetre cave of Kentucky.'

" The turkey is generally esteemed a stupid bird, and, in its tame state, perhaps with truth. Its vigilance and cunning in its native forests, however, often baffle the experience of well trained hunters; and the attention and cunning of the female are noted by Mr. Audubon. The attention of the male to the young is also, in some cases, extraordinary. We have known him regularly attend and protect the female and brood from dogs, or other intruders: and, in two instances, to take the sole charge upon himself, refusing to admit the female to any share of his cares. The same bird frequently drove the hen from her nest, and sat upon the eggs until hatched.

" Mr. Audubon relates a curious anecdote of the turkey, which also illustrates the disposition of the dog.

" ' While at Henderson, on the Ohio, I had, among many other wild birds, a fine male turkey, which had been reared from its earliest youth under my care, it having been caught by me when probably not more than two or three days old. It became so tame, that it would follow any person who called it, and was the favourite of the little village. Yet it would never roost with the tame turkeys, but regularly betook itself, at night, to the roof of the house, where it remained until dawn. When two years old, it began to fly to the woods, where it remained for a considerable part of the day, to return to the enclosure as night approached. One morning I saw it fly off, at a very early hour, to the woods, and took no particular notice of that circumstance. Several days elapsed, but the bird did not return. I was going towards some lakes near Green River to shoot, when, having walked about five miles, I saw a fine large gobbler cross the path before me, moving leisurely along. Turkeys being then in prime condition for the table, I ordered my dog to chace it, and put it up. The animal went off with great rapidity, and as it approached the turkey, I saw, with great surprise, that the latter paid little attention. Juno was on the point of seizing it, when she suddenly stopped, and turned her head towards me. I hastened to them, but you may easily conceive my surprise, when I saw my own favourite bird, and discovered that it had recognised the dog, and would not fly from it, although the sight of a strange dog would have caused it to run off at once.' "

CHOIR OF THE DOMINICAN FRIARY, PORTUMNA;
INTERIOR VIEW.

The flourishing town of Portumna is agreeably situated on the banks of the noble river Shannon, in the barony of Longford, and county of Galway. It has been greatly improved within these few years past, partly by the liberality of its noble owner, the Marquis of Clanricarde, and partly owing to the trade carried on by means of steam navigation. This must have been a place of no small note from a very distant period of time, as being the principal pass whereby the people of North Munster, and they of Connaught, had communication with each other. Portumna, viewed either in a civil or ecclesiastical point of view, will be found to compete with most of our baronial towns, especially in the former; for the members of the illustrious house of Clanricarde took such an active part in the affairs of government, respecting this and the sister kingdom, that to give but a hasty sketch of these momentous transactions, would swell this notice far beyond its proper limits.

Notwithstanding the silence of history as to Portumna's being an ecclesiastical station, previous to the arrival of the English, it is probable that some religious order had settled in a place where there was a town for many centuries before Ireland became subject to the control of the sister kingdom. Had it not been situated on a noted pass of the Shannon, I should not hesitate to say it was an ecclesiastical station, long before the landing of the English; for most of our ancient towns sprung up around religious establishments. I make the above remark because some writers seem as if the first religious house erected at Portumna was in the fifteenth century, for Dominican friars: whereas the Cistercian monks of Dunbrody (a monastery founded in 1182) had a chapel here, dedicated to St. Peter and St. Paul, which depended on their monastery, in the county of Wexford.

At what time Portumna was forsaken by the Cistercians is unknown; but it is very probable that it was given up but a short time when the Dominican friars took possession of it, with the consent of the Cistercians of Dunbrody, and O'Madden the dynast of the place. After having their possessions confirmed by a Bull of the Pope, which bore date 8th of October, 1456, the Dominicans erected a friary and church, which they dedicated to the Virgin, and the original patron saints. Pope Martyn V, a short time after granting the above mentioned Bull, gave indulgences to all those who had contributed to its erection.

About a quarter of a mile to the south of the town, and convenient to the Marquis of Clanricarde's castle, are the extensive ruins of the Dominican friary, and, perhaps, the chapel which belonged to the Cistercians. From being closely surrounded with fine full grown timber, no part of the ruins appear, till of a sudden the east window, which is the one represented in the engraving, discloses itself to the view. The next object to draw the attention, after entering the churchyard, is another beautiful window, which is more florid but less majestic in appearance than the one first seen. Its rich tracery being partly covered with ivy, renders the interior view far superior to the one taken from the outside. It is in the south transept. The friary, which is cruciform, and in the Gothic style, is still in pretty good repair, the walls being nearly all to their original height, except the tower or steeple, which was sprung on four elegant pointed arches, whereof three still remain. One of the two which connected the nave and chancel has been totally taken down; and the other, which is of elegant cut stone, is built up, so as that if a view of it was given, the beautiful window should be left out of the picture. The entrance is in the west end, and by a small doorway, over which is a painted arched window, and from which to the farthest end of the choir or chancel, measures above a hundred feet. The choir is twenty-one feet wide, and the side walls about sixteen feet in height, and served for the parish church till a couple of years ago, when a new one being erected, which does much credit to its architect, it was forsaken and unroofed. The baptistery is built against the north wall of the friary, and was entered by a small door from the choir, which is now built up. The ruined building which I take to be the Cistercian chapel, is joined to the north transept. Was it not for its ancient appearance, I should not doubt its being the church belonging to the friary.— The new church is in the south end of the town, and is a beautiful structure, with stone-sashed windows in the perpendicular style, and a lofty spire. The Roman Catholic chapel is a modern, well-built, and a spacious fabric.

T. A.

THE TUNNEL—KILLARNEY.

About six miles from Killarney, on the new line to Kenmare, there is a tunnel, of which the above is a faithful sketch. It lies about a mile from Hyde's cottage, on the Killarney side, and gives considerable effect to the surrounding scenery, which is of the most picturesque description.

THE HERMIT OF THE LAKES.

It is to be presumed that few persons have visited and viewed the delightful scenery of Killarney—have climbed its mountains, or skirted its lakes, without having heard something of this extraordinary ascetic, who some years since took up his abode in the deserted and mouldering ruins of the abbey of Mucruss,* and who, for reasons known but to himself, became the companion of the lonely dead, relinquishing for ever the society of the living, save when compelled by the cravings of pinching hunger to ask an alms from some neighbouring peasant.

Having in early life visited those delightful scenes, whose varied beauties mock alike the boldest efforts of the pencil and the pen, while ranging along the lakes, or climbing the mountain's ridge, we were accompanied by a youth, whom, although in the costume of the country, *sans* hat or shoes, we found to be extremely intelligent, and well informed in legendary lore, and who, as we sauntered along, by way of amusing us, recounted many a wonderful story of the doings of the good people, or fairies, who he averred were at one period the only inhabitants of which Glena and Mangerton† could boast. Even now, he assured us, on many a clear moonlight night, troops of them were frequently seen cantering down from the mountains on horses not bigger than hares, or sailing on the lakes in vessels made of cockle-shells; while at other times they would join together in the sportive dance on the beautiful green sward with which Mucruss and the surrounding islands were covered.

The evening was fine; the last sunbeam still lingered on the Eagle's Nest; and in order to obtain a more extensive view of the delightful scenery around us, we had left the beaten path, and were endeavouring to gain the summit of Glena mountain, by scrambling up its precipitous sides with the help of the tough roots and impending boughs which sprung from the crevices of the rocks; when on a sudden I observed my guide to start, as if affrighted; and•pointing to a little shallop or boat, which had just issued from a cove that lay beneath us, and contained a being of most extraordinary appearance, he exclaimed, "heaven preserve us, but I fear, there's some bad luck afore us; for there's the hermit of the lakes, and whoever first sees him after his being at yonder mountain, which, yer honour, they calls the Devil's Punch Bowl,‡ is sure to meet with some accident. He has been about no good, I'll warrant him; he goes yonder to converse with a little black man, who they say is the ould boy, though I would not like to wrong him, any how." Scarcely had he uttered these words, when the root by which he was hanging gave way, and not being able to recover his hold, he was precipitated a considerable way down the mountain-side, his progress being at length arrested by the branches of an aged oak, which hung midway in the descent to the bottom. However, not having received any serious injury, he soon regained his former position, exclaiming as he approached me, "and sure, isn't it I that ought to be thankful to the Almighty, that didn't let him do his worst on me; for barrin' that he saved me, the best bone in my body would have been broken. I knew well I should meet with some accident—heaven grant the worst may be over."

Having by this time gained a position where I could with safety turn round and view the individual who had been the cause of such alarm and danger to my guide and companion, I could perceive that there was apparently some ground for the terror expressed. A cap of a conical form covered his head, while a long, black, bushy beard gave to a sharp, haggard, dark countenance an expression of savage gloominess, which even the distance could not obliterate. He was wrapped in a long loose garment, drawn tight at the middle by a belt, from which

were suspended several articles, that my guide informed me were dead men's bones, with which he was used to work his incantations, and practice his black art.

"Do you see that boat, Sir?" said the boy, "that boat was made without the help of human hands, yer honour; it is formed of the coffins of those whose souls are now doing penance; sorra a nail would ye find in it from beginnin' to end, nor was there ever a hammer raised over it—I *seed* it often with my own eyes, yer honour, and I can go bail for the truth of what I say; in fact he is not saucy, for he can both raise the dead, and make the Ould Boy appear in the likeness of a man."

"And where did he come from, or where does he now live?" I enquired.

"And sure, yer honour, nobody knows where he came from, or who he is, and it's I that knows very little about him that's good, only that the neighbours say there is no fear of his being hanged for being a Christhin; and if there was no harm in saying it, I believe myself that he's no very distant relation to the Ould Boy himself—though, yer honour, I would not for the best horse in yer stable, that he should hear me saying so."

Having, on further enquiry, learned that the much-dreaded individual had taken up his residence in the abbey of Mucruss, which my guide informed me was "an illegant ould ruin that every body visited," and which had for many years been a favourite burying place, in the true spirit of juvenile knight errantry, I resolved on exploring it the next morning, and if possible finding out some further particulars relative to the more than mortal who had taken up his abode within its walls. We had by this time wandered a considerable distance, and lost no time in regaining the pathway, in hopes to arrive at the inn (if it might be so called) which I had made my head-quarters, before the shades of night had completely surrounded us. As the evening advanced, fear appeared to lend additional swiftness to the legs of my companion, with whom I was scarcely able to keep pace, and who every now and then looked behind him, as though he dreaded some one was pursuing us. It was late when we arrived, and the evening being somewhat cold, we found that several travellers, who were stopping at the same place, had assembled round a blazing fire of turf and bog-wood, and were, with some neighbouring cottiers, beguiling an idle hour in listening to various spirit-stirring tales of terror with which the courteous landlord was endeavouring to entertain them.

Having taken my seat on a three-legged stool, and Paddy M'Kew, my guide, having also posted himself in the hob or chimney-corner, appeared on thorns until he got an opportunity to communicate the particulars of our adventure. It was quite *à propos*, and drew forth many a story 'learned and long' of the wonderful doings of the Hermit of the Lakes; nor did the miraculous escape of Paddy pass unnoticed.

"And sure it's I that could tell yees a story relating to the ould carle that wud make the hair o' yer head stand upright," said a bluff-looking country fellow, whom from his western accent I deemed, I believe justly, a native of Connaught. Master O'Rourke himself was the very man on whom the Ould Boy played his pranks. One Mr. O'Mulligan was after getting in his harvest, and he proposed to give some of the boys that helped him a bit of a trate, and so he gothered some of the neighbours together in the good ould way, and he gave them lashans of the rale stuff to wash id down wid. So, d'ye see, when they were got pretty well I thank ye, so that they cared no more for seeing the Ould Boy than they wud for seeing wan of their own selves, 'troth,' says Billy M'Comisky, 'it is I that wish we had his reverence, the ould Hermit here; we'd be after making him play some of his strange tricks, just to enliven us a bit; and as he's fond of a drap of the cratur, why it's how I think he would have little objection.' And so it was, as it is aye said, 'speak of the devil and he'll make his appearance;' who should just come round the hill but his reverence—we spied him out of the window where we sat. So out bolts Bill, and says to him, 'I hope yer reverence is well; maybe yer reverence wud like to be after wetting yer reverence's whistle?'

* For drawings and descriptions of this abbey, see last volume of our Journal.

† Very high mountains in the neighbourhood of Killarney.

‡ The name of a mountain in the neighbourhood of Killarney, in which there is an extinct volcano.

'I thank ye, Billy, but I'll take none the-night.' However, after a good deal of pressing, his reverence at length consented; and so in he came, and there he stood like a *statue*, or a spectre, with his eyes fixed on the ground, neither saying aye nor no to one or other of the company; and having drank off a glass of the native, was about to be off, when Billy again says to him, 'may it please yer reverence's grace, as we are all a thriffe hearty, and up for a bit of fun, we have been after thinking that maybe yer reverence would condescind to show us some specimen of your great larning and your supernatheral powers —as we understand yer reverence is well acquainted wid the black art.' So his reverence, wid a great frown, replied, 'Young man, ye know not what ye seek for— could ye stand to see the dead raised?' 'Ay troth, could I—or the Ould Boy himself,' quoth Billy. But I am not good at telling a story, genteels; and maybe you yourself, Masther O'Rourke, would have the kindness just to tell the gentlefolks the story as it occurred, as sure you have the best right to mind it, who was so near losing your life by the doings of the ould chap."

"And sure, Misther Burke, it is you that could tell a story with a grace; but as you are so condescindin', why I will do my best to tell it to the company. So d'ye see, genteels, as Misther Burke has just informed you, Billy M'Comisky was after asking his reverence to show them some of his tricks. So says his reverence to Billy, 'If you have a great desire, I will let you see some of your ould acquaintances.' To be sure he spoke in far more larned and nater language than I can remimber. 'But,' says he, 'mind ye, my lads, if the Ould Boy runs away with one of you, while trying the experiment, you must not blame me for it, but your own curosity. 'Whose afraid,' says Billy. So to work they went; and the boys all commenced, and swept one end of the barn quite clean. And then d'ye see, his reverince axed me could I get him a bible and a pair of mowld candles; and so, says I, 'it's I that could get you as many candles as there are days in the week, if ye wanted them; but I think it is as how there is not a bible or a testament in the parish.' But, aither bethinking myself a bit, thinks I, 'and maybe Masther Fitzhenry, the minister's nephee, would slip us the lend of one for a bit. So off I cuts, yer honours; and maybe it was I that wasn't long in bringing it to the boys, who, by the time I came back had two mowld candles nately sated upon a table, which they had placed right in the middle of the barn, d'ye see, and all round about, which the ould boy (that's the ould hermit I mane) had drawn a ring or circle with a piece of chalk. But I should have tould you they had also a chair placed beside the table, inside the ring, mind ye; and so taking the bible from me, he opened it at a sartain varse, and layin' it on the table, he asked Billy if he could read. 'Indeed I never spelt a lether in my life,' said Billy. 'Och, then, you won't do,' said his reverince; 'is there any one here that can read?' 'So,' says I, 'here am I, your reverince; and I could read, I may say, since the day I was born; for yer honours must know, although I am only a poor man now, I'm come of a good sort d'ye see—there's some of the thick blood of the counthry in my veins after all; and, although I say it myself, that oughtn't to say it, I got the best larning of any boy within ten miles of my father's house, d'ye see. But, as I was after telling ye, when I tould him I could both read and write, his reverince axes me, 'Young man,' says he,—for I was young then, yer honours—young man,' says he—at the same time looking at me with both his eyes, as though he would have pierced them through my very heart, 'd'ye think ye could stan' to hold a conversation with an ould friend of your's who has been dead a while, if I were to bring him to life again?— 'And I'm the boy that could,' says I; for at that time I was neither afeard of ghost or hobgoblin, and besides that, I had taken a hearty sup d'yesce: so down he sets me on the chair, and he gives me a couple of verses to read; and says he to me 'now, Paddy O'Rourke, I know you are not a bad sort of a boy, and I would not wish that any accident should happen to ye; but as you value your life and sowl, do not on any account come outside of that ring that I have chalked on the floor.' 'Never fear me,' says I—although I am bowld to confess I did feel a little twitter of terror come across my mind, just at the moment

they all began to leave me alone, with the bible and the two mowld candles; but out they went, and sure enough, as soon as they got out, what does his reverince do but very carefully locks the door on the outside—a part of the ceremony I did not much like, d'ye see; but maybe it was as how he did not wish to let his black majesty run away with me body and bones; but there I was left; and sure enough I continued roading mighty attentively, when all of a sudden I hears three great knocks upon the barn door, and just liftin' up my eyes a bit, what d'ye think does I see, but the figure upon the wall of a man that I knew right well, who was one of the greatest ould rascals about the country, and who would have been just three months dead, had he lived till next Friday. The sight of Ould Nick himself, with his club foot, could not have frightened me more; and had I been the owner of the squire's great grand estate, which to be sure I may say was mine by right, for it formerly belonged to my great grand uncle; but never mind that now, times may change again, when things will all go to their right owners—as I was saying, if I had been the owner of it at the time, I would willingly have given it to have been at the *right* side of the door; for I was sure and sartain that he would never let me out a livin' man, for having disturbed him from his quiet grave;—but what was I to do? His reverince had laid his biddin' upon me not to stir outside the ring—and besides I had heard him lockin' me in; so I continued with my eyes fixed upon the bible, though sorra a word could I see of what was before me; but just as I was thinking about what I had best be after doin', what should I hear but three other great loud knocks, and again lookin' up—och, genteels, the blood runs cowld in my ould veins as I think of it—I sees the ould lad as large as life, standing with his back against the wall, dressed in his winding-sheet, and his brogues on his feet, and his teeth grinning, and shaking his fist as though he would tear me to pieces. So it was I that didn't know what to do any how—my very knees knocked together with downright terror—when behould you, all of a sudden I hears other three great knocks; and over bounces ould Trevor to the very edge of the ring! exclaiming 'I'm Trevor come to tear you!' What followed I know not; all I recollect is, that in a kind of mad fit I whipped up one of the candlesticks, and after throwin' it at him, I suppose I fainted and fell, as they tould me afterwards they heard a great clatter, and on comin' in, found me lying on the floor, as dead as a door nail; and many a time since have I thanked my stars that I had the good luck to fall inside the ring, for had but the black of my nail been on the outside, I would not have been now here to tell the tale. So my story is finished, genteels; and all that I say is, that I would not undergo the same again for twice as much goold as the whole wide world is worth. So here's to yeer honour's safe journey."

As a kind of *finale* to the story, Burke had just mentioned that he could vouch for the truth of all Mr. O'Rourke had said—and was telling us how after they had left him inside the barn, the old hermit commenced his incantations by walking round the barn three times, at the end of which he gave the three knocks, at the same time muttering some gibberish to himself, that they could not understand—when, in a moment, without any apparent cause, we were all thrown into the most dreadful confusion and dismay, by a tremendous explosion, which seemed to shake the house about us to its very foundation. The large fire around which we were seated was hurled about the floor in a thousand directions, the lights were extinguished, the women and children in the other end of the house uttered a dreadful scream, and several of the company, among whom were the landlord and Misther Burke, were stretched sprawling on the floor. The consternation having a little subsided, and the fire having been again gathered into its place,* one and another once more ventured to look about them and to speak; some imagined they had been making too free with the character of the old Hermit, and that he or his familiar had thus hoped to be revenged.

---

* There are no grates in many of the houses in the country; large piles of turf and wood are heaped on the ground.

Leaving the matter to be adjusted among themselves, I was quietly slipping off to my bed, not well knowing what to think of the matter, when one of the company, a young gentleman who was stopping at the place, beckoned me to follow him to his room, where, in the greatest glee, he informed me the explosion was altogether a contrivance of his—that it had been caused by a small quantity of gunpowder, which he had put into a turf that had been previously bored for the occasion; that he and his companion had purposely introduced the stories relative to ghosts and hobgoblins, in order to give greater effect to the contrivance which he had formed to frighten the simple ones. While I could not but condemn in my own mind the impropriety of a measure which might have been productive of serious consequences, I confess I heartily enjoyed the joke, and could not but give the young traveller considerable credit for having so successfully attained his object; for never did I see a company so completely panic struck as they appeared to be—and I certainly was enabled by the ecclaircissement to retire to rest in a much more pleasant mood than I otherwise should have done; for the whole affair had previously been a mystery to me, and no doubt appeared rather unaccountable. At the same time I determined to visit Mucruss Abbey with the rising sun, and if possible to find out who or what the individual was who had taken up his abode within the confines of its dreary ruins.

I was as good as my purpose; for as the grey dawn of twilight had streaked the eastern skies, I was on my road towards Mucruss, and ere the sun had topped the opposing mountain, I had gained a view of the far-famed Abbey, as it peeped from amidst a grove of tall and stately trees, by which it was surrounded on every side. Even now I well remember I could not but frequently pause to contemplate the grandeur and loveliness of the scenery around me. Chased by the rising sunbeams, the mists of the morning appeared fast flitting away, as if anxious again to mingle in the waters of their great parent, the Atlantic. Before me lay the lovely lake, richly embroidered with innumerable islands, and reflecting from its azure surface the beautifully-diversified scenery around—the waving forest, and the more sombre-shaded mountain from whose stupendous sides the stunted oak or the aged holly, festooned with ivy, sprung spontaneous. My path lay alongside and partly through a wood, and the scenery which frequently burst upon my view was really enchanting;—at one moment the cerulean heaven, which had been for a time obscured, appeared through some opening vista, as reflected in the broad expanse of water which lay beneath me; while at the next step my eye rested on richly planted lawns, or was borne along the hanging woods which boldly swept along the mountain's side.

Wrought by the stillness and solemnity of the scene into a kind of sublime contemplation, and almost forgetting the object of my excursion, I had strolled along to within a very short distance of the Abbey. It was at that time a fine old ruin—a picturesque emblem of greatness in decay—situated on an eminence rising over the lake, and completely surrounded by trees of various growth and species. A pointed door-way, ornamented with various mouldings, showed the entrance to the interior; while innumerable relics of mortality, piled in fantastic groupes on either side the aisle, assured me of the truth of what I had been told by my guide on the preceding day, that it was the *domum ultimum* (until the resurrection) of many who had at one time given life and animation to the scenery around.

As I advanced into the interior of the choir, a feeling of peculiar solemnity appeared to steal over my soul: I experienced a kind of involuntary shudder. The place was gloomy and awful; and the idea that the only being it contained was one whose mysterious character rendered him rather an object of dread than otherwise, created an apprehension in my mind that all my efforts to the contrary could not suppress. I could almost have wished myself exhumed, and once more among those who lived and breathed. Nor were my apprehensions allayed on proceeding towards the cloister, a dismal area of considerable extent, in the midst of which spread an immense

yew, whose stem appeared to be thirty or forty feet in height, and the branches of which formed a canopy so complete, as to render the place gloomy to a degree; the light being scarcely sufficient to point out the mouldering tombstones which lay beneath its shade. Scarcely knowing whither I went, I still proceeded forward; when, on turning the angle of a corridor, which, from the information I had received from my guide, I conjectured might lead to the chamber in which the Hermit had taken up his abode, I observed at the farther end a dim sepulchral light, which seemed as though it proceeded from an expiring lamp or taper. With a palpitating heart I advanced towards it, when in an instant a sudden flash seemed to pass me by, and I was left in almost total darkness. I hastily turned, and was endeavouring to retrace my steps with that expedition which is prompted by fear, when I heard the sound of footsteps quickly following me; but unfortunately in my hurry to regain the cloister, having kept too much to one side of the aisle, my foot was tripped by some relic of mortality, and ere I could recover myself, I fell violently forward, and tumbling over a coffin, which, from having been partially decayed, burst beneath my weight, in an instant I found myself as if in the strict embrace of a lifeless body. Whether from the effect of the fright or the fall I cannot say, but one thing is certain, I was so stunned that I lay for a moment motionless as the corpse beside me, and was only roused from my stupor by feeling myself rudely raised from my position by a gaunt and grisly hand, which I could at the moment scarcely think human, so fierce was the grasp with which I was seized, but which, on approaching the cloister, I perceived to be that of the very person I had seen the evening before in the boat—who, fixing his eyes upon me with a fiend-like scowl, enquired, in a voice which thrilled through every nerve in my body, what had brought me thither?—and ere I could reply, seizing me by the shoulder, and shaking me violently, he exclaimed in terrific accents, "Presumptuous wretch, begone! and know that thou hast done to me an irreparable injury.—The spell is broken—I am undone." Then striking his hand violently on his forehead, as if in agony, "Oh, eternity, eternity! am I now to realize thy horrors?—fearful foreboding! sad reality! lost—lost—lost!"—Here clenching his hands in evident distraction, he remained a moment silent, as if lost in thought; and so petrified was I, that I really felt unable to move from the spot on which I stood. Apparently subdued in feeling, he again addressed me in a much milder mood: "Young man, I forgive your rashness. By your coming here this morning you have fulfilled an augury—you have sealed my doom: but beware! Behold in me the effects of unbounded curiosity, scepticism and impiety! God is just—and I deserve my doom; I myself made the bargain—I bartered my soul——but I will not recal past thoughts—My days are numbered—the future only remains for me." Then again, as if in the most dreadful despair, he exclaimed, "Lost—lost—lost!" As he pronounced these words, whether it was reality or the conjuration of fancy, from the state in which my mind was at the moment, I cannot tell—but I thought I perceived something again flit by me, as if in a flash of fire, and I imagined I heard the word "Away, away!" distinctly repeated. At that moment the Hermit hurried towards the entrance of the Abbey: I followed as fast as my trembling limbs could carry me, and having gained the door, I saw him gliding rapidly along towards the Lake, where he leaped into a boat—in which sat a little black man. In a moment they had gained the middle of the lake—the next they were lost to my view for ever.

Deeply musing on the extraordinary occurrences I had witnessed, and scarcely believing their reality, though evidenced by so many of my senses, I returned to the inn; and but for an injury which I had sustained from the fall I got, could almost have persuaded myself, that the entire was a vision of my brain.

DUBLIN:

Printed and Published by P. D. HARDY, 3, Cecilia-street; to whom all communications are to be addressed.

Sold by all Booksellers in Ireland.

THE
DUBLIN PENNY JOURNAL

CONDUCTED BY P. DIXON HARDY, M.R.I.A.

| Vol. III. | OCTOBER 4, 1834. | No. 118. |

ARDMORE TOWER, COUNTY OF WATERFORD.

The village of Ardmore is situated on the coast of the county of Waterford, about four miles from Youghal, and is remarkable for one of the most perfect round towers to be found in Ireland, the origin of which is attributed to St. Declan, who is said to have been the friend and companion of St. Patrick, by whom he was made Bishop of Ardmore, where he founded an abbey about the year 402, and where his memory is still held in great veneration.

The tower is about ninety feet high, and fifteen feet in diameter at the base; and the door-way is sixteen feet from the ground. Its formation is different from most others, being divided into four stories or compartments, each marked by a projecting course of solid masonry, carried round the building, and each story has a window or loop-hole: the whole structure is well built, and bids fair to withstand the ravages of time for centuries to come.— It is a prominent feature in the landscape, being visible for many miles round, and serves occasionally as a land-mark for vessels at sea.

St. Declan was descended from the family of the Desii, whose territories extended over the southern and western parts of the county of Waterford. He travelled to Italy when young—resided in Rome for several years, and being ordained by the Pope, he returned home; was consecrated Bishop of Ardmore, and survived to a great age; for his immediate successor, St. Ultan, lived until the year 550. He was buried in the churchyard here, in the dormitory, which goes by his name, and which is visited by vast numbers on the 24th of July, on which day his festival is held. Great virtues are attributed to the clay which is supposed to cover his remains, and which being taken away in small quantities from time to time, has gradually exca-

vated the surface to a depth of several feet below the adjacent soil. This dormitory was repaired and roofed, at the expense of Bishop Mills, about one hundred and twenty years ago.

There is also a well bearing the name of the saint, and a stone on the sea shore, which tradition reports to have floated over from Rome with the bells of the cathedral, and which is connected with many superstitious ceremonies.

The present church is but small, being only a part of the chancel of the old one, a portion of the walls of which still remain, covered with ivy; and one of the windows is adorned with curious carvings in freestone, representing the twelve apostles, and various scenes in scripture history.   R. F.

We are informed by our correspondent, E. H., that there are two transverse pieces of wood or metal at the top of the interior of the tower, to which he supposes the bell was attached, which is said to have been so deep and powerful in tone as to be heard at *Glown Moore* or Big Glen, a distance of eight miles. The top of the tower, which suddenly diminishes to a conical point, appears loose, and threatens a momentary fall; but, strange to say, it has withstood the fierce blast of about thirty winters in the same position, before which time it was erect, and surmounted with a cross.

A little further, on the edge of some shelving rocks, which immediately overhang the bay of Ardmore, is the ruin of an old place of worship, called *Thoumpel a Des-hert*, or the old "Temple of Dissart:" at one end of which stood a high gable, ornamented with a well cut Gothic window, which was demolished by a sudden gust of wind about seven or eight years since, and has now nothing more to boast of than the " holy well," in one of the walls, which owes its present neat and enticing appearance to an individual named Hugh Byrne, a private soldier in the Donegal militia, who, after the Irish rebellion of 1798, came here, and passed the remainder of his life in this solitary abode, and was buried beside St. Declan. There is a square door-way in one side of this old building, with an inverted key-stone in the arch, which has been a source of much enquiry and difference of opinion amongst the lower class of the adjacent mechanics, but which may be easily accounted for on inspection. Adjoining this are some silver mine-holes, which at present afford nothing more than pure water.

THE MOWIN' MATCH.

AN IRISH SKETCH FOUNDED ON FACT.

" Ah, thin, Dan, agra, what in the name o' wondher's bringin' you out o' yer bed at this time o' night afther yer hard workin' all day ? a body id think you'd be wantin' some sleep !" exclaimed the careful widow who exulted in the appellation of " Missus Phelim Dawley," to her son, as about midnight she heard him get up and endeavour to steal softly forth.

Dan at first appeared a little posed ; but then rubbing his eyes he muttered in a half sleepy tone—

" Och, wisha, wisha ! bud it's quare"—

" Are you dhramin', child, or what's come over you at all ? Don't you planely persave id's as dark as pitch—an' what's makin' you get up ?"

Dan, who by this time had invented an excuse, gravely answered,

" Why thin, mother, shure enough id's the dramin's bewildhered me entirely. Faix I thought id was mornin'; an' in throth I was wondherin' at meself bein' so lazy at gettin' up bud (a yawn) I'm glad to be in the wrong box, (a yawn) an'll jist turn in agin."

So saying, the sleep-loving youth bade his mother good night, and retired to his nook, for room it could not be called. The careful matron was satisfied at this, and again lay down, and soon fell into a sound sleep ; and the good youth, who was on the watch, no sooner perceived this, than, brogues in hand, he stole across the room, and gently unbolting the door went forth, closing it carefully again. A few stars were twinkling here and there in the sky, and giving but a faint light, by which he might direct his footsteps : however, as his mother's cabin stood beside the road, and he knew every inch of the country, there wasn't much fear of his losing his way.

He proceeded along at a pretty rapid pace, humming some tune, and occasionally whistling, until at length he stopped opposite another cabin, and going to a small window in the back part of it, began to sing the air which he had been trying ever since he left home. The words were very original, and ran somewhat as follows :

" Och, my darlin' Mary ! like a little fairy
  You thrip along the green grass in style ;
An' wor you Dido, or Queen Juno either,
  I'd love you dearly fur yer own sweet smile.
Your lips are the necthor, an' whin you do lecthur,
  Dianya's self couldn't sweeter spake ;
Och, me queen ov beauty, that bates out Vanus,
  If you prove cruel me heart will brake !"

He had got thus far in his tender strain, when " the ould cloak" was chucked out of the orifice which it filled up, and a female face appeared, smiling with satisfied vanity at the complimentary tribute just paid to her beauty ; and before the delighted Daniel could utter a word, she answered his strain somewhat in the same manner, not in a very unmusical voice, and one which he thought sweeter than honey :

" Iv be all this nonsense you think to win me,
  I tell you yer out Misthur Dan, asthore ;
Dianyas' an' Junos' may do fur others,
  Bud not fur me, as I said afore :

I'm a quite colleen, and a plainly spoken,
  So you needn't be thrying all your coortin' art ;
Such flattherree, which yer always croakin',
  Will never make me give you my heart."

" Och, Mary, a lanna, bud id's yerself can turn id," exclaimed the delighted lover, dancing, as if in time to the concluding air :

" always croakin',
  Will never make me give you my heart.

" Whoo—och—musha—it's the natest turned tchune! —Mary, a ra gal, where did you make id out at all ?"

Mary, on the genuine Milesian principle, answered one question by propounding another, which was,

" Ah, thin, you foolish boy you, what brought you here at such an hour as this ?—singin' and gallivantin' undher a poor girl's windee, as iv you wanted to turn her wits.— It 'll be tellin' you somethin' iv me father heers you."

" What brought me out, Mary ! repeated Dan, bringing his voice to the pitch tender ; which, en passant, resembled a key in a rusty lock. " Is id you axes me that, eroo ? Well, that flogs the world : did you never hear tell ov a boy bein' so bewildhered about a bit ov a colleen—eh, mavourneen ? as to venthur out jist to give her a taste ov a saranade, as the gintlemin call id, to make her sleep soundher iv she wor sleepin', and to bid her waken iv she won't."

At this tender and sentimental effusion, Mary did not blush, but her white teeth glittered as she laughingly answered—

" Why, thin, Dan Dawley, you bate my skill, as the gauger said whin the boys put out to say—fur really I didn't think you wor sich a gommoch !"

" Well, well," half soliloquized Dan—" this sartinly bangs—a gommoch ! Och, Mary, asthore, don't you know how you've desthroyed me wid yer pair ov eyes, an' your incomparable beauty—id's murdhered, I believe, I am."

Mary here half drew in her head as she sung in reply,

" Ah, thin, go yer ways, you gay desaver,
  And don't think to move me wid all yer lies ;
Shure yer butthered words are repeated often,
  An' though you pretind, I don't mind yer sighs."

Here the old rag was again thrust into the window, and the voice ceased, and all was silent as before ; for the " spark was quite knocked out ov Dan be her quareness," and he stood for a moment or two irresolutely ; then his pride came to his aid, and he loudly, and with somewhat of exultation, chanted,

" Thin, sense thus you thrate me, so rude and bitther,
  Though a rural famale never born should be ;
No insinuashins shall intoxicate me,
  Thus to be turned off so ungratefullee."

He then twirled his alpeen round his head, gave his caubeen a crush down, disdainfully pulled up his breeches, and loudly humming the latter part of the air, struck off into a path which led across the fields. Scarcely had he gone, till the bundle was a second time chucked away ; and Mary's head appeared peeping forth to discover if he loitered ; but seeing that he did not, she withdrew, saying nought, but in her heart half repenting the useless coquetry which led to his dismissal ; for, be it known unto the reader, Dan Dawley was the boy of all others for Mary Brady's fancy. He had known her long, and paid her every attention ; and the sensible folk observed, that it certainly would be a match whenever Dan " gev over his wild ways, an' reglarly tuk to industhry," a period which would be exceedingly difficult to name.

Love and war are often spoken of together ; and with the rejected Dan Dawley war was now the word ; for he was not such a gommoch as to come out solely for the one, which we will prove plainly to the reader. He scudded on (for his original shambling gait could not be called walking !) for about an hour, and at last stopped opposite a large barn, erected originally beside a dwelling house, but it had long since been levelled, leaving the aforesaid barn standing lone and bare on the brow of a slight hill, and far from any human habitation. At the door of this, a couple of men armed with scythes were standing, who having exchanged the customary salutations of acquaintances, withdrew, and let Dan pass, at the same time saying,

"Id's jist cum in the nick ov time you are, fur yer absence was remarked, an' the masther's spakin' to the boys afore we set off."

When Dawley entered, he at a bird's eye view perceived nearly a hundred men assembled, who were standing, lounging or sitting, just as inclination prompted them; a keg of whiskey was in the centre, beside which stood a tall man, with a ruddy face, and brown curly hair, and he was haranguing them, and did not cease on Dan's entrance, although he perceived him; and he was the leader or masther, as he was called.

"Boys," said he, "I suppose I needn't remind you that whin I had the money I stood to you like a prence, and what more could I do? You know whin the ould house was taken from me, be that rascally Scotch attorney, an' I was sint off athout as much land ov me own as id fill a garden-pot—(I that onst owned, at laste my ancesthors did, the whole counthry!) that I cum an' joined yes in toto, which manes wid a heart and hand, and I have stuck to you since then through thick and thin. Now, boys, I'd have a sperat above remarkin', iv id was an Irishman cum into me property, or a man that id escourage the Irish, but id's not—he's an attorney an' a Scotchman."

Here some, whose national prejudices he had effectually probed, shouted, "enough, enough, Misthur O'Mara, what 'ill we do?"

"Why, thin, boys, darlin', sense your good enough to say so, I'll just tell you, an' id's but child's play to you, although id's justice. He's got over a whole ship load of young larch threes, besides bundles ov others, from Scotland. Mark you—not Irish threes—may I be hanged iv I'd touch a twig ov thim iv they had the Irish sap in thim !

"Who, whoop, hurroo—we know that Misthur O'Mara —we know that."

"He's about six acres ov thim planted, an' I was thinkin' iv we'd jist show him afore mornin' that the Irish air doesn't agree wid Scotch timber, it id be as good a lesson as we could tache him, an' others ov thim too. What do yes say to that?"

"Let us at them—let us at them"—shouted the excited crowd, amongst whom Dan Dawley was not the least conspicuous.

"Well, my lads," continued O'Mara, I knew you'd stand to me, as' so desired you to bring your scythes an' rapin hooks, as they're not two feet above the ground, an' are as tindher as grass. A quare six acres ov hay he'll have in the mornin', I'm inclined to think."

Having thus concluded, he advanced, and gave every man a portion of the whiskey; shaking hands as he passed with Dan, who had the honour of being his foster brother; and then, all being arranged, they set off with wonderful rapidity across the fields in the opposite direction to which Dan had advanced by.

O'Mara had been, at an early age, deprived of both his parents, and thus was left without any control, at the time when the mind is most pliant, and most easily moulded. He got someway connected with some of the boys, with which the county abounded; dashed about his money— drank—gamed—rioted—hunted—and at twenty-eight years of age, owing to his own folly, found himself ejected from his estate, without a penny in his purse, and deeply in debt into the bargain. Such a situation of affairs would have driven any other man but O'Mara mad, but he bore the loss quite philosophically; and when thought would intrude, got drunk if he had the whiskey, and if he hadn't, sang a verse of a popular song, which ran somewhat in this strain,

"The houses and lands may have left me
But joy man with wealth ne'er inherits;
All's lost, but that hath not bereft me
Of pleasure or lightness of spirits.
Then hip—hip—hurrah !
I'll not grieve for the day
That took the estate and the houses away."

He lived on just as usual, only that gradually he found his old rich friends deserted him, and as he asked for the loan of a few pounds pretty often, and had but a bad memory, it is not much to be wondered at. Then he took to the society of the poor ones, and amongst the boys was always the leader, under the old title of " the masthur ;" while in the day he sometimes helped them with their work, not being too proud to put his hand to the plough, and even took part in their frugal but hospitable meal, and thus he managed to do what many young men are sent to college for—namely " to put over his time."

The party which he led, after having travelled about three miles further, at length came upon the verge of the plantation, which extended over fully the number of acres O'Mara had mentioned, and had been planted with infinite cost and labour. He then disposed them silently in a regular row, just as mowers commence; and taking a scythe himself, made the first cut. No sooner was this done than to work they all went, without uttering a syllable, but noiselessly and with vigour, and in a space of time almost incredibly short, the entire plantation was destroyed. O'Mara then drew a paper from his pocket, which he attached to one large tree, that had been left standing purposely, and on which was written, in a disguised hand, and purposely ill spelled :

"Let Mr. Gahagan take notis dat we let no Skotch threes stand on Irish ground.
Signed by ordher,
Captain Starlite,
His ✕ Mark."

Having placed this in the conspicuous position before mentioned, the leader summoned them all together, and at a beck they set off at a quick run till they arrived at another end of the estate, where there were about fifty cart loads of turf drying. He then stopped, and drawing a flint and steel from his pocket struck a light, with which he immediately ignited one of the driest sods, and placing it beneath the mass, yet exposed fully to the high wind, he exclaimed,

"Now, me lads, iv there's any ov you wants to light yer pipe, you'll have a bonfire in an instant, an' maybe whin we go id may warm some poor boy that hasn't the whiskey to keep the cowld out."

At this unexpected feat silence could be observed no longer; so they burst forth into a prolonged shout, that rang like thunder on the silence of the night ; and then perceiving that the mass began rapidly to take the flame, they heaped some of the driest part near it, and, with another hurroo, departed, each separating as he got to a certain spot on the high road.

Dan Dawley and O'Mara went together, as the former had offered him a shelter for the night, and rapidly, as they crossed the fields by the very shortest cut, when they at last reached the cabin and looked round, they perceived that the whole atmosphere was red with the conflagration. In a moment more, chuckling at the success of their project, they both lay down without having a second time disturbed the old woman.

The next morning, when the night's devastation became apparent, the whole neighbourhood was in an uproar; and Mr. Geoghegan, the owner of the property, convened a meeting of his brother magistrates, for the purpose of taking into consideration the best means to be adopted of discovering the perpetrators, and, by a signal example, of stopping effectually such outrages, which began to be too frequent. Suspicion often fixes its lynx eye in the right quarter, and did so in this instance ; for from threats which Geoghegan had heard O'Mara let fall, and from the wild life which he had been latterly living, he said that he had almost no doubt but that he was in some way connected with the mowin' ; and it was proposed by one, and approved by all, that he, together with his constant comrade, the spotless Dan Dawley, should be arrested. They were encountered by the police sent in search of them in a small shebeen house, which they often frequented; and after some insolent language from O'Mara, at such an outrage being committed on his immaculate person, and after Dan "talkin' to one of thim, the rapparee, wid his alpeen," they were at length firmly secured, and led to the mansion of the injured magistrate, which formerly belonged to one of the prisoners, and where almost all the influential men of the county were assembled.

O'Mara, on being led in and confronted with his late attorney, but now the owner of his property, and his foe, preserved a dignified silence, and stood with his arms folded beside Dan, who looked uneasily around, with a half serious, half tipsy glance, that was irresistibly comic, and kept edging farther and farther from the police, who stood near him, till at last he was nearly beside Geoghegan's chair. This gentleman perceiving that he was somewhat far gone, and little knowing that whiskey instead of taking from, gives addition to the cunning of some, began to examine and cross-question him as to how he spent the night, and then found that he could make nothing of him, for his style of parrying, and never giving a direct reply, would puzzle a bench of judges.

"You say," observed one of the gentlemen, "that you were at home all the night; now how comes it that this man swears he heard your voice outside Mary Brady's, a short time before the outrage was perpetrated."

"He say id," indignantly exclaimed Dan, turning an eye of fire on the informer, who was a rival in the favour of his mistress; "the lyin' disciple. Och, give me bud elbow room an' I'll bate the thruth out of him, anyhow."

"Then you positively affirm that you did not leave your home last night."

"Sorry I'd be to conthradict yer worship in that same, an' faix id wasn't an invitin' night be no manner to be out in—I'd rather be sittin be"—

"We don't want to know, Sir, anything about what you'd rather: answer plainly—were you out or not," interrupted Geoghegan, who was beginning to find examining him was hopeless.

"Och, now, yer honor's beginnin' to be angry, I see. The mischief can't stand the gintlemin fur hotness sometimes."

"I'm afraid we'll gain no information from this fellow, Geoghegan," said one of his brother magistrates; "but at all events let us confront him with the girl, as she's now arrived."

Then having called her by name, to Dan's infinite perplexity, Mary Brady stood to be examined. He winked at her in an instant, and that so wickedly, that all present observed it, and ordered him to be led back.

"Wirra sthrue, masther, jewel," he whispered, as he passed the spot where the reckless O'Mara (who was infinitely amused at the entire scene) was standing, "we're sould now in arnest, I'm afeard."

Mary was a modest looking girl, with black piercing eyes, and very red lips, with a certain roguish leer eternally playing about their corners. As she advanced, she looked for an instant on Dan's face, and its ludicrous and imploring expression caused her eyes to brighten with merriment, and her glittering teeth to be seen, as she bit her lip to avoid laughing. However, her answer to the first question effectually dispelled all fear, and Dawley could not conceal the delight he felt at her bewildering the examiners.

"Did you see the prisoner, Daniel Dawley, last night at any hour past eleven," said one of the magistrates who prided himself on his powers of gaining the truth from witnesses.

Her pretty lips affected to pout, and her brows slightly contracted as she answered—

"Oh, Sir, I wondher a gintleman like you 'id attimpt to ask such a question ov a poor girl whose reputashun's all she depinds on. See a man after eleven o'clock—who ever heerd the like."

"This man, Bartle Connor, is ready to swear that he heard his voice under your window."

"Bartle Connor swear that I well, well to be shure, there's no dependin' on any one in this world," exclaimed Mary. "I thought he'd be the last id do so. Musha, musha, I b'lieve the men are all alike."

Bartle was greatly moved at this, and, starting forward, declared that he could not swear to it, but *believed* he heard it; upon which Dan burst out with—

"Why, thin, you ill lookin' spalpeen you, iv you only could say that much, you might have kept your tongue quiet in yer mouth; fur I can tell you id 'ill cost you

somethin'; fur the minut I lay hands on you, highway or lowway, in public or private, I'll make proper smithereens ov yer dirty"—

"Silence, Sir," sternly commanded Geoghegan, upon which Dan immediately ceased.

"Well, my good girl, you are positive in asserting that you did not see Daniel Dawley last night; such pretty lips as those ought to blush if they did not speak the truth."

"Och, an shure well I knew id, an' see id planely now, yer worship's only jestin' wid me. Well your welcum, though id's a shame to make a fool ov a poor girl in such a manner."

"I think," here said Geoghegan, "that we may be justified in committing these men to prison on suspicion, until other circumstances shall arise to prove their innocence, as we can extract nothing in this way."

"Send Dan to preson—is that what yer honour's saying," exclaimed Mary, willing to give the face of affairs another turn—"wisha, thin, id might be the worst day's work ever you dun, in the regard ov losin' a frind; for I heerd him say meself ov yer honour"—

"Say what," eagerly asked he.

"Why that yer honour was a good man, an' just to the poor, an' one agin whom he'd cut off his hand afore he'd rise id—"

"Did Daniel Dawly really say all this?"

"In throth he did, an', more betoken, maybe id was him kep the boys from visitin' you so long, fur all I know."

Geoghegan's greatest pride was to appear popular; and Mary well knew that to tickle his vanity before his brother magistrates, might have the effect of making him more lenient to Dan; nor was she mistaken, for, after some further consultation, he was set at liberty, while O'Mara, in default of finding heavy bail, was detained.

"Give us the five fingers, Mary, a lanna," said he in ecstacy, when they were departing; "Och, bud id's now this heart of mine is entirely yours; an' you may thrate me as you like; bud from this out iv I ever spake an unkind word to you or yours, may I never be happy."

Then turning to his rival, who was a few feet behind,

"As to you, Mr. Bartle Connor, I'd scorn to take a mane advantage of you; so I just peaceably warn you to get together your *back* agin the next *patthern*; fur bad cess to me iv I don't give the Dawleys the wind o' the word, an' bate the sivin sinses out ov every mother's sowl of the Connors I cum acrass: as to yerself you poor atomy ov a crathur, keep out of my way, or I ll be obleeged to dirty my stick wid you!"

To this highflown speech the other disdained reply, but gathering the skirts of his coat " under his arms," he trudged off as if it made no impression; but quite contrary was the case, for since that day "war to the knife" has been the word between the *fagh a ballagh* boys of both the Dawleys and the Connors.

From O'Mara's reckless character, no one would be mad enough to go bail for him; so he was placed in the county gaol until the judges should be going on circuit; and there he was as merry as ever, and as thoughtless; missing only the free liberty of range to which he had been hitherto accustomed. When the trial came on there was no evidence; as although there were upwards of a hundred men employed in *the mowin'*, not one was found to *peach*, and so he was acquitted, much to the delight of his foster-brother, who, "on the strenth ov id," had named that very day for his wedding with Mary, who had at last consented to make him a happy husband.

O'Mara still continued after this to lead the same boisterous life, until at length he was shot in an engagement which some smugglers, whose cause he had thought proper to espouse, had with the excise officers; and Dan and his wife were, along with all the peasantry, mourners at his funeral; for such a disposition as his is always idolized amongst the Irish, as it is partly national; and they don't care for the faults so as the sinner have *a heart.* A cold calculating disposition, no matter how amiable, is always detested, in comparison to a rattling, thoughtless, extravagant one. So saith

DENIS O'DONOHO.

ORNITHOLOGY.

On some of the Birds frequenting Belfast Lough.

BY JAMES D. MARSHALL, ESQ., M. D.

Of the Genus *Totanus*, or sandpiper, four species have been found in our immediate vicinity, viz :—the redshank sandpiper, green sandpiper, common sandpiper, and green-shank.

REDSHANK SANDPIPER.—*(Totanus Calidris.)*

This delicate, pretty-looking bird, commonly known by the name of redshank, is a constant residenter in this part of the country, and except during one or two of the summer months, is always met with on the shores of our bay.

It is one of our commonest species, and any one accustomed to stroll along the shore can scarcely have failed to notice it. Its shrill, piping cry is uttered immediately on taking flight, and the alarm it sounds is so well known to the other species in its vicinity, that the flight becomes general, and the sportsman, with all his caution, is generally outwitted by this wary bird. I have pursued a flock of them for hours round the shores of Island Magee, without being able to approach within gunshot. They collect on the projecting rocky extremities of the small bays, and these are so situated, that the birds cannot fail to notice any attempt made to obtain a nearer inspection of them. There is no lurking place for the fowler, and after following his game from rock to rock, he may be obliged to return fatigued and disappointed.

Bewick says, " that the redshank is usually found solitary or in pairs ;" and in those places where he had opportunities of observing it, this may be perfectly correct, but I should certainly say, that in all the parts of Ireland where I have observed it, I have almost invariably noticed it in flocks, seldom fewer in number than six, and frequently amounting to one or two hundred.

During winter they congregate in large flocks—in spring they separate into smaller ones, and finally into pairs ere they retire to their breeding haunts. About August, however, they are again found united on the shores, having left their summer retreats in company with their respective families. At this season they are generally much tamer than usual, many of them having been only a few weeks excluded from the shell, and consequently totally unaccustomed to the sight of man.

The difference in the plumage of the old and young birds, although not great, has been such as to induce ornithological writers of no ordinary rank, to class the redshank not only under different species, but even as appertaining to different genera. It has been ranged among the woodcock and snipe, under the name of *Scolopax Calidris*, and in other works, *Tringa Gambetta* and *Tringa Striata*. This is only one of the many instances of sub-division of genera and species resorted to by authors, who either had not the opportunities or inclination to investigate the subject. Statements were taken for granted as correct, merely from want of making the proper inquiries, or bestowing on it the necessary portion of time and labour,

The food of the redshank is the same as that of the other waders, univalve and bivalve mollusca, with worms and insects of various kinds. When in search of food they usually gather round a small pool of water left on the bank by the retiring tide, and wading through it, they pick up whatever attracts their notice.

Though I have mentioned this bird as being extremely wary and difficult of approach, yet it may be brought near by imitating its cry or whistle. I have seen a flock of at least two hundred redshanks, which were so wild as to exclude the possibility of bringing the gun to bear on them, brought within twenty yards of the sportsman in consequence of the correct manner in which he imitated their cry. The call must be repeated, as nearly resembling that of the birds as possible ; and when their answer has been returned, the conversation, if I may so term it, must be kept up until they have been brought within the necessary distance.

NORTHERN PENGUIN, OR GAIR-FOWL.—(LE GRAND PINGOIN.)—*Buffon.*

The length of this bird, to the end of the toes, is three feet. The bill is black, and four inches and a quarter long : both mandibles are crossed obliquely with several ridges and furrows, which meet at the edges. Two oval-shaped white spots occupy nearly the whole space between the bill and the eyes : the head, back part of the neck, and all the upper parts of the body and wings are covered with short, soft, glossy black feathers, excepting a white stroke across the wings, formed by the tips of the lesser quills : the whole under side of the body is white : the wings are very short, not exceeding four inches and a quarter, from the tips of the longest quill-feathers to the first joint : legs black, short, and placed near the vent.

From the inability of these birds to fly or walk, they are seldom seen out of the water, and it is remarked by seamen, that they never wander beyond soundings. The female lays only one egg, which she deposits and hatches on a ledge close to the sea-mark : it is of a very large size, being about six inches in length, of a white colour, streaked with lines of a purple cast, and blotched with dark rusty spots at the thicker end.

This species is not numerous any where ; it inhabits Norway, Iceland, the Ferro Isles, Greenland, and other cold regions of the north, but is seldom seen on the British shores.

At a meeting of the London Zoological Society, held during the last month, Mr. G. Bennett read a note on the habits of the *King Penguin Aptenodytes Patachonica (Gmel.)*, as observed by him on various occasions when in high southern latitudes. He described particularly a colony of these birds, which covers an extent of thirty or forty acres at the north end of the Macquarrie Island, in the South Pacific Ocean. The number of penguins collected together in this spot is immense; but it would be almost impossible to guess at it with any near approach to truth, as during the whole of the day and night, thirty or forty thousand of them are continually landing, and an equal number going to sea. They are arranged, when on shore, in as compact a manner, and in as regular ranks, as a regiment of soldiers; and are classed with the greatest order, the young birds being in one situation, the moulting birds in another, the sitting hens in a third, the clean birds in a fourth, &c.; and so strictly do birds in similar condition congregate, that should a bird that is moulting intrude itself upon those which are clean, it is immediately ejected from among them. The females hatch the eggs by keeping them close between their thighs; and, if approached during the time of incubation, move away, carrying the eggs with them. At this period the male bird goes to sea and collects food for the female, which becomes very fat. After the young is hatched, both parents go to sea and bring home food for it; it soon becomes so fat as scarcely to be able to walk, the old birds getting very thin. They sit quite upright in their roosting places, and walk in the erect position until they arrive at the beach, when they throw themselves on their breasts, in order to encounter the very heavy sea met with at their landing-place. Although the appearance of penguins generally indicates the neighbourhood of land, several instances were cited of their occurrence at a considerable distance from any known country.

SIMPLE SCIENCE—ASTRONOMY.

Astronomy is a knowledge of the heavenly bodies with regard to their magnitudes, motions and distances, whether real or apparent, and of the natural causes on which their phenomena depend.

The earth is a body, nearly circular, but not perfectly so, being flat at the poles. It moves round the sun in an orbit nearly circular, and in motion nearly equable in the space of $365° 6^h 9' 11''$; and that the motion is not equable is easily accounted for by the attraction to the sun becoming greater the nearer it goes to it in its opaque orbit. The diameter of the earth is eight thousand miles, and it moves at the rate of nineteen miles in one second. The motion of the moon through the heavens, as well as her appearances at different times, are exceedingly remarkable. When she first becomes visible, at the time she is called new moon, she appears at the western part of the heavens, and seems to be at no great distance from the sun himself: every night she not only increases in size, but moves farther from the sun, until at last she appears in the eastern part of the horizon, just as the sun disappears in the western. After this she gradually moves farther and farther eastward; and, therefore rises every night later and later, until at last she appears to approach the sun as nearly in the east as she did in the west, and rises only a little before him in the morning, as in the first part of her course she set in the west not long after him. All these different appearances are completed in the space of a month, after which they begin in the same order as before.

The periodic time, that is, the time it takes to complete its revolution round the earth, is $27° 7^h 43'$: and it is carried with the earth in its annual motion round the sun. The moon is not a planet, but only a satellite or attendant on the earth. Her diameter is two thousand miles, and her distance from the earth's centre two hundred and forty thousand miles; and she moves two thousand two hundred and ninety miles in one hour, and turns round her axes exactly in the time that she goes round the earth, which is the reason that she keeps always the same side towards us. The phases of the moon are particularly interesting. They prove it to be a spherical body, illuminated by the sun; therefore whilst that half of her which is towards the sun is enlightened, the other half is of course dark and invisible; hence she disappears when in conjunction or between us and the sun, because her

dark side is then towards us: when she is gone a little way forward, we see a little of her enlightened side—a crescent—which is our new moon, which still increases to our view as she advances forward, until she becomes in opposition, (i. e. opposite to the sun,) and then her whole enlightened side is towards the earth, and she appears with a round illumined orb, which we call full moon. The moon has scarce any difference of season, her axis being almost perpendicular to the ecliptic: what is very singular, one half of her has no darkness at all—the earth constantly affording her a strong light in the sun's absence; while the other half has a fortnight light and a fortnight's darkness by turns. Our earth is thought to be a moon to our moon; waxing and waning regularly, but appearing thirteen times as large, and affording thirteen times as much light as she does us. Viewing the moon with a telescope, several curious phenomena offer themselves. A great variety of appearances is exhibited on her disc; there are spots differing very considerably in degrees of brightness. Many of the dark ones must necessarily be excavations on the surface, or valleys between mountains, from the circumstance of the shades of light which they exhibit. There is no reason to suppose that there is any large collection of water in the moon, for if there were, when the boundary of light and darkness passes through it, it must necessarily exhibit a regular curve, which is never observed. It is also probable, from the circumstance of no change being observed on her surface, such as would be produced by vapours or clouds.

That there are lunar mountains is strikingly apparent, by a variety of bright detached spots, almost always to be seen on the dark part, near the separation of light and darkness; these are tops of eminences enlightened by the sun, while their lower parts are in darkness; but sometimes light spots have been seen at such a distance from the bright part that they could not arise from the light of the sun. Doctor Herschell supposes these to be volcanoes—he measured the diameter of one and found it four miles.

Many astronomers formerly denied the existence of an atmosphere at the moon, principally from observing no variation of appearance on the surface, like what would take place did clouds exist, as with us; and also from observing no change in the light of the fixed stars on the approach of the dark edge of the moon; but astronomers now seem agreed that an atmosphere does surround her, although of exceedingly small density when compared with that of our earth. It has been measured by the parallax to be one thousand times rarer than ours, in which atmosphere the inhabitants of this earth could not live many seconds.

The cause of the tides is, the orb of the attracting power, which is in the moon, is extended as far as the earth, and draws the waters, acting upon places where it is vertical—insensibly on confined seas and bays, but sensibly on the ocean, whose beds are large, and when the waters have the liberty of reciprocation, that is of rising and falling—and the presence of the moon occasions an impulse which causes another in her absence. The sun's influence in raising the tides is but small in comparison to the moon's; for though the earth's diameter bears a considerable proportion to his distance from the moon, it is next to nothing when compared to its distance from the sun; and therefore the difference of the sun's attraction on the sides of the earth under and opposite to him, is much less than the difference of the moon's attraction on the sides under and opposite to her; and therefore the moon must raise the tides much higher than they can be raised by the sun.

The diameter of the sun is about 888,000 miles, and its distance from the earth 96,000,000 miles. It moves round its axis in $25° 10^h$, and though to human eyes so extremely bright and splendid, it is yet observed, even through telescopes of but very small power, to have dark spots on his surface of various dimensions; one observed by Dr. Herschell was thirty thousand miles in diameter.—Every spot, if it continues long enough without being dissolved, appears to enter the sun's disc on the east side, and to go from thence with a velocity continually increasing, till it has gone half its way, and then to move slower and slower, till it has gone off at the western side, after which it disappears for about the space of time it spent in crossing the disc, and then enters on the east side again, nearly in the same place, and crosses it in the same track, and with the same unequal motion as before: these spots are not endowed with any permanency, nor are they at all regular in their shape, magnitude, or number, or in the time of their appearance or continuance. Some have been observed to arise and vanish in sixteen hours, while some have lasted seventy days: those spots that are formed gradually are gradually dissolved, while those that arise suddenly are suddenly dissolved. The nature and formation of the spots have been the subject of much speculation and conjecture. Some have thought that the sun is an opaque body, mountainous and uneven, covered all over with a fiery and luminous fluid; that this fluid is subject to edding and flowing, after the manner of our tides, so as sometimes to leave uncovered the tops of rocks or hills, which appear like black spots, and that the nebulosities about them are caused by a kind of froth: others imagined that the fluid which sends us so much light and heat, contains a nucleous, or solid globe, wherein are several volcanoes, which, like Ætna or Vesuvius, from time to time cast up quantities of bituminous matter to the surface of the sun, and form those spots that are seen thereon; and that as this matter is gradually consumed by the luminous fluid, the spots disappear for a time, but are seen to rise again in the same places when those volcanoes cast up new matter: a third opinion is, that the sun consists of a fiery luminous fluid, wherein are immersed several opaque bodies of irregular shapes, and that these bodies, by its motion, are sometimes raised up to the surface of the sun, where they form the appearance of spots, which seem to change their shape according as different sides of them are presented to view: a fourth opinion is, that the sun consists of a fluid in continual agitation; that by the rapid motion of the fluid some parts more gross than the rest are carried up to the surface of the luminary, like the scum of melted metal rising up to the top in a furnace. But Dr. Wilson's opinion has gained more credit than any of the foregoing; for he considers the spots to be hollows in the surface of the luminary, and has even observed the spots to be beneath the level of the sun's spherical surface: he considers that the vast body of the sun is made up of two kinds of matter very different in their qualities; that by far the greatest part is solid and dark; and that this dark globe is encompassed with a thin covering of that resplendent substance from which the sun would seem to derive the whole of his vivifying heat and energy. This supposition will afford a satisfactory solution of the appearance of the spots; because if any part of this resplendent substance shall by any means be displaced, the dark globe must necessarily appear.— The shining substance may be displaced by the action of some elastic vapour, generated within the substance of the dark globe. This is the general opinion of the astronomers of the present day.

Far the greater number of the celestial bodies preserve the same situation with respect to each other—and these are called fixed stars; and although these stars are the only marks by which astronomers are enabled to judge of the courses of moveable ones, yet they seem not to be endued with permanency, but to be perishable and destructible by accident, and likewise generable by some natural cause; and astronomers have supposed that every one of the innumerable multitude of fixed stars are suns, attended by planets and comets, each of which is an inhabitable world like our own, but of course invisible to us. The strongest argument for this hypothesis is, that they cannot be magnified by telescopes, on account of their extreme distance. Hence, therefore, we must conclude that they shine by their own light, and are as many suns; and those who have formed conjectures concerning their distance, thought that some of them were at least 400,000 times farther from us than we are from the sun; and, therefore, we may imagine an innumerable number of universes like to that which we can behold, and extending to infinity.

Besides the sun, earth, moon, and fixed stars, there are ten planets—named Mercury, Venus, Mars, Ceres, Palas, Juno, Vesta, Jupiter, Saturn, and Georgium Sidus. These are vast bodies revolving round the sun, in orbits nearly circular; some at less, some at greater distances than the earth: Jupiter has four satellites, which revolve round like our moon, and are enlightened by the sun. Saturn has seven, and the Georgium Sidus has six. They are all supposed to be surrounded by atmospheres like ours; and there are belts seen round Jupiter which are supposed to be clouds, but appear very permanent. Saturn is encompassed with a broad thin ring, which is exceedingly beautiful; through the space between the ring and the body, fixed stars have been seen. It is illuminated by the sun, and the surface of it appears more brilliant than the planet itself. It is distinctly divided into two parts, which are in the same plane, and revolve round their axis; the outside diameter of the larger ring is 200,000 miles; its width 6,700; the distance between the rings, 2,800; outside diameter of the smaller ring, 180,000, and its width 19,000. The ring is only 1,000 miles thick.

Comets are luminous bodies, occasionally appearing, and generally in the parts of the heavens not far from the sun; they do not appear long together—some only for a few days, others for a few months; but the most striking phenomenon, and what makes them objects of attention to all mankind, is the tail of light which they often exhibit. There have been many comets recorded in history, which are some of them supposed to have returned after a lapse of about ninety years; and calculations are hereby made as to when they may be expected again; but many have been expected which have never appeared. With respect to the tails of comets, little that is satisfactory can be offered in recording the various opinions on the subject. According to Sir Isaac Newton, they arise from a thin vapour, sent out from the comet by the heat of the sun, and supported in the solar atmosphere. Dr. Hamilton supposes the tails of the comets, the Aurora Borealis, and the elective fluid, to be matter of the same kind. According to his hypothesis, it would follow that the tails are hollow; and there is every reason to suppose this from the scarcely perceptible diminution of the lustre of the stars seen through them; but much is yet to be known on this subject.

By the discoveries which have been made in astronomy, we are permitted, as it were, to understand some of the counsels of the Great Creator of the universe. From these we can, from demonstration, overturn the absurd doctrine of blind chance. We see that a supreme intelligence placed and put in motion the planets about the sun in the centre—and ordained the laws of gravitation, having provided against the smallest imperfection that might arise from time: and let us not imagine that only in these vast bodies the supreme care was employed let us not imagine that man, apparently so insignificant, cannot be an object of attention in a world so incomprehensively vast—the protecting hand of the Creator is equally visible in the smallest insects and vegetables, as in the stupendous fabrics which astronomy points out to us. He who formed the human mind so different in its powers and modes of existence from the rest of the works of the creation, has assigned laws peculiarly suited to its preservation and improvement—laws not mechanical but moral—laws not obscurely seen by the light of reason, but fully illuminated by that of revelation.

H—N, T.C.D.

METHOD OF REMOVING HOUSES.

The practice of removing buildings on rollers, so as to widen streets without pulling down, which has been carried on with success for some years in New York, has been received with incredulity by those who have not the means of verifying the fact. Large stores have been carried back ten or a dozen feet—houses have been slewed round, to use a sailor's term, so as to face another street, and all this without in any way endangering the superstructure. When we wish to raise a house a story we unroof and build an attic, not so with brother Jonathan, he builds from the bottom.

We were admiring, says the New York Star—the ease and security with which the handsome two story brick house, 210 Bowery, was raised by screws and blocks to a height so as to enable the owner to build another story under it, and when completed it will be a substantial three story house. The raising of this brick house was done by George Bakewell, 177 Elizabeth-street, and not a wall was cracked or a timber out of place.

KILLESHIN RUINS, QUEEN'S COUNTY.

" Look on its broken arch, its ruined wall,
Its chambers desolate, and portals foul."
CHILDE HAROLD.

The above ruin is situated in the Queen's County, about three miles from Carlow. It is seated on the rising side of the mountain, and when viewed at a distance on a cloudy day, or in the shadowy twilight of evening, enwrapped with its luxuriant wreathing of ivy, it seems, indeed, the fit abode of the spirits of death. The effect is heightened by the gurgling noise of a small stream, which at the bottom of a deep mountain ravine near the church, pursues its way over a series of rocks and falls.

This district it is evident has derived its name from the church ; Kil, in the Irish language, signifying a church.

Cooke notices it in his " Statistical Survey of the Queen's County." After speaking of a bye-road across the mountain, he says " contiguous to this remarkable cut of Killeshin* are the ruins of a church of the same name, which has a very antique and highly ornamental entrance in the Doric order, of really excellent workmanship, and around which is an inscription of very old Saxon characters, but so battered and abused as to be almost totally defaced. Adjoining this church was a Danish rath, encircled with a very deep fosse. This place is remarkable for having once been the chief town in the Queen's County in disturbed times, though not a building now standing bears testimony of it except the ruins just mentioned. Here was the county gaol and court-house, where the assizes were held, and the governor's mansion, which was a fine building ; also a fort and public buildings, of which there is now no trace. The stone stocks and gallows stood the wreck of time the longest ; and their sites are pointed out by the old people, in whose recollection they yet are. But, except the ruins of the church, not a stone building now remains over ground of this once celebrated town, nor the slightest vestige of its entrance."

There are evident traces of the existence of iron ore in this neighbourhood ; among others a spa, at the bottom

* This curious excavation was cut through the solid rock, over a lofty mountain, to the depth of forty feet in some parts, and half a mile in length, by a constant flow of water and the friction of the car-wheels. It was the scene of many a rencontre between the carriers, as, if they should omit to shoot, either through negligence or drunkenness, at the extremity of the defile, probably a meeting would take place, as it often did, when neither willing to put back his horse such a distance, and could not turn about, a battle ensued, when the vanquished gave the way.

of the hill near this ruin ; and also the red colour of the sand-stone rock, (the stones have this colour from the oxide of iron which they contain,) found in the rivulet, and quarries around, bear evidence that such a mineral is to be found here.

Seen from the ruin, Carlow appears to much advantage ; it seems as if on very elevated ground, or rather on the acclivity of a high hill, and the prospect embraces scenery of a picturesque and pleasing description, as the eye rapidly wanders over the " beauties that burst upon the view," while the landscape is studded with neat though small thatched cottages, " whose milk-white walls form an enlivening contrast with the shadowing green, rising like an undulating wave to the mountain's top."

Near the ruin is now a very pretty parish chapel with a tower.   H.

RUINS OF SLETTY CHURCH, QUEEN'S COUNTY.

The above cut illustrates the ruins of the old priory or church of Sletty,* also situated in the Queen's county, near Carlow. This ruin is said to be coeval with the dawning of the light of Christianity in our island. It was of considerable extent, but all that now remains of it are three walls of one apartment, supposed to be the chapel.

It is now and has been for centuries used as a favourite burial place by the people of the neighbourhood ; and it is believed that here rest, uncommemorated and forgotten, in peaceful and humble seclusion, the ashes of its founder.

Tradition and history concur in stating that there was an extensive college formerly attached to this building, where were educated many foreign and native youths. It is also said that a street reached from this place to the then town of Killeshin, a distance of about two miles.

There are two stone crosses erected in the church yard, apparently of the ninth century.

There was some years ago one of those ancient tumuli, being an arched receptacle for the ashes of the Danish dead, discovered in a field adjoining this ruin. The interior was occupied with a number of earthen urns arranged in rows, and each covered with a small round flag. The person who discovered it, supposing that each urn contained gold, was in an ecstacy of delight ; and having raised the flags, to his indescribable astonishment and vexation, he found nothing but a few old burnt bones.   H.

* Sleibtach, or the house near the mountains.

DUBLIN:
Printed and Published by P. D. HARDY, 3, Cecilia-street ; to whom all communications are to be addressed.
Sold by all Booksellers in Ireland.

In London, by Richard Groombridge, 5, Panyer-alley, Paternoster-row ; in Liverpool, by Willmer and Smith ; in Manchester, by Ambery ; in Birmingham, by Drake ; in Glasgow, by W. R. M'Phun ; and in Edinburgh, by N. Bowack.

THE

DUBLIN PENNY JOURNAL

CONDUCTED BY P. DIXON HARDY, M.R.I.A.

VOL. III.   OCTOBER 11, 1834.   No. 119.

SEIR-KYRAN'S CHURCH AND PARISH, KING'S COUNTY.

The place now popularly called St. Kyran's, but properly Seir-Kyran, was anciently denominated Sarger. Seir-Kyran is probably from *Seir*, a heel, meaning Kyran's heel; this parish in shape very much resembling a shoe, with the heel greatly prominent. Its other name, Sarger, is in all likelihood from the Irish, *Saigcoir*, a sawyer, owing to the wooden buildings of which the town was originally composed. Be the derivation of the name as it may, the ancient church is situate in the centre of the parish of the same denomination, about four miles from Birr, in the barony of Ballybritt, and King's County. It is in the ancient district of Ely O'Carroll, which (notwithstanding what Harris says, 'Ware's Bishops of Ossory at Kiaran,') was in ancient Munster, which it is well known extended over part of the modern King's County. Thus Macgeoghagan, Hist. d'Irlande. Tom. 1, fo. 213, describes Ely O'Carroll as "terretoire autrefois de la province de Mumonie," and Colgan AA. SS., says, "In australi plaga et regione Mumonie in plebe quæ vocatur Hele."

At present there is little remaining to indicate the former greatness of this place—a few mouldering walls, built with Pudding-stone, and a stunted stone-roofed tower, partly covered with ivy, about fifteen feet in diameter externally, and twenty feet high, being the only remnants of antiquity appearing above the level of the soil. The vestiges of the numerous deep ditches and high ramparts, which nearly surround the place, and encompass

about ten Irish plantation acres, indicate that it was formerly of importance, and the crumbling ruin of a sod fort, about seventy feet square, is a convincing proof that the occupants in distant ages had an eye to personal security as well as to the worship of the Deity.

These ramparts are in some places double, and seem to have been of that description which Cambrensis alluded to when writing, " Civitates fossatis et muris optime cinnerant."

St. Kyran, who is said to have been born at Cape Clear,[*] or, as Harris[†] has it, at Clear Island, in the ancient district of Corcamluighe, in Munster, in the fifth century, was the founder of this house for Regular Canons of St. Augustine. His father's name was Lugneus, a noble of Ossory, and his mother, Liadian, of Corcamluidghe, or Carberry, in South Munster. It is said[‡] that he met St. Patrick in Italy, who desired him to proceed before him to Ireland, and at a fountain called *Fuaran*, about the centre of the kingdom, to build a monastery where St. Patrick would afterwards visit him. I shall not now stop to enquire whether such a conversation ever took place, but content myself with merely observing, that the ruin I

* 1. Lanig. Ecci. His. 29.   † Ware's Bishops.
‡ Colg. AA. SS.

describe in this article, is actually adjoining the small stream called *Fuaran,** which purls away on the east side of it; and there is also a little to the south of the church, a holy well, neatly faced with stone embankments of a quadrilateral form, and shaded with thorns, well hung with torn scraps of calico dedicated to the tutelary saint.

There is yet to be seen in the middle of the churchyard of Seir-Kyran, a very ancient freestone slab, having a cross and a few Irish letters visible upon it. From the letters legible, (only a few being so,) I am induced to suppose it the tomb of Caomb† Oran, or gentle Oran, who, as he was abbot of Aghaboe, and died in 1066, was probably Bishop of Ossory, and having removed from Saiger, in 1052, at the transfer of the see, his corpse was, in all likelihood, interred in the latter place.

By far the most curious thing at Seir-Kyran's is the round tower, and to which I have never seen a similar one. It is only about twenty feet high, with a conical stone roof, and was evidently erected subsequent to the fabric that once stood beside it, and against the south-east angle of which it was built. It contains a great many loopholes around it. These are three or four inches square on the outside, but are levelled off so as to adjoin each other on the inside. Some of the holes are not on a level with the others. I suppose this tower to have been used for keeping up a consecrated fire in it.— These religious fires were by no means so rare as some suppose. This is not a convenient place for entering upon a dry and lengthened treatise respecting them. The general class of readers of the Dublin Penny Journal would probably spurn such food. Suffice it, therefore, to remark, that the Druids kept fires ignited as emblems of the sun or life. In Toland's History we find that "on a certain evening all the people of the country, out of religious persuasion instilled into them by the Druids, extinguished their fires entirely: that every master of a family was obliged to take a portion of the consecrated fire home, and to kindle the fire anew in his house, which, for the ensuing year was to be lucky and prosperous. He was to pay, however—." Macgeoghagan, Tom. 1, p. 81, writes there was an annual Druidical fire lighted at *Ilachta.‡* in the barony of Clonlisk, and King's County. The same historian says, that this was an institution of the monarch Tuathal-Teuchmar, and that the place it was held in had been cut off Munster by the same king. He adds that it was forbidden to supply fires with fuel on November eve until they were first renewed from that holy fire.— We are informed by early writers that this practice was continued after the introduction of Christianity. We are told that St. Patrick had his consecrated fire, and St. Brigid had at Kildare her perpetual fire. Ware§ informs us that Henry de Loundres, Archbishop of Dublin, put out St. Brigid's fire, *because the custom was not used elsewhere.* It is strange how so learned and laborious a writer as Sir James Ware could have fallen into so great a mistake. In a paper of Mr. Cooke's, of Birr, giving an account of the Barnaari-Cuilawn, (a curious ancient fire-cover in that gentleman's possession,) published in the transactions of the Royal Irish Academy, as read before that learned body the 7th of January, 1822, he shows that relic to have been the cover of a perpetual fire, instituted in the parish of Glankeen, county of Tipperary, by St. Cuilawn, brother to Cormac M'Cullenan, who was King and Bishop of Cashel upwards of nine hundred years ago. In like manner St. Kyran had his consecrated fire at Saiger, in imitation of the Druidical one at Ilachta, which was but a short distance from his monastery. Colgan relates,|| "St. Kyran, the Bishop, resolved that the fire consecrated at Easter should not be extinguished in his monastery for the whole year."— The same authority informs us that "a boy named Chichideus, of Cluain, who belonged to the monastery of Clonmacnoise, having spent some days with St. Kyran at the monastery of Saiger, extinguished the fire, and was killed by wolves as a judgment from heaven; which when his master, St. Kyran, the younger, Abbot of Clonmacnoise, learned, he went to Saiger, to St. Kyran, senior, and was received with great honour, but that there was not then any fire in the monastery, *because the fires all through the place used daily to be kindled from the consecrated fire.*" This story, divested of what relates to the wolves, plainly shows that there was formerly a sacred fire kept up here; and it is most likely the tower I have described was used as the fire-house. Such is at least my opinion, which I offer for the correction of those more learned in these matters.

There is a beautiful demesne called Oakley in this parish. It belongs to George Stoney, Esq., who has expended large sums of money adorning with all the diversities of water and landscape his mansion here, and in doing that which, in a public point of view, is still more creditable, namely, giving employment to the labouring classes. In a fort in this demesne was found, a few years ago, the haft of a pen-knife, of brass, having upon it, in Roman characters, "Success to the King of Prussia—I say for ever, huzza." It was probably brought here by some of the Germans in the year 1798. It is now in the collection of Mr. Cooke, of Parsonstown.

The Roman Catholic chapel in this parish is a tolerable edifice, and the present parish church is not only a plain, but damp and uncomfortable old building. The only thing remarkable about it is its having, projecting from the western gable end, an ancient freestone bust of St. Kyran, which, probably, ornamented the more ancient fabric. The eastern gable is ornamented with an old freestone window-frame, at some distance from which there also projects from the wall a grotesque figure, in freestone, about a foot and a half long, and not unlike, in figure, to a small porcelain Greek idol, in possession of the writer of this account. The above engraving is a representation of it.

KENNY KILFOY—OR MURDER WILL OUT.

It is a custom in several parts of Ireland for the young men of one village to join and perform certain descriptions of work for each other in conjunction. For instance, from a dozen to fifteen young men will assemble, with their spades and *facks,** and completely sow all the potatoes for one family before they stop. They will then proceed to another farm and perform the same task, and so on until all the potatoes belonging to the confederacy are planted. Turf-cutting and reaping are usually performed in this manner. This is generally considered a very good method of performing labour, as it ensures expedition and promotes good feeling in the neighbourhood among the young, besides rendering them better workmen, as there usually exists an emulative pride among them for the best and cleanest work, and the leadership of the field. These meetings are always scenes of feasting and pleasantry; besides, as the farmer considering his work done without an outlay in money, is anxious to give his friends and neighbours the best enter-

* *Fuaran,* a spring.   † Gentle—mild.
‡ Ilachta appears to be situate about Brusna, in Sir Robert Vaugondy's map of Ireland in 1757.
§ Antiq. c. 17. § 6.
|| De vita S. Kierani, c. 35. p. 462.

* Narrow spades with but one foot-rest.

tainment. The rude jest, ever bringing the ready and boisterous laugh, and the loud song are heard over the field the live-long day.

In the beginning of the summer of 1796, a parcel of young men assembled early in the morning on a certain portion of the bog of Allen, adjoining the King's county, to cut the turf of a young farmer named Buckly. They amounted in number to about fifteen, all fine well-limbed and healthy young men, with their *slanes** and wheel-barrows, ready to cut with sinewy arms the black soft soil. The morning was extremely fine, and the young men worked with spirit and activity until about one o'clock in the afternoon, when Buckly's sister and a servant girl were seen approaching the bog, loaded with " the dinner" for the men, and followed by a *gossoon*, carrying two large vessels of milk. The young men ceased working as they approached, and arranged themselves on the heath-covered bank. Among the young men working for her brother, the handsome Essy Buckly had two admirers, who eagerly contended with each other for the honour of her hand at the dance, at fair, or pattern, and who wooed her smiles with the most constant assiduity. She, of course, felt her heart inclined to one, much to the mortification and jealousy of the other. They were both young men, and lived in the same village ; their farms were nearly equal in profit, and subject to the same rent ; and both, with regard to worldly substance, were nearly equal ; that is, both were comfortable in the sense which an Irish peasant understands the thing. Both had a cow giving milk, a few sheep, poultry and pigs ; their corn and potatoes were regularly sowed, and their rent punctually called for by the agent, and generally forthcoming. But still they were not equal in the eye of Essy Buckly. Her favourite, Tom Molloy, in her mind was infinitely superior to his rival, Kenny Kilfoy, for the equality which I have observed between them in *other* things, did not go with Essy as a criterion of their merits *otherwise*. She loved Tom Molloy. He was a dark-eyed, ruddy-faced, black haired, pleasant young fellow ; ever with a smile on his lips, and pleasantry in his look ; always the lightest foot in the dance and the merriest at labour. His rival had the advantage of him in stature, but was not so compactly made or handsomely formed, with light hair and a sallow, colorless face ; his disposition too was sombre ; and he was generally taciturn and reserved. For his own sake he always joined the co-operative labourers ; and though, as his neighbours expressed it, there was ever " the *coatha cour*† about his mouth, and the complaint of one thing or another on his tongue, and though he was always penurious and *garthough*‡ in doing a dacent thing, yet he never thrived better than another. Such were the lovers of Essy Buckly ; and we cannot blame her in her choice of a sweet-heart ; for what young girl would prefer a silent, melancholy lover, without spirit or sprightliness, like Kenny Kilfoy, to a good-humoured, good-hearted, and pleasant handsome young fellow, like Tom Molloy.

The bacon and cabbage was served round on the white, wooden platters, then so commonly in use, by Jack Buckly, the elder brother of Essy ; and the thick milk poured out into the equally white wooden noggins—still the vessel generally used among our peasantry—and the scene was one of happiness and peace. " Rustic labour, toil embrowned." A group of smiling faces, seated on a

---

* Any person acquainted with country work must know what a slane is. For the reader who has not had an opportunity of seeing it, we subjoin a short description ;

Suppose a garden-spade diminished in breadth to one-half, but much lighter and thinner, with a longer and a lighter handle ; then suppose a piece of the same breadth attached at right angles, and on the right side to it, coming from the lower or digging edge about half way up the iron, but sharp at the outer edge, and sloping to a blunt point. This kind of an instrument is used for cutting the soft, compact super strata off the bog into the square form in which it is afterwards dried and burned.

† Words expressive of that draw which a miserable and poor spirit is supposed to give to the expression of the mouth.

‡ Niggardly.

---

high bank richly covered with yellow moss, purple heather, and the long green branches of the " bog-sallow."

" Come, move over there, Kenny," said Tom, who was sitting next his rival, " an' make room for Essy to sit beside me."

" Do you want to shove me into the hole ?" grumbled the stinless Kenny.

" Don't stir, Kenny," interrupted the lively Essy. " I'll just sit down here furninst you 'till I see which o' youz can eat the purtiest."

" Och, thin, iv that's the case," said Tom, " I must turn my back to you."

" Why so, Tom ?" asked Essy ; " I thought you'd give up in nothin' to him."

Kenny smiled grimly, whether through satisfaction or otherwise none could interpret.

" And do you give it up, Tom ?" said Jack Buckly, placing another slice of the bacon upon his platter.

" Oh, faix," said Tom, " he has the best tools ; see what a fine sharp set ov teeth he has, and a beautiful big mouth ; the sorra purthier eather or cleaverer thrincherman on the bog ov Allen this day than you are, Kinny Kilfoy," he added, addressing himself to his rival, with good-humoured comicality.

" Well, sorra take you, Tom, 'said another, " but the dickens can't bate you at jibing."

" Och, I don't mind what *cracked people* sez," grinned Kenny bitterly.

" An' you're right, Kenny," said Essy, mischievously ; " an' the never a betther he is with his romashes—never lets a sober body alone."

" Oh, thin, never heed him you, Essy," smilingly answered Tom, for he saw the choler of his rival rising, and he wished to provoke him or draw him out ; " never heed him—he's vexed enough 'ithout you goin' to vex him more with your sly jokes."

" It's not the likes o' *you* that could vex me at any rate," muttered Kenny, getting more vexed at having his testy humour taken notice of before all his compeers, and her before whom he wished to appear particularly amiable ; " It's not you that could vex me," he added, " barin' you were saucy or impident, and forced me to make you know which was the betther man."

This hint was too much for even Tom's good humour, especially when given before Essy ; and the boys, who felt it in its proper sense, looked to see how such an intimation would be taken. Tom's eyes kindled with a brighter light as he replied, still in his good-humoured way,

" Bar there, Kenny," said he, " I acknowledge that you are an oulder man than me, and that you were a man when I was a *gossoon* ; but I will never say, that now we are both men, that you were ever a taste a betther man, or as good. With regard to what you said afore, about *cracked people*, all I have to say is, that thank God I'm not a moping *omedhaun*, like some body that I could spit upon."

" You may thank that I wouldn't like to spoil the day's work on Jack Buckly," said Kenny ; " and that the dacent girl that I have a regard for is to the fore, or I'd soon let you know the differ."

" It's easy settlin' that," said Tom ; " I'll wrastle you this evening, when the dacent girl that you have a regard for, (mimicking Kenny's drawling tone), an' that cares little about you, I'm thinking, won't be present, and let the best two out of three show who's the man that has a right to brag."

" Aye, that's the fair way," interposed some of the men, who saw a quarrel likely to ensue, and wished to prevent it, by what they considered a harmless trial of strength and dexterity.

The men resumed their work with increased good humour and renovated glee, all except Kenny Kilfoy, who nursed his angry feelings and passions in silence within his own bosom. Their work was soon done, and many a dry or elevated patch in that quarter showed black, being thickly covered with the square sods cut from the deep hole which they left behind them. The sun was not set ; it was yet early evening as they left the bog.

" Well, boys," began Tom Molloy, " many hands makes

the work light; we're done brave and early, and it's as purty a day's work as you need look on."

"We'll have full time," said one, " to thry the three falls here above in the meadow, and be home afther afore the supper time."

"Auch," said another, "sure it's only jokin' Kenny was."

"How's that ?" said another; "sure not maning that it's afraid he is you'd be."

"I never joke 'ithout laughin', boys," said Kilfoy, " an' I'm not in the grinnin' humour much at this present minute."

As soon as they reached the meadow, Tom, who was jogging on before Kenny with another group, tossed off his coat, and addressing Kilfoy, who was crossing the stile—

"Now, Kenny," said he, " let there never be a boast about the best man afther this bout, an' we needn't be the worse friends afther. Come, Pether, lend us your jacket, and throw my thristy here over your showldhers."

He was soon arrayed in the frieze jacket, and kicking off his weighty brogues, he stood in his stocking vamps inside the little circle formed by his companions. He was joined by his rival, whose dark and lowering brow still plainly told of ire unquenched, and passion fierce and burning; and as they stood before each other, Tom stretched forth his hand in a frank and manly manner,

"Come, Kenny," said he, "give us the fist before we begin, to show there's neither spite or anger in regard o' the few words."

"Let every madman and fool shake his own hand," said Kilfoy bitterly, withholding his hand, and looking on the extended one of his rival with a sneer.

"Well, the sorra may care for your good or bad humour," replied Tom, moving towards his opponent, "come on, an' every man do his best."

They grappled, and after a few preliminary movements, the contest became interesting to all parties.

Perhaps there is no exercise so animating and healthy as wrestling, as it is practised in most parts of Ireland, and at the same time so beneficial and conducive to health when conducted fairly. All the agility and strength of the frame are put into requisition; every muscle in the body is strung, and the steadiness of foot—the quickness of eye and limb, and the pliancy necessary to excel, give vigour and elasticity in a surprising degree.

Kilfoy was the strongest man, but he evidently did not possess the action or dexterity of Molloy, who exhibited at every turn that wavy motion of the body, so observable in the tiger and leopard kind, and which gives the plainest indication of strength and agility combined, and which shows the body more like a moving mass of muscle than a composition of flesh and bone. Often did Kenny attempt to toss his opponent, and as often was he foiled by the superior tact and quickness of his adversary, and the spectators, by their looks, gestures, and exclamations, gave vent to their feelings or their admiration.

"By my conscience that was a mighty purty offer of Tom's to dhraw him off."

"Faix he was near getting the sleeshoge on him that time."

"Look at the hump Kenny has on his shouldhers, watching like a badger in a barrel."

"Faix Tom has as purty a stan' as ever I saw with a boy ; as straight an' as light as Sharpfoot the dancin'-masther."

"Bow !—he was near bringing Tom with that strong cross-thrip," said one amateur, starting from a recumbent posture to one knee, as his favourite stumbled from a sudden forcible manœuvre of his opponent.

"A hangnashun ugly thrip that cross-thrip is," remarked another.

"Ha ! he's at it agin—not so well as before though ;" said another.

"Look at Tom how he smiles; watch his eye; he's throwin' himself in the way ov that ugly curl agin," said a young one.

"Never !" said another in a lower voice ; "iv he thries that cross-thrip agin, he's done as sure as his name's Kenny Kilfoy."

Kenny did try the cross-trip again, and as quick as thought his rival drew back ; his foot missed the object, and, in endeavouring to recover his position, his foot was caught, and Kenny Kilfoy measured his length in the green grass. A loud hurroo declared the triumph ov the victor. Kenny rose from the ground more furious than before. He was more enraged than ever, for shame added to his anger. He was certain of victory, and disappointment lent three-fold stings to his former rankling. His friends came round him :

"I was thinking," said one, "that cross-thrip id disappoint you."

"You should have got in on him," said another.

"Close him, Kenny," said a third, "when you go in again; he's too active for you, and you'll have a betther chance, for you're the strongest."

"Standhers-by are always good wrastlers," said Kenny churlishly, shaking off his Job-like advisers, and walking forth again to meet his antagonist. They grappled again; Kenny went more incautiously to work than before. He thripped furiously, and swung his lighter antagonist about in rather an awkward way. Molloy went from side to side with him as he pulled, and escaped his efforts to throw him, until his own violent exertions pretty well fatigued him ; he then commenced annoying, and with a well managed feint he drew his comrade off his guard, and tossed up his heels in a most dexterous manner.

"You're the best man be odds, Tom," said Jack Buckly, "an' Kenny must acknowledge that himself for a good thruth ; but he won't refuse to shake hands I know now, as I won't be easy 'till I see you friends agin."

"Never !" muttered Kenny, with furious emphasis from between his set teeth, and he turned from the group.

"When I offered him my hand," said Tom, " before we began, I did it like a man ; now I wouldn't give him my hand for all he's worth in the world."

Kenny stalked away completely crest fallen, yet with a refreshed and a new burning hate in his bosom. He felt that Tom was beloved by Essy ; and he thought that harmless jest which Tom uttered in the bog was with a design to render him ridiculous before his mistress. He retorted in a way in which he imagined himself sure of drawing his rival into disgrace, and in this too he was foiled. Thus jealousy and shame were heaped upon him, and worked within his moody soul. Yet another trial awaited him, in which he suffered more, but which brought on the most tragic results.

Not far from the village there was a wake on this very night. An old woman, the mother of a neighbouring farmer, and a distant relation of Kilfoy's had "departed" that morning. He would have avoided going, for he knew that the Bucklys and Molloy, and all the witnesses of his defeat would be assembled there, and that the story would be told to many, and that he would be the subject of all tongues, and the marked of every eye. Yet she was his own blood relation that was waking, and would he stay away when strangers would be there ; besides, his absence would be marked, and attributed to a fear of his rival ; and this thought at least he could not bear. His supper was taken in silence, and in a short time after he set out for the wake. He went by the most unfrequented bye-paths, and reached the house just as the darkness was closing around.

To many an Irish wake is a familiar sight : to many more a short description of it, such as it is, in its full costume, as seen in almost every part of Ireland, may not be unacceptable, and we will take this one as for all.— Nearly opposite the door the corpse of the old woman was extended on a large table, which being too short, another smaller was placed at the end, and supported by sods of turf to bring both on a level. Under the head was placed a phangle, or sheaf of straw, but smoothly covered over with a white sheet. The corpse was also covered with white sheets, and on the breast was laid a platter with snuff, which was taken off and handed round the house occasionally. Below the snuff-plate was a bundle of new pipes, half filled with cut tobacco, shook into them rather loosely that it might serve the more. Then a large canopy was formed over the body, with white sheets also, from which others depended, covering the wall, and protecting the corpse from view at head and foot, but leaving it entirely visible in front. Two painted prints were hung over the head; one representing "the nativity," and the other "the crucifixion," while opposite, against the wall, was fastened a large cross, made of two stripes of black velvet placed crosswise.— Then here and there within the alcove was pinned up large bunches of flowers. Such, I believe, is the usual method of "laying out a corpse" in the country places nearly through Ireland. All the stools, forms, &c. in the neighbourhood were borrowed, and the house was thronged with the young and old of both sexes, laughing, chatting, and smoking quite at their ease; but the women invariably decked out in their best muslins and calicoes.

As Kilfoy entered he took off his hat, and kneeling down within side the threshold, he crossed himself, and repeated a few prayers within his breath, and then rose up, without looking at any person, and threw himself carelessly into a seat, and pulled his hat down low upon his brow.

"Ah then, Kenny Kilfoy, but it's gettin' mighty polite and genteel you are," said the light tones of a loved and familiar voice at his side, which made his heart-strings thrill, "an' you sit down without sayin' be' your leave, or lookin' at who's beside you."

It was Essy Buckly. She saw him sunk and cast down—she knew all that past—and with that quick perception, so marked in woman, felt that he was suffering, and that she was the occasion of it; and she thought she had a right to speak cheerfully to him

"An' is it you, Essy, avourneen," said he, "an' are you here alone; an', sure, I didn't see you, or, the Lord forgive me, it's not o' my prayers I'd be thinkin'."

"Oh, yes, Kenny, talk that way av you like," she replied, "but sure it's I that well knows whose nearest your heart. Did I see you the other Sunday whisperin' with Kitty Kinshela, ov the big house, when mass was over? Faix I did; an' a purty cragger you had ov id, Kenny, an' a nice purty girl she is, an dhressed like a lady; it's you that has the dacent notion, an' no blame to you."

Kenny's captious and suspicious temper trembled even under this simple reply. He thought that there was something of irony mingled with the latter part of it; and his already sore heart felt pained by Essy's harmless remarks.

"You may joke, Essy," he answered, "an' you may laugh, iv you like, at me; but iv you knew me—iv you knew my heart—iv you knew all!—I won't say my misery, you wouldn't laugh at me."

"Indeed, Kenny," replied the unthinking girl, struck by his tone and manner, "I wouldn t laugh at you; sure I know you since I was a child, an you're an honest father's an' mother's child; an' I wouldn't laugh at you; but, indeed, I thought you an' Kitty were hand-bound* at least." She added the latter remark in the hope that if it was not the case, that it might serve as a hint to Kenny on more accounts than one.

"I suppose you don't know that Kitty is my cousin, then," said Kilfoy, "an' that 'id be beyant the rules to think ov her in the way of marriage; besides you ought to know that it's a long time since I first tould you how my love was fixed; an' you know I'm not one of your hair-brained kind of people, that has a fair word for every body, an' a laugh an' a soft word for every girl that I meet."

"I know you to be a solid steady boy," replied Essy, evidently at a loss to get rid of a discourse that was growing painful; "but I never thought of any thing in the way of mathrimony, nor never will until—"

Here she was interrupted by the village momus, who had assumed, for the merriment of the company, the character of the parish priest, and was about uniting several candidates for the Hymeneal state, nolens volens; that he might, as he said, "begin the divarshin ov the night."

"Come," said he, "none of your whisperin' behind backs, but come 'till I tie the knot for yous at 'onst."

This was the noted Jack Mulryan, the laughing philosopher of the village. He ever set care at defiance—enjoyed his fun whenever he could make or meet with it—was the master of the ceremonies at every wake in the country—and was the constant leader in every merriment. Jack, with the tail of his great coat pinned about his neck, and a straw hat on his head, tied the young couples as quick as they pleased; and he now summoned Essy and Kenny to have the yoke imposed upon them. Essy refused with much steadiness and reserve, to undergo even the mock ceremony with Kenny, while he, feeling an unusual pleasure at the kindness which he imagined Essy had shown him that evening, pressed her to comply with the humour of Jack, and with the custom to which all usually conform.

She refused; and all the entreaties of Kenny, and the jibes and jests of the mock clergyman could not prevail upon her.

"Come, Essy," said Kilfoy, "you know it can do you no harm; and see all the girls and boys are quite pleasant; do let Jack buckle us, an' don't be afther makin' yourself odd, lest the people say you're gettin' proud."

"No, no," said Essy, "I cannot do it—I will not do it. It is useless for you to tenze me, Mr. Mulryan; and you, Kenny Kilfoy, I am sure it doesn't become you to torment me this way, so it doesn't."

"Mr. Mulryan," said Jack in his bantering strain; "ha, ha—sure it's myself that's growin' the great man. Iv one ov you's calls me Jack to-night any more, after Miss Essy callin' me Misther, pershumin to me but I'll clap yous into the stocks. But," he added, turning to Kenny, "let the colleen alone; you're not the boy, avick, that's for her hand, joke or in earnest. Tom Molloy's the bit ov stuff in fair or market that hits Essy's fancy."

This pointed allusion to his rival, and the persevering coldness of Essy, together with the fresh rushing memory of his shame, contributed to rouse all the bad passions of his heart anew. Turning upon Jack, his sallow face working in varied contortions, and his small, deep sunken eyes flushing with the fire of inflamed rage, he seized him by the collar.

"You fool—you laughin', rhymin', pennyless omedhaun," said he, "how dare you mention Molloy to me?" and he glared and grinned at the still laughing Jack. "But you are a pair ov fools—ger along with you," added he, shaking Mulryan from him.

At the beginning of the above sentence Tom Molloy just entered the wake. Essy was in tears, and he took her hand and placed her quietly, without saying a word, beside an old woman, then turning full to Kenny, who in the madness of his passion had not before observed him,

"You white-livered budogh,"* said he with much excitation, "isn't it a shame for you to be kicking up such ructions in the honest woman's decent wake, and she your own flesh and blood: an' if you had the spark of a man 'ithin in you it's not makin' a wake woman cry, an' callin' a man names behind his back that you daren't before his face."

This was all that was wanting to excite his smouldering passion into full blaze. He made no reply; his face assumed an ashy paleness, the colour fled from his lips, and he rushed to grasp Tom with concentrated fierceness; but Tom, with the eye of the lynx, rushed to meet him, and merely pushing him backward over a long low form, he fell headlong against the table upon which the dead body of his relative was laid. The table, which was rather crazy before, unable to stand such a shock from such a weighty body, broke down, and with a crash covered the unfortunate Kenny Kilfoy with corpse, sheets, and all. The wreck was tremendous: the candles were tumbled about the floor, and put out—the snuff was scattered like a cloud, setting all within its reach into violent sneezing fits; and the heaps of new pipes were smashed into useless fragments. Then the shrieking of the old women, and the darkness were truly frightful. On light being procured, and silence and order someway restored, Kenny Kilfoy was released from the ruin, and the corpse and parapher-

---

* This is a common ceremony among the young people in Ireland, and it is considered even more binding than an oath.

---

* Churl.

nalia in some measure restored to its former appearance. The people rose up to prevent a recurrence of the quarrel, which, however, neither party seemed inclined to renew. Peace was in some measure restored, but there was a strange silence ensued, made doubly remarkable by the previous bustle and noise. Kenny stood with his face turned away from the people, and looking at the corpse. A superstitious feeling had taken possession of his mind; and a kind of horror, mixed with something still more terrible, was expressed in his dark contracted brow and fixed mouth. No person attempted to break the silence. The falling of a corpse was looked on as an unlucky omen, though of what, or to whom, no one could divine; and undefined fear and vague apprehension have ever a mysterious power on the mind. At length an old woman who was seated nearly opposite to where Kilfoy was standing, and who was puffing with might and main from the stump of one of the broken pipes, into which she had crammed the contents of about half a dozen other demolished heads, drawing the pipe from her mouth, and puffing aside the blue smoke, addressed Kenny.

" You ought to pray to heaven,' she said, solemnly and emphatically, " to turn aside any ill luck that's over you —an' it's greatly afraid I am that there's a *crass* afore you, and that thrubble and thribilation 'ill be your lot afore long."

" Keep your *pisherogues* an' your foretellin's till your axed for them,' said he with a scowl, and pulling down his hat he walked out, without looking to the right or to the left, and without opening his lips.

He did not go home; but when he got to a distance from any house, and afar from the sounds of human voices, in a lone field, through which, however, there was a short cut to the village, he threw himself at the foot of a clump of black-thorn and furze mingled, and gave way to every gloomy anticipation and reflection that crossed his mind. The events of that day passed in rapid review before him. The satire and the jest in which Essy and Tom, and her brother joined on the bog—the wrestling match, and the circumstances of the wake. Was he now to be the laughing-stock, and the standing jest-mark of the country side? And then the gloomy apprehensions of fear and superstition about the overturned corpse filled his mind. His heart was a prey to the most conflicting passions. He wished himself dead at one time, and at another he vowed bitter vengeance on the object of his jealous hate. Time passed over quickly, and he 'recked not nor heeded, until at length the sounds of approaching footsteps, and the light sound of voices reached his ear. He listened, and as if pursued by his evil genii, he distinguished the accents of Tom Molloy and Essy, and her brother. They were returning from the wake, and as they drew near he could distinctly hear that he was the subject of their laughter and conversation.

" An' did you mind," said Tom, as they approached where he was, " did you mind when they dragged him out from under the corpse how white he was, an' how he panted, an' how his face twisted. You could swear he was the picther of the dead ould woman."

" Ha, ha, ha," laughed Essy at the comparison, " an' sure there's nothin' sthrange in that, when you know they're near relations."

" Sure enough," said the brother, " you must have given him the father ov a douce to dhrive him that way."

" Psha-at, no," said Tom in a light tone, " just a little push—throth it wouldn't take much to do it, seein' that he's so wake as—"

The rest of the sentence was lost to Kilfoy, but what he heard was sufficient to drive him mad.

The more he thought, the more his dark fancy and imagination wrought his brain to phrenzy, and he started to his feet, and rushed along by another route towards his own house. Revenge was now the overwhelming and master passion in his soul, and a dark and dreadful revenge he determined to wreak.

His cabin lay nearly in a direct line between that of the Bucklys and the cottage of Molloy. He reached it without encountering any person. He rushed in and seized the *slane*, with which he had that day been at work, and, hiding it beneath his great coat, he traversed

the fields with rapid steps, until he hid himself in the shadow of a large ash tree, in a ditch beside the path where he knew his rival must pass upon his return from Buckly's to his own house.

Tom did not remain long with Essy and her brother; he bid them good night, and turned to his own home, and commenced whistling, " speed the plough" in merry thoughtlessness. He never spent a thought upon his quarrel with Kilfoy—his heart was full of joy and love.— Essy had that night promised to be his; and her brother, by his friendly manner, seemed to countenance his addresses to his sister. They could afford, he knew, to give her some trifle that might help them exceedingly beginning the world, and though this was but a secondary consideration to him, still that, and the consciousness of being loved by her besides, rendered his waking dream of anticipated happiness doubly pleasant. With a heart going with all these joyous emotions, he entered upon the pathway where his enemy stood, like the tiger waiting by the stream side for the thirsty antelope. On he came, with his blithe whistle, startling the sleeping birds in the boughs above his head, which flitted with a short chirup, and a whirring flutter, from one branch to another, as he passed beneath. He passed by the ash tree. Kilfoy leaped out, and aimed a dreadful blow at the back of his head. The sudden noise made him jump a little aside, and he received the stroke full on the side of his head, but with the flat part of the slane. He fell, and was in the act of gaining his feet again, when Kilfoy repeated the blow with all his might. He raised his arm to defend his head, but the guard was but feeble when compared to the force of the blow, and the weight of the weapon, and he again fell at his length on the path. Still he was not materially injured, but he felt how it would end, and looked up to the demoniac fury which flashed in Kilfoy's eyes, and his heart and stomach grew sick, either with apprehension or from the blows, and he cried out,

" Oh, Kenny Kilfoy, are you going to murder me ?"

" Ha !" cried the infuriated wretch, " now do you mock me—now who's the best man ? Now tell Essy Buckly that I'm a cowardly, weak, mopin' fool. Now—" and another blow left the unfortunate Molloy silent for ever. The cocked part of the *slane* had penetrated the scull to the depth of several inches, and, as he drew up the weapon, the head of the good-hearted young man clung to it, until the weight of the body detached it. A short, gurgling, choking cry was all that was uttered, and a quivering of the limbs succeeded, and all was still and motionless. This deed was but the work of a few minutes. There stood the murderer and his victim; and, already, the consequences of his crime was felt in his heart, as he gazed at his rival weltering in his hot young blood. A rush of the breeze agitating the boughs into murmurs over his head, seemed to denounce him aloud, and the quivering moon-beams flitting to and fro over the bloody spot, as they streamed through the waving branches, seemed to his already horror-stricken fancy like a thousand dancing lights, flung by unseen hands, to show to the world the cursed deed. He grasped his stiffening hair on each side of his brow with both his hands, and he seemed as if willing to tear the covering from his burning brain, that the chill night breeze might coolly fan it, so tight and hard did he gripe it.

" Now," said he, as the remembrance of the old woman's words rushed into his mind, " now the bad luck is on me. Now the thrubble and the thribilation is my lot for ever," and he gazed fearfully round him, and rushed from the spot.

Early next morning the body of the murdered Molloy was discovered, cold and lifeless, and the *slane* of Kenny Kilfoy lying beside it. The suspicions of all fell directly on him, and the country was traversed in all directions, but the slightest trace of the murderer could not be discovered. He had not slept at home that night, nor had he been seen by any person from the moment he left the *wake*. An inquest was held on the body. The quarrels were stated, and the identity of the slane sworn to; and the jury, without hesitation, pronounced a verdict of " wilful murder against Kenny Kilfoy." It is useless here to describe the anguish of Essy Buckly, the grief of

Tom's little *bocagh*, (brother,) and the sorrow of the whole neighbourhood; for Tom's good-natured and pleasant disposition had endeared him to every one. He was waked according to the usual form, and there never was so numerously attended a wake, or so respectable a funeral seen in the village. As Tom had but one relative, the little cripple abovementioned, who was unable to manage the farm, it was accordingly sold, with all the little live stock and furniture, and with the sum procured the cripple commenced business as a pedlar. He was a cunning, saving, industrious little fellow, who soon improved, and in the course of a few years, his means enabled him to purchase a nag and cart, and to lay in a stock of goods, with which he traversed the country in all directions, and in time became a very wealthy man.

Years rolled away, and still there never was a word heard about Kenny Kilfoy; and the deed and his name were nearly forgotten even in the village. Aby, Tom's brother, but seldom came near his native place. Once or twice a year would he be seen at the spot where his brother was murdered; but regularly, on the morning of the anniversary of the murder, would the villagers behold him, from dawn to sunrise, kneeling on the spot, and, with his long beads depending from his fingers, in the attitude of prayer.

Nearly twenty years passed over in this manner, and still no tidings of Kilfoy could be procured, and it was supposed that he had made his escape to America. Aby Molloy traversed Ireland with his horse and cart, and about the summer of 1813 he attended the fair of Ballinasloe, where, having a great variety of goods for sale, he pleased the country people so well, that he got most of them off his hands at large profits. He then formed the resolution of going down farther into the more distant and remote parts of the province, in hopes to sell out his stock before his return to Dublin for new goods. He passed on from town to town and from village to village, and in the course of some weeks reached the secluded district in the county of Mayo in which is situated the little town of Crossmolina. It was late in the evening when he arrived, and he sought his humble inn for the night. Strange dreams came over him during the night. He thought at one time that he was at the spot where his brother was murdered, and that the earth around was covered with fresh gore. At another he dreamed that his brother came to him, as he beheld him the morning after his death, covered with his own cold and blackened blood, and smiling in his face, the ghastly smile which might be supposed such a hideous face could give, took him by the hand and bid him arise. The terrifying sight would cause him to awake with affright; yet as soon as slumber again visited his wearied frame, the same appalling vision would crowd upon his dreaming fancy. He lay in bed that morning longer than he was wont; his mind was unusually affected, and a gloom was cast over it, which he in vain endeavoured to shake off. On his rising he went to the door to see what appearance the little town had. He looked up and down the street. He looked at the door opposite, for he felt as one feels who has the eye of a stranger fixed on him—(there is a kind of

sympathy excited by the electricity of certain looks)— and what was his horror to behold the identical Kenny Kilfoy, almost unchanged by time, gazing on him with an intense and alarmed gaze. He trembled as he recognised the murderer of his brother. He opened his lips to speak—his tongue was tied in wonder—he hobbled a few steps into the street and extended his arms, but could not utter a word. The murderer disappeared from the door, and he immediately recovered from his surprise, and seeing some military men lounging about a little barracks in the town, he hobbled up, and in hurried accents related the facts. The serjeant of the guard attended him : they entered the house and found the now wretched Kilfoy extended in a paroxysm of fear, and remorse upon his face, on the bed, in a back room.

" There, there," he exclaimed, " there is the man that murdered my brother—take him—take him, he's the murderer."

It may be necessary here to take a retrospective view of the life of Kenny Kilfoy from the night on which he committed the bloody deed. He rushed from the scene of guilt, without noting the direction he took; he travelled at a running rate all that night, and at the break of day he was nearly twenty miles distant from the spot. He perceived some men at a distance going to field-work, and he dreaded to meet the eye of man. He left the road, and took shelter in a screen of fir-trees by the road side. Tired and fatigued though he was, he could not rest. The murdered Molloy was always before his eyes, and when the darkness fell he crept from his biding-place, and resumed his journey ; and though fasting and fatigued, the anxiety of his mind served to bear up his body against the effects of over exertion. He reached Crossmolina in safety, and his mind becoming something easier, he stopped there for some time working with a baker. He was generally abstracted in his manner, and sought active employment as a means of diverting his thoughts from the contemplation of his crime. His attention pleased his employer, and in the course of a few years he acquired a perfect knowledge of the business. His mind became gradually settled, and he felt a security and an ease growing round him. His employer had but one child, a girl, and Kilfoy having saved some money, and being of quiet, sober habits, he was induced to consent to the marriage of his daughter with Kenny. The old man died in a few years after, and at the time of his apprehension, Kilfoy was one of the most wealthy and respected men in the little town. Heaven never blessed him with children, and this he now spoke of as his greatest happiness.

He confessed the murder on being taken by the soldiers, and confronted by Aby, and was then removed to the gaol of Philipstown, where, after undergoing the regular trial the following assizes, he suffered the extreme penalty of the law, acknowledging his crime, the justice of his sentence, and dying truly repentant.

This tale has its foundation in fact, and is an example of the equity of Divine Providence, who, however long crime is allowed to go unpunished, is still sure to detect and punish the guilty.

J. L. L.

ANCIENT BRASS RELIC.

The above is a correct representation of a piece of brass, having a hole in one end, as if intended to be suspended by a string or chain; it is three and a half inches long, and about the tenth of an inch thick. The letters marked thereon are in alto-relievo. It was lately turned up by a plough near the castle of Clonmines, formerly a preceptory of the Knights Templers, in the county Wexford, and

presented by Mr. Sutton, who holds the farm, to Samuel Elly, Esq., of Bannow, in whose possession it now remains. The inscription will afford a subject of enquiry for some of your antiquarian correspondents.

N. B.—The F in the second line has been read by many persons as P. C. H. W.

Wexford, 1834.

ON A NAVAL OFFICER BURIED IN THE ATLANTIC.

There is, in the wide lone sea,
  A spot unmark'd, but holy ;
For there the gallant and the free
  In his ocean bed lies lowly.

Down, down, within the deep,
  That oft to triumph bore him,
He sleeps a sound and pleasant sleep,
  With the soft waves washing o'er him.

He sleeps serene and safe
  From tempest or from billow,
Where the storms, that high above him chafe,
  Scarce rock his peaceful pillow.

The sea and him in death
  They did not dare to sever ;
It was his home while he had breath ;
  'Tis now his rest for ever.

Sleep on, thou mighty dead !
  A glorious tomb they've found thee—
The broad blue sky above thee spread,
  The boundless waters round thee.

No vulgar foot treads here ;
  No hand profane shall move thee;
But gallant fleets shall proudly steer,
  And warriors shout above thee.

When the last trump shall sound,
  And tombs are sunder riven,
Like the morning sun from the wave thou'lt bound,
  To rise and shine in heaven.

NEW MODE OF EMBALMING THE DEAD.

The public journals have already spoken of the new method of embalming, by which Dr. Tronihina, of Palermo, preserves a dead body for two months free from any symptom of corruption. It has been said, that, without opening the body, he prepared a corpse in less than two hours, according to his method, and delivered it to the university, in order to remove every doubt of the efficacy of his proceeding. A letter from Palermo, of the 24th of May, confirms the result of the experiment upon a subject which had been embalmed two months and four days, and was in perfect preservation. Externally, a small incision, about half an inch in length, was observed in the neck ; the face was rather dried, and also the toes, which seemed to be hard, and of a brownish colour ; the pupils of the eyes were covered with a darkish wrinkled skin ; the rest of the body retained its natural colour and the perfect pliability of all the limbs. On opening the skull, the blood issued as red and as fluid as from a person just dead ; the dura mater was white and shining ; the mass of the brain beneath so fresh, that it could scarcely have been believed to belong to the dead : externally it was grey, as usual ; internally, throughout, white ; and the veins as visible, red, and defined as in a quite fresh brain. On opening the chest and abdomen, the heart and lungs were in the same natural state ; and the intestines, which first turn black immediately after death, were precisely those that were in the best state of preservation—white, soft, shining, inodorous, though they contained some fluid matter which should have promoted their corruption. The liver, kidneys, &c. were quite fresh. The attentive silence with which all the spectators (about five hundred persons, in the dissecting-room of the university) had regarded the examination was intermingled with true Italian vivacity, by long and repeated *evvivas* to the doctor.

VILLAGE OF WATERFOOT, NEAR CUSHENDALL.

Having already in a former number described the entire line of coast from Belfast to the Giant's Causeway, we would merely observe, in reference to the little village represented in the above engraving, that it lies between Glenarm and Cushendall—but a short distance from Red Bay, on the one hand, and the romantic vale and cascade of Glenariffe on the other, the prospect to the left being terminated by the lofty conical summit of Crunch-a-Crun —while that to the north is bounded by the beautiful hill of Lurgeidan. On the shores of Red Bay innumerable fragments of the mountains of Carriv-Murphy and Sleive Barighad lie scattered, in promiscuous confusion. Indeed at every step the magnificent scene of desolation assumes new forms, and is finely contrasted by the quiet Vale of Glenariffe, which unexpectedly meets the eye of the traveller, as he journies towards the Causeway.

DUBLIN:
Printed by P. D. Hardy, 3, Cecilia-street.

THE
DUBLIN PENNY JOURNAL

CONDUCTED BY P. DIXON HARDY, M.R.I.A.

| Vol. III. | OCTOBER 18, 1834. | No. 120. |

TEMPLECORAN CHURCH.

These ruins are situate near the little village of Bally-carry, in the parish of Kilroot, on the Antrim coast, which we have already described in our Guide to the Causeway. This spot has been rendered memorable by several interesting particulars. Here, in the year 1611, the first Presbyterian congregation in Ireland was established ; in the adjoining cemetery is the grave of the Rev. Edward Brice, its first minister. The living of Kilroot was the first to which the celebrated Dean Swift was appointed, but which he is said to have resigned from a natural aversion to retirement or solitude.

In Scott's Life of Swift we find the following accounts of this transaction :—

" Swift's life at Kilroot, so different from that which he had led with Sir William Temple, where he shared the society of all that were ennobled, either by genius or birth, soon became insipid. In the mean while, Temple, who had learned, by the loss of Swift, his real value, became solicitous that he should return to Moorpark.— While Swift hesitated between relinquishing the mode of life which he had chosen, and returning to that which he had relinquished, his resolution appears to have been determined by a circumstance highly characteristic of his exalted benevolence. In an excursion from his habitation, he met a clergyman, with whom he formed an acquaintance, which proved him to be learned, modest, well-principled, the father of eight children, and a curate at the rate of forty pounds a year. Without explaining his purpose, Swift borrowed this gentleman's black mare, having no horse of his own, rode to Dublin, resigned the

prebendary of Kilroot, and obtained a grant of it for this new friend. When he gave the presentation to the poor clergyman, he kept his eyes steadily fixed on the old man's face, which, at first, only expressed pleasure at finding himself preferred to a living ; but when he found that it was that of his benefactor, who had resigned in his favour, his joy assumed so touching an expression of surprise and gratitude, that Swift, himself deeply affected, declared he had never experienced so much pleasure as at that moment. The poor clergyman, at Swift's departure, pressed upon him the black mare, which he did not choose to hurt him by refusing, and thus mounted, for the first time, on a horse of his own, with fourscore pounds in his purse, Swift again embarked for England, and resumed his situation at Moorpark, as Sir William Temple's confidential secretary.

" These are the outlines of a transaction, upon which, long after Swift's death, malice or madness endeavoured to fix a construction fatal to his reputation.

" In an edition of the Tatler in six volumes, 1786, executed with uncommon accuracy and care, there occurs a note upon No. 188, which, among other strictures on Swift's history, mentions the following alleged fact : ' Lord Wharton's remarkable words allude, not only to the odium Swift had contracted as the known or supposed author of the Tale of a Tub, &c. but they seem to point more particularly to a flagrant part of his criminality at Kilroot, not so generally known. A general account of this offence is all that is requisite here, and all that decency permits. In consequence of an attempt to ill use one of his parishioners, a farmer's daughter, Swift was carried before a magistrate of the name of Dobbs, (in whose family the examinations taken on the occasion are said to be still extant at this day) ; and, to avoid the very serious consequences of this rash action, immediately resigned the prebend, and quitted the kingdom. This intelligence was communicated, and vouched as a fact well known in the parish even now, by one of Swift's successors in the living, and is rested on the authority of the present prebendary of Kilroot, February 6, 1785.'

" The Rev. Mr. P—r, a successor of Dean Swift in the prebend of ·Kilroot, was the first circulator of this extraordinary story. He told the tale, among other public occasions, at the late excellent Bishop of Dromore's, who committed it to writing. His authority he alleged to be a Dean Dobbs, who, he stated, had informed him that informations were actually lodged before magistrates in the diocese of Down and Connor, for the alleged attempt at violation. But when the late ingenious Mr. Malone, and many other literary gentleman, began to press a closer examination of the alleged fact, the unfortunate narrator denied obstinately his having ever promulgated such a charge. And whether the whole story was the creation of incipient insanity, or whether he had felt the discredit attached to his tergiversation so acutely as to derange his understanding, it is certain the unfortunate Mr. P—r died raving mad, a patient in that very hospital for lunatics, established by Swift, against whom he had propagated this cruel calumny. Yet, although P—r thus fell a victim to his own rash assertions or credulity, it has been supposed that this inexplicable figment did really originate with Dean Dobbs, and that he had been led into a mistake, by the initial letters, J. S. upon the alleged papers, which might apply to Jonathan Smedley, (to whom, indeed, the tale has been supposed properly to belong,) or to John Smith, as well as to Jonathan Swift. It is sufficient for Swift's vindication to observe, that he returned to Kilroot, after his resignation, and inducted his successor in face of the church and of the public ; that he returned to Sir William Temple with as fair a character as when he had left him ; that during all his public life, in England and Ireland, where he was the butt of a whole faction, this charge was never heard of ; that when adduced so many years after his death, it was unsupported by aught but sturdy and general averment ; and that the chief propagator of the calumny first retracted his assertions, and finally died insane."

THE DISSIPATED HUSBAND.

He comes not ; I have watched the moon go down,
But yet he comes not ; once it was not so ;
He thinks not how these bitter tears do flow,
The while he holds his riot in that town.
Yet he will come, and chide, and I shall weep,
And he will wake my infant from its sleep,
To blend its feeble wailing with my tears.
Oh, how I love a mother's watch to keep,
Over those sleeping eyes, that smile which cheers
My heart, though sunk in sorrow, fix'd and deep.
I had a husband once, who loved me ; now
He ever wears a frown upon his brow,
But yet, I cannot hate : oh there were hours
When I could hang for ever on his eye,
And Time, who stole with silent swiftness by,
Strew'd, as he hurried on, his path with flowers.
I loved him then ; he loved me too ; my heart
Still finds its fondness kindle, if he smile ;
The memory of our loves will ne'er depart ;
And though he often stings me with a dart,
Venom'd and barb'd, and wastes upon the vile
Caresses which his babe and mine should share.
Though he should spurn me, I will calmly bear
His madness ; and should sickness come, and lay
Its paralyzing hand upon him, then
I would, with kindness, all my wrongs repay,
Until the penitent should weep and say,
How injured, and how faithful I had been.

EMIGRATION.

In a recent number of our Journal, we extracted from a Canada paper, of the preceding month, some particulars important to persons intending to emigrate : the following is from the *Montreal Daily Advertiser*, and will enable those of the humbler classes to calculate what they may expect as a remuneration for their labour on the other side of the Atlantic :—

We took occasion a few days since to notice a statement which appeared in the *Quebec Gazette*, that wages did not amount to more than ten pence or a shilling a day, with food. We cautioned those who are in any way interested in the matter not to permit the idea to enter into their minds, that the said rate indicated that which prevailed all over the country, particularly in Upper Canada. Since then we have seen the following notice in some of the Upper Canada papers, and as there can be no deception, we insert it :—

Emigrant Office, Toronto, June 13, 1834.
NOTICE TO EMIGRANTS IN WANT OF WORK.—Emigrants in want of employment are informed that the Grand River Navigation Company have advertised for one thousand labourers, who will meet with immediate employment at three pounds, currency, per month, and board. Several hundred labourers are also wanted on the *Welland Canal*, at the same rate of wages. Emigrants desirous of availing themselves of the above offer, should proceed by way of the Welland Canal, and land at Port Robinson. There is also a great demand for mechanics at Hamilton, Dundas, Ancaster and Brentford. Farm labourers are much wanted in the neighbourhood of these towns. For further information emigrants are directed to apply to Mr. Cattermole, at Hamilton.

A. B. HAWKE, *Emigrant Agent.*

Most of our readers are aware that a considerable amount of distress has occasionally prevailed in the cities of Quebec and Montreal among the immigrants of the current year. It is also well known that the rate of wages, in most kinds of employment, are decidedly low, compared with the rates in Upper Canada. The cause of these two states of things is one, namely, the influx of the competitors for employment, with their families, without the means of carrying them to parts of the country where their labour is in demand and well remunerated. Latterly, the emigrant societies—their power of doing being greatly increased by the sums placed at their disposal by the legislature—have done much to mitigate distress, by forwarding immigrants to different parts of the country.

ROSS IN THE OLDEN TIME.

Curious account of the erection of the walls and fortifications of New Ross, in the year 1265, founded on an ancient French poem, supposed from the pen of Father Michael Kyldare, who was an eye witness, and therefore of undoubted authority.

Among the Harleian MSS. in the British Museum is preserved a highly curious volume, towards the close of which occurs an interesting poem, written in the Norman, or ancient French language, contributing, in a remarkable degree, to throw an illustration on the early topography and history of the town of New Ross, county of Wexford, Ireland.

The poem is founded on a quarrel which occurred there between Sir Morice and Sir Walter, A. D. 1265.— This is not a very accurate description, since the object of the writer was not to relate a quarrel between two anonymous knights, but to give a detailed narrative of the erection of the fortifications and walls of Ross, occasioned by the dread felt by the inhabitants, lest the unprotected and open situation of the place might cause them to suffer from a feud, then raging with violence, between two powerful barons, Maurice Fitzmaurice, the chief of the Geraldine faction,[*] and Walter de Burgo, Earl of Ulster, whose deadly wars, in the year 1264, wrought bloodshed and trouble throughout the realm of Ireland. The turbulent violence of the former party proceeded to such a height, that on the interposition of Richard de Repella, (called also Capella Rochel and des Roches), the chief justiciary, the Geraldines not only slighted his authority, but forcibly seized on his person, and placed him, with several others, (among whom was Richard de Burgo, son of Walter,) in confinement.

The very inadequate means possessed by the English sovereigns of quelling this spirit of discord, is sufficiently evident during the whole of the early period of Irish history, and more particularly during the reign of Henry the Third. By the appointment of Sir David Barry, in 1267, to the office of Justiciary, the violence of the Geraldines seems in some degree to have been controuled, and in a measure lessened; but the weakness of the king's representatives, in attempting to subdue the feuds of these turbulent barons, is clearly manifested by the rapid changes which took place during this period in the office of Justiciary, a fresh successor being nominated nearly every twelve months. At length, either from the increasing ascendancy of the Geraldines, or what is more probable, from the policy of the English monarch, Maurice Fitzmaurice was constituted the royal deputy in 1272. He appears to have taken advantage of this mark of favour to revenge himself on the O'Brien's, his hereditary enemies; but being in his own turn betrayed by some of his followers, he was, in the succeeding year, A. D. 1273, taken prisoner, and obliged to give satisfaction for the deaths of his opponents. After a fresh series of similar contests, he died in the town of Ross, A. D. 1286; and the same year proved fatal to his son, Gerald Fitzmaurice, and his son-in-law, Thomas de Clare.

His adversary, Walter de Burgh, who married the daughter of Hugh de Lacy, and in her right inherited the earldom of Ulster, on her father's death, in 1264, was involved in the same scene of bloodshed; and on the cessation of the feud with the Geraldines, laid claim to the territories of Connaught, but being opposed by the O'Connors, and defeated in a conflict, he did not long survive, but after a week's illness, expired in his castle of Galiway, 26th of July, 1271, and was interred in the abbey of Althasil.

These historical data sufficiently confirm the account of the poet, in ascribing the erection of the walls of Ross to this troublesome period; and prove Cambden to have been mistaken when he states that the walls were built by Isabel, daughter of Richard, Earl Strongbow.[†]

So little is known of the early history of New Ross, it is merely described by all topographers as having once been a place of great strength and extent, situated in a large ravine, formed by the junction of the rivers Barrow and Nore. Of its high walls and frowning towers and gates some remains continue until the present day. It was a place of considerable trade so early as the reign of Henry Fifth, and obtained charters from several of the English sovereigns, the earliest of which is supposed to be that of Henry the Fourth. Its port is so capacious that ships of nine hundred tons burden may come up to the quay; but the commerce of the town decreased, subsequently, to such a degree, that in 1776 we only find five or six brigs were to be seen in it. It has since rapidly improved, for upwards of thirty large ships, chiefly employed in emigration, belong to the merchants of the town. The port has also been lately opened, as previously it was in dependance to Waterford.

---

[*] Sir James Ware calls him Earl of Desmond, and says he was drowned in 1268, while crossing from Ireland to Wales; but both these errors are corrected by Cox. The first Earl of Desmond was Maurice Fitzthomas, created by Edward the Third, August 27, 1329.

[†] Grose, in his Antiquities, Vol. 1, page 59, repeats an absurd variation of the same tradition, ascribing the inclosure of New Ross, with a wall, to Rose Macrue, sister of Strongbow, in the year 1310, who is said also to have built Hook Tower, in the same county, and to have been buried at Ross, in the church of St. Saviour's.

THE ARMS OF THE TOWN OF ROSS.

Among the collection of the second Randle Holmes, for the city of Chester, (MS. Harleian, 2173, fol. 42,) is a copy of "a certyficate from the soveraine (mayor) of New Ross, alias Ross Ponte, in Ireland, to show how wee be free with them, and they with the city of Chester, of all customs," 29 Eliz. 1587, A. D. A seal was appended to the document, with the arms of Ross, being a greyhound pulling down a stag, and beneath, a bridge raised on several arches, from which bridge the appellation of Ross Pont was doubtless derived. Round the edge we read, "S. Office :....Superiour, Newe Rosse." In 1257 the Franciscans are said to have settled there; and a convent of St. Augustine's was founded in the reign of Edward the Third. Sir John Devereux subsequently erected the convent of St. Saviour on the site of the Franciscan monastery, and part of it is still appropriated to the use of a parish church. The more modern history of this place is chiefly remarkable for the defence made against the misguided peasantry on the 6th of June, 1798, by the garrison and inhabitants under the command of General Sir William Johnson, Bart.

The author of the poem commences in the following abrupt manner; "I have an inclination to write in romance, if it pleases you to hear me; for a story that is not listened to is of no more value than a berry. I pray you, therefore, to give attention, and you shall hear a fine adventure of a town in Ireland, the most beautiful of its size that I know in any country. Its inhabitants were alarmed by the feud existing between two barons, whose names you see here written, Sir Maurice and Sir Wauter The name of this town I will now disclose to you—it is called Ros—it is the New Pont de Ross." He then proceeds to relate how the principal men of the town, together with the commonalty, assembled to take measures for their safety; and they resolved to surround the town with mortar and stone. They commenced, accordingly, on the feast of the Purification, (February 2, A. D. 1265,) and marked out the fosse or line of circumvallation.—Workmen were speedily hired, and above an hundred each day came out to labour, under the direction of the Burgesses. When this step was taken they again assembled, and determined to establish a bye law, such (says the poet,) as was never heard of in England or France; which was publicly proclaimed the next day to the people, and received with applause; this law was as follows: "That on the ensuing Monday, the vintners, the mercers, the merchants, and the drapers should go and work at the fosse, from the hour of prime till noon." This was readily complied with, and above one thousand men," (writes the poet,) "went out to work every Monday with brave banners, and great pomp, attended by flutes and tabors. So soon as the hour of noon had sounded, these fine fellows returned home, with their banners borne before them, and the young men singing loudly and caroling through the town. The priests, also, who accompanied, fell to work at the fosse, and laboured right well, more so than the others, being young and skilful, of tall stature, strong, and well housed. The mariners, likewise, proceeded in good array to the fosse, to the number of six hundred, with a banner preceding them, on which was depicted a vessel; and if all the people in the ships and barges had been hired, they would have amounted to eleven hundred men," a convincing proof of the importance of the town, at that time, as a mercantile port. On the Tuesday this party was succeeded by another, consisting of the tailors and cloth workers, the tentmakers, fullers, and celers,* who went out in a similar manner as the former, but were not so numerous, amounting only to four hundred men. On the Wednesday, a different set was employed, viz., the cordwainers, tanners, and butchers, many brave bachelors were among them, and their banners were painted as appertains to their craft. In number, I believe, they were about three hundred taken together, little and great; and they went forth, caroling loudly as the others did. On the Thursday came the fishermen and hucksters. Their standards were of various sorts; but on one was painted a fish and a platter; these, five hundred in number, were associated with the wainrights, who were thirty-two in number. On Friday went out the ...... (illegible) in number three hundred and fifty, with their banners borne before them, unto the border of the fosse. On the Saturday succeeded the carpenters, blacksmiths, and masons—in number about three hundred and fifty. Lastly, on the Sunday, assembled in procession the ladies of the town! Know, verily, that they were excellent labourers, but their numbers I cannot certainly tell; but they all went forth to cast stones and carry them from the fosse. Whoever had been there to look at them, might have seen many a beautiful woman—many a mantle of scarlet, green, and russet—many a fair folded cloak, and many a gay coloured garment. In all the countries I ever visited never saw I so many fair ladies. He should have been born in a fortunate hour who might make his choice among them." The ladies also carried banners, in imitation of the other parties; and when they were tired of the duty assigned to them, they walked round the fosse, singing sweetly, to encourage the workmen. On their return to the town, the richer sort held a convivial meeting, "and," as we are told, "made sport, drank whiskey,

* "Celers," mean saddlers, from the French word "selliers."

and sang," encouraging each other, and resolving to make a gate, which should be called the Ladies' Gate, and there would fix a prison. According to the poet, "the fosse was made twenty feet in depth, and its length extended above a league. When it shall be completed," adds the writer, "they may sleep securely, and will not require a guard; for if forty thousand men were to attack the town they would never be able to enter it, for they have sufficient means of defence; many a white hauberk and haubergeon—many a doublet and coat of mail, and a savage Garcon—many a good cross-bow-man have they, and many good archers. Never, in any town, beheld I so many good glaives, nor so many good cross-bows hanging on the wall, nor so many quarrels to shoot withal, and every house full of maces, good shields, and talevases. They are well provided, I warrant you, to defend themselves from their enemies; for the cross-bow-men, in reality, amount to three hundred and sixty-three in number, as counted at their muster, and enrolled in the muster-roll. And of other archers have they one thousand two hundred brave fellows, be assured; and besides these there are three thousand men, armed with lances or axes, in the town; and knights on horseback one hundred and four, well armed for the combat."

The poet then assures us that the object of the inhabitants was by no means to court an assault; but simply for their own protection; "for which," says he, "no one ought to blame them:" they appear, however, to have amply provided for their safety; for the writer continues, "when the wall shall be completely carried round and fortified, no one in Ireland will be so hardy as to attack them; for by the time they have twice sounded a horn, the people assemble and fly to arms, each anxious to be before his neighbour, so courageous and valiant are they to revenge themselves on an enemy. God grant they may obtain revenge, and preserve the town with honour! And let all say amen, for charite! for it is the most hospitable town that exists in any nation; and every stranger is welcomed with joy, and may buy and sell at his will without any thing being demanded of him. I commend the town and all who inhabit it to God, amen." This was done in the year of the incarnation of our Lord, 1265.

CASTLE TOWNSEND.

Cork, August 21, 1834.

Sir—It has often astonished me, that while places far inferior to Castle Townsend are the resort of persons desiring sea-bathing, a spot so well calculated as this has been so long passed by. However, it is now, as it deserves, rising every day in importance, having been for merly composed of but a few fishing huts. It is now a neat, pretty village—a new custom house has been built, and trade is beginning to flourish; slowly indeed, at first, but I have no doubt that it will at length be frequented as a most desirable watering place. The foregoing is a sketch of the parish church, which has been lately built, and is situated in the splendid demesne of Colonel Townsend; it is taken from the opposite side of the bay, which runs up between two hills covered to the water's edge with trees. The harbour is capable of containing large vessels, notwithstanding which it is dangerous on account of rocks, which are under the water. At some future time I shall furnish you with a view of that also, if the present meets your approbation. I remain, Sir, your obedient servant, F. H. T.

Cork, August 25, 1834.

Sir—I send you the view of Castle Townsend Harbour, mentioned in my last communication, and mean in this to describe the different headlands and points, and whatever other parts are worthy of notice. Toe Head, the principal, is a high cliff overhanging the sea, which, although it appears the outside boundary of the harbour, is at least four miles from Castle Townsend. It commands one of the most splendid views I have ever seen—the whole line of coast from Gallyhead to Cape Clear, with the different harbours and bays between them—the view of the sea here is extremely open, and vessels going to America may be seen from this spot as they pass Cape Clear for the last time previous to their leaving the shores of Ireland. Between this and the next hill a bay runs up, called Sandy Cove, where the fury of the Atlantic may be seen at its full height: it is a tremendous sight to behold the waves "dashing against the cliffs with deafening roar," while the spray falls in showers on him who is bold enough to ascend them. There have been several wrecks at Castle Townsend within the last few years. Two ships were lost within the harbour, a few yards from the shore—not one in either of them was saved; the bodies were washed ashore a few days afterwards dreadfully disfigured. There are two rocks at the entrance of the harbour, called the Stags, one of which appears in the present view. The point next it is called Reen, from which the view of the church, which I sent you, was taken.—There is an old castle between that and the neck of land running across the bay; opposite to which is another, in Colonel Townsend's demesne, which was the scene of an engagement during the Irish rebellion—both parties firing across the water. The scene here is remarkably pretty, and, indeed, all the way as far as the top of the bay.—There are the remains of another castle near the old church, but for what purpose built I don't know. It commands the river: a few years since it was in good order, but is now a perfect ruin. Hoping these few particulars may be interesting to the readers of the Dublin Penny Journal, which is at all times interesting to me, I remain, Sir, your obedient servant, F. H. T.

CASTLE TOWNSEND HARBOUR.

DANIEL O'LEARY, THE DUHALLOW PIPER.

Mr. Editor—Some years since, while taking a little excursion through certain wild districts of the south, I had the satisfaction of hearing some of the best Irish airs, played on the best set of "organ pipes," by the best piper in Munster—a rich treat, which I certainly could not have enjoyed had I, like Sir Richard Colt Hoare, Bart., travelled in *my own coach*—or, after the fashion of the famous "Terence O'Toole," of the Dublin Penny Journal, perched "*a top o' the mail*," surveyed the land with eagle's eye, as I glided with eagle's speed by many a tower and abbey grey. No, no, gentle reader—

"If thou on men, their works and ways,
Wouldst throw uncommon light,"

thou must travel as I have done, an humble pedestrian, and learn the unsophisticated feelings of an Irish peasant at his own hospitable hearth. Upon setting forward on my excursion I made some alteration in my usual mode of dress. I doffed my broad brimmer for a hat of narrower leaf. I exchanged the white cravat, which I was accustomed to tie with extreme precision behind, for a gay silk neck-cloth, whose well adjusted knot flowed copiously to the wind; and I laid by my black frock for a "blue body-coat," with a "gilt button," a circumstance which I deem necessary to state for the benefit of the uninitiated in Irish affairs, who may have in contemplation a trip similar to the one to which I allude. Among the peasantry a black coat creates rather unpleasant suspicions, unless they know the wearer to be " one of the clargy,"———without this descriptive mark, men of all avocations may travel with perfect impunity, and a certainty of the most hospitable reception in our wildest glens, proctors and gaugers always excepted. I was under no apprehension of being mistaken for the last mentioned personage, because my person is tall and thin, my face abstemiously pale, and not a single grog blossom expanding its fiery petals on my nasal organ. Furnished with a choice hazel sapling for my hand, and a port folio for remarks, I sallied forth to see the world,

" And know if books or swains report it right."

During my peregrination I gleaned many a tuneful lay and curious legend, which have lived for hundreds of years in the traditions of the land. The results of my wanderings are yet lying by me, and I have not determined whether to print them in a thin quarto, or send them to the Dublin Penny Journal—I think the Journal shall have them.

The glowing sun was going down in the west on a fine evening in the decline of Autumn, as I gained the brow of a hill that overlooks the silver Ariglin, which flows through the western wilds of Duhallow, in the county of Cork, to join the broad Blackwater. It was a glorious scene, where the light and shade of hill and valley were beautifully linked with the evening mist that curled along the winding stream. I sat down to enjoy the free and boundless prospect, beside one of those ancient mounds called Danish forts, and was soon accosted by a man, wrapt in one of those great coats of olden fame, which an English writer formerly designated as " a fit house for an outlaw—a meet bed for a rebel—and an apt cloak for a thief." He had a long pole in his hand, and seemed to be engaged in the business of herding a number of cattle that grazed peacefully in the extensive common below.

" This silent spot," said I, " was once a busy, bustling scene, when the heathen Dane kept garrison here, and subjected to his rule the surrounding country."

" Ah !' said the intelligent herdsman, " it is an error to suppose that all these ancient works are of Danish construction : the Irish must have raised forts also to protect their own possessions, for the Danes were never entire masters of the land at any time. But tradition assigns the erection of this mound to a period when the Danes were without a name in the annals of Europe.— This very fort is said to have been raised by Goul Mac Morna, in the third century, upon separating from Fionn Mac Cool, who resided at Doon, about a mile farther down the Ariglin. The spot where we sit is called in the Irish tongue, " The Fort of the Hill of Parting," and that part of the river which glitters in the last rays of the sun, is named " the Ford of the Glutton," from the death of one of the Fianna which happened there."

' " By what means did this occurrence happen," I enquired.

" When Goul and his adherents retired from Doon to this hill, Fionn, to maintain a friendly correspondence, sent him daily a joint of roast meat ; but one evening, as a certain soldier carried the present to Goul, he was greatly tempted by the delicious flavour of the meat, the richness of which appeared mellowed in the hot sun-beam ; regardless of the consequence, he gratified his appetite, and after depositing the meat at the fort, he returned back towards Doon. When Goul beheld the mutilated ▪•nt, he set an arrow to his bow, in revenge of the insult. The fatal missile overtook the poor glutton, as he crossed the stream, and he fell, pierced to the heart."

" Your legend of the roast meat,' I observed, " has awakened within me a certain sensation, not strictly connected with the romance of the olden day ; and you must now add to the obligations I already owe you, by pointing out the shortest way to the Rev. Father M'Naughtin's."

" You could not reach the priest's before night," he rejoined : " you shall have cead mille failthe, and the accom-

modation my cabin can afford, if you kindly accept them. This path will conduct you to yonder humble mansion in the glen, where the smoke rises above the surrounding alders. I can, likewise, promise you a rich treat of national music, from the chanter of Daniel O'Leary, the first piper in Munster, who luckily has paid us a visit. I shall rejoin you when I turn home the cows."

I thankfully accepted the invitation ; and as I approached the house of this hospitable and well-informed peasant, the large dogs came wagging their tails, and seemed to bid me welcome. It is worthy of remark how readily these sagacious animals adopt the manners of their masters. By my own experience, I can rightly ascertain the manners of the inmates of each particular residence from the temper of the dogs. Thus, at the house of the inhospitable churl, the surly cur annoys the coming traveller : the dog at the " great house" is disdainful and silent, while that of the hospitable cottager is ever friendly.— Within, at the blazing hearth, was seated the piper ; a diminutive man, deformed in person like Willie Wattle's wife, who—

" Had a hump upon her breast,
The twin o' that upon her shouther."

He had a knowing cast of countenance, and a keen, observant eye. When I gave the usual salute, he bid me sit down and take off my shoes, a form of welcome that has prevailed since the earliest times, by which each guest could entitle the last comer to the hospitality of the mansion, on bidding him take off his brogues. O'Leary yoked the pipes to do the stranger courtesy, and, before the arrival of our host, I was gratified to hear " Carolan's Farewell to Music, ' and the beautiful " Aileen a Roon," exquisitely performed. I have listened to much music, but Jack Pigott's " Cosh-na-Breeda," by the winding Bride, and O'Leary's " Humours of Glin," are, in my estimation, the ne plus ultra of bagpipe melody.

In the course of the night our kind host, seeing how much pleased I was with O'Leary's " execution," requested him to favour me with an account of his adventure with the good people in the fort of Doon.

" Ah !" said the piper, " this gentleman has read too much to credit such stories, though, in the ancient times, people saw strange sights ; and seeing was believing."

As I love legendary lore nearly as well as music, I requested the piper to relate his story ; and to show that I was no sceptic in fairy legends, I told the tale of a Cluhericaun* catched by my mother's gossip's grand-aunt, and of a collough-na-luha† at my uncle's house, that picked the pockets of those who sat near the ash-pit. The piper won into an opinion of my orthodoxy, laid the chanter across his knees, and related a tale of which this is the substance.

On a November afternoon Daniel O'Leary was roused from his bed, at his sister's house, in the little town of Millstreet. He had retired to take a nap, for he was engaged during the preceding night at the " Wallis Arms," playing for a party of gentlemen that dined there, and had scarcely fetched half a dozen snores when his repose met the above-mentioned interruption. It was a message from the Squire of Kilmeen, commanding his attendance at the Castle : he had a grand party, and though a fiddler or two were in requisition, Miss Julia Twoomy, one of the young ladies invited, could abide no other music than O'Leary's. In fact, the estimation in which a " dinner ' or wedding is held in Duhallow, is regulated by the circumstance of that piper's absence or attendance there.— Though our friend Daniel disrelished this interruption, he had too much respect for the squire to " refuse going," although the evening was hazy, and he had not quite recovered from the effect of the strong whiskey-punch of

---

* The cluhericaun is a tiny being that mostly practices the shoemaker's craft. When caught he usually shows the fortunate captor a crock of gold, or gives him a purse that is never found empty, as his ransom.

† Collough-na-luha, an old fairy, of light-fingered notoriety. Her station is near the ashes-corner in ancient dwelling-houses ; and it is said that nothing is too hot or too heavy for her in the way of thieving.

the "Wallis Arms." He prepared to depart, and, after "treating" the messenger, was just taking the saddle, (for the squire had sent one of the best horses in his stable,) when a blue-eyed *thackeen* from Knocknagrue, "an ould acquaintance" of O'Leary's passed by, and he directed the squire's servant to walk the horse slowly on before, whilst he whispered a word or two to Nancy Walsh.— They entered the public house at the cross road, and were so agreeably entertained with each other's conversation, over a glass of punch, that it was dark night before they parted. At length, having taken a parting kiss, the piper pursued his way in the hope of soon overtaking the man with the horse, but he reached Tmown, and no servant lingered for him on the bank of its rapid water. Having made his way with difficulty over the high stepping stones, he set forward with accelerated speed in the hope of overtaking him before he reached Blackwater-bridge; for where the broad river rushes through the glen, and sweeps the tall rock at "Justice's Castle," the scene is wild and lonely, and the neighbourhood of that ancient building had, time out of mind, been deemed a favourite haunt of the "good people." As he approached the bridge the moon was rising, and our pedestrian halted to hear if possible the friendly tramp of the horse's hoofs, and he stretched his view along the road which ascended the rising hill, but in vain; he heard no sound save the distant voice of the watch-dog, and no object met his eye but the ivied towers of the castle, surmounting the fir-trees that crowned the rock, and flung their giant shadows athwart the stream, beneath the pale moon-beams that danced like things of life upon the water.

Though Daniel O'Leary was "purty well, I thank ye," yet the punch he quaffed in Nancy Walsh's company could not make him scorn the dangers that superstition taught him to expect in this fairy haunt. Knowing the power of music on these occasions, he yoked the pipes, intending to raise a sacred melody to scare any evil thing that might hover round his path; but, owing to some unaccountable irregularity of idea, after many vain attempts he could bring out no other tune than Carolan's "Receipt for drinking Whiskey." This beautiful air rose sweetly on the night wind as he journeyed along, and when the tune was nearly concluded, he thought he could distinguish the tramp of horses. He ceased his strain, thinking it was the servant that came trotting in the distance behind; but soon perceived the sound multiplied by a hundred hoofs along the road. He now descried the dim figures of horsemen as they approached nearer, and supposing that he had fallen in with a party of *Rockites*, he withdrew a short distance from the road to the shelter of a furze-bush.

As the long procession moved onward, he thought he could distinguish among the horsemen the shapes of persons whom he had known to be long dead, and who he thought were resting in their quiet graves. But his surprise was considerably encreased to behold his friend, Tom Tightly, who conversed with him alive and well that very evening in Millstreet, in the last rank that closed the cavalcade;* and, to complete his astonishment, the horse on which Tom rode was drowned in a bog hole to O'Leary's certain knowledge, about a fortnight before.—From these circumstances the piper was now convinced that these horsemen were the *slua shee*, (fairy host). Tom wore his usual broad-brimmed beaver, that saved his complexion from the summer sun, for he always shone a rustic dandy of the first water. The moon, which that moment emerged from a cloud, gleamed on the large gold ring that circled his fore-finger, and which Tom on all occasions took no small pains to display, for it descended to him through a long line of ancestry, from the sister of *Donall Caum*, whose descendant he was.

"A virrah delish! is it dreaming I am, or are my eyes decaying me all out," says the astonished piper, "Tom

Tightly, if it's yourself that's there wouldn't you spake to the son of your own blood relation, and not lave him to die with the cowld without the benefit of the clargy, by the high road?"

"'Tis a bad day I wouldn't do more than that," says Tom, spurring his horse into the ditch to enable the piper to mount with facility; and at that moment a peal of laughter ran through the whole troop. Had the explorer of an ancient catacomb heard the dead of a thousand years bid him welcome to their silent mansions he could not have experienced greater fear than did O'Leary, when this wild burst of unnatural mirth rose from the ranks of the strange cavalcade upon his mortal ear.—When he mounted, his fear was further encreased to find that neither the horse nor his rider had the solidity of frame common to mere matter; in short, they seemed to form an undefinable something between the shadow and substance of bodies. When they came to the cross road that led to the squire's the horsemen pursued the opposite direction; and when the piper attempted either to alight or expostulate with his friend, Tom, he found both his limbs and tongue equally incapable of motion. They halted at the fort of Doom, near the river Ariglin, where rose a stately building, the brilliant lights of which put to entire shame the lustre of the stars, and the clear full moon. In the great hall appeared a splendid company of both sexes, listening to the music of the full orchestra, where sat musicians bearing instruments, with which the piper was wholly unacquainted; and bards in white robes whose long beards flowed across their tall harps. An elderly man, bearing a long white wand, announced Daniel O'Leary, the Duhallow piper, and immediately three distinct rounds of cheering rose from the crowded assembly, till the fairy castle shook to the sound, and,

"Roof an' rafters a' did dirl."

When the applause had subsided, a beautiful lady rose from her seat, and snatching a certain stringed instrument sang to the music of its chords the following strain, addressed to the astonished piper:

Thy welcome, O'Leary,
    Be joyous and high;
As this dwelling of fairy
    Can echo reply.
The clarseach and crotal,
    And loud Bara-boo,
Shall sound not a note till
    We've music from you.

The bara-boo's' wildness
    Is meet for the fray,
The crotal's soft mildness
    For festival gay:
The clarseach is meeter
    For bower and hall,
But thy chanter sounds sweeter—
    Far sweeter than all.

When thy fingers are flying
    The chanter along,
And the keys are replying
    In wildness of song;
Thy bagpipes are speaking
    Such magical strain,
As minstrels are seeking
    To rival in vain.

Shall bards of this dwelling
    Admire each sweet tone,
As thy war-notes are swelling,
    That erst were their own;
Shall beauties of brightness
    And chieftain's of might,
To thy brisk lay of lightness
    Dance featly to-night.

---

* The peasantry believe that a person may be pursuing his usual occupations whilst a figure exactly resembling him is seen elsewhere engaged in other business, or moving in the ranks of the *slua shee*. This apparition is called the *fetch*, and is said to forebode the death either of the seer or the seen.

* The clarseach is the Irish harp. The crotal was a kind of bell, and the bara-boo an instrument resembling a trumpet.

The wine of Kincorra,*
  The bior of the Dane †
Shall lighten thy sorrow
  Or brighten thy strain ;
In the hall of our feasting,
  Though many shall dine,
We'll deem thee not least in
  The banquet divine.

O'er harper and poet
  We'll place thy high seat ;
O'Leary, we owe it,
  To piper so sweet :
And fairies are braiding,
  (Such favourite art thou,)
Fresh laurel, unfading,
  To circle thy brow.

Thy welcome, O'Leary,
  Be joyous and high ;
As this dwelling of fairy
  Can echo reply ;
The clarseach and crotal,
  And loud barn-boo,
Shall sound not a note till
  We've music from you.

Then a seat that glittered like a throne was prepared for the delighted O'Leary ; and a band of beautiful damsels, with laughing blue eyes, placed a garland of shining laurel round his head. The other performers were completely mute during the rest of the night. Fair ladies poured out the red wine, and pressed their favourite musician to quaff the inspiring beverage. Every new tune elicited fresh applause ; and, when the dancing ended, the lords and ladies all declared that their hearts bounded lighter, and their feet beat truer time to O'Leary's music than ever before. At length, oppressed with wine, and intoxicated with the incense of applause, the piper sunk into profound repose. When he awoke in the morning, he found himself reclining at the same bush to which he had retired to let the horsemen pass ; the pipes were yoked, and his left hand still grasped the chanter. He at first conceived that the scenes of the preceding night, which began to assume a definite shape in his memory, were but the dream of an imagination heated by music, whiskey punch, and his conversation with Nancy Walsh, until he found the unfading wreath yet circling his brow. This wreath of laurel he has preserved, and still exhibits as his fairy meed of musical excellence.

Such was the adventure of Daniel O'Leary. Many opinions are afloat concerning the truth of his narration ; but let sceptics examine, as I have done, this curious wreath of laurel, and consider its complicated braiding, and the piper's unimpeachable veracity in all other respects before they presume to try this singular narrative by the test of their philosophy.   E. W.

ANCIENT IRISH POETRY.

Sir,—Among the notes of that valuable work, "Hardiman's Irish Minstrelsy," are scattered some sweet poetical fragments, many of which are untranslated. I am sure the following versions of two of these little songs (claiming fidelity as their only merit) will not be unacceptable to your readers :

I.

On a bright summer's morn by the side of the King's river, I beheld a stately brown-haired maid : sweeter was her voice than the music of the fairy host ; fairer was her cheek than the foam of waves. Her slender waist like the chalky cliff—her small, light, active foot, gliding with joy over the grassy meads of the desert. I said to her mildly,

"Oh, fair one of the valley ! unless you come with me, my health will depart."

At the birth of this lovely maid, there came a harmonious bee, with a shower of sweet honey on her berry lips. I kissed the fragrant, fair, loving maid ; it was pleasant I vow—but listen to my tale. A sting went from her burning lips like a dart through my heart, which left me without power, (mournful to relate !) Is it not wonderful that I live with an arrow through my heart, and hundreds before me killed by her love.

II.

On yesterday morn, early before the sun, I beheld a maid of resplendent form : the snow and the berry were blended in her beauty, and her small slender body was like the swan on the brook ; and, oh, vein of my heart ! why art thou sad ?

Sweeter was the gentle voice of her joyful mouth, than Orpheus who left the boars feeble ; her large clear eye was like the crystal of the dew-drops, on the verdant grass of summer before the morning sun ; and, oh, vein of my heart ! why art thou sad ?

This last little poem is remarkable in the original for the delightful harmony of its numbers ; and, with the exception of the allusion to Orpheus, its imagery is indigenous. The other bard, however, has displayed more taste in drawing on the fanciful but pleasing mythology of his own country for an illustration of the tuneful voice of his mistress. The earlier bards seldom or never introduce the deities of Greece and Rome in their poems, and the total absence of any such allusions in the Feniau tales, affords in my opinion very strong proofs of their comparative antiquity. A beautiful fragment of one of these curious poems is preserved among the pieces alluded to above, and although it is accompanied by an excellent metrical paraphrase, from the pen of Dr. Drummond, yet I am inclined to think your readers will not be displeased to see it in the more simple garb of a literal translation. It commences by an address from Ossian to Bin Bolbin, a mountain in Connaught.

Thou art sad to-day, oh, Bin Bolbin ! gentle height of the beauteous aspect ! It was pleasant, oh, son of Calpuin ! in other days to be upon its summit ; many were the dogs and the youths ; oft arose the sounds of the chase. There a tower arose ; there dwelt a mighty hero. Oh, lofty hill of contests ! many were the herons in the season of night, and the birds of the heath on the mountains, mingling their sounds with the music of the little bird. 'Twas sweet to listen to the cry of the hounds in the valleys, and the wonderful son of the rock.* Each of our heroes would be present, with his beautiful dog in the slip. Many were the lovely maids of our race that collected in the wood. There grew the berries of fragrant blossom ; the strawberries and the blackberries ; there grew the soft-blushing flower of the mountain, and the tender cresses. There wandered the slender, fairhaired daughters of our race ; sweet was the sound of their song. It was a source of delight to behold the eagle, and listen to her lonely scream—to hear the growl of the otters and the snarling of the foxes ; and the blackbird singing sweet on the top of the thorn. I assure thee, oh, Patrick, that it was a pleasant place. We dwelt on the top of this hill, the seven bands of the Femans. But few are my friends to night ; is not my tale mournful !

I now take my leave, hoping shortly to send you a similar communication.   Iota.

---

* Kincorra, the residence of Brian Poro, on the bank of the Shannon, was famous for its wine cellars.

† Tradition affirms that the Danes made a delicious intoxicating liquor of the mountain heath, called "Bior." The peasant of the present day, when he would assure you of a hearty welcome, says, "were ours the Bior of the Dane, or the wine of Kincorra, it would be poured for you."

* Mac-alla, i. e. the Son of the Rock, is the Irish poetical term for echo. Whoever was the author of this little fragment, he was, (as has been remarked of Milton,) exquisitely alive to the outward creation, to sounds, motions, and forms. Such beautiful descriptions of nature frequently occur in the Irish poems ascribed to Ossian, some of which have been translated by the author of the above article, and will shortly appear before the public in the first series of a work entitled "The Beauties of the Early Bards of Ireland."

DUBLIN:
Printed and Published by P. D. Hardy, 3, Cecilia-street ; to whom all communications are to be addressed.

THE

DUBLIN PENNY JOURNAL

CONDUCTED BY P. DIXON HARDY, M.R.I.A.

| Vol. III. | OCTOBER 25, 1834. | No. 121. |

A VIEW OF THE NORTH WALL, CITY OF DUBLIN

The above engraving will readily be recognised by any inhabitant of our metropolis, as presenting a correct view of that point which may be said to be at once the termination of the city and the bay, and which is usually called the north wall. As we shall have occasion in a subsequent page to describe at length the light-house on the south wall, we feel it would only be needlessly occupying space to notice the one here represented.

THE IRISH PEASANTS—HALLOWEEN.

It was the night of the festival of All Hallows, when every peasant implicitly believes that the fairies and other supernatural beings have double power over the destinies of mortals; I had been out shooting during the day, and was invited by a small farmer, whose cabin was situated near the top of the long mountain at Glen Cullen, to "cum up in the evenin' an' look at the boys an colleens divartin' themselves;" and of course accepted of his invitation. The principal room, which usually served as kitchen, was the spot where the fun was held; and as I entered, a fine handsome-looking youth, with strong athletic limbs, and a good-humoured blue-eyed girl were dancing away on the door, which was taken off the hinges, and elevated on four sods of turf, as a place "fur footin'

id :" all round the room were seats of various kinds, from the high-backed chair of the grandfather, to the three-legged stool of the youngest son ; and many "a dacint boy' was seated on the bare earth beside the boss occupied by his "own little colleen," rather than by accepting of a seat be removed to a distance from her, "an' he not knowin' what design the fairies might have on her."—Large jugs of "raal mountain dew," mixed into punch for the ladies, stood smoking on a table at one extremity, and at the other was the peat fire, blazing brightly, assisted by an occasional poke of *granny's* crutch, who quietly sucked her·"ould pipe," and looked on with much good humour at the pranks of the youngsters. Beside her was seated a thin, pale girl, whose black hair was combed completely back, and fastened with a piece of ribband, and whose brilliant eyes were intently watching two nuts that she had placed in the fire, to burn, as she said, "just for the sake ov thryin' iv her sweetheart id lave her or not." A fair-haired, healthy-looking youth, who was crouched behind her so that she was unaware of his presence, tried in vain to suppress a laugh, as he saw the motionless eagerness with which she watched their blazing; and when the stifled "ha, ha, ha," made his presence known, she turned round and laughed too, while a crimson blush, that was doubly vivid from her paleness of feature, mantled o'er her face and neck. When the couple who were dancing on my entrance grew tired, these two took their places, and though I have often seen the jig danced, never did I see any thing like their style : ease, and grace, and activity, all were united and combined in their movements, and the shouts of applause—the " bravo Larry"—succes, Peggy, *asthore*—it's yerself that can do id," that burst from all those who were standing round, spoke well for the judgment of the lookers-on. By degrees they began to droop, and their place was not taken by another couple when they at length ceased, for the boys then began to help the apples and nuts, with the squares of sweet oaten cake, and the glasses of hot punch, and a cheerful, good-humoured contest took place to determine from whom Peggy, the belle of the room, should take the first apple : but it was soon ended—for Larry, the handsome youth with whom she had been dancing, was the successful aspirant, and the sweetness with which she received it, and the good-natured smile that sat upon her lips, made her look, as one of those present declared, " as purty, ay an purthier, nor the queen o' beauty."

" Shure, then, Peggy, avourneen," said the aged host, who was father to the youth called Larry, and a famous story-teller, " bud id's yerself needn't be ashamed of showin' thim little pins ov your's on any boord in this counthry side, anyhow ; an' I think, whin yer one ov us, between yerself an' Larry, an' the sisthers, they'll want a fine *back* that 'ill bate us at the dancin'."

Peggy blushed at his allusion to her approaching union with his son, and smiled when she felt her hand softly pressed by his as he sat at her side.

" She's the purthiest heel an' toe step I ever seen wid any one, barrin' Biddy Daly beyant in the glin," quietly remarked an old man, who was sitting by the fire ; upon which Larry, fancying this deteriorated from her merit, hastily exclaimed—

" Shure enough, thin, Misthur Cullen, I'll back Peggy any day to tire down an' bate out a dozen Biddy Daly's."

A smile mantled on the father's features at the son's warmth ; and, plucking his pipe from his mouth, and depositing it carefully in his waistcoat pocket, he exclaimed,

" Why, thin, Larry, agra, bud I believe you *have* a dhrop ov the ould hot blood in you afther all. I myself was just such another at the time I met with Teeling's ghost below at the river."

" Whin was that—tell us about, Sur—do Misthur Mullen," here simultaneously exclaimed all, both boys and girls, and the aged host drew closer to the fire, and every one having given their seat a chuck in, after the fashion of playing the interesting game of *cutchecutchoo*, he laid his brawny hands on his knees, and looking complacently on his circle of listeners, commenced.

" Yez must know, boys and girls, that ould Teeling had possession of this house an' bit o' land afore I cum to take id, an' it was said that he berred money some where hereabouts, bud that's more nor I believe ; fur why id a man die as he did in this very room (many a head here looked suspiciously round, and they closed in with one accord to a smaller circle) athout lavin' not only as much as id give him a dacint berrin, an all that, bud also what id get a few pipes an a taste o' whiskey, wid a thrifle of baccy, an' so forth, for his sorrowing neighbours.—Well, whin I cum to take the land, be shure I was tould on all sides that the house wasn't quiet, bud sorra bit of me ever seen a ghost since I cum to the place."

" Did you ever see one before in the house, daddy ?" interrupted an inquisitive scion of the house of Mullen, greatly to his father's annoyance, as he was trying to gloss over that part, as if there was foundation in the report : however this was a poser, so he answered—

" Why no, Tom, *a hagur*, I can't say exactly that I did, bud they spoke ov id anyhow, an' it was generally believed ; bud that's naither here nor there as far as is consarnin' the present story. One evenin' about dusk I was lavin' the fair ov Rafarnam, intendin' to walk home quietly through the mountains, whin I met a frind who insisted on my goen in to take a sup wid him afore I'd start.— Well, sorra one of my whole breed, seed, or gineration evir had the black drop in thim, in the regard o' the licker, an so be coorse I couldn't refuse, an' I went in, an' we had a naggin—quiet, you young rascal—don't be pullin'

your brother's hair ;" this last order was addressed to the same shub-nosed urchin who had a moment before been so inquisitive, and who was now industriously employed in chucking single hairs out of his brother's head, who lay asleep in his mother's lap. " Well, where was I ?" continued the veracious narrator—" oh, ay, we finished our dhrop, an' parted wid a warm shake of the hand ; fur he was a chap I had a regard for ; his sowl's in glory now I hope ; an' off I sets by myself, wid the moon shinin' brightly on the path, and the stars twinklin' an brilliant as diamonds. It's no thrifle of a step, as yez all know, from the fair green to where you enthir on the path through the valley, near where you go up to Misthur White's, an' besides it's all up hill, bud I was young an' active thin, an' didn't mind it, no more nor iv id had been only a couple o' parches. I was whistling cheerily as I wint along beside ov the little throut-straine, an' saw nothin' fur a man to dhread till I cum betune the two great hills where the goiants used to be playin' quoits long ago,* thin it grew mighty dark all ov a suddent, fur a big, ugly black cloud slipped across the moon, an' hid her silver face, an' it was only be the light of the stars I was guided, an' that was no great shakes ; an' jist as I was steppin' across an ould wall, what did I see on the other side bud the ghost of ould Teeling. wid a face like milk, an two blazin' eyes, and a horrid grinnin' mouth—"

" Mercy on us," shudderingly exclaimed one or two of his auditors, while the others listened without daring to breathe.

" He was mounted on his ould black mare, that died long afore him, an' the baste didn't look like the ghost of itself at all at all, fur its skin was smooth, an' it was father nor evir. Well, I didn't know what to say or do, fur the tongue o' me stuck to my cheek, and my heart kep' rappin' an hammerin' away as iv id wanted to brake out, bud at last I plucked up courage, an', sis I,——

" Thin you spoke to id, did you ?" interrupted his son.

" Yis, indeed, Larry a hagur, there was no manner of use in standin' there, glowerin' at him, fur bad cess to the taste of a step he seemed inclined to stir, an' so I made bould, an', sis I,

" ' Misthur Teelin',' sis I, ' iv you'd be plazed to let me pass,' sis I, ' I'd feel particularly obleeged to you,' sis I.

" Wid that, Sur, he gives the ould mare a skelp ov his naked fist, an' id rattled like a hape of bones, an' up she jumps, an' stands on the side ov the hill, tin feet above the path.

" ' Thank you, Sur,' sis I, well pleased at seein him so condiscindin', bud wondherin', at the same time, that he didn't spake to me at all, an' thin turnin' round, an' takin' off me hat, I made a low bow, an', sis I,

" ' Good night, Misthur Teelin,' an' safe home to you, Sur,' sis I, an' set off as fast as my two good legs could carry, an' as the crooked, dangerous road id suffer. Well, all was right till I got within about fifty yards ov me own house, whin I dunna what prompted me to turn round, bud, anyhow, I did so, an' there, close behind me, was ould Teelin' again, an' his mare, who was followin' me all the way, though I nevir heerd the fall ov her hoofs. Sorra a use there was in any further parley thin, fur I seen he was about somethin' that wasn't good ; so seein' I was so near home, though my heart was all thrimblin' like a lafe in a high wind, I makes a sudden dart off, wishin' sweet bad luck to his dirty ould bones, that wouldn't rest quietly in the grave, bud should be comin' up agin to plague an' tormint honest people, who did him no manner ov harm. At this the baste let a murdherin' big shout or screech out of her, the like ov which I nevir heerd before fur curdlin' the blood, an' though I couldn't bear her runnin' I knew she was afther me like the wind. Every step I tuk was twist as long as I could at any other time ; but, howsomdever, jist as I got to my own doore, I feels the cowld hand ov the ghost grippin' me by the neck, an' he lifted me up as iv I wor a child, an flung me down on my face, an' vanished in a flash of lightning. Afther this I

---

* They show a spot on the mountain top here, where they say the giants used to play quoits to the opposite hill.

was so stunned an' stupified wid fear that I lost all recollection, an' whin I woke there was no mare, nor sign ov one present, an' the sun was shinin' like goold upon the glin, an' me ould dog here lickin' my face; bud the wondherfullest thing of all was that me ould woman here never heerd the noise, an' thought I had stopped at the fair all the night."

When Mullon had concluded his story, he looked complacently round, as much as to say, "had any o' yez an adventure to bate out that:" and took the various shrugs of wonder with the air of a man who feels certain that he has deserved applause. His pipe was also a second time replenished, and he puffed away with much self-satisfaction, amid the wondering and fearful looks of the superstitious persons who surrounded him.

"Well, Peggy, my darlin'," said his son Larry to the pretty girl at his side, "in all your born days did you evir hear the aquil ov that?"

"Never, indeed, Larry," was the answer; "bud maybe it's not *all thrue*."

"*Not thrue*," reiterated his father, getting angry at having his veracity for an instant doubted; "it's as thrue as yer sittin' beside ache other this blessed minute; fur didn't I go in the mornin' to the spot where I furst seen thim, an' climb up to the place where the mare jumped whin I civilly axed him to lave the way, an' wasn't the grass all scorched an' withered up, let alone bein' thrampled; an' can't I show yez it any time at all, as id never grew green from that day to this, an' its twenty-five good years sence, an' more, an' iv that's not a convincin' proof, an' you refuse to believe id, why put me down as bein' dotin', that's all."

If there were any persons in the group that had an instant's doubt, this *positive* proof soon banished it, and the aged hero of the tale was viewed with double respect and awe.

By and by various harmless tricks were played off at each other's expense; all the innocent spells too were put into requisition, and the kale stalks were pulled, and much laughter caused by those who were so unfortunate as to get a crooked one.

When the plates containing salt and sand, and pure water, and one a ring, were brought out, much bustle and mystery took place. The maidens tried to find the ring, but did not succeed; and the youths tried sedulously to avoid the sand or earth, as if their lives really depended on it. When it came to Peggy's turn, her hand, as if by some spell, went straight into the plate that contained the ring; and on Larry also advancing, his did the same.— This was instantly prophesied into their being united before the year would be out, and displayed considerable foresight, and prophetic powers on the part of the soothsayers, as the day had been *already* appointed, and was not more than three weeks off.

None of those charms which are wrought in the name of the Devil were attempted, for though *they* are often spoken of as being effected, I think they are seldom tried, as the majority of the Irish peasantry have an awe of those conjurations, which nothing can remove. It was morning ere we parted, and the genuine "good wishes" which followed me on my retirement, came more gratefully to my heart than all the courtly phrases that politeness has invented to take place of sincerity; The pleasure was considerably enhanced from having thus had an opportunity of witnessing the manner in which an evening, pregnant with so much of merriment and sport in the "Land of Cakes," is spent by the Irish peasant.

DENIS O'DONOHO.

In 1784 an ancient tobacco-pipe was found sticking between the teeth of a human skull, at Brannockstown, county of Kildare; and on digging in an elevated field, near the banks of the river Liffey, the labourers found an entrenchment filled with human bones; under the bones lay a number of stone coffins, formed of flag stones, without cement; in each coffin was a skeleton. A battle was fought here between the Irish and Danes in the tenth century.

SUMMER AND WINTER.

Those who are observers of the seasons say, that the last three days of the moon between April and May are infallible presages what summer will be: to know how the winter will turn out, observe the twenty-fourth day of November, and according to it the winter will prove; also observe whether the pigs grub the earth with their heads turned to the north, which foretells a hard and long winter.

The following remarkable occurrence took place some years since at Ballyvaston, on the sea shore, county of Down: a strong wind setting in on the land raised the sandy soil about ten feet from the bottom, and thereby overwhelmed and nearly destroyed a rabbit-warren; by which storm the vestiges of several cottages were discovered, and the hearth-stones and wooden chimney-frames surrounding them appeared. From these traces it is manifest that this place was formerly inhabited.

The venerable Bede, born at Jarrow, in the county of Durham, in youth served his king and country as a soldier; but after, he entered into orders, and applied himself so effectually to study, that he is justly esteemed the greatest scholar of that and many other ages.

LOVE.

(From Crabbe's Life and Poems, just published.)

Love, I have seen a tiger on his prey,
Savage and fond; its capture his intent:
Love, I have seen a sportive lamb at play,
As mild as pure, as soft as innocent:
Love, I have seen a child, who only meant
A short amusement, trifling for an hour;
And now a fox, on secret mischief bent,
And now an owlet, gloating from his bower;
And watchful in his guilt, and gloomy in his power.

He comes in every way that men can come,
And now is garrulous, and now is dumb;
In some takes instant root, and grows apace,
In some his progress you can barely trace.
At first a simple liking and no more:
He sits considering, ' Do I love, or not?'
He seems a pleasing object to explore,
As men appear to view a pleasing spot;
Then forms a wish that Heaven would fix his lot,
In that same place, and then begins regret,
That 'tis not so—but may the prize be got?
Then comes the anxious strife that prize to get,
And then 'tis all he wants, and he must have it yet.
So then he kneels, and weeps, and begs, and sighs,
Hangs on the looks, and trembles in the eyes;
Is all with hope and tenderness possess'd,
Entirely wretched till supremely bless'd.

THE LAND OF MY BIRTH.

Ah! tell me not of a cloudless sky,
Of a perfume breathing air;
Our own sweet fields are of emerald dye,
And, oh, my heart is there!

I love our own soft rose's glow,
And our graceful shamrock's green;
More than the myrtle's shining snow,
Or Dahlia's dazzling sheen.

Though famed Italia's shores may be
The land of song and mirth;
One spot is dearer far to me—
The island of my birth!

M. S. C.

INFLUENCE OF THE MOON ON ANIMAL AND VEGETABLE LIFE.

In considering the climate of tropical countries, the influence of the moon seems to be entirely overlooked; and surely, if the tides of the vast ocean are raised from their fathomless bed by lunar power, it is not too much to assert that the tides of the atmosphere are liable to a similar influence; this much is certain, that in the low lands of tropical countries, no attentive observer of nature will fail to witness the power exercised by the moon over the seasons, and also over animal and vegetable nature. As regards the latter, it may be stated that there are certainly thirteen springs and thirteen autumns, in Demerara, in the year; for so many times does the sap of trees ascend to the branches, and descend to the roots. For example, the *wallaba* (a resinous tree, common in the Demerara woods, somewhat resembling mahogany,) if cut down in the dark, a few days before the *new moon*, it is one of the most durable woods in the world for house building, posts, &c.; in that state attempt to split it, and, with the utmost difficulty, it will be riven in the most jagged unequal manner that can be imagined; cut down another wallaba (that grew within a few yards of the former,) at *full moon*, and the tree can be easily split into the finest smooth shingles of any desired thickness, or into staves for making casks; but, in this state, applied to house-building purposes, it speedily decays. Again—bamboos, as thick as a man's arm, are sometimes used for paling, &c.: if cut at the dark moon they will endure for ten or twelve years; if at full moon, they will be rotten in two or three years; thus is it with most, if not all, the forest trees. Of the effects of the moon on animal life, very many instances could be cited. I have seen, in Africa, the newly littered young perish, in a few hours, at the mother's side, if exposed to the rays of the full moon; fish become rapidly putrid, and meat, if left exposed, incurable or unpreservable by salt; the mariner, heedlessly sleeping on deck, becoming afflicted with nyctolopia, or night blindness, at times the face hideously swollen if exposed during sleep to the moon's rays, the maniac's paroxysms renewed with fearful vigour at the full and change, and the cold damp chill of the ague supervening on the ascendency of this apparently mild yet powerful luminary. Let her influence over this earth be studied, it is more powerful than is generally known.—*Montgomery's History of the British Colonies.*

Jones, Del.

Clayton, Sc.

A Train of Carriages quitting the Station House at Westland Row.

DUBLIN AND KINGSTOWN RAILWAY.

Our readers have already, in several former numbers of our Journal, been made acquainted with such of the details relative to this great national undertaking, as we considered might prove generally interesting. In our 115th number we stated that the carriages would commence running on the 18th of September, and such was the intention of the projectors at the time we wrote the article, circumstances which could not well have been calculated upon, have, however, delayed the opening from that period till the present.* In giving two other sketches of the road—the one taken from the rere of the entrance station—the other a short distance from the entrance to Kingstown harbour, we feel it unnecessary to enter again into any lengthened description of the localities of the district through which the road passes.

* In a demi-official note, which appeared in the newspapers of the day, it is stated that although the engines and carriages, and the lines of rails, have so far been ready for some weeks, that at a few days' notice the transit of locomotive engines and a regular passenger traffic might have been carried on; yet the board have been unwilling to incur the risk of accident which might arise to any of the labourers from the locomotive engines, to which the people of this country are at present unaccustomed; and they have been, therefore, anxious to have all the numerous adjuncts to the railway, such as the stone pavement of the sea embankment, parapets, fences, drains, &c., completely finished, and the principal part of the workmen removed before the road should be opened.

The most strenuous exertions have been made by the contractor to have all completed by the 22d of this month, but though the directors expect that little will remain to be done at that period, they are unwilling, at this late season, still to fix any precise day for the opening, and they wish it be understood that as soon as the traffic can be entered upon with safety, the road will be opened for the conveyance of passengers, of which due notice will be given.

That the work is one which must eventually serve the country, we feel convinced. Whether or not it will eventually confer a benefit on those who have involved their capital in the concern, is a question upon which we have heard very opposite and conflicting sentiments expressed. It is a question, however, upon which we should be sorry to express an opinion, *pro* or *con.* We understand it is the intention of the committee of management to adopt various means of rendering the undertaking productive: the line is ultimately to be carried on as far as Bray; in the mean time omnibuses are to start from different points throughout the city, every half or quarter of an hour, which will convey the passengers to the station-house; while others, again, will ply from Merrion, Black Rock, and Kingstown, in various directions, throughout the surrounding country. There is no doubt that the number of passengers on the road is on the increase every year; and while to the attraction of handsome bathing-lodges and villas, erected along the line, is added the rapidity of travelling, and the freedom from dust and rain which the steam-carriages offer over the present mode of conveyance, a vast addition may be reckoned on; and as by the extension of the line towards Bray and southward, the country between Kingstown and Killiney, and the beautiful valley lying between it and Bray, will doubtless be thickly studded with villas and cottages, much may be expected.

We understand that the rates of conveyance will be as follow:—

	s.	d.
First Class Carriage	1	0
Second do. do.	0	8
Third do. do.	0	6

VIEW FROM THE RAIL WAY AT SALT-HILL.

The entire works, including value of ground, &c, will cost about two hundred thousand pounds; and the computation of probable and anticipated profits are certainly very cheering, when we consider that by the railway, Kingstown, with all its attractions to visiters, lodgers, and residents—of harbour, shipping, bathing, promenades, pure air, scenery, freedom from taxes, &c., will *be as near in point of time to the centre of the metropolis, as as if these were situated within the circular road.* The calculation is also warranted by inference from *facts* having reference to other places. The increase of passengers by the railway from Liverpool to Manchester has been very great; as has also that between Stockton and Darlington, and between Edinburgh and Dalkeith. In the last named place till lately there were but two coaches, each going and returning twice in the day, with the average of not more than five passengers each trip. The number of passengers increased to upwards of five hundred by the formation of a railway six miles in length, although it was constructed with a view solely to the transmission of coal, and although the station house is two miles distant from the centre of Edinburgh, and the carriages are merely drawn by horses, at the rate of eight or ten miles per hour. One day lately the number of passengers going and returning amounted to 8,000.

On Saturday, the 4th instant, the first trial of the steam engine, "Vauxhall," with a small train of carriages filled with ladies and gentlemen, was made on the line of railway from Dublin to the Martello tower at Williamstown. The experiment is said to have given great satisfaction, not only as to the rapidity of motion, ease of conveyance, and facility of stopping, but the celerity and quickness with which the train passed, by means of the crossings from one line of road to another. The distance was about two miles and a half, which was performed four times each way at the rate of about thirty-one miles per hour. The controul over the machinery was complete, the stopping and reversing the motion was effected without a moment's delay.

On the 9th instant a train of carriages, crowded with ladies and gentlemen, proceeded the entire length of the line from the station-house at Westland-row to Salt-hill. There were eight carriages attached to the train; one of the first class, three second, and four of the third class.—

The first trip was made by the locomotive engine, called the Hibernia, and with the many disadvantages attendant on a first starting, the trip from the station-house Salthill was performed in fifteen and a half minutes, and again back to Dublin in twenty-three minutes.

A second trip was made by the Vauxhall locomotive engine, which performed the journey to Kingstown, in fourteen minutes and a half; and back to Dublin in twenty-two and a half minutes.

Several other trials have since been made with the different engines, which have all proved eminently successful. Having joined in one of these trips, we were delighted by the perfect ease and safety with which it was performed; there is so little motion perceptible even when going at the quickest rate, that we could read or write without the slightest inconvenience.

On the probability of the injurious effects which the success of the railway must have on the drivers of cars and carriages along the present line, much has been anticipated. The following statements, from an address to the citizens of Dublin, by Mr. Classon, on his attempt to establish the omnibus system, on a plan similar to that in which it is carried on in London, are so much in point, that we are induced to copy them. To us they show clearly that the fears alluded to are groundless.

" It is stated that the omnibuses would impair the vested interests of the carmen: now, although I do not admit the principle of vested interests in such a case, I utterly deny that the interests of the carmen would be prejudiced; on the contrary, they would be promoted by the introduction of such vehicles, if the carmen will only themselves do what is right, and meet the matter fairly. In establishing this fact, I may assume it as admitted, that low prices induce consumption; and secondly, as equally true, within certain limits, that in articles of every day consumption, the low price is likely to make most money. Is it not manifest that if I sell in a day six articles at a profit of sixpence each, I make more than if I sell but one article in the day at a shilling? This is precisely the case with the carmen; let them agree among themselves to charge no more than sixpence to a single person for a set down within a mile, and they will get six times their present employment. Were the suggestion acted on, twenty omnibuses in Dublin would only be making customers for the cars, by inducing the walkers to become riders at the low price of two pence each seat, and when people once began to take the indulgence of the omnibus, presently they could not do without the cheap run on the car for the cross line that the omnibus did not go. Indeed, I may, I think, assert, that acting on this acknowledged principle of producing cheap accommodation to the public, each and every carman in Dublin would, at least receive two shillings a day, or fourteen shillings a week, more than they do under the present mode.

"Some time since I heard the following anecdote of the far-famed Mr. Bianconi, who has produced such prodigious public accommodation in the south and west of Ireland, and who has thereby raised himself into great eminence and wealth. In the early period of his operations, he determined to run a well appointed car on a certain road, the population and trade of which line he considered might, if he fixed the fares at a reasonable price, justify the undertaking. He was, however, disappointed; his cars went empty. The genius of Bianconi was not to be baffled by temporary disappointment; he resorted to a fair expedient, and started under another name an opposition car, and ran at a ruinously low price. This at once brought the public on the road. One morning the opposition was withdrawn, the rates were then raised to a fair, though low, remunerating price—the public had tasted the sweets of the accommodation, and this spirited individual lives to enjoy the merited fruits of his triumph. One more case, for the sake of the carmen, which I am the more anxious they should consider, as it is a case that not only applies to the introduction of the omnibus generally, but is analogous to the Kingstown railway, and supposed by some about to destroy all the carmen on the Rock road. It is well known that when the Manchester and Liverpool railway was opened, it was supposed that a great North coach proprietor, who ran several coaches from Liverpool to Manchester, would be seriously injured on that line, and although he has been obliged to withdraw all his coaches but one from that road, it is a certain fact, and one which was stated by himself some few months since, that so far from the railway injuring his coaching in the district, he had now more coaches, and better returns, by bringing up the crowds that resort to the railway from different points, than he derived from the Manchester coaches before the railway was in operation. Such is the effect of producing cheap and expeditious accommodation to the public."

We have already said it is not our intention to offer an opinion as to the ultimate success of the speculation in a mercantile point of view; at the same time we cannot but heartily wish that the effort may be crowned with the amplest success; and that encouragement thus given to introduce into our island measures which have tended so much to promote the interests and augment the wealth of other portions of Great Britain, may stimulate our monied men to go forward in many similar undertakings, which shall have the effect of opening up the vast resources of a country rich in mineral wealth, and in those various productions with which the God of providence and of nature has so amply blessed her.

RAILWAYS IN AMERICA.

Perhaps the largest viaduct in the world is that upon which the Columbia and Philadelphia rail-road crosses the river Schuylkill, about three miles above Philadelphia.—At the site of the bridge the stream is about eight hundred and fifty feet wide. On one side the depth of water under the bridge is only four or five feet, but it increases gradually to within twenty yards of the opposite shore, where it is twenty-two feet. The bed of the river is a soft black mud overlaying the solid rock to a depth of from four to ten feet. The bridge consists of seven arches, six piers, and two abutments; five of the arches span 158 feet each, and the remaining two one hundred and twenty-five feet each—making, with the piers, which are thirteen feet broad at top, a total of one thousand and eighteen feet in the clear between the butments.

There are now in the state of New York alone thirty-seven railway companies, all incorporated since the opening of the Liverpool and Manchester railway, whose united capitals make nearly thirty millions of dollars, about six millions sterling.

ANOTHER AERIAL MACHINE.

In addition to the aerial conveyance, which has been so much talked of in Paris, from the idea that a communication may be effected between that city and London in a few hours, another machine, from which still greater expectations are formed, is now exhibiting in the Chaussée d'Antin. It is a sort of terrestrial ship, having three masts. With this curious machine, the inventor, M. Harquet, is said to have travelled from Tours to Paris at the rate of about twenty miles an hour. We have heard it stated, however, that there can be little doubt that this project will prove a complete failure.

SIMPLE SCIENCE—ELECTRICITY.

What does electricity, in general, signify? The operations of a very subtile fluid, which rushes through some bodies with inconceivable velocity. What are these bodies called? Conductors. Does the electric fluid stop at some bodies? It does. These are called non-conductors. What are non-conductors? Glass, and all vitrified bodies; diamonds of all kinds; balsamic and bituminous bodies, as resins, wax, amber, sulphur, &c. By rubbing the coverings of animals, such as hair, wool, feathers, silk, bristles, &c., we seem to collect around them an electrical atmosphere, and thus excited, they will attract bodies of the conductor kind, as gold-leaf, &c. What were the ancients only acquainted with? This property of attraction in amber (electrum.) Is it found to hold with the other non-conductors? It is; hence they are also called electrics. Are conductors electrics? No; they are called non-electrics. Will the rubbing or excitation of these collect or agitate the electrical fluid? No; but if suspended by hair or silk cord, or supported by glass or any of the electrics, at a distance from the wall, floor, &c., (which latter are conductors, and communicate with the earth,) they may be charged with positive or negative electricity, as it is called. What are the conductors or non-electrics? All metals and the greatest part of minerals. Is water a conductor? Yes; and all aqueous and spirituous liquors, and whatever contains in them any of these; as living creatures and animal substances; as leather, bones, shells, &c.; trees and plants; thread, paper, &c. Will glass or any of the electrics become conductors? Yes; when they are moistened; and will not collect the electrical fluid till wiped or dried.— Heat also makes electrics become conductors; while water, being frozen, becomes an electric. When are we insulated? By being placed on a cake of resin, a piece of glass, or on a stool of baked wood, with glass supporters; by the interposition of these electrics or non-conductors between us and the earth, the communication between the electric fluid in our bodies and that in the earth is cut off. When are we negatively electrified, and when positively? Under the above circumstances, the experimenter, by means of his machine, draws from us the electric fire in our bodies; or he charges us with still more of the fire. If a person standing on the floor, touch us at a time when we are negatively electrified what would be the consequence? The fire would be drawn from the earth by our bodies, and rush through him as a conductor; a spark will be seen and heard between us, and both he and we shall feel it. When positively electrified, what is the consequence? The same effects as before, except this difference, the fire will be drawn from us through his body, and pass into the earth, and thus the equilibrium will be restored as before. There are fishes that have the power of giving a shock from their own bodies. Is electricity ever used medically? Yes; streams, sparks, and shocks are all applied to the human body, and have been thought to be very efficacious in removing obstructions, and in rheumatic, paralytic, and inflammatory cases; the most certain or unequivocal appearance of advantage derived to man from the study of electricity, is the protection from lightning, which he obtains by means of iron (or what is still better, copper) rods, raised above the highest part of his house, and extending along the outside down into the ground.   A. G.

KINGSTOWN.

Several circumstances have conduced to render Kingstown a place of considerable notoriety. It was from this place his Majesty, George IV. embarked in 1821; and to commemorate this memorable event, a handsome obelisk, with a suitable inscription, surmounted by a crown, of mountain granite, has been erected on the spot. In order to keep in eternal remembrance the gracious visit of his Majesty to Ireland, the name of this village was changed from Dunleary to Kingstown. The Asylum Harbour will be found well worthy of examination; towards its construction, parliament advanced £505,000, to be repaid by certain duties to be levied off the vessels coming into the harbour. The first stone of this immense work was laid in 1817, by Lord Whitworth, then Viceroy of Ireland.*

The pier extends 2,800 feet, and is at the base two hundred feet in breadth; it terminates in a nearly perpendicular face on the side of the harbour, and an inclined plane towards the sea. A quay fifty feet wide runs along the summit, protected by a parapet eight feet high on the outside; there is a beacon to mark the harbour. Close to the pier-head, there is twenty-four feet depth of water, at the lowest springs, which it is calculated will allow a frigate of 36 guns, or an Indiaman of eight hundred tons, to take refuge within its enclosure; and at two hours flood there is water sufficient to float a seventy-four. To-

wards the shore, the depth gradually lessens to fifteen or sixteen feet. The crowning point of all, however, has been the construction of the railway.

By some, the surrounding scenery has been considered as fine as that which presents itself on entering the bay of Naples. The bay of Dublin is bounded on the north by the bold peninsula of Howth, distant from Dublin about seven miles, and on the south, by a small rocky isle, called Dalky,* separated from the mainland by a deep navigable channel, and crowned at its highest elevation by a Martello tower. The breadth of the bay between these two points is about six and a half miles. Over the low, sandy isthmus of Howth, towers the rocky and picturesque isle, called Ireland's Eye—and beyond that, at a greater distance, the Isle of Lambay. The remainder of the shore on the northern side is low, but all along thickly studded with white-washed houses, placed singly or in groupes to the water-side, from whence a fine country swells into gently rising eminences, clothed with wood and intermingled villas, till the view is lost in the distant horizon.

On the south side, the first objects which meet the view are the Rochetown hills, whose rocky eminences terminate in three summits, several hundred feet higher than the bay. On the northern summit is one of the signal towers of the telegraph; a little below the southern summit a Martello tower commands Killiney bay; and the central and highest summit is crowned with an obelisk. The whole line of coast is rocky and dangerous, but richly ornamented with crowded villages. Behind these, the eye wanders over a delightful variety of villas, woods, and pastures, gradually rising, with easy ascent, from one degree of elevation to another, until terminated at length by the picturesque back ground formed by the Sugarloaf, and the other Wicklow mountains, which are seen extending themselves in a south-westerly direction, as far as the eye can reach.

The light-house, however, which will be perceived standing apparently in the centre of the bay, is an object worthy of inspection. It is an elegant piece of architecture, three stories high, surmounted by an octagonal lanthorn, which is lighted by oil lamps, aided by reflecting lenses. It was erected by Mr. Smith, in 1782, and affords a striking proof that the greatest difficulties may be overcome by genius and perseverance. A stone stair-case, with an iron balustrade, winds round the outside of this extraordinary building, terminating in an iron gallery, which surrounds it at the upper story. This useful and ornamental structure stands at the extremity of a range of building, called the South-wall—which was erected for the purpose of securing the harbour against the sands of the South-bull. The building of this wall was commenced in 1748, and is constructed of large blocks of granite, strongly cemented, and fastened together with iron cramps. It runs in a straight line into the sea the astonishing length of 17,754 feet, or nearly three English miles and a half.

About mid-way on this wall, a fort or battery has been constructed, called the Pigeon-house. The pier at this point is two hundred and fifty feet wide, and on it are built a magazine, arsenal, and custom-house. It is considered a place of great strength, being surrounded with heavy cannon, and commanding the bay in various directions.

From Killiney-hill, about three miles distant, the harbour appears to great advantage. The peninsula of Howth, Lambay, Ireland's Eye, the island of Dalky, and Bray Head, which rises 807 feet above the level of the sea, are also to be seen with much effect from this point. The scenes which here present themselves are altogether of the very finest description.

---

* See "Picture of Dublin," published by Curry and Co.

* The island of Dalky contains about eighteen acres of marsh land. It was formerly dedicated to St. Benedict, and there are still to be seen on it the ruins of a church. In modern times it has been resorted to for purposes of sport and pleasantry. Not long since it was the custom annually to elect a mock king here, with the various officers of state, whose proceedings were recorded in a newspaper, called the Dalky Gazette; this practice has for some years been discontinued.

VIEW OF KINGSTOWN HARBOUR.

Dublin: Printed by P. D. Hardy, 3 Cecilia-street, to whom all communications are to be addressed.

THE

DUBLIN PENNY JOURNAL

CONDUCTED BY P. DIXON HARDY, M.R.I.A.

| Vol. III. | NOVEMBER 1, 1834. | No. 122. |

CASTLE DONOVAN.

RIDES THROUGH THE COUNTY OF CORK.

In our last chapter of these "Rides," we gave for the reader's delectation, the romantic story of Ballinacarrig Castle, accompanied with a view of that interesting ruin as it now stands. Since we wrote our little history, the work of renovation has commenced, in the shape of a substantial wall which Mr. Townshend is erecting, for the purpose of preserving the precincts of the castle from undue intrusion. The neighbouring peasantry had found the castle walls an easy and abundant quarry, from which they often took the materials for their humble dwellings. The quoins of the castle exhibit, near the ground, ample marks of the attacks of its rustic despoilers; but although its beauty is thereby considerably injured, yet such is the solidity and strength of the edifice, that its security has not been affected in the slightest degree. Before we proceed further on our desultory rambles, we must here take notice of an error into which the printer of our last chapter has fallen. He has stated that the mills adjoining the old castle belong to Mr. Neagle : on referring to our manuscript he will find that their proprietor is Mr. John Heazle. The town of Dunmanway, of which we gave a brief description in a former number, lies nearly three miles to the west of Ballinacarrig. On proceeding still further to the west, the traveller has his choice of two roads leading to Bantry. If he move in the exaltation of a carriage of any description, then, by all means, let him take the southern, or mail-coach road; for the wheels and springs of his vehicle would be very unceremoniously discruciated among the picturesque inequalities of the northern route. This southern road, at the distance of a mile from Dunmanway, passes the domain of Dunmanway manor-house, the abode of Mr. Cox. Thence it enters a steep, dark, and lofty defile, which I believe is called Dunmanway Glen. This glen is a mile in length, and is slightly winding. The hills on the northern side exhibit here and there the remnants of former woods of oak and birch. The southern verge of the road overhangs in many parts a rugged and precipitous bank, at whose foot brawls a rapid, sparkling mountain stream. Beyond, ascends the broad shaggy breast of Lisnadinish hill, completely covered with dark purple heath. If this noble gorge were planted with forest trees, it would soon become one of the most picturesque spots in the south of Ireland. Three miles further westward is the solitary public-house of Drimoleague, whence a by-road, very little better than a boheren, conducts the wearied wanderer to the hospitable cottage of the Rev. John R——, priest of the parish of

Drimoleague or Drinah; and here our pen involuntarily stops, to pay a tribute of respect and gratitude to this venerable clergyman. In the year 1828, I was returning from a pedestrian tour to Bantry and Glengariff, when I experienced his kind and unsolicited hospitality, under circumstances which I shall detail before the close of this chapter, and which certainly required the exercise of that Samaritan virtue. His amusing, though eccentric conversation induced me to prolong my stay at his residence for several days, during which I rendered ample honour to his good stories, his excellent cheer, his inimitable port, and hearty welcome.

We will now suppose that the tourist who rejoiceth in the splendor of a wheel carriage has proceeded without any interruption to Bantry; and we will therefore return to Dunmanway, to act in the charitable capacity of guides to the humbler pedestrian. *Him* we would advise to select the old, or northern road, which leaving Dunmanway to the west, passes by Woodbrook, a long, low, white house on the side of a hill, rented by a Mr. Gillman. Thence it proceeds to the lofty hill of Mielane, and surmounting a rising ground beyond this eminence, the vale of Castle Donovan (which forms the subject of our sketch) opens on the sight. It is hard to conceive any thing more wild, more desolate, more lonely, than this savage vale. Yet even this wildness and desolation have a charm for contemplative minds : and where the traveller's reflections are tinged with a melancholy hue, whether from disappointment and sorrow, or from any constitutional tendency, it is chiefly in such scenes as these he will feel the strongest inclination to exchange the delusive and unsatisfying bustle of ordinary existence, for the quiet of seclusion amid the rude, majestic works of nature.

It was late in the autumn of 1828 that I first beheld the rough vale of Castle Donovan. I reached the eminence which commands it from the east, about two in the afternoon of a warm sunny day. Trees there are none in this district, and the heathy covering of the hills was incapable of showing any marks of the advancing season. In the centre of the vale beneath me, was the tall, castellated tower; an extensive marshy meadow lay beyond it, bounded by the steep rocky hills of Mullaugh-Nesha, and its peaked brethren. About half a mile farther on, I diverged from the road to examine the old castle; it is founded on a rough rock whose surface, forming the floor of the vaulted hall of the castle, retains all its original inequalities. Strange notions of comfort must our ancestors have had! Here were men, possessed of a large tract of country, sufficiently wealthy to build several castles; and in this one, the constant residence for many years of a principal branch of the family, the floor of the hall is a bare rock, which never has been levelled, and which is intersected with two or three ridgy indentations, nearly two feet in depth, and extending almost the whole length of the apartment! A spiral stair ascends to the top of the castle. At the first story it opens on a fine large room, about 26 feet long by 22 in width. Perhaps these dimensions are not accurate, as I only attempted to ascertain them by *stepping* the apartment: however I am sure they are not far astray. This room is open to the heavens. The windows of the castle are surmounted by small label mouldings, neatly cut in a dark brown freestone. The offices appear from their fragments to have been formerly very extensive, but little more than their foundations are now visible. Having satisfied my curiosity respecting this old seat of the O'Donovans, I crossed the large marshy meadow, at the expense of wet feet, and ascended the hill called Mullaugh-Nesha. The ascent was toilsome enough, from the alternations of almost perpendicular rocks and slimy marshes which its eastern side presented. Having gained its summit, however, the view well repaid me for the labour of the ascent. To the east was the vale I had quitted, and far in the distance the hills of Corran* and Ballynard, marking the vicinity of

Manche, Kilcascan, and Fort Robert. To the west was indeed a noble prospect. The wide blue waters of the glorious bay of Bantry, their eastern verge still gleaming brightly in the evening sun, while the western side was darkly shrouded in the shadow of the mountains, lay stretched at the distance of some miles from the hill on which I stood, although by a visual deception I could almost have imagined that they washed its base. Then the gigantic mountain barrier which guards the bay from the western storms, and contains within its recesses the enchanting valley of Glengariff, stood forth in all its majesty; Hungarie hill, with its broad bare head, Ghoul mountain, with its narrow, splintered peak; and all the bold eminences receding in disjointed ranks towards the distant bay and river of Kenmare. The impression left upon my mind by this noble scenery, invests with the halo of romantic interest every incident, however trivial, which occurred during my ramble. Standing on the wide heathy summit of Mullaugh Nesha, my attention was arrested by two white dogs, which skipped and gambolled at a little distance. One of them was a pointer, the other a diminutive and silky little King Charles, only fit for a lady's warm hearth-rug, so that I felt some surprise at his strange appearance in a scene so wild, especially as both he and his larger canine friend seemed perfectly the masters of their own motions; the wide summit of the mountain was unbroken and unsheltered for a considerable extent, so that had they been accompanied by any *human* associate, I thought I *must* certainly have seen him. I immediately commenced a brisk pursuit of the dogs. They suffered me to approach them so nearly that they were almost within my reach; and as often as I extended my hand to caress them, the tantalizing animals would utter a short, quick, playful bark, and scamper out of my reach in a moment. This game of pursuit and escape was continued for nearly half a mile, until it led me to the brink of a very small lake, whose black waves seemed astonishingly rough, considering the smallness of its extent and the calmness of the day. Here the dogs appeared suddenly to vanish, leaving me gaping in silent wonderment. I continued my search for the wayward animals along the banks of a larger lake, which lay within thirty paces of the other little sheet of water. The chase, however, was a vain one; and returning to the smaller lake, I was beginning to revolve in my mind the steps I should take to find quarters for the night, when incautiously advancing to the verge of the bank, I fell through a matted canopy of furze and heath into a little natural chasm in the ground, on the very brink of the lake, in which was a turf seat, occupied by one of the strangest-looking mortals I had ever beheld. His person was spare, wiry, and muscular : his legs, bare from the knee to the foot, were mottled red and blue, by the influence of air, fire, wind, and rain, to all which the luckless shins had been alternately exposed from infancy upwards. His face was dark and swarthy, its expression half sinister, half humourous. His dress was as singular as his person. A high-peaked hat, without a brim; a blue jacket, with faded scarlet seams, and tarnished gold buttons; short breeches, of strong pilot cloth, and a leather belt, in which was stuck a broad, sharp knife. The two dogs, which had baffled my pursuit, lay panting at the feet of this personage; at his side was a large basket of provisions. He did not testify the slightest surprise or alarm at my unceremonious entrance, but calmly said in Irish,

"That's a queer way you thought proper to come in, Sir. Now, if *I* was *you*, I'd rather walk in easy at the door of a house than jump down through the chimney."

"Really, my friend," I replied in the same language, "I had not the slightest intention of making so abrupt an entrance; I thought I was standing upon firm ground, and your treacherous furze gave way beneath my feet."

"And you nearly came down on my head," said he.

"Sir, I did not mean to make so free with your head, I assure you," said I.

"You might have knocked my brains out," said he.

"I protest I should have been exceedingly sorry had I done so," answered I.

"But that would have been not the least satisfaction

* The hill of Corran is two miles and a half to the south of Enniskeane village. The summit commands an unrivalled amphitheatre of ocean and mountain, including the Kerry Paps, the Bantry mountains, &c. On the top is the grave of giant M'Gun.

in life to me for the loss of my brains," replied this singular genius, tapping his forehead, " and I'll engage *you* would have been picking them up for the sake of the larning that's in them, and glad to get them too. But since they had the luck to escape, and are still in my brain-pan, what say you to a glass of grog ?"

I thankfully accepted his offer, for the heat and my pedestrian exertions rendered the refreshment very acceptable. Suddenly two shots from a double-barrelled gun were heard in quick succession.

" Well banged, ould father Jack," exclaimed my singular friend ; " I'll warrant there's a brace of grouse down at any rate."

· "Father Jack," repeated I, " pray who is that ?" ·

" My master, Sir," replied this strange being ; " where did you come from at all at all, that you have not heard of him ?"

" Heard of whom, my friend ? I do not know your master's surname yet."

" Father John R——, Sir, parish priest of Drinagh, the best man, the best christian, the best brother, the best friend, the best priest of a parish, and," continued he, approaching the climax with encreasing enthusiasm, " better than all put together, the best sportsman in all Ireland : and now, in arnest, did you never hear tell of him ?"

" No, indeed, I'm ashamed to say," answered I.

" Why then, ashamed you may well be ; are you Turk, Jew, or Connaughtman, never to have heard tell of ould Father John, the best friend of *sowls*, and the bitterest enemy of grouse and *pastrick's*—pop—there goes another bang at the grouse ! I'll engage he'll have his game-bag full to-night !"

" Has he any sportsmen along with him ?"

" Not a christian," replied he, " baring Mr. J. D——, who is as good at the work as any one ; a mortal good sportsman ; a fellow that would walk forty miles without being tired, through bog, moss, and mountain ; hits every thing he shoots at. Father John always begs him to lave *some* for breed ; he's a hearty, fine young gentleman, anyhow ; and free and pleasant—never turns his face from any poor man in distress : may the Lord increase his store, for it is he that would make a right use of it."

The shades of night at length began to close around us ; the sportsmen did not make their appearance, and I quitted my communicative acquaintance to find my way to the cottage of one Mahony, upon one of the mountains, where I had been recommended to take up my quarters for the night. Furnished with some general instruction from Father R——'s servant, regarding the direction in which the cottage lay, I hastened down the mountain, and with the aid of extraordinary exertions, I just reached the bottom as the night set in. The day had been warm, and the evening clear and fine ; but as I reentered the large marshy meadow already alluded to, black clouds chased each other quickly over the mountains, large rain-drops fell at intervals, the wind began to rise, and in less than half an hour I found myself in the centre of the marshy plain, in total darkness, wholly unacquainted with the neighbourhood, and exposed to as pitiless a hurricane of rain and storm as ever wreaked its fury on defenceless mortal. There was nothing to be gained by remaining stationary : so I walked quickly onward, although I knew not in what direction I was moving. At length I reached a tall crag at the foot of a mountain, and casting my eyes earnestly around I could not discern the slightest spark of light in any direction.— Not a dog barked—not a sound was heard, save the howling of the wind and the heavy patter of the rain. The mountain was a formidable barrier to any further progress in that direction ; so I faced about, and pursued my way again across the marsh, until I suddenly plunged up to my middle in a slow muddy stream, which soaked its oozy way through long sedgy grass and *flaggers*. Scrambling from this Stygian pool, I found myself among low, ruined walls, and advancing a few paces further, I discerned in the gloom the tall tower of Castle Donovan.— Never sailor entered harbour with more joy than I felt on entering this old, dark, ruined fortalice ; all it afforded

me, no doubt, was shelter ; but shelter was what I needed most at the time. I was dripping wet, and being rather lightly clad, I soon began to experience a cold shivering, when my attention was diverted from the personal inconvenience I sustained, by the sound of voices approaching the building. They ceased ; and the steps, as of several people, were heard ascending the steep rocky bank to the door of the castle. I presently became sensible that they ranged themselves along the wall against which I was leaning, and some moments of anxious silence ensued. At length the person who stood nearest to me happened, in changing his posture, to become aware that I occupied a corner of the building. Instantly my shoulders were enclosed in a grasp of herculean strength, and a rough voice exclaimed,

" Who is lurking here ?"

" A traveller," answered I, " who entered this ruin to take shelter from the rain."

" Then," returned the voice, while the iron grasp was clutched still deeper in my shoulders, " whoever you are you shall pay dearly for this intrusion."

I struggled to release myself, but I was as a child in the powerful gripe of the unknown.

" Peter," he exclaimed in Irish, " strike a light."

A light was instantly struck from a gun-flint in some tinder ; a bit of *gewsh*, which lay in a corner of the ruin, was lighted, and I saw myself surrounded by a young and handsome lad, a tall patriarchal-looking personage, with a long blue cloak, and the strangely dressed being I had met on the mountain a few hours before.

" Now, Sir," said the blue-cloaked personage, " all waifs and strays belong to the lord of the manor, in which capacity I seize upon you. As soon as the rain subsides you accompany me home, and I think you will do me the justice to say that I provided a better lodging for you than you did for yourself."

Connecting the events of the day with each other I was at no loss to guess that my peremptory friend was the Rev. John R—— : in an hour the hurricane had fallen ; horses arrived to bring the shooting party to his cottage ; I was mounted on the crupper of his steed, and we sped merrily over hill and dale, despite the darkness, until we were received in his hospitable home : there we changed our wet garments, took our seats by a blazing fire, and spent a most social and delightful evening, where we had still more than " the feast of reason, and the flow of soul," as Father John's game-bag was filled with grouse and partridge.

N. B.—These " Rides through the county of Cork," were often performed, *Hibernice*, on foot.

TO A SLEEPING INFANT.

Sleep on, my child, sleep on,
  And be thy dreams of bliss,
That brings again the smile upon
The cheek, now pale and wo-begone,
  In happier worlds than this !

Sleep on, sleep on, my child,
  Thou wilt but wake to care ;
Without is but the trackless wild,
With horrors vast on horrors pil'd,
  Within but blank despair !

How wan thy cheek hath grown,
  The cheek that was so fair !
The cherub look I lov'd is flown,
And famine's bitter blast hath blown,
  Among the roses there !

Sleep on, my child, sleep on,
  And be thy dreams of bliss,
That brings again the smile upon
The cheek, now pale and wo-begone,
  In happier world's than this !

                                 F. F.

ZOOLOGY:

ANIMALS OF THE MONKEY KIND.

Monkies are found only in the warmest parts of the world, and chiefly in the torrid zone. They abound in the woods of Africa, from Senegal to the Cape of Good Hope, and thence to Ethiopia; in all parts of India and its isles; in the South of China; in Japan; and in South America, from the Isthmus of Darien as far as Paraguay. A species or two are also met with in Arabia and the province of Barbary.

On account of the numbers and different appearances of these animals, they have been divided into three classes, and described under the following denominations; viz.—Apes, or such as have no tails; Baboons, or such as have short tails; Monkies, or such as have long tails.

In the ape kind, we see the whole external machine strongly impressed with the human likeness, and capable of similar exertions. They walk upright, their posteriors are fleshy, their legs are furnished with calves, and their hands and feet are nearly like the human.

THE ORAN OUTANG, OR WILD MAN OF THE WOODS.

The oran-outang, or wild man of the woods, is the largest of all the ape kind, and makes the nearest approach to the human figure. One of this kind, dissected by Dr. Tyson, has been very accurately described by him. The principal external differences pointed out by that learned physician, consisted in the great length of the arms, and shortness of the thighs; the thumb is also much smaller, and the palm of the hand longer and narrower, than in man; the form of the feet is very dissimilar, the toes being much longer, and the large toe placed at a greater distance from the others; the forehead is higher, the nose flat, and the eyes much sunk: beside these, the anatomist has enumerated a variety of essential differences in the internal conformation of the oran outang; all of which sufficiently evince, that though he has the strongest affinity to the human form of any other quadruped; yet, as Buffon elegantly observes, " the interval which separates the two species is immense; the resemblance in figure and organization, and the movements of imitation which seem to result from these similarities, neither make him approach the nature of man, nor elevate him above that of the brute."

The oran outang is found in the interior parts of Africa, in Madagascar, Borneo, and some parts of the East Indies.

It is a solitary animal, avoids mankind, and lives only in the most desert places.

The largest of the kind are said to be about six feet high, very active, strong, and intrepid, capable of overcoming the strongest man: they are likewise exceedingly swift, and cannot easily be taken alive. They live entirely on fruits and nuts, will sometimes attack and kill

the negroes who wander in the woods, and drive away the elephants that happen to approach too near the place of their residence. They sometimes surprize the female negroes, and carry them off into the woods, where they compel them to stay with them.

When taken young, however, the oran-outang is capable of being tamed, and rendered extremely docile. One of them, shown in London some years ago, was taught to sit at table, make use of a spoon or fork in eating its victuals, and drink wine or other liquors out of a glass. It was extremely mild, affectionate, and good-natured; much attached to its keeper, and obedient to his commands. Its aspect was grave, and its disposition melancholy. It was young, and only two feet four inches high. Its body was covered with hair of a black colour, which was much thicker and closer on the back than on the fore part of the body; the hands and soles of the feet were naked, and of a dusky colour.

A variety, called the pigmy, is found in Guinea, Ethiopia, and other parts of Africa, much smaller than the last, being not more than a foot and a half in length. It is very tractable, good-natured, and easily tamed; and is supposed to have been the *Pithecos* of the ancients. It lives in woods, and feeds on fruits and insects. Troops of them assemble together, and defend themselves from the attacks of wild beasts in the desert by throwing a cloud of sand behind them, which blinds their pursuers, and facilitates their escape.

THE GIBBON.

The gibbon is distinguished by the extraordinary length of its arms, which reach to the ground when its body is upright, and give it a disgusting appearance. Its face is flat, and of a tawny colour, surrounded with a circle of grey hair, which adds to the singularity of its aspect; its eyes are large and deep sunk; ears round and naked; body covered on all parts with black rough hair, except its buttocks, which are quite naked.

It is a mild, gentle, and tractable animal; feeds on fruits, leaves, and barks of trees; is a native of the East Indies, Sumatra, and the Molucca isles; and measures from three to four feet in height.

THE BABOON.

In the baboon we perceive a more distant resemblance of the human form: he generally goes upon all four, seldom upright, but when constrained to it in a state of servitude.—Some of them are as tall as a man. They have short tails, long faces, sunk eyes, are extremely disgusting, lascivious, and possessed of the most brutal fierceness.

The baboon differs from animals of the ape kind, not only in external appearance, but also in temper and disposition. Fierce and untractable, its disposition seems to partake of the hideous and disgusting deformities of its outward figure. Its body is thick, compact, and nervous; and its strength prodigious. Neither art nor caresses can render it in any degree docile or obedient. It seems to be continually fretting with rage, and seeking every opportunity of showing its savage and vicious propensities. In a state of captivity, it must be kept closely confined; and, even in that state. we have seen one shake the bars of its cage so powerfully with its hands, as to excite the utmost terror in the spectators.

This animal, of which we have given a very faithful representation from the life, was about four feet high when standing on its hind legs: its head was large, shoulders of an amazing strength and thickness, its muzzle was long and thick, eyes small and deep sunk, its canine teeth very large and formidable, and it had pouches in its cheeks: the hair on its head was long, and formed a very elegant toupee from its forehead and each side of its face, which, when angry, it erected: the hair on the body was uniformly of a light reddish brown; the tail short, and darker at the end; buttocks red and naked.

The baboon inhabits the hottest parts of Africa; feeds on fruits, roots, and other vegetables. Numerous troops sometimes make their appearance, plundering gardens and cultivated grounds. They are extremely dexterous in throwing the fruit from one to another, and by this means will do incredible damage in a very short time.

The female brings forth only one young at a time, which she carries in her arms, and suckles at her breast. It will not breed in temperate climates.

It is a curious circumstance, that not only this, but every animal of the baboon and monkey kind we have yet seen, have shewn a remarkable greediness for tobacco, mustard, and even snuff, which they eat without expressing the smallest inconvenience, and always seem extremely desirous for more.

THE DOG-FACED BABOON.

The dog-faced baboon is distinguished by a longer tail than the rest of its kind. In this respect, it seems to bear some affinity to the monkey, and has been mentioned under that denomination by several naturalists.

We may observe here, that, in tracing the progress of animated nature, we are led, by the most imperceptible gradations, from one kind to another. The line of separation seems so faintly drawn, that we are frequently at a loss how to fix the boundaries of one class without encroaching upon that of another; and, notwithstanding the regularity and order which every where prevail among the numerous families that inhabit the earth, the best and most approved systems of arrangement fall infinitely short of precision. They serve, indeed, to direct us to the general characters which form the distinguishing features of each genus, but are very inadequate to discriminate the intermingled shades and nice touches by which all are diversified.

The drawing of this animal was taken from one shown in London under the name of the Persian Savage. Its head was large; muzzle long and thick; eyes small; face naked, and of an olive colour; the hair on its forehead separated in the middle, and hung down on each side of the face, thence down its back as far as its waist; it was long and shaggy, of a bluish grey colour, freckled with dark spots; the hair on the lower part of the body short; its buttocks bare and red.

That described by Mr. Pennant, which seems to agree with this, is represented as very fierce and untractable.

It inhabits the hottest parts of Africa and Asia, lives in troops, and commits great depredations in gardens and cultivated grounds; is above five feet high, exceedingly strong, vicious, and impudent.

THE MONKEY.

The monkey kind are removed still farther, in their resemblance to the human form. Their tails are generally longer than their bodies; and, although they sit upon their posteriors, they always move upon all four. They are a lively, active race of animals, full of frolic and grimace, greatly addicted to thieving, and extremely fond of imitating human actions, but always with a mischievous intention.

In Number 53 will be found an engraving of one of these animals.

So far we have extracted from Bewick's Natural History of Quadrupeds: the following particulars relative to the habits of these animals we copy from an article entitled "The Naturalist," which appeared in a magazine published some time since in Belfast:—

"Apes, baboons, and monkeys, live almost entirely on fruits and grain; though some of them also make use of animal matter. Of these may be mentioned the Oran Outang, which, according to *Gemelli Carreri*, goes down to the sea-coast when the fruits on the mountains are exhausted, and feeds upon crabs and shell-fishes. 'There is,' says he, 'a species of oyster called *taclovo*, which weighs several pounds, and commonly lies open on the shore. The ape, when he wants to eat one of them, being afraid lest it should close on its paw, puts a stone into the shell, which prevents it from shutting, and then eats the oyster at his ease.' The *four-fingered monkey*, (SIMIA *Paniscus*,) shows also considerable address in its mode of feeding upon oysters, which it takes up, and laying them on one stone. with another beats them, till the shells are broken in pieces. Dampier observed them thus employed at the island of *Gorgonia*, on the coast of *Peru*. The cocoa nut is a favourite food with some of the apes, as it is said, that they know both how to extract the kernel, and to drink the juice; but I have not been able to ascertain how this is effected. They most probably break the nut against a stone or tree, and tear out the kernel with their claws; and this opinion seems to be countenanced, by the mode in which the *Chinese monkey*, (SIMIA *Sinica*) is sometimes taken captive. A small hole is bored in a cocoa nut, which is then laid where the monkey may find it; this he no sooner does, than to get at the kernal, he tries to put his paw into the hole, and perseveres till he at last succeeds, when the people on the watch run and seize him before he can get disengaged. This species, when vegetable food fails, lives upon insects, and sometimes on fishes and crabs. The latter it catches by putting the point of its tail between their claws, and as soon as the pincers are closed, it drags them from the shore and devours them.

"Several other species, as the *long legged baboon*, (S. *Fusca*,) the *dog faced baboon*, (S. *Hamadryas*), the *varied monkey*, (S. *Mona*), and others, are fond of insects; and the *yarque*, a variety of the *fox-tailed monkey*, (S. *Pithecia*,) devours bees, and destroys their hives. In a state of captivity, all belonging to this genus are found to eat almost every thing given them; it is remarkable, however, that none of them will touch raw meat, though, when roasted or boiled, they eat it with avidity. They are extremely fond of intoxicating liquors, and this propensity seems to be natural, for the *pigmy apes*, (S. *Sylvanus*,) are taken by means of inebriating liquors placed in the caverns which they frequent; with these they become intoxicated, and, falling asleep, are taken by the hunters.

"If some of this tribe afford instances of ingenuity in taking animal prey, the arts which others practice, to come at their more favourite vegetable food, are no less remarkable. In many parts of Africa the inhabitants are greatly annoyed by them, for they are dexterous thieves, and pillage orchards, gardens, and fields, without mercy. The species most remarkable for this are, the *pigmy ape*; the *baboon*; the *dog-faced baboon*; the *hare-lipped monkey*; the *red monkey*; and the *Chinese monkey* before mentioned. In committing their depredations, some of them remain on the tops of the highest trees or rocks, as sentinels, and, upon any appearance of danger, set up a loud cry that alarms the whole troop; when they all fly off in a moment, taking with them whatever they can carry.

"The *baboons* near the Cape of Good Hope, assemble to rob the orchards in great companies: some enter the garden, while some remain upon the wall; the rest are placed outside, within throw of each other, and extend in a line from the place of pillage to the place of rendezvous. Every thing being arranged, those inside throw upon the wall apples, melons, gourds, and other fruits: from the wall they are handed to those below, and then are pitched from one to another, along the whole line, which usually terminates in a mountain. The *baboons* are so quick-sighted, that the fruit thus thrown is never allowed to fall, and every thing is carried on in profound silence, and with great despatch. When the sentinal is alarmed he gives the signal, and the whole troop scampers off.

"The other species assemble in the same way by hundreds, and do immense damage to the coffee plantations, millet-fields, &c.; and they do more damage than even their thefts occasion, for the *pigmy apes* destroy more than they can carry away. So delicate too is the *hare-lipped monkey* in its choice, that it scrupulously examines every stalk of millet it pulls, and those not suited to its palate it throws on the ground, and roots up others.— It carries off a bunch in its mouth, and one under each arm, and leaps away on its hind feet, but if pursued drops all, except the bunch in its mouth, which does not impede its escape. The *Chinese monkeys* are very fond of sugar-cane. The moment their sentinel, who is placed on a tree, sees any one approach, he cries with a loud voice, *houp, houp, houp,* when immediately they all throw down the canes which they held in their left paw, and make off on three extremities; and if closely pursued, they drop the canes from the right hand also, and seek refuge in the trees. According to Dellon, the *Barbary apes* assemble in troops in the open fields in India, and attack the market women, and plunder them of their provisions.— The *ribbed-nose baboon*, which inhabits Africa, is said to be very fond of eggs, which it sometimes stores up in its cheek-pouches till wanted. When *monkeys* are brought into cold countries they are apt to eat their tails; I have seen one which was kept in a stable, with more than two-thirds of its tail entirely raw, and in most places gnawed into the bone."

The following description of the form and habits of one of the animals first referred to—the *Ourang Outang* —is given by Captain Blanchard;

"He was a native of Batavia: arrived at Boston, where he was intended to be exhibited, on the 1st of June; on the night after, he died. In his appearance he resembled an African; the neck was shorter, and projected more forward. He was three feet and a half high; was covered with hair, except his face, his palms, and soles, all of which were of a negro colour. The hair was inclining to black, somewhat resembling that of a human being; there was little hair on the forehead, it was therefore ample. His ears were small and handsome, lying close upon the head. His eyes were hazel, bright, and deep in the sockets; he had but little hair on the brows; they were prominent. The nose was flat: the lips thicker than a negroe's: the chin and upper jaw were broad and projecting; the chest was full and prominent; the shoulders well set back; the waist small; hips flat and narrow; the arms so long that the nails reached the ankles.'

Captain Blanchard describing his first interview with the animal says, " that while sitting at breakfast he heard the door open behind him, and found a hand placed familiarly on his shoulder; on turning round he was surprised to find a hairy Negro making such unceremonious acquaintance with him. George (the Ourang Outang) sat down to breakfast, took coffee, and was dismissed.— While on ship board he cleaned his house every day from the remnants of food, and with a cloth and water frequently washed it. He washed his hands and face every day. He was docile and obedient, and was fond of play, sometimes of a rough kind. When corrected, he would lie down and cry with a childish voice, as if sorry for his offence. His food was generally rice paddy, sometimes with molasses; but he would eat any thing; he drank claret at dinner. He generally sat on an elevated seat; and walked erect, unless when tired. He sickened on the voyage, got castor-oil with its usual effect, beside vomiting; but the strength of several men could not force him to take it again. He lost his appetite and strength, and at length, much emaciated, terminated his life."

THE ALMANAC.

Sir—The difficulty which your correspondent, J. A., (whose letter dated Milford, appears on the 106th number of the Dublin Penny Journal,) labours under as to what strikes him to be an error in the time given by recent almanacs, for that of sunrise and sunset, principally arises from his not having reflected on the distinction between apparent, solar, and mean time. It is obvious that on the first of February, the day selected, the sun's declination encreases towards the north at the rate of 42.98′ per hour, so that it is more northerly at setting than at rising by about $6 + 20''$. This makes the afternoon semidiurnal arch longer than that of the corresponding forenoon one, and of course the afternoon day-light longer than that before noon, the sun's azimuth at setting being more northerly than his azimuth at rising on the same day.

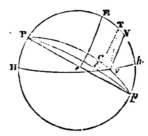

Let H P E V *h p* represent the earth, P the north pole, H v *h* the horizon, and P E *h* the meridian. Suppose the sun at rising on the given day to be at *v*. Then if the declination continued the same, his course, until reaching the meridian, would be along the line *v* V, parallel to the equator, E *e*. But, as the declination is continually on the increase towards the north, the sun, when on the meridian, is found to be at T instead of at V, having proceeded along the dotted line *v*T. In like manner, as the sun descends, his declination is becoming still more northerly, and, at setting, he is found to have receded from the meridian, along the line T *t*, the arch, *v c*, being the difference between his declination at rising and his declination at setting. It is plain, on simple inspection, that the angle, E P *t*, is greater than the angle E P *v*, which is equal to the angle, E P *e*, and, therefore, that as the earth turns on its axis with a uniform velocity, any point upon its surface must take a longer time in moving through the greater angle. Hence it follows that at no period of the year is your correspondent's rule for finding the length of the day and night correct. It is, however, a close approximation when the sun, in either solstice, makes but little variation of declination in a day.

The change of declination is not the only cause of your correspondent's being puzzled. It also proceeds from the difference between apparent, solar, and mean time.— The time set down in recent almanacs is of the latter description, and is that shown by a well regulated clock, at sunrise and sunset. This difference of time amounts on the given day to about 13M. 54¹s., to be added to apparent time, and if this be taken from the hours set down in the almanac, you have 7H. 54M. 6s. for sunrise, and 4H. 26M. 6s. for sunset, which doubled give 15H. 8M. 12s., and 8H. 52M. 12s. the sum of which is 24H. 0M. 24s. The excess of 24s. arises from the sun's motion in the ecliptic, and the obliquity of the ecliptic not being uniform during the twenty-four hours. The sun's declination during the latter portion of the day on the first of February encreases nearly at the rate of one second per hour more than it does in the early part of the same day, which occasions the time from the sun's passing the meridian until his setting, to be longer than the time between his rising and culmination. I hope I have made myself intelligible to J. A., and am, Sir, your well-wisher, B.

WHEN MY OLD CAP WAS NEW—OR IRELAND FIFTY YEARS AGO.

Since this old cap was new,
  Now fifty-two long years;
(It was new at the review
  Of the Dublin volunteers);
There have been brought to pass
  With us a change or two,
They're sorely altered times, alas!
  Since this old cap was new.

Our parliament did sit
  Then in our native land,
What good came of the loss of it
  I cannot understand;
Although full plain I see,
  That changes not a few
Have fallen on the country
  Since this old cap was new.

They are very worthy fellows
  (And much I'd be distressed
To think them else,) who tell us
  That all is for the best;
Though full as ill inclined,
  Now the bargain's closed, to rue,
Yet I can't but call the times to mind
  When this old cap was new.

What rights we wanted then
  Were asked for above board,
By a hundred thousand gentlemen,
  And rendered at the word;
'Twas thus in fair day-light,
  With all the world to view,
We claimed, and gained our right
  When this old cap was new!

But patriots now a days,
  And state reformers, when
A starving people's cry they raise,
  Turn out like trenchermen,
To guzzle o'er their plans:
  Oh, who'd have thought it true,
That men would prate o'er coffee-cans,
  When this old cap was new.

Spouting and swilling slop
  The spooneys pass the day;
Who goeth to the eating-shop
  For what he gets must pay;
Ah! we'd have done the work,
  If it had been to do,
With other tool than spoon or fork
  When this old cap was new.

On the night reforms begun
  By ruffian gangs, that go
A murdering for fun,
  And burning high and low;
And what he wants, not one
  In ten could tell to you;
'Twas differently done
  When this old cap was new.

The nobles of the country
  Were then our neighbours near,
And 'mong us squires and gentry
  Made always jolly cheer!
Ah! every night, at some one's
  Or other's, was a crew
Of merry lords and commons,
  When this old cap was new.

They're altered times entirely,
  As plainly now appears;
Our landlord's face we barely see
  Past once in seven years.
And now the man meets scorn
  As his coat is green or blue;
We had no need our coats to turn,
  When this old cap was new.

Good counsel to propose
  I have but little skill;
Yet ere a vain lament I close,
  In humble trust, I will
Beseech for all his aid,
  Who knows what all should do;
And pray, as I have often prayed,
  When this old cap was new.

God bless that honest gentleman
  And noble prince, the king;
And grant him long the grace to plan
  The best in every thing;
And give unto his ministry
  As kindly hearts and true;
And then the days again will be
  When this old cap was new.

Belfast, September.   E. N. M.

My honest, fine old fellow,
  Though I might be your son's son,
Yet will I venture to advise;
  Mourn not what's past and gone;
But for the blessings that are left,
  Stand the stouter up and bolder;
Or you'll have nothing left at all
  Ere your old cap be much older.

Dublin, November.   A. S.

THE RIGHT OF PRECEDENCE.

The wives of the two presidents of the court of justice and revenue at Cleves, were continually disputing about their respective ranks; and the lady of the president of the court of justice insisted that, in all public places, she was entitled to a rank superior to the other. This provoked her rival so much that she wrote to the king, Frederick the Great, and prayed that he would be graciously pleased to decide which of the two ladies had a right to go first. The king wrote back to her the following answer:

"The greatest fool goes first.

"FREDERICK."

Was this decision remembered it would prevent many angry disputes on the same subject, which seems a never ending source of heart-burnings, &c.

MOATE OF ARDAMINE, COUNTY OF WEXFORD.

MR. EDITOR—While every hamlet or village in England has its rural history, with copper-plate views of its castles, bridges, &c., many of the most remarkable objects in Ireland, well worthy the attention of the traveller, remain to this day unnoticed, even in the statistical accounts of our counties which have been published. One of those objects which have remained unnoticed in the county of Wexford, is the moate of Ardamine, situated on the road leading from the town of Gorey to a small village on the sea coast, called River Chapel; it is a perfect cupola, or half sphere formed of clay, standing on an artificial mound, or platform of earth, about half an English acre in extent; it is the most perfect rath or moate I I have yet met with in this kingdom.

On the north side of the platform stands a stone cross, of a very rude description; and adjoining the moate lies the ancient churchyard of Ardamine. There is a tradition in the adjacent country that there is a stone chamber underneath the upper mound of earth; I believe it has never yet been examined. C. H. W.

Wexford, 1834.

ANCIENT GOLD BALLS.

The above is a reduced sketch of eleven balls of pure gold, which were left at our office by George M'Dermot, of 17 Sackville-street, Esq. They were found by two of his tenants in finishing, or, what is generally called landing potatoes, about twelve inches under the surface, near the ruins of an old chapel, and a fort, on the west banks of the Shannon, near Carrick. They have been submitted to Sir W. Betham, and the Dean of St. Patrick's, and were by the former gentleman, laid before the Royal Irish Academy, at their July meeting, and a paper was read which intimated the opinion, that they were ornamental beads for the neck of a priest or prince of the ancient Irish.— They are formed of thin plates, neatly soldered together, and their whole weight is twenty ounces eight dwts. The centre bead is four inches by two; the smallest, two inches by one; the others graduate in pairs. They are pierced latitudinally, and have evidently been strung. We look with anxiety for the next part of the transactions of the Academy, where no doubt a paper will appear with many full conjectures or accounts of this very extraordinary and interesting evidence of ancient Irish grandeur.

TIMOLEAGUE ABBEY

Is situated about ten miles from Bandon, in the county of Cork, at the entrance to the village of Timoleague; the sea runs up to its walls through Courtmaskerry, a village about three miles distance from the abbey, where the traveller has a fine view of the Atlantic. It is said that Spanish vessels have frequently come up to the walls and delivered their cargoes of wine, &c., for the friars. About a mile from Timoleague, on the road to Clonakilty, is to be seen the remains of a large arch, to which there is many a tale of superstition attached. It is alleged that the abbey was to have been built here, but the work that was done during the day always fell at night—no doubt shaken from its foundation by the strong arm of the good people. The spot where it now stands was at length found to have a peculiar charm, and the work was allowed to proceed unmolested. In one of the aisles there is a wall of sculls, about four feet high, and ten long, which the people hold sacred.

The church in the distance may excite some interest, as it was there the late Rev. Mr. Ferguson, who was murdered near Bandon last year, officiated. S. M.

LINES

On the death of Captain Pierce, who perished off Seacomb, in the Isle of Purbeck, 6th of January, 1786.

The storm is past, and the winds are at rest,
   As he lay on the lonely shore;
But the throb of life is hushed in his breast,
And his spirit is fled to the land of the blest,
   Where the billows are heard no more.

A pillow of stone supported his head,
   Where the waves had left him to die;
The sea-weed his funeral garlands made,
While the bittern shrieked the song o'er the dead,
   And the sea-bird his lullaby!

The full moon rose, like a meteor bright,
   From the billows' watery bed;
And seemed, through the silent calm of the night,
Sadly to smile, with her radiant light,
   On the chill, cold face of the dead.

But the parting beam of that planet died,
   As it gleamed o'er the fitful wave;
Ere the rising surge of the morning tide
Surrounded the corse it wished to hide,
   He sunk in his last, cold grave. C. S. B.

DUBLIN:
Printed and Published by P. D. Hardy, 3, Cecilia-street; to whom all communications are to be addressed.

Sold by all Booksellers in Ireland.

In London, by Richard Groombridge, 6, Panyer-alley, Paternoster-row; in Liverpool, by Willmer and Smith; in Manchester, by Ambery; in Birmingham, by Drake; in Glasgow, by John Macleod; and in Edinburgh, by N. Bowack.

THE
DUBLIN PENNY JOURNAL
CONDUCTED BY P. DIXON HARDY, M.R.I.A.

| Vol. III. | NOVEMBER 8, 1834. | No. 123. |

KILRUDDERY HOUSE.

A GUIDE TO THE COUNTY OF WICKLOW. *

In a "Three Days' Ramble" through the county of Wicklow, which appeared in our 52d number, we gave a bird's eye view of the general beauties of this interesting tract of country. That any sketch of this description, which could be given in a single number of our Journal, must of necessity be a mere outline, will at once be apparent to the reader. In the little volume before us, however, there is every direction which a tourist could require to assist him in exploring this land of glen, and flood, and mountain. That such publications tend greatly to benefit our island, there can be no question. They open up the country to the notice of our English and Scottish neighbours, many of whom we are happy to find, have, during the season, taken advantage of the " cessation of arms" proclaimed by Captain Rock, to come over and see what kind of creatures *the wild Irish* are; and it is gratifying to notice that in general those who came over in this way have returned with a much better opinion of poor Paddy than they had previously formed. They may, indeed, pity his wretchedness, and deplore the misery, and filth, and destitution with which he is surrounded—but in

few instances have we ever heard the slightest charge brought against our peasantry, by strangers travelling through the country, of any thing bordering on rudeness or want of courtesy : on the contrary, the genuine good nature they have evinced when direction or assistance has been required from any of them, even in the wildest districts, has called forth the warmest approbation. To the writings of a Johnson and a Scott, Scotland is greatly indebted for much of her present popularity, as a land, if not overflowing with milk and honey, at least with lovely lakes, and picturesque waterfalls ; and we would again express the hope that some of our writers of talent and observation will turn their attention, more than has hitherto been done, to descriptions of those portions of our island which are at present unknown to the general class of tourists visiting this country. That in many districts of Ireland, altogether unknown to fame, there are scenes as varied, and beautiful, and picturesque as any of those to be met with in the districts to which the attention of tourists is at present directed, we ourselves can affirm from actual observation ; and we trust that ere long the pleasing task of bringing them fairly before the public view will be undertaken by persons competent for it. But our limits and our guide book remind us that at present we must confine our observations to the county of Wicklow, which we are informed, in our author's introductory chapter, "is one of the smallest in Ire-

* Guide to the county of Wicklow, illustrated with five engravings, and a map. New edition, corrected and enlarged. Dublin: William Curry, Jun., and Company ; Simpkin and Marshall, London.

land, lies directly south of Dublin, and contains an area of six hundred and sixty square miles, being thirty three miles in length by twenty in breadth. It is bounded on the east by the Irish Sea; on the west by parts of Carlow, Kildare, and Dublin counties, and on the south by Wexford."

"The aboriginal chieftains of Wicklow, the O'Tooles, O'Byrnes, O'Kavanaghs, and Walshes, are now either extinct or in total obscurity, and their once great domains have passed into other hands.

"The face of the country is extremely varied; in one part rich, level, and fertile; in another, mountainous and barren.

"The visiter will in vain look for either peculiarity of costume, or distinctness of accent : intercourse with the metropolis has destroyed the former, and no county in Ireland is so completely free from the least tincture of peculiarity in dialect."

Having thus introduced our Guide to the reader, we shall, as a kind of map or directory, for such tourists as may be anxious to see all that is to be seen in the county of Wicklow, briefly enumerate the places to which he undertakes accompanying them. Coasting the bay of Dublin, or rather rambling along the shore, through the villages of Black Rock and Kingstown, taking by the way a passing view of the scenery which meets the eye, while standing on Killiney hill, as described in a recent number of our Journal, the traveller is conducted to Bray, by the road which passes Cabinteely-house and the village of Leighlinstown—from Bray to Old Connaught and Kilruddery-house, of which latter place we must needs say something, as forming the vignette or frontispiece of our present number.

"The chief object in conducting our fellow travellers along this road is, to visit the demesne and house of Kilruddery. The grounds are laid out in an old-fashioned, formal style of Dutch pleasure grounds, and are, in this country, quite unique. Amongst the shrubberies are some of the finest evergreens in Ireland. In one place is a circular pond, inclosed by a hedge of beech, nearly 20 feet in height.

"The pleasure grounds higher up the hill are disposed in a uniform manner; from different centres broad green walks diverge, as radii of a circle, inclosed by close beechen hedges, at the end of which run long, straight terraces, carpeted with smooth and soft green moss.— Here the arbutus is seen of an enormous size, and indeed every tree in the demesne appears to wanton in the luxuriance of its situation, for all have outstripped the usual limits of their specific growth.

"The old mansion of Kilruddery becoming unfit for the residence of a nobleman of taste and fortune, was removed in the year 1820, and the present splendid building commenced upon the same site. This beautiful and singular structure is after the design of an eminent artist, W. Morrison, Esq., to whose ingenuity and taste Shelton Abbey, in this county, will bear a lasting and enviable testimony.

"Kilruddery House represents the style of architecture of the latter end of Henry's and beginning of Elizabeth's reign, that style which superseded the florid Gothic, and is now called the old English : many specimens are to be seen in England, but not a single instance in this country. The exterior here is richly decorated with ornamental carving; bower windows are surmounted by open work balustrades, the summits of each pier being ornamented with armorial bearings. The entrance is beneath an octagonal tower, crowned with a cupola, rising in the centre of the north front. Ascending, then, a broad flight of steps, the great hall is entered. This splendid apartment, which rises to the height of the building, is an admirable specimen of the ancient baronial hall, the scene of noble-minded hospitality and grandeur, where minstrels—

'Poured to lord and lady gay
The unpremeditated lay.'

"The walls are wainscotted with oak, to about one-third of their height, at which level a gothic cornice and frieze, filled with armorial bearings, run round the chamber. Above this the light is admitted, on one side, by a row of lofty windows, glazed with stained glass. An open arcade is continued round the remaining sides; the arches of which corresponding with the windows, preserve continuity and uniformity. The ceiling is supported by carved oak-beams, resting on open-work brackets, springing from goshawks, the family crest, carved in dark oak. The grand staircase opens from the hall, and is richly and beautifully decorated. The reception rooms, which are in suite, open on the great hall; they consist of a morning parlour, dining-room, library, and great drawing-room: the last mentioned apartment, which is forty-four feet in length, is subdivided by two skreens of porphyritic columns, supporting a rich entablature. There is, besides, a small drawing-room, with a singularly beautiful pendent ceiling; this elegant apartment terminates the suite, and opens into an extensive conservatory, filled with the choicest plants."

Quitting Kilruddery-house, the tourist is next conducted to the Little Sugar Loaf, thence to the Dargle, Powerscourt, Waterfall, the Glen of the Downs, Belle View, Delgany, Newtown Mount Kennedy, Altadore, Dunran, Devil's Glen, Nun's Cross, Rosanna, Wicklow town, Rathdrum, Avondale, Meeting of the Waters, Castle Howard, Bally Arthur, Shelton Abbey, Arklow, Gold Mines, Ovoca, Glenmalure, Lugnaquilla, Glenmalure Mines, Glendalough, Glenmacanass, Lough Ouler, Lough Nahanagan, Anamoe, Roundwood, Luggelaw, Lough Dan, Military Road from Luggelaw to Lough Bray, Enniskerry, the Scalp, Russborough, and Poul-a-Phuca.

Accurately to describe each and every one of those places, would occupy as many Journals as the places referred to; we shall, therefore, for the present content ourselves with the description given of the valley of Glendalough and the Seven Churches, of which there is an engraving in a following page, referring the reader to the work itself for a description of the other places mentioned.

GLENDALOUGH.

"The valley of Glendalough, commonly called the Seven Churches, is situated in the barony of Ballinacor, twenty-two Irish miles from Dublin, eleven from Wicklow, and five from Roundwood. It is a spacious valley, between one and two thousand yards in breadth, and about two miles and a half in extent, having lofty and precipitous mountains hanging over it upon every side, except on that by which it is entered between Derrybawn on the south, and Broceagh mountain on the north.

"We shall not be accused of under-valuing the wonder-working powers of nature in her exhaustless combinations : we must nevertheless affirm, that the effects of height, depth, and extent; the magic of light and shade, with all that is imposing in form, or exquisite in coloring—all that enchants the sense or transports imagination beyond it : in a word, beauty, and stern sublimity in their most splendid varieties, are ineffective, compared with the moral power of associations belonging to a scene like Glendalough.

"'You pass up the valley,' says the spirited describer, C. O., in introducing whom to the informed reader, we may say, gentlemen, you are acquaintances, we presume, 'through which a stream winds, for about half a mile, and ascending an eminence in the road, see before you, at a quarter of a mile distance, the site of the Bishopric and Abbey of Glendalough. Nothing can be more grand and interesting than this view—interesting from the association of ideas connected with these ruins—interesting from the wild and sublime character of the scenery around. The principal ruins stand on a green eminence that slopes down gradually from the breast of a mountain ridge, separating two deep glens, and terminating in a rich verdant swell just above the churches; the vale to the left is that of Glendalough, 'anglice,' the glen of the two lakes; that to the right neither so extensive nor so deep, nor surrounded with such precipitous mountains, contains some rich lead mines, which are now in full work; at the foot of the eminence on which the ruins stand, the streams, flowing from the glens to the left and right, unite and form the river, which running down by Lara, falls into the Ovoca. The ruins of Glendalough are more interesting from their grouping and position than from any grandeur in their separate parts. Here is a lofty and perfect round tower, and here is one of the old stone-roofed buildings, similar to that on the rock of Cashel, and at St. Doulough's, near Dublin, which is called Kevin's kitchen. From the round tower, which is one of the finest I have seen, there is a full view up the two glens, and down the valley towards Lara— you enter the churchyard surrounding those buildings by an old ivied Saxon arch, which is now only kept from falling by the ivy that surrounds it. I repeat that there is nothing in these buildings peculiarly interesting—it is their extraordinary position, in the midst of the lonely mountains, placed at the entrance of a glen singularly deep and secluded, with its two dark lakes winding far in gloom and solitariness, and over which deep vale hang mountains of the most abrupt forms, in whose every fissure, linn, and gorge, there is a wild and romantic clothing of oak, and birch, and holly.'

"On the southern side of the vale are the hills of Derrybawn and Lugduff, in the latter of which is St. Kevin's bed, a natural excavation in the front of a perpendicular rock, thirty feet above the surface of the lake.

"Between Lugduff and Derrybawn is a stream of peculiarly clear and cold water, dangerous to bathe in, as the sun has no influence on its surface at any period of the day, from the thickness of the woods overhanging it, and from the narrowness and depth of the dell. A little to the east is an extraordinary fissure, where the horizontal strata of mica slate, composing the mountain's brow, are cleft perpendicularly, and one part of the hill appears to have sunk below the level of the other; this is called the Giant's Cut. I believe," says the author from whom we quote, " such an appearance is called in miner's language a fault, and in every instance where it occurs, the strata fall down more or less, and then at a lower level continue their course, at the same angle with their horizon.— This fault or break in the stratification, looking as if the side of the hill was cut in two, and the continuity destroyed by some sharp instrument, has given rise to a legend, which of course had its place in Mr. Irwin's catalogue.

LEGEND OF FIN M'COOL.

"'That's Fin M'Cool's job—the cut above us he made with his own two-handed sword.'—'No bad specimen, Irwin, of his arm's strength, or his steel's temper; but on what occasion pray?' 'Look, your honour, across the lake, and you can't but see, on the brow of Comaderry, a big white rock. Well, Sir, upon a day, as Fin M'Cool was resting and cooling himself with an odd whiff of a pipe, up there above us, on Derrybawn; who should come, but Brian Borou, King of Munster, and he sits him down just opposite, on the big white rock of Comaderry, and the king cries out to General Fin—" bright morning to you Fin, ma bouchal; sure I'm come from giving the Danes the greatest leatherin' that ever the villains of the world got, since they came from the East sea—troubling and racking poor Ireland—the villains!—I've finished their job at Clontarf,' or, as the place is spelt in English, the Bull's field, near Dublin—' ah, it's there I've bullied them—I'll be bound it's little more nose-rent they'll ever again gather in green Erin—and Fin, my tight youth, as I have done a good hand's turn for Ireland, now's your time; for I have got the hard word that those thieving Danes, fairly beat as they were by me on Clontarf, have got a magician from out of Norway to come and gother all the giants that were ever in the known world, from Goliah of Gath to Gog and Magog; and he has them all in a camp on the Curragh of Kildare. So Fin, my son, you're the only man in all Ireland, you and your Fions, to go against these big, factious, and heathenish fellows, who have no fear of God, or of his sacred saints, Patrick, or Bridget, or Kevin, before their eyes. But Fin, my dear man, though I send you, as it is proper I should, being king commander of all Ireland, I'm in dread that I'll never lay my two eyes on you again—for these monstrous fellows must and will cat you up, even supposing you were twice as game and stout as all the world knows you are.' 'Never you fear me,' replies Fin—

'I've a bit of a sword along my leg that never yet failed, or let me come off in fight or ruction second best.' Well then, says Brian Borou, King of Munster, 'I'd give the best cow on all the corkasses of Clare, to see you try that good sword upon a giant's skull.'—' Troth then, now,' says Fin, laughing, the good natured fellow ! 'more's the pity, for the sake of your Majesty's fun, that I have not the head of one of the fellows under my fist, until I'd give you a pattern of what I could do—but, any how, you shan't want for a holy show'—so he ups with his sword, and taking advantage of the fall of the hill, he hits the mountain such a skelp, that he just gushed it down and left it as you now see.'

DESCRIPTION OF JOE IRWIN, THE GUIDE.

" Leaving my horse at a wretched inn near the bridge, I was accosted as I proceeded towards the churches, by a queer-looking old fellow, attired in what once was a military frock coat, that might have been scarlet, but now by some dirty dye had assumed the hue of bog-water; this hung in stripes about his heels, with an old shapeless felt on his head, such as country boys call a cobbeen—his countenance was not less uncouth than his attire—a leering cautious cunning in the wink of his eye, a hooked miserly formed nose, a huge mouth, whose under lip hung loose and pendulous. The expression of the whole outward man denoted practised confidence, cunning, and meanness. Addressing me with the assurance that denoted his calling—

"' Here I am, Joe Irwin, the best and only guide to the Churches—I'm the boy that can show your honour all, and tell you all ; sure it's I that's in the book.'

"' What book ?'

"' Why Doctor Wright's book, that tells the quality all about the county of Wicklow—sure I'm down there, printed off in black and white—and sure it was nobody else but I, that showed the Duchess of R—— all and every thing about the churches—'twas I, my own self, that handed her, all as one as if I was her Duke, into Kevin's bed—and there I brought also, the great Sir Walter Scott, who, though he be short of one leg, is an active and proper man sartainly, and very free, and dacent, and generous, as I may say, to a poor body. It was just at this hill where we now stand, that the Duchess ordered her coachman to draw up, and the darling lady looked out amongst us all, as we stood around, and a posy she was, with her cheeks as red as poppies among the corn; a proper woman too, as to size, as becomes a Duchess—so my dear life, out she drew her book, and then she axed " where is the guide that is down in this book, for no other will my Grease have," says she; so says I to myself, " now's your time, Joe Irwin, to step forward, for your the boy for her money ;" so out I started from among the poor crathurs who were about the coach, for they all knew, sure enough, that I was the man in the book ; so taking off my hat, and not forgetting to make a bow and a scrape of the heel, " I'm the boy you want, my Grease," says I ; " I know the ins and outs of every thing here, and can tell yees all about St. Kevin, and King M'Thoul, and Cathleen, and the dog, and the serpent, and the willow apple, and any thing else your Duchess pleases." " Come along then," says my Duchess, " you're the man for my money ; and so let all the other spalpeens sneak off about their business, for not a mother sowl shall be a follower or get a penny of mine, but the man that's down in the book, and that's yourself, honest Joe Irwin.' "

" And now for Saint Kevin, ' Come,' says I to Mr. Irwin, my guide, as I sat down to rest myself under the shade of the old archway—' tell me, as you know all about Glendalough, tell me something about it in old times.' 'With all the veins of my heart, Sir. St. Kevin was born not long after St. Patrick ; his father was a blood cousin of King M'Thoul, or O'Tool, for it's all one in the Irish : he was the prettiest child ever born, they say, in Ireland, so beautiful that an angel from heaven came down, kissed him, and christened him himself, and called him Comgan, or Kevin, which signifies in Irish, the pretty boy. As he grew up he did not throw any discredit upon his christening, for he learned Latin as fast as another would sup milk, and instead of playing commons or pitch-and-toss like other boys, he was always counting his beads ; and instead of spending his time a courting, as any other pretty gentleman would, he resolved to be a clergyman, and was full of holy thoughts ; so he one day came up here, on a visit to his blood relation, King M'Thoul, who owned all these mountains and vallies, and was now grown old, and, as a body may say, a little the worse for the wear, in mind as well as body. " How," says young Kevin to King M'Thoul, " does your lordship now spend your time, seeing you are grown too old to hunt the bucks and boars through the glen ?" " Why it's no other way I spend my time, than seeing my geese swimming about the lake : and once on a time I had the greatest sport you ever saw with the gander, for he used to take flight about all those hills, and come back again to his old master ; but now he has grown old too, and can fly by no manner of means." " What will you give me," says Kevin, " if I make him fly again for you ?" " Why I'll give you," says the easy, soft-hearted king, " all the ground he flies round, even suppose he flew round the whole glen." So blessed St. Kevin took the old gander in his hand, and bid him fly away. And, my dear life, away he went, round he flew the whole valley, up even to the tops of the hills, enclosed the place where the churches now stand, and the fine meadows along the river, and then came back to St. Kevin. " Now," says the saint, " King M'Thoul, be as good as your word ; give me this place, and I will dedicate it to God." And the king, if he were sorry, kept his grief to himself, and putting a handsome fece on the thing, he made over to the saint, for ever and a day, this valley, and all belonging to it : and so then he began to build these fine churches, and that great tower.'

" We shall conclude our notice of Saint Kevin with another amusing extract, from the lively and characteristic writer who has already stood us so much in good stead.

LEGEND OF GARADH DUFF.

"' Having rested myself sufficiently, I proceeded with my guide through the grave-yard towards the largest of the ruined churches, which is called the cathedral. In passing along, Mr. Irwin directed my attention to an old grave-stone with a round hole in it. " This, Sir, said he, " is the tomb of Garadh Duff, or Black and Yellow, the horse-stealer, whom St. Kevin killed for telling him a lie. It happened as follows :—Black and Yellow one day was coming over the ford, there above, not far from Lough-na-peche, riding a fine black mare, with a foal at her foot ; and meeting the saint, blessed Kevin asked him, " where, Garadh, did you get that fine beast ?" " Oh, I bought her from one of the Byrnes." " That's a lie, I know by your face, you thief." " Oh, may I never stir out of this spot," says Garadh, " if what I say is not true."" Dare you tell me so : now in order to make a liar, and a thief, and a holy show of you to the world's end, I'll fix your foal and mare there in that rock, and the print of their hoofs shall remain for ever, and you yourself must die and go to purgatory." " Well," if I must die," said the thief, " please me, holy father, in one thing, bury me in your own churchyard, and leave a hole in my tombstone, so that if any stray horse or cow should pass by, I may just push up my arm and make a snap at their leg, if it was nothing else but to remind me of my humour, and that I may keep my temper during the long day of the grave.'"

" We recommend the tourist to visit the curiosities of Glendalough in the order of the following description :

" The first ruin on the road side, on the north of the vale, is usually called the Ivy Church ; it was a small chapel, originally roofed with stone, at one end of which are the remains of a round tower, perfectly detached from the body of the church, although only by a distance of a few feet. The ruins of this church are too imperfect to detain the tourist long.

" At the distance of about a quarter of a mile are the supposed ruins of the famous city of Glendalough. The origin of this city, and its celebrity as a seat of learning, are attributed to Saint Mochuorog or Mocorog, a Briton. A little paved space, of a quadrangular form, now called the market place, indicates its site ; from this a paved causeway led to Hollywood, on the borders of the county of Kildare, through the vale of Glendason. This little Appian way, which is yet visible, was composed of blocks

of hewn stone, placed edge-wise, and was about twelve feet in breadth.

" Not far from the village is a rivulet, called St. Kevin's Keeve, which is said to possess miraculous powers.

" Near the cathedral stand the ruins of a small building, probably used as a sacristy, or place where the relics and religious vestments were preserved. Visiters are recommended to turn round three times in this closet, as a preventive of future head-aches. In the confused heaps around these buildings, a stone is pointed out, bearing three figures ; that in the centre represents some religious person, on whose right hand is a pilgrim, leaning on his staff, and on the left, a sinner extending a purse of money as a commutation for penance.*

" Several remnants of crosses lie scattered up and down, the most remarkable of which is that standing in the cemetery of the cathedral, eleven feet in height, and formed of one solid block of granite. Certain miraculous properties are attributed to this : but it is first necessary that the votary should completely embrace the stone, making his hands meet at the opposite side. The stranger naturally walks up to the *front* of the cross, and throwing his arms about the stone, attempts to unite his hands ; this he will soon find impracticable, from the great breadth of the flat front ; but upon changing his situation, and standing close up to the narrow *side* of the shaft, the object will be easily accomplished.

" To the west of the cathedral stood our Lady's Church : this could not have been a very extensive structure originally, but from the traces still discoverable, it appears to have been built with more architectural taste and knowledge than the others. The doorway must have been admirably executed : in the lintel was wrought a cruciformed ornament, not unlike the flyer of a stamping press. The walls, as high as the doorway, are of hewn stone of a large size, and the remainder of a rag stone, admirably cemented. The eastern window was like that of the cathedral, but it is now in a ruinous condition.— There are several recesses in the wall, in which females, particularly those lately united in the hymeneal bonds, are advised to turn round three times : the advantages of this ceremony will be satisfactorily stated by the guide.

KEVIN'S KITCHEN.

St. Kevin's Kitchen is now the most perfect of the Seven Churches, it is roofed with stone, and has a steeple

* This is Ledwich's explanation, which is much ridiculed by Dr. Lanigan.

at one end, a perfect miniature of the round towers. It was lighted by one window, the architrave of which was of freestone, richly sculptured, but want of good feeling and of good taste, permitted this enriched moulding to be carried away, and bruised into powder for domestic purposes. The interior measures twenty-two feet nine inches in length by fifteen in breadth : its height is twenty feet, and the thickness of the walls three feet six inches. At the eastern end, an arch, the chord of which measures five feet three inches, opens a communication with a smaller chapel, ten feet six inches in length by nine feet three inches in width, having also a small eastern window. The several lower courses of the walls are of a coarse mountain granite ; their thickness is three feet, and height about twelve ; the door is six feet eight inches high, two feet four inches wide at the top, and four inches wider at the bottom, the stones running the entire thickness of the wall.

"The belfry, which rises from the west end of the church, is a round tower, about fifty feet in height ; it is accessible by a small aperture in the ceiling, over which, between the cove and the roof, is a large dark void ; it was lighted by a small loop-hole, near the summit. The roof of the church, which is still perfect, and very curious, is comprised of thin stones or flags, neatly laid, and with a very high pitch ; the ridge of the roof is thirty feet, while that of the double building at the east end is only twenty.

"Beneath the dark, frowning cliff of Lugduff, on a little patch of arable land, almost inaccessible, except by water, are the ruins of a church, called Teampull-na-Skellig—i. e. the Temple of the Desert or Rock ; it is also called the Priory of the Rock, and St. Kevin's cell. Here the saint used to seclude himself for the Lent season, and spend his time wholly in penitence and prayer. It was at a window of this cell, while in a supplicating attitude, and with one hand extended, that a blackbird is said to have descended, and dropped her eggs in St. Kevin's hand.— Tradition states, that the saint never altered the position of his hand or arm, until the poor creature had hatched her eggs, which is the reason that all representations of St. Kevin exhibit him with an outstretched hand, and a bird perched upon it.

"Near the Rhefeart church is a Cairn or circular heap of stones, round which pilgrims perform their appointed penance.

"Our description of the most eastern church, perhaps the most important, and which is nearest to the entrance of the vale, has been intentionally postponed, because the visitor generally enters at the northern side of the valley, and making a circuit, takes his leave by the south ; this is generally called the abbey, and was dedicated, like the cathedral, to St. Peter and St. Paul. St. Kevin's well lies near the pathway leading from the Rhefeart church to the abbey. The abbey appears to have been the most masterly specimen of the art of building amongst this extensive collection of architectural remains ; it originally consisted of two buildings parallel to each other, and of curious and beautiful workmanship ; the eastern window was ornamented with rich sculpture. Several of the carved stones were removed and used as key-stones for the arches of the bridge at Derrybawn, but some very curious devices are still to be seen ; on one is an engraved wolf, with his tail in his mouth, the whole figure within a triangle. The wolf was an old inhabitant of Glendalough, and not totally extirpated until 1710 ; the triangle may have some reference to the Trinity, which we know was illustrated by the trefoil or shamrock by St. Patrick. On another stone, two ravens are represented pecking at a skull, a mere emblem of mortality. Runic knots may be discovered on several stones : on one is seen a wolf, the tail of which is entwined in the hair of a man's head ; and on others, wolves, or rather wild beasts in general are represented devouring human heads, all simple emblems of mortality.

"These specimens are quite unique in Ireland.

"Why there were exactly seven churches, can be explained only by stating, that the ancient Irish attached some peculiar merit to this number; witness the Seven Churches at Clunmacnois, Iniscathy, &c , and the seven altars at Holy Cross and Clonfert, &c.

ROUND TOWER AND VALLEY OF GLENDALOUGH.

"There is one monument of antiquity, of more remote date, most probably, than the churches themselves, not yet noticed, although the visiter never loses sight of it during his peregrination through the extensive vale of Glendalough, that is the round tower. The use of these extraordinary buildings are not yet fully ascertained.*

"Before taking leave of these interesting ruins, we will draw again upon the never failing descriptive talent of our able assistant, C. O.

"'A cemetery is often an interesting, sometimes even a beautiful spot. I suppose not here, such a dank, noisome enclosure as a city churchyard; neither do I contemplate that finished specimen of Parisian affection, Pere la Chaise. But I summon to my fancy the burying ground of some English village, surrounding a parish church, gray and time-touched, like its venerable vicar; but, like him also, firm, orderly, and upright; a shady place, where—

'The rude forefathers of the hamlet sleep,'

under chesnuts that witnessed the Norman invasion, and yews that supplied, during the wars of the Plantaganets, the tough bow for the formidable archery of England; or I would rather ponder on such a spot as this at Glendalough—surrounded as it is by mighty mountains, dark winding glens—all its lakes, and streams, rocks, and waterfalls, in keeping and accordant association with a place of ruins—ruins that testify of altars and of a priesthood overthrown—a work-shop made desolate—a people scattered and peeled; where the long, continuous shadow of the lofty and slender round tower moves slowly from morn till eve, over wasted churches, overturned oratories, shattered crosses, scathed yew trees, and the tombs, now undistinguishable, of bishops, abbots, and anchorites—walking its round as time centinel, and telling forth to the Ancient of Days, how many suns have run their diurnal and annual course since these holy men of old had descended to their graves.

"'I certainly did feel strongly impressed with the scene around, and entered into abstracted communion with the " Genius loci," and my imagination had Coemgen, and Moliba, and Aidan, and their successors, Malachy and Laurence O'Toole, passing before me, and mourning over this their sanctuary, their mountain-retreat for ascetic contemplation, now trodden under foot by the ruthless spoiler, and become curious for its desert loneliness and hoary desolation—where the carrion crow croaks hoarsely from the briared chapelry, where she has made her a nest—and where the fox, the martin, and the wild cat now find their hiding places.— Such were the imaginings that came thick upon me, as I walked across the churchyard of Glendalough. And, after all, they were unfounded fancies I was then possessed of. For it was not the work of the reformation to cause these ruins—it was not the church-spoiler of Henry or Elizabeth's day—nor yet the curse of Cromwell, that swept all here into desolation; as we have the best authority for supposing, that long before the changes brought about by Protestantism, or even before the suppression of monasteries, this place had become a ruined and deserted scene. An archbishop of Tuam, cited by Ware, writing 616 years ago, mentions, that this place, though from ancient times it was held in great veneration on account of St. Kevin, had now become so deserted and desolate, that instead of being a retreat for churchmen, it had become a den of robbers, and the resort of thieves—so much so, that more homicides and crimes are committed in this valley than in any other place in Ireland.'

"After a complete inspection of the churches and their appendages, a natural curiosity of more than usual interest remains to be visited; this is St. Kevin's bed. This wonder-working couch is a small cave, capable of contain-

ing three persons at most, in the front of a rock, hanging perpendicularly over the lake; the approach is by a narrow path along the steep side of the mountain, at every step of which the slightest false trip would precipitate the pedestrian into the lake below; certainly the guide endeavours to infuse an additional degree of confidence into his followers, by assuring them, that since the fate of the fair Cathleen, at which period St. Kevin prayed that none might ever find a watery grave in that lake, no mortal has ever perished there. There is one place in particular where all the eloquence of the guide is sure to be exerted to encourage the party, and where it frequently proves unsuccessful, that is, the ledge of the rock called the Lady's Leap. After passing this rubicon, the landing-place immediately above the cave is soon reached, without difficulty; but the visiter must descend with caution, his face turned to the rock down which he climbs, while the guide directs which way he is to turn, and where to plant his foot, until at last he reaches the mouth of the sainted bed.

"The bed is about thirty feet from the surface of the water, and the front of the rock, for the whole of its height or depth, perfectly perpendicular. Those who are not disposed to confide in the efficacy of St. Kevin's prayers, for the safety of his posthumous visiters, can see the cave distinctly from the opposite side of the lake; and if there should be any person entering at the time, it will mark out the path and its dangers more distinctly than even those actually engaged in the task can themselves perceive.

"We are now under the necessity of leaving for a while the beaten track, in order to introduce our reader to scenery less familiar to the tourist's foot, and not so much within the showman's catalogue.

"'After picking our way,' writes our friend C. O. faithful as ' Old Truepenny' in Hamlet, but a trifle more companionable on a mountain side, ' through miry ways and sundry sloughs, and leaving the first lake called Lough-na-Peche (or Piast) behind us, we arrived at the ravine dividing the hill of Derrybawn from the higher and more precipitous mountain of Lugduff. Here is one of the most delightful spots I know any where. A wild waterfall tumbling from the mountain to the south, through a ravine fringed with all sorts of appropriate timber—Lugduff rising before you in dark grandeur, very like some views I have got of Turk mountain at Killarney; beneath you the upper lake, winding dark and deep up the glen; just at your feet the still, translucent basin of Poolanass, in whose crystal depths, as in condensed ether, hundreds of trout are disporting – I do not think any of the waterfalls of Killarney more interesting than this.'

"'A good steady boat hove in sight, freighted not only with Joe Irwin, but also with a strange gentleman, who, like us, had come to see Kevin's bed, &c. and he also had brought his guide.'

STORY OF TIM DWYER.

"In the boat the story of Dwyer is narrated :— Tim Dwyer was worth a ship-load of him—a stouter fellow never pointed a pike—a fleeter foot never lifted a brogue —a clearer head or eye never measured danger, or planned an escape. Many a day and night he lay within the face of yon hill—Kevin's bed was his retreat and his sleeping place, until it was made too hot for him. Government hearing that this was his haunt, sent down the Highlanders; they thought that because they were mountain men, they would be the only match for the boys. But soon Tim Dwyer showed the Sawnies a trick or two worth larning—not but that the petticoats were fine fellows, and if they knew the mountain passes, and the caves, and the bogs, and the toghers, they maybe would have snaffled Dwyer—but every cock crows best on his own dunghill—so Dwyer and his boys made a show of them. Dwyer, gentlemen, was one summer's morning lying fast asleep in the bed, and a serjeant's guard of the Highlanders was patroling along the other side of the lake just opposite to us; the party was commanded by serjeant Donald M'Bane, who is remembered here to this day, as one of the best shots that ever rammed down a

---

* " A recent antiquarian appears to have thrown the light of historical evidence upon this 'vexata questio' of the learned brotherhood. His essay, which was honoured with a prize and medal by the unanimous decision of the Royal Irish Academy, is not yet before the public. We cannot, therefore, avail ourself of his reasons; but are, we believe, correct in stating his conclusion to be, that these towers were belfries and places of strength attached to ecclesiastical edifices. His arguments, it is generally said, are free from conjecture, and founded on authentic history, as well as the actual sites, positions, and architectural characters of these remarkable ruins."

bullet; some people were even led to believe he could shoot a man round a corner. Well—this keen, canny Sawney, thought he saw something in the bed, and he ups with his terrible gun, and sure enough he was near giving Dwyer his billet for the other world—for the ball grazed his thigh, cut away the skin upon his ribs, but did no real injury, except tapping a little of his blood; and now my poor fellow thought it high time for him to bolt, and so, naked that he might run light, he took to his well-known pass up the face of Lugduff. The Highlanders, like sporting fellows, immediately grounded their muskets, and, bayonet in hand, started off in pursuit: some making after him by the head of the lake, towards Glencoela; others turned to the left, and made their way over the stream by Polanass. In the meanwhile Dwyer was toiling up the face of the mountain, and they could see a streak of blood running from shoulder to flank, and down the white limbs of the clean-skinned fellow; when half way up the hill, he turned him round to look after the Scotchmen, and saw that all had turned either to the right or left of the lake in making towards him, and had left the whole of Comaderry side without a man. Dwyer at once changed his plan, bounced and bounded down the face of the hill, plunged into the lake at Templenaskellig, swam across the water before you could say Jack Robinson, and took possession of all the Scotchmen's muskets and cartridge boxes—and now maybe it was not he that shouted, and crowed, and triumphed, as one after another he pitched the guns and ammunition into the lake; you could hear his huzzas rattling and echoing through the hills, as if the mountains clapped hands with joy, and tossed the triumph from one to another; he then very leisurely lounged away towards Toulenagee mountain, and so off towards his old haunts under Lugnaquilla.

"Our space does not allow of the sequel of Dwyer's story—the more as we cannot omit the description of an ascent into Kevin's bed, which follows:

"'By this time we had rowed under Kevin's bed, and landing adjoining to it, ascended an inclined stratum of the rock to a sort of ledge, or resting place, from whence I and some others prepared to enter the bed. Here the guides make much ado about proposing their assistance; but to any one who has common sense and enterprise, there is no serious difficulty; for by the aid of certain holes in the rock, and points which you can readily grasp, you can turn into this little artificial cave, which in fact is not bigger than a small baker's oven; and were it not that it hangs some twenty-five feet perpendicularly, over the dark deep lake, this cavity, not larger than many a pigstye I have seen excavated in the side of a bank, could not attract so many visiters. I, and two young men who followed me, found it a very tight fit when crouched together in it: at the further end, there is a sort of pillow and peculiar excavation made for the saint's head, and the whole of the interior is tattooed with the initials of such as have adventured to come in. Amongst the many, I could observe those of Sir Walter Scott, Lord Combermere, &c. &c.; and we were shown the engravings of certain blue stocking dames, as for instance, Lady M——n, who had made it her temporary boudoir. Just where the left shoulder of the saint may be supposed to have rested, I took leave to inscribe a little c. o., conceiving it might be well to have an entry on the saint's bead-roll, along with the gallant and gifted individuals who are registered therein. And yet, after all, while reclining here, some sceptical doubts did intrude, whether any but a madman or an outlaw could ever have thought of making it his resting-place.'

MELANCHOLY EVENT.

"'Not long ago, as some of our party informed me, a sad event took place in consequence of a superstition. A lovely young woman, the pride of the vale in which she lived, and not a year married to a youth, every way worthy of her, came to the patron, attended by her mother and only sister, and large with her first child: after going the usual rounds about the churches, she was led by her mother towards the Bed; and though she and her sister expressed strong repugnance towards the duty, the superstitious old crone urged them forward, and actually pushed them on to the enterprise. Though midsummer, the day, as frequently happens in these mountains, was dark and blustery; storm clouds enveloped Lugduff, and the waves of the windlashed lake sent their spray even up to the level of the Bed, and from the cliffs and fissures of the precipices around, fitful sounds, as it were wailings of grief and agony, came down. On such a day there could be no approach to the Bed by water, and they must take the path overhead, unsheltered, steep, and slippery: perhaps the young woman's peculiar situation unnerved her—but she felt dizzy, and trembled exceedingly; still the old voteen goaded her on, and just as they gained the point of the path, over the Bed, a gust from the mountain swept against them, and the eldest lost her presence of mind and footing; with a shriek she went down, dragging her sister after her into the depths of the lake; for a moment they rose, and their white garments were seen mixing with the foam—and then sunk for ever!'

"C. O. next describes the still more difficult exploit of the turning stone: 'Understanding well enough Joe's motive for drawing me off from his offensive rivals, I attended him towards a precipice not far from Kevin's bed, along the face of which, and some fifteen or twenty feet from the water, a ledge runs about four inches broad, at the end of which there is a shelf somewhat wider, and on which, according to tradition, if a person turns round three times, having faith, he will never go to hell. Having a clear head and active body, I ventured on and accomplished the experiment, but as my faith was neither full nor active, I am inclined to look to some surer safeguard from the wrath to come.'

"A little further on, the oldest of the Seven Churches is met, Templenaskellig, where St. Kevin 'kept his Lents,' according to the trusty Joe.

LEGEND OF CATHLEEN AND ST. KEVIN.

"The fair Cathleen was descended of an illustrious race, and endowed with rich domains: having heard of the fame of St. Kevin, at that time a youth, she went to listen to his religious admonitions; but unholy thoughts crept in amidst the telling of her beads, and she became enamoured of the youthful saint. Tradition says, it was the intention of the saint to have built his abbey in the valley of Luggelaw, on the margin of Lough Tay; but that the repeated visits of Cathleen, while he sojourned there, induced him to remove to some retreat where he might be freed from her interruptions, and he ultimately decided upon Glendalough.

"Just when he had established his religious seminaries, and supposed himself at rest for the remainder of his mortal career, the beauteous but unhappy Cathleen renewed her visits. Determined to avoid the temptations of so much innocence and fidelity in one so fair, and to spare her tender feelings, the saint withdrew to his stony couch in the inaccessible front of Lugduff. Day after day Cathleen visited the wonted haunts of her beloved Kevin, but he was no where to be found. One morning as the disconsolate fair was slowly moving along the church-yard path, the favourite dog of St. Kevin met and fawned upon her, and turning swiftly, led the way to his master's sequestered home. Here then follows the most uncharitable part of the saint's conduct, for, awaking and perceiving a female leaning over him, 'although there was heaven in her eye,' he hurled her from the beetling rock. The next morning, says one traditionary historian, the unfortunate Cathleen, whose unceasing affection seems to have merited a better fate, was seen, for a moment, on the margin of the lake, wringing her flowing locks, but never was heard of more.

This tale is the subject of Moore's Melody:

By that lake whose gloomy shore
  Sky-lark never warbles o'er.
Where the cliff hangs high and steep,
  Young Saint Kevin stole to sleep.
"Here at least," he calmly said,
  "Woman ne'er shall find my bed."
Ah! the good saint little knew
  What that wily sex can do.

'Twas from Cathleen's eyes he flew
  Eyes of most unholy blue!

She had lov'd him well and long,
  Wish'd him her's nor thought it wrong.
Wheresoe'er the saint would fly,
  Still he heard her light foot nigh ;
East or west, where'er he turned,
  Still her eyes before him burned.

On the bold cliff's bosom cast,
  Tranquil now he sleeps at last ;
Dreams of heaven, nor thinks that e'er
  Woman's smile can haunt him there.
But nor earth, nor heaven is free
  From her power, if fond she be;
Even now, while calm he sleeps,
  Cathleen o'er him leans and weeps.

Fearless she had tracked his feet,
  To this rocky wild retreat !
And when morning met his view,
  Her mild glances met it too.
Ah ! you saints have cruel hearts !
  Sternly from his bed he starts,
And with rude repulsive shock,
  Hurls her from the beetling rock.

Glendalough ! thy gloomy wave
  Soon was gentle Cathleen's grave.
Soon the saint, (yet ah too late,)
  Felt her love and mourn'd her fate.
When he said, ' Heaven rest her soul !'
  Round the lake light music stole ;
And her ghost was seen to glide
  Smiling, o'er the fatal tide !

" The reader is now probably content to quit Cathleen, St. Kevin, and Glendalough, and will be disposed to pardon the numerous fables brought within his view, when he is informed, that no where else have they a collective existence."

Such is the description which our guide gives of the valley of Glendalough, and as our readers must by this time have perceived that the little volume not only furnishes a faithful directory to the beauties of Wicklow, but is also replete with legends and stories connected with the places it describes, we feel it unnecessary to pen a line in the way of recommendation. The work possesses this advantage over the generality of guide books, while it must prove extremely interesting to those who purpose making the tour of Wicklow, it may be read with pleasure and satisfaction by the fireside among the social circle. With the exception of one little volume, " The Northern Tourist, or Stranger's Guide to the North of Ireland"—(and we must of course at all times be admitted to make this exception, being ourselves personally concerned)—the present Guide Book to the county of Wicklow is the best thing of the kind we have ever seen.

We have noticed one or two trivial errors with regard to the present proprietors of demesnes and resting places on the road, but these do not materially affect the general accuracy of the work ; they should be carefully looked after in future editions. The volume contains several well executed engravings, from one of which we have copied the design in our first page.

THE SCALP, COUNTY OF WICKLOW.

In our 82d number, already referred to, will be found a correct description of this very extraordinary natural pass through the mountains which divide the counties of Dublin and Wicklow. " It is situated about two miles from Enniskerry, on the road to Dublin. The opposite hills appear to have been rent asunder by some tremendous convulsive shock, and being composed of granite strata, the internal structure, when exposed to view, presents the secret recesses of nature in an awful and appalling point of view. Enormous masses of granite, many tons in weight, are tossed about in the most irregular manner, and so imperfect and unfinished was the effort of nature in creating this gulf, that the opposite sides of the pass are distant only the breadth of a narrow road from each other ; in some places enormous masses actually interrupt the continued regularity of the limit of the road."

DUBLIN :

Printed and Published by P. D. Hardy, 3, Cecilia-street ; to whom all communications are to be addressed.

THE

DUBLIN PENNY JOURNAL

CONDUCTED BY P. DIXON HARDY, M.R.I.A.

| Vol. III. | NOVEMBER 15, 1834. | No. 124. |

LISCARROLL CASTLE, COUNTY OF CORK.

The town of Liscarroll is situated in a mountainous part of the county of Cork, and is a very inconsiderable, dirty town. In it are the ruins of a very large and strong castle, built, as is generally supposed, by King John, though some attribute it to some of the Strongbonian adventurers.

In the latter end of the month of August, 1642, it was besieged by the Irish army, under Lord Mountgarret, consisting of seven thousand men; and on the second of September, after a siege of thirteen days, it surrendered. However, the very next day, the Earl of Inchiquin came to its relief, attacked the Irish army, and after a very severe contest defeated them, and slew fifteen hundred men. It was again taken, in 1646, by Lord Castlehaven, with an army of five thousand men.

The castle is an oblong square, two hundred and forty feet by one hundred and twenty, and was flanked by six great towers, two square and four round and the walls were thirty feet high. The south entrance was defended by a strong fort, of which very little now remains, as may be seen by the above drawing, which represents the south side. There are some subterranean passages near the castle, the entrances to which are now mostly filled up.

There was, about twenty years ago, an extraordinary well, or rather hole, somewhere near this town, the depth of which was so great, that if a stone were let fall from the brink, it would not be heard to plunge into the water below for sixteen seconds afterwards; but though I made every enquiry, I could not find it, neither did any person there know anything about such a curiosity. It was called "Kate's hole." Perhaps some of your correspond-

ents could give some information about it, as it certainly did exist, for I find it mentioned in two books of very good authority.　　　　　　　　　　　W. A.

MRS. VAN BUCHELL.

In 1775 died the wife of that eccentric empiric, Dr. Martin Van Buchell, and the singular mode employed for the preservation of her body merits notice. On her death taking place, he applied to Dr. Hunter to exert his skill in preventing, if possible, the changes of form usual after the cessation of life. Accordingly the doctor, assisted by Mr. Cruikshank, injected the blood-vessels with a coloured fluid, so that the minute red vessels of the cheeks and lips were filled, and exhibited their native hue; and the body, in general, having all the cavities filled with antiseptic substances, remained perfectly free from corruption, or any unpleasant smell, as if it was merely in a state of sleep. But to resemble the appearance of life, glass eyes were also inserted. The corpse was then deposited in a bed of thin paste of plaster of Paris, in a box of sufficient dimensions, which subsequently crystalised, and produced a pleasing effect. A curtain covered the glass lid of the box, which could be withdrawn at pleasure, and which box, being kept in the common parlour, Mr. Van Buchell had the satisfaction of preserving his wife for many years, frequently displaying the beautiful corpse to his friends and visiters. A second marriage, some years afterwards, having occasioned family differences, it was found expedient to remove the preserved body.

153

"THE GAEL AND CYMBRI."[*]

In directing the attention of our readers to this learned, ingenious, and interesting work, on the ancient history of our country, we feel it is due to them, as well as to the author, to apologize for having allowed it to remain so long unnoticed. The truth is, that when we first took it up, we considered the subject to be one requiring such a depth of research—such an acquaintance with the works and opinions of other writers on the same or similar subjects, and such an extent of space to be devoted to its consideration, that we felt a kind of instinctive disinclination to enter seriously on its review, until at least, we had prepared ourselves in some measure for the task. On carefully perusing the volume, however, we have been agreeably surprized to find that the subject has been treated in that plain and popular manner which brings it down to every comprehension: that it may be perused with satisfaction and pleasure not only by the professed antiquarian and scholar, but by every individual who may take an interest in the early history of nations, or who may wish to gain information concerning the particular people by whom the British islands were at first colonized.

We have been particularly induced to notice Sir Wm. Betham's work at the present moment, from having observed, in a recent number of the "Printing Machine," an article purporting to be a review of the work, written by an individual who certainly can know very little of the men and manners even of the time in which he lives, otherwise he would not make such a mistake, as to insinuate that the work was the production of an *enthusiastic Irishman!*—or that it was any thing of that national vanity, of which Irishmen are accused, prompted its publication. For ourselves, though Irish to the back bone, we will freely confess that to us one great recommendation which the volume possessed was, its not being written by an Irishman, who might be accused of partiality to his country; and it did indeed afford us pleasure to find that the subject had been taken up by a cool, calculating, steady Englishman, properly qualified to form a correct opinion upon it, and who would not be biassed by those preconceived ideas relative to the greatness of the ancient Irish, which, like an *ignus fatuus*, had led so many former Irish writers into the morasses and quagmires of Irish history. While the reviewer in the "Machine" is forced to admit that Sir W. Betham, in his work, " has collected together many rays of historic light, tending to strengthen the received opinion that the language and many usages of the Irish people are of high antiquity, and of eastern origin,' with a fixed predetermination not to allow of any thing that might be favorable to the arguments which Sir Wm. brings forward relative to the early greatness of Ireland, he dismisses the work without further notice, as having been written by an Irishman, " in the truly *exaggerated spirit of national vanity* ;" and then, with a flourish of trumpets, introduces a nice little theory of his own, which he denominates " a *philosophical explanation* of the grounds or origin of the general illusion respecting the ancient celebrity of Ireland,' in which the Elysian fields of Homer, the Atlantes of Plato, and the happy isles of Hesiod and Plato, the Cimmerian and Hesperian world, with a thousand other lofty imaginings, are largely descanted on— while the origin of the Gael and Cymbri, the subject on which the volume has been written, is never once alluded to or touched on, no more than if the question had never been proposed. This is certainly reviewing with a vengeance. We should suppose it is the new system recommended by the Society for the Diffusion of Useful Knowledge, or at all events we may take it as a specimen of reviewing by steam. But, to return to the book before us ; we believe it will be generally admitted that to separate the fable from fact in the early records of any nation is an utter impossibility. However careful the ancients among any people may have been to hand down to posterity a faithful record of events

by the means of merely *oral* tradition, it is evident that during the lapse of ages much of falsehood would be mingled with the truth. With respect to the traditions of the bards and senaechies of Ireland, although, as Spencer somewhere quaintly observes, there is much of truth in their songs and stories, which a well-eyed man may discover and find out, there is also much of fiction ; and it is only when we bring the records of any people to the test of written history, and draw our deductions from correct analogy, and a proper rendering of various authors, that we can ever hope to come to a just and legitimate conclusion : in this way, it would appear to us, our author at first set about and finally accomplished his work. That there are many and serious difficulties in the way of considering the subject of which he treats, will be readily admitted. It is one which has engaged the pens of many able writers, and yet, after all, we hitherto appear to have been left nearly as much in the dark as ever.— The very advertisement from the Royal Irish Academy, which in some measure brought forth the present work, proves this :—" Who were the Scoti, and at what period did they settle in Ireland ?" is the question they proposed for a prize ; and even should Sir W. Betham's book not be considered as going the full length of an answer to the query in its various bearings, it must be admitted as doing much towards opening up the ground for exploring those caverns in which the secrets of the early history of our country have hitherto lain hid.

Sir William, in treating his subject, commences with first principles, and argues from facts, and were there no other merit in his book, this, we would think, should call forth the high approbation of all who wish to see the subject fairly investigated. He tells us—

" The examination of the language, laws, religion, customs, and institutions of the people of Gaul, who were declared by Cæsar, to have called themselves Celtæ, was the first object of my attention, and the result of that investigation has established, it is conceived, beyond the possibility of doubt or question, that the Irish, Britons, and Gauls, of Cæsar's day, all spoke the same language, had the same origin, religion, laws, institutions, and customs, and were, in fact, but different branches of the same people. Thus far one branch of the question has been, I conceive, effectually answered—the Scoti, or Irish, were Celtæ.

" The other question still remained—' WHEN DID THEY SETTLE IN IRELAND ?' This could not be answered without first solving the problem of ' WHO WEAR THE CELTÆ ?' It was not sufficient to rest *on the probability* of their settling in the British islands from Gaul, although that alternative has hitherto been the *dernier resort* of most English writers, who, rejecting altogether the Milesian story as fabulous, have had no other way of accounting for the peopling of those islands, than in frail wicker coracles, covered with skins, from the nearest coast of the continent

" ' *Who and whence were the Celtæ* ?' involved investigation into the history of all the ancient people of Europe, but it was not long before that question was also satisfactorily answered ; a strong affinity was palpable between the Celts and the Phenicians—their language, religion, and institutions, not only appear to have been similar, but identical ; they not only traded with, but colonized Spain, the British Islands, and Celtic Gaul, expelling or extirpating the previous inhabitants, and planting therein their own people. Thus is the second question answered, and the long sought problem solved.

" Another question arose out of this investigation, viz. were ' *the Welsh the ancient Britons who combated against Cæsar, and, after the fall of the Roman province of Britain into the hands of the Saxons, took refuge in Wales, and there maintained their independence, and handed down their language, laws, and institutions, to their descendants ?*'

" I had always considered the affirmative of this proposition true, and, although a slight acquaintance with the Welsh language, led to the conclusion that it varied essentially from the Gaelic, still it appeared but *a variance*, and I considered the two languages, in their origin, essentially the same. Finding, however, discrepancies and anomalies in the notion of the Welsh being the ancient Britains, which appeared irreconcileable, I determined, in the first instance, to examine, more particu-

---

[*] Or an inquiry into the Origin Religion, Language, and Institutions of the Irish Scoti, Britons, and Gauls. And of the Caledonians, Picts, Welsh, and Bretons. By Sir W. Betham, Ulster King of Arms, &c.: London : Thomas and William Boone, New Bond-street. Dublin : Curry and Co.

larly, the construction of the Welsh language, and was surprised to find that it differed totally from the Gaelic, and had not, in fact, the slightest affinity, unless it could be considered an affinity that a few words are to be found in each tongue, which have the same or similar meaning."

"Having thus ascertained that the Welsh and Gael must have been a totally distinct and separate people, and therefore, that the ancestors of the Welsh could not have been the Britons, who fought with Cæsar, as they were undoubtedly Gael, the question then arose—" who were the Welsh, and when did they become possessed of Wales?'"

"Thus did another difficulty present itself, of no small magnitude, which, however, was eventually surmounted. Lhuyd and Rowland, two of the most eminent Welsh writers, had unwillingly been coerced into the opinion, that a people, who spoke the Irish language, were the predecessors of the Welsh in Wales, and gave names to most of the places in that country and all parts of England; and that Welsh names of rivers and places, were only to be found in the eastern and southern parts of Scotland : therefore, it appears clear, that the Picts, who inhabited that country, must have been the ancestors of the Welsh, and that they conquered Wales, Cornwall, and Britanny, on the fall of the Roman empire ; and calling themselves *Cymbri*, they were a colony of the *Cimbri*, a people who once inhabited the neighbouring coasts of Jutland, the ancient Cimbric Chersonesus, the country opposite the land of the Picts.

"The origin and history of the Gael and Cymbri is thus placed on its true basis, and that is now in harmony, which, heretofore, was confused, anomalous, and contradictory.

"It has been my object to adduce evidence, perfectly free from even the suspicion of Irish predilection or bias ; it will be found that few Irish authorities have been quoted, except the Gaelic language itself. Even for the Irish history, the account given by Nennius and Giraldus Cambrensis, have been preferred to Irish MSS. or Keating's history, although it should be admitted, in candour and fairness to that learned writer, that his real history, in the original, is very superior to the spurious English translation, published by Dermot O'Connor. The Milesian story, however, will eventually be found grounded in truth ; and, although but a faint and imperfect sketch, it is the true history of the first settlement of the Celtæ in Europe.

"The following pages are now laid before the critical and intelligent, with no small portion of anxiety ; they appear to me to demonstrate, that ancient colonies of Phenicians settled in Spain, Ireland, Britain, and Gaul, long before the Christian era, and that they called themselves Gael, and Gaeltach, or Celtæ, and that the Irish, the Gael of Scotland, and the Manks, are now the only descendants of that ancient people who speak their language.

"The Phenician language has been, for two thousand years, unknown, that is, *with any certainty* : at all events, so imperfectly understood, that all attempts to explain even the shortest inscription, found upon coins, medals, or marbles, have been but vague and uncertain guesses.— Spanheim, Bochart, and Gebelen, have endeavoured to render them intelligible through the Hebrew, but their attempts have been abortive, or very imperfectly successful ; though kindred tongues, the affinity of the Hebrew with the Phenician is too distant to be useful for such a purpose. The Phenicians, although co-descendants of Shem, through Eber, with the Jews, had so much intercourse with other nations, that their language became very much mixed and changed, while the Hebrew remained stationary and pure.

"The discovery that in the Irish a people still exist *who speak the language of the Phenicians*, is of the first historical importance, for by it Phenician inscriptions may be decyphered, and the extent of their commerce and navigation traced by the ancient names of places in the world known to the ancients.

"The Irish character has been used in this work to express the Gaelic words, because the Scottish method of using an *h* instead of a point, to eclipse or render mute the preceding consonant, gives an uncouth and awkward

appearance to the word itself, and would render it unpronounceable, according to the power of that letter in any other language. An alphabet of the Irish letters, and a brief explanation of the power of the points, is, therefore, given.

"The alphabet consists of the following seventeen letters :—

a b c ꝺ e ꝼ ᵹ ꝉ l m n o p ꞃ ꞅ ꞇ or u
a b c d e f g i l m n o p r s t u

ċ ḋ ᵹ̇, having a point over them render them mute.
ḃ and ṁ change their power to *v* consonant.

ꞃ̃ signifies that the letter is doubled, and is the same as *nn*.

"These few observations are sufficient to explain the sound of the Irish words used in the following essay.— The only letters which differ much from the Roman, are ꝺ *d*, ꝼ *f*, ᵹ *g*, ꞃ *r*, ꞅ *s*, and ꞇ *t*, but even in these the variation is so very slight, that the knowledge of them will be easily acquired."

From the foregoing extracts the reader will be able to judge of the ground taken by Sir W. Betham : it would be impossible, however, in the brief space we could allocate to the article to give even a synopsis of the various points of argument ; we must, therefore, refer to the work itself, merely allowing our readers to judge of the correctness of our author's reasoning from the analogy of language, by the following extracts :

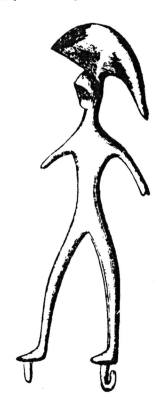

" BRONZE FIGURE OF A PHENICIAN SOLDIER,

" Found in a bog in Ireland about two years since. It is exactly similar to the Etruscan bronzes found in Italy.

"It has already been stated that the Phenicians, the first discoverers of the British Islands, gave them their original names, and also conferred the subordinate denominations on the smaller islands, promontories, estuaries, mountains, rivers, &c. It will naturally be objected, and justly, that the Phenicians, before they had approached the British coasts, had discovered, and of course named the countries situated on the coasts of the Mediterranean, with the islands, promontories, estuaries, rivers, mountains, and straits thereof, and also the coasts of Spain, Portugal, and Gaul. It may, therefore, be necessary before it will· be admitted, that the Gael and Phenicians were the same people—that there should be an equally striking conformity and analogy, in the Gaelic language, between the meaning of those names, which are acknowledged generally, and almost universally, to have been conferred by that people, as of those of the British Islands and Gaul. This is such obvious and just criticism, that I would say if we do not find those names in the Gaelic etymons, exactly descriptive and accordant with their peculiar situation, character, and circumstances, in so striking and palpable a manner, as scarcely to admit of question or doubt ; the names of Britain and Gaul being Gaelic, only prove an identity between the inhabitants of those countries, as different branches of the Gael, but do not go far enough to establish an identity, or even a connexion between them and the Phenicians. But, if the names of the coasts and islands of the Mediterranean and of Spain, or a great majority of them, are evidently and palpably Gaelic, we may fairly, and without encroachment, conclude that language to be the genuine remains of the ancient Phenician tongue, and the Celtæ, colonies of that enterprizing people, whose merchants were princes, and the honourable of the earth.

"It will not be expected that *every name* to be found in the Mediterranean, or in Spain, should be explained, or even be capable of being rendered into Gaelic ; *some*, no doubt, had a different origin, nor would it be advisable to fatigue the reader by an unnecessary detail of etymologies, as the most striking will sufficiently establish the desired position ; the mind becomes bewildered instead of being instructed by injudiciously multiplying proofs. The collation of all the names might and would be useful in a gazetteer, or geographical work, but here would be out of place.

"We will begin by first examining the names of the cities of the coast of Phenicia itself—and first the chief city.

Tyre—Ꜩ)ɼ—*The land, or the country,* by way of eminence, *the home* of the Phenicians, their pride and glory —like Rome to the Romans. Tyre was called THE CITY. Ꜩ)ɼ is sometimes spelled Ꜩ)oɼ, in ancient MSS.— Christian Mattheus, derives Tyre from the Hebrew ⲧⲣ which signifies a *stone* or *rock*, because it was built on a *rock*.

"*Sidon, or Saida*—ɼɑꝺoɑ—*a seat,* or site. Sidon, though second to Tyre in glory and greatness, is said to have been the elder city, and the first settlement or *seat* of the Phenicians on the Mediterranean.

Palmyra—pɑlɑɼ, *the palace*—m)ɲe, *of pleasure,* or *diversion*—pronounced *Palmire.*—*Tadmor* is ⲧɑ)ʒ— *house*—and moɲ, *great*—the great house or palace.

"*Italy*—Ꝺⲧ, *corn*—ⲧɑlɑm, *country—the land of corn, or agriculture,* pronounced *Itala.*

"The *Tiber.* This is evidently the Gaelic and Phenician ⲧ)bɑɲ, a *well, fountain, spring, stream.*

"*Dalmatia*—ꝺɑl, *a share, a tribe, a country possessed by a tribe*—mɑ)ⲧ, *good excellent.* The excellent, or good share, or allotment, pronounced *Dalmait.*

"*Sardinia*—ɼɑɲꝺ, *the greater or larger*—)n)ɼ, *island ;* the greater island with reference to Corsica, pronounced *Sardinis.*

"*Corsica*—coɲɼɑꝺ, *the coast,* or the island near the coast.

"*Malta, or Melita*—melⲧ, *banishment*—or the place of banishment.

"Those names could not have been accidentally so descriptive, they must have been given by a people speaking the language which so clearly expresses their peculiar circumstances. There is no straining, cutting down, or changing letters or syllables, the words declare their origin as palpably as that *Cape of Good Hope,* or *Desolation Bay,* were names given by the English."

Under this head many other names are given, to which are added a vast number of the names of the rivers and former inhabitants of Spain, Portugal, and the Mediterranean. He has also as a further evidence collated the Carthagenian speeches in the Penulus of Plautus with the Irish ; and having thus, as he contends, successfully established the fact of the identity of the Gaelic and Phenician language, and that the Gael or Celtæ were a Phenician colony, goes on to prove that the ancient Britons and Gauls of Cæsar's day spoke the Gaelic language, and were the same people as the Irish ; and this he does by an investigation of the language, religion, institutions, manners, and customs of the Celtæ of South Britain and Gaul in the time of the Romans. As we have already said, to the book itself we must refer those who wish for further information on the subject ; and we think there are few such who will not feel gratified and informed by its perusal.

THE BOASTER OUTBOASTED.

A few months since one of those self-important specimens of the sense and talent of the sister isle, yclept "riders," happened to be in a neighbouring town—and entering into conversation with some gentlemen in a coffee-room, amongst other topics he enlarged on the superior success of his countrymen in the improvement of manufactures, alleging, as a proof of his assertion, that in the manufactory to which he belonged, it was only necessary to place the fleece of wool on the machine, and immediately it became a piece of fine cloth. "All that is wonderful," replied one of the bye-standers, "but still it is not equal to our own manufactory here in Carrick-on-Suir, where we place the live sheep at one end, while at the other is produced a dish of roast mutton, and a ready made coat." Yours, &c., C. D.

Wexford, September, 1834.

INTERIOR OF MALAHIDE ABBEY.

The above ruin immediately adjoins the ancient Castle of Malahide, the property of the Talbot family, situated between six and seven miles from the metropolis, in a N. E. direction. In 1641, Thomas, the then Lord Talbot, having been outlawed in consequence of the part he took in the rebellion of that time, his castle and lands remained for seven years in the possession of Miles Corbet, the regicide, who is said to have unroofed the chapel for the purpose of using the materials in covering a barn or outhouse, and thus it has ever since remained.

ANIMAL SAGACITY.

The following curious circumstance occurred about twenty-four years ago, in the neighbourhood of Belfast :

A Mr. F. having a water-dog, about a year old, which his father conceived had the effect of drawing too much of his attention from business, advised that the dog should be disposed of. This was promptly complied with, and Neptune, (such was the dog's name,) was given to his father's head mill-wright, a Mr. Scott, who resided at a place about three quarters of a mile distant. Although Nep. appreciated the favours of his new owners with evident manifestations of the warmest gratitude, he did not forget his old master, to whom he was in the habit of paying an occasional visit. Some time after our hero had taken up his abode in the house of the overseer, it came into the head of his mistress to send a present of a few fine young ducks to Mrs. F. They were accordingly forwarded, and duly acknowledged. On the following morning, however, it was discovered by Mrs. Scott, to her great surprise, that all the ducks were back again, safe and sound, at her own door. This created some enquiry and amazement ; for, as ducks are bad travellers, and their wings not being grown, they could not fly, it could not be surmised how they had got back. Off the ducks were packed a second time ; but lo ! next morning, they were again home at Mrs. S.'s door. This was too bad. The girl was strictly examined, who deposed that she delivered them all to the cook. The cook was examined, whose testimony agreed with the girl's. The ducks, however, were once more restored to Mrs. F., who ordered two to be killed for dinner, to break the charm. This left seven, there being nine at first. All was now right, but fairies or witches are not just so easily mastered.— On the following morning the seven ducks had once again taken up their station at Mrs. S.'s door. Back they went a fourth time, and now effectually to prevent their return, the heads were cut off the entire. This was a settler to all witchery. The mystery, however, of how nine young ducks could make their way through three close-barred gates, and travel nearly a mile in the short space of a summer's night, continued for several months. It was at last explained. One day a gentleman passing Mr. S.'s door, observed the dog, Neptune, and recognised him to be one he had met on the road several months before, ere sun-rise, driving ducks, and carrying a lame one in his mouth, which was unable to travel. This at once unravelled the mystery, and cleared the "good people" or fairies of the crime of transporting them. The circumstance is certainly true as it is strange. That Neptune knew his mistress's ducks, and *stole* them home to her three several nights, is placed beyond any doubt ; and it now remains for the philosopher to define the "*thinking substance*" by which the sagacious animal was actuated to the performance of so extraordinary an achievement.

R. M.

TAGHMON—COUNTY OF WEXFORD.

I send you a rough outline of a stone cross, now standing in the church-yard, near the village of Taghmon, in the county of Wexford.

An abbey was founded in, or near this village, about the year 599, by St. Munnu, from whom the town derives its name, being formerly called Teach-Munnu, or Teagh-mun, no remains of which can now be traced.

ANCIENT RELICS IN BANNOW CHURCH, COUNTY OF WEXFORD.

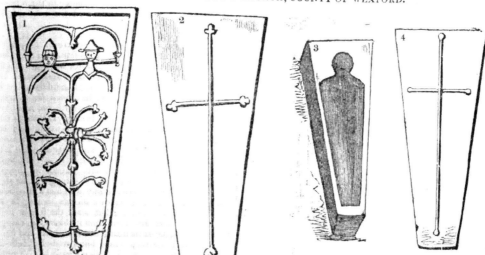

Sir—Perhaps among the ruins of the Irish Herculaneum, none can so well claim the attention of the antiquarian and stranger, as those tombs which lie in undisturbed repose, within the walls of Bannow church, of which the above are copies.

No. 1 represents, on the upper part, a knight and lady in a recumbent posture, their heads resting on a pillow, beneath separate canopies ; on the lower appears a cross, of a very highly ornamented order : the inscription being in relievo, is nearly effaced, and quite illegible, though the letters, D S S, are deeply engraven on the band of the knight's helmet.

2. A simple cross, ornamented with similar flowers as the former, but no inscription whatever is visible.

3. A stone coffin, remarkable for having a place for the head excavated—its length is about six feet.

4. The lid of a stone coffin, generally supposed to have covered the preceding, but from which opinion I differ, as the coffin is of blue lime-stone, and this a slab of grey sand-stone ; it bears neither date nor inscription.

It is rather curious that none of the stones are sunk in the ground, but are on a level with the surrounding grave-yard.

C. D.

Wexford.

ROMANCE OF IRISH HISTORY.

THE FAITHLESS BRIDE OF BREFFNI.

CHAPTER I.

Oh, why was given to man the power
    To break the bonds that beauty wove ;
To tear asunder in an hour
    The hearts for ever joined in love.
                    *
Alike the time—no matter where ;
And oftner in the heartless glare
Of pleasure and of revelry :
The widowed heart will turn and sigh
O'er dreams that now 'twere sin to bless,
Though time can't make it love the less
                    ORIGINAL POEM.

" Such," says Geraldus Cambrensis, an historian who flourished in the twelfth century, " is the variable and fickle nature of woman, by whom all mischief in the world (for the most part) doth happen and come, as may appear by Marcus Antonius, and by the destruction of Troy."

That the destruction of Troy and the " soft Triumver's" defeat were caused by woman, I allow ; but that Ireland, as Cambrensis infers, was lost by woman, I deny. " 'Tis true, and pity 'tis 'tis true," that on her the fault fell ; but the reader will perceive that it was worldly aggrandizement on the one side, and the basest of human passions on the other, that caused the fall of Ireland, and not lovely woman.

It was the eve of a winter's day, in the year 1168—the cheerless beams of a November sun were struggling through the broken windows and ruined walls of the fragment of a ruin, long since forgotten, beneath which a young man was moving rapidly backwards and forwards over the matted grass and half-sunken stone : there was a sullen calmness depicted on his dark, manly features, but it was the calmness of despair. Every now and then he would start from his walk, madly toss his clenched hands in the air, and a deep curse would hover on his quivering lips : again he would stop, and fold his arms over his breast, quietly deliberate within himself, and again resume his walk. His feelings at length overcame him, and covering his brow with his hand, he sunk down on a broken piece of masonry.

The person we have thus introduced to our readers was Dermot M'Murchad, King of Leinster ; in earlier days and happier hours he had become acquainted with Dearbhorgil, the lovely daughter of the King of Meath. She was a delicate and gentle being, of a soft and sensitive turn of mind ; her pensive blue eye ne'er beamed with aught but love and tenderness ; and her figure, though small, was sylph-like, and exquisitely formed. Her retiring modesty shrunk from the glare of the noon-day sun, in which gaudier, though less beautiful flowers, would be glad to bloom. M'Murchad was young and ardent— though not of the gay, thoughtless disposition of most youth : two such beings, coming in contact, could hardly fail to raise a mutual passion. It was so. M'Murchad loved her dearly and faithfully ; she was the beau ideal of his young fancy—that something to be loved, " that one want," for which he had so often sighed.

'Twould be useless to follow M'Murchad and the object of his ' love's young dream,' through the endless variety of endearing scenes that filled up the first years of their acquaintance—those little trifling attentions which to all, save the two beings engaged, appear as nothing.— Time flew on, and Dearbhorgil must lose the companion of many a happy hour ; yet, ere he departed, he received the vows of a young and trusting heart, and gave his in return : but what availed their plighted faith against the commands of her father. O'Rourk, prince of Breffni, came to woo the fair Dearbhorgill ; his wealth and power, as is the case in the present day, obtained the preference ; and the King of Meath forced his daughter to name the day that was to make her for ever miserable. M'Murchad heard of her intended marriage, but he did not believe it, or if he did it was in that fitful manner in which a troubled dream appears to our memory in the morning. This was the cause of the phrenzy in which we first introduced him to our readers.

As he sat, thoughtful, and, as it were, unconcious of the things around, a heavy sigh fell upon his ear. He listened for a moment, then started to his feet, but could see nothing. Oppressed with a superstitious dread, he turned to leave the ruin, when to his terror and astonishment, he perceived a figure descending from the air towards him, surrounded with a glow of light. As it approached, M'Murchad perceived it to be a beautiful female, clothed in loose drapery, that floated gracefully round her aeriel form, and in her he also recognised a spirit that was inimical to his family, and always appeared when some misfortune was to befal them. Placing himself in a posture of defence, he drew his sword, and awaited the spirit's coming, though now and then he raised his left hand, and passed it across his eyes, so as to hide from them the fearful apparition. In the mean time, the figure almost hovered over him, holding gracefully, and at the same time twining a wreath of flowers above her head. She dropped the wreath on him when it was finished, and fluttering round him, sung in clear, thrilling notes the—

PROPHECY.

I've cast a charm, and made a spell,
    As I sate in the lily's snow-white bell ;
I've begirt my ancient enemy
    In a tangled web that he cannot see :
'Tis round him by night, and round him by day,
And never will leave till hope fall away.

Hunted by blood-hounds, he'll part, he'll part
    From the guilty idol of his heart.
Forced from home and kindred to fly,
A foreign land will receive his sigh :
Yet again will he come with steel-clad band,
To claim and hold his forfeit land.

The king and the chieftains of Erin unite,
    Swift to save, but swifter to smite ;
'Tis rain—'tis rain—the earth is red
With the gore of the patriot hearts that bled ;
But though sceptered and crowned, I can see, I
        can see !
M'Murchad must live but in misery !

At the end of this wild chaunt, the figure uttered close to M'Murchad's ear, the words ' I rejoice—I rejoice !' and as she winged her flight towards her home in the broad— the blue—the starlit sky, he still heard the echo of her last words ' I rejoice—I rejoice !

*   *   *   *   *   *

The wedding-day of Dearbhorgil soon arrived ; her prayers and entreaties were of no use, and her father led the reluctant girl to the altar, placed himself her hand in that of a man she could never love—of one who, at the moment she was pledging the nuptial vow, she hated and despised. So much for the King of Meath :. we have seen *his* fatherly love, and his sacrifice to the god of wealth and ambition. Now let us turn to the Prince of Breffni. O'Rourk may have loved Dearbhorgil ; but he who would buy the " loathing virgin," from her father's arms to bless himself, deserves not the name of a man ; and, after all, what is he possessed of ?—A mere, lifeless, violated form—the heart he can never confine : it will still wander in thought through the world with him who first taught it to sigh. O'Rourk may be compared to one who sees a beauteous flower ; he plucks it, and places it on his bosom, to let himself and others admire it ; but, alas ! the fragile child of summer, thus cruelly torn from its blooming companions, and the home of its heart, will soon fade, and leave nothing in its possessor's hands but a wasted, inanimate stalk. Thus appears O'Rourk, in the most lenient point of view, and let the reader judge by whom was Ireland lost.

*   *   *   *   *   *

The Prince of Breffni had been some days absent on a pilgrimage to St. Patrick's Purgatory. He took a numerous train of vassals with him, and left but a small guard of honor with his queen. O'Rourk and she had now been some years married, and all thoughts of M'Murchad were supposed to have long faded from her heart. But, alas, it was far otherwise ; they know not the heart of woman who think that time will banish the remembrance of her first love, though "accident, blind contract, or the strong necessity of loving," may partially, or for a time, make her seem to forget it; still, in the solitude of her bosom, will she weep over happier hours and brighter prospects—now faded for ever. The plighted heart of Dearbhorgil could know no more happiness; the world, with its praises and its dispraises, was no consideration to her; dead to shame, and all else around, except the thought of the bereaved M'Murchad, she formed the resolution of eloping with him, and for this purpose a private correspondence was carried on between them.

"Why looks my lady so sadly and reproachful at yonder sun? Is his flight less swift than it was wont to be?" asked the companion and attendant of the Princess of Breffni, as they wandered one evening over the flowery fields of her fair domains.

"Not so, girl;" replied the princess, "but thou knowest that I sent my faithful page, Lorcan, on a commission; he should—he ought to be here by this. I hope no misfortune has fallen upon him," her voice growing more agitated every moment.

"None in the slightest, my gracious princess," cried a beautiful youth, bounding from a thicket, and kneeling at the feet of Dearbhorgil.

She gave an exclamation of surprise, but soon checked herself, and, assuming a careless air, asked if he had completed his commissions, and if he had to let her hear all about them.

"Well, your majesty must know," said the favoured youth, "that the rare birds you expected are not yet arrived; your beauteous flowers are safe; the silks, satins, diamonds, jewels, &c., and though last, not least, the little white mouse; (and he looked expressively in her face;) I feared to leave behind, so tied them to my saddle bow; they are yonder," his eyes glancing in the direction of some trees.

Dearbhorgil understood him; but, notwithstanding, she lost her self-possession; and, in the agony of her mind, she exclaimed,

"He! Where! Oh, lead me to him—my own, long-loved—"

"Which," interrupted the crafty page, in time to prevent a total discovery; "is it the beautiful bird, or the diamonds, or the silks, or the flowers, or—that my princess would wish to see."

The lady perceived the page's intention, and he again resumed.

"They are all removed by this to the palace; would your grace move in that direction, and let your lady proceed before, to announce your coming, and have the things in readiness for your inspection?"

Dearbhorgil nodded approval, and accordingly the lady was ordered onwards, while the page conducted his mistress, at an easy pace, towards the palace.

CHAPTER II.

One touch to her hand, and one word in her ear,
When they reached the hall-door, and the charger stood near;
So light to the croup the fair lady he swung,
So light to the saddle before her he sprung;
She is won—we are gone over bank, bush and scaur—
They'll have fleet steeds that follow, quoth young Lochinvar
LADY HERON'S SONG.

The sun had for some time been sunk behind the range of hills that surrounded the palace, or rather resident fortress of the Prince of Breffni; and the golden sea he had left behind him was resting, as it were, on the summit of a few hills, that shot their peaky tops above the rest of their companions; grey evening was melting into indistinct shadows and brown masses, the various romantic points of the landscape, as the princess and her guide were slowly moving onwards; presently they approached a thicket, through which a sandy path led, by a circuitous way, to the palace; and turning the angle of the walk, what a sight met the eyes of Dearbhorgil. There stood M'Murchad, leaning, in an agonised position, against a tree, with one hand covering his face. On hearing steps approach he stood out from the tree; but oh, how altered since last she saw him: the brightness of his eyes was gone; his countenance, between its usual haggard, dejected look, and the wild joy that rushed through him on seeing Dearbhorgill was awful in the extreme: a mixture of madness and joy. One bound, and he was beside the object of his guilty affection—she rushed into his arms, and they remained for some moments in each other's embrace.

Short was the time M'Murchad had to greet his long lost Dearbhorgil; gently taking her hand, he drew her closer to his bosom—one embrace—one guilty kiss, and he hurried her off the ground.

A few moments brought him to the place where his small but faithful band of warriors were resting after the fatigue of their late hard riding. Placing his lovely and almost lifeless burden before him on his strong black war-steed, and marshalling his warriors, he dashed forward at a rapid pace for his capital of Ferns, and arrived safely, and without pursuit, which was more than he expected. The domestics of O'Rouark were few, and without a leader; and when the princess was missed, all was consternation and dismay; one flew here, and another there, so that the band that could be mustered would be too small to pursue the Leinster king, did they even know the rout he had taken. Word was soon sent to O'Rouark, who returned, foaming with madness at his loss and dishonour. It could not be long kept a secret as to where Dearbhorgil was conveyed, and with whom she was.— O'Rouark applied to the monarch, Rhoderick O'Conor, who summoned an assembly of the different kings of Ireland, the result of which was that M'Murchad was declared a traitor, his kingdom forfeit, and assistance was given to O'Rouark to drive his rival from the throne of Leinster. Accordingly both sides prepared to take the field. A short time enabled the monarch, Rhoderick, to take the command of a numerous army. The opposite sides soon met, and many skirmishes took place. A general battle ensued, and ended in the total defeat of Dermot M'Murchad. His troops gave way from the first; though when danger was darkest, and death reigned triumphant, there was the King of Leinster, striving to infuse into his dastard soldiers the hope he himself had long ceased to cherish. When the fate of the day was decided, M'Murchad and a chosen troop of horsemen hurried off the field; he was perceived by Rhoderick, who immediately put himself at the head of his own body-guard of horse, and dashed after the fugitive.

O'Conor had known what it was to love; he had seen the ill-fated Dearbhorgil, and loved her; pressed his suit to her own ear with all a lover's warmth, and was rejected. He was told in that kind, gentle way, which, though it be a death-blow to our happiness, deprives the refusal of half its bitterness; and in the place of love friendship usurps the heart. 'Twas thus with O'Conor; he was of a high and noble disposition, and scorned to urge his suit where he knew that the heart was already engaged. He offered his aid and friendship to Dearbhorgil, and it was accepted. He strove to forward his rival in her father's opinion, and when O'Rouark first addressed the King of Meath for his daughter's hand, O'Conor strenuously opposed him.

As a traitor, and a disgrace to royalty, Rhoderick could not but abhor M'Murchad: but as the lover, and the favoured one too, of Dearbhorgil, he could not hate him. Such were the different feelings that agitated his breast as he set forward in the pursuit.

O'Conor's men were not long in joining the pursued; and a desperate combat took place, which lasted a full hour, hand to hand and hilt to hilt; they fought, for their numbers were nearly equal, till at length the greater part of M'Murchad's men were either killed or wounded, and he was left almost alone to continue the combat. At this moment O'Conor's voice was heard commanding his men to take, but not kill the King of Leinster; and accordingly they began to surround the ill-fated man, who, his horse being killed, still fought with desperate valour on foot. Surrounded on every side, he gave up all hopes of making his escape, and sooner than fall into his enemies' hands, he determined to sell his life as dear as possible. Thus did he combat on, the soldiers doing their utmost to take him, and death being the reward of those who attempted it.

A herculean officer now approached, boasting how soon he would make the traitor surrender. Dashing the spurs into his charger, one bound brought him almost on top of M'Murchad, and his double-edged sabre flew within an inch of his head. Then turning his horse again, he caught the crest of M'Murchad's helmet; in this position he was entirely in the power of the "guardsman," who was greeted for his capture by a loud shout from his comrades; but M'Murchad, by a dexterous spring, loosed himself from the gripe of his enemy, and sprung up behind him on his war-steed, shortened his sword in his hand, and a powerful thrust laid the officer dead in his own saddle, and made M'Murchad master of the strongest and fleetest horse in his enemies' army, who all stood as if they had been spell-bound. M'Murchad, taking advantage of the surprise and fear that appeared visible in the countenances of all the soldiers around, dashed the spurs into his prize, soon effected an opening among his enemies, and fled fleetly along the plain. Though darkness favoured his flight, fate seemed against him; his pursuers, roused from their fear by the voice of the King of Ireland, were again close upon his heels. He was in the act of leaping a high wall, when a shaft from one of them laid his brave steed dead. This was, indeed, the severest blow that could be inflicted on M'Murchad, but there was no time to think; so clambering over the wall the best way he could, he got behind some furze, with which the place abounded. Here he could hear his pursuers galloping rapidly in the direction in which he was; their shouts rang fearfully in his ears, as they were borne along by the night wind. They were now close to him, coming down like a mountain torrent; there was a tremendous clang of sabre-scabbards against spurs, ringing of chains, bridle-bits—a confused hum, and then a total silence. M'Murchad knew there was a halt, for the stone wall had stopped them in their career. Favoured by darkness M'Murchad fled, and escaped to England, thence he went to Normandy, where Henry the Second was; and his subsequent history is too well known to need a repetition.

T. A. G—M—N.

THE ABANDONED.

"No; pleasures, hopes, affections gone;
The wretch may bear, and still live on,
Like things within the cold rock, found
Alive, when all's conjealed around."—MOORE.

Why is that languid eye unlit with hope?
And why that listlessness of aspect worn?
Is there within no thought of pride to stir
The soul's quick tumult—to awake its fires;
No passionate feeling, from whose kindling power
The face becomes irradiate. Alas!
Foul treachery has been at work; and guile,
Accursed guile hath wreaked this mischief dark.
Is there no thunderbolt of vengeance, winged
With most abiding wrath, to strike with fire,
And pain unyielding, and intensest heat
The base and perjured one who wrought the deed!
No voice of execration dire to blast,
With accent meet, remorse's keenest pang,
To raise and sting the recreant's soul with fears,
Dreadful and deep, as are the woes he gives;
And shall he not, for that despairing grief,
Which, like the fever-flame, consumes an heart,
Too weak and gentle to abide its force,
Be given to feel a punishment as strong?
Shall not each tear in judgment rise against him,
E'en as the primeval martyr's blood to heaven?
Shall not each sigh become a furnace-breath,
Burning hereafter with volcanic heat
Unquenchable; and fraught with utter ruth!
Victim of guile! and is thy lot thus desolate?
Though meek-eyed resignation fain would beam

From out each glassy orb—its light is faint,
Like the dim taper's ray, when in some pile
Of ancient ruins, from afar it shines;
The child of gentle impulse—innocent mirth;
Whose laugh was music, and whose smile was peace—
Is changed, and fearfully. The maid is changed:
Where is her voice of welcome, like the sigh
Of winds that blow through summer's golden bowers?
'Tis quelled in silence; in its stead remains
The look of agony—the gaze of tears;
Nor do they flow, as though their source was full—
But few, and burning, as though life itself
Came forth in each; as though each falling drop
Was blood-distilled from out her broken heart.
There is a perfidy to friends—to man,
When social compact, or when private tie
He breaks, to further his ambitious plans;
But this, the consummation of that guilt
Whereby weak woman, who looks up towards him,
As the fond child unto the parent's care,
Is left undone, heart-withered, and betrayed;
Is twice condemned—is more than doubly wicked;
Dishonour, cruelty, deceit, neglect,
Combine to perfect this especial crime.
Triumph thou false one! while thine hour is fair;
There *will* be moments when the gall of wrath
Shall parch thy vitals; when the writhing pangs
Of fiery conscience, and the icy grasp
Of chill despair shall each thy soul torment.
Thou shalt be wretched—keenly, deeply wretched;
And for the mental murder thou hast wrought,
Ten thousand darts, with fiery poison tinged,
Shall pierce thy soul—nor shall its pains expire;
No; they shall live with thee—be thine existence;
While the poor martyr, whom thou'st given to bleed,
With all her wounds, in heavenly balsam steeped,
Shall taste the plenitude of sacred bliss.
For though her spirit falsehood's arm hath crushed,
She can forgive, and o'er the ruin smile;
Her hope is not of earth—she therefore prays,
While yet her glimmering ray of life is seen,
For him, the murderer of her joys and peace.
Calm be the setting of her lovely beam;
'Twas given to shine upon some brighter scene,
Which oft, amid the desert wastes of life,
Like to the Oasis of Afric's clime,
Delights the traveller on his painful way.

R. G. M.

ANECDOTE OF STRONGBOW AND HIS SON.

When Strongbow was marching to Wexford, through the barony of Idrone, to relieve Fitzstephen, he was briskly assaulted by O'Rian and his followers; but O'Rian being slain by an arrow, shot at him by Nichol the monk, the rest were easily scattered, and many of them slain. It was here that Strongbow's only son, a youth about seventeen years old, frighted with the numbers and ululations of the Irish, ran away from the battle, and made towards Dublin; but being informed of his father's victory, he joyfully came back to congratulate him; the severe general, however, having first reproached him with cowardice, caused him to be immediately executed, by cutting him off in the middle with a sword. So great an abhorrence had they of dastardliness in those days, that, in imitation of the old Romans, they punished it with a severity which, how commendable soever it may be in a general, was nevertheless unnatural in a father.

EPITAPH ON STRONGBOW, EARL OF CHEPSTOW, AND HIS
SON, IN CHRIST CHURCH, DUBLIN.
"Nate ingrate mihi pugnanti terga dedisti
Non mihi sed genti Regno quoque terga dedisti."

DUBLIN:
Printed and Published by P. D. HARDY, 3, Cecilia-street; to whom all communications are to be addressed.

Sold by all Booksellers in Ireland.

In London, by Richard Groombridge, 6, Panyer-alley, Paternoster-row; in Liverpool, by Willmer and Smith; in Manchester, by Ambery; in Birmingham, by Drake; in Glasgow, by John Macleod; and in Edinburgh, by N. Bowack.

THE
DUBLIN PENNY JOURNAL

CONDUCTED BY P. DIXON HARDY, M.R.I.A.

Vol. III. NOVEMBER 22, 1834. **No. 125.**

Mr. E. Heyden, Del.   Clayton, Sc.

LISFINNY CASTLE.

The castle of Lisfinny is situated on the side of a gentle declivity, rising from the margin of the river Bride, which here enters the boundary of the county of Waterford, a little to the west of the town of Tallow. It is supposed to have been originally erected by the earl of Desmond, who had several castles in the same county. It is at present pretty perfect, and does not appear to have undergone any material change for the last fifty years. The surrounding scenery has of late been much improved by Captain E. Croker, whose good taste and judgment has discerned the necessity of planting, the luxuriance of which will in a few years not only very much relieve the cold appearance of the back ground, but will also prevent the eye from being pained by resting on some tasteless buildings in the immediate vicinity of the ruin.

The castle is a strong square tower, eighty-four feet in height, and was originally divided into three compartments, one arched floor of which at present only remains perfect. A rugged winding stair-case still occupies one angle of the building, and is sufficiently perfect to admit of ascending to the top. A square aperture is also formed in the east side, and is diminished one-third of its width at every floor with which it communicates; this is known as the *murdering hole*, but is nothing more than a conducting passage, intended for the discharge of dirt or other nuisance in case of being besieged. Looking back some ten or twenty years, the writer can well remember when the old building afforded a source of amusement and pleasure to many a thoughtless urchin from the neigh-bouring town, some of whom might be seen, heedless of danger, climbing the interior of the rugged walls, determined at any hazard to gain the upper or green-room—while others, still more enterprising, would surmount the summit, and stand on their heads on the *Tailor's Bench*, a name given to a transverse flag which crowns the utmost height of one angle of the building, and from which may be seen a very varied and extensive tract of country—a continued glen, which for upwards of twenty miles is watered by the delightful river Bride, which passes rapidly at the foot of the castle, and immediately becomes navigable, but whose ever varying course only admits of being seen in the distance like so many silvery lakes, and is bounded on either side by neat, and in many instances elegant villas and well-cultivated hills. Immediately in front of the castle is the town of Tallow, which of late years has rather an improving appearance.

E. H.

CURE FOR THE AGUE.

The following is said to be an infallible remedy for the ague:

Let the party affected procure a sound onion. On the approach of the fit, cut the onion in two equal parts, apply one to each wrist, with a bandage tolerably tight, to remain on during the paroxysm; it is then to be removed.

In no instance, during a period of thirty years, have I known a return of the complaint. G. J.

CROFTON CROKER'S FAIRY LEGENDS.*

What a strange, wild, eccentric, and superstitious people we Irish are!—abounding in legends and stories, which, no matter how extraordinary or improbable, meet with implicit belief. With us every ruin has its fearful story and its "wondherful sperit"—every green and mossy mound its race of fairies, or *good people*—every well, its cure and charm—every lone glen, its blood-freezing tale of midnight murder, and every lake its legend of enchantment or witchcraft. Here, if all is to be believed which is told us, *poochas*, ghosts, and evil spirits, are perpetually playing their mischievous pranks, and there is hardly one amongst the peasantry but has had his adventure, which if pressed he will relate, with many a " bless me sowl," and fearful shrug of the shoulder. From all and every one of those tellers of stories who have entered the field of Irish legendary fiction, or attempted to delineate the feats and frolics of the fairy tribes who in olden time were wont to disport themselves over the green hills and vallies of this our Emerald Isle, it must be admitted Crofton Croker has " borne off the bell ;" that he is the greatest *story-teller* in Great Britain is admitted by all ; and however questionable such a character might be considered by the cold-blooded natives of our sister island, there can be no question, that in this land of saints and sinners, one could not confer upon him a recommendation which would prove a readier passport, or give him a better introduction to every class of the community, from the inhabitants of the ancient palace of kings, to those of the mud walled cabin at the side of a ditch. In the little volume before us we have his three large tomes, which we believe originally cost two or three guineas, compressed into one which costs only five shillings : and who would not give five shillings for such a volume? The stories are arranged under the following heads, which may be considered as a kind of classification of the various descriptions of these wonder-working spirits, who at one period were thought by the people of Ireland to have such an influence in the direction or superintendence of their affairs : The Shefro; The Cluricaune; The Banshee; The Phooka; Thierna na Oge ; The Merrow ; The Dullahan ; The Fir Darrig. To these are appended several other stories, under the title of " Treasure Legends," or " Rocks and Stones." As a finale to each chapter, Mr. Croker has appended a short description of the particular fairy who figures in the story. From these we select the following, as affording the reader some insight into the character and habits of these celebrated little personages.

The name Shefro (variously written Sɩa bɲuᵹ, Sɩᴄbɲoᵹ, Sɩᵹbɲoᵹ, Sɩoᵹbɲoᵹ, Sɩoᵹbɲuᵹ, &c.) by which the foregoing section is distinguished, literally signifies a fairy house or mansion, and is adopted as a general name for the Elves who are supposed to live in troops or communities, and were popularly supposed to have castles or mansions of their own.—See *Stewart's Popular Superstitions of the Highlands*, 1823, pp. 90, 91, &c.

" The Irish," according to the Rev. James Hely's translation of O'Flaherty, " call these *Sidhe*, aërial spirits or phantoms, because they are seen to come out of pleasant hills, where the common people imagine they reside, which fictitious habitations are called by us *Sidhe* or *Siodha*."

The main point of distinction between the Cluricaune and the Shefro, arises from the sottish and solitary habits of the former, who are rarely found in troops or communities.

The Cluricaune of the county of Cork, the Luricaune of Kerry, and the Lurigadaune of Tipperary, appear to be the same as the Leprechan or Leprochaune of Leinster, and the Loghery-man of Ulster ; and these words are probably all provincialisms of luaᴄaɟɩman, the Irish for a pigmy.

" Banshee, correctly written beanᴄɟᵹe, plural mudɲɟᵹe, she fairies or women fairies, credulously supposed, by the common people, to be so affected to certain families, that they are heard to sing mournful lamentations about their houses at night, whenever any of the family labours under a sickness which is to end in death. But no families which are not of an ancient and noble stock are believed to be honoured with this fairy privilege."— *O'Brien's Irish Dictionary.*

For accounts of the appearance of the Irish Banshee, see " Personal Sketches, &c. by Sir Jonah Barrington ;" Miss Lefanu's Memoirs of her Grandmother, Mrs. Frances Sheridan, (1824.) p. 32 ; " The memoirs of Lady Fanshaw," (quoted by Sir Walter Scott in a note on " The Lady of the Lake,") &c.

Sir Walter Scott terms the belief in the appearance of the Banshee, " one of the most beautiful" of the leading superstitions of Europe. In his " Leters on Demonology," he says that " several families of the Highlands of Scotland anciently laid claim to the distinction of an attendant spirit, who performed the office of the Irish Banshee," and particularly refers to the supernatural cries and lamentations which foreboded the death of the gallant Mac Lean, of Lochbuy.

The *Pouke* or *Phooka*, as the word is pronounced, means, in plain terms, the Evil One. " Playing the puck," a common Anglo-Irish phrase, is equivalent to " playing the devil." Much learning has been displayed in tracing this word through various languages, vide Quarterly Review [vol. xxii.] &c. The commentators on Shakspeare derive the beautiful and frolicksome Puck of the Midsummer Night's Dream from the mischievous Pouke.— Vide Drayton's Nymphidia.

The Irish Phooka, in its nature, perfectly resembles the *Mahr* ; and we have only to observe, that there is a particular German tradition of a spirit, which sits among reeds and alder bushes ; and which, like the Phooka, leaps upon the back of those who pass by in the night, and does not leave them till they faint and fall to the earth.

THE BROTHERS GRIMM.

The Irish *Merrow*, correctly written moɲúaᴅ or moɲúaᴄ, answers exactly to the English Mermaid, being compounded of muɟɲ, the Sea, and Oɟᵹ, a maid. It is also used to express a sea-monster, like the Armoric and Cornish *Morhuch*, to which it evidently bears analogy.

Dullahan or Dulachan (ᴅublaᴄal) signifies a dark sullen person. The word *Durrachan* or *Dullahan*, by which in some places the goblin is known, has the same signification. It comes from *Dorr* or *Durr*, anger, or *Durrach*, malicious, fierce, &c.—*M.S. communication from the late Mr. Edward O'Reilly.*

The correctness of this last etymology may be questioned, as ᴅub black, is evidently a component part of the word.

The Death Coach, or Headless Coach and Horses, is called in Ireland " *Coach a bower ;*" and its appearance is generally regarded as a sign of death, or an omen of some misfortune.

" The people of Basse Bretagne believe, that when the death of any person is at hand, a hearse drawn by skeletons (which they call *carriquet au nankou*), and covered with a white sheet, passes by the house where the sick person lies and the creaking of the wheels may be plainly heard."—*Journal des Sciences*, 1826, communicated by Dr. William Grimm.

Fir Darrig, correctly written Feaɲ Deaɲᵹ, means the red man, and is a member of the fairy community of Ireland, who bears a strong resemblance to the Shakspearian Puck, or Robin Goodfellow. Like that merry goblin, his delight is in mischief and mockery ; and the Irish spirit is doubtless the same as the Scottish *Red Cap*, which a writer in the Quarterly Review (No XLIV. p. 358), tracing national analogies, asserts is the Robin Hood

---

* Fairy Legends and Traditions of the South of Ireland. London : John Murray, Dublin : W. F. Wakeman.

of England, and the Saxon spirit Hudkin or Hodeken, so called from the hoodakin or little hood wherein he appeared—a spirit similar to the Spanish Duende. The Fir Darrig has also some traits of resemblance in common with the Scotch Brownie, the German Kobold, particularly the celebrated one, Hinzelman), the English Hobgoblin (Milton's "Lubber Fiend"), and the Follet of Gervase of Tilbury."

The stories in our present number we select not so much for being the best, but for best suiting the limited space of our little publication. In reference to other stories in the work, we may observe, that in his pruning for the present edition,.it had been well if Mr. Croker had left out some of those passages, which will go far to strengthen religious superstitions, and which, we have no doubt, will be considered highly objectionable by a particular class of our readers.

"THE LORD OF DUNKERRON.

The lord of Dunkerron[*]—O'Sullivan More,
Why seeks he at midnight the sea-beaten shore?
His bark lies in haven, his hounds are asleep;
No foes are abroad on the land or the deep.

Yet nightly the lord of Dunkerron is known
On the wild shore to watch and to wander alone;
For a beautiful spirit of ocean, 'tis said,
The lord of Dunkerron would win to his bed.

When, by moonlight, the waters were hush'd to repose,
That beautiful spirit of ocean arose;
Her hair, full of lustre, just floated and fell
O'er her bosom, that heav'd with a billowy swell.

Long, long had he lov'd her—long vainly essay'd
To lure from her dwelling the coy ocean maid;
And long had he wander'd and watch'd by the tide,
To claim the fair spirit O'Sullivan's bride!

The maiden she gazed on the creature of earth,
Whose voice in her breast to a feeling gave birth;
Then smiled; and, abashed as a maiden might be,
Looking down, gently sank to her home in the sea.

Though gentle that smile, as the moonlight above,
O Sullivan felt 'twas the dawning of love;
And hope came on hope, spreading over his mind,
Like the eddy of circles her wake left behind.

The lord of Dunkerron he plunged in the waves,
And sought through the fierce rush of waters, their caves;
The gloom of whose depth studded over with spars,
Had the glitter of midnight when lit up by stars.

Who can tell or can fancy the treasures that sleep
Intombed in the wonderful womb of the deep?
The pearls and the gems, as if valueless, thrown
To lie 'mid the sea-wrack concealed and unknown.

Down, down went the maid—still the chieftain pursued;
Who flies must be followed ere she can be wooed.
Untempted by treasures, unawed by alarms,
The maiden at length he has clasped in his arms!

They rose from the deep by a smooth-spreading strand,
Whence beauty and verdure stretch'd over the land.
'Twas an isle of enchantment! and lightly the breeze,
With a musical murmur, just crept through the trees.

The haze-woven shroud of that newly born isle,
Softly faded away, from a magical pile,
A palace of crystal, whose bright-beaming sheen
Had the tints of the rainbow—red, yellow, and green.

And grottoes, fantastic in hue and in form,
Were there, as flung up—the wild sport of the storm;
Yet all was so cloudless, so lovely, and calm,
It seemed but a region of sunshine and balm.

' Here, here shall we dwell in a dream of delight,
Where the glories of earth and of ocean unite!

Yet, loved son of earth! I must from thee away;
There are laws which e'en spirits are bound to obey!
' Once more must I visit the chief of my race,
His sanction to gain ere I meet thy embrace.
In a moment I dive to the chambers beneath:
One cause can detain me—one only—'tis death!'

They parted in sorrow, with vows true and fond;
The language of promise had nothing beyond.
His soul all on fire, with anxiety burns:
The moment is gone—but no maiden returns.

What sounds from the deep meet his terrified ear—
What accents of rage and of grief does he hear?
What sees he? what change has come over the flood—
What tinges its green with a jetty of blood?

Can he doubt what the gush of warm blood would explain?
That she sought the consent of her monarch in vain!
For see all around him, in white foam and froth,
The waves of the ocean boil up in their wroth!

The palace of crystal has melted in air,
And the dies of the rainbow no longer are there;
The grottoes with vapour and clouds are o'ercast,
The sunshine is darkness—the vision has past!

Loud, loud was the call of his serfs for their chief;
They sought him with accents of wailing and grief:
He heard, and he struggled—a wave to the shore,
Exhausted and faint bears O'Sullivan More!"

LOCOMOTIVE ENGINES ON THE DUBLIN AND KINGSTOWN RAILWAY.

In a former number of our Journal, while describing the line of railway, we took occasion incidentally to notice, that there had been six Locomotive Engines built expressly for the company here—three by Messrs. Forrester and Co., of Liverpool, and three by Messrs. Sharpe, Roberts, and Co., of Manchester. The engraving in our present number gives a correct representation of one of those manufactured by the latter house. For the following description of the engine we are indebted to Mr. E Heyden, to whom we would take this opportunity of expressing our acknowledgments for several other communications and drawings of an interesting character.

Before describing the Locomotive Engine itself, it may be necessary, for the sake of those readers who have not had an opportunity of seeing a railway, to premise that the engine does not move by means of a line of cogs and corresponding cogged wheel, which is the generally received opinion of persons who have not had an opportunity of seeing a Locomotive at work, but is propelled by the adhesion caused by its own weight on the rail, which pressure of adhesion must be more than the exact power necessary to move the train of attached carriages; otherwise, although the engine may be set to work, it will not move forward. If, for instance, an over-proportionate train of coaches be attached to the engine when set in motion, the steam-power will, in some degree, raise the engine; the wheels will then slip or revolve without moving the machine, and so continue until either an additional weight be placed over the wheels of the engine, or the train of carriages be made less.—Each engine may be estimated at about ten tons weight, and is calculated to draw a train of carriages from sixty to eighty tons weight, at the rate of twenty miles per hour: each railway coach may be estimated at two and a half or three tons; they are fourteen feet long by six feet wide, and are capable of accommodating according to the different classes, eighteen, twenty-four, and thirty-five persons respectively, beside luggage.

In order to explain why the engine is capable of propelling so great a weight at the rapid speed we have mentioned, although in a former number we have endeavoured to describe the construction of the road or plane upon which the vehicles move, it may be necessary here again to observe—first—That a railway is nothing more than a common road, made as nearly level and straight as possible, upon which are laid two or more lines of wrought iron tracks set in stone blocks, upon which the wheels of a coach or other machine may move with a degree of steadiness and facility. Second—that the rail

---

[*] The remains of Dunkerron Castle are distant about a mile from the village of Kenmare, in the county of Kerry. It is recorded to have been built in 1596, by Owen O'Sullivan More.—(More is merely an epithet signifying the Great.)

tracks are higher than the road, and of a convex surface; thereby obviating the inclined planes and other obstacles, which a machine moving on the common turnpike road has ever to encounter. Third—That the periphery or outer rim of the wheels, which move on the track, are flat on the bearing surface, with a flange on the inside of each wheel, which occasionally touches the track, and prevents the machine from moving off the rail. Fourth—that the rail-track has not a continued bearing from *end to end* of the line, but is supported at every three or four feet by metal beds set in granite blocks, which are perforated and plugged generally with hiccary wood, to receive pins for making fast the metals; from which arrangement it is evident that the rail tracks are so many continued lines of elasticity, and as the bearing of the wheels, when in contact with the rails, are diminished to points, thus, undoubtedly, diminishing the friction to the slightest possible degree on the periphery of the wheel, and, thereby, consequently affording the greatest facility to the moving body.

We shall now proceed to describe the Locomotive Engine, of which we give a drawing in the opposite page. The frame, A, on which the works are constructed, is made of strong wrought iron; it is 15 feet long, by 7 feet in width, and is supported by four springs, (concealed within the frame) on an equal number of wheels, which revolve with the axle: along the centre of this framing is placed a wrought iron boiler, B, of a cylindrical form, at one end of which is the furnace, C, from which the caloric or heat is conveyed through the water in the boiler by a number of pipes or tubes, which form the communication with the chimney placed at the other end; these tubes in the engine here represented amount to upwards of ninety, and are about an inch and a half in diameter. On the top of the chimney is placed a wire net capping, D, to arrest the ignited particles of coke which are carried through the tubes by the rapid draught necessary to maintain the intense fire required in the furnace, and which is caused by the waste steam after it has performed its work in the cylinders, being allowed to rush upwards through the flue, and so escape into the atmosphere, which it does with great force. At the furnace end, where the engineer and assistant stand, are placed three gauge-cocks, E, for ascertaining the quantity of water in the boiler. Also the levers, F, by means of which the motion of the machine either backward or forward, is perfectly under control, and may be almost immediately directed as occasion requires. On the boiler are placed two safety valves; one of these, G, is under the control of the engineer, so that he can regulate the elastic force of the steam; but the second valve, H to which he has not access, is previously adjusted for the maximum pressure or force required. He is by this arrangement effectually prevented from endangering the safety of the boiler by exposing it to a greater elastic force than it is capable of resisting. From the upper part of the boiler, tubes or conducting pipes, convey the steam to the slide-valve box, K, which in this engine is of a peculiar form, invented by Mr. Roberts: this box is connected to the cylinders, L, which are made fast to the framing before mentioned, at either side of the boiler. The slide-valve box is a reservoir from which the steam by the action of the valve, regulated by the motion of the whole machine, is alternately admitted into the upper and lower chambers of the cylinder, the pressure or elastic power of the steam thus acting upon the upper and lower faces of the piston, forces it alternately upward and downward, and then passes off by the under tube, R, called the ejection or waste-pipe, into the chimney, as before described.

The piston-rod, M, passes through a stuffing-box, placed on the upper external surface of the cylinder, and is packed with oiled cotton or hemp, through which the rod moves freely without admitting the least possible portion of steam to escape. On each side of the engine-framing is also introduced a bell-crank movement, N, which receives motion from the piston by a connecting rod at one end, and gives motion to the hind wheels by a similar connecting rod, O, which is attached to the crank-pin fixed to the nave of the wheel, at a distance from 'ts centre equal to

half the stroke of the piston, and therefore causes it to revolve on the principle of a common spinning-wheel.[*] Attached to this bell-crank movement may also be seen through the eliptic aperture, a rod, P, which is continued on to the force-pump, Q. and by a lesser stroke than the piston, with a well-proportioned pump, sends the requisite quantity of water into the boiler, to supply the place of that converted into steam: this water is drawn through a flexible tube from the tender, (which is a separate machine for carrying a supply of fuel and water, and is necessarily attached to every Locomotive Engine). The crank-pins on the nave of each wheel are so disposed as never to be both at their dead points at the same time, or, in other words, they are at right angles with each other.

In the tubes, I, which we before mentioned, as the conductors of the steam from the top of the boiler to the cylinder, are placed regulators, the nature of which may be easily conceived, by imagining the principle of a common water-cock; these may be turned so as entirely to cut off the communication between the cylinders and boiler, and by shutting in the steam, stop the machine altogether, or let it flow more or less as speed or occasion may require. In manufacturing engines an apparatus, termed a governor, actuated by the machinery, regulates the speed of the engine; but in Locomotives, the engineer has this duty to perform.

Having thus far given an outline description of the Locomotive Engine, we will now endeavour to explain the ingenious principle upon which the boiler (where alone there could be any risk of explosion) is constructed, and point out how unfounded are the fears of those who apprehend such an accident. To describe it in terms familiar to every capacity, we will suppose a long barrel or cylinder of any description, closed at each end, and divided by two internal partitions into three unequal spaces; one of these spaces or chambers, between one of the partitions and the external end, may represent the furnace—the other, the opening to the flue or chimney; the space between these partitions contains the water to be converted into steam, for which purpose a number of tubes convey the heat, arising from combustion in the furnace, immediately through the water; and as the caloric liberated in the furnace by combustion, has no other means of escape than through these tubes along with the rarified air, and being thus exposed to very extensive surfaces, it is transmitted with the utmost rapidity to the water. These tubes are made of thin sheet copper or brass, and are the only parts of the boiler exposed to the action of the fire, or subject to any wear, but being entirely surrounded by water on their outsides, they are effectually protected. We have seen tubes taken from Locomotive Engines after having travelled thirty thousand miles without being seriously worn; should, however, a fissure from expansion of the tubes by intense heat, or by any other equally unforeseen or uncontrollable cause lead to the breaking of a tube, no other inconvenience could possibly be felt than delay, as the water and steam would immediately rush from the boiler into the furnace, and extinguish the fire; in fact, we know such an occurrence not to be uncommon on the Liverpool and Manchester railway, and the passengers are no otherwise sensible of it than from the train ceasing to move.

The carriages when propelled, are continually striking, or to use a *technical* phrase, buffing against each other, the effect of which is most materially felt when either starting or stopping, and in order to prevent this repeated concussion, a buffing and drafting apparatus has been ingeniously attached to a large spring in the centre of each carriage, which entirely counteracts the effect that the first impetus of an engine would otherwise occasion, and which would be both annoying and dangerous.

---

[*] We may here remark, that the larger the working wheels are, the greater will be the speed, and the less the power; and, *per contra*, the less the wheels the less will be the speed and the greater the power: the wheels under the *Hibernia engine*, which we are at present describing, are five feet high, which is the size found, from experience, best calculated as a medium between speed and power.

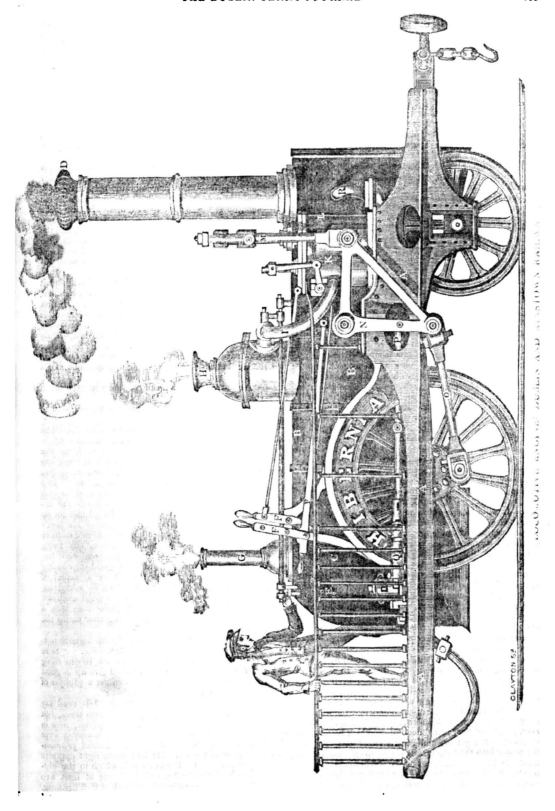

LOCOMOTIVE ENGINE, HODGES AND MIDGLEY'S PATENT.

DUBLIN AND KINGSTOWN RAILWAY.

Mr. Lardner, in his Lectures on the Steam Engine, has the following passage, p. 195, fourth edition. Speaking of the Liverpool and Manchester Railroad, he says, " I cannot conclude my observations on this great national undertaking, without expressing my regret that the directors have not thrown its advantages more open to the population among whom it has sprung up. No visitor can examine the details of the works without being struck with the circumstance, that the bulk of the persons engaged upon them, in almost every capacity, are strangers to the soil and to the surrounding population, and appear to be brought from another part of the kingdom to reap benefits to which the local population have a moral right —a right which, I am persuaded, the body of directors and proprietors would, if consulted individually, have respected."

It is only necessary to draw attention to these observations, as the opinion expressed in the conclusion is, we are satisfied, fully applicable to the gentlemen connected with the Dublin and Kingstown Railroad. The moral right of our local population should be the more regarded, as it is one of the poorer classes, and that to a large extent, which will be thrown out of the regular line of employment, and forced to seek some other road for its industry. It is easy to tell such that every progression in machinery is a national advantage, and though individuals suffer, the general good is promoted—though labour is diminished in one way, it is greatly increased in others. The Manchester railroad interfered with, and quickly did away, the numerous coach-owners, with their train of drivers, guards, hostlers, &c. on that road—yet what are some of its results with respect to labour?—the communication being so easy, the number of passengers, as well as the quantity of goods, has greatly increased, and is daily increasing ; hence porters, omnibuses, waggons, &c., in all parts, not only of Liverpool and Manchester, but of the intermediate towns, &c. The men engaged on the road itself amount to seven or eight hundred, while from the quickness of conveyance to the best markets, numbers of vegetable gardens, dairies, &c., have sprung up along the line. We say nothing of our Irish produce ; any thing which carries it quicker from its own country may be objected against—yet it is something for a cattle jobber, as I knew of one lately, to offer a beast in the Liverpool market for twenty pounds in the morning, and three or four hours after sell him in Manchester for twenty guineas. It would occupy too much space, otherwise the cotton manufacture presents the most striking results ; every improvement in the machinery tended to diminish the immediate manual labour ; one after the other the old descriptions of workmen were superseded, yet, owing to the cheapness of production, the increase of consumption, and the extension of commerce, indirect labour has been multiplied beyond estimation. Somebody says, and says truly, that Cæsar, when Emperor of Rome, had neither a clean shirt to his back, nor glass in his windows— the peasant of England has both—such are the results of her machinery. Fifty years ago a gentleman, from the time he left the nursery, wore a wig, rising through all the degrees from bob to full bottom—the very children strutted about in the grandsire's old ones, cut down by the village Bassegio from seventy-fours to frigates. In the march of improvement of that day, it would have been just as rational for the wig-makers to have petitioned parliament to compel gentlemen to wear wigs for ever, as in the present day to prevent the use of machinery ; yet the wigmakers might cry out, " Othello's occupation's gone." However, people set their sons' now to something better than stitching hairs together, and gentlemen's heads look all the neater into the bargain. It is easy to offer such arguments to the people, but examples are better than arguments, and the employment of the local population will go farther to remove any ill feeling towards the railroad, and will lessen the poverty which must for a while result from many individuals being thrown out of their occupation, and which makes it an act of injustice to introduce strangers. I am acquainted with the neighbourhood, and am sorry to see strangers already employed; it is not too late to remedy this in a great degree, and some observations to the purport might be beneficial.   G.

FAIRIES OR NO FAIRIES.

Continued from our Notice of Crofton Croker's Fairy Legends.

John Mulligan was as fine an old fellow as ever threw a Carlow spur into the sides of a horse. He was, besides, as jolly a boon companion over a jug of punch as you would meet from Carnsore Point to Bloody Farland. And a good horse he used to ride ; and a stiffer jug of punch than his was not in nineteen baronies. May be he stuck more to it than he ought to have done—but that is nothing whatever to the story I am going to tell.

John believed devoutly in fairies ; and an angry man was he if you doubted them. He had more fairy stories than would make, if properly printed in a rivulet of print running down a meadow of margin, two thick quartos for Mr. Murray, of Albemarle-street ; all of which he used to tell on all occasions that he could find listeners. Many believed his stories—many more did not believe them— but nobody, in process of time, used to contradict the old gentleman, for it was a pity to vex him. But he had a couple of young neighbours who were just come down from their first vacation in Trinity College, to spend the summer months with an uncle of theirs, Mr Whaley, an old Cromwellian, who lived at Ballybegmullinahone, and they were too full of logic to let the old man have his own way undisputed.

Every story he told they laughed at, and said that it was impossible—that it was merely old woman's gabble, and other such things. When he would insist that all his stories were derived from the most credible sources—nay, that some of them had been told him by his own grandmother, a very respectable old lady, but slightly affected in her faculties, as things that came under her own knowledge—they cut the matter short by declaring that she was in her dotage, and at the best of times had a strong propensity to pulling a long bow.

" But," said they, " Jack Mulligan, did you ever see a fairy yourself ? "

" Never," was the reply. " Never, as I am a man of honour and credit."

" Well, then," they answered, " until you do, do not be bothering us with any more tales of my grandmother."

Jack was particularly nettled at this, and took up the cudgels for his grandmother ; but the younkers were too sharp for him, and finally he got into a passion, as people generally do who have the worst of an argument. This evening—it was at their uncle's, an old croney of his with whom he had dined—he had taken a large portion of his usual beverage, and was quite riotous. He at last got up in a passion, ordered his horse, and, in spite of his host's entreaties, galloped off, although he had intended to have slept there, declaring that he would not have any thing more to do with a pair of jackanapes puppies, who, because they had learned how to read good-for-nothing books in cramp writing, and were taught by a parcel of wiggy, red-snouted, prating prigs, (" not," added he, " however, that I say a man may not be a good man and have a red nose,") they imagined they knew more than a man who had held buckle and tongue together facing the wind of the world for five dozen years.

He rode off in a fret, and galloped as hard as his horse Shaunbuie could powder away over the limestone. " Sure enough," hiccuped he, " the brats had me in one thing —I never did see a fairy ; and I would give up as good five acres as ever grew apple-potatoes to get a glimpse of one—and, by the powers ! what is that ?"

He looked, and saw a gallant spectacle. His road lay by a noble demesne, gracefully sprinkled with trees, not thickly planted as in a dark forest, but disposed, now in clumps of five or six, now standing singly, towering over the plain of verdure around them, as a beautiful promontory arising out of the sea. He had come right opposite the glory of the wood. It was an oak, which in the oldest title-deeds of the county, and they were at least five hundred years old, was called the old oak of Ballinghassig. Age had hollowed its centre, but its massy boughs still waved with their dark serrated foliage. The moon was shining on it bright. If I were a poet, like Mr. Wordsworth, I should tell you how the beautiful light was broken into a thousand different fragments—and how it filled the entire tree with a glorious flood, bathing every particular leaf, and showing forth every particular bough ;

but, as I am not a poet, I shall go on with my story. By this light Jack saw a brilliant company of lovely little forms dancing under the oak with an unsteady and rolling motion. The company was large. Some spread out far beyond the farthest boundary of the shadow of the oak's branches—some were seen glancing through the flashes of light shining through its leaves—some were barely visible, nestling under the trunk—some no doubt were entirely concealed from his eyes. Never did man see any thing more beautiful. They were not three inches in height, but they were white as the driven snow, and beyond number numberless. Jack threw the bridle over his horse's neck, and drew up to the low wall which bounded the demesne, and leaning over it, surveyed, with infinite delight, their diversified gambols. By looking long at them, he soon saw objects which had not struck him at first; in particular that in the middle was a chief of superior stature, round whom the group appeared to move. He gazed so long that he was quite overcome with joy, and could not help shouting out, "Bravo! little fellow," said he, "well kicked and strong." But the instant he uttered the words the night was darkened, and the fairies vanished with the speed of lightning.

"I wish," said Jack, "I had held my tongue; but no matter now. I shall just turn bridle about, and go back to Ballybegmullinahone Castle, and beat the young Master Whaleys, fine reasoners as they think themselves, out of the field clean."

No sooner said than done, and Jack was back again as if upon the wings of the wind. He rapped fiercely at the door, and called aloud for the two collegians.

"Halloo!" said he, "young Flatcaps, come down now, if you dare. Come down, if you dare, and I shall give you oc-oc-ocular demonstration of the truth of what I was saying."

Old Whaley put his head out of the window, and said, "Jack Mulligan, what brings you back so soon?"

"The fairies," shouted Jack; "the fairies!"

"I am afraid," muttered the Lord of Ballybegmullinahone, "the last glass you took was too little watered: but, no matter—come in and cool yourself over a tumbler of punch."

He came in and sat down again at table. In great spirits he told his story; how he had seen thousands and tens of thousands of fairies dancing about the old oak of Ballinghassig; he described their beautiful dresses of shining silver; their flat-crowned hats, glittering in the moonbeams; and the princely stature and demeanour of the central figure. He added, that he heard them singing, and playing the most enchanting music; but this was merely imagination. The young men laughed, but Jack held his ground.

"Say," said one of the lads, "we join company with you on the road, and ride along to the place, where you saw that fine company of fairies?"

"Done!" cried Jack; but I will not promise that you will find them there, for I saw them scudding up in the sky like a flight of bees, and heard their wings whizzing through the air." This, you know, was a bounce, for Jack had heard no such thing.

Off rode the three, and came to the demesne of Oakwood. They arrived at the wall flanking the field where stood the great oak; and the moon, by this time, having again emerged from the clouds, shone bright as when Jack had passed.

"Look there," he cried, exultingly; for the same spectacle again caught his eyes, and he pointed to it with his horsewhip; "look, and deny if you can."

"Why," said one of the lads, pausing, "true it is that we do see a company of white creatures; but were they fairies ten times over, I shall go among them;" and he dismounted to climb over the wall.

"Ah, Tom, Tom;" cried Jack, "stop, man, stop! what are you doing? The fairies—the good people, I mean—hate to be meddled with. You will be pinched or blinded; or your horse will cast its shoe; or—look! a wilful man will have his way. Oh! oh! he is almost at the oak—God help him! for he is past the help of man."

By this time Tom was under the tree and burst out laughing. "Jack," said he, "keep your prayers to your-self. Your fairies are not bad at all. I believe they will make tolerably good catsup."

"Catsup!" said Jack who when he found that the two lads (for the second had followed his brother) were both laughing in the middle of the fairies, had dismounted and advanced slowly—"what do you mean by catsup?"

"Nothing," replied Tom, "but that they are mushrooms (as indeed they were); and your Oberon is merely this overgrown puff-ball."

Poor Mulligan gave a long whistle of amazement, staggered back to his horse without saying a word, and rode home in a hard gallop, never looking behind him. Many a long day was it before he ventured to face the laughers at Ballybegmullinahone; and to the day of his death the people of the parish, aye, and five parishes around, called him nothing but Musharoon Jack, such being their pronunciation of mushroom.

I should be sorry if all my fairy stories ended with so little dignity; but—

> "These our actors,
> As I foretold you, were all spirits, and
> Are melted into air—into thin air."

LEGEND OF THE BANSHEE.

The Reverend Charles Bunworth was rector of Buttevant, in the county of Cork, about the middle of the last century. He was a man of unaffected piety and of sound learning; pure in heart, and benevolent in intention. By the rich he was respected, and by the poor beloved; nor did a difference of creed prevent their looking up to "the minister" (so was Mr. Bunworth called by them) in matters of difficulty and in seasons of distress, confident of receiving from him the advice and assistance that a father would afford to his children. He was the friend and the benefactor of the surrounding country—to him, from the neighbouring town of Newmarket, came both Curran and Yelverton for advice and instruction, previous to their entrance at Dublin College. Young, indigent, and inexperienced, these afterwards eminent men received from him, in addition to the advice they sought, pecuniary aid; and the brilliant career which was theirs, justified the discrimination of the giver.

But what extended the fame of Mr. Bunworth far beyond the limits of the parishes adjacent to his own, was his performance on the Irish harp, and his hospitable reception and entertainment of the poor harpers who travelled from house to house about the country. Grateful to their patron, these itinerant minstrels sang his praises to the tingling accompaniment of their harps, invoking in return for his bounty abundant blessings on his white head, and celebrating in their rude verses the blooming charms of his daughters, Elizabeth and Mary. It was all these poor fellows could do; but who can doubt that their gratitude was sincere, when, at the time of Mr. Bunworth's death, no less than fifteen harps were deposited on the loft of his granary, bequeathed to him by the last members of a race which has now ceased to exist. Trifling, no doubt, in intrinsic value were these relics, yet there is something in gifts of the heart that merits preservation; and it is to be regretted that, when he died, these harps were broken up one after the other, and used as firewood by an ignorant follower of the family, who, on their removal to Cork for a temporary change of scene, was left in charge of the house.

The circumstances attending the death of Mr. Bunworth may be doubted by some; but there are still living credible witnesses who declare their authenticity, and who can be produced to attest most, if not all of the following particulars.

About a week previous to his dissolution, and early in the evening, a noise was heard at the hall-door resembling the shearing of sheep; but at the time no particular attention was paid to it. It was nearly eleven o'clock the same night, when Kavanagh, the herdsman returned from Mallow, whither he had been sent in the afternoon for some medicine, and was observed by Miss Bunworth, to whom he delivered the parcel, to be much agitated. At this time, it must be observed, her father was by no means considered in danger.

"What is the matter, Kavanagh?" asked Miss Bunworth; but the poor fellow, with a bewildered look, only uttered, "The master, Miss — the master —he is going from us;" and, overcome with real grief, he burst into a flood of tears.

Miss Bunworth, who was a woman of strong nerve, enquired if any thing he had learned in Mallow induced him to suppose that her father was worse.

"No Miss," said Kavanagh; "it was not in Mallow———"

"Kavanagh," said Miss Bunworth, with that stateliness of manner for which she is said to have been remarkable, "I fear you have been drinking, which, I must say, I did not expect at such a time as the present, when it was your duty to have kept yourself sober; I thought you might have been trusted: what should we have done if you had broken the medicine-bottle, or lost it? for the doctor said it was of the greatest consequence that your master should take the medicine to-night. But I will speak to you in the morning, when you are in a fitter state to understand what I say."

Kavanagh looked up with a stupidity of aspect which did not serve to remove the impression of his being drunk, as his eyes appeared heavy and dull after the flood of tears; but his voice was not that of an intoxicated person.

"Miss," said he, "as I hope to receive mercy hereafter, neither bit nor sup has passed my lips since I left this house; but the master—"

"Speak softly," said Miss Bunworth; "he sleeps, and is going on as well as we could expect."

"Praise be to God for that, any way," replied Kavanagh —"but oh! Miss, he is going from us surely—we will lose him—the master—we will lose him, we will lose him!" and he wrung his hands together.

"What is it you mean, Kavanagh?" asked Miss Bunworth.

"Is it mean?" said Kavanagh: "the Banshee has come for him, Miss; and 'tis not I alone who have heard her."

"'Tis an idle superstition," said Miss Bunworth.

"May be so," replied Kavanagh, as if the words 'idle superstition,' only sounded upon his ear without reaching his mind—"May be so," he continued; "but as I came through the glen of Ballybeg, she was along with me keening, and screeching, and clapping her hands, by my side, every step of the way, with her long white hair falling about her shoulders, and I could hear her repeat the master's name every now and then, as plain as ever I heard it. When I came to the old abbey, she parted from me there, and turned into the pigeon-field next the berrin ground, and folding her cloak about her, down she sat under the tree that was struck by the lightning, and began keening so bitterly, that it went through one's heart to hear it."

"Kavanagh," said Miss Bunworth, who had, however, listened attentively to this remarkable relation, "my father is, I believe, better; and I hope will himself soon be up and able to convince you that this is all but your own fancy; nevertheless, I charge you not to mention what you have told me, for there is no occasion to frighten your fellow-servants with the story."

Mr. Bunworth gradually declined; but nothing particular occurred until the night previous to his death; that night both his daughters, exhausted with continued attendance and watching, were prevailed upon to seek some repose; and an elderly lady, a near relative and friend of the family, remained by the bedside of their father. The old gentleman then lay in the parlour, where he had been in the morning removed at his own request, fancying the change would afford him relief; and the head of his bed was placed close to the window. In a room adjoining sat some male friends, and, as usual on like occasions of illness, in the kitchen many of the followers of the family had assembled.

The night was serene and moonlight—the sick man slept—and nothing broke the stillness of their melancholy watch, when the little party in the room adjoining the parlour, the door of which stood open, was suddenly roused by a sound at the window near the bed: a rose-tree grew outside the window, so close as to touch the glass; this was forced aside with some noise, and a low moaning was heard, accompanied by clapping of hands, as if of a female in deep affliction. It seemed as if the sound proceeded from a person holding her mouth close to the window. The lady who sat by the bedside of Mr. Bunworth went into the adjoining room, and in the tone of alarm enquired of the gentlemen there, if they had heard the Banshee? Sceptical of supernatural appearances, two of them rose hastily and went out to discover the cause of these sounds, which they also had distinctly heard. They walked all round the house, examining every spot of ground, particularly near the window from whence the voice had proceeded; the bed of earth beneath, in which the rose-tree was planted, had been recently dug, and the print of a footstep—if the tree had been forced aside by mortal hand—would have inevitably remained; but they could perceive no such impression; and an unbroken stillness reigned without. Hoping to dispel the mystery, they continued their search anxiously along the road, from the straightness of which and the lightness of the night, they were enabled to see some distance around them; but all was silent and deserted, and they returned surprised and disappointed. How much more then were they astonished at learning that the whole time of their absence, those who remained within the house had heard the moaning and clapping of hands even louder and more distinct than before they had gone out; and no sooner was the door of the room closed on them, than they again heard the same mournful sounds! Every succeeding hour the sick man became worse, and as the first glimpse of the morning appeared, Mr. Bunworth expired.

We could scarcely hope in our humble way to give a correct idea of the spirit of the engravings. The above, which we have copied from the vignette to Treasure Legends, tells the story in itself. There is also a fund of humour in the tail-pieces.

DUBLIN:
Printed and Published by P. D. Hardy, 3, Cecilia-street; to whom all communications are to be addressed.

THE
DUBLIN PENNY JOURNAL

CONDUCTED BY P. DIXON HARDY, M.R.I.A.

| VOL. III. | NOVEMBER 29, 1834. | No. 126. |

A PAGE FOR OUR JUVENILE FRIENDS.

It is now nearly twelve months since we devoted an entire number of our little work to the gratification and instruction of our juvenile readers, with a promise of an occasional page from time to time. The engravings in our present number may, therefore, be considered as especially intended for their amusement: the designs, although miniatures, they will perceive are good of their kind. They are from the pencil of an eminent artist, and from their variety, they will, we doubt not, be to many of our young friends an agreeable change from our monotony of old castles, moates, and monasteries. To describe them were a work of supererogation—as each one does, what every picture ought to do—speak for itself.

AMERICAN MANNERS IN 1833.

Translated from a German work by a Correspondent of the Athenæum.

BROADWAY, NEW YORK.

Broadway, the principal street in New York, is one of the noblest in the world. It is always thronged with carriages—but the equipages are not so brilliant as the European; the coachmen and footmen are invariably blacks, and the whole concern is merely hired; for not a creature has carriage and horses of his own, excepting those who keep them to let out on hire. The liveliest part of this street is the middle. The beginning of it is formed by the neat but not spacious dwellings of the oldest wealthy families. Those who have enriched themselves in later times, and these are almost exclusively native Americans, were therefore obliged to build their magnificent habitations in the third mile of the street. Here they stand, at first intermixed with wretched houses, then with sheds and huts, and, finally, quite detached, and further apart, scattered among heaps of rubbish, on vacant spots that have never been levelled. A mile in advance are the streets *to be* occupied by future generations, scarcely indicated on the wild, uneven, rocky soil, upon which here and there a crippled forest-tree owes its existence to the victory of indolence over the love of gain.

The shops and the throng of people next claim our attention. The Parisians, it is well known, are masters in the art of tastefully decorating their *magazines*, as they pompously style the most petty shops—of setting off their goods to the best advantage, and displaying them in the most striking and attractive manner: in this accomplishment, the people of New York are not a whit behind them; and when you see the troops of dressy ladies and officious gentlemen parading the streets and pouring into the shops, you have not the least doubt that a great deal of business must be done; but I was soon convinced of the contrary. All the shops which I entered were full of ladies; the master, as well as the shopmen, was busily engaged in taking down parcels of goods, opening and tying them up again. Each lady wished to see everything, to learn the price of everything, when it arrived, by what ship, from what place, and the like. It is amusing to see the fair querists tumbling over the silks and ribbons with their delicate hands, unrolling everything, asking a thousand questions whilst examining the quality; at last laying the stuffs in folds, the ribbons in bows, forming the most elegant draperies, nay, extemporizing whole tableaux with astonishing celerity. When this is over, they leave the shop, promising to call again, and go into the next to repeat the same game, which is kept up from eight in the morning till two in the afternoon. At that hour every body goes to dinner; they eat much and quick, then rest for an hour, and by half-past four the Broadway is again in full bloom.

In spite of the good example, I could not help buying, whenever I went into a shop, some trifle or other, for which, of course, as a foreigner, I was obliged to pay double price; but the lesson which I learned at the same time, amply indemnified me. For the first thing I bought I was asked one dollar and fifty cents. I laid a bank note of two dollars on the counter. The shopkeeper immediately put it into his till, and went to attend to something else. When I reminded him that he had not given me the change, he coolly asked whether I was sure that I had paid him. I was speechless at this impudence, when a gentleman interfered, and said with a French accent, "The lady has paid—for I saw her." Upon this the shopkeeper, without betraying the least embarrassment, gave me back twenty cents; I told him that he ought to have given me fifty. He reckoned for some time, and then handed me six more cents. Hoping to shame him out of it, I requested him to lend me the slate, and wrote down for him the little account. He immediately rubbed out what I had written, made figures for a couple of minutes, and gave me a few more cents, saying, "Now it is quite right." It was not right by a great deal; but, being disgusted, I turned away, made an obeisance of acknowledgment to my unknown protector, and was preparing to leave the shop, when he addressed me. "I see," said he, in French, "that you are a stranger. Permit me to inform you, that in this country a person never pays even the smallest trifle, without taking a bill and receipt in one hand, while he pays the money with the other: and even then it is highly advisable to have at least one witness to the transaction. Whoever has no time to lose provides himself with change, so that he can pay the exact sum; for it is a principle with the people here to make a profit by everything, and of course by giving change." I thanked him for the hint.

The pedestrians in the Broadway confine their perambulations to its west side: it is not the fashion, and it would be considered vulgar to walk on the other. Still the carriage-way is crossed here and there by broad stripes paved with large flag stones, like the foot pavement, to keep up the communication. In crossing these stripes, the drivers of carriages are expected to be very cautious. The most urgent business would not induce an American to shorten his way by crossing the street at any other place, that, should he suffer any injury from a carriage, he may have a right to claim compensation from the owner. The precipitate crossing of the street, therefore, indicates the foreigner. Independently of this voluntary regulation of street police, the stranger, on his part, immediately discovers the genuine American among the streaming masses. A long, pale face, that appears to be stuffed out on one side by a quid of tobacco; lips embrowned by the same herb, deep-seated, large, light, gray eyes: a thoughtful brow, furrowed by the incessant arithmetical exertions of the brain; a decent, but negligent dress. Such is the picture of the native American.

The American, when sitting, may be distinguished at the slightest glance from the native of any other country in the world. If you see a pair of legs stuck up against a window, they belong to some American dandy, who sits rocking himself upon his chair, smoking a cigar or chewing tobacco, and is employed, to a certainty, in trimming his nails with a pen-knife. If you pass coffee-houses, hotels, pastry-cooks, taverns, and such like places, the street is full of chairs on which loll human bodies, while the legs belonging to them are shored against the wall, or against the pillars that support the awning, spread over the whole breadth of the pavement in front of houses of that kind. From the windows beneath the awning dangle as many boots and shoes as can find room at them. Such feet as cannot here find a point of support, usurp the back of a chair that is already occupied, and completely bar the way. At such places the tobacco juice is squirted about like a fire of rockets.

Among the fair sex may be seen many extremely interesting, but mostly pale faces. The stature is not contours charming; but a fine bosom, and the colours of youth and health are universally wanting. The costume is Parisian, but highly exaggerated, and the most amiable creatures run about like maniacs. In their toilette they are extremely economical. At the end of April the fashions are fixed for the year. Every one then procures a dress and a dress bonnet, in the form of which only regard is paid to the fashion, and which is in general made of some cheap stuff. The low prices result from the bad quality of the foreign goods, made up expressly for this market; and hence, rich and poor, white and black, are all dressed alike. You see nothing but *elegant* people; and as in both sexes one imitates another, and all have the greatest resemblance to each other in character, it may be asserted with truth, that whoever has seen and heard one American, has seen and heard all.

*   *   *   *   *   *

AN AMERICAN HOTEL.

He invited us in; it was the landlord himself, and to our great joy, we found ourselves in the Hotel de Commerce. Under such circumstances, we could not be particular about price; still my husband did not omit to settle that point before-hand, a precaution which, in America, ought never to be neglected. It was agreed, that for board (without drink) and lodging we should pay one dollar a day per head, without distinction of age; and we were then conducted up handsomely carpeted stairs, to a spacious apartment, also covered with a magnificent carpet. It was soon evident that carpets constituted the principal luxury.

No sooner had we retired to rest, and closed our weary eyes, than we were roused by a fresh alarm. Gleaner opened the window. Gracious heaven! what a tumult! fire-engines, with their endless water-pipes, drawn by hundreds of sturdy Americans—the lights of numberless torches—the clang of trumpets—the shouts of people— all failed to waken a creature in the house; the neighbours, also, were quiet; so we, too, would have gone to sleep again, but, on opening the windows, such a host of gnats, three times as large as those of Europe, had penetrated into the room, that we could scarcely breathe.— They tormented us horribly, and next morning we were all lamentably stung. The sufferings to which we were thus exposed, rendered us indifferent to what was passing abroad; so that in this first painful night we could hear a third alarm of fire with truly American phlegm, without being tempted to open the window again. On the other hand, we waited impatiently for the first dawn of light, in hopes that our nocturnal persecutors would then allow us some rest. This they actually did, probably needing it themselves, for they must have been weary with the work which they had done upon us.

We went down to the breakfast-room, where we found the long table covered with a variety of hot and cold meats and fish, and surrounded by about thirty guests.— Each helped himself to what stood before him. One began with salad, then eggs, and then he took a slice of roast beef, washing it down with coffee, and following that up with cold fish; while his neighbour reversed the order. Before we could recover from the astonishment, everything in the shape of eatables was consumed. So much the more was I surprised to hear calls from all sides for forks, the use of which I could not divine; as I had already seen that the American has no need of them for eating, but uses his knife alone, with wonderful dexterity. A waiter brought several plates full of forks, and set them in the middle of the table. The gentlemen— what signification these genuine republicans attach to this term, I really do not yet know—immediately fell upon the forks; each secured one, rose, and repaired to some part of the room where he could support his feet against the wall. Some even put their legs upon the table, and in this posture began at their ease to pick their teeth and pare their nails. When this operation was finished, each drew from his waistcoat pocket a bit of tobacco prepared for chewing, shoved it with his finger high up beneath the cheek, and hurried away to business.

Our host now came to us. "If," said he, "you would not rise from the table hungry, you must fall to immediately. I have frequently the most distinguished gentlemen in the country, with their whole families, at my table, but the meal never lasts longer than ten minutes.— But let me ask," proceeded our comforter, "have you not slept with your windows open?" I was just bursting forth into bitter complaints of the past night, when the landlord resumed with a smile—"it is a pity that the mosquitoes should have used you so ill the very first night; but they will let you alone the sooner; you cannot get rid of the persecution of these insects till they have had the last drop of European blood out of you. In two years, not a mosquito will touch you any more than a native American." "Aha!" cried Gleaner, rather peevishly, "so then a foreigner must part with everything, even with his blood!" "Just so," replied our host, dryly, and a foreboding shudder came over me.

ON THE BEST BOOKS FOR ATTAINING A CORRECT KNOWLEDGE OF THE IRISH LANGUAGE.

In compliance with the request of our correspondent, J. C. Y., we subjoin a list of a few elementary books; the first on our list we would especially recommend as decidedly the best book for a learner:

Owen Connellan's Gospel, according to St. John, in Irish, with an interlined English translation, a Grammatical

Praxis, and an appendix of Familiar Conversations, which may be had of Tims, Dublin; Hamilton and Adams, Paternoster-row, London: Thady Connellan's English Primer, Guide to the Irish Language, Irish and English Spelling Book, Irish Grammar, Irish English Dictionary, English Irish Dictionary, and his other elementary books, published by Walls, Temple bar; Hatchard, Rivingtons, &c., London. The best grammars are—Dr. Neilson's of Belfast, and that published by John Barlow, of Dublin, in 1808; the latter a very learned and able work, by the late Mr. Halliday, who was certainly one of the best Irish scholars of modern times. This work, we fear, is out of print: The Common Prayer, in English and Irish, of which there are many editions; Watts, London; Grierson, Dublin; &c.—the last the best: The New Testament, Watts, London; Grierson, Dublin; and the Bible Societies: The Holy Bible, do. do.: The first volume of Keating's History of Ireland, by the late William Halliday, in opposite pages, Irish and English. There is no good English-Irish Dictionary; the Irish-English Dictionaries—O'Brien's, of which a new edition has lately been published, consisting chiefly of the words in the Sacred Scriptures—O'Reilly's, which is a much more extended and useful work: Armstrong's Scottish-Gaelic Dictionary contains both English and Gaelic, and Gaelic and English; and as the Gaelic and Irish are but dialects of the same tongue, with very slight and almost imperceptible variations, this book is a most useful assistant to the Irish scholar: The magnificent Gaelic Dictionary, published by the Highland Society of Scotland, is a very learned and elaborate work, but for all useful purposes we consider Armstrong's sufficient.

We rejoice to find the Irish language exciting curiosity in England; to the grammarian and lexicographer it will afford a valuable mine of etymological wealth, and will supply the radicals for many words which have baffled enquiry hitherto in the most ancient as well as the modern languages of Europe; also the meaning of numerous names of the prominent geographical features of Europe— the promontories, estuaries, rivers, mountains, cities, &c. Indeed, we cannot do better than refer to the volume by Sir W. Betham, which we noticed in our 124th number, for proof of this assertion, where the reader will find many names collated and explained in a manner which clearly and satisfactorily demonstrates them to be Irish. That the similarity could have been the effect of chance, appears to us not only improbable but altogether impossible. Sir William Betham maintains, and to our mind has most satisfactorily proved, that the ancient Irish were a colony of Phenicians; the names, therefore, were Phenician, and should not in fact be called Irish, as they were mostly given before the Phenicians settled in Ireland.

ANECDOTE OF FREDERICK THE GREAT, KING OF PRUSSIA.

Frederick the Great had heard that a corporal in his regiment of body-guards, who was well known as a remarkably handsome and brave young man, wore out of vanity a watch chain, suspended from a leaden bullet in his fob. The king had the curiosity to enquire into the circumstance himself; and an opportunity was contrived that he should meet the corporal as by chance.

"Apropos, corporal," said the king, "you are a brave fellow, and prudent too, to have spared enough from your pay to buy yourself a watch."

"Sire," replied the soldier, "I flatter myself that I am brave; but as to my watch, it is of little signification."

The king, pulling out a gold watch, set with diamonds, said, "By my watch it is five—what o'clock are you, pray?"

The corporal, pulling out his bullet with a trembling hand replied—"My watch neither tells me five nor six, but shows me clearly the death I am to die in your Majesty's service."

"Well, then," returned the king, that you may likewise see the hour among the twelve, in which you are to die in my service, I will give you mine."

THE COMIC OFFERING.

BY LOUISA HENRIETTA SHERIDAN.

Among a number " of old friends, with new faces" the " Comic Offering" for 1835 presented itself to our notice ; and although, from the elegance of their outward trappings, as well as from the intrinsic value of their inward contents, some of the others seemed to bespeak our earliest attention, still, being at the moment in a mood rather to have our fancy tickled than our mind or our imagination deeply impressed, we turned mechanically, we might say instinctively, to Miss Sheridan's little work, which we find is equally full of fun and frolic as her last year's " Offering." Indeed, were it merely for the humour and point in the engravings, we might fairly recommend it to the patronage and support of our laughter-loving countrymen. As it is an old adage, however, that example goes far beyond precept, we shall allow our readers to judge of its merits by giving them, in our rude way, a copy of *four* out of *sixty designs*, with which the little work is embellished ; and by adding to these, one of the *least* comical, though certainly not *worst* stories in the volume, together with a specimen of the poetry, we think they will be able to form a tolerably correct opinion.

Organic remains !

" Eyes right !"
" Please, Sir, I cawn't !"

Offer of a *hand !*

Delivery by the Post !

THE MYSTERIOUS LODGER—A FACT.

BY THE AUTHOR OF "THE MAN WHO CARRIED HIS OWN BUNDLE."

An uncommonly dull season at the demi-semi-fashionable bathing town of Scratchby had concluded, leaving things in a more melancholy state of stagnation than it had found them ! The few migrating idlers who had ventured thither, fled before the chilling blast of an early autumn; the proprietors of furnished villas and apartments were in despair. Tradesmen scarcely dared look at the gazette, lest they should behold their own names among the bankrupts; the milliners walked about with rueful looks, dressed in their own unsold finery, wondering how it was to be paid for ; and the owners of bathing machines were ready to drown themselves off their own steps !

Dismal November, with all its fogs had set in ; and if

November in London be proverbial for its gloom, what must it be in a little ill-built smoky town, on the eastern coast of England, where people have nothing to amuse them but watching the arrival of herring-boats, or the departure of sprat-fishers, the flight of sea-gulls, or the periodical ebb and flow of the tide!

The most inveterate gossips of Scratchby became at length weary of propounding to each other the question, "What news?" on account of the eternal reply, "No news!"—when a sudden excitement was given to their suspended animation, by hearing that a stranger had actually arrived—how, when, or whence, no one knew; but he occupied the best apartments at the principal hotel, rose at twelve, breakfasted at one, dined at eight, excommunicated steel forks, ordered dishes with unheard of names, and called for wines, the mention of which made the landlord's wig stand on end! Moreover he burned wax-lights, and read no newspaper but the Morning Post: "by all which tokens it was plain that he was a person of consequence," said the landlady, who had once filled the situation of lady's maid in a nobleman's family.

The landlord said he was quite satisfied respecting guests, if they paid their reckoning, which the stranger had insisted on doing every night; the young ladies of the house thought it very singular that the gentleman had no baggage; yet his dress was scrupulously neat, and fresh every day, though no one could discover what became of the clothes he took off!

Yet, notwithstanding this disqualifying circumstance, the young ladies were sure he was somebody extraordinary. He was so tall and thin, and interestingly sallow, and had such expressive dark eyes: besides he wore no cravat. Had it been ten years sooner, he *must* have been Lord Byron, or the Great Unknown, or Prince Leopold looking out for a second wife at Scratchby; as it was, they only ventured to surmise him into the ex-duke of Brunswick, one of the Buonapartes, or some titled sentimentalist, in search of disinterested love. It is the disposition of the world at large, much more the word *in little*, to surmise the *worst* of every one: but the mysterious lodger, though a man without a name, and without baggage, was evidently the master of a well-filled purse, which in these virtuous days compensates for the lack of every thing else! The report of this having transpired, there was a meeting of the Scratchby exclusives, to debate whether the mysterious lodger should be admitted to the society of "the head persons of the borough," at which the majority considered mine hostess's standard of aristocracy as quite orthodox; and "the breakfast at one, dinner at eight, French dishes, Rhenish wines, silver forks, wax lights, and the Morning Post," must be indubitable symptoms of high breeding!

After the adventure of Lord A—— B——'s incognito, these worthies were disposed to look upon every pedlar, who carried a smaller pack than usual, as a peer of the realm in disguise. So they came to the conclusion, that the mysterious lodger at the Mermaid was an itinerant of rank, whose friendship it would be desirable to cultivate, and they would favour him with a visit: but as it is *rather* awkward to call on a person without even knowing his *name*, they summoned mine host of the Mermaid, and put him to the question ordinary and extraordinary —— Mine host professed his ignorance respecting his lodger, observing that it would be wastly impertinent to question any one who behaved so *genteelly* as to pay his reckoning every night. "Besides," added he, "had it been a possible thing for *any* one to do, our mistress, Sir, would have found out his name before he had been in the house six hours, for she is a special person at secrets."

"It is only a walk to the post-office, at the worst," soliloquized Mr. Fox, the recorder, taking up his hat.

"Yes, yes, sure to find it out there," rejoined the sagacious mayor, nodding his head, and all the corporation nodded their heads also, while the great man of the town, Mr. Loftus, the banker, whistled, "We are a' noddin."

Mr. Fox presently returned with a blank countenance. "The gentleman at the Mermaid had never received a letter!"

The exclusives were now in greater perplexity than

ever respecting the incognito "who breakfasted at one, dined at eight," &c. &c.

"You shall wait upon him with the subscription book of the reading-rooms, Mr. Hawk," said the mayor, after a pause, "and request him to add his name to the list."

"And if he ask what papers and periodicals we take, be sure to say, the Morning Post, St. James's Chronicle, and the Courier; Blackwood's Magazine, and the Quarterly," added Mr. Loftus.

"We'll write by this day's post, and stop the Times, and the Traveller, and the Star," said Mr. Fox, "and we'll order John Bull, and the Tory County paper."

"Very good," observed the town clerk; and do you, Boniface, present my compliments to your lodger, and say I wish to speak to him."

Mine host, who had formed a shrewd idea of his guest's peculiarities, undertook the office with any thing but alacrity.

His mysterious lodger was reposing at full length on a hard narrow sofa, with a crumpled red-and-yellow chintz cover, dosing over the Morning Post, when he entered and delivered Mr. Hawk's message.

"Hey, what d'ye say? a new sort of fish in town?" yawned the object of universal interest.

"No, Sir; Mr. Hawk, the town-clerk's compliments, and he will be happy to speak to you."

"What does he want? let him send his business."

"Send his business! why, to be sure, Sir, you don't know what sort of a gentleman our town-clerk is."

"No, nor do I wish to acquire any knowledge of him; I am acquainted with too many troublesome persons already!"

"Well, Sir, to be sure, Sir, it's all very true, Sir, but pray, Sir, what am I to say to Mr. Hawk, Sir?"

"Any thing you like, except that I shall be happy to see him—for I have an especial dislike to busy bodies!"

"And you wish him to send his business, Sir."

"No, I do not wish to be plagued with it, but, if he insists upon it, I suppose I must."

Mine host descended to the committee below, and, with some amendments, repeated the ungracious speeches of his mysterious lodger.

Mr. Hawk looked white; the corporation and the mayor looked at Mr. Loftus.

"Person of consequence, no doubt," observed the latter, who did not rightly understand the difference between persons of consequence, and consequential persons. "Here, landlord, take the book of subscribers to the gentleman, and say Mr. Loftus and the gentlemen of Scratchby desire their compliments, and hope he will do them the honour of adding his distinguished name to their society at the reading-room."

"Society at the reading-room!—add my distinguished name, (what do they know of that I wonder?)—to such a set as this!" muttered the mysterious lodger, glancing his eye quickly over the list of the little great of Scratchby; then contemptuously tossing the sacred book from him, he resumed the study of the Morning Post.

The message, if message it could be called, was repeated to the eagerly-expecting conclave.

"Are you certain he observed *my* name?" demanded Mr. Loftus.

"And mine? and mine? and mine?" inquired the mayor, Mr. Fox, and every member of the corporation, and genteel resident in the town, from class A, down to about class G.

"Don't you think we had better commit him as a vagrant or ill-disposed person, Mr. Worshipful?" said the attorney, hesitatingly.

"And then you can *compel* him to give some account of himself," observed the offended town-clerk.

"Of what can we accuse him?" asked the chief magistrate.

"Of being a Radical," said Mr. Loftus.

"But he reads the Morning Post," rejoined the curate.

"All art and grimace," said Mr. Hawk. "I'll wager any thing that he has some of Cobbett's thrash in his possession, if he were now searched."

"Farmer Rickman's stacks were fired the night before last, you know, gentlemen, by some maliciously-disposed person, whose *name is unknown*," said the attorney, significantly.

"And whom are we to suspect, unless it be a suspicious person?' rejoined Mr. Hawk.

"Very true," said Mr. Loftus, "and it was only yesterday that I received myself a threatening letter, signed 'Swing.'"

"Indeed!" exclaimed the whole conclave.

"Then, Sir," said the attorney, "you may depend this mysterious lodger at the Mermaid is neither more nor less than that *ignis fatuus* villain, Swing himself, and, perhaps, cousin germain to the Irish Captain Rock, whom no one has yet been able to catch."

This speech was received with universal applause; and the corporation were now far more desirous of hanging the mysterious lodger, than they had been a few minutes before of cultivating his acquaintance. Mine host was summoned and cross-examined as to his guest's mode of spending his time; when, to their infinite satisfaction, Mr. Boniface admitted that the party suspected went out about six o'clock on the evening the conflagration took place; and, though he had ordered dinner at the usual hour, did not return until after midnight.

"A plain case, a plain case," was murmured through the room.

"Have you ever observed any thing of a suspicious nature lying about in his apartments?" queried Mr. Fox.

"No, Sir," replied mine host; "no, Sir, not so much as a nightcap; and our Betty is of opinion he does not wear such a thing."

"Had you not better summon Betty, Mr. Mayor, to give her evidence?" asked Mr. Fox.

"Certainly, by all means," responded Mr. Worshipful; and Mrs. Betty, smirking and curtesying, yet frightened at the awful presence, entered the room.

"Well," said the mayor, with an encouraging nod, "what have *you* to say of the suspicious character who has taken up his abode in this house?"

"Why, lawk, Sir, I doesn't wish to say any thing against the gentleman, though he be rather a spicious person, as you say."

"Mr. Hawk, take down, that Betty Brown, the chambermaid, considers him a very suspicious character," said the mayor.

"Oh, pray, my honours, don't go to set down any thing that I should say against the gentleman's character," exclaimed Betty, in great agitation. "I am sure he has always behaved in the genteelest manner to me, giving me a shilling every evening when I brings him his night candle, and what was still genteeler than that, when he gave me half-a-crown the day of the fire, to go and buy him a sixpenny box of Lucifers, he wouldn't take none of the change, but said, 'Molly, never mind the change, it will do to buy you a ribbon, for you are a very honest girl in bringing me back so much money, for I never got a box of Lucifers so cheap before, and I use a good many,' says he."

"*Now*, gentlemen," exclaimed the mayor, "I think we may congratulate ourselves on being instrumental in bringing such a notorious delinquent to justice. You find, by his own voluntary confession to Betty, that he has long been addicted to the infernal practice of purchasing Lucifers to assist in his demoniacal amusement of incendiarism. I say that hanging is too good for such a villain."

"Very true," observed Mr. Loftus, "and it is a pity the laws will not admit of his being burned alive."

"Sir," I quite agree with you," said Mr. Hawk; "but, Mr. Mayor, you had better commit him on strong suspicion of having been the author of the late conflagration."

"Very good," replied the mayor; "but I must summons him before my worshipful self first, you know, and examine him myself on the charge of having maliciously and wilfully set fire to neighbour Rickman's stack."

So a summons was issued without further delay; but to their infinite disappointment, the constable who had been dispatched with it, after searching every nook and corner of the hotel, returned with the information, "that he was no where to be found!"

"Absconded by all that's circumstantial!" exclaimed Mr. Hawk.

"Lawk, gentlemen," simpered Betty, "he is only gone out for a walk as he do every day into the country, to look about him a bit, and he's sure to be home to dinner, because he have ordered some of his heathen messes, to be ready by eight o'clock; for I heard him tell our *missus*, he chose some '*mutton-go-tawney*' soup, and a homlet, and some *petticoat lays*, which are nothing in the world but some lamb-chops, and a *stew-flea* by way of pudding; so you may be sure, my honours, he will be home to eat such a dinner as that; for if he don't I am sure nobody else will."

"It is my opinion that this person ought to be pursued in all directions, without loss of time," said Mr. Hawk.

And so thought the mayor, and every member of the corporation who was possessed of a horse, or could afford to hire one, or knew how to play the equestrian: and within half an hour all the cavalry of Scratchby was in motion, with Mr. Loftus at their head; for Mr. Worshipful, though a *mayor*, was a poor manager of a horse, and preferred bringing up the rear in his comfortable stanhope.

Although there were several bowery green lanes in which a fugitive might have sought temporary shelter from the formidable pursuit of the civil authorities, they disdained to diverge from the straight line of the turnpike road, and had not proceeded more than three miles before they overtook the object of their suspicion; nay, more, detected him in the very act of striding across the pales of Sir Mowbray Mortimer's park!

Mr. Loftus being a resolute man, instantly leaped from his saddle, and with the town clerk, the recorder, the constable, and one or two of the most courageous members of the corporation, succeeded in surrounding, and taking into custody, the suspected incendiary, whom, though an elegant and fashionably dressed man, they loaded with every vituperative epithet which their indignation at his evil deeds could suggest.

The mysterious lodger protested against the violence and illegality of their very extraordinary proceedings, in terms which indicated his familiarity with the technicalities of the bar, to the infinite astonishment of his arch enemies—the town clerk, and the recorder, who were not prepared to find a professional brother in a villainous incendiary.

The mayor now coming up, insisted (as he had passed the bounds of his own jurisdiction) on taking the object of their suspicions before Sir Mowbray Mortimer, who being a very active J. P, (and moreover, a strict manorist!) was not very likely to look favourably on the trespass and character of the mysterious lodger.

Sir Mowbray hastened to give audience to these bustling civilians and *incivilians*, secretly wondering for which of his sins he was punished with the infliction of a visit from such a set of intolerable bores! However, as the aristocracy are "the politest" people in the world, he received the Scratchby *consequentials* with all the courtesy of "a person of consequence," and, instead of asking their business, waited for them to unfold it.

"Sir Mowbray Mortimer, sir," commenced the mayor, "I dare say you are surprised to see me here so far out of the bounds of my jurisdiction; but, Sir, as a brother magistrate, I beg to state that I and my corporation left Scratchby this afternoon in pursuit of the celebrated incendiary, Swing, whom we happily caught on your manor, Sir Mowbray, in the illegal and felonious act of striding over your park pales!"

"Indeed, Sir!" said Sir Mowbray, whose curiosity now began to be excited; "and where is he?"

"Sir, he is waiting, handcuffed, in the hall, under charge of Dick, the constable."

Sir Mowbray having signified his wish to see the object of suspicion, Dick, the constable, was desired to bring his prisoner forward; the latter advanced with greater alacrity than could be expected from a person under his circumstances—but what was the surprise of his captors when they heard Sir Mowbray greet him with,

"Why, my dear Littleton, what riots have you been engaged in, since you were last here, to entitle you to those bracelets?" laughing, and pointing to the handcuffs.

"So far from engaging in riots, my dear fellow, responded the prisoner, "that, as I had heard what bellicose people the men of Scratchby were, I eschewed their society altogether till the arrival of my fellow commissioner, Mr. Boreham Brushall, might enable me to inquire into the abuses of this corporation with sufficient effect. But in the mean time, Mr. Mayor and the rest of them having determined to be beforehand with me, I suppose, accuse me of being no less a person, Mortimer, than that notorious will-o'-the-wisp, Mr. Swing !"

"On what grounds, may I ask, have this worshipful assemblage brought this accusation against my friend here, who is the Honourable Blackstone Littleton, of the Inner Temple, one of the commissioners empowered by ministers to inquire into the abuses of corporate bodies ?" asked Sir Mowbray, as soon as he could conquer his risibility.

"Will Mr. Littleton be pleased to account for his absence from the Mermaid between six in the evening, and an hour past midnight on the night of the conflagration on Farmer Rickman's premises ?" said Mr. Hawk, the only one who was not struck speechless by the ominous name and business of the mysterious lodger.

"Mr. Littleton did me the honour of dining with me at seven that evening, and kindly remained here till nearly the hour you mention ;" said Sir Mowbray.

"But, sir, the purchase of the box of Lucifers still remains to be explained," said the abashed, yet pertinacious town-clerk.

"Sir," replied Mr. Littleton, "I always use Lucifers to ignite my cigars, for which purpose I purchased a box of these articles on the day of which you speak. I happen to have it about me, gentlemen, and beg to produce it for your satisfaction, still unopened. And now, gentlemen, I hope when I, in conjunction with my colleague, Mr. Brushall, (whom I expect to-morrow) proceed to inquire into corporation abuses, you will be able to return as satisfactory answers to our queries, as I have done to yours !"

The mayor and corporation, who had dreaded the long threatened advent of these commissioners of inquiry, worse than the cholera, stood aghast at the adventure, while Dick, the constable, scarcely needed their sign to release the wrists of this important personage from the handcuffs.

"Indeed, Sir," apologized Mr. Fox, "if you had only been kind enough to add your name to the list of the reading-room, we should have been aware who you were, and conducted ourselves with proper respect."

"I am sure, Sir, if we had taken you for a gentleman, it would have been very different," whined the mayor.

"And if you had suspected me of being a commissioner of inquiry," said Mr. Littleton, "I suppose I might have purchased Lucifers enough to put the whole county in a blaze, without being called to an account for it—so that I had not thrown too much *light* on *your* proceedings."

For the benefit of such of my readers as may be curious respecting the development of minor mysteries, I beg to state that Mr. Commissioner Littleton's portmanteau having been mis-sent, he was reduced to the necessity of borrowing articles of dress of his friend, Sir Mowbray Mortimer, at whose mansion he had regularly performed his mysterious toilet, while he had been the "mysterious lodger" at the Mermaid !

.

A MARRYING MAN.

BY MRS. ABDY.

Never warn me, my dear, to take care of my heart,
When I dance with yon Lancer, so fickle and smart ;
What phantoms the mind of eighteen can create,
That boast not a charm at discreet twenty-eight ;
A partner, 'tis true, I would gladly command,
But that partner must boast of wealth, houses, and land ;
I have looked round the ball-room, and, try what I can,
I fail to discover one Marrying Man !

Time was, in the pride of my girlhood's bright dawn,
All but talented men I regarded with scorn,

Wits, authors, and artists, then beaued me about,
Who might each have passed muster at Lady Cork's rout ;
In duets, I had always a second well skilled ;
My album with sonnets and sketches was filled ;
I went on the brisk " march of intellect" plan,
But the " march" countermands ev'ry Marrying Man !

How oft, when mamma would sage counsels impart,
Have I pouted and wept at her hardness of heart ;
She cared not for genius—her idol was pelf ;
Now I've grown just as icy and hard as herself.
Alike I am rock to the handsome and wise,
To wit and to waltzing, to singing and sighs,
Nay, Phœbus himself would come under my ban,
For *he* certainly is not a Marrying Man !

Finding London a failure, I varied my path,
I " took tea" with the painted old ladies of Bath ;
At Hastings, the hills laboured panting to reach ;
At Ramsgate, sat out with a book on the beach ;
At Cheltenham walk'd to the band's matin sound,
At Brighton, " missed aim" on the archery ground !
Through each place pointed out by the " Guide," have I ran,
But the Guide would not point to one Marrying Man !

That object seems still the philosopher's stone,
Another " ninth statue," a new " Great Unknown ;"
I have tried all the schemes and manœuvres of old,
And must strike out some measure decisive and bold.
I'll try a *deep* plan in the diving-bell soon,
Or, with Green's assistance, I'll visit the moon !
Yes, yes—sure the last's an infallible plan,
If the " Man in the Moon" be—A MARRYING MAN !

MONASTERY OF CLONARD IN THE COUNTY OF MEATH.

This now insignificant spot, which is situate near the river Boyne, in the barony of Moyfeurath, and county of Meath, was formerly a place of great splendour and considerable importance. It was heretofore called Cluainraird, which signifies the retirement on the western height, and more anciently Rossfinnehuill. However inconsiderable it appears at present, it was once famed as a bishop's see, and boasted of an abbey of regular canons as well as of a nunnery for regular canonesses, dedicated to the Virgin Mary.

St. Kyran, the son of Bœtius and Dasercha, who was called the son of the artificer, and in the year 548 founded the famous abbey of Clonmacnoise, in the King's County, having received a grant of that place, together with Inis-Aingin and one hundred churches in Meath, from Dermid, the son of Cervail, monarch of Ireland, a short time before his death, which took place in 519, bestowed Clonard upon St. Finian. Finian, who was of high descent, and eminent as a divine and philosopher, founded here an abbey, and dedicated it to St. Peter. He also established a school here, at which were instructed several men remarkable for learning and piety. In the year 548 he died of the plague, on the 12th of December, on which day annually he is commemorated at Clonard.

From the annals of the abbey of Clonard we collect the following, as the most remarkable of the vicissitudes to which it was exposed. In the year 838 the Danes destroyed it and put the clergy to the sword. These ruthless invaders also destroyed it in 889. King Congalagh, in 949, exempted it from cess and other charges. In 1136, the people of Brefney (now the county of Leitrim and part of Cavan) not only rivalled but surpassed the Danes in the ruthlessness of their conduct towards this religious house ; for they not only ravaged and sacked the abbey, but stripped naked O'Daly, then chief poet of Ireland, leaving him in that situation. They at the same time carried away *the sword* of St. Finian, an instrument which, indeed, could have been better suited to the hands of such freebooters than to those of the inmates of a peaceful monastery. Dorunald O'Doin Fhiacha, lord of Teaffia, became a great penitent, and died here in 1141 ; and a great part of the abbey, and all the library was consumed by accidental fire in 1143. The abbey and town were despoiled and burnt in 1170, by M'Murcha, aided by Earl Strongbow and the English; and having been afterwards rebuilt, they suffered a similar fate in the year 1175, about which time Walter, son of Hugh de Lacy, erected a monastery here, under the invocation of Saint Peter, for Canons Regular of St. Augustine.

The nunnery was founded and endowed by O'Melaghlin, King of Meath, who dedicated it to the Virgin Mary, before the arrival of the English. About the year 1195, when Agnes was abbess, Pope Celestine the Third confirmed the possessions of this nunnery, which, having afterwards become reduced to great penury, became a cell to the nunnery of St. Brigid of Odra or Odder.

As to the bishopric of Clonard, it was, before the year 1152, united to that of Trim and others, all of which were annexed to Meath about the commencement of the following century.

Having thus far traced the former state of this place, once celebrated for religion and learning, we now return to its present situation. There is not at this day a vestige remaining of former magnificence; and even the curious tomb which Seward and Archdall say once was here, has vanished by the ruthless plans of some modern vandal.

The present church is a wretched looking edifice, and in still more wretched repair. It consists of an oblong rectangular choir, about fifty feet long by twenty-four broad, having a tasteless steeple fifty feet high at the west end, on one side whereof is stuck an old corbel stone, with an antique-shaped head carved upon it, which they call the head of St. Finian. On the outside of the eastern end is a plain stone slab, serving as the door to a vault that lies under the communion-table, and was made by order of Lady Jane Loftus. Mr. Loftus, of Killyon, and his mother, as also Sir Thomas Ashton, of Ashfield, all in the county of Meath, are interred here. Upon an old gravestone in the churchyard is the following epitaph:

" Here *lyethe* the body of
Digby Waddington, Esqr.
Son and *here* of Sr Henry Waddington Knight who dyed the
1st day of July 1622 aged 3
yeares "

Within the church is a handsome marble cœnotaph to the memory of Edward Barlow, Esq., of Mullingar; and enclosed within an iron paling, as you enter the churchyard are three monumental stones, one of which commemorates the departure of Surgeon Edward Barlow, late of Mullingar, who, after having been in care of the county of Westmeath infirmary for fifty-six years, died, aged eighty-one years. The second stone tells the reader that John Barlow, physician, late of Moate, died in 1817, at the age of fifty-nine years; and that his son, Edward Barlow, of Dublin, also a physician, died, aged thirty-one, in 1815. The third tomb announces, that Dr. John Barlow, the father of the first mentioned Edward and John sleeps beneath it. On beholding the lasting abodes of these once eminent practitioners, and the triumph which death has here attained over the skill of Esculapius, I could not avoid involuntarily reflecting how feeble are the efforts and inventions of man, when they are directed against the immutable laws ordained by Divine Providence.

The ancient town is said to have been to the S. E. of the present church, to the west of which is one of those elevated burial mounds or tumuli, frequent in Ireland.— This piece of monumental antiquity nourishes a large tree which grows upon its summit. An attempt seems to have been made heretofore to perforate this mound, but with what success I was unable to learn.

With the exception of what has been already mentioned, the only remnants of antiquity about Clonard are a square stone vessel, once used as a depository for holy water, but now half buried in clay and weeds, and an ancient baptismal font, which stands in a neglected state in the steeple of the church, and is about thirty inches high by as many in breadth.

This venerable font, of which the above is an engraving, is exceedingly curious, and worthy of better care. It is formed of limestone or marble, and on the inside of the shape of a convex demisphere. The outside is an octagon, composed of square panels, beneath which are eight other panels that diminish in size towards the base. The upper panels are ornamented as follows: One exhibits, in relief, a representation of the Virgin and Child, upon the ass, flying to Egypt. The next is divided, per pale, into two compartments, the first of which exhibits Joseph leading the ass, whose halter is brought over from the former panel; the second compartment of this panel contains a grotesque figure, holding a book, and having its lower extremity terminating in a true lover's knot. A third panel has St. John, baptizing our Saviour, who is standing in a river, while the baptist pours water upon his head out of a vessel with his right hand; with the left he holds the arm of Christ, who has his arms placed across his breast in an attitude of devotion. A fourth panel is divided, per pale, having in each compartment a grotesque human figure with wings, and holding a shield with both hands. The fifth panel is like that last described; and the sixth differs from them merely in the second figure's holding an open book instead of a shield. The seventh panel is also divided per pale: on the first compartment is the figure of a saint with wings, and holding in his right hand a loose belt, which encircles his waist. This is probably for St. Augustine, as the hermits of the Augustinian order wore a leathern belt. The corresponding compartment contains St. Peter with the key. The eighth panel is divided into two, like those already described. On the first part is a bishop with a crozier, probably St. Finian; and on the other is a figure with long robes and a book, in the clothing of a Regular Canon of St. Augustine, to which saint, Walter, son of Hugh de Lacy, had dedicated the monastery. In four of the lower panels, consecutively, are represented angels holding shields, and in the other four are trees or shrubs. The base, which consists also of eight sides, is ornamented with leaves and flowers.

I cannot conclude without animadverting upon the want, or rather culpable neglect, of decency, which mocks the venerable relic of bygone days that I have described in this article. The church is dangerously damp: the steeple, when I saw it, was used as a *turf-house*; nay, one of the pews in the aisle, was, at the time I visited Clonard, filled up to the top with turf; and the ricketty and filthy-looking communion-table would be a disgrace to the meanest kitchen in the country.

DUBLIN:
Printed and Published by P. D. HARDY, 3, Cecilia-street, to whom communications are to be addressed.
Sold by all Booksellers in Ireland.

THE
DUBLIN PENNY JOURNAL
CONDUCTED BY P. DIXON HARDY, M.R.I.A.

| Vol. III. | DECEMBER 6, 1834. | No. 127. |

GENERAL POST-OFFICE, DUBLIN.

This noble building, one of the finest structures of the kind in Europe, stands on the west side of Sackville-street. It is 223 feet in front, 150 in depth, and 50 feet (three stories) in height, to the top of the cornice. In front is a grand portico, 80 feet in length, consisting of a pediment, supported by six massive pillars, of the Ionic order. This pediment is surmounted by three finely executed statues, representing Hibernia resting on her spear and harped shield; Mercury, with his caduceus and purse; and Fidelity, with her finger on her lips, and a key in the other hand. The tympanum of the pediment is decorated with the royal arms, and a fine ballustrade surmounts the cornice all round the top, giving an elegant finish to the whole. This superb edifice is built of mountain granite, except the portico, which is of Portland stone. The expense was something more than fifty thousand pounds.

The first stone of this magnificent edifice was laid by his Excellency, Earl Whitworth, on the 12th of August, 1815. With the exception of the Board-room, which is rather an elegant apartment, and in which there is a white marble bust of Earl Whitworth, there is no object worthy the notice of the tourist in the interior. The departure of the coaches from the office, would by some be deemed rather an interesting exhibition. Ten or twelve mail-coaches leave Dublin every evening for different parts of Ireland. They all assemble at the General Post Office every evening, a little before seven o'clock, and having received the bags, each in their turn, set out for their different destinations. This nightly exhibition generally attracts a crowd of spectators, when the sound of the horns, the prancing of the horses, and the last adieus of friends, form altogether a very interesting and animated picture.

As a public convenience of the highest utility, the Post-Office, in its present improved state, must be considered as one of the most useful and important establishments in any country. In civilized nations, even amongst the ancients, it appears that the interests and feelings of mankind very early pointed out the necessity of some regular mode of communication between distant places. After the fall of the Roman empire, however, no posts seem to have existed in Europe until about 1475, when Louis XI. established them for the conveyance of state information throughout France. In England letters were conveyed by special messengers, until a system of postage was established in the reign of Elizabeth, which was conducted by individuals for their own profit. Things continued in this state until 1643, when Charles I. ordered his Post-master for foreign parts to run a post between London and Edinburgh; and similar regulations were soon after made for Ireland, by Chester and Holyhead. The system was much improved during the Protectorate of Cromwell, when regular packet-boats were established between Chester and Dublin, and Milford and Waterford. The rates of postage at that time were—for every single letter within eighty miles of London, two pence; beyond that distance to any part of England, three pence; to Scotland, four pence; and to Ireland, six pence. In 1711, a Post-master General was appointed for all the British dominions; but in 1782, when the independence of Ireland was acknowledged, its Post Office became a separate establishment, and has continued to be so, notwithstanding the Union. It is, however, in contemplation to join it with the London establishment.

The introduction of mail-coaches has not only greatly improved the system of the Post Office, but has been attended with the greatest advantages to the general interests of Ireland. Previous to their introduction, the state of the roads was such, that it commonly took five or six days to perform a journey from Dublin to Cork, and it is said that persons, in those days, deemed it a matter of more serious importance to undertake a long journey through Ireland, than many do at present to undertake a voyage to America. The first mail-coaches commenced running from Dublin to Cork and Belfast on the 5th of July, 1790. A regular improvement in the state of the Irish roads has continued from that time to the present, and they are now allowed to be amongst the best in Europe.

"THE AMULET."

In our usual course of noticing the Annuals—one at a time—as among the best of the present year's production we turn to the "Amulet," which, within a modest and unassuming binding, possesses more of beauty and excellence than is to be met with in several of its competitors, who wear a much more attractive and splendid exterior. Of the ten elegant engravings with which it is embellished we prefer the "Gipsy Mother," by Wilkie; and "The Watches on the Beach," by Timbrell. As to the general contents of the work we cannot say much : scarcely one of the stories reach mediocrity, while the poetry is of a very common place order. The volume has one good quality, however ; several of the sketches furnish information, in a pleasing form, on subjects well calculated to interest the general reader. Of those the description of "The Water-Mole of Australia," by George Bennett, Esq., will serve as an instance ; while "The Gipsy Mother," by Mrs. Hofland, may be taken as a fair specimen of the stories in the work.

THE GIPSY MOTHER.

"Mercy!—mercy! Oh I have mercy on him!—he is young, very young. I will kneel to you for mercy."

Such were the words, uttered almost in the shriek of terror, yet by a voice of singular sweetness, which arrested the steps of William Hughes, as he was dragging towards the horse-pond a young gipsy boy, whom he had caught in the fact of stealing his mother's poultry. The depredations had been of late numerous, and much greater than the little farm could bear. William was very angry, and justly bent on punishing the culprit ; but he paused at the cry of distress. The gipsy girl forced her way through the brake, and stood before him in all the agitation fear and affection could inspire, again fervently imploring his pity.

"We have neither father nor mother to teach us any thing. I am his elder—but it is seldom boys obey girls. I will watch over him and guide him : he will never, *never* come here again if you will forgive him now."

William did not believe this, although he had known instances of promises being kept by the tribe ; and he was also aware that the pleader would have preferred the ducking he meditated, to the transportation he might cause. But he could not bring himself to inflict the punishment she would unquestionably share so acutely ; and he contented himself with giving a slight shake and a heavy threat to the culprit, who bounded far away the moment he was released, leaving his still trembling sister to receive the reproaches too likely to be poured upon her head, and through her on that of all her tribe.

But Ayeshe's gratitude was so fervently, yet modestly expressed, her sensibility was so genuine, and her helplessness so deprecating (as one of a degraded and reprobated caste), that William said not a word beyond that of warning her against approaching his father's premises ; adding in a softened tone, as he perceived the liquid lustre of those eyes which still swam in tears, and the pearly whiteness of teeth displayed by her still pleading lips :—

"Of course, I mean, keep the boy away : of yourself, my girl, I never knew harm of any kind."

William strode away rapidly towards the house ; but the steps of the gipsy maiden were slow and disconsolate. And, when she had re-passed the stile, and crossed the meadow, often did she peer through the hedge to see if he were indeed inclosed within the walls of his father's dwelling ; if he were indeed beyond the ken of eyes which she thought could discover him in the depths of the earth, and offer him the fond homage of her thanks, her admiration, and (though she knew it not) her love.

Neither Benoni nor Ayeshe were again found near Farmer Hughes's barns ; but never did William go forth to the field, or the market, without seeing, in some green dell or narrow lane, the slight form, beaming eyes, and blushing cheek of the young gipsy. Never did she essay to offer him any sample of her art as a fortune-teller ; never did she appear employed on any vagrant errand : either she was seated, making cabbage-nets or baskets for sale, or she was walking steadily forward towards some of the neighbouring hamlets. It was impossible not to return the "good-morrow," so gently whispered—not to acknowledge the grateful recognition of one evidently so well disposed.

Thus, naturally and blamelessly, commenced an acquaintance which, by degrees, on the side of William, ripened into friendship ; for his heart had need of a confidant, since times were hard, and his father's flock was too numerous for the pasture. Thence the transition to love was soon made ; and, alas ! from love to error.

There was not a man of better character in that part of Sussex which he inhabited than Farmer Hughes, nor one whose family had hitherto done more credit to their father's precept and example. Bitter was the agony of William, when he felt himself to be the first who should bring shame on the house where he had been held the especial darling ; bitterer still the pang of separation from a fond, loving, tender creature, who, however the world might despise and reject her, he knew to possess an understanding and capacity beyond any female in his circle of companions, and whose only fault, so far as he had seen, was that of having loved *him* too well.

Still, there was "a great gulf between them," and it was but right that he should feel the value of his own situation as the son of an honest man, religiously brought up, efficiently educated, whom younger brothers looked up to for example, and sisters considered their protector. Could he hope, or even desire, that his family should receive amongst them a creature brought up among profligate pilferers, ignorant of the common decencies of life, averse to labour, unconscious of honesty, and deemed by all a *heathen* and an *outcast* ? Must he wring, perhaps *break*, the heart of his mother, and bring "his father's grey hairs with sorrow to the grave," by an union with one at whom every finger in the parish would point with contempt ? Yet, could he forsake her ? She asked not, expected not, the reparation others (no better perhaps) would have demanded ; but did not her submission, her silence plead ?

Such were the thoughts continually racking the heart of William, whilst yet the guilty secret rested in his own bosom ; and to his corroding cares was added the hourly dread of discovery. Happily for him the whole neighbourhood were engrossed by a subject of such absorbing interest, that neither his untimely walks, haggard looks, nor impoverished appearance, excited curiosity ; though within a short time he had been the smartest-frocked youth in the parish at church, and the best appointed player on the cricket-ground.

At this period that truly patriotic nobleman, the earl of Egremont (whose comprehensive charity at once embraces the widest objects of benevolence, and stoops to the minutest details) was providing the means of emigration to Canada for numbers of persons who found no market for their labour on his over-populated lands. Farmer Hughes had not the happiness of being his lordship's tenant, for his small farm belonged to a small proprietor ; but, as he was situated in a district belonging to him, and had in his large family at least two sons who might go out with great advantage, and were likely, from their age and abilities, to share the beneficent intentions of one whose bounties flow in no narrow stream, he was amongst the most anxious inquirers on the subject, especially as his son Frank, a youth about sixteen, ardently desired to embark in the projected enterprise.

Whilst all around him were thus engaged, William, the altered, abstracted William, had beheld his son—had pressed his lips on the "velvet cheek" of infancy—and felt in one strangely mingled emotion the charm of paternity, the bliss of loving, and the self-reproach of having already injured a dear and innocent being, whom it was not less his duty to protect, than it would have been his rich recompence to cherish. Tears were in the eyes, and anguish in the heart, of the young father; but he suffered not his feelings to appear. And Ayeshe was too happy in her babe to have room for regret: her very being was absorbed in the creature to which she had given existence. A new world seemed to have been granted to her prayers; and never queen rejoiced more proudly in her empire: of shame she had no sense, of want she had no fear; and in the delicious *present* all care for the *future* was banished.

But a change soon came over this spirit; and deep thought, solicitude to very heart-ache, sat on the brow of the young gipsy mother. When William saw this, he imputed it to the desertion of her brother, who had deeply resented her conduct, as "unworthy of a daughter of their tribe, which held aloof from contamination with strangers." But the good old woman, whom he had induced to receive and attend her, imputed it to conversation she had overheard relative to the departure of many young men, his own name and his brother Frank's being mentioned as those whom their father desired to settle in life through this medium.

"Does she believe, then, that I am capable of forsaking her, and my poor child, without even preparing her for my departure?"

"No; she fears that you will refuse to go, and offend your father: it is the fear of bringing harm on you that afflicts her. Even in her sleep she is troubled for you, and urges you to set out; and she has some scheme always working in her mind by which she hopes to help you, or at least comfort you."

William could believe this; for never had one selfish wish escaped the lips of Ayeshe. But much was he startled when, on his next visit, he learned that she had set out the day before, with her babe in her arms, and her bundle in her hand, neither signifying the place where she was going, nor the time when she might return; saying only that she would be neither disgrace nor hinderance any longer to her beloved William, who might trust her safely with his child.

A day and night had passed, but she could not have gone far; and William lost not a moment in setting out to seek her. But neither dell nor dingle, coppice nor shed, the haunts of her people, nor the hiding-places of her solitude, gave indications of her having been there of late; and he returned to his father's house under such perturbation of spirit that, when the younger branches of the family had retired, his over-burthened heart flung itself, by full confession, on the compassion of his parents.

His mother wept over his sad story, and wished "she could have taken the little one;" his father was grave and sorrowful, rather than austere: after long ruminating on the case, he observed, that "one of two ideas had unquestionably influenced the poor girl—generosity towards William, since by withdrawing herself she had given him a liberty necessary for his welfare; or, an incapability of confining herself any longer to the habits of domestic life. Under either circumstance, although it was his duty to repent the past, he might consider himself relieved, and so far happy."

This William held to be impossible; but he found great comfort in the kindness of his parents, and his mind assented to much of the reasoning they used to soothe and re-assure him. He believed that *both* the causes mentioned co-operated to produce Ayeshe's conduct, since he well knew her disinterested love and capability of self sacrifice, and also her enthusiastic attachment to the woodland haunts of her childhood, her passionate admiration for the beauties of nature, and of the changes and conflicts of the elements. Often had he listened, with

surprise and delight, to the bursts of untutored eloquence which broke from her lips, when she hailed the first tufts of violets or primroses that had met her eye—described the effects of a spring shower, or the awful impressions of a thunder storm; and at such moments became conscious of the sympathies which drew her so closely to his heart as to obliterate all that was revolting in her situation.

By entering into his feelings, and aiding him in his enquiries, his father became to him the friend and companion he required; and by degrees his sense of loss subsided, and his interest in the general duties of life returned. He listened attentively to the letters received from the first emigrants from his own village, and to the suggestions of his young brother; and though he was dearer than ever to his parents, they saw too clearly that he would never completely recover his spirits and energies whilst he remained at home, and doubted not his abilities and success if he went abroad; they therefore hailed with pleasure the slow indications he now gave of following in the track of many of his young companions.

In the spring of 1833, the same bounty was renewed, and the same stirring among the poor and enterprising was afloat; and William, with his father, set out to Petworth, a distance of about sixteen miles, in order to inquire how far the brothers might be permitted to share in the benefits offered by his lordship's munificence. They went soon after sunrise, and reached the village of ———, which was about two miles from the park, about eleven, not sorry to find themselves at the curate's house, as he had married a distant relation of the farmer's and would not only receive them hospitably, but probably give them information on the subject of their enquiries.

They were received courteously by the clergyman's daughter, who said, "As it was a prayer-day her father was then in the church;" to which place, after taking a draught of beer, the elder Hughes followed him, but the young man sat down to enjoy a shady parlour; and finding the late occupant did not return thither, he took the liberty of looking at a book she held on their entrance, and had left open at the place where she was reading; it was the second page of the story of "Grace Huntley" in the "Amulet" of that year.

William read, and read, not only with his eyes, but his mind, his very soul; audible sobs, quick gushing tears, succeeded; his intended voyage, his long-nurtured resolution, his present situation, were alike forgotten. Grace Huntley on the one hand, and his own infant child on the other, possessed him wholly; and at length, dropping the book, he exclaimed, "And did *she* do this?—a poor, weak, trembling, and loving woman! Could she thus wrench away the fondest, strongest chords of existence to save her child from sin, even after that child had been contaminated? and shall I suffer my innocent babe to become the associate of the vile from its birth? No! I will rather search every corner, from sea to sea, to seek and snatch it from perdition; and God grant I may save its mother also!"

The energy with which these words were pronounced drew the attention of the curate's daughter from the kitchen, where she was employed at the moment; and the sounds she had heard, aided by the flushed cheek and evident emotion of William, communicated the idea of his being angry at being left alone, and the good girl began eagerly to apologize.

"My father will be here presently, I am certain: it is true I ought to have told you that his absence would be longer than usual, because he had a christening to perform."

William, whose thoughts were "running to and fro through all the earth," mechanically echoed the words, "a christening!"

"Yes; a very extraordinary one, being, not only that of an adult (which rarely occurs), but that of a gipsy."

"A gipsy!" reiterated William with more animation.

"Yes; she came to this place last year, about harvest, alone, and having the appearance of being worn down with long travel. She never attempted to gain money by the usual arts of her people, but appeared singularly desirous of being received amongst our poor as one of themselves, and especially to obtain the best knowledge; for this purpose she crept into the church, where she generally sat behind a pillar. She then loitered much about the school-house, asking many questions of the children; and, finally, made an acquaintance with me, which led to one with my father. She has been now many months under instruction from us both, and has, indeed, well deserved our care; or, of course, she would not have been admitted by my father into the church of Christ, especially under her circumstances; for, alas! poor thing!—oh, here they come, both your father and mine."

William was utterly unable to speak, yet felt as if more than life depended upon the answer to a single question; and whilst the curate was warmly shaking him by the hand, and praising him for the step he was about to take, he was utterly unable to arrange his thoughts, or command his feelings, so as to utter one word in reply. The good man imputed this to a natural feeling in one who knew that his poverty influenced him, rather than his wishes, in the affair of which his father had spoken; and to relieve him, addressed his daughter, saying,

"Well, Anna, the deed is done; your poor *protege* is become one of us now; and I humbly trust, nay, doubt not, will be found hereafter one of those who were 'brands snatched from the burning.' At her own request she has taken your name at the font: remember this when you see her, and do not call her Ayeshe."

"Ah!" cried William, " my conscience, my heart surmised the truth! Oh, Sir, what shall I say? You have christened my poor wanderer; you have instructed her to that end; for which may the God you serve especially bless you? And now will you marry her to me?"

"Do it!—I pray your worship, do it? I intreat it, who am his father; for never did I feel so much for any living creature as I did just now for that young woman. I am, I fear, a proud man; I should not like William's marriage to be *talked about;* but I do wish him to take a wife with him, for surely ' it is not good for man to be alone' in the desert; and who so proper to be his helpmate as her to whom he owes atonement, and who has so anxiously sought to render his faith, her faith—his God, her God?

" ' Let him that hath sinned, sin no more,' is, of course, my language. Be assured, farmer, that I will publish the bans, marry them in my own church, and your parish be none the wiser. I doubt not that this poor girl will prove an excellent wife; but we must respect the prejudices which guard conduct, and not induce our villagers to seek connexions among vagabonds : years may pass, and not produce another Ayeshe."*

To William she was produced at this moment by her young benefactress, who had beckoned him into her father's study, and he beheld her, not only with a fond approbation, but a delight he had never known before; for, under the improving hand of her female friend, her personal appearance had been, on this eventful day, altered exceedingly for the better. The gipsy-cloak and head-gear were discarded for the neat and delicately clean habiliments of the Sussex peasantry, and her fine features and happy countenance were seen in all their beauty.

But who shall paint the altered mind—the joy, the gratitude, the sense of heavenly interference which naturally possessed a being so singularly situated? Ayeshe had cherished, nay, she had lived on the hope of one day following William, and presenting to him a son whose virtues and endowments should not only ensure love from the father, but win for herself a purer regard than she had yet inspired. To effect so high and sacred a purpose, she had sought the instruction which eventually rendered her the participator of those blessings desired for her child.

But never had she dared to hope for the happiness now promised—to become William's lawful wife with the consent of his parents—to offer her child to their caresses—to sail with him over the wide ocean far beyond the voice of reproach or the smile of scorn—to labour with him and for him, the blue skies above them, the free breeze blowing over them, and the green woods around them—to prove her own powers of aiding life in a situation new to him, and her acquirements in things long valued by him; each was such a sweet, deep, heart-moving joy, that she felt almost oppressed by the sense of her own blissful emotions.

All things went well with our petitioners: William was married to Anna the day before they sailed, and the greater part of his family accompanied them to the seaport. The parting was necessarily painful, not only to one who bade adieu to many dear ties, but to her who felt, in no common measure, veneration and gratitude for those who had looked on her in her low estate; therefore,

" Some natural tears she dropped, but wiped them soon;"

for she beheld her son in his dear father's arms, and remembered that she was no longer a gipsy-mother.

ANCIENT CROSS IN THE CHURCHYARD OF ST. MARY'S, NEW ROSS.

Sir—I send you a rough draught of a cross with the inscription, which is cut on a tomb-stone in the churchyard of St. Mary's, at New Ross, in the county of Wexford; the interlacing in the foundation of the cross is extremely curious, and the word Novæ, or new, before Ross, is a circumstance worthy of notice at so early a period as 1487.

Here lies Patrick Conway, burgess of the town of New Ross, who died Anno Domini, 1487.

In the same churchyard there is also a similar cross on another stone, but not in as good preservation as the former; it bears the following inscription in old English character:

Hic jacit Denis *Idam* and his wife, Joan Hanroke, whose families this tomb received, 1577.

The word *Idam* is disputed.   C. D.

Wexford, September, 1834.

* The original Ayeshe had not the fault of this, but all her merit; since she crept out of the most infamous neighbourhood in London to obtain instruction, and became a Christian, previous to her marriage.

DULEEK CHURCH, COUNTY OF MEATH.

This venerable ruin is situated about twenty miles from the metropolis, a little to the left of the mail-coach line to Drogheda, in the village of Duleek, on the Nanny-water. The ruined *Abbey-Church*, with its majestic tower is, with justice, perhaps, supposed to have been the first stone edifice, of its kind, erected in Ireland. St. Cianan, or Kenan, is said to have founded the abbey about 488: it was frequently plundered by the Danes, as well as by the Irish in their intestine wars; notwithstanding which, it contained great riches at the Dissolution, and was possessed of a very large property in lands and tithes. The bodies of Brien Boromhe, and Morogh, his son, both slain at the battle of Clontarf, were brought by the monks of Swords to this abbey, and from thence conveyed to Louth by those of St. Cianan.

Athcarne Castle, romantically situated in the midst of trees, not far from the Nanny-water, which flows by its north side, is a large square building, defended at the angles by towers; the whole in good preservation. To the west, adjoining the main building, are offices, which appear to be of the same date. The principal entrance, which is on the south side, is through a pointed arch. The houses and plantings in the neighbourhood form an agreeable contrast to the barren and uncultivated appearance of the country through which the traveller has had to pass during the preceding eighteen or twenty miles of his journey, in the route from Dublin to Drogheda. It is said King James slept in the castle on the night previous to the battle of the Boyne.

THE WATER-MOLE OF AUSTRALIA.

(Continued from our notice of " The Amulet ")

It was on a beautiful evening, in the month of October, the commencement of summer in Southern latitudes, that, arrived in a district lying to the south-west of Sydney, and distant about two hundred miles from that seat of the Colonial Government, I approached the banks of the Yas river, in the interior of Australia. The scenery here is of the most picturesque description: the open forest country and wooded hills; the neat cottage and garden, with the grain of a vivid green just bursting into ear, the tranquillity around being only occasionally disturbed by the lowing of cattle, bleating of sheep, or the gay and blithesome notes of the feathered tribe. The silver stream of the Yas continued its silent course, its banks adorned by the beautiful pendulous Acacias, which, at that season,

were profusely covered by their rich golden and fragrant blossoms; while the lofty and majestic gum-trees, the graceful manna, or the dark "swamp oak," added to the variety and beauty of the landscape.

The sun was near its setting, when at a more quiet part of the river I sought the burrows of those shy animals, the " water-moles," the *ornithorynchus paradoxus* of naturalists, known also as the platypus or duck-billed animal.

Those only who are accustomed to view, and investigate the varying productions of nature—whether in the peculiar forms and habits of the animal, or the brilliant and animating varieties of the vegetable world—can appreciate the true feelings of enjoyment experienced on seeing in their native haunts creatures which before were known merely from vague description.

Perhaps no animal on its first introduction into Europe gave rise to greater doubts as to its being a production of nature, or excited deeper interest among naturalists respecting its habits and economy, than this paradoxical creature, which, from its external appearance, as well as internal anatomy, may be correctly described as forming a connecting link between the bird and the quadruped.

The animal, when seen in a living state running along the ground, conveys to the spectator an idea of something supernatural, and its uncouth form produces terror in the minds of the timid: even the canine race (except those accustomed to bring them out of the water when shot) stare at them with erect ears, and the feline race avoid them, still, although of such a " questionable shape," it is an animal of perfectly harmless, although restless, disposition.

Among the colonists in Australia it is known by the name of " water-mole," from some resemblance it bears to the common European mole. By the aboriginal tribes at Bathurst, Goulbourn Plains, Yas, Murrumbidgee and Tumat countries, it is designated by the two names, Mallangong and Tambreet, the latter being more in use with them than the former.

The above print may assist the reader in forming a correct notion of the peculiar shape and character of the animal. The body is depressed like the otter, mole, and beaver. It is covered by long and thick dark brown hair, underneath which is a short and very soft fur, resembling the two distinct kinds found on the seal and otter; on the abdomen, breast, and throat, the fur and hair is of much finer quality, and more silky in its nature. In young specimens the under surface of the tail is covered by hair of a beautiful silvery white; this is lost, however, in the adult; the under surface of the tail in such, having merely a few coarse hairs scattered over it. This circumstance induced many to suppose that the animal uses its tail as a trowel, in a manner similar to the beaver; but from an examination of their burrows, I have no doubt that the hair is rubbed off by the attrition of the tail on the surface of the ground. The tail is flat, broad, and inclining on each side abruptly off at the termination, beyond which the long hairs project. The hair on the upper part of the tail is of a dark colour, long, and coarse, and destitute of the peculiar glossy appearance of the other parts of the body. There was no variation in the colour of the fur in all the specimens I have seen; the under short fur is of a greyish hue. The whole of the under surface of the body is of a ferruginous colour, varying in intensity according to age. The legs are short, feet pentadactyle, webbed, and in the fore feet the web extends a short distance beyond the claws, is loose, and falls back when the animal burrows. The head is flat; and from the mouth two lips, or mandibles, project, resembling the beak of a Shoveller-duck; the lower mandible is shorter and narrower than the upper, and its internal edges are channelled with numerous striæ, resembling, in some degree, those seen in the bill of the duck. The colour of the superior mandible above, when seen in an animal recently taken out of the water, is of a dull, dirty, greyish black, covered with innumerable minute dots, and the cartilaginous continuation around the mandible is uniformly smooth and soft. The eyes are very small, but brilliant, and of a light brown colour; they are situated rather high up the head. The external orifice of the ear is situated at the upper part of the external angle of the eye; the orifice is easily discovered when a living specimen is examined, as the animal is then seen frequently to open and close it; but remaining collapsed in dead specimens, it is not readily perceived by persons unacquainted with its exact situation. From this orifice a semicircular cartilaginous canal is continued, which terminates at the base of the skull, and probably increases the intensity of sound, giving the animal an acute auditory power. The size varies; but the males are usually found to be, in a small degree, larger than the females; the average length being from eighteen to twenty inches.

When the fur is wet the animal has a soiled and far from attractive appearance, resembling more a lump of dirty weeds which are often seen floating about the rivers, than any production of the animal kingdom; it would therefore often escape observation, but for its paddling motion in the water; such was its appearance when lying dead on the surface, or when drifted by the stream against the stump of a tree, or among the reeds and bulrushes growing profusely near and upon the banks of the river.

When the Ornithorynchus is captured, it makes great efforts to regain its liberty, and its loose integuments cause it to be retained with difficulty, for the animal feels as if it was contained in a thick fur bag, under which are very powerful cutaneous muscles. During its struggles to escape it makes no attempt to bite, but occasionally emits a low growling noise. The aborigines use them for food. The methods employed in their capture are by digging them out of the burrows, or by spearing them. They dig up the burrows at certain seasons of the year, when the young are nearly full grown, and at that time they consider them excellent eating, and often capture the old animal at the same time.

THE SPIRITS' LAND

BY THE AUTHOR OF "SELWYN."

Oh, beauteous are the forms that stand
　Beyond death's dusky wave,
And beckon to the spirits' land,
　Across the narrow grave!

No damp is on the freed one's brow,
　No dimness in his eye,
The dews of heaven refresh him now,
　The fount of light is nigh.

The parent souls that o'er our bed
　Oft poured the midnight prayer,
Now wonder where their cares are fled,
　And calmly wait us there.

The dearer still—the close entwined
　With bands of roseate hue:
We thought them fair; but now we find
　'Twas but their shade we knew.

'Tis sweet, when o'er the earth unfurled
　Spring's verdant banners wave,
To think how fair yon upper world,
　Which knows no wintry grave.

'Tis sweet, when tempests earth deform,
　And whirlwinds sweep the sky,
To know a haven from the storm,
　When worlds themselves must die;

To know that there in safety rest
　The tranquil barks of those
Who, soaring on life's billowy crest,
　Attained to heaven's repose;

To know that brethren fondly wait
　Our mansion to prepare—
That death but opes that mansion's gate,
　And, lo! our souls are there!

IRISH AND DANISH RATHS.

Sir—As a constant reader and admirer of your cheap and excellent Journal, I feel not a little gratified at the increasing prosperity thereof, as announced in the preface of the second volume: and I entertain a sanguine hope, that so valuable a periodical will always meet with, and continue to be held in, the estimation which it so highly deserves.

You will, perhaps, allow me to intrude on your columns a few observations concerning the raths, or, as the country people call them, forts, (Irish leara:) so thickly scattered throughout Ireland, and said to have been constructed by the Danes. In reference to these singular habitations, one circumstance strikes me very forcibly, as being (to myself at least) a very unaccountable difference in their formation—namely, that in several parts of Ireland, in Kerry for instance, all, or most of them, are open, each having a small door or inlet in the centre; while in other parts, as the county of Limerick, no passage to the interior is visible in any of them. Some years since I had the curiosity to visit about twenty of these forts, in the neighbourhood of Killarney, and several more in other parts of Kerry; and found in each an opening in the centre, like a small arch; most of them having also stone steps descending to the bottom. I have visited many more in the counties of Cork, Limerick, and several other parts, but could never find the least trace of a passage to the inside. There is a very large one at Killilagh, six miles S. E. of Newcastle, county of Limerick; and about ten years ago, a gentleman who resided there caused it to be dug up by a number of his labourers, in order to explore the interior, which, however, after digging to a considerable depth, they failed to find. For several miles round this place there is scarcely a townland without one of these forts, but no entrance appears to any of them.

Mr. Editor, these remarks may appear trifling, or worth little notice; but, perhaps, they would, if inserted, elicit some valuable information from other quarters respecting these Danish forts, as they are called. In the hope, therefore, that some of your able correspondents will favour us with an explanation on this subject, I request you will give these lines a place in the Penny Journal.

T. G.

EXTRAORDINARY CIRCUMSTANCE.

The chaplain in Lady Ware's family had dreamed that on such a day he should die; but being by all the family laughed out of the belief of it, he had almost forgotten it, till the evening before at supper. There being thirteen at table, according to an old conceit, that one of the family must soon die, one of the young ladies pointed to him, that he was the person. Upon this he recollected his dream, and became disconcerted, and Lady Ware reproving him for his superstition, he said he was assured that he was to die before morning; but being perfectly well, he was not attended to. It was Saturday night, and he was to preach next day. He retired to his room, and sat up late, as it appeared by the burning of his candle; he had been preparing notes for his sermon, but was found dead in his bed the next morning.

ROMANCE OF IRISH HISTORY.

HELEN O'DONNELL.

Helen O'Donnell, daughter of the earl of Tirconnell, was considered the most beautiful and accomplished young lady of the time: a graceful mien, lovely countenance, and a benignity of disposition like hers did not fail to attract the young nobles of Ireland. Helen, on the other hand, was not without feeling particular attachments: there was one fortunate suitor, the elegant young chieftain of Fermanagh, who was blessed with her regard. Maguire had spent his minority in Spain, and, added to an uncommonly graceful deportment, he had received a good education, and acquired all the habits of gallantry for which that court was so famed. The earl of Tirconnell favoured the suit of the young chief, and all were happy: but that "the course of true love never did flow smooth," her short and eventful history furnishes another proof.

The celebrated Shane O'Neill, earl of Tyrone, came on a visit to his brother chief, O'Donnell, to arrange for a general attack on the English border. All the chieftains of Donegal belonging to the sept of O'Donnell as well as of Maguire assembled at Ballyshannon, to greet the patriot chief, who had so gallantly defended his country from the inroads of the English.

The entertainments were such as might be expected from a prince of the O'Donnells. The days were passed in hunting the red deer on the neighbouring mountains of Barnesmore, or shooting the wild sea-birds on Lough Erne, and the nights in song and merriment: but all these and other amusements were lost on the chief of Tyrone: he had seen Helen O'Donnell—he had conversed with her—he had conceived a passion for her—nay, he had even proposed for her—but was politely refused by her father, who stated the fact of her being betrothed to the young chief of Fermanagh. O'Neill appeared satisfied, but he was far from being so; within his breast there kindled a flame of passion and jealousy which threatened dreadful consequences. Shane O'Neill was not accustomed to have his desires thwarted; he therefore determined to punish alike the innocent and the guilty, as some atonement for the offence he thought he had received.

One evening after the banquet, Maguire left the hall, and proceeded to seek his intended bride in the garden of the castle. Helen came forward to meet her lover; she had her little Spanish hat and feathers on, and her crimson scarf.

"Reginald," said she, with a maiden playfulness, "why did you delay so long. Come, let us walk near the lake, 'twill be long ere the evening closes, let us enjoy the scene."

"Let me bear your harp, Helen," said Reginald, as he bowed acquiescence. They walked a considerable distance from the castle, along the banks of the little river which flows from Lough Erne. Conversation and music at intervals stole the hours away. At length they rested on a verdant slope near the lake. The view was enchanting. 'Twas summer: nature was dressed in her liveliest apparel—the sun had retired behind the mountains, but his last rays resting on the valley threw a splendid radiance over the entire scene.

"Reginald, shall I sing you a wild scrap I composed lately?" said Helen, as she touched the strings of her harp. The young chief willingly consented, and she proceeded—

Hail to my birth-place on high,
  Hail to the noble and free;
Hail to my home, near the sky,
  Where the wild deer away,
  Dash through heather so gay,
Oh this, this is liberty!

Hail to my own land above,
  Towering so gallantly;
Hail to the land that I love,
  Where the eaglets roam,
  Where all find a home,
Oh this, this is liberty!

Then hail to my birth-place once more;
  I shall never again quit thee,
But list to the waterfall's roar;
  'Tis my tansie so wild,
  I'm liberty's child,
And I love, I love liberty!

Helen ceased to sing, but her fingers still wandered among the strings of her little harp, when Reginald stopped short and listened.

"Helen, did no you hear a noise among the brushwood yonder?" Scarce were the words spoken, however, when from the spot rushed Shane O'Neill and four of his clansmen. Reginald Maguire threw aside the harp, and drew his sword; clasping the lifeless form of Helen with his left arm, he defended himself gallantly; but she was torn from him in an instant: he rushed on O'Neill, but the contest was of short duration; the powerful Tyrone soon laid him dead at his feet, and followed his vassals; who, at some little distance, had their horses in readiness for instant flight. The inanimate form of Helen O'Donnell was placed on the horse, in front of Tyrone, and all being ready, they proceeded at full speed out of Donegal, and were not long in reaching their own border, where, for the present, they might have no fear of pursuit.

As soon as the barbarous ingratitude of Shane O'Neill was made known to O'Donnell, he instantly summoned his chiefs, and, aided by those of Fermanagh, marched to attack Shane's castle, which stood on the banks of Lough Neagh. O'Neill drew out to give them battle, and, after a desperate fight, which lasted three hours, he beat them completely over his border with immense loss.—O'Donnell was defeated, but not satisfied: he, without delay, sought aid from the English, who did not let so favourable an opportunity pass of working their own ulterior schemes. Both English and Irish armies combined, proceeded to his country. Shane O'Neill met and entirely defeated them. He now marched towards Dundalk; and, after gaining another signal victory at Ravensdale, he laid siege to the town; but the clans of Hy Nial, (for such was their ancient name) although irresistible in the field, were not at all fitted for defending or attacking fortresses. He was, therefore, forced to break up the siege, and fly into the mountains of Ravensdale.

The Scotch, who occupied Carrickfergus, immediately in his rear, now attacked him: he twice defeated them. In the first action he killed with his own hand their chief, James M'Donnell; and, in the second, took his brother, Surly Boy, prisoner; but all the bravery of the men, and spirit of the chief, could not resist the increasing enemy. Shane O'Neill therefore determined to throw himself on the mercy of his Scotch enemy, in preference to any other. For this purpose he took with him his prisoner, M'Donnell, and, with two of his chiefs, set out for northern Clanneboy, where the Scotch, to the number of six hundred, were encamped, under the command of Alexander M'Donnell, called the younger, brother to Surly Boy, Shane's prisoner, who had now received his liberty.

When Shane O'Neill entered the camp of Alexander M'Donnell, he was received with much courtesy; but, whilst in the act of making conditions, he and his chiefs were stabbed to death by the Scotch from behind.

Shane's head was now severed from his body, and sent as a present to the deputy in Dublin, where it was stuck on a pole over the gates of the castle.

The two sons of O'Neill who were left to guard the castle, thought it prudent to restore Helen O'Donnell to her father, and beg a peace. This young and beautiful lady, shocked at the dreadful scenes she had witnessed, shortly after retired for ever from the busy scenes of life; and no entreaties of the young and the ardent could ever tempt her again to mix in them.

HINDOO SHARK FIGHTER.

The boat was on its progress down the Hooghly when a huge shark was seen swimming round it: the combatant, on the offer of a small reward for his dexterity, holding the rope, on which he had made a sort of running knot, in one hand, and stretching out the other arm, as if already in the act of swimming, stood in an attitude truly picturesque, waiting the re-appearance of the shark. At about six or eight yards from the boat the animal rose near the surface, when the native instantly plunged into the water, a short distance from the very jaws of the monster. The shark immediately turned round, and swam slowly towards the man, who, in his turn, nothing daunted, struck out the arm that was at liberty, and approached his foe. When within a foot or two of the shark, the native dived beneath him—the animal going down almost at the same instant. The bold assailant in this frightful contest soon re-appeared on the opposite side of the shark, swimming fearlessly with the hand he had at liberty, and holding the rope behind his back with the other. The shark, which had also by this time made his appearance again, immediately swam towards him; and while the animal was apparently in the act of lifting himself over the lower part of the native's body, that he might seize upon his prey, the man making a strong effort, threw himself up perpendicularly, and went down with his feet foremost, the shark following him so simultaneously that we were fully impressed with the idea that they had gone down grappling together. As far as could be judged, they remained nearly twenty seconds out of sight, while we stood in breathless anxiety, and it may be added horror, waiting the result of this fearful encounter. Suddenly the native made his appearance, holding up both his hands over his head, and calling out, with a voice that proclaimed the victory he had won while underneath the wave—'_tan—tan!_' The people in the boat were all prepared—the rope was instantly drawn tight, and the struggling victim, lashing the water in his wrath, was dragged to the shore and dispatched. This truly intrepid man received only a cut on the left arm, apparently from the fin of his formidable enemy.—(_From Montgomery Martin's History of the British Colonies, Vol. I.—Asia._)

ANCIENT TOMB IN TINTERN CHURCH, COUNTY OF WEXFORD.

Sir—In the old church of Tintern, in the county of Wexford, adjoining the once famous abbey of Tintern, stands a tomb belonging to the ancient family of the Colcloughs. The crest and arms were formerly attached to the tomb, but have been removed. In copying the inscription I have followed the exact spelling, as I think it somewhat curious.   C. D.

In obitum egregei virei Antoni Colcloughe, milites
Pristine sublimi proavorum stemate ducta
Et sereis magnis orta ab imaginibus
Atque superba manus variis ornata tropheis
Hæc sortis fragili sola parentur ope
Ast sincerus amor patriæ vox consona vulgi
Et verus vero candor honore niteris.

Neschia vel duris flecti constantia rebus
Non aliena sed hæc nostra vocare licet
Vterum plura daret sors et mature vicessim
Certarunt uno cuncta viator habes.

Here lieth the body of Syr Anthony Colclovghe Knight El-dest Sune of Richard Colclovghe of Volverton in Stafford Shire Esqvre, who came first into this Land the 31 Yeer of Henry ye 8. and then was Captayn of the Pensioners in which place, and others of greater Charge, He continved a most faythfvl Servant dvring the Life of Edward the VI. and Qven Mary and vntill the xxvi Yer of ovr most noble Qven Elizath, and then died the 9th of December 1584—he left by his Wife Clare Agere Dowgher of Thomas Agere Esqvre, Seven Sonns, Francis, Ratlife, Anthony, Syr Thomas Colclovghe, Knight, John, Mathew, Lenard, and four Doghters, Jaqnet, was maried to Nichlas Walsh Esqvier of the Privie Covnsal and one of the Justise of the Kings Bench Irland, Frances maried to William Smethwike Esqvre, Clare, maried to William Snead of Brodwall in Staferd Shier Esqvre, Elenor died Ivnge.

CROMLEACH—COUNTY OF DOWN.
FINN'S FINGER STONE.

On a part of the extensive estates of the Marquis of Downshire, situate in the parish of Clonduff, and county of Down, about two miles from Hilltown, and ten from Newry, on the old line of road which formerly led from the latter town to Downpatrick, stands, or rather rests, one of those ancient monuments of antiquity, called Cromleachs. The top stone measures in length fifteen feet, and in breadth ten feet seven inches, and all nearly the same depth or thickness—about five feet six inches. Its greatest breadth is within four feet of the east end. It is supported by three stones, which measure, two of them six and a half, and the other eight feet high by three feet in width and about ten inches in thickness.—One end now rests on the ground, though, not more than thirty or forty years ago, it was also supported by stones nearly of the same height as those in front, which were loosened by persons in search of supposed treasure, and afterwards carried away for building. In the memory of several persons now living in the neighbourhood, it was surrounded by stones which formed a circle, a large row of the same running from it in an easterly direction; they were nearly the size and shape of those which support it: but, were, however, some time since, also carried off; and had it not been for the late noble marquis, who caused some trees to be planted around it, it would also have shared the same fate. On the south side, and partly under it, is a kind of cell, formed of three stones, like those that support it, two being placed on their edges, and the third being laid over them, with one end resting on the ground, thus forming an apartment about eight feet long, and three wide, and about three feet in height; it is now converted into a sty for pigs. A few years ago, on some persons removing a part of this cell, in it was found a beautiful urn, containing ashes and small bones, which immediately crumbled to dust on their being touched and exposed to the air; this urn had beautiful figures cut on it; and likewise a representation of the sun or moon: it also shortly went to pieces. I have still in my possession a portion of it, as also an arrow of flint that was beside it. A great quantity of bones have been raised here, from time to time, of a gigantic size, which confirm the inhabitants in the opinion that this cell was the bed of Finn M'Coul, and that he was buried convenient to the stone: 'tis sometimes called Finn's finger-stone; and the marks of his fingers are shown, where 'tis said he caught it by, and threw it from a mountain called Spalga, a distance of nearly four miles, to the place it now stands; and, afterwards, lifting and setting it up on stones, gave rise to the name it now goes by, i. e. _Cloch-thogbail_, lifting or lifted stone.   J. R.
Hilltown Constabulary.

DUBLIN:

Printed and Published by P. D. Hardy, 3, Cecilia-street; to whom all communications are to be addressed.

THE
DUBLIN PENNY JOURNAL

CONDUCTED BY P. DIXON HARDY, M.R.I.A.

| VOL. III. | DECEMBER 13. 1834. | No. 124. |

GATE-HOUSES OF BALLYSAGGARTMORE CASTLE.

E. Hayden, del.   Engraved by Clayton

VIEW OF THE AVENUE LEADING TO BALLYSAGGARTMORE CASTLE.

BALLYSAGGARTMORE CASTLE, NEAR LISMORE.

Sir—Permit me through the medium of the Dublin Penny Journal an opportunity of giving the public a brief description of the situation and scenery of Ballysaggartmore, the much improved residence of Arthur Keiley, Esq. situate one mile west of Lismore, on the north side of the river Blackwater. The porter's lodge at the entrance to the avenue, is composed of cut mountain granite or freestone, of a whitish colour, variegated with a brownish strata, which gives the whole a rich and pleasing appearance; it consists of a double rectangular building, in the castellated style, flanked by a round tower at either end, through which is a passage, and a carriage-way of twelve feet in the centre, over which is a *perpendicular pointed* arch, enriched with crockets, and terminated with a finial; the buildings at either side of the gateway, although similar, form a variety in themselves; and the situation is so disposed as not to be seen until very near the approach: the gate is composed of wrought and cast iron; and is, I will venture to assert, the most perfect gothic structure, formed principally of wrought iron, in the kingdom.* It was executed by a native mechanic, and cost about one hundred and fifty pounds.

Passing onward through the avenue, the road, which is perfectly level, leads through a beautifully romantic wood, neatly planted with all the varieties of fir, and other forest timber; and is naturally enriched by a limpid mountain stream, which, after passing over some very considerable rocks, and gliding down the glen, falls immediately into the Blackwater; over this stream, which in winter is often very rapid, stands the bridge, of which the prefixed engraving is a correct representation, consisting of three gothic arches, surmounted with richly embrazured battlements. A group of towers, embracing almost every shape and style of Gothic architecture, is erected at either end of the bridge; and the roadway leads under two very pretty obtuse Gothic arches. The greatest novelty in the whole is a round tower, erected on one of the arches. The stone used in the building has an agreeable reddish tint, and is all *vermiculated*, or, in other words, is a rusticated structure, which gives it somewhat the appearance of antiquity; this and the gate-house, was designed and built under the inspection of Mr. John Smyth.

Almost adjoining the bridge is a pretty tunnel, through which a road is conducted from the town to the upper grounds; and the avenue, which leads onward to the house, has nothing more to boast of than a continuation of neatly disposed wood and shrubbery.

E. H.

INDIA, PRIOR TO THE BRITISH OCCUPATION.

Timour was justly denominated the "firebrand of the universe"—the greatest wholesale butcher that humanity ever heard of; he plundered and massacred without distinction of religion or sex, and his track was marked by blood, desolation, famine and pestilence. Aurungzebe was little better towards the Hindoos; Tippoo Snib circumcised all the Brahmins he could get hold of, and it is said sixty thousand Christians were subjected by him to the same operation. After Abdallah captured Delhi in 1761, he ordered a general massacre, which lasted seven days! his guards were not even then glutted with slaughter, but the stench of dead bodies drove them out of the city; a great part of the buildings were reduced to ashes, and thousands who escaped the sword suffered a lingering death by famine, sitting upon the ruins of their smoking tenements. Thus a city extending thirty-four miles in length, and containing *two millions* of inhabitants, became almost a heap of ruins. The historians of the day have handed down to posterity the most appalling description of human suffering, of women and men whipped naked through the streets with wanton tortures—citizens fleeing from their dearest friends, as from beasts of prey, for fear of being devoured amidst general starvation: women feeding on their own children, and infants sucking at the breasts of their deceased mothers; fire and sword seemed to contend for pre-eminence in the work of havoc and destruction; the work of war and blood was perpetual; human heads piled in pyramids, and the streets of cities and towns rendered impassable by heaps of slain; the country in many places exhibiting few signs of being inhabited, save in the bones of murdered bodies, and the smouldering ruins of villages and temples; all law and religion trodden under foot, bonds of private friendship as well as of society broken, and every individual, as if amidst a forest of wild beasts, could rely upon nothing but the strength of his own arm, or the deep villainy of his nature."—*British Colonies.*

YOUTHFUL HEROISM.

In one of the battles during the American war, 1777, Lieutenant Hervey, a youth of sixteen, received several wounds, and was repeatedly ordered off the field by the Lieutenant Colonel of his regiment; but the gallant lad would not leave the ground while he could stand, and see his brother-soldiers fighting beside him. A ball striking one of his legs, his removal became necessary; and in the act of conveying him away, another wounded him mortally. In this situation the surgeon recommended him to take a dose of opium, to avoid several hours of life of extreme torture. This he immediately consented to do; and when his Colonel entered the tent, with Major Harnage, who were both wounded, they asked whether he had any affairs they could settle for him? His reply was, that being a minor, every thing was already adjusted; but he had one request, which he retained just life enough to utter—"Tell my uncle (Adjutant-general Hervey) I died like a soldier."

THE BACHELOR AND THE HUSBAND.

I hate old bachelors on system,
I always have, and will resist 'em.
Ladies attend—your cause I plead—
And if, while these brief lines you read,
A blush of approbation rise,
Or a bright tear bedew your eyes,
That blush, that tear I proudly claim,
For they to me are more than fame.
What! wed—and be a slave for life!
Fettered by fondness!—vexed by strife!—
Yes—better 'tis in marriage bound,
Trace e'en in chains its narrow round,
Or peep through iron bars of home,
Than celibacy's desert roam,
Where barren boundless heaths extend,
Without a comfort or a friend.

Comfort! we're free—we do not need 'em.
But yours is the mere outlaw's freedom.
Snatching the fierce, unsocial joys,
Of Cherokees, or Chickesaws.
Like toad immured for many a year,
Breathing self's sullen atmosphere.
But he whom social feelings warm,
Whose bosom homebred raptures charm,
Who knows one dear companion shares
His happiness, and soothes his cares,
And reads, while tears delicious rise,
His history in his children's eyes.
By pity touched, his feelings flow,
Unfrozen by the chill of woe;
Though friendship cool, and fortune chide,
Still onward rolls the genial tide:
He feels what wealth can ne'er impart,
The yearnings of a softened heart.

* Indeed if the sketch of a Gothic gate, furnished by Mr. Loudon in his "Encyclopedia on Cottage and Villa Architecture," page 1004. fig. 1799, be the neatest he could adduce, as that at Ballysaggartmore far exceeds it, he should give it in his next edition.

PHENOMENON RESPECTING TIDES.

It has sometimes happened that tides have risen in various places to an unusual height, without any apparent adequate cause, deducible from the relative positions of the moon and the earth. The following is submitted as an explanation of this curious fact :—

If, from the extremities of any given portion of this habitable globe, two strong winds should continue to blow for any considerable time in opposite directions, (for instance, one to the north, and the other to the south,) it is manifest that *that part* of the atmosphere which is contained in the intermediate space, must, by this long continued subduction of its matter, be much lessened in density and weight, and of course the earth or water immediately below it sustain a relative smaller degree of pressure than usual. Now, the quantity of air withdrawn by these contrary winds must necessarily add to the weight of the atmosphere in those places towards which it has been carried. Suppose it, therefore, to press with this additional weight on that part of the ocean on which it rests ; much water will of course recede from thence to that portion of the sea which had been lightened of so much of its incumbent atmosphere. It will be impelled hither from two distinct points, by two contrary impulses—viz, from north and south. If this event should happen about the time of high tide, the swell of the sea will be enormous. The mercury will of course sink at the time and place of these unusually high tides ; for the air, lessened of its weight and pressure, becomes unable to support it at its average height. Succeeding storms may, in such cases, be expected —for the reflux of the air into that part of the atmosphere which had been stripped of so large a portion of its elastic matter, must be rapid in the extreme, and of course generate tempests and whirlwinds. That contrary currents of air frequently prevail in the atmosphere, at the same time and place, is manifest from the rapid carry of the clouds, which are often seen moving towards diametrically opposite points of the heavens.

THE COCOA-NUT TREE OF CEYLON, ITS VARIOUS USES.

" From Columbo to Tangalle, a distance of one hundred miles along the sea-shore, plantations of cinnamon amidst groves of cocoa-nut trees, skirt the whole coast for ten miles from the bordering of the tide, which laves the very roots of those graceful and indispensable palms, the cocoa-nut being, in reality, the most valuable product of the island. I recollect hearing in Ceylon an enumeration of ninety-nine distinct articles made from this tree ; among the principal were—1. *Arrack* (the spirit under this name, made from the cocoa-nut blossom, is far superior to the Batavian arrack, made from Rice), which is distilled from the sweet juice of the incised flower-stock, termed, 2. "*Toddy*," in itself a delicious wholesome beverage, when drank fresh drawn before the morning sun has caused fermentation to commence. 3. *Jaghery*, a coarse, strong-grained, but peculiar flavoured sugar, (well adapted for crystilization, or refining in England), made in abundance from toddy. 4. *Vinegar*, equal to any made from white wine, also prepared from the toddy, and used in making exquisite 5. *Pickles* from the young shoots. 6. *Coir* or ropes, so strong and elastic, and having the peculiar property of being best preserved for use in sea water ; (hence their adaptation for mooring, and other purposes, to which they are now applied in Mauritius harbour and elsewhere, as also for running rigging in the Indian shipping.) 7. Brushes and brooms of various descriptions.— 8. Matting of excellent quality. 9. Rafters for houses. 10. Oil of much value, and now used in England for candles as well as lamps. 11. Gutters or waterspouts, or conveyances, for which the hollow stem or trunk is so well adapted. 12. Thatching for the peasantry ; the shady broad leaf being admirably suited for the purpose. To particularize further, would, however, be tedious, suffice it to say, that the natives of the Maldive islands send an annual embassy to Ceylon, the boats conveying whom are entirely prepared from this tree, the persons composing the embassy, clothed and fed on its products, and the numerous presents for the governor of Ceylon, are all manufactured from this queen of the palms"—*Martin's British Colonies.*

LUIDHEAUN CRUADHTAN FOR DHIOM-HAOINEAS.*

Some few years since, amongst many passengers that landed from a Liverpool vessel, after a rough voyage, was a sun-burned, well-looking man, seemingly about forty ; on coming on shore, he fervently thanked God for again finding himself on Irish ground, adding, that he had trod many a weary step with a heavy heart since he had left it. He accompanied the rest of the voyagers to one of the best inns—the term *hotel* was not then used. On arriving there the head waiter glanced at him with the supercilious expression that is not uncommon even now amongst those gentry—the brethren of the knife and fork—when they suppose the person cannot satisfy their rapacity, and turned him over to the care of an underling, a fine lad. The stranger ordered dinner, and a retired room ; and, after dinner, desired the attendant to bring whiskey, lemons, &c., to make punch ; saying, it was a long time since he had tasted his native liquor. "Come, my boy, here is a glass of wine for you ; you have attended me well, but I am sorry to see one so young in your situation—a bad school for you, how old are you ?"

" Fifteen, *if you please, Sir,* next Michaelmas."

" Ah, my !" exclaimed the stranger with a sigh ; " young, indeed, to be left to yourself ; have you no friend that could do better for you ?"

" My mother is living here also."

" Your mother—that is well ; no doubt she is careful of you ; and your father—where is he ?"

" I never saw him, Sir. My mother says he is dead," replied the lad in confusion.

The stranger concluded from the boy's manner that he was illegitimate, and asked no further. When left to himself he began to think over the events of his past life, and few pass such a retrospect without mixed sensations of weal and wee. " I have had my trials," said he, " who is without them ? God be praised for all !—here I am again, a richer man than ever I could have expected to have been ; and sweet is the wealth that has been acquired innocently, by honest fair labour, under the help of God. I have now but one wish to have gratified ; but on that hangs all my future happiness. If she be dead or married, what will become of me ? yet if ever woman was to be trusted it was herself."

Time passed unheeded, as the stranger mused on his own affairs, till the clock striking eleven, roused him.— "Come, there's no use in thinking ; a night's rest will do me more good than all my waking thoughts. I will ring for the little waiter ; I like that lad, and must not lose sight of him if my own matters go on well. He has a handsome Irish face, with all the freshness of youth and innocence. Alas ! I have not seen such for a long time ; yet his features are familiar to me too, though I cannot remember who I have seen like him ; in a dream, perhaps"—here the lad entered, rubbing his eyes.

" Did you ring, Sir ?"

" Ay, my poor child, I have kept you up too long ; but all shall be settled tomorrow. Is my luggage in my room ?"

" Yes, Sir, and a good fire there."

" Well, my boy, show me the way."

The housemaid, a handsome woman, was settling the luggage as the stranger entered ;" the lad left the light on the table and withdrew ; the housemaid was about to follow—

" That waiter is a fine lad ; who is he ?"

" My son, please your honour ; and, though I say it, a better boy never lived, goodness be praised for it."

" Your son," said the stranger, looking sharply at her ;

---

* Hardship attends idleness.

" why you seem too young to be his mother; you are then married ?"

"I am—I was," she replied with a sigh, and moved towards the door.

"Stop a minute; the lad is like you: is he also like his father ?"

Instead of replying, she asked whether he wanted any thing more in his room, and was again leaving it.

"Not in such haste," said the stranger; "nay, don't be alarmed. I have taken a fancy to your son, would you let him go with me ? I would be careful of him as my own."

"Thank your honour kindly."

"What is your name ?"

"Jessy Mahony."

The stranger started; but recovering, asked in a faint voice—

"Is that your husband's name ?"

"It is: and a good husband he was; of a poor man, a better never lived."

"I knew one Mick Mahony abroad, perhaps he was your husband."

"Oh, that I could say it was! but that is *unpossible*; I saw his corpse after he was drowned; oh, could I have but one sight of my Mick again, I could die happy."

The stranger caught her in his arms. "Dear Jessy, I am your Mick Mahony. I was not drowned; but Peter Dunne was, that trapped me on board the trading vessel. He took my clothes; but God is just; and Peter got so drunk with the money he got for kidnapping an able seaman, such as I was then, that he tumbled into the Liffey. I saw him fall. Meanwhile Jessy pondered over what she had heard, and knew not what to think. The corpse was in her husband's clothes, but so disfigured from lying in the water, that otherwise she could not have thought it her husband; but then there was no account of him; and the circumstance of a body being found of her husband's size, coloured hair, and in his clothes, made her certain that her poor Mick had perished. She glanced at herself in the mirror. "I might be known for the wife Mick left;" she thought, "but can this strange coloured man, with white hair, be my clean-skinned, black-haired, youthful Mick? Though my heart warms to him, I will be cautious. It's not long since Biddy Casey was tricked by a man that set up for her husband, just returned from foreign parts ?" Mick Mahony seemed to understand his wife's scruples, and thought how he could remove them.

"Why woman, have you forgotten all your Irish, that I taught you when we were courting, and you but a slip of a girl; do you forget how often you and lame Joan would try to keep me from my work to give you a lesson ?"

"I do, I do remember it well, but what did you say to us when you wanted to put off my lesson till evening, when your work would be finished ?"

"*Luidheaun cruadhtan for dhiomhaoineas*," said he eagerly.

"My own *darlint* Mick, and no other," exclaimed Jessy, transported with joy.

HIBERNICUS.

"FRIENDSHIP'S OFFERING."

We have often been astonished, while turning over the pages of the Annuals, that among them all we should meet with so little good poetry, and that the prose pieces should so very generally be without real merit. It would appear, indeed, as though the editors of by far the greater number of them, depended for their success on the excellence of the pictorial department. Now we really cannot see why this should be the case: an entire year is allowed for the selection—and surely, if it were sought for, there would be found talent sufficient to supply the demand of even a greater number of annuals than are now published. We must not be misunderstood, however, as directing our observations to the work before us; on the contrary, we have not in any of the next year's annuals, which we have yet looked into, observed as much of what may be truly termed poetry, as is to be found among the pieces in the "Friendship's Offering;" and while to this we add,

that one or two of the stories are good, and that several of the plates are really beautiful, it will be seen that we award it a high place amongst its competitors for popular favour. The "Client's Story," by no means the worst tale in the volume, is, it will be perceived, imitative, or at least very much in the style of the stories of a Physician in Blackwood. It wants, however, the vigour and feeling of the writer in *Maga*. The following is a fair specimen of the poetry. The engraving from which our wood-cut is taken is very effective:

THORNY-BANK FARM.

About a mile from the king's highway, stood
A pretty farm-house, half embowered in wood.
In front were corn-fields, and behind a grove
Of beech, whose murmurs told the cushat's love;
On this side was the farm-yard, and on that,—
Some fifty yards beyond a verdant plat—
A pond for goose and duckling; there they swam
Down to the sluice which filled the miller's dam—
The snowy gander, with a swan-like pride,
And mother-goose, with goslings by her side.
The roof was thatch, by osiers interlaced;
With climbing shrubs the lattices were graced;
And whoso looked and saw the smoke ascend,
Thought almost how this earth with heaven might blend;
For industry was blessed with sweet increase,
And Love made there abode with plenty and with peace.

James Fleming had two daughters, Jess and Jane:
And, with such treasure, how could he complain,
Although no stalwart son was his, to heir
Paternal fields and in his labours share.
Small had his outset been, when he, on life
Just entered, took Maud Turnbull for his wife;
And now some thirty years had passed away,
On either head the tresses waxing grey,
While sprang beneath their eyes these daughters fair
In age unequal, but a handsome pair,
Loved with o'erflowing love, and nursed with tender care

When life was young with me, a school-boy gay,
There spent I many an autumn holiday;
And roaming idly, mind and body free,
Figured what Paradise of old might be—
As to the evening woodland came along
The reaper's carol, and the milkmaid's song;
While, overhead, the green ancestral trees
Shook their broad branches to the cooling breeze.
Then, home returning, round the cheerful hearth
We gathered, old and young, in smiling mirth,
To listen to the tale, or legend old,
Of love-lorn damsel, or of outlaw bold,
Of burial aisle, and phantom with its shroud,
Which all believing, Jane would read aloud,
For she was younger, and we closer drew,
As through the pane the night-breeze drearier blew,
Then to our sleep went panting; every sound
Seeming to say that spectres flitted round !

Last autumn—now my hairs are sprent with grey—,
To Thorny-Bank alone I bent my way,
And gazed around. No Thorny-Bank was there—
But a trim mansion, with its gay parterre
And painted rails;—the pond was now a lake;
And classic swan succeeded homely drake;
Improvement stood on tiptoe stiff and starch,
And here indeed her walk had been a march.
—And ask ye for the Flemings—where were they,
My kind protectors in life's early day ?
All gone—A tombstone in the field of graves,
By whose neglected side the nettle waves,
Tells where and when the honest Flemings bade
Adieu to life, and here their dwelling made.
Jess also sleeps beside them; soon or late
Death comes, and hers was an untimely fate:
She never had been strong—and oft the bloom
On woman's cheek speaks louder of the tomb
Than rosy health ;—'twas so with her : decay
Marked her an early, and an easy prey;
For slighted love lent, too, a poisoned dart,
And a frail frame contained a broken heart.

Jane—once the household pet—had linked her lot
With one whom worldly fortune favoured not,
So, after years of struggle, toil, and care,
With children five, the love-united pair,
With wreck of substance forced afar to roam,
In wild Canadian forests sought a home.

Thus Thorny-Bank is Thorny-Bank no more:
Yet vagrant fancy sees it as of yore,
With its old inmates.—Times have changed, and I,
Like my old friends, must shortly look to die;
Nor leave, like them, more during trace behind
Than dew on herb, or music on the wind !

Δ

THORNY-BANK FARM.

THE CLIENT'S STORY.
BY THE AUTHOR OF "SPAIN IN 1830."

It was late one Saturday evening in December, when I received a letter, which, on opening, I found to be from Walter Moreton: and the purport of the letter was, to request my immediate presence at Cambridge, in the capacity both of a friend and of a lawyer. The letter concluded thus : " Do not delay your journey many hours after receiving this. My urgency will be explained by the change you will perceive in yours, Walter Moreton."

I had known Walter Moreton in youth, and in manhood : we had been intimate, without having been altogether friends ; and the attraction which his company possessed for me, arose rather from the shrewdness of his remarks than from any sympathy of feeling betwixt us. Of late years, I had seen comparatively little of Moreton : I knew that he had married ; that he had been in straightened circumstances ; that his father-in-law had died, and had left a large fortune to his wife ; that she had died, and left him a rich widower ; that he had married a second time, and that he was now the father of three children. From the tenor of the letter I had received, I could scarcely doubt that Walter Moreton had been seized with some dangerous illness, and was desirous of settling his worldly affairs. My old intimacy with Moreton would of itself have prompted me to obey his summons ; but the requirement of my professional aid of course increased the celerity of my obedience. Early next morning, therefore, I put myself into the Cambridge Coach ; and after dispatching a hasty dinner at the Hoop, I walked to Walter Moreton's house in Trumpington-street.

I was prepared for a change, but not certainly such a change as that which presented itself. Walter Moreton could not have been forty, but he seemed a broken-down man ; grey haired, thin visaged, and cadaverous. His expression too was changed ; there was an uneasy restlessness in his eye ; his lips had grown thin ; and he appeared moreover, to be under the influence of extreme nervousness.

He received me with apparent kindness ; thanked me for my ready compliance with his wish ; and informed me at once that he had need of my professional services in the disposal of his property ; but I had no difficulty in perceiving, from a certain reserve and distractedness of manner, that something beyond the mere making of a will had brought me to Cambridge. I did not of course make any observation upon the change which I observed in his appearance ; but expressed a hope that his desire for my professional assistance had not arisen from any apprehensions as to the state of his health ; to which he only replied, that his health was not worse than usual, but that it was always well to be prepared ; and he added, " Come, Thornton, let us to business ;" and to business we went.

I need scarcely say, that I was prepared for instructions to divide the father's fortune according to some rule of division—or, perhaps, of some capricious preference, among his children—two sons and one daughter, children yet of a tender age—and to secure a life-rent interest to his wife. Great, therefore, was my surprise when Mr. Moreton, after mentioning a few trifling legacies, named, as the sole successors of his immense fortune, two individuals unknown to me, and of whose connexion with the testator I was entirely ignorant.

I laid down my pen, and looked up :—" Mr. Moreton," said I, hesitatingly, " you have a wife and children !"

" I have children," said he ; " but God preserve them from the curse of wealth that does not belong to them."

" Moreton—Walter Moreton," said I, " you are over scrupulous. I know, indeed, that this large fortune b' come to you through your first wife; but it was her's to give; she became the sole heiress of her father, when his three sons of a former marriage were unfortunately drowned in the ——"

"Hush, Thornton!" interrupted he hastily; and in a tone so altered and so singular that it would have startled me, had I not at the moment been looking in his face, and seen the expression that passed over it, and the convulsive shudder that shook his whole frame. I perceived there was a mystery, and I resolved to be at the bottom of it.

"Moreton," said I, rising and approaching him, and laying my hand gently on his shoulder, which slightly shrunk from my touch. "We were once companions, —almost friends; as a friend, as well as a lawyer, you have sent for me. There is some mystery here, of which I am sure it was your intention to disburden yourself. Whatever the secret be, it is safe with me. But I tell you plainly, that if you are resolved to make beggars of your innocent children without giving a sufficient reason for it, some other than Charles Thornton must be the instrument of doing it.

"Thornton," said he, in a grave tone, and without raising his eyes—"there is a mystery—a fearful mystery; and it shall be told this night. That done, neither you nor any man can be the friend of Walter Moreton; but he will have no occasion for friendship. Reach me some wine, Thornton, and pour it out for me; my nerves are shattered—another glass—now, sit down—no, not there —ay, ay—one other glass, Thornton."

I took my place in a large high-backed chair, as Walter Moreton directed me; and he, placing himself a little out of my view, spoke as follows:

"It is now upwards of ten years, as you know, Thornton, since I married my first wife, the daughter of Mr. Bellenden—old Bellenden the lawyer. She, you also know, was the child of a former marriage—and that the large fortune of my father-in-law which in the end came— no matter how—to me, belonged to him, or rather to his three sons, in right of his second wife, who was also dead at the time of my marriage. I could not have indulged any expectation that this fortune would ever reach me; for although I knew very well that, failing my wife's three half brothers, it came entirely into her father's power, yet there could be no ground for any reasonable expectation that three healthy boys would die off, and make way for Agnes. Mark me, Thornton, I did not marry for money; and the thought of the succession which afterwards opened, never entered into my mind. I will tell you, Thornton, the first occasion on which the hope dawned upon me. There was an epidemic in this part of the country; and my father-in-law's three sons were seized with it at one time. All the three were in the most imminent danger; and one evening when the disease was at its height, and when my wife seemed greatly distressed at receiving a message that it was doubtful if any of the three would survive till morning—'And if they should die;' said I, within myself! This supposition constantly recurred—and was so willingly entertained that I lay awake the whole of that night, planning within myself the disposal of this large inheritance; forgetting, at the time, that another life, that of my father-in-law, stood betwixt us and the succession. Next morning, however, a favourable change took place, and eventually the three youths recovered: but so strong a hold had the hopes, which had been thus suddenly created, taken of my mind, that in place of their being dissipated by the event, which naturally deprived them of any foundation they ever had, I was not only conscious of the keenest disappointment, but felt as if an untoward accident had defrauded me of something that was all but within my reach. 'How near I have been to affluence,' was a constantly recurring thought; and when I heard every morning, that this person was dead, and that person was dead, a feeling of chagrin was invariably felt. You are perhaps incapable of understanding these feelings, Thornton; and so was I, until the events took place which gave birth to them."

Moreton paused a moment; but I did not interrupt him; and, after passing his hand over his forehead, and filling out with an unsteady hand another glass of wine, he proceeded:

"You must understand, Thornton, that these were mere thoughts, feelings, fancies: if I had stood beside the sick beds of these boys, when the flame of life was flickering, I would not have blown it out; if two phials had stood by, one containing health and the other death, do not suppose I would have administered the latter.— no; I was no murderer, Thornton, no murderer—then!

"You know something of the river here; and of the passion for boating. The three boys often indulged in this exercise; and it sometimes happened that I accompanied them. One day about the end of August, we had spent the day at Eel-pits, and it was not far from sunset when we set out to row back to Cambridge. It was a fine calm evening when we left that place, but it soon began to rain heavily; and in the scramble for cloaks and umbrellas, which the suddenness and heaviness of the shower occasioned, the boat was all but upset; but it righted again, and served only as matter of mirth to the boys: though in me a very different effect was produced. More than a year had elapsed since the presence of the epidemic had given rise to the feelings I have already confessed to, and the circumstance had been nearly— but not altogether forgotten. At that moment, however, the thoughts that at that time had continually haunted me recurred with tenfold force. 'If it had upset!' I said within myself, while sitting silent in the stern—'If it had upset!' and the prospect of wealth again opened before me. The three boys, Thornton, were sitting shouting, and laughing, and jesting, and I sat silently in the stern, putting that question to myself. But it was only a thought, a fancy, Thornton; I knew that no one but myself could swim; but any thing premeditated was as far from my thoughts as yours. I only contemplated the probable results of an event which was nearly taking place.

"Well—we continued to row; and it soon fell dusk— and the moon rose; and we continued to ascend the river—ours the only boat upon it—till we were within less than two miles of Cambridge. I had occasionally taken a turn at the oar; but at that time I sat in the stern; and still something continually whispered to me, 'if the boat had upset!' I need not tell you, Thornton, that little things influence the greatest events; one of those little things occurred at this moment. I had a dog in the boat, and one of the boys said something to it in Latin. 'Don't speak Latin to the dog,' said another, 'for its master does not understand Latin.' 'Yes he does,' said the eldest, 'Mr. Moreton understands dog Latin.' This was a little matter, Thornton, but it displeased me. There was always a good deal of assumption of superiority, especially on the part of the eldest, on account of his university education; and little annoyances of this kind were frequent. It was precisely at this moment that something dark was seen floating towards us: it chanced to come just in the glimpse of the moon on the water, and was seen at once by us all; and as it approached nearer, till it was about to pass within an oar's length of the boat.——You have heard the story, Thornton— you said, if I recollect, that you knew the three boys were"——Here Moreton suddenly stopped, and hastily drained the wine he had filled out.

"Drowned in the Cam," said I: "yes I knew of this misfortune; but I did not know that you were present."

"I was—I was—present!" said Moreton, laying a peculiar emphasis on the word. "Ay, Thornton, you've hit the word—I was present—but listen. I told you the dark object floated within an oar's length of the boat; at once the three boys made a spring to the side of the boat, extending arms and oars to intercept it; and—in an instant the boat was keel uppermost!"

Moreton pronounced the last words rapidly, and in an under tone, and stopped; he raised the wine-decanter from the table, but let it drop again. Moreton had yet said nothing to criminate himself: the incident appeared, from his narrative, purely accidental; and I therefore said, "Well, Moreton, the boys were unhappily drowned; but it was the consequence of their own imprudence."

"Thornton," said he, "you are there to hear a confession; I am here to make it: 'tis of no use shrinking from it: fill me a glass of wine, for my hand trembles. Now, two of the boys, the two youngest, I never saw, as God is my judge, I believe if I had seen the youngest, I would have done my uttermost to save him. I suppose they sank beneath the boat, and floated down below the surface. The eldest, he rose close to me; we were not twenty yards from the bank; I could have saved him.— I believe I *would* have saved him, if he had cried for help. I saw him but for a moment. I think, when I struck out to swim, I kicked him beneath the water—undesignedly Thornton, undesignedly : but I did not turn round to help him; I made for the bank, and reached it—and it was then too late. I saw the ripple on the water, and the boat floating away ; but nothing else. Thornton, I am his murderer !"

When Moreton had pronounced this word, he seemed to be somewhat relieved, and paused. I imagined his communication had ended; and I ventured to say that although it was only justice that the inheritance which had become his should revert to the heirs of those who had been deprived of it—supposing them to have been deprived of it by his act—it was proper to consider the matter coolly ; for there was such a thing as an over sensitive conscience ; and it was, perhaps, possible that, in the peculiar circumstances attending the awful event, his mind had been incapable of judging correctly; that he might have too much coupled the fancies which had preceded the event, with the event itself; and that want of presence of mind might have been mistaken for something more criminal. I confess that, in speaking thus, although I believed such reasoning might in some cases be correctly applied, I had little hope that it was so in the present case. There was a deliberateness in the mode of Moreton's confession that almost commanded belief; and besides, Moreton was no creature of imagination. He had always been a shrewd and strong-minded man : and was in fact, all his life, a man of realities.

"Oh, no, Thornton," said he, "I am no fancier: believe it to be as I have told you. But if you ever could have doubted, as I do not believe you do, your doubts would have been dispelled by what you have yet to hear. I am not going to give you a narrative of my life ; and shall say nothing of the time that immediately followed the event I have related. The fortune became my father-in-law's; and my wife became an heiress. But my present circumstances were no wise changed. Brighter prospects led to increased expences; and embarrassments thickened around me. You know something of these, Thornton; and tried, as you recollect, ineffectually, to extricate me from them. Meanwhile, my father-in-law, who speedily got over the loss he had sustained, spoke of his daughter—of Agnes, my wife—as a great heiress, and boasted and talked much of his wealth, though it made no difference in his mode of living. 'Not one shilling, Walter, till I die,'—was constantly in his mouth : and not a shilling, indeed, did he ever offer, although he well knew the pressing difficulties in which we were placed. I once, and only once ventured to ask him for some advance; but the answer was the same. 'Not a shilling, Walter, till I die : patience, patience—it must all go to Agnes.'

"Must I confess it, Thornton? yes—I may confess any thing after what I have already confessed. The words, 'not a shilling till I die,' were continually in my ears.— The event that had placed fortune within my power frequently recurred to my memory : and with it, the conviction that I was no way benefitted by it : the nearer vicinity of wealth only made the want of it more tantalizing. The 'ifs,' and fancies, that had formerly so frequently arisen in my mind, had all been realised. The crime—ay, Thornton, the crime—that had placed an inheritance within my view, seemed the blacker since no advantage had attended it : and the oft-repeated 'not a shilling till I die,' repeated, and repeated with a complacent chuckle, and on occasions the most inopportune, begot within me an insatiable longing for—ay, why mince the matter ?—for the moment when the saying should be fulfilled.

"You recollect very well, Thornton, my application to you in December, 182—, six years ago You recollect its extreme urgency, and the partial success which attended it, sufficient, however, to keep me from a jail. You might well, as you did, express your surprise that my wife's father should suffer such a state of things to be; but he could suffer any thing, save parting with his money —he was a miser—the love of riches had grown with

their possession ; and, I believe, he would have suffered me to rot in jail rather than draw upon his coffers.

"It was just at this time, or at most a week or two subsequent to it, that Mr. Bellenden was attacked by a complaint to which he had been long subject—one requiring the most prompt medical aid ; but from which, on several former occasions, he had perfectly recovered. Agnes was extremely attentive to her father ; and on Christmas evening, as we were both on the way to the sick-chamber, we met the family surgeon leaving the house.

"'You are, perhaps, going to spend some time with my patient ?' said Mr. Amwell.

"'My husband,' said Agnes, 'means to spend an hour or two with my father : I have a particular engagement at present, and am only going to ask how he does.'

"'I have some little fears of another attack,' said Mr. Amwell ; 'do not be alarmed, my dear madam, we know how to treat these things ; promptness is all that is required. It will be necessary, my dear Sir,' said Mr. Amwell, addressing me, ' to lose no time in sending for me, should Mr. Bellenden experience another attack ; all depends upon the prompt and free use of the lancet. There is no occasion for any alarm, madam. The good old gentleman may live to eat twenty Christmas dinners yet.'

"Mr. Amwell passed on, and we entered the house, and ascended to the sick chamber. My wife remained but a few minutes—she had some particular engagements at home : and as she left the room, she charged me to lose not a moment in calling Mr. Amwell, should there appear to be any occasion for his aid. She shut the door, and I seated myself in a large chair near to the bed.

"Mine was a singular situation. I, who for many years had had my hopes directed towards a great inheritance—I, who had seen, and rejoiced to see, the most formidable obstacles removed, and who had myself been instrumental in removing them, was now watching the sick bed of the only individual who stood between me and the succession—an individual too, whose death I had looked forward to and had allowed myself to hope for. I could not help smiling at the singular situation in which I was placed ; and as I looked towards the sick bed, and heard only the uneasy breathing of the old man in the silence of the room, I felt—very like a criminal.

"There was a table near to me with several phials upon it. I took them up one by one, and examined them. One was labelled, ' laudanum.' While I held it in my hand, all the demon was within. My pecuniary difficulties seemed to augment ; the excellence of wealth to increase ; the love of enjoyment grew stronger; and my estimate of the value of an old man's life weaker. At this moment, the sick man asked for drink. Thornton ! —need I hesitate to confess that I was strongly tempted— but I resisted the temptation ; I held the fatal phial for a few moments in my hand ; laid it down, pushed it from me, and assisted the old man to his needs. But no sooner had I done this, and reseated myself, than I began to accuse myself of inconsistency. These, thought I, are distinctions without any real difference. A youth, who stood betwixt me and fortune, was drowning; and I did not stretch out my hand to save him : there are many kinds of murder, but in all the crime is the same.

"I had nearly proved to my own satisfaction that I was a fool, when certain indications that could not be mistaken assured me that Mr. Amwell's fears were about to be realised, and they instantly were, to the fullest extent. Mr. Amwell's parting words recurred to me : ' all depends upon the prompt use of the lancet.' My heart beat quick ; I rose—hesitated—re-seated myself—rose again—listened—again sat down—pressed my fingers on my ears that I might hear nothing—and leaned my head forward on the table. I continued in this posture for some time, and then started up, and listened. All was silent ; I rang the bell violently ; opened the door, and cried out to call Mr. Amwell instantly, and returned to the chamber—which I believed to be no longer a chamber of sickness, but of death ; and re-seated myself in the chair, with a strong persuasion that the last obstacle fortune had been removed. But, Thornton, again I knew that I was, a second time, a murderer!"

Here, Mr. Moreton paused, and leaned back in his chair, apparently exhausted. I again thought his communication had ended; and although I could not now address him as I had addressed him before, I was beginning to say that to make absolute beggars of his children could not be an acceptable atonement for crime—when he interrupted me, heedless, apparently, of my having addressed him.

"In a few minutes, Mr. Amwell entered the room. He approached the bed, bent over it, turned to me, and said, 'I fear it is too late, Mr. Moreton.'

"'Perhaps not,' said I; 'at all events make the attempt.'

"Mr. Amwell of course did make the attempt; and in a few moments desisted; shook his head, and said, 'A little, and I have reason to believe only a very little too late,' and in a few minutes I was again left alone.

"Thornton, since that hour, I have been a miserable man."—Another long pause ensued, which I did not attempt to break; and Moreton at length resumed.

"Since that hour, I say, Charles Thornton, I have never known a moment's peace. My wife's tears for her father fell upon my heart like drops of fire; every look she gave me seemed to read my innermost thoughts; she never spoke that I did not imagine she was about to call me murderer. Her presence became agony to me. I withdrew from her, and from all society—for I thought every man looked suspiciously upon me; and I had no companion but conscience—ay, conscience, Thornton—conscience that I thought I had overcome; as well I might, for had I not seen the young and healthy sink, when I might have saved? and how could I have believed that ?......but so it was, and is: look at me, and you will see what conscience has made of me. Agnes sickened, and, as you know, died. This I felt as a relief; and for a time I breathed more freely; and I married again. But my old feelings returned, and life every day becomes more burdensome to me. Strange, that events long passed become more and more vivid—but so it is. The evening on the Cam, and the death-chamber of old Bellenden, are alternately before me.

"Now, Thornton, you have heard all. Are you now ready to frame the will as I directed? I am possessed of a quarter of a million, and it belongs to the heirs of those for whom it was originally destined."

Some conversation here ensued, in which my object was to show that, although the large property at Moreton's disposal ought never to have been his, yet, if the events which he had related had not taken place, it never could have come into the possession of those for whom he now destined it. I admitted, however, the propriety of the principle of restitution to the branches of the family in which it had originally been vested, but prevailed with Mr. Moreton, in having a competency reserved for his own children and for his wife, who married in the belief that he was able to provide for her. And upon these principles, accordingly, the testament was framed and completed the same evening.

It grew late. "Walter Moreton," said I, rising to take leave, "let this subject drop for ever. When we meet again, let there be no allusion to the transactions of this evening."

"Thornton," said he, "we shall never meet again."

"There are remedies, my friend," said I—for could I refuse to call the wretched man before me, friend?—"there are remedies for the accusations of conscience: apply yourself to them; if the mind were relieved by religious consolations, bodily health would return. You are yet little past the prime of life; I trust we may meet again in happier circumstances. Conscience, Moreton, is not given to us to kill, but to cure."

Moreton faintly smiled. "Yes, Thornton," said he, "There are remedies; I know them, and will not fail to seek their aid. Good night!"

I returned to the inn, and soon after retired to bed; as may easily be believed, to think of the singular revelations of the evening. For some time these thoughts kept me awake; but at length I fell asleep. My dreams were disturbed, and all about Walter Moreton. Sometimes he was swimming in the river, or standing on the bank pointing with his finger to a human head that was just sinking; sometimes he was sitting by the bed-side of old Bellenden, examining the phials, and walking on tiptoe to the door, and listening; and sometimes the scene of the past evening was renewed, when I sat and listened to his narrative. Then again, he had a phial in his hand, and uncorked it; and in raising it to his mouth, it seemed to be a small pistol, and just at this moment I awoke.

The last scene remained forcibly and vividly on my mind. It instantly occurred to me that he might have meditated suicide, and that that was the remedy of which he spoke. I looked at my watch; it was an hour past midnight. I hastily dressed, and hurried to Trumpington-street. There was a light in one of the windows. I knocked gently at the door; and at the same time applied my hand to the knob, which yielded. I hurried up stairs, directed by the situation of the light I had seen, and entered the room. Moreton stood near to the bed, beside a small table; a phial was in his hand, which at the moment I entered, he laid down. I sprang forward and seized it. It was already empty. "Ah, my friend!" said I—but farther speech was useless. Moreton was already in the grasp of death.

ANCIENT STONE OR FLAG.

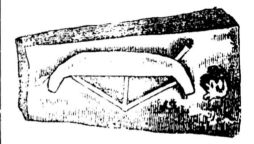

The above is a correct representation of an ancient stone or flag, in the graveyard of the abbey of Selskar, (a drawing of which appeared in the Journal some weeks since,) on the surface of which some hieroglyphics are pourtrayed. It may be seen by the drawing that a piece is broken off the end of the stone; the upper figure seems to represent a man's head, and it is probable that the other is a bark or vessel, with which the individual, whose remains it once covered, had likely some connexion.

P. M. O.

Wexford, 1834,

HEARTBURN.

This is an uneasy sensation of heat about the pit of the stomach; sometimes attended with flatulence and difficulty of breathing, with retching. It generally proceeds either from bile, debility of the stomach, or a too frequent use of acid food, which ferments on the stomach. Those, therefore, who are subject to heartburn should avoid all fat substances, acids, &c. Violent exercise, after a full meal, is also injurious. If it arises from indigestion, a dose of rhubarb will be necessary, and afterwards the Peruvian bark, or any stomachic bitter infused in wine or brandy, and taken as a strengthener. When the disorder arises from acidity in the stomach, two teaspoonfuls of magnesia in a cup of mint-water will generally alleviate the pain; but a larger dose will not be hurtful, should that not prove sufficient.

DUBLIN:

Printed and Published by P. D. HARDY, 3, Cecilia Street; to whom all communications are to be addressed.

Sold by all Booksellers in Ireland.

In London, by Richard Groombridge, 6, Panyer-alley, Paternoster-row; in Liverpool, by Wilmer and Smith; in Manchester, by Ambery; in Birmingham, by Drake; in Glasgow, by John Macleod; and in Edinburgh, by N. Bowack.

THE

DUBLIN PENNY JOURNAL

CONDUCTED BY P. DIXON HARDY, M.R.I.A.

| Vol. III. | DECEMBER 20, 1834. | No. 129. |

A SWISS COTTAGE.

Who that has heard of the scenery of Switzerland, of its serrated mountains—here piercing the clouds, and wearing an eternal covering of snow—and at a little distance overhanging some romantic valley, clad in nature's richest verdure, and decked with many a rustic cottage, but has longed to see some of those scenes of happiness and peace so glowingly described by former, and even by recent travellers. The above engraving, we have reason to conclude, is a faithful representation of a Swiss Cottage. We have copied it from a beautiful engraving on steel, which stands as a vignette to a work in course of publication,* descriptive of scenery in Switzerland, and from which we quote the following lively sketch of the general character and condition of the inhabitants, and of the scenes which first present themselves to view, as the traveller, quitting the fertile plains of France, and following the highly picturesque passage of the Jura, enters the cantons of Switzerland.

"Whoever has travelled much," says the author, "and compared the various attractions presented to him in the course of his peregrinations, will generally be found to admit that if there be any country that merits more attention than the rest, *that* country is SWITZERLAND. He may have traversed the fertile plains of Italy, and become familiar with the vestiges of her ancient grandeur : he may have coasted the "shipless shores" of Greece, and felt his mind kindling with enthusiasm, while he dwelt

upon those scenes and associations which have thrown such hallowing lustre over her soil and history ; but in both, the contemplation is more or less tinted with melancholy, and the proud memorials of the past exhibited in humiliating contrast with the present. In both the human mind, half divested of its original attributes, groans under the pressure of despotism, or expends its once elastic spirit in trivial pursuits and occupations. Every where he deplores the degradation of intellect, the traces of ungovernable passions, and the baneful influences of a grovelling superstition. This, indeed, may admit of many isolated exceptions both in districts and individuals—the rule, nevertheless, is general. But quitting these, let the traveller enter Switzerland by what point he may, how different is the picture which engages his contemplation ! Here the energies of the human mind are presented to him in full operation. Every where he observes the regenerating influence of freedom ; the equal protection of rights and extension of privileges ; an equable distribution of the public burdens ; a strong practical morality ; an unwearied industry, and love of independence ; united with a patriotism which, from its very intensity, has become proverbial. Here the peasant, fearing no avaricious lord, no spiritual inquisitor, enjoys the fruits of his labour in peace, sweetened and improved by the free and full toleration of his religion.

"Although subdivided into so many cantons, and inhabited by a people who present so many distinct features in their customs, dress, religion, language, and municipal laws, Switzerland, nevertheless, furnishes ample proof

* Switzerland, by William Beattie, M. D. Illustrated by W. H. Bartlett, Esq.
VOL. III.—NO. 25.

that she is actuated by one sole pervading spirit; where every canton contributes with friendly emulation to improve her domestic policy, and to strengthen her political relations. Here, commerce is fast extending her ramifications—a process which is greatly facilitated by the medium of her lakes and rivers. Her towns appear like so many national hives, where science, arts, and mechanism are industriously prosecuted, and generally secure independence. In the lower valleys agriculture is carried to great perfection, while the higher are devoted to pastoral purposes, and present to the eye of a stranger a life of cheerful and patriarchal simplicity.

"Here also, the business of public education is conducted with remarkable industry and success. Institutions for the advancement of this most important branch of political economy have become universal in the Protestant cantons, where they are liberally conducted, and, under the vigilant guardianship of men whose labours in the good cause do honour to human nature, they may be viewed as the best guarantees of that prosperity which exalteth a nation. Here virtue is not merely "its own reward," but being honoured by public approbation, it is imitated, and becomes an object of generous competition; while vice, kept in constant check by the powerful influence of good example, is but rarely productive of capital offences. Timely reprobation and correction are salutary measures; and the legislative authorities acting upon these principles, and animated by a humane and lively solicitude for the moral welfare of the people, have directed their efforts to the *prevention*, and consequently have greatly diminished the necessity for the *punishment*, of crime. It is thus that, in a moral estimate, Switzerland may be said to take as decided precedence over other nations as she does in her geographical position—the most elevated country in Europe.

"Such, briefly, are the moral features of Switzerland; but, that they are universal, is not to be inferred. Religion alone, by its various and irreconcilable tenets, has a powerful effect in their development; and from the Lake of Constance to the Lake Maggiore, the traveller observes many striking contrasts and modifications, and such as, from the distinctions above stated, the reader will readily suppose. But after unprejudiced observation and much familiarity with the country, we will cheerfully admit that there is infinitely more to command our admiration than to provoke our censure.

"But as these reflections may appear rather foreign to a work more ostensibly devoted to the "sublime and picturesque" scenery of Switzerland; and as the literary portion must necessarily be brief and limited, we proceed to our task, *con amore*, and shall now conduct the reader through those scenes which may be truly said to embrace whatever is most striking in Helvetian landscape; most characteristic of its peculiar grandeur and magnificence; and on which the struggles and triumphs of a high-minded and heroic people have conferred an especial immortality.

PASSAGE OF THE JURA.

"On quitting the plains of France, and passing through St. Laurent on the road to Morey, we behold the gradual development of the Jura mountains, which form the grand and imposing barrier between France and Helvetia on one hand, and Germany and Helvetia on the other. As we advance, our attention becomes more and more rivetted by the scenery before us, and the silence of contemplation is often interrupted by enthusiastic bursts of admiration. By degrees every individual feature assumes a more imposing aspect; points less distinct appear to advance; those in advance, to increase in magnitude, till the dwarf seems to shoot up into the stature of the giant, and every step gives additional life and prominence to the landscape.

"The Jura, unlike the other and loftier mountains of Switzerland, is clothed from base to summit with luxuriant pine forests. Here, you observe them advancing in isolated promontories and outposts; there, grouped into a congeries of hills, or shooting up in serrated and precipitous ridges; but towards the base, variegated by intricate and romantic valleys, and labyrinths of rich meadow land, which give striking ornament and relief to the sombre forests in which the whole chain is enveloped. This passage of the Jura abounds in every variety of scenery;—the simple and picturesque, the savage and the sublime, follow one another in such rapid succession, and are assembled in such remarkable juxta-position, as to defy all description or classification. The ascent is full of interest, and the impression not a little strengthened by the sense of personal risk which the traveller must at times encounter before he can accomplish his task. Winter is the season when it is to be seen in all its wildest magnificence, for then the snow-sledges supersede almost every other vehicle of locomotion, and, preceded and followed by horses and mules in long procession, with a constant tinkling of bells, present at first sight a most novel and picturesque effect.

"After pursuing for some leagues a steep, rugged, and circuitous route, winding, at one time, along a deep ravine, or the deserted bed of some ancient torrent; at another, under the threatening verge of precipitous rocks, we reach the immediate frontier of Helvetia.

THE ALPS.

"From La Vattay, a town shut up in the deep obscurity of pine forests, and enjoying most perfect seclusion, a shelving, terraced road conducted us up the Dole,[*] whose isolated summit presents one of the boldest features in the Jura. Here, at an immense elevation above the valley, a new world opened upon us, and we unexpectedly found ourselves on the almost perpendicular side of the mountain. The pine-covered precipices upon which we stood gave us a full command of the wild undulating forest scenery around, which plunged, as it were, into an extensive plain, where gleaming spires, villages, and chateaux, swam beneath us like a floating cloud. Stretching away in far perspective to the shores of the Leman—from which a pale, transparent vapour crept slowly upward, dilating as it ascended—the vast forms of confused and blended mountains towered, range above range, in shadowy grandeur: while, loftier still, and lifted into the serene purple of an evening sky, the eternal Alps burst suddenly upon our view, and by an irresistible fascination, held us for a time in fixed and silent admiration.

"The sublimity of this scene has been acknowledged by general acclamation, and the glowing colours with which it has been invested by the author of *Eloise*, are far from exaggerated. It was from a similar point that Rousseau, after his pilgrimage and sojourn in Italy, hailed these stupendous landmarks as the unchangeable features of his country, and gave vent to those powerful emotions which he has recorded with so much pathos and simplicity.

"Whether we dwell upon the picture of beauty expanding before us, or lift our eyes to the glorious frame-work in which it is set, our hearts are strangely touched, and overflow with sentiments hitherto unfelt. Amazement, admiration, and delight, melt and captivate the mind by a new and unwonted impulse, and call forth that homage which perhaps no other scene in existence could so effectually command. It exhibits in one glorious view the divine attributes of omnipotence and beneficence. The first we behold exemplified in those everlasting barriers which every where bound the horizon, and enclose the landscape like a curtain; of the latter we have abundant evidence in the Eden-like valley before us, where every field is fertile, every tree fruitful; where the ornamental and the useful go hand in hand, and where every thing seems to foster life and administer to the luxuries of man.

"The unique character of the landscape before us is greatly enhanced by the classic Leman which occupies the centre, and whose shores, rising as they recede, present an assemblage of features singularly striking and animated. Every where the labours of man have encroached upon the asperities of nature, and left upon all the stamp of his enterprise; while his empire is only limited by that frozen line of demarcation which sepa-

---

[*] Or *Dolaz*—4,000 feet above the Lake of Geneva, and commanding the Alpine Chain to the extent of 100 leagues.

rates his social existence from the awful solitudes of the Alps.

"As we descend the Jura, the scenery which characterises these shores differs materially, and presents itself in striking and mutual contrast. On the Savoy side of the lake, it is bold, variegated, and abrupt: beetling cliffs overhang, and green promontories jut out into the lake. Terraced vineyards occupy the acclivities, and corn-fields the valleys and gentler slopes; while towns, hamlets, isolated châteaux, and villas rise in white clusters along the shore, or sprinkle the heights in picturesque and solitary beauty. Beyond these, vinyards and corn fields merge into green pastures; the cheerful cottage is superseded by the *châlet*; valleys are contracted into deep ravines; orchards are succeeded by ridges of dark pines, and every thing demonstrates a new and less kindly region. Higher still, cataract and avalanche claim undisputed possession: man retires from the vain and ineffectual struggle, and the process of vegetation is suspended. The chaos of the Alps commences, and numerous *aiguilles*, stationed like advanced outposts, lead in lofty succession to the sovereign Blanc, whose unchangeable aspect presents one of the boldest emblems of eternity which the material world can supply. The opposite, or Lausanne side, exhibits nothing of this sublimity; but it offers every combination of the beautiful and picturesque, while at the same time, it is the granary, as well as the garden, of Switzerland. From the Jura to the lake, though comprising a distance of only three leagues, it embraces every feature that the human eye delights to contemplate—a naturally favoured, fertile, and highly cultivated soil; an appearance of universal cheerfulness and comfort; an industrious and healthful population, fully alive to the blessings of independence, and indefatigable in every means best calculated to render such blessings permanent.

"While we slowly continued our descent, the twilight met us from the east, and gave to the already enchanting picture that gorgeous finish, which has called forth the remarks of so many tourists, and excited the admiration of all. Travellers in these and other parts of Switzerland are not unfrequently charged with enthusiasm, and with embellishing their scenes by drawing on the imagination; but where is the imagination that could conjure up a scene fit to compete with that which now opened upon us? Here also, what so often implies incredulity or exaggeration, was literally true—every thing appeared à *couleur de rose*.

MONT BLANC.

"Over the heights above Lausanne, the clouds assumed what meteorologists term a cirro-cumulated form; the extreme edges of which were richly tinted with bright gold, and faded in the circumference into deep crimson. From the bay of Morges, at the same instant, to the rocks at Meillerie, the bosom of the lake glowed like a topaz; while every white sail crossing the magic circle, assumed the same bright livery, till it glided away to the eastward, where the water retained the deep sapphire tint. Looking back on the extreme ridge of the Jura, it appeared to rest on a sky of fire; while the light which now penetrated its recesses, was a new and amusing phenomenon, and played and flashed through its pines in a thousand fantastic coruscations.

"In sympathy with these, and as the rich saffron faded gradually from the lake, the mountains, one after another, and according to their elevation, took on the same glowing tint, which continuing to ascend as the sun went down, gradually invested the side of Mont Blanc, and at last, like a golden diadem, settled upon his head. Of the beauty of the scene which followed, we feel it impossible to convey any adequate idea; and must apologize for having attempted to describe scenes, which only lose by description, and impress every writer with a deep and humiliating consideration of his own inefficiency. To all who have been actual spectators of these phenomena, description will necessarily appear irksome and unsatisfactory; but for the sake of our untravelled readers, we have ventured to record *first impressions*, on crossing the JURA, and if these have been sketched but faintly, they have, so far as they go, been sketched with fidelity."

ST. GOTHARD'S CLIFF.

Hast thou viewed St. Gothard's cliff,
  Where th' awful avalanches ride,
Hast thou, as a light wing'd skiff,
  Seen the dread lavanges glide?

Hast thou ever marked a stranger
  O'er the baseless fabric stray;
Heedless of the threat'ning danger
  Hast thou seen him urge his way?

Has thy bosom felt a glow,
  Mixed with transport, pain, and fear?
Hast thou felt a pleasing wo?
  Hast thou shed a silent tear?

Throbbed not high your trembling heart,
  While you viewed the awful scene;
Did young hope a ray impart,
  Did not terror intervene?

Thus through *fancy's* vista gazing,
  Youth beholds a prospect fair;
Pleasure's brightest phantoms blazing,
  Show the vision beauteous rare.

Soon upon the baseless scene
  Care obtrudes his haggard form,
Rends the breast with anguish keen,
  Late in ecstacy so warm.

Fear its every terror lending,
  Still we view the wanderer stray,
Yet fond *Hope*, in pity bending,
  With its halo gilds the way.

                H.

RECOLLECTIONS.

It was a lovely night in the summer of 1833, when the splendid frigate, M——, homeward bound, having passed the long ship's-light, and with a rattling breeze was fast closing the Lizard, that as merry a set as ever formed a mess, were enjoying themselves together; and, although all felt happy at the prospect of soon meeting the warm and affectionate welcomes of their dearest connexions and friends, unseen for years, yet there was visible on all a look of sorrowing gloom at the idea of being so shortly to separate from each other, perhaps for ever.

"Ned, my old fellow," said one, " don't forget to let me know when you're shipped again."

"And Bill, my boy," said another, who had been the life of our mess, " I wish the old M—— had three years more of it." Even poor Peter Pillbox, our assistant-surgeon, who for his seriousness and eccentricity, had been the butt of us all, could not suppress a starting tear.

At the first glimmering of day, the boatswain's whistle sounded shrilly through the ship; while the hoarse calls of starboard and larboard-watch, shake reefs out of top-gallant-sails—rig out studding-sail-booms—idlers, wash decks, &c., made all alive. The M——, with a fine leading wind, bowled along at a splendid rate; and early in the day we rounded Ram's-head, passing mount Edgecumb, and came to anchor under the lee of the magnificent break-water, which forms the entrance to Plymouth sound.

All obstacles of detention being removed, I made a start in the Brunswick steamer, for Portsmouth, and joined my old uncle's and aunt's family circle, being received with the most affectionate cordiality. The old gentleman had always a parental fondness for me, having passed with him the earliest years of my life, and I felt quite indigenous to a home where I had spent such happy times; although, I confess, that for Paddy-land, my native country, I had a far warmer regard. Days and weeks passed on in uninterrupted rounds of pleasure. My cousins were constantly planning parties to the island, pic-nics' to Alverstoke, which, with the lots of pretty girls, the life of a sailor on shore, the time passed most delightfully. Oh, how happy was I then!—free from care, and with a heart as free. I laughed and joked with all,

Aye, indeed, I repeat my heart was free; for lovely and beautiful as many of my fair English friends were, not one made the slightest impresssion. I may be considered partial—I may judge severely—but I thought that too many did not possess that reserve, that winning modesty of manner, which grace the fair daughters of Erin : yet, to be just, they are generous, they are warm-hearted in the extreme. Three months had elapsed in the repetition of these amusements. I began to weary of them; and, with gladness, accepted an offer to join the mess of an old friend, who commanded the S—— revenue-cutter, about to sail for a three week's cruise, between Beachy-head and the South Foreland ; and, although the month of November was not the most tempting season, yet the change to me was gratifying. The monotony of a life on board a revenue vessel is dull in the extreme. Dodging from headland to headland—standing off and on, as the weather permits—and nothing to relieve the stupid series, but the hopes that fortune may propitiously throw in their course some unfortunate smuggler.

My time passed pleasantly enough, my friend being a most jovial, merry-hearted fellow—abounding in anecdote, and having seen an immensity of service ; he had tales of his adventures in all quarters of the globe.

We had been five days on our station : the weather had been very threatening, with stiff breezes from the N. W. and W. N. W., accompanied with showers of sleet and rain; but we still kept our berth; information having been given of a smuggling lugger, that was expected off this part of the coast. On the sixth morning the sun shone luridly with a red and angry glare; the sea was fast rising and rolling with a long and heavy swell ; while the wind whistling shrilly through the shrouds, gave us warning to expect plenty of dirty weather. To the southward and westward, heavy dark masses of clouds were collecting. The men were not idle during the day—every thing was made snug. The boom was lashed down, topmast housed, halliards and stays all made taut, the bowsprit reduced to the third reef, and the guns and the carronades were doubly lashed.

[Cutter close hauled, blowing hard, with a strong running sea.]

"Mr. Baxter," said Captain B—— to the chief mate, "lay her to; and tell Thompson to keep a sharp lookout, and mind what lee-way she makes."

She was now under double-reefed foresail, fore-sheet to windward, and helm hard-a-lee. The S—— was a fine sea-boat ; and, although the sea was increasing, and ran along with great rapidity, she did not labour much. The short day was now near its close : the sky had a wild appearance, and the white fleecy clouds were shaded with a sombrous copper tinge. The wind had shifted to the W. S. W., and vented its spite in violent gusts, while the scud, widely spreading, was driving with great velocity from that quarter. We were now made tolerably snug for the night, Beachy-head bearing W. by N. eleven miles.

"Bill, my lad," said Captain B——, "we shall have more of it before the night's over ; let's turn down and have some grub. Mr. Baxter we shall be glad of your company, to soil your platter with us."

I never was in better trim for it. Half drowned with rain and spray, and fagged with the hard day we had had, I attacked an excellent hot dinner as voraciously as a young alligator. We had now comfortably settled ourselves over our grog, regardless of the howl-

ing of the gale, the rolling of the vessel, and the hissing of the sea over her deck, as she occasionally shipped one, when Baxter, who prided himself in having a fine powerful voice, gave us one of his old favourites—

The wind blew hard, the sea ran high,
The dingy scud drove cross the sky :
All was safe stow'd, the bowl was slung,
When careless, thus Ned Haulyard sung :
    A sailor's life's the life for me,
    He takes his duty merrily ;
    If winds can whistle, he can sing,
    True to his country and his king ;
    He gets beloved by all the ship,
    And toasts his friend, and drinks his flip.

Baxter had scarcely finished the first stanza of his song, when a tremendous lurch a-starboard, accompanied with a heavy sea breaking right over her quarter, rather discomfited us; at the same time a rush of water along the deck partly forced its way down the companion, and presented itself most unceremoniously in our cabin, setting us all afloat.

"Hallo, my boys, a fresh hand to the bellows," said

Captain B——; but a roar of merriment from some of the men at others, who had got a sweet drenching, satisfied us that no mischief had been done on deck. Tom Hayter, our coxswain, now pushed in his ugly bushy phiz, saying,

"Mr. Baxter, Mr. Thompson would be glad as how you'd come on deck, Sir."

"How's the night going on, Tom?" said Captain B——.

"Bad enough, Sir; blowing great guns, and there's a terrible sea rising. This berth won't do, Sir; she's drifting in with the land."

"How does the light bear now?"

"About W. by S. ½ S., Sir."

We were quickly prepared, and soon on deck; and a most uncheering prospect presented itself. The wind had increased to, a perfect gale, the sea was running very high, and was, literally, all on fire; having that luminous appearance that I have often observed in hard weather, when the wind has been from the southward or westward. The night was pitchy dark; not a star to be seen; and the moon being in her last quarter, we were not blessed with her mild light, so cheering to poor seamen. Beachy revolving light occasionally gleamed murkily through a thick and heavy mist. Thompson, the second mate, with his night-lantern, was busily engaged directing the men in opening the lee-ports, to give a freer egress to the sea, now constantly breaking over us. His little rotund figure, equipped in his dreadnought watch-coat, with his souwester, presented a laughable appearance. Punchy Dick, as the men named him, was a good humoured little fellow, a capital seaman, and, notwithstanding he was over sixteen stone, was amazingly active, and could scud with his little fat pins along the deck with wonderful celerity.

"Hard night this, Mr. Thompson," said Captain B——.

"Hard enough, Sir; I think it would be as well to look for snugger quarters."

"Captain B—— and Baxter soon decided on running for the Ness; and as the ebb-tide would be setting to the south-west in two hours time, we should have been terribly hobbled in our present berth. The men were called aft to set the try-sail; and the S——, now with a double reefed foresail and her spitfire, (seventh or storm-gib) scudded away, reeling at a glorious rate. It was now eight o'clock; and we calculated we had about a run of thirty miles before we could get inside the Ness. The helm was well manned; and a good look-out being kept, she did not in yawing ship many seas. Abreast of Hastings we could see the lights flickering along the shore; and as I stood on one of the carronades abaft the lee-shrouds, I thought of the many pleasant evenings I had spent in Portsmouth at such an hour, when playing ecarté with my old uncle, or Vingt-un with my merry cousins; and, perhaps, many in Hastings were then enjoying themselves in the happy society of their family, regardless of the storm that raged. About midnight we were close in with Dungeness-light. The sea was terribly high and broken, the ebb-tide making strong. We had shipped several seas, when Captain B—— suddenly caught my arm.

"Bill, my lad, look out now."

At the same time Baxter's stentorian voice,

"Hold on, my lads; mind your starboard helm now."

The "ay, ay, Sir," had scarcely been given, when a tremendous fellow came right over our weather-quarter, broke the fish-blocks from the weather-davits, carried the gig clean away, and swept every thing loose off the deck. I was streamed at full length like a dog-vane, but having a crab's-claw hold of the weather back-stay. I soon righted. The S—— quickly freed herself; and now scudding with tremendous velocity, pass the Head we soon got into comparatively smooth water, and she was again hove too. The watch being set I turned into my berth, and was soon forgetful of all that had passed.

An unusual bustle on deck, and the flapping of the main-sail, roused me from my sleep. The day-light faintly appeared through the bull's eye over my birth; and Ben, our platter-scrubber, was busying himself in the cabin.

"Hallo, Ben, what's going forward?"

"Getting under veigh, Sir; there be a hodd-looking vessel to luard; it's a fine morning, Sir—not blowing so fresh."

I rattled on my duds, and was on deck in a giffy. The men were swaying away at the throat and peak-halyards, when Captain B—— hailed me, pointing over the lee-bow—

"There, Bill, there's something for our night's work."

About four miles to leeward a suspicious-looking lugger, had been lying-to, and she seemed to have carried away her main-mast during the night's gale, only a few feet of the stump remaining above deck. She was well-manned, and was equally on the alert, as she was now scudding away gaily under her fore and mizen-lugs.

"Bear on her well, Tom," said Captain B—— (to Hayter, who was at the helm), as the S—— smoked along, under a double reefed mainsail, foresail, and her fourth gib, while she crumbled the sea in a mass of foam from her bluff-bows. As the mist of the morning cleared, the wind freshened, and again showed a disposition to treat us roughly. The S—— had as much canvass as she could stagger under, and rolled on her course through a tumbling sea, with tremendous impetus.

"We're gaining on her, Sir," said Baxter ; "but she goes snug under her sail ; she doesn't feel the loss of her main this wild weather—she scuds well."

The deck had been righted from the mishaps of the night ; the guns cleared, and all ready for running alongside. The men, on the strength of the prize, had treated themselves to an additional quid, and were lining the weather-bow, grinning their trite remarks, and eyeing their victim like cormorants. We had run E. by N. about thirteen miles: the lugger now scarcely one a-head ; when suddenly, as a forlorn hope, she hauled her wind, and stood S. E. by S., intending, as we afterwards learned, had she beaten us on a wind, to have made for Ambleteuse. In no time the sheets were hauled aft, and the S—— sprung to the wind ; and, as she showed her beam to the breeze, she heeled deeply, and buried her lee-chains and the square-sail-yard well in the water, while it occasionally rushed along the deck in a line with the fifth plank. The lugger now flew through every sea, while the S——, pitching her bows heavily under, sent a continued shower of spray over us. In less than three quarters of an hour we were nearly within gun-shot. We could see about twenty sturdy fellows along her deck.— She had two carronades. A gun was fired, and our ensign run to the peak, to bring her to ; but unheeding, she still kept her course.

"We'll bring you to manners yet, my gay boys," observed my friend, as he cried out, " clear away one of the long guns ; forward, my lads."

All was quickly ready.

" Fire !"

And the ball marking its line with a cloud of spray, fell short of the lugger's weather-quarter.

"Try it again, my lads—take out the coin."

The muzzle being now more elevated, and the cutter eased a point off the wind, to bring the gun to bear better, the word,

" Steady—mind the weather-roll—fire."

All was confusion in the lugger ; the ball had struck the bolt rope of the leech of the fore-lug, carried away the sheets and blocks, and the sail was split and flapping in the wind. The cutter gained rapidly on her, running right in the lugger's wake. Her men had quickly rove fresh sheets, and again had the lugger belayed aft—but she had lost too much. We were now almost aboard of her, when Captain B—— hailing, threatened to run her down unless she bore to.

"Bear on, you Philistine villains," sung out an old weather-beaten ruffian, who appeared to be her captain, and who had been standing near two of the men at the helm during the whole run.

The words had scarcely been uttered when the lugger, in a heavy pitch, again burst the sheets from the lug, and before the cutter could sufficiently answer her helm, her bowsprit ran across the lugger's mizen out-rigger, and right over the taffrail, on her lee-quarter. With the shock the lugger was thrown dead in the wind. Crash went the out-rigger, and away went our topmast-fore-stay and gib-halyards.

"Forward, my lads ; bear a hand and clear away," roared Captain B—— ; and fifteen of our men, armed with their cutlasses, with Punchy Dick and myself, were along the bowsprit, and on the lugger's deck in a shake.

In the next moment Baxter's powerful voice was heard,

" Clew up the main tack ; heave the helm hard up ; ease off the main-sheet ; haul the fore-sheet to windward ; ease away the yard-lifts and braces ; haul away on the after starboard-brace ;" all was quickly done as said ; and the S—— bore round, and passed clear of the lugger's lee-gang-way in fine stile, without further damage.

The lugger's men, muttering curses, offered no resistance. The wreck of the mizen was soon cleared ; and Punchy Dick had gone forward with some of our men to the fore-lug, which was now a-back. I also unluckily followed ; for in a heavy lurch, a sea broke over, upset poor Dick, who struck me in his fall, and sent me skimming along the deck, until I was brought to by the carronade. This would have been all fine fun, had not my side struck violently against one of the iron prise-bolts on the cheek of the carriage, and so completely took away my breath, that I was for some time unable to rise. Although writhing with pain, I could scarcely refrain from bursting into a fit of laughter, at the awkward but feeling condolence expressed by poor Dick for the accident ; when suddenly one of the lugger's men seized my hand with a forcible grasp, while the large tears fell fast down his manly, but care-worn and weather-beaten features ; and he uttered in smothered accents,

" Ah, thin, Masther William, is it yourself I see ?"

He could say no more, but continued sobbing and shaking my hand, clasped in both with his own. I looked—my heart sickened. The recollections of former years burst through my mind—I gave way to my feelings.—It was poor Lanty that was before me.

The cutter had hauled her wind, and brought-to a short distance from us. The men having found the bowsprit sprung, had bent her sixth gib, and rove fresh hal-yards. As the cutter's sails again filled, she threw out a signal for the lugger to follow. Mr. Thompson had taken charge of the prize, which we found to be the Morning Star of —— ; having a part of her cargo of tubs of Hollands, ankers of Brandy, and a few bales of tobacco, that they had been unable to land before the gale set in. It was still blowing very fresh, which made us keep good way, although having but the fore-lug on her. The lugger's men had been ordered below, with the exception of poor Lanty, who gave me some account of himself since we last parted.

" It is now nearly eleven years, Mr. William, since the time I tuk my lave ov ye on Annagierah-bridge.* Och, and that was the sorrowful day to me ; nevir did the remimbrance ov the dhreary, dhreary night I spent in Kilmurry† lave my sinses ; but, och, my sweet Kate, she's an angel in heaven, and 'tis ovten have I prayed that I might be wid her," and he brushed his swollen eyes with the back of his huge hand : " however the thoughts of the throuble of my poor mother made me hasten my way to Kerry, to the coast near Ventry, where my father's frinds wanst lived ; but she had died there broken-hearted. She had gone to a land of sthrangers, and she found no frind there to cheer her ould days, or to close her eyes dacently in her last ind. I then went to Iunismore,‡ and stopt there until a smuggling schooner took me as a hand : but hating ever to come to my own country agin, I changed in Flushing, aboard a vessel thrading to England, and have until the present moment been always at sea in different crafts, and many's the thought has crossed me ov the pleasint days we had together, but they are gone, and God is good whatever our inds may be."

Poor Lanty's wayward fate was too painful a subject to dwell on. I made no allusion to former scenes, but endeavoured to cheer him ; and as he was likely to be sent on board a ship of war, I exerted my reasoning powers to impress upon him, that by steadiness and good conduct he might lay up a store of comfort for his old days, and that his mind being properly directed in an honest line of duty,

* About four miles from Miltown Malbay, on the main road to Kilrush, over the river Annagivagh.

† Kilmurry, Ibrickan, a small hamlet on the coast, two miles south of Miltown.

‡ Inuismore, one of the Blasket islands,

might again be restored to a tranquil state; and, indeed I was glad that his lawless career was stopped. I had not turned my eyes for some time to the cutter, now close a head, under easy sail, until I heard the man in her chains heaving the lead, sing out, " quarter less five," and found we were running in for Folkstone.

As the cutter was likely to be detained for some time in getting a new bowsprit spar, and my side being very painful, I took a last farewell of poor Lanty, (begging of my friend, Captain B——, to interest himself about him,) and starting for Canterbury, and via London to Portsmouth, again established myself with the old gentleman. My side still continuing painfully swelled, obliged me to place myself under Surgeon G——'s treatment, who, with a long phiz, attacked it with a formidable array of leeches, cupping glasses, blisters, &c., with the pills at night, the draught in the morning, and sounding his retreat each day with " you must keep yourself perfectly quiet." As my limbs were thus to remain inactive until further orders, I employed myself in tracing the following Recollections, brought so forcibly to mind.

(To be continued.)

RECREATIONS IN MATHEMATICS AND NATURAL PHILOSOPHY:

CONTAINING AMUSING DISSERTATIONS AND ENQUIRIES CONCERNING A VARIETY OF SUBJECTS CALCULATED TO EXCITE CURIOSITY AND ATTENTION.

When we at first undertook the management of the Penny Journal, we promised to mingle as much as possible the *utile* with the *dulce*—in plain language, to convey as much useful information as we possibly could in an engaging and agreeable form. How far we have adhered to this determination we leave our readers to judge. In furtherance of the same object, we now purpose, from time to time, extracting from a very valuable though scarce work, " Hutton's Recreations in Mathematics and Natural Philosophy," such portions as we may deem calculated at once to amuse and inform our general class of readers; and we feel persuaded that to those to whom the subjects which we may bring forward are familiar, no apology will be requisite, as they will be ready to appreciate the benefit of extending useful knowledge in an engaging manner among individuals not possessing advantages they themselves enjoy. As nothing can be more useful in the general concerns of life than an intimate acquaintance with arithmetic, and a ready way of calculating, and as such exercises will not be an unprofitable employment to a number of our youthful readers during the Christmas holidays, we shall commence with that department of useful science. The questions proposed in one number shall be answered in the next, thus leaving time sufficient for solving the problems, and obviating the necessity of answers being forwarded to us. We shall now merely state a few particulars, which may be interesting to the reader, of James Ozanam, the first author of the " Mathematical Recreations," translated by Hutton.

He was born at Boligneux, in Bressia, in 1640. Having considerable genius, as well as much industry, he made very great progress, though unassisted by a master, and at the juvenile age of fifteen years he wrote a mathematical treatise. While very young he removed to Lyons, and, for a maintainance, taught the mathematics, with tolerable success: but his generosity soon procured him a better residence. Among his pupils were two foreigners, who, being disappointed of some bills of exchange for a journey to Paris, mentioned the circumstance to him: finding that fifty pistoles were necessary to enable them to accomplish their purpose, he immediately supplied them with the money, even without their note for it. On their arrival at Paris, they mentioned this generous action to M. Dugusseau, father of the chancellor; who being struck with this trait in his character, engaged these young gentlemen to invite Ozanam to Paris, with a promise of his favour He embraced this opportunity with eagerness, and, at Paris, the employment of giving instructions in mathematics soon brought him in a considerable income. He

wrote a great number of useful works. Among these we cannot help mentioning his Treatise on Lines of the first Order, and on the Construction of Equations, published in 1687: the Mathematical Dictionary, published in 1690: the Course of Mathematics, 5 volumes octavo, published in 1693: the Mathematical and Philosophical Recreations, first published in 1694, in 2 vols. 8vo: and the Elements of Algebra, in 2 vols. 8vo. published in 1702.

Ozanam possessed a mild and calm disposition, a cheerful and pleasant temper, an inventive genius, and a generosity almost unparalleled.

CURIOUS ARITHMETICAL CALCULATIONS.

Under the head of " Arithmetical and Geometrical Progressions, and of certain problems which depend upon them," the first question proposed is—

I. If a hundred stones are placed in a straight line, at the distance of a yard from each other; how many yards must the person walk, who undertakes to pick them up one by one, and to put them into a basket a yard distance from the first stone?

II. A gentleman employed a bricklayer to sink a well, and agreed to give him at the rate of three shillings for the first yard in depth, five for the second, seven for the third, and so on increasing till the twentieth, where he expected to find water: how much was due to the bricklayer when he had completed the work?

III. A gentleman employed a bricklayer to sink a well to the depth of twenty yards, and agreed to give him twenty pounds for the whole; but the bricklayer falling sick, when he had finished the eighth yard, was unable to go on with the work: how much was then due to him?

IV. A merchant being considerably in debt, one of his creditors, to whom he owed 1860*l.* offered to give him an acquittance if he would agree to pay the whole sum in twelve monthly instalments; that is to say, 100*l.* the first month, and to increase the payment by a certain sum each succeeding month, to the twelfth inclusive, when the whole debt would be discharged. By what sum was the payment of each month increased?

. As we have already said, the answers to the foregoing shall appear in our next, which will preclude the necessity of any communication to us on the subject; and here we would take the opportunity of expressing our sincere acknowledgments to those friends who have favoured us with articles on various subjects fitted for our little miscellany. We trust that we shall be excused for not replying to or noticing the numerous communications forwarded to us, as it would absolutely require more time to answer the various letters we receive than we could altogether afford to the conducting of the Journal. We shall at all times feel much obliged for useful hints and suggestions, and grateful for the communications of our friends, who may rest satisfied that their favours are not overlooked—but, if considered suitable for our pages, shall appear as opportunity offers. The impossibility of inserting articles immediately after they come to hand, will be evident when it is recollected that we have at all times several numbers of the Journal in advance, in order to meet the English and Scottish markets; and, with regard to postage, it will, perhaps, be sufficient to remind our correspondents that sometimes a single postage will take away the profits of several dozens of Journals —*Verb. sat.*

CURIOUS DISCOVERY IN FRANCE.

As some workmen were digging upon the high road, at Homaizeé, a village about five leagues from Poitiers, they found the skeleton of an elephant, in perfect preservation. The bones were placed horizontally upon a sort of bench of calcareous stone, and occupied a space of more than ten feet (French) in length, by a foot and a half in breadth.

DEVOTION OF FRIENDSHIP.

DEAR SIR—The description of the scenery around Glendalough, in a recent number of your Journal, recalled to my memory an instance of friendly devotion which occurred some time since, in that interesting though secluded district; and while we read with pleasure and delight, sketches of heroism and devotedness in the inhabitants of a sister island, which have been touched off with such fidelity by the pen of a late eminent writer, we should surely be disposed, in our estimate of the real merit of similar actions, performed by individuals in our own land, to overlook the cause in which they were at the time engaged. Under these feelings I enclose, for insertion in your Journal, the following lines, written shortly after the transactions to which they refer had taken place. You will readily perceive they are a juvenile production, something in the style of the "Border Ballads." With best wishes for the success of your little periodical, I am, dear Sir, yours truly,

G. D.

DWYER AND M'ALISTER.

A TALE OF 1798.

Oft mid rebellion's blood-stained lines
　The noblest deeds of honour glow,
As the fair sun the brighter shines
　When storms around him darkness throw.

The outlaw in his cavern wild,
　High o'er the still lake's smooth expanse,
Where rocks magnificently piled,
　Conceal him from pursuers' glance,

May still possess an heart that's form'd
　In brilliant honour's purest mould,
As softly by affection warmed,
　As when in danger, stern and bold.

I sing M'Alister, the brave,
　Whose deeds are worthy of a song;
To snatch them from oblivion's grave,
　And bid them live both late and long.

M'Alister, the faithful friend
　Of him who waged th'unequal war,
And led his band from end to end,
　Of Wicklow's mountains, famed afar.

The golden lure was held in vain,
　The price of Dwyer's devoted head;
Nor hope of pardon or of gain
　An outlaw from his honour led.

Beset, pursued o'er hill and dell,
　Through shady wood and rocky glen:
By murderous foes—ah! shame to tell,
　For they themselves were highland-men.

From mountain-top to deepest vale,
　Where caves conceal the chosen band;
Through the soft shades of dark Imail,
　They hurl the dreadful fire-brand.

An hospitable roof remote,
　Where whilome dwelt Glendalough's saint;
As evening's gentle vapours float,
　Received the outlaw weak and faint.

But still the staunch hounds closely press,
　To find their undiscovered haunt;
And by the tracks of blood they trace
　Those foes whom they could never daunt.

That blood had warmed the truest breast,
　Ah! then, why was it idly shed?
It was to save their chief, distrest—
　The blow was aimed at Dwyer's head.

M'Alister, with fury burning,
　Received instead the deadly blow;
When quickly on the foeman turning,
　The gallant chieftain laid him low.

Then o'er the wild heath swiftly bore
　His faint and wounded friend along,
And marked each step with trickling gore,
　That on the heath-bells trembling hung.

And now within the peaceful cot,
　Released from toil, as each suppose;
Refreshing rest they, wearied, sought,
　And stretched themselves in soft repose.

When—hark! the bugles thrilling blast
　Aroused them from their slumbers sweet;
Betrayed! they cried, come now, at last
　Like heroes we our death shall meet.

In crowds the kilted Scots surround
　The outlaw'd rebel's calm retreat,
The cliffs with echoing shouts resound—
　The valiant band for death await.

The flaming brand is tossed on high,
　The crackling thatch now blazes wide—
The curling smoke ascends the sky—
　The lake reflects her burning side.

The gallant band in mute despair
　Around their chosen leader stand;
Resolved in death his fate to share,
　And nobly perish hand in hand.

Within they feel the scorching flame,
　Abroad they dread the highland ball;
The polish'd bag'net's lightning gleam—
　The blazing roofs' destructive fall.

At length the solemn pause was broke.
　M'Alister, in feeble tone,
His honour'd leader thus bespoke,
　Whose life he prized beyond his own:

" The window which o'erhangs the deep
　A friendly passage opens wide;
'Tis but the rocky crag to leap,
　To meet the still lake's dimpling tide.

Then gliding o'er the silvery wave,
　To reach the shore each effort bend,
Whilst I the Scottish ruffians brave,
　And sell my life to save my friend.

The thund'ring volley aimed at me,
　A favouring moment will obtain:
Oh, snatch that moment and be free,
　Nor let your friend's death be in vain."

He said, and darted forth with speed,
　Like arrow from the twanging bow;
Nor would his friend's remonstrance heed,
　But rush'd to meet the deadly blow.

That instant roared the fatal peal;
　Its flashes lit the mountain side;
The hero felt the leaden hail,
　And like a hero nobly died.

Now forth the furious Dwyer sprung,
　Along the craggy steep descent;
His valiant heart with anguish wrung—
　His noble soul on vengeance bent;

Nor meanly sought his single life,
　But stood exposed to Scottish view;
Resolved his death should end the strife,
　Ere flames devour his faithful crew.

The Scotsmen turn to seize their prey,
　And quickly take too certain aim;
Though wounded, still he stands at bay,
　Until his band rush from the flame.

Then bounding o'er the rugged rock,
　They safely reach the tangled wood;
Where thickest shades pursuers mock,
　The grateful outlaws panting stood.

And now the pressing danger o'er,
　They stretch along the blooming heath;
And each a solemn vengeance swore
　To take for their companions' death.

DUBLIN:
Printed and Published by P. D. Hardy, 3, Cecilia-street; to whom all communications are to be addressed.
Sold by all Booksellers in Ireland
In London, by Richard Groombridge, 6, Panyer-alley, Paternoster-row; in Liverpool, by Willmer and Smith; in Manchester, by Ambery; in Birmingham, by Drake; in Glasgow, by John Macleod; and in Edinburgh, by N. Bowack.

THE
DUBLIN PENNY JOURNAL
CONDUCTED BY P. DIXON HARDY, M.R.I.A.

VOL. III.	DECEMBER 27, 1834.	No. 130.

Mr. A. Nichol, del.   Clayton, sc.

STALACTITE CAVERN AT MITCHELSTOWN.

STALACTITE CAVERN AT MITCHELSTOWN.

Shortly after the discovery of this extraordinary subterranean work of nature, we presented our readers with an engraving of one of the stalactite caves, from a drawing made by a friend, who was among the first of those who explored its recesses. Although a hurried sketch, it served the purpose of attracting public attention to the spot. Since that time the cavern has been visited by thousands, and we are at this day enabled to give three faithful sketches, taken expressly for our Journal, by our talented friend, A. Nichol, Esq. to whose pencil, as our readers must be aware, we are already indebted for several of the very best designs which have appeared in our pages. Anxious that the public should be made acquainted with the real character and extent of this justly celebrated cavern, we have procured several descriptions from persons who have inspected it. The accuracy of the following communications may be relied on. The first is by Mr. Nichol, who sketched the designs in the engravings; the second is from an intelligent gentleman who recently visited the Cave; and the third, a most minute and scientific description, with the accompanying map, we extract from the first volume of the Journal of the Dublin Geological Society, and which was read at a meeting of that learned Society, by Professor Apjohn—the map by Mr. T. Kearney; and from the entire, we should hope the reader will be able to form something like a correct estimate of the magnificence and extent of the Cave. We have been the more anxious on this point, from having observed in either the "*London Literary Gazette*" or "*Athenæum*," (we cannot now recollect which) some observations rather calculated to throw discredit on the accounts which had been given of its great extent. In reference to which, we should suppose, that the simple circumstance stated by Mr. Nichol, (of the accuracy of which there can be no question,) will afford ample evidence—that although the Cave was visited by forty persons during the two days he was making his drawings in it; and though all that time he was surrounded by four boys holding large candles for him, which might naturally be expected to attract the notice of visitors, he did not see, and apparently was not observed by any one of the number.

Of the extraordinary magnificence of the place, we presume some idea may be formed from the engravings in our present number; and yet, after all, we have reason to think, indeed we know it to be the case, that the Cavern contains several very spacious apartments, which have never yet been seen by strangers who have visited it.

MR. NICHOL'S DESCRIPTION OF THE CAVERN.

DEAR SIR—Having been on a tour in the south of Ireland this summer, I was induced to visit the justly celebrated Kingston Cavern, which is situated about midway between Caher and Mitchelstown, in the county of Tipperary, and was first discovered on the 3d of May, 1835, by a person of the name of Condon, and two boys, sons of Mr. Shelly, proprietor of the inn on the new road, within one short mile of the Cave. It is on the farm of a poor man of the name of Gorman, who realizes something handsome by acting as guide to persons visiting the place. The entrance is through a narrow passage about three feet in height; and the following are the circumstances which led to its discovery: Condon and the above-named boys having heard of a hole where the labourers were quarrying, determined on exploring it; they therefore procured light and entered the passage, (which was much narrower at that time than it is now,) and after proceeding a considerable distance with great caution, they at length arrived at the brink of a perpendicular precipice, which appeared to put a stop altogether to their farther progress. Their anxiety and determination, however, to explore this subterranean wonder, increased with the difficulty of attaining it; and after various conjectures, as to how they ought to proceed, they at length procured a burning turf, tied to a string, which they dropped to the lower part of the precipice, measuring about sixteen feet. Afterwards, lowering each other down by means of ropes, they proceeded with lighted candles along the narrow and rocky passage—the grandeur and novelty of the place, together with its apparent endless extent, mas-

sive columns and pyramids of spar, stalactites, &c. succeeding each other in endless variety, and the desire of discovery, attracted them onwards, till their lights were nearly burnt out. It was then the danger of attempting a return in the dark struck them; they hastened back, but long before they arrived at the cavern's mouth, the lights had expired, and they sat down in despair. They remained in this alarming situation until midnight. At length the father of the boys and some other friends came in search of them, and found them in the middle cave. Such is the singular way in which this astonishing phenomenon of nature was discovered, which might otherwise have remained unknown for ages.

On arriving at the entrance as above described, you descend the precipice by means of a ladder, and proceed in a stooping position for a considerable distance, surrounded by enormous blocks of grey limestone, some thirty or forty tons weight, apparently hanging by the corners overhead; whilst some hundreds are scattered around, presenting one of the most striking pictures of savage grandeur it is possible to conceive; it is too horrible to be described—to be understood it must be seen. Such is the entrance to the middle cave. This is generally allowed to be the most beautiful part of the entire Cavern, presenting to the eye nine columns of brilliant spar, the most remarkable of which is called the Pyramid. It is highly ornamented towards its base, with tiers of transparent crystalizations, resembling icicles, surrounded by hundreds of stalactites and stalagmites, of various sizes and of the most fantastic forms, and tremendous rocks, which are here strewed about in the wildest confusion. A petrifaction called the Table, will also be here pointed out by the guides—an enormous body of spar, about thirty feet in circumference, ornamented much the same as the pyramid. There is nothing, however, in this part of the Cavern, more striking than what is termed the Four Courts—(why it should have this name I cannot say.) Here the spar assumes the most fantastic appearances—parts resembling the columns of the Giant's Causeway, with pillars rising from the ground to the ceiling; to the left is an immense body of spar, resembling some huge animal, covered with brilliant crystalizations, and supported by two or three graceful pillars, formed by the junction of the stalactite from above with the stalagmite below. The next object worthy of notice here, is a magnificent massive column, whose base may be, I dare say, twenty or thirty feet in circumference, to which the guides have given the name of Lot's Wife.

You now proceed to Kingston Gallery, the most remarkable compartment of any yet visited, representing a very long Gothic aisle, composed entirely of spar, with a large block of crystalized matter, resembling a mutilated statue, standing on a pedestal, with magnificent transparent curtains hanging across the passage; it has all the appearance of a gallery of snow, partially melted and frozen again, the melted parts assuming the most fantastic and beautiful forms. Having explored the Cavern as far as I have already described, and bestowed on its unrivalled wonders the most enthusiastic admiration, the guides told me of a part which was little visited, owing to the difficulty of access, called the New Discovery; so the spirit of curiosity was again awakened within me, and I determined on seeing it. We proceeded a long distance in a stooping position, at times crawling on our hands and knees; at others, going sideways, where the passage was narrow. At length, after amazing fatigue, together with being literally covered with mud, we came to a place where rocks seemed to block up the passage. This, however, was not the case: we were enabled, by lying down flat on the bottom of the passage, and catching hold of some of the projecting rocks, to draw ourselves through. A short way farther on is the New Discovery, and it is certainly one of the most astonishing and beautiful things I ever beheld: in the centre rises a noble pillar of the most brilliant, glittering spar, (owing I suppose, to its not having been discoloured by the torches.) On the left is a number of the finest curtained crystalizations that I have seen in the entire Cavern, apparently partially drawn, exhibiting the most graceful folds, the stains giving an effect which would be almost incredible, so closely does it resemble the most beautiful hanglings; above are seen a row of splendid stalactites, as regular as the pipes of an organ; whilst in the foreground rise a number of fine stalagmites. This part is filled as you advance, with curtains, pillars, and petrifactions, of every size and form, and many of the rarest and most beautiful specimens of spar are to be found in this part of the Cavern. It would be hard to say what the extent of the Cave would be in this direction. I had not time to explore it farther. On looking at my watch I found, to my astonishment, that it was eight o'clock, having been in it for about ten hours; and to give an idea of the place to persons who have not visited it, there were strangers, I was told, exploring it that day to the number of forty, and I did not meet with a single person.

I was informed, while in the neighbourhood of the Cavern, that there were four scientific gentlemen, a short time since, from the Institure in Paris, measuring and making drawings of it, one of whom said he considered it one of the finest things of the kind in Europe. I am, dear Sir, yours, &c.   A. N.

———

The following is from a correspondent who recently visited the Cave:

As some very exaggerated and incorrect accounts respecting this magnificent place, have got into circulation, I am desirous to put your readers in possession of such information as, while it may serve to stimulate them to visit it, shall not, at the same time, excite ideas of magnitude not to be realized on actual inspection.

The entrance is rather difficult, but capable of being much improved by the judicious outlay of a few pounds. After arriving, by the assistance of a ladder, at the foot of a precipice, you proceed on a gradual descent, over a succession of large and very rugged rocks, and through an uninteresting and gloomy passage, for about a hundred yards, when the Cavern rather suddenly expands on every side, and some of its beauties become conspicuous. This, which may be considered the first resting place, and from which numerous passages or smaller caverns branch off in different directions, is the largest space or chamber yet discovered in the Cave. Its diameter, (not, of course, measuring inside the entrances to any of the minor passages,) is about sixty to eighty feet, giving, at the utmost, a circumference considerably under a hundred yards; yet this, though falling so very far short, as it does, of some of the extravagant reports which have gone forth about it, presents, nevertheless, a most magnificent and imposing appearance; and would doubtless lead a casual observer to estimate its size at double what it really is. The roof here is perhaps thirty feet high towards the centre, and in many parts ornamented with stalactites, which depend from it in great variety of size and shape. From this you are introduced successively into the smaller caverns or " halls," as they are termed, abounding, as most of them do, in scenes of indescribable splendour; but of which, to attempt anything like a just description, capable of communicating to the reader a correct idea of what will (should he visit the place) strike his astonished eye, would be in vain indeed. If we were to point the visiter's attention to any one above another of the various forms which the calcareous deposit assumes in this Cavern, it would be to that which resembles *drapery*, hung from the rugged, black limestone rocks, in the most graceful forms and folds; clothing them in some places with sparkling robes of beautiful white, and in others of a rich honey yellow colour, while some of the dependent sheets are elegantly veined or striped with a purplish brown colour, which appears to great advantage when the lights are held behind. In one place you are shown what is termed the "river;" being, however, only a pool of limpid water amongst the rocks; in another part you are introduced to the "well," a scene which reminds of the fanciful descriptions of "fairy land." The "bedchamber" is also pointed out to you, where the drapery appears in great perfection; and you should not overlook the smaller pools of water, which are frequently to be met with, and which you will find in general are limpid, with exquisitely beautiful, though minute crystals. In other parts you will find the scene greatly diversified; all around you being more or less coated with a viscid kind of clay, of

the consistence of soft putty, and which greatly retards your progress for a time—again, your course lies over a bed of extremely fine sand.

If we were to venture an opinion as to the length of the Cave between its extreme points, as far as is yet known, we would say it was under a quarter of a mile, though from the great exertion required in clambering through it, the distance appears much greater.

Perhaps we keep within the bounds of correct description in presuming that this great national curiosity exceeds in splendour any thing of the sort in the British empire; and we strongly suspect, that in this particular it ranks next to the famous grotto at Antiparos.

Visiters going to the Cave may be accommodated at Gorman's cottage, where they can put up their horses or carriages, change their dress, and make all preparations necessary for their *descent;* and under *his* care they may rest satisfied they will not be led into needless danger. We warn our friends against employing *any one* as a guide, &c. without the special recommendation or advice of Gorman, as they will be sure to have offers enough from people who have nothing whatever to do with the place, and have repeatedly forced their way into it, when he was absent or engaged, to the great annoyance of visiters, and the dilapidation of the spar, &c.; so that we again say, employ none but Gorman's people, and then, on coming out, you have none but the one payment or settlement to make if you please.

Lord Kingsborough, on whose estate the Cave is, and who may be said to be the proprietor, in fact, of all its contents, has been repeatedly in it, and has given the charge of it to Gorman, with strict injunctions to preserve the spar, &c. as free from spoliation as possible; and we would here respectfully suggest to his lordship, the absolute necessity which exists for enclosing the entrance with a small building, which would enable whoever may be in charge of it, effectually to prevent the intrusion of mischievous people, which is almost impossible at present; and if suffered to remain as it now is, we much fear the consequences.

We need hardly inform our readers that the Cavern is on the road from Burnt Court to Mitchelstown, about a mile from the north west corner of Lord Lismore's beautiful demesne at Shanbally, and thirteen from Clonmel; and parties taking early breakfast at the latter place, may view the Cave satisfactorily and return to dinner; or, if they prefer taking provisions with them, they will meet with civility and accommodation from Gorman and his wife, as far as lies in their power to afford.

DOCTOR APJOHN ON THE MITCHELSTOWN CAVE. FROM THE DUBLIN GEOLOGICAL JOURNAL.

The townland of Coolnagarranroe, in which the cave is found, lies in the valley which separates the Galtee and Knockmildown chains of mountains, the former constituting its northern, the latter its southern boundary. The prevailing rock at this extremity of the Galtees is conglomerate, which occasionally passes into sandstone, while that which composes the opposite chain of hills possesses a structure intermediate between that of sandstone and schist, and includes few, if any, rounded or water-worn pebbles. The material of the interposed valley is compact grey limestone, and this rock, in the townland already mentioned, forms two small, rounded hills, within both of which cavities of considerable magnitude exist. One of these, namely, that occurring in the western elevation, has been known from the remotest antiquity, and repeatedly explored; the other, which was only discovered on the 2d of May, 1833, by a man of the name of Condon, while quarrying for stones, is that which has since attracted so much attention, and respecting which I purpose making a few observations.

The hill within which the newly discovered cave exists, rises to the height of about a hundred feet above the Caher and Mitchelstown road; and the entrance to it, which is at the bottom of a quarry, is somewhat less than halfway up, or about sixty feet from the summit. The mouth of the adit is covered by an iron grating placed over it by a man of the name of Gorman, the occupier of the farm, and kept in its place by a hasp and padlock.

with a view of preventing the descent of any but those who, by the payment of a small fee, acquire the right of visiting his subterranean wonders. Upon getting within the grating, a narrow passage of about four feet in height and thirty-three in length, and sloping at an angle of about 30° with the horizon, terminates in an almost vertical precipice, fifteen feet in depth, down which the visiter passes by means of a ladder. Advancing forward from the foot of the ladder the floor resumes its original angle of inclination, which it maintains for the distance of about twenty-eight feet. It now becomes nearly horizontal, and continues so for 242 feet, or until the opening into the lower middle cave is reached. The bearing, however, of this passage, which was hitherto due south, becomes, at 150 feet from the mouth of the middle cave, south east. The height of the entrance varies a good deal, the limits being from three to seventeen feet; its average breadth from the ladder to the point where the bearing takes a more easterly direction, is about nine, and from this point to the entrance of the cave, twenty-seven feet. The floor,

from the foot of the ladder forwards, is everywhere strewed with blocks of limestone; and the roof, which is very irregular, exhibits scarcely any sparry productions.

The lower middle cave, at which we have now arrived, is one of very considerable magnitude. In shape its ground plan resembles a mattrass or bottle with cylindric neck and globular bottom, the diameter of the latter being ninety-five, and the length and diameter of the former seventy-two and forty-two feet respectively. The vertical section of its wider end is that of a dome or hemisphere, the apex of which has an elevation above its base of thirty-five feet. Stalactites of a small size depend from the roof, and a sheeting of sparry matter is observable all along the joints of the limestone, and covers beneath many parts of the floor, where it is usually superimposed upon a very fine red clay, which would appear to have been washed down by water filtering from above before the interstices of the arch were sufficiently closed by calcareous incrustations. The floor of this cave is strewed with large tetrahedral blocks of limestone.

Nichol, del.   Clayton, sc.

THE CROWN CAVERN.

From the southern extremity of the chamber just described, a passage, varying in height from five to ten, and in breadth from seven to fourteen feet, and sixty feet in length, leads to one of somewhat greater magnitude, and of much greater interest, which is known under the name of the upper middle cave. The horizontal section of this natural excavation may, neglecting its irregularities, be considered as a semiellipse, the axes of which are respectively 180 and 90 feet, the major pointing directly east and west. A vertical view or section, corresponding to the line connecting the northern extremity of the minor and eastern extremity of the major axis, shows the roof nearly horizontal, and raised twenty feet above the floor.

This is the most remarkable part of the entire cavern, for the magnitude, beauty, and varied and fantastic appearances of its sparry productions. Immediately upon entering the cave, on the right hand, and attached to the

wall, is found the organ—a huge calcareous growth, which is conceived to bear some resemblance in shape to the musical instrument from which its name is borrowed. Nine great pillars of carbonate of lime occur in this same compartment, rising from the floor to the ceiling; of these the lower third is usually of great diameter, and very irregular in form, while the remaining, or upper portion, usually exhibits the shape of an inverted cone, the base of which is in the ceiling, while the vertex is in connexion with the lower portion of the pillar. In some instances I observed, (but am not sure that it was in this part of the cavern,) that the upper cone had not come in contact with the stalagmite below, though, should the calcareous deposition proceed as heretofore, there can be no doubt that such junction will be finally achieved. The most remarkable pillars in this cave are those known among the guides under the names of *Drum* and *Pyramid,* the former of which occurs fifteen feet south of the organ; the latter at the eastern end of the chamber. The base of the former is not simple, but composed of stalks cemented together, and having leaved or foliated edges; some of these edges are of great extent and thinness, and when struck gently, vibrate so as to produce an agreeable sound. The pyramid, a pillar fourteen feet in height, rests upon a base of great dimensions, and its shaft is distinguished by the circumstance of its tapering upwards towards the ceiling. The other pillars are of inferior size, but some of them possess a symmetry and beauty superior to those just described. In addition to the pillars, stalactites and stalagmites every where abound; the former depending from the roof, the latter springing from the floor of the cavern. They are of every length, from an inch to three or four feet; and they, or rather the greater number of them, together with the pillars, usually correspond in position to the vertical joints of the limestone beds composing the roof of the chamber. Before leaving this part of the cavern, I should not omit to mention, that S. S. W. from the *Pyramid*, and at the distance of twenty feet, there is a rectangular sparry production, raised some feet above the floor, to which, from its shape, the name of *Table* has been applied.

Nichol, del.   Clayton, sc.

THE FOUR COURTS.

From the upper middle cave there are two exits beside that already mentioned, one of which takes an easterly, the other a southerly direction. The former, which augments gradually from four to fifteen feet in breadth, terminates at the distance of 110 feet, in a cul de sac; but about twenty feet from this extremity, there is sent off, in a northern direction, an arm which conducts to the cellar cave, and what is called the *River*. When visited by us, this *river*, which is very difficult of access, appeared to be but a stagnant pool; (or, if the water is ever in motion, such phenomenon was not at the time to be observed;) in the winter season, however, there can be little doubt, as shall be hereafter shown, that this, as well as several other parts of the cavern, is subjected to the action of running water.

The southern exit conducts, by a steep and rugged passage, about fifty feet in length, first ascending, then descending, to what is called the *long* cave — a designation calculated to convey erroneous notions respecting the nature of this part of the cavern. In point of fact, it consists of several galleries, two of which pursue an E. N. E. and W. S. W. direction, and are intersected by several others at an angle of about 105°, or as nearly as possible that of the primitive crystal of carbonate of lime. The east and west galleries average a width of about fourteen feet, and have, the one a length of 190, the other of about 350 feet. Of the cross galleries, which are all exactly parallel to each other, and have a direction N. N. W. and S. S. E.; the largest is that which faces the entrance from the upper middle cave, and may be considered a prolongation of it; its breadth is fourteen, and its length about 140 feet. The second possesses the same length, but its continuity is interrupted, the entire of the intervals between the lanes it intersects not being traversed by it. It extends somewhat further south, and sends off to the west two branches of about thirty-eight feet in length. Two other galleries, having the same direction with these, are so small, that by the careless observer they may be considered as fissures, and they are so marked upon the map. Throughout the entire of these passages, the fine red clay already described as occurring in the lower middle cave, is very abundant, and in many places is sheeted over with thin spar. Calcareous concretions of other kinds also occur, but not in such quantity, or of such beauty, as in the upper middle cave. From this statement, however, I should except the eastern extremity of the largest of them, where several specimens of singular beauty are found, and where, upon the sides of the gallery, the spar exhibits the graceful and brilliant undulations of the richest drawing-room hangings. The dimensions assigned to these galleries must not be received as representing their actual extent: to none of them did we find an absolute termination; and the accompanying chart merely gives the limits at which, in consequence of the difficulties opposed to our progress, further investigation was abandoned.

We shall now, returning to the lower middle cave, examine the outlets of its N. E. extremity. From this quarter of it a branch is sent off to the south, 40 feet in length and 6 in breadth, from the centre point of which there is an offset of about the same dimensions, which takes a N. E. direction, and is crossed at the termination by another gallery parallel to the first, and which has probably, as shall be hereafter shown, a subterranean connexion with that prolongation of the upper middle cave in which the river is found. The cross passage just described is encrusted on both sides with sparry productions: fewer in number, however, and of inferior beauty to those which occur in the galleries it connects.

The second outlet of the upper end of the lower middle cave, expands in a N. N. W. direction, into a cavity of an elliptical shape, 90 feet in length and 45 in breadth, its S. S. E. half being divided into two by a wall of limestone 45 feet in length, and about fifteen in breadth. On the western side of this wall, and between it and the side of the cave, occur four or five magnificent pillars, and at the south angle a small cavity, composed entirely of spar, which was described to us under the name of the *bed-chamber*; it is entered on the north side, through a narrow hole; and from it, but through a smaller and more difficult passage, it is possible to return into the lower middle cave. The portion of the bed-chamber cave to the east side of the stony partition, exhibits nothing remarkable until we reach its N. E. extremity; here, three magnificent stalagmites are encountered, and a pillar of unusual magnitude extending from the floor to the ceiling, and which has received from the guides the name of Lot's wife. This huge stalactitic production occurs at the commencement of an avenue twenty feet long, and about ten wide, at the termination of which three distinct adits present themselves. One of these faces directly the avenue just described, and leads to the Garrett cave; the other two, which are on the left hand, and distant from each other about seven feet, constitute the respective entrances to the grand Kingston gallery and Sand cave.

The Garrett cave extends 255 feet in an easterly direction, with a sweep to the south; its breadth at the commencement being 15, and augmenting gradually until, at its widest part, it becomes 55 feet. The floor, which is every where covered with blocks of limestone scattered in the greatest disorder, is not horizontal, but ascends by a considerable angle, so as, at its remote extremity, to come within a few feet of the ceiling: there is no department of the entire cavern in which pillars, stalactites, and stalagmites of spar are more numerous or more beautiful. The more remote or upper portion, also, of this chamber, is distinguished by the enormous number of small stalactites of from six inches to a foot in length, depending from the ceiling, and studding it at almost every point. The ceiling also, in one part of the cave, would appear to have recently fallen, the floor being covered with a confused pile of fragmented rocks, and the corresponding portion of the roof being destitute of stalactitic productions.

Upon returning to the entrance of the Garrett cave, and ascending by a steep and rugged passage into the most westerly of the two adits already mentioned, we find ourselves within the grand Kingston gallery—the most remarkable compartment of the entire excavation. It is a perfectly straight hall, 175 feet in length and 7 in breadth, with a direction about one point to the west of north. The arching of this gallery is in the Gothic style, and its walls are every where glazed with spar, in some places red, in others mottled, but no where of a perfectly white colour. This gallery, at the distance of 126 feet from its entrance, was originally blocked up by a thin

diaphragm or sheet of spar, but it is now perfectly continuous throughout, a passage having been some time ago broken in the partition, through which one individual at a time can pass. Immediately beyond this partition, a large pillar is met with in the centre of the gallery—about 15 feet further on, another of the same magnitude—and some distance beyond this, and in a line, four others of inferior size. The grand gallery terminates in a rectangular cave, 52 feet wide and 30 long, from the north of which there is a passage in the same line with the grand gallery, and which admitted of being explored to the extent of 87 feet.

From the rectangular cave just described, and which is situate about twelve feet lower than the floor of the Kingston gallery, there is a passage leading back to the entrance of the Garrett cave. This passage, which is called the Sand cave, from the quantity of this material which covers its floor, is, for two-thirds of its length 12 and for the remainder three feet wide: it is perfectly parallel to, and of the same length with the Kingston gallery, but placed at a somewhat lower level.

On the east side of the rectangular cave in which the Sand cave and gallery terminates, there are two long and narrow entrances, which pass directly E. N. E., the northern one bending at the distance of about thirteen feet to the south, so as to meet the other. From this point they constitute a single passage, which proceeds directly south, and then, bending westward, opens into the Sand cave at about forty feet from its northern point of commencement. This winding channel expands and contracts in its progress, so as to form a string of small cells called closets, amounting, as we were informed, to about twenty in number: these closets, however, though laid down in the map, we did not personally examine. In the Sand cave there are no sparry formations; and, indeed, nothing of any interest which has not been mentioned, save a collection of water in a calcareous basin, within a few feet of its southern termination.

From the preceding brief description, the newly discovered cavern, it will be seen, is not a single excavation, but is composed of a number of chambers, some of greater, some of less magnitude, connected by rugged and narrow passages, the floor of these being generally covered with prismatic blocks of limestone, and the sides and ceiling loaded with calcareous incrustations. Pillars also of the same material as has been already described, often connect the floor and ceiling; and the masses of limestone on the floor, are, in many places, covered with spar, giving rise to stalagmitic productions of the most varied and fantastic appearance. The length of the entire cavern, from the entrance to the extremity of the long cave, which corresponds with the line of section given in the map, is seven hundred feet; but a line passing through the grand gallery, and extending to the northern and southern limits of the entire series of cavities, would measure 870 feet. Another line, drawn from the entrance to the farthest extremity of the Garrett cave, has an east and west direction measuring 572 feet, which may be considered as giving the greatest breadth of the cavern, or as comprehending its eastern and western boundaries. The floors of the different chambers, included in the annexed section, namely, of the lower middle, upper middle, and long caves, are very nearly horizontal, and depressed about 55 feet below the grate through which the cavern is entered. The depression of the Kingston gallery below this point is but 47 feet, and that of the eastern end of the Garrett cave but 19. This latter chamber is, therefore, that which comes closest to the surface, and the thickness of the intervening strata is, it may be observed, diminished not only by its actually greater elevation, but also by the circumstance of this portion of the cavern corresponding, not to the apex, but to the north-eastern slope of the hill.

In glancing at the accompanying ground plan, several portions of the cavern are observed to be parallel, all running S. S. E. and N. N. W. Three of these are in a line, namely, the Sand cave to the north, and off-sets from the lower and upper middle caves to the south: between these different passages there can be no doubt that there is a subterraneous communication, and that, at certain seasons of the year, they are traversed by running water. It is worthy of remark, that at the time of our visit, water was found at two points on this line, namely, at the junction of the Sand and Garrett caves, and at the prolongation of the upper middle cave, where the river has been already described as occurring. It may be also not uninteresting to mention, that the line of direction just specified, corresponds with that of the dip of the limestone beds which compose the hill.

MAP OF MITCHELSTOWN CAVES.

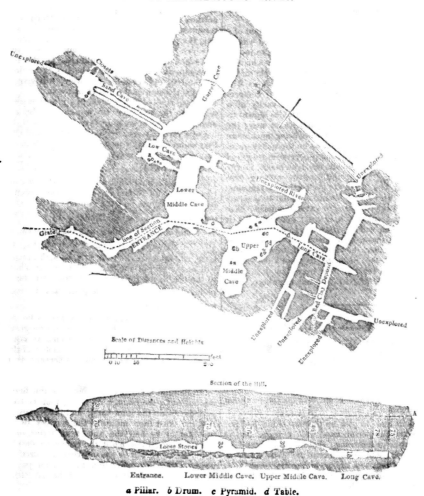

a Pillar. b Drum. c Pyramid. d Table.

The figures on the Map express the depth in feet below the line of section A.A.

ON THE FORMATION OF SPARRY PRODUCTIONS.

The manner of formation of sparry productions in limestone caves is so generally known, that it is scarcely necessary to advert to the subject here. Water filters through the roof, containing carbonate of lime held in solution by carbonic acid, and this gas, gradually passing with some water into the atmosphere, the calcareous salt is deposited. The atmosphere within the cavern was, as might have been anticipated, found saturated, or nearly so, with moisture: for though its temperature was not lower than 50°, the pulmonary halitus condensed into a visible cloud, and the body, under slight exertion, became bathed with perspiration; but it did not, it is fair to conclude, contain any unusual per centage of carbonic acid, for it supported, in the ordinary manner, both respiration and combustion. What then becomes of the carbonic acid, the development of which is the immediate cause of the deposition of spar? Why does it not accumulate so as finally to create an irrespirable atmosphere? These are interesting but difficult questions, and the following is put forward only as a conjectural solution of the difficulty. These caves are usually traversed by running water, and as this, at common temperatures, combines with one volume of carbonic acid, the gas may be considered as in a continual process of absorption and removal. It is a peculiarity, also, of æriform fluids, as Dalton has shown, that however different in density, they will, when placed in contact, blend together so as finally to constitute an equable mixture. Now, as the roofs of limestone caverns are seldom, if ever, so tight at every point as to be altogether impermeable to gases, we perceive in the law which regulates their diffusion, additional means for effecting the elimination of the carbonic acid.

There is a circumstance connected with the structure of stalactitic spars, which must have been frequently noticed, though it would not appear to have attracted much attention, for I do not recollect having seen any allusion to it in books—*all the smaller stalactites are hollow along the axis, but those of a larger size are solid throughout.* This fact, however, it is not difficult to explain. If a drop of a solution of supercarbonate of lime be conceived depending from some prominence in the roof of a cave, the evaporation necessarily takes place from its external surface; and in virtue of this, it will be shortly invested with a film of spar which will, in a great measure, protect its interior from a continuance of the process. The afflux of additional calcareous solution, will augment the thickness of the film first formed, and the greater part of the fluid trickling from above, being carried to the lower extremity, of the stalactite already formed, its prolongation downward in a vertical direction, is easily understood.

To the completion of this theory it would obviously be necessary to explain—1st. Why the stalactite, while small, does not become sealed up at the vertex; and 2dly. Why, when its bulk is augmented, its internal cavity is obliterated.

The reason why the drop with which the formation of a stalactite commences does not become covered with a coating of spar at its lowermost point, appears to me to be, that the hydrostatic pressure of the solution which is constantly flowing down from above, and dropping on the floor of the cave, removes it mechanically as fast as it is produced. The other fact is still more easy of comprehension. The fluid which fills the fistulous cavity of a small stalactite, as well as that which trickles down its external surface, gradually lets fall particles of spar; the deposition, however, in the former case, being much more slow, owing to the obstacle presented by the sparry envelope to evaporation. A real and progressive growth of the internal surface, does nevertheless take place, in virtue of which the diameter of the fistulous opening constantly diminishes, and the cavity itself finally disappears.

Before closing this paper, I should not omit to mention that no bones, either of existing or extinct animals, have as yet been found within the cavern; nor indeed is it likely that any such will be discovered; as, until accidentally perforated through the quarry, it would appear to have been altogether impervious, and therefore inaccessible as a den or place of shelter to those kinds of animals whose osseous remains have been found in such abundance in the cave of Kirkdale, and elsewhere.

CURIOUS ARITHMETICAL CALCULATIONS.

RECREATIONS IN MATHEMATICS AND NATURAL PHILOSOPHY:

CONTAINING AMUSING DISSERTATIONS AND ENQUIRIES CONCERNING A VARIETY OF SUBJECTS CALCULATED TO EXCITE CURIOSITY AND ATTENTION.

The following are answers to the four queries proposed in our last number:

I. It is evident that, to pick up the first stone, and put it into the basket, the person must walk 2 yards, one in going and another in returning; that for the second he must walk 4 yards; and so on, increasing by two as far as the hundredth, which will oblige him to walk two hundred yards, one hundred in going, and one hundred in returning. It may easily be perceived also, that these numbers form an arithmetical progression, in which the number of terms is 100, the first term 2, and the last 200. The sum total, therefore, will be the product of 202 by 50, or 10100 yards, which amount to more than five miles and a half.

II. This question may be easily answered, by the rules already given; for the difference of the terms is 2, and the number of terms 20; consequently, to find the twentieth term, we must multiply 2 by 19, and add 38, the product, to the first term 3, which will give 41 for the twentieth term.

If we then add the first and last terms, that is 3 and 41, which will make 44, and multiply this sum by 10, or half the number of terms, the product 440 will be the sum of all the terms of the progression, or the number of shillings due to the bricklayer when he had completed the work. He would therefore have to receive twenty-two pounds.

III. Those who might imagine that two-fifths of the whole sum were due to the workman, because eight yards are two-fifths of the depth agreed on, would certainly be mistaken; for it may be easily seen that, in cases of this kind, the labour increases in proportion to the depth. We shall here suppose, for it would be difficult to determine it with any accuracy, that the labour increases arith-

metically as the depth; consequently the price ought to increase in the same manner.

To determine this problem, therefore, 20l. or 400 shillings must be divided into 20 terms in arithmetical progression, and the sum of the first eight of these will be what was due to the bricklayer for his labour.

But 400 shillings may be divided into twenty terms, in arithmetical proportion, a great many different ways, according to the value of the first term, which is here undetermined; if we suppose it, for example, to be one shilling, the progression will be 1, 3, 5, 7, &c., the last term of which will be 39; and consequently the sum of the first eight terms will be 64 shillings. On the other hand, if we suppose the first term to be $10\frac{1}{2}$, the series of terms will be $10\frac{1}{2}$, $11\frac{1}{2}$, $12\frac{1}{2}$, $13\frac{1}{2}$, $14\frac{1}{2}$, which will give 112 shillings for the sum of the first eight terms.

But, to resolve the problem in a proper manner, so as to give to the bricklayer his just due for the commencement of the work, we must determine what is the fair value of a yard of work, similar to the first, and then assume that value as the first term of the progression. We shall here suppose that this value is 5 shillings; and in that case the required progression will be 5, $6\frac{11}{19}$, $8\frac{1}{19}$, $9\frac{14}{19}$, $11\frac{6}{19}$ $12\frac{7}{19}$ &c., the common difference of which is $\frac{30}{19}$, and the last term 35. Now to find the eighth term, which is necessary before we can find the sum of the first eight terms, multiply the common difference $\frac{30}{19}$ by 7, which will give $11\frac{1}{19}$, and add this product to 5 the first term, which will give the eighth term $16\frac{1}{19}$; if we then add $16\frac{1}{19}$ to the first term, and multiply the sum, $21\frac{1}{19}$, by 4, the product, $84\frac{1}{19}$, will be the sum of the first eight terms, or what was due to the bricklayer, for the part of the work he had completed. The bricklayer therefore had to receive $84\frac{1}{19}$ shillings or 4l. 4s. $2\frac{10}{19}d$.

IV. In this problem the payments to be made each month ought to increase in arithmetical progression. We have given the sum of the terms, which is equal to the sum total of the debt, and also the number of these terms, which is 12; but their common difference is unknown, because it is that by which the payments ought to increase each month.

To find this difference, we must take the first payment multiplied by the number of terms, that is to say, 1200 pounds, from the sum total, and the remainder will be 660, we must then multiply the number of terms less unity, or 11, by half the number of terms, or 6, and we shall have 66; by which if the remainder 660 be divided, the quotient 10 will be the difference required. The first payment therefore being 100, the second payment must have been 110, the third 120, and the last 210.

QUERIES IN GEOMETRICAL PROGRESSIONS.

A courtier having performed some very important service to his sovereign, the latter, wishing to confer on him a suitable reward, desired him to ask whatever he thought proper, promising that it should be granted. The courtier, who was well acquainted with the science of numbers, only requested that the monarch would give him a quantity of wheat equal to that which would arise from one grain doubled sixty-three times successively. What was the value of the reward?

A gentleman taking a fancy to a horse, which a horse-dealer wished to dispose of at as high a price as he could, the latter, to induce the gentleman to become a purchaser, offered to let him have the horse for the value of the twenty-fourth nail in his shoes, reckoning one farthing for the first nail, two for the second, four for the third, and so on to the twenty-fourth. The gentleman, thinking he should have a good bargain, accepted the offer: what was the price of the horse?

DUBLIN:
Printed and Published by P. D. HARDY, 3, Cecilia-street; to whom communications are to be addressed.
Sold by all Booksellers in Ireland.
In London, by Richard Groombridge, 6, Panyer-alley, Paternoster row; in Liverpool, by Willmer and Smith; in Manchester, by Ambery; in Birmingham, by Drake; in Glasgow, by John Macleod; and in Edinburgh by M. Bowack.

THE

DUBLIN PENNY JOURNAL

CONDUCTED BY P. DIXON HARDY, M.R.I.A.

| Vol. III. | JANUARY 3, 1835. | No. 131. |

" Blow high, blow low," or March in the Metropolis.

The Return to Town—a Scene in October.

THE COMIC ALMANACK FOR 1835

Is really worthy of Cruikshank. In several of the illustrations, which are lithographed on tinted paper, there is a fund of humour worth the price of the entire calendar; and which would actually some few years since, printed on larger paper, have cost that price. The little work, with the exception of the mere calculations contained in an ordinary almanack, is a severe tho' well deserved satire on the empiricism and impostures of such worthies as Mr. Francis Moore, and his notorious allies, the quack doctors, who have so long gulled honest John Bull with their *postulates* and *pills*.

The humour in the engravings we have endeavoured to transfer to our wood-cuts; they have, however, necessarily lost a considerable portion of the spirit in the transfer. They are evidently "Scenes from Nature," and "Life in London," during the months of *March* and *October*;—those for the other months are equally good.

In the letter press there are numerous excellent hits at the men and manners of the age—*ex. g*, under the head

"HUMBUGGUM ASTROLOGICUM PRO ANNO 1835."

COURTEOUS READER—Stepping in the steps of my late worthy and much lamented prototype, Francis Moore, deceased, I herewith present you with my hieroglyphic, "*adapted to the* TIMES." "Its interpretation is in the womb of time," and those who do pry with curious eyes into the mysteries of the stars, will, in due season, divine the hidden meaning thereof. Yet may I observe, that by the rules of art, I have discovered, that a *fiery planet*, which has been for some time located in the *upper house*, and has been for a long while ceive divers juveniles, of eighty years old and upwards, seated on stools, with horn-books in their hands. The man in the Moon is also very busy, striving to metamorphose his sticks into *brooms*, to sweep away the cobwebs of ignorance therewith. Moreover, I do observe about half a million miles of cast-iron rail-road, in the direction of the earth, by which I do opine an inclination towards this planet. But there doth appear a great consternation amongst the other constellations, more especially in the *Upper House*, where *Libra* hath got into fiery opposition with *Mars*; and *Saturn* (who hath grown *Grey*) hath, in striving to part them, lost the skirts of his coat, and is glad to put up with a *Spencer*, whereby is clearly shadowed forth a fierce encounter between two great commanders. Let those, who think little of law and justice, read the ten thousand volumes of the Abridgment of the Statutes, and tremble!

PROCEEDINGS OF LEARNED SOCIETIES.

At the Philosophical Institution, held at the Pig and Tinder Box, in Liquorpond-street, a letter was read by Sawny Suck-Egg, Esq, on the possibility of extending the realms of space, and adding to the duration of eternity. In the same essay, he also satisfactorily proved, that two and *too* do *not* make four; that BLACK is very often white; and that a Chancery suit has shewn to many a man, that what has a beginning does not necessarily always have an end.

A successful method of converting stones into bread has been transmitted to the New Poor Law Commissioners, and a three-and-sixpenny medal presented to the ingenious discoverer thereof.

Zoological Society at Hookem Snivey.—A new animal has been transmitted from No-Man's-Land, which has been named the Flat-Catcher. It bears some resemblance to the human species, as it walks on two legs, and has the gift of speech. It seems quite in its element when among *pigeons*, and preys ravenously on the *gulls* that hover about watering places, getting hold of them by a kind of fascination, which throws its unconscious victims entirely off their guard, when it never fails to make them bleed profusely; after which, it suffers them to depart.

A laborious investigator has discovered, that there are exactly nine millions one hundred and sixty-four thousand five hundred and thirty-three hairs on a tom-cat's tail, which he defies all the zoologists in Europe to disprove. He also maintains, that a bull sees with its horns, and a rat with its tail, although he admits the possibility of their doing so without them.

It was stated at the last meeting of this institution, that one of its members had observed a tremendous water-

lord of the ascendant, has come in fiery opposition with *Scorpio*; while *Taurus* hath flung a quartile ray at both of them.

ASS-TROLOGICAL PREDICTIONS.

I now proceed to put on my conjuring cap, and show forth the wonders of the stars.

On looking at the moon, through my 500-horse power telescope, which magnifieth the planets ninety-seven millions of times larger than life, I discern, that the march of intellect hath already travelled to that luminary; for I do distinctly perceive.

spout from one of the plugs in Thames-street; and sensible shocks of an earthquake had been felt at Puddle-dock.

Society of Antiquaries.—Among the antiquities presented at the last meeting was one of Cleopatra's corns, and the celebrated *Needle* with which she darned her hose; also, a gas-pipe, found at Herculaneum, and the fragment of a steam-carriage, dug out of the ruins of Palmyra.

Entomological Society in GRUB-*street.*—A very animated conversation took place on the natural history of the flea, involving many curious conjectures, such as, whether it had ever been known to have attained the size of the elephant; whether it was of the same species with the hog-in-armour and the rhinoceros, or was to be classed among the *Jumpers;* how high and how often it leaped; whether it always looked before it leaped; and whether it leaped highest in Leap Year; the further discussion of all which queries was deferred till the said Leap Year.

The Horticultural Society of Seven Dials has been presented, by the Society of Antiquaries, with the identical pumpkin converted by the fairy into Cinderella's chariot.

Premiums have been awarded by various learned bodies to the following :—

To Henry Broom, for the application of the crab motion, and the "do-as-little-as-possible" principle, to the state engine. To Lord Durham, in conjunction with the above, for an improved mode of progression for the said engine, namely, by each pulling the opposite way. To Signor Paganini, for an improved mode of extracting gold from catgut scrapings, and of skinning flints. To Miss Harriet Martineau, for a new preventive check-string for the regulation of the fare (*fair*.) To the proprietor of Morison's Pills for the discovery of the *perpetual motion.* To the Society for the Confusion of Useful Knowledge, for their successful endeavours in be-*Knight*-ing the public intellect.

ADVERTISEMENTS EXTRAORDINARY.

Brutish Humbug College of Health.—The wonderful efficacy of the MORISING PILLS becomes every day more conspicuous. The discerning Public swallows 'em' like winking; and we defies all opposition, and the *Weakly* attempts of our enemies, to *Dispatch* us. We tells those as calls us quacks, that, under the blessing of Divine Providence, we glories in our ignorance; and takes every opportunity of exposing it, for the benefit of our suffering fellow-creatures. And we have found them a *sovereign* remedy for ourselves, that; having, for a long while, been afflicted with an emptiness of the chest, and a great deficiency of the *yellow stuff*, all which terrible symptoms have speedily disappeared; so we feels in duty bound to propagate our pills to the remotest prosperity.

The following are selected out of several millions of cases, furnished by a single agent, in a most sensible letter, to prove the never-to-be-enough-wondered-at wonderful efficacy of the Hy-gee-wo-ian Medicines.

MOST RESPECTED SIR,

Having been appointed your agent, and, therefore, influenced, like yourself, by the most disinterested motives, I make it a point to recommend them on all occasions, and always in sufficiently large doses, on which I observe you lay peculiar stress; and very justly; for does it not follow, as a matter of course, that if six pills do a certain quantity of good, six thousand must, as a natural consequence, do six thousand times as much more good, and the patient must be six thousand times the better for them? There are some censorious folks who insinuate, that the more pills I sell, the more money I get by them; but I need not assure you, that, in this respect, my motives are quite as disinterested as your own. Yours, ever to command,

FRANCIS FLETCH'EM.

P.S.—Please to send me a dozen wagon loads of No. 1 Pills, and the same of No. 2 Pills, as early as possible. I hand you the following cases, which have come under my own knowledge.

To the Haggent for the Morising Pils.

ONERR'D SUR,

THIS hear kums 2 akwaint you that havein Lst my happy-tight i tuk to takein your Morising Pils witch i only begun with takein 5 hundred hat a time witch had the blessed defect of turnin me inside out and I felt in a wery pekooliar citywation witch discurraged me 2 parsewere and i tuk 1 thousen hat a doze by witch I was turnd outside in by witch my happytight was kwite discuvvered witch was a grate blesin for my whife who is bigg in the famylyat way with 12 smal children with grate happytights all threw your pils and I ham now Abel to wurk and yarn my 12 shillin a weak So no more hat presnt from your tunbel Servt to command

GREGORY GUDGEON.

No. 9, Nobody-knows-where Street, Jericho,
Feb. the 32d, 1836.

SIR—I BEG to inform you, that a poor man was blown to atoms by the explosion of the Powder Mills on Hounslow Heath. His affectionate wife, who happened to be passing at the time, carefully picked up the fragments, and placed them together; and, by administering a dose of the Universal Medicine, he was able to walk home, and eat a hearty dinner of bacon and cabbage.

If any person should doubt the truth of the above statement, I beg you will refer them to me, when I will fully satisfy all inquiries. I am easily *found out*—as *every body knows me.* Your obedient servant,

GILES GAMMON.

No. 1, Blarneygig Place, Salisbury Plain,
next door to Stonehenge.

P.S.—I forgot to add, that the poor woman, in the hurry of the moment, made a small mistake, by placing the head of a donkey, which had been blown off by the explosion, upon her husband's shoulders, instead of his own; but she says it is of very little consequence, as very few of his acquaintance could perceive any difference.

THE "WISDOM OF OUR ANCESTORS."

"The way to be certainly loved, is to take the marrow of a wolf's left foot, and make of it a sort of pomatum, with ambergris and cyprus powder, carry it about one, and cause the person to smell of it from time to time."—*Albertus,* p. 12.

"To prevent differences and a divorce betwixt a man and his wife, take two quails' hearts, the one of a male, the other of a female, and cause the man to carry about him the male, and the woman the female."—*Thiers,* t. 1, p. 389.

The humbug prophecies of Francis Moore are thus turned into ridicule:

PROGNOSTICS FOR JANUARY.
Weather likely to be cold,
If the frost is very old:
If no snow should chance to fall,
Then, perhaps, no frost at all.

FOR FEBRUARY.
Rain or hail, snow or sleet
In this month you're sure to meet.
If you don't why then you wont:
Perhaps there won't be one nor t'other,
Why then 'twill happen in some other.

MORAL TO THE FOREGOING.

While we venerate what is deserving of veneration let us not forget, that quackery, knavery, bigotry, and superstition always merit exposure and castigation.

COMFORTS OF THE SEASON.

Chilblains sore on all your toes,
Icicles hang from your nose;
Rheumatis' in all your limbs;
Noddle full of aches and whims;
Chaps upon your hands and lips,
And lumbago in your hips.
To your bed you shiv'ring creep,
There to freeze, but not to sleep;
For the sheets, that look so nice,
Are to you two sheets of ice;
Wearied out, at length you doze,
And snatch, at last, a brief repose;
Dream all night that you're a dab,
Lying on fishmonger's slab.
While indulging in a snore,
There comes a rap at chamber door;
Screaming voice of Betty cries:
"If you please, it's time to rise."
Up you start, and, on the sheet,
Find your breath is chang'd to sleet;
Tow'rds the glass you turn your view,
Find your nose of purple hue,
Looking very like, I trow,
Beet-root in a field of snow.
You would longer lie, but nay,
Time is come—you must away,
Out you turn, with courage brave,
Slip on drawers—and then to shave!
Seize the jug, and in a trice,
Find the water chang'd to ice:
Break the ice, and have to rue
That you've broke the pitcher too.
Water would not run before;
Now, it streams upon the floor,
Threat'ning with a fearful doom,
Ceiling of the drawing-room.
In the frenzy of despair,
You seize you don't know what, nor care,
Mop up all the wet and dirt,
And find you've done it with your shirt,
Your *only* shirt all filth and slosh,
For all the rest are in the wash.
Into bed you turn again,
Ring the bell with might and main,
Stammer out to Betty, why
'Twixt the sheets you're forc'd to lie,
'Till, pitying your feelings hurt,
She dabs you out another shirt.

Thus far then, good reader, have we copied the sayings of Rigdum Funnidos, Gent. For the remainder of the "right merry cuts" and pleasant conceits of Mr. George Cruikshank, we refer you to the little work, which is well worth its price.

Thirty days hath September, April, June and November, February, twenty-eight alone, all the rest have thirty-one.

THE
ALMANACK OR CALENDAR

FOR THE YEAR OF OUR LORD,

1835,

BEING

THE THIRD AFTER LEAP YEAR, THE FIFTH YEAR OF THE REIGN OF KING WILLIAM IV. AND THIRTY-FIFTH YEAR OF THE UNION.

EXPLANATION OF THE MARKS.

* High Tides at Dublin Bar. † Nights of the greatest moonlight. || Bank Holidays. § Courts do not sit.
[See the following pages.]

JANUARY, 1835.

Week Days, and Remarkable Days.

1	Thursday, Circumcision
2	Friday
3	Saturday
4	2Sunday past Christmas
5	Monday
6	Tuesday, EPIPHANY
7	Wednesday
8	Thursday
9	Friday
10	Saturday
11	1Sunday past Epiphany
12	Monday, Term begins
13	+Tuesday, Hilary Quarter Sess. Dublin
14	+Wednesday
15	+Thursday, City Record Court sits
16	Friday, Quarter Assembly Dublin
17	Saturday
18	2Sunday past Epiphany
19	Monday
20	Tuesday, Civil Bill Court sits
21	Wednesday
22	Thursday
23	Friday
24	Saturday
25	3Sunday past Epiphany, Conv. St. Paul
26	Monday
27	Tuesday
28	Wednesday
29	Thursday
30	Friday, King Charles I. martyr.
31	Saturday Fast, Term ends.

First Quarter, Tuesday, 6 day, 15 minutes past 9, afternoon
Full Moon, Wednesday, 14 day, 51 minutes past 5, afternoon
Last Quarter, Wednesday, 21 day, 31 minutes past 6, afternoon
New Moon, Wednesday, 28 day, 46 minutes past 8, afternoon

FEBRUARY, 1835.

Week Days and Remarkable Days.

1	4Sunday past Epiphany
2	Monday, Purification
3	Tuesday
4	Wednesday
5	Thursday
6	Friday
7	Saturday
8	5Sunday past Epiphany
9	Monday
10	Tuesday
11	Wednesday
12	+Thursday
13	+Friday
14	+Saturday, Valentine
15	Septuagesima
16	Monday
17	Tuesday
18	Wednesday
19	Thursday
20	Friday
21	Saturday
22	Sexagesima
23	Monday, Fast
24	Tu. St. Matthias, Queen's B. day kept
25	Wednesday
26	Thursday
27	Friday
28	Saturday

First Quarter, Thursday, 4 day, 10 minutes past 7, afternoon
Full Moon, Friday, 13 day, 34 minutes past 5, afternoon
Last Quarter, Friday, 20 day, 26 minutes past 4, morning
New Moon, Friday, 27 day, 3 minutes past 0, afternoon

MARCH, 1835.

Week Days and Remarkable Days.

1	Quinquagesima, St. David
2	Monday, Bristol Fair
3	Shrove Tuesday
4	Ash Wednesday
5	Thursday
6	Friday
7	Saturday
8	1Sunday in Lent
9	Monday
10	Tuesday
11	Wednesday, Ember Week
12	Thursday, Gregory M.
13	+Friday
14	+Saturday
15	2Sunday in Lent
16	Monday
17	Tuesday, Saint Patrick
18	Wednesday
19	Thursday, Equal Day and Night
20	Friday
21	Saturday
22	3Sunday in Lent
23	Monday
24	Tuesday, Fast
25	Wednesday, Annunciation
26	Thursday
27	Friday
28	Saturday
29	4Sunday in Lent, Mid. Lent Sunday
30	Monday
31	Tuesday

First Quarter, Saturday, 7 day, 47 minutes past 2, afternoon
Full Moon, Saturday, 14 day, 42 minutes past 9, afternoon
Last Quarter, Saturday, 21 day, 1 minute past 1, afternoon
New Moon, Sunday, 29 day, 17 minutes past 4, morning
Spring Quar. begins Sat. 21 day, 31 minutes past 7, morning

APRIL, 1835.

Week Days and Remarkable Days.

1	Wednesday
2	Thursday
3	Friday
4	Saturday
5	5Sunday in Lent
6	Monday
7	Tuesday
8	Wednesday
9	Thursday
10	Friday
11	+Saturday
12	6Sunday in Lent, Palm Sunday
13	+Monday
14	Tuesday
15	Wednesday, Term begins
16	Thursday, Battle of Culloden, 1746
17	Good Friday
18	Saturday, Fast
19	Easter Sunday
20	E. M. Curr. Races, Civil B. Court sits
21	Easter Tuesday
22	Wednesday
23	Thursday, Saint George
24	Friday
25	Saturday, Saint Mark, Evangelist
26	1Sunday past Easter, Low Sunday
27	Monday
28	Tuesday, Quarter Sessions Dublin
29	Wednesday
30	Thursday, City Record Court sits

First Quarter, Monday, 6 day, 6 minutes past 9, morning
Full Moon, Monday, 13 day, 51 minutes past 6, morning
Last Quarter, Sunday, 19 day, 48 minutes past 10, afternoon
New Moon, Monday, 27 day, 55 minutes past 8, afternoon

MAY, 1835.

Week Days and Remarkable Days.

1	Friday, St. Philip & Jas. Qr. Ass. Dub.
2	Saturday
3	2Sunday past Easter
4	Monday
5	Tuesday
6	Wednesday
7	Thursday
8	Friday
9	Saturday
10	3Sunday past Easter
11	Monday
12	+Tuesday
13	Wednesday, Term ends
14	Thursday
15	Friday
16	Saturday
17	4Sunday past Easter
18	Monday
19	Tuesday
20	Wednesday
21	Thursday
22	Friday
23	Saturday
24	5Sunday past Easter, Rogation
25	Monday
26	Tuesday
27	Wednesday, Fast, Term begins
28	Ascension day, King's Birth day kept
29	Friday, Restoration of Charles II.
30	Saturday
31	Sunday after Ascension

First Quarter, Tuesday, 5 day, 18 minutes past 10, afternoon
Full Moon, Tuesday, 12 day, 48 minutes past 2, afternoon
Last Quarter, Tuesday, 19 day, 13 minutes past 1, afternoon
New Moon, Wednesday, 27 day, 7 minutes past 1, afternoon

JUNE, 1835.

Week Days and Remarkable Days.

1	Monday
2	Tuesday
3	Wednesday
4	Thursday
5	Friday
6	Saturday, Fast
7	Whit. Sunday
8	Whit. Monday, Curragh Races
9	+Whit. Tuesday
10	+Wednesday, Ember Week
11	+Thursday, St. Barnabas
12	Friday
13	Saturday
14	Trinity Sunday
15	Monday
16	Tuesday, Battle of Dettingen, 1743
17	Wednesday, Term ends
18	T. Corpus Christi, B. Waterloo, 1815
19	Friday
20	Saturday
21	1Sunday past Trinity
22	Monday, Longest day
23	Tuesday, Fast
24	W. St. John Baptist, Midsummer day
25	Thursday
26	Friday, King's Accession
27	Saturday, Fast
28	2Sunday past Trinity
29	Monday, St. Peter
30	Tuesday

First Quarter, Thursday, 4 day, 40 minutes past 7, morning
Full Moon, Wednesday, 10 day, 20 minutes past 10, afternoon
Last Quar. Wednesday, 17 day, 11 minutes past 3, morning
New Moon, Friday, 26 day, 55 minutes past 1, morning
Sum. Quar. begins Mon. 22 day, 30 minutes past 4, morning

JULY, 1835.

D.M.	Week Days and Remarkable Days.	Sun rise. H M	Sun set. H M	Dublin Bar Mrn. H M	Dublin Bar Aftr. H M	Moon rises. H M	Moon sets. H M
1	Wednesday, Battle of the Boyne, 1690	3 38	8 29	2 6	2 27	9m20	11a38
2	Thursday, Dog Days begin	3 38	8 28	2 48	3 13	10 42	11 53
3	Friday	3 39	8 28	3 38	4 6	0a 2	—
4	Saturday	3 40	8 27	4 34	5 7	1 26	0m 7
5	3 *Sunday* past Trinity	3 41	8 27	5 40	6 16	2 52	0 21
6	Monday, Chester Fair	3 42	8 26	6 53	7 27	4 23	0 37
7	Tuesday	3 43	8 26	8 2	8 34	5 52	0 58
8	†Wednesday	[illegible]	[illegible]	[illegible]	[illegible]	[illegible]	[illegible]
9	†Thursday	3 45	8 24	10 5	10 32	8 26	2 12
10	†Friday	3 46	8 23	10 59	11 24	9 19	3 14
11	Saturday	3 47	8 23	11*49	—	9 56	4 29
12	4 *Sunday* p. Trinity, B. of Aughrim, 1691	3 48	8 22	0*11	0*33	10 21	5 52
13	Monday	3 49	8 21	0 53	1 14	10 40	7 14
14	Tuesday, Quarter Sessions, Dublin	3 50	8 20	1 33	1 53	10 55	8 35
15	Wednesday, Swithin	3 52	8 19	2 12	2 31	11 6	9 53
16	Thursday, City Record Court sits	3 53	8 18	2 49	3 7	11 18	11 6
17	Friday, Quarter Assembly Dublin	3 54	8 16	3 27	3 48	11 30	0a17
18	Saturday	3 55	8 15	4 13	4 39	11 43	1 29
19	5 *Sunday* past Trinity	3 57	8 14	5 9	5 39	11 58	2 40
20	Monday, Civil Bill Court sits	3 58	8 13	6 13	6 48	—	3 51
21	Tuesday	4 0	8 11	7 22	7 56	0m18	5 8
22	Wednesday	4 1	8 10	8 25	8 55	0 45	6 11
23	Thursday	4 2	8 9	9 19	9 44	1 21	7 11
24	Friday, Fast	4 4	8 7	10 6	10 29	2 9	8 1
25	Saturday, St. James	4 6	8 6	10 49	11 10	3 10	8 38
26	6 *Sunday* past Trinity	4 7	8 4	11*30	11*50	4 23	9 5
27	Monday	4 9	8 3	—	0*9	5 41	9 27
28	Tuesday	4 10	8 1	0 29	0 48	7 3	9 46
29	Wednesday	4 12	7 59	1 8	1 27	8 25	10 1
30	Thursday	4 13	7 58	1 46	2 6	9 48	10 13
31	Friday	4 15	7 56	2 27	2 49	11 12	10 25

First Quarter, Friday, 3 day, 16 minutes past 2, afternoon
Full Moon, Friday, 10 day, 11 minutes past 6, morning
Last Quarter, Friday, 17 day, 19 minutes past 3, afternoon
New Moon, Saturday, 25 day, 49 minutes past 4, afternoon

AUGUST, 1835.

D.M.	Week Days and Remarkable Days.	Sun rise. H M	Sun set. H M	Dublin Bar Mrn. H M	Dublin Bar Aftr. H M	Moon rises. H M	Moon sets. H M
1	Saturday, Lammas Day, B. Nile, 1798	4 16	7 54	3 11	3 37	0a32	10a41
2	7 *Sunday* past Trinity	4 18	7 53	4 3	4 36	2 4	11 6
3	Monday,	4 20	7 51	5 [illegible]	5 48	3 32	11 26
4	Tuesday	4 21	7 49	6 [illegible]	7 7	4 56	—
5	Wednesday	4 23	7 47	7 47	8 22	6 10	0m 2
6	Thursday	4 25	7 45	8 58	9 38	7 9	0 56
7	†Friday	[illegible]	7 43	[illegible]	[illegible]	[illegible]	[illegible]
8	†Saturday	4 28	7 41	10 48	11 10	8 22	3 24
9	†8 *Sunday* past Trinity	4 30	7 39	11 33	11*52	8 43	4 49
10	Monday	4 32	7 37	—	0*12	8 58	6 12
11	Tuesday, Dog Days end	4 33	7 35	0*29	0 47	9 13	7 30
12	Wednesday	4 35	7 33	1 4	1 21	9 24	8 46
13	Thursday, Queen born, 1792	4 37	7 31	1 37	1 54	9 37	10 0
14	Friday	4 38	7 29	2 10	2 26	9 49	11 14
15	Saturday, Assumption V. M.	4 40	7 27	2 44	3 2	10 2	0a26
16	9 *Sunday* past Trinity	4 42	7 25	3 24	3 47	10 20	1 38
17	Monday	4 44	7 23	4 16	4 46	10 45	2 49
18	Tuesday	4 45	7 21	5 21	5 58	11 16	3 58
19	Wednesday	4 47	7 19	6 37	7 16	11 58	5 0
20	Thursday	4 49	7 16	7 50	8 24	—	5 54
21	Friday, King born, 1765	4 51	7 14	8 52	9 20	0m54	6 37
22	Saturday, Fast	4 52	7 12	9 44	10 9	2 4	7 8
23	10 *Sunday* past Trinity	4 54	7 10	10 29	10 50	3 22	7 31
24	Monday, Saint Bartholomew	4 56	7 8	11 10	11 30	4 46	7 52
25	Tuesday	4 57	7 5	11*49	—	6 9	8 7
26	Wednesday	4 59	7 3	0*8	0*26	7 34	8 19
27	Thursday	5 1	7 1	0 45	1 4	8 58	8 32
28	Friday	5 3	6 58	1 24	1 44	10 23	8 47
29	Saturday	5 4	6 56	2 5	2 28	11 51	9 0
30	11 *Sunday* past Trinity	5 6	6 54	2 52	3 20	1a21	9 29
31	Monday	5 8	6 51	3 48	4 22	2 49	9 59

First Quarter, Saturday 1 day, 24 minutes past 7, afternoon
Full Moon, Saturday, 8 day, 14 minutes past 3, afternoon
Last Quarter, Sunday, 16 day, 50 minutes past 8, morning
New Moon, Monday, 24 day, 56 minutes past 3, morning
First Quarter, Monday, 31 day, 27 minutes past 0, morning

SEPTEMBER, 1835.

D.M.	Week Days and Remarkable Days.	Sun rise. H M	Sun set. H M	Dublin Bar Mrn. H M	Dublin Bar Aftr. H M	Moon rises. H M	Moon sets. H M
1	Tuesday, Bristol Fair	5 10	6 49	4 57	5 38	4a 5	10a48
2	Wednesday	5 11	6 47	6 20	7 1	5 7	11 50
3	Thursday	5 13	6 44	7 43	8 17	5 52	—
4	Friday	5 15	6 42	8 52	9 20	6 25	1m 4
5	†Saturday	5 17	6 39	9 48	10 9	6 48	2 26
6	†12 *Sunday* past Trinity	5 18	6 37	10 31	10 50	7 5	3 51
7	†Monday, Curragh Races, R. M.	5 20	6 35	11 10	11 27	7 19	5 11
8	Tu. Nativity, King & Queen Cr. 1831	5 22	6 32	11*44	11*59	7 31	6 28
9	Wednesday	5 24	6 30	—	0*15	7 42	7 42
10	Thursday,	5 25	6 27	0 30	0 45	7 52	8 56
11	Friday	5 27	6 25	1 0	1 16	8 6	10 9
12	Saturday	5 29	6 23	1 32	1 49	8 23	11 21
13	13 *Sunday* past Trinity	5 31	6 20	2 7	2 26	8 43	0a33
14	Monday	5 32	6 18	2 47	3 9	9 11	1 44
15	Tuesday	5 34	6 15	3 36	4 3	9 49	2 50
16	Wednesday, Ember Week	5 36	6 13	4 40	5 17	10 39	3 48
17	Thursday	5 37	6 10	5 59	6 42	11 43	4 33
18	Friday	5 39	6 8	7 19	7 57	—	5 8
19	Saturday, Fast	5 41	6 6	8 26	8 55	0m57	5 33
20	14 *Sunday* past Trinity	5 43	6 3	9 18	9 42	2 18	5 53
21	Monday, St. Matthew	5 45	6 1	10 3	10 24	3 44	6 11
22	Tuesday	5 46	5 58	10 43	11 3	5 9	6 25
23	Wednesday	5 48	5 56	11*22	11*41	6 36	6 38
24	Thursday	5 50	5 53	—	0*1	8 3	6 53
25	Friday, Equal Day and Night	5 52	5 51	0*21	0 42	9 34	7 9
26	Saturday,	5 53	5 48	1 3	1 25	11 5	7 30
27	15 *Sunday* past Trinity	5 55	5 46	1 47	2 12	0a33	8 0
28	Monday,	5 57	5 44	2 38	3 8	1 55	8 43
29	Tuesday, St. Michael	5 59	5 41	3 39	4 15	3 5	9 40
30	Wednesday	6 0	5 39	4 52	5 35	3 55	10 54

Full Moon, Monday, 7 day, 25 minutes past 2, morning
Last Quarter Tuesday, 15 day, 19 minutes past 3, morning
New Moon, Tuesday, 22 day, 1 minute past 2, afternoon
First Quarter, Tuesday, 29 day, 42 minutes past 6, morning
Harvest Quar. begins Wed. 23 day, 24 minutes past 6, afternoon

OCTOBER, 1835.

D.M.	Week Days, and Remarkable Days.	Sun rise H M	Sun set. H M	Dublin Bar Mrn. H M	Dublin Bar Aftr. H M	Moon rises. H M	Moon sets. H M
1	Thursday	6 2	5 36	6 18	6 57	4a28	—
2	Friday	6 4	5 34	7 37	8 8	4 55	0m12
3	Saturday	6 6	5 32	8 39	9 3	5 13	1 35
4	16 *Sunday* past Trinity	6 8	5 29	9 27	9 47	5 26	2 55
5	†Monday	6 9	5 27	10 7	10 26	5 39	4 12
6	†Tuesday, Quarter Sessions, Dublin	6 11	5 24	10 43	10 58	5 52	5 26
7	†Wednesday	6 13	5 22	11 13	11*29	6 2	6 41
8	Thursday, City Record Court sits	6 15	5 20	11*45	11*59	6 13	7 54
9	Friday	6 17	5 17	—	0*13	6 27	9 5
10	Saturday, Chester Fair	6 18	5 15	0 28	0 43	6 45	10 19
11	17 *Sunday* past Trinity	6 20	5 13	1 0	1 18	7 9	11 31
12	Monday, Curragh Races	6 22	5 10	1 37	1 57	7 43	0a40
13	Tuesday	6 24	5 8	2 18	2 40	8 29	1 39
14	Wednesday	6 26	5 6	3 7	3 35	9 26	2 29
15	Thursday	6 28	5 3	4 10	4 45	10 33	3 7
16	Friday, Quarter Assembly, Dublin	6 29	5 1	5 25	6 6	11 50	3 35
17	Saturday	6 31	4 59	6 43	7 21	—	3 57
18	18 *Sunday* past Trinity, Saint Luke	6 33	4 56	7 51	8 22	1m13	4 16
19	Monday	6 35	4 54	8 46	9 11	2 38	4 30
20	Tuesday, Civil Bill Court sits	6 37	4 52	9 33	9 55	4 4	4 44
21	Wednesday, Battle of Trafalgar, 1805	6 39	4 50	10 15	10 36	5 33	4 58
22	Thursday	6 41	4 48	10 56	11*17	7 3	5 13
23	Friday, Irish Rebellion, 1641	6 43	4 45	11*38	11*59	8 36	5 33
24	Saturday	6 45	4 43	—	0*22	10 10	5 59
25	19 *Sunday* past Trinity, Crispin	6 46	4 41	0 46	1 11	11 40	6 37
26	Monday	6 48	4 39	1 36	2 3	0a57	7 31
27	Tuesday, Fast	6 50	4 37	2 30	3 0	1 54	8 40
28	Wednesday, Saints Simon and Jude	6 52	4 35	3 30	4 5	2 35	9 59
29	Thursday	6 54	4 33	4 40	5 19	3 2	11 22
30	Friday	6 56	4 31	5 59	6 35	3 21	—
31	Saturday, Fast	6 58	4 29	7 12	7 41	3 34	0m43

Full Moon, Tuesday, 6 day, 35 minutes past 4, afternoon
Last Quarter, Wednesday, 14 day, 27 minutes past 9, afternoon
New Moon, Wednesday, 21 day, 52 minutes past 11, afternoon
First Quarter, Wednesday, 28 day, 21 minutes past 3, afternoon

NOVEMBER, 1835.

D.M.	Week Days and Remarkable Days.	Sun rise. H M	Sun set. H M	Dublin Bar Mrn. H M	Dublin Bar Aftr. H M	Moon rises. H M	Moon sets. H M
1	20 *Sunday* past Trinity, All Saints	7 0	4 27	8 11	8 35	3a47	1m58
2	Monday, All Souls, Term begins	7 2	4 25	8 59	9 19	3 58	3 14
3	†Tuesday	7 4	4 23	9 39	9 56	4 9	4 28
4	†Wednesday, King William III. born	7 6	4 21	10 13	10 29	4 22	5 42
5	†Thursday, P. Plot, 1605	7 8	4 19	10 45	11 1	4 34	6 56
6	†Friday	7 10	4 17	11*18	11*33	4 50	8 7
7	Saturday	7 11	4 16	11*48	—	5 13	9 19
8	21 *Sunday* past Trinity	7 13	4 14	0*4	0 21	5 42	10 29
9	Monday	7 15	4 12	0 38	0 56	6 22	11 33
10	Tuesday	7 17	4 10	1 16	1 36	7 14	0a26
11	Wednesday, St. Martin	7 19	4 9	1 57	2 18	8 17	1 8
12	Thursday	7 21	4 7	2 42	3 7	9 30	1 39
13	Friday	7 23	4 5	3 37	4 7	10 48	2 2
14	Saturday	7 25	4 4	4 44	5 22	—	2 20
15	22 *Sunday* past Trinity	7 27	4 2	5 59	6 36	0m 9	2 37
16	Monday	7 29	4 1	7 9	7 42	1 31	2 50
17	Tuesday	7 30	3 59	8 8	8 35	2 57	3 9
18	Wednesday	7 32	3 58	8 59	9 23	4 25	3 16
19	Thursday	7 34	3 56	9 46	10 10	5 58	3 32
20	Friday	7 36	3 55	10 33	10 56	7 33	3 54
21	Saturday	7 38	3 54	11*20	11*45	9 8	4 28
22	23 *Sunday* past Trinity, Cecilia	7 40	3 53	—	0*10	10 35	5 17
23	Monday	7 41	3 51	0 35	1 1	11 45	6 20
24	Tuesday	7 43	3 50	1 28	1 53	0a34	7 39
25	Wednesday, Term ends	7 45	3 49	2 18	2 44	1 6	9 4
26	Thursday,	7 46	3 48	3 11	3 40	1 29	10 28
27	Friday	7 48	3 47	4 10	4 42	1 45	11 48
28	Saturday	7 50	3 46	5 14	5 48	1 57	—
29	*Advent Sunday*	7 51	3 45	6 22	6 54	2 8	1m 5
30	Monday, St. Andrew	7 53	3 44	7 27	7 53	2 19	2 17

Full Moon, Thursday, 5 day, 50 minutes past 9, morning
Last Quarter, Friday, 13 day, 3 minutes past 2, afternoon
New Moon, Friday, 20 day, 4 minutes past 10, morning
First Quarter, Friday, 27 day 20 minutes past 8, morning

DECEMBER, 1835.

D.M.	Week Days and Remarkable Days.	Sun rise H M	Sun set. H M	Dublin Bar Mrn. H M	Dublin Bar Aftr. H M	Moon rises. H M	Moon sets. H M
1	Tuesday	7 54	3 44	8 20	8 43	2a31	3m30
2	Wednesday	7 56	3 43	9 6	9 26	2 42	4 41
3	†Thursday	7 57	3 42	9 47	10 4	2 58	5 56
4	†Friday	7 59	3 42	10 21	10 38	3 17	7 8
5	†Saturday	8 0	3 41	10 56	11 13	3 43	8 18
6	2 *Sunday* in Advent	8 2	3 41	11*31	11*49	4 20	9 34
7	Monday	8 3	3 40	—	0*7	5 8	10 22
8	Tuesday, Conception V. M.	8 4	3 40	0 25	0 43	6 6	11 7
9	Wednesday	8 5	3 39	1 1	1 20	7 16	11 40
10	Thursday	8 7	3 39	1 40	2 0	8 32	0a 7
11	Friday	8 8	3 39	2 21	2 42	9 51	0 28
12	Saturday	8 9	3 39	3 6	3 31	11 11	0 46
13	3 *Sunday* in Advent	8 10	3 39	4 1	4 31	—	1 0
14	Monday	8 11	3 39	5 5	5 39	0m32	1 9
15	Tuesday	8 12	3 39	6 14	6 49	1 54	1 20
16	Wednesday, Ember Week	8 13	3 39	7 22	7 56	3 20	1 38
17	Thursday	8 14	3 39	8 25	8 56	4 53	1 54
18	Friday	8 14	3 39	9 23	9 51	6 26	2 20
19	Saturday, Fast	8 15	3 40	10 17	10 44	8 0	2 57
20	4 *Sunday* in Advent	8 16	3 40	11 10	11*37	9 31	3 54
21	Monday, St. Thomas	8 16	3 40	—	0*[illegible]	10 29	5 11
22	Tuesday, Shortest day	8 17	3 41	0*29	0 52	11 5	6 37
23	Wednesday	8 17	3 41	1 16	1 38	11 32	8 3
24	Thursday	8 18	3 42	2 0	2 21	11 49	9 27
25	Friday, CHRIST BORN	8 18	3 43	2 43	3 4	0a 2	10 47
26	Saturday, Saint Stephen	8 18	3 43	3 26	3 49	0 16	—
27	1 *Sunday*, past Christmas, St. John	8 18	3 44	4 12	4 42	0 [illegible]	0m 4
28	Monday, Innocents	8 19	3 45	5 12	5 45	0 37	1 18
29	Tuesday	8 19	3 46	6 19	6 53	0 49	2 30
30	Wednesday	8 19	3 47	7 28	7 58	1 4	3 44
31	Thursday	8 19	3 48	8 29	8 58	1 23	4 56

Full Moon, Saturday, 5 day, 10 minutes past 5, morning
Last Quarter, Sunday, 13 day, 20 minutes past 4, morning
New Moon, Saturday, 19 day, 49 minutes past 8, afternoon
First Quarter, Saturday, 26 day, 8 minutes past 7, afternoon
Winter Quar. begins Tue. 22 day, 54 minutes past 11, morning

STAMP DUTIES.

ON BONDS. *Stamp.*

Any bond, conditioned, for the payment of any Sum not exceeding £92. 6s. 1½d. -								£0	10	0
Exceeding				And not exceeding						
———	£92	6	1½	-	£184	12	3¼	1	0	0
———	184	12	3¼	-	276	18	5½	1	10	0
———	276	18	5½	-	461	10	9¼	2	0	0
———	461	10	9¼	-	923	1	6½	2	10	0
———	923	1	6½	-	1,846	3	1	3	10	0
———	1,846	3	1	-	2,769	4	7½	4	0	0
———	2,769	4	7½	-	3,692	6	1¼	4	10	0
———	3,692	6	1¼	-	4,615	7	8¼	6	0	0
———	4,615	7	8¼	-	-	-	-	10	0	0

BILLS OF EXCHANGE AND PROMISSORY NOTES.

Not exceeding										
———	£9	4	7½	-	-	-	-	0	0	6
Exceeding				And not exceeding						
———	9	4	7½	-	27	13	10¾	0	1	6
———	27	13	10¾	-	46	3	1	0	2	0
———	46	3	1	-	92	6	1½	0	3	0
———	92	6	1½	-	184	12	3¼	0	4	0
———	184	12	3¼	-	461	10	9¼	0	5	0
———	461	10	9¼	-	923	1	6½	0	8	0
———	923	1	6½	-	2,769	4	7½	0	15	0
———	2,769	4	7½	and upwards			-	1	5	0

RECEIPTS,

Amounting to				And not amounting to						
———	5	0	0	-	9	4	7½	0	0	2
———	9	4	7½	-	18	9	2¼	0	0	4
———	18	9	2¼	-	46	3	1	0	0	8
———	46	3	1	-	92	6	1½	0	1	0
———	92	6	1½	-	184	12	3¼	0	2	0
———	184	12	3¼	-	461	10	9¼	0	3	0
———	461	10	9¼	and upwards			-	0	5	0
A Receipt in full of all demands				-	-	-	-	0	5	0

TERMS FOR THE YEAR 1835.

Hilary Term,	Begins Mon. Jan. 12,	Ends Sat. Jan. 31
Easter Term	——— Wed. April 15,	——— Wed. May 13
Trinity Term'	——— Wed. May 27,	——— Wed. June 17
Michaelm. Term,	——— Mon. Nov. 2,	——— Wed. Nov. 25

CITY of DUBLIN QUARTER SESSIONS for 1835.

City of Dublin Quarter Sessions, Tuesday, 13 January, Tuesday, 28 April, Tuesday, 14 July, Tuesday, 6 October.

CUSTOM-HOUSE HOLIDAYS, 1835.

24th February, 17th April, 28th May, and 25th December.

HOLIDAYS KEPT AT THE STAMP-OFFICE.

17th April, 28th and 29th May, 13th Aug. 8th Sept. 25th Dec.

REIGNING SOVEREIGNS OF EUROPE.

Kingdoms.	Sovereigns.	When born.	Accession.
England	William IV.............	Aug. 21, 1765	1830
France	Louis Philippe I.........	Oct. 6, 1773	1830
Russia	Nicholas I..............	July 6, 1796	1825
Spain	Maria Isabella..........	Oct. 10, 1830	1833
Portugal	Donna Maria II.	April 4, 1819	1826
Prussia	Frederick William III..	Aug. 3, 1770	1797
Holland............	William I...............	Aug. 24, 1772	1815
Belgium............	Leopold I...............	Dec. 16, 1790	1831
Denmark	Frederick VI.	Jan. 28, 1768	1808
Sweden and Norway	Charles (John) XIV....	Jan. 26, 1764	1818
Austria	Francis II..............	Feb. 12, 1768	1792
Popedom	Gregory XVI...........	Sept. 18, 1763	1831
Sardinia............	Charles Amadeus	Aug. 16, 1800	1831
Naples and Sicily ..	Ferdinand II.	Jan. 12, 1810	1830
Turkey	Mahmoud II.	July 20, 1785	1808
Hanover	William IV. of England	Viceroy, Duke of Cambridge	

SHORTEST METHOD OF CALCULATING INTEREST AT FIVE PER CENT.

Multiply the number of days by the pounds of the principal sum; then divide the product by 365. The quotient will be the amount in shillings: the fractional remainder, if any, will give an idea as to the pence sufficiently near for all practical purposes. If the amount of interest at any other rate is required, calculate as above, and take the proportion of the result; for instance, deduct one-fifth, and you have the amount at the rate of four per cent.

ECLIPSES OF THE SUN AND MOON AND TRANSIT OF MERCURY, IN 1835.

In the year 1835 there will be two Eclipses of the Sun, one of the Moon, and a Transit of Mercury. The only one of these visible at Dublin will be the Eclipse of the Moon on June 10.

May 27.—Annular Eclipse of the Sun, invisible at Dublin. This eclipse will be visible more or less to the inhabitants of Africa and South America, and the Southern parts of Europe.

At the Cape of Good Hope this Eclipse—

Begins .... 3h. 49m. 36 s. }
Ends........... 4h. 4m. 7 s. } Mean time at the Cape.

Magnitude of the Eclipse=0.003 (assuming the diameter of the Sun 1, or unity) on the Northern limb.

June 10 *and* 11.—Partial Eclipse of the Moon, visible at Dublin:

First contact with dark shadow .. 9 h. 42 m. .... aftern.
Middle of the eclipse............ 10 h. 10 m. .... aftern.
Last contact with dark shadow . 10 h. 39 m. .... aftern.

Magnitude of the Eclipse=0.07 (assuming the diameter of the Moon 1, or unity) on the Northern limb.

At 8 h. 51m., just 44 minutes after the first contact with the penumbra, the Star θ Ophiuchi will be occulted (or disappear) behind the Moon, and will reappear at 9h. 57m. about fifteen minutes after the first contact with the dark shadow.

Nov. 7.—Transit of Mercury over the Sun's disk. This interesting phenomenon will occur after sun-set in this country.

Nov. 20.—Total eclipse of the Sun, invisible at Dublin. This eclipse will be visible in the southern parts of Asia and Europe, the whole of Africa, except Egypt, and the north-eastern part of South America. A very small portion of the Sun's disk may probably appear eclipsed between nine and ten o'clock, A. M. in the South of Ireland, Devonshire, Cornwall, and Pembrokeshire. The line on which the eclipse will appear total, crosses Madagascar and Africa obliquely in the direction of Sierra Leone.

At the Cape of Good Hope this Eclipse—

Begins .... 11 h. 10 m. 12 s. }
Ends...... 1 h. 8 m. 0 s. } Mean time at the Cape.

Magnitude of the Eclipse=0.30 (asuming the diameter of the sun 1. or unity) on the Northern limb.

From the Christian Almanack, elegantly printed, and containing much useful information, we copy the following Diagram or figure, explanatory of the nature of eclipses, with the annexed observations:

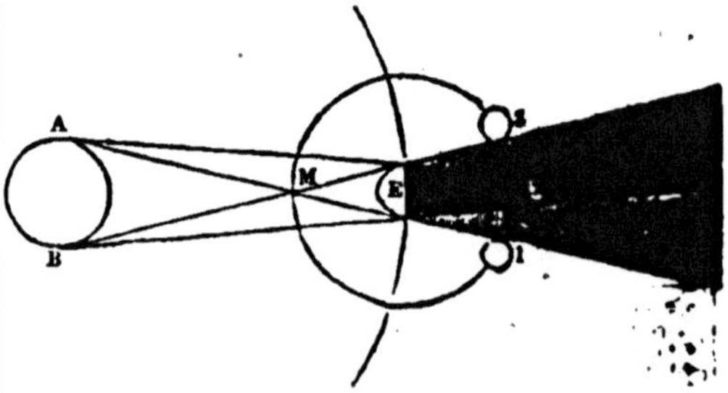

Let A B represent the Sun, E the earth; and the circles 1 2 3 the Moon at three different portions of her orbit or path round the earth. The lines drawn from the Sun represent the direction of the rays of light which illuminates one half of the earth, and forms both the dark shadow and penumbra.

Shadows formed by opaque bodies are the consequence of the rays of light moving in straight lines. As the globe we inhabit is opaque, it casts a shadow. The form of any shadow depends upon that of the body which casts it, together with the magnitude of the source of light. Now the earth being a globe and the diameter of the Sun being so much larger than that of the earth (about 110 times,) the form of the shadow cast by the earth must necessarily be a cone, as is represented by the dark shadow in our engraving; and as a further consequence of the greater diameter of the Sun, the lighter shade (called the penumbra) will also be cast.

When the Moon in her course round the earth arrives at No. 2, it is then in opposition to the Sun, and is called *Full Moon*, and if at the same time its position be such, that a line passing through the Sun and the earth would pass through the Moon also, then a lunar eclipse must take place; that is, the Moon must pass through the earth's shadow. This might be expected to take place once a month, that is once in each journey of the Moon round the earth; but as the Moon's orbit or path is oblique, or inclined to the ecliptic, in which the Sun always appears, the Moon, when full, will sometimes pass above the shadow, and sometimes below it; at other times only a small portion of the Moon will enter the shadow, in which case a partial Eclipse takes place, as the one described above for June 10th.

In a lunar Eclipse, when the Moon arrives at the point marked No. 1, it is called the first contact with the penumbra; at No. 2, the middle of the Eclipse, it is then invisible, or if visible, of a deep copper colour; and at No. 3, the last contact with the penumbra.

A solar Eclipse can only happen at new Moon being at that part of her orbit which is next the Sun, as at M; it is then said to be *new*, or in conjunction with the sun. The Moon being also an opaque body, its dark side will then be turned towards the earth, and the shadow which it casts will pass over part of the earth, or in other words, part of the earth will pass through the Moon's shadow; therefore, to a spectator on the Moon the earth will be partially eclipsed, and to a spectator on the earth the Sun will be eclipsed. This phenomenon would also occur every new Moon, but for the obliquity of the Moon's orbit before spoken of.

ON THE APPEARANCE AND MOTIONS OF COMETS.

None of the celestial bodies have given rise to more speculation and conjecture than Comets. Their strange appearance has in all ages been a matter of terror to the vulgar, who uniformly have looked upon them as bad omens, and forerunners of war, pestilence, &c. Others, less superstitious, supposed them to be meteors raised in the higher regions of the air.

Aristotle conceived them to be meteoric bodies; Kepler huge animals, that swam round the sun like fishes; and Bodin imagined that they are spirits, which, having long dwelt on the earth, are about to be translated to the skies. Kepler discovered, from his own observations and those of his master, Tycho, that the comets did not, as had been supposed, move in straight lines, but in paths concave towards the sun, and he conceived that their orbits were parabolas.

The tails of comets have given rise to various conjectures; but though it is apparent that they are in some way connected with the sun, we know as yet absolutely nothing of either their cause, or their uses.

Mr. Whiston has conjectured that the deluge, of which, in the sacred writings, we have the only authentic record, but of which the annals of most nations have traditionary accounts, was produced by the near approach of a comet, whose atmosphere had been attracted by the earth; and he further surmises, that the final catastrophe foretold in the Scriptures may be produced by the approach of a comet prodigiously heated in its perihelion. We pretend not, however, on such subjects as these, to penetrate the secrets of Almighty wisdom, which can produce its own ends, by means of which we have no conception.

Much attention is at present paid to this branch of astronomy; and the consequence has been, that a visit of a comet to our regions is found to be an event of very frequent occurrence. In the year 1825 not less than five different comets were observed.

In seeking for information on this interesting subject, we turned to the report of the proceedings at the recent great meeting of the British Association in Edinburgh, in the hope that some new or important point had been discussed by the 'cognoscenti' on the occasion. The following, however, was the only paragraph which we could discover, bearing any relation to the subject: we copy it from the *Literary Gazette, Sept.* 13.

" At the Assembly Room, after the chairmen of the sections had delivered their reports, Dr. Hamilton delivered a discourse on Comets, particularly Halley's and Encke's, which was well adapted to a mixed auditory, though rather too long. He was followed by Mr. Whewell, on the same subject, who blended astronomy and humour so curiously together, that we hardly knew whether he was in earnest or jest—only that we never met with jokes illustrated by diagrams.

" The theory of Comets has yet to be discovered; but these vague philosophical sports are quite right for an evening meeting of ladies and gentlemen."

The following particulars appear to contain all that is yet known as to the form or movements of these eccentric heavenly messengers.

Fig. 3.   Fig. 4.   Fig. 1.

Fig. 2.

Comets viewed through a telescope have a very different appearance from any of the planets. The nucleus, or star, seems much dimmer. They are to appearance surrounded with atmospheres of a prodigious size, often rising ten times higher than the nucleus, and have often likewise different phases, like the moon.

The head of a comet, seen through a good telescope, appears to consist of a solid globe, and an atmosphere, that surrounds it. The solid part is frequently called the nucleus; which, through a telescope, is easily distinguished from the atmosphere or hairy appearance.

A comet is generally attended with a blaze or tail, whereby it is distinguished from a star or planet; as it is also by its motion. Sometimes the tail only of a comet has been visible at a place where the head has been all the while under the horizon; such an appearance is called a beam. Whether the tail of a comet is caused or not by the heat of the sun, it is always observed to grow larger as it approaches, and to diminish as it recedes from that luminary.

The tails of comets often appear bent.(fig.1 and 2.) This is probably owing to the resistance of the æther: which, though extremely small, may have a sensible effect on so thin a vapour as the tail consists of. This bending is seen only when the earth is not in the plane of the orbit of the comet continued. When that plane passes through the eye of the spectator, the tail appears straight, (fig.3): if the eye be a little out of the line, the tail will appear short, (fig.4.)

From observations made on the great comet of 1680, Sir Isaac Newton found that these bodies, like the planets, move round the sun in elliptical orbits. This comet was seen for twenty-one days in its passage towards the sun, and for nearly three months as it receded from that luminary. The most careful observations were made to determine its place, and the conclusions deduced from these observations are confirmed by observations made on all that have been well observed since.

There is now no question among astronomers, that comets are opaque bodies enlightened by the sun. Their perihelion distances from the sun are exceedingly various, some being not more than one-fifth, and others upwards of four times the mean distance of the earth. Their diameters, too, differ very greatly. Their apparent diameters of course vary with their distance; and some have supposed that those apparently preternatural darknesses, of which several are recorded in history, may have been caused by the interposition of a comet between the earth and the sun, at a time when, from its proximity to the earth, its apparent diameter was greater than the sun's, and when its apparent motion was in the same direction as the sun's. The diameter of the comet of 1744, when at the distance of the sun from us, was about one minute, hence its real diameter was about three times that of the earth. The diameter of their atmosphere is however often ten or fifteen times as great as that of the nucleous.

HALLEY'S COMET.

The following particulars relative to this comet are given by Sir John Herschell:—

" The comet of Halley is so called from the celebrated Edmund Halley, who on calculating its elements from its perihelion passage in 1682, when it appeared in great splendour, with a tail 30 degrees in length, was led to conclude its identity with the great comets of 1531 and 1607, whose elements he had also ascertained. The intervals of these successive apparitions being 75 and 76 years, Halley was encouraged to *predict* its reappearance about the year 1759. So remarkable a prediction could not fail to attract the attention of all astronomers; and, as the time approached, it became extremely interesting to know whether the attractions of the larger planets might not materially interfere with its orbital motion. The computation of their influence from the Newtonian law of gravity, a most difficult and intricate piece of calculation, was undertaken and accomplished by Clairaut, who found that the action of Saturn would retard its return by 100 days, and that of Jupiter by no less than 518, making in all 618 days; by which the expected return would happen later than on the supposition of its retaining an unaltered period, and that, in short, the time of the expected perihelion passage would take place within a month, one way or other, of the middle of April, 1759. It actually happened on the 12th of March in that year. Its next return to the perihelion has been calculated by Messrs. Damoiseau and Pontécoulant, and fixed by the former on the 4th, and by the latter on the 7th of November, 1835, about a month or six weeks before which time it may be expected to become visible in our hemisphere; and, as it will approach pretty near the earth, will very probably exhibit a brilliant appearance, though to judge from the successive diminutions of its apparent rise, and the length of its tail in its several returns since its first appearances on record, (in 1305, 1456, &c.,) we are not now to expect any of those vast and awful phenomena which threw our remote ancestors of the middle ages into agonies of superstitious terror, and caused public prayers to be put up in the churches against the comet and its malignant agencies."

The 'Almanach de Gotha pour l'Année 1835' observes, that though the Comet has varied very much in its appearances, as regards its brilliancy, the length and form of its tail, &c., still it has been found to diminish gradually. We cannot determine under what form it will appear next year, but it will probably be less brilliant than in 1759. If its light be not too feeble, it will appear during the month of August, in the East, about midnight, and must be looked for in the constellation *Taurus*. It will move so very slowly, that it will not have reached *Gemini* before the middle of September, when it will be visible for a great part of the night. Following a north-east course, it will reach *Lynx* early in October, when on account of its great northern declination, it will be nearly in our zenith, and will neither rise nor set. Afterwards its motions will be more rapid, so that about the 6th of October, it will have passed *Ursa Major*, and on the 11th, will be below Corono Borealis, and only visible in the morning, and for a short time in the evening. After the 21st of October it will not be visible in the morning, and will set early in the evening. In the month of November it will be seen for a short time at sunset, and will then disappear. In the month of December it will re-appear on the western side of the sun, and be visible for a short time in the morning.

Sir Thomas Brisbane has received a communication from Mr. Rumker, his former able assistant at the Paramatta Observatory, stating it as his opinion, that with a good telescope the Comet may possibly be seen much earlier than is generally expected.

The foregoing chart indicates the path of this Comet amongst the fixed stars. The elements of the orbit given by M. de Pontécoulant are as follows:—

Passage of the Perihelion, Nov. 7.

Passage of the perihelion on the orbit 307ª 1ª 15ª

Longitude of the ascending node 55 30 0

Ratio of the eccentricity to the semi axis major 0.967324

Semi axis major 17.94770

Motion retrograde.

Dublin: Printed by P. D. Hardy, 3, Cecilia-street, to whom all communications are to be addressed.

THE

DUBLIN PENNY JOURNAL

CONDUCTED BY P. DIXON HARDY, M.R.I.A.

| VOL. III. | JANUARY 10, 1835. | No. 132. |

RUINS ON THE ROCK OF CASHEL.

For a minute description of these interesting ruins, we refer the reader to the 66th number of our Journal. We take the present opportunity, while giving a drawing of another portion of the ruin, of correcting a slight error in the description which we then gave of some of the buildings on the rock. It was stated that the materials of the Round Tower alone formed an exception to those used in the other buildings; it appears, however, that the little Norman chapel, which it will be seen by the above sketch, stands nearly opposite the tower, is of the same material with that erection; it is a kind of freestone, none of which is found within several miles of the place. All the other erections on the rock are of limestone, a circumstance which may in some measure serve to fix the dates at which the various buildings were erected, or at least to afford presumptive evidence that the tower was erected at the same period with the little chapel.

THE DEEPEST MINE IN GREAT BRITAIN.

The following interesting account of the sinking of a mine near Sunderland, as given in the *Durham Advertiser*, we would strongly recommend to the notice of the landed proprietors of this country. From time immemorial Ireland has been celebrated as—

> "rich in store
> Of veiny silver, and of golden ore,"

while, in nearly every district of the country, the baser metals are to be had in abundance, and that coals of the very best description might also be had, there can be no doubt, if but one-twentieth part of the labour or capital were expended in mining for them which has to be laid out in England. We trust the proprietors of the soil in Ireland will learn wisdom from experience, and by turning their attention to the subject so forcibly brought before them in the following article, determine to try an experiment, if, indeed, that can fairly be called an experiment, of which there can be no doubt—that by sinking mines in this country they would not only eventually enrich themselves, but conduce most essentially to the comforts of the people, by giving them constant employment.

"The shaft at present sinking at Monkwearmouth Colliery, near Sunderland, has attained a considerably greater depth than any mine in Great Britain, (or, estimating its depth from the level of the sea, than any mine in the world.) Pearce's shaft at the Consolidated Mines in Cornwall was, till lately, the deepest in the island, being about 1470 feet in perpendicular depth, of which 1150 are below the surface of the sea. The bottom of Woolf's shaft (also at the Consolidated Mines) is 1230 feet below the sea; but its total depth is less than that of Pearce's shaft. The bottom of the Monkwearmouth shaft is already upwards of 1500 feet below high water mark, and 1600 feet below the surface of the ground. It was commenced in May, 1826. The upper part of the shaft passes through the lower magnesian limestone strata, which overlap the south eastern district of the great Newcastle Coal-field, and which, including a stratum of "freestone sand" at the bottom of the limestone, extended, at Monkwearmouth, to the thickness of 330 feet, and discharged towards the bottom of the strata the prodigious quantity of three thousand gallons of water per minute—for the raising of which into an off-take drift, a double-acting steam-engine, working with a power of from one hundred and eighty to two hundred horses was found necessary. The first unequivocal stratum of the coal formation, viz., a bed of coal 1½ inches thick, was not reached till August, 1831, (being about three hundred and forty-four feet below the surface,) after which the tremendous influx of water which had so long impeded the sinking operations was "stopped back" by cylindrical "metal tubing" or casing, fitted (in a series of small portions) to the shaft, and extending from below the above bed of coal to within twenty-six yards of the surface. The sinking now proceeded with spirit—still, no valuable bed of coal was reached, although the shaft had passed considerably above six hundred feet into the coal measures, and much deeper than had hitherto been found requisite for reaching some of the known seams. It became evident that the miners were in unknown ground. A new "feeder of water" was encountered at the great depth of one thousand feet, requiring fresh pumps and a fresh outlay of money. The prospects of the owners became unpromising in the eyes of most men, and were denounced as hopeless by many of the coal-viewers! still the Messrs. Pemberton (the enterprising owners of this colliery) continued, and in October last reached a seam of considerable value and thickness, at the depth of 1578 feet below the surface, and presuming that this newly discovered seam was identified with the Bensham seam of the Tyne, (or Maudlin seam of the Wear), they are rapidly deepening their shaft, in anticipation of reaching the Hutton, or most valuable seam, at no distant period, but which (if their anticipations are well founded) will be found at a depth approaching three hundred fathoms from the surface ! In the mean time, however, workings have very recently commenced in the supposed Bensham seam. A party of scientific gentlemen descended into these workings on Saturday last, and aided by every facility and assistance which could be afforded to them by the Messrs. Pemberton, made several barometric and thermometric observations, the detail of which will be *deeply* interesting to many of our readers. A barometer at the top of the shaft (87 feet above high water mark) stood at 30.518, its attached thermometer (Fahrenheit) being 53. On being carried down to the new workings (1584 feet below the top) it stood at 32.280, and *in all probability higher than ever before seen by human eye!* the attached thermometer being fifty-eight. Four workings or drifts had been commenced in the coal; the longest of them being that "to the dip," twenty-two yards in length and nearly two in breadth—to the end of which the current of fresh air for ventilating the mine was diverted—(and from which the pitmen employed in its excavation had just departed) was selected for the following thermometric observations. (Temperature of the current of air near the entrance of the drift, 62 Fahrenheit; near the end of the drift 63; close to the face or extremity of the drift, and beyond the current of air, 68.) A piece of coal was hewn from the face; and two thermometers placed in the spot just before occupied by the coal (their bulbs being instantly covered with coal dust) rose to seventy one. A small pool of water was standing at the end of the drift. Temperature of this water at eleven o'clock, seventy; three hours later sixty-nine and a half. A register thermometer was buried eighteen inches deep below the floor, and about ten yards from the entrance of the drift; forty minutes afterwards its maximum temperature was sixty-seven. Another register thermometer was similarly buried near the end of the drift, and after a similar period indicated a maximum temperature of seventy. It was then placed in a deeper hole and covered with small coal; some water oozed out of the side of this hole to the depth of six or eight inches above the thermometer, which, upon being examined after a sufficient interval of time, indicated a temperature of seventy-one and a half.

A stream of gas bubbles (igniting with the flame of a candle) issued through the water collected in this hole; the bulbs of two very sensible thermometers were immersed under water in this stream of gas, and indicated a temperature constantly varying between 71.5 and 72.6. A thermometer was lowered to the bottom of a hole drilled to the depth of two feet and a half into the floor of another of the workings, and the atmospheric air excluded from it by a tight stopping of clay: this thermometer being raised after the lapse of forty-eight hours, stood at 71.2. Other experiments, in the prosecution of these inquiries, are contemplated."

"THE JUVENILE FORGET-ME-NOT."

EDITED BY MRS. S. C. HALL.

This is not only a very pretty, but a very interesting little book, for little people. Its merit does not rest on the beauty of the engravings. The stories are in general well adapted for the class of readers for whom it is intended; and several of the pieces of poetry, besides being instructive, are *poetical*. We shall give a specimen of each.

A GHOST STORY.

IN A LETTER FROM WALES.

MY DEAR FRED—When I promised to write to you, I little thought I should have such an adventure to relate —such a ghost—yes, a real ghost story to tell you. I think it long till the holidays are over, to tell it to all the boys in our room at once: it beats George Amherst's stories all to nothing; and then as papa says, it does so well show the folly of being afraid. But, I say, Fred, my boy, only think of a lady in white coming to my bedside —oh! I shall not easily forget it; but, mind, you never catch me believing again in any of your tales of ghosts, hobgoblins, or whatever you please to call them. I mustn't spoil my story before I can tell it. I was, you know, going to describe all about Wales, and the Welsh people; but I can think of nothing else, talk of nothing else, and write of nothing else, than the ghost which haunted the new house. It is in a most beautiful spot, to be sure; yet, I own, I was a little disappointed, because I did not think, till I came, of the difference in the scenery between North and South Wales. I was expecting to see the long chain of brown dusky mountains, of stupendous cliffs, and frightful precipices, with a cottage here and there interspersed; instead of which we are surrounded by fertile hills. The house papa has bought, stands on one, the base of which is washed by a beautiful winding river, and when the tide is full in, it is a glorious prospect;—but a great deal more about all this when my story is told. The accommodations at the village inn were so miserable that my papa ordered some furniture from the neighbouring town, resolving to have two or three rooms fitted up in the house. The people of the inn stared aghast as he announced his determination.

"La, Sir, you surely be joking! sleep there, Sir?"

"Yes, indeed," said papa, "I was never more in earnest in my life."

"You will excuse my making so free, but, indeed, you *cannot* sleep *there*, Sir."

"Why not?" asked papa.

"Because, Sir—because they say the house is haunted."

"By whom, my good friend?"

"By the lady, Sir."

"By what lady, pray?"

"Why a lady who, they say, was murdered there many long years ago."

"And do you really believe these things?"

"La, Sir! to be sure I do. Who that comes to so foul an end could rest quiet in a grave?"

"But for what purpose do you suppose the spirits of those who are gone are permitted to disturb the innocent here? If those who killed the lady were still on earth, perhaps their guilty consciences might lead them to fancy her before them."

"I know nothing about that, Sir; but sure and am I, that there she walks every night; and no one has since slept twice in the house. There was one man, Sir, disappeared with her, and never was seen again from that day to this : five years ago, Jem Coleman once fancied he saw him on the deck of a vessel a few miles out at sea, but he was gone in a moment ; he did put his boat out, and rowed to the vessel, and asked if they had Bad Barney, as we used to call him, on board , but they only laughed, and said they never knowed such a person ; so, sure and certain, it was his troubled spirit."

" But has the house never been let ?"

" It goes with the land, you see, but nobody can live in it; but the land fetches such a good price, it quite makes up for it. Indeed, Sir, as sure as you stand there, you will never lie quiet in your bed."

" Indeed I do not admire having my rest broken ; but even if I am disturbed, I shall not lay it to the poor ghost ?"

" Well, Sir, seeing is believing, you know ; and trust me if ever you go there a second night—and what's more, I am sure nobody in the village will go with you."

" Never mind," said papa, " I have my own two servants, and my son, which, I trust, will be sufficient ; if it is only a lady ghost, I presume she will not use any violence towards us ; and even if she does, I think we should be more than a match for her. Can you tell me of any mischief she has done ?'

" I think it is enough if she frightens people out of their wits ; but, sure, you won't take the young gentleman with you ? '

" That I leave to himself ; he is old enough to judge which he had best do. He has been taught to fear nothing while he knows he has acted rightly, and to believe himself in all places and circumstances under the immediate protection of God ; and, young as he is, he would not, I think, very easily be persuaded to believe in a ghost."

" Well, Sir, you really are very hard of belief, almost as much so as Bill Simpson, who used to swear he feared neither God nor devil ; but he never dared the ghost a second night, nor was he ever after heard to boast of his unbelief, but went regularly to church, chapel, ay, and prayer-meeting too, for matter o' that."

" Indeed," said papa, " you begin to make me think very well of the lady ghost, and almost desirous of her acquaintance."

" Well, to be sure, you be a merry gentleman, and not very soon frightened ; but if your courage doesn't come down a peg or two afore this time to-morrow, my name is not Mary Jones."

Had not papa cut the matter short, I know not when poor Mrs. Jones's persuasions would have stopped ; and it was soon plain that she did not drop the subject when she left the room, as our intention of sleeping on Castle Hill was soon spread all over the village, which, certainly, was not very large. You would have laughed to see the women standing in groups, with their knitting in their hands, whispering together, and looking at us as if we were going to be sacrificed.

You will wonder how I felt all this while—why, rather queer, Fred. I will own, but still determined to go through all, if only for the sake of having a good story to tell the boys when I return to school. Without papa I know I never could have gone, but when one sees another not afraid, we are not so much so ourselves : I did sit for a few minutes thinking where the ghost could or would take us to if she attempted to spirit us away, and, though half afraid he would laugh at me, I ventured to ask papa ; he tried to conceal a smile, but could not, as he told me to reflect a moment whether it were possible, if she really were supernatural, for her to do such a thing.

" Let me," continued he, " put one question to you, Henry : Out of all the marvellous stories you have ever heard, do you remember one of them to have been related by any really religious, well-educated person ? Are they not always represented to have been seen by the ignorant and superstitious ?"

" Why, yes, papa, they certainly are," replied I.

" And have they not been described to be perfectly harmless—merely embodied for a moment, then vanishing in the air—for this obvious reason, because their disappearance could no other way be accounted for ? You

never hear of any good resulting from the disclosures they make. And were they even empowered to unveil the future, have we any business to penetrate that which God, in his infinite wisdom, forbids us to know ? And happy is it for us that his goodness has so ordained ; for if bad is to come, would not the knowledge of it render the intervening time miserable, which might otherwise be one of enjoyment ? and if we had the certainty of future happiness, how unfitted should we be for present duties in anticipating its arrival !"

But I shall fill my sheet with papa's remarks, and not have room for the best part of my story ; so I shall skip over all that passed till we went to our rooms at night.— There was a little tent-bed for me by papa's—now mind, Fred, not one word to the boys when we get back, but, indeed, I could not help it—I crept out of my own into his. The two men-servants were in the adjoining apartment. We, at least I, lay a long time awake, trembling no more than I could possibly help, and was just beginning to feel a little heavy, when I heard the village clock strike one. It was a bright moonlight night ; I could hear the splashing of the water as the tide kept ebbing and beating over the rocks. Papa had fallen into a sound sleep—this I was sure of, from the noise he made. As I lay, I fancied I heard a sort of rumbling and creaking ; and, though I felt a little alarmed, I could not for the life of me keep my head under the bed-clothes ; so I ventured to look towards the door, which kept opening a little and a little wider, with the noise of a chair I had placed there, as there was no key in the door I crept closer to papa, who, out of deference to the ghost, ceased snoring, or rather awoke, though he lay still, and spoke not. Presently, in came a lady, all in white, sure enough, with long black hair flowing all over her shoulders; a large muslin veil hung over her head, which was thrown back ; her face was of an unearthly hue—very, very pale and ghastly.— She was extremely ugly, and held something in her hand which emitted a faint blue flame. She advanced with a noiseless step to the foot of the bed, when she began singing something in the Welsh dialect. She then came to the side where I lay, making such horrid faces ! I shall never forget her looks. She was just turning away, when papa, snatching a pistol from behind his pillow, called out, " pray, madam, don't leave us yet, though I have nothing to offer you but a little gunpowder, and have not time to make it into tea ; so you must excuse taking it thus."— Saying this, he fired a pistol—not exactly at the ghost, but near enough to frighten her terribly. She gave a most violent shriek, and attempted to dart through the opposite door, which led into the room where the men slept.

" That door, ma'am is secured ; and through this, by which you entered, you pass only through my other pistol, which you will excuse my pointing at a lady ; but unless you this moment declare your purpose and your errand, its contents are lodged in your body."

Then the poor woman, falling on her knees, and throwing off part of her ghostly attire, confessed her only object was to drive people from inhabiting the house ; which, with a subterraneous passage leading out to the sea through the rocks, was partly occupied by a gang of smugglers, whenever they wanted to deposit their cargoes. The ghost lady was daughter to one, and was shortly to be the wife of another—the very Bad Barney, who was reported to have been carried away, but who, in fact, joined the gang ; and it was really he who was seen on the deck of the vessel, but he had assumed a different name ; and as to the man whose reform was represented by Mrs. Jones to be effected in the haunted house, the whole gang set on him as fiends, pretending to be sent for him.

The woman confessed, that in one or two nights the whole party would be in, as the spring tides had begun. These confessions were extorted by fear and surprise, so unexpected had papa's firmness been. She acknowledged to have been completely thrown off her guard. As she recovered from her terror, and began to recollect herself, she was much alarmed lest her desperate associates should wreak their vengeance on her for betraying them ; but papa promised her liberty and protection for herself and father after a certain time.

The next day notice was given to the proper authorities, and a certain number of officers and soldiers of the Preventive Service, with others from the Custom House, were all stationed ready. Towards sunset a vessel was descried making towards the place. It was beautiful to see how she cut through the water, and, though heavily laden, carrying every sail she could hoist. Still she glided on in fine style.

Of the rest I can only tell you by hearsay, as papa said it was any thing but a proper scene for boys to witness. The end was, that although great resistance was made, the smugglers were secured to a man, and their cargo also—

the old man and his daughter set at liberty, as papa hopes, to get an honest livelihood—and we were left in quiet possession of our house and grounds.

Thus has papa, by a little presence of mind, rid the country of a nuisance; and I know I have learned a useful lesson, and seen the folly of indulging in idle fears.—But so prejudiced are the country people, that, though he has found one ghost to be human, they will believe as firmly as ever in supernatural appearances. Believe me ever yours, HENRY.

— Bolster, Esq. Cork, Del. Clayton, Sc.

DOOR-WAY OF AGHADOE CHURCH, KILLARNEY.

AGHADOE.

The engravings in this and the following pages, taken by different artists, represent, very accurately, the ancient Romanesque door way of the ruined cathedral of Aghadoe an architectural relic of high antiquity, and interesting not only for its beauty of detail, but for the light which it reflects upon the state of national taste and art of the period to which it belongs, probably the sixth or seventh century.

It stands upon a bare green eminence, a mile and a half to the north-west of Killarney, in the county of Kerry, and in the ancient territory of the Eoganacht Lochlein, the patrimony of the M'Carthy More, and The O'Donoghue, in their day stalworth men-at-arms, and hunters of the red deer. The prospect from this place, over the enchanting lower lake, is of a magnificent description, decidedly one of the best that can be obtained: it is broad, extensive, and various, and speaks highly for the good taste of those old religious men who selected the situation for their respective fanes—the Druid, the erector of the *Turaghan*, or the Christian missionary, who raised the Cathedral.

It was morning when, accompanied by a friend, I visited this elevated upland. What a contrast between the cold

comfortless ruin, whose interior was yet in deep shadow, and the luxuriant scenery spreading far around! Before us lay the lake, one bright, sparkling, inland sea, with its dark boundary of towering mountains sloping away to the horizon. Ross Castle stood glittering in the early sunbeams, with its finely wooded peninsula, running into the lake, and that little gem of the waters, the fairy islet of Innisfallen, appearing like a shining emerald in the bosom of the wave. Turk, and Mangerton, and Glenna were still, dark, and sombre; the sun had not yet smiled on their brown sides, whilst Mucruss, amid its thick monastic groves, enjoyed all the blush and brilliancy of the hour. Truly all that the imagination can conceive of the wild, and romantic, the magnificent and beautiful, is here brought before the eye, and dull and insensible must be that mind which would not feel it luxury to gaze upon such a landscape. My companion's spirit was up and soaring: he himself declared he was spell-bound as he looked out upon the blue waters of O'Donoghue, and viewed his fairy kingdom; all the varied and vivid associations hanging over that wide spread scene, with its castles, towers, monastic shrines, and sainted isles, passed in rapid succession before his teeming fancy. I could scarcely restrain my smile, as, contrasting his warm enthusiasm with my own more staid emotions, I heard him, with tremulous tone, sing out—

" Of all the blue lakes where day-light leaves
His lingering smile on golden eves,
    Fair lake, fair lake, thou'rt dear to me !"

The remains at Aghadoe consist of a round tower, a small ruinous cathedral, and a round castle, called the " Bishop's Chair." This last stands on the hill side, about 260 feet to the south-west of the church, and is in a very dilapidated state—one of its windows is round-headed.

It would be hard to make off the form of the others. We can only conjecture the age of its erection by analogy. The old Saxon castles were generally round, and built upon a tumulus, as at Pontefract, in Yorkshire, &c. We have at Shannad, in the county of Limerick, one of a similar rotund form, based upon a tumulus. It is said to have been built by an earl of Desmond, but this I do not credit. Like the round fortalice at Aghadoe, it never possessed an arched apartment, or stone stair, and, indeed, seems to have belonged to the same period, probably the ninth or tenth century. These towers I would regard as interesting specimens of the early Irish fortress.

A. Nichol, Esq. del.   Clayton, Sc.

DOORWAY.

The cathedral and remains of the round tower stand upon what may be called " The Table Land" of the hill, surrounded by a thickly tenanted burying-ground.

The former is a low oblong building, consisting of two chapels of unequal antiquity, and forming at present a nave and choir. These are divided by a solid wall, through which had once been a communication, but closed up before the destruction of the building. The whole church is about eighty feet long by twenty feet broad. The choir, or more modern division, was lit above its altar by a double but exceedingly narrow acute or lancet window, sloping inwards. Another window in the south wall, five feet high by three feet in breadth, assisted with its twilight to illumine the gloom of this ancient chamber. It contains

within it three tombs. The greater part of the south wall of the nave has fallen. This chapel was lit by two small round-headed windows—one in the north wall, now closed up—the other in that part of the south still standing. The ornamented door-way is placed in the western wall. It is a semicircular arch, springing from small round pillars, each about three feet in height, surmounted by simple capitals. The face of the arch, or architrave, displays two courses of the chevron or zig-zag, in low relief, as also the toothed moulding, and a series of beads or bosses in mezzo-relievo. The parts between the pillars and jambs are wrought into fanciful fretwork, which, as well as the sculpture of the entire, is executed with the utmost care and very superior taste. On the whole, the architectural style of this chapel, whilst it refers to the seventh or eighth century, proves it of higher antiquity than the eastern chapel or choir, which belongs to the thirteenth century.

The turaghan or round tower, stands fifty-four feet from the north-west angle of the church, and is called " the pulpit" by the peasantry : all that remains of this ancient structure formed only a part of the basement, not reaching even to where once stood the door. The height is about twelve feet. It measures in its outer circumference fifty-two feet; its diameter within the walls is six feet; and the thickness of the walls three feet and a half. Its masonry is greatly superior to that of the church; the stones are large, regular, and well-dressed. The cut-stone or facing of the north-west side has been all taken away for the erection of tombs in the adjacent burying-ground. Within and without, spoliation has been at work effectually, aided by those worst of pests, the gold seekers; fellows whose unhallowed dreams are most fatal to our antiquities. This tower must have fallen before the last century, but no notice of it in its erect state has survived. The re-erection or repair of one of those beautiful structures is a thing that has never yet been attempted in Ireland ; and, I am afraid, will not for many a long day to come. Our tastes are not sufficiently in advance yet to become conservative of antiquities ; and yet the towers deserve our care. Laying aside their beauty, behold how useful, as food for speculation, have they been. What ink has been poured forth in revealing what has not been yet revealed—their origin and use: what latent absurdities of mind and vagaries of the fancy have they not brought forth. Why, if we had not the round tower, we would never have the volume of the learned O'Brien, and the heaven-born discovery of the *Lingam* in form, and the " cupboard" for use, to hold Dutch figures sacred to that very decent deity, the Indo-Irish *Budha*. Neither should we ever have heard of Simon, the Stylite, affording, as a model to our anchorites, his *square, solid* pillar, wherefrom, by way of making a close copy, they erected a *round, hollow* tower ; but the Stylite theory was, as I shall submit, but an *approach* to the truth. The builders of our towers looked a little higher than the pillar of the Egyptian anchorite : read the 11th of Joshua, according to the Vulgate, and, lo, what a light gleams upon us ! how the eye unscales ! Therein it is said, " Jacob worshipped on the top of his staff."* Here it is clear that the staff answered the sire of " Judah and his brethren," as the pillar did the Stylite; of which pillar the said staff was the undisputed prototype. The Irish, from first to last, were Jacobites. They copied the patriarch's staff one day—on the next they borrowed his very pillow. The curious may, for a small gratuity, see the latter to this hour in Westminster abbey. Let them look at any one tower, from Antrim to Ardmore, and they will see a faithful fac simile of the patriarchal staff.

General Vallancey has stated that within the church in the north-west corner was a brown rough stone, with a few Ogham characters inscribed. It was about seven feet long, but he thinks might once have been longer. The inscription, too, he thought imperfect, but took no trouble about explaining it. This stone has since been removed, and, it is said, used in the erection of a vault or tomb, in the adjoining burying-ground.

The loss of this ancient relic could be but badly spared, though, I believe, Ogham inscriptions are by no means few over the country; yet, of these, our antiquaries have hitherto actually discovered (and imparted their discoveries to the world, not more than three or four. This bare fact exhibits both the zeal and qualification of this very self sufficient but do-little race. Nothing is more certain than that the Pagan Irish inscribed frequently the " Ogham

* Anxious to afford every facility to the investigation of the subject of Round Towers, we give the theory of our Correspondent as he himself lays it down, without pledging ourselves in any way for its accuracy. We had hoped long since to have been enabled to lay before our readers the theory advanced by Mr. Petrie, in his Essay on this long contested question, which gained for him the prize of the Royal Irish Academy. It is scarcely fair to keep it so long from the public.

Name" of the dead on *Dallans*. Many inscriptions of this, as well as other kinds, remain, which a little research would bring to light ; but they are enduring the common fate of our Irish literature—suffered to lie unknown, unsought, and neglected. The writer of this article has himself seen several of these inscribed Dallans, ascertained the existence of others, and assisted in presenting one of them lately to the Cork Institution, where it may now be seen. On some future occasion he may present a memoir, accompanied by drawings, to the readers of the Journal.

In conclusion, I understand that it is intended to erect a new church at Aghadoe. No site certainly could be better chosen ; but, I trust there will be no meddling with, or displacing of the old structure. We should all be desirous that antiquity should be honoured, and all its associations, historical and legendary, preserved ; room enough there is for a new church, beside the poor old, but time-honored and interesting ruin.　　　J. W.

VICISSITUDE OF FORTUNE—VIZIER ALLY.

SIR—Presuming that the generality of your readers must feel interested in the extraordinary vicissitude of fortune which this young man experienced, I beg to enclose, for insertion in your Journal, the following brief statement of facts as they occurred; and am, Sir, your obedient servant,　　　A CONSTANT READER.
December 28, 1834.

Among the deaths mentioned in an old Calcutta newspaper, is that of Vizier Ally, once Nabob of Oude ; but being deposed by the East India Company, was subsequently, and in consequence of the treacherous murder of Mr. Cherry and others, at Benares, confined for life in a room made to resemble an iron cage, in Fort William, where he lingered out an imprisonment of seventeen years, three months, and four days. He died at the age of only thirty-six years.

Vizier Ally was the adopted son of Asuf-ud-Dowlah, late Nabob of Oude. His mother was the wife of a Forash (a menial servant of low description.)

His reputed father, Asuf-ud-Dowlah, was a wealthy and eccentric prince. Having succeeded to the Musnud of Oude, by the assistance of the East India Company, he professed great partiality for the English. Mild in manners, polite and affable in his conduct, he possessed no great mental powers : his disposition was kind, considering his education, which instilled the most despotic ideas. He was fond of lavishing his treasures on gardens, palaces, horses, elephants, European guns, lustres, and mirrors. He expended every year about two hundred thousand pounds in English manufactures. This Nabob had more than one hundred gardens, twenty palaces, twelve hundred elephants, three thousand fine saddle-horses, fifteen hundred double-barrel guns, seventeen hundred superb lustres, thirty thousand shades, of various forms and colours ; several hundred large mirrors, girandoles and clocks ; some of the latter were very curious, richly set with jewels, having figures in continual movement, and playing tunes every hour ; two of these clocks cost him thirty thousand pounds. Without taste or judgment, he was extremely solicitous to possess all that was elegant and rare : he had instruments and machines of every art and science, but he knew none. He sometimes gave a dinner to ten or twelve persons, sitting at their ease in a carriage drawn by elephants. His haram contained above five hundred of the greatest beauties of India. He had an immense number of domestic servants, and a very large army, besides being fully protected from hostile invasion by the Company's subsidiary forces. His jewels amounted to eight millions sterling. Amidst this precious treasure, he might be seen for several hours every day, handling them as a child does his toys.

Usuf had no legitimate children. He was in the habit, whenever he saw a pregnant woman, whose appearance struck his fancy, to invite her to the palace to lie in ; one of those was the mother of Vizier Ally.

The sprightliness of Vizier Ally, while yet an infant, so entirely engrossed the affections of the old Nabob, that be determined to adopt him. In conformity with this resolution, the youth received an education suitable to a prince who was destined to succeed to the Musnud. He is said, however, to have developed, at this period, a propensity to delight in the sufferings of the brute creation. The affection of the old nabob towards his adopted son still increasing, he lavished upon him every mark of regard.

To give an idea of the splendour which attached to his youth, and from which he fell, the following account of his wedding is taken from Forbes's Oriental Memoirs.

At thirteen his marriage took place, and was celebrated at Lucknow, in 1795, and was one of the most magnificent in modern times. The nabob had his tents pitched on the plains, near the city of Lucknow ; among the number were two remarkably large, made of strong cotton cloth, lined with the finest English broad-cloth, cut in stripes of different colours, with cords of silk and cotton. These two tents cost five lacs of rupees, or above sixty thousand pounds sterling; they were each one hundred and twenty feet long, sixty broad, and the poles about sixty feet high ; the walls of the tents were ten feet high; part of them were cut into lattice-work, for the women of the nabob's seraglio, and those of the principal nobility to see through. His highness was covered with jewels, to the amount, at least, of two millions sterling. From thence we removed to the Shumeeana, which was illuminated by two hundred elegant girandoles from Europe, as many glass shades with wax candles, and several hundred flambeaux. When seated under this extensive canopy, above one hundred dancing girls, richly dressed, went through their elegant dances, and sung some soft airs of the country, chiefly Persic and Hindoo-Persic.

About seven o'clock the bridegroom made his appearance, so absurdly loaded with jewels, that he could hardly move. The bride was ten years old ; they were both of a dark complexion, and not handsome.

From the Shumeeana we proceeded on elephants to a most extensive and beautiful garden, about a mile distant. The procession was grand beyond conception : it consisted of about twelve hundred elephants, richly caparisoned, drawn up in a regular line, like a regiment of soldiers. About a hundred elephants in the centre had houdahs, or castles covered with silver ; in the midst of these appeared the nabob, mounted on an uncommonly large elephant, within a houdah covered with gold, richly set with precious stones. The elephant was caparisoned with cloth of gold. On his right hand was Mr. George Johnstone, the British resident at the court of Lucknow ; on his left the young bridegroom. The English gentlemen and ladies, and the native nobility, were intermixed on the right and left. On both sides of the road, from the tents to the garden, were raised artificial scenery of bamboo-work, very high, representing bastions, arches, minarets, and towers, covered with lights in glass lamps. On each side of the procession were dancing-girls, superbly dressed, on platforms supported and carried by bearers. These platforms consisted of a hundred on each side of the procession, all covered with gold and silver cloths, with two girls and two musicians on each platform.

The ground from the tents to the garden, forming the road on which we moved, was inlaid with fireworks : at every step of the elephants the earth burst before us, and threw up artificial stars in the heavens, besides innumerable rockets, and many hundred wooden shells that burst in the air, and shot forth a thousand fiery serpents, these, winding through the atmosphere, illuminated the sky, and, aided by the light of the bamboo scenery, turned a dark night into a bright day. The whole of this grand scene was further lighted by above three thousand flambeaux, carried by men hired for the occasion.

In this manner we moved on in stately pomp to the garden, which we entered, after descending from the elephants. It was all illuminated by innumerable transparent paper lamps or lanterns, of various colours, suspended to the branches of the trees. In the centre was a large edifice, to which we ascended, and were introduced into a grand saloon, adorned with girandoles and pendant lustres of English manufacture, lighted with wax-candles. Here we had an elegant and sumptuous collation of European and Indian dishes, with wines, fruits, and sweet-meats ; at the same time about a hundred dancing-girls sung their lively airs, and performed their native dances.

Thus passed the time until dawn, when we all returned to our respective homes, delighted and wonder-struck with this enchanting scene, which surpassed in splendour every entertainment of the kind beheld in this country. The affable nabob rightly observed, with a little Asiatic vanity, that such a spectacle was never before seen in India, and never would be seen again. The whole expence of this marriage feast, which was repeated for three successive nights in the same manner, cost upwards of three hundred thousand pounds sterling.

When Vizier Ally was recognised by Asuf as his successor to the throne, great opposition was manifested by the old nabob's family. He was, however, on the death of the latter, upheld by the English government, and placed on the throne.

After being placed upon the throne, he shewed a turbulent, restless, and intriguing temper, and broke his faith with the English government ; the consequence of which, was his being deposed from the Musnud, and Sadut Ally, brother of the late nabob, was placed on it.

A pension was assigned to Vizier Ally of two lacs of rupees per annum, about twenty-five thousand pounds ; but it was considered necessary that he should reside near the presidency, that he might be more under the eye of government. He, therefore, proceeded from Lucknow to Benares, where Mr. Cherry, the Company's resident, was to make arrangements for his going to the presidency.

Shortly after his arrival at Benares, Mr. Cherry invited him to breakfast. He came, attended by a large armed retinue : which Mr. Cherry disregarded as being hostile, although he had had a caution.

Vizier Ally complained much of the Company's treatment of him ; and, on a signal being given, several of his attendants rushed in, and cut Mr. Cherry and Mr. Graham to pieces. They then proceeded to the house of Mr. Davis, with the view of massacreing him also ; but fortunately he had some intimation of his danger before they arrived, and got his family to the top of the house, and posted himself at the summit of a narrow, circular stone stair-case. Here the ruffians pursued him, but with a hog-spear he defended himself for a long time, killing several, which blocked up the passage, till he was rescued by a party of the Company's troops, which came to his assistance. The followers of Vizier Ally killed another European gentleman at Benares.

Vizier Ally made his escape into the territory of the Rajah of Berar, a powerful and independent chief, who refused to give him up, unless under a promise of his life being spared. This the English government acceded to, and he was brought to Calcutta, and confined in the garrison of Fort William, in a kind of iron cage; and here he died, after an imprisonment of seventeen years and a few months, as above mentioned.

HOLLY AND IVY.

Reviewing the many strange and apparently unmeaning customs which characterize a people, the superficial observer will see only what may be laughed at, as ridiculous and absurd ; whilst the antiquarian or philosopher, diving beneath the surface, and comparing the present with the past, is frequently enabled to separate, in wisdom's crucible, the dross from the finer metal, and thus to trace these customs to their true origin.

Ireland is a spot peculiarly marked by such customs ; some derived from the earliest annals of Druidism—others coeval with Christianity, all richly deserving the enquiry of the critic, or the ingenious conjecture and research of the antiquary. The antic mummeries of a rude, unpolished peasantry—the boisterous and hearty mirth that at certain periods of the year bursts forth through every impediment, levelling the barriers that modern refinement would interpose, and giving full scope to the strong ebullition of national feeling, show, that in sunshine or storm—in times of dearth or plenty—in the calm and sluggish stillness of debasing servitude, or the hurricane of political agitation—under every vicissitude or clime, the Irish peasant is the Irish peasant still—the light-hearted, generous, enthusiastic lover of his father-land—the ardent panegyrist of the olden time, and the scrupulous observer of the various fetes of fun and superstition handed down through a long series of years; no matter how inconsistent with reason or common sense they may be—whether the cause of their institute be remembered or forgotten.

From the fire of Baal, at Summer's dawn, to the Brideog, of Bridget's night—from the startling rites of all-Hallowed-eve to the pancake tossing of Shrovetide, we have seen comments and discussions, from Vallancey, to the present day; but why, in the festivals of Christmas, the Holly and Ivy should, in preference to all other shrubs, adorn the house or embower the dresser; or, huddled together, and hung with ribbons, become the throne of a Murdered Wren, no attempt has yet been made to explain. I shall, therefore, Mr. Editor, with your permission, endeavour to throw some light upon the transaction.

It appears to me a very reasonable supposition that, in a season of universal gladness, sensible and mercurial people, who knew the value of the senses as conduits of information, would avail themselves of the opportunity of blending instruction with amusement, and thus point out to the aoróg of that day, whilst they carolled and gambolled round the object of their delight, its grand and mysterious associations. Like the Jews and Egyptians, the Irish were extremely fond of figure and hieroglyphic; and like the old Fire-worshippers of Persia, in their May-eve fire, (Baalteine is the name of May) worshipped Baal or the Sun, who was considered the supreme dispenser of life and light to this nether world. On the introduction of Christianity, as may be well conjectured, they naturally looked around for suitable emblems to represent the objects of their new faith. As an illustration of the Trinity, the Shamrock was immediately adopted; whilst the Wren, embedded in Holly and Ivy, might not be considered an inappropriate type of the incarnation. Indeed they could scarcely have chosen a more expressive symbol of the wondrous humility of the Deity in taking the helpless form of infancy than the Wren, the smallest and most despicable of the feathered race in our island. The chilling wind and piercing cold of winter, with the various circumstances of poverty and humiliation which attended a Saviour's birth, are not inaptly denoted by the prickly roughness of the Holly, which circles the poor persecuted Wren, hunted down, as was its Creator, by the unreflecting votaries of false, misguided zeal. But, whilst the Holly reminds us of the stings and crosses of a wicked and contankerous world, the smooth unruffled surface of the Ivy must also bring to our recollection the peace and goodness announced in the mild tenets of the Gospel to man, and the value of a good conscience, which, though bound up too often through life's journey with the holly of turmoil and disappointment, yet strengthens and supports its possessor, like the Ivy that clasps and shelters some aged oak or venerable pile, adding lustre to its beauty, and protecting it from ruin.

The bush then is emblematic of the crib of Bethlehem; the ribbons that embellish it represent the swaddling clothes that wrapped the tender limbs of the Redeemer; and the glad and merry notes of the wren boys, chaunting the praises of "the king of all birds," may denote, though feeble and immeasurably distant indeed, the sweet melody of the angelic choir announcing the glad tidings of redemption; and, to pursue farther the illustration, the rich offerings of gold, frankincense, and myrrh, of the Eastern wise men, may be typified by the willing contributions given in honour of the little feathered monarch to his numerous and devoted followers, who generally retire at the close of e'en, to enjoy that social happiness which, to them, as individuals, their comparatively cheerless dwellings are too often incapable of affording:

"For Christmas comes but once a year,
And when it comes it brings good cheer."

Such, Mr. Editor, is, I conceive, a true interpretation of these annual displays; which, however solemn and instructive their origin may have been, yet, now-a-days, form a portion of these superstitious observances that, in many places, disgrace our country, being succeeded by scenes of vice, riot, and intemperance. However, there can be no doubt that the character of our people is fast improving—education is making rapid strides—the thirst for information is abroad, and crime must necessarily give way to the steady advance of that light and genial instruction which is now spreading over every portion of our island.   A WREN BOY.

Cork, Nov. 1834.

THE SNOW STORM.
(From " The Juvenile Forget Me Not.")

BY J. OGLE.

Thick clouds ascending slowly climb'd the sky—
The red round sun had set—a storm was nigh;
The village children's evening task was done,
And all were happy in their homes—but one:
She saw the clouds uniting far and near,
While darkness thickened, and she sighed for fear.
With starting tears, and lips apart, she ran
To reach her home, ere yet the storm began.
But ah! the winds arise, the tempest breaks,
Fast whirls the snow in broad contiguous flakes;
O'er roofs, and trees, and field, and road, 'tis spread—
Pale, cold, and noiseless—emblem of the dead!
The lonely church presents a solemn sight--
The tower, the yew, the graves, are clothed in white:
Beneath that soil, poor child! thy mother lies,
Nor feels the storm that round thee falls and flies.
Oh, haste thee, maiden!—haste thee on thy way,
Observe the path, nor let thy footstep stray;
And tread with caution where the single beam
Extends—a dang'rous bridge across the stream;
Forget the miles between thy home and thee,
Lest terror rob thee of the power to flee.
In such a night the stoutest hearts might fail,
When hopeless horror, cold, fatigue, assail.
Before the fire, with warm expanded hands,
Expecting thee, thy sister smiling stands;
While, as the flickering flames arise and fall,
The girl's huge shadow dances on the wall.
Thy grandam longs in vain to aid thee child,
So weak with age is she, the night so wild;
Nor has she near one sympathising friend,
To guide and guard thee to thy journey's end.
Tow'rd the old clock her anxious gaze is cast,
That shows the hour of thy return is past;
And as the gusts against the lattice beat,
She thinks each sudden sound the sound of feet.
That night the shepherd strove to cross the plain,
And save his distant flock—but strove in vain.
Deep lay the drift, the snow flew fiercely still,
And sheep by twenties perish'd on the hill.
Full half his flock, he knew, must needs be lost;
His fingers slowly counted up the cost.
The dog's caress, his angry hand forbade—
His head was busy, and his heart was sad.
The mails were stopp'd, or wandered from the road—
The plunging horses fail'd to move the load.
And where the wind blew freely o'er the moor,
Three feet of snow had block'd the widow's door;
Nor can a helpless child, when tempests rave,
And spread beneath his feet the traveller's grave,
Endure what manhood well might bear to brave;
And if a wand'rer fall, the ruthless skies
Will wind the sheet of death before he dies;
The brain will swim, and fatal torpor creep
O'er all the limbs, and seal the eyes in sleep.
Thus, when the moon mid clouded radiance rose,
And lit the paleness of the bleaching snows,
Deep, deep beneath their surface, smooth and fair,
They hid the gentle maid they would not spare.
That night her father, on the southern seas,
Was sailing, homeward bound, before the breeze;
With helm in hand he stood, and, musing, smiled,
He thought to meet—ah, how he mourned his child!

DUBLIN:
Printed and Published by P. D. HARDY, 3, Cecilia Street; to whom all communications are to be addressed.
Sold by all Booksellers in Ireland.
In London, by Richard Groombridge, 6, Panyer-alley, Paternoster-row; in Liverpool, by Willmer and Smith; in Manchester, by Ambery, in Birmingham, by Guest; in Glasgow, by John Macleod; and in Edinburgh, by N. Bowack.

THE
DUBLIN PENNY JOURNAL
CONDUCTED BY P. DIXON HARDY, M.R.I.A.

| Vol. III. | JANUARY 17, 1835. | No. 133. |

THE CITY OF ARMAGH

View of College-street, Armagh, taken from the road leading to the Observatory.

M. Barns, del.

Bruce, Sc.

THE CITY OF ARMAGH.

In the 24th number of the Penny Journal will be found a correct engraving of the Cathedral of this ancient city, as it then stood, with a brief sketch of its history. In now presenting to our readers a striking representation of one of its leading streets, we shall take the opportunity of mentioning some further particulars relative to the present condition and former history of the city itself, for the greater proportion of which we are indebted to Dr. Stuart's valuable History of Armagh.

The city of Armagh, which is situated in the province of Ulster, is not only the capital of the county of that name, but likewise the ecclesiastical metropolis of Ireland. It stands on the sloping sides of a gently ascending hill, and is generally esteemed to be the best built and finest inland town of which our island can boast. The streets are well laid out and regularly built, and the city is adorned with several public buildings, erected in a chaste and elegant style of architecture. It is surrounded on every side by a highly improved picturesque country. A traveller who enters it from the rural village of Richhill, will be much pleased with the tasteful improvements which partly encircle the family seat of the Richardsons; but he will be delighted with the more romantic and magnificent demesne of Sir Capel Molyneux. In Castledillon, every advantage of hill and dale, wood and water, are united; and art has most judiciously perfected the grand outline which nature had so nobly drawn. Near the centre of the lands is an extensive lake, on which various species of wild fowl sport undisturbed. Hills, crowned with woods and interspersed with lawns, surround the lake, and the spires of Grange and Armagh churches, beheld through vistas, render the scene more picturesquely beautiful. As we approach Armagh in this direction, the deanery, the observatory, the Primate's obelisk, demesne and palace, and the city itself, surmounted by its ancient Gothic cathedral, burst at once upon the view, giving to the surrounding landscape, "rich by nature and improved by art," a nameless and indescribable charm.

The approaches to Armagh, both from the west and from the north, are also beautiful. The improvements at Glasslough demesne, the ancient seat of the Leslie family —the noble edifice erected by the earl of Caledon, and the surrounding plantations—the rural mansion of Woodpark—the groves of Elm-park and Knappa—the rich and highly improved lands of the Maxwells—the undulating hills, interspersed through the country, whose summits are crowned with forest trees—these, and an uninterrupted succession of sylvan scenes, afford the purest satisfaction to the tourist, as he passes from the county of Monaghan to the ecclesiastical metropolis of Ireland. In the vicinity of Armagh, the rural habitations, and the light and lofty mills, erected near the winding banks of the river Callan, give cheerfulness and animation to the landscape. The roads which lead from Dungannon and its vicinity, pass through a rich and well-wooded country. The improvements in Viscount Northland's demesne—those of John Henry Burges, Esq. near Castle-Caulfield—the neat and simply-elegant dwellings of the colony of Friends (Quakers,) who inhabit Grange—the rural villages of Moy, Charlemont, and Blackwatertown —the romantic hills, rocks and glens, which encircle the ruined castle of Benburb – the navigable river Blackwater, which forms a grand and noble boundary betwixt two populous counties—the bleach-greens which adorn its margin, deepening to the eye the verdure of the adjacent lawns, by contrast with the splendid robe of white which mantles their surface—these diffuse around the whole country an air of tranquillity, successful industry and domestic happiness, on which the imagination of the patriot and of the philanthropist dwells with pure and uninterrupted delight.

The ancient cathedral which crowns the summit of Druimsailech-hill, is at once the most central point, and the most conspicuous object, in the city of Armagh. Towards this venerable church, some of the streets seem to converge, like radii, to a common centre—others ascend, in more oblique directions, from the base of the hill, and are intersected by those of greater magnitude, which encircle the town. The citizens' houses are neatly built with calcareous stone, and generally slated. Numerous public edifices, erected with hewn limestone of a very vivid colour, and finished in a chaste style of architecture, unite beauty with utility, and give peculiar interest to the city. The sites of these edifices have been so judiciously selected, that the buildings are not concealed from view by contiguous dwelling-houses, nor degraded by the neighbourhood of any uncouth or despicable objects. They are each possessed of unity and elegance, and being distinctly visible, in various directions, are at once ornamental to the town itself, and to the surrounding country.

Formerly the country abounded with lakes, marshes, and unreclaimed bogs. In the city of Armagh itself, there was, at the beginning of the eighteenth century, a small lake, containing many eels. It was called Lake Lappan, and was situated behind the site of the old sessions-house, at the foot of Market-street. In the seventeenth century, deep woods and thickets, impervious to the sunbeams, prevented the free circulation of the air, and kept the surface of the earth in perpetual moisture. At present the ground is greatly denuded of trees, the bogs are drained, few swamps exist, and the atmosphere is pure and healthy.

Few remains of antiquity can be discovered in Armagh or its immediate vicinity. In our memory, the last fragment of the Culdean buildings were pulled down, and the habitable part of the Augustinian monastery, dedicated to St. Peter and St. Paul, was levelled to the earth.

Camden says, the ruins of the ancient palace of Eamhain Macha or Eamania, which both he and Speed, who wrote in 1614, call Owen Maugh, were visible near Armagh, in his time. O Halloran, a modern author, speaks positively of their existence in his day. We, however, have not been able to discover any such ruins. The townland, indeed, on which the building stood, can be accurately ascertained. In the primate's demesne, contiguous to the city, are the remains of an ancient abbey, situated nearly south-east of the cathedral. In the middle of the last century, the ruins of this venerable edifice were very extensive, and even yet some of the arches are in good preservation.

Camlets, as well as woollen and linen cloths, were manufactured at Armagh in the seventeenth century. At present, however, the great mass of the population in the adjacent districts is employed in the linen trade and in agriculture.

The new sessions-house, a portion of the front of which is seen in our engraving, was erected in the year 1809, and is situated a little to the north-west of the public walks, now denominated "The Mall." Thus situated, it is seen to considerable advantage, and has a striking effect. It is built with hewn limestone, with a handsome portico in front.

From time immemorial the city of Armagh has been the scene of many a deadly feud and bloody engagement —in wars, waged at one time between the Irish chieftains themselves—at others, between the Irish, Danes, and Ostmans—and afterwards between the natives of the country and the invading armies of Scotland and England: at several times it was taken, plundered, and set fire to by various armies of Danes, Ostmans, and English, and even by some of the Irish chieftains themselves. That the ancient college of Armagh was founded by St. Patrick, and continued for a long time one of the most celebrated seminaries of literature in Europe, is now generally admitted. From time to time, it received the patronage of the kings of Ireland, and even Roderick O'Connor, the last of its native monarchs, made a grant to the professors of this college, in the year 1169. From this school many learned men, not only of the Irish nation, but students from every part of Christendom, issued forth to instruct their respective countrymen, and to diffuse knowledge throughout Europe. Some of these scholars became martyrs for the truths of Christianity.

The annals of Ulster state, that in the year 1162, an ecclesiastical synod, assembled by Gelasius at Cleonad, decreed that no persons should be permitted to teach or publicly lecture on the science of theology, except those who had studied at the Armagh academy. Hence all

assertion made by Florence Macarthy, that seven thousand pupils were, at one period, to be found in that college, is by no means incredible. From this synodical decree, we may fairly infer, that the school had retained its high character from age to age, and was at all periods the chief seminary of literature in this kingdom. Hence it is probable that the Irish philosopher and mathematician, Feargall, known on the continent by the names of Virgil and Solivagus, was educated here. So early as the year 748, this eminent man maintained the sphericity of the earth, the existence of the antipodes, and the plurality of worlds, as is manifest from a letter written by Pope Zacharias to Bishop Boniface, on that subject. Here, also, it is probable that Erigena derived those liberal sentiments in religion and philosophy, which rendered him illustrious on the continent in the ninth century.

Foreign students were gratuitously furnished, in the Irish colleges, with lodging, diet, clothes and books, and we have the authority of Bede and Alcuin, as well as of Erric, of Auxerre, and of the writer of the Life of Sulgenus, that numbers of Saxons, Gauls, &c. flocked to Ireland for instruction. This account is corroborated by Camden, Spencer, Llhuid and Roland. It is certain, that whoever wished to perfect himself in Theology, and in the other sciences, deemed it necessary to reside in some of the literary seminaries of this country. Hence Camden quotes the following passage from the Life of Sulgen:—

" Exemplo patrum commotus amore legendi
Ivit ad Hibernos, Sophia mirabile claros.''

He alleges, also, that the ancient English even learned the form of their letters from the Irish. Indeed the Irish language seems to have been formerly held in considerable repute, even by British monarchs; for when Aidan preached in that tongue to the Northumbrians, King Oswin himself interpreted his discourse to the people. When any learned man on the continent had disappeared, it was generally said of him—" *Amandatus est ad disciplinam in Hibernia.*" Aldelm, an author of the seventh century, the very first of the English nation who wrote Latin poetry, was a pupil of the Hibernian Scot, Maidulph, as Camden testifies. Aigilbert, the first bishop of the Western Saxons, and afterwards bishop of Paris, and Alfred, king of Northumberland, were educated in Ireland.

The sciences and liberal arts, taught in the Irish colleges were Theology, Grammar, Rhetoric, Logic, Arithmetic, Music, Geometry and Astronomy.

The study of their vernacular tongue was not neglected by Irish scholars. A glossary of that language was written by Cormack Mac Cuillionain, king of Munster and bishop of Cashel, who was slain at the battle of Bealach Muchna, A. D. 908. A very ancient copy of this work, on vellum, is deposited in the library of Sir William Betham, and another in the collection of the learned Irish lexicographer, Edward Reilly. There is some probability that the ancient Danes, as well as the Saxons, acquired their knowledge of letters from Ireland; and Wormius admits that his countrymen have an old alphabet called Ira Letur, or Irlandorum Literæ.

To Hibernian Scots, the literati of Europe owe the introduction of scholastic divinity, and the application of philosophic reasoning to illustrate the doctrines of theology, as we learn from the works of Benedict, abbot of Aniam, in Languedoc, a writer of the eighth century.

Giraldus Cambrensis (no favourer of the Irish) seems to have been quite enraptured with their music, which was taught scientifically in their colleges. Their skill, he says, was " incomparably superior to that of any other nation."

The Irish literati of the middle ages did not confine their useful labours to their own colleges, but formed various literary, hospitable and religious establishments, in foreign countries. In the council of Meaux, A. D. 845, it was decreed that complaints should be made to the king of the ruin of hospitable houses, *particularly of those of the Irish nation, founded by benevolent natives of that country.* In the seventh century, Columban, an Irishman, founded the abbey of Luxevil, in Burgundy—a second at Fontanelle—and a third at Bobio, near Naples. Gall, another Hibernian, founded the abbey of Stinace, or Stinaha, near the lake Constance. In the sixth century, Columba, the Irish Culdee, founded the famous monastery of Hi, or Iona, and converted the Picts.—Arbogast, an Hibernian Scot, about the year 646, founded an oratory in Alsace, where Hagenau was afterwards built. Maidulph erected the monastery of Ingleborne, where, about the year 676, he instructed the English youth in classic literature. Fursey founded a monastery at Cnobersburgh, now Burgh castle, in Suffolk, about the year 637, and shortly afterwards, the abbey of Laigni, in the diocese of Paris. He died on the 16th of January, 648. It is unnecessary to pursue this subject further. We may, however, remind our readers that Charlemagne, of France, placed the university of Paris and that of Ticinum, (i. e. Pavia,) the two first formed establishments of the kind on the continent of Europe, under the care of two Irishmen, Albin and Clements, as best qualified to preside over institutions, at once so novel and so useful.

In the immediate neighbourhood of the city are several very extensive public walks, well planted, and judiciously laid out. To those in the primate's domain admission may be gained by obtaining a ticket from his agent—while to the grounds belonging to Captain Algeo, and Leonard Dobbin, Esq. M.P. the public have free admittance without any ticket, or leave asked or given—a line of conduct well worthy of imitation by gentlemen in every part of the country, and well calculated to induce kindly feeling between the various classes of the community. The following description of the walks in Mr. Dobbin's ground we extract from an article published some time since in a Belfast paper :

DOBBIN'S VALLEY.

The Irish tourist who keeps the highway loses much of the beauty of the country; and I would advise the traveller to Armagh to turn in at the handsome gate which stands on the left, on his approach to that city, by the Richhill road. Should the elegant little lodge and neat planting invite him into the valley, the clack of the mill will soon lead him down to the river; and there is little probability of his turning on his step till he winds round the lake, into which an artificial embankment has widened the Avonmore—now sauntering down straight alleys of closely planted firs and larches, through whose embowerings the sun can scarcely penetrate—now bursting out into the lake and open lawn, and again winding along close by the bed of the rocky stream, pendent over which are the entwining branches of trees of various kinds, springing from rocks that scarce seem to afford sufficient soil for the nurture of the moss and the wild flowers with which they are enamelled. The stranger will scarcely credit that all the variety can be contained in the scope of ground which, on ascending any of the neighbouring eminences, he may see beneath him. His surprise will be nothing diminished on being told that a few years ago this spot, now so beautiful, presented nothing but a rude glen, with a little stream idly brawling among rocks and briars. These natural advantages, which a taste less refined and accurate would altogether have overlooked, have been beautified by the owner almost into a fairy land; and with a liberality which reflects on him the highest credit, the grounds have been thrown open to the public. Were a desire to embalm his memory the object this gentleman had in view, he could not have hit upon a more infallible expedient. Long after he is gathered to his fathers will this valley be called by his name. Associated as it is with the sunniest hours of their existence, the youngest of those who now roam through its labyrinths will often make it the theme of their discourse in the evening of their days, even though time and neglect should long before have reduced the place to its original wildness.

At the time in which I visited this valley the whole scenery appeared to peculiar advantage; heavy torrents of rain had swoln the rivulet, for the stream is nothing more, although the hyperbole of the aborigines has dignified it with so magnificent a name—thundering beneath a bridge of unplaned fir it poured down a perpendicular and artificial fall, and continued its brawling course over rocks and stones, foaming and chaffing at every little obstruction.

Before the woods in the neighbourhood of Armagh were felled, the country abounded with pheasants and wolves, and wolf-dogs were to be found in every farm house. There were then few partridges, and neither magpies nor frogs in the country. Fynes Moryson, who was in the kingdom from 1799 till 1603, says, " Ireland had neither singing nightingale, nor chattering pie, nor undermining mole, nor black crow, but only crows of mingled colour, such as we call Royston crows. They have such plenty of pheasants, as I have known sixty served up at *one feast*, and abound much more with rails, but partridges are somewhat *scarce*." At present partridges, black crows, and magpies, are numerous; but pheasants can scarcely be found. Wolves, which were indigenous, and thence styled by the Irish " Mac-tir,"—" son of the earth," have totally disappeared, and, we believe, there is not now a wolf-dog in existence. The late Dr. Robinson, (a pupil of the celebrated Boorhave,) who lived near Tynan, had two immense wolf-dogs, which we have seen accompanying him in the year 1779. These were the last remains of the Ulster wolf-dogs: but Lord Altamont, since Lord Sligo, had some wolf-dogs, about twenty years ago, at Westport. These are since dead, and the present Lord Sligo has, we believe, introduced in their stead a kind of double-nosed Grecian water-dogs, larger than Newfoundland dogs; and

another species which, in head, resembles a wolf, and, in the hinder parts, a fox. Since we have incidentally mentioned some of the animals which formerly abounded in Ireland, we may be permitted to add, that the first *frog* which was ever seen in this country made its appearance in a pasture field near Waterford, about the year 1630, and is noticed by Colgan, in a work printed in 1647. It had probably been conveyed from England in some vessel. It was viewed with horror by the Irish; but it did not continue its species. Frog-spawn was afterwards placed, it is said, about the year 1696, in a moist place in the college park, Dublin, from which our fields have been colonized by these croakers. Formerly there were black rats in this country, and brown rats were unknown; and Hollinshead says, " the towne of Ardmagh is an enemie to rattes, and if any be brought there, presentlie it dieth, which the inhabitants impute to the prayers of St. Patrick."—It may be worth remarking, that at the Irish feasts, to which Moryson alludes in the above passage, the lights used were made of the pith of rushes twisted together, with a small part of the skin, to preserve cohesion. This was saturated with unctuous matter, and formed into a taper about the size of a man's waist, from which issued a splendid flame, visible at an immense distance.—*See Annals Donegal, A. D.* 1557.

HOTEL AND POST-OFFICE—PILLTOWN.

PILLTOWN.

We this day present our readers with two views of the village of Pilltown, copied from drawings taken on the spot. The one is the hotel and post office of the place, as seen from the road; the other, the market-house and street of the hamlet, immediately in front of the inn, and as it appears from the hall door. There are few neighbourhoods in Ireland which exhibit within a narrow compass, scenery at once so varied and delightful. Nature and art have gone hand in hand in its embellishment; and the benefits to be derived from the residence of a landlord, were never more faithfully pourtrayed, than in the village of Pilltown. It is situated in the southern part of the county of Kilkenny, on the north side of the river Suir, between the city of Waterford and the town of Carrick, three miles from the latter, and ten from the former place. The principal street is about half a mile in length. The houses, mostly of modern construction, have small gardens of flowers and evergreens in front, enclosed from the pathway. The cottages are distinguished for an external neatness and internal cleanliness, which we very seldom see in Ireland. The entire of the village belongs to the Ponsonby family, who became possessors of a considerable tract of the southern portion of the county of Kilkenny, besides grants in the counties of Carlow and Leitrim, at the time of the Cromwell conquest. The splendid demesne of the earls of Bessboro immediately adjoins, on which is built the family residence of the Ponsonbys.

The gentleman who filled the responsible office of agent to the Bessboro estate, about twenty years ago, was a man of considerable taste, in the extended signification of the word. He was a lover of pictures, and an encourager of the fine arts, generally speaking, and was extremely anxious to improve and beautify the spot over which he had, at the time, an almost absolute controul,

He was particularly remarkable for cherishing native talent; and during his reign, (for reign it might almost be called,) Pilltown and its immediate neighbourhood produced several young artists of no inconsiderable merit in their respective branches of the fine arts. Some, indeed, with the fatality attendant on Irish genius, have, since then, verified the description of the poet,

"Unhallowed they sleep in the cross ways of fame,"

while others, (and some of them are still living,) have acquired a fair share of local celebrity for their cleverness and talent. Under the dynasty of the person we allude to, a spirit for outward improvement at least, was diffused throughout the bosoms of most of the tenantry, which the fostering care and encouraging eye of the proprietor himself, has since matured and preserved, practice and theory having gone on hand in hand under his prudent direction. About eight years ago, Lord Duncannon, eldest son to the earl of Bessborough, visited for the first time, this portion of the possessions of his ancestors, bringing his family with him. The change which immediately took place for the better in the entire appearance of the place, and in the condition of the inhabitants, was strikingly great. There were rack rents and middlemen before, which not all the external beauty of the place could atone for. These were both at once, and without delay, abolished. There were occasionally village tyrannies: these were put a stop to. The poorest labourer was taught to feel, that though he was subject himself to the controul of the laws, he had also a protection in them from oppression. In his arrival also, an incentive was given to industry—to improvement, an example—to morality, a reward; and to vice a powerful and stern check. But to return to our description of the place: a mountain stream empties itself into the Suir, about a mile and a half from the hamlet, capable of floating boats of seventy tons or upwards, when the tide swells the waters of this Pill, from which the village takes its name. Immediately behind the market-house is a commodious quay and dockyard, to which the navigation of the Pill only extends. A bridge or viaduct has been built within the last few years, (over another stream which flows into the Pill from an angle of the demesne,) for the purpose of cutting off a short rocky hill on the Waterford road, which now runs on straight by the right hand corner of the hotel, instead of turning by the small gate pier to the right, in the foreground of the engraving. The view of the market-house exhibits the road leading to Carrick, through the principal part of the village, which lies up amongst the trees in the distance.

MARKET-HOUSE—PILLTOWN.

At the very extremity of this end stands an unfinished tower, erected to perpetuate the memory of one of the Ponsonby family, who fell in the last war. Midway in the village is built a pretty school-house for the Protestant children; while the upper part of the market-house serves a similar purpose for the Roman Catholics.

The hotel, of which we have given a view, is pregnant with a considerable degree of interest in itself. Its proprietor, Mr. Redmond Anthony, evidently imbued with the spirit of the late agent of the estate, has been engaged for many years in the formation of a museum; and the collection of paintings, minerals, fossils, gems, statuary, medals, armour, antiques of every description, and from every country, with which he has enriched the little gallery, in the turreted angle of the building, immediately over the Post-Office, might fairly challenge many museums of great pretensions and extent, to an examination. Numerous articles of Irish antique, of great value, and rarely to be met with, carry us off in imagination to the days

"When Malachi wore the collar of gold."

Besides a specimen of this collar, numerous varieties of old Milesian and Danish jewellery, general ornaments, spear heads, battle axes, armours, &c. adorn some of the compartments of a rich Japanese cabinet. Turkish, Chinese, Indian, Polar, and European travellers, would here recognize articles of the costume, arms, natural curiosities, &c. of their respective lands; and even the wild chief of the American woods, might start at beholding his calumet, mocassins, scalps, wampum belts, bows and arrows, &c. amongst all the extraordinary products of other climes with which this emporium abounds. Could the chivalrous knights of the 15th century again assume their mortal coil, their arms, defensive and offensive, might here be once more assumed; and the fowler of the Birman empire might find in an Irish village beneath the Walsh mountains, the gilded and richly ornamented bow, and the timber-topped, ball-headed arrows, with which he brings down his variegated and glittering game, with unharmed plumage. Here are to be seen specimens of shark, sword-fish, tortoise, boar, lynx, alligator, &c. of other lands. Amongst the various medals and coins, there is one of Alexander the Great, which was found, together with a considerable number of others of different dates and countries, under the foundation of the northern gateway of the Abbey of Ferns, county of Wexford. J. Aspin, in his Systematic Analysis of Universal History, speaking on the subject of coins and medals, observes, that " few studies are of more importance to history, than that of coins and medals. Amongst the Greeks and Romans no war was declared, no peace concluded, no colony founded, no magistrate entered upon his functions, no prince ascended the throne, but a medal was struck commemorating the event; they are, therefore, in the absence of other documents, of the first importance to the chronologer in enabling him to fix the dates of such events as they were designed to perpetuate. The medal of Alexander, to which we allude, has on the obverse, the head of that prince in fine relief, crowned with the chaplet of ivy leaves and berries, which was the symbol of Bacchus, and which Alexander assumed on his conquest of India. There is also a ram's horn, (the symbol of strength and power ascribed to Jupiter Ammon, whose son Alexander was ambitious of being thought) twisting round from the back of the ear. This horn was also an attribute of Bacchus, and it might be, that he took it together with the chaplet; or it might be the goat's, which was the symbol of Macedon. However, the former is the most probable supposition. On the reverse is the figure of Hercules, clad in the skin of the Nemean lion, and having the club in his hand." Aspin says the figure of Hercules is common on the coins of Alexander the Great. Partly round the margin, and on the exergue,* is a Greek legend in very old characters, and in the Doric dialect, the first two words of which run from left to right, in the usual manner, while the last word is from right to left. Now, Froelick, quoted by Pinkerton, remarks, " coins of the most remote antiquity may be distinguished by certain infallible characteristics;" amongst which he enumerates " their not being exactly round—of a globous swelling shape—antiquity of the alphabet—the letters being retrograde, or *the first division of the legend in the common style*, while the rest is retrograde." The coin in question possesses both these signs. Formerly, Mr. Anthony allowed every person free privilege to inspect his gallery: a small sum is now charged, which is applied to the funds of the Fever Hospital of Carrick-on-Suir, by which means the institution is benefitted to the amount of about £50 per annum.

There is a Farming Society established here under the superintendence and patronage of Lord Duncannon, which has been of very great advantage to the country generally.

THE GHOST AND THE TWO BLACKSMITHS.

Upwards of forty years ago, in the beautiful little village of Randalstown,

> " Wham ne'er a town surpasses
> For honest men and bonnie lasses,"

there lived a blacksmith, named James Walker; he was an industrious, honest man, and regularly attended the Presbyterian house of worship—but still he had his failings. He occasionally took a little too much of the mountain-dew, to quench the spark in his throat, but was accounted a most excellent workman notwithstanding. About a mile and a half from the village, on the road lead-

ing to Ahoghill, lived another blacksmith, called Harry Donnell. Harry was in most respects a similar character; for he too had a similar failing, with this exception, that though he had to pass through Randalstown to the chapel, he made it a point never to be seen tipsy on Sunday. At any other time, when he came to the village, James and he were sure to have a drop. During their potations, however, they never meddled with religion, wisely observing, that it was a subject too sacred for discussion over the bottle. Their time was generally employed in discussing the most improved methods of shoeing horses, making spades and plough-irons, &c.; and whatever improvement any of them had made or found out, it was freely imparted to the other.

It happened one year, in the latter part of autumn, that Harry had been detained longer than usual from seeing his friend; but having got his corn in, and the potatoes secured from the coming frosty blast, he resolved to go to the village to purchase some iron and coals and other articles, but more especially to see his friend, James, and have a glass. He left home in the afternoon of one of the dreary days in November, telling his family not to be uneasy if he should delay longer than usual, being almost certain he would get company home.

As he walked along the road, his eye wandered with delight down the sloping vale of the river Main, where the *then* comfortable farmers resided in independence, and hospitality sat smiling at their board; but, alas! the times are altered *there* now. He soon reached the town; and having made his purchases, and arranged all to his mind, he called at the shop of his friend, James, from whom he received a hearty shake of the hand, with an expression of surprise at his being so long absent.

They immediately went to the sign of the Black Bull, —were shown into the little parlour, where a rousing turf-fire was blazing in the grate, at which they sat down—called for half a pint of spirits, and in a short time a smoking jug of punch was on the table, which they speedily quaffed, discoursing on their usual topics; and the jug was again and again emptied and replenished, till the toll of the curfew informed them it was nine o'clock. Harry then remarked that it was time he was home, adding a wish that he was past *Drumarory Bush.** " where," he said, " so many *fearsome* things had been seen, and about which so many alarming stories had been told." This led them into a discussion on the existence of ghosts, fairies, and other aërial beings: James arguing that there were no such things, and Harry as firmly maintaining that there were. At last, James, seeing that all his arguments had no effect in convincing Harry, or in removing his fear, proffered to accompany him beyond the dreaded bush; protesting that he feared neither ghost, nor fairy, nor even emissary of the ould boy himself. Harry thankfully accepted his company; and, when matters were thus arranged, they repaired to the bar, to pay the reckoning; after which Harry remarking, that it would be very dangerous to go out in so cold a night after drinking warm punch, without a taste of *raw spirits*, called for another naggin, during the drinking of which their former subject was renewed at the bar, and was attentively listened to by all who surrounded the kitchen fire. At last Harry and James set off; James still protesting that he was as little afraid of passing Drumarory bush as any other bush. Their discourse ran mostly on the same subject till,

> " The *dreaded* bush was drawing nigh, ●
> Whar *ghosts* and *witches* nightly cry;"

but, to their great inward satisfaction, all was quiet. Scarcely had they proceeded a few paces further, when a

---

* *Exergum, Exergue*, (from the Greek "*ex ergou*," out of the work,) is the bottom of a coin, commonly separated from the field by a line, upon which the figures of the reverse stand. When the letters run round the margin, or on the exergue, they are denominated a legend; but when they occupy the field they are called an inscription.

* Drumarory Bush was a large hawthorn, that grew on the edge of the road, one half mile out of Randalstown in going to Ahoghill, and was famous in country story, as the haunt of fairies, witches, and evil spirits; and even the devil himself was said to be seen at it; so that it was a place very few liked to pass at a late hour. In fact, the writer, when a boy, durst not pass it alone after night-fall. It is now cut down, so that its place is no more to be found; but a little above where it stood is a rise in the road, still called *Drumarory Brae.*

blazing light sprung up and seemed to dance about the bush with great rapidity; this put them to a stand. James said, "In God's name we'll see what it is;" but they had not gone more than a few steps when something clad in white stooped on the road, giving a wild unearthly scream; and just opposite to them they heard another still more terrific. James's philosophy instantly forsook him; and both took to their heels back to the town; but still, as they ventured to peep round, they saw the white ghost, and the light following, till they came opposite Feehoge, where the apparition and light glided down a dark avenue, and disappeared. Over-exertion and terror made them now slacken their pace; but they soon renewed it, on hearing a foot coming fast behind them; they stopped, however, on hearing a human voice cry out, "If you are Christians or men, I entreat you to stand, for I am frightened out of my senses by a ghost." This person soon joined them; and, to their great joy, they found it was Jamie Irons, the barber of Randalstown, who declared he would faint, or perhaps die, unless he would soon get a glass of whiskey. This he was promised, as they were now at the head of the town. They came to the same inn, called for a pint of spirits, of which Jamie got a large share, and related to the amazed inmates their strange adventure—Irons confirming it by declaring, that as he was coming up Feehoge avenue, a white woman or ghost, followed by a blazing light, passed him, and afterwards glided, without any noise, through the orchard-hedge.

The whiskey soon restored their wasted spirits; and Jamie seeing no chance of any more liquor coming in, began to remark that it would be a pity Harry should be detained in town all night. That as there were now three of them, he proposed they should go to Drumarory, and see Harry past; offering himself as a *rulette*. To this they agreed; and, taking another glass, they set off; Irons, as he promised, being some perches in advance. They soon arrived at the bush—but nothing was to be seen or heard, save the distant swells and falls of the river Main: so leaving Harry on the top of Drumarory Brae, the two returned to town. Harry being now in full spirits, and, as he thought, out of all danger, began to grow quite courageous—swearing that he could beat any fellow who durst oppose him on the road—nor was he afraid of the very Old Boy. The whiskey was now taking full effect. In this way he went on till he reached Seymour's-bridge, a mile out of town, where there was, and still ought to be, a school-house; against the gable of which he leaned himself, in order to rest; when, looking towards the west, across the road, he saw on the height opposite, a man, in the attitude of challenging him to fight! Harry instantly stepped on the road, ordered him to come down, and keep less vapouring, or he would soon make him repent it; to this the man seemed to pay no attention, but still kept taunting him as formerly. At this, Harry losing all patience, made a race at him; but forgetting there was an old gravel-pit, generally full of water, on a level with the road, and directly opposite, he plunged into it over head and ears, and would probably have been drowned had he not been providentially rescued by a young man coming down the road at the time, who heard the plunge. When brought out, he could hardly be persuaded that what he took for a man in the attitude of fighting was nothing but a large *rag-wort* waving in the wind. He, however, resolved, in future, never to be drunk after night in Randalstown, or stay there late, which resolution he faithfully kept till the day of his death.

The story of the ghost and the two smiths passed current in the town and country; and was firmly believed by almost every one; and there are still some people living in that neighbourhood, who would yet vouch for its authenticity; but the truth is, Jamie Irons, as he informed the writer, was the ghost himself: he was, perhaps, the greatest man for tricks of this sort, ever bred in the county of Antrim; and, though his countenance was indicative of nothing but wisdom, and the utmost gravity, so that he was seldom seen to smile, yet he was of a most playful and merry disposition, and delighted in humbugging every one that he knew was self-conceited or too opinionative. On the night mentioned, he was sitting at the inn's kitchen-fire; and, when James Walker so fre-

quently protested that he feared no ghost or evil spirit, he resolved to put his courage to a fair trial. Getting, therefore, a white sheet, a keenoge,* and a bunch of splinters of bog-deal, such as is used by fishers at night, he proceeded before the two smiths to Drumarory; and, with the assistance of a person he brought for the purpose, performed, as can be easily imagined, the above deception on the blacksmiths.   J. G.

Ballymena.

THE CHIEF OF CLANAWLY.†
A LEGEND OF THE SOUTH.

BY EDWARD WALSH.

There's a feast in the hall where Clanawly's chief dwells,
And waking of wild harps, and sounding of shells;
Unclasp'd are the helmets—the wavy plumes now
Bend graceful no more o'er the warrior's brow;
The chiefs are all waiting—did any behold
The princely M'Auliff, proud lord of the wold?

The night breeze sings cold o'er Clonfert's ancient tomb,
Daloo ripples dark in his wavy woods' gloom;
The guests are impatient—"M'Auliff doth hunt
The red mountain deer as a chieftain is wont,
Or urging the chase of the wolf from the plain
To his lair in the cliff, does M'Auliff remain?"

Ah, no! for his tall dogs in idleness howl;
Beyond them the gaunt wolf may fearlessly prowl;
The long hunting spear, and the loud hunting horn,
No more in the chase o'er the wide heath are borne ·
For the chase of the grey wolf, or red mountain deer,
Doth least in the thoughts of the chieftain appear.

For Ellen, the heiress of all that divide
The bank of Daloo from the Allo's loud tide,

---

* *Keenoge* or *Cunea*, is a turf-coal, rolled tightly in tow or flax, so that you may carry it a long way in your pocket without its kindling; but when opened out to the air, it instantly becomes, as it were, alive again, and will kindle any combustible.

† Castle M'Auliff, the seat of the chiefs of Clanawly, rose on the bank of the river Daloo, to the left of the road leading from Newmarket to Millstreet, and about a mile from the former. It was a strong building, and towered proudly on a tall cliff that overhung the stream; but the ruin which time and the fire of the invader failed in accomplishing, modern vandalism has completed; and its grass-grown foundations can now hardly be traced. M'Auliff's territory was a mountainous tract, and it yet bears the name of "M'Auliff's dark Mountains." The last lord of Clanawly was attainted in the rebellion of 1641, with M'Donough of Kanturk, prince of Duhallow, whose uncle M'Auliff was. The popular legends of this race are very curious. M'Auliff, the legend concerning whom we have attempted to portray, rescued the beautiful daughter of a neighbouring chieftain from the "power of faery," in the manner related in the text; and a wild and spell-bound destiny seems to have awaited his posterity by that lady, whom he afterwards married. His son on a certain day, overpowered by the fatigues of the chase, lay down to rest upon the margin of a clear well, which is yet shown as you enter Newmarket from the west: he drank of the water, and falling asleep, awoke in some hours greatly endued with the spirit of prophecy. These prophecies he uttered in Irish verse—they are yet preserved among the peasantry of Duhallow, and are extremely curious. In one of them, with a mournful prescience, he alludes to the extinction of his own race. This was fulfilled about the year 1828, by the death of a well-known character in the neighbourhood of Newmarket, called John M'Auliffe the Active, the last of that noble line: he spent a poor, precarious life—a wanderer in the extensive territory of his ancestors. Meelan, the daughter, I believe, of the last chief of Clanawly, was, on her wedding night, conveyed by supernatural agency to a tall cliff on the right bank of the Daloo, over against the ruined church of Clonfert. A huge excavation in the steep still bears her name, and the peasantry affirm, that often, while the shadows of night are falling fast around, her plaintive tones of lament are heard to wake the echoes that sleep round the rock of her enchantment.

Is dead. Oh! bethink ye that bosom's dismay,
Which consigns all it loves to the cold reptile's sway:
And never did Love's brilliant fetter entwine
More true heart's, M'Auliff, than Ellen's and thine!

There's wringing of hands—and the mourner's shrill cry,
And the wild *ullalu* of the keener are high;
And the handmaids have strew'd early flowers on the grave
Where Kilcorcoran's alders in solitude wave:
But an old, hoary wizard of visions hath told
A tale which the chieftain forbears to unfold!

And whispers are heard, that fair Ellen survives
Where spells of the fairy bind enchanted lives—
That the bier where the mourners had pour'd their despair,
Held nought but the semblance of young Ellen there!
I wist not what tale did the grey wizard tell—
The breast of the chief holds it closely and well.

But nightly, since Ellen was wrapt in her shroud,
Though the lightning may gleam and the fierce storm be loud,
And though Daloo's dark water his green valley fills,
Increas'd by the streams of his cloud-cover'd hills,
Through blue flash, wild tempest, and wilder wave's flight,
He seeks yon lone crag on the pine-covered height.

There's a feast in the hall—but he climbs the rude steep
When the shadows of darkness are silent and deep;
The breeze that had swept yonder home of the dead,
Was bending the pine on that peak's rugged head,
Where rose through the gloom, on his wonder-struck eye,
A palace where fairies hold festival high!

The essence of all that gives colour to light,
Did with treasures of earth in that structure unite;
And the spirit of music, exalted, refin'd,
Like a spell, round the heart of the listener entwin'd,
As he enter'd the portal, and pass'd on to where
Gay pleasure was reigning—for woman was there!

And wine-bowls of brightness the banquet did crown;
In mantle and mail sat old chiefs of renown.
The white bearded harper's wild melody rings,
While the fierce *Eye of Battle** arose on the strings,
And shouts of the brave from the mail-covered throng,
Came blent o'er the board with that wild battle song!

There were bright eyes of beauty, and bosoms of snow,
And maids that were *stolen* long ages ago;
And sea-nymphs that came from their home in the main;
And fairies of ocean, and fays of the plain;
But the chieftain's eye wander'd the bright circle round
In search of young Ellen—and Ellen it found!

The voice of the harp and the hero had fled,
When the mortal appear'd at the feast of the dead;
But *one* who in stature resembled a god,
Cried, "Welcome, O chief, to the crystal abode!"
"Thrice welcome, M'Auliff!" the banquet guests cried ·
"Thrice welcome, M'Auliff!" the echoes replied.

And he who in stature resembled a god,
To the lord of Clanawly right courteously strode,
And led him to where stood a canopied throne,
That with gold and rich jewels all gloriously shone;
Then signed to the harper, who sweetly and well,
Poured the charm of his voice with the clarseach's soft spell.

"All hail, potent lord of Clanawly!—to thee
Thy home long be sacred, thy mountains be free;
May the falchion, thy fathers to victory bore,
Flash vengeance on tyrants till thraldom be o'er.

* Ross Catha, or the Eye of Battle, was a warlike air, to the music of which the warriors moved to the fight. It was likewise in high repute at the festive meetings of the chiefs; and, it is said, that its thrilling notes were capable of rousing their military ardour to the highest pitch of excitement.

The heroes are met, at the clarseach's loud call,
To share the glad feast, in the banquetting hall;
But often they gather'd, in mantle and mail,
At glory's proud call, for the right of the Gail.

These red bowls of brightness, our banquet-guests drain,
In flavour exceed the famed boir* of the Dane;
And the chiefs of Kincora ne'er honoured such wine,
As o'er this glad board pours its current divine.

We've maidens like those whose thrice-beautiful eyes,
Lur'd angels to earth, from their home in the skies;
And voices are here, at whose magical will
The tempests of ocean were silent and still.

With the fair and the brave share the banquet of joy,
With music and wine the glad moments employ;
And sirens of sweetness shall warble for thee,
In this hall of our feasting, their songs of the sea.

Then hail, potent lord of Clanawly! to thee
Thy home long be sacred, thy mountains be free;
May the falchion, thy fathers to victory bore,
Flash vengeance on tyrants till thraldom be o'er."

M'Auliff then rose, to the brave and the bright:
"In the hall of Clanawly there's feasting to night;†
To stay in your palace, that banquet to shun,
My fathers would blush for the shame of their son.
I'll dance but one measure, then quickly retire,
To head the glad feast in the home of my sire.

He bow'd to young Ellen—she blush'd, and looked down;
Some beauties grew pale, and some maidens did frown.
Such graceful young dancers 'twere seldom to see,
His stature so noble—so beauteous was she.
"High Heaven defend us," he whispering said,
"There's danger, dear maid, in this measure we tread!"

As quick gleam their steps on the diamond-paved floor,
One hand grasps the lady—they rush to the door—
And one the black dagger,‡ whose spell-rending steel
The power of faery would tremble to feel!
Then clasps his fond maid in his ardent embrace,
And, gaining the portal, escapes from the place.

There were rushing of lady and chief from the hall
And wailing and woe, would the bravest appal;
But the cock's sudden clarion gave notice of day,
And the hall and the fairy-guests faded away.
So constant in love, and in danger so bold,
Have ye heard of a chief like the lord of the Wold?

* Tradition affirms that the Danes made a delicious intoxicating liquor, called Boir, of the mountain brath. Kincora, the residence of Brien Boro, on the bank of the Shannon, was celebrated for its wine-cellars; and, when the peasantry would assure you of a hearty welcome to their fire-side, they say, in their expressive manner, "were ours the boir of the Dane and the wine of Kincora, they should be poured for you."

† To eat or drink at such feasts as this would be the surest way of subjecting himself to fairy spells; and M'Auliff was, doubtless, glad of a fair excuse for evading such influence.

‡ The *Skien Dhu* or black dagger, had irresistible power over the strongest enchantments: its efficacy, even to this day, in destroying fairy spells and killing ghosts, is most devoutly believed; and, to use a phrase of Lord Byron's, "most incredibly attested."

DUBLIN:
Printed and Published by P. D. Hardy, 3, Cecilia-street; to whom all communications are to be addressed.
Sold by all Booksellers in Ireland.

In London, by Richard Groombridge, 6, Panyer-alley, Paternoster-row; in Liverpool, by Willmer and Smith; in Manchester, by Ambery; in Birmingham, by Guest; in Glasgow, by John Macleod; and in Edinburgh, by N. Bowack.

THE
DUBLIN PENNY JOURNAL

CONDUCTED BY P. DIXON HARDY, M.R.I.A.

| VOL. III. | JANUARY 31, 1835. | No. 134. |

TOWN OF CARRICKFERGUS.

Having taken occasion in several numbers of our first volume, to give some of the most interesting particulars of the early history of this ancient town, it may at present be sufficient to observe, that travellers *en route* to the Giant's Causeway, would do well to devote a little more time than is generally spent in this place, to an inspection of the Castle, and the remains of the walls and trenches by which the town is surrounded, as affording a tolerably fair specimen of the style of fortification from 1640 to 1746, in the northern portion of the island.

Carrickfergus is the assize town of the county. It was at a very early period considered rather an important situation, and was the scene of several sanguinary conflicts. We are informed by Mr. M'Skimmin in his History of Carrickfergus, that the walls, which were flanked with seven bastions, are still pretty entire, about six feet thick on the top towards the land, and about eighteen feet high, coarsely but strongly built in that manner called grouting; the corners of the bastions of cut yellowish free-stone, different from any stone found in this neighbourhood. The land side was also strengthened by a wet ditch, now nearly filled up. There were four gates, anciently distinguished by the following names: Glenarm or Spittal gate, Woodburn or West gate, Water gate, and Quay gate. Spittal gate, now North gate, and West gate, now Irish gate, were formerly entered by drawbridges: the drawbridge and deep trench of the latter remained within memory, and part of the arch over the former is yet standing. Water gate and Quay gate were defended by battlements over them.

Adjoining, on the south of the town, is an ancient cas-

tle belonging to the crown, occupied as a military garrison, and magazine to the northern district. It stands on a rock that projects into the sea, so that, at common tides, three sides of the building are enclosed by water. The greatest height of the rock is at its southern extremity, where it is about thirty feet, shelving considerably towards the land, the walls of the castle following exactly its different windings. Towards the town are two towers, called from their shape half moons, and between these is the only entrance, which is defended by a strait passage, with embrasures for fire-arms. About the centre of this passage was formerly a drawbridge; a part of the barbican that protected the bridge can still be seen. A dam west of the castle, is believed to have been originally made to supply the ditch at this entrance with water. Between the half-moons is a strong gate, above which is a machicolation, or aperture, for letting fall stones, melted lead, or the like, on the assailants. Inside this gate is a portcullis, and an aperture for the like purpose as that just mentioned; the arches on each side of this aperture are of the Gothic kind, and the only ones observed about the building. In the gun room of these towers are a few pieces of light ordnance. A window in the east tower, inside, is ornamented with round pillars; the columns are five feet high, including base and capital, and five inches and a half in diameter. The centre column seems to be a rude attempt at the Ionic; the flank columns have the leaves of the Corinthian; their bases consist of two toruses. Within the gates is the lower yard, or balium; on the right are the guard room and a barrack; the latter was built in 1802. Opposite these are large vaults, said to be bomb proof, over which are a few neat apartments occupied by the officers of the garrison, ordnance storekeeper, and master gunner. A little southward are the armourer's forge and a furnace for heating shot; near which, on the outer wall of the castle, is a small projecting tower, called the lion's den.

Southward, on the right, is the passage into the inner yard or upper balium, by a gate with a semicircular arch, above which is a long aperture, circular at the top. Inside, this aperture opens considerably; and, on each side, are niches in the wall, apparently to protect those who defended the gate—northward of which are several like apertures, and on the south, a square tower, near which is a small door, or sally-port, with semicircular arch, and ornamented. The openings above this gate, and in the wall, appear to have been originally intended for the discharging of arrows; the top of the wall overhead seems to have been formerly garrated for a like purpose.

Within this yard, which is encompassed by a high wall, is a small magazine, built a few years since, several storehouses, and the keep, or donjon, a square tower ninety feet high. Both the south and east sides of this tower face the inner yard, its west wall forming a part of the outside wall of the building: its north wall faces the outer yard. The walls of the keep are eight feet ten inches thick; the entrance is on the east by a semicircular door in the second story. On the left of the entrance is a small door, now built up, by which was formerly a passage in the south-east corner, by helical stone stairs, to the ground floor and top of the tower. In this passage were loop-holes for the admission of air and light; and opposite each story a small door that opened into the different apartments. At present the ascent to the top is partly by wooden stairs inside. The ground story of the keep is bomb proof, with small slits looking into the inner yard. It is believed to have been anciently a state prison, and is now the principal magazine in this garrison. Several rooms in the other stories are occupied as an armoury, and for other military stores. On the top of the tower are two small houses; that on the south-east corner covers the mouth of the passage; the other, on the south-west corner, seems to have been intended for a sentinel.

The tower is divided into five stories; the largest room was formerly in the third story, with semicircular windows. It was called Fergus's dining-room, and was twenty-five feet ten inches high, forty feet long, and thirty-eight broad. Within the keep was formerly a draw well, thirty-seven feet deep, the water of which was anciently celebrated for medicinal purposes. This well is now nearly filled up with rubbish.

The following notice of this castle is given in a survey by George Clarkson in 1567 : " The building of the said castle on the south part is three towers, viz., the gatehouse, tower in the middle thereof, which is the entry at a draw-bridge over a dry moat; and in said tower is a prison and porter lodge, and over the same a fair lodging, called the constable's lodging; and in the courtain between the gate-house and west tower in the corner, being of divers squares called Cradyfergus, is a fair and comley building, a chapel, and divers houses of office, on the ground, and above the great chamber, and the lords lodging, all which is now in great decaie as well in the couverture being lead, also in timber and glass, and without help and reparation it will soon come to utter ruin."

THE LITTLE NURSE.

A SKETCH FROM THE WICKLOW HILLS.

* * * * * * *

Shall we not seize the time and ride
By Avon's stream, by Lara's side,
To yon lone vale where, hid from day,
The miner works his venturous way,
Wresting from earth her glittering hoard,
Beneath primeval ruin stored ;
Heap piled on heap, as wave on wave,
Of worlds succeeding worlds the grave.

Such were the concluding lines of an invitation once sent me, to join a few scientific friends on a tour through the Wicklow hills. An amateur in geology was the Laureate of the party. The events of this little excursion are among the pleasantest recollections of my life ; but in the following sketch of our first day's progress, I have omitted much, especially in details of scenery, rendered familiar by the pens of more professed tourists; and indeed my chief inducement to arrange these notes for perusal is, that they include an affecting and somewhat novel incident in the history of domestic life.

The first object of our excursion was the great lead mine of Luggenure, opening, as our geologist informed us, on the side of a lofty hill, and driven downwards to a great depth through the solid rock. To reach this point we started with the earliest dawn, and ere sunrise were upon a road which, winding at the base of Sugarloaf mountain, leads by a very gradual ascent to the plain of Calory, on its south-western side. Here our botanist, Mr. Neville, who has preserved beyond the close of his half century, all the freshness of spirit and much of the activity of youth, insisted on climbing the mountain in quest of some of the rarer species of Fern which he expected to find among the rocks near the summit. The geologist, hammer in hand, backed this proposal: our painter anticipated a glorious view from the peak ; and Dr. James and myself, having no hobbies of our own, were content to enjoy it with him.

Accordingly, where the road wound through the valley of Glencormac, we quitted our vehicle, and, sending it forward to meet us at the opposite side, began to climb the shoulder of the hill, although the loose rocks upon its steep and shattered side, seen through the grey twilight, appeared doubly grotesque in form and threatening in position. Before we had reached the top, the east began to redden, and a light breeze arose : the clouds broke up suddenly, like the ice in a northern spring, and the blue sky, bright and distant, became visible through the openings. A wreath of white mist still rested on the low range of hills stretching to our right, from the waterfall and wooded heights of Powerscourt to the eastern boundary of Lake Dan, concealing their outline, and waving like a curtain along their sides : the monarch Djouce alone heaved his broad summit into the clear blue sky, and, cut off by the mist from the adjoining hills and the plain below him, seemed a portion of some brighter world. One by one the cabins scattered over the lower grounds began to send up their thin columns of smoke, and figures could be seen moving through the fields as we descended slowly towards a dark speck on the road below, which we hailed as our vehicle. Mr. Neville had found his fern, but the geologist had been less successful as to certain sandstones, and the mist had interfered with our draughtsman's view. Not the less cheerily did we resume our way. We had started as philosophers, and were determined to support that character in all its senses.

The sun was up, and the world awake and stirring, as we passed the bridge over the Avonmore, and entered the romantic valley of the Seven Churches. The bare and rocky glen of Luggenure now lay open to our right ; but instead of proceeding at once to the mine, we advanced into Glendalough, and again crossing the river nearer to where it issues from the lake, wandered for some time among those ancient ecclesiastical buildings now in ruin, the number of which within so small a space, renders it probable, independent of local tradition, that here was one of those seats of learning and religion which gave celebrity to this island in the earlier ages of Christianity. We then rowed across the lake to gain a nearer view of the rock from which St. Kevin saw the waters close over his Kathleen, and also of the cave or "bed," which he is said to have made his home. Our painter was so delighted with the land view from the lake, that on our return he spread forth his drawing materials upon a rock, and commenced a sketch. As I stood beside him watching the progress of his work, I could not but reflect how nearly to a state of nature this once thronged and cultivated valley had returned ; and, except in the vague traditions of the place, how entirely the memory of those who once taught and worshipped here had perished. The ruined walls remain, and traces of ancient husbandry can still be discerned on the steep sides of the surrounding hills : but of the sage or the saint—those lights of a barbarous time—no authentic memorial has survived : they have bequeathed to us no living work—no monument of their intellectual strength or beauty—no pillar of the mind to lift its head above the flood of time, and point to the vale of Glendalough.

I was awakened from this dream of the past, by the near approach of an old woman who had been for some time making slowly towards us. She stopped for a moment before the painter, then made a low courtesy, and said in a hesitating manner, " Maybe your honour's not the gintleman? They told me at the inn that there was a strange doctor gone to the Bed."

" I'm a strange fellow, no doubt," said the artist, without raising his head, " but not exactly the one you want. There, old woman," looking up, and pointing with his pencil, " there stands your man of physic—that laughing gentleman in black."

Dr. James, who was standing at a little distance, with Mr. Neville, jesting on the geologist and his pre-adamite worlds, turned on hearing this. " Well, granny, what's the matter with you—don't mind that daubing fellow."

" Och, its not with me that the matter is, your reverence, (your honor I mane, if I could spake); I'm ould, acushla, and there's no cure for that. But it's a poor little child that's anexpicted—the crathur's in the scales since morning, and it 'ud be the height of a charity to cast your opinion on it ; and the poor sister——"

" Can you tell me the child's complaint ?"

" Och, God help it, it can t complain, and it not nine months ould ; and I'm only a neighbour, and the little sister's not a jidge."

To a further question, however, she explained that the infant had " an impression on it heart," to remedy which they had " baided it in potato water," and put " black wool on it chist," and given it a drop of punch " to rise it little heart ;" but " in spite of all," last night it was " smothered entirely."

James now expressed his readiness to visit the child, and the old woman moved off, followed by our whole party. She directed her steps towards a point at some distance, where smoke seemed to issue from the side of a sloping bank ; keeping up as she hobbled before us, a sort of broken rambling soliloquy, of which, from time to time, I could catch, " the greatest of Christian charities—skilful looking gintlemen, God bless them—the height of poverty and exile—the poor little sister, not twelve years ould—this pain in my back——"

She was interrupted by a group of little girls, who were dancing or rather jumping, hand in hand, around one of their companions, chanting some merry but monotonous rhyme. They now suddenly broke up their sport to crowd about her, and enquire eagerly, " How was 'Statia's child ?—would it live?—would it die ?" The old woman held on her way, saying, " Don't stop me, jewels ; don't you see the gintlemen—bad enough, bad enough it is."

We now approached a cabin of very small dimensions, lodged, for the advantage of shelter, in an excavation of the high bank of gravel which rose behind it. The thatch was much decayed, and where attempts to repair it were visible, rushes from the neighbouring lake had supplied the place of straw. There was no chimney, the smoke issuing through a hole in the roof ; and the aperture intended for a window was partly closed by a large slate. Before the door, several young children—plump, rosy, and ragged—were shouting in great glee, and dragging about a goat, which the tallest boy made many unsuccessful attempts to ride. This urchin wore a trowsers, the legs of which, torn through their entire length, fluttered in streams behind him as he ran. Another little fellow waddled about in a man's waistcoat, worn as a surtout, and covering him to his heels. A cheque apron thrown on as a cloak, helped out the attire of a third ; while two young ones sprawled in the sun, with scarcely any pretensions to apparel. The old woman pushed through them, muttering, " God help yes for childer ! ye've no better wit," and led the way into the cabin, where a sadder scene presented itself.

On the floor, in one of those large baskets used here by the peasantry, for straining their boiled potatoes, and

now applied to the purpose of a cradle, lay the sick child. Beside it, on a very low stool, sat a little girl, whom I judged to be the sister mentioned by the old woman. She seemed about eleven or twelve years old, and might be considered handsome, even for this region of personal as well as picturesque beauty ; but her figure was small and slight, and there sat an anxious and careworn expression on her pretty features, which strangely contrasted with their extreme youth, and seemed to denote a premature acquaintance with sorrow or suffering. She looked up as we entered, and cast an enquiring glance on our conductress, but did not rise.

" 'Statia, jewel," said the old woman, " it's a doctor that's in it ; and I brought him to see the poor brother ; and, with God's help, who knows what he may do ?"

The little girl instantly rose. Her cheek, which before was very pale, became deeply flushed ; and as James bent over the cradle, feeling the infant's pulse, and watching its hurried breathing, she stood opposite to him, her figure leaning forward, her little hands clasped, her bright eyes keenly and eagerly fixed, as if to catch from his first glance some presage of her brother's fate.

" Sir," said she, " will it live ?"

The doctor seemed unprepared to answer this question, or, willing to evade it, he remained silent for a moment, and then inquired for the mother.

" We have no mother, Sir," said Anastatia ; " she died the night he was born."

" Well, my dear, whoever nurses the child—any one to take directions."

" I nurse him, Sir—there's nobody else."

As this announcement called forth a general expression of surprise, the old woman explained to us, that the father of this family (having six children besides the new-born infant, when bereft of his wife,) had been unable, from extreme poverty, to employ a nurse. The neighbouring women, therefore, had taught little 'Statia to feed the child, " And well," added she, " has she fed him and cared him, day and night, hour and time—sure the half of the crature's not in it—she's worn off the face of the earth."

The child's appearance, as in his feverish sleep he tossed about his large ruddy limbs, bore testimony that the feeding, at least, had not been neglected.

" And can it be possible," said I, " that you have reared this fine boy without assistance ?"

" Yes," said she, mournfully, as she bent down to arrange the coverings he had thrown aside—" I reared him. He never had a nurse but me, and now he's going—"

Here the old woman threw in her mite of consolation. " And 'Statia, dear, if it's going, sure it's going to God : and wont it be better done for, than ever you could do for it."

The poor little nurse turned impatiently away, and burst into tears. She was, no doubt, sufficiently instructed to be aware that the old woman had spoken truth. But this infant, while he claimed from her a mother's care, had awakened, even thus early, a mother's love. He was to her in place of the toys and recreations of her youth : her pet—her plaything—her own ! She had watched over him till her young cheek had become pale, and her childish form wasted, and now " he was going—" going to the coffin, and the deep dark grave.

I was so much moved by the poor girl's distress, that, although quite ignorant in the matter, I tried to cheer her with some hope of her brother's recovery. But the doctor's silence had not escaped her.

" O Sir," said she in a whisper, " that gentleman don't think so—you don't know how bad he is."

James now assured her that there was still a chance of recovery, which, however, would depend on his being able to bleed the child ; and for this purpose directed the old woman to take him upon her lap : but 'Statia interposed—

" He wouldn't stay with you, Molly—he's quiet with no one but me."

She now seated herself beside him, and I remarked the expert and matronly air with which she lifted her young charge from the cradle, and adjusted him on her lap for the operation—holding out his arm, and hiding his face in her bosom, that he might not see the strangers.

" Now, Sir," said she, " he's ready. Children, stand from the gentleman's light—boys, stay outside, I bid you".

When the lancet appeared, I observed that she shut her eyes, and turned her head aside: yet, although her whole frame shook, she held him firmly till the operation was over.

The child bled rapidly and became faint; and we had some difficulty in convincing her that he was not dying. After a few minutes, however, the relief he had experienced became manifest. The eldest boy was now directed to follow us to the inn for some medicine which the doctor had in his valise, and we were leaving the cabin, when a gaunt, ragged figure, carrying a spade on his shoulder, appeared coming towards it. On learning from Molly that this man was the father of the family, Dr. James went up to him, and explained what had been done for the child, adding, that although somewhat relieved, he was by no means out of danger. The poor man sighed deeply.

"Welcome," said he, "be the will of God. But that little crature you saw there, 'ill break her heart after him; and she's all the mother I have for six of them. If anything happens *her* I'm totally defeated."

We said what we could to cheer him, and promising to visit the child on our return, set forward for Luggenure. Before us stood the celebrated round tower, rising, like a huge pillar, to the height of 110 feet in the centre of the valley. The history of these singular structures is still enveloped in the mist of ages; and the researches of the antiquarian have tended rather to show what they *were not*, than to throw light upon their real origin and use. The most probable opinions connect them with some form of pagan worship—possibly of the Phenician idols—the gods of Canaan brought into this remote island by the scattered remnant of that mighty, but ill-fated race. Their "high places" were certainly *buildings*, and were not always seated upon hills, for they were at one time to be found in *all* the cities of Israel; and there also was one in the valley of Hinnom. They may therefore have been "high" only with respect to the grove which it was usual to plant around them. As I turned from this monument of human frailty, towards the hovel we had just quitted, I thought how much heavier might have been the burden of its poor inmates, but for that purer faith which had overthrown the idol, and left its high place desolate in the midst of Christian temples. The poor peasant, who in his sorrow yet "welcomed the will of God," must have turned for help to the frantic and cruel rites of the heathen: his sweet child might have bent her knee at the profligate shrine of Baal, or her brother have torn from her arms to pass through fire to Moloch.

I must not lengthen this paper by a description of Luggenure; especially as I did not enter the mine myself. The painter, who did, (his sublime and beautiful lie above ground, and he is somewhat fastidious in his dress,) after ten minutes disappearance, suddenly scrambled out, denouncing it as "a den, Sir; a mere hole—deep, dirty, dark, and dangerous." Our geologist, on the contrary, was enchanted, and saw worlds piled on worlds at every step of his descent.

It was evening when we returned to the sick child, and to our inexpressible satisfaction, found him so much relieved, that the doctor considered his danger nearly over. I may add, that before we left the neighbourhood he had perfectly recovered.

Years have since rolled by, and I have seen little 'Statia in the bloom of womanhood, surrounded by those children to whom—herself a child—she had been as a mother. The elder boys were then sufficiently grown to be able to assist their father, and add somewhat to the comforts of their cabin. The latter had improved in its furniture, and was enlarged by an additional room. She did not recollect me, till I reminded her of the scene I have described, and enquired for the child. She then blushed and smiled, and beckoned to a rosy boy, who came prancing across the floor, and jumped upon her lap—"Paddy," said she, "did you ever see that gentleman before?"   J. M.

The Croup, one of the most dangerous and rapid of the diseases of children, may in many instances be effectually checked by the external application to the throat of equal parts of camphor, spirits of wine, and hartshorn, well mixed together.

CASTLEKNOCK.

Thus often shall memory, in dreams sublime,
　Catch a glimpse of the days that are over;
Thus sighing, look through the waves of time,
　For the long faded glories they cover.
                                        MOORE.

Outside the town of Castleknock, and situated in the demesne of Mr. Guinn,* are two steep hills, one a plain circular knoll, formerly called Windmill hill, crowned by a circular building, which was erected by Mr. Guinn for an observatory, but afterwards let go to ruin; the other, bearing the venerable remains of an old castle, from which the town takes its name. Scanty as the remains are of this "ruin of a ruin," they must strike the eye of the traveller with reverence: the many scenes that are associated with it, of chivalry and of glory—of feudal pomp and revelry, and, perhaps, many a foul and midnight murder, must leave an impression on his mind, as he treads on the ground on which "the Bruce" of yore strode in his might, not easily to be obliterated. Well may he sigh as he gazes on the ivy branches that cluster round the aged walls, in hopes of preserving them from the fate of their former lords,

"For the long faded glories they cover."

Tradition says that this castle was a royal residence of the Danes. I have seen an old Irish verse in which it is called "Royal Castlenoc." Grose says it is a respectable old ruin, and was given by Strongbow to his friend, Hugh Tyrrell, from which time it remained in the same family till the invasion of Edward Bruce who took it and its lord, Hugh Tyrrell, and family, prisoners, but ransomed them after. It was again taken by Colonel Monk in 1642, who killed eighty rebels, and hanged many more. In 1649 the Earl of Ormond appeared before it. After the Restoration it fell into decay. Its situation is bold and commanding in the extreme, and the view from its walls very extensive; it is said that the hill of Maynooth can be seen from it. On the east side, the remains of the entrenchments have given place to an indistinguishble mass of steep earth: but on the opposite side they are almost perfect, though mount and fosse are now both alike covered with tall trees. The only perfect open about the building is a little postern door in one of the battlement walls, to the west. The ruin shown in the drawing, I presume, was a round tower or keep, and appears to have been battered from the opposite hill. The open in the centre, I think, was a gate or door, as it appears to have been arched. In the thickness of the walls was a winding passage, not a stairs, from the bottom to the top of the castle. The inhabitants say that you could go by that passage to the foundation of the walls, which are said to

* I believe it now belongs to the Rev. Gentlemen of Maynooth College.

be level with the surrounding country, where there is an immense chamber, of which there is the following Tradition.

When St. Patrick was preaching Christianity through Ireland, he came to Castlenoc, then in the possession of a Danish king, called Morrishtae, whom he endeavoured to convert; but the Dane, not wishing to be *bothered* by the pious saint, and unwilling to be inhospitable, after listening for some time, and giving sundry nods of approval, as the saint would come to a colon or semicolon, at length fell fast asleep in his great arm chair, or, as it was then called, his throne. St. Patrick preached on for some time, until he was astounded by a most unchristian snore from the poor Dane; and then his rage knew no bounds: he tore his beard and acted several *ramashes*, and in the height of his passion, prayed that the uncircumcised king should sleep in the same place and posture till the day of judgment; and there, it is said, he remains to the present hour. Such is the legend related by the village schoolmistress.

> I cannot say how the truth may be,
> I tell the tale as 'twas told to me;

but this much I know, that the owner of the Castle before Mr. Guinn, attempted to open this chamber and the vaults which are said to be under the entrenchments all round the ruin, and actually found a flight of stone steps leading to the vaults, when a panic struck his labourers, that the sleeping king might come on them, and they instantly fled in the utmost confusion. The excavation was soon closed up. Money to an incredible amount is said to be buried in the Windmill hill, which was a rath. There are other traditions concerning this Castle, too long for this concise notice.

An abbey was founded in this town by Richard Tyrrell, in the thirteenth century, and dedicated to St. Bridget. There is also a well dedicated to her here, and she is said to visit it every seven years, dressed in white.

The winding passage is shown in the engraving by the two dark opens, at the top of which, tradition says, there was a beautiful well for the use of the garrison, but now dry. I cannot say where the celebrated window, spoken of by Stanihurst, is situated; perhaps it is the open which I have taken for a gate. T. A. G—m—n.

THE GIANT'S GRAVE.

In that part of the county of Donegal which borders on Fermanagh, (a short distance from the high road leading from Ballyshannon to Enniskillen,) there is a very extraordinary remnant of antiquity, called by the peasantry, "The Giant's Grave." It is in shape somewhat like the vaults of the present day, though of very gigantic proportions. There is a low entrance at the southern end, formed by an enormous projecting block of stone, supported by two others; the roof seems to have fallen in, as the inside is filled up with large stones, overgrown with brambles and underwood. The sides are composed of immense limestone flags, each side having been originally formed of one stone, of such a size, that it was used for a ballcourt before reduced to its present dimensions; and it is remarkable there is no limestone in the immediate neighbourhood—a proof that the people of those days must

have been well acquainted with the mechanical powers; or, if not, have possessed strength commensurate with the size of the occupier of this grave. The owner of the farm filled a limekiln with stones broken from this flag; and (as the peasantry generally mix up their superstitions with every thing of the olden time) he informed me, "no power on earth could burn one of them." I asked whether he would assist me in opening the grave; but he declared at once he would have nothing to do with it; for that a few years since, two men endeavoured to do so, in hopes of finding treasures, but they had hardly struck their spades into the sacred ground, when they found their feet miraculously fastened to their spade shafts, so closely, that they could not, by any efforts, shake them off. This giant had an armour-bearer, whose tomb, situated at the top of an eminence not far distant, has been proved not to possess the same sanctity or miraculous powers as his master's, it having been opened by the owner of the ground, who discovered an earthen urn, containing some ashes, (supposed to be the ashes of the heart,) and several bones of an enormous size. The lower jaw bone was quite perfect, and so large, that it went with ease over the jaws of the biggest headed labourer present. G. H. R.

Ballyshannon.

SELSKER ABBEY.

In a recent number we gave a drawing of a curious stone coffin, found in the vicinity of Selsker Abbey. The engravings which precede and follow, are said to afford a more correct idea of the ruins of the abbey itself, than the drawings which appeared in our 109th number. It is said to have been erected by those Danes who became converted to the Christian religion. The buildings are of blackish stone; the tower in the centre is large, though much decayed at the top; it is supported on arches resting on plain square piers, with the exception of one, which is octagonal.

THE ABBEY.

A RUSSIAN LITERARY CHARACTER.

The Imperial Academy of St. Petersburgh has just printed a book of Poems, written by Elizabeth Kulmann, a young girl, who died at the age of seventeen. This girl possessed very remarkable talents. She was not only acquainted with Greek and Latin, but spoke several modern languages. Among her works is said to be an excellent translation of the Odes of Anacreon.

RECREATIONS IN MATHEMATICS AND NATURAL PHILOSOPHY.

The following are answers to the two queries proposed in our 130th Number.

1. The origin of this problem is related in so curious a manner by Al-Sephadi, an Arabian author, that it deserves to be mentioned. A mathematician, named Sessa, says he, the son of Daher, the subject of an Indian prince, having invented the game of chess, his sovereign was highly pleased with the invention, and wishing to confer on him some reward worthy of his magnificence, desired him to ask whatever he thought proper, assuring him that it should be granted. The mathematician, however, only asked a grain of wheat for the first square of the chessboard, two for the second, four for the third, and so on to the last or sixty-fourth. The prince at first was almost incensed at this demand, conceiving that it was ill-suited to his liberality, and ordered his vizier to comply with Sessa's request; but the minister was much astonished when, having caused the quantity of corn necessary to fulfil the prince's order to be calculated, he found that all the grain in the royal granaries, and that even of all his subjects, and in all Asia, would not be sufficient. He therefore informed the prince, who sent for the mathematician, and candidly acknowledged that he was not rich enough to be able to comply with his demand, the ingenuity of which astonished him still more than the game he had invented.

Such then is the origin of the game of chess, at least according to the Arabian historian Al-Sephadi. But it is not our business here to discuss the truth of this story; our business being to calculate the number of grains demanded by the mathematician, Sessa.

It will be found by calculation, that the 64th term of the double progression, beginning with unity, is 9223372036854775808. But the sum of all the terms of a double progression, beginning with unity, may be obtained by doubling the last term and subtracting from it unity. The number, therefore, of the grains of wheat equal to Sessa's demand, will be 18446744073709551615. Now, if a standard pint contains 9216 grains of wheat, a gallon will contain 73728, and, as eight gallons make one bushel. if we divide the above result by eight times 73728, we shall have 31274997412295 for the number of the bushels of wheat necessary to discharge the promise of the Indian king; and if we suppose that one acre of land is capable of producing in one year, thirty bushels of wheat. to produce this quantity would require 1042499913743 acres, which make more than eight times the surface of the whole globe; for the diameter of the earth being supposed equal to 7960 miles, its whole surface, comprehending land and water, will amount to very little more than 128467889177 square acres.

Dr. Wallis considers the matter in a manner somewhat different, and says, in his Arithmetic, that the quantity of wheat necessary to discharge the promise made to Sessa, would form a pyramid nine miles English in length, breadth, and height; which is equal to a parallelopiped mass, having nine square leagues for its base, and of the uniform height of one league. But as one league contains 15840 feet, this solid would be equivalent to another one foot in height and having a base equal to 142560 square leagues. Hence it follows, that the above quantity of wheat would cover, to the height of one foot, 142560 square leagues; an extent of surface equal to eleven times that of Britain, which, when every reduction is made, will be found to contain little more than 12674 square leagues.

If the price of a bushel of wheat be estimated at ten shillings, the value of the above quantity will amount to £15687498706147 10s. a sum which, in all probability, far surpasses all the riches on the earth.

2. By calculating as before, the 24th term of the progression 1, 2, 4, 8, &c will be found to be 8388608, equal to the number of farthings the purchaser ought to give for the horse. The price therefore amounted to £8738 2s. 8d. which is more than any Arabian horse, even of the noblest breed, was ever sold for.

Had the price of the horse been the value of all the nails, at a farthing for the first, two for the second, four for the third, and so on, the sum would have been double the above number, minus the first term, or 16777215 farthings, that is £17476 5s. 3¾d.

Judging by the same system of calculating, it is not astonishing that the race of Abraham, after sojourning two hundred and sixty years in Egypt, should have formed a nation capable of giving uneasiness to the sovereigns of that country. We are told in the sacred writings, that Jacob settled in Egypt with seventy persons: now if we are to suppose that among these seventy persons, there were twenty too far advanced in life, or too young, to have children; that, of the remaining fifty, twenty-five were males and as many females, forming twenty-five married couples, and that each couple, in the space of twenty-five years produced, one with another, eight children, which will not appear incredible in a country celebrated for the fecundity of its inhabitants, we shall find that, at the end of twenty-five years, the above seventy persons may have increased to two hundred and seventy; from which, if we deduct those who died, there will, perhaps, be no exaggeration in making them amount to two hundred and ten. The race of Jacob, therefore, after sojourning twenty-five years in Egypt, may have been tripled. In like manner, these two hundred and ten persons, after twenty-five years more, may have increased to six hundred and thirty; and so on in triple geometrical progression: hence it follows that, at the end of two hundred and twenty-five years, the population may have amounted to 1377810 persons, among whom there might easily be five or sixhundred thousand adults fit to bear arms.

If we suppose that the race of the first man, making a proper reduction for those who died, may have been doubled every twenty years, which certainly is not inconsistent with the powers of nature, the number of men, at the end of five centuries, may have amounted to 1048576. Now, as Adam lived about nine hundred years, he may have seen, therefore, when in the prime of life, that is to say, about the five hundredth year of his age, a posterity of 1048576 persons.

QUERIES IN GEOMETRICAL PROGRESSION.

1. A club of seven persons agreed to dine together, every day successively, as long as they could sit down to table differently arranged. How many dinners would be necessary for that purpose?

2. Fifteen Christians and fifteen Turks being at sea in the same vessel, a dreadful storm came on, which obliged them to throw all their merchandize overboard; this however not being sufficient to lighten the ship, the captain informed them that there was no possibility of its being saved, unless half the passengers were thrown overboard also. Having, therefore, caused them all to arrange themselves in a row, by counting from 9 to 9, and throwing every ninth person into the sea, beginning again at the first of the row when it had been counted to the end, it was found that after fifteen persons had been thrown overboard, the fifteen Christians remained. How did the Captain arrange these thirty persons so as to save the Christians?

"THE FORGET-ME-NOT."

This, the last of the Annuals for 1835 which it is our intention to notice, when formed into rank with the numerous class of publications of a similar order, which have recently appeared before the public, must be allowed to pass muster with considerable credit. We are compelled to say, however, that while it contains nothing which can in any way be offensive to a correct taste, or a cultivated understanding, there is nothing whatever of that impress of genius which we should expect to find in such a publication. No doubt, in several of the illustrations there is considerable cleverness, but in none of them can we discover anything which we could pronounce as an effort of real genius; and the same remark may be applied to the prose and poetry throughout the volume. Now, if we mistake not, it was with an intention of enabling artists of genuine talent to bring before the public efforts of the pencil or the chisel, that the Annuals were at first established. How far this was the case in earlier years we will not pretend to say, assuredly is by far the greatest number of those for 1835, there is little of either genius or talent; and we are of opinion, that unless a greater effort is made, during the present year, to effect the object for which they were originally designed, there will be a considerable falling off in the sales of most of them. That "The Forget-Me-Not" for the year 1835, is fully equal to its predecessor, we do not deny; but we think it might be much improved, and we are anxious that it should be so, as it has all along been a favourite with us. The following simple story, "A Night Alarm," we insert, as an excellent example of the manner in which many of those extraordinary circumstances of supernatural intervention, which have from time to time been attested as matters of fact, could be explained in a very simple natural way. "In the soft and melodious tones," succeeded "by the harsh and grating sounds," our readers will readily recognize "the Banshee," as described in several of our former numbers. "The Snow," by C. Swaine, Esq. we consider as pretty a specimen of the poetry as any to be found in the volume.

A NIGHT ALARM.

BY MRS. LEE.

It was eleven o'clock, and four young and lovely sisters had assembled in one room to hear the contents of a letter, which had arrived that morning from a distance. No matter what the letter said, but it may be presumed that it was unusually interesting; and the quickly approaching marriage of one of the parties might lead to an easy divination of its nature, were it necessary to the following narrative. The groupe thus collected was worthy of the most skilful painter, and, although any artist might have been improved by the attempt, the most consummate feeling and execution could alone have done justice to it.

As it most probably never will be painted, it may as well be described. The owner of the letter was in bed, but the broad lace border of the close cap could not hide the deep expression of that dark grey eye, or the admirable delicacy of that chiselled nose; the long and taper fingers, too, as they held the letter, bespoke an elegance of form well suited to the features. Another sister, half reclined on the foot of the bed, held the candle, the pale broad light of which discovered a countenance whose expression made even its regularity forgotten: every sentence of the letter was reflected in that ever varying face; everything that was good and tender, everything that was sad or joyous, might there be found, and nothing but what was unfeminine or bad could fail to meet with its corresponding image there. A third sister had suspended the brushing of her long glossy hair to listen to the tale; the intelligent look, the high commanding forehead, showed the mind of lofty and fixed purpose, and, as she rested one elbow on the pillar of the bed, she unconsciously displayed a form of faultless proportions. The party was completed by an arch rogue on her knees, whose beaming black eyes, half hidden by her raven ringlets, and whose delicate little foot, peeping from beneath the long dressing-gown, half excited a regret that she was more concealed than the rest.

The attention of all was deeply engaged, and nought was heard but the low and gentle voice of the reader, when a faint vibration of the window beneath, caused a cessation and a glance of inquiry from one sister to the other.—"It was only the wind," said the standing beauty, and the reader resumed her happy occupation. After a few more lines, the noise was repeated with greater force than before, and the kneeler sprang on her feet. "What can it be?" said she, in a scarcely audible tone. A long silence followed, and again came the sound, deeper and louder than ever, and it continued till the whole of the large dining-room window seemed to wring with the unaccountable tones, and to shake in every pane.

The house was built in the shelving part of some high cliffs, a succession of which bordered a lovely little bay on the eastern coast of England. It was not many yards from the sea; no habitation, except the station-towers of the preventive service, stood nearer than a quarter of a mile; the village was even more distant: a small old church, in which the sabbath was celebrated by a primitive sort of service, stood on the top of a neighbouring hill, and nothing could be more tranquil or retired than the whole scene. It was perfectly refreshing to contrast it with the common-place, bustling, time-killing, dissipated, and frivolous resorts of those who seek but to get rid of themselves. And so secure was it deemed, from its retirement, that there was not even a fastening to the gates at either end of the shrubbery.

"Let us call papa," continued the raven-haired lass, "for I am certain it is some one breaking into the dining-room."

"Nonsense," observed the damsel of the brush; "no one would think of coming in here, and papa has been fishing all day, so we must not wake him on uncertainty. Look out, and see if any one is on the lawn."

No one, however, dared venture to go near the window; and, while all were considering what to do, the noise was reiterated with such force, that every rod of iron in the drawing-room balcony, close by, seemed to vibrate with the efforts made on the ground-floor.

"This is too much," said the hitherto silent candle-bearer; and one and all rushed into the gallery behind the room, not excepting the recumbent nymph.

They proceeded together to the chamber of a friend who was staying with them, and knocked at her door. On opening it, four long pale faces, huddled close to each other, presented themselves: but the visiter, being accustomed to such alarms in London, easily divined the nature of this unusual summons. The matter was whisperingly explained, and all five returned to the apartment where the noise had been heard, placed the candle in the gallery outside, and, shutting the door, waited in breathless silence. Expectation was soon realised, and courage was then assumed to look out into the garden; but all there was quite still.

It was then thought expedient to call the man-servant, who, with his wife, slept in another part of the house. Such efforts are always made in a body by females, and, therefore, the five ladies called the man, but his wife alone answered, saying that it was a false alarm—perhaps it was the puppy trying to get in—perhaps it was the wind: in short, it was any thing but a house-breaker. A moment's reflection seemed to convince the party that this fear was absurd; for, being only an occasional residence, no property of value which could afford temptation was kept there. But the noise was there, and whence could it proceed?

A walk along the cliffs, taken on that very evening, had discovered some haunts of smugglers, and very recent indications of their presence were found; besides which, one of the ladies had seen two men stealing along where there was no path, just at dusk, and, of course, they could have no good motive. Smugglers, therefore, were suggested as the primary cause of the alarm; and the idea of these lawless people having been closely pursued by the preventive men, and having taken refuge in their grounds, was much more tolerable to the ladies than that of housebreakers.

Whatever may be the cause, there certainly is in the female breast, a feeling of sympathy, or kindness, or interest of some sort, towards smugglers, and the first impulse is to assist them: but in the present instance horrors were conjured up, which entirely banished the little female partiality on which these men might otherwise have reckoned. Supposing it were possible for them to lodge their goods in the house, for the sake of concealment, the officers would soon arrive—a struggle would ensue—some would be wounded; their papa never would connive at the escape of a smuggler. But, in the midst of these deliberations and reflections, shake went the window—ring went the balcony—screech went the boat upon the shingles (as they thought)—and away rushed the ladies to the door of the sleeping host, begging him to rise immediately and see what was the matter.

The good-humoured readiness of the father, and his speedy appearance, showed that no hesitation need have been made in asking his help. The fears were soon related; the noise was listened for, but in vain; the house was inspected, the females following at a respectful distance, though, of course, ready to attack any body who might endanger the safety of papa : but there was neither a trace of kegs nor of bales in the dining-room, nor were footsteps to be perceived on the soft gravel or dewy lawn in the garden ; no puppy, even—for every animal on the premises, except the human species, was buried in profound sleep. Nothing uncommon was to be seen, except a lighted candle in a lantern, standing on the kitchen hearth, which certainly looked like the attention of a wife towards an absent husband, and confirmed the ladies in their suspicions that there was connivance with smugglers somewhere.

What the master of the house thought no one ever knew, for he was not a man to betray his feelings without a necessity for doing so. He quietly asked his daughters and his guest if they were satisfied that all was safe, and advised them to retire to rest : but a keen observer might have discovered a lurking expression of mischief in his eyes, which told that they were spared only till he had an opportunity of venting his tormenting observations. He himself soon gave audible proofs that he had resumed his slumbers, and, when their tongues were weary with conjecture, the ladies thought proper to go to bed also.

The reader of these pages, however, will be little versed in female weaknesses, if he or she supposes that they sought solitary repose. Could one bed have held the five they would all have shared it ; but, as the dimensions of the beds in the house would not admit of this arrangement, the five were distributed in two, and nought was heard throughout the night except some stealing footsteps outside, which there was no doubt proceeded from the returning man-servant, after his carousal in the village.

In the course of the ensuing summer, a near relation of the proprietor of this beautiful spot, with his wife, children and servants, went to the same house, for the sake of the sea air. After a few days' stay, the husband left his family, and in a few days returned. He fancied that he saw an unusually grave expression on the countenances of his lady and her attendants. "Is all well ?" he exclaimed. "Quite well," was the reply ; and the expression was so slight, that he could not make any remark upon it.

The evening closed in, and, taking their station in the dining-room, the lady occupied herself with her needle, and the gentleman began to answer the letters which had awaited his arrival. An unbroken silence ensued, which was interrupted by a low and gentle sound ; the needle fell from the lady's fingers, in half a minute the noise was increased to a shrill, grating vibration, and gradually subsided into the softest and most melodious tones that ever issued from an Eolian harp. Occasionally it stopped, then rising to its utmost strength, the whole window shook, and the bars of the balcony above ran like echoes to the sounds beneath.

"We have heard this before," said the lady, starting up. "I would not tell you of it when you first came in, because I wished you to receive the full impression of this mystery. We have searched in every direction ; we have listened and watched ; we have done every thing in our power to account for it, but in vain : and my servants are more than half persuaded that it is supernatural."

She was interrupted by a return of the noise : it recommenced with a harsh, grating sound, and appeared now to come from the ceiling—now from the window—and now from the earth. At times it was so loud, that the lady and gentleman thought it was a boat hauled ashore, and flew to the window. A bright moonlight rendered every thing visible ; but nothing of the kind was to be seen. The sound gradually ceased, as if retiring to a distance ; and, for the first time in his life, the husband felt a superstitious feeling creeping over him, and began to think that there was more reason than he chose to acknowledge in the suppositions of his servants.

On the ensuing day, every endeavour was made to find out the cause of this mysterious music ; but it baffled all research and defied every conjecture. The evening advanced. and all remained perfectly quiet ; the lady and gentleman went into the next room to partake of some refreshment, and the music recommenced, exactly in the same manner as before. The gentleman returned alone to the larger room, without a light, and, seating himself in the middle of the room, so as to be able to see all round him, determined not to go to bed till he had fully investigated the matter. He at length felt sure that the tones proceeded from the window, and, approaching it, he anxiously watched the shore and the sea, by the occasional and fitful gleams of moonlight. After five or ten minutes, the most heavenly tones seemed to proceed from behind him ; and, turning his head quickly round, they at the same moment appeared to come from the window beside him. A feeling of awe, and perhaps terror, now assailed him, but he argued that, if he did not now convince himself of the fact, whatever it might be, he should be for ever disturbed with the recollection of the circumstance ; and, mastering his half-formed fears, he went to the window, and leaned his head against it. The music then seemed to be close to his face, and, for a moment, he recoiled ; but, fixing his eyes on the same pane of glass, he beheld a dark speck upon the window. He tried to lay hold of it, but it eluded his grasp, and the tones continued with more beauty than ever. At length he struck the window smartly, and all was still.

He immediately procured a candle, and, calling his wife and servants, proceeded with them to the inspection of the mysterious spot. The music became loud and shrill, but the light discovered that all these vibrations—these Eolian sounds—these harsh gratings—these awful and heavenly tones—these attempts at robbery—and these frightened smugglers were occasioned by —— a simple snail, which was crawling across the pane. As it drew nearer to the centre of the pane, the sounds became deeper and fuller, as it approached the edge, they were shrill as a fife. The occasional touching of its shell, in its course, and the greater or less sliminess of the animal, produced the vibrations and harsh gratings, the former of which were increased according to their vicinity to the frame-work ; and, as there were several snails crawling along at the same time, in different parts of the same window, and in different windows, the varied positions of the sounds at the same moment was easily accounted for.

About the time that the above circumstance happened, the sister-in-law of the writer was startled, while at work at a window which opened into a garden, by the shrillest sound she ever heard, and which she said afterwards she could only compare to the crowing of a cock close to her ears. For a few moments she was bewildered by it, but her active endeavours to ascertain the cause proved it to be also a snail. She placed snails on the window purposely, and heard all the varieties of vibration caused by the state of the animal, the size of the pane, and the distance from the framework.

THE SNOW.

The silvery snow !—the silvery snow !—
Like a glory it falls on the fields below ;
And the trees with their diamond branches appear
Like the fairy growth of some magical sphere ;
While soft as music, and wild and white,
It glitters and floats in the pale moonlight,
And spangles the river and fount as they flow ;
Oh! who has not loved the bright, beautiful snow !

The silvery snow, and the crinkling frost—
How merry we go when the Earth seems lost ;
Like spirits that rise from the dust of Time,
To live in a purer and holier clime !
A new creation without a stain—
Lovely as Heaven's own pure domain !
But ah ! like the many fair hopes of our years,
It glitters a while—and then melts into tears !

DUBLIN :

Printed and Published by P. D. Hardy, 3, Cecilia-street ; to whom all communications are to be addressed.

Sold by all Booksellers in Ireland.

In London, by Richard Groombridge, 6, Panyer-alley, Paternoster-row ; in Liverpool, by Willmer and Smith ; in Manchester, by Ambery; in Birmingham, by Guest ; in Glasgow, by John Macleod ; and in Edinburgh, by N. Bowack.

THE
DUBLIN PENNY JOURNAL

CONDUCTED BY P. DIXON HARDY, M.R.I.A.

Vol. III.	JANUARY 31, 1835.	No. 135.

OLD MONKSTOWN CHURCH.

With an engraving of the new church of Monkstown, which appeared in the 106th number of our Journal, we gave the only particulars relative to the old church, (a representation of the ruin of which we give above,) which appeared to us at all interesting to our readers. The place is supposed to have derived its name from a number of monks who took up their abode in it, and who, at a very early period, erected a place of worship there. The ruin stands between the castle and the new church, but a short distance from the Black-rock and Kingstown, and forms rather a picturesque object in the landscape.

MY UNCLE—A PORTRAIT.

"This fellow now is like an over ripe melon—rough outside with much sweetness under it."—THE MOUNTAINEERS.

Imagine a short, burly-faced man, in a pepper-and-salt coat, red waistcoat, light Kerseymere breeches. and short gaiters; his hat beauishly inclined, a slight degree from the perpendicular, over his right ear—the left scantily covered with a few gray hairs, suspiciously disguised with powder; an eye of varied expression: dignified when glancing at an inferior, courteous in salutation of an equal, and "mighty engaging entirely" when ogling a 'colleen dhess.' Imagine, too, a prominent paunch, and consequential air, which the ever present reflection of being worth a plum never fails to impart, and you have a tolerably fair portrait of my uncle, Mr. Darby O'Gallagher, citizen and bachelor.

Your plodding city tradesmen of the last century, never suffered their imaginations to stray to green fields and rural felicity, till they had worn out the pith of existence in acquiring a competence. They built substantial mansions

in narrow alleys, and immured themselves and their progeny in their brick warrens, till their thirst for money-getting was sufficiently quenched to prompt the wish for retirement; and then they very prudently withdrew from the turmoils of traffic, to die of ennui and nothing-to-doishness in a dull country village. My honoured kinsman, though somewhat tinged with antiquated notions, and gone-by prejudices, was yet wise enough to leave off bargain-driving and stock-jobbing, before he lost all relish for rurality; but having passed life's meridian unburdened with connubial cares, he found, after a few months' possession of his snug cottage in the Groves of Blarney, that the prattle of children, and the music of a woman's tongue, might have proved less annoying than chewing the cud of his own musings, nodding over a newspaper, or contemplating the stagnant veridity of a duck pond. He grew tired of gazing on hedges, and listening to the cawing of crows and the whistle of cow-boys. The blue sky and green fields—his grotto and hermitage—his thickset hedges and flower-decked arbours, became alike indifferent to his unpoetic imagination; and he sighed for the busy bustle of the weigh-house or corn-market, and the grateful hum of the chamber of commerce. Pent up in his green solitude, he felt convincingly how dreary a thing it was to lead the life of a bachelor; and then he fell to reflecting how silly it was of him some twenty years back, to break off his courtship with Miss Biddy Brady, the rich saddler's daughter, for disliking his pea-green coat; and that if he had bridled his anger, he might have secured the dear creature for himself, instead of holding the stirrup, like a fool as he was, to fat Fergusson the ironmonger, or 'Goulnaspurra, who vaulted in his place, and galloped off with the prize. All this, however, was now past praying for, and though he had retired, that was no reason why he should be hypped to death with the blue devils in Blarney; he therefore made up his mind to drive to Cork once a day to look round and see how the world wagged, scrupulously resolved to drive no more bargains for time or tallow, but merely to peep at the "busy Babel," and occasionally secure an old friend to share his gig, with dinner and bed, at his rural domicile. Besides, there were other causes beyond the mere sense of loneliness, to induce him to adopt this plan : among the rest he missed his morning drisheen and comfortable basin of turtle. He had, to be sure, a tolerable cook ; his guests praised her fabrications highly ; but still she was never able to match the ' ne plus ultra' soups of Best or M'Evers.

As he had no one to please but himself, his scheme was soon put into practice, and a new gig was ordered, a vehicle, by the bye, he had little fancy for, and in which nothing but the prejudice of the old school against riding in a stage coach, could have induced him to peril his neck. I had the honor of initiating him into the noble science of driving ; an acquirement which he never thought of living to see a gentleman taking pride in. He was immensely awkward at first—the clumsiest Phæton that ever took a fancy to horse flesh. His fat, fleshy knuckles grasped the reins with a most ungraceful air, and he brandished the whip like a Drumcolliher carman. However, he was highly delighted with his new toy ; and I shall never forget the glee with which he bundled into M'Dowell's, and shook hands with a dozen of his cronies after a twelve-month's absence. Even the waiter came in for a share of his regards—" What, Joe ! what—here still, eh, Joe ? Not in business yet, eh ? And Kitty, the bar-maid, too, I declare ! Well, Kitty, how d'ye do ?—not married yet, I see. Joe and you make a match of it, eh ? Can set up Joe's coffee house then you know." A new dawn seemed to have gleamed on the old gentleman's existence. He grew fat and frolicsome, and had snug little dinners and small revels at his ' rus in urbe,' till, like Falstaff, he grew out of all compass—out of all reasonable compass. Self-willed, as old bachelors usually are, he would no longer suffer me to drive, and my equestrian services were dispensed with—" Young hair-brained fellows, like you," he said, " are not fit companions for sedate elderly folks." The fact was, he had no mind that I should witness the nightly orgies of his retirement, and I had no inclination to partake of them. It happened one morning, after a night's roucawn in Cork, with a select few, that he attempted to drive home, half, or perhaps all, in the band. The tit that ran in his gig was a fine blood mare of my own choosing, and I often told him, that if he did not wish to be thrown from his seat, the whip and her hide should be kept at a respectful distance. "Attempt," said I, " to brush a fly off her neck, and depend on it, she'll break yours." Well, what does my sagacious kinsman do, but just as he came to that deep descent on the old Blarney road, called Faggot hill, a little beyond Clogheen chapel, where any man in his senses would have held the reins tight, he lays half a dozen lashes on the mare's flank—away scampers Bess, helter, skelter—off flew the wheel—snap went the shafts, and out tumbled my uncle Darby. The mare was stopped with difficulty, the gig was dashed to pieces, and uncle was conveyed home to bed. The old boy was more frightened than hurt—all his limbs were sound, and he had no bruises ; but terror performed the work of reality, and introduced him, for the first time in his life, to the pleasures of the gout. His temper was not the mildest in the world, and he indulged freely in the popular remedy of expletives. To be tied down to his arm chair was punishment enough, but to be tortured into the bargain, would have excited cataraphobia in a less irritable temperament than his. I received a note from him a day or two after his accident, written in much apparent pain, if I may judge by the hieroglyphics jumbled together in its composition. It was couched in the following terms :

" Bob, you scoundrel, why dont you come to me ? I am dying, you undutiful cub, and you wont stir a peg. I've had a sad accident, Bob—spilt from that kickshaw cockleshell, the gig—all my bones broken. Confound that mare—your buying, Bob—on purpose, I believe, to break my neck. Got the gout, too, Bob ; and a bad gout it is, as Doctor Leary declared it—the gout, you villain, and you know it, and wont come. Yes, here I may die ; nobody cares for me—nobody cares for an old bachelor. Bobby, my boy, come to your poor lame uncle—you rascal, if you dont set out directly I'll cut you off to a shilling. Your loving uncle,   DARBY O'GALLAGHER."

My sensations on perusing this epistle were none of the most agreeable ; not that I disliked the old gentleman ; but I was so well aware of the testiness of his temper, that I felt my dependence on him at this moment stronger than ever. I knew that it hung on a thread, and that, square my behaviour as I would, I could hardly hope to please him. Besides I had a tale to unfold, on the reception of which the future happiness of my life depended ; and if the variable wind of his weathercock disposition, should happen to set in the wrong quarter, a long farewell to all the fairy pictures of felicity my imagination had painted. I have already glanced at the old man's attachment, in his younger days, to Miss Biddy Brady, who wedded his rival. The lady certainly acted a little precipitately in the affair ; for had she waited the ebullition of my uncle's passion, he doubtless would be the first to make overtures of peace. However, she promptly decided on giving her hand to the ironmonger, and left her quondam beau to recover his surprise and chagrin as he might. Since then he cherished a bitter dislike to the ironmonger, and drove from his mind the oft-recurring image of Biddy, with the epithets of jilt, coquet, and inconstant. Now it happened, by the most singular chance in the world, that the daughter of this couple was introduced to me at a ball—that grand mart, time out of mind, for the exchange of hearts ; and, as a matter of course, I fell in love. I hope none of my readers will take offence at this old-fashioned method of imbibing the tender passion ; for I can assure them that, even now, hearts are sometimes lost in ball-rooms, as well as in the days of Sir Charles Grandison. I skip over the honied hours that preceded my offer and acceptance. Two obstacles alone opposed our union—the consent of her parents and of my uncle, on whom a too-generous and ill-fortunate father left me dependant. It was agreed that I should write to the former, and make a viva voce appeal to the latter. Mr. and Mrs. F. were good sort of people, anxious to see their daughter happy ; and they wrote in reply, that if my uncle gave his consent, theirs should not be withheld. It was at this critical juncture his letter reached me. Oh ! thought I, the miseries of dependance, and on an old bachelor, the testiest animal in the world ! Old bachelors are a sort of wild beasts; they carry their untamed ferocities about to the annoyance of their fellow creatures, whilst a married man, in ninety-nine cases out of a hundred, is the gentlest creature imaginable. Marriage, like the gentle arts, " emollit mores nec sinit esse feros"—it prevents men from degenerating into brutes—and, by constant collision with woman's milder mind, gives them a portion of her tender spirit, and humanizes the soul : these reflections were engendered by the fear that the old animosity of my uncle to the very name of Fergusson, might stand between me and my hopes. I glided up the stairs that led to his apartment ; and, as I held in dubious suspense the handle of the door, endeavoured to screw my courage to the sticking place ere I turned it round, and ventured into his presence. The effort was made—the door opened : by the side of the fire, half encircled with an old-fashioned screen, sat my uncle Darby, in a capacious arm-chair ; his legs enveloped in flannels and fleecy hosiery ; his hands resting on the elbows of the chair ; his countenance flushed with pain and vexation ; and his eyes glaring at the glowing embers in distracted vacancy. As I advanced, with the best look of condolence I could, he raised his head and exclaimed,

" So you are come at last. A pretty, dutiful nephew—a tender-hearted kinsman. Yes—here I might be, and languish till doomsday. Even my own brother's son cares nothing for me ; no, not an atom. Well, Sir, what do you stand there for, like a stock fish ?—why don't you get a chair ?"

" Sir," I replied, mechanically obeying him, " I assure

you I never heard of your accident till the receipt of your letter, and I set off on the instant."

" Dare say you did—don't think it though. Hoped to find your old uncle at his last gasp, I've no doubt. Disappointed, mayhap ; shall live long enough yet to tire you out. Sound at the core, Bob—no chance for you these twenty years. Took care of myself when young, and did not waste my health or money in drinking and raking. No Tom and Jerrying in those days."

" I should hope, Sir, my conduct would acquit me of any undutiful wish towards an uncle who has always proved so kind to me."

" Eh—well—perhaps it would, as you say I hav'nt deserved it, Bob. Don't think you are hard-hearted ; never did. You are tolerably well as the world goes ; only a little flighty. Young men, now a-days, are not as they were when I was a stripling. Bobby, my boy, just shift this leg on the cushion. Why, you scoundrel, you've crippled me. You villain, do you suppose my toes have no more feeling than a horse's hoof ? Did you think you were handling a bed-post ?"

I stammered out an apology, attributing my inadventure to my anxiety to relieve his pain. This soothed him a little.

" Why, look ye Bob ; you know I am naturally good-tempered, but it would provoke the patience of a saint to be thus cooped up like a capon, roasted, as I am, by a slow fire ; drenched with drugs, and fed upon slops. But tell me what are you doing ? How do you like the law ? Fancy you like the play-house better. Prefer hopping at the Clarence-rooms to studying Coke upon Littleton—eh ?"

" Sir, I never go to balls."

" Never go to balls !—more shame for you. Dare say you never said a civil thing to a lady in your life."

" I trust, Sir, I have not been deficient in due attention to the fair sex."

" Pshaw ! I don't believe you. I know you are a shy cock ; no more gallantry than a goose ; no more spirit than a tom-tit—an animated ice-berg. Oh ! when I was a youngster, the spark of a bright eye acted on me like a spark in a powder-barrel—I was in flames in a moment. Dare say you never formed a single attachment. Sorry for it. Should like to see you married, Bob."

" Perhaps, Sir, you could recommend me a wife."

" Not I, Bob ; I never played the part of match-maker in my life. You must beat up your own game, lad, and run it down yourself."

" Then, my dear uncle, to confess the truth, so far from being the cold composition you imagine me, I am actually engaged to a lady."

" The deuce, you are ; and pray who is she ?"

I hesitated and changed colour.

" What are you stammering at ? You're not ashamed of telling her name surely."

" Oh, no, Sir. Her name is—her name—that is, her name is—Miss Julia Fergusson."

He stared at me a second or two in mute surprise.

" Fergusson ! No relation, I hope, to fat Fergusson the ironmonger."

Here was a crisis ! It was in vain to repent my precipitancy. Sincerity was all I had to trust to, and I confessed she was his daughter. The effect was fearful. He never uttered a word ; but I could see the workings of pride, passion, and resentment, as they alternately displayed themselves in the fiery glances of his eye, the flushings of his cheek, and the quivering of his lips. Opposite to his window there grew a sturdy oak ; he turned his eyes towards it, and thus addressed me with unassumed coolness,

" Bob, look at that oak. When your strength shall be able to bend its trunk, you may hope to bend my wishes to your will. Fergusson ! I detest the name, and all who bear it ; and sooner than you should wed her I would follow you to your grave."

There was something so appalling in his manner as he uttered this denouncement, that I was unable to reply: But I was spared the effort, by the sudden opening of the door, and the entrance of an old friend of my uncle's, who

stopped suddenly, struck by the expression of both our countenances.

" Hey day," said he, " what's the matter ?—uncle and nephew at loggerheads !"

" Here's Bob," replied my kinsman, " has dared to acknowledge a passion for the daughter of fat Fergusson, the fellow that—"

" Married your adorable, because you were too sulky to ask her hand for yourself. Well, what is there so wonderful in that ? Julia Fergusson is a fine girl, and deserves a good husband."

" Very likely—but do you suppose I would ever give my consent to her union with my nephew ?"

" And why not ? Let me tell you the Fergussons are a respectable and worthy family."

" But their blood shall never mingle with mine."

" Look ye, O'Gallagher, you are an unforgiving fellow : your blood would suffer no contamination by such a union ; and I can tell you this, that whatever animosity you may bear them, they always speak in the highest terms of you. Mrs. Fergusson, to this day, says you are the best-hearted man she ever knew."

My uncle's features here assumed a more complacent aspect.

" Answer me one question," said he, " can you deny that she jilted me ?"

" I can. You might have had a regard for her, but it does not follow that she was in love with you ; and surely she had a right to marry the man of her own choice."

" Humph ! Well, I care little about that now. I hate animosity as much as any man ; and Bob knows it was always my wish to see him happy ; and if I thought they really wished to renew the acquaintance—"

I interrupted the sentence by putting into his hand the letter I just received.

He was much agitated on perusing it ; and I could see a tear in the corner of his eye. He wiped it away with the back of his hand, and bid me reach him the writing apparatus. In a few minutes a letter was written announcing his wish for a reconciliation, and giving consent to the marriage. Our hearts were too full to speak. My uncle reached out his hand to his friend. He shook it heartily :

" You've acted," said he, " like yourself. This is as it should be."

I quitted the room to dispatch the letter, and in three weeks time became the husband of the ironmonger's daughter. ROBERT O GALLAGHER.

Cork, Nov. 1834.

RECREATIONS IN MATHEMATICS AND NATURAL PHILOSOPHY.

The following are answers to the two queries proposed in our last Number.

1. It may be easily found that the required number is 5040, which would require 13 years and more than 9 months.

2. The method of arranging the thirty persons may be deduced from these two French verses :

Mort, tu ne failliras pas
En me livrant le trepas.

Or from the following Latin one, which is not so bad of its kind :

Populeam virgam mater regina ferebat.

Attention must be paid to the vowels A, E, I, O, U, contained in the syllables of these verses ; observing that A is equal to 1, E to 2, I to 3, O to 4, and U to 5. You must begin then by arranging 4 Christians together, because the vowel in the first syllable is o ; then 5 Turks, because the vowel in the second syllable is u ; and so on to the end. By proceeding in this manner, it will be found, taking every ninth person circularly, that is to say, beginning at the first of the row, after it is ended, that the lot will fall entirely on the Turks.

The solution of this problem may be easily extended still farther. Let it be required, for example, to make the lot fall upon ten persons in forty, counting from twelve to twelve. Arrange forty ciphers in a circular form, as below:

then, beginning at the first, mark every twelfth one with a cross; continue in this manner, taking care to pass over those already crossed, still proceeding circularly, till the required number of places has been marked; if you then count the places of the marked cyphers, those on which the lot falls will be easily known: in the present case they are the 7th, the 8th, the 10th, the 12th, the 21st, the 22d, the 24th, the 34th, the 35th, and the 36th.

A captain, obliged to decimate his company, might employ this expedient, to make the lot fall upon those most culpable.

It is related that Josephus, the historian, saved his life by means of this expedient. Having fled for shelter to a cavern, with forty other Jews, after Jotapat had been taken by the Romans, his companions resolved to kill each other rather than surrender. Josephus tried to dissuade them from their horrid purpose, but not being able to succeed, he pretended to coincide with their wishes, and retaining the authority he had over them as their chief, to avoid the disorder which would necessarily be the consequence of this cruel execution, if they should kill each other at random, he prevailed on them to arrange themselves in order, and, beginning to count from one end to a certain number, to put to death the person on whom that number should fall, until there remained only one, who should kill himself. Having all agreed to this proposal, Josephus arranged them in such a manner, and placed himself in such a position, that when the slaughter had been continued to the end, he remained with only one more person, whom he persuaded to live.

Such is the story related of Josephus by Hegesippus; but we are far from warranting the truth of it. However, by applying to this case the method above indicated, and supposing that every third person was to be killed, it will be found that the two last places on which the lot fell were the 16th and 31st; so that Josephus must have placed himself in one of these, and the person he was desirous of saving, in the other.

QUERIES IN GEOMETRICAL PROGRESSION.

1. A man has a wolf, a goat, and a cabbage, to carry over a river; but being obliged to transport them one by one, on account of the smallness of the boat, in what manner is this to be done, that the wolf may not be left with the goat, nor the goat with the cabbage?

2. Three jealous husbands, with their wives, having to cross a river at a ferry, find a boat without a boatman; but the boat is so small that it can contain no more than two of them at once. How can these six persons cross the river, two and two, so that none of the women shall be left in company with any of the men, unless when her husband is present?

CASTLETOWN HOUSE, COUNTY OF DUBLIN.

The superb and elegant seat of Colonel Conolly, M.P., two miles beyond Leixlip, and ten from the Castle of Dublin. This noble edifice, erected in the Grecian style of architecture, is generally considered as one of the finest in the kingdom. It is built entirely of hewn stone, and contains a range of thirteen windows in each of the three stories. A colonade, supported by nine columns on each side, joins the house to the two wings, which are each two stories high, and seven windows in breadth. The apartments are elegantly finished; the grand stair-case is very magnificent, and ornamented with brass balus- trades. The demesnes and plantations about the house are extensive and beautiful.

Here may be seen, amongst many other natural productions, the largest *cedar* and *vine tree* perhaps in the kingdom. The view from the house (owing to the quantity of full grown timber) is rather limited to the neighbouring objects. The river winds through the lawn in many a fantastic form, as if it were consciously struggling to avoid the manufacturing uses and dirty sewers by which it is contaminated in its entrance into the city.

Tullow, Sept. 1834.   E. H.

RHEBAN CASTLE, COUNTY KILDARE.

Rheban was, in the second century, one of the inland towns of Ireland. The Castle stands on the western bank of the Al Berba, Birgus, or Barragh, (the boundary river,) now the river Barrow. It was built, or greatly enlarged, in the early part of the thirteenth century, by Richard De St. Michael,* when this and Dunamase, an adjoining district, were erected into a barony, and granted to him in fee, of which he was created baron. Rheban was found of consequence to the first English settlers, who repaired and strengthened the castle, as also the opposite one of Kilberry, both intended to protect a ford on the river. The name of this castle was anciently Raiba, or Righ-ban, that is, the habitation of the king; and though now in ruins, some idea can be formed of its former grandeur. Its massive walls—its mullioned windows, with its imposing situation, show it to be a place designed to awe the surrounding country, and forcibly call to mind the days when the chivalrous De St. Michael held his court here in feudal splendour, and lorded it over the petty chieftains of the borders of the Pale.

In 1325, in the absence of the English settlers, Rheban, Dunamase, and all their dependencies, were taken by O'Moore.

In 1424, Thomas Fitzgerald, lord of Offaley, and afterwards seventh earl of Kildare, marrying Dorothea, daughter of Anthony O'Moore, received in dower the manors of Rheban and Woodstock.

In 1642 the marquis of Ormond took Rheban from the rebels, after an obstinate resistance.

In 1648 it was taken by Owen Roe O'Neal, who was afterwards defeated by Lord Inchiquin, and compelled to surrender Rheban and Athy.

Near the Castle is a very high conical mount, thought to have been a sepulchral mound, raised over some king or chieftain, and though artificial in a great degree, there was, nevertheless, advantage taken of a natural height, as may be seen by the undisturbed beds of gravel that are now taken from it for road purposes.

Rheban is situated in the parish of Churchtown and union of Athy, about two and a half miles north west of the latter.   ENNA.

---

* This Richard De St. Michael founded a monastery in Athy on the west (his own) side of the river for crouched friars, under the invocation of St. John. A burial ground and some remains still exist. There was another religious edifice erected by the families of Boesel and Hogan, at the east entrance of the town, and dedicated to St. Michael, which is erroneously stated to have been the one founded by De St. Michael, lord of Rheban. A coincidence between the names of the supposed founder and the monastery, called as it is St. Michael's, may have led to the mistake. St. Michael's is built on an eminence, agreeable to the custom of selecting the site of all religious houses, intended to be dedicated to St. Michael, on the highest ground, from a notion, perhaps, of the superior order of the archangel.

RECOLLECTIONS,

(Continued from our 129th Number.)

SCENES IN CLARE.*

" Lives there a man, with soul so dead,
Who never to himself hath said—
' This is my own, my native land ?'"

It was early in the summer of 1822, that I arrived on a visit to a near relative, who had very comfortable country quarters, and some property in the neighbourhood of Miltown Malbay, county of Clare. He was married to an amiable lady, and they were made happy by having around them a young and promising family. Mr. —— was a younger brother, of a highly respectable family in that county; and, as he chiefly resided on his property, he was, by his kindness to his tenantry, very popular, and much beloved. Being a thorough sportsman, he had held out every inducement to tempt me from home, to try his native sports in all their wildness and diversity. He had not exaggerated—for never before did I feel such admiration—such delight—such pleasure; whether in contemplating the grandeur of the bold and magnificent coast, with the formidable billows of the Atlantic thundering on its cliffs and shores—its wild, inland scenery of mountain, lake, and trackless bog, or the devotedness and affection of his tenantry and retainers. Oh! none but those who have witnessed those devoted, those warm-hearted feelings of the peasantry towards a kind and indulgent landlord, can form any idea how perfect a little monarch he is among them. Yet these are the poor—the despised Connaughtmen. But, I fear, that within these few years, from absenteeism, illiberal landlords, and harsh agents, much of that fine spirit is passing away. I was very young at the time, but, being of a strong wiry frame, and trained to hardy exercises, I soon became inured to the fatigues of the bogs; and could, with confidence, cross in safety the most dangerous bogach.† The summer passed delightfully. We had fished all the lakes‡ within our reach, and many were the fine salmon and white-trout that graced our bags from the Anna, Annagieragh, Cri, and Dunbeg rivers.§ Now knowing the country tolerably well, and being able to attempt a smattering in Irish, I would often venture by myself to a considerable distance, when my friend was otherwise employed, in exploring every part with eager delight, to gain fresh additions to my collection of curiosities, plants, and stuffed birds.

Natural history and botany were to me sources of endless delight and amusement; and I had always endeavoured to cultivate practically those interesting studies, when rambling with my gun among the wild mountains and bogs, or along the rocky coast; and often, when visiting the many small romantic lakes, so numerous in

---

* Although Clare is now incorporated with Munster, the natives still consider themselves as belonging to Connaught. Indeed, in their habits, manners, and language, there is a striking difference between them and their Kerry neighbours on the opposite side of the Shannon.

† A morass or quagh—There are patches of verdant grass and Sphagnum (bog-moss) offering such temptations of sure footing to the uninitiated, that they frequently sink into a watery pit of many feet in depth before they are aware. They are sometimes highly dangerous. Sphagnum obtusifolium (blunt leaved bog-moss) is so retentive of moisture, that it is used to pack up live plants to send to a distance—Sphagnum palustre of Linnæus.

‡ The lakes in Clare are very numerous, and abound in trout, being generally free from that scourge to their race, the pike. Many of the lakes are large, and have very fine trout, weighing from three to eight and nine pounds; but the otters are very destructive to them. Dromore and Inchiquin are fine sheets of water, and that beautiful lake in the barony of Tullagh, Loco Graoine or Loce ua Griane, the bright or sunny lake, or lake of the sun, commonly called Lough Graney

§ These rivers are within a range of seven miles to the south of Miltown, and empty themselves into the Atlantic. In the autumn and spring they are stored with salmon and white-trout, and in the autumn floods afford great sport. Salmon have been caught in Dunbeg (or Cooraclare river) as large as twenty pounds.

Clare, (when the day had turned too bright or calm, " to timpt the throut to taste the steel,") have I zealously examined every nook and bank for those beautiful plants that abound along their margins, and decorate every little inlet. Often have I admired the flowering rush (Butomus Umbellatus)[*] with its proudly erect stem, and beautifully crowned-head of many rose-coloured flowers, and the common reed, (Arundo Phragmites)[†] so strong and stately, opposing a formidable barrier along the sedgy shore, and presenting a graceful appearance with its large, handsome, drooping panicles. With what delight have I watched from amid their concealing protection, the pretty feathered teal (Anas Crecca) escape, with whirring wing, while the stately swimming mallard, (Anas Boschas) with his mate, portraying anxious care, collect together, with warning cry, their flapping offspring; and with what disappointment have I marked the heavy pampered trout, roll sluggishly at the well-dissembled fly, and mock my utmost art to lure him from his too luxurious retreat. An admirer of nature, in such wild scenery, can never feel himself alone; for even, across the pathless bog, what a beautiful appearance the common, and the broad-leaved cotton grass[‡] (Erisphorum Augustifoluim, and Polystachion) present, or called by the country people, Canach,[§] or Cana's snowy down, having long tufts of pendulous spikelets, gaily dancing in every light breeze, and exhibiting a dazzling lustre with its cottony plumes of purest white. I had been fishing in the lake of Buailidh-beag,[||] and had for a while rather good sport, but from rain being overhead, the trout did not continue long to rise merrily. The lake is surrounded with wild romantic rocky hills, and many are clothed with the pretty little ever-green shrub (Vaccinium Vitis Idœa,[¶] red whortleberry, or cowberry, so lively with its box-like leaves; and the (Vaccinium Myrtillus) bilberry or whortleberry, and called by the peasants Fraochans and Braoilleogs. The lake is well stocked with trout, and some are of good size, but much smaller flies than those used on the other lakes answer better. It is very small; of an oblong square; and so formal with its straight banks, that it appears the work of art. I had tied up my rod, and was ascending a steep hill, which rises abruptly on the north side of the lake, when my attention was arrested by a howling kind of shout, " go dé do gno annso !"[*] which was again repeated in much wilder notes. On looking up I perceived a strange figure, more like to a satyr than a human being. He had his bristighe[†] girdled with a sugàn,[‡] while his breast and shoulders were bare, and so discoloured with soot and smoke, and his features were so completely hid by his long matted hair, that I was quite at a loss to discover to what class and order the creature above me belonged. But the mystery was soon elucidated, for near to where he was standing, I observed a cabin,[§] and issuing from its doorway occasional puffs of smoke, which gave me to understand what was going forward there.

" Oh ! oh ! my gay fellow," " Bail o Dia ort"[||]—I must get some of the good stuff; but before I could well satisfy him of my friendly disposition, a light active figure came bounding down the steep part of the hill towards us, and crying, as he firmly sprung along the uneven rocky tract,

" Eist do beal, Eist do beal,[¶] Morteein ; sure it is the masther's frind at —— ;" and doffing his cáibin,[**] (which scarcely confined his fair luxuriant curly hair) begged that I would refresh myself with Blas braou[††] poteen.

" Sure the nevir a one more welcome, Lanty, than the same masther or his kind, but the likes ov sthrangers in these parts doesn't make us altogether comfortable at times," said Morteein.

Being now treated with the most friendly respect, and with that warmth of welcome which characterises the Irish peasant, I entered with Lanty and Morteein, and was gratified in seeing a still at full play, while a creature of as equally uncouth appearance as Morteein, was drawing off the Coachan[‡‡] into a large tube or receiver.

" Eogham," said Morteein, " give us a dhrop ov the best ;" and Eogham bolg-chosach,[§§] as he was called, waddled round with great self-satisfaction, and handed me a

---

[*] A highly ornamental plant, flowering from June to August. It is perennial, having a white tuberous root. It forms a very showy addition to an aquarium.

[†] Growing on the borders of lakes, having a gracefully wavy appearance, and even, during the storms of the winter months, appears beautifully undulating with the breeze. It is the tallest of our four grasses, being six feet or more high, sheltering many aquatic birds—flowers in July—panicles dye woollen green. The culm forms a durable screen in gardens against the wind, and is used for thatching, and as a foundation for plaster floors. The inner membrane of the culm forms a very sensible Hygrometer.

[‡] In Mr. Kater's Hygrometer, the Hygroscopic substance is the beard of the grass, known in the Canarese language, by the name of Oobeena Hooloo, being the Andropogon contortum of Linnæus. It is found throughout the Mysore country in the month of January, which is the proper time to gather it, that it may be fit for use.

The Andropogon Nardus, nard or spikenard, is the Indian plant, so highly celebrated by the ancients for its perfume. Sir W. Jones, mentions that it is a very fragrant grass, growing on the banks of the Ganges, and in some places covering whole acres; when crushed, it diffuses a strong odour. There are many species of Andropogon, all exotic grasses of easy culture.

[§] Ceannbhan mona or Ceanach-na-mona, flowering from April to July.

[||] Buailidh or Buaili, means a kind of sheeling or hut, built for herdsmen that attend cattle that are put to depasture on the mountains during the summer season—beag, is little. There are three small lakes to the S. E. of Miltown, having good trout. Coire, Fainleog, and Buaili beag. Fainleog, or more properly Ainleog, means swallow-lake.

[¶] Flowering in May and June. The Vitis Idœa having racemes of terminal drooping, campanulate flesh-coloured flowers. The Myrtillus, drooping urceolate flowers, greenish, with a rose-coloured tinge, and of a waxy appearance.

The leaves of the red whortleberry are frequently used, and substituted in commerce for those of the red-bear-berry (Arbutus Uva Ursi). They bear a near resemblance, but the differences are highly important. The leaves of the Vitis Idœa are roundish obovate; edges, revolute; fine cartilaginous towards the point ; fine sawed and dotted beneath. Those of the Uva Ursi are longish obovate ; edges, pretty even, perfectly entire, reticulated beneath, (being veined underneath like net-work) and without any points. The green leaves of the Uva Ursi are powerfully astringent, possessing Tannin and Gallic acid. These principles are not found in the leaves of the Vitis Idœa.

In England the berries of the Vaccinium Myrtillus are gathered in autumn for making tarts ; in Devonshire they are eaten with clotted cream ; in Poland they are ripe in July, and, being mixed with wood-strawberries and eaten with new milk, are considered a great delicacy. In the highlands of Scotland they are eaten with milk, and made into jellies. They may be successfully cultivated in a shady border of bog earth. The fruit of the vaccinium vitis idœa, is somewhat acid and bitter, but makes very good rob or jelly, which in Sweden is eaten with all kinds of roast meat, and forms a sauce for venison, which is thought superior to currant jelly. In Wales we have experienced it to be an excellent addition to roast mutton. It requires the same cultivation as the former.

The broad-leaved whortleberry, (vaccinium amœnum) is cultivated at Enghein, in the Duc D'Aremberg's garden, and the fruit used in the same way as the cranberry.—Loudon.

[*] The Irish given here is such as is generally spoken in Clare, but the words are sometimes far from being either pure or grammatical. Go dé do gno annso ?—What is your business here ?—pronounced by them, Gui thay tho gnow in suigh.

[†] Breeches.

[‡] As sugaun, a straw or hay-band or rope.

[§] As cabaun, a hovel or hut.

[||] Success from God on you ; or the meaning sometimes intended to be conveyed by the country people—God bless the work ; pronounced by them generally, as Bal o Yhea arth.

[¶] Hold your mouth, or hold your prate, Martin ; pronounced Est tho voil.

[**] As Caubeen, a hat.

[††] Taste a drop of poteen.

[‡‡] Singlings. Whiskey in the first process of distillation.

[§§] Bandy-legged Owen. These kind of names are very generally applied : as Seumas bolg-shuileog, goggled-eyed James ; Eoine barach, lame Johnny ; maoileadanach Matha, baldheaded Matthew.

Cupàn* of rich Uisge beatha,† as Lanty said would warm one's heart. I tumbled it off with Go soirbige Dia duit,‡ and took my leave of worthy Morteein and Eoghan. Lanty now accompanied me; and as the clouds were gathering heavily and gloomily, threatening plenty of rain, we hastened our steps to the banks of the Anna. On passing through the defile of hills, that surround Bualidhbeg, the scenery is exceedingly solitary and wild; a long stairs or causeway of stones, irregularly laid, afford in the wet season an insecure footing, through a morass, to the Lake of Fainleog. At the foot of the hills I noticed the Alpine Club Moss, (Lycopodium Selagenoides || with its shining light-green leaves; and the marsh shieldfern (Aspedium Thelypteris).¶ Poor Lanty bounded along with great glee by my side; it was the first time that we had met, although we had often heard of each other. His laughing blue eyes beamed with pleasure, and he displayed such a row of pearly teeth, when his countenance brightened with his lively remarks, that I was quite prepossessed with his comely and honest features. He was at that time of a light form, but his limbs were firm and strongly knit.

"That was a fine Bradàn,** Masther William, ye killed last week in Dunbeg, out wid the masther," said Lanty; "and if there comes a frish in the river, after the rain, we'll have plinty of new fish up. Larry Maroney says there's a power outside, if there war but high tides enough to let'em get in."

"And who told you, Lanty, that I killed the salmon?"

"Kate Brennan," replied Lanty, in a half kind of sly roguish smile."

"So Kate told you, did she? I twig you now my lad; and how comes it, Lanty, that you never go to the house; for although I have been nearly three months in this part of the country, I have never seen you with the girls."

"Throth and that same has been a sore trouble to me, Masther William, and its long sorry I'd be to say or do a hand's turn against Kate's father; but big Mick Brennan is a Fear gàn cri,†† and has done me a cruel site of mischief with the masther and misthress; but he's a snug man, and one ov the masther's best tinants, and ov coorse they'd mind him afore the likes ov me."

"Well, Lanty, I'll settle all that for you; and the next time the master goes out fishing you shall come with us: never mind big Mick; I'll bring you to the dance, when the boys and girls meet again, for Kate often said to me how much she wished her poor Lanty was with them."

"The Lord bless ye, and may good luck attend ye, Master William; and 'tisn't the first time ye gave consolation," uttered poor Lanty, as his countenance beamed with grateful delight. Being close to home, we parted, and he bounded off with a lighter heart than the poor fellow had had for many a day.

Mick Brennan, called Mick Mor,‡‡ (from his large size, rented a snug farm from my friend: he was a comfortable and independent man, and stood high among the other farmers, as Mick was considered the most knowledgeable man among them in tillage, and in keenness at the fairs. He had been a widower for some years, and had only two children, both daughters, Kate and Peggy. Poor Kate! often have I lamented thy sad fate. She was a min cailin,§§

and was then in her nineteenth year. Her slender, active form is still before me—how well do I recollect, even as it were but yesterday, the mild flashing of her bright dark eye; her clear complexion and pretty features, and her raven hair so neatly braided o'er her fair forehead. And she was mild and gentle-hearted. Kate was not of a sorrowful disposition; but since the death of an affectionate mother, whom she had dearly loved, her natural vivacity had settled into an evenlike seriousness of manner, which gave to her pleasing countenance a doubly interesting appearance I had always esteemed and admired that gentleness of disposition and modesty of manner—the proudest ornaments that adorn a woman. Her little sister Peggy was much younger, and quite of an opposite disposition, being all life and archness, full of tricks and playful mischief; and it required all Kate's motherly controul to keep her roguish glee restrained. She was her father's pet, and a sad bradóg;* yet she was of an amiable disposition, and loved her sister Kate with all her heart. Mick Brennan was an intelligent and honest man, but being of a very churlish and ungracious temper, I seldom visited his house, although it was very near to my friend's; but Kate and Peggy were constantly at the masther's, to see old Matha, who was really a good old man, and had always some kind saying and advice for the cailins. Matha was the piobaire† of the family, and the best in that part of the county. Occasionally, (and particularly on holiday evenings,) the boys and girls assembled in the great kitchen, and enjoyed themselves in dancing their moneen jigs and reels. My friend and his lady were exceedingly kind to their neighbours, and it gave them the greatest pleasure to witness the glee, and wild flow of spirits of the happy boys, with their lasses. We sometimes joined in the jigs; and many a one have I danced with poor Kate. Oh! how strongly is painted to my view, my friend's large and comfortable kitchen, with ou'd Matha sitting in his easy rush chair, tuning his piob-mhala;‡ while the boys were quietly stealing in, and the cailin deas§ in their scarlet cloaks and silken snoods, with their glossy braided hair, would, as they entered, gently lisp, "Dia annso,"|| and casting a sly glance around to see if their favoured baitslear¶ had arrived. I had often wondered I had never seen Lánty, at these happy meetings; his name was familiar with the cailins, and he was called by them a buachail gleoite.** He also had a most excellent character, from his obliging disposition, and for his warm affection for his mother, the Widdy Power. It was from little Peggy I had gleaned their early history; and she had often expressed her fears, lest her obdurate-hearted father should discover the strong, the deep affection that existed between her dear Kate and Lanty. By her arch playfulness and lively wit she had always lulled her father's suspicions of the many happy meetings she had been accessary to with the affectionate pair. Lanty's mother had been living for many years in Clare, but belonged to Kerry, from the neighbourhood of Ventry. Her husband having been killed in a tight between two factions, she left her native county with her only child, Lanty, and settled near Milltown. The Widow Power had a brother, Denis Hoolahan, a noted smuggler, and who was then on board a large smuggling cutter, called the Big Jane. This vessel was frequently off the coast, and Denis would sometimes land to see his sister, the widdy, and bring her his accustomed present of tobacco and tea. She had a small extent of ground, sufficient for her cow and goats, and a crop of paities; and with Lanty's assistance, who cultivated a little garden, and now and then added to their store a good bradán, or a dish of throuts, they were enabled to live tolerably comfortable.

---

* A Cup.
† Literally, Water of life; from whence, Usquebaugh.
‡ That God may prosper you.
§ Stepping stones.
|| The fine dust of the common club moss, (lycopodium clavatum,) or properly the seeds of the plant, when diffused or thrown in the air, takes fire from a candle, and burns with a flash. It is used in the London theatres to produce artificial lightning. The pollen is desiccative, and useful for ichorous excoriations.
¶ Polypodium thelypteris, growing two feet high, having lanceolate leaves, of a pleasant green.
** Bradaun, a salmon.
†† A heartless man, or a man without a heart.
‡‡ Big Mick.
§§ A gentle or mild girl. Is deas an cailin, She is a pretty girl.

---

* A sly trickish girl.   † Piper.
‡ Pipes, or literally a bag-pipe. Piobaireachd, playing on the pipes.
§ Pretty girls.
|| God, here; or, meaning to convey the salutation, God save all here. Also, Dia duibh, God save ye. Bail o Dia duibh, Blessing of God to ye. Duibh is pronounced as yeib.
¶ Bachelor or sweetheart, or lover.
** Handsome boy. Buachail gleithe, Handsome, clean, boy.

Kate's father had some intimation of the courtship that she had been carrying on with Lanty, and he had strongly and angrily forbidden it; but her affection was then too deeply rooted to be controuled by her parental duty. Mick Brennan had moreover spoken to my friend, and had represented Lanty's conduct in so unfavourable a light, that he was thence considered an unwelcome intruder. But it is not alone, said Peggy, Lanty's not being so snug as ourselves, but that her father had a most inveterate dislike to him and the widow, on account of their Kerry origin.● I had never visited the widow's cottage; it was situated much off the main road, and the only approach was by a cosan,† across several fields. It overlooked the little river Anna,‡ which winds its course through luxuriant meadows, falling down through a barrier of rocks, about half a mile from the sea, and pursuing its way amid romantic cliffs, rocks, and sandy hills, empties itself (rushing when swollen with heavy rains) over masses of stones into the Atlantic, on Cassino beach.§ Here the billows of the Atlantic roll in with all their fury; and, when impelled by the western storms, throw up enormous cubes of limestone rock, and blocks of great weight are strewn over the beach.‖ Dripping from a cliff that overhangs the beach is an excellent chalybeate spa, called the lua rhua, or red water spring, from the red appearance given to the water, when streaming down a little channel in the bank, composed of a reddish clayey strata.¶

The rain had been so continued since I last saw Lanty that I had not the opportunity of going to his cottage until the following Sunday; and being obliged to keep close quarters, I had amused myself in tying flies, and in the mean time I had settled every thing with my friend and his lady, in re-establishing Lanty to their favour again. When our fieldsports or excursions into the country, did not take us from home, we always dined early. In the evening before the girls and boys had assembled for their usual dance, I crossed the fields to the Widdy Power's; and never were there two more delighted, than the widdy and Lanty. She was a neat, bustling old woman, and exerted herself to be mighty civil—"And it's ourselves

that's proud, Masther William, that yez have found the way to our abode at last," said the widdy, as she kicked the ould dog from the fire, and gave the turf an additional poke; whilst the hins and ducks were made to fly in double quick time, to their quarters, not forgetting the ould goose, hobbling to its nist under the dresser.

"Maybe yez 'il sit down and tak an air ov the fire;" and the busy old body wiped the cathair luachraigh● with her apron.

Lanty stood grinning with delight, and as I was afraid that I had much discomposed the widdy's domestic arrangements, I took my leave; observing that I had called for Lanty to bring him to the house, and that I would often call and see her.

By the time I returned, most of the boys and girls had met; and, when I presented Lanty, it was evident from the warmth of greeting, how much the poor fellow was liked; and never will I forget the modest, beamy look of gratefulness poor Kate bestowed on me, as I placed Lanty by her side. Matha too joined in the pleasure felt by all; and, as he vigorously plied the bellows to the drone, his ould eyes sparkled with a determination to give us a regular bout. Matha gave us his best collection; and as I futted it to the Fox-hunter's Jig, Highland Mary, and the Sean Ban Bochd,† with many a Catlinòg,‡ I felt more happiness with those joyous innocents, in all their native wildness, than ever the crowded brilliancy of the ball-rooms of the great could afford. As for Lanty, I thought we should never have been able to stop him: he danced all the cailins regularly down, and we had at last to put a stopper on ould Matha's bellows.

It was early of a fine morning, in the month of September, that I summoned Lanty to attend us on a fishing excursion to Croidhe or Cri River. After the late rains the river was in high order, and, with a fine westerly breeze, we promised ourselves excellent sport. Our ceadlongadh§ was prepared, and, oh, what a feast we did make! What horror would have been depicted in the countenance of a gentle city belle, had she, when gracefully entering the breakfast parlour, in her morning dress of studied elegance, viewed our prodigal arrangement of broiled salmon and white-trout, beef-stakes, Cru-phutog,‖ pratees and milk, griddle-bread, butter and crame, and eggs by the score, while a huge Corcran,¶ surrounded with well-lit turf (kept simmering on the hearth) supplied us with the purest of Souchong. Such is the fare of the early-rising sportsman, to strengthen himself for the manly exercises of the day—such the mode of life of the western country squire, who, with his rod, his gun, and his dog, pursues a daily round of sports, braced with health and free from care; while the lovely citizen, negligently sipping her Mocha, plans her visiting and shopping rounds, and studies the most becoming costume that may, the approaching night, display her charms, and add new conquests to the admiring crowd of her obsequious beaux.

(To be continued.)

● A singular circumstance occurred some years since in Kilrush, strongly evincing the kind of feelings of distinction existing between the Clare and the Kerry people. It had long been an annoyance to their Clare neighbours, the number of beggars that were constantly passing from Ballylongford across the Shannon to Kilrush. Complaints against this practice were so frequently made to a worthy magistrate of the latter place, that he at last ordered all the beggars that were in the neighbourhood to be collected, and sent back to Kerry, in the revenue pinnace. The old cockswain, Jack M'C——, (a Clare man,) who had the charge of them, on landing them at Carrigfoill Castle, raised his hand, with great vehemence saying, "Go; and if ever you're caught in Ireland again, 'tisn't this way we'll serve ye."

† Footpath.

‡ A very handsome bridge has since been erected near the mouth of the river, connecting the new line of road between Milltown and Kilrush.

§ The face of this cliff is much altered since I first saw it; many portions have crumbled away, and it is singular to remark how very unobserving the residents are of these changes along the coast; and of the serious ravages periodically made by the sea upon some of the most formidable cliffs and rocks.

‖ Mr. Dutton, in his "Survey of Clare,"in remarking on the force of the waves in stormy weather; states, that limestone rocks of ten or twelve feet in diameter, are thrown up on ledges of rock several feet high at Doolen; and at the same place may be seen a barrier of water-worn stones, some of them many tons weight, thrown up twenty feet across a small bay.

¶ Dr. Hibbert, who visited the Isle of Stenness, one of the Shetland Islands, in 1818, mentions that he measured a block, that had been dislodged from its bed by the waves, and removed to a distance of thirty feet, and found it to be seventeen feet and a half by two feet eight inches deep. It was afterwards shivered to fragments, and some were carried still farther, from thirty to one hundred and twenty feet. A block, nine feet two inches by six feet and a half, was hurried up a slight acclivity to the distance of one hundred and fifty feet.

● Cathair-luachraigh, a rush chair, or chair made of rushes.

† The poor old woman— pronounced Shan Van Vagh.

‡ A young girl—as, buachail òg, a young man or lad; fear òg, a young married man; bean òg, a young married woman.

§ Breakfast.

‖ Black pudding; or, literally, a blood pudding.

¶ Large pot. Before the establishment of the water guard along the western coast, smuggling was carried on to such an extent, and tobacco and tea were so plentiful, that it was no uncommon occurrence for the more wealthy farmers (who all connived at these illegal proceedings) to boil half a stone of tea at a time, in a large kettle or pot, for their breakfast.

DUBLIN:

Printed and Published by P. D. Hardy, 3, Cecilia Street; to whom all communications are to be addressed.

Sold by all Booksellers in Ireland.

In London, by Richard Groombridge, 6, Panyer-alley, Paternoster-row; in Liverpool, by Wilmer and Smith; in Manchester, by Ambery, in Birmingham, by Guest; in Glasgow, by John Macleod; and in Edinburgh, by N. Bowack.

THE
DUBLIN PENNY JOURNAL
CONDUCTED BY P. DIXON HARDY, M.R.I.A.

| Vol. III. | FEBRUARY 7, 1835. | No. 136. |

A. Duncan, Esq. del.   Clayton, sc.

BALLYMOON CASTLE, COUNTY OF CARLOW.

A. Duncan, Esq. del.   Clayton, sc.

View of the South-East and South-West sides of the interior of Ballymoon Castle, County of Carlow, with
Mount Leinster in the distance.

BALLYMOON CASTLE.

Ballymoon Castle, situated in the parish of Dunleckney, barony of Edrone East, and county of Carlow, is supposed to have been built about the year 1096. The ruins are very spacious. They form a square, measuring about one hundred and twenty feet on each side. It was formerly surrounded by a moat, now almost filled up. The interior has totally fallen into ruins—some traces of cross-walls remaining here and there, and the bases of a few pillars, scarcely distinguishable. There are two square towers—in the south, one, and in the north, another. The windows, mere loop holes, are in good preservation, about five feet in height, four inches broad, and of a crucifix form at top. The entrance is on the west, by a cut-stone arched gateway, the upper part of which has fallen from its place. The main walls, which are about 31 feet in height, are not less than eight feet thick, and are covered with earth and grass. The centre appears to have been at all times an open, uncovered area. The architecture is of great strength and durability. To the right, on entering, is a pointed arch; inside which, and *in the main wall*, are some stone steps leading to a loop-hole. From this circumstance, some idea may be formed of the extraordinary solidity of the structure.

Cromwell, amongst other similar depredations, is said to have battered it down; although, from its low situation, and the heights surrounding, it could never have been very formidable to an invading enemy. Some curious specimens of armour, &c., and a beautiful set of diamond beads was found some years back, in digging amongst the ruins.

In an historical tale, written, as is supposed, by Ossian, about the year 296, is the following passage : "But the intrepid hero, Conon, was not at this bloody battle; for, going to the adoration of the sun the preceding May, he was cut off by the Leinster troops, though he but a single knight of Connaught; and his body lies interred on the north-west side of the dreary mountain of Callan, and over a flag is his name inscribed in the Ogham."—The Ogham was a character sacred to the Druids, the alphabet of which is still preserved. The tomb of Conon was discovered in 1785, by the Right Honorable W. B. Conyngham, in company with Mr. O'Flanagan, who was sent from Dublin for that purpose, by the Royal Irish Academy. The tomb is placed on a kind of tumulus, and lies on an eminence above a small lake. This stone has long been celebrated in the county of Clare : it is of granite ; and the inscription is interpreted—" Beneath this flag is interred Conon the turbulent and swift-footed." Callan mountain is in Irish, " Altoir na Goiene," or altar of the sun. The Irish names of places have always some reference to locality or historical facts ; changing their names is therefore injudicious, as it destroys the records of the past.

Saint Piers founded a church and blessed a well at Llanberis in North Wales. The well now bears his name, and miraculous qualities were attributed to it. But the most singular circumstance connected with its history in later times, is, that here a large trout has continued for upwards of twenty years, and become so familiar, that it will take a worm from the hand of a poor woman, who seems to have adopted that privilege as her own.

ON RINGS.

According to the accounts of the heathen mythology, Prometheus, having been delivered from the chains by which he was fastened to Mount Caucasus for stealing fire from heaven, in memory or acknowledgment of the favour he had received from Jupiter, made himself of one of those chains a ring, in whose collet he represented the figure of the rock where he had been detained ; or, as Pliny relates, set in it a bit of the same rock, and placed it on his finger. But we otherwise learn that the use of rings is very ancient, and that the Egyptians were the first inventors of them, and had in them the figures of their gods, or other hieroglyphics. Pyrrhus, king of Epirus, wore a ring, reputed inestimable on account of its agate, which *naturally* represented an Apollo holding his lyre, and seated in the midst of the Muses. This king having been conquered by the Romans, they kept his ring in the temple of Concord, as the most precious article they had belonging to him. It was thought that this ring was a talisman. Polycrates, king of the isle of Samos, possessed a ring with an invaluable emerald set in it. This king having been during his whole life favoured by fortune, was willing to make a visible trial of it, by throwing this ring into the sea; but by a very surprising incident, he found the ring in the stomach of a large fish that was the next day served at his table. This ring was also reputed a talisman, and was reposited at Rome in the royal treasure in the temple of Concord, with that of Pyrrhus. The Roman knights were distinguished from the senators by their gold rings. In the time of the war between Carthage and Rome, Hannibal, as a token of the signal victory he had gained over the Roman army at Cannæ, sent to Carthage three bushels of rings, taken from the fingers of the nobles and Roman knights, who were slain on the field of battle. Though the first inhabitants of England, Ireland, and Scotland, and the ancient Gauls, were accustomed to wear their rings on the middle finger, use at last prevailed among all nations, to place them on the finger next to the little one of the left hand; which thence has the name of anomlong, or ring finger; because, as Macrobius in his Saturnalia, Appion in his Egyptians, and after him Gellino, say, that there is a small nerve, according to the opinion of the Egyptians, which proceeds from the heart to this finger. Thumb rings were formerly worn, and portraits of Anne Bullen, and of the great O'Neal, earl of Tyrone, are represented with them.

         A.

THE CHOUGH AND CUCKOO.

ADDRESSED TO MODERN TRAVELLERS.

A cuckoo once, as cuckoos use,
Went out upon a winter's cruise,
Return'd with the returning spring—
The birds about him form'd a ring,
As fluttering from his foreign flight,
They saw him formally alight,
With pride elate, with travel stiff,
Upon the top of Dover cliff.
They bid him welcome 'cross the main,
T'old England safe return'd again ;
When, eying scornfully the strand,
" Old England ! yes, the land's a land !
But believe me, gentlemen," says he,
" We passage fowl that cross the sea,
Have vast advantage over you,
That keep your native shores in view.
The season passed I took a jaunt
Among the isles of the Levant.
Then 'twas my chance some weeks to be
In that choice garden, Italy :
But, underneath the sky's expanse,
No climate like the south of France !
You've often heard, I dare to swear,
How plenty ortalons are there ;
'Tis true ; and more delicious meat,
Upon my word, I never eat :
Their eggs are good—it was ill luck
The day I had not ten to suck.
Yet, notwithstanding, to my goût,
The bird's the sweeter of the two."
Thus prating, malapert and loud,
A dry old chough, among the crowd,
Stopp'd short his insolent career
With, " What a chattering pie is here ?
You travell'd, Sir ; I speak to you
Who've pass'd so many countries through ;
Say, to what purpose is't you roam,
And what improvements bring you home ?
Has Italy, on which you doat,
Charged your monotony of note ?

Or France, that boasts so fair a sky,
Taught you less clumsily to fly ?
I cannot find that both together
Have alter'd you a single feather :
Then tell us not of where you've been,
Of what you've done, or what you've seen ?
For you, and all your rambling pack,
Go cuckoos out—come cuckoos back.''

ELECTIONEERING ANECDOTES.

At the close of an election at Lewes, the Duke of Newcastle was so pleased with the conduct of a casting voter, that he said, " My dear friend, I love you dearly : you're the greatest man in the world ! I long to serve you ! What can I do for you ?" " May it please your Grace, an exciseman of this town is very old. I wish to succeed him as soon as he shall die." " Aye, that you shall with all my heart. As soon as he is dead, set out to me, my dear friend : be it night or day, insist upon seeing me, sleeping or waking. If I am not at Claremont, come to Lincoln's-inn-fields ; if I am not at Lincoln's-inn-fields, come to court ; if I am not at court, never rest till you find me ; nay, I'll give orders for you to be admitted, though the king and I were talking secrets together in the cabinet." The voter swallowed everything with ecstacy. The exciseman died the following winter. As soon as the Duke's friend was apprised of it, he set off for London, and reached Lincoln's-inn-fields about two o'clock in the morning. The king of Spain had, about this time, been seized by a disorder, which some of the English had been induced to believe, from particular expresses, he could not possibly survive. Amongst these the Duke of Newcastle was the most credulous. On the very first moment of receiving this intelligence, he had sent couriers to Madrid, who were commanded to return with the utmost haste, as soon as the death of his Catholic Majesty should have been announced. Ignorant of the hour in which they might arrive, the Duke gave the strictest orders to send any person to his chamber who should desire admittance after he had retired to rest. When the voter asked if he was at home, the porter answered, yes ; his Grace has been in bed some time, but we were directed to awaken him as soon as you came." " Ah ! heaven bless him ! I know that the Duke always told me that I should be welcome by night or by day. Pray show me up." The happy visiter was scarcely conducted to the door, when he rushed into the Duke's bed-chamber and, transported with joy, cried out, " My lord, he's dead."

" That's well, my dear friend ; I am glad of it with all my soul. When did he die ?"

" The morning before last, and please your Grace."

" What ! so lately ? Why, my worthy good creature, you must have flown—the lightning itself could not travel half so fast as you. Tell me, you best of men, how I shall reward you ?"

" I beg that your Grace would please to remember your kind promise, and appoint me to succeed him."

" You, you blockhead ! you, king of Spain ! What family pretensions can you have ? Let's look at you ?"

The astonished Duke drew back the curtain, and recollected the face of his electioneering friend ; but it was seen with rage and disappointment ; the voter was at first dismissed with all the violence of anger and refusal. At length, the victim of the Duke's passion became an object of his mirth, and, when he felt the ridicule that marked the incident, he made the voter an exciseman.

Sir Francis Blake Delaval represented the borough of Andover, in the British parliament in 1771, and, it is related, he obtained his election by a very singular manœuvre. He got a culverin, and, at the time of polling, he discharged five hundred guineas, which, flying among the voters, soon determined their choice. This might literally be called bombarding the town, and taking it by surprise. Such a *coup de main* would succeed at most elections.

NAPOLEON AND THE TYROLESE.

During the campaign of 1809, Napoleon arrived at Brünn, in Moravia. He had to pass the Old Gate : a steep ascent leads to this gate, contiguous to which stand several houses. One of these houses was occupied by a mechanic, as a dwelling and workshop. Among his journeymen there was a native of Tyrol, an industrious and worthy fellow, but, like all his countrymen, a furious enemy to Napoleon and the French. On the morning that the Emperor rode the Spielbergh, the Tyrolese was missing. His comrades were just talking of him, when the apprentice entered the shop, and mentioned that he had seen the Tyrolese at the window of the loft. This awakened curiosity, and the master went up to the loft to look after the man. There he found him kneeling at the window, with a gun ready cocked lying before him, and his eyes fixed on the road by which Napoleon must necessarily pass. As the house stood on the declivity of the hill, consequently lower than the gate, the Emperor on horseback, at the moment when he came up to the gate, would have been nearly on a line with the window where his humble foe had posted himself ; and the distance would have been so small, that scarcely any marksman, and least of all a Tyrolese, could have missed his aim. A few minutes after the master had disarmed his workman, Napoleon passed the gate, and rode down the hill.

THE COMMON FOWL AND PHEASANT.

In the autumn of 1826, a wanderer of the pheasant tribe made his appearance in a small valley of the Grampians, the first of his family who had ventured so far north in that particular district. For some time he was only occasionally observed and the actual presence of this *rara avis* was disputed by many ; wintery wants, however, brought him more frequently into notice ; and in due season, proofs still more unequivocal became rife. When the chicken broods came forth, and began to assume a shape and form, no small admiration was excited by certain stately, long-tailed, game-looking birds, standing forth amongst them, and continued to grow in size and beauty, until all doubts of the stranger's interference with the rights of *chanticleer* effectually vanished. These hybrids partake largely of the pheasant character ; and as they are of a goodly size and hardy constitution, a useful and agreeable variety for our poultry yards may be secured in a very simple and economical manner.—A. F.—*Quart. Journ. Agric.*

RECREATIONS IN MATHEMATICS AND NATURAL PHILOSOPHY.

The following are answers to the two queries proposed in our last Number.

1. He must first carry over the goat, and then return for the wolf ; when he carries over the wolf, he must take back with him the goat, and leave it, in order to carry over the cabbage ; he may then return, and carry over the goat. By these means, the wolf will never be left with the goat, nor the goat with the cabbage, but when the boatman is present.

2. The solution of this problem is contained in the two following Latin distichs :

It duplex mulier, redit una, vehitque manentem,
Itque una ; utuntur tunc duo puppe viri.
Par vadit et redeunt bini, mulierque sororem
Advehit ; ad propriam fine maritus abit.

That is : " two women cross first, and one of them, rowing back the boat, carries over the third woman. One of the three women then returns with the boat, and remaining, suffers the two men, whose wives have crossed, to go over in the boat. One of the men then carries back his wife, and leaving her on the bank, rows over the third man. In the last place, the woman who had crossed enters the boat, and returning twice, carries over the other two women."

This question is proposed also under the title of the three masters and the three valets. The masters agree very well, and the valets also ; but none of the masters can endure the valets of the other two ; so that if any one of them were left with any of the other two valets, in the absence of his master, he would infallibly cane him.

DOCILITY AND FACULTIES OF DOMESTIC ANIMALS

Birds of prey teach their young not only to fly at and seize their prey, but also to catch it dexterously on the wing. M. Dureau Delamalle has observed falcons and hawks training their young in this manner. I lodged, said he, from 1794 to 1798, in one of the combles of the Louvre. The building was not then finished, and contained many birds of prey, which, not being molested in a city where it was not permitted to shoot them, were quite tame. My window looking into the square court of the Louvre, I had many opportunities of seeing the birds. At the time when the young were beginning to fly, I have often seen the old birds coming with a dead mouse or sparrow in their talons, hovering over the court, and calling to the young birds which remained in the nest. The latter came forth on hearing their parents, and fluttered under them in the court. The old birds then rose perpendicularly, apprizing their scholars of the circumstance by a loud cry, and let fall the prey, on which the young birds precipitated themselves. At the first lessons, with whatever care the old birds dropped the mouse or sparrow, so as to fall near the young ones, it was seldom that the latter caught the object; and, when they failed, the old birds came down like a ball, and carried it off before it had reached the ground. They then ascended to repeat the lesson, and never allowed their pupils to eat the prey until they had caught it in the air. When the young birds had become perfect at this exercise, the old ones brought them living birds, and repeated the above manœuvre until the former were able to catch them, and had consequently learned to provide for themselves.

BRITISH PEARL FISHERY ON THE RIVER CONWAY.

It may not be generally known that a pearl fishery exists at the present time in any part of Great Britain. The pearl muscle (Mya margaritifera) is found in abundance in the river Conway, in North Wales, and is collected by many of the natives, who obtain their livelihood entirely by their industry in procuring the pearls. When the tide is out, they go in several boats to the bar at the mouth of the river, with their sacks, and gather as many shells as they can before the return of the tide. The muscles are then put in a large kettle over a fire to be opened; and the fish taken out singly from the shells with the fingers, and put into a tub, into which one of the fishers goes bare-footed, and stamps upon them until they are reduced into a sort of pulp. They next pour in water to separate the fishy substance, which they call *solach*, from the more heavy parts consisting of sand, small pebbles, and the pearls, which settle in the bottom. After numerous washings, until the fishy part is entirely removed, the sediment is put out to dry, and each pearl separated on a large wooden platter, one at a time, with a feather: and when a sufficient quantity is obtained, they are taken to the overseer, who pays the fisher so much per ounce for them. The price varies from 1s. 6d. to 4s.; there are a number of persons who live by this alone; and where there is a small family to gather the shells and pick out the fish, it is preferable to any other daily labour. The pearls are generally a dirty white, sometimes blue, but never, it is believed, green or reddish.

A. Duncan, Esq. del.   BALLYLOUGHAN CASTLE.   Clayton, sc.

The ruins of Ballyloughan Castle, situated in the parish of Dunleckny, and barony of Idrone East, show it to have been a place of considerable strength and importance. Although at present roofless, the walls are in good preservation. It is of a square form, having two towers in the front; from the outer extremity of one of which to that of the other, being a distance of forty feet. The walls, about five feet thick, are in some places fifty feet high; they are of rude stone work, built in the most permanent manner. Fourteen stone steps conduct to the second floor, which rests on an arch. There are two flights of steps higher up, but they are in a state of dilapidation. An apartment about seven feet in height, with two windows, seems to have been in each of the towers: between the towers was the chief entrance, of arched, cut stone.

The appearances of the ground adjacent would indicate that the castle was formerly surrounded by a ditch. At a distance of eighteen yards to the west, stands another ruin, about thirty feet square. It has one stone-cased window, with holes for iron bars. The walls are five feet in thickness, and the structure is about twenty feet in height. About forty yards from the main building, to the north, is another ruin of small dimensions.

It formerly belonged to the Kavanaghs; and was occupied by Donagh Kavanagh, (second son of Murragh Ballagh, styled king of Leinster,) at the end of the sixteenth century. Shortly afterwards it passed into the possession of the Bagenal family, but is now on the property of Henry Bruen Esq.

TRIM CASTLE.

Trim Castle, standing on the banks of the Boyne, forms a pleasing object in the landscape. Sir R.C. Hoare says that it "is almost the only building in Ireland that deserves the name of *castle*." It was originally erected by Hugh de Lacy, to secure his large possessions in Meath, or, as Camden asserts, by William Peppard, previously to the grant of Meath to De Lacy, and continued during successive centuries to be the most important stronghold of the English Pale. According to an historical fragment by Maurice Regan, published by Harris, in his 'Hibernica,' Hugh de Lacy, on completing the building, departed for England, leaving it in the custody of Hugh Tyrrell, 'his intrinsicke friend.' The king of Connaught, taking advantage of De Lacy's absence, assembled all his powers, with a view to its destruction; and though Tyrrell, advised of his coming, dispatched messengers to Strongbow for assistance, and though the earl marched towards Trim in all haste, yet Tyrrell, seeing the enemy at hand, and thinking himself too weak to resist their numbers, abandoned the castle, and burnt it; upon which the Irish monarch, satisfied with the success of his expedition, returned home. Strongbow, however, pursued him, and, falling upon the rear of his army, slew 150 of the Irish; which done, he retired to Dublin, and Hugh Tyrrell to the ruined castle of Trim, to re-edify it before Hugh de Lacy should return from England. The castle was built in a much stronger manner, upon the ruins of the old one. Here, in 1399, Richard II. who was then in Ireland, hearing of the progress of the Duke of Lancaster in his English dominions, imprisoned the sons of his rival and of the Duke of Gloucester; the former of whom was afterwards drowned on his passage to England. In 1423, Edmund Mortimer, earl of Meath and Ulster, who had possessed the inheritance of Trim, and, as Lord Lieutenant of the island, had enjoyed more than customary authority in that office, died of the plague in this castle.

Lord Barrymore built a fine house at Castle Lyons, county of Cork, formerly called Castle Lehan, on the foundation of O'Lehan's castle. In throwing down some of the old walls of the castle, a chimney-piece was discovered with the following inscription, "Lehan O'Cullone hoc fecit, MCIIII." which proves that stone buildings were much earlier in Ireland than some modern antiquarians allow them to have been.

THE PATTERN OF THE LOUGH.

"Old times are changed, old manners gone."—Scott.

"The patthern," as it is pronounced by the peasantry, is the remnant of an ancient and religious custom which is now very much on the decline, or nearly extinct. At least, it is so changed and deformed from its original design, as scarcely to retain any marks of what it once was intended for. In the early ages of Christianity in Ireland, it signified a festival or holiday, instituted in honor of the patron saint of the parish or district, and hence called a pattern or patron saint's day. Formerly the people assembled at sun-rise, at a certain place, and performed certain kind of prayers, called *stations*, which occupied some time, and consisted of certain forms of prayer, recited on the knees, and in companies—one person giving out, and all the rest responding; and this is repeated at several places, fourteen being the usual number. The pattern was usually held in the vicinity of a holy well, near a chapel, on a hill side, where grew a lonely tree, or such other place, consecrated by custom from times long past away: but now the good intention and the prayers are all forgotten—and "divarshin and dhrinkin" are the only ostensible motives for which old and young assemble. Tents are pitched around the scite, as in a fair, for the sale of whiskey, and all the pipers and fiddlers, for miles around, are collected—and courting, dancing, drinking, and fighting prevail until the close of the day. This custom, I have said, is on the decline through Ireland; and, during a few years back, several patterns, in different places, have ceased altogether.

This custom was not peculiar to this country; for, during the primary stages of Christianity in England, *wakes* were instituted for nearly similar purposes as our Irish patterns. The people assembled near the churches on the eve of the patron saint's day, and erected bowers of green branches, (if it was summer weather) which they decorated with flowers, in a gay manner, and remained there all the night, praying and singing hymns. Hence it was termed "the wake," from the people being awake all night. The next day, as a thing of course, was devoted to feasting and rejoicing, being a holiday, when the devotees made amends, by their mirth and good cheer, for the penance and mortification done and endured during the former night's vigil. The wake is still held through England; but, like the Irish, they have dispensed with the religious part of the ceremony, and only hold the holiday and the festival. The amusements, considering the different temperament of the people of both nations, are nearly the same. As races, running in sacks, *eating cakes for a wager*, playing single-stick for a collection, dancing, drinking, &c. &c. are carried on with that system and in that dull spirit of method and rule, so different from what we know in Ireland. Yet, if their sports want the life, spirit, animation, and eccentricity of ours, they also want that character of violence and bloodshed which too frequently are seen to stain even the most trifling of the amusements of our peasantry.

We must come to the province of Leinster, where, I believe, above all other parts of this island, the patterns are still most frequently held. On the banks of the beautiful *Lough Ouel* or *Houel*, situated within two small miles of the town of Mullingar, there is still a pattern held on the first Sunday in August, called, among the country people, the "Pattern of the Lough;" and the Sunday on which it falls is as marked among the festivals of the year as Easter Sunday or Christmas Day, and usually referred to by the title of "Lough Sunday." The tents are usually pitched on the Saturday previous, in a field adjoining to that in which the great crowd collects; and the principal attraction is the swimming of horses in the lake. Early on the Sunday morning the multitudes assemble from all quarters of the country; some for the purpose of amusement or meeting friends who live at a distance; others to settle the preliminaries of a marriage contract; a great many, because it is the custom, and because others go; but the greater number to meet and fight the people of an adjacent barony, or to revenge some real or imaginary quarrel or insult. Swimming horses in the lake is a fa-

vourite feat, and affords much amusement to the spectators. It is also attended with considerable danger; and
scarcely a year passes but some life is lost on the occasion. Matches are made; and as none but the most resolute young men and the most expert swimmers dare engage in the exercise, the sport becomes very exciting.
Yet accidents more frequently occur from the terror and
want of capability in the animals so unused to such im-
mersions and such efforts, in an element of which they
are much in dread, than in the want of resolution, presence of mind, or agility in the riders.

There resided near the lake a young man of the name
of Donoghoe, who, for many years, was very successful in
the lake matches, and even when he had to manage inferior horses to those against him, by his skill, adroitness,
and quickness, always came off the winner of the prize.

At the time my story commences, the year 1818, Peter
Donoghoe was solicited, by a sporting gentleman in the
neighbourhood, to swim a horse for him at the ensuing
pattern, which he agreed to do. Peter, like all successful
men, took a pride in his fame; and he could not bear the
thoughts of not having "a baste" to swim on Lough Sunday; and, indeed, he was seldom without having his wish
gratified. He accompanied the gentleman to his house—
examined the animal—was highly pleased with his appearance, and recommended a certain kind of keeping
and feeding to be practised before the pattern, but, above
all, laid his strict prohibition against any thing like plunging him into the water, by way of preparing or inuring the
horse for the watery struggle.

"Why, Peter," said the gentleman, "I have always
understood 'twas better to give him a taste of it by degrees, so that he might not be taken by surprise, or too
much in dread when entering the lake."

"Oh, by no manner ov means at all, Sir," said Peter,
"they always get a dislike to the wather, and the more
they get ov id the more they hate id; bud you see, Sir,
whin a sperited baste, like that, is dashed in o' the suddent, an' has a man on his back that he feels can manage
him, an' whin he knows he can masther the wather himself, he'll get stout an' bould, an' shwim like a pig, 'tall
the waves cuts his throat."

"I believe you are right, Peter," said the gentleman;
"but what do you think of 'Cock o' the Heath?'" [the
name of the horse.]

"You may depind that I'm right, Sir," replied Peter;
"an' it stan's to reason; bud I'm fearing the young cock
is too flighty—that he's not studdy (steady) enough. Nothin' like a studdy baste, your honour, for the lough."

"Then, perhaps, you wouldn't like to ride him, or is it
afraid you are, Peter?" asked the gentleman. This last
observation struck Peter on the tender point; a glow of
indignation crossed his brow as he turned his keen eyes
upon the gentleman, and replied,

"Afeerd, your honor! afeerd to bring a baste into the
lough! No, no; it's not Pether Donoghoe that id be
afeerd to bring a puckawn gont into the very middle ov
id; leave him to me, your honour; iv he's flighty, I'll
manage him, I'll be bail; an' you may call me a coward
an' a boast while I live, Sur, iv I don't bring him through
the wather like a say-gull."

The taunt conveyed, and the stain which he thought
was so near being affixed to his good name, nerved Peter
for the ride in the waves; and he set about preparing and
training himself for the day, with all the eagerness and
anxiety of his soul. Three times a day he sought the
lough, and played fearlessly in its limpid waters; throwing
the stone and wrestling with the young men of the neighbourhood, after his day's work, were practised, to give
nerve and strength to his arm and elasticity and firmness
to his frame and limbs, and hope was high in his bosom
when the "Lough Sunday" drew nigh.

Peter was the only son of a widowed mother, and the
sole support of two sisters and this one parent. He was
their pride, and their glory; and even the sisters looked
forward to Peter's triumph on the lough with delight and
joy. But the mother, though she did not approve of
such dangerous amusements, said nothing to induce him
to forego them. She had seen many a sad example of the
temerity of the young, daring, and thoughtless; and she

dreaded, even in idea, that any accident would deprive
her of her darling—the prop of her old age, and the light
of her aged eyes. Yet still she did not wish to oppose
him in what she knew afforded pleasure to him she loved
so well. Peter, too, had even a tender attachment; for,
like most Irishmen, love, at a very early age, had made
deep inroads in his heart. And as women are fond of the
brave and the generous, Peter found himself loved in
turn, with as pure and as tender a flame as ever the heart
of woman could boast of. Yet Peter's was a particular
situation: he loved his mother and his sisters; they
could not think of Peter's marrying, lest he might be induced to neglect them; and the father of his sweet heart
Cicely, being a man of means and substance, would
sooner see his daughter a cold corpse before him than behold her in the arms of a cottier—a mere day-labourer.
Peter was true to Cicely, and Cicely was true to Peter.
Though many village belles displayed their finery, arts,
and charms to catch Peter, yet Peter was deaf and blind
to all their allurements; and though many an advantageous
offer, as it is called, was made to the father of Cicely, yet
no inducement could make her think of another. Thus
they lived without a hope of being united, yet still determined to live single for ever, unless fortune or fate favoured their single-hearted attachment.

At length the "Lough Sunday" came round. 'Twas a
bright and a beautiful morning, and Peter was up at the
dawn, and preparing for the sport. His heart was throbbing with expectation, for it was the greatest match that
was ever made of that kind in the country, and an immense concourse of spectators was expected: besides,
Peter had that day to contend with a powerful rival. His
mother was up as soon as himself, and trouble and uneasiness were painted on her countenance. She seemed
seeking for an opportunity to begin a conversation, yet
did not know how to open it. Peter remarked her as
she sat opposite him, while taking his frugal breakfast,
consisting of oatmeal bread, butter, and sweet milk.

"Ah thin, mother," said he, "there's somethin' the
matther wid you—sure it's not sick you'd be this mornin'?"

"Why thin, I'm not sick or sore, Peter, alanna," replied the mother; "but it's as you say, there's somethin'
the matther wid me this mornin' abow (above) all the
mornin's in the year."

"You got up too early, mother, may be," said Peter;
"and you know that doesn't agree with you."

"It's not that either, awoughal,"* said the mother;
"but it's somethin' that's at my heart—somethin' that's
hangin' over me, an' I dunna what."

"Och, rouse yourself, mother—it's only down in the
sperits you are," said Peter, "and don't let any thing
come over you that way."

"Oh bud, Pether," said the anxious mother, "I had
such a quare dhrame last night, an' the thoughts ov id
stick to me still, that you can't tell how throubled I am
about you."

"About me, mother! Oh, then, never fear for me, anyhow—there's no danger ov me; them that's born to be
hanged 'ill never be dhrowned, you know. Ha, ha, ha!"
and he endeavoured to make light of the old woman's apprehensions. His mother shook her head mournfully, as
she rejoined,

"Ah bud, Pether! dhreams like mine never come for
nothin'; an' if you take your mother's advice you won't
go to the patthern this day."

"Oh, sure I knew what you were about, mother," replied Peter; "you're too much afraid, an' you're too
fond ov me—bud never fear for me."

"Yes—bud, Pether, asthore, I never axed you afore;
an' if you knew the blackness that's on my heart, you
wouldn't go agin my will;" and the old woman looked im-
ploringly at her son.

"Aye—bud what would Misther Mac——— say,
afther I promisin' that I'd ride his baste 'ithout fail; an'
sure you wouldn't ax me to make a behay† ov myself

* A provincialism—alias, ma bouchal, my boy.
† I don't believe this word is either Irish or English, but
yet is generally used among the people. "His making a
behay of himself"—i. e. "he's making himself ridiculous,"
is a common expression.

through the counthry for a coward, an' a brag, an' a liar, an' a desaver—what I never was."

"Ah, bud the horrid dhrame, Pether," replied the mother, as if more in communication with the fears of her heart than with any outward or extrinsic passion or object.

"All *pisherogues*,* mother. Here, Kitty—where's my green hankercher to tie round my head?" and he stood up to prepare to go out. His sister handed him a green silk handkerchief, which he handed back, saying, " why don't you spit on id, an' wish me luck and safe back as you used to do?"

Here the mother seized his hand with an affectionate and impulsive movement.

"Take your poor mother's advice, Pether, jewel," said she with a tone and expression that chilled even his heart; "I never advised you to do wrong, an' don't make light ov my words. Stay away from the getherin' this Sunday; there's misforthin afore you, iv you go; an' God brake hard fortune below your feet; bud grant me this one request—don't go."

"Aw, mother," said one of the sisters, " one would think twasn't to a man you were tawkkin'; sure there's nothin' to happen him more than another."

The old woman didn't heed the remark of her daughter; she was too much absorbed in her own feelings to hear them; for seeing Peter still preparing to depart, she fell on her knees before him and exclaimed, with all the passion of a prophetess,

"Pether, Pether, stay at home this day for the sake ov the Almighty, and for the sake of the mother that bore you, an' don't go agin my warnin'. Mind, I now warn you, that there's somethin' afore you—and that you'll lave your poor ould mother to sorrow and desolation iv you don't take her advice. Pether, would you like to see your mother goin' from door to door? Pether, would you like to see her thrustin' to the hand of the stranger for her bit —an' to the cowld corner of the sthrangers' barn for her bed? Pether, would you like to see your mother in her last day, like the baste of the field, 'ithout a hand to close her eyes in charity? I know you wouldn't, my own kind-hearted, good, an' ginerous *bouchal adowna*. I know you wouldn't—an' you'll take your mother's advice an' stay at home this one day."

At this moment Cicely entered the cottage, and casting a quick glance around her to where Peter was standing in gloomy silence beside his mother, ·

"Thank God," she exclaimed, " he is not gone yet."

This was the first time she had ever stood beneath the roof of him she loved. His mother and sisters gazed on her in wonder—for her manner was wild, and she looked like one who had come in haste upon some errand of desperation. She did not notice them; but approaching Peter, who held out his hand to welcome her, she looked into his face with a mingled and undefined meaning.

"You're welcome, Cicely," said he, " what's the matter wid you—you look so frikened?"

"Oh, Peter!" said the fond girl, " I had the shockin'-est dhrame about you last night that ever was in the world; an' my heart's so sore, that I could not help comin' over to tell you not to go to the lough to-day."

"Why that's the very thing that my mother sez," said Peter; " 'pon my word I b'lieve yez med a match ov id; do you's always dhrame be couples, that ways, I wondher?"

"Oh, Pether!" said the anxious maiden; "you don't know the way my heart is, or you wouldn't spake that way to me."

"Well, then, Cicely, I thought you were sinsible, but let us hear what you dhramt about," and he sat down on a kind of three-legged chair; and his mother and sisters formed an attentive group around them.

"Well," began Cicely, "I thought that I saw you swimmin' the horses in the lough, and that a big monsther,

twice as big as the horse, follyed you ; and that all the people shouted to you to take care of the monsther who come up to you, and pulled you off the horse, and that you screeched and stretched your hands to the people to save you, but that 'twas no use; and that the monsther pulled you, horse an' all, down to the bottom, and that the whole lake was covered with blood."

"Heaven pursarve us!" said the mother, " bud that's my very dhrame—the very dhrame I dhremt; there's somethin' in id, Pether, dear; now won't you take your mother's an' this dacent little girl's advice, that wouldn't advise you ill; don't go to-day."

". Well, well, but the nonsense of women bests the puck antirely," said Peter, rising contemptuously; " an' is this all the foundation you's have for all this fuss and botheration. Why, sorra doubt but by and bye you's 'ill be for wantin' me to walk on my head instead ov my heels."

His mother and Cicely endeavoured to persuade him to remain at home for that day, but in vain. The scorn of the boys, and the sneers of the girls would be directed against him. His word and promise would be broken; besides, his vanity and fame were engaged, and could he leave the triumph to another. Cicely, after a short time, gave up the argument, and offered no more opposition to her lover's wish. The mother was not so easily conquered; she was more impressed, and felt more acutely and keenly the terrors of her forebodings, and the consequent miseries that awaited herself.

The gathering was already immense as Peter Donoghoe entered the pattern, where a number of his young companions collected around him. A spacious and gently sloping hill side, leading, without any abrupt declivities, to the sandy beach of a small bay, formed by the lake at its foot, was the place where the multitudes collected. The girls, decked in all their smiles and beauties, and decorated with their gaudiest ribbands—the boys putting on their gayest and most gallant demeanour along with their Sunday clothes. Here and there they paraded in couples from standing to standing, and from booth to booth. At the door of almost every tent a musician had pitched his stool, and doled out, in no stinted measure, jigs, reels, and hornpipes, to the votaries of the merry-heeled deity. While not unfrequently a fight, in which some scores were engaged, would arise and subside in so very short a space as scarcely to cause the slightest confusion, unless among those personally concerned. But what appeared the most novel sight, and seemed to draw the general attention of the pattern, were a pair of ballad-singers—wandering minstrels—who, having a ring accorded to them by common consent, sung out the tenderest strains to catch the stray halfpenny pieces among the soft-hearted boys and girls. The song was one of true love—a theme ever dear to the heart of an Irish peasant, and might run in nearly the following style and words, as far as memory serves at the present time :

THE TRUE LOVER'S GARLAND.*

As I walked forth one mornin' fair, in the pleasant month
    of spring,
To see the *flagrant* flowers, and view the wild birds sing;
'Twas then I spy'd a maiden fair, a makin' pit'yous moan,
All in a shady *harbour*, an' by herself alone.

I gintly stept up to her, an' thus to her did say,
"Oh, fairest of all creatures I come tell to me, I pray,
What thrubble, care, or sorrow, disturbs your gentle heart
Or has your own thrue lover been forced from you to
    part?"

She sez, " kind Sir, to answer you it's now I do intend;
In hopes some time hereafter that you might prove my
    friend;
My thrue lover, Johnny Doyle, is now on the ragin' say,
An' it was my cruel father that sent the boy away."

---

* Foolish, superstitious practices or belief—applied generally as a term of contempt to a belief in dreams, signs, or superstitious faith in charms or incantations—things common among the peasantry.

* This is truly in the manner of the love ditties now popular among our peasantry, at least in the English language. It is only fair, however, to remark, that where the Irish language is used and understood, the songs in that tongue are of a very superior description, as may be seen from the translations which we have before us.

"If Johnny Doyle was your thrue love, as I do now
    suppose,
The truth to you, fair creature, I quickly must disclose ;
He's wedded to a lady fair, an' dhrest in rich array,
With lands and money plenty in the South Amerike.

But cheer up gallant lady, and come along with me,
And your true love, for ever, so faithful I will be ;
And to my own counthry you'll come, where I'll make
    you my wife,
And think no more of Johnny Doyle—he's married now
    for life."

"Go away, false-hearted young man, if what you say be
    thrue,
It only does my sorrow, my grief, and pain renew ;
For I have vowed to wed but him, an' my thrue vow I'll
    keep
Until kind death will close my eyes in the last quiet sleep."

"Then turn about, fair Nancy, an' look on me, I pray,
Have you forgot your Johnny Doyle, that was so long
    away ;
And now comes back to his thrue love, from the wild,
    stormy main,
With goold and riches plenty, an' we'll never part again ?"

But soon a general movement to the water's edge announced that the swimming was about to take place, and
thousands crowded down to the strand to witness the
horse-race in the waters. Four fine animals were already
prepared for the struggle in the waves, and they waited
but for the fifth, which soon made its appearance, led by
Peter Donoghoe. It was a young and fiery animal, in
high condition, and required all Peter's dexterity and
strength to manage and curb him, frightened as he was by
the noise and rush of the multitude. The place where
the swimming was to take place was from one point of the
little bay mentioned above, round a small boat anchored
at some distance in the deep water, and back to another
point not far distant from where they started. The hill
swept easily round the bay, forming with its crowd a living amphitheatre, and far away, in the deep blue water, a
small island, covered with trees, arose, the only land-mark
from the swelling waves until the eye rested on the distant and woody shores which bounded the prospect.

The men were stript to the waist, and without shoes or
stockings, and at a given signal they mounted their respective animals and drew up in a line on the beach. At
another signal they plunged at once into the water, and
the animals, unused to the liquid element, and frightened
at the sudden immersion and the loud shouts that rung
around them, plunged violently, and some endeavoured
to return to the shore ; and one timid animal, despite all
the endeavours of his rider, a powerful young man, who
encouraged, coaxed, and applied the whip by turns,
struggled back, and bounded, trembling with terror, to the
strand, and snorting with joy and shaking his long mane,
he dashed away recklessly with his rider through the
crowd. The other four were urged into the deep, and
on they steered their way, with scarcely any part over the
water but their swelling nostrils and starting eyes, and the
heads of the men, bound with their handkerchiefs of different colours. Two were lagging far behind—but Peter
Donoghoe and the rival he so much dreaded were in a
line. They were nearing the boat, and as this was the
critical moment which was apt to decide the race, every
nerve was strained, and every exertion made to turn it
first. Every foot of vantage gained by either was hailed
by the loud cheers of the men on the hill ; and, as they
drew near, the horses were side by side—that of Peter
nearest to the grand object ; and just as he was on the
point of dexterously wheeling round, his opponent, by a
violent movement, forced the animal he was guiding directly across his way, driving Peter and his horse against
the boat. The shock was terrible ; for the feet of the
horses mingled and clashed in the water beneath, and
Peter was stunned by the force with which he was driven
against the boat ; and in the plunging of the animals to
get free of each other, the horse he bestrode received a
kick from that of his opponent, which broke one of its
fore legs. The animal neighed fearfully and instinctively,

as he sunk beneath the blue and bubbling waters ; and
one shrill shriek of terror broke the silence on the hill,
as the green handkerchief of Peter disappeared beneath
the agitated surface. The other man looked about in
terror as they went down, and the boat rolled into its
former situation over the spot. The victor came on shore,
panting with terror, and not a single shout hailed his triumph. Boats were immediately put out, and, with much
difficulty, and after a length of time, the lifeless body of
Peter Donoghoe was extricated from beneath the horse
at the bottom.

It were useless here to enter into a description of his
mother's frantic grief, or the deep and settled sorrow of
poor Cicely—of the loud anguish of his sisters, or the lamentations of the multitude ; for as he was generally beloved, so he was universally lamented. His mother, as she
had prophesied, lived to eat her bread from the charity of
the stranger : and Cicely lived for some years after him—
but no more like the former light-hearted sweet girl than
her own shadow in the sun-beams. She pined away day
by day, and at length passed away like a spirit from the
earth ; and, on a "Lough Sunday," she was buried in the
old churchyard of the island in Lough Ouel. J. L. L.

PALMYRA.

The moon is full, and o'er me bends
    The deep though dark blue sky—
Around me spreads the desert waste,
    The desert breezes sigh,
And o'er my path, like dreamy shape,
    What seems of elder time ;
A ruin'd pile all silent stands,
    In solitude sublime.

Oh, city of the wilderness !
    Thy palms above thee weep
Where now—the boast of vanished years—
    Thy beauteous marbles sleep.
The night bird in thy palaces,
    Is echoed by the blast ;
And dim thy silent pillars rise,
    Like spectres of the past.

Oh ! where are now thy great of old—
    Thy famed of other days ;
Whose glory wakes the harp and song,
    And tires the tongue of praise ?
The hands that swayed thy sceptre, where—
    That reared thy sculptured pride ?
A voice is breathing from thy dust,
    That murmurs they have died.

Thy gates were opened east and west—
    The pulse the press of life ;
Were busy then in triumph's hour,
    Or fierce in mortal strife :
Now deeply rests the level sand,
    Where stirred that living crowd ;
And death is not more silent than
    The dwellings of the proud.

Yet never in thy days of pride,
    'Midst all the pomp of power,
Could'st thou so touch the musing soul,
    As in this thrilling hour ;
More lovely now in thy decay,
    All desolate and lone,
Than when the trumpet shook thy towers,
    And kings were on thy throne.
               BEAUREGARD.

DUBLIN:
Printed and Published by P. D. HARDY, 3, Cecilia-street ; to whom
    all communications are to be addressed.
Sold by all Booksellers in Ireland.

In London, by Richard Groombridge, 6, Panyer-alley, Paternoster-row ;
  in Liverpool, by Wilmer and Smith ; in Manchester, by Ambery ; in
  Birmingham, by Guest ; in Glasgow, by John Macleod ; and in Edinburgh, by N. Bowack.

THE
DUBLIN PENNY JOURNAL
CONDUCTED BY P. DIXON HARDY, M.R.I.A.

| Vol. III. | FEBRUARY 14, 1835. | No. 137. |

E. Hayden.

Clayton, sc.

GLENCAIRNE ABBEY.

Glencairne Abbey, situated on the same margin of the river Blackwater with Lismore Castle, from which it is about three miles distant, is a pretty edifice, in the abbey style, and forms a prominent feature amongst the many beautiful and truly picturesque objects with which the banks of the above river are ornamented. It belongs to the family of the late Henry A. Bushe, Esq., by whom it was finished; and we regret to remark, that notwithstanding the bold situation, and the judiciously designed and highly finished compartments of the interior, yet (owing to the original projector) the exterior of the walls, with the exception of the buttresses, are a composition of plaster in imitation of limestone, which, although at present wearing so very pleasing an appearance to a superficial observer, must, in a few years, inevitably moulder to decay.

We the more readily make the above remark, as the immediate and surrounding country abounds with limestone, which might be procured at no great expense, and thus prevent the defects to which plaster must be liable.

E. H.

THE RUINED FORGE.

A December evening was falling fast, when a traveller left the inn of Kilworth to pursue his journey over the solitary mountains which divide the counties of Cork and Tipperary. He was a man of middle age, of an athletic frame, silent in his manner, and of a singularly stern and forbidding aspect: he was apparently a stranger in the country, and his whole appearance bespoke him a traveller rather for business than pleasure. He was wrapped in a horseman's large cloak, well mounted on a powerful black horse, and carried pistols in his holsters. As he was leaving the village his horse lost a shoe, which compelled him

to halt at a neighbouring forge. The smith was a man little liked by his neighbours; and many strange reports respecting his former avocations were afloat in the country. The traveller and he took but little notice of each other until the horse was shod; but, when the smith was receiving payment, a large scar on the stranger's right hand, attracted his attention; he raised his eyes to his face with an expression of surprise, but the instant he caught the dark, stern visage of the traveller, bronzed by the ruddy light of the forge, the blood fled from his cheek; and, with a half-smothered cry of horror, he dropped the money on the ground. The eyes of the stranger literally flashed fire, and his dusky figure, half seen by the flickering light, seemed to dilate with very rage.

"Hush!" said he, in a deep voice that the smith recognised right well. There was a dead silence.

The smith looked fearfully round, as if he thought the very walls had ears; then wiping the sweat from his forehead with the back of his hand, he exclaimed, in an agony of terror,

"Are you come to me at last? Och, an it's little thim that's watchin' for ye know's who they're watchin' for; an' must I go wid ye?"

"Is not the time come?" said the stranger sternly.

"Sure enough," said the smith with a grin—"it's come, sure enough. You'll be met on the road," added he in a lower voice, "for, as I tould ye, there's thim waitin' that thinks to stop ye; an' the loadin' of yer pistols is drhawin; an' the road over the mount'in is set."

The brow of the stranger grew dark as midnight, but he spoke not a word: he drew his pistols from the holsters. The smith had told him truth; the charge was gone, but the priming was untouched. The smith followed him with an anxious eye, as he turned towards the fire and deliberately loaded them again: a faint and ghastly smile curled his lips for a moment, contrasting strangely with the deep gloom of his brow. The very heart of the smith died within him. The stranger replaced his pistols; and walking slowly to the door of the hut, looked forth into the night. It was dark and gloomy; the moon had not yet risen; the clouds were gathering together in shapeless and heavy masses above the tops of the lofty mountains; and the wind came by with that moaning and melancholy sound which forebodes a coming storm.

"In an hour," said he, "the moon will rise; till then I will remain here; and, at twelve to-night, you shall see me again."

So saying he closed the door, fastened his horse to the wall, and, wrapping himself in his cloak, sat down on a stone bench opposite the fire; the smith took his at some distance, and both relapsed into perfect silence. At length the moon appeared struggling with the huge and shadowy masses of clouds that racked along the sky. The stranger again looked forth into the night; then turning to his horse, tightened the girths, and led him to the door. The smith watched him in silence. The stranger, before he mounted, again turned slowly towards him, fixing his eyes upon him with that strange expression I have already endeavoured to describe. The wretched smith hid his face in his hands, nor did he stir until the sound of the horse's hoofs, as they rang hollowly on the frosty ground, assured him that the stranger was gone. He watched him as long as he was in sight, his tall dark figure still taller and darker in the moonlight, as his horse strode at a rapid pace along the mountain road At length he disappeared in the distance; and the smith returned to his hut. He closed and barred the door, accumulating every possible fastening with the quick and nervous haste of one under the influence of overpowering fear; but suddenly stopping—"Och! its all of no use—and, sure, I know it · I might as well sthrive to keep out the wind;" with that he sat or rather sank down on the seat he had left.

The traveller meanwhile was pursuing his road, and had reached the top of the mountain; he reined his horse, and cast his eyes around; the prospect was wild and dreary to the last degree: a wide extent of barren and uninhabitable bog lay on either side of the road, its monotonous uniformity broken only by patches of snow or piles of rocks; lofty mountains of the same cheerless and dreary character occupied the distance; and the only vestige of human habitation was a ruined and roofless cabin, which stood by the road side, at a short distance; its low black walls scarcely distinguishable even in the moonlight from the bog, of which they had once been a part. The traveller drew his right hand pistol from the holster, cocked it, and, gathering up the reins, proceeded at a slow and steady pace, keeping a watchful eye upon the ruined hut, yet not so as to attract attention. As he passed the door a man sprang into the road: he had a blunderbuss in his hand; but, while he was actually in the spring, the traveller laid him dead at his feet. He replaced his pistol, and deliberately alighted from his horse. The moon had broken from between the clouds, and was shining bright and clear; he turned the dead man on his back; the pale, clear light fell full upon his face; his eyes were fixed and staring; and, though he expired without a groan, the parting pang had left a horrible expression on his livid features. The stranger bent over his victim; his dusky form and sallow brow half in light, half in shade: he gazed on him intently; and as he looked, he laughed until the very rocks rang back to the echo of his ghastly mirth. He left the dead man where he lay, and, remounting his horse, returned to Kilworth: it was almost twelve when he again reached the inn. He knocked loudly and long; at length the door opened.

"Where is your master?" said he to the waiter.

"In bed, Sir, these two hours."

"Call him," said the stranger, "I must see him instantly."

There was something of mockery in his tone as he spoke.

"I durst not," said the waiter, evidently disconcerted; "I could not rouse him now for any one."

"You are right, friend," said the stranger. "It will take a louder voice than your's to waken him now; but,

if you have a mind to try your skill, you will find him on the top of yonder mountain. So saying, he turned his horse from the door, leaving the waiter rivetted to the spot. Of the rest of that fatal night nothing is known: in the morning the body was found, and a warrant was issued for the apprehension of the smith, but his forge was closed—his cabin deserted—and he was heard of in that quarter no more. I myself have seen that ill-omened forge; it is in ruins. The grey-headed peasant who pointed it out told me the singular story I have related: he remembered well the very night. When he had done he lowered his voice, and, by way of making his assurance doubly sure, tendered an unbidden though solemn oath, that he himself had often heard, when passing that spot in the deep gloom of a winter night, the clang of sledge and anvil sounding from the RUINED FORGE.

November 29, 1834. H. J. B.

LIFE IN AMERICA.

It is not customary in New York to give dinners; from economical motives, the houses are so arranged as not to admit of it. When the homely family meal is over, and they have duly picked their teeth, the men continue to sit and drink, but the females withdraw to their bed-room, and commence their potations. At this time they admit no visitors, unless, perhaps, most intimate friends of their own sex. The answer then given is, "that the ladies are asleep," which means, that they wish not to be disturbed while they secretly indulge in spirituous liquors, and smoke their cigars. Social parties, not having a political tendency, are not to the taste of the Americans: the restraints which decorum imposes in such companies are absolutely incompatible with their notions of liberty. In the great seaports, and in Washington, there are occasionally tea-parties: from national vanity, people sometimes submit to this trouble, in order to give foreigners a high opinion of the extreme refinement of manners and the high polish of the Americans. A few days after my introduction to the reverend doctor, I received an invitation to such a party.

Whenever a lady entered, all the gentlemen at once offered her their seats with low bows; and each person on entering shook hands with all present, who then waited in profound silence till the party was complete. The mistress of the house then counted her guests, and began to prepare tea. During tea, fish, cakes, smoked meat, and, fruit were eaten promiscuously, and washed down with every sort of wine and liqueurs. The feasting over, the married ladies seated themselves together; the men slunk away to the windows and other corners, shuffled about with their feet, slowly crossed their legs, and at length assumed their favourite position by clapping them against the wall. One or other secretly slipped the beloved quid into their mouths, and began to chew, to spit, and to talk, politics in a low tone. The younger females stood in a group in the middle of the room, and inquired of one another, how many quarters each had taken lessons on the piano. Almost every one of them had several school medals, the rewards of diligence in the different departments of learning, hanging round her neck from long and broad ribands: the mothers explained to one another the purport of these decorations, and when that subject was exhausted, they took up the absolutely inexhaustible topic of the preceding Sunday's sermon; and this afforded each occasion to display her exquisite sensibility, profound wisdom, and refined morality, which, if they did not entertain the company, at least kept it together till past twelve o'clock. Another group was formed by the young *elegants.* Having taken their pen-knives from their waistcoat pockets, they were trimming their nails, while the young damsels leered coquettishly at them. At length the boldest of them, putting up his knife, and having convinced himself of his amiability by a self-complacent glance at the mirror, and ascertained that his cravat was the stiffest and his waistcoat the whitest, he shuffled in three strides, in which he stumbled only twice, across the carpet to the young ladies, drew a chair to the piano, and with a thousand obeisances invited the damsels to play. The latter set on foot an inquiry, which of them had learned music the longest; it turned out that one of them had taken eight quarters' lessons, and she was forced to play. 'Yankee Doodle' was the first air, of course: then followed 'Buy a broom,' and lastly, the equally celebrated old French song, 'Ah, vous dis-je, cherè maman,' was thrummed. When all the young ladies had played the same tunes, and the daughter of the house, a fine girl of seventeen, had jagged a solo, to which she sang the music herself, while five school-medals flying about gave her many a bruise, till, breathless and exhausted, she was obliged to desist, the company expressed their applause by a general stamping of the feet, and then broke up.

An American city has no other promenade but the streets. On the sabbath all the streets are closed with chains, in order to deprive the inhabitants of the pleasure of walking or riding. In New York alone, they have so far relaxed from this rigid morality, as to leave the chains down for a couple of hours in the day. Games of chance are deemed immoral in this country, and are never tolerated in any company. The sale of playing-cards and dice is prohibited; billiards and draughts are forbidden, and chess is not known; and yet a nation so fond of lucre cannot but be fond of games of chance. The Americans in fact play as deeply as they drink. Faro-banks and billiard-tables, are almost publicly kept; and the inspector and municipal authorities are induced, by a sufficient fee, to wink at the violation of the law. Sometimes, indeed, they take the delinquents by surprise, but when they have pocketed the legal penalty, and what they can squeeze out besides, they are quiet for a while.— *Translated from the "Morgenblatt," by "The Athenæum."*

THE SPIRIT OF LOUGH DERGART.*
A LEGEND OF THE SHANNON.
BY EDWARD WALSH.

By Lough Dergart's wave, where rude winds roar,
A dark spirit dwelt in time of yore:
And fishermen, fraught with wild affright,
Still shun the curst haunt of the water-sprite.

For often he lur'd the home-bound skiff
To the eddy beneath the haunted cliff,
Where the sailors' last shriek, and the rocks' reply,
Were blended in air with his fiendish joy.

Full often, beneath his evil eye,
The 'witch'd herd would fall—the harvest die;
And death-dealing shafts the fiend would fling,
As he sported in air on the tempest's wing!

Some horror-fraught deeds of this evil thing,
No legend would say, no bard would sing;
For nothing of ruth could round him dwell,
Who sprung from a witch and a fiend of hell.

His artifice bore to an early tomb,
A maid in the pride of beauty's bloom:
I wept o'er her fate long days ago,
And I'll weave in my lay the tale of wo.

This maiden would oft her pathway take
To church by the side of that lonely lake;
And the water-sprite thought, with fell design,
"O! that I could make yon maiden mine!"

When the sabbath bell toll'd with tone profound—
Though wicked ones hate the sainted sound—
He seeks the bless'd fane; and his angel eye
Of magic would steal a young maiden's sigh.

He shone, a gay knight of noble mien—
The sedge of the lake, his armour green;
And the mantle that flow'd o'er his shoulders, he
Had form'd from down of the willow tree.

He made a light boat of the wild waves' spray,
To bear to dark doom his fated prey;
And the long lily-leaves the wide lake bore,
Were the white-bosom'd sails the bright bark wore.

---

* Lough Dergart is a large lake formed by the waters of the Shannon, equidistant between Banagher and Limerick. In a novel called the "Monk," there is a legend much resembling this: but I have given the story exactly as tradition has preserved it among the fishermen that inhabit the banks of Lough Dergart.

The high bounding boat soon leaves the land;
The helm well obeys the green knight's hand:
No mortal e'er saw in time gone by,
A bright bark so brave—such chieftain high.

And thus have I seen some bright barks brave,
All gallantly glide o'er life's wild wave—
How dark were the hearts could say my song,
Of the loud-laughing crew that sail'd along!

He bounds from the well-moor'd bark to shore,
And God's holy house his feet explore,
Where matron and maid admired the mien,
And the blue, laughing eyes of the chieftain green.

He strode up the aisle with stately air,
And sat him beside his maiden fair;
When he press'd her white hand, her eyes betray'd,
And the glow of her cheek, the conquest made.

"My castle is gay in yon lake-girt land,
Where tall forests wave to the breezes bland:
Be queen of that isle and mine own for aye—
To death I'll decline if thou answer 'Nay.'"

She falter'd consent—and the nuptial rite
Fast bound the fair maid and the elfin knight;
But the setting sun's gleam o'er blue waves spread,
Soon lighted the bride to her watery bed!

The fresh'ning gale blew the light boat on,
The false castle's towers in the distance shone,
And the falser green knight did thus address
His bride 'mid the waters' loneliness.

"Some brave barks lightly walk the waves when prospering gales pursue,
And things of life that tread the deck may oft such passage rue;
For things of life in bravest barks may tempt the treacherous main,
And quit the shore to which no gale may bear them back again.

"The wise ones say that dangers deep the smoothest waves o'ershade,
And legends tell that genius dark would sigh for mortal maid:
If so, thy blissful bridal bed may be the oozy cave—
A water-sprite the gay green knight to whom the vow you gave!

"Yon forests high where breezes sigh, and yonder turrets tall,
Where the mild moon-beam sheds yellow gleam, are potent magic all!
At my command uprose that land, and shone those turrets fair;
Lo! from the lake their flight they take, and vanish into air.

"My own beloved bride! for thee I doff this gay disguise,
With all my native loveliness now feast thy raptur'd eyes:
This form uncouth may give thee joy when you're bound with potent spell,
Where gnomes of horrid shape appear, and things of darkness dwell!

"Why shriek?—the tie that made us one, no earthly power can rend;
Beneath the deep my court I keep, then let us quick descend.
This day of doom, when yearly come, shall view the tall bark ride,
And thou be seen those arms between, thus sink beneath the tide."

Then blended the boat with its kindred foam,
Then sunk the dark sprite to its watery home,
Then shriek'd the lost maid as her garments white
For an instant were stay'd by the breeze's flight.

Once every year, by sacred doom,
A bark o'er the wave is seen to come,
And the maiden's last shriek is heard to break
The loneliness of the moon-lit lake.

Ye maidens! beware of false ones' sighs,
And shun the warm gaze of eager eyes;
When whispers soft vows some gay green knight,
Be warn'd by the tale of the water-sprite.

E. Towell.   Clayton, sc.

CASTLE HYDE CHURCH.

E. Towell.   Clayton, sc.

CASTLE HYDE.

CASTLE HYDE CHURCH AND CASTLE.

On the banks of the Blackwater river, in the county of Cork, about two miles to the west of Fermoy, stands Castle Hyde, the residence of John Hyde, Esq. Situated in the midst of a picturesque and well-wooded demesne, this mansion presents at once a pleasing and grand appearance, standing as it does on the margin of a beautiful river, whose varied windings never fail to afford subjects in variety for the pencil of the artist, and "sites" sufficient to induce the boldest efforts of architectural design.

The mansion consists of a fine suit of rooms, a spacious hall, and circular stair-case, well executed Portland stone stairs, three stories high, which terminate at the attic in a domical and well-finished ceiling. Off the principal hall, at either side, are spacious corridores, at the termination of which are two neat circular rooms, finished in perfect accordance with the rest, adding much to the extent—in all the most perfect uniformity has been observed, altogether making it a commodious and extensive house. On a rock to the rere, and immediately to the right of the house, are the relics of one of those monuments of antiquity, to which the name claims reference, and of which little more remains than the walls, to the height of one story, of a richly ivyed tower ; it consists but of one apartment, in which is a doorway, a few openings, and an oven, rather perfect considering the dilapidated state of the walls. Access to this apartment is from the spacious and well-disposed gardens, which boast a most delightful aspect, and from which may be seen, to the west, the boldly situated castle, crag, &c.

Attached to the demesne is a neat church, part of which being an addition to the original building, is from the design of G. R. Pain, Esq., of Cork. The interior is neat and ornamental ; the stained glass in the window has a brilliant and lively effect, together with a handsome groined ceiling, ornamented with stucco centre-pieces, &c. The pews and gallery are of oak, grown on the demesne, all of which are neat and in good repair.   E. H.

THE NATURALIST'S LIBRARY—ORNITHOLOGY—VOL. IV.

Of the former volumes of this work we have had occasion to speak in terms of high approbation. With the exception of the Memoir of Sir Thomas Stamford Raffles, which is very interesting, we can say little for the volume before us. We have already given it as our opinion, that such works should not be confined to mere dry scientific detail. Numerous anecdotes, and many interesting particulars relative to the birds might readily be collected, and by being introduced, would naturally fix the attention of youthful readers, the principal class for whose benefit such publications are intended. In the former volumes of the Naturalist's Library, we were pleased to find that this was the case. In the present volume there is a very brief demi-scientific description of thirty-two kinds of grouse. To sportsmen this may be interesting—to the general reader it certainly is not. It is but fair to say, however, that the very excellent Memoir of Sir Stamford Raffles, which is given in the foregoing part of the work, will, to the minds of many, make ample amends for the deficiencies in the latter. To Sir Stamford, as many of our readers must be aware, the British Naturalist is indebted for a Zoological establishment, which has already rivalled the utility, and emulated the magnificence, of the Continental institutions.

The name of Sir T. Stamford Raffles is intimately connected with the political history of the East, and it is no less so with that of its natural productions. It will be seen that the researches of this naturalist were not confined to one branch of the science, but every department, both of the history of the inhabitants of those islands, and their natural productions, were carefully studied.

MEMOIR OF SIR THOMAS STAMFORD RAFFLES.

To furnish even a sketch of Sir Stamford's life would carry us far beyond our limits. From the following extracts the reader will be able to form some idea of the labour and fatigue which men of talent and energy experience in the following out of their literary, scientific, or philosophic pursuits—in their endeavours to add to the stores of general knowledge. Little do readers imagine, when glancing over such volumes as the one before us, how much time, and care, and anxiety the information they contain may have cost men of superior minds and information, in collecting facts or making discoveries in the various departments of natural history or science to which they may have turned their attention. As an introduction to the extracts which we purpose giving, we shall merely mention that Sir Stamford, the son of Benjamin Raffles, one of the oldest captains in the West India trade, was born at sea on the 5th July, 1781, off the harbour of Port Morant, in the Island of Jamaica. Little appears to be known of his family, except its antiquity, and that its earlier members passed through life with unblemished reputation. Of his youth previous to the age of fourteen, when he entered into active business, few traits seem to have been recollected, beyond a sedateness of temper, and perseverance in his studies superior to that of his school-fellows, with a vivid apprehension of the incidents which occurred. During this period he studied under the charge of Dr. Anderson, who kept a respectable academy near Hammersmith ; and, at the early age we have mentioned, he was placed as an extra clerk in the East India House.

When we consider the very portion of his early life, wherein he could regularly gain the rudiments of a common education, we must be surprised at the variety of acquirements which he afterwards displayed, or rather, perhaps, at the industry by which they were attained. During his sedentary occupation as a clerk, he employed his leisure in attending to several branches of literature, and he obtained a tolerable knowledge of French, which a retentive memory enabled him to retain, and afterwards to use with much advantage, in his various duties of diplomacy. His power of acquiring languages was great, and in his after engagements gave him advantages and influence over the native powers of the East, which could not have been obtained unless by a free intercourse, and which a knowledge of their language could only give.

It would scarcely have been expected that a young man, placed in so apparently friendless a situation, should have made to himself patrons. A friend had, however, marked him ; and upon the occurrence of a vacancy in the establishment of the East India House, the appointment was given to the young and studious Raffles, in preference to many who were thought at least to have possessed more interest. In 1805 the Directors determined upon sending out an establishment to Penang ; and Mr. Ramsay, then secretary, having observed his talents for diplomacy, his application, and his quickness, recommended him to the office of assistant secretary. In September following, Mr. Raffles first set foot in the East, the theatre in which his acquirements and industry were to be shown forth. During the voyage out he had nearly mastered the Malayan language ; and, from the illness of the secretary, he was at once obliged to enter upon all the duties and difficulties of his office, a task of great responsibility, but which he executed to the satisfaction of his employers.

While at Malacca he first saw and mixed with the varied population of the Eastern Archipelago, heard the dialects, and became interested in their origin ; and to this singularity and variety may be attributed the first desire to investigate the history and antiquities of this people. In these pursuits he was assisted by the researches which now occupied Mr. Marsden, whose constant application upon the occurrence of difficulties, and innumerable queries, forced and kept up the interest of a subject to which he was already deeply attached. It was at Malacca, also, where he first gained the acquaintance and friendship of Dr. Leyden.

The capture of Java was terminated in 1811, and by all, much of the merit of planning and conducting the expedition is attributed to Mr. Raffles. The services which he had performed were so highly judged of by Lord Minto—the performance of any trust to be reposed in him was so confidently anticipated—that he at once appointed Mr. Raffles Lieutenant-Governor of Java and its dependencies. " The charge was of the most extensive, arduous, and responsible nature, comprising on the island of Java alone, a population of six millions, divided into thirty-six residencies, under powerful chiefs, who had long been desirous of throwing off the European yoke, and who were by no means disposed to submit quietly to the rule of their new governors."

For some time his cares and duties were so heavy, that every moment was required for their fulfilment, but ere long the pursuits of natural history and antiquities began to fill his moments of leisure. In a letter to his first and old friend, Mr. Ramsay, written in the same year with his establishment in the government, after mentioning the surmounting of several difficulties, he says, " By the next opportunity I shall have the satisfaction of forwarding to the authorities in England, several reports from Dr. Horsfield, and other scientific gentlemen, on the natural history of the island; and as the Batavian Literary Society have solicited that I should take that institution under the protection of government, I trust that by uniting our efforts with those of the Asiatic Society in Bengal, very considerable light may be shortly thrown on science and general knowledge. The numerous remains of Brahminical structures in every part of the island, prove beyond a doubt, that a colony of Hindus settled on this island about the first century of the Christian era; and the materials of which they are constructed, induce the belief that this colony must have emigrated from the Coromandel coast. The beauty and purity of these structures are entirely divested of that redundancy of awkward and uncouth ornaments and symbols which are found in India."

During his residence in England, Mr. Raffles gained additional friends, and formed new attachments; he regained his former health, and early in the year of his arrival married Sophia, the daughter of Mr. Hull, an Irish gentleman. His leisure was occupied in writing his History of Java, of which we shall afterwards speak; and upon presenting it to his Majesty, George IV., (at that time Prince Regent), he received the honour of knighthood.

In November, 1817, Sir Stamford Raffles, accompanied by his lady, sailed for his new residency; and, after a tedious voyage, arrived safely at Bencoolen. The condition of this establishment at the time of his arrival must have been very desolate. In a letter to Mr. Marsden, he thus describes their uncomfortable situation : " This is without exception the most wretched place I ever beheld. I cannot convey to you an adequate idea of the state of ruin and dilapidation which surrounds me. What with natural impediments, bad government, and the awful visitations of Providence, which we have recently experienced in repeated earthquakes, we have scarcely a dwelling in which to lay our heads, or wherewithal to satisfy the cravings of nature. The roads are impassable; the highways in the town overrun with rank grass; the government-house a den of ravenous dogs and polecats." The administration seemed to have been little better; a listless idleness had taken hold of the native inhabitants, gaming and cockfighting prevailed, and the Malayan character exhibited in its very worst aspect; while the murder of Mr. Parr, a former resident, had given rise to complete distrust amongst the European inhabitants; " an appearance of general desolation appeared."

By the energy and prudent measures adopted without delay by Sir Stamford, the aspect of affairs and of the country became soon improved, and confidence, to a certain extent, was restored between both the native and European population. To pursue this object still farther, it was necessary that a general knowledge of the island should be obtained, and Sir Stamford resolved to make some excursions to the interior. Accounts of these he has given in a series of letters to his friends; and as they contain much interesting information regarding the natural history of the island and its productions, we shall here notice some of the more important discoveries which were made.

The first excursion extended only to the nearest range of hills which had not previously been visited by Europeans; and on a part of the range, " The Hill of Mists," he selected a situation for a country residence, not very favourable, if we may judge from the name, but it commanded an extensive view of the lower country, and was subjected to a less degree of heat. The second was to the southern residencies, and the Passumah country, and is remarkable for the discovery of the gigantic parasitic

flower, destined to hand to posterity the names of its discoverers—Rafflesia Arnoldi. [*]

" On the next morning, at half-past five, we commenced our journey towards Passumah on foot, the party consisting of myself, Lady Raffles, Dr. Arnold, and Mr. Presgrove, the resident at Manna, with six native officers, and about fifty coolies (porters), carrying our food and baggage. Our journey lay near the banks of the river during the whole day, but frequently over high cliffs, and almost entirely through thick forests. On approaching Lebu Tappu, where a village once stood, we fell in with the tracks of elephants. They were very numerous, and it was evident they had only preceded us a short time. We here passed over much ground, which at one period must have been in cultivation, but which had long been in a state of nature. After breakfasting at Lebu Tappu, under the shade of the largest tree we could find, we proceeded on to a place called Pulolebar, where we were to sleep. This also had been the site of a village, but no trace of human dwelling or cultivation was to be found; we reached it at half-past four in the afternoon, having walked for upwards of eight hours. We immediately set to work, and erected two or three sheds to sleep in, collecting the materials from the vegetation around us. The river here was broad but very rocky; the scenery highly romantic and beautiful. During the night we were awakened by the approach of a party of elephants, who seemed anxious to inquire our business within their domains. Fortunately they kept at some distance, and allowed us to remain unmolested. The natives fancy that there are two kinds of elephants—the Gaja bermakpong, those which always go in herds, and which are seldom mischievous, and the Gaja salunggal, or single elephants, which are much larger and ferocious, going about either singly or only two or three in company. It is probable the latter kind are only the full grown males.

" I must not omit to tell you, that in passing through the forest, we were, much to our inconvenience, greatly annoyed by leeches; they got into our boots and shoes, which became filled with blood. At night, too, they fell off the leaves that sheltered us from the weather, and on awaking in the morning we found ourselves bleeding profusely. These were a species of intruders we were not prepared for.

" The most important discovery throughout our journey was made at this place. This was a gigantic flower, of which I can hardly attempt to give any thing like a just description. It is, perhaps, the largest and most magnificent flower in the world, and is so distinct from every other flower, that I know not to what I can compare it. Its dimensions will astonish you; it measured across, from the extremity of the petals, rather more than a yard; the nectarium was nine inches wide, and as deep, estimated to contain a gallon and a half of water, and the weight of the whole flower fifteen pounds.

" The Sumatra name of this extraordinary production is Petiman Sikinlili, or Devil's-siri (betle) box. It is a native of the forests, particularly those of Passumah, Ulu, Manna.

" There is nothing more striking in the Malayan forests, than the grandeur of the vegetation. The magnitude of the flowers, creepers, and trees, contrasts strikingly with the stunted, and, I had almost said, pigmy vegetation of England. Compared with our fruit-trees, your largest oak is a mere dwarf. Here we have creepers and vines entwining larger trees, and hanging suspended for more than one hundred feet, in girth not less than a man's body, and many much thicker; the trees seldom under one hundred, and generally approaching one hundred and sixty to two hundred feet in height.

" From Pulo Laber we started at half-past five, and halted at eight to breakfast. At eleven we reached the Sindangaré river, where we took some refreshment, and in the evening, about half-past five, reached Barong Rasem.

" The day's journey was most fatiguing, and not less than thirty miles, entirely through a thick forest, and over stupendous mountains, one of which, called the Sindangan mountain, could not have been less than between four and five thousand feet high. Neither on this nor on the

[*] Dr. Arnold, who accompanied Sir Stamford in many of his excursions, but lately fell a victim to the climate.

preceding day was there vestige of population or cultivation; nature was throughout allowed to reign undisturbed, and from the traces of elephants in every direction, they alone, of the animal kingdom, seemed to have explored the recesses of the forest.

"We got on, however, very well; and though we were all occasionally much fatigued, we did not complain. Lady Raffles was a perfect heroine. The only misfortune at this stage was a heavy fall of rain during the night, which penetrated our leafy dwelling in every direction, and soaked every one of the party to the skin. We were now two days' march beyond the reach of supplies; many of our coolies had dropped off; some were fairly exhausted, and we began to wish our journey at an end. We, however, contrived to make a good dinner on the remaining fowl, and having plenty of rice and claret, did not complain of our fare.

"On the next morning we started in better spirits, having been met by one of the chiefs of Passumah, who came to welcome our approach, and to assure us if we walked on foot we should reach a village in the afternoon. For the first part of the day, our route was still over stupendous mountains, sometimes in the beds of rivers for miles, and at all times difficult; but about noon we came into a country that had once been cleared, and again fell in with the Manna River, which we crossed on a raft previously prepared for the purpose, many of the chiefs and people of Passumah having assembled to meet us. We had still, however, a very steep ascent to encounter; but no sooner had we attained the summit, and bent our steps downwards, than our view opened upon one of the finest countries I ever beheld, amply compensating us for all the dreariness of the forest, and for all the fatigues we had undergone; perhaps the prospect was heightened by the contrast, but the country I now beheld reminded me so much of scenes in Java, and was in every respect so different to that on the coast, that I could not help expressing myself in raptures. As we descended, the scene improved; we found ourselves in an immense amphitheatre, surrounded by mountains ten and twelve thousand feet high; the soil on which we stood rich beyond description, and vegetation luxuriant and brilliant in every direction. The people, too, seemed a new race, far superior to those on the coast, tall, stout, and ingenuous. They received us most hospitably, and conducted us to the village of Nigri-Cayu, where we slept.

"At Tanjung Alem, we remained two nights. We found the villages in this part of the country most respectable, many of them having more than five hundred inhabitants; the houses large, and on a different plan to those on the coast; each village, which may rather be considered as a small town, has a fosse or ditch round it, with high palisades. We passed the site of two or three towns, which were represented to have been destroyed by the petty hostilities between the chiefs.

"The utmost good humour and affection seemed to exist among the people of the village; they were as one family, the men walking about holding each other by the hand, and playing tricks with each other like children. They were as fine a race as I ever beheld; in general about six feet high, and proportionably stout, clear and clean skins, and an open ingenuous countenance. They seemed to have abundance of every thing; rice, the staple food of the country, being five times as cheap as at Bencoolen, and every other article of produce in proportion. The women and children were decorated with a profusion of silver ornaments, and particularly with strings of dollars and other coins, hanging two or three deep round the neck. It was not uncommon to see a child with a hundred dollars round her neck. Every one seemed anxious for medicine, and they cheerfully agreed to be vaccinated. The small-pox had latterly committed great ravages, and the population of whole villages had fled into the woods to avoid the contagion.

"We now thought of returning to the coast, and on the 25th set off for Manna by a different route to that by which we had arrived. Our first day's journey was to Camumuan, which we reached a little before six in the evening, after the hardest day's walk I ever experienced. We calculated that we had walked more than thirty miles, and over the worst of roads. Hitherto we had been fortunate in our weather; but before we reached this place, a heavy rain came on, and soaked us completely. The baggage only came up in part, and we were content to sleep in our wet clothes, under the best shade we could find. No wood would burn; there was no moon; it was already dark, and we had no shelter erected; by perseverance, however, I made a tolerable place for Lady Raffles, and, after selecting the smoothest stone I could find in the bed of a river for a pillow, we managed to pass a tolerably comfortable night. This is what is here called the Ula Pino road; and we were encouraged to undertake long marches, in the hope of only sleeping in the woods one night, and in this we fortunately succeeded.

"The next day we reached Merambung, where we got upon a raft, and were wafted down to the vicinity of Manna in about seven hours. The passage down the river was extremely romantic and grand; it is one of the most rapid rivers on the coast: we descended a rapid almost every hundred yards.

"After proceeding from Manna to Cawoor, we returned by the coast to Bencoolen, where we arrived on the 3d of June, to the no small astonishment of the colonists, who were not inclined to believe it possible we could have thought of such a journey."

The party having thus returned in safety to Bencoolen, the attention of Sir Stamford was occupied for a month in the concerns of the company; but he contemplated other excursions, and, in July 1818, commenced his inquiries regarding the ancient Malayan city, Menangkabu, celebrated for the richness of its ores and mineral productions. He embarked for Padang, accompanied as formerly by Lady Raffles, having upon the journey also, the company and assistance of Dr. Horsfield. The journal of this expedition, written at the time of its execution, and sent home to his friends, is extremely interesting, but from its length, would occupy too much space here.

In most of his excursions he was accompanied by Lady Raffles, who entered warmly into his pursuits, and delighted in exploring those fairy isles, the lands of eastern fable and magnificence, celebrated by all mariners as the most gorgeous water scenery in the world:

"So strong the influence of the fairy scene."

"It is impossible," writes Lady Raffles, "to convey an idea of the pleasure of sailing through this beautiful and unparalleled Archipelago, in which every attraction of nature is combined. The smoothness of the sea, the lightness of the atmosphere, the constant succession of the most picturesque lake scenery; islands of every shape and size clustered together; mountains of the most fanciful forms crowned with verdure to their summit; rich and luxuriant vegetation extending to the very edge of the water; little native boats with only one person in them, continually darting out from the deep shade which concealed them, looking like so many cockle-shells wafted about by the wind. Altogether, it is a scene of enchantment deserving a poet's pen to describe its beauties."

Circumstances occurred which required his return to England, previous to which, however, he was the means of reorganizing a Society of Arts at Batavia.

This state of rural happiness and employment in benefiting the country was now, however, about to terminate. A succession of sickly seasons occurred, which ravaged the population, and we may almost be surprised that Sir Stamford and his lady were preserved among the many losses they sustained. Their three eldest children fell victims in succession to the climate, and it was resolved that they should consent to separation from their fourth and only surviving daughter, rather than she should run the risk of encountering the malaria. To these diseases his bosom friend and companion in research also fell a victim, and while under these severe dispensations, a voyage to Singapore was undertaken finally to arrange the settlement, and to prepare for his departure from the East, after a residence of much labour, anxiety, and satisfaction, of much affliction and much happiness.

"We embarked on the 2d instant in the Fame, and sailed at daylight for England with a fair wind, and every prospect of a quiet and comfortable passage.

"The ship was every thing we could wish, and having

closed my charge here much to my satisfaction, it was one of the happiest days of my life. We were, perhaps, too happy, for in the evening came a sad reverse. Sophia had just gone to bed, and I had thrown off half my clothes, when a cry of fire, fire! roused us from our calm content, and in five minutes the whole ship was in flames! I ran to examine whence the flames principally issued, and found that the fire had its origin immediately under our cabin. Down with the boats. Where is Sophia? Here. The children? Here? A rope to this side. Lower Lady Raffles. Give her to me, says one: I'll take her says the captain. Throw the gunpowder overboard. It cannot be got at; it is in the magazine close to the fire. Stand clear of the powder. Skuttle the water-casks. Water! water! Where's Sir Stamford? Come into the boat, Nilson! Nilson come into the boat. Push off—push off. Stand clear of the after part of the ship.

" All this passed much quicker than I can write it. We pushed off, and as we did so, the flames burst out of our cabin window, and the whole of the after part of the ship was in flames. The masts and sails now taking fire, we moved to a distance sufficient to avoid the immediate explosion; but the flames were now coming out of the main hatchway, and seeing the rest of the crew, with the captain, still on board, we pulled back to her under her bows, so as to be more distant from the powder. As we approached we perceived that the people on board were getting into another boat on the opposite side. She pulled off—we hailed her; have you all on board? Yes, all save one. Who is he? Johnson, sick in his cot. Can we save him? No, impossible. The flames were issuing from the hatchway. At this moment, the poor fellow, scorched, I imagine, roared out most lustily, having run upon deck. I will go for him says the captain. The two boats then came together, and we took out some of the persons from the captain's boat, which was over-laden; he then pulled under the bowsprit of the ship, and picked the poor fellow up. Are you all safe? Yes, we have got the man—all lives safe. Thank God! pull off from the ship. Keep your eye on a star, Sir Stamford. There is one scarcely visible.

" The captain then undertook to lead, and we to follow, in a north north-east course, as well as we could, no chance, no possibility being left, that we could again approach the ship ; for she was now one splendid flame, fore and aft, and aloft, her masts and sails in a blaze, and rocking to and fro, threatening to fall in an instant. There goes her mizen-mast; pull away, my boys. There goes the gunpowder. Thank God!—thank God!

" My only apprehension was the want of boats to hold the people, as there was not time to have got out the long boat, or to make a raft; all we had to rely upon were two small quarter boats, which, fortunately were lowered without accident; and in these two small open boats, without a drop of water or grain of food, or a rag of covering, except what we happened at the moment to have on our backs, we embarked on the ocean, thankful to God for his mercies! Poor Sophia, having been taken out of her bed, had nothing on but a wrapper, neither shoes nor stockings. The children were just as taken out of bed, where one had been snatched after the flames had attacked it: in short, there was not time for any one to think of more than two things. Can the ship be saved? No. Let us save ourselves then. All else was swallowed up in one grand ruin.

" To make the best of our misfortune, we availed ourselves of the light from the burning ship to steer a tolerably good course towards the shore. She continued to burn till about midnight, when the saltpetre she had on board took fire, and sent up one of the most splendid and brilliant flames that was ever seen, illuminating the horizon in every direction to an extent of not less than fifty miles, and casting that kind of blue light over us, which is of all others the most horrible. She burnt and continued to flame in this style for about an hour or two, when we lost sight of the object in a cloud of smoke.

" Neither Nilson nor Mr. Bell, our medical friend, who had accompanied us, had saved their coats; but the tail of mine, with a pocket handkerchief, served to keep Sophia's feet warm, and we made breeches for the children

with our neckcloths. Rain now came on, but, fortunately, it was not of long continuance, and we got dry again. The night became serene and starlight; we were now certain of our course, and the men behaved manfully ; they rowed incessantly, and with good heart and spirit, and never did poor mortals look out more for daylight and for land than we did; not that our sufferings or grounds of complaint were any thing to what had befallen others, but from Sophia's delicate health, as well as my own, and the stormy nature of our coast, I felt perfectly convinced we were unable to undergo starvation and exposure to sun and weather many days, and, aware of the rapidity of the currents, I feared we might fall to the southward of the port.

" At daylight we recognised the coast and Rat Island, which gave us great spirits; and though we found ourselves much to the southward of the port, we considered ourselves almost at home. Sophia had gone through the night better than could have been expected, and we continued to pull on with all our strength. About eight or nine we saw a ship standing to us from the roads; they had seen the flames from shore, and sent out vessels to our relief; and here, certainly, came a minister of Providence, in the character of a minister of the Gospel, for the first person I recognised was one of our missionaries. He gave us a bucket of water, and took the captain on board as a pilot. The wind, however, was adverse, and we could not reach the shore, and took to the ship, where we got some refreshment and shelter from the sun. By this time Sophia was quite exhausted, fainting continually. About two o'clock we landed safe and sound, and no words of mine can do justice to the expressions of feeling sympathy and kindness with which we were hailed by every one.

" The loss I have to regret beyond all, is my papers and drawings—all my notes and observations, with memoirs and collections, sufficient for a full and ample history, not only of Sumatra, but of Borneo, and almost every other island of note in these seas; my intended account of the establishment of Singapore; the history of my own administration; eastern grammars, dictionaries, and vocabularies; and last, not least, a grand map of Sumatra, on which I had been employed since my arrival here, and on which, for the last six months, I had bestowed almost my whole undivided attention. This, however, was not all; all my collections in natural history, all my splendid collection of drawings, upwards of two thousand in number, with all the valuable papers and notes of my friends Arnold and Jack; and, to conclude, I will merely notice, that there was scarce an unknown animal, bird, beast or fish, or an interesting plant, which we had not on board; a living tapir, a new species of tiger, splendid pheasants, &c., domesticated for the voyage; we were, in short, in this respect a perfect Noah's Ark.

" All—all has perished; but, thank God, our lives have been spared, and we do not repine.———"

After this heavy dispensation we might suppose a person desponding, it was not so with Sir Stamford; and in no event of his life did he exhibit so much energy. He had seen the labours of twenty years, his collection of drawings, manuscripts of his own, and of his companions, who had fallen victims to their researches, the greater part of his private property, the presents of his friends, and testimonials of his services, all swept away, reduced to ashes in a few hours. But truly thankful for the preservation of his family, and as soon as he had again placed them in a situation of comfort and safety, do we find him endeavouring to repair the vast losses he had sustained.

The anxiety of Sir Stamford and Lady Raffles, after these severe trials, to reach England, naturally increased, and another ship was engaged, in which they again embarked on the 8th of April. They experienced a most tempestuous passage, but arrived in safety among their anxious friends.

His establishing of the Zoological Society of London on his return home, and subsequent decease is already known to our readers.

DUBLIN :

Printed and Published by P. D. Hardy, 3, Cecilia Street, to whom all communications are to be addressed.

THE
DUBLIN PENNY JOURNAL

CONDUCTED BY P. DIXON HARDY, M.R.I.A.

| Vol. III. | FEBRUARY 21, 1835. | No. 138. |

J. F. W. del.   Clayton, sc.

Cottage at Futler's Gift, near Drimoleague, Parish of Drinagh, County of Cork, residence of Rev. J. Ryan.

J. F. W. del.   Clayton, sc.

View of Mielane and Shaghy mountains taken from Kilcascan. 1828.

RIDES THROUGH THE COUNTY OF CORK—THE PRIEST'S FIRESIDE.

At the close of the last section of our rambling narrative, the reader will remember we were snugly ensconced in our chair, by the hospitable fireside of Father R——, of Drimoleague. The windows were closely curtained—a roaring fire blazed and bickered up the chimney—the table displayed a cloth of snowy purity, and was further graced with a sirloin of real *Kerry* beef, (the native of course of the mountains of *Cork*) delicious ham and chickens, beefsteaks of unrivalled tenderness, and a couple of flanking decanters of excellent brown sherry, and port of no contemptible antiquity; of the vintage, as our host assured us, of 1811. What a dinner for sportsmen and tourists' and its zest was increased by the cordial welcome which displayed itself in the evident delight our reverend entertainer felt at the relish we evinced for our quarters, and the good things they afforded.

"That old ruin of Castle Donovan," said Father John, " has sheltered me ere this, when benighted on a sporting excursion. Those are incidents, however, which don't occur more than once or twice in the life of a sportsman. A man must possess some ingenuity to contrive to be benighted in an interesting manner every time he goes out shooting."

"I wonder that it ever should be *your* case, Sir," said I; "for you are doubtless acquainted with all the farmers' cabins in your parish, and the worst of them all, one would think, should afford better accommodation than that cut throat old castle. There are a couple of gaps in the rocky floor like graves. I stumbled over them this evening in the dark, and almost broke my legs."

"Why the castle certainly did not appear to much advantage to *you*," replied the priest, "and yet it afforded most capital quarters for sportsmen on the occasion I allude to. All depends on the *cuisine*, as we say in France. As you say, Sir, a man would more naturally go in quest of comfort in some inhabited cabin, than in an old fortalice, whose only inmates are jackdaws and fairies ; but it happened then, as it happened to-night, that I was shooting at night-fall on the top of Mullaugh Nesha, and I thought that by coming across the marshy meadow I might meet my horse and servant at the road near the castle. Then came the rain, hail, and wind—any port, you know, in a storm ; so I e'en preferred the dry though rugged floor of the old castle, to being bogged up to my hips in the manure which composes the floor of Bonaparte Howlaghan's cabin, in the next furze brake.'

"Bonaparte Howlaghan!" repeated I, "an odd mixture."

"Bonaparte is a sobriquet," answered the priest, "which the fellow has acquired from his noted political enthusiasm."

"But tell me,' said I, "reverting to the subject from which we were straying, "how did it happen that the castle ever afforded you comfortable quarters? Surely you had better entertainers than the jackdaws and fairies?"

"So we had I warrant you," replied Father John, "we were host and guest ourselves in our own proper person. Sir, it was in the year ——9, or thereabouts, when I first became priest of this parish, that two or three sporting English tourists, with pens, ink, paper, pencils, pallettes, double-barrelled guns, and all that, beat up my quarters about this time of year. They were quite made up for writing books, taking views, and knocking down grouse and partridge. So they graciously solicited my poor aid in both their literary and sporting capacity, and you know it would not have given them a favourable specimen of Irish courtesy and ho-pitality to refuse their request. Accordingly I escorted them to Mullaugh Nesha, Cnocnabruish, Wheeough, Oulteen, and all our uphonious hills and eminences. They desired peculiarly accurate information regarding the topography, and were not a little perplexed on finding that few of the people knew any thing of English ; and those who did had a particular way of computing distances, which did not convey much instruction to the Englishers. They asked my friend Bonaparte how far it was to a farm-house where I meant to spend the night, and Bonaparte answered it was six mountains off.'

"'But pray how many miles?' persisted the Englishman.

"'Ogh," said Bonaparte, "we knows nothing about miles in Drinagh. We always reckons distance by the rocks and the bogs. We say sich or sich a place is three rocks away, or hauf-a-dozen bogs, or six mountains off, or something of that sort. Miles! Indeed, honey, a man would be kicked that talked of miles in Drinagh ; and it's well for yous, a pair of foreign jintlemen, that you happened to ax a man of my edicashun and jintility. Miles! arrah sure we have neither miles nor mile-stones here, but the rocks and the mountains, which are heaven's own finger-posts and land-marks, planted by the hand of nathur!'

"You may guess that my English friends felt inclined, after such a sublime declaration, to confine their inquiries to me. However I allayed their apprehensions by assuring them that Bonaparte was a humourist, and a shrewd one too, and merely meant to amuse himself at their acquaintance with our character and customs."

"But the castle, Mr. R——" interposed I, "you must not forget the old castle."

"Oh, aye," said the priest, "and a glorious night we spent there. I was croosting grouse like blackberries on the top of Mullagh Nesha till nightfall, and Regan's cabin, where I had intended to pass the night, was seven miles away among the mountains. My servant had been ordered to have my horse, and also a pair of steeds for the Englishmen, at the road near Castle Donovan, in case we should think proper to return to my house. About seven o'clock we resolved on returning, and on arriving at the old ruin, we found that our drunken dog of a messenger had not brought the message to my servant : the wind howled, the rain was like a water-spout with occasional volleys of hail-shot ; there was no help for it ; in we went ; our clothes were not very wet, as the storm had only just commenced ; we struck a light, and were well supplied with gewsh for firing by Bonaparte.* I undertook to cook for the party ; our game-bags were full, to say nothing of our other provender. I picked, drew, washed and dried the grouse. I'll warrant you I was not unprovided with my sporting stewpan. I placed on the bottom of it a slice of my own Drinagh bacon, half fat, half lean, (the fat like mother of pearl, so exquisitely transparent). I clapped down my grouse upon that, breast upwards, sprinkled them with flour from my dredging-box—shred half a dozen shalots ; (Baxter says three are enough, but I think six improve the flavour ; in fact it all depends upon taste) I threw in the shredded shalots along with three table-spoonsful of mushroom catsup, and half a table-spoonful of walnut catsup. I added a pinch of red pepper and some salt. I had not any port, which was a shocking oversight, because the flavour is considerably heightened by a wineglassful. Well, Sir, all this while one of the Englishers was cooking away with his own apparatus, in a style that clearly showed he was no novice, I promise you. He manufactured a brace of hares in glorious style, while my stewpan was simmering on the fire ; and the other chap was arranging his portfolio of landscapes on the floor, mincing out a song about Daniel O'Connell, to the tune of 'Patrick's day in the morning,' but the fellow's cramped English throat could not drive out the *keöl†* in the slashing, dashing, tearaway style that Bonaparte Howlaghan did, who took up the song the minute the Englishman stopped or was run dry. I was half an hour teaching him to pronounce the name of our heath-clad hill of Wheeough, but he could not come nearer to it than 'Wee-aw, wee-aw,' till Boney desired him to whistle as if he was calling in his black setting spaniel bitch : and the effort thus made afforded him more practical instruction in bringing the aspirate into operation, than my obtuser genius would ever have devised. On the whole, he made a very respectable effort to pronounce the word Wheeough—that is, for an Englishman. In the final guttural he was far, very far from perfection. Boney, who at that time had a vile unchristian habit of fighting at fairs, from which I

---

* Begwood. The splinters are substitutes for candles with the poor.

† Music.

tion h
e how fa
d the mi.
ntains off.

have since had some trouble to reclaim him, had a huge oak stick, with a knob of lead at the end, to which stick he gave the awful name of *Baus gaun Saggart.*[*] Whenever Boney was seen to display some incipient impatience, and wheel Baus gaun Saggart half a dozen times round his head, mischief was assuredly brewing. The slighter and smaller of the Englishmen, (the portfolio gentleman) struck with the formidable appearance of the weapon, inquired its name and use, with the purpose of transferring a drawing and description of it to his book, under the head of '*Irish weapons.*'

"'Pray, Mr. Awlegan,' said he to Boney, 'what is the use of your large stick, may I ask?'.

"'To thrash rapscallions wid, and smash their skulls!' roared out the giant Boney—(I should rather say the *Boney* giant)—and he spoke with the enthusiastic zest of an anticipated slaughtering match.

"'Bless me!' ejaculated the soft voice of the little Englishman, 'what a formidable purpose! Now, ow do you use this heavy stick, Mr. Awlegan? I can ardly lift it!'

"'This way,' shouted Boney, whirling the stick a dozen times round the Englishman's head with such force as to whirr through the air like a whole covey of partridge rising. The evident terror of the Englishman was excessively diverting. He crouched and cowered, and at last exclaimed,

"'I request you may not smash *my* skull, Mr. Awlegan?'

"'Niver fear,' responded Boney, flinging down the stick, 'I only thought you'd like a thrifle of instruction, my boy.'

"'Oh, thank you, Mr. Awlegan, I'm sure I'm much obliged—much obliged, indeed. What do you call the weapon, Mr. Awlegan?'

"'Is it the stick?' answered Boney; 'why I calls it Baus gaun Soggarth,' (with a most ferocious expression and attitude) 'which manes, d'ye see, death without clargy.'

"'Death without clergy!' exclaimed the Englishman, 'bless me, very characteristic—very ferocious I meant to say. May I trouble you, Mr. Awlegan, to repeat its Hirish name once more?'

"'The throuble's a pleasure,' said Boney, exceedingly gratified at the interest excited by his implement of war. 'Baus gaun Soggarth, Sir, is the name of him.'

"'Bosken sogga! bless me! Thank you, Mr. Awlegan,' and down went a drawing of the stick into the book, and the formidable name, as well as the writer was able to catch it. At this moment, we, the cooks, completed our culinary labours, the enjoyment of which suspended for a while the inquiries of the tourist and the reminiscences of the sportsman."

"Really, Mr. R——," said I, "you spent a most amusing evening in the old castle. But for a night spent among your mountain fastnesses, and beneath the shelter of a feudal ruin, methinks it passed off too quietly."

"Especially," said Mr. Thomas D——, "as your party included so ferocious a personage as Bonaparte and his *Baus gaun Soggarth.*"

"Why, indeed," said the priest, "an incident occurred which rather alarmed the literary Englishmen. While we were seated on gewsh logs at our dinner, which was spread on a table sent from Bonaparte's cabin, the report of a gun was heard outside the castle walls, and a ball, which entered at a loop-hole, whistled over our heads.

"'Heaven defend us!' exclaimed he of the portfolio, 'we shall all be murdered.'

"'Never mind it,' says I, 'it's nothing in life but a little rebellion, maybe, or some such thing. Finish your sherry, man! I'll engage that wag, Boney, fired the shot just to help your digestion; it's twice as good, a start like that, as one of Thompson's dinner pills.' As I spoke, Boney, who had gone out a few minutes before, walked into the apartment, and picking up an object which lay on the floor near the wall, exhibited a starling, which the lights and bustle had frightened from its nest

in the wall; and which Boney had shot through the loop-hole."

"'Wasn't that nate killing?' exclaimed Boney triumphantly. I just whipped off his head with the ball in two two's. There's a power of the cratures, Father John, fluttering hither and over about the ould castle; for the boys have lit splinters up stairs, and, without a doubt, the birds are bothered entirely with the lights?'

"This pacific explanation of the shot, which had terrified the poor little Englishman to such a ludicrous degree, secured in some sort to restore him to tranquillity. However he was not himself for the rest of the night.

"Now, Mr. W—— and Mr. T. D——," exclaimed our worthy host, "you are doing my vintage of 1811 less than justice," and he hospitably urged us to do honour to his excellent wine. I complied; but Mr. T. D—— appeared wrapt in such a reverie as might envelope the consciousness of Nimrod. At length Mr. R—— exclaimed, "what are you thinking of, Thomas?"

"I was thinking," replied Mr. T. D——, with enthusiasm, "how delightful it is to stand on the patch of smooth green grass before Dan Mahony's cottage at the mountain, on a clear frosty October night, after a good day's sport, with your game-bags exceedingly plethoric, and your dear faithful dogs barking and leaping in an ecstacy round you! and the cold clear moon sailing broad and round, high over the top of Mullaugh Nesha, and the rough rocky fragments which lie scattered through the heath, glancing white in the moonlight; and the short quick baying of the dogs echoing through the dark hills, which are rich with to-morrow's sport—oh, it is rapture ineffable!"

"Now, gentlemen," said Mr. R——, "I must leave you for a couple of hours for my breviary; I trust you will pass the time agreeably during my absence,' and he left the room.

"There," said Mr. T. D——, "goes one of the best natured men in Ireland. I always experience an elation of spirits at his snug retired mountain-dwelling here, which I do not feel any where else. It is a sweet spot in the months of May and June, when the bees are buzzing under those old sycamore trees in the garden hedge, and the little orchard is laden with its fragrant blossoms. I have sat there often reading, and have thought how happy might a person of moderate desires be in such a retirement."

"You are a juvenile philosopher," said I.

"No, Mr. W., I do not pretend to any philosophy, unless it be such to wish for a mountain box in the neighbourhood of first rate coursing, fishing, and shooting."

"And would you prefer such a residence to the Gothic turrets of R——?"

"Yes—for *game* I certainly would; for we have only owls and jackdaws in the battlements; and yet I should not abuse R—— neither, for there is very fair cock-shooting in the woods there, and hares enough too, and we've snipe on the inches; but *here* there's twenty times the sport."

In such bold and disjointed chat the time passed until Mr. R. returned. Something, which I do not now remember, led us to the subject of Prince Hohenlohe and his wonderful cures.

"I can't say that I believe in them," said our host, "not," added he, checking himself, "that I mean to deny that God could work a cure through the agency of you, or me, or any man; but I want proof, Sir—I want proof that he has done this, and I am not satisfied with what we have been given."

"Have you not been playing Prince Hohenlohe yourself in a small way here?" asked Mr. T. D. with a smile.

"Ah, ha!" said Mr. R. "and who has been telling you about old Molly M'Grider? Mr. W.," (addressing himself to our humble selves) "you shall have the story, since our sporting friend has thought fit to allude to it. Poor old Molly was dumb for many years, and a mad beggarman persuaded her husband that *I* could work a miracle in restoring her speech. I assured the poor people that my horse was just as able to work miracles as I was, but all would not do.

"'Your *raverence* must thry your hand at the *maracie*, as far as you can,' said old Pether.

---

[*] *Death without clergy.*

"'Take care, now, Peter,' said I, 'for if I should succeed, which is very improbable, you will, in all likelihood, be very impatient to get me to work the counter-miracle of making your wife dumb again.'

"'Ogh, no, plase your raverence,'said Peter; 'just set her once talking, and I'll be the happy man.'

"'Very well,' said I, 'I'll do my best.'

"So I cleared them all out of my kitchen except Molly, and locked the door. I then heated the poker in the fire, and when it was red hot I made a feint to run at Molly with it, exclaiming, 'talk now, you old goose, or I'll ram this poker down your throat.'

"'Oh, heaven defend me,' roared Molly; upon my word, gentlemen, she spoke, and has had her speech since : but the worst of it was. that my very unexpected success has established my miraculous fame among my parishioners, so that my sanative abilities are repeatedly referred to, in spite of all my lectures on the subject of the nerves, and the effects of fear, surprise, or any other external shock upon the nervous system."'

At this moment the trampling of a horse in the lane was heard, and presently afterwards a summons for the priest arrived ; a sick call to the cottage of a farmer two miles off amongst the mountains. Instantly Mr. R. donned his hat and cloak.

"Is it possible," I said to Mr. T. D.," sotto voce, "that he will think of going this inclement night ?"

"God forbid I should refuse," said Mr. R. earnestly ; "the poor man is extremely ill, and we would, indeed, be unfaithful shepherds of the flock, did we refuse to attend them in their need at any moment's warning. Were I dangerously ill myself—were my spirit near passing to the presence of its Creator, I should deem but poorly of the zeal of that priest who should refuse to attend my summons to administer the last comforts and consolations which the church has appointed for the dying Christian. I know this sick man well. I have always instructed him to rest his hope on Christ ; and in Him I do believe he will depart." So saying, this humble mountain priest sallied forth with a cheerful alacrity. on what must appear to many a very uninviting mission. Mr. T.D. immediately retired to rest. *We* followed his example ; nor did we awake till the morning's sun had risen high in the heavens.

J. F. W.

CONNA CASTLE, COUNTY OF CORK.

Mr. E. Heyden, del,

Clayton, sc,

From three to four miles west of Tallow stands Conna Castle, on a high limestone rock, which rises almost perpendicularly from the river Bride. The exterior of the building is tolerably perfect. It presents a square tower, about eighty feet in height. The first arched floor, called *The Earl's Room*, is accessible by a winding staircase of cut limestone, which, for neatness of execution, far exceeds any I have before seen in the ancient towers of the south. From this room may be seen, to the west, a tract of finely diversified country : immediately under is the village of Conna ; a little beyond which is seen a rising ground, called *Gallows Hill*, the spot where, we are told, Cromwell stationed his army, and held council for the execution of the defending army, and from whence he battered the castle, apparently with little effect. Over the entrance is a covered aperture in the wall, which communicates with the upper room, and is evidently for the purpose of letting fall missiles, or boiling water or lead, on an enemy attempting to force the doorway ; this conducting aperture is, with few exceptions, peculiar to the ancients' defensive towers, and similarly situated in each. In the river side of the castle is a large square opening, continued from the base to the top, such as is mentioned in the description of Lisfinny Castle in a former number of your Journal. Dr. Smith, in his History of the county of Cork, thus mentions—"A mile west of Maguly is Connough

Castle, which belonged to Thomas Fitzgerald Roe. It was demised to Sir Richard Boyie by Sir James Fullerton, anno 1603. Near it is a stone bridge over the river Bride. This castle is a high square tower, built on a steep rock, and commands an extensive prospect over the adjacent country. More west is the small parish church of Knockmourne, in repair,* the only remains of an ancient corporation, which was entirely burned down by the White Knights, with many other churches and villages, in Desmond's rebellion."

* A few tattered walls, covered with ivy, now alone remain to shew the design of its former site.

HANNAH MORE'S COTTAGE.

COWSLIP GREEN.

From " The Christian Keepsake and Missionary Annual for 1835," edited by Rev. W. Ellis.

Although scarcely coming within the legitimate scope of our notice, we deem it but just to say of this new candidate for popular favour, that it deserves every encouragement from those who would wish to see the arts and sciences become the handmaids of religion. We are informed that it is devoted to the interest of benevolence and piety, on the broad principles of sacred charity. Most of the engravings are of a very superior order, and several articles throughout the volume will be read with interest by individuals of every sect and party. The above engraving, Cowslip Green, which we copy from the vignette title page, is an untenanted cottage, in the beautiful valley of Wrington, and was, many years since, the residence of the late Mrs. Hannah More. The description which follows is from the pen of the Rev. Henry Thompson, M. A. We do think *England* might have furnished Mr. Ellis much better poetry than any we notice in the volume:

Light rests around each honour'd spot,
    Trod by the wise and good ;
The scutcheon'd hall, the ivied cot,
    The heartless solitude.

Nor in the mimic form so near,
    Nor in the breathing page,
Seem we to contemplate or hear
    The holy and the sage.

As when with reverent step we trace
    The path their lives went down ;
Ling'ring by each old storied place,
    Renowned in their renown.

Rude husbandry may lay the land
    In fertile ruin round ;
Or Eden, reared by beauty's hand,
    Bloom o'er that charmed ground.

Or desolation, blank and lone,
    There frown in sullen sway ;
Still the pure light lives quenchless on,
    Through change and o'er decay.

There the rapt soul, from earth removed,
    Communion soars to hold
With each great mind that dwelt or rov'd
    Amid these haunts of old.

Sweet dream ! but soon to melt in air ;
    Yet, did we rightly deem,
That dream might shape substantial wear,
    When life shall be a dream.'

Go, pilgrim ! and when earth's dull truth
    Falls deadening round thy track,
And memory wooes the light of youth
    To thy dark bosom back.

And, musing o'er the visioned hour,
    Spent in this sainted glade,
Fain would'st thou prove again the power
    Thy willing soul obeyed.

Ask why around this still retreat
    Such holy gleams abide,
And faith may win, like influence sweet,
    Home to thine own hearth-side.

Go, "through an atmosphere of love.'
    Gaze with a heart resign'd
On all around thee and above,
    Thy Saviour and thy kind.

Live to His glory and their weal ;
    So while friends fall away—
While heart's best lov'd and trusted feel
    Estrangement's icy sway ;

While die or part, the faithful few
    One friend shall still be near ;
One fadeless hope, to meet the true,
    Blest in His presence dear.

Thus though thy wanderings ne'er again,
    These solemn scenes explore,
Thou still shalt tread, nor tread in vain,
    The lucid steps of More.

* " She lived and walked in an atmosphere of love."—Mr. Harford's Obituary Sketch.

Nor shall dim fancy's dreams alone
That holy presence bring;
When meet earth's myriads round the throne
Of heaven's descending King.

Where shine the spirits of the just,
From imperfection free.[*]
There hope, with no delusive trust,
With that lov'd saint to be.

CAPTAIN DEMPSEY, THE HERMIT OF DUBLIN.

Who that was resident in Dublin between the last forty and fifty years but remembers Captain Dempsey?—a tall, sinewy man, with high cheek bones, sunkon eyes, and self-resigned aspect, and over whose chin no razor had passed for years. His beard was of a brownish hue and very bushy. He wore in general a long plaid mantle tied at the neck, and hanging loosely over his shoulders—a broad hat, with a singularly round crown; two patches of leather sewed on his knees, and large silver buckles in his shoes. His finger was adorned with several rings—not for their lustre, it was evident, but in remembrance of some dear friends; for at times he would be seen to make a sudden stand in the streets, look on them with a wild stare, then, as if collecting his scattered senses together, let the day be never so wet, drop on his knees, offer up on each ring a prayer in silence, then precipitately rise and proceed on his journey, although through a crowd of gapers and shouts of idle boys. Patrick-street was his favourite haunt, and he seemed to have a particular taste for herrings, as he was seldom ever observed to return home without a few of them under his cloak.

His habitation was a wooden hut, in one corner of a piece of waste ground, at the lower end of Townsend-street, near the old depot. The door was at the top, to which he ascended by blocks of wood nailed at the outside at regular distances. The door or window, we may call it either, overlooked the sea: there would he sit for hours together in seeming pensiveness. When his mind would be tranquil, which was often the case, he was very conversant, and so condescending to the enquiry of the curious, that he would seem gratified in satisfying the inquisitive demands of the meanest boy. But if any of his fits of insanity should visit him, he would clap the door in the face of the person to whom he was speaking, and retire to a place he had under ground, in which was a little altar, and two tin lamps constantly burning. Sometimes his door would be shut for several days, until the fit worked off him, for which the neighbours charitably watched, and as soon as he again appeared and resumed his accustomed station, would bring him such refreshments as his weak frame required. The chief point requisite in the visitor appeared to be to keep his mind and eyes from his rings; for if he once dwelt on them all discourse was over, and ten chances to one but the door of his little habitation would be so quickly dashed in the face of the visitor, as to strike him violently in the face.

I had the curiosity to ascend his Crusoe-built hut one day. I found him in one of his best humours; and to introduce myself the better, I presented him with a few red herrings and some white biscuits, which he thankfully received, viewing and smelling the former with seeming gratification. After a little roundabout discourse, I collected from him the following short sketch of his life and cause of retirement. No doubt I got it in piecemeals, through his wanderings, but I have endeavoured to link it together with as much care and probability as I could.

He mentioned that his father bound him an apprentice to his uncle, who was master and owner of seven good trading ships. His first trip was to the West Indies, where he remained for two years, trading from one island to the other. On his return he was caressed by many friends—at one merchant's house in particular. "Oh!" he said, with a heavy sigh, "I saw an angel, as it were, rising out of the sea—so lovely, so endearing, so complaisant:

[*] "The spirits of just men made perfect."—Heb. xii. 23.

I saw her eyes—I still see them following my steps over the sea-green carpet. Three weeks only did I enjoy this heaven-sent bliss. I went on another trip. My uncle took ill of the yellow fever at Jamaica, and died. He bequeathed all he possessed to me when of age, as I was then only eighteen. The mate of the vessel was his executor, under whose care he placed me. We sailed home. I no sooner stood on terra firma, than I would make to where the needle of my soul directed; but whatever lesson the mate received from my dying uncle, or whatever the mate put into his mind, I could never learn, but I would not be let go unless he was present with me. I cared not—he came—I saw my leading star—she received me with inexpressible joy. Her father hinted his intention of going to settle in Scotland, and that he would put the adorable Lydia (for that was her name) under my protection, and leave her with her aunt until himself should follow. My heart sprang, and my pulse beat high at the honour, nay the blessing, he was going to confer. I mildly bowed, and said she should be taken care of. Next day she went on board with two female servants. We made our destined port too soon. I often wished for contrary winds to drive us half seas over. On landing, Gretna was our object. Our plot was discovered by the mate. He ordered me to my cabin, and said I should not quit the vessel without his permission. I stamped—I thought I had sufficient authority to set him adrift—I was mistaken. 'You shall see who'll be master,' he said, as he took my angel by the hand, and led her off. How did I subdue my rage?

"He then wrote to her father, exulting in himself how he had discovered the plot. But I had my satisfaction so far. Instead of her father thanking him, he replied, that his child knew well how to conduct herself, and was sorry he had taken such trouble. In fact, her father would be well satisfied had such taken place, as I was under age, and could not get his consent. I saw my love again. We exchanged gifts, the emblem of never-ending affection. We weighed anchor—made our destination. I there received letters stating that one of my best ships had been wrecked off Wales. I felt not the loss, as I enjoyed only the name of owner. On my return home, to darken the gloomy tale as black as pitch. I was informed that my beloved Lydia had taken shipping in her in order to meet me at my landing, and went down with the whole crew.

"I wept—I cursed every ship I had—I cursed the waves as I saw them break against the beach. I hurried away in another vessel of my own that had just cleared out of port, and bound for Bologne.

"The mate, as soon as he found me gone, drew large sums of money in my name, then taking in a general cargo, set sail for Gibraltar, where he sold ship and all. However, he had some slight spark of humanity left, for he deposited a small box, containing my uncle's will, and other papers of value in a merchant's hands. I was now come of age—I had five ships left, and a considerable sum of money due to me. I strove to shake off the melancholy that depressed my spirit too long. Proposals were made me by a wealthy merchant in Glasgow with his daughter. The young lady, no doubt, was one that might gain the affections of any man—But, oh, Lydia——I was to be married, when hearing of my mother's illness, without hope of her recovery, I hastened to visit her in her last moments, and commit her dear remains to the earth. I returned to my intended bride; but again my cup of sorrow was brimming over—she had been poisoned by some base wretch, who long expected her hand. She was in her last pangs. 'Twas only now I felt love for her strike me with the same power it did for Lydia. When she raised her languid eyes, and stretched forth her arms, as fair as alabaster, to receive and bid me a last, a long farewell. O —— her sunken eyes, as they stared, can I ever forget the tender look. . . . . . .

"In about a month after her decease, I resolved on quitting the land of all my woes for ever. So regulating my affairs, and appointing a steady agent, I set sail for America. We had a favourable wind for several days, till on the night of the 2d of September, 1776, we were wrecked on the coast of Newfoundland. Every soul on board perished, save myself and a cabin boy. When drifted to shore almost exhausted to death, and unable to crawl from the spot we gained, the boy observed a light in the window of a small house at no great distance. I despatched him with news of our sad disaster. Two men servants came to my assistance. I was brought to the house, and every refreshment given. I was now poor, aye, very poor indeed. Next morning I wrote to a merchant living about twenty miles distant for a supply of money. He attended to my demand.

"All this time I saw not the owner of the house, but was attended by a servant. So thinking it some house of public entertainment, I called for my bill.

"'What, Sir!' said the servant, 'would you offend the lady of the house?'

"'From the debt I owe,' I replied, 'no money, 'tis true, would acquit me; but may I be allowed to see her, that I may return thanks for her kindness.'

"'You can, Sir, this afternoon,' said the servant, 'and she expresses much desire to see you, but not until evening;' so bowing he left me.

"I viewed my sea-beat trim, and felt that I was not fit to appear in a lady's presence. The servant I despatched for a cloth broker, and had myself new rigged in less than two hours.

"The appointed hour arrived. I was ushered by a female servant to a well-fitted apartment, and showed to a seat. In a few minutes a lady entered, dressed in black, and thickly veiled. I rose to salute her—she returned it in silence. She then made several attempts to speak, but her breathing seemed short and stiffled. The boldness of a tar came on me.

"'Madam, your veil so drowns your voice, that I cannot catch a word you say. Excuse me, Madam;' so stretching my hand I suddenly raised her veil, and as suddenly let it fall again. Lydia stood before me. I sprang to embrace her. She spurned at my ecstacy, and threw me back with her hand.

"'Stand back, Robert!' she exclaimed; 'touch not polluted lips,' and she burst into tears.

"Strange amazement seized my soul—I stood motionless—I dare not approach her. At last, recovering from the first shock, I cried out, 'Tell me, tell me quickly. Lydia, the cause of this strange action. You that I thought for ever lost, and now'—

"'So I was, and so I am,' she replied, 'lost! lost! lost!'

"After a mutual silence, she turned her eyes, those eyes so full of tenderness, towards me, and spake thus:—

"'Of course you felt the loss of your ship, and know every circumstance attending it. After it went down, myself and another female got into a small boat. We tossed about from wave to wave until near daylight, when we were picked up by a vessel outward bound. The storm continued, and she was obliged to pursue her voyage. We still expected, day after day, to meet a vessel bound homeward. We did at last—one bound for France. Into her myself and servant entered. I was treated for about five days with all marks of politeness and respect. At last he proved a monster, and I fell a victim to his brutal lust. My maid suffered the same fate by the sailors; but rather than live under this hopeless affliction, this redeemless dishonour, she flung herself overboard and perished. But I, the object of divine vengeance, still live. I am here in the brute's dwelling, which to me is a wolf's den: and now the fiery rays of revenge quicken hotter in my breast. The only buoy that sustained my soul, and preserved me from sinking in the unfathomable depths of despair, was, that ever since the wretch placed me here, he offered me no more violence; but 'tis fear, not honour, urges him to do so; and if possible, to hide the crime and save his neck. I seldom see him; and though he has placed a watch over me, he might save himself the trouble—I do not want to escape. I am happy in my mind, that all the world imagines I lie at the bottom of the deep —let them think so still.'

"I could subdue my fury no longer. My blood boiled—my sinews began to brace, that I thought they'd crack.

"'Where is the brute now?' Where will I find him, that I may gnaw his entrails like a shark?'

"'Peace, hasty man,' replied my soul-torn Lydia, wiping the tears away from her eyes, 'suppress your rage a moment; let the revenger learn patience from the injured.' This checked my rage. I sought an embrace. I was again denied. I implored her on my knees to quit her savage prison. She glided out of the room in the twinkling of an eye.

"In a few minutes I received a note from her, telling me that as I held dear the remembrance of what she once was, not to leave the house until her design would be accomplished; and that very evening, at the same hour, I might come into her presence.

"I now turned into my own room. Who could pourtray my tortured mind. I paced the floor the live long night, laying down plans of revenge, but on whom I knew not.

"Morning broke at last. I despatched my boy with a letter to my friend, from whom I had received the money, requesting him to direct the first vessel homeward bound to touch at the point and take me in, but on no account to let my name be known."

Here he suddenly cast down his eyes. I thought that he was about to end his narrative, but he as suddenly raised them again.

"Ay; my correspondent obeyed my wish. Three days after I saw a vessel nearing the shore. I saw the jolly-boat rowing to shore. Lydia saw it too. I heard her scream—I still hear her scream. I ran to her apartment. I raised her head. I gave her the first—a senseless kiss. She opened her rolling eyes, and again screamed horribly.

"'He comes. The wretch—the brute now comes. Fly, Robert, and leave me.'

"'I will, Lydia,' I cried with mad joy. So snatching a hanger that caught mine eye, I rushed forward—met the wretch—the very master of the vessel sent for me—the despoiler of all I loved on earth. He fell on his own threshold. As I stood over him with fiend-like grin, I started again. Fresh joy burst on my remaining sense, when I beheld no other than my perfidious mate—the robber of my youth—my poor uncle's trustee. Hau! hau! haw!"

After an immoderate fit of laughter he began again.

"I rushed into Lydia; but scarce had time to meet her when the crew of the jolly-boat was at my heels. I stood for some time in my own defence, until one of them who had known me interfered. However I was taken to prison. Lydia came forward with a sailor, who proved to the brutal treatment she received, and I got other evidence of his robbery. I was acquitted. Lydia! Lydia! Lydia!" he exclaimed with all the workings of despair, and was again going to break off, when, fortunately, a ship under full sail met his rolling eye, and forced the nautical man to pour out—

"Just such another," said he, pointing to her, was my Mermaid; see how she stems the tide."

"And was that the name of the ship," said I, in order to come round again to the subject, "that you first lost."

"No," he said, "but the one I first sailed in with my uncle; the one that carried all the treasure I adored on earth—my Lydia."

"And after you were acquitted, captain, did you leave Lydia behind!"

"Leave Lydia behind! No, foolish youth," he said, gathering his mouth to a sarcastic grin. I seized my hard sought prize. I offered her my hand, with full assurance that the misfortune would but make her more dear to me. But no; her soul could not be polluted, although in a frail earthly frame; she was still as pure as the morning dew.

"'Nay, Robert,' she replied to all my entreaties, 'never shall you be pointed at. While you now sympathise, and the first impulse of your love rekindled, all is well; but as soon as the matrimonial chain would attain its full weight, perhaps—and for me to escape this trial—a trial worst of all. I shall ever love, but never give my—I have no hand to give. Oh, Robert Dempsy! if you bear the shadow of your former love, hide me, and provide for me in some lone retreat, where the insulting eye of the human race can never see me.'

"As she ended I looked on her with tender surprise. Methought every feature shed the lustre of an angel.

" "Yes, yes,' I cried, and grasped her struggling in my arms; you shall possess your wish while blood flows in those veins. I shall be your protector—your lover—and no more: and yet I will live in hopes of other joys when your mind becomes more tranquil. Speak, Lydia, speak; say where you chuse for your retirement.'

"She did, with tears of gratitude bursting from her soft dark eye. A vessel bound for Ireland received us both. Yonder, yonder was her chosen spot, he said, as he pointed with his finger to Clontarf. There she lived for thirteen short years. There she died, and was buried by the sea shore—the lamented stranger. For thirteen years she was the beacon of my soul. With brother's love alone I came and went. From east to west nothing was too precious or dear for her. Aye—thirteen years I implored—I adored her. At last she left the world and me a wanderer. She was interred before I could once more gaze upon her. I looked for all the gifts I bestowed, thinking she preserved them. So she did—but 'twas in heaven. Every rarity I gave her was turned to money. The poor wanted it. She did not. I heard it all. I learned enough. No directing star to guide my vessel of mortality, the binical of my reason was overturned. The squall of grief was too sudden and severe. My agents made away with my property. French privateers took more. The sea swallowed up the rest. But ah!" he said with an air of triumph, "they could not devour all without myself—my Lydia's first gift. I hold it more dear than ship's treasure, or even myself. There it is.' So saying he cast his eye on his hand, while he placed his finger on the upper ring—then in succession—"my Lydia—my mother—my intended bride, Mary—and"—he made a pause. I immediately dropped from my hold. The door was shut. I saw or heard no more.

In about a month after the interview I called to see him. I saw him, but did not find him so conversant. However I picked out as much matter as he did not before explain. His whole soul seemed absorbed in the contemplation of the one object—his early love, who he seemed to look upon as an angel of light.

He lived about two years after this, and died in 1802. His death was unknown for a whole week. 'Twas thought he was in one of his frantic fits. When his hut was opened, he was found in his place of prayer under ground.

Thus ended Captain Robert Dempsy, born at Cork, 1742. It seems many documents were found in his hut, but whether destroyed or preserved I cannot say, but hope, one day or other, the possessor will give them to the public.   T. E.

THE VEGETABLE WORLD.

In all places where vegetation has been established the germs are so intermingled with the soil, that whenever the earth is turned up, even from considerable depths, and exposed to the air, plants are soon observed to spring as if they had been recently sown, in consequence of the germination of seeds which had remained latent and inactive during the lapse of perhaps many centuries. Islands formed by coral reefs, which have risen above the level of the sea, become, in a short time, covered with verdure. From the materials of the most sterile rock, and even from the yet recent cinders and lava of the volcano, nature prepares the way for vegetable existence. The slightest crevice or inequality is sufficient to arrest the invisible germs that are always floating in the air, and affords the means of sustenance to diminutive races of lichens and mosses. These soon overspread the surface, and are followed, in the course of a few years, by successive tribes of plants of gradually increasing size and strength; till at length the island, or other favoured spot, is converted into a natural and luxuriant garden, of which the productions, rising from the grasses to shrubs and trees, present all the varieties of the fertile meadow, the tangled thicket, and the widely spreading forest. Even in the desert plains of the torrid zone, the eye of the traveller is often refreshed by the appearance of a few hardy plants, which find sufficient materials for their growth in these arid regions; and in the realms of perpetual snow which surround the poles, the navigator is occasionally startled at the prospect of fields of a scarlet hue, the result of a wide expanse of microscopic vegetation.—*Roget's Bridgewater Treatise.*

CURIOUS FISH POND.

At Port Nessock, in Wigtonshire, a large salt water pond has been formed for cod. It is a bason of thirty feet in depth and 160 feet in circumference, hewn out from the solid rock, and communicating with the sea by one of those fissures which are common to bold and precipitous coasts. Attached to it is a neat Gothic cottage for the accommodation of the fishermen, and the rock is surmounted all round by a substantial stone wall three hundred feet in circumference. From the inner or back door of the lodge a winding stairway conducts to the usual halting place—a large flat stone, projecting into the water, and commanding a view of every part of the aquatic prison. When the tide is out the stone is left completely dry, and here a stranger perceives with surprise a hundred mouths simultaneously opened to greet his arrival. The moment the fisherman crosses his threshold the pond is agitated by the action of some hundred fins, and otherwise thrown into a state of anarchy and confusion. Darting from this, that, and the other corner, the whole population move as it were to a common centre, elevate their snouts, lash their tails, and jostle one another with such violence that on a first view they actually seem to be menacing an attack on the poor fisherman in place of the creel-full of limpets he carries. Many of the fish are so tame, that they will feed greedily from the hand; while others again are so shy that the fisherman frequently discourses of their different tempers as a thing quite as palpable as the fins they move by. One gigantic cod, which answers to the name of "Tom," is considered as the patriarch of the pond, and forcibly arrests attention. This unfortunate (who passed his youth in the open sea) was the first prisoner in Port Nessock Pond; and within the last six months of his sojourn he has gradually increased in bulk and weight. He is now wholly blind, from age or disease, and has no chance whatever in the general scramble. The fisherman, however, is very kind to him, and it is affecting as well as curious to see the huge animal raise himself in the water, and then, resting his head on the flat stone, allow itself to be gently patted or stroked, gaping all the while to implore that food which he has no other means of obtaining. Cod is the prevailing species in this pond; there are also haddocks, flounders, and various other kinds.

COMMON HONEY BEE.

At a late meeting of the Verulam Philosophical Society, Kenton Moore, Esq., vice-president, in the chair, the secretary (C. Dewhurst, Esq.,) read some interesting observations on the natural history and management of the apis mellifica, or common honey bee, wherein he detailed a plan of securing the honey without depriving the bees of life, and which is now generally adopted in the county of Suffolk, and originated with his father, the Rev. C. Dewhurst, at Bury St. Edmund's. It is as follows: The hive which is employed by this gentleman is similar to the common one, but with an opening in the roof, of about four inches diameter, with a moveable top, and which is pegged down during the period the bees are filling the hive. As soon as the hive is full, Mr. Dewhurst then carefully removes the top, (while the bees are absent) and then places a wooden box of about eight inches square in its place, and into which the bees work; when this box is full of honey, it is removed, and another substituted, and by repeating this process, great quantities of honey may be yearly obtained, without the least loss or injury to the community.

DUBLIN:
Printed and Published by P. D. Hardy, 3, Cecilia-street; to whom all communications are to be addressed.
Sold by all Booksellers in Ireland.
In London, by Richard Groombridge, 6, Panyer-alley, Paternoster-row; in Liverpool, by Wilmer and Smith; in Manchester, by Ambery; in Birmingham, by Guest; in Glasgow, by John Macleod; and in Edinburgh, by N. Bowack.

THE

DUBLIN PENNY JOURNAL

CONDUCTED BY P. DIXON HARDY, M.R.I.A.

Vol. III.   FEBRUARY 28, 1835.   No. 139.

WEST END OF ST. PATRICK'S CATHEDRAL, DUBLIN, (partially rebuilt).

ST. PATRICK'S CATHEDRAL, DUBLIN.

The foregoing view of the west end of the Cathedral Church of Saint Patrick, Dublin, exhibits the best piece of Gothic architecture in the kingdom. The stones are from the Tullamore quarry, and are of the most durable description; and the workmanship has been executed by the Firm of Henry, Mullens, and M·Mahon, which, in addition to the north transept recently rebuilt by them, it is but justice to say does great credit to the Firm, who, we are informed, have manifested more zeal for renovating the Cathedral agreeably to its original style of architecture than to any pecuniary profits to themselves. The restoration of this ancient door and window will remain a lasting testimonial to future ages of their taste and abilities as builders as well as a specimen of Irish architecture. The great window has been erected at the sole expense of the Very Rev. Henry Richard Dawson, the present dean of the Cathedral, for which he pays six hundred pounds. The door and other repairs, by the Dean and Chapter, to be paid for by instalments out of the Economy Fund, as circumstances will permit. The great western door now stands six feet under the level of the small modern one that has been removed. You now enter by an easy flight of steps, descending from the street in front of the Church, which has been sunk to the original level of the door when the Cathedral was first built, the street in front having been raised from time to time upwards of six feet, to prevent the frequent inundation of the Poddle river, which runs in front of the church; but those inundations have of late years been enirely prevented, by removing mills and other obstructions, and frequently cleaning the bed of the river. It is hoped that the munificent example of the Dean will be followed by the Archbishop of Dublin and the dignitaries and prebendaries of the Cathedral, together with the Knights of St. Patrick, by putting in a new window each, at their own expense, thereby restoring to its pristine grandeur this venerable pile, which has nearly stood the lapse of seven hundred years, having been built by John Comyn, the first English Archbishop of Dublin, shortly after the conquest, when King John was lord of Ireland, in 1190. Since that period the Cathedral has suffered in common with other public buildings in Ireland during the civil wars. It was suppressed, and its revenues seized on by Henry the Eighth. During the reign of Edward the Sixth, the Cathedral was appropriated to the Courts of Law, and the Manses of the Canons to the officers of those courts, but was again restored by Philip and Mary in as full and ample a manner as it had been enjoyed at any time before its dissolution, during the civil wars between the parliament and King Charles the first, when Cromwell was in Dublin, he made the Cathedral a stable for his horses, and it has caused much surprise how so many of the monuments escaped the destruction of his fanatic soldiers. After the restoration it was again converted to the pious purposes of its original founders; and a new charter, with additional grants of land made by King Charles to the Vicar Choral. The interior of the Cathedral, during the last twenty years, has been much improved and large sums of money expended on the organ, which is reckoned the best in the kingdom. Much still remain to be done towards restoring this ancient structure, the funds of which are so small, the Dean and Chapter have had to borrow money on interest for the purpose of executing these late necessary repairs.

"A FOREST ON FIRE."

From the vicissitude of season which takes place in the temperate clime we inhabit, the inhabitants can form but a very faint idea of many of the miseries experienced by settlers in less favoured lands. Among others the frequent fires which take place in the forests, and which, sweeping like a flash of lightning, or with the effect of a tornado, devastate the entire country for miles around. The following awful description of one of these "forest fires" we copy from that justly celebrated work relative to the Birds of the united states of America, from which our readers will remember we some weeks since quoted the interesting account of the "Habits of the Turkey." M. Audubon relates it as from the mouth of an individual who witnessed it, and thus described its effects:

"About twenty-five years ago, the larch or hackmitack trees were nearly all killed by insects. This took place in what hereabouts is called the 'black soft growth' land, that is, the spruce, pine, and all other firs. The destruction of the trees was effected by the insects cutting the leaves, and you must know that, although other trees are not killed by the loss of their leaves, the evergreens always are. Some few years after this destruction of the larch, the same insects attacked the spruces, pines, and other firs, in such a manner, that before half a dozen years were over, they began to fall, and tumbling in all directions, they covered the whole country with matted masses. You may suppose that, when partially dry or seasoned, they would prove capital fuel, as well as supplies for the devouring flames which accidentally, or perhaps by intention, afterwards raged over the country, and continued burning at intervals for years, in many places stopping all communication by the roads, the resinous nature of the firs being of course best fitted to ensure and keep up the burning of the deep beds of dry leaves of the other trees.

*　　*　　*　　*　　*

"'I dare say that what I have told you brings sad recollections to the minds of my wife and eldest daughter, who, with myself, had to fly from our home, at the time of the great fires. I 'felt so interested in his relation of the the causes of the burnings, that I asked him to describe to me the particulars of his misfortunes at the time.

*　　*　　*　　*　　*

"'It is a difficult thing, Sir, to describe, but I will do my best to make your time pass pleasantly. We were sound asleep one night, in a cabin about a hundred miles from this, when about two hours before day, the snorting of the horses and lowing of the cattle which I had ranging in the woods suddenly awakened us. I took yon rifle, and went to the door to see what beast had caused the hubbub, when I was struck by the glare of light reflected on all the trees before me, as far as I could see through the woods. My horses were leaping about, snorting loudly, and the cattle ran among them with their tails raised straight over their backs. On going to the back o the house, I plainly heard the crackling made by the burning brushwood, and saw the flames coming towards us in a far extended line. I ran to the house, told my wife to dress herself and the child as quickly as possible, and take the little money we had, while I managed to to catch and saddle the two best horses. All this was done in a very short time, for I guessed that every moment was precious to us.

"'We then mounted, and made off from the fire. My wife, who is an excellent rider, stuck close to me; my daughter, who was then a small child, I took in one arm. When making off, as I said, I looked back and saw that the frightful blaze was close upon us, and had already laid hold of the house. By good luck, there was a horn attached to my hunting clothes, and I blew it, to bring after us, if possible, the remainder of my live stock, as well as the dogs. The cattle followed for a while; but, before an hour had elapsed, they all ran as if mad through the woods, and that, Sir, was the last of them. My dogs, too, although at all other times extremely tractable, ran after the deer that in bodies sprung before us, as if fully aware of the death that was so rapidly approaching.

"'We heard blasts from the horns of our neighbours, as we proceeded, and knew that they were in the same predicament. Intent on striving to the utmost to preserve our lives, I thought of a large lake, some miles off, which might possibly check the flames; and urging my wife to whip up her horse, we set off at full speed, making the best way we could over the fallen trees and the brush heaps, which lay like so many articles placed on purpose to keep up the terrific fires that advanced with a broad front upon us.

"'By this time we could feel the heat; and we were afraid that our horses would drop every instant. A singular kind of breeze was passing over our heads, and the glare of the atmosphere shone over the day light. I was sensible of a slight faintness, and my wife looked pale. The heat had produced such a flush in the child's face, that when she turned towards either of us, our grief and perplexity were greatly increased. Ten miles, you know, are soon gone over, on swift horses; but, notwithstanding this, when we reached the borders of the lake, covered with sweat and quite exhausted, our hearts failed us. The heat of the smoke was insufferable, and sheets of blazing fire flew over us in a manner beyond belief. We reached the shores, however, coasted the lake for a while, and got round to the lee side. There we gave up our horses, which we never saw again. Down among the rushes we plunged by the edge of the water, and laid ourselves flat, to wait the chance of escaping from being burnt or devoured. The water refreshed us, and we enjoyed the coolness.

"'On went the fire, rushing and crashing through the woods. Such a sight may we never see! The heavens themselves, I thought, were frightened, for all above us was a red glare, mixed with clouds of smoke, rolling and sweeping away. Our bodies were cool enough, but our heads were scorching, and the child, who now seemed to understand the matter, cried so as nearly to break our hearts.

"'The day passed on, and we became hungry. Many wild beasts came plunging into the water beside us, and others swam across to our side and stood still. Although faint and weary, I managed to shoot a porcupine, and we all tasted its flesh. The night passed I cannot tell you how. Smouldering fires covered the ground, and the trees stood like pillars of fire, or fell across each other. The stifling and sickening smoke still rushed over us, and the burnt cinders and ashes fell thick about us. How we got through that night I really cannot tell, for about some of it I remember nothing. * * *

"'Towards morning, although the heat did not abate, the smoke became less, and blasts of fresh air sometimes made their way to us. When morning came, all was calm, but a dismal smoke still filled the air, and the smell seemed worse than ever. We were now cooled enough, and shivered as if in an ague fit; we removed from the water, and went up to a burning log, where we warmed ourselves. What was to become of us I did not know. My wife hugged the child to her breast, and wept bitterly; but God had preserved us through the worst of the danger, and the flames had gone past, so I thought it would be both ungrateful to Him and unmanly to despair now. Hunger once more pressed upon us, but this was easily remedied. Several deer were still standing in the water, up to the head, and I shot one of them. Some of its flesh was soon roasted; and, after eating it, we felt wonderfully strengthened.

"By this time the blaze of the fire was beyond our sight, although the ground was still burning in many places, and it was dangerous to go among the burnt trees. After resting awhile, and trimming ourselves, we prepared to commence our march. Taking up the child, I led the way over the hot ground and rocks; and, after two weary days and nights, during which we shifted in the best manner we could, we at last reached the 'hard woods,' which had been free of the fire. Soon after we came to a house, where we were kindly treated for a while. Since then, Sir, I have worked hard and constantly as a lumberer; but thanks be to God, here we are safe, sound, and happy.'"

EMMA.

E 'en as the ray that decks the lucid tear,
　Which, in the summer's morn, bedews each tree;
M y little girl—as sweet, as mild, as dear—
　The smiles of *innocence* we owe to thee:
M ay they adorn thee when thy childhood's past—
　T hy loving parents pride and hope, to see,
A nd that those smiles we gaze on then may last,
　Are all, sweet little one, we wish for thee.

TAMBOURGI.

THE TWO MARRIAGES.

He had wooed her in the spring time, when both of them were young,
With love's first passion in his heart, its ardour on his tongue;
He had won her, they were wedded, when the beautiful and bright,
In summer morning's sunshine, were bursting into light;
When music waked around them, and spoke in every tone,
He clasp'd her to his bosom—his beautiful, his own!

The crimson rose was blushing through her sparkling gems of dew,
And the treasures of her odour came on every air that blew;
The deep deep azure o'er them as stainless was and bright
As their own young spirits, kindling in love's ecstatic light;
And thus, ere sorrow shadow'd o'er their sunny morn of life,
And when every pulse was glowing, he had ta'en her for his wife.

Oh the summer waves of pleasure how rapidly they glide,
While it seems the fullest flowing, 'tis the swiftest ebbing tide;
For rapture was not meant for earth, and joy it may not last—
One tranced moment round the soul their glory they may cast;
Yet, oh, 'tis but a moment, in a world so false and vain,
Where the links the soonest riven are the brightest in the chain.

*　　*　　*　　*　　*　　*　　*　　*

The funeral knell hath sounded, and the shroud is round her cast;
He hath looked upon that heavenly face, the last time, aye, the last.
Oh for the sickening anguish that comes when all is o'er,
When the sunlight that had blessed and warmed is gone for evermore.

His heart and home are desolate; his path is now alone
Mid scenes where memory broodeth o'er her sad and silent throne:
And, oh, though sweet the odours that come back from vanished years,
The loveliest, they are but distilled from withered flowers by tears:
His soul within him drooping, he sought the crowded hall,
And wandered, like a spectre, through the garish midnight ball;
Bright glances flashed around him, and lovely forms were there,
Whose fairy footstep's falling, seem'd as noiseless as the air;
But he turned them from their smiling, for his heart could not reply
To mirth, it could but echo back the lone and stifled sigh.

He stood within the casement—the moon was dim and cold,
As slowly through the murky clouds in solitude she rolled;
When softly o'er his saddened ear a voice of music stole,
And breathed along each sorrowing chord within the mourner's soul.
He turned, and, lo, a gentle form, with brow and cheek so pale,
They reflected back untinted the snowy moonlight's veil;
Her moistened eyes are gleaming with a soft and tender ray,
While she seeks to win his spirit from its heavy thoughts away.
Oh! the heart of man is changeful, he hath turned him to the maid;
And the power of beauty's magic o'er his soul again hath played,
Again he bends him at her shrine, again he breathes the vow;
But oh, how coldly spoken, how uneloquently now.

He hath wooed her, they were wedded, when the year was near its close,
And the last pale leaf was scattered of the autumn's lingering rose;
When the fitful breeze came sighing, and the forest leaves were sere,
And nature seemed as mourning o'er the beauteous summer's bier.
He kneels before the altar—hath his heart responded true?
Doth memory call no vision up to haunt the bridegroom's view?
The vows that *he* had spoken, can he plight them there once more
With all the truth and ardour that he plighted them before?

Oh, no, that may not, cannot be; such thought is idle, vain,
To that which *first* inspired his voice—*this love* is but a name.
'Tis true *her* young heart's fondness was devoted all to him,
But the altar where that heart was laid its fire was wasted, dim.
He might bid her at the board and hearth the vacant place to fill,
But a lingering longing in the *heart* will speak it vacant still:
Though her voice be sweetly tuneful, it will vibrate on a string
That ever echoes mournfully, " 'twas thus she used to sing,"
'Twas thus the first enchantment round my youthful heart was thrown,
And, aye, that charm remaineth first, clearest, best, alone,

Oh, yes, the love that's lighted in the morning of our years,
Ere the bosom hath been tainted by the world's cares and fears;
When the gush of youthful feeling is as pure as it is warm
From the soul's deep sunlit fountains, ere they're ruffled by a
storm,
Though dimmed be all its lustre, it will linger to the last,
As the summer warmth pervades the night, though the sun-
beams be past.   M. M'D———TT.

A FORTUNATE ESCAPE.

In 1751, the following affair happened at Bedlam. Several patients, who were suffered to walk about the
house, being in the kitchen one morning when the doctor
was there, complained to him of the badness of their
broth; and said that they were determined not to suffer it
any longer, for, as the cook was absent, they would rectify
it themselves; and immediately seized him, and were
going to put him into the boiling copper. The doctor
told them, with great presence of mind, that his clothes
would spoil the broth, and desired leave to strip; which
was granted, and he was accordingly reduced to his
breeches and shirt, when some person knocked at the
door, which the madmen had fastened. The doctor called
out, that no one could be admitted, as he was undressing
to get into the copper to be made broth of. The person
outside immediately comprehended the doctor's situation,
and roared out—fire, fire; at which the patients were so
terrified that they opened the door, and ran up stairs, by
which means the doctor escaped.

GREAT WINDOW, ST. PATRICK'S CATHEDRAL.

(For description see preceding page.)

MAGLASS CHURCH, COUNTY OF WEXFORD.

About six miles south of the town of Wexford, stands
the very interesting ruin of the church of Maglass, commonly called the abbey, situated in the barony of Forth;
it was divided into a nave and chancel by a large Saxon
arch, which has fallen during the last year; in the eastern
gable there are two arches for the bells; and where the
altar formerly stood is a large circular niche, evidently
intended for the figure of a saint or a crucifix; it is the
only one of the kind I have met with in this county. The
church appears to have been erected towards the end of
the thirteenth or beginning of the fourteenth century. It
stands on the summit of one of the old Danish mounds,
on the side of the road leading from Wexford to the village of Kilmore. In this churchyard is interred the headless remains of the unfortunate Bagnal Harvey, who was
executed on the bridge of Wexford in the year 1798.

It is a rectory and vicarage divided, but without any
church at present in the parish.

A singular instance of local attachment was for many
years witnessed by the villagers resident near the church;
an old goat took up his abode on the platform under the
belfrey, of which neither the severity of the weather or
the annoyance of the village urchin, could make him give
up the possession, until death at length brought the reverend tenant to the same abode as the proud abbot who
paced through the venerable arches of this once beautiful
building.

The ruin stands on the estate of John Grogan Morgan,
Esq., one of those resident landlords who make this county
the most improved in Ireland.   C. H. W.

DOORWAY OF MAGLASS CHURCH.

THE "RULING PASSION."

Some years ago, in the flag-ship at Bermuda, a seaman was employed in painting some part of that vessel; the paint, which was white-lead, had been mixed with a proportion of rum, as a substitute for spirits of turpentine, as a drying liquid: at the close of the day, when the work had been finished, the man who had performed it, could not resist the temptation of draining the remaining liquid from the pot, and although he must have been sensible of its deleterious quality, as being impregnated with poisonous matter, he drank it off, and very shortly after paid the forfeit of his life for the rash act. On inspection it was found that the stomach had not been affected, but that the brain was in a high state of inflammation. In further illustration of this point, we may here mention a ludicro-serious anecdote that came within our own knowledge. A foremast man on board his Majesty's ship ——, in all requisite qualities a valuable seaman, while lying on his back in his hammock, almost in the last stage of existence from a disease produced by habitual drunkenness, was informed by the surgeon, that unless he refrained from drinking he would certainly die within a month. On the day following the surgeon was going on shore, and as he passed the patient's hammock, the latter thus addressed him : " I say, doctor, as you are going ashore, you may as well order my coffin, for I can't give up the grog."—*United Service Journal.*

RECOLLECTIONS—SCENES IN CLARE.
(Continued from our 135th Number.)

Having our rods and tackling all complete, we started for the river, which we found in capital order ; the water being of that fine beer-coloured tinge, on the clearing of a flood, which generally insures a good reception of our flies among the finny tribe. We fished from about two miles above Cri-bridge down to the sand hills of Mountrivers ; and what a glorious day we had of it ; such tumbling of trout, and the occasional rolling of a weighty fish, as the sharp whirrh-rrh-rrh of our wheels, and the swift cutting through the water of the line, as the rod bent steadily to the strain, made us sure of a good one. What delight there is in gaffing a fine *peal*,* as he shows his broad silvery side, exhausted by the skilful turnings to his opposing movements. I had on my foot-link two small *peal-flies,*† especial favourites of mine when the new fish

---

* Salmon, salmon-peal, and white trout, force their way into the rivers from the sea, in great numbers, in the latter end of July, August, and September—particularly when the autumnal rains cause a greater flow of water. They are at that time in the highest season—being far more delicate of flavour, and of greater firmness than after their seasoning to the fresh water. They are then termed new fish ; their scales being of a most brilliant silvery appearance. They rise very fearlessly and merrily at the artificial fly, taking it w th great eagerness. The salmon that remain in the rivers after the spawning season, are termed red salmon, having undergone a considerable change in colour, flavour and appearance ; and if detained beyond the usual periods of their return to the sea, become sickly, pine, and die. In April, and the early part of May, the salmon fry descend the rivers in immense shoals to the sea. The skerling of the Usk and Wye, in Monmouthshire, is the samlet or salmon-peal. Ray observes in his work, " Wisdom of God manifested in the Works of the Creation," " that salmon will yearly ascend rivers even to four and five hundred miles, only to cast their spawn, and secure it in banks of sand till the young be hatched and excluded, and then return to sea again." The same instinct prevails, in a singular manner, with the land-crab or violet-crab, (Cancer ruricola) which, in South America, inhabits mountainous woods contiguous to the sea. Annually, in prodigious numbers, they migrate to the sea, performing a wearisome journey of some months ; and after washing off their spawn, set about on their return home, where they burrow in the mountains. It varies in colour, but is generally of a blackish violet ; it is from four to six inches wide, and walks sideways, like the sea-crab. The flesh is considered good, notwithstanding it feeds on the highly poisonous berries of the Hippomane Manchinella, manchineel tree, being very fond of them. The wood of this tree is very beautiful, but the saw-dust is so acrid and poisonous, that sawyers and carpenters are forced to work upon the wood with gauze masks.

† Stretcher tied on treble F. hook ; tipped with gold tinsel ; tailed with guinea-fowl and golden pheasant's feathers; body, of

are in the river ; and with them I fished during the morning without changing. The river, for nearly a mile to its mouth, runs through flat marshy meadows, having good deep water, and some excellent stands for a salmon or

---

orange silk, ribbed with gold twist, and a deep copper-coloured grouse hackle and jay's hackle, laid over together ; winged with golden pheasant's feathers, Guinea fowl's, and brown turkey's feathers mixed, and a few sprigs of the tail feather of the gold pheasant ; head finished off with the whirl of a black ostrich feather. Dropper tied on treble F., tipped with gold twist, tailed with dark mallard's feather and blue macaw ; body, Deoigh a dhu and crotal-coloured mohair mixed, ribbed with gold twist ; a deep morone coloured hackle or fiery brown, full under the shoulder, and winged with golden pheasant's feather, dark brown turkey feathers, and blue macaw. Deoigh a dhu or dubh, means fire black, or, termed by the natives, fiery brown ; they are very partial to the colour. The crotal colour is a kind of deep brick or cinnamon colour, being a most excellent shade either for lake or salmon-fishing. It is dyed with the rock border-moss, (Parmelia Saxatilis) found on stones and the bark of trees. It is called, in Irish, crotal or crostal. It dyes the French colour, Feuillemort. The navel border-moss (Parmelia Omphalodes) dies wool of a lasting dull crimson or purple colour, termed, in Irish, corcur. The country people use it in Scotland. The celebrated dyeing rock-moss (Rocella tinctoria) is a whitish lichen, growing upon rocks in the Canary and Cape Verd Islands, from whence it is imported, being named there Orseille, Orchill. It is found also in Guernsey and Portland Island. It is sold, as manufactured by the Dutch, in a kind of paste, called litmus, (orseille en pâte) in square masses of about half an inch in breadth and thickness, being hard and brittle, having the appearance of a violet-coloured earth, with white spots. The thallus, or frond of the lichen, when moistened with a volatile alkali, dyes a beautiful but perishable purple, and gives a fine bloom to other colours. By the addition of a solution of muriate of tin, the colour becomes more permanent, but changes to a scarlet. M. du Fay says, that a solution of orchil in water, applied on cold marble, stains it of a durable and beautiful violet or purplish blue colour, sinking deeply into the marble. It appears to make the marble more brittle. Litmus is used as a test for acids, the paper stained with it becoming red when an acid is present. The original colour is readily restored again by ammoniacal gas. Water absorbs nearly six hundred times its own weight of this gas, combining with it with explosive velocity, forming saturated ammonia. Copper is always detected by ammonia changing the water in which the copper exists to a beautiful blue. Prepared orchill is the substance principally made use of for colouring the spirits of thermometers. The solution of muriate of tin is a valuable mordant in dyeing in giving permanency to colours. Linen or woollen boiled in it, and then placed in a solution of cochineal, becomes a permanent scarlet, but if afterwards put into solution of potash it changes to a permanent crimson. Recent muriate of tin is a very delicate test of mercury.

Tartarinodine (Rinodina tartarea) found on rocks, and collected by dyers, the rocks being scraped once in five years ; when prepared by grinding, and the addition of ammonia and alum, is used to dye woollen yarn or give a bloom to other colours. It is called cudbear, the Lichen tartareus of Linnæus.

In the transactions of the Royal Geographical Society of London, mention is made of a singular tree, growing in the Cocos or Keeling Isles, (situated in the Indian Ocean) whose root, when grated and infused in a lye of potash, yields a beautiful scarlet dye. Its fruit, when cut, resembles plum-cake, and is used as a pickle.

Ammonia is not only highly useful to the sportsman, chemically, in assisting to give brilliancy and permanency (in dyeing) to his salmon and trout colours, but it is also highly valuable to him medicinally, particularly in those feverish inflammatory attacks and colds, brought on by excessive fatigue and long continuance in damp clothes. Where medical aid cannot immediately be procured, (which at the time I allude to was frequently the case, no medical person being nearer than Ennis or Kilrush, the former being seventeen, the latter twelve miles distant) I have found very heavy colds, accompanied with severe shivering fits, when attended to early, quickly yield to the use of the solution of acetatia of ammone, (aqua acetatis ammoniæ) known by the old name of spirit of mindererus—the sufferer being kept very warm, and taking half an ounce of the solution in a warm drink, every two or three hours, until a sensible perspiration is produced. Its effect proves more powerfully sudorific when preceded by an emetic—dissolving two grains of Tartarized antimony in four ounces of distilled water, and two table-spoonsful of the mixture being taken every half hour, until vomiting is caused.

peal. Its banks are lined with the bull-rush,* (Scirpus Lacustris) and the yellow iris (Iris pseudo-àcorus†) :

" Where waves the bulrush as the waters glide,
And yellow flag-flowers deck the sunny side."

Along the coast here, the sands blown in by the western winds, present a high range of hills, and being made firm by the growth of a variety of grasses and plants, form an impenetrable barrier to the encroachments of the ever rolling and restless Atlantic. Here the Arundo Arenaria,‡ with its creeping binding roots, is an invaluable guardian, displaying its rigid culm with long, narrow, and light glaucous green leaves. The Carex Arenaria, and the common birds-foot trefoil (Lotus Corniculatus)§ are also highly useful—the latter having decumbent stems growing to a great length, and their strong roots penetrating deeply into the sand. The pretty gold-coloured flowers of the Lotus Corniculatus, and its thickly set green leaves, retain the finest verdure in the hottest and driest summers. This plant and the white clover (Trifolium repens)* grow very extensively on these sand-hills, and form the principal food of the innumerable rabbits that burrow there. There are also many valuable agricultural grasses, &c., growing spontaneously ; such as the perennial darnel or rye-grass, (Lolium perenne)† crested dog's-tail-grass, (Cynosurus Cristatus,)‡ called also thraneens or trathnin, meadow soft grass, (Holcus lanatus)§ common purple trefoil or red clover, (Trifolium pratense) and the black medick or nonsuch (Medicago lupulina). The common ragwort or rag-weed, (Senecio Jacobœa)‖ grows in great abundance, having stems three feet in height, crowned with large golden yellow flowers in corymbs, from which it is named, by the peasants, Buachail an buidhe, the boy with the yellow head. Numerous plants of the yellow or ladies' bed-straw, (Galium verum)¶ Yarrow, (Achillea Millifolium,)** sea-holly,(Eryngium maritimum)†† purple sea-rocket, (Cakile maritima)‡‡ and the sea-side gromwell, (Lithospermum maritimum)§§ are growing about the hills and on the shore. That pretty little flower, the pansy violet or heart's-ease, (Viola tricolor) enlivens the sandy fields with its brilliant colours, in conjunction with the scarlet pimpernel or poor man's weatherglass (Anagallis Arvensis).‖‖ The pansy bears a variety of names, from a fancied resemblance in the throat of the flower ; such as,

---

As a diaphoretic, it is perfectly safe, not being attended with the risk in serious inflammatory cases, where other more powerful sudorifics might increase the mischief. Externally, when diluted with rose-water, it forms a good collyrium for weak and slightly inflamed eyes ; and, as a lotion, for sprains, bruises, and superficial inflammation. The solution of acetate of ammonia can be simply prepared by taking one ounce of the sub-carbonate of ammonia, and two pints of diluted acetic acid, or as much as may be sufficient ; add the acid to the ammonia until it ceases to effervesce, or till the mixture has no effect in changing the colour of Litmus paper. In this process the ammonia of the sub-carbonate is disengaged, and passes over to the acetic acid, forming acetate of ammonia, which remains in solution, while the carbonic acid escapes. Twenty-five drops of the acetate of ammonia, in a glass of any sweetened liquid, has been employed to relieve headaches caused by hard drinking, and even to dissipate drunkenness.

It is far from my intention to arrogate any medical opinion, but merely to state that such simple remedies as I have mentioned, have often proved very serviceable in an early stage of severe cold, where distance and great loss of time prevented the opportunity of getting a regular practitioner. The only person at that time in the country was poor Dr. H——, a wretched itinerant quack. The poor man, who in disposition was as harmless as he was unfortunate, terminated a miserable career, after visiting a patient, being found dead on the road side, from the effects of excessive intoxication.

* Bull-rushes, the stalks growing sometimes eight feet high, and being at the base as thick as a finger, constitute a considerable article of trade in England, being used for matting and making the bottoms of chairs. Coopers employ them for filling up spaces between the seams of casks.

† Iris palustris, marsh fleur de-leuce. Roots are very acrid when fresh, and warm when dry, bearing very nearly the same medicinal properties as the galangale root (kæmpferia) the dried root of which is brought from China ; but it is not now noticed in the British Pharmacopœias. In the Paris Codex it is termed maranta galanga. It is an aromatic and acrid root, hot, stimulant, and also errhine. It is medicinally used in dyspepsia, and the root chewed in paralysis of the tongue.

‡ Arundo Arenaria, also Ammophila Arundinacea, (common sea-reed) Ammophila being derived from αμμος, sand, and Θιλος, a lover It is extensively employed in Norfolk in preserving the banks of sand from the inroads of the sea, and called there sand marram (Psamma Arenaria.) It is also planted on the north coast at Liverpool for the same purpose. Queen Elizabeth was so sensible of its importance, that she prohibited the extirpation of it. In Holland the Dutch fortify their sandy barriers by the propagation of this reed and the upright sea-lime-grass (Elymus Arenarius). That industrious nation have much to contend with to keep their sea-boundaries secure from the breaking in of the sea, and the destructive ravages of the teredo navalis—(ship-worm)—the teredines in vast numbers working their way into the piles that support the dikes, and threatening their total demolition, when the precaution of sheathing them with copper, or a composition of tar and glass, has been neglected. Although the teredo is a native of equatorial seas, yet, by adhering to the bottom of ships, it has become quite naturalized in Holland, as also in England.

Mr. Lyell states that one of the most memorable irruptions of the sea in Holland occurred in 1421, where the tide, pouring into the mouth of the united Meuse and Waal, burst through a dam, in the district named Bergse-Veld, and overflowed twenty-two villages, forming that large sheet of water called the Bies Bosch. No vestige even of the ruin of these places could ever afterwards be seen, but a small portion of the new bay became filled up and formed an island.—*Principles of Geology.*

§ Horned birds-foot trefoil and milk-vetch. Herb in moist meadows, makes excellent hay ; flowers turn green in drying, like those of indigo.

* The white clover (Trifolium repens) is the seamar bhan, seamrog or shamrock.

† Lolium perenne is an excellent grass for agriculturists. It may be sown with a crop of oats and red clover ; the clover and the loliumwill produce a plentiful crop the following season, furnishing a good fodder for cattle. Meadow fox-tail grass (alopecurus pratensis) is the best early grass for farmers.—Mr. J. T. Mackay.

‡ Found to be one of the best grasses for making ladies' bonnets.—J. T. M.

§ A good grass for low damp grounds.—J. T. Mackay.

‖ S. Jacobœa, dyes wool a deep green, and alummed wool, yellow.

¶ The flowers of the Galium verum, or true cheese-rennet, smell like honey—are antispasmodic, and, with allum, dye a fine yellow. They coagulate milk when boiled in it. In Scotland the Highlanders employ the plant with the leaves of the stinging nettle, (urtica dioica) and a little salt, as a rennet to curdle milk. The root is dark green; boiled in a solution of alum it dyes a fine red.

** Common yarrow or milfoil, with small cream-coloured or rose-coloured flowers, yielding an essential oil ; infusion of the flowering plant is stimulant and stomachic.

†† The roots are well tasted when candled, and act as a stimulating tonic.

‡‡ Bunias Cakile of Linnæus.

§§ Pulmonaria maritima of Linnæus— growing with numerous procumbent branched stems, bearing flowers in racemes, of a beautiful purplish blue. It is also named sea mertens (Mertensia Maritima) and sea bugloss. The whole plant is very glaucous, narcotic; and it has been remarked that the flavour resembles that of oysters.

‖‖ A pretty native annual, having small brilliant scarlet flowers, with a purplish pink eye in the centre of each corolla— called poor man's weatherglass, because the corollas never expand in rainy weather or when the air is moist ;

" The hollow winds begin to blow,
The clouds look black, the glass is low ;
  *   *   *   *
Closed is the pink-eyed pimpernel.—Dr. JENNER.

Collected before the flowers expand, the powder has been prescribed in doses of one scruple in epilepsy and mania. It is narcotico-acrid poison. The smaller kind of birds seek the seed with great avidity. Anagallis fruticosa, latifolia, monelli, and linkfolia, are pretty little biennials, and are exceedingly ornamental in a conservatory. They are of easy culture, and increase in peat-sand and vegetable mould.

Curtis says, that trefoil, wood-sorrel, mountain ebony, senna, African marigold, &c., &c., are so regular in folding up their leaves before rainy weather, that they seem to have a kind of instinct or foresight similar to that of ants,

love in idleness; call me to you; kiss me ere I rise; and from its colours, three faces under a hood, and herb-Trinity. The word pansy is a corruption of the word pensée, thought; In Hamlet, Ophelia says—

"And there are Pansies, that's for thoughts."

In the French floral language this favourite flower means, "think of me," pensez à moi. In the fields near the river, coltsfoot (Tussilago farfara)* is met with, and a variety of other valuable and useful plants. We finished our day in famous style, each of us having a weighty bag of good white trout, from one to three pounds each, and a few salmon peal, nearly five pounds each. Our friend Jemmy Aymes, at the cross roads, supplied us with a sup of comfort, and we gaily trudged our way home, anticipating, for the next, a treat with the salmon in Dunbeg.† Again we were on the road to Dunbeg, with our rods, but we were sadly disappointed; the day brightened, and was cloudless, and the wind not lying fair on the river, but one poor salmon rewarded our toil, although numbers splashing in mockery at our flies, gave us an invitation for another day. The Dunbeg river, or Cooraclare, as it is frequently called, is rather deep, and in some parts of good breadth, having excellent salmon-stands the whole run from Ballydoneen-bridge, on the Ennis and Kilrush road, down to its mouth. It rises in Mount Callen, and forms in its course Lough Dulogh or Dhuloce, the black lake, in the barony of Ibrickan, and continuing a run of near sixteen miles, passing by the village of Cooraclare,‡ disembogues itself into the Atlantic at Dunbeg. Dunbeg bay is unsafe for vessels or boats of any size, from the numerous rocks which bar its entrance. At the river's mouth are the castles of Dunmor and Dunbeag. They are situated on the south side of the creek, and distant from each other about half a mile: Dunmor, or the big fortress, being at the entrance on the sea-shore and Dunbeag, or the little fortress, on a rising ground overlooking the creek, and close to the village.

Underneath the Castle of Dunmor§ extend several caverns, and the tide from the Atlantic forcing a passage into them, occasions at times most awful and unearthly sounds. Tradition hands down that one of its possessors was remarkable for his treachery and cruelty, it being his practice to lower his guests and captives through trap-doors into the caverns or vaults, where they were destroyed on the flowing of the tide. The occasional roarings of the water the superstitious imagined to be the moanings of the spirits of the murdered victims—

"Beneath, terrific caverns gave
Dark welcome to each stormy wave

That dash'd, like midnight revellers, in;
And such the strange, mysterious din,
At times throughout those caverns roll'd;
And such the fearful wonders told
Of restless sprites, imprisoned there."*

A range of sand hills along the coast present a similar appearance to those at Mount Rivers.

Time passed rapidly on; the fishing season had gone by; our rods were laid aside for our guns; and mountain, bog, and shore resounded with their sharp reports:

"For winter came; the wind was his whip:
One choppy finger was on his lip:
He had torn the cataracts from the hills,
And they clank'd at his girdle like manacles."†

Without these amusements the dreary winter months would be insupportably dull. In that part of the country grouse and partridge are scarce; but hares, snipe, and all kinds of wild fowl and sea-birds are in abundance. The winter seasons generally are wet; and very frequently tremendous gales of wind from the west and north-west prevail, lasting for several days with unabated violence:

"Oh, wild west wind! thou
For whose path the Atlantic's level powers
Cleave themselves into chasms; while far below
The sea-blooms and the oozy woods, which wear
The sapless foliage of the ocean, know
Thy voice, and suddenly grow gray with fear,
And tremble and despoil themselves."‡

To the admirers of the sublime and terrible, a walk along the coast, or standing on the verge of some high cliff, would excite in them feelings of the deepest sense of their own insignificance, and of the awful power of the Almighty and all-wise Ruler of the universe, when they behold the mountainous billows of the Atlantic Ocean§ rolling in, and its surges breaking on the beach, lashing the rocks with terrific roarings, and oftentimes sending its spray far over cliffs several hundred feet in height. Ah! well might they then exclaim, in the sublime language of Pope,

"Not God alone in the still calm we find,
He mounts the storm, and rides upon the wind."

Or as Thompson, in his Winter, beautifully expresses,

"'Till Nature's King, who oft,
Amid tempestuous darkness dwells alone;
And, on the wings of the careering winds,
Walks dreadfully serene."

---

* Common coltsfoot. The leaves and flowers are considered of great efficacy as a demulcent and expectorant in coughs. The dried leaves, with powdered asarum, (Asarabacca) form the basis of cephalic snuffs, and are frequently smoked like tobacco, for the relief of asthma. A strong decoction has been found serviceable in scrofulous cases: the down, on the under surface of the leaves, is used as tinder.

The tussilago fragrans, a frame perennial from Italy, is a very desirable plant for a green house, being much valued for the delightful fragrance of its flowers during the winter season. It grows in any soil—increases like the common tussilago—and one plant will perfume the whole room.

† Dunbeg river is not now so famous for its salmon; for, since the time alluded to here, a kind of weir has been run entirely across it, near the village, which prevents the greater number of salmon from getting up in the proper season, unless very heavy floods come at the time. Of late there has been no spirited fly-fisher in that part of the country to compel the owners of the weir to adhere to the fishery regulations, viz.—to keep a free passage open from Saturday night until Monday morning. Mr. James O'Gorman was the best and the most fair fly-fisher in that part of the country; he has killed great numbers of salmon, and some were very weighty fish.

‡ Deriving its name from the castle situated on the hill beside the village. It means the Court of Clare, having belonged to the Lord Clare, who fled from the country after the battle of Aughrim.

§ Dunmor and Dunbeag. Dunmor Castle, Mr. Dutton states, was inhabited at the time he made his survey of Clare; but when I visited those castles, their only tenants were wild pigeons, starlings, and a solitary owl. The weather being exceedingly calm, I had not the opportunity of witnessing those awful sounds so much spoken of.

* Lalla Rookh—Fire worshippers.
† Shelley.
‡ Shelly's Ode to the West Wind.
§ The following vivid and interesting accounts from Dr. Hibbert's description of the Shetland Islands, published in Edinburgh in 1822, are extremely applicable here:

"These Isles are exposed continually to the uncontrollable violence of the Atlantic, for no land intervenes between their western shores and America. The prevalence, therefore, of strong westerly gales causes the waves to be sometimes driven in with irresistible force upon the coast, while there is also a current settling from the north. The spray of the sea aids the decomposition of the rocks, and prepares them to be breached by the mechanical force of the waves. Steep cliffs are hollowed out into deep caves and lofty arches; and almost every promontory ends in a clustre of rocks, imitating the forms of columns, pinnacles and obelisks."

Again he observes, "But the most sublime scene is where a mural pile of porphyry, escaping the process of disintegration that is devastating the coast, appears to have been left as a sort of rampart against the inroads of the ocean: the Atlantic, when provoked by wintry gales, batters against it with all the force of real artillery; the waves having, in their repeated assaults, forced themselves an entrance. This breach, named the Grind of the Navir, is widened every winter by the overwhelming surge that, finding a passage through it, separates large stones from its side, and forces them to a distance of no less than one hundred and eighty feet. In two or three spots, the fragments which have been detached are brought together in immense heaps, that appear as an accumulation of cubical masses, the product of some quarry."

The mean depth of the Atlantic Ocean is calculated to be about three miles. Young's Nat. Phil. Lect. xlvii.

Although the stupendous cliffs* along the coast of Clare appear a formidable ocean boundary, some being elevated to four hundred and even to six hundred feet, and frowning with haughty grandeur on their furious opponent; yet the Atlantic is making serious inroads, and, with the storms of each winter season, huge masses are crumbled and swept away, while the sand-banks, united in the close embraces of the Ammophila Arundinacea, put to defiance its wildest attacks, and form an impassable limit.

Frost is sometimes very severe, and at times attended with heavy falls of snow, but never lasting long, so much humidity existing in the air from the vicinity of the sea. I remember being out one very cold freezing day in January with Lanty, on the salt marsh of Annagieragh, close to the lake, and stealing nearly waist deep in snow and water to get within shot of some shell-drakes, and being almost blinded with the sharpness of a thick, driving sleet, that a flock of wild swans dashed into the water, about sixty yards from where I was lying. How my heart beat for the prize, as, with deadly aim, I levelled my long duck-gun; but the invaluable improvement of detonating locks was not then known in that part of the country. I had the extreme mortification, after snapping two or three times, to see them majestically rise, and skim far away to some mountain lake. I have since often thought of the fatigue, the wet, the cold, that I have endured for mere amusement; and were I compelled to have gone through such hardships in the earning of a livelihood, I doubtless would have complained of the severity of my destiny.

[Our intelligent correspondent has given a list of Birds, among which are many rare and beautiful water-fowl, which he says are not seen in other parts of Ireland; and which he either shot or met with along the coast of Clare, and particularly in parts of the Shannon near its mouth, and about the caves of Ballybunian, on the Kerry side. To this list he has appended many scientific observations and remarks, which, we have no doubt, will be esteemed important by persons who take an interest in such studies. The entire will appear in a volume about to be published.

---

* Captain Portlock, in his valuable paper on the study of Geological Phenomena in Ireland, read before the Dublin Geological Society, on the 11th of April, 1830, in alluding to the disintegration or wearing down of the surface of the earth by atmospheric agents, and of the powers of atmospheric waters in eroding mountain rocks, provided their substance be loose and porous; continues—"Leaving atmospheric agents, we meet another (powerful to destroy) in the ocean; and, after reading all the instances of its ravages collected together by Mr. Lyell, we might almost tremble for the safety of Ireland. But, if we resist alarm, we may indulge curiosity, and study with effect the sublime cliffs of Clare, or those equally picturesque of Donegal, exposed as they both are to the full sweep of the western ocean."

Webster, in his Geological Transactions, mentions many serious occurrences of the encroachments of the sea on the south coast of England, and of the wearing away of the cliffs. A portion of the promontory of Beachy Head was so undermined, that a mass of chalk, three hundred feet in length, and seventy to eighty feet in breadth, fell, in the year 1813, with a tremendous crash: similar slips have since been frequent.

The wild majestic grandeur of the cliffs of Clare is indeed sublime; their lofty range extending from Loophead to Baltard, with Caoi na Faoileann and Cathoair Crohane overtowering all—

"like giants stand,
To sentinel enchanted land."

How great is the effect produced upon the mind, when standing upon their dizzying summits, with the boundless mass of the waters of the Atlantic before us, and here and there the fishing eagle, (sole lord of those aerial heights) sailing round in easy curving lines, with all the majesty of his species; and now, with a loud rushing sound, plunging for its prey into the sea with the certainty of a rifle. In the language of Blair, "It produces a sort of internal elevation and expansion; it raises the mind much above its ordinary state; and fills it with a degree of wonder and astonishment which it cannot well express."

The cliffs of Caoi na Faoileann, or sea-gull's house or retreat, are four hundred and sixty feet in height; those of Moir or Moghur, at the Hagshead, exceed six hundred feet—one particular pinnacle being one hundred and twenty fathoms.

Our kind friend has also added to the present portion of his article on Clare, with which he has so obligingly favoured us, what by botanists, we have no doubt would be esteemed a very valuable appendix, a scientific description of most of the grasses and plants to be met with in that district. As the general class of our readers cannot be considered sufficiently scientific to enjoy this description of reading, we have preferred allowing them to appear in the volume to which we have referred, rather than introduce them into our columns. We have great pleasure, however, in extracting the following well-merited meed of praise to Mr. Mackay, Botanical Demonstrator, and Lecturer on Botany and Horticulture in the Botanic Garden of Trinity College; freeing us from the charge made by Mr. Lyell, that scarce any thing is known of the natural history and botany of this country.]

"There is a legend that St. Patrick expelled all reptiles from Ireland; and certain it is that none of the three species of snakes common in England, nor the toad, have been observed there by naturalists. They have our common frog, and our water newt, and, according to Ray, the green lizard. Schultes, the botanist, observed, a few years since, in his tour in England, that there were two great islands in Europe of which the flora's were unknown—Sardinia and Ireland; he might, perhaps, have added the fauna* of the latter country.† The latter is but too true; but, I am happy to add, that Mr. or Herr Schultes, or whatever he may be, was most ably answered‡ and silenced by that indefatigable and scientific botanist, J. T. Mackay, Esq., Curator of Trinity College Botanic Garden, Dublin. To this gentleman I feel deeply indebted for the exceeding delight and pleasure I have derived from attending to his admirable botanical demonstrations; and for the much valuable information he at all times most willingly and anxiously gave; and I am proud to have the ▓▓▓▓▓▓ of announcing that he has nearly comple▓▓▓ shortly give to the public a "Flora Hibern▓▓▓ ing all the phænogamous and cryptogamou▓▓▓ country, with their correct habitats. From ▓▓ ▓▓▓ observer, and from one of such long known experience; a publication of the kind will not only be invaluable to all interested in the delightful science of botany, but it will also rank high as a national work. Indeed, Mr. Mackay's catalogue, published in 1825, contains the only correct habitats of our indigenous plants, that has yet appeared. In regard to that part of the quotation from Mr. Lyell, "they have our common frog," it brings to my mind an amusing article given by Mr. O'Reilly in his excellent Irish Dictionary—the word frog is the original Irish, and described by him as "an animal not found in Ireland before the reign of William the Third of England, whose Dutch troops first introduced it amongst us."

---

* Fauna. The various kinds of animals, &c., peculiar to a country constitute its fauna, as the various kinds of plants constitute its flora. The term is derived from the fauni, or rural deities in Roman Mythology.

† Lyell's Principles of Geology, 3d vol. page 451, 3d Edition, 1834.

‡ Loudon's Magazine of Gardening, for April. 1831.

§ Cryptogamous, a name applied to a class of plants, such as ferns, mosses, sea-weeds, and fungi; in which the fructification or organs of reproduction are concealed, derived from κρυπτος, kryptos, concealed, and γαμος, gamos, marriage. Mr. Mackay possesses a rich collection of Cryptogamous plants.

Phænogamous, are the flowering plants whose ▓▓▓▓▓ are distinct and visible.

DUBLIN:

Printed and Published by P. D. Hardy, 3, Cecilia-street, all communications are to be addressed. Sold by all Booksellers in Ireland.

In London, by Richard Groombridge, 6, Panyer-alley, ▓▓▓▓; In Liverpool, by Wilmer and Smith; in Manchester, by Ambery; in Birmingham, by Guest; in Glasgow, by John Macleod; and in Edinburgh, by N. Bowack.

THE
DUBLIN PENNY JOURNAL

CONDUCTED BY P. DIXON HARDY, M.R.I.A.

| Vol. III. | MARCH 7, 1835. | No. 140. |

A. Duncan, Esq. del. Clayton, sc.

VIEW OF THE LIGHT-HOUSE, SOUTH WALL, DUBLIN.

A. Duncan, Esq., del, Clayton, sc.

PIGEON-HOUSE, LOOKING FROM THE LIGHT-HOUSE.

LIGHT-HOUSE AND PIGEON-HOUSE, SOUTH WALL, DUBLIN.

The Light-House stands rather a little to the south side of the bay of Dublin. It is an elegant piece of architecture, three stories high, surmounted by an octagonal lanthorn, which is lighted by oil-lamps, aided by reflecting lenses. It was erected by Mr. Smith, in 1782, and affords a striking proof that the greatest difficulties may be overcome by genius and perseverance. A stone stair-case, with an iron balustrade, winds round the outside of this extraordinary building, terminating in an iron gallery, which surrounds it at the upper story. This useful and ornamental structure stands at the extremity of a range of building, called the South-wall—which was erected for the purpose of securing the harbour against the sands of the South-bull. The building of this wall was commenced in 1748, and is constructed of large blocks of granite, strongly cemented, and fastened together with iron cramps. It runs in a straight line into the sea the astonishing length of 17,754 feet, or nearly three English miles and a half.

About midway on this wall, a fort or battery has been constructed, called the Pigeon House. The pier at this point is two hundred and fifty feet wide and on it are built a Magazine, Arsenal, and Custom-house. It is considered a place of great strength, being surrounded with heavy cannon, and commanding the bay in various directions. There is always a large detachment of artillery stationed here, for whose accommodation a barrack has been erected. At this place there is also a basin, for packets and other vessels of a similar description, nine hundred feet in length, and four hundred and fifty in breadth ; but since the formation of the harbours of Howth and Kingstown it is but little frequented.

CAPE CLEAR LIGHT-HOUSE.

Sir—As some of your inland readers scarcely know what species of structure a light-house is, I send you the following account of the one erected at this station, upon the accuracy of which they may rely.

It may be well here to mention, that round the coast of Ireland there are no less than thirty-six light houses. Some are harbour lights, others floating; some revolve at different periods, others stationary ; and some are furnished with stained glass, which varies the colour of the light.

Many have been the contrivances in former days to warn ships of danger or direct them in their course, by means of fires, &c.; but it remained for modern days to adopt proper methods of constructing houses, in which the lights might be so varied as to assure the mariner of the safety of his course, and prevent the recurrence of shipwrecks. It may be interesting to some also to state that all foreign vessels are obliged to pay the sum of one halfpenny per ton for every light-house or floating light which they may have passed, or be about to pass, along the coast. British and Irish vessels, on a foreign voyage, and foreign privileged vessels, one farthing per ton for every light-house or floating-light which they may have passed or be about to pass. Coasters, one farthing per ton for every light-house or floating-light, which they may have passed. If in ballast, one-eighth of a penny per ton only.

In reference to Cape Clear I may observe that it is an island, three miles long and one and a half wide, containing nine hundred and sixty-nine inhabitants. On the south side of this island is the light-house, a very fine building, erected about the year 1817, by the Ballast Board of Dublin. It is a circular tower of cut granite—the workmanship of which is remarkably well executed. It is about thirty-six feet high from the base to the balcony, which surrounds the lantern, and from high water-mark four hundred and forty-eight feet. On the inside are three flights of winding stone steps. The floors are very curiously constructed, being formed of large stones—the centre one, which is circular, supported by those adjacent, into which it is grooved, and lead in the interstices. In the upper part, or lantern, are sixty four panes of the best plate glass, of near a quarter of an inch in thickness ; the frame, in which the glass is placed, is metal, with copper screwed over. The cupola, or roof, is of copper, painted white, and ornamented with a weather-cock.

The light is produced by twenty-one lamps, which are placed in the foci of large reflectors of the parabolic form : they are of copper, with silver fronts ; the whole of which are supported by a branch which revolves by machinery, much resembling that in a clock, but on a large scale, enclosed in a brass-pannelled case, and put in motion by a metal of three hundred weight. The light appears once in every two minutes, and is seen at the distance of six or seven leagues—in its brightest state, like a star of the first magnitude, and gradually becoming less luminous, is eclipsed, there being three sides, with seven lamps on each, and three angles ; the sides shew brightest, and the angles dark. There is consumed each day, on an average, seven hundred and fifty gallons of spermaceti oil. It is lit at sun-set, and extinguished at sun-rise. It bears to Misen-head N. W. ¼ W. nine and a half miles.

Annexed to the light-house, by a corridor or hall, is a square tower, which was formerly occupied by a naval lieutenant and midshipman, with a party of soldiers, and used in making telegraphic signals. The assistant light-keeper resides in it at present, and the principal, in a dwelling-house, built by the Ballast-board, convenient to the tower. There are out-houses and yards, &c., and the whole enclosed by a wall, with a gate opening to the road, which leads to South Harbour, a small cove at the S. W. part of the island.　　　R. WILSON, jun.

Dec. 1834.

The following additional particulars relative to the Island of Cape Clear have also been sent to us by Mr. W.:

On the north-west point stand the ruins of a castle, built on a wild point of a cliff in the sea, called *Duna-nore*, i. e. the Golden Fort. There is a very narrow and dangerous passage, about a yard broad and ten yards in length, to this castle. It and the island formerly belonged to O'Driscoll, and were taken on the 22d of March, 1601, by Captain Harvey, who soon after obliged Sir Fineen O'Driscoll to submit to Queen Elizabeth.* Some time ago, a priest and another person went to see this castle : the latter stirring one of the lower stones, they had scarcely left it two minutes when the whole top part fell down ; the stones were fast together after falling, and remain there still in masses.

There are four fresh water loughs—three towards the west of the island, two of which are full of reeds, which are used by some of the Capers to thatch their houses; the other, they say, is enchanted, and that if an oily barrel, a dirty jar, a rusty key, or any thing else be put into it, it would become as clean as ever.

On the south side of the island there is a cove, called South Harbour, where a vessel may anchor in safety when the wind is not south. On the opposite side there is another, called North Harbour, where there is a pier and basin for the safety of the fishing boats, the largest of which contain from ten to twelve tons. At this harbour (which is called in Irish *Tra Kieran*, i. e. Saint Kieran's strand) stand the ruins of a church, dedicated to St. Kieran, and near it is the burying ground ; there is also a pillar of stone, with a cross rudely cut—of this stone it is said, that the saint was the workman. Here the people collect on St. Kieran's day, to do penance ; there is a *holy well* near it. This St. Kieran was the first bishop of Saiger. Archbishop Usher says, he was born in this island.†

Towards the middle of the island is the chapel, a long narrow thatched building, and as destitute of any ornament as a barn. The priest lives in the island during the winter months, and in the summer stops at Sherkin, an island which lies between the cape and the main land

The houses are built of stone, with mud for mortar, and are mostly thatched with straw, which is artfully kept down by nets covering the whole roof; these nets are made of ropes of straw, the meshes not quite a foot square ; to the ends of these stones are tied, which hang down round the eaves. There is no turf on the island, but there is a kind of mud at the west lakes, which a few of the inhabitants work together with their hands and dry ; turf is brought from the mainland, and sold on Sundays and holidays.

The inhabitants are very poor, and generally a simple

---

* From Smith's History of Cork.　　† Idem.

honest people; most of them are strong and healthy, being seldom invaded with disorders, and die generally of old age, chiefly owing to their temperate living, hard labour, and clearness of the air. They are kind to each other, and courteous to strangers; they are excellent pilots for that part of the coast.

Cape is famous for its springs of fresh water, which are reckoned to be superior to any in Ireland; it was brought to Dublin, and tried by Andrew Blake Kirwan.

The ground is chiefly manured with sea-weed, which is cut from off the rocks, by means of an implement resembling a scythe, composed of a long pole with a hook affixed. The women take as active a part in the cultivation of the ground as the men; their food chiefly consists of potatoes and fish, which are boiled together in one pot; they like onions, leeks, and garlick, which are eaten raw. Both men and women are very fond of tobacco; they delight in dancing, and have the bagpipes played in a field on summer Sunday evenings. They marry at a certain season, which is after Christmas. On the whole island there are but two trees, which are situated in the pound at South Harbour.

The game on the Cape are—wild duck at the lakes—green and grey plover, very few partridge, snipe, pigeons, and a great number of sea birds in the cliffs—also rabbits.

There are a number of cows, and but half a dozen horses; the sheep are very small, being fed on the most barren part of the island—they are kept for the sake of the fleece, of which they make frieze for clothing. There is a school on this island for poor children, situated near the chapel.

BELL-ROCK LIGHT-HOUSE.

The Bell-rock, or Cape, is a dangerous ridge of sunken rocks, lying about twelve miles east from the point of Fife-ness, and an equal distance south from Arbroath harbour, between the openings of the Firths of Tay and Forth. The ridge extends about a mile in length, and half a mile in breadth; the top of the rock only being seen a few hours at low water in spring tides. This rock not only renders the navigation of the Tay and Forth very hazardous, but is also highly dangerous to all vessels navigating coast-wise. Every year, formerly, vessels of great value were wrecked upon it, and there is reason to suspect that many which were supposed to have foundered at sea, have suffered on this dangerous reef. It is a remarkable fact that hardly a single instance has been known of a vessel being saved which had the misfortune to strike upon this rock. Captain Brodie of the royal navy placed a beacon on it some years ago, but though the greatest care was taken to have it properly secured, the first storm broke the chains, and the beacon was driven ashore. Previous to the erection of the noble light-house now placed there, it was commonly remarked that, even if it were practicable to erect it upon such a sunken rock, no one would be found hardy enough to live in an abode so dread and dreary, and that it would fall to the lot of the projectors themselves to possess it for the first winter. The bill appointing commissioners for this great undertaking, however, passed both houses of parliament late in the session of 1806. In the following summer a vessel was fitted out as a floating-light, and moored off the Bell-rock. Mr. Stevenson, engineer for the commissioners of the northern light-houses, modelled the first design, which was submitted to the opinion and advice of Mr. Rennie, and subsequently adopted.

The Bell-rock Light-house is a circular building, the foundation stone of which is nearly on a level with the surface of the sea at low water of ordinary spring tides; and consequently at high-water of these tides, the building is immersed to the height of about fifteen feet. The two first or lower courses of the masonry are imbedded into the rock, and the stones of all the courses are dovetailed and joined with each other, forming one connected mass from centre to circumference. The successive courses of the work are also connected by joggles of stone; and to prevent the stones from being lifted up by the force of the sea, while the work was in progress, each stone of the solid part of the building had two holes

bored through it, entering six inches into the course immediately below, into which oaken tree nails, two inches in diameter, were driven, after Mr. Smeaton's plan at the Eddystone. The cement used at the Bell rock, like that of the Eddystone, was a mixture of pozzolano, earth, lime, and sand, in equal parts, by measure. The building is of a circular form, composed of stones of the weight of from two tons to half a ton each. The ground course measures forty-two feet in diameter, and the building diminishes, as it rises to the top, where the parapet wall of the light-room measures only thirteen feet in diameter. The height of the masonry is one hundred feet, but including the light-room, the total height is one hundred and fifteen feet. The building is solid from the ground course to the height of thirty feet, where the entry-door is situate, to which the ascent is by a kind of rope ladder with wooden steps, hung out at ebb-tide, and taken into the building again when the water covers the rock; but strangers to this sort of climbing are taken up in a chair, by a movable crane projected from the door, from which a narrow passage leads to a stone stair-case thirteen feet in height. Here the walls are seven feet in thickness, but they generally diminish from the top of the stair case to the parapet-wall of the light-room, where they measure one foot in thickness. The upper half of the building may be described as divided into six apartments for the use of the light-keepers, and for containing light-house stores. The lower or first, formed by an inside scarfement of the walls at the top of the stair-case is chiefly occupied with water tanks, fuel, and the other bulky articles; the second floor is for the oil, cisterns, glass, and other light-room stores; the third is occupied as a kitchen; the fourth is the bed-room; the fifth, the library, or strangers' room, and the upper apartment forms the light-room. The floors of the apartments are of stone, and the communication is made by means of wooden ladders, excepting in the light-room, where every article being fire-proof, the steps are made of iron. There are two windows in each of the three lower apartments, but the upper have each four windows. The casements are all double, and are glazed with plate-glass, having besides an outer storm-shutter, or dead light of timber, to defend the glass from the waves and spray. The parapet wall of the light-room is six feet in height, and has a door which leads out to the balcony or walk formed by the cornice round the upper part of the building; which is surrounded by a cast iron rail, wrought like net-work. This rail rests upon butts of brass, and has a massive coping, or top rail, of the same metal. In the kitchen, there is a grate or open fire-place of cast iron, with a smoke tube of the same metal, which passes through the several apartments of the light-room, and heats them in its passage upwards. This grate and chimney merely touch the building, without being included or built into the walls, which, by this means, are neither weakened, nor liable to be injured by it.

It is of an octagonal figure, twelve feet across, and fifteen in height, formed with cast iron sashes, glazed with large plates of polished glass, measuring about two feet six inches by two feet three inches, each plate being a quarter of an inch thick. The light-room is covered with a dome roof of copper, terminating in a large gilded ball, with a vent-hole in the top. The light of the Bell-rock is very powerful, and is readily seen at the distance of six or seven leagues, when the atmosphere is clear. The light is from oil, with Argand burners placed in the focus of silver plated reflectors, measuring twenty-four inches over the lips; the silvered surface or face being hollowed or wrought to the parabolic curve. That the Bell-rock light may be easily distinguished from all other lights upon the coast, the reflectors are ranged upon a frame with four faces or sides, which, by a train of machinery, is made to revolve upon a perpendicular axis once in six minutes. Between the observer and the reflectors, on two opposite sides of the revolving frame, shades of red glass are interposed, in such a manner, that during each entire revolution of the reflectors, two appearances, distinctly differing from each other, are produced; one is the common bright light familiar to every one, but, on the other, or shaded sides, the rays are tinged of a red colour. These red and bright lights, in the course of each revolution, alternate with intervals of darkness, which, in a very beautiful and simple manner, characterise this light.

In foggy weather two large bells of about twelve hundred each, are tolled day and night by machinery. Vessels who cannot see the lights, thus get warning to put about. The establishment at the Bell-rock, consists of a principal light-keeper and three assistants. At Arbroath, the most contiguous town on the opposite coast, a suite of buildings has been erected, where each light-keeper has three apartments for his family. Here the master and mate of the light-house tender have also accommodation for their families; a plot or piece of an enclosed garden ground is attached to each house. Connected with these buildings there is a signal tower erected, which is about fifty feet in height. At the top of it there is a room with an excellent five feet achromatic telescope, placed upon a stand. From this tower, a set of corresponding signals is arranged, and kept up with the light-keepers at the rock. Three of the light-keepers are always at the light-house, while one is ashore on liberty, whose duty it is for the time to attend the signal room; and when the weather will admit of the regular removal of the light-keepers they are six weeks at the rock, and a fortnight ashore with their families.

The attending vessel for the Bell rock, and the light-houses at the isle of May and Inchkeith, in the Firth of Forth, is a very handsome little cutter of about fifty tons register, carrying upon her prow the model of the light-house, and is appropriately named the Pharos. She is stationed at Arbroath, and is in readiness to proceed for the rock at new and full moon, or at spring-tides, carrying necessaries, and the light-keeper on leave, to the rock and returning with another. This vessel is navigated by four men, including the master, and is calculated for carrying a boat of sixteen feet keel, or of sufficient dimensions for landing at the rock in moderate weather. The master and mate are kept in constant pay, and have apartments in the establishment ashore: the former, acting as a superintendent, has the charge of the buildings and stores kept at Arbroath.

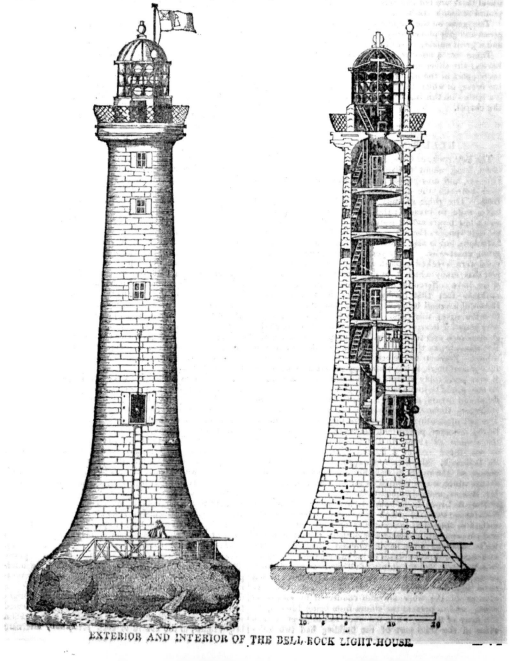

EXTERIOR AND INTERIOR OF THE BELL ROCK LIGHT-HOUSE.

THE REBELLION OF SILKEN THOMAS.

FROM THE "HIBERNIAN NIGHTS' ENTERTAINMENTS," IN THE DUBLIN UNIVERSITY MAGAZINE.

Acting upon our avowed determination not to meddle with politics or religion in the conducting of the Dublin Penny Journal, we have conscientiously abstained from noticing any of those periodicals which may be considered as the organ of a party, however talented or deserving of encouragement, considered in a literary point of view. Having, however, observed in several of the recent numbers of the Dublin University Magazine, articles which must be interesting to Irish readers generally, we have been induced to copy one of them into our little work; and we feel persuaded, that the following account of the "Rebellion of Silken Thomas," will be read with a kind of melancholy pleasure by every description of reader. For the opinions put into the mouths of some of the actors by the author, in scenes he has represented, we do not hold ourselves accountable. We may observe, by the way, that the story is one of a number related in order to while away the time during the imprisonment of Henry Roe O'Donnell, and several other youths, in Dublin Castle, some short time after the period of the rebellion referred to.

"Come, then, Turlogh Buy," cried Hugh, "tell us how *Tomás-an-teeda,* the bold Fitzgerald, set our Saxon lords by the ears in the late king's reign."

"With all the veins of my heart, noble princes," replied Turlogh; "and the readier, because I know a tale made on that very event, by a gentleman who was present in it. It will be a longer story than I have told you yet; for it contains the fortunes of some others, besides the arch rebel himself."

"It is a pity the Clan-Gerald was not of Irish blood," said Hugh; "they have ever been a race of brave gentlemen, and sharp thorns in the side of the invaders."

"They are more Irish than English, by ten generations to one," replied Henry; "and it is the same with Mac William Burk, and the Clan Butler. But let us to our tale; and, Turlogh, take time, and run it not into such close compass as to lose the best of your matter, as you did in the Captive of Killeshin. *Dar Columb!* your knight and lady had not words enough together to justify a colleen's courtship with a *buachal na mo!*'

"Ah, noble Henry," cried the old man, "'tis long since I sat, myself, by the side of a colleen dhas, talking the sweet words of honey that I spoke too easily ever to remember:—it is not what a man says readiest in the reality, that he tells freest in its recounting. Could your nobleness repeat all that the *duine Uaisle Oge* said to the daughter of Mac Mahon that summer evening in the wood of Truagh, when"——

"Say no more, Turlogh," cried Henry, blushing; "I'll let you off with the courtship; for I see O'Donnell burning to be at blows, and my brother Art longing to hear of the silk jackets of *Tomás-an-teeda's* gallowglass."

"Then we will suppose the courtship over, and introduce the lovers without more ado," said Turlogh with a smile, and addressed himself to his tale.

"In Dublin, near to Dame's Gate, lived, in 1534, a wealthy merchant, by name Paul Dudley. His house, built on the bank of the Liffey, overlooked a wharf at which one or more of his barques might usually be seen receiving or discharging cargo. Merchandize and nautical stores lay piled or scattered about the busy area of the court-yard, and the arched entrance resounded to the tramp of draught horses and the rattling of ponderous waggon wheels. Thus, towards the river, all was business and bustle; but southward, between his house and the secluded street it fronted, was a quiet garden, well planted and enclosed, and stretching in broad parterres and deep shrubberies almost to the city wall.

"It was a bright June morning, and the sun shone sweetly on the flowers and foliage; the birds sang in every tree; and a thrush, notwithstanding the presence of two persons on the rustic bench below, warbled loudly from her accustomed branch, over the great honeysuckle arbour. The occupants of the summer-house were a young man and fair girl; they had sat there so long, that the birds were grown familiar with them. They were lovers, as the maiden's conscious blushes and the eager looks of the cavalier confessed. Their loves were sanctioned, for they betrayed no clandestine apprehension; their looks were those of two of heaven's most favoured creatures, perfectly happy in mutual confidence and affection.

"'And now, my sweet Ellen,' said the wooer, 'now that I have heard from your own lips that you are mine for ever, my joy is so complete, that I think I can never be unhappy again.'

"'Indeed, Sir John,' said his companion, 'I knew not that you were unhappy; had you known my heart, you would have had little cause to be so.'

"'Dear Ellen,' he cried, 'you make me belie myself: I am again unhappy; for I feel that you suspect me of having doubted you. No, dearest, I could not distrust your true heart; I could never fear for you; but I confess I did dread, lest, in my absence, some other might find means to influence your father against our union; and although I would deem myself rich enough in your love alone, to disregard all other fortunes for my own part, yet, trust me, I would rather see my right hand cut off, than know you subjected to one harsh word or unkind look from your parent on my account. If that villain, Parez, has poisoned your father's ear, as I have reason to suspect, I vow by Saint Bernard'——

"'Thou hast been deceived:—in sooth, Sir John, and on my word, some one hath belied my father to thee,' cried the lady earnestly; 'Master Parez's suit sped not worse with me than with my father. He is a plain man, and a trader'——

"'Nay, dear Ellen, forgive me,' said the knight; 'I feel I have done your father wrong; he has still shown himself a kind friend to me; and doubt of his good-will could never have found a place in my thoughts, if I had not been at a distance from you; for when absent from you, Ellen, there was but one bright image in my mind; all the rest was dark and wretched.'

"'I have long wished, Sir John,' said the lady, scarcely attending to all the knight had addressed to her, 'to tell thee more of my father; and, I pray thee, think me not importunate to dwell on this. Indeed, Sir John, thou knowest him not. They say he hath preferred thee to others, for the sake of ennobling his riches by thy lineage; indeed they do him great wrong. He loves thee for thyself; believe me he doth. He is not a man to make many fair professions; but, blunt as thou hast thought him, he bears a warm and a true heart towards thee. It was but yesterday I heard him urge thy deserts on the Archbishop, with whom he has much influence.'

"'Dear Ellen,' said the knight, 'I feel it all, and love you the better for what you have said. For your father's good offices with the Archbishop, he has my gratitude; but I fear the friend of Lord Thomas Fitzgerald has little chance of favour with the old enemy of Kildare. I would I knew how the brave earl speeds at the court of England!'

"'I know little of the cause of anger between the Archbishop and the Lord Deputy,' said the lady; 'but I have heard such whispers among the Primate's friends who frequent my father's house, for loans and aids of ships and merchandize, as make me tremble, both for the Earl and his son, whom he hath left in his stead. Would to heaven, you were no longer associated with young Lord Thomas!'

"'Lord Thomas is a brave and generous gentleman,' cried the knight; 'his father, the Earl, was my youth's friend and protector; their noble house has ever been allied both by blood and mutual service to mine own, and I were a recreant and base churl to shrink from their quarrel, whether it be with bishop or king! Forgive me again, sweet Ellen, that I forget your father's friendship for the Primate in my own love and loyalty to the bold Geraldine.'

"Ellen Dudley yielded him her hand in token of the easily accorded pardon; but the truth was, she had spoken as much on the impulse of her judgment as of her feelings, and an involuntary predilection for the cause of her lover's friends, was already converting her forgiveness to sympathy, if not approval, when her father appeared at the upper end of the garden coming towards them from the house.

"Paul Dudley was an aged man, of a careful aspect, attired in sad coloured apparel somewhat faded, such as a rich citizen could afford to gratify his humility on. He advanced, and welcomed his elected son-in-law, with a grave cordiality suitable to his age and character: 'Sir John, thou art welcome,' he said, 'I am heartily glad to see thee again. Thou wilt excuse my delay, for I had with me certain contractors, when I heard of thy arrival, whom I might not sooner leave. Ellen, my child, go gather a dish of cherries, while I and Sir John fetch a walk here in the sunshine.'

"Ellen retired with a glance of glad meaning at her lover, and the knight and merchant walked arm-in-arm down the garden. 'Sir John,' said Dudley, 'I am a man of few words. When my daughter marries, I mean that she shall be lodged as suits the station of a lady; mine is a spare and frugal household, and would ill suit a nobleman's necessary retinue. I have, therefore, purchased a more commodious dwelling, with lands enough for its honourable maintenance, which shall be thine on thy wedding-day. Disert Castle is a strong pile, and I look to see it well manned against the Irish. The chief service of thy tenure will be to protect the Archbishop's rangers, and furnish a riding-out of twenty horse men yearly, on Saint John's day, to the prior of Kilmainham.'

"'Master Dudley,' said the knight, 'I will be frank with thee; when friends were scarcest with my father, the Earl of Kildare stood by him with purse and countenance, aye, even to the peril of his own head; when I was left an orphan he had me cared for as if I had been his own son; by his bounty I am educated as becomes my birth; from his honoured hand I hold my degree of knighthood. I cannot render service to the enemies of such a benefactor. On my honour, Master Dudley, it gives me pain to seem thus disposed to cavil at thy most generous proffer; but if thine own father had had so true a friend, and that friend so bitter an enemy, say, couldst thou thyself, if sought to take such service, act otherwise?'

"'Say no more, Sir John—say no more—the tenure shall be altered; thou shalt hold in capite, and serve none but the king. I am not a man to be easily moved from my purpose; yet surely I can see a hardship, and peradventure feel for an honourable scruple; nay, I would the more readily redress the one, Sir John, because I respect the other.'

"The merchant spoke with an honest sincerity which could not be mistaken; a tear glistened in the knight's eye as he grasped his hand—'Master Dudley, I thank thee from my heart. By my honour, I am even more beholden to thee for this consideration than for the bounty it confirms. I will hold Disert for the king right joyfully; aye, and call me churl if I keep not such goodly garrison as will make the passes of the pale, when thou shalt come to see me, as safe for thy trotting nag as the highway over Hoggin Green.'

"'Enough,' said Dudley, 'I know well that thou bearest no ungrateful mind; but there is another matter touching which I would now talk with thee. Thou art young and ardent; when there are as many grey hairs in thy beard as in mine, thou wilt not hold thy manhood's interest so light when weighed against thy youth's friendships; but I am not accustomed to waste words on idle hints; I will tell thee plainly, thy attachment to Kildare and his faction will plague thee yet, if you keep it not in more discreet bounds. The Earl, I tell thee, is in disgrace at court; his son, our ruffling Deputy, has offended every lord of the council here, by his pride and violence; not a day passes without injury and complaint; the king is enraged against both father and son, and Sir William Skeffington is striving hard to get the sword of office to himself. Now, I will not say to thee, as others might, that a wise man should keep clear of a falling house, and that thou oughtest to desert thy friends in this extremity: for I think there is in thee that constancy and nobility of nature which would spurn so unworthy a course, even if I

did give thee that base advice. No; if by the reverse of fortune Lord Thomas or his father stand in need of such help as one of thy estate may lawfully bestow, spare not my coffers in their service; for I would not have a child of mine lie under painful obligation where gold might lighten the burthen on his mind; but what I ask of thee is this—while thou shrinkest not from rendering all the kindly gratitude and lawful aid that a man may yield to his benefactor, without trenching on his duty to his king, shun the society of these rebellious conspirators who surround Lord Thomas, keep thy allegiance free from all contamination of traitorous suggestions; but, above all, if the frantic pride of the young Deputy do drive him into open treason, let no power of mistaken friendship or chivalrous devotion persuade thee for a moment to lend connivance or countenance to an attempt so desperate!—I am a peaceful man, loyal to the king, and desirous of good order in the state; thou art about to become my son, and the successor to my riches; do what reasonable, what lawful friendship requires, but bring not destruction on an honest house, and disgrace on the grey hairs of one who is willing to love thee as his own son!'

"'On my honour, Master Dudley, I know not why thou shouldst distrust my loyalty. I am the servant of the king; I have both given and taken hard blows under his banner; against whom have I ever fought, if not against his enemies? God forbid that my noble benefactor should ever need the service of my sword against our common Sovereign; but, by your hand, Master Dudley, this is some calumny of the Earl spread by his and the Lord Thomas's enemies. I never heard of other design among either them or their retainers, than to support the royal authority, or defend themselves against their private enemies; and I freely promise thee I will not strike a stroke on their behalf in any other quarrel.'

"'It is enough,' said the merchant, 'I trust to thine own candour and generosity; there is that in my heart which tells me thou wilt not deceive me.'

"'A man overwhelmed with obligation must make his promises with as bad a grace as his acknowledgments; I can but say, Master Dudley, I thank thee, and will do my best to show myself not unworthy of thy good opinion.'

"'And that is all I ask,' cried Dudley; 'I am now satisfied in all things. Go to my daughter, Sir John, and settle what day you please to end the wooing. God bless them both!' he exclaimed, as the knight disappeared down the green alley which led to the orchard; 'and God be praised who has bountifully given me two such children to bless! Surely my heart should be at ease at last. Here are the two now dearest to me in this world happy; all around me is pleasant and cheerful—strange! I have not marked the singing of the birds for many a year until to-day! Ah, Paul Dudley, what hast thou been dreaming of so long, not to know what a comfort thou hadst at hand at the sunny walks of thine own garden? By my faith, I feel young. I cannot tell how. What need have I of a staff?—lie there, thou halt companion!'—and he cast away his gold headed cane, and walked up and down, smoothing the grey locks from his forehead and turning up his face to the breeze with a long, unwonted sense of buoyant enjoyment.

"The tramp of horses sounding from the street roused Dudley from a train of happier anticipations than had perhaps occupied his thoughts since the eve of his own nuptials; but ere he had inquired who were the new comers, his child and destined son were seen approaching.

"'Oh, my dear father,' cried Ellen, as he folded her fondly in his arms, 'how can we thank thee for all thy goodness?' and she hid her blushing face on his breast.

"'Love each other, my children,' cried the happy old man, 'love each other, and I am well repaid!' So saying he joined their hands, and blessed them fervently.

"It was while Paul Dudley was thus ratifying his approval of his daughter's marriage, that an armed man advanced from the house towards the arbour, in front of which they stood. Whether it was that his aspect was habitually forbidding, or that he disliked his present errand, the stranger wore a black look from the moment he entered the garden; but when, on turning into the walk that gave him a full view of the scene before the summer-house, he caught the first glance of Ellen Dudley, in the arms of another, and her father standing by, he stopped for a moment, and drew back as if his eyes had been blasted—griping to his dagger, and actually reeling, like a man stunned by a heavy blow. In an instant, however, he recovered himself: his hand slid down from his belt, and his brow relaxed into comparative smoothness: still, as he advanced, there was a cloud on his dark features, and an inequality in his step, that told of the recent fit of passion. When Dudley saw him coming towards them, he advanced to meet him, although, from the evident dislike that marked his manner, it was plainly more for the sake of taking his scowling eyes off the knight and lady, than from any wish to show him a marked courtesy.

"'Master Parez,' said he, 'I bid thee a good morrow: hast thou any commands for me?'

"'I come, Master Dudley,' replied the ominous stranger, 'on an errand that will not much increase thy love for me. I bear a packet for the hands of yonder knight, whom I have sought in vain at guard-room and barbican, and now find toying with fair damsels in thy arbour. I have besides a message, by word of mouth, for Sir John Talbot.'

"'Ah, Master Parez,' said the merchant, 'thou art the man to do thy errand, without scruple for place or time. But go on, man; give the knight the letter, and say what thou hast to say; for, though I be hurried, yet I would have thee take a cup of wine with me before thou goest, till I tell thee of some danger to thy friends that it behoves thee to know.'

"'I thank thee, Master Dudley,' said Parez; 'but no wine shall cross my lips to-day; and as for the Lord Deputy's danger, let his enemies look to themselves." With this churlish answer on his lips, he advanced to the knight, and said, 'I have sought thee in vain, Sir John, both at the Newgate and at thy company's quarters, and would not have broken in on thy privacy here, had my orders not been so urgent as they are. The Lord Thomas Fitzgerald commends him to thee, and sends thee for thy perusal this letter, which Sir John de la Hyde had this morning of him to whom it is addressed—a friar, whose friend writes from London, as thou mayest read.'

"As Parez spoke, his eyes were fixed on Sir John Talbot with an expression of mixed malignity and triumph. The knight bent a fixed glance on him, in return, as he took the packet from his hands; but was soon too deeply interested in its contents to care whether his angry rival scowled or smiled upon him. But scarcely had he read half through the first page, when the colour fled from his cheeks, and large drops of perspiration burst out over his forehead. 'Parez!' he cried, and gasped a moment for utterance; then, as the blood rushed back to his brow, he seized the messenger fiercely by the arm—'Parez! if I thought you came here to triumph over my ruin, I would instantly despatch thee.'

"'I came here to do my duty, Sir John Talbot,' replied Parez, subduing a coarse smile that was already beginning to attest how much he enjoyed the agony of his rival; 'and, that duty done, I wait to know whether thou art equally prepared to do thine.'

"'Thou, at least, shalt never report me a recreant!' cried Talbot. 'Leave me: I know what thou wouldst say: I will be with Lord Thomas in an hour.'

"'An hour, Sir John! My Lord did not expect to find his friends so slack at this pinch.'

"'Parez, leave me. You have your revenge: you see me ruined. If there be a heart in your breast, stay not here to torture me! if you love your life, Christopher Parez, go! I will follow you.'

"Parez's eye glanced for a moment to the arbour, where Ellen Dudley had sunk, pale as ashes, on a seat: but, at a motion of the knight's hand to his dagger, accompanying a fiercer repetition of the command to withdraw, he turned sullenly upon his heel, and retired. Talbot's energy, before which the ignoble nature of Parez had thus quailed, deserted him as he turned to the arbour, where Ellen Dudley, with a beating heart, awaited the issue of their ominous conference. She rose in alarm as he entered.—'Thou art pale, Sir John; thy hands are cold as ice.

Mother of mercy! what has the wretch done to make thee look so ghastly?'

"'Ellen, I am a ruined man! They have murdered the Earl.'

"'Who have murdered? what Earl? for pity's sake, do not look so!'

"'The King has murdered the Earl of Kildare, Ellen; and Lord Thomas has—has sent to let me know.'

"She laid her hand on his, which was clenched and convulsively pressed on his knee. 'Oh, Sir John,' she said, 'believe me how well I feel for thy affliction; but take comfort; it pains my heart to see thee grieve so sorely: perhaps this news may be untrue.'

"'No, no, Ellen; it is all too sure: it has been too long and too deeply planned to leave any chance of failure when the blow was to be struck. The letter is positive; Kildare was beheaded in the tower on Saint Swithin's eve.'

"'Alas, what had they against him? was he not ever a loyal subject of the king?'

"Treason, Ellen; they charged him with treason, which his heart could no more conceive than it could malice or untruth. But I cannot talk of this now: my soul cries for vengeance within me when I think of it.'

"'Dear Sir John,' said Ellen, 'I feel, and from my heart I deplore, this misfortune; but do not, I beseech you, look so despairingly: you have lost a generous benefactor; but believe me, you have found new friends, if not so noble or so powerful, fully as willing to serve and love you.'

"'Ellen, I have lost both.'

"'Oh, no, no; say not so; do me not that wrong; do not so wrong my father.'

"'If I have done you wrong, Ellen, you are the truest hearted, but alas, the most hapless maiden that ever clung to man in his misfortunes! You know not to whom you would vow your fidelity. Yet I call heaven to witness that nothing short of this could have driven me to be what I am. It was murder, cold-blooded and cruel murder; and if ever rebellion was justified before heaven, it is ours against that treacherous and cowardly tyrant, who has thus wantonly spilled the blood of the kindest and most gallant gentleman that ever drew sword in his ungrateful cause.'—She looked piteously in his face, and burst into tears.—'You may weep now, Ellen; the worst is told—I am a rebel. The friends of my slaughtered benefactor are up in arms, and I will not fail them in this extremity. God, who knows my heart, knows with what grief and wretchedness my soul is filled since I made up my mind to leave you—you, who were my comfort in all sorrow before, on whom every hope that I had to cheer me in this world was fixed—for, Ellen, I feel at this moment that I have loved you far more dearly than the thoughts of a man who has not felt such grief as mine to-day could ever have conceived. Dear, indeed, as my own soul, far, far dearer than my life, is the love of Ellen Dudley in my heart's core for ever. But, Ellen, my love were worthless and unworthy, and I a wretch debased in the eyes of all brave men, if I loved not honour better than either life or love. I go, Ellen, dearest; I must leave you—I may never press these lips again; I may never again fold that true heart to mine. Speak, my beloved; tell me, are you then lost to me for ever?'

"'Never, dearest! I will never forsake you,' she murmured through her sobbing—he clasped her closer to his breast, and bent over her, kissing away her tears.

"At this moment voices sounded from the garden. 'I tell thee Sir, Sir John cannot have said so! It is scarce half an hour since he promised me with his own lips to abjure for ever the broils and treasons of thy turbulent faction.' It was Paul Dudley, high in wrath, disputing the passage of Parez to the arbour. When the lovers heard their voices, they tore themselves asunder. Ellen sat down, almost fainting, in the green recess; but Talbot came forth, prepared to go through with the sacrifice—for he felt that it was little better—come what might.

"'Sir John Talbot,' cried Dudley, when he saw him, 'here is a traitor in arms against the king, avowing his rebellion, and seeking to implicate thee in the same villainy; nay, boasting that thou art his abettor in the treason.'

"'There is little in common between me and Master Parez,' replied Talbot; 'yet in this cause we are companions.'

"'In what cause, Sir John? What means this conniving between thee and an open rebel?'

"'Master Dudley, Master Dudley,' cried Talbot, 'knowest thou that the noble Earl of Kildare is basely murdered by that arch-heretic and cruel tyrant, who was yesterday my king; and dost thou marvel that I am in arms for vengeance on my benefactor's enemies?'

"'If thou be in arms against the Royal Majesty, thou art a forsworn traitor, Sir John Talbot!' cried Dudley: 'thou hast deceived me, and villain, thou hast stolen the affections and ruined the peace of my child! for with my own hands I would rather strangle her, than see her wedded to an outlawed robber, as thou and thy traitorous associate will shortly be. Ho, Giles and Watkin, Jeniko and Gregory! stand by your master, ye knaves; lay hands on the rebels—ten pieces of gold to him who secures the traitor Talbot!' and, weaponless as he was, he threw himself upon the armed knight as boldly as if he had himself been cased in steel and bounding in the vigor of youth: but his men, seeing the house surrounded by Parez's troop, and confident that, however their enraged master might rave against his old favourite, he did not at heart desire his injury, held back; and the weak old man, exhausted by contending emotions, and overcome by unusual personal exertion, fell, almost powerless, into the arms of him whom he had sought to pull to the ground.

"'Forgive me, Master Dudley; forgive me, my father!' cried Talbot, as he consigned the tottering merchant to the arms of his daughter, who had come from her retreat the moment she heard her father's voice summoning his servants to ineffectual violence, and now half forgot her own grief in alarm for her parent's safety.

"When Dudley heard himself called by the name of father, and saw the knight, when that appeal obtained no answer, turn away as if he could not bear the contemplation of his humiliating helplessness, he was stirred with strong feelings of affection and pity. 'Come back, come back, and I will forgive thee every thing,' he cried, while tears burst from his eyes, and his voice trembled with emotion. 'Thou art still my son, if thou wilt but shun thine own destruction. Return, return to thy allegiance; it is not yet too late to repent and save thyself! Oh, Sir John, for thine own sake, for pity to my grey hairs, and, as a last appeal, as thou wouldst not break the heart of this innocent girl, do not yield to this madness, to this fearful and dishonouring sin!'

"'May God have pity on me!' cried Talbot: 'this is a sore trial to put a man's heart to.'

"'Give the word to mount,' cried Parez, who had stood silent through the scene, but now spoke loudly and scornfully. 'What answer shall I bear to Lord Thomas, Sir John Talbot? Shall I say that you refuse to join?'

"'You shall bear no base account of me to-day?' cried the unhappy gentleman, and without trusting himself with another look at the wretched two he left behind, hurried to the court-yard, where a horse stood ready saddled for his use."

(To be continued.)

THE NATURAL HISTORY OF BIRDS.*

This is a little work very much to our mind. Its object is, we are informed, "to render the study of that portion of nature of which it treats more inviting, more easy, and more instructive, especially to the young, and still more especially to those who devote the intervals of business or labour to that most delightful of all sports—self-improvement, but who may not have the means of procuring, or time for studying, works of greater magnitude and more lofty pretensions."

We have more than once before, in noticing works of a similar genus, taken occasion to state our opinion as to the description of books best calculated to induce the young and the uninformed, not only to commence, but to continue, the acquisition of Natural History; and we perfectly agree in opinion with our author, that "very many, if not all, of our introductory works, not on this particular branch of knowledge only, but on every branch, go the wrong way to work, and by this means, instead of removing the difficulties which belong to the subject, encumber it with many others, which arise entirely from the mode of treating it."

There can be no question, speaking generally of all classes, that to induce all to *learn* that which is useful, "the natural desire for knowledge has only to be preserved alive, and enticed by that which is pleasant: all will learn, not only voluntarily, but in spite of opposition.

"That such would be the case, if the young were not sickened with mechanical trifles in which there is no occupation for the mind, and condemned to drudge at that in which they can see no usefulness and find no pleasure, is not only probable, but demonstrated in the cases of those who have been spared the weariness of the spirit, and also saved from those errors into which the unoccupied minds of the young are so prone to fall."

And that such is the object of the little work before us, is obvious; we therefore recommend it to all who are anxious to obtain an easy introduction to the delightful study of Natural History.

THE ROSE.

Air—"My heart and lute."

The rose, the sweetly scented rose,
　The pride of summer's bloom—
Beyond all other flow'rs it glows
　In beauty and perfume.
'Tis come in hey-day loveliness,
　In all its bright array;
While summer's smiles of radiance bless,
　And ev'ry scene is gay.

Meet type of tend'rest feeling, all
　That vivid feeling warms,
All hearts alive to beauty's call,
　Must own thy graceful charms.
I hail thee, queen of lovely flowers—
　"The light that gilds the page"
Of nature's bland and florid hours,
　Proclaim'd from age to age.

Besides thy bloom's most beauteous glow,
　Or yet thy fragrant spell,
I've reason why I love thee so,
　Sweet rose, that I'll not tell.
Reign o'er my bower, thou peerless gem,
　That bygone joys recall;
The tide of thought 'twere vain to stem—
　I own its magic thrall.

Dear, dear to mem'ry is the spread
　Of thy young beauty's tint;
Though youthful bliss, alas! be fled,
　How sweet the bright imprint.
Then hail, my charming, lovely rose!
　The pride of summer's bloom!
Thou art the dearest flower that blows,
　For beauty and perfume.

C. M. C.

Kilkenny.

DUBLIN:
Printed and Published by P. D. Hardy, 3, Cecilia-street; to whom all communications are to be addressed.
Sold by all Booksellers in Ireland.
In London, by Richard Groombridge, 6, Panyer-alley, Paternoster-row; in Liverpool, by Wilmer and Smith; in Manchester, by Ambery; in Birmingham, by Guest, 91, Steelhouse-lane; in Glasgow, by John Macleod; and in Edinburgh, by N. Bowack.

---

* The Natural History of Birds. By Robert Mudie.—London: Orr and Smith, Paternoster-row.

SILKEN THOMAS RENOUNCING HIS ALLEGIANCE.

THE REBELLION OF SILKEN THOMAS.

FROM THE "HIBERNIAN NIGHTS' ENTERTAINMENTS," IN THE DUBLIN UNIVERSITY MAGAZINE.

(Continued from our last Number.)

" Talbot mounted, in the silence of rage and sorrow, and as the troop wheeled out of the court-yard and turned up to the Dame's-gate, struck his horse fiercely with the spur, and dashed out in front; he could not bear the eyes of those around him, for his own were swimming in grief and indignation. When he reached Castle-street, he was so far in advance of his company, that he found himself obliged to pull up till he should learn which way they intended to take. He looked up and down the busy thoroughfare before him, all alive with the bustle of secure prosperity; stalls, shops, and warehouses, far as the eye could reach, teeming with a peaceful and industrious race, toiling on in happy ignorance of the impending calamities which he was even then lending his aid to hasten, and for a moment his heart failed him; but as he looked up at the fortress, and saw on the brow of the barbican, the sharp outline of the spikes on which the heads of the Leinster rebels were bleaching in the blue sky, he thought, with a shudder and a thrill of anguish, of his own friend's kindly features clotted with the blood from the block, and exposed to the insults of his enemies, over the gates of London, and the thirst for revenge, which then seized his whole soul, consumed whatever lingering attachment to his allegiance might have been revived by his first contemplation of the peaceful security around him. By this time Parez was again by his side, and the troop wheeled down to the right, passed the castle at a trot, and drew up in line opposite the gate into Thomas-street. The citizens crowded round, admiring their gay accoutrements and martial order, for as yet there was no suspicion of

rebellion in their minds, and the men themselves, in general, were ignorant of the purpose for which they were assembled. Presently the crowd collected round the gates began to break up and line the causeways at either side, and a gallant cavalcade was seen through the open arch, advancing from Thomas-court towards the drawbridge. 'Way for the Lord Deputy,' cried two truncheon bearers, dashing through the gate, and a shout rose on all sides, that Lord Thomas was coming. Trumpeters and pursuivants at arms rode first; then came the macebearer with his symbol of office, and, after him, the sword of state in a rich scabbard of velvet, carried by its proper officer. Lord Thomas himself, in his robes of state, and surrounded by a dazzling array of nobles and gentlemen, spurred after; the arched gateway was choked for a moment with tossing plumes and banners, flashing arms and gleaming faces, as the magnificent troop burst in like a flood of fire upon the dark and narrow precincts of the city. But, behind the splendid cortege which headed their march, came a dense column of mailed men-at-arms, that continued to defile through the close pass, long after the gay mantles and waving pennons of their leaders were indistinct in the distance.

" Talbot, still high in passion, as the pomp drew near his position, kept his eyes fixed on the face of the young Geraldine. Lord Thomas's brow was flushed, and he glanced fiercely from the castle to the river, as he listened to the urgent representations of an elderly knight by his side. But when his eye fell on Talbot, where he sat reining back his charger to give room for the cavalcade, a haggard smile crossed his agitated features, and he called him by his name, and extended his hand to welcome him.

" ' Talbot!' he cried, 'I thank thee! I knew thou wouldst not fail me in trouble; for he who is gone for failed thee in time of need—may my race be forgotten, and my name be a watchword of reproach, if I make not the day of his death the blackest in the English calendar!—ha, Sir John, knowest thou that I mean to hold the island against Henry?'

"'My lord,' replied Talbot, 'I have not yet heard your lordship's design; but be it what it may, I will back the quarrel of your father's son as long as I can hold my sword.'

"'My own design and my desire,' said Lord Thomas, is to fling a bold defiance in the teeth of the council, rendering up office and allegiance together, and opening the war as becomes an associate of the royal princes whom I look to have for my allies.'

"'My Lord, this is madness,' cried the old knight at his side; 'ride up to Bermingham tower with that sword and mace before you, and the king's chief castle is won without a blow; renounce your allegiance before the council, and White will have his draw-bridge raised and his cannon pointed, before we can so much as make good our passage back from Mary's-abbey.'

"'Sir Oliver,' replied the young lord, 'thou art my uncle, and God forbid I should make light of thy advice; but it shall never be said of Thomas Fitzgerald, that he struck his first blow against Henry Tudor in the dark! What would they say at Rome, or at Madrid?'

"'My lord,' cried a gentleman who rode near him, 'what we do here is the question, not what they may say there. If we can, by the use of Henry's authority, make head against his friends till succours from the Pope and Emperor arrive, trust me, our allies will never ask whether we won the quarters where we lodge them by strength of hand, or virtue of the king's writ.'

"'Sir Richard Walsh,' exclaimed Lord Thomas, 'but that I know none here would cheaply see my father's son dishonoured, I would say that some among us bent on turning this brave adventure to a rascal conspiracy!'

"'You do us wrong, my lord,' cried Sir Oliver Fitzgerald, colouring deeply; 'but I urge you no further; conduct the war as you will. Yet although I withdraw my unpalatable advice, I will not hold back my hand; for I would rather strike ten blows in your quarrel, than waste another word on your headstrong folly.'

"'Pardon me, my dear kinsman,' cried the young noble, earnestly grasping his uncle's hand; 'and you, Sir Richard, and those other knights and gentlemen who have advised me otherwise, forgive me for what I have said; but, trust me, this is the nobler, this is the worthier course. Nor do I think I stand alone in preferring the honourable chances of open warfare, to the petty successes of surprise or treachery. Sir John Talbot, am I not in the right?'

"'I for one,' cried Talbot, 'would think our cause dishonoured in the eyes of all brave men, if your lordship turned the sword, which you have sworn to use for the benefit of the king's government, against those who committed it, on the faith of that oath, into your lordship's hands.'

"'Pooh!' cried Burnet of Belgriffin, 'who talks of a breach of faith, and he already forsworn in his oath of allegiance?'

"'There is no faith to be kept with heretics,' said an ecclesiastic of the party; 'Henry is a rotten sheep, to corrupt the flock of Christ—anathema esto!'

"'He stuck upon no point of honour when he put the Earl to death, after bringing him to London on a solemn pledge of safety!' exclaimed Sir Dominick Le Poer.

"'The end, my children, justifies the means,'' again urged the churchman.

"'Treachery for treachery!' cried Parez; 'it is but equal justice.'

"'My Lord!' exclaimed Talbot, drawing up, and Lord Thomas checked his horse at the same moment, so that the whole party were brought to a sudden halt—'I said I would back the quarrel of your father's son: I am ready to make good what I have said at peril of my body, but I tell those knights and gentlemen, that I would rather my hand were rotted off than that it should ever draw blade in the cause either of plotting conspirators or of priestly bigots!'

"'What!' cried Le Poer, scornfully, 'this is somewhat early for desertion; if any man here be afraid to join in our revolt, he is at liberty to withdraw himself at once; there is no need of splitting straws for an apology.'

"'Sir Dominick Le Poer,' said Talbot, 'if you mean me, I will tell you plainly, the chief fear I have in this adventure is, being joined in it by one whom I once saw turn his back upon his friends, when blows were plentier than good advice, in the gap of Garrycaltrim.'

"'The cause never yet prospered that was begun by blaspheming the ministers and church of God,' exclaimed the angry ecclesiastic, before Le Poer could reply to this biting retort.

"'Before heaven, priest,' cried Sir Oliver Fitzgerald, 'I like thy doctrine as little as he—thou and Master Parez are bad advocates among cavaliers of honour: I am, in truth, already half of the opinion of my noble kinsman and his valiant friend. Heaven forbid that either falsehood or treachery should ever be charged on Oliver Fitzgerald, though thou and thy whole church were to be saved from perdition by their means!—nephew, I counsel the use of thy authority only so far as thy conscience can clearly carry thee; if it goes a hair's breadth against thy honour as a knight and gentleman to take advantage of the castle for thy proclamation of revolt, lead on to Mary's-abbey, and we will bid these proud lords defiance!'

"'And so say I,' cried Sir John De la Hyde. 'And I'—'and I'—'and I,' re-echoed from a dozen gentlemen around, whom indecision, or dislike of disagreement had hitherto kept silent.

"'Come on, then, friends and kinsmen!' cried Lord Thomas, turning his horse's head towards the river; 'we will never leave it to our enemies to say that we have played any but a fair and manly part by them.' The dissentient party yielded reluctantly, and the whole cavalcade wheeled down to the Liffey. Sir Oliver, as they crossed the bridge, cast a wistful eye over the battlemented range wall, on the towers of the castle, frowning in massive security behind them; but the time was past; for, even as he gazed, he saw the long levers of the draw-bridge rise high against the sky above the curtain of the barbican.

"'White has caught the alarm, so good by to Dublin Castle!' cried Burnel, bitterly.

"'Ay,' answered Le Poer, sharply, 'will a point of honour, think you, weigh down that draw-bridge, or a sharp gibe cut open that portcullis? Yet we told them how this would be.'

"'It is a judgment and a sign'—began Travers, the churchman; but Sir Oliver cut him short. 'Spur on to the Abbey, gentlemen, or the tidings will have reached the council before us.'

"The gates of Mary's-abbey soon received the leaders of the revolt, and ere the last of their followers had ceased to pour into the echoing court-yard, Lord Thomas and his friends were at the door of the council-chamber. The assembled lords rose at his entrance, and way was made for him to the chair of state.

"'Keep your seats, my lords,' said he, stopping midway between the entrance and council table while his friends gathered in a body at his back. 'I have not come to preside over this council, my lords. I come to tell you of a bloody tragedy that has been enacted in London, and to give you to know what steps I have thought fit to take, in consequence.'

"'What tragedy, my lord?' said Alan, the archbishop of Dublin; 'your lordship's looks and words alarm me: what means this multitude of men now in the house of God? My lord, my lord, I fear this step is rashly taken; this looks like something, my lord, that I would be loth to name in the presence of loyal men.'

"'My Lord Archbishop,' replied Thomas, 'when you pretend an ignorance of my noble father's murder'—

"'Murder!' cried the Lord Chancellor Cromer, starting from his seat, and all at the council table uttered exclamations of astonishment or horror, save only Alan and the Lord High Treasurer—'Yes, my lord,' the young Geraldine continued, with a stern voice, still addressing the Archbishop, 'when you pretend ignorance of that foul and cruel murder, which was done by the instigation and traitorous procuring of yourself and others, your accomplices, and yet taunt me with the step which I have taken' rashly, it may be, but not, I trust, unworthily of my noble father's son, in consequence; you betray at once your treachery and your hypocrisy.'—By this time the tumult among the soldiery without, who had not till now heard of the death of the Earl, was as if a thousand men had been storming the abbey. They were all native Irish, and to a man devoted to Kildare. Curses, lamentations, and cries of rage and vengeance sounded from every quarter of the court-yard; and some who rushed into the council-hall, with drawn swords, to be avenged on the authors of their calamity, were with difficulty restrained, by the knights and gentlemen around the door, from rushing on the Archbishop and slaying him, as they heard him denounced by their chief, on the spot. When the clamour was somewhat abated, Alan, who had stood up to speak at its commencement, addressed the Chancellor.

" 'My lord, this unhappy young man says he knows not what. If his noble father, which God forbid, should have come under his Majesty's displeasure—if he should, indeed, have suffered—although I know not that he hath—the penalty of his numerous treasons'—

" 'Bald priest, thou liest!' cried Sir Oliver Fitzgerald; 'my murdered brother was a truer servant of the crown than ever stood in thy satin shoes!'

" 'Alan, and the Lord Chancellor Cromer, also an Archbishop, and Primate of Armagh, rose together; the one complaining loudly of the wrong and insult done his order; the other beseeching that all present would remember they were Christians and subjects of the crown of England; but in the midst of this confusion, Lord Thomas, taking the sword of state out of the hands of its bearer, advanced up the hall to the council table, with a lofty determination in his bearing, that at once arrested all eyes. It was plain he was about to announce his final purpose, and all within the hall awaited what he would say in sullen silence. His friends and followers now formed a dense semicircle at the foot of the hall; the lords of the council had involuntarily drawn round the throne and Chancellor's chair; Thomas stood alone on the floor opposite the table, with the sword in his hands. Anxiety and pity were marked on the venerable features of Cromer, as he bent forward to hear what he would say; but Alan, and the treasurer, Lord James Butler, exchanged looks of malignant satisfaction.

" 'My lord,' said Thomas, 'I come to tell you that my father has been basely put to death, for, I know not what, alleged treason; and that we have taken up arms to avenge his murder. Yet, although we be thus driven by the tyranny and cruelty of the king into open hostility, we would not have it said hereafter that we have conspired like villains and churls, but boldly declared our purpose as becomes warriors and gentlemen. This sword of state, my lords, is yours; not mine. I received it with an oath, that I would use it for your benefit; I should stain my honour if I turned it to your hurt. My lords, I have now need of my own weapon, which I can trust; but, as for the common sword, it has flattered me not; a painted scabbard, while its edge was already red in the best blood of my house; ay, and is even now whetted anew for further destruction of the Geraldines. Therefore, my lords, save yourselves from us as from open enemies. I am no longer Henry Tudor's Deputy—I am his foe. I have more mind to conquer than to govern—to meet him in the field than to serve him in office. And now, my lords, if all the hearts in England and Ireland, that have cause thereto, do but join in this quarrel, as I look that they will, then shall the world shortly be made sensible of the tyranny, cruelty, falsehood, and heresy, for which the age to come may well count this base King among the ancient traitors of most abominable and hateful memory.'

" 'Croom aboo!' cried Neale Roe O'Kennedy, Lord Thomas's bard, who had pressed into the body of the hall, at the head of the Irish soldiery. He was conspicuous over all by his height, and the splendour of his native costume. His legs and arms were bare; the sleeves of his yellow cothone, parting above the elbow, fell in voluminous folds almost to the ground, whilst its skirts, girded at the loins, covered him to the knee. Over this he wore a short jacket of crimson, the sleeves just covering the shoulders, richly wrought and embroidered, and drawn round the waist by a broad belt,

set with precious stones, and fastened with a massive golden buckle. His laced and fringed mantle was thrown back, but kept from falling by a silver brooch, as broad as a man's palm, which glittered on his breast. He stretched out his hand, the gold bracelets rattling as they slid back on the thickness of his red-haired arm, and exclaimed in Irish—' Who is the young lion of the plains of Liffey, that affrights the men of counsel, and the ruler of the Saxon, with his noble voice? Who is the raked-up ember of Kildare, that would consume the enemies of his people, and the false churls of the cruel race of clan-London? It is the son of Gerald—the top branch of the oak of Ofaly—it is Thomas of the silken mantle, *Tomás an teeda, Ard-Righ Eireann!*'

" 'Righ Tomas go bragh!' shouted the soldiery, and many of the young lord's Anglo-Irish friends responded—'Long live King Thomas!' but the Chancellor, Archbishop Cromer, who had listened to his insane avowal with undisguised distress, and who had already been seen to wring his hand, and even to shed tears at the misguided nobleman and his friends thus madly invoked their own destruction, came down from his seat, and earnestly grasping the young lord by the hand, addressed him:

" 'Good, my lord,' he cried, while his venerable figure and known attachment to the house of Kildare, attested as it was by such visible evidences of concern, commanded for a time the attention of all present: 'Good, my lord, suffer me to use the privilege of an old man's speech with you, before you finally give up this ensign of your authority, and pledge of your allegiance. I have known the friendship of your noble father, and I am bold to say, there is no man in this presence, saving yourself, my Lord Thomas—for loth indeed I would be to have to call you so soon my lord of Kildare—who would more deeply deplore any injury that might befal him. But this report of his death, whereon your lordship would ground your anger, what is it at best but an obscure rumour? My lord, I cannot credit it. We of the council have had no tidings of such severity either designed for the Earl of Kildare, or practised against him. Yet, if it be the case that God has permitted the heart of the King to be turned against his servant, and that you, my lord, are thus suddenly called upon to support the name and honour of your noble family, trust me, you ought now rather to be considering how best you could discharge the grave duties of the head of such a house, and how best restore it to the dignity of its half-forfeited loyalty, than thus to run to hopeless arms in the desperate certainty of utterly destroying all that you have left worth the retrieving.'——

" 'Chorp an dioul! What says the Saxon Ollamh?' said one of the galloglass to his neighbour.

" 'By the axe in my hand, Phelim Gorm,' replied the other, 'it seems to me that he is making a rann in praise of the old Earl—my heavy curse on them that brought him low!'

" 'What!' cried Phelim Gorm, 'have the Saxons got fileas among them, as well as doctors and brehons?'

" 'If he be not a bard,' replied the galloglass, 'he is a rhymer, and is crying the keene—see if the tears be not running down his cheeks! *A yeah yeelish! mo vrone, mo rilleah, agus mo lenn ghairt!*'

" 'Oh, my lord,' the voice of Cromer was now heard exclaiming, 'the name of a king is sacred, but odious is the name of rebellion: the one derived from heaven, and by God defended, the other forged in hell, and executed by Satan. My lord, this is no private broil, in which you might, with little hurt, give way for a time to your passion: this is a quarrel which concerns the crown, that touches the nobility, that appertains to the whole commonwealth, and therefore it behoves you well before you jeopardize so many and so weighty interests, first, to see that the cause of your quarrel is certain, and then to ask whether the advantage to be gained be not outweighed by the calamity and wretchedness which this attempt, if persevered in, must produce.'

" 'It is no keening, Con,' said Phelim Gorm, 'he is pronouncing some heroical oration in praise of the Ierna Oge—*farrah! Tomás-an-teeda aboo!*'

" 'That I cannot tell,' replied Con; 'but, be he bard

or, rhymer, he wears a glibb and coolun longer than the wildest of O'Connor's kerns.'

"'Tis not rightly trained,' observed Phelim; 'and to my eye it does not seem like a man's natural hair; but, ababoo! what says he now?'

"'My lord,' continued Cromer, 'while the gale blows full in your sails, doubt not that divers will cleave to you, and feed upon you as crows upon their carrion; but when the storm begins to bluster, then will these same summer friends leave you like a goodly bark stranded at the ebb, or driven by the tempests ashore. Then will come impeachment, and conviction, and attainder—your arms reversed, your manors confiscated, your castles razed, your name dishonoured! Weigh then, my lord, the nobility of your ancestors; remember your late father's exhortation, forget not your duty to your prince, but above all, have pity on the wretched state of your poor country. Think with what heaps of curses you will be loaded, when the barbarous soldier, let loose in those wars, shall plunder the poor subject, consuming the widow's portion and inheritance of the fatherless, wasting the country, length and breadth; ay, and so endangering the whole realm, that they are not yet born who shall last smart for it. My lord, the king is a vessel of grace and mercy, and your offence is not yet over-heinous: cleave to his clemency—it is not yet too late. Oh, my lord, I pray you in most humble wise, for the love of God, for the duty you bear your prince, for the regard you bear your country, and the respect you would have for your own safety, abandon this headlong folly, and return to your allegiance!'

"'My Lord Chancellor,' replied Thomas, 'I came not here to take advice, but to give you to understand what I purpose to do. As loyalty would have me know my prince, so duty compels me to reverence my father. I thank you heartily for your counsel; but it is now too late. As to my fortune, I will take it as God sends it, and rather choose to die with valour and liberty, than live under King Henry in bondage and villainy. Wherefore, my lord, I thank you again for the concern you take in my welfare, and since you will not receive this sword out of my hand, I can but cast it from me, even as here I cast off and renounce all duty and allegiance to your master.' So saying, he flung the sword of state upon the council table. The blade started a hand's breadth out of its sheath, from the violence with which it was dashed out of his hands. He then, in the midst of a tumult of acclamation from his followers, and cries of horror and pity from the lords and prelates around, tore off his robes of office, and cast them at his feet. Stripped thus of his ensigns of dignity, Lord Thomas Fitzgerald stood up, amid the wreck of his fair fortune, an armed and avowed rebel, equipped in complete mail, before the representatives of England and Ireland. The cheering from his adherents was loud and enthusiastic, and those without replied with cries of fierce exultation.

"'Farrah, farrah!' shouted Neale Roe O'Kennedy, in a voice of thunder; 'it is Thomas of the shirt of iron, that has leaped forth from his silken livery, like the bright steel from its sheath of velvet! like the brand from its cloak of ashes! like the red flaming and consuming fire of heaven out of the scattered clouds of the sky!—The sword of Erin is sharp, heavy, and piercing; the ember of the raked-up wrath of Erin is red, smoking, and terrible; the flash of the avenging thunderbolts of Erin is swift and sure, strong and sudden, burning and blasting, and wasting, and inevitable!—Ring around him, sons of Gerralt! shout for the *Mac an Earla More!* Throw by your hunting spears, ye children of the chase: we must soon follow our game with battle-axe and claymore to the wild dog's den; cast away your bows of chase, ye hunters of the plains of Leinster, we must hunt a prey to-day with the shots of guns and cannons in the nest of dragons and in the lair of the dun Saxon lion! *Farrah, farrah! Croom aboo!'*—and crying the Geraldine war cry, he rushed into the court-yard, his red locks flaming over the heads of the clansmen like a torch.

"By this time the lords of the council were dispersed by the doors at the throne end of the hall, for Lord Thomas, with the same chivalrous generosity that induced him openly to withdraw his allegiance, had permitted them to escape unmolested, as from a solemn parley. His friends now gathered round him to consult on their proceedings.

"'My lord, if we get not the first word with his Holiness and the Emperor,' said Sir Oliver Fitzgerald to his nephew, 'that pestilent fellow, Alan, will have the start of us, and mar our hopes of succour from the continent.'

"'Right, uncle,' said Thomas—'it shall be looked to; but first let us summon White to deliver up the castle.'

"'Your lordship will hardly handle the keys of Dublin castle now without blows,' said Le Poer.

"'Well, then, if we must take them by strong hand, let us fall to without delay,' cried Thomas.

"'The citizens are ill-affected towards us,' observed Sir Richard Walsh; 'I question much whether they will suffer us to place our batteries within the walls; and from Sheep-street and the south, across the city ditch, we would assault the place to a manifest disadvantage.'

"'Ha!' cried Sir Oliver, 'it is true; the porking churls do hate us heartily; yet if we do not get their good will, by fair means or by foul, White may baffle us for a good six weeks yet.'

"'I'll tell you what, my lord,' said Burnel, 'although I advised against this course, I will do what a true man may to aid you out of it. From my poor house of Ballgriffen, I hold, as it were, the keys of Fingal, the granary of Dublin. Now, my lord, send a flag to the citizens, and give them to understand that if they refuse your lordship's artillery a friendly reception, I will close the doors of their market-house, while a bushel of corn remains in Meath.'

"'It is well said,' cried Lord Thomas. 'Let us send to the knaves as Master Burnel advises. Parez, wilt thou and Sir John Talbot do me this service?'

"'Willingly, my lord,' said Parez; and Talbot, conscious of his having been the chief adviser of a course that was already beginning to be beset by gratuitous difficulties, and unwilling to exhibit farther dissatisfaction, also consented. His dislike of Parez was, if possible, increased since he had heard his dishonourable sentiments in the dispute about giving up the sword, and his passions, ruffled as they had been by successive excitements, were still unallayed, and with difficulty kept under. As they received their instructions, he could plainly perceive that all those who had been opposed to him in that dispute, regarded him with evident distrust; while many of the rest, beginning to feel the difficulty into which their rashness had hurried them, hung back, or muttered their acknowledgments of late repentance.

"Again, riding side by side, with dark brows and averted glances, the rivals silently and sullenly proceeded on their mission. The gates at the farther end of the bridge were closed, and a gun was run out from the embrazure above as they advanced.

"'Give the word, or I shoot!' cried a bulky citizen, showing his linstock above the breech of the falcon.

"'Base churl, who trusted thee with a gun, that know not a flag of truce from a royal standard?' cried Talbot. 'Open thy gates, sirrah porker, we come with terms for your burghers.'

"'Churl! porker!' exclaimed the angry citizen, vainly striving to bring the piece to bear upon Talbot's men, who were now close under the walls—'Traitor and rebel! I'll teach thee to revile the city authorities! Heave her up, my masters—I'll blow the bankrupt coxcomb into the Liffey!'

"'Stop thy hand, good Master Harvey,' cried Talbot, with a smile; 'the recoil of the piece will burst thy girdle; on my honour, master draper, I knew you not; else I had not used those unworthy terms; but I have been chafed to-day, and need thy forgiveness.'

"'Ah, Sir John, Sir John, what desperate course is this thou hast taken to,' cried the appeased trader; 'where shall I now look for payment of the last suit of velvet, thou attainted spendthrift?'

"'This, at least, is not yet confiscated,' cried Talbot, flinging him his purse. 'There is my debt, and a broad piece beside for top-knots to thy wenches; but, Master Harvey, open the gates, and give us speech of your burghers without more delay.'

"'What hast thou to say to the loyal citizens of Dublin?' demanded a voice which made Talbot start in his saddle, as Paul Dudley showed himself over the battlement above the gateway, with others of the aldermen and burghers.

" ' Do you refuse our flag any more convenient conference than this, Master Dudley?' said Parez, for Talbot had turned his head away, and could make no answer.

" ' If you like not this,' replied the loyal merchant, ' you shall have a louder from our cannons' mouths—what seek ye ?'

" ' Passage to the castle, to summon the constable to surrender; and free quarters to besiege him if he refuse.'

" ' Tell your traitorous master that he shall have no passage through the streets of Dublin, but over the bodies of its slaughtered citizens,' was the reply.

" ' Then hear what I am commanded by my master to tell you,' said Parez, and he repeated the threat, as it had been made by Burnel, of stopping the supplies from Fingal and Meath. There was a moment's evident consternation among the citizens, that spoke of slenderly victualled stores; but Paul Dudley stood forward and said, ' You have your answer. You get no footing here, though we should eat our belts ! Come, brother citizens, be of good cheer : I have in my warehouses some twenty hogsheads of powdered beef, at the service of the city, if need be.'

" And I,' cried another alderman, ' so far as an hundred pounds' worth of pork and flour can go in our supply, will freely open my stores to the wants of our garrison.'

" ' Want nothing for wine, while the ten tuns in my cellars at Preston's Inns can feel the spiggot,' cried a third; but Talbot, who had listened with mingled feelings of remorse and admiration, advanced again to the gate as his party were retiring.

" ' For the love of heaven,' he cried, ' hear me one word before we go ! As I hope for mercy, Master Dudley, I had rather lose my right hand, than see the people of this fair city suffering as they must suffer, notwithstanding all your private means, if this resolution of yours be persisted in. My worshipful masters, you who have wives and little ones at home, think, I beseech you, what it is to see them we love perishing of famine'——

" ' I have a daughter at home,' said Dudley, ' and I would rather see her dead for hunger, than let a rebel plant one gun within our walls !'

" Talbot shuddered, and for a moment shrunk back; but he was not yet repulsed. ' Citizens of Dublin, heed

not what he says,' he exclaimed ; ' it is anger against me has made him mad. You will starve before three weeks, if you listen not to our terms. Oh ! Master Dudley, do not think that I came on this errand with my own will. I tell you, that my heart is wrung with anguish when I think of the hard fate that brings me here ! Relent in time—'tis you alone who leads the rest in this. Oh ! Master Dudley, relent, I pray you, by the love you bear the one you love best.'

" ' Traitor, name her not,' cried Dudley, ' or not even your flag shall protect you !—go with your new associates—go !'

" ' There was a time, Master Dudley'——

" ' That time is past—hence, traitor !'

" ' Heaven send you better counsel, I pray from the bottom of my heart,' cried Talbot to the burghers ; and after another appealing look to Dudley, met by a rigid frown that forbade all hope of reconciliation, he turned, silently, from the gate, and rode back to Mary's Abbey with his party.

" ' Well, Sir John, what say those scum of the city ?' were Lord Thomas's first words, as he entered the hall, where the rebel leaders were still in consultation.

" ' My lord, it grieves me to say, they obstinately refuse us admittance.'

" ' Then may White sleep sound to-night,' cried Le Poer ' for no flag of ours will wave on Dublin castle this bout.'

" ' What, Sir John,' cried Lord Thomas, · did you urge the cutting off of their supplies ?'

" ' We did, my lord,' replied Parez, ' but they aver they are well victualled. I would to God we had taken the other course !—but no matter—'tis useless to repine when the time has gone by.'

" ' By my honour, Sir John Talbot, it was bad counsel you gave,' said Sir Richard Walsh.

" ' I begin to see again that it was so,' exclaimed Sir Oliver ; ' but 'tis too late to grieve for what cannot now be helped.'

" ' Judgments are prepared for scorners, and stripes for the backs of fools,' muttered Father Travers.

" ' Gentlemen,' cried Lord Thomas, ' at my door lie the blame, if blame has been deserved. Leave off, now, idle regrets, and let us proceed with the disposition of our forces.' "

(To be continued.)

LEA CASTLE, QUEEN'S COUNTY.

Lea Castle was built about the year 1260, by the Anglo-Norman family De Vesey, in the usual style of the military architecture of the day, and was intended to protect the Pale on the north and north-west. It consisted of a quadrangular building of three stories, flanked by round bastions, of which but one at present remains. In the rere was the inner ballium, in which was a tennis-court and tilt yard. The outer entrance, which is still in good preservation, consisted of a gate, defended by a portcullis; and the whole was surrounded by the bawn, in which cattle were secured during the night.

The north side was protected by the river Barrow, which supplied with water a wide ditch that extended round the other sides; and the mount on which the castle was situated being thus formed into an island, obtained the name of " Port na hinch," or the " Castle of the Island."

In 1284, the Irish princes, jealous of the encroachments of the English, attacked and burnt the castle; but it was soon afterwards repaired, and taken possession of, by De Vesey, who was then Lord Justice of Ireland.

In 1307, the Irish renewed their hostilities, and considerably injured the castle. It was afterwards fully repaired by Fitzgerald, who erected a church, with a steeple and bells, in the village, but which, in 1315, was destroyed by the Scotch army under Robert Bruce.

For the next hundred years Lea frequently changed its proprietors; and its history is but a mere catalogue of attacks, surrenders, and reprisals.

In 1533, we find it again in possession of the Fitzgeralds, the head of which family was the celebrated Earl of Kildare, who was appointed to " govern all Ireland, as all Ireland could not govern him.' He, though entrusted with the government of the country, disregarded the administration of the laws, but as it contributed to his own personal influence and authority. Thus, he furnished the Castle of Lea with guns and ammunition out of the royal stores, in opposition to the express commands of his Majesty.

In 1598, the Castle of Lea was taken by the Irish chieftain O'More, who, having established a garrison, marched with a considerable force, and successfully attacked the Earl of Essex, then Chief Governor, at the pass of Ballybrittas. From the quantity of feathers taken from the gay soldiers of the English favourite, the field of action was called " The Pass of the Plumes."

On the breaking out of the rebellion of 1641, Lea was garrisoned by the rebels, but was shortly afterwards taken possession of by the loyalists, who, in commemoration of the event, planted in the market-place a young ash tree, which during the period of its existence, (one hundred and seventy years,) attained an immense size, and was universally known as " The Tree of Lea."

Its girth by some is stated to have been 29 feet, while a manuscript which is in the possession of a gentleman in Portarlington, mentions it to have been eleven yards, and that the shade formed by its foliage exceeded sixty feet in diameter. The tree having lost one of its principal boughs during a storm, went rapidly to decay: and the hollow trunk, having for some time served a poor woman for a cow-house and piggery, sunk, like an aged patriarch, beneath the weight of years, respected and lamented by the inhabitants of the village.

In 1642, Lea was taken by Lord Castlehaven; and in 1650, by the parliamentary forces under Colonel Hewson and Reynolds, and finally dismantled.

The last person who took up his abode at Lea was a noted horse-stealer, (Dempsey,) who converted the extensive vaults under the castle into stables, and for several years successively carried on his nefarious trade. From the dexterity he evinced in committing his depredations, he acquired the Irish name of " Shamas a Copparil," or " James the Horse;" and as the peasantry, especially of Ireland, are fond of " the wild and wonderful," his history furnished the subject of many an evening tale.

RAILROADS IN THE UNITED STATES.

From a recent file of American papers, we find that the progress of railroads in the United States is estimated as follows: In Pennsylvania, there are fifteen lines completed, and sixty-seven in contemplation; in New York there are six completed, and twenty-seven in contemplation; in the state of Ohio, twelve are in progress, but none yet brought to a perfect state of completion; in Massachusets, there are also several in progress; and the

great railroad from Baltimore, through Maryland, to the Ohio river at Wheeling, a distance of 275 miles, is rapidly approaching to a close. Altogether there are forty-seven railroads completed, and one hundred and thirty seven commenced, or in contemplation. Besides the great line to the western states from Baltimore to Wheeling, it appears that corresponding lines are projected from Philadelphia and New York; these being required in order to preserve an equality of advantages with Baltimore, in the trade to the great regions of the Ohio river. In the line from Philadelphia to Pittsburg, it is boldly determined upon, to tunnel through the Alleghany mountains, the circuit being otherwise so expensive, as to render that great labour the cheaper course to be pursued. It is to be observed, however, that these railroads have not the solidity, and probable strength and durability of the railroads of this country. The rails are laid down upon wood, and not upon stone, as in the Manchester and Liverpool railroad, and others which our readers may have seen. This plan has been adopted in consequence of the abundance of timber upon the lines of country through which the railroads pass, and the less quantity of labour required for preparing that material, in a country where wages are so high. It is calculated that the wood work must be renewed upon an average once in the course of seven years. Perhaps, as truly, and indeed the whole science of locomotion, are evidently yet in infancy, this cheaper mode of proceeding may be in reality the more judicious, since less capital is thus endangered by the introduction of improved steam carriages, or other still cheaper and more advantageous locomotive power. The iron-work is all imported from Great Britain, the iron of the United States being too soft for this and other purposes where much friction is produced. For this reason, the government has very judiciously allowed railroad iron to be an exception to the Tariff regulations of the country; it being now exempt from all duty. Altogether, the progress of the railroad system in the United States opens out a wide and extraordinary scene of speculation as to its effects upon the destinies of that great nation. Through this invention, the people of regions lying hitherto far away from all effectual control, will be brought into the solid union of the social bond; and the fear that the United States were too large for one government, will become an unencumbered and visionary folly.—*Athenæum.*

AN IRISH OTTER.

At a recent meeting of the Zoological Society, London, Mr Ogilby called the attention of the members to a specimen of an Irish otter, taken near Newtownlimavady. On account of the intensity of its colouring, which approaches nearly to black, both on the upper and under surface; of the less extent of the pale colour beneath the throat, as compared with the common otter, [*Lutra vulgaris*, Linn.] as it exists in England; and of some difference in the size of the ears, and in the proportions of other parts. Mr. Ogilby has long considered the Irish otter as constituting a distinct species; and he feels strengthened in this view of the subject by the peculiarity of habitation and manners. It is, in fact, to a considerable extent a marine animal, being found chiefly along the coast of the county of Antrim, living in hollows and caverns formed by the scattered masses of the basaltic columns of that coast, and constantly betaking itself to the sea when alarmed or hunted. It feeds chiefly on the salmon; and as it is consequently injurious to the fishery, a premium is paid for its destruction; and there are many persons who make a profession of hunting it, earning a livelihood by the reward paid for it and by disposing of its skin. Mr. Ogilby stated his intention of comparing it minutely with the common otter as soon as he should be enabled to do so by the possession of entire subjects, and especially of attending to the comparison of the osteological structures.

BASALTIC COLUMNS.

A range of basaltic columns has been discovered on the south side of Colmonny Hill, in the parish of Connor, three miles N. E. of Antrim. The columns are as regularly formed as those of the Giant's Causeway—they are in general hexagonal—they incline from the perpendicular towards the north at an angle of about 17 degrees, the columns at either side leaning towards the centre. The space of ground already opened is about 40 feet in breadth, and 14 deep; the columns appearing at present being about 12 feet in height. It is the opinion of a scientific friend, (as far as he could judge from a hurried observation,) that these columns form probably part of a great whin dyke, running southward from the northern shores of Antrim, and that they will not be found to extend much beyond the width now exposed in view, either towards the east or west. This will, in some degree, soon be ascertained. In the mean time, the discovery of such regular basaltic columns so far inland may form to the geologist a subject of interesting speculation.—*Belfast News Letter.*

CATCHING A TARTAR.

The Galtee mountains, in the county Tipperary, are frequented by a large species of the eagle, which have been an uncommon annoyance to the farmers, in the destruction of their lambs and poultry; there is also a rabbit-warren convenient, which the eagles often visit in search of prey, and kill great numbers, in defiance of every means resorted to for the purpose of destroying them. A few months ago, one of these enormous birds was observed to pounce upon a large cat which was sleeping upon the roof of a thatched cabin, and to carry her off, (taking her, it was supposed, for a rabbit.) The eagle arose right upwards, and the spectators continued to watch him until he soared beyond their sight. About ten minutes after, he was seen to descend, apparently struggling with his intended victim. At last he fell to the earth, not fifty paces from the spot where he lifted the cat, so weakened through loss of blood that he died almost immediately, his throat and breast having been desperately cut in the struggle. The cat was little or nothing the worse.					N.

SINGULAR SAGACITY OF TWO MULES.

About two miles from the town of Ballymahon, in the county of Longford, resides a gentleman, who has in his possession two mules of the Spanish breed. They will regularly go to a pump placed in the yard, and while one applies his mouth to the spout, the other works the handle by alternately raising and depressing his shoulder. When one has satisfied his thirst, he exchanges places with his companion, and returns the service he has received. Improbable as this may appear to some, it is an absolute fact; and the person who gives the account of it, has received it very recently from the owner of the mules, and from several members of his family.					W. C. L.

CHURNING IN CHILE.

In Chile, butter is packed in sheep-skins, with the wool side out, and would be very good in spite of appearances, were it not so much salted. The operation of churning is performed by a donkey. The cream is put into large gourds or dry skins, placed on his back, and then the animal is kept trotting round the yard till the butter is made. In this art they seem not to have advanced a single step since its discovery; for we are told that a countryman some where lost a large jug of cream by carrying it for a distance on a hard trotting horse, which accident led to the important invention of churns and butter. A friend told me that he had presented, some years ago, a Yankee churn to a family residing near the capital, and taught them to use it. So long as it was a novelty they were pleased, but at the end of a few weeks they decided that the donkey made butter just as well, and consequently threw it aside.—*Three Years in the Pacific.*

ORTHOGRAPHICAL TRANSMOGRIFICATION.

A blacksmith lately made out a bill against one of his customers, in which a charge was *intended* to be made for *steeling two mattocks*—i. e. putting steel to the iron points of the instruments. But the son of Vulcan, who had been more used to wielding a sledge hammer than studying Doctor Johnson, actually wrote the following item: " *To stealing two mad ducks, 2s !*"

THE EXILE'S SONG.

By the side of the Ganges, whose mystical wave
Oft serves as a tomb to the exile and slave,
I mourn, but in vain, for the dear belov'd few
That bound me for ever, dear Erin, to you.

In vain does the East all its treasures display,
Or the free Asiatic enliven the day;
My bosom still beats for the dear belov'd few,
That mourn'd my departure, dear Erin, from you.

Unchanged is my heart, though my spirit 's subdu'd;
The sunshine of hope, oftentimes will intrude,
And tempt me to sigh for the dear belov'd few,
That bound me for ever, dear Erin, to you.

When the woes of the care-worn exile shall cease,
And the mandates o' death bring a final release,
O! the last throb of nature's eternal adieu,
Shall be mingled in blessings, dear Erin, for you.

Farewell, honour'd land of my forefathers' birth;
Dear isle of delight—heaven's favoured on earth!
To thy green mantled bowers and mountains of blue,
Dear Erin, my country! for ever adieu!

					J. D.

WOODSTOCK CASTLE, ATHY, COUNTY KILDARE.

——— " Thy walls that rise sublime,
In proud defiance of all conquering time."

———

Strength and duration in one glance combined,
High thoughts awaken in the soaring mind;
For man, frail tenant of a day, an hour,
Exults in dreams of long-enduring power;
While noble piles, in ancient models cast,
Teach him a sacred lesson of the past.
Bid him bend o'er the gulf of former days,
Or pierce the future with his ardent gaze.—*M. Cross.*

To have the recollection of the days that are long gone over stirred up in our minds, and to dwell upon them with affectionate interest, may appear weak in the eyes of true philosophy. Yet to dwell fondly on the history of scenes that are for ever fled, if it be a weakness, it seems to be one of the most pardonable weaknesses of our nature—a frailty as universal as it is interesting. It is a sobering reflection which we are naturally affected with, and by it the best sympathies of our nature are often awakened. When contemplating the mouldering remains of the edifices of our forefathers, associations press on the mind, linked as they are with the present and the past, that often convey instructions of no ordinary kind. Perhaps the Castle of Woodstock, the subject of our present notice, may be classed amongst others as affording evidence of the justness of this remark.

From its vicinity, Woodstock Castle has partaken of nearly all the changes that befel Athy. Standing on the western bank of the river Barrow, it was designed to command the principal ford on this part of the river, in conjunction with White's castle, situate on the opposite bank, a little lower down—the ford lying between. The time this castle was built is unknown. Tradition assigns it to about the year 1290, and that a descendant of the earl of Pembroke was its first master; whilst our antiquaries, with more reason, seem inclined to attribute the erection of the present structure to Thomas Fitzgerald, lord of Offaley, and afterwards seventh earl of Kildare, who, on marrying Dorothea, the daughter of Anthony O'Moore, of Leix, received in dower the manors of Woodstock and Rheban, in which family it still remains. The plan of the building was originally a regular square; in after times an addition was made to it of a square tower, joining the south side, and built in uniformity with the front facing the river. The walls are of great thickness, and, considering the attacks they have been exposed to, in good preservation. The mullioned windows are much admired, and were elegantly executed. In viewing the interior from what can be collected from the remains, we are struck with the curious arrangements of ancient architecture. A fine arched gateway, and part of the outer court-wall yet remain. Some short time since a stone, of which the following cut is a representation, was discovered in the ruins, and carefully preserved by Holmes Bigham, Esq., the present occupier of the adjoining land; it is the only piece of sculpture of interest that has, even in a mutilated state, survived, from the barbarous taste of disfiguring pleasure-grounds and grottoes with relics, that can be only useful where they were rendered interesting by time.

The ford which the castle commanded, and from which Athy derives its name, was called Athelehac, or anciently Athlegar, the ford towards the west; also, Ath-trodan, or the cattle ford. It was here the great battle was fought, in the third century, between the people of Munster and those of Leix, under Laviseagh Cean Mordha.

In 1642, the Marquis of Ormond took Woodstock from the rebels; and subsequently, in 1647, Owen Roe O'Neal surprised it, and put the garrison to the sword; his victory, however, was but of short duration: for Lord Inchiquin compelled him, in a little time after, to surrender it and Athy.

The lordship of Woodstock and Castlemitchell was set by the Earl of Kildare to Daniel Hutchison, alderman, for ninety-nine years, from May 1st, 1657, at 100l. the first forty-one years, yearly, and 200l. a year during the rest of the lease, with six fat wethers or three pounds.

ENNA.

WOODSTOCK CASTLE.

The writer accidentally met with the following verses, connected with Woodstock Castle, which, he believes, are original, but appear to have suffered much in transcribing:

Woodstock, famed in Irish story,
    Raising high its tow'ring head;
Still proclaims its former glory,
    Near old Barrow's crystal bed.

O'er its walls, where ivy creeping,
    Loves to wave its sombre green;
Forth, beneath the foliage peeping,
    Many a sculptured stone is seen.

Where the silken standard flying,
    Once its waving folds display'd;
Now the breeze, in murmurs sighing,
    Mourns the havoc time has made.

Oft, within those dark recesses,
    Perish'd many a chief of old;

While the blood-stain'd floor confesses
    Horrors human tongue ne'er told.

Woodstock's lord once lov'd a fair one,
    And did court her to his arms;
Daughter of a neighbouring baron,
    Blest with beauty's softest charms.

But her sire had pledg'd his daughter
    To a gentle knight hard by,
Who with tender love had sought her—
    Call'd Sir Kemelin, of Athy.

Vengeful thoughts seized Woodstock's bosom,
    When denied the blooming maid;
Yet to none did he disclose 'em,
    But his plot in secret laid.

Straight he made him preparation,
    Solemn tourney to proclaim;
And forthwith sent invitation
    To many a noble knight and dame.

To partake at Woodstock-hall,
    Mask and dance, and pageant gay;
All within the castle's wall,
    On St. John's high holiday.

Gladsome rose the wished for morn,
    Rob'd in cloudless golden light;
Loudly blew the bugle horn,
    Banners grac'd the castle's height.

And many a lady passing fair,
    All bedecked in rich array;
And many a brave knight from afar
    Passed through Woodstock's gate that day.

Ah! who is he whose vernal cheek
    Blooms high in health and beauty's pride;
Whose blue eyes, love's soft language speak
    To the fair lady by his side?

'Tis Kemelin—flower of chivalry—
    And Eva with the golden hair;
Of Rheban's youth the bravest he,
    And she the Curragh's maid most fair.

Festive mirth, its joys imparting,
    Beamed around the splendid scene;
Till at midnight hour departing,
    Hied them o'er the distant green,

"Kemelin," quoth Lord Woodstock, "stay
    With thy lady here this night;
False Tyrconnell may thee betray—
    'Tis said he owes thee mortal spite."

"Much I thank thee, courteous baron,
    Though my heart ne'er felt dismay;
Yet, to calm this trembling fair one,
    Here, beneath thy roof, I'll stay."

Sad and dismal was the hour,
    Darker frown'd the low'ring gloom;
When, yielding to a villain's power,
    Kemelin seal'd his tragic doom.

From that fatal moment, never
    Eva to her friends returned;
Mystic was her fate for ever—
    Long the hapless fair they mourned.

But, upon the seventh morn,
    Kemelin's floating corse was found,
Down the river's current borne,
    Pierced with many a ghastly wound.

Near the river stands a mound,
    O'er it the tall poplars wave;
Water-lillies spring around,
    And this, I heard, is Kemelin's grave.

And still the banshee, wand'ring round,
    Loves to raise her plaintive song;
When each swift revolving year,
    Brings the feast of good St. John.

T. FRENCH.

DUBLIN:
Printed and Published by P. D. HARDY, 3, Cecilia Street; to whom all communications are to be addressed.

THE

DUBLIN PENNY · JOURNAL

CONDUCTED BY P. DIXON HARDY, M.R.I.A.

Vol. III.   MARCH 21, 1835.   No. 142.

CALLAN ABBEY.

CALLAN CHURCH.
(For Description see other side.)

CALLAN.

CALLAN, a small town, about eight miles from Kilkenny, situate on a stream called the King's River, was formerly a place of note, possessing three castles, all now in ruins: the place in every other respect appears in the same dilapidated state to which it was reduced in the time of Cromwell. A Friary for Augustinian Eremites was founded here, by James, father to Peter, Earl of Ormond, who died on the 16th of April, 1467, and was interred here. The tower and walls of this friary still remain; and it is probable that the bones of the founder were laid in the wall, under two Gothic arches which yet stand near the east window. The nave of the church, with its fine lateral aisles, still remains in good preservation: the choir is now the parish church; and the cemetery of the founder's family, overgrown with moss and ivy, adjoins the choir.

ROMANCE OF IRISH HISTORY.
THE BRIDAL.

Courtstown Castle, the seat of the noble family of Grace, whose proud towers are now no more, and whose powerful lords are now mingled with the dust, and long have been forgotten, except by the antiquary, and the casual eye of the tourist, who in visiting the venerable cathedral of St Cannice in Kilkenny, may cast a glance on the dilapidated tomb of the Graces, with its marble statue and its rampant lion. Rudely as it is carved on the unpolished marble still it calls to mind the days in which the rude retainers of that noble house bore their lords, with all the pomp of feudal grandeur, through the lofty arches of that gloomy aisle, to be gathered to their fathers, or when that rampant lion waved from the top of the keep of Courtstown, in defiance of all its enemies, or fluttered over the heads of the soldiers of Grace in the last battle they ever fought for their country. The ancient banner of that ancient house never waved its silken folds on a more happy occasion than when the young and beautiful Catherine Archer was to wed the eldest son of the Baron of Courtstown. The preparations for the coming bridal was the sole business of the inhabitants of Courtstown for some time. Nothing was heard but the clang of craftsmen erecting palisades, and the noise of armourers repairing and making armour; while many a young heart beat high with the hope of distinction at the coming banquet, and many an aged minstrel was invited to lend his assistance at the nuptials of the youthful pair.

Alas, poor mortals! how often, in the midst of splendour, pomp, and gaiety, would the heart fall, and the dance cease, and the rose leave the cheek of beauty, and the tear rise in the laughing eye, and fall upon the breast throbbing with grief, which but a moment before had been the abode of all that could make it happy—if they but knew what a week would bring forth.

The wished for day at length arrived, and never did the morning break over the hills of Tullaroan with greater beauty and brightness, and never did the "glorious lamp of heaven" shine with a brighter light on the massive, though elegant, towers of Courtstown, than it did on that morning, when with light and merry hearts the bridal party left its noble domains, and turned their horses' heads towards the walls of Kilkenny.

The lofty round tower, which forms such a remarkable object in the same noble cathedral of St. Cannice, was already visible to the bridal party, nor were they long till they reached its gates, where they were met by the monks of St. John by whose abbot the ceremony was to be performed. The gallant train wended slowly through the gloomy arches of that spacious aisle, which at that time was the finest in Ireland, and which then looked doubly beautiful, as it was graced by a splendid window, subsequently demolished by the soldiers of Cromwell, in the true spirit of tyrannical bigotry. The rays of the summer sun, glancing through the gorgeous and gilded sashes, threw the reflection of its brilliancy on the cold marble, making the armorial bearings seem as if they had been fresh coloured by the hands of the artist. The ceremony had commenced, and the Lord of Ormonde and the Count de Burgess stood near the altar, and seemed to regard the proceedings with more than common interest.

"Without doubt, De Burgess," said Ormonde, "she is a lovely girl. Among all the beauties that surround her, she seems to be the most beautiful."

"But why gets the bride so suddenly pale? Look, Ormonde, look—see that foul raven on the bridegroom's bonnet;" and as he spoke, the bird of ill-omen flew upwards, while its hoarse and croaking voice resounded among the arches, and entered its accustomed haunts in the lofts of the cathedral tower. This ominous event damped for a while the general mirth; but on the venerable abbot speaking a few encouraging words, and bestowing a fervent blessing on the youthful pair, the general harmony was restored.

The sun had not yet long passed its meridian, when the party set out in gallant array for the castle of Kilkenny, where refreshments awaited them; and as they rode along the high street of Kilkenny, many an humble citizen left his business to gaze on the passing train.

The noble castle of Kilkenny, whose lofty towers look down in the limpid waters of the "stubborn Nore," as if gazing at their own splendour, was now entered; and its lofty gateway never gave entrance to a more noble company. First came the Lord of Ormonde, the Count de Burgess, and the Graces; then followed, in long succession, the Sweetman, the Fitzgerald, the Horselail, the Shortal, and numerous others. The long and splendid gallery, the beautiful towers, and the noble gateway, were each admired; and after the banquet, in which the noble Butler had vied with the princely Grace in hospitality, again the guests set out for Courtstown, and again the Butler and De Burgess rode together.

They had now began to penetrate the forest which intervened between Kilkenny and Courtstown—the last rays of the sun still lingered on the horizon—and now they had gone half way through its recesses, when suddenly there was a rustling among the branches, and an arrow whistling among them, electrified the party; and amidst the shrieks of the women, and the execrations of the men, the gallant young bridegroom fell from his horse a lifeless corpse.

There was a general cry of "Treason, treason—we are beset!" The noise of the stringing of cross-bows, the whissing of bolts, and the clang of arms, for a while drowned the shrieks of the women; but when the first panic had subsided, all eyes were turned on Catherine. She stood gazing on the corpse, but no tear flowed from her dark eye, and no sound escaped from her compressed lips. Her brother Henry, a fine youth of fifteen, stood with his arms round her.

"Oh, Catherine, Catherine!" said he, "why do you not speak—why do you not cry? Oh, Catherine, do not look so wildly!"

"Henry," said she, "for shame; those tears become you not. Remember that you now wear a sword—revenge, first—then we will have time for tears. My lord of Ormonde, and all you noble lords who have done honour to my unfortunate lord, this is the deed of the traitor Cantwell—he cannot be far off. Oh, noble Ormonde, lead the chase! I saw his dark and ruffian countenance among the trees just as that fatal arrow whissed past me."

"Then, I swear, lady, this sword will never find its sheath, until his body hangs on that oak, be he taken dead or alive. I did not think the outlawed traitor dare do this. Come, my gallant comrades, there is a lady with tears in her eyes, who will stand by and see them. Come, De Burgess, come Sweetman, come all: but stay—let you, De Burgess, remain with the Lady Catherine, and also let you, followers of Grace, stay and protect your lady. If odds overpower us we will shout, 'Butler aboo—to the rescue!' And now forward, my brave comrades—death to the Cantwell." And with shouts of revenge the little party dashed among the surrounding trees.

The lovely Catherine bent over the body of her husband, the other ladies also surrounded it, and all wept but the bride, whose eyes, hot and dry, refused a single tear. She looked up at length, and softly said, 'Henry,' he was not there. "Oh, Henry, Henry, if that traitor Cantwell know you, he will take thy life! Oh, Ormonde, may thy sword protect him." The manly figure of De Burgess, who stood by with folded arms, his head sunk on his breast, and the dark plumes of his Spanish hat shading his face, now caught her attention, and raising her head, "Sir Knight," said she, "my brother." She said no more; and De Burgess was just turning to follow the pursuers, when he heard the sudden cry of "Grasneaboo —to the rescue, to the rescue," and he perceived that they were attacked. A tall knight, in sable armour, with one black plume in his helmet, seemed the leader. On him De Burgess immediately flew, although without armour of any description to protect him, and nothing but his short hunting sword in his hand. The odds were too fearful—the gallant knight soon lay upon the ground, and all resistance was almost at an end, when Ormonde, Sweetman, and the rest, rushed into the fray, and soon Ormonde made the sable knight "bite the dust;" and placing his foot upon his throat, "Yield thee, Cantwell, or this moment thou diest!"

" I will not yield, Ormonde, to you, at least, thou false knight. I will never yield."

"Then die," said Ormonde: "but no; the death of a true knight thou shalt not die—that oak shall be thy end. Secure him, soldiers!" and the victorious party bound him, and then unloosing his helmet, displayed the savage features of Cantwell.

"Traitor!—and more than traitor, murderer—what was thy motive for that?" said Ormonde, pointing to the body of Edward.

"He loved Catherine Archer," said Cantwell, "and I loved her, and he won her—her, for whom I would have forsaken all; and did forsake all—he got her."

"Do your business, minion," said Ormonde to a kern who with rope in hand stood by; "it is almost dark, you must use despatch."

"Ormonde," said Cantwell, "my sins be on your head, if you grant me not time to say a prayer."

Ormonde pointed to the corpse again. Cantwell was silent, and in a few moments his body was quivering from the tree.

P. A.

THE LAUREL TREE,
(IN KILFANE VALLEY, COUNTY KILKENNY.)

Behold the blooming laurel, of emerald sheen so bright,
Though all around is drooping, it cheers the wand'rer's sight,
To hill and vale bestowing a gleam of gladness dear,
The only thing now blowing, of all that flourish'd here.
It bends to kiss the streamlet, and brighter seem the rills
That sport in curves around it, than aught the fount distils;
It glistens in the meek ray of winter's transient sun,
As if Sol in its full sway upon its beauty shone—
Nay, lovelier it seems, now a golden lustrous plume,
While fragile summer rivals look drear or in the tomb.
The gay laburnim 's hoary, the rose more sombre still,
And all the verdant glory, that deck'd yon sloping hill,
Have cast their summer dresses; in dullness all appear;
Yet still the laurel 's blooming to greet the new-come year.
Nor violet, nor primrose, now delight us on the gale,
(How oft in this lone vale I've stood their sweetness to inhale;)
Nor ev'n the spangled daisy, that makes each scene look gay—
All, all that told of summer, alas! have met decay:
Like h pe, the laurel 's smiling through ev'ry season's change;
Not hope that lives beguiling, and fond hearts would estrange
From all but earthly pleasures—Oh, no! but hope that cheers
Through every change of fortune, and dries the mourner's tears.
C. M. E.

STATE OF SOCIETY IN LIVERPOOL.

"Life in London" we have had sketched for us in a thousand different forms. The following outline of the present state of society in Liverpool, is the first description we have seen in print of the manners and habits of this commercial town. We copy it from a work just published, "Sketches of a Seaport Town," by H. F. Chorley.

SOCIETY IN GENERAL.

"To say, that in a place singularly destitute of nobility, its inhabitants have themselves substituted an aristocracy of wealth in place of one of family, is, perhaps, some little beyond the precise truth; and yet, it comes nearer to the truth than any other form of words that could be used. There is as much subdivision into sets and sects, as much

exclusiveness, with all its train of bad consequences, as in the wider and nobler circles of the metropolis—and over all, and through all, a mercantile spirit at work, which is singularly unfavourable to the development of mind. There is, indeed, scarcely any inducement for a man to exert and improve the powers with which he has been gifted, if, valuing every thing by the standard of pounds, shillings, and pence, he feels that his standing is secure, that he may talk wisdom or folly, as he will, and still be looked up to in society, as a person of consequence and authority;—nay, that he is in most circles more popular as he is, than he would be were he to bear the character of a hard reader, or a deep thinker. The withering influence of fashion, has also its share in depreciating the standard of intelligence. Our circles are not wide enough to allow of individuals setting up as characters; in which case alone does she tolerate any originality of thought, word, or deed—she therefore imposes upon her subjects a uniformity of conduct and manner; trammelling them as effectually within their artificial ordinances, as the conjuror, when he confines the chicken within his magic circle of chalk. But it seems to me, that we are fallen on particularly cheerless times, as respects ease or enjoyment in general society.

THE MEN.

"As far as concerns the Men, the age of dandyism has, thank Heaven! passed over: the delicate youths who put their hair in *papillotes*, and ironed their cravats upon their necks, are now striving in the mart of business, for their rising families, or shivering over their cheerless bachelor hearths, remembering days and glories gone by, when it was at once their occupation and their pleasure to rival the caprices of fair ones as fanta-tic and *manieré* as themselves. But though the present race of men may be less finical than the last—poor society is no gainer by their increase of manliness. If they are less sedulous attenders of balls than their predecessors, they are more constant at dinner parties; and at these they love to herd together, to talk the strong talk of emptiness—of their dogs, and horses, and amours—and to settle the great questions of the day, over which statesmen are racking their brains, and for the full understanding whereof, philosophers are patiently drawing their conclusions from the experience of the past, in a few stout words, against which there can be no appeal. As to pursuit of any kind, beyond the above mentioned amusements, it is almost utterly unknown among them, and even should any one be followed in secret, it is not to be alluded to in conversation, if its follower would keep clear of the artillery of idle tongues, ever ready to satirise what their owners do not comprehend.

THE LADIES.

"On the other hand, the present system of female training, has its share in making society a burden, instead of an excitement and an exercise to those who understand something better than vapid talk about the nothings of the day, or the more racy amusement of quizzing your *vis-à-vis* in a quadrille. While fashion attacks any tendency to bluism with her most blighting ridicule, and inculcates a cold *posé* demeanour, under which every natural impulse and feeling is to be impenetrably concealed; education has parcelled out the time of her victim, and carried her at set hours from French to history, from history to music, from music to metaphysics, and so on, without ever stopping to study the natural biases and talents born with her. What a marvellous discrepancy is there between these two codes! Routine (for it is dishonouring education to allow her counterfeit to assume her name) ordains that the young lady of the nineteenth century shall know every thing: fashion values her in proportion as she talks as if she knew nothing—routine crams her with book-learning—fashion teaches her to sneer at clever people; and thus, between the two, the natural buoyancy of girlhood, which never stayed to consider whether the laugh was a tone too loud, or the step a thought too quick, or the talk a shade too confidential, is as completely crushed as if it had never existed; and there seems now no longer any intermediate step between the child on her way to school, and the well tutored, well-dressed women, armed at all points for society, and equally proof against enjoyments and annoyances."

IRISH ORNITHOLOGY.

A very rare and beautiful specimen of the gull tribe, at least in this country, (*Lary Calarractus,* or Squa Gull,) has been lately shot by J. Martin, Esq. of Galway, and sent to A. Bushe, Esq. of Fitzwilliam-street, Dublin. Glennon, of Suffolk-street, with his usual ability, has preserved and restored it to its appearance when in the full enjoyment of its voracious propensities. It is, we believe, the first of the kind that has been shot for many years by any of our country sportsmen. The specimen of which we write was a female, and weighed a little more than two pounds. The length two feet five inches, extent four feet seven inches. It was shot when in the act of killing a sea-gull. It is remarkable that the œsophagus was of an equal width from the throat to the bottom of the sac, where it ended in a strong gizzard, which was filled with feathers and half digested flesh, with the windpipe of a bird quite perfect. The colour of the flesh was a deep purplish red, and cuts as coarsely as the flesh of a horse—the tongue long and soft, and ending in a horny substance, and split about one-fourth of an inch. Two rows of tubercles, like teeth, on the palate, extending nearly to the nostrils—a soft naked ligamental muscle surrounded the gape of the mouth, the economy of which seemed to be to enable the animal to open its jaws to the extent of five inches, thus affording it the capacity to swallow a middling sized bird at once. The bill is very strong, and much hooked at the point, black, as also the legs, which are studded with long horny tubercles, like shagreen; toes long, and webbed to the claws, hooked, and very sharp, thus enabling it to grasp and hold its prey. The tail consists of twelve feathers, two middle ones a little longer than the rest. From the great quantity and length of the feathers, the size of this bird amounts to that of a small eagle. All the feathers are white at the roots, those on the back of the head, neck, back, and wings, have a dash of a ferrugineous colour, widening towards the top or point. This specimen differs from any other of the same species which has ever met the eye of the intelligent curator into whose hands it has fallen, having, when its wings are expanded, a white band across the quill feathers.

COLLEGE OF KILKENNY.

COLLEGE OF KILKENNY.

The College of Kilkenny is an institution of great public utility. We are informed by Stanihurst, that "a Grammar School was founded in the weste of the church-yard by Pierce, or Peter Butler, Erle of Ormond and Ossorie, and his wife, the lady Margaret Fitzgerald." Peter White, some time Fellow of Oriel College, Oxford, was a distinguished master of this early establishment; and Stanihurst was himself educated at Kilkenny, under this preceptor.

In the year 1684, we are informed by Dr. Ledwich, "the Duke of Ormonde granted a new charter to the College of Kilkenny, of a certain house in John's-street, with the adjacent park, for a school-house." The duke, at the same time, bestowed some rectories and tithes for the use of the establishment, and rendered it subject to a regular code of statutes.

This laudable institution experienced some changes, during the troubled state of public affairs in the latter years of the seventeenth century. King James II. erected this establishment into a royal college, consisting of a rector, eight professors, and two scholars, in the name of more; to be called "the Royal College of St. Canice, Kilkenny, of the foundation of King James." New rules were then drawn up by Dr. Phelan, the Catholic bishop of Ossory; but these were of short prevalence. On the retreat of James, this institution, with others of still greater importance, returned to the channel from which it had been for a time diverted.

According to the original terms of foundation, the master was to be nominated by the Dukes of Ormonde; but, owing to the attainder of James, Duke of Ormonde, in 1715, the right of presentation lapsed to the provost and fellows of Trinity College, Dublin. Although the term of *College,* as applied to this establishment, is entirely a title of courtesy, the grammar-school of Kilkenny is a distinguished ornament and advantage to the south of Ireland, and demands to be named amongst the chief public schools of the empire. The house having sunk to decay, was lately rebuilt, by the aid of parliamentary grants, amounting to £5064. Amongst many celebrated persons who have received the early part of education at this school, may be mentioned Swift; Congreve; Farquhar; Mr. Harris, the continuator of Ware; Provost Baldwin; and Dr. Berkeley, Bishop of Cloyne. Dr. Edward Jones, afterwards Bishop of Cloyne, was master of this school in 1670. Dr. Henry Ryder, master in 1680, was promoted to the see of Killaloe.

THE REBELLION OF SILKEN THOMAS.

FROM THE " HIBERNIAN NIGHTS' ENTERTAINMENTS," IN THE DUBLIN UNIVERSITY MAGAZINE.

(Continued from our last.)

" In the arrangements that followed, Talbot found to his cost the effects of the distrust with which the leaders now regarded him. While the main body of Lord Thomas's forces returned to Kilmainham, or went to garrison the Earl's numerous castles in Kildare and Ofaly, he was assigned a petty post at Artane, a poor village beyond Clontarf, with orders to intercept provisions or succours coming to the city by way of Howth or the Skerries. Hardly concealing his indignation, he put himself at the head of his little party, and departed for his obscure post, where he took up his position among the wretched cabins before nightfall. He could not go to rest; he traversed the clay floor of his hut with hurried and irregular steps, or flung himself, hopeless of sleep, from the coarse couch to the coarser bench. At length, wrapping his cloak around him, he rushed out, and strove to allay the bitterness of his reflections by walking in the open air. The night was dark and stormy, and the gale, sweeping in from the bay, sounded along the leafy flats of Clontarf with the roar of an aerial sea. He breathed more freely as he heard the tossed branches struggling with the blast overhead. ' Blow on,' he muttered—' strip them while they are green; I was blighted before leafing time.—Dogs and traitors! this is a fair return they make me for preserving them from eternal infamy! Oh, weak, weak, Lord Thomas; weak nephew, and weaker uncle!—and Travers, the hypocrite, and Le Poer, the dastard, and Parez, the sneering villain! Why was I born to bring shame on an honest man's grey hairs, and sorrow on an angel's heart, for the sake of such associates? Forgive me, noble Gerald! forgive me, that I had forgotten thee and thy cruel wrongs! Oh, if the departed spirit can hear the complaint of wretches upon earth, look down upon the child of your bounty, driven out from happiness and home for your sake, and forgive him if he has forgotten your wrongs in his own misfortunes.'

" With such thoughts shaping themselves into bitter exclamations, he roamed on through a groaning alley of elms and beeches, their swinging tops hardly distinguishable from the sky. Ere long he found himself in an open knoll, from which, through their darkness, the lights of Dublin were visible beyond the Liffey. Softer emotions swelled upon his bosom as he stood to gaze and speculate whether any of these could be the taper in Ellen Dudley's chamber. He thought of her last look as he had left her with her infirm parent in her arms that morning: he pictured her now sitting weeping and disconsolate, the bridal favours he had bound in her hair lying withered at her feet; or by the side of her angry father, listening, with timid dutifulness, to his severe commands.—' I will go to her, let loyalists and rebels do the worst!' he exclaimed, and rushed down the eminence towards Dublin. Careless of his path, he pushed on through thicket and ploughed land, fording the Tolka at Drumcondra, and holding his course right for the light on Newman's Tower. On the Liffey bank opposite was a solitary cabin. Talbot knocked loudly at the door: ' Ho, Connor Bawn!' he cried; ' Connor Bawn Kelly, rise and ferry me to Finn's Castle stairs. It is I, Sir John Talbot.'

" ' *Ababoo!*' cried the ferryman ; ' is your nobleness in trouble, that you seek a ferry at this hour of the night ?'

" ' I am Connor; I am in arms with *Tomás-an-Teeda*, and in need of help.'

" ' *Yeah yeelish!* and the old Earl has had foul play among the Saxons. May God lay his heavy hand on them that did it! Ay, surely I will row your nobleness across, if the night were blacker than their hearts that could do hurt to the kind Mac Gerralt!'

" Connor came forth with his oars, and they pushed his shallop down to the stormy water's edge. It was so black above, that they could hardly see the walls as they pulled through showers of spray across the river. In the darkness, and among the noises of the winds and waters, they crossed unchallenged. Connor moored his boat silently in shelter of the little pier from which the stairs descended; and Talbot stole along the base of the rampart, till he came to where Paul Dudley's house abutted on the river bank. He climbed the wall of the courtyard by the gates, thence clambered to a buttress of the garden wall, which was overgrown with ivy, surmounted it, and, dropping down upon a flower plot inside, found himself under Ellen Dudley's window.

" ' Ellen! Ellen Dudley!' he whispered, tapping upon the glass; ' come to me, for heaven's sake! I have dared everything to see you.'

" ' Mother of mercy!' he joyfully heard her exclaim, ' I hear his voice even now !'

" ' You do, dearest; come to the window. I am safe now, and you need fear nothing.'

" When the first fond words of welcome and tenderness were over, Ellen said—' Sir John, why did you come to the gates this morning in company with Parez? My father took it as an avowal of your having abandoned all desire of reconciliation; he is mortified and enraged beyond measure; for, indeed, he still hoped to have reclaimed you, and all might still have been well had you not made your participation in this revolt too prominent : but his anger against you now is as great as the love he bore you then. Heaven grant you may not be found here while it lasts !'

" ' Ellen, I would rather have faced ten men-at-arms than have met your father as I did upon the bridge to-day ; but I could not refuse to obey the command which committed that galling service to me and him you named : yet, if I had thought Paul Dudley was to have-been the man we were to treat with, I would—on my honour I would—have remonstrated with Lord Thomas, though I have to-day got both blame and ill-will for one expostulation too much already.'

" ' But, oh, Sir John, where do you come from now ? or what, for pity's sake, is to become of you and this wild broil ?'

" ' 'Tis scarce more than an hour since I left my post in the woods of Artane, where I have been stationed to guard the northern passes to the city. I have been slighted, Ellen,' he continued bitterly, ' by those about Lord Thomas : I am housed in a hut, and sent to deal with the cattle-drovers and clowns who would bring their commodities to your market, while Parez is appointed to command the Earl's chief castle of Maynooth, and force the nobles of the western pale to submission.'

" ' It is ungrateful and ungenerous in Lord Thomas to sanction such an insult. You were well worthy the highest command he had to bestow,' cried Ellen, at once partaking in her lover's indignation. ' But alas !' she added, with a sigh, ' I should be better contented that you will thus have a less share in the misery your revolt will bring upon so many innocent beings: for—and I do not know whether I should tell you this; but, trusting to your honour, I will confide it to you—boldly as our citizens spoke of their resources to-day, when pride and emulous loyalty sustained their hearts, and lent confidence to their looks, I heard my father, when he came home, confess, and that with tears in his eyes, that if the passes from Fingal and Meath be closed, we will have famine among us before a fortnight.'

" ' Good heaven !' cried Talbot, ' had I known this, I had not so easily been dismissed this morning : but you, at least, shall want for nothing, while I have hands to bring it to you. The ferryman is at my devotion : neither you nor one of your father's house shall want, come what may.'

" ' It is not for ourselves I feel,' said Ellen ; ' but thinking of the poor people who are unprovided for, and must suffer first and longest, makes me sick at heart.'

" ' Oh, trust me, Ellen, it will never come to that ; they will open their gates before they are brought to such a pass.'

" ' Alas, Sir John,' she replied, ' you little know the firmness of their leaders : they have sworn to hold out while there is food for a man within the walls.'

" ' Ellen,' said Talbot, earnestly, ' you must come with me. Poor as my cabin is, it will still be a safer home for you than here : wretched as my fortunes are, better even such, than to sicken here over scenes that will but blight your youth's promise, and haunt your memory with miserable recollections through all your life after. I did not come to night to ask you to fly with me; nothing but this could make me offer to share such poverty as mine with her I love best : but, Ellen, that shame is gone, and I will not blush to bear you to whatever refuge I can offer from the horrors that await you here.'

" Her voice had a tone of stronger feeling as she replied—' Sir John, you could not love me as you say you do, if you believed I would do this.'

" His heart smote him at once—' Oh, Ellen, forgive me ! You are, indeed, his only stay : to leave him in this time of danger and affliction is what I could not have asked you to do ; but, before heaven, I had forgot even his existence in the tumult of my thoughts. Such a day and night are enough to make a man forget all but his own miseries.'

" ' No ; in this peril and distress,' said Ellen, ' I cannot leave my father.'

" ' But Ellen, dearest ; if—and yet God in mercy forbid !—but if your father should be taken away—oh, believe me, believe me, I would not give you this pain, Ellen, if any suffering of mine could avail to save you—but, my own love, and my heart's betrothed, will you not fly with me if left alone in such a scene of suffering and danger?'

" ' When I plighted you my troth, Sir John,' she replied, but she was weeping while she spoke, ' I never meant that peril or misfortune should prevent my being true to what I said. I cannot, and you will not ask that I should, leave my father now : but when his danger is over—oh ! my heart is full—I cannot, indeed I cannot, help this weeping—but it is what my heart has been foreboding till I feel as if I had prepared myself to expect it ; and oh, sweet mother ! what more were needed to complete my misery ?—But forgive me, Sir John—and think it not, I beseech you, unmaidenly in me to confess this—when my father's danger is over, I will be true to my plighted troth to you, through whatever may befal.'

" ' Ellen dearest, I repine not at all I have suffered, when I hear you thus secure the only hope that was worth my preserving. You shall see me often ; and heaven speed an end to this siege, till I can claim the fulfilment of the dear words that you have blessed me with. But hark ! I hear footsteps in the street : ha ! they knock ; and there is a stir towards the river. Adieu, sweet Ellen ; may good angels watch over you and all you love till I come back. I must away. Oh, farewell !' and he hastened to escape. He descended the buttress and court wall in safety, until within a few feet of the ground, when, his foot slipping on a bar of the gates, he fell heavily among some loose planks lying below.

" ' Who goes ?' cried a sentry upon the walls next Newman's Tower, and a dog in the courtyard began to bark furiously.

" ' Treason, ho !' shouted some one from the house windows. Ere the words were out, the report of the sentry's matchlock roused that whole quarter of the walls. Talbot, stumbling over the broken ground between the rampart and the soft bank of the river, ran for Finn's Castle stairs at the top of his speed, for he plainly heard Paul Dudley's gates thrown open behind him, and the voices and footsteps of men in pursuit. Another flash from the walls showed him Connor Kelly in the stern of his boat, sheltering himself behind the little pier, and hastily throwing off the tackling by which he was moored.

" ' Treason ! treason !' resounded from the walls overhead—' the e's a spy's boat at the stairs ; fire into her with the demi-culver !—lights and linstocks, ho !'

" ' Leap light, a-cushla,' cried the boatman, in a low voice, as Talbot sprung on board the swinging skiff; ' leap light, or you will go through and through her.— Ah ! chorp an Chroist, the plank's started ! Dar Kiaran, she's clean gone ; but keep up your heart, duine deelish— if we pull free, we'll get across before she fills.'

" ' Hush, Connor ; I trust there's no harm done ; it was my fault I know ; but pull,' cried Talbot, dropping his cloak, and stretching himself to the oar.

" ' Keep her head to the swell, Sir Shawn ;' cried Connor ; ' the seam gapes a finger's breath at every stroke.'

" ' They are pointing the culver, Connor ; bear up out of the range of the shot.'

" ' Pull for your life, Sir Shawn ! The Buachal ghosta has a worse wound in her keel than either culver or falcon will put in her to-night.'

" ' Give fire !' cried a voice from the battlements, and the shot drove up the water in a white jet over the seas, a dozen yards a-head ; but the flash showed the centre of the Liffey running in a line of sharp breakers, close under their bow.

" ' I mind their shot no more than a buachaleen's snowball,' said Connor ; ' but this swell—this swell ; it is shaking the broken creature to pieces. Lay yourself to to the oar, a vic deelish ! never mind their matchlocks : pull, pull, for the love of God ! the cott is filling—she is filling fast,' and Talbot, who now felt the water above his ancles as he sat, perceived that she no longer rose to the waves, but rolled heavily in the hollow of every sea.

" ' Throw off your brogues, Connor Bawn,' he cried, ' we must swim for it.'

" ' Pull, Shawn Uaisle, pull !' still cried the boatman ; ' ten strokes more, and I am safe ; ten strokes more for the love of God, and I am in my depth !'—Talbot did not say a word, but with a full heart he strained at the tough ash, till his sinews cracked ; it was all in vain, the boat settled down heavier and heavier ; the oar broke in his hands, and as he fell back, the swamped shallop sunk, and left nothing but the angry waters about him and her ill fated owner. He seized Kelly by the shoulder :— ' Hold up, Connor ; keep a fast hold of the oar ; there's a barge pulling for us from Dudley's wharf. I see her between me and the sky ; hold up, Connor Bawn, and you are safe.'

" ' Let me go,' gurgled the drowning man ; ' I have neither wife nor child— Shawn Uaisle, you must not be taken !—Let me go !—I'd rather drown than let them take you, a vic deelish ma chree ! May the great God—a yeah vore, the water's choking me !—bless—bless the work !—Let me sink, Shawn deelish !—I can die easy in the cause. Tomas, Tomas-an-teeda, Righ Tomas go bragh !—Croom, croom, aboo !' and in spite of Talbot's most desperate exertions, he was wrung out of his grasp, and rolled over and beaten down by the rushing waters, although within ten yards of the shallows, where, if he could have set his foot, his life had been saved. The barge he had seen approaching, swept by within an oar's length in the darkness.

" ' The culver shot sunk them,' cried one.

" ' I did not strike within a spear's cast of them ; they swamped in the stream swell,' said another.

" ' You are sure it was Kelly ?' asked a third.

" The first speaker answered : ' I saw him as plainly as I saw the gunner's face in the flash ; but who he was that was with him, I cannot tell.'

" ' Pull back, my men,' cried the questioner, ' pull back to the traitor's house ; we will make a bonfire of it, that the rebels may read the proclamation of their treason by, from Chapelizod to Clontarf !'

" Talbot, who had been striking out for the little quay, where Connor kept his boats, now yielded to the current of the river, and was carried past unseen, while the crew of the barge pushed across on their savage errand. He made for the beach, about a hundred yards lower down, where a ditch, running from the river side, afforded him a screen from observation. It was fortunate for him he did so, for ere he was well clear of the oozy exposed beach, the flames from the thatch of the devoted dwelling were casting gleams of pale light over the flat he had to traverse. Presently the fitful flashes broke into a red glare, that showed every object around as plainly as the sun at noon ; and the destroyers raised a shout that made his blood run cold, as shuddering, he crept closer under his shelter. He blessed God that there were no shrieks of fatherless children ; no moans of a widowed mother to cry to heaven from under the blazing rafters ; still, when he thought of the generous sacrifice made for his sake, by him who had so long, in honesty and peace, inhabited those desolated walls, and who might now be rolling to the sea, an unanointed corpse, with all his sins and failings fresh upon his head, he could not restrain the anguish that rushed upon his soul, and the tears burst from his eyes. Dripping and spent, he lay panting in his concealment, till he saw the incendiaries retire to their barge; the river and the walls beyond started out into a moment's renewed splendour, as the falling roof sent up its last jet of red sparks and flame, but in another minute the darkness closed down again on the smoking ruin, and Talbot might pursue his way without dread of observation. He reached Artane before morning, but it was not till after day-break that sleep closed his weary eyes, and gave him a temporary forgetfulness of all the strange events and conflicting emotions of that momentous day.

Week after week rolled on, and Talbot was not summoned from his monotonous solitude, to take part in any of the more active services of the revolt. He dared not seek another interview with Ellen; and had he dared, he had no longer the means of accomplishing it. The haunting misery of his thoughts was the reflection, that he was aiding in the infliction of want and suffering on those he loved; this gnawed upon his soul continually, and, joined to the disgust and indignation which he felt at Lord Thomas's neglect, and the slights of the leaders, threw him into deep melancholy, and made his life utterly wretched. One afternoon, while sitting in his hut, and brooding in fierce impatience over his misfortunes, he was roused, for the first time since he had taken post in that lonely station, by a party of horse from Ballgriffen, with Burnel at their head.

" ' Ha, Sir John, how goes the game here in the woods?' cried he, ' by my faith, we must not let you waste your time in this lonely inaction—mount, my good friend, there is work to be done this evening at Kilmainham.'

" ' To horse, men !' cried Talbot, buckling on his sword, but made no other answer.

" ' By Saint Doulagh, Sir John, you speak wondrous short; but no matter; I come to ask the aid of your sword, not to waste time in idle talk, but if you like not the service, you have but to say the word.'

" ' Master Burnel, lead on: I need me to be reminded of my duty.'

" They rode to Oxmantown-green in silence, and prepared to cross the Liffey. As they passed the ford, they heard a sudden and sharp firing between the city and Kilmainham Castle. The shouts and din of a fight were distinctly audible as they hurried up the opposite bank. The noise came from the little wood of Salcock, about a quarter of a mile across the country a-head.

" ' Spur on, gentlemen,' cried Burnel, ' it is the churls who have sallied to drive a prey, at blows with our friends from Kilmainham and Inchicore.'—They put spurs to their horses, and dashed across the plain to intercept the retreat of the citizens. It was a calm sunny evening, and the landscape lay green and glittering before them; the birds were even twittering among the straggling trees, but the heart of the wood was convulsed with a struggle desperate and deadly; for the firing had now ceased, and, as the party went at a hand gallop down the alleys of Salcock, they could hear, louder and louder, at every bound, the tumultuous hubbub of a contest, hand to hand. At length they burst in upon the scene of action; it was a level green among the trees, through the stems, and under the branches of which the setting sun poured his radiance on as bloody a spectacle, for its extent, as ever met the eye of day. The little round of pasture was covered with dead and dying, among whom the survivors, so locked and mingled, as hardly to be distinguished, reeled to and fro in one body, shaking the ground with their tramp, and thrusting or striking in the earnest silence of savage determination. But though the men on either side fought without war cry or clamour, the crush and collision, and the redoubling clang of blows made a fearful din. The appearance of Burnel's reinforcement decided the day. At their first charge, both citizens and rebels were driven off; for they were so grappled, that no man could tell at which side his own friends pushed or resisted. It was a pitiable sight, when the ground was cleared, to see the wan wretches who had been driven to the field by hunger, bleeding among the rushes, as in a shambles, beside the bodies of the cattle they had hoped to

consume; for, at the first attack of musquetry, both man and beast had fallen where they stood. Burnel's troop now charged through the glades in pursuit; for some more desperate than the rest, had made a stand among the trees, and were again beginning to ply their matchlocks. As Talbot followed with his men, across the open space where the dead lay thickest, his eye caught an object on the ground, that made him pull up with such a strain, as nearly threw his horse upon his haunches. A sword of rich workmanship, which he had often admired, over the mantel-piece of Paul Dudley, lay broken in two, among the long grass. He leaped from the saddle, and turned the prostrate man that lay nearest, on his back. It was the loyal merchant; but so disfigured with wounds—so wasted by toil and suffering, that his own son could hardly have known his features at the first look.

" ' Oh, my God !' cried Talbot, raising the passive body, and propping it against his knee, ' can this be the good old man—can this indeed, be the loyal and kind Paul Dudley?' The fainting merchant slowly opened his eyes, and gazed upon the scene of carnage; but when, on looking up, he saw the face of Talbot bending over him, he closed them again with a convulsive effort that told how sick a pang the sight had cost him, and groaned deeply.

" ' He is not dead,' exclaimed the knight; ' it is his cumbrous coat of mail that is smothering him ! What, ho, ye knaves, dismount ! there is blood enough shed !— villains, come back and help me to undo the wounded gentleman's gorget !—his life is worth more than all we have lost to day ! If you let him die among your rude hands, I will strike my dagger through some of your bodies !—There—lift him up—let the air to his face—ah, this Milan shirt, it is choking him !—Oh, heaven ! that he should have been driven to load his aged limbs with such a weight of iron !—water, ye dogs, bring water in your helmets; there is a brook in the hollow—haste, haste for your lives !' .

" Just then, a horseman, reeking from the slaughter, galloped into the little plain :—' Sir John Talbot, your troop is wanted in the wood. Lord Thomas has sent to know why you delay ?—The loyalists have made another stand : three of our captains are slain : mount, Sir John Talbot, this is no time for hanging back.'

" ' I care not who stands, or who falls, here I stay, sir, till I see this aged gentleman cared for,' cried Talbot; ' and as for hanging back, I tell thee, Christopher Parez, that if I were not supporting the head of a man I love too dearly, to leave for so light a cause, I would drive the falsehood down thy dishonourable throat !—villian, see to what you have brought us !'

" ' Sir John Talbot,' cried Parez, ' the blade that is glued to its scabbard by an 'if,' gives me little apprehension ; I scorn the threats of a braggart.'

" ' Put thy knee under his head, Art; thou wert ever the kindliest of thy company,' said Talbot, in a low voice, as he transferred his charge to the hands of one of his troopers, ' and if I fall, carry him in a litter to the priory hospital, and tell the almoner it was my last request that he should be kindly nursed.' Then rising, he drew his sword, and motioned to Parez to follow him a little apart from the spot where Dudley lay. Parez, whose weapon was out, and already steeped in blood, turned pale when he saw himself summoned to a more equal combat than that in which he had so cheaply fleshed it ; he seemed to debate with himself whether he ought not to charge upon his enemy, and trample him under his feet; but casting his eyes on the soldiery around, he abandoned a design so perilous, and sullenly followed his adversary on foot. They engaged with all the hate that rivalry and mutual insult can kindle in the human breast; but both were clad in complete armour, and for some time their deadliest strokes fell harmless on the cold iron. The clang was like that of the armourer's hammer, and for a while the eyes of the spectators were dazzled with the equal comminglement of their weapons. But, ere long, Parez was giving back, under the incessant battery which Talbot showered, swift as whirling sleet, upon his head ; he reeled—staggered—and then in desperation rushed in, and they closed with a clash of their breastplates, like twenty pair of cymbals. Both were strong men, and both tugged for life or death, for they knew that, once down, the dagger of the uppermost would soon make its way where the sword had failed. Down they went at length, with a sidelong flash in the sun, and a crush of plate and mail that sent the sound of its heavy dint an arrow flight into the woods around. They rolled and grappled for a moment, and none could tell which was uppermost; when, in the height of the struggle, Lord Thomas Fitzgerald and his company galloped in upon the ground. Talbot had at last got the advantage, and planted his knee upon his prostrate adversary's breast, his dagger was out, and he was holding down Parez's right hand with his left, and calling on him to beg his life, while the other with the gauntlet of that hand which was at liberty, was shielding his throat where he expected the descending blow—

" ' For shame, gentlemen, for shame! hold your hand, Sir John Talbot ! I am your general, and I command you, hold your hand !' cried Lord Thomas, as he leaped from the saddle, and seized the arm of the knight, whom he dragged bodily off his enemy.

" ' My lord, this is my private quarrel; I will let no man stand between me and my just vengeance !' cried Talbot, fiercely, shaking himself free, and rushing upon his antagonist again; but Burnel, De La Hyde, and the rest came between, and held him back by main force. Parez got up with a countenance black as night, the cold sweat standing in beads upon his forehead, and every joint trembling with rage and shame. ' I will be avenged yet —I will, by him that made us both !' he exclaimed, and turned away.

" Lord Thomas now addressed Talbot, ' Sir John, Sir John, what mean you by this conduct ? Are you weary of the service ? Would you return to your allegiance ? In God's name, say so at once, if you wish it; but baulk us not by seeming to be our friend, and acting in such a time of need so like an enemy.'

" ' My lord, I am not your enemy,' cried Talbot, ' but I had neither been a man or a Christian had I passed him that loved me as a father loves his son, and he perishing upon the field where your lordship's troops were already victorious. I drew this sword, my lord, against King Henry for the sake of the father of my orphan childhood; for his sake I have borne the displeasure of the only other friend I ever had; of one who would have been a second father to me if my loyalty to you had not rejected the bounties he would have poured upon me, and outraged the love and kindness that was already mine. My lord, that ill-requited friend lies yonder bleeding to death; his only child will soon be fatherless as she is motherless already—my lord and gentlemen, I am betrothed to Dudley's daughter, and I will not see him die deserted, though I should lose my own life by his side !' and he strode forward to the spot where Dudley lay, all yielding a passage, and many at the moment crying that he was in the right. As he knelt down again by the side of the dying man, the troopers and captains who had heard him, drew back with compassionate delicacy, and left them alone among the dead.

" ' Master Dudley, will you give me your forgiveness ?' said the knight, and took the merchant's cold hand in his.

" Dudley opened his eyes and looked mournfully upon him. ' I am going fast, Sir John,' he whispered faintly; ' I bear no anger against any man.'

" ' Shall I call to them to send a priest ?' asked the knight, raising him higher in his arms.

" ' I am shrived—I die at peace with the world—I did not think you loved me so well, Sir John,' said the old man, and was silent. Talbot could not speak; but his tears fell on the face of the dying merchant, as he lay in his arms quite still for about a minute. At last he sighed deeply, and looked again in the face of his supporter, while his hand, cold as it was, faintly returned the pressure. ' Ellen, my child,' he murmured in a voice hardly audible, but Talbot bent over him and caught every sound. ' She has none now to protect her—take her—my wealth is in jewels—take all, and may God bless you !' Talbot's heart was in his throat; he could make no reply, and both were again silent, but the merchant with a last effort

roused himself, and cried in a clear voice—My son, with the last breath I shall ever draw, I say, abandon this rebellion—give it up whenever you can without dishonour, and save the race of an honest man from shame !' He fell back as he spoke, and after a feebly drawn sigh or two, expired.

" Talbot laid him softly down, and called his men to bear the body to Kilmainham; but De La Hyde, when he saw him rise, advanced, and taking him by the hand, said, ' Talbot, time presses; we can wait no longer. You are to return to Artane in company with Burnel. On my honour, I am sorry for this; but they all insist upon it, and Lord Thomas has been forced to consent. Ah ! the brave old man, he's gone; but you may leave him without fear; he shall have Christian burial; I give you my hand upon it, he shall.'

" ' De La Hyde, I thank thee ; I am content; but for the others, I did not look for this at their hands.'

" ' Parez's account of the affair has enraged them beyond measure, and Travers is there denouncing heretics and blasphemers; but they and Lord Thomas are now gone, and Burnel awaits you. Farewell, you have my word that I will see him cared for.'

" Talbot wrung De La Hyde's hand, and with a bursting heart, leaped upon his horse, and led his troop off the field.

(To be continued.)

A DEAF AND DUMB POET.

One of the youngest American poets, JAMES NACK, is *deaf and dumb!* This singular boy has a precocity that would be remarkable in a child who had the full possession of its powers. He lost the use of his senses while an infant, and can of course have little of memory in his ideas of sound. When quite a lad he published a volume called " The Legend of the Rocks, and other Poems." The following, from a piece called " The Minstrel Boy," though not the best specimen of his productions, is most interesting, from its allusion to his misfortunes :—

Amid a throng in deep attention bound,
    To catch the accents that from others fall,
The flow of eloquence, the heavenly sound
    Breathed from the soul of melody, while all
Instructed or delighted, list around,
    Vacant unconsciousness must *me* enthral;
I can but watch each animated face,
And there attempt th' inspiring theme to trace.

Unheard, unheeded are the lips by *me*,
    To others that unfold some heaven-born art,
And melody—Oh, dearest melody !
    How had thine accents, thrilling to my heart,
Awaken'd all its strings to sympathy,
    Bidding the spirit at thy magic start !
How had my heart responsive to the strain,
Throbb'd in love's wild delight or soothing pain.

In vain—alas, in vain ! thy numbers roll—
    Within my heart no echo they inspire;
Though form'd by nature in thy sweet controul,
    To melt with tenderness, or glow with fire,
Misfortune closed the portals of the soul;
    And till an Orpheus rise to sweep the lyre,
That can to animation kindle stone,
To me thy thrilling power must be unknown.

DUBLIN:
Printed and Published by P. D. HARDY, 3, Cecilia-street; to whom all communications are to be addressed.
Sold by all Booksellers in Ireland.
In London, by Richard Groombridge, 6, Panyer-alley, Paternoster-row; in Liverpool, by Wilmer and Smith ; in Manchester, by Ambery; in Birmingham, by Guest, 91, Steelhouse-lane; in Glasgow, by John Macleod ; and in Edinburgh, by N. Bowack.

THE

DUBLIN PENNY JOURNAL

CONDUCTED BY P. DIXON HARDY, M.R.I.A.

Vol. III.   MARCH 28, 1835.   No. 143.

QUEEN ELIZABETH ENGAGED IN HAWKING.

The Engravings in our present Number we have copied from "The Graphic and Historical Illustrator," by E. W. Brayley, Esq.—a work which reflects the highest credit on its talented editor, and which must have succeeded, were works of genius and research always certain of success. We are informed by Mr. Brayley, that in the publication of "the Illustrator" his wish was " to extend the influence of antiquarian lore, to correctly delineate the national manners of the olden times, to disseminate just principles on architecture and the arts, to elucidate points of history of dubious authenticity, to investigate our provincial dialects, and finally, to supply instructive entertainment for an intellectual and high-minded people." By the failure of his publishers, however, his intentions were frustrated; and a work which must have proved of the greatest interest, not only to the antiquarian and scholar, but to the archi-

tect and builder, was thus strangled in its infancy. Many of the engravings are excellent; while several of the essays on chivalry and ancient English manners and customs, bring back the mind, in a train of pleasing reminiscences, to scenes of heroism and noble daring, over which the mind still lingers with pensive pleasure.

QUEEN ELIZABETH HAWKING.

The above engraving, representing Queen Elizabeth engaged in hawking, and surrounded by her courtiers and attendants, is copied from 'a tracing made from the first edition of Turberville.

" 'Hawking.' observes Henry Peacham, 'was a sport utterly unknown to the ancients; yet it appeareth, by Firmicus, that it was known twelve hundred yeeres since.' Where it was first exercised, and at what precise era it came into vogue, is uncertain, 'but it is mentioned by a Latin writer of the fourth century, and is affirmed by some to have been borrowed by the Romans from the Britons, as early as the reign of Vespasian.' 'In England,' says Mr. Pennant, 'I cannot trace the certainty of falconry till the reign of King Ethelbert, the Saxon monarch, in the year 860, when he wrote to Germany for a brace of falcons, which would fly at cranes and bring them to the ground, as there were very few such in Kent.' The unfortunate Harold is pictured going on an embassy of the utmost importance, with a dog under his arm, and a hawk on his wrist; and even females of distinction were occasionally thus represented. 'Alfred the Great, who is commended for his proficiency in this, as in all other fashionable amusements, is said to have written a treatise upon the subject.'

"'A knowledge of hunting and *falconry,*' Warton describes 'as an essential requisite in accomplishing the character of a knight;' and in such high repute was it held by our nobility, for several centuries, that its tenacious support 'may be traced through the statute laws, and swelling the pains and penalties of criminal jurisprudence.' In the 34th of Edward III. it was made felony to steal a hawk; and to take its eggs, even on a person's own ground, was punishable with imprisonment for a year and a day, besides a fine at the king's pleasure. In the reign of Elizabeth, although the term of confinement was reduced to three months, the offender was compelled to find security for his good behaviour for seven years, or to remain in prison till he did. At the beginning of the seventeenth century, Mr. Smith informs us that a goshawk and tassel hawk were sold for 100 marks, and that in the reign of James II. Sir Thomas Monson gave £1000 for a cast of hawks.

"The twelfth century appears to have been the season when falconry attained the zenith of its popularity. Not only kings and nobles, but high-born maidens and dignified ecclesiastics pursued this favourite amusement. Even Becket, the archbishop of Canterbury, when despatched on an embassy to the court of France, by Henry the Second, carried hawks and hounds with him of every description.

"For a long period, no person of high rank was represented without his falcon. 'In travelling, in visiting, in affairs of business or of pleasure, the hawk still remained perched upon the hand, which it stamped with distinction.' Nay, to such excess was this practise carried, that the nobility attended divine service with their hawks and hounds.

"'To part with the hawk,' says Mr. Smith, 'even in circumstances of the utmost extremity, was deemed highly ignominious. By the ancient laws and capitularies of France, a knight was forbidden to give up his sword and his *hawk*, even as the price of his ransom. These two articles were too sacred to be surrendered, although the liberty of their owner depended on them.' Boccacio's ninth story affords a beautiful illustration of this usage.

"Federigo degli Alberighi becomes enamoured of a lady of Florence, called Monna Giovanna, ruins his fortune by a succession of tournaments, feasts and banquets in honour of his mistress, who rejects his suit,—retires to a little farm, by the produce of which he contrives to procure a bare existence, and carries nothing with him but his favorite falcon. His mistress in the mean time marries, and is left a widow with one son, who conceives a great admiration for Federigo's bird, and falling ill, intreats his mother to obtain it for him; she answers, 'How can I send or go to ask for his hawk, and what alone mayntains him in the world? Or how can I offer to take away from a gentleman all the pleasure he has in life.' Overcome however, by her child's importunity, the fond dame, at length, consents.

"This promise brought a beam of joy into the boy's countenance, and the same day he showed evident signs of amendment. The next morning, Monna Giovanna, taking with her another lady as a companion, proceeded to Federigo's humble habitation and inquired for him. He was beyond measure surprised when he heard that Monna Giovanna was asking for him, and ran in great joy to meet her. As soon as she saw him approach, she gracefully moved to meet him, and respectfully saluting him, said, 'Federigo, I come to recompense you in some sort for the evil you have received at my hands, at a time when you loved me more than was wise on your part; and the recompense I intend is to make myself and my companion your guests at dinner to-day.' To which Federigo with great humility replied, 'Alas! Madam, I do not recollect to have received any evil at your hands, but so much good, that if it were ever in my power I should be happy, for the love I have borne you, and more so for the honour of this visit, to expend my fortune a second time in your honour;' and thus speaking, he respectfully led her into his house, and thence conducted her into the garden; and there, not having any other person to introduce her to, said, 'Madam, this good woman, the wife of my husbandman, will wait on you whilst I prepare our table.' But, alas! living in a state of poverty, he had no provisions to set before his guests, nor money to procure any—this almost drove him to desperation: at last, observing his beloved falcon, the only vestige of his former splendour, resting on its perch in his chamber, and seeing no other resource, he killed his favourite bird, and causing the wench carefully to roast it, placed it before the ladies. When they had risen from table, after some agreeable conversation, Monna Giovanna made known the purpose of her visit. Federigo hearing her request, and seeing he could not gratify it, became unable to reply. At length he told her the sad truth, and produced the feathers and beak and talons of the poor bird. The lady reprehended him for killing so fine a falcon for such a purpose; but at the same time, however, highly commending, in her own mind, his magnanimity, which it had not been in the power of fortune to abase. The sequel may be supposed, her boy died, and after having indulged her sorrow for some time, her brothers, seeing that she was left extremely rich, entreated her to marry again. 'I should willingly,' she replied, 'if it were agreeable to you, remain in my present state, but if you insist that I marry, I will assuredly take no one for my husband but Federigo degli Alberighi.' On which her brothers, smiling, replied, 'What folly is this! would you marry a man who is a beggar?' To this she answered, 'Brothers, I well know that the matter is as you state it, but I choose rather a man that hath need of wealth, than wealth that hath need of a man.' Mr. Smith, who merely alludes to this story, remarks upon it, 'the author doubtless intended to impress us with the *most exalted* notion of Federigo's gallantry and devotion to his mistress.'

"In England, falconry continued in high repute till about the time of the civil wars, when 'its fall was sudden and complete.' 'An inquiry,' says a writer in the *Censura Literaria*, 'of how it became neglected, can, I believe, only be answered with conjecture.' Peacham says, 'it can bee no more disgrace to a great lord to draw a fair picture, than to cut his hawke's meat;'—and this nauseating courtesy established between the owner and the hawk, and apparently in part a necessity, to make the bird answer to the lure, might first occasion its falling into neglect and almost total disuse.' Smith attributes its downfall to the invention of gunpowder; but, probably, the puritans may be charged with undermining this, as well as the village May-games and our other national amusements. Only a partial trace of this ancient amusement remained in the seventeenth century. It is now a question, whether there is one reclaimed foreign hawk in the western part of the kingdom; but there may be a few English hawks annually trained in the neighbourhood of Bridport, in Dorsetshire, for the taking of land-rails in the hemp and flax fields near that town, in which, during some seasons, they are very plentiful."

THE TOURNAMENT.

The following account of the Tournament, extracted from the same work, will be interesting to our readers:—

"Gorgeous pageantries, rich caparisons, knightly gallantry, and, above all, the beauty of high-born maidens, combined to grace and glorify the ancient Tournament. Our ancestors were weak or vain enough to believe, that this martial sport was derived from the funeral games celebrated by Æneas, in honour of his father, Anchises; yet few marks of similarity can be traced between them, and as Mr. Mills justly observes, 'the knights might have discovered in the nature and tendency of circumstances, and the practice of their known and immediate forefathers, sufficient matter for originality. War was an art in the middle ages, and a long and painful education preceded the practice of it. It was the delight as well as the occupation of the world; for fame, fortune, and woman's love could only be obtained by gallant bearing. Hence we find that thoughts of war were not abandoned in times of peace, and that some softened images of battle formed the grace of festive solemnities.'

"The tournament was admirably calculated to rouse and nourish the chivalric spirit of Europe; and while it trained the youthful aspirants for actual combat, it veiled the horrors of strife and bloodshed with the courtesies and amenities of peace.

"On very solemn occasions, the monarch, purposing to hold 'a passage of arms,' dispatched his heralds to every Christian court, who challenged every true and amorous knight to hasten to the place appointed, and break a lance for God and his lady-love. To those who made long journeys for this chivalric purpose, safe conduct through hostile countries was always granted. The champions, who generally arrived some time before the Tournament, affixed their armorial bearings above the entrances of the tents assigned them, and placed their silken pennons beside their names, so that if any one of them had behaved unknightly, the delinquent might be judged by the presiding maidens, and (if proved guilty) his banner stricken down from its place.

"'None,' says Mills, 'could tourney who had blasphemed God, or offended the ladies; he who had been false to gratitude and honour; he who had violated his word, or deserted his brother in arms in battle, was unworthy of appearing in the splendid show; and the high courtesy of chivalry was maintained by the law, that no one could tourney who, without warning, assailed his enemy, or by indirect means had despoiled his territory.'

"The above regulations, however, were frequently not complied with. We read of *unknown* knights performing exploits at nearly every recorded tournament. Some, who had just commenced their career of glory, concealed their names with the diffidence and timidity of novices. Sometimes *kings* disguised themselves to make personal trial of the prowess of their knightly servants. Troops of warriors in the garb of Arthur and his famous knights, plunged into the lists; and history informs us, that at a Passage of Arms, held A. D. 1428, at Valladolid. in Spain, the king of Castile was attended by twelve knights, who called themselves the Holy Apostles.

"The place of combat was termed the *Lists.* It was surrounded by ropes, or railing, and splendid galleries, which were hung with velvet, gold and silver cloths, and richly-woven tapestry. Youthful maidens awarded the rewards and punishments, and were the supreme judges of the tournament. They generally, however, deputed their power to a knight, who, on this account, was called the *Knight of Honour,* and he bore on his lance a ribbon, or some other mark of female favour.

"On the morning of the eventful day, the proud, and the brave, and the beautiful, repaired to the place appointed. The ladies wearing military girdles, overlaid with gold and gems, and leading the fiery steeds of the knights they loved; while martial music, and the song of the minstrel, floated merrily on the breezes. Froissart tells us, that in the reign of Richard II. on one of these occasions, there came out of the Tower of London, first, threescore coursers, apparelled for the lists, and on every one a squire of honour, riding at a gentle pace, and next issued threescore honourable ladies, mounted on fair palfreys, each lady leading by a chain of silver a knight, sheathed in jousting harness, and that they proceeded in this manner through London to Smithfield.

"When they reached the lists, the constable was wont to examine the weapons of the assembled warriors, and the points were removed from their lances, or covered by broad pieces of wood, called *rockets.* Such precautions were not unnecessary, for Tournaments had so often terminated in real encounters, that an oath was imposed on every knight, that he would frequent the tourney solely to learn military exercises; he was only allowed to use the broad sword, and spectators were not permitted to bear any arms whatsoever. The tilting armour was light and costly, and their helmets and spears were usually decorated with the favours of the lady-loves of their possessors, and every courteous knight bore the device of the queen of his affections.

"No sooner had the arms been examined, than the heralds shouted, 'A l'ostelle, à l'ostelle—to achievement, knights and squires, to achievement!' and the knights, having bowed to the ladies, retired within their tents. Again the trumpet sounded, and the cry of 'Come forth, knights, come forth!' rent the air; the warriors simultaneously came forth from their pavilions, and vaulting on their chargers, each awaited the signal for encounter, by the side of his banner.

"The hum of the plebeian beholders, and the merry laughter of the joyous 'damoiselles'—nay, every sound was hushed, and the heralds anxiously expected the sign of the *Knight of Honour*: the moment it was given, 'Laissez aller!' broke the silence, the ropes which separated the hostile bands were slackened, and with the speed of lightning, and the crash of thunder, the gallant champions met each other in full career. They were closely followed by their squires, who not only supplied them, in case of need with fresh arms and horses, but were the bearers of encouraging words and favours from the lovely maidens present.

"'One encounter,' says Mr. Mills, 'seldom terminated the sport; lances were broken, horses and knights overthrown, and the tide of victory flowed to either end of the lists.' Each warrior invoked his dame, as though she were his patron saint, and strange as it may seem to our female readers, this most dangerous scene of the Tournament afforded the greatest interest to the fair spectators, who, with sparkling eyes and glowing countenances, encouraged and enjoyed the mimic war. The ladies leant over the gilded balconies, waved their snowy kerchiefs, and called their knights to bear them bravely if they would win their love, and the elder swordsmen cried, 'On, valiant knights, fair eyes behold you!' At every noble achievement, the poursuivants-at arms blended their acclamations, 'Honour to the sons of the brave;' the minstrels echoed them in the loudest notes of their martial music, and the chivalrous spectators replied by the cry, 'Loyauté aux dames!' When every knight had done some gallant deed,[*] or became disqualified for further action, the lord of the tourney dropped his warder, and the heralds shouted 'Ployez vos banniers,'—fold your banners,—and thus the tourney ended.

"Then followed the festival:—divested of their armour, and robed in costly garments, with hawk on wrist, and attended by their faithful stag-hounds, the champions crowded round the festive board, which was sometimes a round table, in honour of Arthur and his companions, or else the long feudal table, with its raised upper end, or dais. Each sate by the side of his lady-love, and the minstrels chaunted spirit-stirring songs in praise of valour and courtesy; 'and when the merriment was most joyous, the heralds presented to the ladies the knights who had worthily demeaned themselves—she who, by the consent of her fair companions was named *La Royne de la Beaulté et des Amours,* delivered the prizes to the kneeling knights,' and addressed to each a few words of thanks and laud, concluding with the wish, that such a valiant cavalier

---

[*] The old English ordinances, stating what feats of arms were most honourable, and the contrary, have been preserved; the following are extracts from them:—"First, whoso breaketh most spears, as they ought to be broken, shall have the price. Item, whoso hitteth three times in the helm shall have the price, Item, whoso meeteth two times coronel to coronel, shall have the price. Item, whoso beareth a man down with stroke of spear shall have the price.

"How the price should be lost—First, whoso striketh a horse shall have no price. Item, whoso striketh a man, his back turned, or disarmed of his spear, shall have no price. Item, whoso hitteth the toil or tilt thrice, shall have no price. Item, whoso unhelms himself twice shall have no price, without his horse fail him."

would have much joy and worship with his lady. ' The victory was entirely owing to the favour of my mistress, which I wore in my helmet,' was the usual answer of the knight. ' As Tournaments were scenes of pleasure, the knight who appeared in the most handsome guise was praised ; and to complete the courtesies of chivalry, thanks were rendered to those who had travelled to the lists from far countries.'

"The prizes were not unfrequently bestowed on the listed field, and the conquerors rode slowly round the enclosure till they came before the throne of the Queen of the festival.

'They press to see the victor who advances,
    Youngest, yet bravest son of chivalry,
Unrivalled breaker of a hundred lances,
    In single fight, with warriors bold as he,
    And lauded for his peerless courtesy ;
In every land, the dazzling sun shines on,
    Where feats of arms receive their meed of praise,
    And halls re-echo with the poet's lays,
Or wandering minstrel's soul-entrancing song. * * *

* * Still as he passes by
    Each stately gallery,
And sees what forms are there, he bares his head,
    And all his auburn hair
    Floats in the breezy air
Like lambent flames from wings of angel shed ;
    And in that single glance
    Of his proud countenance,
His mind has concentrated all its meaning ;
    So god-like 'tis—that none
    Behold unmoved, and with the will of one
They shower down flowers, half o'er the gold rails leaning.'

" The Tournament sometimes continued for three days : on the second morning, the squires encountered instead of the knights : these also were escorted to the lists, and rewarded by high-born ladies. On the third, there was usually a *mêlée* of *knights and squires*, to whom prizes were distributed, as on the first day. The festivities concluded with music and dancing, and the knights lavishly remunerated the heralds."

MOCK TOURNAMENT AT NUREMBERG, IN 1446.

BURLESQUE TOURNAMENTS.

" Notwithstanding the number of authors whose pens, dipped in ancient lore, have made chivalrous deeds the theme of their writings, it has scarcely been noticed that the TOURNAMENT, the darling delight of our ancestors, (that imposing spectacle, at which all that was gallant, noble, and courteous, assembled to vie in attraction, or prowess,) was often made the subject of *Ridicule*. So gross were the ideas in by-gone days, that the same persons could not only tolerate the mummery too often attached to religious observances, but also its burlesque imitation. At one time they would enforce the strict and ceremonious regulations prescribed to insure obedience and respect, and at another admit of their deterioration by buffoonery and make-game :—at this moment giving respectful heedance to all the pomp and circumstance of feats of honour and knighthood, and at the next, allowing of their being made the butt of ribaldry and merriment to the most vulgar minds. The Lord of Misrule and his attendants were sometimes of the lower class, who performed the *saturnalia* of their day ; and the Mock TOURNAMENTS were celebrated by those who were ex-

cluded from the privileges that admitted the high born to that envied amusement. But then these were permitted by the rest of society, who shared in the enjoyment experienced by the others.

" The Burlesque Tournaments were carried to a much greater extent on the Continent than in England, and yet they formed part of the splendour and show of our own Lords of Misrule, for whom, as we find by records still existing, were provided 'certain maskes with their furniture, and coates of canvas painted like shirts of mail, and bases, barbes, and caparisons, with trappours made, garnyshed and sette out, and complete furniture for iiij challengers and their xx horses, well appoynted and prepared to use in and for the tryumphe and justes, with long fools' cotes of white and red baudekyn.'—When these mock encounters first began is not easy to decide: they were known certainly as early as the commencement of the reign of Henry VI. and had probably grown out of the *Troy* game, and such like harmless sports; and it would seem that the *behourds* or mock lances, made of reeds, were used when actual armour was not worn for protection."

THE COURT FOOL.

"Amongst the pleasing reveries that crowd a cultured mind at ease, few are more kindly entertained than those that savour of the daily doings of our old English households: they may be likened to links in the social chain that unite the present and the past, and hold affiance to the love of our country.

"Would that our chroniclers of old, had given us, for every page of coronations, royal weddings, births and deaths of princes, with knightly tournaments, and wars their prototypes, and all that appertains to courts, and camps, at least another page, touching the more genial events of common life.

"Chaucer has shown us what men were in his time; society abounded in character then, as now. Every city, town, and village, performed its daily drama, in which each one played his part.

"Who more holy than the prior? who more jovial than the monks? When not at mass, they might be found at the hosteiry hard by, teaching mine host how to choose good sack, and mine hostess how to season venison pasty; he being somewhat of a homely wit, and she a buxom dame. Then the bench bore corpulent justices, and bodies-corporate grew fat at the mayor's feast. Then attorneys-at-law, scrupulous to the very letter, o'er the parchment, met neighbour, neighbourly at the inn. Barons were then right lordly, maintaining open hospitality, and their ladies courteous and bounteous to the poor. Esquires were brave abroad, frank, generous, and noisy as their beagles; when at home, cracking fair maiden's ear-strings with loud tallihoes: self-grudging misers there were, and self-loving extortioners; but these were shunned. Then there were humourists of every degree, in high life, and in low; each wearing his humour as a badge. The schoolmaster and the rhymer; the priest and poticary, the sexton and the pinder; the smith and the cord-wainer; the miller and the malster; the tanner and the tinker; the weaver and the tailor; the millwright, carpenter, and mason; little confraternities, neighbours in good fellowship. Yea, a congregate of character, the thrifty and the thriftless; the sober and the sottish; the joyous and the moody; the phlegmatic and warm-hearted; the sprightly and the grave, all mingling, and helping to drive on the daily system of life, through all its social ramifications, and congenial dependencies.

"That these diurnal doings were done in days of yore, we know; but, vain would now be our regret, at not knowing more of these the daily doings of our worshipful forefathers."

THE COURT FOOL.

"Amongst other eccentrics of former days, was that merry wight, ycleped Jester, and his no less sprightly coeval, the Motley-fool; whose frolics, gibes, and jeers were the delight and the talk of all, whilst few, even among the writers contemporary, had the kindness to record their witty sayings, for the entertainment of posterity.

"Master John Heywood was one of those cognomened Jester, a character not to be confounded with that of Patch, or Fool. Killegrew, a man of letters also, was commonly so designated, as one of the leading wits of Charles the Second's court.

"Heywood doubtless was a master-wit; it were sufficient to establish this to know, that he was the delight of Sir Thomas More, who frequently entertained him at his seat at Chelsea, and exchanged many a lively joke with Master John. He himself, indeed, kept a Fool in his own house, whose portrait was introduced by Holbein into his celebrated picture of the More family."

The above wood-cut, we are informed, is a fac simile of a portrait of a Court Fool, selected from a group of those prankish wights, sketched by the masterly hand of Albert Durer.

THE REBELLION OF SILKEN THOMAS.

FROM THE "HIBERNIAN NIGHTS' ENTERTAINMENTS," IN THE DUBLIN UNIVERSITY MAGAZINE.

(Continued from our last Number.)

The preceding sketch of the Rebellion of Silken Thomas, containing the principal facts of that extraordinary history, we have given verbatim from the February number of the University Magazine. The second portion of the narrative in the number for March, has run to such a length, however, and without being yet finished, that we feel compelled to refer those who may wish for further particulars to the Magazine itself—confining ourselves to a mere summary of the events as grouped together in this interesting story of Irish rebellion.

The citizens of Dublin, after considerable resistance, having given the insurgent forces access to the Castle, Sir John Talbot lost little time in visiting the dwelling of Master Dudley, which he finds empty, Archbishop Alan having on that day set sail for England, taking with him old Dudley's daughter, the fair Ellen. Talbot, returning to his quarters in the greatest distress of mind, is the means of saving the Archbishop and his beloved one from being shipwrecked on the coast.

" The citizens of Dublin were now less obstinate in refusing to give the insurgent forces access to the Castle through their gates; and negociations for that purpose were again opened. On the evening of the first day of the truce that succeeded, Sir John Talbot, wrapped in his cloak, passed into the city, unobserved among the multitude that flocked from all quarters with provisions for the famished inhabitants, for the poorer classes had already suffered dreadfully from hunger. The streets were thronged with gaunt crowds, some laughing, some weeping—mothers and their children, their faces smeared with the raw oatmeal which they ravened up from the sack mouth, tottering upon the causeways; then the rebel soldiery, flushed with their success, and insolent in their anticipated triumph, shouting and singing in the streets, and the disheartened loyalist, on the Castle walls, replying with faint cheers at intervals, and every now and again, the sound of a solitary shot against the batteries, begun in Preston's Inns, fronting the barbican, together made a bewildering hubbub, like the noises in a dream. Talbot treaded the intricate throng, with hurrying steps and a beating heart. Each pale face that passed him seemed like a spectre glaring through the twilight: the confused noises that surrounded him fell on his ear like a general lamentation. When he reached Dudley's court, doors and windows were barred, and all was silent as the grave. 'Ah!' he exclaimed, 'here is an altered household; my poor Ellen, this shock will have broken her heart! but still, I bear her some comfort; she will need it now more than ever;—but, surely, they cannot have left the house!' he cried, as the echoes of the heavy knocker died away in the silence of the empty court-yard. His heart sunk as he listened in vain for any indication of reply; his first idea was, that they had perhaps gone to Kilmainham; but this he rejected, unconscious of any reason, and walked with a quick but unsteady step round to the garden side. He clambered over the wall; the flowers were trampled and tangled, and the place did not look like itself. He ran to Ellen Dudley's window; there was no reply but the echo. The thought that all had perished of famine then fell upon his soul with the coldness of death; he tore open the window and rushed in. The chamber was empty, the hall was dark and silent—yet, his first fear was groundless; they were all gone; but he dared not ask his heart whither, for the presentiment of some undefined calamity, admitted nothing but suggestions of horror. He opened a door, and passed like a sleepwalker into the court-yard; then staggered out upon the wharf. Here, on the shank of a broken anchor, sat an old serving-man gazing down the river.

" 'Friend! where, tell me for mercy sake, are they gone?' cried he, and laid his hand upon the man's shoulder, for he felt as if he would drop.

" 'Some to Skinner-row for meal, and some to the Bridge foot for sheep,' replied the sailor; 'we are all discharged now, since the old master was slain at Salcock.'

" 'But his family—his daughter—where is she? she has gone to the house of some of her father's friends, has she not?'

" 'No, master; she has gone with the Archbishop.'

" 'With the Archbishop! what right had the Archbishop to take her away? Is not Archbishop Alan with White in the Castle?'

" 'He left the Castle this morning, master, for he feared it could not hold out against the rebels, now that they have got within the city walls; and when he came here and found the poor young lady almost heartbroken, with neither father nor mother, nor any friend to protect her, and the household broken up, and she without brother or sister:'——

' "Speak out, Sir! speak! what has Alan dared to do with Master Dudley's daughter?'

" 'The Archbishop has taken young mistress Ellen with him; and right glad any friend of the house ought to be to know she is in such holy keeping. I hope in God's mercy, they will be safe in Bristol before to-morrow night; why, Sir, I have been watching them here, and praying them a good passage for the last hour and better.' As he spoke he pointed down the river, where a bark was dimly visible in the twilight, beating out into the open bay.

" 'A boat, a boat!' cried Talbot, casting off his cloak; 'we can overtake them, yet! the wind is all against them!—traitor priest, you shall not rob me, false prelate! I will have her back, though I break thy crosier for it!—Ten rose nobles for a boat! call Connor Kelly; where is the bouhchal ghasta?—ah! I am raving. Friend, for the love of heaven, help me to get a boat; I will give ten pieces of gold to be put on board yonder ship.'

. " 'They are far beyond the reach of pursuit,' no open boat could live in the sea that is now running on the bar. The Archbishop's bark, that is a stout vessel of an hundred tons, will have enough to do to clear the Bulls.'

" '——————! and she is to be carried off before my eyes!—ho, sirrah, is the Archbishop's vessel armed?'

" 'Better manned and armed than any other that has left the port since the troubles begun: you may make up your mind to let them go where they will this bout, master.'

" Talbot stood for a minute silent, with clenched hands and swelling heart, gazing blankly on the receding sail; at length he demanded, 'Went she with her own will?' and then, before the man had time to make an answer, burst into exclamations of rage against the Archbishop. 'She never went with her will! Alan has forced her off, and I swear, if he has, I will be avenged, if he were thrice a bishop!—dog priest!' and he shook his clenched hand furiously at the distant vessel; 'I will meet thee yet—I will! and if thou hast dared to practice any villainy on that pure and innocent lady, that neither sanctuary nor altar shall shield thee from the vengeance of a desperate man!—went she with her will? I say again, sirrah!"—But the man had risen in horror and alarm, and was closing the wicket of the court-yard behind him, as Talbot turned to repeat the question. Uttering many an exclamation of furious purport, he paced up and down the deserted wharf, sometimes stopping and straining his eyes to catch a glimpse of the dim sail; then turning abruptly, as if he could not bear the sight of it; and then again searching the grey distance to take another last look, blank and despairing; but the indistinct outline had melted ere long, into the wide misty horizon, and he was left alone among the deep shades of evening with the rising winds whistling desolately along the unmanned ramparts overhead, and sweeping up the bare expanse of the river into black and angry tumult at his feet. With a heart full of rage and sorrow, he returned by the water's edge, and re-crossed the bridge as the darkness of the night set in.

" The night fell black and stormy, and, as he rode back to Artane. He pulled up, and, half unconsciously, turned his face to the sea. A pale line of light marked the sweep of the surf, but all beyond was dark as midnight.

'A wild night for your voyage Ellen dear,' he cried; ' they had hard hearts that could force you on the sea such a night as this !' As he spoke, a flash suddenly broke through the gloom in the offing. He held his breath and listened, while the tear trembling on his eye-lid was dried up in the absorbing intensity of his gaze : he heard nothing but the breakers and the growling of the trees—could it have been the fire glancing from his eyeballs?—no—there was another flash! and he now heard plainly over the mingling roar of waves and woods, the report of a gun. 'The Archbishop is making signals of distress !' he exclaimed ; ' he is driving ashore—I may save her yet !' and, dashing the spurs into his horse's flanks, he never drew bridle till he reached Artane—' Up, up,' he cried ; ' twenty men arm, and follow me—to the strands, to the strands—bring ropes and tackle, and make for the stranded ship ;' and, heading seaward, he again urged his horse through brake and furrow at desperate speed to the shore. While he descended to the sea, flash after flash gave momentary glimpses of the driving wreck, as she came broadside on before the waves ; but when the sound of his horse's feet was lost at last upon the sands, the bark became visible with the light of signals. Her black hull now heaved high against the obscure horizon; and now nothing was to be seen above the weltering seas but the bulwarks, and the torn rigging streaming from the stump of her broken mast. Their last gun, fired when they were driving within fifty yards of the beach, showed the crew, crowding the deck, all ghastly as phantoms in the sudden light ; and, while the flash was still before Talbot's eyes, a shriek rang from the quivering planks, and the remnant of mast and tackle went over board as she took the ground. The water was shallow to the very verge of the shelf on which she struck ; for she had driven in the channel of the Tolka, which there flows into the bay, and the tide had been for a short time on the ebb ; so that Talbot, who knew the ground, and was a practised swimmer, did not hesitate to dash into the surf and make straight for the wreck. The violence of the breakers drove him back twice ; but after a hard struggle, he made good the third attempt, and was the first man to climb the side of the stranded vessel. It was so dark he could not tell the face of a man on board ; but hearing a voice he knew in the waist, he went thither, and found the Archbishop, surrounded by his servants, holding on under shelter of the bulwark, and loud in prayer.

' " My lord archbishop, where is that young gentlewoman you took away from Dudley's court this morning ?' were Talbot's first words.

" ' Sir John, O Sir John Talbot, I am here !' cried a weak voice from the hatches, and ere the words were well spoken, Ellen Dudley was in his arms.

" By this time the soldiery from Artane had reached the strand, and some riding into the surf, had thrown the ends of coiled ropes on board, while others were buffeting the waves, and striving to climb on deck. When the Archbishop's people saw the means of escape at hand, they crowded to the side of the vessel ; but Talbot, still supporting his almost speechless burthen, called to the sailing master, and demanded how long the hull could bear the beating of the seas without risk of going to pieces. The seaman replied that there was no danger for another hour, at the least.

*   *   *   *   *

" Ropes were now stretched from the beach, and a party of his men who had been ordered to remain, stood up to the middle in the water, holding lights, and ready to receive his burthen in their arms, but Talbot plunged among the breakers with Ellen clasped to his own breast, and bore her himself in safety to the dry land. The wreck was now deserted, and the crew dispersed. He left a guard upon the beach to prevent plunder, then placed his precious charge upon his own horse, sprang on before her, and, attended by a few gallowglass, set forward once more for the city. As they rode along, the sense of her entire dependance on her companion grew stronger every moment in the heart of Ellen Dudley. Riding, with her arms clasped around him, she felt that, without him, she

would be as weak as the ivy without its sustaining oak.

" While these thoughts passed through her mind, Talbot did not cease to urge upon her every representation that could render them more influential ; so that when at last as they approached the end of their journey, he besought of her to let their hands be joined on the next day, she could only reply by entreating of him in return, that he would consent to abandon the insurgent cause, and fly with her to Waterford, whence they might make their escape to the Continent in safety.

" ' Ellen,' said Talbot, when, with tears and intreaties, she had so far stipulated, ' when I asked you to desert your father, you told me that I could not have loved you as I said I did, had I believed that you would have yielded to that solicitation. Can you love me, and believe that I would thus abandon my honour ? Your father, with the last words he ever spoke, besought me to give up the cause ; and I vowed in my heart—for, alas, he could not have heard my answer, had I spoken it—that when I could, without dishonour, leave the island, I would. It was all he asked, and I promise it to you as to him. I have been basely treated ; but although others may play an ungrateful and foul part by me, I cannot suffer their dishonour to justify mine. I would, dear Ellen, I was free to fly with you ; but I cannot, I dare not. Still, even as I am, I can afford you protection. We may, at least, be happy in ourselves : this war cannot last long ; we must soon either be secure in victory, or free to save ourselves as we best can, without scruple. And now, since heaven's will is manifest in your restoration to me—for surely the hand of Providence was visibly put forth on our behalf this night—since winds and waves have conspired to return you to my arms ; now, too, that our union has been once more sanctioned, and the blessing again bequeathed us, wed me at once, Ellen dear, and come what may, I shall at least be loyal to the love I will bear you to the last.' His suit prevailed, and ere they parted, Ellen Dudley had consented that the next day should see her united to him in the bands of wedlock."

Having left his fair charge with a kinswoman of his own in the city, he returns to his quarters where he finds the Archbishop Alan sound asleep, and retires to rest himself in an adjoining apartment ; but in a short time is aroused from his slumbers by a noise and tumult, occasioned by the murder of the Archbishop, in the adjoining chamber. An extraordinary scene ensues, in which Lord Thomas Fitzgerald, Travers, Sir John, and his old enemy Parez—are brought into collision, in which Sir John is accused of being the murderer, and which ends in his withdrawing himself altogether from the malcontents.

" ' My lord, before I go, I again claim the combat.'

" ' Sir John Talbot, heaven forbid that, if there was a doubt upon any man's mind of your guilt, I should deny you the right of that appeal ; but the thing is manifest : and whether or no, till the war is over, no officer of mine shall venture his life in such a dispute. Master Parez, put up your sword : we have had over much brawling to-night ; I will give you some more profitable use for your weapon, till you cool, or this—I tell you, sirrah, you are my lieutenant, and shall strike no stroke to-day.'

" ' Then, my lord,' said Talbot, ' farewell ; farewell, Sir Oliver ; Art—Barry Oge—Redmond—farewell, my true, brave fellows ! You are soon to have another captain—but if you think I did this act, my exhortation would weigh little.'

" ' Noble Sir,' said Art, ' I would take your word for it, if there were the oaths of ten men against you !'

" Talbot's eye kindled proudly ; he took the son of Connogher by the hand. ' Art,' said he, ' I thank you for that word more than for all the good service you have done under me ! Farewell, Art ; obey your next captain as you have me. I shall never ride at the head of a battle of gallowglass again !'

" ' A vic, vic deelish ma chree !' cried the poor fellow, the tears running down his cheeks as he spoke,' stay with us—we will never do good without you. If you go, astore —noble Sir John, if you go, I will go with you !'

" ' We will follow him over the ridge of the world !' exclaimed Barny Oge.   *   *   *   *

" Back, Back ; do as I desire, and God bless you all ! —*banaght leat go bragh !*' and without bestowing another look on those he left behind, he put spurs to his horse and galloped off the ground. The master-feeling in his mind was exultation. He had kept his word with Dudley : he was clear of the rebellion ; and he felt a calm assurance that, he knew he was so without dishonour, the imputation of Pazez could never prevail against him. On that charge, indeed, he scarce bestowed a thought, but acted over and over, in imagination, the triumph he had gained against him as mere hostile antagonist. ' My way is now clear,' he cried. ' Ha, ha ! I could scarce have wished it better ! No man can blame me for any tittle of what I did ; I was right—by my honour, I was right throughout ! to-night has quit me of my score of all their slights and insults. Ay, if he had done me injury ten times as great, that look I gave him pays for all ! How the catiff writhed ! As I am a Christian, I have had fair revenge ! Ah, Ellen, you little dream this morning that we will be on our way to Waterford, as you wanted last night, before either of us is a day older. It will delight her poor heart to hear it. Thank heaven, that I have the good news to carry her ; it will be like the first burst of sunshine after a storm of thunder.'

" By this he was at the Tolka. As he rode through, he bethought himself of the blood upon his hands and clothes. He dismounted, and washed his person clean of the pollution ; but his buff coat was so saturated, that he could not remove the stains. The thought then, for the first time, struck him, that there might be danger in showing himself. Travers was gone, no doubt, to Dublin, and would certainly repeat the accusation he had so strenuously aided in having brought forward. Innocent as he was, to be taken up with proofs of guilt so strong against him—nay, in his present circumstances, to be apprehended at all—was not to be thought of without a pang that went to his heart like a knife. Yet into Dublin he should and would go ; a few hours would make Ellen his wife ; they might then depart together, and be out of the reach of pursuit before another day. But to leave the country with this stain upon his name—that sent another pang that thrilled in his breast as sharply as the first. Well, he was at least conscious of his own innocence, and Ellen would believe him that he was so : what more could an outlawed man expect ? But he must make sure ; he must not run the risk of being taken ; his clothes must be changed ; the bearded lip must be left bare, and the long dark curls, that played upon his shoulder, must be thinned and shortened. Seeing the necessity, he lost no time in making preparations to comply with it. He rode to the house of one in whom he could confide, announced his purpose, and dispatched a messenger to the city for such habiliments as he thought most suitable to the character he meant to assume—that of a native gentleman of some account.

" The messenger delayed—the hour appointed for the ceremony was approaching—arrived—elapsed—and he could not go out of doors, his entertainer with friendly violence resisting his attempts to run all hazards, and urging on him every reasonable ground why he should rather wait till he might go in safety, than expose his bride to a calamity so much more serious than an hour's disappointment. The dress at last was procured, and Talbot left the house so altered that he hardly knew his own shadow on the wall. His trowsers of grey plaid, tight to the leg, were strapped under light brogues of unstained leather : his coat, of the fine frize of Waterford, was buttoned to the throat ; the standing collar closely fitting at the neck, while the full skirts descended from a broad belt round the waist, in plaited folds barely reaching mid-thigh. Over this was cast his mantle, dark brown, short, and of the Spanish cut, with fringed edges, and a warm collar of silk thrums. His hat alone was English, for, to have appeared in the blue barrad of the country, after cutting of crommeal and coolun, would, in Dublin, have excited the animadversion of the citizens. Thus equipped, Sir John Talbot, with rapid steps, sought the city gates ; the English furniture of his horse had pre-

vented him from riding. He posted up from the bridge, unmindful of the approving glances of many a Saxon burgers's daughter, admiring the tall Irishman ; hurried past Christ's Church and down Nicholas-street, shouldering aside the throng of the market with the step of a man well accustomed to have way made for him—' Way there, you knave,' cried he to one fellow, blocking up the narrow passage with his cart.

" ' Mercy, Teague !' replied the man of English blood, with a stare, but took no further notice.

" ' Out of my way, rascal !' cried Talbot, seizing him by the collar, and flinging him to one side : the fellow, who fell among the potato dealers' baskets, rose cursing furiously, but he had no wish to try the strength of the audacious native's arm a second time.

" ' He is mere Irish,' said another ; ' stick your knife into him, Peter—what about the thirty shilling ?—we'll club for the fine, if it be ever levied.'

" ' Not I,' replied Peter, ' Irish as he is, I would not take his life by subscription !'

Meanwhile, Talbot was at Nicholas-gate ; another minute placed him at the door of Dame Keating's house, when he received a note, appointing a meeting at the cathedral.

" Talbot had scarce read the whole till he was on his way thither. The sun was shining brightly on the huge tower, and making all the flying buttresses stand out like bars of silver from the dusk bulk of the building. Fair as the scene was to a man leaving Nicholas-gate with the open field before him, and the great cathedral in the midst, with all its battlements and pinnacles tipped with the sunbeams and glittering against the blue sky, Talbot bestowed scarce a look upon its beauties, but hurried round to the great western doorway, and entered the cathedral, panting for haste, and half forgetful of the accustomed observances of his religion.

" Talbot was gazing up the long bright vista as the dean himself withdrew, his robes shining like flashes of fire, as he crossed each bar of the sunshine lying across the narrow passage from every window, when, with a joyful start, he found those whom he sought, by his side.

" ' Dear kinswoman !' he cried, extending his hand to Dame Keating, but she drew back in dignified amaze, and even Ellen, who was leaning blushing on her arm, looked at him a moment in equal ignorance ; but a few words explained all. ' Ah Ellen,' he cried, when he had done so, ' you did not think I would so soon fulfil my promise ; well, I have left them without dishonour, although I would rather we had parted better friends ; but come, my love, lean now upon me. Dear father, take to your blessed work, for I feel as a suppliant at heaven's gates till the words are said.'

" ' Come in then, my children ; I have little time to lose,' replied Father Keating, leading them into his little oratory, which was scarcely sufficient to give them all room ; ' I have,' said he, ' some farther duties to attend to to-day ; something has happened, I know not what, but I will have to take a part ; the dean signified as much to me as he was going out ; so kneel down, my children, for I must tie this knot with what speed I may.' The ceremony was performed, and Talbot and Ellen arose, man and wife.'

The finish of the story is promised in the Magazine for April, and, we doubt not, many of our readers will purchase the number, were it merely to follow the fortunes of Sir John Talbot, and his newly plighted spouse, Ellen Dudley.

. We should, perhaps, mention that the Engraving to this article in our last number, was copied from the vignette to one of the volumes of M'Gregor's " True Stories of Ireland." We would take this opportunity of apologizing to those of our Correspondents who have kindly favoured us with Drawings, whose names may, by some oversight, have been omitted. Among others, we may mention that the sketch and description of Lea Castle, which appeared in the same number with the engraving of Silken Thomas, was kindly presented by Mr. Robert Patterson of Belfast.

THE

DUBLIN PENNY JOURNAL

CONDUCTED BY P. DIXON HARDY, M.R.I.A.

| VOL. III. | APRIL 4, 1835. | No. 144. |

AFRICAN SKETCHES.

SHOOTING THE SPRINGBOK.

BULLOCK-WAGGON CROSSING A MOUNTAIN.

AFRICAN SKETCHES.
BY THOS. PRINGLE.

We should, perhaps, apologize to the publishers and our readers, for having allowed this very interesting volume to remain so long unnoticed. The truth is, we have frequently to regret that the contracted limit of our little periodical prevents our paying attention to works of merit forwarded to us immediately on their publication. Wishing to maintain for our Journal that character of *nationality* which it has hitherto supported, we have invariably given precedence to matters connected with, or having reference to, Ireland; and we trust this will be a sufficient excuse for any apparent neglect of other works, which might to some appear as claiming an equal share of our attention.

There can be no question, that few things can be better calculated to expand the mind, or to enlarge the ideas, than an acquaintance with the men and manners of other climes. It is for this young men of family and fortune are sent forth on their travels; and although many such frequently return little improved by what they may have seen or heard, still there are others, and those not a few, who do derive material benefit by observing what is passing around them, in the various districts of earth in which they may sojourn for a time. What travel does for some, reading and study perform for others. By the art of printing, individuals whose circumstances would not permit them to travel into other countries, are enabled to contemplate and study the habits, and manners, and customs of the various inhabitants of the earth, with nearly the same correctness and perspicuity as those of their more highly favoured fellow beings, whom fortune has enabled to wander whithersoever their fancy led them.

The work before us, treating of an interesting portion of our globe, of which little, comparatively speaking, is really yet known, will be perused with pleasure by readers of every class. Mr. Pringle, it would appear, was one of the first of those who availed themselves of the encouragement given by Government to emigrants disposed to settle in Africa. Early in 1820 he arrived at the Cape of Good Hope, having been strongly recommended to the notice of Government by the late Sir Walter Scott. He was evidently a man of considerable mind, and accustomed carefully to observe what was passing around him. His narrative has altogether such an air of *vraisemblance*, as at once to impress the reader with the conviction that he must really have seen and heard the various matters which he so well describes. There are one or two little things, indeed, which, having before observed given verbatim in other works, induced us to pause for a moment on this point. Such, for instance, is an account of a lion hunt in page 257 of the work, which our readers will find quoted in the 93d number of our Journal, from the " Naturalist's Library," where it is related as having occurred to Mr. Thompson—the favourite riding horse of each having been killed in a similar manner, with various et ceteras proving the account to be that of one and the same occurrence. But *n'importe*—the work is not only very readable, but highly entertaining. The sketches of men and manners are well touched off; while various " hair breadth 'scapes" from "perils by flood and field," keep up the reader's attention from the beginning to the end. Mr. Pringle does not pretend to any great scientific research in his description of natural history. He has, nevertheless, endeavoured to give as much useful information in this way as may serve the purpose of the general reader. Indeed we question very much, whether general readers will not derive more real information, relative to the actual habits and dispositions of the various animals described in the volume, from the desultory descriptions, brief hints, and outline sketches of Mr. Pringle, than they would from the works of those who go more fully and scientifically into such subjects.

As it would be impossible for us, within the limits of our brief space, to accompany the author through the entire of his residence in Africa, we shall for the present confine ourselves chiefly to those portions of his work which bear on the natural history of, and those customs and practices peculiar to, the country, which are described in our engravings, and which, we may observe *en passant*, are copied from a work, published some few years since on a similar subject, by another writer. We must, however, allow the author himself to describe his new settlement:—

" We struck our tents on the 15th of June, which is about the middle of winter in the southern hemisphere. The weather was serene and pleasant, though chill at night—somewhat like fine September weather in England. Our travelling train consisted of seven waggons; all, except one which was driven by a slave, being conducted by the owners or their sons, Dutch-African farmers. These vehicles were admirably adapted for the nature of the country, which is rugged and mountainous, and generally destitute of any other roads than the rude tracks originally struck across the wilderness by the first European adventurers; and which are repaired by throwing merely earth and faggots into the gulleys and beds of torrents, which, during heavy rains, sometimes render them impassable. Each waggon is provided with a raised canvas tilt to protect the traveller from sun and rain; and is drawn by a team of ten or twelve oxen, fastened with wooden yokes to a strong central trace (*trektow*), formed of twisted thongs of bullock's or buffalo's hide. The driver sits in front to guide and stimulate the oxen, armed with a whip of enormous length; while a young Hottentot, running before, leads the team by a thong attached to the horns of the foremost pair of bullocks.   *   *   *

" We passed over an extensive tract of mountainous country at the Zureberg, where the roads appeared to us most frightful and perilous. Certainly no wheel carriage used in England could have survived them; but our African charioteers jolted us along with great *sangfroid*, and without any material disaster. Sometimes we had two teams, of twelve oxen each, yoked to one waggon, to drag our loads of iron-ware up the steep hills; and then there was tremendous shouting, and barbarous flogging of the poor animals. But these are ordinary occurrences in Cape travelling. We saw very few inhabitants of any class, and few wild animals, except antelopes and quaggas in the distance. The features of the country changed alternately from dark jungle to rich park-like scenery, embellished with graceful clumps of evergreens; and from that again to the desolate sterility of savage mountains, or of parched and desert plains, scattered over with huge ant-hillocks and flocks of springboks. Here and there a solitary farm-house appeared near some permanent fountain or willow-margined river; and then again the wilderness, though clothed perhaps with verdant pasturage, extended for twenty miles or more without a drop of water.   *   *   *

" It were tedious to relate the difficulties, perils, and adventures, which we encountered in our toilsome march, of *five days* up this African glen;—to tell of our pioneering labours with the hatchet, the pick-axe, the crow-bar, and the sledge-hammer—and the lashing of the poor oxen, to force them on (sometimes 20 or 50 in one team) through such a track as no English reader can form any adequate conception of. In the upper part of the valley we were occupied two entire days in thus hewing our way through a rugged defile, now called Eildon-Cleugh, scarcely three miles in extent. At length, after extraordinary exertions, and hair-breadth escapes—the breaking down of two waggons, and the partial damage of others—we got through the last *poort* of the glen, and found ourselves on the summit of an elevated ridge, commanding a view of the extremity of the valley. 'And now, mynheer,' said the Dutch-African field-cornet who commanded our escort, ' *daar leg uwe veld*—there lies your country.'

" The 2d of July was our first Sunday on our own grounds. Feeling deeply the importance of maintaining the suitable observance of this day of sacred rest, it was unanimously resolved that we should strictly abstain from all secular employment not sanctioned by absolute necessity; and at the same time commence such a system of religious services as might be with propriety maintained in the absence of a clergyman or minister. The whole party were accordingly assembled after breakfast, under a venerable acacia tree, on the margin of the little stream which murmured around our camp. The river appeared shaded here and there by the graceful willow of Babylon, which grows abundantly along the banks of many of the African streams, and which, with the other peculiar features of the scenery, vividly reminded us of the pathetic lament of the Hebrew exiles :—' By the rivers of Babylon, there we sat; yea we wept when we remembered Zion. We hanged our harps upon the willows in the midst thereof.'

" It was, indeed, an affecting sight to look round on our little band of Scottish emigrants, thus congregated for the first time to worship God in the wild glen allotted for their future home and the heritage of their offspring. There sat old ——, with his silvery locks, the patriarch of the party, with his Bible on his knee,—a picture of the high-principled, grave Scottish husbandman; his respectable family seated round him. There was the widow ——, with her meek, kind, and quiet look—the look of one who had seen better days, but who in adversity had found pious resignation), with her three stalwart sons, and her young maiden daughter placed beside her on the grass. There, too, were others, delicate females—one of them very nearly related to myself—of whom I need not more particularly speak. There was ——, the younger brother of a Scottish laird, rich in blood, but poor in fortune, who, with an estimable pride, had preferred a farm in South Africa, to dependence on aristocratic connexions at home. Looking round on these collected groups, on this day of solemn assemblage, such reflections as the following irresistibly crowded on my mind : ' Have I led forth from their native homes, to this remote corner of the globe, all these my friends and relatives for good or for evil ?—to perish miserably in the wilderness, or to become the honoured founders of a prosperous settlement, destined to extend the benefits of civilization and the blessed light of the Gospel through this dark nook of benighted Africa ? The issue of our enterprise is known only to Him who ordereth all things well . " Man proposes, but God disposes." But though the result of our scheme is in the womb of futurity, and although it seems probable that greater perils and privations await us than we had once calculated upon, there yet appears no reason to repent of the course we have taken, or to augur unfavourably of the ultimate issue. Thus far Providence has prospered and protected us. We left not our native land from wanton restlessness or mere love of change, or without very sufficient and reasonable motives. Let us, therefore, go on calmly and courageously, duly invoking the blessing of God on all our proceedings ; and thus, be the result what it may, we shall feel ourselves in the path of active duty.' With these, and similar reflections, we encouraged ourselves, and proceeded to the religious services of the day. * *

" In our journey from Algoa Bay, we had seen in the distance a few herds of large game, chiefly of the antelope tribe ; and we found our highland valley to be pretty well stocked with the animals mentioned in the beginning of this chapter. But we had as yet seen none of the beasts of prey that inhabit the country, with the exception of one or two jackals, although we had once heard the peculiar growl, or garr, of the Cape tiger (or leopard), and been serenaded nightly by the hungry howl of the hyæna, almost all the way from the coast. We were not allowed, however, to continue long without a closer acquaintance with our neighbours of the carnivorous class. The lion introduced himself, in a mode becoming his rank and character, a few nights after our arrival at Glen-Lynden.

" The serene weather with which we had been favoured during our journey, was succeeded on the 3d of July by a cold and wet evening. The night was extremely dark, and the rain fell so heavily that, in spite of the abundant supply of dry firewood which we had so luckily provided, it was not without difficulty that we could keep one watch-fire burning. Having appointed our watch for the night (a service which all the male adults, masters as well as servants agreed to undertake in rotation), we had retired to rest, and, excepting our sentinels, were all buried in sleep, when about midnight we were suddenly roused by the roar of a lion close to our tents. It was so loud and tremendous that for a moment I actually thought a thunder-storm had burst upon us. But the peculiar expression of the sound—the voice of fury as well as of power—instantly undeceived me, and instinctively snatching my loaded gun

from the tent pole, I hurried out—fancying that the savage beast was about to break into our camp. Most of our men had sprung to their arms, and were hastening to the watch-fire, with a similar apprehension. But all around was utter darkness ; and scarcely two of us were agreed as to the quarter whence the voice had issued. This uncertainty was occasioned partly, perhaps, by the peculiar mode this animal often has of placing his mouth near the ground when he roars, so that the voice rolls, as it were, like a breaker along the earth ; partly, also, to the echo from a mountain-rock which rose abruptly on the opposite bank of the river ; and, more than all, to the confusion of our senses in being thus hurriedly and fearfully aroused from our slumbers. Had any one retained self-possession sufficient to have quietly noted our looks on this occasion, I suspect he would have seen a laughable array of pale or startled visages. The reader who has only heard the roar of the lion at the Zoological Gardens, can have but a faint conception of the same animal's voice in his state of freedom and uncontrolled power. Novelty in our case, no doubt, gave it double effect, on our thus hearing it for the first time in the heart of the wilderness. However, we resolved to give the enemy a warm reception ; and having fired several volleys in all directions round our encampment, we roused up the half-extinguished fire to a roaring blaze, and then flung the flaming brands among the surrounding trees and bushes. And this unwonted display probably daunted our grim visiter, for he gave us no further disturbance that night.

" A few days afterwards some of our people had a daylight interview with a lion—probably the same individual who had given us this boisterous greeting. They had gone a mile or two up the valley to cut reeds for thatching the temporary huts which we proposed to erect, and were busy with their sickles in the bed of the river, when, to their dismay, a huge lion rose up among the reeds, almost close beside them. He leaped upon the bank, and then turned round and gazed stedfastly at them. One or two men who had guns seized them hastily, and began to load with ball. The rest, unarmed and helpless, stood petrified ; and, had the lion been so disposed, he might easily have made sad havoc among them. He was, however, very civil—or, to speak more correctly, he was probably as much surprised as they were. After quietly gazing for a minute or two at the intruders on his wild domain, he turned about and retired ; first slowly, and then, after he was some distance off, at a good round trot. They prudently did not attempt to interfere with his retreat. * *

" Besides the lion, there are not fewer than five species of the genus felis found in the colony, which are known by the local names of tiger, berg-tiger, luipaard, tiger-bosch-kat (serval ?), roode-kat (caracal ?), and wilde kat (felis capensis). The first of these, which is the real leopard (felis leopardus) is considerably the largest and most formidable. The berg-tiger has not, so far as I know, been distinctly classed by naturalists. The animal called luipaard by the Dutch-African colonists, and generally considered to be the felis jubata, is far inferior to the real leopard, both in size and beauty.

" The South-African leopard differs from the panther of Northern Africa in the form of its spots, in the more slender structure of its body, and in the legs not being so long in proportion to its size. In watching for his prey the leopard crouches on the ground, with his fore-paws stretched out and his head between them, his eyes rather directed upwards. His appearance in a wild state is exceedingly beautiful, his motions in the highest degree easy and graceful, and his agility in bounding among the rocks and woods quite amazing. Of this activity no person can have any idea by seeing these animals in the cages in which they are usually exhibited in Europe, humbled and tamed as they are by confinement and the damp cold of our climate.

" The African leopard, though far inferior to the lion or Bengal tiger in strength and intrepidity, and though he usually shuns a conflict with man, is nevertheless an exceedingly active and furious animal, and when driven to desperation, becomes a truly formidable antagonist. The Cape colonists relate instances of frightful and sometimes fatal encounters between the hunted leopard and his pursuers. The following is a specimen of these adventures.

It occurred in 1822, in the interior of the colony, and is here given as it was related by an individual who knew the parties engaged in it.

"Two African farmers, returning from hunting the hartebeest, roused a leopard in a mountain ravine, and immediately gave chase to him. The leopard at first endeavoured to escape by clambering up a precipice; but being hotly pressed, and wounded by a musket-ball, he turned upon his pursuers with the frantic ferocity peculiar to this animal on such emergencies, and springing upon the man who had fired at him, he pulled him to the ground, biting him at the same time on the shoulder, and tearing one of his cheeks severely with his claws. The other hunter, seeing the danger of his comrade, sprang from his horse, and attempted to shoot the leopard through the head; but, whether owing to trepidation, or the fear of wounding his friend, or the quick motions of the animal, he unfortunately missed. The leopard, abandoning his prostrate enemy, darted with redoubled fury upon this second antagonist, and so fierce and sudden was his onset, that before the boor could stab him with his hunting knife, the savage beast struck him on the face with his claws, and actually tore the scalp over his eyes. In this frightful condition the hunter grappled with the leopard, and, struggling for life, they rolled together down a steep declivity. All this passed far more rapidly than it can be described in words. Before the man who had been first attacked could start to his feet and seize his gun, they were rolling one over the other down the bank. In a minute he had reloaded his gun, and rushed forward to save the life of his friend. But it was too late. The leopard had seized the unfortunate man by the throat, and mangled him so dreadfully that death was inevitable; and his comrade (himself severely wounded) had only the melancholy satisfaction of completing the destruction of the savage beast, already exhausted with the loss of blood from several deep wounds by the desperate knife of the expiring huntsman.

"Of the ferocity of the Cape leopard, another example occurred in the case of the Moravian missionary Mr. Schmitt, whom I met at Enon. This worthy man had gone out with a party of Hottentots at another Moravian station to hunt some hyænas which had been very destructive to their flocks; and with one of the Hottentots, entered a thicket in pursuit of a tiger-wolf that they had wounded. Their hounds, however, instead of the hyæna, started a leopard, which instantly sprang on the Hottentot and bore him to the ground. Mr. Schmitt ran forward to the aid of the man, with his gun cocked; but before he could find an opportunity of firing, the animal left the Hottentot and flew with fury at himself. In the scuffle he dropped the gun, but luckily fell above the leopard with his knee on its stomach. The animal seized him by the left arm with its jaws, and kept striking him with its paws, and tearing the clothes in tatters from his breast. Schmitt, however, being a powerful man, succeeded, after receiving another severe bite or two, in seizing the leopard by the throat with his right hand, and held it down, in spite of its desperate struggles, for a few minutes; until, just as his strength was giving way, one of the Hottentots on the outside of the jungle, who heard his cries for help, came to his rescue, and shot the ferocious beast right through the heart, so that its death was quite instantaneous. Had any life been left, its dying struggles might still have proved fatal to Mr. Schmitt. As it was, he was so terribly lacerated, that for several weeks his life was in the greatest danger. The Hottentot who was first attacked, was less severely wounded; but his face was so much torn by the animal's talons, that his eyes were filled with blood, and he was unable to render any aid to the missionary who had so generously come to his rescue.

THE HYÆNA—MODE OF CATCHING THEM IN TRAPS.

"I have cursorily noticed in my diary the depredations of the hyænas in our folds, and our success in catching them in traps. For this contrivance we were indebted to the Hottentots. The trap was built of large loose stones, with a hanging door of wood or stone, upheld by a stick, the lower end of which is baited with a dead dog, or the entrails of a sheep. By this simple contrivance we speedily entrapped several of the depredators that had so much harassed us; and after having killed them with spears, their carcases were thrown out on the open plain. The smell of the *hyæna crocuta* is so rank and offensive that scarcely any animal will come near the carcase. When they are once fairly killed, even dogs leave them with disgust. Yet none of those we destroyed ever remained two nights undevoured. Their own voracious kindred uniformly came in the night and devoured them, leaving scarcely a remnant of the skull and larger bones to show where the rest had found a sepulchre.

" Of all the beasts of prey that inhabit South Africa, the common spotted hyæna (*hyæna crocuta*), called by the colonists the *tiger-wolf*, is the most voracious and destructive to the flocks. Were the courage of this animal equal to its strength, it would be exceedingly formidable, even to man himself—at least in a country where it exists in such numbers; but, happily, its cowardice is not less characteristic than its voracity. Though they are sometimes met with in packs or troops of twenty or more, I never heard of an instance of their attacking mankind either by day or night, within the colony. At the same time it ought to be remarked, that their awe of civilized man is probably greatly increased by his possession of the firelock; for among the Caffer tribes the same animal is found so much bolder, that he not unfrequently attempts to enter the huts of the natives, and even occasionally devours children and infirm people. But in the latter case, his audacity cannot fail to be greatly increased by the wretched superstitions which induce those people to expose the bodies of their dead to be entombed in the maw of this universal devourer, and which cause them to regard the hyæna himself as a sort of sacred animal.

" One of the chief functions of the hyæna in the economy of nature appears to be that of carrion-scavenger, an office which he divides with the vulture. The lordly lion, the imperial eagle, always kill their own game. The hyæna and vulture come after and gather up the offals.

This animal devours not only the remains of dead carcases, but also the hide and the bones, leaving nothing but the skull and a few of the larger joints, which baffle even his enormous strength of jaw.

" Three other species of hyæna are distinguished in the colonial nomenclature, as the *strand-wolf*, *berg-wolf*, and the *wilde-hond*. The strand-wolf is found exclusively on the coast, as its name denotes. It is larger than the tiger-wolf, and is said to be a dark grey colour. The berg-wolf, or mountain hyæna, is also large, and of a lighter hue. I have only seen the latter at a distance, and the strand-wolf not at all; but their habits I was told are very similar to those of the tiger-wolf. The *wilde-hond*, or wild-dog, (*hyæna venatica*,) is an animal with which the colonists are but too well acquainted. It was first accurately described, and classed as a hyæna, by Burchell. It forms in fact the connecting link between the wolf and hyæna families, and in its habits and physical conformation partakes of the character of both. These animals always hunt in packs; they are swift of foot, and though not so powerful, are much fiercer than the other species of hyæna. When they break into a fold, or fall upon a flock of sheep in the field, they frequently kill and mangle ten times as many as they could possibly devour : they are consequently much dreaded by the farmer. Some of them have been occasionally tamed by the colonists. The *laughing-hyæna*, which I have repeatedly heard, but never seen, is reported by the colonists to be a distinct species, smaller than the three preceding; and is considered (I know not with what justice) to form a sort of link between the hyæna and jackal families.

MARE AND FOAL ATTACKED BY A WOLF.

" The following incident in buffalo-hunting, may serve as a specimen of this rough pastime : it was related to me by a Dutch-African farmer, who had been an eye-witness of the scene some fifteen years before. A party of Boors had gone out to hunt a herd of buffaloes, which were grazing on a piece of marshy ground, interspersed with groves of yellow-wood and mimosa trees, on the very spot where the village of Somerset is now built. As they could not conveniently get within shot of the game without crossing part of the *valei* or marsh, which did not afford a safe passage for horses, they agreed to leave their steeds in charge of their Hottentots, and to advance on foot; thinking that if any of the buffaloes should turn upon them, it would be easy to escape by retreating across the

quagmire, which, though passable for man, would not support the weight of a heavy quadruped. They advanced, accordingly, and, under covert of the bushes, approached the game with such advantage, that the first volley brought down three of the fattest of the herd, and so severely wounded the great bull leader that he dropped on his knees, bellowing furiously. Thinking him mortally wounded, the foremost of the huntsmen issued from the covert, and began reloading his musket as he advanced to give him a finishing shot. But no sooner did the infuriated animal see his foe in front of him, than he sprang up and rushed headlong upon him. The man, throwing down his heavy gun, fled towards the quagmire ; but the beast was so close upon him that he despaired of escaping in that direction, and turning suddenly round a clump of copsewood, began to climb an old mimosa tree which stood at the one side of it. The raging beast, however, was too quick for him. Bounding forward with a roar, which my informant described as being one of the most frightful sounds he ever heard, he caught the unfortunate man with his terrible horns, just as he had nearly escaped his reach, and tossed him into the air with such force that the body fell, dreadfully mangled, into a cleft of the tree. The buffalo ran round the tree once or twice, apparently looking for the man, until weakened with loss of blood he again sunk on his knees. The rest of the party, recovering from their confusion, then came up and despatched him, though too late to save their comrade, whose body was hanging in the tree quite dead."

AMERICAN PENITENTIARIES.

In some recent numbers of our Journal we enabled our readers to judge of the present state of society in the United States. We have heard much of the improved condition of their prisons and prison discipline—the following extract from the "Report of William Crawford, Esq. on the Penitentiaries of the United States," printed by order of the House of Commons, will serve as a specimen of the way in which brother Jonathan manages these affairs. That solitary confinement is productive, in many instances, of great benefit, has been established beyond the possibility of a doubt. It is evident, however, that great circumspection is required in the mode of administering this species of punishment.

PHILADELPHIAN PENITENTIARY.

"This penitentiary is situated about a mile from the city of Philadelphia. The site occupies about twelve acres. It is built of stone, and surrounded by a wall thirty feet in height. Every room is vaulted and fireproof. At each angle of the boundary wall is a tower for the purpose of overlooking the establishment. In the centre is a circular building, or observatory, from which several corridors radiate: they are under complete inspection. The cells are ranged on each side of the corridors, in the wall of which is a small aperture and iron door to each cell: through this aperture the meals of the prisoner are handed to him without his seeing the officer, and he may at all times be thus inspected without his knowledge. Other openings are provided for the purposes of ventilation and warmth. Heated air is conducted by flues from stoves under the corridors. In the arched ceiling of each cell is a window for the admission of light. The cells are eleven feet nine inches long, seven feet six inches wide, and sixteen feet high to the top of the arched ceiling. The cells on the ground floor have double doors leading into a yard, eighteen feet by eight feet, in which the convict is allowed to take exercise for an hour daily. The walls of the yard are eleven feet high. Prisoners are not allowed to walk at the same time in adjoining yards; and when in the yards, are inspected by a watchman placed for that purpose in the tower of the observatory. * * * On the admission of a convict he is taken into an office at the entrance of the penitentiary, and subjected to the usual course of examination. His person is cleansed, and he is clothed in a uniform. He is then blindfolded and conducted to his cell. On his way thither he is for a short time detained in the observatory, where he is admonished by the warden as to the necessity of implicit obedience to the regulations. On arriving in his cell, the hood is removed, and he is left alone. There he may remain for years, perhaps for life, without seeing any human being but the inspectors, the warden and his officers, and perhaps occasionally one of the official visitors of the prison. For the first day or two, the convict is not allowed to have even a Bible, nor is any employment given to him for at least a week, a period during which he is the object of the warden's special observation. The prisoner soon petitions for an occupation. It is not, however, until solitude appears to have effectually subdued him, that employment of any kind is introduced into his cell. * * * *

"So strict is this seclusion, that I found, on conversing with the prisoners, that they were not aware of the existence of the cholera, which had but a few months before prevailed in Philadelphia."

SYSTEM OF SOLITARY CONFINEMENT AT AUBURN AND ELSEWHERE.

"A trial of solitary confinement, day and night, without labour, was made at Auburn in the year 1822, for ten months, upon eighty of the most hardened convicts. They were each confined in a cell only seven feet long, three feet and a half wide, and seven feet high. They were on no account permitted to leave the cell, during that long period, on any occasion, not even for the purposes of nature. They had no means of obtaining any change of air, nor opportunities of taking exercise. The most disastrous consequences were naturally the result.

"Several persons became insane; health was impaired, and life endangered. The discipline of the prison at that period was one of unmixed severity. There was no moral nor religious instruction of any kind communicated within its walls, nor consolation administered by which the convict was enabled to bear up against the cruelty of this treatment. Nor was a trial of the same description, which took place in the State of Maine, conducted under more advantageous circumstances. The night-rooms or cells at this prison are literally pits entered from the top by a ladder, through an aperture about two feet square. The opening is secured by an iron grate, used as a trap-door; the only other orifice is one at the bottom, about an inch and a half in diameter, for the admission of warm air from underneath. The cells are eight feet nine inches wide, and nine feet eight inches high. Their gloom is indescribable. The diet, during confinement, was bread and water only. Thus immured, and without any occupation, it will excite no surprise to learn that a man who had been sentenced to pass seventy days in one of these miserable pits hung himself after four days' imprisonment. Another, condemned to sixty days, also committed suicide on the twenty-fourth day. It became necessary to remove four others, who were unable to endure this cruelty, from the cell to the hospital repeatedly, before the expiration of the sentence. It is said that similar experiments have been made in Virginia, and that various diseases, terminating in death, were the result. The cells in which the prisoners were confined have been since disused: they are, in fact, dungeons, being on the basement story, and so dark as to require a lamp in visiting them. In damp weather the water stands in drops on the walls. The cells were not warmed at any season of the year. A prisoner's feet were actually frozen during his confinement."

Such is the system pursued by the "wise men of the West," to work reformation in the minds of rational beings!

AN ADVENTURE.

"It is many years since a gentleman happened to take up a night's lodging in a room which overlooked a churchyard, situated in the midst of a small town. Whether he was a stranger, a visitor, or a resident there, I cannot, at this moment, call to mind; nor do I mention the name of the town, for obvious reasons. The gentleman was young, strong, and by no means visionary—so that if he looked out of his window before he retired to rest at midnight, it was most probably to speculate upon the weather. Once having looked, however, he could not withdraw his gaze—his eyes were rivetted upon the church—for he perceived, to his great surprise, that a light was burning within it, casting a dull gleam from the windows which surround the altar. He watched for a few moments in silence, and, it may be supposed, with as much awe as curiosity, until he was certain that there could be no deceit—for the light remained burning in the same place. He was resolved to ascertain what so singular an appearance could mean; but he would not go alone—perhaps he durst not—perhaps he wished for the company of other witnesses besides himself. One or two neighbours were called up, and the keys of the church-yard procured, after some delay. There burned the light still; and, though their eyes were anxiously fixed upon it as the gate creaked upon its rusty hinges to admit them, it neither faded nor moved. They approached the building—the windows were so high that to gain any view of what might be passing in the interior, it was necessary to have recourse to a ladder; this, too, after some delay, they obtained. They applied it to the large window of the chancel; and there was some deliberation as to who should first ascend. The gentleman who had given the alarm at last volunteered the service, and, with a panting breath, and a brow covered with beads of dew, reached the top and looked down—the rest huddling together behind him, and pressing closely one upon the other. The sight he saw was sufficient to shake the courage of the stoutest. The communion-table had been uncovered, as for the rite, and drawn to a short distance from the wall. Two candles had been brought from the vestry, lighted, and placed thereon; three figures were seated round it, playing at cards! They were young men of licentious habits and notorious impiety; and their flushed countenances and disordered clothes, showed that their present audacious act of sacrilege had been planned at some debauch. But there was a fourth at the table—that fourth a corpse, which had that day been buried in a vault within the church! It had been dragged from its grave by these blasphemous rioters to assist at their game, as if they were resolved that no horror should be wanting. You may think how ghastly the dead face looked when contrasted with their rude and glaring countenances; how chilling was its motionless silence in return to their infernal ribaldry. Those who beheld looked long ere they could believe that living men could dare to perpetrate so enormous a crime. Other inhabitants of the neighbourhood were presently collected; the church door unlocked; and the gamesters interrupted—who could have dared to wait until the game was played out? They were immediately taken into custody; and it was further discovered that the criminals belonged to some of the most respectable families of the place. How they had gained an entrance, or what had tempted them to so fearfully wicked an act, was never known—or, if it was known, was never told; for, in consideration of their families, the matter was hushed up, the miscreants allowed to escape from ——, to re-appear there no more!"

FORCE OF IMAGINATION.

Some years ago a celebrated physician, author of an excellent work on the force of imagination, being desirous to add experimental to his theoretical knowledge, made application to the minister of justice, to be allowed an opportunity of proving what he asserted by an experiment on a criminal condemned to death. The minister complied with his request; and the criminal agreed to the proposal, counting himself happy in being freed from the painful exhibition of a public execution. At the time appointed, the physician repaired to the prison, and the patient having been extended on a table, his eyes bound, and every thing being ready, he was slightly pricked near the principal veins of the legs and arms with the point of a pen. At the four corners of the table were four little fountains, filled with water, from which issued small streams falling into basins placed there to receive them. The patient, thinking it was his blood that trickled into the basins, became weaker and weaker by degrees, and the remarks of the medical men in attendance, in reference to the quality and appearance of the blood (made with that intention,) increased the delusion, and he spoke more and more faintly, until his voice was at length scarcely audible. The profound silence which reigned in the apartment, and the constant dropping of the fountains, had so extraordinary an effect on the brain of the poor patient, that all his vital energies were soon gone, although before a very strong man, and he died without having lost a drop of blood.

MEELAN; A LEGEND OF THE SOUTH.
BY EDWARD WALSH.

———————— " Enchantments drear,
Where more is meant than meets the ear."—*Milton.*

'Tis night, and the moon, from her star-clad height,
  Flings her marble of silver hue
O'er Clonfert's green graves; and all sparkling bright
Daloo, in her gleam-beams, a sheet of light,
  Where murmur its waters blue.

How gloom from afar, o'er the soothing scene,
  The tall cliff and wavy wood;
And mournful and grey are the rude rocks seen,
As heaves the green turf in huge mounds between,
  Where Castle M'Auly stood.*

Here frown'd the dark turrets in lordly pride,
  Here smil'd the gay chieftain's hall,
The clansmen here marshall'd in order wide,
When war-fires high blazed on the mountain's side,
  For battle at glory's call.

Here ne'er shall the string of the clarseach wake;
  The songs of the hall are o'er;
No more shall the voice of the victor break,
When home, o'er the mountain, their wild way take,
  The kern† and crahadore.‡

The clansmen, who battled with Saxon foes,
  The chief of the lordly dome;
The bard, at whose call the stout clansmen rose,
In death undistinguished all calm repose—
  They are gone to their silent home!

Lo! yonder, where moss-grown the grave-stones lie,
  M'Auliffe sad-sought the tomb;
He fell not in battle by victor high,
Heart-broken he yielded his latest sigh
  For Meelan, his daughter's doom!

Daloo, while thou glidest thy groves between,
  Shall the maids of thy sun-lit glade
Twine horror-fraught tales of the nuptial scene
With the olden lays, echoed through woodland green,
  For Meelan, the gold-haired maid.

And mild as the lambkin, that crops the lea,
  And pensive as cowslip's pale,
She oft sought the valley alone—for she
Was woo'd by a chieftain of high degree
  In yonder dark lonely dale.

O'Herly was gallant, and brave, and gay;
  And chronicles ancient tell,
That Malachy bid his fair daughter say,
Who'd kiss her pure cheek on the nuptial day—
  Her choice on O'Herly fell.

Fond pair! you have woven in fancy's loom
  Sweet garlands of pleasure gay;
Dark destiny withers your garland's bloom,
Yet could beauty, could merit, revoke the doom,
  Not yours were this plaintive lay.

The glad nuptial morn arrives; and, lo!
  The high notes of joy resound:
The guests are in waiting, a glorious show—
The bards' raptur'd voices all sweetly flow,
  To join the wild harp's soft sound.

As blooms the young rose in the sun-beams clear,
  With bright pearly dew besprent;
So fair Meelan shone, through the smile and tear,
When the young chieftain soothed each maiden fear,
  As they to the altar went.

How glorious the pomp of the lordly train,
  That leads the young pair along;
What silver-shod coursers proud paw'd the plain—
Clonfert never saw, in her sacred fane,
  So gallant, so fair a throng.

To view the gay pageant the deep crowds press'd,
  Warm hearts in hot wars turmoil;
Whose lips, warmly praying, the bright pair bless'd,
As they went where the priests were in surplices dress'd,
  To the altar, along the aisle.

* The castle of M'Auliff, the Chief of Clanawly, stood over the Daloo, on the left hand side of the road to Blackwaterbridge. The foundations are now scarcely visible.
† Kern, an Irish foot soldier.
‡ Crahadore, the taker of spoils.

The hollow wind whistled the tombs among
  The owl, from her ivy tower,
Her harsh nightly notes on the day-light rung,
When young Meelan whispered. with faltering tongue,
  Consent to the nuptial power.

The marriage ring wax'd as the moonbeam pale,
  And deep was her dark heart's fall,
As the loud tempest gather'd adown the dale,
And the bride and the bridegroom sad-sought the vale,
  That led to M'Auliff's hall.

The hollow winds whistle—the owlet's cry—
  The marriage rings paly glow ;
The gloom of the moment—the unconscious sigh—
The lowering dark cloud of the boding sky
  Proclaim a sad tale of woe !

The sun hath gone down o'er the mountains steep,
  And tinges its glades with gold ;
The voice of the banquet is loud and deep—
The last and the latest that hall shall keep—
  Clanawly shall e'er behold !

Poor bride ! and the handmaids thy chamber spread,
  And show'd the gay fragrant flower ;
Thou wilt press with thy lover no nuptial bed—
Borne off by enchantment so drear and dread,
  From bridegroom and bridal bower !

The revelry rose on the night's dull ear,
  The vaulted hall loudly rung,
When Meelan discover'd, in wildest fear,
A stranger was seated beside her near,
  As " twelve" the strict warder sung.

His flowing locks mock'd the dark raven's plume ;
  His carriage, commanding high,
Bespoke the proud chieftain ; but silent gloom
O'erspread every bosom around the room,
  Though none knew the reason why.

His bright eye keen flashed with unearthly fire,
  No mortal might meet its glow ;
The guests of the banquet with cold hearts retire,
The bards' fingers ceas'd o'er the trembling wire,
  His presence such fears bestow.

Ye guests of the banquet surcease your dread,
  Right courteous the stranger tall ;
He fills o'er the table the wine bowl red ;
He pledges the bride with low bending head—
  The bridegroom and chieftains all.

He leads the young bride in the circling dance,
  Most regal his robes were seen ;
The banquet-guests view'd him with eyes askance—
The bride, O ! she trembled beneath his glance—
  Though graceful and gay his mien.

How quick gleam her steps on the marble floor,
  And gentle her light foot's sound
In the hall which her white foot oft trod before,
As she led her gay handmaids that marble o'er
  To move in the mazy round.

'Tis done—When the murmurs applausive ceased,
  The chief led the blooming bride
Where Malachy, 'mid the high chieftains placed,
Presided supreme o'er the nuptial feast,
  Then sat by the maiden's side.

" Thy light step, fair bride," the dark stranger said,
  " But echoed the music's sound :
With fair, blooming beauties the dance I've led—
Their charms would have vanished, their light step fled,
  Wert thou in the mazy round.

" I love a young maid—and her grace is thine,
  And thine are her tresses long,
And thine is her dark eye of light divine—
And, O ! if thou listen to strains of mine,
  I'll sing to my fair a song."

She bowed—and he rais'd some enchanted tone
  Ne'er warbled by mortal tongue ;
If golden-harp'd seraphs to earth had flown,
The voice of the stranger would seem their own—
  And these were the strains he sung :

THE SONG OF THE SPIRIT.

" Thou knowest where yon mountain uprears its huge head,
Where the hoarse torrent roars down its rude, rocky bed,
There stands my bright palace—high dwelling of air—
And the bride of my bosom shall smile on me there !

" Where the hues of the rainbow, all glorious, unite,
Festooning the hall in gay vapours of light,
Whose diamond-starred pavement now sparkles in sheen,
Far brighter than gems the deep grottos of Lene.*

" The soft bridal bed my beloved shall share,
I've pluck'd from the pinions of spirits of air ;
And the fairies of ocean, by strong spell beguil'd,
Shall soothe her to slumber with melody wild.

" I know where the waters of loveliness flow,
Whose pure draught can beauty immortal bestow ;
And the rose of her cheek, and the snow of her brow,
Shall live through wreck'd ages, as peerless as now !

" My chariot the wild winds—my pathway the sky—
O'er wide earth and ocean unfettered I fly ;
And my bright bird of beauty can wing her quick way
On the zephyr's soft pinion, as light fancy may !

" I know where the diamonds of brightness have birth,
In the caves of old ocean and dark womb of earth ;
I'll choose for my fairest the rarest of all,
To deck as she pleases the crystal-built hall.

" 'Tis the night of my bridal—I've pass'd it with you :
The morning-star blazes—ye chieftains, adieu !
When yearly this dark night of wonder shall be,
Remember the bridal—and think, think, of me !

" High lord of the castle ! dark chief of the Wold !†
The banquet of feasting I leave. But behold !
I'll snatch to my bosom the maid of my vow—
M'Auliff's bright daughter, that maiden art thou !

" 'Tis vain, O rash bridegroom ! nor tempt my high power
I've deck'd for the Meelan the gay nuptial bower !
My train are in waiting—impatient I fly—
My chariot the wild winds—my pathway the sky"

Then rose through the castle the wild guest's fright,
  As his strong arm he twin'd her round,
And wing'd through the wide-yawning roof his flight :
But ne'er was the bride since that fear-fraught night,
  Or the mysterious stranger, found.

To yonder rude cliff, called from Meelan's name,‡
  Through many an olden day—
Where rises the hall of enchanted fame,
Invisible save to the wizard's beam—
  The mountain-sprite bore his prey.

At night when the cottagers calm repose,
  And silent the grove and green,
Fair Meelan is oft at that dark hour's close,
While swells the sad tale of her fate and woes,
  Near her rock of enchantment seen !

---

* Loch Line, or the Lake of Killarney, remarkable, among its other natural curiosities, for diamonds. Tradition tells, that a carbuncle of immense value lies in the bosom of the lake, guarded by enchanted spells.

† The father of Meelan, and last lord of Clanawley, was remarkable for his austere dark temper. His territory was a mountainous tract, and are yet called " The Dark Mountains of M'Auliff."

‡ Meelan's Rock is a natural excavation, in a huge steep that crowns the right bank of the Daloo, over against the ruined church of Clonfert.

DUBLIN:

Printed and Published by P. D. Hardy, 3, Cecilia-street ; to whom all communications are to be addressed.
Sold by all Booksellers in Ireland.

In London, by Richard Groombridge, 6, Panyer-alley, Paternoster-row ; in Liverpool, by Wilmer and Smith ; in Manchester, by Ambery ; in Birmingham, by Guest, 91, Steelhouse-lane ; Glasgow, by John Macleod ; and in Edinburgh, by N. Bowack.

THE

DUBLIN PENNY JOURNAL

CONDUCTED BY P. DIXON HARDY, M.R.I.A.

| Vol. III. | APRIL 11, 1835. | No. 145. |

THE BECHUANA BOY.

AFRICAN SKETCHES, BY THOMAS PRINGLE.
SECOND NOTICE.

In our notice of a portion of this interesting volume in our last, we believe we did not mention that about one-third of it consists of poetic sketches. While as *poetry*, they could not be ranked beyond mediocrity, as descriptive, touching sketches, connected with Africa, they justly claim a fair portion of the reader's attention. Of this the following will afford an illustration. It is, as the reader will perceive, a description of the engraving which we have given, and which stands as a frontispiece to the volume.

THE BECHUANA BOY.

I sat at noontide in my tent,
    And looked across the desert dun,
Beneath the cloudless firmament
    Far gleaming in the sun,
When from the bosom of the waste
A swarthy stripling came in haste,
With foot unshod and naked limb ;
And a tame springbok followed him.

With open aspect, frank yet bland,
    And with a modest mien he stood,
Caressing with a gentle hand
    That beast of gentle brood ;
Then, meekly gazing in my face,
Said in the language of his race,
With smiling look yet pensive tone,
" Stranger—I'm in the world alone !"*

"Poor boy !" I said, " thy native home
    Lies far beyond the Stormberg blue :
Why hast thou left it, boy ! to roam
    This desolate Karroo ?"
His face grew sadder while I spoke ;
The smile forsook it ; and he broke
Short silence with a sob-like sigh,
And told his hapless history.

"I have no home !" replied the boy :
    " The Bergenaars—by night they came,
And raised their wolfish howl of joy,
    While o'er our huts the flame

* " ' *Ik ben alleenig in de waereld !*' was the touching expression of Marossi, the Bechuana orphan boy, in his broken Dutch, when he first fell accidentally under my protection, at Milk River in Camdeboo, in September, 1825. He was then apparently about nine or ten years of age, and had been carried from his native country by the Bergenaars. He was sold to a Boor

(for an old jacket !) only a few months previously, when the kraal or hamlet of his tribe had been sacked by those banditti in the manner described in the text. The other incidents of the poem are also taken from his own simple narrative, with the exception of his flying to the desert with a tame springbok—a poetical licence suggested to me by seeing, a few days afterwards, a slave child playing with a springbok fawn at a boor's residence.

" This little African accompanied my wife and me to England ; and with the gradual development of his feelings and faculties he became interesting to us in no ordinary degree. He was indeed a remarkable child. With a great flow of animal spirits, and natural hilarity, he was at the same time docile, observant, reflective, and always unselfishly considerate of others. He was of a singularly ingenuous and affectionate disposition : and, in proportion as his reason expanded, his heart became daily more thoroughly imbued with the genuine spirit of the Gospel, insomuch that all who knew him, involuntarily and with one consent, applied to this African boy the benignant words of our Saviour—' Of such is the kingdom of heaven.' He was baptised in 1827, and took on himself (in conjunction with Mrs. P. and me) his baptismal vows, in the most devout and sensible manner. Shortly afterwards he died of a pulmonary complaint under which he had for many months suffered with exemplary meekness."

Resistless rushed ; and aye their yell
Pealed louder as our warriors fell
In helpless heaps beneath their shot :
—One living man they left us not !

" The slaughter o'er, they gave the slain
　To feast the foul-beaked birds of prey ;
And, with our herds, across the plain
　They hurried us away—
The widowed mothers and their brood,
Oft, in despair, for drink and food
We vainly cried ; they heeded not,
But with sharp lash the captive smote.

" Three days we tracked that dreary wild,
　Where thirst and anguish pressed us sore ;
And many a mother and her child
　Lay down to rise no more.
Behind us, on the desert brown,
We saw the vultures swooping down :
And heard, as the grim night was falling,
The wolf to his gorged comrade calling.

" At length was heard a river sounding
　'Midst that dry and dismal land,
And, like a troop of wild deer bounding,
　We hurried to its strand—
Among the maddened cattle rushing ;
The crowd behind still forward pushing,
Till in the flood our limbs were drenched,
And the fierce rage of thirst was quenched.

" Hoarse-roaring, dark, the broad Gareep
　In turbid streams was sweeping fast,
Huge sea-cows in its eddies deep
　Loud snorting as we passed ;
But that relentless robber clan
Right through those waters wild and wan
Drove on like sheep our wearied band :
—Some never reached the farther strand.

" All shivering from the foaming flood,
　We stood upon the stranger's ground,
When, with proud looks and gestures rude,
　The white Men gathered round :
And there, like cattle from the fold,
By Christians we were bought and sold,
'Midst laughter loud and looks of scorn—
And roughly from each other torn.

" My mother's scream, so long and shrill,
　My little sister's wailing cry,
(In dreams I often hear them still !)
　Rose wildly to the sky.
A tiger's heart came to me then,
And fiercely on those ruthless men
I sprang.—Alas ! dashed on the sand,
Bleeding, they bound me foot and hand.

" Away—away on prancing steeds
　The stout man-stealers blithely go,
Through long low valleys fringed with reeds,
　O'er mountains capped with snow,
Each with his captive, far and fast ;
Until yon rock-bound ridge we passed,
And distant stripes of cultured soil
Bespoke the land of tears and toil.

" And tears and toil have been my lot
　Since I the white man's thrall became,
And sorer griefs I wish forgot—
　Harsh blows, and scorn, and shame !
Oh, Englishman ! thou ne'er canst know
The injured bondman's bitter woe,
When round his breast, like scorpions, cling
Black thoughts, that madden while they sting !

" Yet this hard fate I might have borne,
　And taught in time my soul to bend,
Had my sad yearning heart forlorn
　But found a single friend :
My race extinct or far removed,
The boor's rough brood I could have loved ;
But each to whom my bosom turned
Even like a hound the black boy spurned.

" While, friendless thus, my master's flocks
　I tended on the upland waste,
It chanced this fawn leapt from the rocks,
　By wolfish wild-dogs chased :
I rescued it, though wounded sore
And dabbled in its mother's gore ;
And nursed it in a cavern wild,
Until it loved me like a child.

" Gently I nursed it ; for I thought
　(Its hapless fate so like to mine)
By good UTIKO* it was brought
　To bid me not repine—
Since in this world of wrong and ill
One creature lived that loved me still,
Although its dark and dazzling eye
Beamed not with human sympathy.

" Thus lived I, a lone orphan lad,
　My task the proud Boor's flocks to tend ;
And this poor fawn was all I had,
　To love, or call my friend ;
When suddenly, with haughty look
And taunting words, that tyrant took
My playmate for his pampered boy,
Who envied me my only joy.

" High swelled my heart !—But when the star
　Of midnight gleamed, I softly led
My bounding favourite forth, and far
　Into the desert fled.
And here, from human kind exiled,
Three moons on roots and berries wild
I've fared ; and braved the beasts of prey,
To 'scape from spoilers worse than they.

" But yester morn a Bushman brought
　The tidings that thy tents were near ;
And now with hasty foot I've sought
　Thy presence, void of fear ;
Because they say, O English chief,
Thou scornest not the captive's grief :
Then let me serve thee as thine own—
For I am in the world alone !"

Such was Marossi's touching tale.
　Our breasts they were not made of stone :
His words, his winning looks prevail—
　We took him for " our own."
And one, with woman's gentle art,
Unlocked the fountains of his heart ;
And love gushed forth—till he became
Her child, in every thing but name.

In our last we observed, that although Mr. Pringle in
his outlines of natural history did not at all *affect* the man
of science, from his brief sketches of the various animals
which came under his observation, more information might
be obtained relative to their manners and habits, than
may be frequently gained from works professing to treat
scientifically of such subjects.

THE ELEPHANT.

Of the peculiar habits and instincts of the elephant
much has been written. The following, evidently sketched
from nature, we venture to affirm will afford a juster idea
of the character of this lord of the forest, as seen in his
own domain, than could be gathered from any work on
zoology yet published.

" We slept one night at the mouth of a subsidiary dell,
which I named Elephant's Glen, from the circumstance of
its wooded recesses being then inhabited by a troop of
those gigantic animals, whose strange wild cry was heard
by us the whole night long, as we bivouacked by the river,
sounding like a trumpet among the moonlight mountains

---

* " Utiko, a term now in general use among many of the South
African tribes for the Supreme being, is derived from the Hottentot word ' Tiko,' which is said literally to signify ' The
Beautiful.' It has been adopted by the missionaries to denote
the true God."

Here I had the good fortune to fall in with a troop of elephants—a truly magnificent spectacle.

" Next day, we followed the course of the Koonap over green sloping hills, till the increasing ruggedness of the ravines, and the prevalence of jungle, compelled us to pursue a Caffer path, now kept open only by the passage of wild animals, along the river margin. The general character of the scenery I have already described. During the forenoon, we had seen many herds of quaggas, and antelopes of various kinds, which I need not stop to enumerate; but after mid-day, we came upon the recent traces of a troop of elephants. Their huge foot-prints were every where visible; and in the swampy spots on the banks of the river it was evident that some of them had been luxuriously enjoying themselves by rolling their unwieldy bulks in the ooze and mud. But it was in the groves and jungles that they had left the most striking proofs of their recent presence and peculiar habits. In many places paths had been trodden through the midst of dense thorny forests, otherwise impenetrable. They appeared to have opened up these paths with great judgment, always taking the best and shortest cut to the next open savannah, or ford of the river ; and in this way their labours were of the greatest use to us by pioneering our route through a most intricate country, never yet traversed by a wheel-carriage, and great part of it, indeed, not easily accessible even on horseback. In such places the great bull elephant always marches in the van, bursting through the jungle as a bullock would through a field of hops, treading down the brushwood, and breaking off with his proboscis the larger branches that obstruct the passage, whilst the females and younger part of the herd follow in his wake.

" Among the mimosa trees sprinkled over the meadows, or lower bottoms, the traces of their operations were not less apparent. Immense numbers of these trees had been torn out of the ground, and placed in an inverted position, in order to enable the animals to browse at their ease on their juicy roots, which form a favourite part of their food. I observed that, in numerous instances, when the trees were of considerable size, the elephant had employed one of his tusks, exactly as we would use a crow-bar—thrusting it under the roots to loosen their hold of the earth, before he attempted to tear them up with his proboscis. Many of the larger mimosas had resisted all their efforts; and, indeed, it is only after heavy rains, when the soil is soft and loose, that they can successfully attempt this operation.

" While we were admiring these and other indications of the elephant's strength and sagacity, we suddenly found ourselves, on issuing from a woody defile, in the midst of a numerous herd of those animals. None of them, however, were very close to us ; but they were seen scattered in groups over the bottom and sides of a valley two or three miles in length ; some browsing on the succulent spekboom, which clothed the skirts of the hills on either side ; others at work among the young mimosas and evergreens sprinkled over the meadows. As we proceeded cautiously onward, some of these groups came more distinctly into view ; consisting apparently, in many instances, of separate families, the male, the female, and the young of different sizes ; and the gigantic magnitude of the chief leaders became more and more striking. The calm and stately tranquillity of their deportment, too, was remarkable. Though we were a band of about a dozen horsemen, including our Hottentot attendants, they seemed either not to observe, or altogether to disregard, our march down the valley.

" Captain Fox, who had only recently arrived from England, was very desirous of seeing an elephant hunt ; and the Hottentots, who were well experienced in such pastime, eagerly solicited permission to attack a group that were browsing in a thicket about a quarter of a mile distant; but it was judged imprudent as well as useless to make any such attempt. The sun was sinking fast towards the horizon ; we had recently passed through a long succession of intricate and difficult defiles ; a pass of the same description lay just before us ; and the hills on either side rose steep, and rugged, and shaggy with an impenetrable forest of evergreens. To have commenced an attack, in

such a situation, with our small guns and leaden bullets, on any part of a herd whose total number exceeded fifty elephants, would have been not only ineffective, but dangerous in the extreme. I confess, too, that when I looked around on these noble and stately animals, feeding in quiet security in the depth of this secluded valley—too peaceful to injure, too powerful to dread any other living creature—I felt that it would be almost a sort of sacrilege to attempt their destruction merely to furnish sport to the great destroyer man ; and I was glad when, after a brief consultation, it was unanimously agreed to leave them unmolested.

" While we were conversing on this subject, as we rode leisurely along through a meadow thickly studded over with clumps of tall evergreens, I observed something moving over the top of a bush close a-head of us, and had just time to say to the gentleman next me—' Look out there !' when we turned the corner of the bush, and beheld an enormous male elephant standing right in the path within less than a hundred paces distance. We halted and surveyed him for a few minutes in silent admiration and astonishment. He was, indeed, a mighty and magnificent creature. The two engineer officers, who were familiar with the appearance of the elephant in his wild state, agreed that the animal before us was at least *fourteen feet* in height ; and our Hottentots, in their broken Dutch, whispered that he was ' *een groot gruwzaam karl—bania', bania' groot !*'—or, as one of them translated it, ' a hugeous terrible fellow, plenty, plenty big !'

" The elephant at first did not seem to notice us ; for the vision of the animal is not very acute, and the wind being pretty brisk, and we to the leeward of him, his scent and hearing, though keen, had not apprised him of our approach. But when we turned off at a gallop, making a circuit through the bushes to avoid collision with him, he was startled by the sound of our horses' feet, and turned towards us with a very menacing attitude, erecting his enormous ears, and elevating his trunk in the air, as if about to rush upon us. Had he done so, some of us would probably have been destroyed; for the elephant can run down a well-mounted horseman in a short chase ; and besides, there was another ugly defile but a little way before us, where the only passage was a difficult pass through the jungle, with a precipice on one side and a wooded mountain on the other. However, the ' *gruwzaam karl,*' fortunately, did not think proper to give chase, but remained on the same spot looking steadfastly after us ; well pleased, no doubt, to be rid of our company, and satisfied to see his family all safe around him. The latter consisted of two or three females, and as many young ones, that had hastily crowded up behind him from the river margin, as if to claim his protection, when the rushing sound of our cavalcade startled their quiet valley.

" I counted altogether fifty-three of the herd, and there were probably a few more concealed by the tall copsewood.

" To give the reader some idea of the peril of encountering the African elephant when enraged, I may here insert the following account by my friend Lieutenant Moodie, of the 21st Fusileers, of his remarkable escape from under the feet of one, only a few months previous to the period of the above excursion.

" ' The day previous to my adventure I had witnessed an elephant hunt for the first time. On that occasion a large female was killed, after some hundred shots had been fired at her. The balls seemed at first to produce little effect, but at length she received several shots in the trunk and eyes, which entirely disabled her from making resistance or escaping, and she then fell an easy prey to her assailants.

" ' One of our servants came to inform us that a large troop of elephants was in the neighbourhood of the settlement, and that several of our people were already on their way to attack them. I instantly set out to join the hunters; but, from losing my way in the jungle through which I had to proceed, I did not overtake them, until after they had driven the elephants from their first station. On getting out of the jungle I was proceeding through an open meadow on the banks of the Golana, to the spot where I heard the firing, when I was suddenly warned of approaching danger, by loud cries of ' *Pas-op !*'

—'*Take care!*'—in Dutch and English, coupled with my name; and at the same moment I heard the crackling of broken branches, produced by the elephants bursting through the wood, and the tremendous screams of their wrathful voices resounding among the precipitous banks. Immediately a large female, accompanied by three others of a smaller size, issued from the edge of the jungle, which skirted the river margin. As they were not more than two hundred yards off, and were proceeding directly towards me, I had not much time to decide on my motions. Being alone, and in the middle of a little open plain, I saw that I must inevitably be caught, should I fire in this position, and my shot not take effect. I therefore re-reated hastily out of their direct path, thinking they would not observe me, until I should find a better opportunity to attack them. But in this I was mistaken, for on looking back I perceived, to my dismay, that they had left their former course, and were rapidly pursuing and gaining ground on me. Under these circumstances I determined to reserve my fire as a last resource; and turning off at right angles in the opposite direction, I made for the banks of the small river, with a view to take refuge among the rocks on the other side, where I should have been safe. But before I got within fifty paces of the river, the elephants were within twenty paces of me—the large female in the middle, and the other three on either side of her, apparently with the intention of making sure of me; all of them screaming so tremendously, that I was almost stunned with the noise. I immediately turned round, cocked my gun, and aimed at the head of the largest—the female. But the gun, unfortunately, from the powder being damp, hung fire, till I was in the act of taking it from my shoulder, when it went off, and the ball merely grazed the side of her head. Halting only for an instant, the animal again rushed furiously forward. I fell—I cannot say whether struck down by her trunk or not. She then made a thrust at me with her tusk. Luckily for me she had only one, which still more luckily missed its mark; but it ploughed up the earth within an inch or two of my body. She then caught me with her trunk by the middle —threw me between her fore feet—and knocked me about with them for a brief space—I was scarcely in a condition to compute the number of minutes or seconds very accurately. Once she pressed her foot on my chest with such force, that I actually felt the bones, as it were, bending under the weight; and once she trod on the middle of my arm, which, fortunately, lay flat on the ground at the time. During this rough handling, however, I never entirely lost my recollection, else I have little doubt, she would have settled my accounts with this world. But owing to the roundness of her foot, I generally managed, by twisting my body and limbs, to escape her direct tread. While I was still undergoing this buffetting, Lieutenant Chisholm, of the royal African corps, and Diederik, a Hottentot, had come up, and fired several shots at her, one of which hit her in the shoulder; and at the same time her companions, or young ones, retiring, and screaming to her from the edge of the forest, she reluctantly left me, giving me a cuff or two with her hind feet in passing. I got up, picked up my gun, and staggered away as fast as my aching bones would allow; but observing that she turned round, and looked back towards me, before entering the bush, I lay down in the long grass, by which means I escaped her observation.

"'On reaching the top of the high bank of the river, I met my brother, who had not been at this day's hunt, but had run out on being told by one of the men that he had seen me killed. He was not a little surprised at meeting me alone and in a whole skin, though plastered with mud from head to foot. While he, Mr. Knight, of the Cape regiment, and I, were yet talking of my adventure, an unlucky soldier of the Royal African corps, of the name of M'Clane, attracted the attention of a large male elephant, which had been driven towards the village. The ferocious animal gave chace, and caught him immediately under the height where we were standing—carried him some distance in his trunk—then threw him down, and bringing his four feet together, trod and stamped upon him for a considerable time, till he was quite dead. Leaving the corpse for a little, he again returned, as if to make

quite sure of his destruction, and kneeling down, crushed and kneaded the body with his fore-legs. Then seizing it again with his trunk, he carried it to the edge of the jungle, and threw it among the bushes. While this tragedy was going on, my brother and I scrambled down the bank as far as we could, and fired at the furious animal, but we were at too great a distance to be of any service to the unfortunate man, who was crushed almost to a jelly.

"'Shortly after this catastrophe, a shot from one of the people broke this male elephant's left fore-leg, which completely disabled him from running. On this occasion, we witnessed a touching instance of affection and sagacity in the elephant, which I cannot forbear to relate, as it so well illustrates the character of this noble animal. Seeing the danger and distress of her mate, the female before mentioned (my personal antagonist), regardless of her own danger, quitted her shelter in the bush, rushed out to his assistance, walked round and round him, chasing away the assailants, and still returning to his side and caressing him; and when he attempted to walk, she placed her flank under his wounded side and supported him. This scene continued nearly half an hour, until the female received a severe wound from Mr. C. Mackenzie, of the Royal African corps, which drove her again to the bush, where she speedily sank exhausted from the loss of blood; and the male soon after received a mortal wound also from the same officer.

"'Thus ended our elephant-hunt; and I need hardly say, that what we witnessed on this occasion, of the intrepidity and ferocity of these powerful animals, rendered us more cautious in our dealings with them for the future.'

"At the upper extremity of the White River valley, I found a solitary farm-shieling. Here the proprietor's wife complained bitterly of the annoyance that she and her family received from the nocturnal visits of the elephants. They were, she said, 'too big to wrestle with.' They came out of the forest by night, trod down her little corn-field, devoured her crop of maize, pulled up her fruit trees, and tossed about, as if in wanton malice, articles that they could neither devour nor totally destroy; and only a few days previously, her husband, on returning home at a late hour, had made a narrow escape from one of those animals, which met him on the road and chased him several times round his waggon. She added, however, that they were far less dangerous than they had been when she and her family first came to reside in this wild though beautiful valley; and pointing to a rocky mound at a little distance, which rose abruptly from the grassy meadows, and overhung a pool of the river, she said that on the summit of that rock, not many years since, her husband used to lie concealed among the brushwood, and shoot the elephants as they passed down the glen in numerous herds, even at mid-day.

"The following curious illustration of the peculiar sagacity of this animal was brought under my notice at this place. A few days before my arrival at Enon, a troop of elephants came down one dark and rainy night close to the outskirts of the village. The missionaries heard them bellowing and making an extraordinary noise for a long time at the upper end of the orchard; but knowing well how dangerous it is to encounter these animals in the night, they kept close within their houses till day-break. Next morning, on examining the spot where they had heard the elephants, they discovered the cause of all this nocturnal uproar. There was, at this spot, a ditch or trench, about five or six feet in width and twelve in depth, which the industrious missionaries had recently cut through the bank of the river, on purpose to lead out the water to irrigate some part of their garden ground, and to drive a corn-mill. Into this trench, which was still unfinished and without water, one of the elephants had evidently fallen, for the marks of his feet were distinctly visible at the bottom, as well as the impress of his huge body on its sides. How he had got in it was easy to imagine, but how, being once in, he had ever contrived to get out again, was the marvel. By his own unaided efforts it seemed almost impossible for such an animal to have extricated himself. Could his comrades, then, have assisted him? There appeared little doubt that they had; though by what means unless by pulling him up with their trunks, it would not be easy to conjecture. And in corroboration of this supposition, on examining the spot myself, I found the edges of this trench deeply indented with numerous vestiges, as if the other elephants had stationed themselves on either side, some of them kneeling, and others on their feet, and had thus, by united efforts, hoisted their unlucky brother out of the pit."

THE STRIPED HYÆNA.

AFRICAN SHEEP.

THE ANTELOPE.

THE FOUR-HORNED ANTELOPE.

THE PRONG-HORNED ANTELOPE.

In our former notice of Mr. Pringle's work, we gave several particulars relative to the hyæna—and as there is very little of a distinctive character in the African sheep, from those of other countries, to claim a particular notice—we pass on to the Antelope. We are informed by Mr. Pringle, that "this family of animals consists, in South Africa, of not fewer than nineteen or twenty distinct species, ranging in size from the *blaawbok*, or pigmy antelope, which seldom exceeds ten inches in height, to the *eland*, as tall as the common ox, though more slender in its shape, and weighing from 700 to 1,000 pounds. This last-named animal, which is the *antelope oreas* of naturalists, is, I believe, now nearly extirpated in every part of the colony.

"Of the numerous family of antelopes which inhabited our glens and mountains, I shall only particularly mention the gnu, which is now become rare in most parts of the colony. Though shy, they appeared to have a large share of curiosity; bounding away when approached, and then returning again, in a sweeping circuit, to gaze on the traveller or huntsman; spurring up the dust with their hoofs, tossing their manes, lashing their sides with their long tails, and performing other evolutions not a little amusing. They are said to be strongly affected if a red flag be exhibited to them, but I never had an opportunity of trying the experiment. They are fierce and dangerous when wounded. I tried to rear a young one which a hunting party brought home with them (the poor animal following the horsemen when its dam was shot), but it soon pined and died. They have been frequently tamed by the boors, when thus caught young; but are said, when grown up, to become mischievous. The animal appears to form an intermediate link between the antelope and the bovine families."

PADDY CORCORAN.

" Welcome home, Paddy; and sure and a purty time you wor away from us," was shouted out as Paddy Corcoran hopped before his own cabin door, he evidently appearing as one who was after seeing hard service—his swelled face and black eye giving sure evidence that he did not go and return from his usual excursion without meeting with something beyond his every day manner of life. Paddy, as far as could be judged from his *one* perfect eye, which beamed as bright as all *well watered* eyes generally do, winked with great significance to a bloated, dapper little man, who whispered him—" And have you the Queen's own (smuggled whiskey) along wid you, Paddy dear ?"

Paddy Corcoran was a *regular hager* or carman between his own native town, and the capital of the same county, who once a week received commissions to gratify every taste, and satisfy the different wants which the capital could supply; and although Paddy was as irregular as the different houses of call on the road could make him, yet his horse, true to its paces whether with or without its owner, was in due course received by a crowd of expectants, who thronged around Paddy's dwelling to feast their eyes with the newest importations; and frequently the contents of the cargo were fully distributed ere Paddy made his appearance, whose arrival was often facilitated by his being picked up from off the road by some more sober neighbour, as he drove along.

At this moment the dapper little man whom we have mentioned, gave a knowing wink, which was immediately recognised by Paddy, who followed him; and as he was well-known to sell a good "dhrop," and as Paddy's arrival was a sure indication that there was no fear of being disappointed, and a strong chance of "hearing all about it," some half a dozen of the boys brought up the rear, until they stopped before a house, over the door of which was inscribed " Entertainment for man and beast," into the taproom of which they entered, and rapping for a pint of the " raal sort," invited Paddy to sit and partake of " what's going ;" who nothing loth, and finding himself again in his own town, and amongst the neighbours, after taking a hearty swig of the tumbler, became himself again ; and the boys, itching to have the particulars of Paddy's adventures, continued priming him to the " spaking" point, which, from his present *dry* condition, required some time to *soak* the following account of his distant travels.

" And, och, boys, it's meself that's glad to see you and Judy, and the childer, once more agin, and good luck to ye. Never, whiles the world's a world, did Paddy Corcoran 'spect to suffer the murdhering he's after getting, or his two eyes to behould what he did behould. Sure, boys, yeerselves seed me leaving this last Wednesday, full and hearty, and many's the commission myself had to town for the neighbours; but bad cess to the tay (tea) which the quality dhrinks, it has been sore tay to me at any rate. When I got to the big town, I called to deliver my messages. I wint to the grocer's for the tay, who tould me that he could not give it thin, as the river was so full iv the rain, that the boats couldn't come up.

" ' But, Paddy,' ses he, ' maybe you would go yerself for it ; and as t'other neighbours has goods lying also at the mouth of the river, I will get a load for ye to bring back with ye.'

" ' Wisha, Sir,' sez I, ' any thing in honesty to earn a penny ; and as I have no business home widout the tay, I may as well, wid a blessing, go for it.'

" So off I sets, laughing wid myself what a fine sthory I'd have to tell ye when I came back, boys; and, sure enough, I had the fine sthory to tell—but I'm laughing at the wrong side of my mouth. Well, as I was tellin' ye, off I sets of a beautiful morning ; and sure and sartin, a delightfuller road I couldn't have of it. The very birds wor glad to see me, and the small crathurs, wid their whistlin', seemed to say, ' You're welcome out this fine morning, Paddy Corcoran!'—' Och, success to ye, my darlints, and

more power to yer windpipes,' sez I, ' for iligant nightingales, and the curse of Cromwell attind the farmer that 'ud begridge ye a morsel from his corn-fields; and the nixt house I come to,' sez I, ' I'll drink yer health, and a welcome.' And shure enough, as luck 'ud have it, I was jist beside a cozy little one, where I wint in and calls for me mornin', barrin' the one I tuck before I come out.

" ' But, Paddy,' sez I, ' as you are in a sthrange country, maybe ye doesn't know where the best is to be had.'

" Wid that, myself begins to consider; but as I didn't know how many was on this road, ' Why, thin,' sez I, ' I had betther thry this one at any rate, for fear of a disappointment.' So myself did, and a good dhrop it was, too.

" Well, boys, if you wor to see Paddy Corcoran, wid all the birds in the air singing above him, and all the fishes in that beautiful river dancing up and down about him, and the fine road under him, shure ye might say he was as happy as the son of an Irish king : but wait a bit, till ye hear what befel him hereafter. On and on I wint, and och, the counthry that was afore me, and the mountains at one side of me, and the beautiful river at the foot,— ' Shure,' sez I, ' this beats Banagher ; and them fine boats, too—yurrah, where are they goin' in sich a hurry.' And och, as I wint along, and still sees mountains upon mountains, till ye'd think they'd ritch the ind of the world, wid big forests upon them that looked like hanging from the sky, wid purty houses in the middle of them—thinks Paddy to himself, where are ye now?—and it's myself couldn't tell. And I begins to conshider—' Did ye ever hear tell of any place likes it, at all at all. Wisha, thin, I have it,' says I, ' this is the charming place that the gorsoon was reading about. This is Killarney,' sez I, ' and it's myself must sthop at Killarney ;' and shure I was in luck agin, for what should I see but ' Licensed to sell Spirits :' and never a fear had I now what they sould, as I determined to thry every house of that sort along the road, that when I come back, or iver wint the road agin, I would know where to get the best sup—and a sthrong sup I got there to my sorrow, for I couldn't keep aisy for roaring and bawling, ' I'm come to Killarney !' And murdher in Irish, over the way in the big mountains a hundred voices cried out, ' Paddy Corcoran's come to Killarney !' ' Well, that's mighty odd,' sez I ; and jist as I said it, up comes a sthrapping fellow, and axed me what call had I to the Larneys. ' Nothing at all, avick,' sez I : ' be all accounts the Larneys is dacent people, though myself hasn't their acquaintance.' ' He's a Connaughtman,' sez one. ' He's a Kerryman,' sez another. ' Arrah, be aisy,' sez I. Wid that the sthrapper calls out, ' Does ye want to kill a Larney, whiles the dhrop of their blood is in my body? Hurrah for the Larney,' sez he ; and he ups wid his stick and welted me, till I was kilt entirely—' Oh, bad cess to the tay,' sez I, ' I'm getting it widout sugar or milk ! Och, Judy and the childher, never more will my eyes behould ye ; nor no wake nor funeral, nor no neighbours to cry over me. Och, don't murther me entirely, sez I ; and myself knows nothing more about it, till I opened my eyes in the Peelers' barracks.

" ' Gintlemen,' sez I to them, ' is it fair that a poor man should get this usage for nothing at all at all ?'

" ' You'll get more of it, to your sorrow,' sez the strapper agin : ' let me see who will touch one of the Larneys.'

" ' Oh, boys, sez one of the Peelers, who must be a great scholard, ' sure Paddy manes the Lakes of Killarney.'

" And wid that the honest people seed I had no spite to them, and we shuck hands, and made it up at the nixt public-house ; and agin I was on the road, wid this thumpin' black eye and broken face that ye sees upon me—givin' the promise to myself that sorra a sup would enter my mouth, till I arrived at my journey's ind ; and myself hadn't long to keep it, for soon I sees the town afore me. As myself intered it, I began to look about very cutely for the house I had the letter to—but all the shutters wor up. ' And sure this isn't Sunday,' sez I ; ' warn't to-day Turday since I left the big town. Sure it can't be a holiday, aither,' sez I, for the *doors* would be open at any rate— It must be Sunday ! And och, millia murdher, I sees

be kilt this three days by the Larneys !—There's no help for misfortunes,' sez I, ' and myself will put up the baste, and get prayers at any rate.' So myself did put up at the stage ; and glad I was to see the ostler was a Mullinahone boy.

" ' Arrah' cushla,' sez I, ' trate the poor baste kindly, till I goes to hear Mass.'

" ' There's no Mass to day,' sez he.

" ' Why, what day is this ?' sez I, beginnin' to doubt.

" ' And what day wud it be,' says he, ' but Tursday.'

" ' And what is the shops shut for, thin ?' sez I.

" ' Och,' sez he, ' the great big man over the way, that sould the blankets, is dead.'

" ' Is there more nor one,' sez I, ' bekase all the shops is shut ?'

" ' Is that all you know about it ?' sez he; ' why, whin a Christian dies here, all the town goes to his funeral.'

" ' Thin ye are ov the right sort here,' sez I ; ' and it's myself will go and see yer town,' sez I, ' till the funeral is over.'

" And out I walks to see the boats; and shure myself wondhered to see them called after Christians—Mary and Sally, and a power of other names.—' Well, this is quare enough,' sez I.

" ' Welcome to town, Paddy Corcoran,' sez a voish behind me.

" I turns about, but as I did not know it, I thought it was spaking to the boatman afore me—and thinks I, there's more Paddy Corcorans nor one.

" ' Welcome to town, Paddy Corcoran,' sez the boatman, that was now behind me.

" ' Well this bates any thing, any how,' sez I.

" ' Welcome to town, Paddy Corcoran,' said the crew of them.

" ' Well, shure enough, it's myself they mean !—but how does they know me ? Perhaps the great Counshellor O'Connell tould them the plumper I gave to the little county mimber in spite of my landlord. So for fear of being axed to take any thing, myself will take myself away,' sez I ; and wid that I walks away from them. But sich a shout of ' Welcome to town, Paddy Corcoran !' was raised after me, that away I runs intirely from them.

" ' Welcome to town, Paddy Corcoran !' sez a dacent man, as he passed me.

" ' Arrah, avick,' sez I, ' does you know me ?'

" ' To be shure I does,' sez he ; ' and how is the wife and childher ?'

" ' Bravely,' sez I ; ' and, maybe,' sez I, ' as we're in a sthrange country, we wouldn't be after taking a dhrop together.'

" ' Never say it twice,' sez he; and away we goes opposite.

" ' Welcome to town, Paddy Corcoran !' sez a power of voishes around me.

" ' Be the powers of pewter, here's more of my counthrymen,' sez I ; ' and never be it said that Paddy Corcoran will iver deny them. Come along, boys, and Paddy will thrate ye all.'

" ' Welcome to town, Paddy Corcoran !' sez the publican.

" ' Welcome to town, Paddy Corcoran !' said all the place ; and ' Welcome to town, Paddy Corcoran !' was shouted in every direction, till myself didn't know what to think of it. Howsomiver, I was determined to do the ginteel, and called for lashins of whiskey.

" ' Welcome to town, Paddy Corcoran !' was still the shout ; until myself roaring out, ' Welcome to town, Paddy Corcoran !' which every sup I tuck made it more difficult to say, I sees the tables, stools, pots, tumblers, and fifty candles, wid all in the room, and myself along wid them, whirl around ; and sorra a bit I knows what happened after, till I found myself shuck by a gintleman, who axed me was I Paddy Corcoran.

" ' Plase your honour, Sir,' sez I, ' sure all the town knows that already, and all the neighbours you sees about me,' (raising myself on my elbow ;) but, och, botheration, never a one did I see, but myself and the gintleman.

" ' Paddy,' says he, ' the goods you come for yistherday is ready.'

" ' No, yer honour,' sez I, ' 'twas to-day.'

" ' Why, it's now but morning,' sez he.

" ' Och, murdher, murdher, Sir,' sez I, ' let it be any day you plase, if, wid a blessin', I once agin sees daylight sittin' on the roof of my own cabin.'

" Wid that up I leaps, and, shure enough, if the gintleman didn't cry, wid laughing—' Welcome to town, Paddy Corcoran !'

" ' None of yer blarney, Sir,' sez I ; ' I'll have nothin' more to say to counthry acquaintances. Paddy has suffered enough already by rason of this place.'

" ' No wonder, Paddy,' sez he, ' whin your name is behind your back,' taking a paper from off it, wid ' Welcome to town, Paddy Corcoran !' written in big letters upon it.

" ' Och, may great big bad luck attind that Mullinahone boy up yonder, that played me sich a trick,' sez I. ' And ten thousand blessins on yer honour, and dispatch me quick.'

" ' Very well, Paddy,' sez he.

" Wid that I calls for the reck'ning, and, wurrah ! wurrah ! sich a bill for quarts of whiskey and gallons of porther, that would sail a boat down to the say intirely. Out I was obligated to pull all the change about me, and much more nor that, that Peggy Clancy gev me to buy the sthraw bonnet and the shoes. Well, whin I had my loading ready, off I sets; and whin I was going out of town, ' Welcome to town, Paddy Corcoran !' was fresh as iver. ' Badershin,' sez I, and left them, sore and sorrowful ; and wid a heavy heart I fetched my load to the big town, and the very birds and fishes themselves seemed to frit for me ; and wid a dhry mouth and empty pockets home I come. And here I am, determined niver to visit foreign parts agin."
H.

HINTS ON PERSPECTIVE DRAWING.

The following hints on Perspective Drawing will not be lost on those of our kind correspondents who from time to time favour us with designs for our Journal :—

" It is probable that we have now a far greater number of amateur draughtsmen than any age has known—naval, military, and private tourists, male and female ; and their published travels contain an immensely greater display of sketches and descriptive plates than heretofore ; and their private portfolios, of elegant drawings. The utility of this practice is not ill appreciated in society ; and the pleasure it affords to the tourist and to the reader is very generally acknowledged. It is therefore somewhat surprising that the study of perspective should prevail so little. Is it the fault of the books, the teachers, or the scholars ? Is it the fear of the undertaking, or want of perception of its value, that indisposes amateurs to undertake this study? It must be acknowledged that some of our first masters have been careless of perspective up to a certain degree ; but the neglect appears in general in the subordinate parts only of their pictures ; still their inattention, even in this degree, has left an example, which, being on the indolent side, is too readily followed by artists of inferior talent ; and it deceives the eye and habituates it to incorrect representation.

" Notwithstanding, however, this unperceived morbid habit, good perspective is always pleasing. The untutored eye catches the effect, and perceives unexpectedly the resemblance to nature. Who is not delighted by the magic of the dioramas ? But (without more than mentioning those specimens of the art) who does not feel pleased with a true representation of even the simplest scene, where the surface of a road-side pond appears level and flat—where the street in a country town appears to open to the spectator as though he could trot along the hard ground where the boy's hoop seems balanced as it runs on the pavement ? While, on the other hand, however finely a picture may be coloured, or however beautifully pencilled a drawing, how lost is the effect when the artist has not taken the pains to consider where his horizontal line is, or has not known to what points his vanishing lines should tend ! The spectator feels at once, though he may not know why, that the figures appear not to stand on the ground ;—that the two sides, whether of a cathedral or a cottage, look like one long face ;—that the water slopes;—or that even a round tub appears bigger on one side than the other.

"Perspective is the first requisite—the *sine qua non* of picture. Picture is the representation of *space* and *bulk* on *superfices*. It consists in *form, light and shade*, and *colour*; but form comes first—drawing. Now the form of one and the same object varies infinitely, in the infinite variety of positions in which it is viewed; and the representation of that form, *according to that position*, is perspective; which, therefore, is the first essential of picture."—*Philosophical Magazine.*

SWEET-SCENTED CHINA ROSE.

The following mode of propagation is easy and expeditious:—Put a plant or two into the hot-house in January or February, and there will soon be some young shoots: as soon as they have three or four leaves, take them off, no matter how tender or succulent, *but never remove or shorten a leaf.* Having prepared your cuttings, put them into sand, with a glass over them, in the same heat as the plants, and in three weeks they will be ready to be potted off. Thus continue taking fresh cuttings, or topping the cuttings already struck, till there are as many as you want. I propagated upwards of one hundred plants in one season, from a small plant which only afforded three cuttings at the commencement.—*Gardener's Mag.*

SAVINGS' BANKS.

According to Mr. Pratt, the number of depositors in savings'-banks in England and Ireland, between November 1831 and November 1833, increased 45,755; and the additional amount deposited was £1,403,464. The total number of depositors in all the banks was 475,155, and the whole amount deposited, £15,715,111. The increase in England in the above period, amounting to eight per cent, and in Ireland (a fact no less gratifying than extraordinary, considering the state of that distracted country) to twenty-five per cent.—*Literary Gazette.*

Effectual Means of curing a Cut, Bruise, or Burn, is said to be the inside coating of the shell of a raw egg. Apply the moist surface to the wound; it will adhere of itself, leave no scar, and heal any wound, without pain.

STOCKHOLM.

STOCKHOLM.

In giving views of places, our engravings have in general been confined to Ireland. We have been induced to copy the above from an engraving at the head of a mercantile letter from Stockholm, in order to recommend to the mercantile men of our own country the adoption of a similar heading to their letters. It would not only prove a very efficient means of promoting the fine arts amongst us, were our merchants thus to give encouragement to young men of talent to sketch and engrave designs of our principal buildings, but would also afford to strangers at a distance some idea of the beauty and proportions of those elegant edifices with which the city is adorned.

Stockholm is not only the capital of Sweden, but the principal emporial of the entire country. It is the great centre of import and export; and has a fine harbour, with great depth of water. Its chief exports consist of iron, steel, copper, tar, and timber, which are, generally speaking, of a superior quality. It is situated at the junction of the lake Maelar with an inlet of the Baltic. It stands on three islands—the situation being extremely picturesque. The central island constituted the old city, and is still the most busy part of the town. Its quays are bounded by a stately range of buildings, the residences of the principal merchants. It also contains the palace and other public buildings; but its houses being high, and its streets narrow, it has rather a gloomy appearance. The other divisions of the city, called Sodermalen and Naormalen, though not having so many public buildings, are better laid out, and more attractive in their appearance. On an eminence called the Mount of Moses, nature and art have combined their powers to render the scene effective. It displays an assemblage of rocks, houses, plantations, ships, and water, in all the variety of romantic scenery.

DUBLIN:
Printed and Published by P. D. Hardy, 3, Cecilia-street; to whom all communications are to be addressed.
Sold by all Booksellers in Ireland.
In London, by Richard Groombridge, 6, Panyer-alley, Paternoster-row; in Liverpool, by Wilmer and Smith; in Manchester, by Ambery; in Birmingham, by Guest, 91, Steelhouse-lane; in Glasgow, by John Macleod; and in Edinburgh, by N. Bowack

THE
DUBLIN PENNY JOURNAL

CONDUCTED BY P. DIXON HARDY, M.R.I.A.

Vol. III.   APRIL 18, 1835.   No. 116.

NATURAL HISTORY.

1. The Lizard.   2. The Crocodile,   3. The Aligator,   4. The Chamæleon,   5. The Siren,   6. The Salamander,

NATURAL HISTORY.

Wonderful are the works of the great Creator; and in many instances mysterious to the finite comprehension of man. For what purpose such creatures as those represented in the foregoing page, which we have copied from an engraving in the London Encyclopædia, would ever have been formed, is a question which bids defiance to the speculations of philosophy; and must remain unanswered till the veil of mortality be removed, and the light of another world be brought to bear upon the mysteries and motions of the globe we now inhabit.

The various animals represented in the engraving may be said to belong to the same class—a genus of amphibia, belonging to the order of *Reptilia*. They are, no doubt, all, *by name*, familiar to our readers. Who has not heard or read of

THE CHAMÆLEON?

" A lizard's body, lean and long—
A fishes head—a serpent's tongue ;"

With a cylindrical, crooked tail; which can dilate and contract its size like the frog; and, if we can believe all that has been written upon it, can assume at pleasure the various colours of the rainbow. It is a native of Africa and Asia, and has been the subject of much contention among naturalists.

The head of a large chamæleon, is almost two inches long, and thence to the beginning of the tail it is four inches and a half. The tail is five inches long, and the feet two and a half. The thickness of the body is different at different seasons; for sometimes from the back to the belly it is two inches, and sometimes one; for he can blow up and contract himself at pleasure. This swelling and contraction is not only of the back and belly, but also of the legs and tail. The chamæleon will continue blown up for two hours together, and then grow less and less insensibly; for the dilatation is always more quick and visible than the contraction. In this last state he appears extremely lean; the spine of the back is sharp, and all his ribs might be told; the tendons of the arms and legs might also be seen distinctly. The skin is very cold to the touch; and, notwithstanding he seems so lean, there is no feeling the beating of the heart. The surface of the skin is unequal, and has a grain not unlike shagreen, but very soft, because each eminence is as smooth as if it was polished. The head is like that of a fish, being joined to the breast by a very short neck, covered on each side with cartilaginous membranes resembling gills. There is a crest directly on the top of the head, and two others on each side above the eyes, and between these there are two cavities near the top of the head. The muzzle is blunt, like that of a frog : at the end there is a hole on each side for the nostrils; but there are no ears, nor the sign of any. The jaws are furnished with a bone in the form of teeth, of which he makes but little use, as he lives by swallowing flies and other insects without chewing them ; and hence arose the vulgar notion of his living upon air, because he was never seen to eat. The form, structure, and motion of the eyes, have something very peculiar; for they are very large, being almost half an inch in diameter, of a globular figure, and stand out of the head. They have a single eye-lid like a cap, with a small hole in the middle, through which the sight of the eye appears, no bigger than a pin's head, and a shining brown, encircled by a little ring of a gold colour. But the most extraordinary thing relating to the eyes is, that this animal often moves one when the other is entirely at rest; nay, sometimes one eye will seem to look directly forward and the other backward, and one will look up to the sky when the other regards the earth. The four feet are all of equal length; but those before are turned backwards, and those behind forwards. There are five toes on each paw, which have a greater resemblance to hands than feet. They are all divided into two, which gives the appearance of two hands to each arm, and two feet to each leg; and though one of these parts has three toes, and the other but two, yet they seem to be all of the same size. These toes he together under the skin; their shape, however, may be seen through the skin. With these paws the chamæleon can lay hold of the small branches of trees like a parrot. When he is about to perch, he parts his toes differently from birds, placing two behind and two before. The claws are little, crooked, very sharp, and of a pale yellow, proceeding but half way out of the skin, while the other half is hid beneath it. He always wraps his tail round the branches of trees, and it serves him instead of a fifth hand. Some naturalists believe the change of colour to depend upon the feelings of the animal, or upon the different degrees of heat or cold to which it is subjected. It seems similar to blushing, and is probably produced by the greater or less quantity of blood sent into the minute vessels, assisted also by the distension of their immense lungs, which, being expanded with air, render the animal nearly transparent. Previously to the chamæleon's assuming a change of colour, it makes a long inspiration, the body swelling out to twice its usual size ; and, as this inflation subsides, the change of colour gradually takes place. According to D'Obsonville, the blood of the chamæleon is of a violet blue colour; the vessels and cutis yellow; the epidermis transparent : hence, he conceives, that, in consequence of more or less blood being sent to the external arteries, all the shades of colour which the animal presents may be produced.

THE ALIGATOR.

So very great is the resemblance between the aligator and the crocodile, that many naturalists suppose them to be but a variety of the same species. Others, on a closer inspection, have pronounced the American crocodile to be altogether a distinct species from the aligator of the Nile.

The alligator arrives at a size not much inferior to that of the crocodile, specimens having often been seen of eighteen or twenty feet in length. Though the largest and greatest numbers of alligators inhabit the torrid zone, the continent abounds with them ten degrees more north, particularly as far as the river Neus, in North Carolina, in the latitude of about 33°, beyond which they have not been found, which latitude nearly answers to the northernmost parts of Africa, where they are likewise found. They frequent not only salt rivers near the sea, but streams of fresh water in the upper parts of the country, and in lakes of salt and fresh water, on the banks of which they lie lurking among reeds, to surprise cattle and other animals. In Jamaica, and many parts of the continent, they are found about twenty feet in length : they cannot be more terrible in their aspect, than they are formidable and mischievous in their natures, sparing neither man nor beast they can surprise, pulling them down under water, that, being dead, they may with greater facility, and without a struggle or resistance devour them. As quadrupeds do not so often come in their way, they almost subsist on fish ; and as, by the close connexion of the vertebræ, they can neither swim nor run away, but straight forward, and are consequently disabled from turning with that agility requisite to catch their prey by pursuit, therefore *they do it by surprise in the water as well as by land.*

THE CROCODILE.

The crocodile has a compressed jagged tail, five toes on the fore, and four on the hind feet. This is the largest animal of the genus. A young one that was dissected at Siam, an account of which was sent to the Royal Academy at Paris, was eighteen feet and a half long ; the tail was no less than five feet and a half, and the head and neck above two and a half. He was four feet nine inches in circumference where thickest. The hinder legs, including the thigh and the paw, were two feet two inches long ; the paws, from the joint to the extremity of the longest claws, were above nine inches. They were divided in o four toes ; of which three were armed with large claws, the longest of which was an inch and a half, and seven lines and a half broad at the root. The fore legs had the same parts and conformation as the arms of a man, but were somewhat shorter than those behind. The hands had five fingers, the last two of which had no nails, and were of a conical figure, like the fourth toe on the hind paws. The head was long, and had a little rising at the top ; but the rest was flat, especially towards the extremity of the jaws. It was covered with a skin, which adhered firmly to the skull and jaws. The eye was very small in proportion to the rest of the body ; and so placed within its orbit, that the outward part, when shut, was only a little above an inch in length, and ran parallel to the opening of the jaws. The nose was placed in the middle of the upper jaw, near an inch from its extremity, and was perfectly round and flat, being two inches in diameter, of a black, soft, spongy substance, like the nose of a dog. They had twenty-seven dog teeth in the upper jaw, and fifteen in the lower, with several void spaces between them. They were thick at the bottom, and sharp at the point; being all of different sizes, except ten large hooked ones, six of which were in the lower jaw, and four in the upper. The mouth was fifteen inches long, and eight and a half broad, where broadest; and the distance of the two jaws, when opened as wide as possible, was fifteen inches and a half. The skull, between the two crests, was proof against a musket ball, which only rendered the part a little white that it struck against. The skin was defended by a sort of armour, which, however, was not proof against a musket-ball. They have no tongue, but in place of it a membrane, attached by its edges to the two sides of the under jaw. In the stomach of one of these animals, dissected before the English consul, they found the bones of the legs and arms of a woman, with the rings which they wear in Egypt as ornaments.

These animals are seen in some places lying for hours, and even whole days, stretched in the sun, and motionless; so that one not used to them might mistake them for trunks of trees covered with rough and dry bark: but the mistake would soon be fatal: for the seemingly torpid animal, at the near approach of any living creature, instantly darts upon it, and carries it to the bottom. In the times of an inundation they sometimes enter the cottages of the natives, where they seize the first animal they meet with. The crocodile, however, except when pressed with hunger, or with a view of depositing its eggs, seldom leaves the water. Its usual method is to float along upon the surface, and seize whatever animals come within its reach; but, when this method fails, it then goes close to the bank. There it waits in patient expectation of some land animal that comes to drink; the dog, the bull, the tiger, or man himself. It seizes the victim with a spring, and goes at a bound much faster than such an unwieldy animal could be supposed to do; then, having secured the creature both with teeth and claws, it drags it into the water, instantly sinks with it to the bottom, and in this manner quickly drowns it. Sometimes it happens that the creature, wounded by the crocodile, makes its escape; in which case the latter pursues it with great celerity, and often takes it a second time. In these depredations, however, this terrible animal often seizes on another as formidable as itself, and meets with desperate resistance. Combats often occur between the crocodile and the tiger. All tigers are continually oppressed by a parching thirst, that makes them frequent great rivers, whither they descend to drink. On these occasions they are seized by the crocodile, upon whom they turn with the greatest agility, and force their claws into his eyes, while he plunges with his fierce antagonist into the river. There they continue to struggle, till at last the tiger is drowned. A negro, however, with no other weapon than a knife in his right hand, and his left arm wrapped round with a cow-hide, will often venture boldly to attack this animal, in its own element. As soon as he approaches the crocodile, he presents his left arm, which the animal swallows, but as it sticks in his throat, the negro has time to give it several stabs below the chin, where it is easily vulnerable; and the water also getting in it at the mouth, which is held involuntarily open, the creature soon expires. The natives of Siam are particularly fond of the capture of crocodiles, which they take by throwing three or four nets across a river, at proper distances; so that if the animal breaks through the first, it may be caught by one of the rest. When first taken it employs the tail, which is the grand instrument of strength, with great force; but, after many unsuccessful struggles, the animal's strength is at last exhausted.

All crocodiles breed near fresh waters, though they are sometimes found in the sea. They produce their young by eggs, and for this purpose the female chooses a place by the side of the river, or some fresh water lake, to deposit her brood in. She always pitches upon an extensive sandy shore, where she may dig a hole without danger of detection from the ground being fresh turned up. The shore must be gentle and shelving to the water, for the greater convenience of her going and returning; and a convenient place must be found near the edge of the stream, that the young may have a shorter way to go. When all these requisites are adjusted, the animal is seen cautiously stealing up on shore to deposit her burden. The presence of a man, a beast, or even a bird, is sufficient to deter her at that time; and, if she perceives any creature looking on, she infallibly returns. If, however, nothing appears, she then goes to work, scratching up the sand with her fore-paws, and making a hole pretty deep in the shore. There she deposits from eighty to one hundred eggs, of the size and form of a tennis-ball, covered with a tough white skin like parchment. She takes above an hour to perform this task; and then, covering up the place so artfully that it can scarcely be perceived, she goes back to return again the next day. Upon her return, with the same precaution as before, she lays about the same number of eggs; and the day following also a like number. Thus having deposited her whole quantity, and having covered them closely up in the sand, they are soon vivified by the heat of the sun; and at the end of thirty days the young ones begin to break open the shell. At this time the female is instinctively taught that her young ones want relief; and she goes upon land to scratch away the sand and set them free. Her brood quickly avail themselves of their liberty; a part run unguided to the water; another part ascend the back of the female, and are carried thither in greater safety. But the moment they arrive at the water, when the female has introduced her young to their natural element, the male becomes their formidable enemy, and devours as many of them as he can. The whole brood scatters into different parts at the bottom; by far the greatest number are destroyed, and the rest find safety in their agility or minuteness. The eggs of this animal are not only a delicious feast to the savage, but are eagerly sought after by every beast and bird of prey. All along the banks of great rivers, for thousands of miles, the crocodile propagates in such numbers as would soon overrun the earth, were not the vulture appointed by Providence to counteract its fecundity.

THE SALAMANDER

Has a short cylindrical tail, four toes on the fore feet, and a naked, porous body. This animal has been said, even in the Philosophical Transactions to live in the fire: but this is a mistake. It is found in the southern countries of Europe. Whilst the hardest bodies cannot resist the violence of fire, the world have endeavoured to make us believe, that a small lizard can not only withstand the flames, but even extinguish them. This lizard, which is found in so many countries of the ancient world, and even in very high latitudes, has been very little noticed, because it is seldom seen out of its hole, and because for a long time it has inspired much terror. One of the largest of this species, preserved in the late French king's cabinet, is seven inches five lines in length, from the end of the muzzle to the root of the tail, which is three inches eight lines.

It was long believed that the salamander was of one sex; and that each individual had the power of engendering its like, as several species of worms. This is not the most absurd fable which has been imagined with respect to the salamander; but, if the manner in which they come into the world is not so marvellous as has been written, it is remarkable in this, that it differs from that in which most other lizards are brought forth, as it is analogous to that in which the chalcide and the seps, as well as vipers and several kinds of serpents, are produced. On this account the salamander merits the attention of naturalists much more than on account of the false and brilliant reputation it has so long enjoyed. M. de Maupertuis, having opened some salamanders, found eggs in them, and at the same time some young perfectly formed; the eggs were divided into two long bunches like grapes, and the young were enclosed in two transparent bags; they were equally well formed as the old ones, and much more active. The salamander, therefore, brings forth young from an egg hatched within its belly, as the viper; and her fecundity is very great; naturalists have long said that she has forty or fifty at once; and M. de Maupertuis found forty-two young ones in the body of a female salamander, and, fifty-four in another. The young ones are generally black, almost without spots; and this colour they preserve sometimes during their whole lives in certain countries, where they have been taken for a distinct species.

THE GREEN LIZARD.

The green lizard of Carolina is so denominated from its colour. This species is very slender, the tail is near double the length of the body, and the whole length about five inches. It inhabits Carolina; where it is domestic, familiar, and harmless. It sports on tables and windows, and amuses with its agility in catching flies. Cold affects the colour; in that uncertain climate, when there is a quick transition in the same day from hot to cold, it changes instantly from the most brilliant green to a dull brown. They are a prey to cats and ravenous birds. They appear chiefly in summer; and at the approach of cold weather retire to their winter recesses, and lie torpid in the hollow crevices of rotten trees. A few warm, sunshiny days often so invigorate them, that they will come out of their holes and appear abroad; when on a sudden, the weather changing to cold so enfeebles them, that they are unable to return to their retreats, and die of cold.

THE SIREN.

Notwithstanding the fabulous history of the Siren, recent naturalists have classed the species in no higher a grade than that of muræna, which includes *eels* of every description.

The sirens, or sirenes, in fabulous history, were celebrated songstresses, who were ranked among the demigods of antiquity, as half women and half fish. Some say that the Syrens were queens of the islands named Sirenusæ, and chiefly inhabited the promontory of Minerva, upon the top of which that goddess had a temple, built by Ulysses. Others tell us of a certain bay, contracted within winding straits and broken cliffs, which, by the singing of the winds and beating of the waters, returns a delightful harmony that allures the passenger to approach, who is immediately thrown against the rocks, and swallowed up by the violent eddies. Horace calls idleness a siren. But the fable may be applied to pleasures in general, which, if too eagerly pursued, betray the incautious into ruin.

Browne, in his "Vulgar Errors," observes, "Few eyes have escaped the picture of a mermaid, with woman's head above, and fishy extremity below, answering the shape of the ancient Sirens that attempted upon Ulysses—

    " ' Did sense persuade Ulysses not to hear
        The *mermaids'* songs, which so his men did please,
      That they were all persuaded, through the ear,
        To quit the ship, and leap into the seas ?' "

The following description of a Mermaid, is given by a Correspondent of the Magazine of Natural History :—"A few years back a mermaid was shown in London. This specimen was said to come from Japan. I can aver that it came from the East Indies ; for, being at St. Helena in 1813, I saw it on board the ship which was bringing it to England. The impression on my mind was, that it was an artificial compound of the upper part of a small ape with the lower half of a fish; and being allowed to examine it as closely as I pleased externally, my attention was directed, by the aid of a powerful glass, to ascertain the point of union between the two parts. I confess I was somewhat staggered to find that this was so neatly effected, that the precise line of junction was not satisfactorily apparent. I speak of it in its best state of preservation; perhaps now the imposture can be more easily detected. A short time back, the skeleton of a mermaid, as it was called, was brought to Portsmouth, which had been shot in the vicinity of the island of Mombass. This was allowed to be submitted to the members of the Philosophical Society, when it proved to be the Dugong. The anatomy and natural history was illustrated by some of the members present, and briefly noticed in the Annual Report for 1826-7, p. 21. To those who came to the examination with preconceived notions of the fabulous mermaid, it certainly presented, as it lay on the lecture-table, a singular appearance. It was, if I recollect right, about six feet long: the lower dorsal vertebræ, with the broad caudal extremity, suggested the idea of a powerful fish-like termination ; whilst the fore legs, from the scapula to the extremities of the phalanges, presented to the unskilful eye an exact resemblance to the bones of a small female arm. The cranium, however, had such an *outre* brutal form, that even the most sportive imagination could never have supposed it to have borne the lineaments of the ' human face divine.' It is now, I believe, in London."

THE BOA CONSTRICTOR.

THE ANACONDA.

THE BOA CONSRICTOR AND ANACONDA.

These immense animals, many of which measure from thirty to forty feet in length, are in zoology a genus of the order "*serpentes*," of the class amphibia. The boa constrictor has a very thick body, of a dusky white colour, is marked on the back with twenty-four large, pale, irregular spots, having its sides beautifully variegated with pale spots, and its tail of a dark colour.

The head is covered with small scales, and has no broad laminæ betwixt the eyes, but has a black belt behind them. The tongue is fleshy, and very little forked. Above the eyes, on each side, the head rises high. The scales of this

serpent are all very small, roundish, and smooth. It frequents caves and thick forests, where it conceals itself, and suddenly darts out upon strangers, wild beasts, &c. When it chooses a tree for its watching place, it supports itself by twisting its tail round the trunk or a branch, and darts down upon sheep, goats, tigers, or any animals that come within its reach, twists itself several times round their body, and by the vast force of its circular muscles, bruises and breaks all their bones. After the bones are broken, it licks the skin of the animal all over, besmearing it with a glutinous kind of saliva. This operation is intended to facilitate deglutition, and is a preparation for swallowing the whole animal. If it be a stag, or any horned animal, it begins to swallow the feet first, and gradually sucks in the body, and last of all the head. After this serpent has swallowed a stag or a tiger, it is unable for some days to move; the hunters, who are well acquainted with this circumstance, always take this opportunity of destroying it. The Indians, who adore this monstrous animal, use the skin for clothes, on account of its smoothness and beauty. There are several of these skins preserved, and to be seen in the different museums of Europe. The flesh is eaten by the Indians and Negroes of Africa.

The Anaconda is supposed to be the Boa of Linnæus. It is the name given in the island of Ceylon to a large and terrible rattle-snake, which frequently devours the unfortunate traveller entire and alive. It is itself eaten by the natives of the country.

Mr. Pringle, in his African Sketches, mentions several curious particulars relative to a species of these animals, which he met with during his residence in that country :—

" I must not omit to say something also of the serpents, a class of the animal creation for which Africa is so renowned. The species commonly accounted the most dangerous at the Cape are the *cobra-capella* (which is not the *cobra di capello* of India), the *puff adder* (*vipera inflata*, Burch.) and the *berg-adder* (or mountain snake. The first of these is exceedingly fierce and active, and sometimes, it is said, attains the formidable length of six or seven feet; I have, however, never met with any of much more than five. The cobra has been known to spring at a man on horseback, and to dart himself with such force as to overshoot his aim. The puff-adder, on the other hand, is a heavy and sluggish animal, very thick in proportion to its length, and incapable, when attacked in front, of projecting itself upon its enemy. To make amends, however, it possesses the faculty of throwing itself backward with perilous and unexpected effect. But its disposition is inert, and unless accidentally trod upon, or otherwise provoked, it will seldom attack mankind.

" There is another species of serpent a good deal dreaded by the natives, from whom I obtained the following account of it. It is about three feet in length: its bite, though poisonous, is not fatal; but its peculiar property is the faculty it possesses of spouting its venom in the face of an assailant, or of any person approaching it within three or four paces, when the wind is in its favour. From this singular faculty. it is called by the Cape colonists the *spuig-slang*. or spirting-snake. If the venom enters the eyes, towards which the animal is supposed by instinct to squirt it, immediate blindness ensues. Several instances of permanent loss of sight from this cause were mentioned to me by intelligent Hottentots, whose veracity I had no reason to question.

" During my residence in the Cape Colony and in the course of various journeys through the interior, I met with a considerable number of snakes; yet I do not recollect of ever being exposed, except in one instance, to any imminent danger from these reptiles. On the occasion referred to I was superintending some Hottentots, whom I had employed to clear away a patch of thicket from a spot selected for cultivation, when one of the men suddenly recoiling, with signs of great alarm, exclaimed that there was a *cobra-capella* in the bush. Not being at that time fully aware of the dangerous character of that species, I approached to look at him. The Hottentots called out to me to take care, for he was going to spring. Before they had well spoken, or I had caught a view of the reptile, I heard him hiss fiercely, and then dart himself towards me amidst the underwood. At the same instant, instinctively springing backward to avoid him. I fell over a steep bank into the stony bed of the Lynden; by which I suffered some severe bruises, but fortunately escaped the more formidable danger to which I had too incautiously exposed myself. The Hottentots then assailed the snake with sticks and stones, and forced him (though not before he had made another spring and missed one of them still more narrowly than myself) to take refuge up a mimosa tree. Here he became a safe and easy mark to their missiles, and was speedily beaten down, with a broken back, and consequently incapable of further mischief. The Hottentots having cut off his head, carefully buried it in the ground, a practice which they never omit on such occasions, and which arises from their apprehension of some one incautiously treading on the head of the dead snake, and sustaining injury from its fangs; for they believe that the deathful virus, far from being extinguished with life, retains its fatal energy for weeks, and even months, afterwards. This snake measured nearly five feet in length.''

THE ROCK OF CASHEL.

In some of our previous numbers, we gave views of detached portions of these very interesting ruins. The fore-going will afford a correct idea of the entire buildings, as they stand together.

THE CLANDESTINE MARRIAGE.

AN IRISH ETCHING, BY DENIS O'DONOHO.

To what fearful consequences one false step may lead us! How vain are then the regrets we feel, and how bitter the remorse! The path of sin once entered on, it is hard to withdraw from its seducing maze; and we may contemplate at an immeasurable distance the peaceful scenes of virtue we have lost, and feel the barrenness of the vice we have preferred!

"Good morra, Phelim! How goes id wid you the day?" said Bill Gerrity on meeting with his old boon companion, Phelim O'Donoho, at the cross-roads, near the ancient village of S——.

"Good morra an' good loock," responded he; "faix an' I'm purty hearty, thank you, an' I hope I find you the same. How is the sister, an' all the people? I hope this fine weather's bringin' round the ould chap!"

"All well, Phelim, a hagur; an', glory be to God! thrivin', and gettin' on betther an' betther every day."

"Is there any gossip at all at all, Bill, since I seed you last? Are any ov the girls marrid, or is there an incrase in any ov the families?"

"Sorra a haporth worth spakin' ov."

"How's Jim Courtney, an' Ellen, the beauty of the world? Is she off yet, or are the boys fightin' about her as usual—foolish crathurs?"

"Ah, thin, Phelim, are you in arnest all out in axing that—an' hav'nt you heerd about her? Och, I see you're takin' a wind at me. Well, you're welcome to yer joke."

"Here about her? Welcome to me joke?" reiterated Phelim. "Be the——no, I won't curse; bud, may the pipe burst in me mouth, iv I'm jokin'!"

"Well, that bates still-huntin'! An' so, Phelim, you raally don't know about Ellen Courtney, an' her runaway match?"

"No, Bill darlin', in throth; bud tell us about id at wanst—or stay tall we see iv we have the price ov a naggin among us, an' we'll take a dhrop in Missis Mulligan's here, iv you're not undher a vow!"

Having then clubbed, and found that all was right in that particular, the cronies entered Missis Mulligan's residence, which was a mud cabin, newly covered with thatch and whitewash, where "Enthertainmint for man an' baste," was written by "the ganius ov the village," with a few lines of poethry appended, describing the good fare to be had within. For this specimen of his abilities the ganius received a glass of the native whenever he passed; which began to be so often, that the widow, for so was Missis Mulligan, was "obleeged to hould her hand:" and then the infuriated poet teemed with indignation at the ingratitude of the world, and the heartlessness of its inhabitants. Poets are certainly not only threadbare and sensitive in coats, but also in feeling!

Bill's disclosure could be in no wise interesting to the reader, if we did not stop every moment to explain; and so deeming it more explicit at once to relate it in our own way, we shall adopt that resolve.

Ellen Courtney was the only daughter of "ould Jim," as her father was familiarly called; and as her mother was snatched away before she was old enough to estimate her loss, and he had not married a second time, when she grew up a little, he was the only being her heart had to turn to, with its load of young affection. From her very infancy she was indulged in every whim; and the old man's very existence was centered in her. They were hardly ever asunder, and as her temper was naturally gentle, mild, and amiable, and her heart open and generous, all her thoughts, feelings, and impulses, were freely confided to his keeping; and he, loving her as he did, could sympathise, consult with, and advise her, with the freedom of one more her equal in years! Ellen was a pretty child, with mild bright eyes and yellow hair, curling naturally around her healthy, blooming face; as she advanced in years, her childish beauty seemed to ripen, and become doubly engaging, and at eighteen a host of admirers told of her charms being appreciated by others, and a more studied arrangement of her simple dress, with a certain coquettish pout about the corners of her mouth, of their being equally appreciated by herself.

Ellen's fault—a fault that was visible in her every turn —was vanity of self, and thirst for admiration. If she had fifty lovers, she had smiles for them all, and could listen to their unstudied compliments with untiring pleasure; and so Ellen, at an early age—too early an age for such a failing—had settled down into what might be termed a regular coquette. Her father had amassed together what might be termed a considerable fortune for a person in his rank of life; and as it was well understood that she had no other relations to interfere in the succession, a host of interested admirers was buzzing about her, as well as those who were caught by her attractions.

One of those, named Corney Brady, was the most constant in his attendence; and though not favoured at all by the old man, appeared otherwise with Ellen: and, in fact, the only serious quarrel ever she had with her father, was on his telling her peremptorily to cease all communication with him—an advice which she heeded for a time, and then disobeyed, as inclination led her to act so. Corney Brady was singularly handsome and prepossessing in appearance—was always smartly dressed—and sometimes sported trinkets and other costly articles, at which his rivals dared not attempt to approach. No one knew who he was; and yet he was saluted and spoken to by all, for he had a certain off-handed, free air, that soon made acquaintance; and though they could not exactly recollect where they saw him first, still Corney certainly was at the last wake, and Corney certainly sided with them at the last wrestling match, and threw his man: and thus his intimacy was admitted by the young and old—the former wondering sometimes how he lived, as he always appeared to have little to do, and the latter shaking their heads at his approach, and hoping all was as it should be. He had no settled place of residence in or about the village, and it was at the ale-house he generally took up his quarters for the night—where, as he sported his money liberally, he enjoyed that "freedom at an inn," which Shenstone has so celebrated.

There was a certain air of mystery thus thrown about him, and as his manner was different at times, and full of strange inconsistencies, Ellen felt, she knew not why, a preference to his society above that of all the rest. To whatever place of merriment, wedding, or wake (for both are equally so!) she went, she was sure to meet him; and there was that in his large, black, admiring eyes, and the gentle fervour of his expressed thoughts, which silently, and almost unconsciously, banished the doubts which her better reason suggested, and made her forget the warnings and advices of her father. He was at last so incensed at perceiving that she was inclined to disobedience, that he forbid entirely any intercourse between them; and she, deeming him harsh, scarcely hesitated to break through the admonition. One false step led on to another, till at length a clandestine correspondence was established; and so infatuated did she at last become, that she left her home, her father, and all, and eloped with the man he had desired her to avoid, trusting in his representations, and relying on his promises!

When her father rose on the following morning, and found no daughter ready to receive him at the breakfast-table, a chill rushed upon his soul, and he ascended, with forced calmness to her room—but it had been unoccupied during the night. He then sat down, and covering his face with his hands, wept with that deep and bitter agony which the aged must feel before they are moved to tears. The daughter in whom he trusted had deceived him— he suspected the man who was the companion of her flight—and he could not tell, but that even at that moment she was a guilty one, unworthy of all his love and fondness!

Ellen was overpersuaded against her better reason, when she consented to steal from the roof beneath which she had always found shelter, and meet the man whom her father had desired her to shun; and even as she went, a voice within, which would not be stilled, told her that she might yet repent. It was a gloomy, dark night, and a slight drizzling mist was falling heavily on the ground, as she drew near the place of appointment; and her very soul trembled, as she did not perceive any one apparently waiting. However, immediately after she forgot all in the warm embrace with which she was received by Corney, who was accompanied by another man, who held two shaggy mountain ponies for them to ride. Having taken her seat, and resigned the rein entirely to this man's guidance, Corney gave the word, and they set off at a smart pace, the man who held her rein running by the pony's side with untiring lightness and vigour. She perceived shortly after, that they had struck off from the regular path, and followed a kind of uneven mountain-track, which they pursued for some time; while Corney subdued the agitation of her mind, by his expressions of tenderness, and assurances of safety.

Suddenly they made a full stop, when they came in front of a low, half-ruined hovel, through the small window of which a bright light was glancing; and as the clatter of the animals' hooves was heard, the door instantly opened, and an aged woman, with grey hair and sharp pinched features, made her appearance. Ellen then was assisted by Corney to dismount; and having led her in, and placed her before a cheerful turf fire, he pressed her lips, and welcomed her to his home. She then felt a double misgiving within her, at the idea of his residing in such a lonely, deserted spot; and as the first tinges of fear and conscience began to be made apparent, she fervently wished that she had never left her father. A few minutes afterwards and Corney, who together with the old woman had retired for a moment to the inner room, again made his appearance, accompanied by the same man whom she had before seen, and another clad in a suit of dingy black much the worse for the wear, and bearing a small clasped volume in his hands. He was introduced to her as Father Philemy; and shortly after joined their hands, and blessed them, the witnesses to the marriage being the man before mentioned, and the old crone, from whose forbidding features the timid Ellen shrank with ill-concealed disgust and fear. The ceremony, such as it was, being over, she was again left alone with Corney; and though he did every thing in his power to render her situation comfortable, she could not but feel that she had acted wrong, and that she would willingly return again to her father. Such was the wedding night of Ellen Courtney!

On the very evening following that of her marriage, her husband, telling her that he was obliged to leave her for a short time, went out, and did not return even when night had fallen. She grew very uneasy, and went repeatedly to the door to watch for his approach; and at length, about eleven, she perceived some one coming up the narrow road, and her heart bounded with expectation—but it was a stranger—a tall, dark, villanous looking man, who appeared extremely agitated and hurried. He started on perceiving her, and then unceremoniously brushing by her, entered the cabin, and she heard him curse the old woman who was sitting inside.

"*Thonna mondhoul!* who's the white-faced *colleen* standin' there now? It is some ov Corney's ould thrick's, I'll ingage!"

"Hoosh! hoosh! *be dhu husth*, Jack!" the crone muttered in reply; "yer absince previnted yer knowin'—he's marrid to her—she's"——

"*He marrid!* hah! hah! hah!" laughed the man, while the timid listener's flesh actually crept—"the tiger marrid to the lamb!—ha, ha, ha! Bud who is she?"

The answer was in a whisper too low for Ellen to hear; and soon after the intruder came forth, and bending a look of curiosity on her from beneath his shaggy brows, stalked rapidly away up the mountain, towards the very wildest part of that region where all was rock and bog.

Shortly after this her husband made his appearance, and she ran forward joyously to meet him, half-forgetting the alarm she had felt at the whispers she had overheard, and the appearance of the man who had just departed.

When they had entered the cabin, and were sitting by the fire together, her thoughts returned, and she fixed her eyes on him and asked—

"Corney, I don't know what to think ov a man who come in a few minutes ago, an' cursed about me bein' here, and wint up the mountain there, as if he was afther committin' some crime, an' was flyin'!"

"What man was here?" suddenly asked he of the crone, not minding to answer her.

"Only Jack Lonergan himself," answered she, "goin' acrass the hills to buy wool fur the spinnin'."

"Oh, Ellen," then said he, "he's a quite crathur as iver was born, an' a fosther brother ov mine into the bargain; an', you know, we're not all to be taken be our looks!"

"That's just what my father used to say ov you, Corney, little thinkin' that I niver minded him, or was a disobedient girl, who loved a sthranger well enough to lave his side for *him!*" and her eyes filled, in spite of herself, with tears, as she thought of that father now abandoned and in grief. "Bud whin may I go to kneel at his feet, an' ask him to forgive us!"

"To-morrow, darlin! iv you plase," said Corney, half abstractedly, for he had been musing ever since she had began to speak. Those fits, even in the days of her courtship, were usual with him; but now she could not bear to see him thoughtful, and so playfully tapping his cheek, she exclaimed, in gay light tones, while the tears summoned up at the idea of her father yet were watery in her eyes—

"Why, Corney *asthore,* what's the matther wid you? —you don't seem glad to see Ellen. You often said, iv you'd be a day away you'd die; an' now you've been nearly so, au' are as silent as iv you'd been robbin' a priest."

This banter she in a moment perceived was any thing but well received, and so she grew serious, and he continued silent, and she placed her hand in his, but it returned no pressure. Her heart grew full. She recollected all that she had heard of man's treachery: and the hour, the lone hovel, the strange visitor, the priest that united them —all formed so sombre a picture, that she held in her breath to try to repress a heavy sob, but could not, and burst into a passion of tears. Corney was moved at this, and passed his arm round her, and drew her to his breast, and addressed her in words of endearment, which fell like balm in an instant on her heart; and so well did she love him, that in a moment again the sensitive girl had dried her eyes, and was conversing with him in tones of deep, though subdued, happiness, and hazarding various conjectures as to the reception she should meet with on the morrow. Corney pleaded fatigue, and they retired early to rest, her heart relieved completely of those busy fears which fancy had conjured up, and anticipating a joyful meeting with her father; and a life passed with all its cares equally divided between him and her adored husband.

The following morning, attended by her husband, Ellen sought her father's house; and she being his only child, and it her first offence, is it to be wondered at, that his arms were opened to receive her, and that she obtained a full pardon? The old man did not utter a syllable of reproof, for reproof would *then* be useless; but as he strained her to his breast, he blessed her, and prayed that she might never live to repent her choice, or regret her acting against his sincere and uninterested advice.

Brady came home to live at the old man's house, and assisted in the cultivation of his farm; and for a few months—short and happy months to Ellen—was attentive to his duties, and affectionate in his manners, as her father could wish him to be. But after this a sudden change came over him, and he began to drop hints of a wish to settle for himself, and about his wife's fortune, and was rather pressing in his demands on his father-in-law's purse. Ellen strove to shut out from her mind an idea that would sometimes intrude, of his being actuated by interested motives from the first; and now at his continual pressing her to ask her father for money, she became alarmed: and as he began to have long intervals without seeing her, during which no one knew where he was, a terrible certainty of her suspicions would intrude on her, turning her heart's joy to bitter, bitter tears.

One evening, after an unusually long absence, he entered the sitting room, where she was alone, and flung himself sullenly into a chair without speaking. Upon which she approached, and laying her hand on his shoulder, gently asked if any thing was the matter.

"Yes!" he harshly answered, without turning his eyes to look at her—"you know there is—I want money, an' yer father won't give id. Bud why do I tell you this?— what do you care!"

" Oh! Corney, *this* from you!" said the poor girl. " Have I deserved it at *your* hands ?—indeed, indeed, I haven't !"

" What do you mane ?" said he, with a deep contraction of his brows.

" What do I mane, Corney? Do you ask me this? Didn't I lave me father fur you ?—didn't I give up every thing fur you? an' you say afther, I don't care. Oh, dear Corney, you're changed an' akthered since thin !"

" Well, well, I can't help that. I didn't think then that it would turn out as it has. I thought yer father id give some ov his useless goold to make us happy; bud I was desaved, an' so let him keep id, an' you may encourage him—I don't care."

" Oh, Corney! Corney!"

" Yes, you encourage him! Don't I know you do ?" he cried, in increasing passion, and energy of manner— " what else id make him 'refuse me bud that ?—I'll wring id out ov him at last, an' no thanks to you, though !"

" Oh, me dear husband," cried the affrighted girl, " don't say that! I'm afeard ov you whin you spake so, an' think bad ov you, bud I can't help id. Listen to me now—listen to yer own Ellen—listen to the wife who loves you! I'll go an' ask him fur what you want—on me knees I'll ask him, an' he won't refuse. Bud Corney, dear Corney, don't spake to me any more as you've spoken now, or you'll kill me—indeed you will !"

Her father here entered; and perceiving that something was the matter, inquired into it : and Brady, who appeared to have been drinking, was doubly violent, and his wife could do nothing but weep, so it ended in high words and a quarrel : and Corney, in a storm of passion, left the house, vowing never to return, and cursing with a vehemence that made the old man shudder. Such were some of the events consequent on Ellen's clandestine marriage.

Three or four days elapsed, and still he returned not, and Ellen wept in anguish over the wreck of her heart's imagining of happiness. When the sixth day came, and brought no sign of Corney, she determined in the quiet of her chamber, that she would go seek him, and ask if he intended to abandon her; for she felt that with all his unkindness she still loved him, and that he still was her husband. This scheme she communicated to none, even to her father, for she knew that he would interfere to prevent her; and so at nightfall she stole silently from the house, and took the path which led to the hovel in the mountains, where they had been wedded, and where something told her that she yet might hear of him. The night continued rapidly to become more dense as she proceeded; and by the time that, weary and jaded, she had attained the bridle-road leading from the direct one, it was dark as pitch—not a single star being discernable in the heavens, and the dull heavy winds moaning loweringly and with a dismal monotony. Her soul sustained itself through all this as she continued to advance: and after an hour's tiresome walking, she at length stood outside the cabin, where she paused. The little window was covered with a board within, so as almost to exclude the light; yet through a couple of chinks a few rays still beamed, and the loud noise of many voices was heard arguing within. She approached the window on tiptoe, and peered long and intensely through one of the narrow slits; and if all emotion had suddenly become numb within her bosom, her face could not in a moment have become more rigid sallow, and utterly bloodless. The fell, the horribly dark solution of all her fears and anxieties was now exposed to her, and she stood like a statue, scarcely daring to sigh lest she should be overheard—detained as if by some spell, and congealed, as it were, with motionless agonising astonishment and awe!

At a low table, on which were two large pistols and a black bottle, sat the same ruffian fig ire which she had seen for a moment before, and there were two others equally desperate in appearance, and who were also armed. Opposite the first one, with his back turned towards the place where she stood, was Corney, his hand grasping a rude drinking vessel, in which he appeared to be pledging his comrades, and his voice drowning theirs completely.

" Yis, boys !" he shouted; " I'll do id, never fear—an', maybe, thin we won't baffle all purshute, as we've long

done. Whoo! there's nothin' I'd stop at wid such fellows as you to back me."

" Don't lave him in a situation to be able to inform !" said the deep voice of the ill-looking ruffian opposite— " Do the job nately !"

" Come, boys !" again said Corney, who was just getting merry, " don't let the bottle stand. Here's my wife's health !—ha, ha, ha !—*my wife !*"

A general laugh and cheer followed this, and the poor trembling listener turned quietly round, unable to bear more, and with the scalding tears streaming down her cheeks, walked slowly in the direction from which she had come—her hopes were all blasted, her joy of soul utterly and irremediably destroyed! She had in the madness, it might be called, of passion, united herself to a ruffian—a robber, and maybe a murderer; and dreadful indeed was the conflict in her bosom as she proceeded towards her once happy home; and willingly would she have given worlds could she recal the events of the last few months, and tear the image of Brady from that heart where she found, and shuddered at the perception, that his image was still enshrined! Oh! it is often thus with us—we would change when it is too late; and find that the indulgence of our passions brings nought but tears and bitter unavailing repentance!

Her aged parent had missed her, and stood at the door looking for her return. He welcomed her with joy, and she shortly retired to rest, though not to sleep. About midnight, the old man, who had sat up watching her, was startled by hearing a rustling sound proceeding from below, where his money and valuables were; and taking the candle, he went forth to ascertain the cause. Ellen, rising up in the bed, pushed her hair from off her ears, and listened to the same noise which had alarmed him. In a second more, she heard the horrid sound of an old man's cry of terror, and her blanched lips trembled convulsively, and her whole frame shook as she arose; and, scarcely knowing what she did, she descended.

The moment she entered the lower room, she perceived her father cast on the ground, while a tall figure, grasping a pistol, stood over him, holding it to his head, and demanding the key of the money-chest. She sprang with the sudden energy of despair, and seized the uplifted arm; upon which the ruffian turned round, and disclosed the features of her husband! He spurned her back—but she still clung to him, and grasping the barrel of the extended pistol, supplicated for her father's life. But as the old man began to rise, he shouted fiercely—" Then die, since you won't let go yer hoult !" and pulling the trigger, the ball entered her breast, and with a piercing sharp cry of agony she fell on her father, bearing him to the ground with her, while a gush of blood spouted over his face. He moaned deeply, and then lay as insensible, and to appearance as dead, as his murdered daughter.

In the morning the old man and his daughter were found in the same position. The aged domestic, who had not heard the shot, was the first to make the discovery. She stood horror-struck; till at last hearing the old man moan, she assisted him to rise, and having placed him in an arm chair, went out to alarm the neighbours. They found the box that contained his hard earnings broken open and rifled; but they remained in uncertainty till the arrival of the magistrate. When the bereaved father recovered sufficiently to give evidence, a thrill of horror pervaded the entire assembly at his declaring the murderer to be his own son-in-law, Corney Brady; and police were immediately dispatched in search of him, while the people remained to do all in their power to soften the old man's affliction—but, alas, the blow was too deep for mortal power to heal! Ellen, the victim of false passion, was interred in the same grave that was shortly after opened to receive her broken hearted father. And the neighbours still relate the story of her fate, as a warning to their children against indulging their own inclinations, contrary to the advice of the experienced. Brady was never discovered, though every exertion was made : but the just hand of an all-seeing Providence *could not* have let him grow gray-headed in his guilt.

Dublin : Printed and Published by P. D. Hardy, 3, Cecilia Street; to whom all communications are to be addressed.

THE
DUBLIN PENNY JOURNAL
CONDUCTED BY P. DIXON HARDY, M.R.I.A.

VOL. III.　　　　　APRIL 25, 1835.　　　　　No. 147.

THE HORSE.

THE HORSE.

In our notices of animals, foreign and domestic, we should suppose that a few observations on that noble animal the Horse, will not be unacceptable to a large proportion of our readers. To enter into a minute detail of the many excellent properties possessed by the various breeds of horses, would lead us far beyond our space.

It has been remarked by an able writer, "that the breed of horses in Great Britain is as mixed as that of its inhabitants; the frequent introduction of foreign horses has given us a variety that no other single country can boast: most other countries producing only one kind; while ours, by a judicious mixture of the several species, by the happy difference of our soils, and by our superior skill in management, has brought each quality of this noble animal to the highest perfection. In the annals of Newmarket may be found instances of horses that have literally outstripped the wind. Childers is an amazing instance of rapidity; his speed having been more than once exerted equal to eighty-two feet and a half in a second, or nearly a mile in a minute. The species used in hunting is a happy combination of the racer with others superior in strength, but inferior in point of speed and lineage: a union of both is necessary; for the fatigues of the chase must be supported by the spirit of the one, as well as by the vigour of the other. No country can bring a parallel to the strength and size of our horses destined for the draught; or to the activity and strength united of those that form our cavalry. In the late campaigns, they showed, over those of our allies, as well as the French, a great superiority both of strength and activity; the enemy was broken through by the impetuous charge of our squadrons; when the German horses, from their great weight and inactive make, were unable to second our efforts. The increase of our inhabitants, and the extent of the manufactures of Britain, together with the former neglect of internal navigation to convey those manufactures, multiplied the number of horses; an excess of wealth, before unknown in these islands, increased the luxury of carriages, and added to the necessity of a culture of these animals: their high reputation abroad has also made them a branch of commerce, and proved another cause of their vast increase."

The following remarks, intended to guide the purchaser in the selection of the particular kind of animal he may require, are copied from a valuable little work, a second edition of which has recently been published.*

---

* Advice to Purchasers of Horses. By J. Stewart, Veterinary Surgeon, and Professor of Veterinary Surgery in the Andersonian University. Glasgow: W. R. M'Phun.

"EXTERIOR CONFORMATION OF THE HORSE.

"There are some peculiarities in the form of the horse, which admirably fit him for one kind of work, but at the same time render him useless, or nearly so, for another. The racer, with his light airy form, delicate limbs, rapid movements, and fiery spirit, is eminently an animal of speed; but yoked to a heavy waggon along with a stout cart horse, he appears comparatively weak and worthless. Though one horse, from his conformation, is best fitted to carry, and another to draw, and another still to do both with decency, yet there are certain points, which it is desirable to have in all horses, for whatever work they may be designed. Such, for example, is a large nostril. which is a good quality in all, and does not, like some others, become a bad one, when the horse is applied to a different purpose. But then, it is one of far more consequence in a horse wanted for quick work, than one whose pace need never exceed a walk. In the one case, it is absolutely requisite, but in the other, is only a secondary consideration.

"The horse in most general use, is a compound of the speed of the racer and the power of the draught horse: and it is the different proportions in which these qualities exist, that make one a hunter, another a hackney, &c. To explain how a certain form makes one horse fleet, and another powerful, would, in most cases, lead to an anatomical consideration of the whole machine, so that in the majority of cases, I can only state the fact. The muscles are the organs of motion, and in proportion to their development the animal is strong; but the bones being the levers upon which the muscles act, that strength, and the horse's action, must be considerably increased or diminished, according as the bone they are attached to is longer or shorter than is usual. The strength is likewise much, and, generally speaking, the extent of action more, influenced, by the *position* of the bone, as in the case of the shoulder blade, which by being long, and slanting from the withers forwards and downwards, gives the horse extensive action as well as strength, while a more upright position (and if upright, it *must* be short likewise) of the same bone, confines the action of the whole limb, and reduces the power of the muscles. The bones, besides, sustain and give form to the whole structure, and add considerably to the weight: consequently their bulk in the draught horse is not a serious objection, for he does much of his work by throwing his weight into the collar, and as it were pushing it before him.

"Notwithstanding the importance of conformation, it is not all that is required. Experience reminds us, that many seemingly faultless animals have lamentably disappointed the expectations their figure had raised, while others, as insignificant in appearance as may be, have surprised good judges by their extraordinary and unlooked for performances. Hence, many horsemen exclaim, that 'there are good horses of all shapes.' The fact is, a great deal depends on the quantum of nervous energy or 'bottom' which the animal possesses, and it is the union of this energy with good conformation that makes many horses invaluable. Its absence or presence, however, is not likely to be discovered by the purchaser, without a trial: and to avoid disappointment in this respect, it is therefore advisable to obtain one prior to purchase. The horse should be set to the work he will be called on to perform, and if he is intended for the saddle or single harness, he should have no companion on his trial, for many horses work well in company, that are downright sluggards when alone.

"Some horses have an unpleasant way of going, or are difficult to manage, or have some vice which is only displayed at work. These are so many more reasons for having a trial prior to striking a bargain. But if that cannot be obtained, some sort of conclusion regarding the animal's spirit may be drawn from his general appearance. The way he carries his head—his attention to surrounding objects—his gait—and the lively motion of his ears, may all or each be looked to as indicative of 'bottom' or willingness to work. It is only, however, in a private stable, or in that of a respectable dealer, that these *criteria* can be depended upon.

"In considering the conformation of the horse, it is convenient to divide him into Head and Neck, Trunk or Carcase, and Extremities, or the Hind and Fore Legs. Under these heads I shall note what are deemed the most essential points, and only those: for there can be no occasion for dilating upon the subject as is usual, when attention is directed to such trifles as, 'the ears should be well placed, small, pointed, erect, covered with thin skin, the eyelids thin, the muzzle thin, and well supported,' &c. Such an account might consistently close by saying, that the horse should have four feet as well as four legs. Until men can make horses as they say they *should* be, the purchaser must content himself if he gets one with those qualities which are most important in fitting him for his destined work, and whose general appearance will do his master no discredit.

"THE HEAD AND NECK.

"The head, as being a part not at all contributing to progression, should, in the saddle horse, be small, that it may be light—the nostrils expanded, to admit plenty of air, and the space between the branches of the lower jaw, called the channel, should be wide, that there may be plenty of room for the head of the windpipe. In the draught horse, a heavy head is not, as far as utility is concerned, an objection, for it enables him to throw some weight into the collar, and hence, excepting its ugliness, it is rather an advantage if he is used entirely for draught. But it makes the saddle horse bear heavy on the hand of the rider, makes him liable to stumble, and, when placed at the end of a long neck, is apt to wear out the four feet and legs by its great weight. The neck of the saddle horse should be thin, not too much arched, and rather short than long, for the same reason that the head should be light: and in the draught horse, it may be thick, stallion-like, and sufficiently long to afford plenty of room for the collar, and for the same reason that the head may be large in this animal. The windpipe should be large, and standing well out from the neck, that the air may have an easy passage to and from the lungs. The horse used for both carrying and drawing, should have a head and neck neither too light nor too heavy. The advantage of a heavy head and neck to a draught horse, is illustrated by the practice of some carters putting a boy on the shoulder of a horse, when starting a load in deep ground. By enabling him to throw the boy's weight besides his own into the collar, it assists him materially.

"THE TRUNK OR CARCASE.

"That the saddle horse may be safe and have extensive action, it is necessary that the withers be high. This advantage is indicated by the horse standing well up before; and it is usual in showing a horse to exaggerate the height of the forehand, by making him stand with his fore feet on a somewhat elevated spot. A horse with low withers appears thick and cloddy about the shoulder. In the ass and mule, the withers are very low, and the shoulders very flat, and this is the reason why they are so unpleasant to ride, and why it is next to impossible to keep the saddle in its proper place without the aid of a crupper. High withers, however, are not essential to the racer or the draught horse. The former does all his work by leaps, and that is performed best when the horse stands somewhat higher behind than before: neither are high withers necessary to the draught horse: but in the roadster they are as important as the safety of the rider is, for a horse with a low forehand is easily thrown on his knees. In the draught horse, this tendency towards the ground is obviated by the support the collar affords.

"The *chest* should be deep and wide in all horses, but especially so in one intended for quick work, in order that there may be plenty of room for those important organs, the lungs. When the chest is deficient in capacity, the horse has neither strength nor endurance; and is in stable language termed 'washy.' Such horses have in general more fire than vigour, and being showy, may carry a lady well enough, but are comparatively worthless for effective service. A narrow chest is indicated by the fore legs standing close to each other.

"The *barrel* behind the girth should approach as nearly

as may be to a cylindrical form, that there may be plenty of room for the digestive organs.

"The *back* should not be too long nor too short, for though length is favourable to an extended stride and rapid motion, yet it makes the horse weak, and unable either to draw or carry any considerable weight. On the other hand, if the back be too short, the horse's action must be confined, and short-backed horses in general make an unpleasant noise when trotting, by striking the shoe of the hind foot against the shoe of the fore one : and though they are in general very hardy, and capable of enduring much fatigue, and of living on but little food, yet a back of middling length is better by far than one immoderately short or long.

" The back should be nearly straight ; when it is curved downwards, the horse is termed 'saddle-backed,' and though he is very easy to ride and pleasant in his pace, yet he is weak, and unable to carry a great weight. Sometimes, instead of being sunk, the spine is arched upwards, and the horse is said to be 'roach-backed.' He is the very reverse of the saddle-backed horse in every respect.

" The *croup*, or space between the termination of the loins and the root of the tail, should be considerable, and in a horse intended for quick work, it should run more in a horizontal than a perpendicular direction. In the Irish horse, this part is short, and instead of proceeding almost directly backwards, suddenly droops; and though such a conformation does not unfit him for trotting, or drawing, or even leaping, and is even an advantage for an upright leap, yet he cannot in the gallop compete with the English horse, whose croup is long, and very little inclined downwards.

" The *quarters* are never too extensive from before backwards, nor deep from above downward, nor are they ever too much spread out laterally. A great deal is done by the hind legs, and the quarters should in every case be as expanded and well furnished with muscles as possible. When the haunch bone projects more than usual, the horse is said to be 'ragged hipped,' and is commonly objected to for it. But as this bone, by spreading well out, affords plenty of room for the attachment of muscles, it cannot be said to be a fault. When it appears so, the loins are the seat of that fault. They are too narrow.

" THE FORE LEG.

" In the saddle horse, and where safety is desirable, the position of the fore leg is worthy of attention. It should be placed well forward, and descend perpendicularly to the ground, the toe being nearly in a line with the point of the shoulder. The pasterns should neither be turned in nor out. When they are turned inwards, the horse is in general very liable to cut the fetlock joint by striking the opposite foot against it. The draught horse may be excused though he leans a little over his fore legs, but the saddle horse will be apt to stumble if he does so.

" The *shoulder* should, like the hind quarter, be extensive, well covered with muscle, and in the saddle horse, where rapid and extensive action is required, it should slant from the withers to the breast. The neck should join the shoulder in such a manner as to seem to run into it. But the draught horse's shoulder should be, and usually is, more upright, that the collar may sit well upon it. The setting on of the neck is more distinct in the draught than in the saddle horse, the shoulder bone being more upright; and the muscles taking a different direction make the shoulder swell out abruptly, and form a seat upon which the collar conveniently rests.

" The *elbow* should be wide from before backwards—the space between it and the knee rather long, and well supplied with muscles—the knee should be broad from before backwards, and *straight* : when it is bent forward, the horse is said to be 'bent before,' and it is, in general, a symptom that he has endured some hard work, and his surefootedness cannot be depended upon. When the knee is bent backwards, it is called a 'calf knee,' and though it is an ugly fault, I am not aware that it is any thing more, although it is possible there may be a little loss of power in the muscles that bend it. Below the knee the leg should be fine, and flat in back and front, and broad from

before backwards. The back tendons should stand equally well out from the knee to the fetlock.

" The *pasterns* in the very heavy draught horse, are, in general, short and nearly upright : and it is necessary that they should be so, in order to uphold his huge frame ; but in the racer, they are long and slanting, in order that, by giving way at every step of the animal, the shock accompanying rapid motion may be destroyed. The purchaser must, therefore, look for a horse, whose pasterns have the proper degree of obliquity for the purpose the horse is to be used for. If the pastern be too long, the leg is very liable to strain, and even the horse to break down when urged to the top of his speed. If it be too upright, the action of the horse is stilty, and very unpleasant to the rider. And besides that, such horses are, from the concussion they are liable to, very subject to diseases of the bones below the knee, such as ring bones, splints, &c.

" The *foot* should be as nearly round as possible, smooth, and displaying no signs of brittleness by pieces being broken and chipped off by the nails; the sole should be but moderately concave; when flat it is objectionable, and particularly so in the heavy, high actioned horse, for there is then a probability of its becoming convex.

" THE HIND LEG.

" I have already spoken of the quarter. The part between the stifle and hock joint, commonly called the thigh, should be long, and, above all, supplied with abundance of muscle.

The *hock* should be broad from before backwards, because when it is so, it shows that a lever (the point of the hock) is long, and, consequently, the muscles that act upon it will have more power to extend the leg. And as it is by the extension of the leg that the animal is projected in the gallop and leap, it is of importance that the hock be broad, and the point projecting backward, in the horse wanted for quick work. The hock should likewise in the same animal be well bent under him. When the hocks lean towards each other, the horse is said to be 'cat-hammed,' or 'cow-hocked.' It is most common in ponies; but setting aside its ugliness, it is not a serious defect : indeed it is commonly thought to make the animal a good trotter. It is certain, that a hock bent outwards is more objectionable, for the weight of the carcase is then like a person placed between two stools. Below the hock, the back tendons and the pasterns should be the same as in the fore leg.

" Short as this account of the conformation of the horse is, it might have been still shorter, for it is a fact, that the existence of one good point is in general sufficient to ensure the possession of another or others. A good shoulder, for instance, rarely goes without good withers, a deep chest, and a well-turned fore leg : but as it sometimes does, I have briefly particularised all that is commonly deemed most essential in the formation of a good useful horse."

THE CHIMNEY SWALLOW.

The following curious account of a settlement of Chimney Swallows, we extract from "An Account of the Habits of the Birds of the United States," by J. Audubon, recently published :

"Immediately after my arrival at Louisville, in the State of Kentucky, I became acquainted with the hospitable and amiable Major William Croghan, and his family. While talking one day about birds, he asked me if I had seen the trees in which the swallows were supposed to spend the winter, but which they only entered, he said, for the purpose of roosting. Answering in the affirmative, I was informed that on my way back to town, there was a tree remarkable on account of the immense numbers that resorted to it, and the place in which it stood was described to me. I found it to be a sycamore, nearly destitute of branches, sixty or seventy feet high, between seven and eight feet in diameter at the base, and about five for the distance of forty feet up, where the stump of a broken hollowed branch, about two feet in diameter, made out from the main stem. This was the place at which the swallows entered. On closely examining the tree, I found it hard, but hollow to near the roots. It was now about four o'clock afternoon, in the month of July. Swallows were flying over Jeffersonville. Louisville, and the woods around, but there were none near the tree. I proceeded home, and shortly after returned on foot. The sun was going down behind the Silver Hills; the evening was beautiful: thousands of swallows were flying closely above me; and three or four at a time were pitching into the hole, like bees hurrying into their hive. I remained, my head leaning on the tree, listening to the roaring noise made within by the birds as they settled and arranged themselves, until it was quite dark, when I left the place, although I was convinced that many more had to enter. I did not pretend to count them, for the number was too great, and the birds rushed to the entrance so thick as to baffle the attempt. I had scarcely returned to Louisville, when a violent thunder storm passed suddenly over the town, and its appearance made me think that the hurry of the swallows to enter the tree was caused by this anxiety to avoid it. I thought of the swallows almost the whole night, so anxious had I become to ascertain their number, before the time of their departure should arrive.

" Next morning I rose early enough to reach the place long before the least appearance of day-light, and placed my head against the tree. All was silent within. I remained in that posture probably twenty minutes, when suddenly I thought the great tree was giving way, and coming down upon me. Instinctively I sprung from it, but when I looked up to it again, what was my astonishment to see it standing as firm as ever. The swallows were now pouring out in a black continued stream. I ran back to my post, and listened in amazement to the noise within, which I could compare to nothing else than the sound of a large wheel revolving under a powerful stream. It was yet dusky, so that I could hardly see the hour on my watch, but I estimated the time which they took in getting out at more than thirty minutes. After their departure, no noise was heard within, and they dispersed in every direction with the quickness of thought.

"I immediately formed the project of examining the interior of the tree, which, as my kind friend, Major Croghan, had told me, proved the most remarkable I had ever met with. This I did, in company with a hunting associate. We went provided with a strong line and a rope, the first of which we, after several trials, succeeded in throwing across the broken branch. Fastening the rope to the line we drew it up, and pulled it over until it reached the ground again. Provided with the longest cane we could find, I mounted the tree by the rope, without accident, and at length seated myself at ease on the broken branch; but my labour was fruitless, for I could see nothing through the hole, and the cane, which was about fifteen feet long, touched nothing on the sides of the tree within that could give any information. I came down fatigued and disappointed.

"The next day I hired a man, who cut a hole at the base of the tree. The shell was only eight or nine inches thick, and the axe soon brought the inside to view, disclosing a matted mass of exuviæ, with rotten feathers reduced, to a kind of mould, in which, however, I could perceive fragments of insects and quills. I had a passage cleared, or rather bored through this mass, for nearly six feet. This operation took up a good deal of time, and knowing by experience that if the birds should notice the hole below, they would abandon the tree, I had it carefully closed. The swallows came as usual that night, and I did not disturb them for several days. At last, provided with a dark lantern, I went with my companion about nine in the evening, determined to have a full view of the interior of the tree. The whole was opened with caution. I scrambled up the sides of the mass of exuviæ, and my friend followed. All was perfectly silent. Slowly and gradually I brought the light of the lantern to bear on the sides of the hole above us, when we saw the swallows clinging side by side, covering the whole surface of the excavation. In no instance did I see one above another. Satisfied with the sight, I closed the lantern. We then caught and killed with as much care as possible more than a hundred, stowing them away in our pockets and bosoms, and slid down into the open air."

INCH CASTLE, CO. KILDARE.

The castle which our woodcut represents, is situate about three miles north-east of Athy, in the parish of Moone, and union of Timolin, and barony of East Narragh and Rheban. It was built by De Veacy, in the reign of King John, and afterwards enlarged by the sixth earl of Kildare, about 1420. There is but one of the towers now remaining, yet, from the extensive foundations, it must have been a place of considerable importance. The land in the neighbourhood lies remarkably flat, with the exception of two ridges that run nearly parallel northward from the castle, with a marsh lying between them.

It was on those heights the armies of Ormond and Mountgarrett, in 1642, marched in sight of each other the evening previous to the battle of Kilrush; that of Ormond on the high grounds of Ardscull, Fontstown, and Kilrush; whilst the rebel army, under Mountgarrett, and attended by the Lords Dunboyne and Ikerrin, Roger Moore, Hugh Byrne, and other leaders of Leinster, proceeded in the same direction, along the height of Birtown, Ballyndrum, Glassealy, and Narraghmore. Mountgarrett having the advantage in numbers, and anxious for battle, out-marched Ormond's forces, and posted himself on Bullhill and Kilrush, completely intercepting Ormond's further progress to Dublin: a general engagement became unavoidable. The left wing of the Irish was broken by the first charge; the right, animated by their leaders, maintained the contest for some time, but eventually fell back on a neighbouring eminence, since called Battlemount; here they broke, fled, and were pursued with great slaughter across the grounds they had marched over the day before. This victory was considered of so much consequence, that Ormond was presented by the English Government with a jewel, value £500.

Indeed the country for miles around Inch Castle has many historical connexions; to the east can be seen the much spoken of Rath of Mullimast, the ancient Carmen, or the enclosed place, which was the *Naasteighan*, where the states of the southern parts of Leinster met. It is situated on a high and gently sloping hill, and near it are sixteen little conical mounts, on which, it is supposed, the chiefs sat in council. Carmen was anathematized in the sixth century, and the place of assemblage of the chiefs, was then removed to the present Nans, one of the shire towns of the county. It takes its present name, Mullimast or *Mullach Mastean*, (the moat of decapitation) from the base conduct of some adventurers in the sixteenth century, who having overrun part of the neighbouring country, were resisted by the Irish chieftains that had properties on the Leix (Queen's county) side of the river Barrow. However, in order to have a final settlement of their differences, it was proposed by the adventurers, that a conference should be held at Carmen, which was agreed to; and on New Year's day, 1577, the chiefs of the Barrow side repaired to the place, where they were treacherously made prisoners and beheaded. Sixty years since a hole was shewed, where it was said the heads of the betrayed were buried; at that period it was twenty feet deep; it is now nearly closed. The successful assassins took possession of their victims' properties, and the barony bears the name of Slieve-Maugue, or the Hills of Mourning to this day.

A little to the north of the castle is also to be seen the Moat of Ardscull, Ascull, or Arstoll, anciently *Rath ais-Cael*,[*] corruptly Rath-ascull. In 1315, the Scots, under Robert Bruce, gained a battle here, and plundered the neighbourhood. The rath stands where the battle was fought, and commands a great extent of country. Hammond le Crose, Sir William Prendergast, and John, Lord de Bonneville, on the part of the Irish; and Fergus Andressan and Sir Walter Murray, of the Scottish party, were slain in this battle and buried in Athy.

About a furlong to the south of Inch Castle, is a small mound or tumulus, rendered interesting by the following tradition:

During the memorable year, 1439, when the plague was silently and awfully depopulating the country, a member of the family of Mac Kelly was in possession of the castle and the surrounding lands. His son, Ulick, was taken ill, and, as was customary, removed to the fields, where a shed was prepared for the occasion. Within a quarter of a mile was the little village of Bally-kil-bawn, (now Ballycolane) where Onny Moore lived with her brothers, and she, also, had been one of the many victims to Ulick Mac Kelly's deceit and treachery; but latterly she became the constant visitor of the *White Church*, whose inmates' lessons of peace and good will had not fallen uselessly on Onny's ears. She could look with calmness on the solitary she had made, with less of a vengeful, and more of a pardoning spirit; and to her, the mortality that raged was divested of half its terrors. It was early on the morning after Ulick was placed in the sick shed, that she was observed to cross the small river, and make her way through the marsh that almost surrounds the castle—and her purpose could be only known to one—she had not revealed it to any. For a few days after, if the inhabitants on the other side of the moor chanced to look .to the sick corner, Onny could be seen in a sitting posture, a few feet from the opening of the tent, with her face turned towards it; and, after many days, when the raven and magpie were found to be the only visitants of the place, the token in those times that the work of death was done, some neighbours ventured near, and found the one putrified in the tent, and the other in her wonted position, but lifeless. The bodies with the shed were reduced to ashes, and a mound raised upon the spot, on which there yet remains seven very old white-thorn trees. Report points it out as a place of no small superstitious dread, and even at this time a female form is said to be often seen sitting near the hill, having a gentle motion from side to side, something in the manner of a woman when oppressed with sorrow.

Connected with the above story, are the following fragments of a ballad, communicated to the writer by a very old person, who remembers it to have been a favourite wake-house song in the neighbourhood:

" Oh ! hear me sogarth's[†] of Kilbawn,[‡]
  Oh ! listen to my sorrows ;
The clouds hang heavy o'er the home,
  Of Onny's harden'd brothers.

---

[*] There appears to have been much mistake in attributing the erection of raths to the Danes; the word signifies a pledge. Long before the invasions of the Danes they were constructed by the Irish chieftains and their dependants, and called raths or pledges, for the fealty and due subordination of the adjacent country. Had raths been erected by the Danes, they would have been prostrated on their expulsion; but, instead of being objects of aversion, they are held in the greatest reverence by the country people. Baron Finglass, who wrote in the year 1510, says, (Brev. of Ireland). "That the English statutes, passed in Ireland, are not observed eight days after passing, whereas those laws made by the Irish on their *hills*, are kept firm and stable, without breaking through them for any favor or reward." This may show, even at that time, the uses to which they were applied.

[†] Priests.

[‡] Whitechurch: it was once called Cean-pul-a-snauta ; the remains still exist near the road side, opposite Ballycolane ; from its stile of architecture it appears to be of great antiquity.

And heavier still, the clouds that lower,
  On Ulick's father's land;
For there, in sadness, lies a flower,
  Strew'd by Ulick's hand.

* * * * *

On moon-light nights the shadow flits
  Across the *ghaise* and moor ;
And at the *cairn* in silence sits,
  Until the midnight hour.

* * * * *

The bittern's[*] only moan is heard,
  Along the waving reeds ;
But the shadow still is feared,
  As Onny's restless shade."

The town of Inch, including Ballycolane, Turnerstown, Foxhill and Glanbane, in all about 1060 acres, was set by the Earl of Kildare to Sir W. Burrows, for twenty-one years, from the 1st May, 1662, for one hundred pounds per annum, a fat ox, or four pounds.

The chiefs of this country were Hy Caelen or Mac Kelly; and it is said that the last master of the castle, Girode-crone Mac Kelly, defended it during his life time with reckless determination.

Several of the foregoing particulars, amongst other sources, are taken from a valuable and interesting work, by the late Captain Thomas J. Rawson, of Cardenton, entitled "A Statistical Survey of the County of Kildare," with an introduction to its ancient history.

ENNA.

METAL IMAGE, FOUND NEAR CLONMEL.

IRISH ANTIQUITIES.

The above engraving is taken from a correct drawing of a curious metal figure which has been lately found in

---

[*] The moor that almost surrounds Inch Castle was remarkable, within the memory of persons yet living, for the number of bitterns found in it; at present the snipe or heather-bleat is the principle occupant.

the neighbourhood of Clonmel, many feet under the surface, where it must have remained from a very remote period. It is conjectured that it has been a Druidical idol.

In height, this curious relique is fifteen inches; its weight twenty-four pounds. It is rather a singular coincidence, that a similar one, but only nine inches high, weighing sixteen pounds, and with the addition of a shield and spear, fell into the hands of the possessor of this antique, a few years ago, from whom it passed into the splendid museum of Henry C. Sirr, Esq. Dublin Castle. This latter one was noticed in the Dublin Literary Gazette of the 10th of April, 1830, which had also, a wood-cut of the antique. Both figures are fac-similes, with the exception above mentioned. This one, however, has two pedestals supporting the figure over a kind of arch, which the other had not. It is in three quarters relief, and the back is quite flat and mural. The present owner of this curiosity is Mr. R. Anthony of Pilltown, of whose gallery and cabinet we gave a short sketch a few months back. The first one to which we allude, was found in the bog of Ballykeerogue, county Waterford. What makes both more extraordinary, is, their being formed of metal, apparently cast.

"A JOURNEY TO FRANCE."

Reader, were you ever in *La Belle France?* Whether or not, you shall have a story something similar to Lover's famous tale of the "Gridiron." You know all about that legend of course ; but mine, however, is a true history founded on facts.

Edward Coppinger, of the city of Dublin, Gent. towards the close of the seventeenth century resolved to undertake a journey to France. His friends considered him mad— still go he would. The occasion was—he had expended large sums of money in law, for the recovery of his wife's marriage portion, which was detained by an unprincipled scoundrel of the name of George Charles Jermyn ; but as it would be tedious and uninteresting to follow up the dry monotonous details of the law, let it suffice to say, that when the affair had almost come to a close, the agent of this gentleman (who was all this time on the Continent) died. It then became necessary to serve the principal with an order of law to appoint another solicitor. To accomplish this object, every means that could be resorted to was used, but without success—money was lavishly expended, but to no purpose. Heart-sickened with each successive failure, with the prospect of beggary staring him in the face, and burthened with a large family, Mr. Coppinger ventured on going to France, and ferreting out his opponent. Fancy an elderly man, weakened by repeated attacks of gout, just rising from a bed of sickness, with a debilitated frame, and not possessing the most remote knowledge of the language, going to a country remarkable for its extent, and, to a stranger, the intricacy of its numerous towns and villages. Having made the necessary preparations, he embarked on board the packet from Plymouth for Havre de Grace. Arrived at Havre, he laughed at the difficulties he had so fearfully anticipated, as, from the concourse of English, he found himself quite at home. I should have apprized the reader before, that he had heard Mr. Jermyn resided in Tours under a fictitious name. When he arrived at his destination, he proceeded with all due caution, lest his enemy might be aware of his approach. Before breakfast the morning after his arrival he took a walk, determined, if possible, to have a peep at the domicile of his opponent. After walking some time, admiring the prospect, but more admiring his own sagacity, he stopped before a very handsome villa, and accosting a boy who was philosophically munging a piece of flat cake bread—

"Tell me, my lad, whose house is that?"

"Je ne sais, Monsieur," replied the garçon, understanding the gesture which accompanied the question, rather than the question itself.

The answer at once recalled Mr. C.—"The deuce take your gibberish," said he "can't you answer me like a Christian—whose house is that?"

This observation attracted the attention of a gentleman passing by, who very politely inquired, could he be of any

assistance, at the same time begging pardon for laughing— "But really I could not refrain," continued he, "your remark was so singular."

Mr. Coppinger thanked him, and replied, "I have quite forgotten where I am—I was inquiring who that beautiful villa belonged to."

"It is at present unoccupied. It was inhabited by Mr. Jermyn a long time ago. The air did not agree with him, and he left it, since which time it has remained unset. I presume you are going to make some stay here. My name is Allen—here is my card—I shall be happy to be of use to you."

Mr. Coppinger thanked him, gave his address, and requested he would call on him. He then returned to the hotel with a bursting heart, in an almost indescribable state of disappointment and distress. All his high fed hopes had fled ; and bitterly did he think of the prospects that were in store for him. He thought of the jeers and laughter that awaited his unsuccessful return. He thought of the family he had left after him, and of their anxious prayers for his safe return. With them, at least, he knew his success was but a secondary consideration ; and for their sake he inwardly determined to undergo every privation, to encounter every danger, and make use of every exertion that man could make for the success of his undertaking. Scarcely tasting the breakfast set before him, he inquired of the host, who tolerably well understood English, owing to the influx of strangers.

"Can you inform me, or find out, where Mr. Jermyn is gone to? I am a particular friend of his, and would like to see him much. If you can procure the information for me, I will reward you for your trouble."

"Monsieur is ver good—tres bon en verité. Mais quant a moi ; je ne sais. Bah ! excusez moi, you no know what I say. Monsieur Jermyn is gone long time—il-y a plus de trois ans qu'il à quitté, et depuis ce temps, pas de nouvelles ! Mais, you no listen, you no understand. I vill bring M. Allen, il est Angleterre—he vill do what you vant. Monsieur est fort poli."

Mr. Coppinger, who had been pacing the room during the Frenchman's harangue, in despair of understanding him, at once acceded to the proposal, and begged he would lose no time. In a short time Mr. Allen made his appearance, and from him he learned that Mr. Jermyn had departed quite suddenly, after selling his furniture. No one knew where he was, but it was conjectured he had gone to England, or to some part of Normandy.

"He is a man," added Mr. Allen, "eccentric and retired in his habits, and not much prone to indulge idle curiosity ; so that taking every thing into account, I rather imagine you will be unlikely to meet with him."

This was the only information could be procured. On Mr. Allen's suggestion, Mr. Coppinger purchased a book of French and English dialogues ; and after staying two or three days in Tours, he mounted the diligence, not knowing, and not caring, where its destination was. On he went for the length of the day, silent as the grave ; for the best possible reason, he had no one to address that understood him. He had paid what they demanded from him on starting, so he met with no interruption, save when his passport was twice examined. At night they stopped at a small town, where they slept. On getting up the next morning, he found himself in a strange place, without a being to understand a sentence from him. After an untasted breakfast, with the big tear standing in either eye, he walked towards the seashore, which he perceived from the window. After walking about until wearied with disappointment and vexation, he bent his steps towards the inn. When he arrived, he was delighted to see a gentleman standing at the doorway who from his appearance he thought to be his countryman. He immediately accosted him—

"Sir," said he, "by your manner I take you to be an Englishman—I beg you may confirm the surmise by your language. For the last two days I have not heard the sound of my own voice."

"Then, Sir," responded the other, "make amends for your silence—indeed I am delighted to see one of my countrymen. We must be better acquainted."

On a little further conversation, Mr. Coppinger found this stranger friend to be a Colonel Wharton, who had seen compelled to leave Ireland owing to some disturbances, and who, getting into the French service, had attained the rank of colonel. Many were the questions he asked, numerous the inquiries he made after absent friends—some were alive, some were dead, some were inhabitants of foreign climes; and the soldier felt so grateful for news thus unexpectedly told, that he panted for an opportunity to oblige his new found friend. Mr. Coppinger opened his whole heart to him. He told him how his property was maliciously withheld from him, and how he had undertaken his present journey to find out his opponent, having in vain employed persons conversant with the country and its language; and finally, he told him his settled resolve, to lay his bones in a foreign land, rather than not accomplish his design. Colonel Wharton warmly sympathized in his object.

"I know," said he, "numerous families residing in and about France. Tell me the name of the person you seek, possibly I may be able to assist you; at all events I will put you in the best way of succeeding."

Mr. Coppinger warmly thanked him for the interest he took in his affairs. and replied—"His real name is Jermyn; but I understand he travels under an assumed title, or name. However, he resided in Tours some time back, and during his residence there he lived openly. I cannot imagine why he should assume any other name than his own, being a man of most independent fortune, and high respectability—it cannot be for the purpose of avoiding me."

"My dear friend," at once exclaimed the other, "say no more; I know the person you allude to—nay more, I know him well. I also know where he at present resides; so set your mind at rest on that point. It will be necessary for you to retrace your steps. You must go into the heart of Normandy, to the little town of V—d—m—e. Mr. Jermyn lives some distance from it; but that town will be the theatre of your operations, so far as preparation is concerned. And I here advise you of the difficulties you have to encounter. Do not imagine when you have found out his retreat, all your difficulties are at an end—no such thing. Mark me!—I know this man. You will encounter opposition. He will get rid of you. Listen to me—he will not stop at murder, through the agency of assassins who are ever ready for a trifling recompense to do the behests of unprincipled men who may employ them. You must be very wary. Indeed, the more I reflect on it, the more I would recommend you to give it up altogether. Well, well, since you are so very determined, all we can do is to give you the best instructions. Fortunately, there is a particular friend of mine in the college at V—d—m—e, Mr. Gilman, Professor of English. I will give you a letter to him, and I have no doubt he will give you all the assistance in his power.

Having arrived at V—d—m—e, Mr. Coppinger lost no time in delivering his letter of introduction, when Mr. Gilman informed him that undoubtedly he could give much assistance, but regretted that he had to deal with a dangerous man.

"I know little personally of him," said he; "he resides about six leagues from this, under the name of Colonel Dumont. He has taken a very handsome chateau, with a large tract of land attached to it. There also lives with him a Frenchman, whose nephew is at our college. Report speaks of these gentlemen as very mysterious, if not dangerous, characters. No visitors or strangers of any kind are admitted. They never come to town; and the country people say, they have huge dogs, and ferocious looking retainers, or servants. For what object all this precaution is used, I cannot conjecture; however, it leads me to suppose you will encounter danger of some kind. If after this you are still determined to proceed, I will think of the means to be used in accomplishing your object; but I would strongly advise you to give up the matter. The more I think on it, the more certain I am, that you will have cause to repent your temerity. For why (unless the man be of desperate character) should he wrap himself up in so much mystery?"

Mr. Coppinger listened with marked attention to all Mr. Gilman advanced, and then replied—

"I confess, what you have said has alarmed me, but still my determination remains unchanged; and I have only to hope you will take me under your protection, and I am sure I must succeed."

"Since that is the case, let us think of the means. Mons. D—l—p—t's nephew goes home once a month—a cab is sent in for him generally. On two occasions, by some accident or other, the cab was not sent for the boy, but he was sent out by his uncle's directions in a hired vehicle. We will try and find out the man who went home with him. This, I think not only the most likely mode, but also, I fear, the only method you have of reaching him. The sooner you start the better, for should this Colonel Dumont learn that a stranger is in the town, he will be much more circumspect, and extremely cautious how he admits any person even on his ground—for this, I must tell you, has been the subject of much remark. Now let us set to work. Come, till we look for this man."

And accordingly they both sallied out, nor were they long in finding the object of their search. This man agreed to go with Mr. Coppinger, and was directed to be at the hotel at eight o'clock the following morning, in order to be at the chateau by twelve. This point arranged, little more was to be done. The time previous was occupied in procuring arms of offence and defence. A case of pistols and a double edged dagger were purchased, and then Mr. Coppinger retired for the night, which he spent in no very pleasing anticipations. He made his will, with a presentiment hovering over him of never returning to his home. With this very pleasant feeling, he impatiently waited for the time of action, which would be a relief. The time did come, and punctual with it was the cab that was to take him to the chateau. Mr. Gilman breakfasted with him, and gave directions to the driver to wait Mr. Coppinger's return from the chateau—the moment he should return, to gallop back as fast as possible—but in case, after a lapse of half an hour, he did not come back, he was to go in and inquire for him. A handsome gratuity awaited the punctual performance of those directions, which he promised faithfully to execute to the best of his ability. Every thing being now ready, off they started.

During the three hours drive, Mr. Coppinger's mind was too much involved in plans and strat.gems to give way to any foreboding. When they entered on Colonel Dumont's ground, the first object that attracted their attention was a young boy coming towards them, with a satchell slung across his shoulder—the horse was pulled up.

"Ah! comment vous-porter, vous Pierre Mons D—l—p—t est-il-chez lui?" enquired the driver.

"Oui, mais il dort encore. Monsieur désirerait avoir l'honneur á le saluer. Qui est-ce? Je ne sair en verite."

The dialogue concluded, on they went again

In a quarter of an hour they stopped before a large handsome building, the driver got out and rung a bell which sent fort a peal almost deafening; a man came to the gate and stared with surprise; he opened the gate and admitted them without saying a word; they then drove into an inner court yard, and stopped before a large handsome entrance—immediately on stopping, a tall soldierly looking man came out. He had a pair of mastiffs in a leash, and they could see two men, with big staves in their hands, far back in the hall. He asked in a gruff, disagreeable voice, "Que demandez vous, Monsieur?"

"Colonel Dumont," replied Mr. Coppinger, getting out of the cab.

"C'est bien, il n'est pas chez lui."

Mr. Coppinger did not understand his reply, and shook his head. Mons. D—l—p—t, satisfied that it was not him he wanted, now directed one of his servants to show Mr. Coppinger to Colonel Dumont. The servant went on to the other side of the chateau—Mr. Coppinger took care to follow close at his heels. "Restez ici un moment," said his conductor, showing him into a room. Mr. Coppinger had no idea of waiting there though—he still followed, much to the man's surprise. Every door he passed he opened. In one he observed some females sewing—they started, and he shut the door hastily. The man appeared much enraged—"Il n'y est pas, je vous dis," said he. At last he came to the right door. As he was about to open it, Mr. Coppinger pushed him aside, and went in. And there he beheld George Charles Jermyn, alias Colonel Dumont, in the act of—what, reader?—why shaving to be sure. The man all this time maintained his position at the door, without moving. Mr. Coppinger perceived this, and at once stepped forward with both hands out, (he knew Jermyn would not recognise him, not having met for fifteen years previous)—

"Ah, Mr. Jermyn," said he, "I am delighted to see you! Don't you know your old friend?"

"Indeed I do," said Mr. Jermyn, "though I don't recollect your name;" and they shook hands cordially together. The man on observing this retired.

Mr. Coppinger then produced his document, and very quietly handed it to Mr. Jermyn. This produced rather a startling effect.

"Sir, I don't understand—what's the meaning of this? Come, Sir," he exclaimed, with a fearful oath, "you must not stir! Explain this!"

"It is merely to appoint a law agent. And now, Sir, having completed my business, good morning, Sir."

"Not so soon, if you please," and he sprung towards the bell and Mr. Coppinger, who was standing close beside it. A pistol flashing on his view checked Mr. Jermyn's career. He started back.

"What do you mean, Sir?"

"Move one step, and it will be your last. Be quiet—I have not ventured so far without sufficient precaution."

Mr. Jermyn sat down, every limb quivering with ill-concealed passion. Mr. Coppinger stood on a chair, produced his dagger, and cut the bell pull as high as he could reach. He then left the room, locked the door, the key of which fortunately was outside, and hurrying down stairs, got into the cab, and drove off—they got outside the gate, and then put the horse to his speed. In less than three hours Mr. Coppinger was at the Diligence office taking his place, Mr. Gilman standing by his side

embracing him. While receiving Mr. Gilman's congratulations, a gig was seen thundering along the road, drawn by a powerful black horse, whose speed, urged by severe chastisement, was astounding. On he came, and dashed far up the street before his course could be checked. At length he was pulled in, and Mr. Jermyn alighted from the gig, went into the office, and, of course, met Mr. Coppinger. His face grew livid with passion at the rencontre.

"Sir," said he, "I have followed you, to insist on your telling me who you are."

"Well, then," interrupted Mr. Coppinger, "I am sorry you have had so much trouble, as I will tell you nothing about me."

"This gentleman has served me with an order of law," said Jermyn, turning to Mr. Gilman, "who is he?—Do you know him?"

"Mr. Gilman, will you oblige me by writing Mr. Jermyn's—I beg pardon, Colonel Dumont's acknowledgment of the fact in my pocket-book—he might forget it."

"Certainement, vous n'avez pas tort," said Mr. Gilmas. Mr. Jermyn was thunderstruck—"Ne le sais pas, et tu seras content." Seeing Mr. Gilman writing without minding him he grew outrageous.

"Mr. Jermyn, there is no use in getting into such a passion—submit quietly, it is the best thing you can do."

As Mr. Gilman said this, the coachman came in, "Messieurs, il est temps de partir. Vite, vite, s'il vous plait—allons, Messieurs." And on they went; and Mr. Coppinger returned to his native land in safety, and has now the satisfaction of reciting his wonderful adventures to his friends, one of whom was your humble servant.   J. C.

*** This story is founded on facts—indeed, every word is true—nor is there one incident which did not occur. Should you think it worthy of publication, it will be immediately recognised by a large portion of your readers.
                                                                    J. C.

THE RUINS OF RIVER LYONS, KING'S COUNTY.

This once splendid mansion, finely situated in the vicinity of Philipstown, was, in 1760, the residence of Henry Lyons, Esq. one of the representatives for the King's County in the Irish Parliament. He was a gentleman highly esteemed, and was married to the Honourable Miss Rochford, daughter to the Earl of Belvedere.

Dublin, Printed and Published by P. D. Hardy, 3, Cecilia-street; to whom all communications are to be addressed. Sold by all Booksellers in Ireland.

THE
DUBLIN PENNY JOURNAL

CONDUCTED BY P. DIXON HARDY, M.R.I.A.

Vol. III.	MAY 2, 1835.	No. 148.

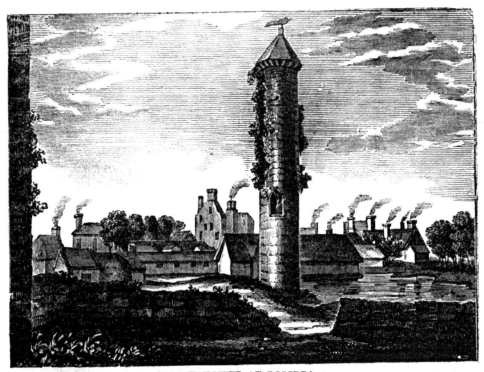

ROUND TOWER AT ROSCREA.

ROUND TOWER AT ROSCREA

This tower is eighty feet high, and fifteen feet in diameter, with two steps round it at the bottom. At fifteen feet from the bottom is a window, with a regular arch, and at an equal height is another window with a pointed arch. If this latter is not a more recent addition, which it probably is not, it certainly reduces the date of this tower to the twelfth century, which is rather earlier than the time allowed for the use of this arch.

Anciently a great annual fair was held here on the festival of St. Peter and St. Paul, for fourteen days. The Danes, in the year 942, formed a design to surprise and pillage the merchants assembled here; but they were defeated, with the loss of Olfinn their commander, and four thousand men slain. When the English arrived in this isle, they soon extended their power into Munster; and as they proceeded, secured themselves by strong castles and garrisons. After some contests with Mortogh, king of North Munster, they obtained Roscrea; and in 1213, founded a strong castle in it, as a barrier against the attempts of the natives on that side. This ancient fortress is at present in a good state of preservation, and no small ornament to the town, as is seen in the back ground of this view.

A.

THE WAKE.

The period at which we commence our sketch, was one when a spirit of insubordination and resistance to the authorities began to manifest itself all through Ireland, but more particularly in the southern parts. There outrage was followed by outrage; some were even committed in the broad day; and any one who was considered to differ in opinion with the midnight legislators, was sure of a hostile visit. The peasantry doggedly resisted every description of impost or taxes, but more particularly tithe; and large parties, headed by some leader, scoured the country round each night, taking up arms, and swearing the terrified inhabitants against paying any government demands, particularly that one set apart for the use of the clergy. If any individual dared to disobey this command, a notice signed "Captin Moonshine," or "Captin Cardher," or some other fantastical appellation, was sure to be found nailed to his door; and if he did not comply with its order of departure from his house and lands, he was generally either mutilated, or forced by nightly visits eventually to leave the country. Such was the state of the south at this period, that although government had sent down troops to suppress all outrage, the same practices were still carried on; and such was the daring ingenuity of the disturbers, that they had almost entirely escaped detection.

On a bright and sunny day in June, large bodies of the peasantry were observed collecting in different parties on the heights surrounding the little town of W——. They all seemed incited by some common purpose, and as they met, exchanged salutations, if not altogether silent, at least only consisting of a muttered "God save you," or "good morra." The majority of the multitude was composed of strong, able-bodied men, whose bent brows, and frowning features, had something very fearful in appearance, and yet there were women, and even children too, amongst them, each evidently accompanying a father or a husband. By degrees they continued to advance, till at length they assembled in considerable numbers at the market-place, and thronged up all the avenues surrounding the town. There they stood in little knots together, conversing in whispers, and keenly watching the proceedings of a military party, who occupied the centre round which they had collected. This last named body consisted of thirty mounted dragoons and a young officer, who were guarding about eleven or twelve head of cattle seized the day before for non-payment of tithe. They had collected there for the purpose of setting them up at auction, and were somewhat disturbed by the appearance of the multitude, who evidently had assembled for no friendly purpose. It was a strange and unusual sight in that little town; the armed troopers, with their proud and pawing war horses, eyeing with much appearance of hatred and distrust the sullen, dark body of men before them, and the loosely clad, athletic-limbed peasantry, gradually increasing in number, their silence resembling a deep volcano, ready to burst into fury and destruction. The deep, indistinct buzz of voices, the lowing of the cattle, the snorting of the troopers' horses, and the clanging of their arms and accoutrements, that glittered in the noonday sun, had a bustling and martial sound, quite strange to the peaceable inhabitants of the town. *They* might be seen mingling amongst them, and watching their movements with deep and fearful interest.

Cow after cow was set up, and yet there appeared no bidder; and at each failure the multitude nearest them set up a wild shout of derision, which was echoed by their companions in the rear, while the muttered curses of the troopers, and the impatient manner in which they checked the curvetting of their steeds, spoke of feelings and passions with difficulty restrained. At this period, a figure slowly moved from behind the mounted party, and advanced to their front. He was clad in a loose coat of blue frieze, open at the breast, corduroy breeches, and woollen stockings; his hat was pulled deeply on his brow, and his keen, suspicious eyes glanced round about, with habitual caution, mingled with not a little fear. As soon as he was perceived, the whole multitude seemed as if actuated but by one impulse; they drew closer to the dragoons, grasped their sticks firmly in their hands, and set up a roar of hatred and invective absolutely frightful from its wild bitterness. Occasionally, too, curses loud and deep were heard above even their wildest shouts, such as " Bad loock attind the murdhering procthor"—" Och, tin thousand curses descind on you, Dinis Kelly"—" Atin' an' dhrinkin', sleepin' an' wakin', no pace to the vile informer," &c. &c, which he heard with a slight shudder, and a deeper frowning of his shaggy eye-brow.

After a little, another cow was brought forward, but the voice of the setter up could not be heard, so loud had the murmured curses of the multitude continued. However, he that they had dubbed Dinis Kelly bid for it, and it was knocked down to him at a few shillings. As he began to drive it from the place where it was standing, a shower of execrations was poured upon him from the crowd, and a few large stones were flung by the hinder party, one of which felled him to the earth, and another of which struck the young officer commanding the detachment. The troop immediately formed into order, facing the large, dark mass of human beings, whose demon shouts, and terrible curses, still made fearful uproar, while the trembling proctor, with his head streaming with blood, conceiving from this movement that they were about to desert him, in abject accents implored them to stay. Their leader having consulted for a moment or two with a grey-headed serjeant, the second in command, walked his horse slowly to their threatening front, and desired them to disperse in quiet; upon which the mass opposite to where he stood opened a little, and an individual advanced from their uneven ranks, and stood grasping a blackthorn stick within about three yards of the youthful commandant. He was a true specimen of the bold and hardy peasant—his frame was firmly and regularly moulded, and the flashing of his proud eye told of a spirit that quailed not at the fear of man.

" Sassenagh," he began, " you ordher us to disparse in quiet, an' it aint the fear ov your swords or pistols ill make us obey; bud as we mane no harum to you or yours, iv you surrindhur to our keepin' that thrimblin' thraitor, Dinis Kelly, we'll separate athout farther annoyin' or inthermpin' you."

Here a loud cheer from his companions told that he had spoken their sentiments; and the being of whom he spoke, on hearing his demand, listened with an intense eagerness, as if his welfare in this world and the next depended on the answer.

" Denis Kelly," answered the officer, " is here under my protection, and I dare not disobey my orders by deserting him. But, whether or no, I would not give him up to men seemingly thirsting for his blood. Again I desire you to disperse quietly—we are well armed, and can enforce obedience."

A low scoffing sound proceeded from the dark body, as their leader answered—" Agin I tell you, we don't dhread yer power, nor fear yer shinin' arms; bud we must get a grip ov the thievin' procthor that's shiverin' an' shakin' there forenint us—as unasy as a hin on a hot gridle."

A low laugh passing through the crowd testified their enjoyment of his simile, and he continued in the same sneering tone—

" Just sind him across to us as we wish, an' we'll throuble you wid no more ov our company. Don't you see how aiger we are to welcum him, an' the *omedhaun*, not knowin' his own intherest, thryin' to avoid us."

" One word for all," was the reply, " while life lasts, I will never disobey my commander's orders; so Denis Kelly is, and will be, safe from your, I fear, murderous designs."

" Gintly, agra !" interrupted the peasant, still preserving his sneering manner, " you misundherstand us a thrifle. We don't mane to take his life, the coward ! bud jist merely to lave our mark on him by way of tachein' him to behave betther for the future. Jist to sthrip him ov a taste ov his ugly nose or ears; bud by no manner ov manes to desthroy his beauty out and out, which takin' his life might chance to do. So don't you stan' in our way, an' it 'ill be a great improvemint to him intirely."

" Your insolent manner shall not sway me," was the rapid answer : " while I can wield a sword, he never shall be in your power."

" Then sorra a fut ye'll lave this till we saize him, an' no thanks to ye," impetuously exclaimed the spokesman, throwing off all reserve; upon which the blood rushed in a tumult to the young officer's cheek, and exclaiming, " insolent scoundrel, dare you threaten ?" he made his horse spring forward to overturn the speaker; but he, bounding lightly aside, with one blow of his cudgel, given with lightning-like celerity, sent the uplifted sword many feet into the air, and retreated again to his party, while their shouts of exultation and defiance, seemed to rend the very skies. The whole mounted party upon this advanced, and the peasantry did not move an inch, but the shouting ceased, and they remained in sullen silence as if awaiting an attack. The officer, who had again recovered his sword, made a second effort to move the mob to obedience, but without effect; and as their menacing appearance was increasing every instant, he gave orders to his own men to form a square with the proctor in the centre, and they slowly retrograded from their numerous opponents. For every inch of ground they moved away, the whole multitude regularly advanced another; and as they left the town, and came upon the high road, they perceived that the fields on each side were filled with men, advancing as if to impede their progress. The dangers of the handful of troops seemed momentarily to increase; and the occasional shouts of the multitude sent a chill to their very hearts. As to the being they protected, he seemed almost paralysed with fear, and at every wild cry he shuddered, as if he heard his death knell. His feelings were easily seen from the wistful glances that he cast from side to side, and the look of ill-suppressed agony, with which he viewed the rudely chiselled stone that told of their being many miles from succour. At length they arrived at a part of the road which was deep and narrow, besides being flanked by a high wall on one side, and a thick hedge at the other. There the first symptoms of an attack began to manifest themselves, as a huge shower of stones, and other missiles, descended on the troopers from each side of the road, while loud cries of " give up the thraitor"— " Turn out the black procthor," &c. were heard above the loud hurroo with which the shower of missiles was accompanied. The escort suddenly stopped, unslung their car-bines, and faced round to the crowd; when their officer again advanced a little, and desired, nay entreated them to retire. The same individual that had before held par-ley with him, who seemed their principal, if not their only leader, also advanced a little in front of his party, and made answer,

" Let us take Dinis Kelly, an' thrate him as we plase, an' thin we'll retire athout molestin' you."

" You have already heard my sentiments on that point," was the determined answer, " he never shall be surren-dered up.'

" We tould you we didn t intind takin' his life, bud only a bit ov him, jist by the way ov a thriflin' keepsake," again quietly observed the peasant; " an' it 'ill be betther for you not to attimpt to stop us, so take the thing asy, an' hand him over here."

" I perceive you are determined on violence," said the officer, retiring to the front of his own party, " and now desire you to depart for the last time, or I will order my men to fire."

A shower of stones more violent than the former one, was the answer to this last remark; and he gave the word of " ready" and " present," in a cool, unshaken tone of voice. Ere the last, fatal word passed his lips, he looked once more towards the crowd, and they all were stationary, seemingly wavering a little whether to advance or not, till the same voice that had spoken their sentiments shouted—

" Hurroo, boys, give the bloody sodgers another volley," and then another rush of stones flew like hail amongst the troopers. He hesitated no longer, but gave the word, " fire." There was a loud report, a bright flash, and three of the foremost of the assailants, fell desperately wounded; while their former spokesman, who headed them, suddenly stopped in his career, clenched his outstretched hands, with convulsive violence, and fell to the earth, his heart's blood gushing from the wound.

The vaunting crowd were actually paralysed with sur-prise. They thronged round the body of their leader, and of the three other wounded, and gazed upon them with a kind of stupid stare. Some hastily retreated—others, but they were very few, made a movement as if for revenge: but the majority felt all their evil passions as if suddenly quelled by some unseen power, and with deep and bitter grief surrounded the body of their leader—lately exulting in the consciousness of strength, now a lifeless mass, cold, still, and feelingless! After some slight interruption, and a couple of harmless vollies, the soldiers were suffered to depart; and the younger and more hot-headed, who had followed them for the purpose of revenge, returned to their companions, crest-fallen and silent. There was a litter of boughs hastily constructed for the wounded, and another for the dead, and in a few minutes more the en-tire group had departed. The calm sun still shone with unclouded beauty. All was peace below, and there was no mark, save a small pool of black blood, to tell that a human being had been writhing there in the last dreadful agonies of departing life—the keen and fearful throe with which the spirit leaves its tenement of clay !

It was the interior of a large barn, that stood within a few miles of the spot where the sanguinary occurrence we have just related took place. Groups of men and wo-men sat in different companies around the walls, which had been originally whitewashed, but time, the destroyer! had then given them a dingy appearance, which suited well with the gloomy aspect of the place. The light at the upper end was exceedingly brilliant, but the lower came under the expressive denomination of " darkness vi-sible;" and the effect of the entire was very fine—one half of the figures distinctly seen, and the other sitting in the deep shade, save when now and then a pale ray of moon-light streaming through the open door, lit up their rugged features. It was a scene only to be met with in our na-tive land—a genuine Irish wake ! At the upper end of the barn, supported on a low and hastily constructed frame, lay the body, " dacintly dhressed wid clane linen," and already placed in the coffin. The features were strongly marked and regular, bearing no trace of agony or torture; but they looked doubly pale from the bright glare of twelve candles placed at regular distances, six on each

side. The lid was laid athwart the coffin so as to form the appearance of a cross, and on a bright plate in its centre was rudely engraven, " Bryan Murphy, aged 27"— he was the leader of the peasants, whose melancholy death we have before spoken of. On the lid were several sau-cers, containing pipes, tobacco, and snuff, which as soon as emptied were regularly replenished; and that was pretty often, as at a wake every peasant takes care to fill his horn snuff-box and tobacco pouch, they being luxuries he does not meet with every day. There were four or five aged females sitting about the coffin, conversing in low tones, and sometimes giving utterance to a deep, melan-choly, and by no means unmusical wail, as the merits of the deceased chanced to come under discussion. They were the keeners, but were not then employed in their vocation, as they were talking of the circumstances under which Bryan had met his death, and hazarding various conjectures as to whether it would be revenged. Large jugs of punch, composed of the " raal stuff," that " niver grew wake at the sight ov a murdherin' gauger," were oc-casionally handed round by the more youthful of the party; and many a comely " boy," and black-eyed " col-leen," was sitting apart from the group, and " coortin away quite cozily." Their parents, in the mean time, perhaps, were pledging each other to the happiness of the young folk—that is, when no obstacle intervened, and when the boy, besides being " clane an' likely," was steady and industrious, while the colleen, " havin' got the dacint rarin' an' broughtin' up, an' the idication," in addition to it was careful and thrifty, besides " havin' a thrifle ov goold" to purchase a cow or pig. The occasional excla-mation of " Arrah, Jim, be asy !" uttered half pettishly, half in good-humour, whenever it reached the ear of the aforesaid parents, caused a smile to pass over their quiet features; and the feeling that prompted that smile, often stealing to their hearts, reminded them of their own young days, to which era they looked back with pride, and a something like regret. About the centre of the barn, on an elevated seat, was Murdock, the blind piper, and near him almost all the youthful of both sexes were posted. They were busily engaged in supplying him with punch, knowing from experience that when a trifle elevated he played with double vigour; and sure enough, having drank as much as would float a small navy, he seized his pipes, and after one or two discordant symphonies, began " the wind that shakes the barley." A tight-limbed boy immediately bounded forward, half leading, half dragging a cherry-cheeked and seemingly reluctant girl; and then with a kind of introductory or animating whoop, began " tatterin' away fur the bare life." His partner, the mo-ment she " felt the boord undher her," lost all affecta-tion of modesty, and " welted the flure" with as much rapidity of motion, and precision, as if her life depended on keeping time. Then the shouts of " Hurroo, the little darlin' "—" maybe she doesn't thrush it in style"—" throth, she'll tire you"—the laughter and the good-humoured taunts occasionally interchanged—made it appear one merry-making scene, and as if such a thing as grief were not in the world. But by degrees the shouts grew less and less frequent, the laughter less loud; and when the cessation of the music told that the dance had ended, each swain led his drooping partner to a seat. The remarks of the elder party as they passed them by, were in this strain —" Deuce take the boy in the country equil to him, any how"—" Jist observe the purty crathur athout the sign of hate on her, an' she afther tirin' down a pair ov them— musha, good loock attind her !"—while a thought of what they formerly had accomplished themselves, gave their faces a placid serene expression.

The bustle and the laughter grew more and more bois-terous as the potteen began to be profusely distributed, till suddenly every sound of merriment ceased, and every eye was fixed intently on a figure that stood for a moment at the opened door, with the moonlight streaming full on her white dress, and then slowly approached the coffin, speak-ing not as she passed along. It was Ellen Murphy, the wife of the deceased, who when her husband was brought home, all pale and bloody, seemed as if she had received a death-stroke—she did not utter a single exclamation—did not shed a single tear, but one heart-breaking sob burst from her quivering lips, and she fell into the arms of her brother, senseless and seemingly without life. She had remained in that state during the two days that, according to custom, they kept the body, the slightest breathing alone telling that she yet lived; and the reader may judge of the surprise of all at seeing her entering the barn. Her attendant had stolen to take a "peep at the fun," and at that precise moment awaking from her stupor, every thing was revealed to her at one instant's thought, so rising from her bed, she hastily huddled on some loose clothing, and appeared as we have described.

Her head was bending over the pale fixed features of her husband, and her long coal-black hair, which was dishevelled and unbound, floated along the white drapery that shrouded the body of the dead. A thick choking sob, with a low wail of bitter grief, occasionally burst from her lips, and at length rising her head, she flung back her dark hair and revealed her pale and marble features, agonized and full of deep distress: then she began a wild chaunt or keening in her native tongue, her body swaying to and fro "like a reed shaken by the wind," as if in harmony with her song of grief. The conclusion of each sentence was caught up by the keeners on each side, and prolonged with a deep and melancholy cadence. It ran as follows—

"Oh! husband of my heart! you have left me now in sorrow—I mourn beside thy cold form."—"My heart is breaking—it will soon cease to beat, and I'll be laid low."—"Beside my love I'll rest ere long, and the green grass will grow above my head."—"Strong was your arm in the fight, and yet your heart was soft—you would not harm a child."—"Proud was I once to be your choice, but now you are cold and dead, ullah!"—"I'll never see thy smile again, to warm me like the summer noon-day sun."—"Your little child will cry out 'Father,' but you will not be there to stop his mouth with kisses."—"You have gone from me for ever. I care not for life, since you have ceased to live."—"Oh! husband of my soul! would I were laid beside thee, with the cold cold earth for my pillow."—"Oh! pulse of my heart! I will not live to see thy name forgotten: we will rest in the same deep silent grave, ullah."

There was something irresistibly touching in her overwhelming grief, and in the deep pathos of her melancholy chant, that gradually became lower and lower, till at length, with one wild, prolonged, quivering wail from the keeners, it entirely died away, and all again was silence. Then after a little commenced the buzz of voices, and at intervals the merry laugh—for such is the mercurial nature of the Irish feelings, that sadness rests on them but for a season. But the dance was not again resumed, neither was the bustle so loud as before, as "it wouldn't be dacent afore the widow." She—poor bereaved one! sat like a statue, unmindful of all around her—life, passion, and feeling all concentred in one wistful gaze upon the features of the silent dead: he was her all, and without him she felt that she was alone in the wide world—alone and in misery!

Bryan Murphy was decently interred on the following day, and his afflicted widow survived him but a very few months.   OSCAR.

MARKET PLACE OF ATHLONE

Athlone is a considerable town, situated about seventy miles north by west from Dublin. It has been rendered rather an important station as commanding the passage of the Shannon, on which it is situated, and by means of which it communicates with the Grand Canal. It is partly in the county of Westmeath, and province of Leinster, and partly in the county of Roscommon, and province of Connaught; the divisions made by the Shannon, being united by a well-built bridge. The place was formerly rich in antiquities: but they were nearly all destroyed during the civil wars; the castle still remains, defended by numerous guns. We are informed by Archdall, that an Abbey was founded here for Cistertian monks, under the invocation of St. Peter. Other writers give the dedication to St. Benedict, and say it was founded for monks of his order. In a table of the procurations of the church of Elphin, this is called the Monastery de (Iunocentia. In that part called the *English Town*, situate on the east coast of the Shannon, a monastery was founded for Conventual Franciscans by Cathal, or Charles Croibh Dearg O'Connor, Prince of Connaught, who, not living to finish the building, it was completed by Sir Henry Dillon. The country round Athlone is flat, and has few natural beauties to recommend it.

Athlone sends one member to Parliament. It gives title of Earl to the Dutch family of Ginckle, as a reward for the services performed by the General of that name in the year 1691. It is the station of a large military force and numerous staff. Lines have also been thrown up on the bank of the Shannon; but, though they might serve to protect the place in the event of any sudden popular commotion, they could oppose no effectual barrier to a regular force. There is a celebrated chalybeate spring in the vicinity.

A BRIEF DESCRIPTION OF AN ANCIENT BUILDING, SUPPOSED TO HAVE BEEN A TEMPLE OF THE SUN, ON GREENAN MOUNTAIN, DONEGAL.

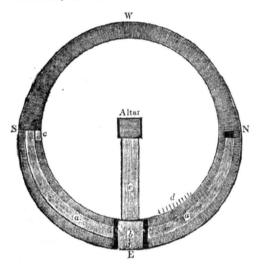

SKETCH PLAN OF GREENAN TEMPLE.

a. a. The two passages in the wall.
b. The entrance.
c. Communication from the south passage into the area.
d. The stairs leading to the top of the wall.
e. Flagged passage to the altar.

Londonderry, December, 1834.

SIR—In the account of Burt Castle, No. 64, Vol. II. of your interesting miscellany, there is a brief allusion to a Temple of the Sun on Greenan mountain in that neighbourhood. The ingenious author of that very accurate account, was not aware, I am sure, of the existence of a very particular and minute description of that highly interesting remnant of antiquity, written by a very elegant scholar and gentleman of much antiquarian research, particularly in matters connected with Ireland, Colonel Blacker. The detail is given in a letter addressed to that very respected prelate, the Hon. Dr. Knox, the late bishop of this diocess. A few copies only were printed, for private circulation among the friends of the writer. One of these I was fortunate enough to procure; and considering it well suited to the purposes of your Journal, request your acceptance of it, and remain, your obedient servant,
G. H.

To the Editor of the Dublin Penny Journal.

My Lord—If your antiquarian research keeps pace with your taste in modern improvements, I know of none to whom I could with greater propriety address the following observations. But however this may be, your Lordship has an official claim to priority of information on the subject of any ecclesiastical remains discovered within the range of your diocess.

The epithet "ecclesiastical" may sound strange when applied to scenes of Pagan adoration; but your Lordship cannot but be aware that it is made use of by Giraldus Cambrensis, when speaking of those round towers, which, together with the Arenæ of sun-worship (one of which I am about to describe), serve to establish, in my humble opinion, the Eastern origin and habits of Ireland's early inhabitants.

The mountain of Greenan, in the county of Donegal, rises from the southern shore of Lough Swilly. immediately in rear of the island of Inch, from which it is separated by a channel of no great breadth, and, in one part, passable at low water for cattle, &c. The ascent, for about a mile, is tolerably gradual, till, within a few hundred yards of the summit, it, as it were, starts up somewhat precipitously into a circular apex of many acres in extent, crowned by the pile which I have just mentioned my intention of attempting a description of.

That this spot was, in former days, consecrated to the purposes of sun-worship, is sufficiently evident from its name : Greenan, or, more correctly, Grian-an, signifying, literally, "the place of the sun," or "appertaining to the sun."

To the casual observer, the first appearance of the edifice is that of a truncated cairn of extraordinary dimensions ; but, on a closer inspection, particularly since the clearing away of fallen stones, &c. which took place under my directions, in May last, it will be found a building, constructed with every attention to masonic regularity, both in design and workmanship. A circular wall, of considerable thickness, encloses an area of eighty-two feet in diameter. Judging from the number of stones which have fallen on every side, so as to form, in fact, a sloping glacis of ten or twelve feet broad all round it, this wall must have been of considerable height—probably from ten to twelve feet—but its thickness varies : that portion of it, extending from north to south, and embracing the western half of the circle, being but ten or eleven feet, whereas, in the corresponding, or eastern half, the thickness increases to sixteen or seventeen, particularly at the entrance. To discover this entrance was one of the first objects of my attention, and having directed a clearance to be made as nearly due east as possible, a passage was found, in breadth about four feet, flagged at the bottom with flat stones, equal in width to the opening itself, and fitted with great regularity : this passage was covered with flags of very large dimensions, which, however, we found fallen in ; the main lintel, on the inner side, was formed of a single stone, six feet three inches in length, and averaging fourteen inches square in thickness. Within the wall, to the right and left of this entrance (though not communicating with it), are carried two curious passages, about two feet wide by four in height, neatly covered at top with flags, in the same manner as the entrance. These passages extend through half the circumference of the building, terminating at the northern and southern points : that running southward was found to communicate with the area, or interior of the place, by an aperture extremely disproportioned to the passage itself, being merely wide enough to permit the entrance of a boy ; this aperture is due south, and the passage, as it approaches the eastern part of the building, becomes gradually narrow, being not more than six inches wide at its termination, adjoining the entrance. The approach to that gallery or passage, wending northward, appears to have been from above, there being no signs of an aperture communicating with the area, as in the case of the other passage just mentioned ; whereas, on clearing away the fallen stones, to the northward of the main entrance within the building, we discovered a staircase, eighteen inches wide, leading from the level of the area to the top of the wall, very similar to those shown in the model of the Staig Fort, near Kenmare, to be seen in the museum of the Dublin Society. This passage extends to the northern point, but, different from the other, it carries its breadth the entire way. On either side of the entrance passage, a few feet within, appears a square niche, or what masons would call a double reveal, of four inches deep : at first sight it seemed as if they had been the entrances to the two passages already mentioned, and which had been for some cause built up, but on examination this was found not to be the case ; they were evidently formed at the original building of the wall, and I am inclined to think may have served for the purpose of enabling those within to close the passage from above by means of something in the nature of a portcullis. From a careful examination of the wall, in different places throughout its circumference, it appears to have been parapeted, the space between the parapet and the interior of the circle being (as was usual in amphitheatres) allotted to spectators, and accessible by the stair-case already noticed. In the centre of the area are the remains of the altar, or place of sacrifice, approached from the entrance of the building by a flagged pathway, which was discovered on raising the turf by which it is overgrown: around these are the ruins of a square building, but of comparatively modern construction—in fact, the place was resorted to by the Roman Catholics in the vicinity, for the purposes of worship, until some forty years back, when a small chapel for their accommodation was erected at the foot of the mountain—a certain proof of the traditionary sanctity of the spot. It is a well known fact, that the early propagators of Christianity in Ireland were too wise, too good judges of human nature, to expect that men could be induced all at once, and without the possibility of relapse, to abandon forms, to desert, perhaps to destroy fanes hallowed to them, however mistakenly, by a thousand endearing associations : instead, therefore, of insisting upon, or attempting to accomplish anything of the kind, they retained the place of worship, while they changed the object of adoration. Hence we see the Christian Church and the symbol of atonement reared beside the tower of the Guebre. The fane of Baal became the temple of Jehovah. The Milcom of the Ammonite, the Ashtoreth of the Sidonian, gave place to the St. Columb and the Madonna of the Catholic; and for many an age the sacred fire continued to burn unquenched, for a Christian vesta, in St. Bridget of Kildare! The change extended from the hill and the altar to the valley and the fountain, and the poor devotee who tells his beads at the holy well of Fahan, or of Malin, little dreams that his Pagan ancestor held the same spring in equal reverence, under a different name and tutelage. Surely, my Lord, it is not unreasonable to conclude that a place of worship, so considerable as Greenan appears to have been, must have come in for its re-consecration, and continued more or less in the odour of sanctity, until the period I have mentioned.

The stones of which the building is formed are of the common grey schistus, but evidently selected with considerable attention as to size; and considering their exposure to the Atlantic storms for so many centuries, the decomposition is wonderfully small. In those parts of the wall which have been protected by the accumulation of the debris from above, the chisseling is yet sharp and the squareness perfect. The circumstance of its being a stone building adds considerably to the antiquarian interest which Greenan is calculated to excite; for, with the exception of the Staig Fort above mentioned, I am not aware of any other similar edifice being discovered in Ireland. Places of Sun-worship abound. Among the most remarkable may be instanced the Moat of Granard (or Grian-ard, the eminence of the sun), in Longford; and Greenmount (or Grian-mont, the mount of the sun), in Louth: the latter of which, situated as it is, close adjoining the most frequented road in Ireland, is passed daily, hourly, by travellers and tourists of all sorts, without exciting an observation. The virtuoso who will "compass sea and land" to see a few mouldering pillars, once sacred to Jupiter and Minerva, traverses the great Belfast road, wholly unconscious that he is passing almost within the shadow of one of the most perfect remains of Pagan sun-worship which this, or perhaps any other country in Europe exhibits. But both of these, as well as others of a minor description, are mounds (stupendous ones, certainly) of earth. Any that are of stone are, in point of architectural pretension, little beyond the ordinary cairn; nor do they appear to aim at a higher designation. One of the principal, I believe, exists in Antrim, at no great distance from Templepatrick, and is known by the name of Cairn Graney, or "the cairn of the sun."

I was a good deal surprised to find that the very existence of this building was unknown to so many of my acquaintances in Derry, which it stands within four miles of—and some of whom are persons of research and much

historical information; still more was that feeling exhibited by learning that it had (as far as I have been able to discover) escaped the particular observation of the surveying officers of engineers, who had actually a station on the walls of it: to be sure trigonometrical accuracy is one thing, and antiquarian lore another. In this respect, however, it has only shared the fate of numberless objects of curiosity and interest with which the county of Donegal abounds, but which have remained unexplored, or at least undescribed, until very lately, when my friend, the Rev. C. Otway, gave to the world his highly interesting, as well as delightfully written "Sketches" of some portion of the scenery around Kilmacrenan—to the fidelity of which, in a descriptive point of view, I am enabled to bear the fullest testimony. I sincerely wish he had crossed the Swilly to Greenan.

But, to return from this digression, it only remains to be mentioned, that the building was encircled by a double foss, the first about twenty yards from the wall, the second at a like distance beyond the first—both may be distinctly traced throughout the entire of their extent—and the visitor can hardly fail to observe that the turf between the building and the first foss is remarkable for the superiority of its verdure over any portion of the surrounding mountain grass lands.

Such, my Lord, is Greenan—a visit to which is of easy accomplishment, and will well repay the exertion; for, even putting Antiquarianism out of the question, the view from the place, on a clear day, is one of the finest that can be imagined. The boundless Atlantic—the grand estuaries of Foyle and Swilly—the Alpine scenery of Donegal, from Barnesmore to Birdstown—the basalt cliffs of Magilligan, and a large portion of Derry and Tyrone, are all placed beneath the eye, as in one vast map. To this may be added an additional gratification, if the visitor has the good fortune to be acquainted with a certain worthy friend and connection of mine, whose hospitable mansion lies embowered near the base of the mountain and to whom I am indebted for the assistance and facilities which have enabled me to attempt the foregoing description.

I have the honour to remain your Lordship's very obedient servant,

W. B.

Carrick, June, 1830.

ACCOUNT OF SOME SUBTERRANEAN CHAMBERS DISCOVERED NEAR CARRIGTOHILL, COUNTY OF CORK, AND AT BALLYHENDON, NEAR FERMOY, IN THE SAME COUNTY.

"Admiralty, 31st January, 1835.

"Sir,—In compliance with the wish expressed by T. G. in No. 127 of the Dublin Penny Journal, for information respecting the circular entrenchments, termed Danish Forts, so numerous in the South of Ireland, I beg leave to transmit to you a copy of a communication on this subject, made a few years since to the Society of Antiquaries, and which you are at liberty to send to your correspondent, or reprint in your Journal.

"With every good wish for the success of your publication, I remain, Sir, your very humble servant,

"T. Crofton Croker.

To the Editor of the Dublin Penny Journal.

Barnes, Surrey, Dec. 17, 1829.

My dear Sir,—When at Cork, in the early part of the present year, I was informed that some subterranean chambers had been recently discovered on a farm named Garranes, in the parish of Carrigtohill, about nine miles east of that city.

By the kindness of Mr. Cummins, the proprietor of the ground, I was afforded an opportunity of examining these chambers, in company with Mr. Robert O'Callaghan Newenham, whose pencil has so skilfully illustrated the picturesque antiquities of Ireland. They are situated within one of those circular entrenchments, popularly (but I am inclined to think incorrectly) termed "Danish Forts." The diameter of this entrenchment is one hundred and twenty feet; and at the third of that space from the south side appeared a circular pit, about seven feet in depth, and measuring five feet and a half in diameter.

From this pit (which probably had been a chamber, the roof having fallen in,) two holes, resembling the entrances to fox-earths, descended at an angle of about twenty degrees into chambers of a depressed beehive-like shape, excavated from the soil, which is a stiff clay mixed with gravel. These holes or passages (in size barely sufficient to allow a man to creep through them) respectively led to a chamber formed, as I have just described, without any masonry, and from each of these a like communication led to a third chamber, from which there was a similar passage into a fourth. Here terminated our examination, in consequence of finding that the passage into a fifth chamber was blocked up with large stones, two or three of which we removed, but from the confined space the workman was placed in, it would have been impossible for us to have opened this communication without more time and labour than we had it in our power to devote to the investigation.

The dimensions of the chambers varied from seven to eight feet in diameter, and in form they were between the oval and the circle. I annex a plan,* as it will convey at a glance a better idea of their relative situations than can be done by description; and also a section of the entrenchment, with measurements.†

When the discovery of these chambers was made, a considerable quantity of charcoal was found in them, and the fragment of a quern or hand-mill.

It may not be irrelevant to mention, that on Mr. Cummins's farm at Garranes there are five circular entrenchments or forts, all of which we visited. At the distance of about fifty yards from one of these, on the descent of a hill, a spot was pointed out to us, as the entrance of a passage or tunnel leading into chambers beneath the fort; but it had been closed up for many years by the falling in of the earth. Our informant, who was an old man, stated, that when a boy he remembers to have gone some way into this passage, and that the sides were lined with very large stones, upon which great flags rested and formed the roof.

We caused an excavation to be made here for a short time, but we were obliged to abandon the undertaking, without discovering the entrance, although from the vast quantity of charcoal turned up, there appeared to be little doubt that the information given to us was correct.

Within a circle of five miles round Garranes there are no less than fourteen circular entrenchments remaining. They are called by the country people, when speaking of them in Irish, as far as I can perceive, indifferently "Lis" and "Rath," and in English, "the Danes' Fort," or "the old Fort." The tradition of the peasantry is, that the Irish, after the battle of Clontarf, when the Danes retreated to these subterranean chambers for security, kindled large fires at the entrance, the smoke of which either suffocated those within, or compelled them to crawl forth; and thus were the invaders destroyed. Another popular notion is, that by means of these forts, which are said (and with some foundation) to have been constructed within view of each other, a communication was kept up by the Danes throughout the country. This was effected by means of fires, one or more of which were lighted to convey certain pieces of intelligence.

I have repeated these traditions because they are so general, and have no doubt that they originated from the frequent discovery of charcoal in and about the entrenchments. To me it appears probable that these works were thrown up by the native Irish around their little wigwam settlements, as a defence against any sudden attack from an enemy or from wolves, and that subterranean chambers or cellars were formed for granaries, or as secure depositories in time of danger for their rude property.‡ That

so many of these entrenchments should remain in nearly a perfect state, is to be attributed to the gross superstition of the peasantry, who regard them as "Διμιϑ" (haunted) places, inhabited by "sheoges," "good people," or fairies, and believe that some severe misfortune is sure to befal the person who meddles with them.

I beg to add the copy of a letter which I have received from Mr. Newenham, containing some further particulars respecting the subterranean chambers of the south of Ireland:

"Since writing my last letter I have been exploring under-ground chambers by the dozen, and find them, to my surprise, much more frequent than even we had imagined. My first dive was into one set on the lands of

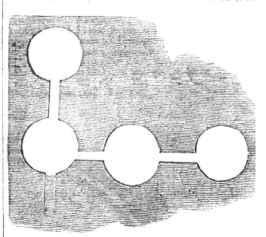

Ballyhendon, within two miles of Fermoy, precisely similar in formation to those we examined near Carrigtohill. On coming out I gave my guide a couple of shillings, which so pleased his numerous friends, that they flocked round me, each offering to lead me to others; so that you would have thought the whole country resembled a bee-hive. I chose out a few of the most intelligent, and followed them. In the course of an hour I visited five sets, within a circuit of two miles, those on Mr. Joyce's farm

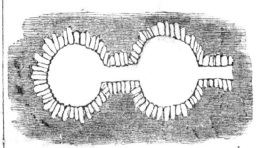

as well as a set at Kilcrumpher, differ from the others in

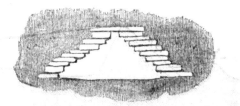

being built or lined with stone. We had candles and spades, so that every corner was explored, but no discovery made, except decayed bones and charcoal. The bones appeared to be those of the ox, but little remained except the joints. In the inner chamber of those on Mr

---

* Figure I.   † Figure II.
‡ This conjecture is supported by the following passage in Tacitus, who describes a similar practice among the old Germans: "Solent et subterraneos specus aperire, eosque multo insuper fimo onerant, suffugium hiemi, et receptaculum frugibus, quia rigorem frigorum ejusmodi locis molliunt: et si quando hostis advenit, aperta populatur, abdita autem et defossa, aut ignorantur aut eo ipso fallunt, quod quærenda sunt." Cap. 16.

Joyce's farm, I perceived a small square aperture, as if to admit air: it did not rise perpendicularly, but sloped upwards at an angle of about seventy degrees. A fourth excavation, near the third at Kilcrumpher, consisted of long galleries only; at least we could discover no chambers. The fifth at Ballyhooly was too much choaked up to admit of examination. None of these were connected with ancient entrenchments or forts, though there appeared several in the immediate neighbourhood, and the remains of two cromlechs. There were also three natural caverns, in which there were marks of fire.

"Some of these excavations had been discovered forty years ago; others recently and accidentally. The country people say that they discover new chambers every year, all of the same shape and size. They are impressed with a belief that the Danes used them to hide in, when the Irish wished to drive these invaders out of the country. Finding the accounts given me of those I had visited so correct, and having ascertained that these chambers were all so nearly alike, and that nothing was to be found in them, I did not think it worth while to visit more."

Believe me to be, my dear Sir, your very humble servant,

T. CROFTON CROKER.

P. S.—I have just received a letter from Doone Glebe, in the county of Limerick, giving an account (which I regret is conveyed in such general terms) of the levelling of a "Danish Fort" in the neighbouring mountains, on some ground belonging to Mr. White. About fourteen feet from the surface, in the centre of the Fort, a number of silver coins were found, and a spur of gold, which is said to be in Mr. White's possession. Several stone jars were also discovered in subterranean chambers, but they were all broken or lost by the falling in of the earth, except one, which Mr. White sent to Mr. Coote. This is of a light brown mottled stone-ware, highly ornamented; and a drawing of it, with the measurements, has been forwarded to the Gentleman's Magazine. One of the broken jars was described as "a beautiful royal purple vase, resembling very fine China."*

To Nicholas Carlisle, Esq. &c. &c.

---

* I have since seen one or two of these jars, and they do not appear to be of more ancient manufacture than the time of Elizabeth. They are what were called "Grey-beards" at that period.   T. C. C.

31st Jan. 1835.

Figure I.

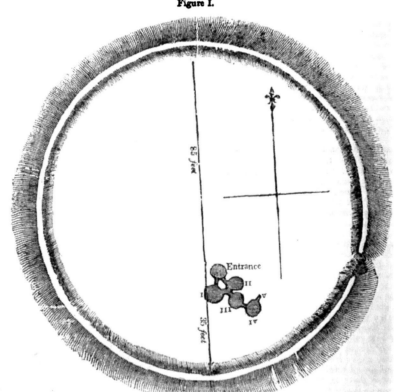

Figure II.

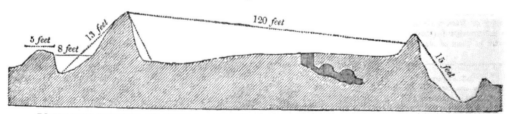

PLAN AND SECTION OF SUBTERRANEAN CHAMBERS AT CARIGTOHILL, NEAR CORK.

Dublin: Printed and Published by P. D. Hardy, 3, Cecilia-street; to whom all communications are to be addressed. Sold by all Booksellers in Ireland.

THE
DUBLIN PENNY JOURNAL

CONDUCTED BY P. DIXON HARDY, M.R.I.A.

| Vol. III. | MAY 9, 1835. | No. 149. |

ARCHITECTURE.

Amongst all the arts which the inventive ingenuity of mankind has at different periods originated, to administer to the wants and weaknesses of human nature, this must surely be ranked in the very highest class : not only does it contribute in the first degree to the blessings and comforts of civilized life ; not only does it give a tangible shape, a " local habitation and a name" to the soft endearments of home—but it affords likewise a pregnant subject for the eye of taste to dwell on ; and is largely instrumental in exciting that refined and imaginative pleasure which springs from the contemplation of abstract beauty and proportion.

Architecture is divisible into a number of different branches, according to the styles adopted by the various nations practising it, and according to the several eras in which it has been practised. An intelligent French writer on architecture, of the present day, gives us the following enumeration :—Egyptian, Indian, Persian, Phenician, Hebraic, Chinese, Greek, Roman, and Gothic, to which list may be added, the Etruscan, the Moorish or Saracenic, the Saxon, and the English. With regard to epochs, the characteristics arising from these may be ranged under four great heads, namely, ancient architecture, that of the lower empire, that of the middle ages, and modern architecture.

By the means of architecture we are furnished with a test from which may be inferred the comparative cultivation and progress of intellect between man arrived at a high state of civilization and his ruder forefathers ; and the opinion of Plato should not be forgotten, that even the study of politics and legislation began with the building of cities. The lofty and stupendous pyramids, obelisks, and temples of Egypt, bear witness to the truth of history and tradition which represent the grandeur and numerical strength of the ancient dwellers on the banks of the Nile. The relics of ancient Athens attest the veracity of those authors who attributed to its population a refined and elegant taste, and an unsurpassable perception of beauty and harmony.

Great caution must be observed in speculating on the state of this art among the nations of antediluvian celebrity. It may, we think, safely be conceded, that they did possess a system of architecture ; but it was probably of a very rude and unsophisticated description.

" Anciently," says Vitruvius, " men lived in woods, and inhabited caves ; but in time, taking example perhaps from birds, who with great industry build their nests, they made themselves huts. At first they made these huts, very probably, of a conic figure ; because that is a figure of the simplest structure ; and, like the birds, whom they imitated, composed them of branches of trees, spreading them wide at the bottom, and joining them in a point at the top ; covering the whole with reeds, leaves, and clay, to screen them from tempests and rain.—Thus :

" But finding the conic figure inconvenient on account of its inclined sides, they changed both the form and con-struction of their huts, giving them a cubical figure, and building them in the following manner : having marked out the space to be occupied by the hut, they fixed in the ground several upright trunks of trees, filling the intervals between them with branches closely interwoven and covered with clay. The sides being thus completed, four large beams were placed on the upright trunks ; which, being well joined at the angles, kept the sides firm, and likewise served to support the covering or roof of the building, composed of many joists, on which were laid several beds of reed, leaves and clay.—Thus :

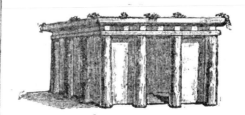

" Insensibly mankind improved in the art of building, and invented methods to make their huts lasting and handsome, as well as convenient. They took off the bark and other unevennesses from the trunks of trees that formed the sides ; raised them, probably, above the dirt and humidity, on stones ; and covered each of them with a flat stone or slate to keep off the rain. The spaces between the ends of the joists were closed with clay, wax, or some other substance ; and the ends of the joists covered with thin boards cut in the manner of triglyphs. The position of the roof was likewise altered ; for being, on account of its flatness, unfit to throw off the rains that fell in great abundance during the winter season, they raised it in the middle ; giving it the form of a gable roof, by placing rafters on the joists, to support the earth and other materials that composed the covering.—Thus :

" From this simple construction the orders of architecture took their rise. For when buildings of wood were set aside, and men began to erect solid and stately edifices of stone, they imitated the parts which necessity had introduced into the primitive huts ; insomuch that the upright trees, with the stones at each end of them, were the origin of columns, bases, and capitals ; and the beams, joists, rafters, and strata of materials that formed the covering, gave birth to architraves, friezes, triglyphs, and cornices, with the corona, the mutules, the modillions, and the dentils.

" The first buildings were in all likelihood rough and uncouth ; as the men of those times had neither experience nor tools : but when, by long experience and reasoning upon it, the artists had established certain rules, had invented many instruments, and by great practice had acquired a facility in executing their ideas, they made quick advances towards perfection, and at length discovered certain manners of building, which succeeding ages have regarded with the highest veneration."

Perhaps the earliest cultivators of architecture, as a fine art, were the Assyrians, whose empire was founded by Nimrod, the builder of the far-famed Nineveh. From Assyria the arts passed into Egypt, one of the most ancient nations in the world, and to which, it is probable, we may fairly attribute the rise of the habits and pursuits of cultivated life into a tangible and definite form. The Egyptians were ignorant of the construction of the arch, and were consequently compelled to provide for its absence by an accumulation of clumsy pillars and heavy architraves, extremely offensive to the eye of a just taste.

The different kinds of edifices peculiar to the Egyptians are: the subterranean grotto; the pyramid; the obelisk; the labyrinth, that immense collection of halls, of which Herodotus, Pliny, and Strabo, have left us descriptions; the monolithal chamber (constructed of a single stone); and their stupendous temples covered with hieroglyphics, paintings, and sculptures, and preceded by ranges of carved animals, of sphinxes, or of obelisks.

It is in the country of its origin that those colossal wonders, the pyramids, are situated. The largest of the three, which is some leagues distant from Cairo, forms a square, each side of whose base is 660 feet; its external circuit being, therefore, 2640 feet, and is nearly 500 feet in height.

The monuments of ancient Indian architecture which remain to gratify the ardent spirit of inquiry awake at the present period, consist chiefly of excavations from the rock. Of this description we meet with spacious halls and lofty columns, and solemn temples, constructed in such a manner as to excite in the beholder the strongest emotions of admiration and surprise. One of the most remarkable specimens of these Indian excavations is to be found in the little island of Elephanta; perhaps so called from the circumstance of an elephant of black stone, of the size of life, being encountered near the landing-place. The elevated situation of this temple, wrought in a hill of stone, and approached through a quiet and solemn valley, is very striking and impressive. It forms nearly a square of from 130 to 135 feet, and is about fourteen feet and a half in its interior height. The roof is supported by ranges of columns, disposed with sufficient regularity; and upon the walls gigantic figures are sculptured in relievo.

The ruins of ancient Persian architecture, although they do not indicate any great superiority as products of art, are yet remarkable when we consider the former greatness and splendour of the empire in which they were erected. The most distinguished are those of Perseopolis, once famous for containing a magnificent palace, the relics of which for a long while comprised forty pillars or columns, and were thence denominated by the inhabitants of the country chehul minar, or tschil minar, i. e. the palace of forty columns. They are constructed of a species of deep grey marble, very hard, which is susceptible of a beautiful polish, and thence becomes almost black. These noble ruins are now the shelter of birds and beasts of prey.

Our next inquiry into the earlier stages of architecture leads us to take a glance at the productions of the Phœnicians. This primitive people, who possessed the arts of civilization at an extremely remote epoch, had several large cities, famous for their riches, manufactures, and extended commerce. There is reason for supposing that the Phœnician architects were much in the habit of employing timber instead of stone, Mount Lebanus, among other places, furnishing them with an abundant supply of the former material; and hence we are led to a consideration of Hebraic architecture, inasmuch as Phœnician artists were doubtless engaged in the building of Solomon's temple, a great portion of which was in all probability constructed of wood.

The Hebrews, or Israelites, acquired a considerable degree of civilization during their residence in Egypt. After their deliverance from captivity, it was suggested to them to construct a place which they might dedicate to the worship of God. Owing to the necessity prescribed by their wandering kind of life, this assumed the shape of a spacious tent, and was denominated the tabernacle. The whole structure, according to the best authorities, covered a space of 100 biblical cubits, by 50 cubits wide; and the enclosure, five cubits high, was formed of wooden columns with brass bases and silver capitals, having curtains of tapestry suspended between them. These columns were sixty in number; twenty on each side, which lay north and south, and ten on each end, which faced the east and west. The Jews used this moveable temple for a length of time after the conquest of Palestine.

Under the reign of Solomon the grand temple was erected, preparations for which had been made by David, that monarch's father.

The summit of Mount Moriah formed a plain of 36,310 square feet. They began by levelling the top and sides of the mountain, against which they afterwards built a wall of freestone 400 cubits high. The circumference of the mountain at the foot was 3000 cubits. Upon the plain was built the temple, divided, like the tabernacle, into two divisions, by a partition of cedar. Under the second, or the sanctuary, it appears they preserved the treasures of the temple. The exterior walls of the temple were of stone, squared at right angles, and ornamented with the figures of cherubim, palm-leaves, flowers, &c. sculptured probably in the stone, like the Egyptian hieroglyphics. The roof was covered with plates of gold, and in the interior decorated in the richest manner; the Hebrews following the custom at that time of all civilized people in ornamenting their temples, they used a great quantity of gold and precious stones. Besides this temple, Solomon erected many other works, as the walls of Jerusalem, several public granaries, stables, &c.

Of Chinese architecture, the original types and models appear to have been pavilions or tents, and evidences of this derivation are constantly visible in almost all their buildings. The materials chiefly employed by them are various kinds of wood, together with bricks and tiles, burnt or dried in the sun. The prevailing style of Chinese architecture, as has been observed by Mr. Elmes, "must be familiar to every one who has drank from a China tea-cup, or who has seen many of the signs of grocers' shops, Sir William Chambers's pagoda in Kew Gardens, or Mr. Nash's pavilion at Brighton."

But the most gigantic work of Chinese architecture is their celebrated wall, compared with which those of the Picts, the Romans, &c. sink into great inferiority. This stupendous fabric exceeded 2000 miles in length, and comprised 45,000 towers. We must not omit noticing, likewise, the science and mechanical skill displayed in the laying out of their canals, as well as in the construction of their bridges. But, taken altogether, there is little to recommend this light and weak style to the eye of the enlightened connoisseur.

Cadmus, who flourished about 1500 years before the Christian æra, is reported to have introduced the arts and sciences into Greece, between 500 and 600 years after the building of the walls of Babylon. He built a city called after the celebrated one in Egypt, Thebes, and it is not at all probable that he was satisfied with borrowing merely the name. The kingdoms of Athens, Argos, Sparta, and Thebes, were successively founded by Cecrops, Cadmus, Inachus, &c.

Art having begun to shed its beams steadily over these distinguished, though at first unimportant, colonies, their radiance was soon diffused throughout the whole country, and a taste gradually sprung up, the correctness and loveliness of which has been subscribed to by all subsequent ages; and which, not seeking to astonish by gigantic and useless productions, selected the choicest materials of preceding styles, and founded thereon that exact proportion, that perfect harmony of parts, which soon rendered the disciples of the Egyptians as completely their masters as ours.

The principal orders in the Grecian architecture are the Doric, the Ionic, and the Corinthian, each of which shall be considered in course. To these may be added the use of the arch.

The first material used by the Greeks in their sacred buildings was timber; next brick, the art of making which they learned from the Egyptians; subsequently stone was employed, as in the temple of Apollo, built by Amphyction;

and, ultimately, the most enduring as well as the most beautiful of all substances applied to the purpose was abundantly introduced, namely, marble.

Almost coeval with the rise and progress of architecture in Greece is the formation of the Etruscan school. The Etruscans are by some antiquarians said to have been originally a Grecian colony ; and to have received, as a matter of course, the arts and sciences from the parent state.

In the most ancient specimens of this school we find abundant use made of the arch, the construction of which was evidently well known to their architects. Their columns differed in shape and proportion from those of any other nation, and Vitruvius has awarded to them the honour of having formed a new order, which, however, is only a variation, and by no means an improvement on the Grecian Doric.

In noticing the best examples of Roman architecture, produced at its most flourishing period, we observe, in addition to the square plans of the Greeks, circular temples crowned with domes. The Corinthian order was evidently the favourite one, and was practised with great skill and success, particularly when not tortured into their own modification of it—the composite.

The most prominent features of the pure Grecian style are invention, elegance, and a severe beauty, at the same time not destitute of richness, which has left to succeeding ages the finest models for imitation. If we turn to the Roman school, which succeeded it, we are struck by the display of splendour, vastness of extent, carelessness of expense, and redundancy of ornament.

The triumphal arches of the Romans constitute a leading feature in their architecture. In the designing of these nothing was overlooked which might tend to perpetuate the fame of the conquerors.

The Saracens, in their buildings in Egypt, appear to have availed themselves, in a very small degree only, of the style of the aboriginal inhabitants. Their style may be justly regarded as the immediate precursor of the Gothic, and is distinguished by the lofty boldness of its vaultings; the slenderness of its columns; the peculiar mixed form of its curves; the variety of its capitals ; and the immense profusion of its ornaments. The greatest peculiarity, however, lies in the small clustered pillars, and pointed arches, formed by the segments of two intersecting circles. The genuine style of Gothic architecture is grand, characteristic, and impressive. What it wants in chasteness and simplicity is made up by solemnity, and a grace peculiarly its own. The elements of this style are spires, pinnacles, lofty-pointed windows, and elevation, as opposed to the horizontal line of the Greeks.

Of the progress of the science of architecture in this country, especially the Saxon, the Norman, and modern Gothic, we shall have occasion to speak more at length in an early number.

The Doric Order obtained its name from the Dorians, a nation of ancient Achaia, from whom it unquestionably received those parts and proportions, by means of which it has been distinguished from subsequent orders. The character of the Doric is robust and masculine, and it has hence been termed the Herculean order. From its peculiar character, this order is well calculated for town-halls, gates of cities, and other public buildings destined for purposes of utility rather than ornament. Among the ancients it was almost uniformly executed without a base. However this be, persons of good taste will grant, that a base gives a graceful turn to the column, but is likewise of real use, serving to keep it firm on its plan ; and that if columns without bases are now set aside, it is a mark of the wisdom of our architects, rather than an indication of their being governed by prejudice, as some adorers of antiquity would insinuate.

The following are the proportions of the principal parts of this order. The whole height of the entire order is divided into five equal parts, one of which is the height of the pedestal ; and the remaining four, which are assigned to the column and entablature, are likewise to be divided into five. One of these belongs to the entablature, and the remaining four being divided into eight equal parts, one of them will be the inferior diameter of the column.

The Ionic Order is said to have been first used in the temple of Diana at Ephesus. This column is more slender and graceful than the Doric. Its ornaments are in a style of composition partaking at once of the plainness of the latter and the richness of the Corinthian. Its general effect is that of simple elegance.

The proportions of the principal parts of the Ionic columns are as follow : the height of the entire order is divided into five equal parts. One of these parts is assigned to the height of the pedestal ; and the remaining four are divided into five, for the column and entablature. One of these is appropriated to the entablature, and the remaining four are for the column, including its capital and base. These four being divided into equal parts, one is assigned for the inferior diameter. The cornice is fifty-four minutes in height, and its projection the same. The drip in the under side of the corona is channelled out one minute deep, and two minutes from the front ; and before the cyma reversa, one minute.

The shaft of the column is sometimes fluted, and sometimes plain. Twenty, or twenty-four are the number of flutes allotted, not only to this, but to every other order. In general, however, twenty-four are preferable. The plan of the flutes may be rather more than a semicircle, as they will then appear more distinct. The fillets, or intervals between them, must not be broader than one-third of the flutes, nor less than one fourth ; and it should further be observed, that in the capital of rich compositions, over each flute is placed an ove or egg.

The Corinthian Order is evidently derivable from the architecture of Egypt, adapted, refined, and nationalized. Cecrops, the founder of Athens, was an Egyptian ; and Dædalus, the earliest Athenian artist, visited the shores of the Nile to study the principles of the fine arts. Added to these facts, it is likewise well known that the Greeks borrowed their laws, manners, and customs, from the Egyptians, and purified them in the alembics of their own brighter genius.

The following are the general proportions of this order : the whole height of the entire order is divided into five equal parts, and one is given for the height of the pedestal. The remaining four are divided into five equal parts ; one is assigned for the entablature, and the remaining four are assigned to the height of the column, including its base and capital ; which are again divided into ten equal parts, one of which is for the inferior diameter. The base is thirty minutes, and the capital seventy in height. The cornice is sixty minutes in height, and fifty-eight in projection.

Of the Tuscan Order little historical can be said ; neither is there any regular example of it among the remnants of antiquity.

The Composite Order is obviously derived from the Ionic and Corinthian, but it cannot, we think, in any case, be applied with superior effect to the latter. It was first employed by the Romans in the triumphal arches erected by them to exhibit to posterity their dominion over their conquered provinces.

The Composite unquestionably derives its origin from that constant solicitude after novelty which always renders the mind of man restless in enlightened and highly cultivated ages. The desire of variety and novelty, stretched to a point beyond the judicious, engaged the Roman architects to combine with the proportions and enrichments of the Corinthian order the angular volute of the Ionic, and thus to compose a new order.

The following are the general proportions of this order : the height of the entire order is divided into five equal parts, one of which is appropriated for the height of the pedestal, and the remaining four for the column and entablature. These four parts being again divided into five, one is for the entablature, and the remaining four for the height of the column, including its base and capital. The height of the column is divided into ten equal parts, one of which is given to the inferior diameter. The base is thirty minutes, the capital seventy, in height, adorned with acanthus leaves, and volutes, drawn by the same method as those of the Ionic : and the plan of the capital is similar to that of the Corinthian order.

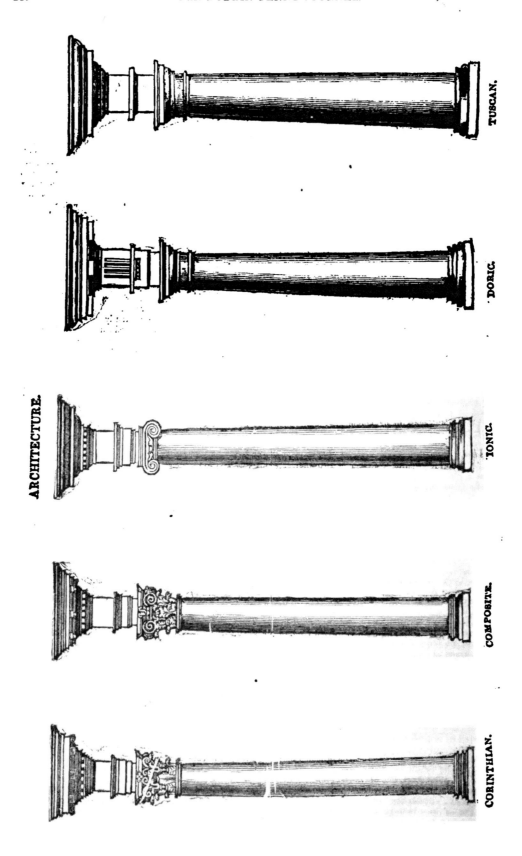

COMPOSITE ARCH. CORINTHIAN ARCH.

DORIC ARCH. IONIC ARCH. TUSCAN ARCH.

COMMON
GOTHIC ARCH. SAXON ARCHES.

The foregoing sketch and engravings, for which we are principally indebted to the article on "Architecture" in the London Encyclopædia, (being the best that we could find upon the subject,) will enable those of our kind correspondents who occasionally furnish us with drawings, to state the particular order to which the building belongs, as well as afford the general reader an idea of the description of building, &c. he may meet with from time to time in the Journal.

THE INCONSTANT.

AN IRISH SKETCH.

Gentle reader, have you ever in the course of your wanderings, passed through the pretty little picturesque town of Cullen? It is, without any exception, the neatest and cleanliest collection of residences to be found in our Emerald Isle. It must be admitted, indeed, that we Irish, take us for all in all, are as partial to mud and dunghills as those over modest and unobtrusive animals yclept pigs.

Where will you see a genuine Irish cabin that has not its stagnant pool, in which perchance the rising generation of children and ducks perform daily, nay hourly ablutions? and which the owner might remove with little trouble— "bud thin what id becum ov the crathurs for a place to swim in?" Where will you see a regular "pisant" without his face being innocent of washing, and perfectly free from the imputation of over exactness? unless, indeed, he is about to pay a visit to a *fair* or a *fair one*, for then the knobs of mud are carefully scraped off his brogues, and they present a shining, well-greased appearance, while his visage is shaved and polished with the most scrupulous nicety—as "the boy id like to show dacint afore the colleen." Where will you see——but stop—stop! whither are we wandering? This is no place for dissertations on a subject so trite as Hibernian carelessness of appearance, or in other words, of Irish filth! We were speaking of the town of Cullen. It is a few miles beyond Slane, beautifully situated and all that—(for we decidedly eschew descriptions of places), and presenting to the eye an elegantly arranged set of—we don't know what to term them, as they are above the appellation of cabins or cottages, and do not aspire to the dignity of houses—however, they are pretty residences enough, some having woodbine and passion-flower growing into their little casements, and others with their fronts of spotless white, dazzling the eyes as they catch the blazing beams of the mid-day sun.

On a beautiful evening in October, when the western heaven was in all the glory of sun-set, a pretty girl might be observed to leave one of those whose trelliced lattice was peering out from the overhanging wreaths of jasmine. She looked round cautiously, to see that she was not particularly observed, and then tripped lightly on to the extremity of the town, exchanging many a nod and " good evenin' to you" as she passed. There is a romantic and beautiful demesne situated at some little distance from Cullen, which we believe is now the property of Lord Oriel, who resides in the town, contributing much by his presence to its neat and orderly arrangement—at the period of which we speak there was much more of wood in it than at present, and it was a favourite haunt of all those who had a taste for the wild beauties of nature, or whose hearts had been susceptible to the shafts of the little winged god. Thither she bent her footsteps, and had scarcely entered the precincts of a large shrubbery that afforded a delightful shade at mid-day from the scorching sun, when a fine but fiery looking youth bounded forward to meet her, and having exchanged salutations and drawn her arm within his, they continued their walk together. He had been evidently for some time expecting her arrival, for the frown of uncertainty which was scarcely banished by the joyous smile that lit up his features on her approach, told of the impatience with which he had been waiting.

" Well, Maggie, anillich," said he as they proceeded along, " I'm shure you kep' me waitin' long enough, any how—you promised you'd cum an hour ago."

" Indeed an' that's thrue for you, Tom," answered she in a sweet low tone, " an' I was frettin' fur fear you'd go off athout seein' me, fur my father was watchin', as iv he knew you wor in the town—bud how comes id that you're not in rigimintals, as you have been sence you wor so foolish as to list ?"

" I thought these id be less remarkable, Maggie ; bud isn't it cruel ov you to reproach me wid turnin' sojer, whin you knew how I was situated ?"

" Reproach you, Tom," she eagerly interrupted, turning round her eyes so as to look fully at him—" Dear knows I meant it not that-a-way, bud its the thought ov our bein' obleeged to separate that makes me spake warmer nor usual."

" Oh, Maggie darlin' !" bitterly exclaimed he, pressing her hands convulsively in both of his, " why must I be forced to lave you, an' go wandher thro' the wide world, whin others, that once had no bether prospects than myself, can stay at home an' be happy ?"

The deep feeling with which this sentence was uttered brought tears into her eyes, and still thinking of his enlistment with sorrow, she sobbed, though not reproachfully—

" Iv you hadn't been so hasty, Tom, all might be well."

" Hadn't been so hasty !" reiterated he, stamping on the ground, and pressing her hands so tightly as to hurt them—" What could I do? Where could I turn to ? Who could I ask assistance from ? livin' as I was depindant on a step-father who hated me—atin' a male that I knew his heart grudged tho' his hand gev id—athout other kith or kin to look up to fur shelther. Oh Maggie, Maggie, don't—don't say I was hasty whin you think ov that."

On hearing him speak thus, her emotions could be no longer repressed, and she turned her face to his shoulder and burst into tears. At this the passion which had arisen instantly became stilled, and he strove to comfort her in a soothing tone of voice, that contrasted with the late harshness, seemed soft and even melodious.

" Maggie, Maggie, don't cry so !" exclaimed he—" I couldn't help spakin', fur I'd choke iv I didn't say id !— Bud never fear, we'll be happy yet, Maggie—I ll gain a fortune worthy of my good little girl, an' thin no power can separate us."

She raised her head from his shoulder, and a bright and beautiful beam of anticipated joy danced in her soft black eyes, even at the moment when the last tear-drop fell from their silken fringe. Her heart was full of hope, that sweet enchantress, who whispers consolation in the ear of the despairing—and her newly awakened joy found utterance in broken accents that breathed a world of tenderness and truth.

The final, long, and lingering farewell was breathed again and again—the severed ring was divided, and one sunny lock that a moment before had decked her snowy brow, was given as a remembrance—yet they still remained—too agitated to speak, and as if neither dared to be the first to move ! At length, pressing both her hands to his lips and to his heart, he faltered out, " Heaven bless my darlin' Maggie !" and then suddenly released them, and rushed away, as if not daring to trust his firmness any longer. She stood for a moment, looking in the direction where he had disappeared, as if rooted to the spot, and then sighing heavily, moved listlessly in the opposite direction.

The following morning the entire population of Cullen seemed assembled outside the small—barrack, we believe we may call it—where a troop of soldiers were getting ready for departure. The women wept, and the men pressed each other's hands warmly as the order was given to march, and many a heart was sad as the military looking array passed down the principal street. When they came opposite the house which Maggie had left the evening before, the lattice was opened, and her figure was seen bending forth through the thick clusters of jasmine and woodbine, which she pushed aside with her hand :— at this one of the soldiers, who was in the rear, turned round and waved his hand, while a tear fell hotly on his manly cheek. Another moment passed, and they were hidden from view by a turning in the road, and a choking sob burst from her bosom as she left the window, and sitting on her low pallet, with its spotless coverlid pressed both her hands to her burning eyes, and wept in silence over her young heart's bereavement. Such, reader, was the parting of Maggie and her lover!

Maggie, as we shall in future call her, as we hate formal Margaret, was the youngest and prettiest of Mr. Keenan's two daughters. He was for many years a widower, and latterly had scarcely felt the loss of his wife in the society of her and Jane, the elder sister; for as they were both warmly attached to him, they made it the study of their lives to render him as happy as possible. The first disagreement they almost ever had was on the discovery of the attachment between his younger daughter and Tom Higgins, the dependant on the bounty of his stepfather, who was always hated by Keenan, though we believe he himself could not assign any reason for his strange antipathy. This youth, in early life, was so unfortunate as to lose his father, who died suddenly, leaving a widow and child both unprovided for ; and on her second marriage, shortly after, began to feel the miseries of dependance—we say began, because it was not until a new family gradually sprang up around him that he encountered the real slights and neglects that every one in a like situation is almost certain of having to endure. He was naturally very high spirited, and of a violent and hasty temper, and so was doubly disqualified to endure the thousand petty insults that were daily heaped upon him. He was poor—a mere dependant, and did not know whither to fly—and on a recruiting party coming through the town, goaded with hourly mortifications, he followed and enlisted.

Poor Maggie wept bitterly when she heard of this step being taken ; but he himself did not know the extent of the sacrifice until one month after the regiment he had joined was ordered on foreign service. But then repining was useless—go he must, and his bitterest pang was the thought of being parted from her for such a long period of time, and not knowing but that he might never return. When Maggie's father heard of his departure, he was delighted, as knowing the fickle nature of most female minds —observe, ladies ! we do not say of all—he deemed that she would soon cease to remember the absent lover in the presence of another of his choice, whom he was determined to provide. We are but simple narrators of facts and so shall not attempt to pry into the gradual change that came over her as time and distance placed their bar between her lover and his home. At first she grew pale, and thin, and melancholy—then her colour begun slowly to return, and her dress to be arranged on Sundays as neatly and with as much care as ever—then her easy vivacity of manner and cheerfulness returned, and then—oh, womankind!—she was more than once seen listening with an evidently pleased ear to the whispers of Pat Daly, a young and thriving farmer, whom her father favoured on account of his wealth. Six short months elapsed, and rumour was busy with a whispered tale of her approaching marriage; and in the middle of the seventh the day was actually appointed, and every preparation made for a "raal rattlin' splicin' match."

It was the night previous to the day appointed for the ceremony to take place—the silver moon smiled along the blue vault of heaven, and shed a bright beam of light through the open casement where Maggie sat, with her cheek leaning on her hand, unmindful of the chill night air, and deeply musing. Her face looked, indeed, lovely in that pale cold light, and the clusters of her bright hair being flung back from her temples, hung gracefully on her neck. It appeared as if, in the silence of the night, she had sat down to think of him who was far away, and whose form used to be always present to her mind. A conflict of various feelings agitated her once peaceful bosom, and it heaved with deep sighs as she drew forth a small black ribbon, to which was fastened a broken ring. It was the pledge of truth and faith—a pledge that she was on the point of breaking—and as she gazed on it, an unbidden tear dimmed her sight, and fell hot and scalding on the hand that held it forth: it was one of the last sincere tributes that came from her very soul to the shrine of unrequited and undecayed affection, for at that moment a light finger was laid on her shoulder, and her sister's cheerful voice rang in her ears as she exclaimed—

"What in the name ov wondher are you dhramin' ov, Maggie, an' I here this five minits, an' you never knew id?"

She passed her hands rapidly across her eyes, to brush off her tears—smiled, but her smile was wan, and passed not the lip; and at last, unable any longer to feign what she did not feel, she stood up, and putting her arms round her sister's neck, hid her face in her bosom, and wept silently and without restraint. Jane, not knowing the feelings that urged them forth, and deeming they were but the tears of weakness generally shed by females about to leave their home and trust in the protection of a stranger, was not much alarmed, and soon succeeded in calming her; and then placing her sitting on a low chair, she knelt at her feet and soon busied herself in the opening of a box that contained the white and stainless wedding dress which had just arrived as a present from Pat Daly.

"There—there!" she rapidly uttered as she turned over the contents—"look at that, Maggie—isn't it a nice dhress? I'm shure you'll look elegant in id—an' these white roses too fur yer hair—musha! bud he 's the nate taste anyhow;—look, Maggie, what nathural looking flowers they are—let me fix thim in for a minit, jist till we see how they'll do. Oh! you're killin' entirely now, an' ill be glad yet you didn't throw yerself away on that poor Higgins."

While Jane was running on thus, she had fixed the flowers in her sister's hair, and held up a small glass for her to see the effect of them, and Maggie, in the eagerness of dress and vanity, had forgotten almost her late sad musings, and was as anxiously employed as her sister in the arrangement of her luxuriant curls. But the mention of his name called up again all the feelings of her heart, and she let her hands droop by her side, and grew pale as she asked—

"Tell me, Jane—do you think I am doin' right in thryin' to forget him whom my very heart burns for, even at this minit?"

Her sister looked at her for a moment with astonishment, for her voice was hollow, and she looked, with the white flowers in her hair, as pale as though she were dressed out for the grave.

"Maggie! my dear Maggie! what makes you look so?

Why do you spake in such a way? What has come over you so suddenly?—is there any thing the matther?"

"No, sisther, nothin'—nothin' to signify—only I feel a pain here—here," and she placed her hand upon her heart. "I know I should not have so soon larned to forget him—he wouldn't be so wid me, I dar say: bud no matther, it can't be helped now—hand me that cup of wather, Jane, an' don't say you saw me cry. I'm a wake, foolish poor girl."

If she felt any further emotion that night, it was concealed effectually, for she laughed and chatted gaily with her sister as they were preparing for rest, and soon sank into a gentle slumber.

Next day, amid the admiring gaze of many a "nate counthry boy," and the envying glance of many a village beauty, Maggie Keenan was led to the altar of the pretty little church which is such an ornament to Cullen. Her blushing cheek burned with maiden shame as well as the pride of conscious loveliness, and as she breathed her responses, and felt her fingers tremble in the warm clasp of her excited lover, we will venture fearlessly to assert that not a single corner of her heart was sad with thoughts of the absent one to whom she was behaving so faithlessly. Oh, what a wild, wondrous, and incomprehensible article is the heart of woman!

Feasting and fighting, drinking and dancing, with all the festivities generally attendant on a wedding, concluded the affair; and Maggie, between the adulation she received from every side, and the happiness she saw going on around her, felt as if in an absolute delirium or bewilderment of joy, and laughed, and danced, and made merry with the wildest hearted who were present. There was no "small still voice" within to make her feel the pain of a broken vow, for nothing was there to remind her of the absent one—all was pleasure—every eye met hers with a bright and laughing glance, and every heart seemed resolved, if only for one night, entirely to fling care aside. Such, reader, was the wedding of Maggie Keenan.

Years passed rapidly by, and she became the mother of a lovely boy, who was the sole pledge of their mutual affection, and in the new cares of her wedded life almost totally would have forgotten her absent lover, but for the piece of broken ring, which, with a feeling she could not account for, she still continued to wear about her person. Rumour said that he had fallen a victim to the plague; and it was generally believed, from his long silence, that he was dead. However, as where there is one opinion there always will be found some one to differ from it, others asserted that he was living still, and would yet return. His step-father had died shortly after his departure, and the farm he held was managed now by his eldest son, with whom Higgins was always a favourite, and who was one of the most anxious in his enquiries after him, but who could not by any means find out where he had been ordered to.

On a scorching day in the middle of the month of June a few idlers were loitering about the door of a public place of entertainment whose sign still swings in Cullen, listlessly observing every one's approach, and speculating on their different purposes. Suddenly they were silent as a tall figure, evidently worn with the toil of travelling and stooped with fatigue, approached the door round which they were clustered. He wore a faded military uniform, with three stripes on the arm that denoted his rank, and had a scar on his right cheek that showed he had seen some service; but his face was pale and sallow, and his lips blue and thin. "God save you, Sir," said one of the group as he drew near. "God save you kindly," he rejoined: "can you tell me if Mr. Keenan is livin' here still, an' if he's in good health?"

"Sorra healthier ould cock undher the sun, sur, as a body may say," was the answer. "Ever sence his daughter's weddin' he looks as iv he'd taken out a new lase."

At the mention of his daughter's wedding the fiery blood burst into the soldier's cheek, and his lip quivered, while his eye blazed and his brow lowered; but habitual caution gave him a command over his features, and in a calm easy manner he asked—

"Which of his daughters did you say was married?"

"Faix, Miss Maggie to be shure; an' more shame fur

that same, as they say she promised she'd have poor Tom Higgins, who's been gone off this many a day."

The mention of this so rudely and suddenly came like a thunderbolt upon the stranger—he clenched both his hands—uttered a heart-rending ejaculation, and sank powerless on the seat. Surprised at such emotion in a stranger, they examined his lineaments more narrowly, and discovered that, though much changed, it was Tom Higgins himself that stood before them. Upon this, many a hand was outstretched, but not received, and their greetings of welcome were not responded to, for he sat sternly silent, with his arms folded and his eyes fixed on the earth. While they viewed him with astonishment he suddenly sprang up, and asking the way to her residence, which was on the banks of the river outside of the town, he strode off in that direction, as rapidly as if he were fresh and unfatigued.

As he went along, the agonizing expression of his face was indeed fearful, and his lips moved rapidly as he uttered various hasty and unconnected expressions, such as—

"Married—married!—can it be possible! My Maggie! to decave me thus—afther all my labour and my toil, to return and find her false!—To return full of fondness and joy, and find——but no: I hate her—I loathe her, and she shall hear it—I'll tell her so, and fly to the end ov the earth."

When he came in sight of the cabin, he left the beaten track, and almost ran along the banks of the river in his eagerness—it was, although midsummer, nearly full of water, and the breeze was not strong enough to agitate its surface even into the tiniest ripples. As he went along, he heard the cheerful voice of a child singing, and caught a glimpse of a female form approaching the spot from whence the sounds issued: then suddenly he heard a quick heavy plash, and one wild and agonizing shriek! It was his Maggie's voice—he would have recognised it in the midst of a thousand, and fearing he knew not what, he rushed on with renewed speed. When he suddenly emerged from behind a clump of trees, Maggie—for it was she indeed—perceived him, and springing madly forward, she caught the hand that shrunk from her touch, and screamed wildly,

"Oh my child—my child—save my child!"

A demon gratification at her misery for a second parted his lips with a smile, but then he heard the bubble of the poor boy struggling for his life, and looked upon the distorted lineaments of those features he once so fondly loved, and all his better feelings returned, and he cried—

"Yes, Maggie, thy child shall be saved!"

Then springing into the river just as the boy was sinking, he rescued him, and brought him safe to land.

"The God who witnessed that action will reward you, for I cannot!" sobbed the grateful mother as he laid her frightened but not insensible boy in her arms, and kneeling down beside him, kissed his cherub lips, and parted from his forehead his wet and glossy hair. As he stooped, a ribbon which was round his neck loosened, and some weight at its centre bore it down and it fell upon her lap. She shrieked wildly when she saw it, and gazing intently at his features, muttered inaudibly, "It is him!" and sank back breathless and unconscious—that ribbon bore the piece of broken ring!

He looked with agony on her pale, pale features, and as the little boy cried out, "Mother!" he stooped down and pressed his lips to hers with one long and burning kiss—then raising her gently up, he bore her to the cottage, followed by the child, and was met at the door by her sister. Shocked as she was at Maggie's death-like appearance and the child's dripping clothes, she hardly cast a glance on Higgins till she had laid her sister on the bed—then she turned round, but he was gone!

The ducking the little boy received by his accidental fall had no effect, but Maggie had a violent fever, brought on by the agitation she had suffered, but again recovered; and though she lived many years after, was never observed to laugh with the same gaiety as before, for her spirits had sustained a decided shock. Higgins was never seen afterwards by either of the sisters, for he exchanged into a regiment going to Jamaica, and was believed to have perished there.   DENIS O'DONOHO.

TO ERIN.

(From the Belfast Magazine.)

My country!—too long, like the mist on thy mountains,
 The cloud of affliction hath sadden'd thy brow:
Too long hath the blood-rain empurpled thy fountains,
 And Pity been deaf to thy cries—until now.

Thou wert doom'd for a season in darkness to languish,
 While others around thee were basking in light;
Scarce a sunbeam e'er lighten'd the gloom of thy anguish;
 In "the Island of Saints," it seem'd still to be night.

Of thy children, alas! some in sorrow forsook thee,
 They could not endure to behold thee distress'd;
In "the land of the stranger" did other's o'erlook thee,
 Unworthy the life-stream they drew from thy breast.

And the song of the minstrel was hushed in thy bowers;
 For Discord's dire trump, thy lov'd harp was thrown by;
While, strong as the ivy that strangled thy towers,
 The gripe of oppression scarce left thee a sigh!

That is past—and for aye let its memory perish;
 The day-spring arises, while heaviness ends;
Wake, Erin! forbear thy dark bodings to cherish—
 The wheel hath revolv'd, and thy fortune ascends!

Yes—thy cause hath been heard—men hath wept at thy story—
 Alas! that a land of such beauty should mourn!
Have thy children ne'er grac'd the high niches of glory?
 Was kindness ne'er known in their bosoms to burn?

Yes, rich as the mines which thy teeming hills nourish,
 Are the stores of their genius which nature imparts;
And sweet as the flow'rs in thy valleys that flourish,
 The fragrance of feeling that breathes from their hearts!

When stung to despair, in their wildness what wonder
 If sometimes their souls from affection might rove?
That frenzy subsiding, their feelings the fonder
 Will seek their own halcyon channel of love?

Let the past be forgotten!—Yet shalt thou, fair Erin,
 Fling off the base spells which thy spirit enslave;
Thou shalt, like the sea-bird, awhile disappearing,
 Emerge with thy plumage more bright from the wave.

Once more 'mong the verdure and dew of thy mountains
 The shamrock shall ope its wet eye to the sun,
While fondly the muse shall recline by thy fountains,
 And warble her strains to the rills as they run.

And plenty shall smile on thy beautiful valleys,
 And peace shall return, the long wandering dove;
And religion, no longer a cover for malice,
 Shall spread out her wings o'er an Eden of love.

Then tuning thy mild harp, whose melody slumbers,
 As high on the willow it waves in the breeze,
Let poesy lend thee her liveliest numbers,
 To sound thy reveillie, thy anthem of praise.

And say unto those that have left thee forsaken—
 "Return, oh return, to your lone mother's arms!
Other lands in their sons can a fondness awaken;
 Shall Erin alone for her race have no charms!

"Oh, blush as ye wander, that it e'er should be taunted,
 That strangers have felt, what my own could not feel;
That, when Britons stood forth in my trial undaunted,
 My children slunk back, unconcerned in my weal!

"Oh! if yet in your bosom one last spark ye treasure
 Of love for the land of your sires—of your birth—
Return! and indulge in the soul-thrilling pleasure,
 Of hailing that land 'mong the brightest on earth!"

Then joy to thee, Erin! thy better day breaketh;
 The long polar night of thy wo speeds away,
And, as o'er thy chill breast the warm sunlight awaketh,
 Each bud of refinement evolves in the ray.

Yet remember—the blossom is barren and fleeting,
 As long as the canker of strife, unsubdued,
With its poisonous tooth at the core remains eating—
 If e'er thou art glorious, thou first must be good.

Dublin: Printed and Published by P. D. HARDY, 3, Cecilia Street, to whom all communications are to be addressed.

THE
DUBLIN PENNY JOURNAL
CONDUCTED BY P. DIXON HARDY, M.R.I.A.

| Vol. III. | MAY 16, 1835. | No. 150. |

THE GREATER SUGAR-LOAF MOUNTAIN.

In our 82d Number will be found a correct, though hasty, outline of a three days' tour through the County Wicklow. Having in that article, in our sketch of the Wicklow mountains, particularly described the Greater and Lesser Sugar Loaf, we shall now merely observe, that while their conical summits attract the eye of the traveller at a very considerable distance from almost every point of observation, they are seen to the greatest advantage while the traveller is passing through the Scalp on the road to Enniskerry. In a little work* published since the appearance of that number of our Journal, the following vivid description of the place is given :—

" Immediately over the park and woods of Kilruddery, rises the lesser Sugar-loaf, one of the most conspicuous ornaments of the scene. As such we may leave it to speak for itself; our business is to conduct our reader to avail himself of the advantages which it offers to the enterprising visitor, whose taste, time, and alertness, induce him to seek for the less trite points of view over this broad and diversified vale. This hill affords the best inland prospects. Somewhat more than half way up, looking towards the south and west, an elevated natural terrace, of smooth, short, grassy sheepwalk, runs round the hill, from which, if the hill be ascended on the south-east side, the varying prospect opens with fresh magnificence, and new combination at every perch. First, looking across a broad, deep, and shadowy glen, the greater Sugar-loaf raises its

imposing form, against the south. As a picturesque object, it varies according to the position of the sun, or the varying disposition of the heavens. We have seen it from this point, upon a cloudless noon, across the clear gray interval of interposing air, vast, shadeless, but clothed in its garb of mountain hues, with, perhaps, some three or four figures in the distance, toiling up its sultry side. Again we have seen it from the same point, upon some shadowy day, standing like a mountain monarch amidst its levee of subject hills, attired in its splendid robe of beams, which seemed to fall down over its graceful shoulders, from a superb tiara of clouds overhead, among which the sun lay like a chrysolite of purest fire. For these effects the pedestrian must choose his day : we recommend the shadowy, as harmonizing by far the best with the general character of the scenery. Some steps further, the prospect opens far into the depth of wood and far-off mountains, forming the background of the rich and lordly demesne of Powerscourt. A few steps more disclose the north western range from Enniskerry, or rather from the Scalp, to the sea—broad, varied, and spotted with cultivation and ornamental planting. Having reached a wall which runs up the northern side of the acclivity, we would advise the pedestrian to press up the hill, and look down over Kilruddery, which lies mapped beneath. He may then look round about him wherever else it pleases him, north, south, east, or west. This hill is rendered pleasing by the freshness of its vegetation : the bilberry plant here intermingles its bright green with the rich russet of the heath ; and there is a lonely and untrodden aspect, which awakens meditation, or, if not, at least gives a pleasurable sense."

* Guide to the County of Wicklow. Dublin : Wm. Curry, Jun. and Co. 1835.

VOL. III.—NO. 46.

381.

SCENE IN A PRIVATE MAD-HOUSE.

FROM THE MONTREAL HERALD.

" The following lines, descriptive of a scene in a private mad-house, are from the pen of M. G. Lewis, Esq. They were published in the National Intelligencer, about eight years since, the editors of which paper introduced them with these remarks :—' If any one can read the following lines without shuddering in sympathy with the supposed captive, he must have a heart dead to every human feeling. The perusal of them had the more effect upon us, from the conviction we have for some time entertained, that insanity, when superinduced (not natural)—when it is an affection of the mind, and not a defect of organization—is often the consequence of the treatment of the disease ;—not merely of the estrangement of friends—of seclusion from the world—of coercion—but of the horrible dread of being thought mad by others. We recollect hearing of the case of an enlightened physician, who was carried by his friends to an asylum for the insane, after exhibiting symptoms of an alienation of mind. " My God ! am I come to this ? Never shall I leave these walls !" And he died within them not many days after.'

" Stay, jailer, stay, and hear my woe !
    She is not mad who kneels to thee ;
For what I'm now too well I know,
    And what I was, and what should be.
I'll rave no more in proud despair—
    My language shall be mild, though sad ;
But yet I firmly, truly swear,
    I am not mad—I am not mad !

" My tyrant husband forged the tale
    Which chains me in this dismal cell ;
My fate unknown my friends bewail—
    Oh ! jailer, haste, that fate to tell.
Oh ! haste, my father's heart to cheer :
    His heart at once 'twill grieve and glad
To know, though kept a captive here,
    I am not mad—I am not mad !

" He smiles in scorn, and turns the key—
    He quits the grate—I knelt in vain ;
His glimmering lamp, still, still I see—
    'Tis gone ! and all is gloom again.
Cold, bitter cold !—No warmth ! no light !—
    Life, all thy comforts once I had ;
Yet here I'm chained, this freezing night,
    Although not mad—no, no, not mad !

" 'Tis sure some dream, some vision vain ;
    What ! I—the child of rank and wealth—
Am I the wretch who clanks this chain,
    Bereft of freedom, friends, and health ?
Ah ! while I dwell on blessings fled,
    Which never more my heart must glad,
How aches my heart, how burns my head—
    But 'tis not mad !—no, 'tis not mad !

" Hast thou, my child, forgot, ere this,
    A mother's face, a mother's tongue ?
She'll ne'er forget your parting kiss,
    Nor round her neck how fast you clung ;
Nor how with me you used to stay :
    Nor how that suit your sire forbade ;
Nor how—I'll drive such thoughts away—
    They'll make me mad—they'll make me mad !

" His rosy lips, how sweet they smiled !
    His mild blue eyes, how bright they shone !
None ever bore a lovelier child !
    And art thou now for ever gone ?
And must I never see thee more,
    My pretty, pretty, pretty lad ?
I will be free ! unbar the door !
    I am not mad—I am not mad !

" Oh, hark ! what mean those dreadful cries ?
    His chain some furious madman breaks.
He comes—I see his glaring eyes—
    Now, now, my dungeon grate he shakes.

Help ! help !—He's gone !—Oh, fearful wo,
    Such screams to hear, such sights to see !
My brain, my brain !—I know, I know,
    I am not mad—but soon shall be.

" Yes, soon—for, lo you ! while I speak,
    Mark how yon demon's eye-balls glare !
He sees me—now, with dreadful shriek,
    He whirls a serpent high in air.
Horror !—the reptile strikes his tooth
    Deep in my heart, so crushed and sad,
Ay, laugh, ye fiends !—I feel the truth—
    Your task is done—I'm mad ! I'm mad !

NIAGARA FALLS.
(Written during a Thunder Storm.)
FROM THE SAME.

" Among the many productions to which the impressive sublimity of the Falls of Niagara have given birth, the following is deserving of a high place. It was copied from the Public Album at the Falls, during the late visit of the editor to that place.

" Niagara—Niagara—careering in its might,
The fierce and free Niagara shall be my theme to-night ;
A glorious theme—a glorious home, Niagara are mine ;
Heaven's fire is on thy flashing wave, its thunder blends
    with thine.
The clouds are bursting fearfully, the rocks beneath me
    quiver.
But thou, unscathed, art hurrying on for ever and for ever ;
Years touch thee not, Niagara, thou art a changeless thing—
For still the same deep roundelay thy solemn waters sing ;
The great, the proud, of other lands, the wisest and the
    best,
Must speak and think of little things—they have not seen
    the West—
They have not seen the glorious West, nor in the forest
    dwelt,
Where nature's ever present God is most intensely felt—
There is a chainless spirit here whose throne no eye can
    reach,
Awakening thoughts in human hearts too deep for human
    speech.
This is the shrine at which the heart is tutored to forget
Its former joy, its future hope, its sorrow and regret,—
For who that ever lingered here a single hour or twain,
Can think as he hath thought, or be what he hath been
    again.
Where'er the wanderer's foot may roam, whate'er his lot
    may be,
'Tis deeply written on his heart that he hath been with
    thee."

VISIT TO A WORK-HOUSE IN ENGLAND.

Whether or not the tax which, in England, obliges every man to provide a home for the destitute, be an evil or a good, certain it is that very many, but for such institutions as the parish workhouse, would not have where to lay their heads ; and that numbers are kept in comparative ease and comfort, who, were it otherwise, would be wanderers on the wide world, existing on the pitiful morsel which the hand of charity might now and then fling to them. Preservation from want is an Englishman's birthright. In all his troubles, or sorrows, he is never without the certainty that his death-bed will not be a dunghill, or the knowledge that his dying lips will be moistened in the hour of struggles. Those thoughts suggested themselves to my mind, when, a short time ago, I visited the workhouse of a parish, a little distant from the crowded portion of London ; among the aged, the sick, and the desolate, to seek materials for contemplation.

It is not my intention to dwell on the internal management of the house ; in which, as in most others, selfishness had taken up his abode with charity. All my wish, and all my object, in passing through the wards, was to notice its hapless, or its happy, inmates. The first who attracted my attention, and who came under the latter class, was a young woman who had been bed-ridden from childhood. She was the victim of many diseases ; yet their power had not been able to chase from her cheek the placid smile which dwelt there, and spoke of the tranquillity that dwelt within, while the body suffered. Her countenance was serene and beautiful, though very pale; but there was a slight moisture on the upper lip that betokened the pain under which she laboured. Her employment for years (for years she had been an inmate of the workhouse) had been to teach children; and she was, at the moment I entered, surrounded by her youthful pupils. I perceived a reverend gentleman, who, as I afterwards understood, was the clergyman of the parish, going through the wards, to drop, as he passed, that cordial, which gives hope and consolation to the poor and destitute. I knew by the blessings which followed him as he went by, that he was not one of those who

> " As surely as our church is vacant, flock
> Into her consistory, and at leisure
> There stall them, and grow fat."

Nor was he one of those clerical coxcombs who can never touch the sick, but with a glove on hand, who hasten from the death-bed to the card-table; and who never dream that their days in this world should be spent in preparing themselves and others for a better. But he was one of those who love to go on their master's errand; whose most delightful task is to soften the pathway on earth, by pointing out the road to heaven; and who are happier in the salvation of one soul, than a monarch in the acquisition of a new kingdom.

He sat down by the invalid's bed, assisted her in the instruction of her young pupils; and gave her hints, now and then, how she should instil into their minds the principles of religion and virtue, in order that they might " remember their Creator in the days of their youth, so that, when they become old, they may not depart from them."

In another ward lay a poor Irishman, who was by special favour an inmate of the workhouse; for his is not like the Englishman's—a right. The reverend visitor drew near, and accosted him with, " And how is it with you, Tim?" " Ah! God be wid you, an' all belongin' to you, it's bad enough sure, thank God," replied Tim. " And why so?" asked the clergyman. " Becase, yer honour, I'm alone in the cowld world, and there'll be nobody to weep for me when I'm under the sod—no wake for poor Tim, now Judy's gone, and the childhre, and all." " And where are Judy and the children, Tim?" " Dead, dead, yer honour, and the cabin wid 'em. 'Twas the great flood that swept all away. I was off to the mountain; and, when I came down, they were cowld corpses afore me; many was the cry over the counthry for the poor things, and I—I never saw luck nor grace since. And 'tis little the neighbours thought my father's son would be in a poorhouse, among strangers, God bless 'em, any way, they wouldn't let a poor Irishman starve among 'em."

In another room lay a woman in the last stage of a consumption; and, apparently, in the agonies of death. The clergyman paused, took her hand, bent down, and whispered, " Is all peace?" And she replied, " All is peace." She meant that all was tranquil within, for the convulsive motion of her fingers showed that it was not so with the suffering body.

In the next ward was a man bowed down by the weight of years. When the clergyman approached him, he scarcely raised his head to receive the salutation, and his reply was a thankless murmur. There was a sort of restless agony in his manner, which appeared the result of despair rather than disease, and bespoke him one of those who had seen better days, but who had not borne adversity as the blow which chastens, but does not fell—who had never learned that the wind is tempered even to the shorn lamb; and who, instead of being resigned in the hour of sorrow and suffering, was ungrateful both to God and man. The hollow eye, that looked forth from under a scowling brow, seemed to watch with a suspicious eagerness every one who passed him; and the bitter sneer on his lip betrayed the feeling with which he regarded even those who gave him food. I left him as one who was equally unfit to live or die, and grieved for a being whose mouth was filled with curses even on the brink of the grave.

In the next bed lay a father, beside whom his two children stood. The one was looking earnestly in his face, and the other appeared to be counting the veins which ran through his wasted hand. It was a strong contrast to the scene I had just witnessed—to the man who lay near him. The one was like a tree blasted by the lightning—the other, although falling to decay, looked with hope to the flourishing progeny which grew up around him. He smiled when the reverend visitor addressed him, and pressed the offered hand to his pale lips. " I have been talking to my poor children of their mother, Sir," said he, " and have been teaching them those lessons which must bear fruit when they are indeed orphans. I know they will heed me, and walk in the ways of righteousness, and obtain peace. There is one who will be a friend to them when I am gone, who will not leave them nor forsake them, and whom death cannot sever from their youth or age. I am sure they will be good children—will you not, Mary?" said he, addressing the little one who was gazing on his countenance. " I will, father," sobbed the poor girl; " but you will not die, as my mother did; there will be no one to love us then." Her almost infant brother was looking on the group, apparently unconscious of any care. He was at that age when sorrow is seen not in perspective—before the heart contemplates aught of suffering in the world on which it has but newly entered. And I, a stranger, felt more for his fate, than he who was going into the world without a friend, save Him, of whom it hath been said, He " never saw the righteous forsaken, nor his seed begging their bread."

Near this group lay an old veteran sailor, who had seen almost every part of the habitable globe; and who was passing away from earth carelessly, as one who is embarking on a long voyage, and who cares little for the result. " It matters not to me, Sir," said he to the reverend visitor, " I have weathered many a gale, and I can bear this; 'tis time for me to weigh my anchor and depart. I have seen good and evil days, and my shattered hulk must sink at last. Many of my old comrades are gone before, and there are but few to come after me. Some have died in the battle, and some in the flood, but they are almost all gone. I shall go down bravely, in my own country, and not, like my old shipmates, lie buried in a foreign land."

In the next ward, among many others, who were almost at the bottom of the hill of life, was a very old woman, who sat in her bed, knitting. Her grand-daughter was beside her, smoothing her pathway to the grave, by reading from that book which teaches all, that, though they live in sorrow, they may die in peace. There was in the venerable and time-worn countenance of the old woman, so much of that happy expression which, more forcibly than words, bespeaks one over whom the grave could have no victory, and for whom death could bear no sting; that I felt assured the smile which graced her cheek while living, would dwell upon it when dead.

These were the few I selected from the many who were worthy of more lengthened observation. I found what I had anticipated, that a parish workhouse is not barren of instruction; and I departed, quoting the words of the wise man—" It is better to go to the house of mourning, than to the house of feasting."[*]

A POINT OF HONOUR.

There was something very noble in the reply of the banished Queen of Denmark, who was suffering, charged with a crime of which her answer alone would prove her innocence, when solicited by her husband to return, and be reconciled, " No!" she replied, and she sacrificed a throne to the majesty of her resentment—" No! if the accusation is just, I am unworthy of his bed; if it is false, he is unworthy of mine." Her accuser, who could send her a homeless wanderer into the world, was unable to deprive her of the consciousness of her integrity—and that feeling supported her.

DEATH RATHER THAN DISHONOUR.

During the Irish "reign of terror" in 1798, a circumstance occurred, which in the days of Sparta would have immortalized the heroine; it is almost unknown, no pen has ever traced the story. We pause not to inquire into the principles which influenced her; suffice it, that, in common with most of her stamp, she beheld the struggle as one in which liberty warred with tyranny. Her only son had been taken in the act of rebellion, and was condemned by martial law, to death; she followed the officer, on whose word his life depended, to the place of execution, and besought him to spare the widow's stay; she knelt in the agony of her soul, and clasped his knees, while her eye, with the glare of a maniac, fell on her child beside him. The judge was inexorable, the transgressor must die. But, taking advantage of the occasion, he offered life to the culprit, on condition of his discovering the members of the association with which he was connected. The son wavered—the mother rose from her position of humiliation and exclaimed, "My child, my child, if you do, the heaviest curse of your mother shall fall upon you, and the milk of her bosom shall be poison in your veins." He was executed—the pride of her soul enabled her to behold it without a tear—she returned to her home; the support of her declining years had fallen—the tie that bound her to life had given way—and the evening of the day that saw her lonely and forsaken, left her at rest for ever. Her heart had broken in the struggle.

ing round to Bray-head, from which the graceful cones of the greater and lesser Sugar-loaf, etherially tinted through the half dozen miles of intervening air, terminate the view. Turning round and looking along the coast, a scene of inexpressible richness, variety, and grandeur, bursts upon the eye: beneath is Kingstown, no longer the poor residence of fishermen, but a large town, or rather an infant city, built in the most ornamental style, and still enlarging into the dimensions of maturity: stretching away beyond its picturesque pier, the most splendid bay in Europe spreads for miles its vast and lake-like level, adorned with all imaginable objects that can animate and diversify: the towns and shining outlets—the piers, docks, batteries, and beacons—the sail of every form, the darkening curve of steam, the cloud-like canopy of Dublin—and Howth,

" Like leviathan afloat on the wave,"

shutting in the bay at the distance of a dozen miles."

We give a representation of the obelisk, to remind the tourist to whom he is indebted for the comfortable seat which the room affords. We are induced also to present him with a view of Malpas Castle, the house of the late Mr. Boucher, by whom the obelisk was erected.

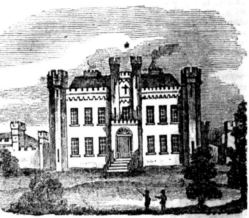

MALPAS CASTLE.

Here, with permission, may be visited, in a field behind Mount Druid demesne, a druidical circle, with the high priest's chair and sacrificing stone. The visitor will also observe a pillar raised to the memory of the late Duke of Dorset, on the spot where he was killed by a fall from his horse in hunting.

OBELISK ON KILLINEY HILL.

Who is there living in Dublin, that has read the description of Killiney in our 113th Number, but has visited that delightful spot, so rife in fine views and pleasing prospects? And who is there that has visited Killiney, and ascended its summit, that has not felt gratified and pleased at being allowed to rest his wearied limbs, after toiling up the hill, in the little reception room in the obelisk, which was some time since raised by Mr. Boucher, to commemorate *nothing!* but to point out to the stranger in search of the picturesque, a spot from which he can at once obtain, by merely turning on the pivot supplied by the heel of his shoe, some of the finest views of maritime and inland scenery to be met with in our island.

" Approaching from the Dublin side, and ascending the hill, a sudden view is gained of Killiney bay, with its glittering semicircle of water and smooth zone of sand sweep-

THIS PILE
Was raised to mark the fatal spot where, at the age of 21,
GEORGE JOHN FREDERICK,
The Fourth Duke of Dorset,
Accidentally lost his life, 14th Feb. 1815,

SKETCHES IN IRELAND.

We have had some experience in the *trade* of publishing, and of all the works which have issued from the Irish press, none have more surprised us, or more completely set us at *fault* in our calculations, than Carleton's " Traits and Stories of the Irish Peasantry," and " Sketches in the North and South," the little volume from which we copied into a former Journal the " true story" of the Irish way of " bilking an exciseman." In no other work have we ever observed such graphic illustrations of Irish life and manners as in the " Traits and Stories ;" and never were there better sketched or more faithful representations given of some of the wildest and most romantic scenery of our island, enlivened by full length pencil sketches of the aborigines of the country, " the *raal* Irish," who are still to be met with in some of the more remote districts, than in the " Sketches in the North and South," published anonymously, but well known to be from the pen of the Rev. Cesar Otway. The former work, although, we believe, it is now three years since it first made its *debut,* has only yet reached a *third* edition, while the latter still appears in its *original* binding.

We avail ourselves of the opportunity presented by the appearance of the third edition of the " Traits and Stories," to give an extract, prefaced by a *fac simile* of one of the wood-cuts. We have *heard* and *read* much of encouragement to *Irish talent* and *genius.* We have observed very little of it put into practice ; and sorry we are to have it to say, least of all from *Irishmen.* Had a similar publication to that from which our extract is taken been brought out in Scotland, the poorest peasant in the country would have possessed himself of a copy.

" George, my love, is the pig also from Ireland ?"

PHIL PURCEL, THE PIG-DRIVER.
AN OUTLINE.

" Phil Purcel was a singular character, for he was never married ; but notwithstanding his singularity, no man ever possessed, for practical purposes, a more plentiful stock of duplicity. Every body knew that Phil was a knave of the first water, yet was he decidedly a general favourite. Now as we hate mystery ourselves, we shall reveal the secret of this remarkable popularity ; though, after all, it can scarcely be called so, for Phil was not the first cheat who has been popular in his day. The cause of his success lay simply in this—that he never laughed ; and none of our readers need be told, that the appearance of a grave cheat in Ireland is an originality which almost runs up into a miracle. This gravity induced every one to look upon him as a phenomenon. The assumed simplicity of his manners was astonishing, and the ignorance which he feigned, so apparently natural, that it was scarcely possible for the most

keen-sighted searcher into human motives to detect him. The only way of understanding the man was to deal with him : if, after *that,* you did not comprehend him thoroughly, the fault was not Phil's, but your own. Although not mirthful himself, he was the cause of mirth in others ; for, without ever smiling at his own gains, he contrived to make others laugh at their losses. His disposition, setting aside laughter, was strictly anomalous—the most incompatible, the most unamalgamatible, and the most uncomeatable qualities that ever refused to unite in the same individual, had no scruple at all to unite in Phil. But we hate metaphysics, which we leave to the mechanical philosophers, and proceed to state that Phil was a miser, which is the best explanation we can give of his gravity.

" Ireland, owing to the march of intellect, and the superiority of modern refinement, has been for some years, and is at present, well supplied with an abundant variety of professional men, every one of whom will undertake, for proper considerations, to teach us, Irish, all manner of useful accomplishments. The drawing-master talks of his profession ; the dancing-master speaks of *his* profession ; the fiddler, tooth-drawer, and corn-cutter (who, by the way, reaps a richer harvest than we do) since the devil has tempted the schoolmaster to go abroad, are all practising, in his absence, as professional men.

" Now Phil must be included among this class of grandiloquent gentlemen, for he entered life as a Professor of Pig-driving ; and it is but justice towards him to assert, that no corn-cutter of them all ever raised his profession so high as Phil did that of pig-driving. In fact, he elevated it to the most exalted pitch of improvement of which it was then susceptible.

" In Phil's time, however, pig-driving was not so general, nor had it made such rapid advances as in modern times. It was then simply pig-driving, unaccompanied by the improvements of poverty, sickness, and famine. The governments of those days were not so enlightened as the governments of these. Political economy had not taught the people how to be poor upon the most scientific principles ; free trade had not shown the nation the most improved plan of reducing itself to the lowest possible state of distress ; nor liberalism enabled the working classes to scoff at religion, and wisely to stop at the very line that lies between outrage and rebellion. Many errors and inconveniencies, now happily exploded, were then in existence. The people, it is true, were somewhat attached to their landlords, but still they were burdened with the unnecessary appendages of good coats and stout shoes—were tolerably industrious, and had the mortification of being able to pay their rents, and feed in comfort. They were not, as they are now, free from new coats and old prejudices, nor improved by the intellectual march of politics and poverty. When either a man or a nation starves, it is a luxury to starve in an enlightened manner ; and nothing is more consolatory to a person acquainted with public rights and constitutional privileges, than to know the principles upon which he fasts and goes naked.

" From all we have said, the reader sees clearly that pig-driving did not then proceed upon so extensive a scale as it does at present. The people, in fact, killed many of them for their own use ; and we know not how it happened, but political ignorance and good bacon kept them in more flesh and comfort than those theories which have succeeded so well in introducing the science of starvation as the basis of national prosperity. Irishmen are frequently taxed with extravagance, in addition to their other taxes ; but we should be glad to know what people in Europe reduce economy in the articles of food and clothing to such close practise as they do. Our governments and our landlords appear to be trying such an experiment upon our great power of living upon a little food, as the man did who entertained the warm expectation of being able to bring his horse to live without it ; but who, when he had brought him to one straw *per diem,* found that the animal was compelled to decline the comforts of such economy, by dying in his own defence. In our ignorant days we had a trade, but no Custom-house ; and now, in our enlightened days, we have a Custom-house, but no trade.

" An old bachelor uncle of ours in the country, seduced

by the plausibility of a tailor's puff in the metropolis, sent him, in reliance upon what he professed in it, his height and weight for a suit of clothes. The clothes came; but as the old gentleman happened to be wry-necked, wore his head in fact upon one of his shoulders, and was a little hump-backed, into the bargain—points which he either forgot, or declined mentioning—it is unnecessary to say, that the clothes did not fit.

"'I ought to have known,' said the old gentleman, 'from the peculiarity of my make, that no tailor could fit me without taking my measure.'

"In like manner may we say, that England is legislating for us without taking our measure; and that her laws, consequently, are a bad fit, considering the unconscionable price we pay for them.

"There was, in Ireland, an old breed of swine, which is now nearly extinct, except in some remote parts of the country, where they are still useful in the hunting season, particularly if dogs happen to be scarce.* They were a tall, loose species, with legs of an unusual length, with no flesh, short ears, as if they had been cropped for sedition, and with long faces of a highly intellectual cast. They were also of such activity that few greyhounds could clear a ditch or cross a field with more agility or speed. Their backs formed a rainbow arch, capable of being contracted or extended to an inconceivable length; and their usual rate of travelling in droves was at mail-coach speed, or six Irish miles an hour, preceded by an outrider to clear the way, whilst their rear was brought up by another horse-man, going at a three-quarter gallop.

"In the middle of summer, when all nature reposed under the united influence of heat and dust, it was an interesting sight to witness a drove of them sweeping past, like a whirlwind, in a cloud of their own raising—their sharp and lengthy outlines dimly visible through the shining haze, like a flock of antelopes crossing the deserts of the east.

"But, alas, for those good old days!—This breed is now nearly a curiosity—few specimens of it remaining except in the mountain parts of the country, whither these lovers of liberty, like the free natives in the back settlements in America, have retired to avoid the encroachments of civilization, and exhibit their Irish antipathy to the slavish comforts of steam-boat navigation, and the relaxing luxuries of English feeding.

"Indeed, their patriotism, as evinced in an attachment to Ireland and Irish habits, was scarcely more remarkable than their sagacity. There is not an antiquarian among the members of that learned and useful body, the Irish Academy, who boasts such an intimate knowledge of the Irish language in all its shades of meaning and idiomatic beauty, as did this once flourishing class of animals. Nor were they confined to the Irish tongue alone, many of them understood English too; and it was said of those that belonged to a convent, the members of which, in their intercourse with each other, spoke only in Latin, that they were tolerable masters of that language, and refused to leave a potato field or plot of cabbages except when addressed in it. To the English tongue, however, they had a deep-rooted antipathy; whether it proceeded from the national feeling, or the fact of its not being sufficiently gutter-al, I cannot say: but be this as it may, it must be admitted that they were excellent Irish scholars, and paid a surprising degree of deference and obedience to whatever was addressed to them in their own language. In Munster, too, such of them as belonged to the hedge-schoolmasters, were good proficients in Latin; but it is on a critical knowledge of their native tongue that I take my stand. On this point they were unrivalled by the most learned pigs or antiquarians of their day; none of either class possessing, at that period, such a knowledge of Irish manners, nor so keen a sagacity in tracing out Irish roots.

"Their education, it is true, was not neglected, and their instructors had the satisfaction of seeing that it was not lost. Nothing could present a finer display of true

* We assure John Bull, on the authority of Phil Purcel, that this is a fact,

friendship, founded upon a sense of equality, mutual interest, and good-will, than the Irishman and his pig: the Arabian and his horse are proverbial; but had our English neighbours known as much of Ireland as they did of Arabia, they would have found as signal instances of attachment subsisting between the former as between the latter: and, perhaps, when the superior comforts of an Arabian hut are contrasted with the squalid poverty of an Irish cabin, they would have perceived a heroism and a disinterestedness on the side of the Irish parties that would have struck them with greater admiration.

"The pigs, however, of the present day are a fat, gross, and degenerate breed; and more like well fed aldermen than Irish pigs of the old school. They are, in fact, a proud, lazy, carnal race, entirely of the earth, earthy. It is one comfort, however, that we do not eat but ship them out of the country; yet, after all, it is not surprising that we should repine a little on thinking of the good old times of sixty years since, when every Irishman could kill his own pig, and eat it when he pleased.

"The education of an Irish pig, at the time of which we write, was an important consideration to an Irishman. He, and his family, and his pig, like the Arabian and his horse, all slept in the same bed; the pig generally, for the sake of convenience, next the stock. At meals the pig usually was stationed at the scrahag, or potato-basket; where the only instances of bad-temper he ever displayed broke out in petty and unbecoming squabbles with the younger branches of the family. Indeed, if he ever descended from his high station as a member of the domestic circle, it was upon these occasions, when, with a want of dignity, accounted for only by the grovelling motive of self-interest, he embroiled himself in a series of miserable feuds and contentions about scraping the pot, or carrying off from the jealous urchins about him more than came to his share. In these heart-burnings about the good things of this world, he was treated with uncommon forbearance: in his master he always had a friend, from whom, when he whined out his appeal to him, he was certain of receiving redress: 'Barney, behave, avick: lay down the potstick, an' don't be batin' the pig, the crathur.'

"In fact, the pig was never mentioned but with this endearing epithet of 'crathur' annexed. 'Barny, go an' call home the pig, the crathur, to his dinner, before it gets cowld an him.'—'Barney, go an' see if you can see the pig, the crathur, his buckwhist will soon be ready.' 'Barny, run an' dhrive the pig, the crathur, out of Larry Neil's phatie-field; an', Barny, whisper, a bouchal bane, don't run too hard, Barny, for fraid you'd lose your breath. What if the crathur does get a taste o' the new phaties—small blame to him for the same!'

"In short, whatever might have been the habits of the family, such were those of the pig. The latter was usually out early in the morning to take exercise, and the unerring regularity with which he returned at meal time, gave sufficient proof that procuring an appetite was a work of supererogation on his part. If he came before the meal was prepared, his station was at the door, which they usually shut to keep him out of the way until it should be ready. In the mean time, so far as a forenoon serenade and an indifferent voice could go, his powers of melody were freely exercised on the outside. But he did not stop here: every stretch of ingenuity was tried by which a possibility of gaining an admittance could be established. The hat and rags were repeatedly driven in from the windows, which from practice and habit he was enabled to approach on his hind legs; a cavity was also worn by the frequent grubbings of his snout under the door, the lower part of which was broken away by the sheer strength of his tusks, so that he was often enabled, by thrusting himself between the bottom of it and the ground, to make a most unexpected appearance at the hearth, before his presence was at all convenient or acceptable.

"But, independently of these two modes of entrance, i. e. the door and window, there was also a third, by which he sometimes scrupled not to make a descent upon the family. This was by the chimney. There are many of the Irish cabins built for economy's sake against slopes in the ground, so that the labour of erecting either a gable or side-wall is saved by the perpendicular bank that re-

night after the site of the house is scooped away. Of the facilities presented by this peculiar structure, the pig never failed to avail himself. He immediately mounted the roof, (through which, however, he sometimes took an unexpected flight,) and traversing it with caution, reached the chimney, into which he deliberately *backed* himself, and, with no small share of courage, went down precisely as the northern bears are said to descend the trunks of trees during the winter, but with far different motives.

" In this manner he cautiously retrograded downwards with a hardihood which set furze bushes, brooms, tongs, and all other available weapons of the cabin at defiance. We are bound, however, to declare, that this mode of entrance, which was only resorted to when every other failed, was usually received by the cottager and his family with a degree of mirth and good humour that were not lost upon the sagacity of the pig. In order to save him from being scorched, which he deserved for his temerity, they usually received him in a creel, often in a quilt, and sometimes in the tattered blanket, or large pot, out of which he looked with a humourous conception of his own enterprise, that was highly diverting. We must admit, however, that he was sometimes received with the comforts of a hot poker, which Paddy pleasantly called, ' givin' him a *warm* welcome.'

" Another trait in the character of these animals was the utter scorn with which they treated all attempts to fatten them. In fact, the usual consequences of good feeding were almost inverted in their case ; and although I might assert that they became leaner in proportion to their good feeding, yet I must confine myself to truth, by stating candidly that this was not the fact, that there was a certain state of fleshlessness to which they arrived, but from which they neither advanced nor receded by good feeding or bad.

" At that point, despite of all human ingenuity, they remained stationary for life, received the bounty afforded them with a greatness of appetite resembling the fortitude of a brave man which rises in energy according to the magnitude of that which it has to encounter. The truth is, they were scandalous hypocrites ; for with the most prodigious capacity for food, they were spare as philosophers, and fitted evidently more for the chase than the sty —rather to run down a buck or a hare for the larder, than to have a place in it themselves. If you starved them, they defied you to diminish their flesh ; and if you stuffed them like aldermen, they took all they got, but disdained to carry a single ounce more than if you gave them whey thickened with water. In short, they gloried in maceration and liberty ; were good Irish scholars, sometimes acquainted with Latin ; and their flesh, after the trouble of separating it from a superfluity of tough skin, was excellent venison so far as it went.

" Now Phil Purcel, whom we will introduce more intimately to the reader by and by, was the son of a man who always kept a pig. His father's house had a small loft, to which the ascent was by a step-ladder through a door in the inside gable. The first good thing ever Phil was noticed for, was said upon the following occasion. His father happened to be called upon, one morning before breakfast, by his landlord, who it seems occasionally visited his tenantry to encourage, direct, stimulate, or reprove them, as the case might require. Phil was a boy then, and sat on the hob in the corner eyeing the landlord and his father during their conversation. In the mean time the pig came in, and deliberately began to ascend the ladder, with an air of authority that marked him as one in the exercise of an established right. The landlord was astonished at seeing the animal enter the best room in the house, and could not help expressing his surprise to old Purcel :

" ' Why, Purcel, is your pig in the habit of treating himself to the comforts of your best room ?'

" ' The pig is it, the crathur ? Why, your haner,' said Purcel, after a little hesitation, ' it sometimes goes up of a mornin' to waken the childhre, particularly when the buckwhist happens to be late. It doesn't like to be waitin', the crathur ; and sure none of us likes to be kept from the males mate, your haner, when we want it, no more than it, the crathur.'

" ' But I wonder your wife permits so filthy an animal to have access to her rooms in this manner.'

" ' Filthy !' replied Mrs. Purcel, who felt herself called upon to defend the character of the pig, as well as her own, ' why one would think, Sir, that any crathur that's among Christyeen childhre, like one o' themselves, couldn't be filty. I would take it to my dyin' day, that there's not a claner or dacenter pig in the kingdom, than the same pig. It never misbehaves, the crathur, but goes out, as wise an' riglar, jist by a look, an' that's enough for it, any day—a single look, your haner, the poor crathur l'

" ' I think,' observed Phil, from the hob, ' that nobody has a betther right to the run of the house, whedher up stairs or down stairs, *than him that pays the rint.*'

" ' Well said, my lad !' observed the landlord, laughing at the quaint ingenuity of Phil's defence. ' His payment of the rent is the best defence possible, and no doubt should cover a multitude of his errors.'

" ' A multitude of his shins you mane, Sir,' said Phil, ' for thrath he's all shin.'

" In fact, Phil from his infancy had an uncommon attachment to these animals, and by a mind naturally shrewd and observing, made himself as intimately acquainted with their habits and instincts, and the best modes of managing them, as ever the celebrated *Cahir na cappul* did with those of the horse. Before he was fifteen he could drive the most vicious and obstinate pig as quietly before him as a lamb ; yet no one knew how, nor by what means he had gained the secret that enabled him to do it. Whenever he attended a fair, his time was principally spent among the pigs, where he stood handling, and examining, and pretending to buy them, although he seldom had half-a-crown in his pocket. At length, by hoarding up such small sums as he could possibly lay his hands on, he got together the price of a ' slip,' which he bought, reared, and educated in a manner that did his ingenuity great credit. When this was brought to its *ne plus ultra* of fatness, he sold it, and purchased two more, which he fed in the same way. On disposing of these, he made a fresh purchase, and thus proceeded, until, in the course of a few years, he was a well-known pig-jobber.

" Phil's journeys as a pig-driver to the leading seaport towns nearest him, were always particularly profitable. In Ireland swine are not kept in sties, as they are among English feeders, but permitted to go at liberty through pasture fields, commons, and along roadsides, where they make up as well as they can for the scanty pittance allowed them at home during meal times. We do not, however, impeach Phil's honesty ; but simply content ourselves with saying, that when his journey was accomplished, he mostly found the original number with which he had set out increased by three or four, and sometimes half-a-dozen. Pigs in general resemble each other, and it surely was not Phil's fault if a stray one, feeding on the roadside or common, thought proper to join his flock and see the world. Phil's object, we presume, was only to take care that his original number was not diminished, its increase being a matter in which he felt little concern.

" He now determined to take a professional trip to England, and that this might be the more productive, he resolved to purchase a drove of the animals we have been describing. No time was lost in this speculation. The pigs were bought up as cheap as possible, and Phil set out, for the first time in his life, to try with what success he could measure his skill against that of a Yorkshireman. On this occasion, he brought with him a pet, which he had with considerable pains trained up for purposes hereafter to be explained.

" There was nothing remarkable in the passage, unless that every creature on board was sea-sick, except the pigs ; even to them, however, the change was a disagreeable one, for to be pent up in the hold of a ship was a deprivation of liberty which, fresh as they were from their native hills, they could not relish. They felt, therefore, as patriots, a loss of freedom, but not a whit of appetite ; for, in truth, of the latter no possible vicissitude short of death could deprive them.

" Phil, however, with an assumed air of simplicity, absolutely stupid, disposed of them to a Yorkshire dealer, at about twice the value they would have brought in Ireland though as pigs went in England it was low enough. He declared that they had been fed on *tip-top* feeding : which was literally true ; as he afterwards admitted that the tops of nettles and potato stalks constituted the only nourishment they had got for three weeks before.

" The Yorkshireman looked with great contempt upon what he considered a miserable essay to take him in :

" ' What a fule this Hirishman mun bea,' said he, ' to think to teake me in ! Had he said that them there Hirish swoine were *badly* fed, I'd ha' thought it fairish enough on um ; but to seay that they was oll weal fead on *tip-top* feeadin' ! Nea, nea ! I knaws weal enough that they was noat feade on nothin' at oll, which meakes them looak so poorish ! Howsomever. I shall fatten them, I'se warrant —I'se warrant I shall !'

" When driven home to sties somewhat more comfortable than the cabins of unfortuate Irishmen, they were well supplied with food which would have been very often considered a luxury by poor Paddy himself, much less by his pigs.

" ' Measter,' said the boor who had seen them fed, ' them there Hirish pigs ha' not teasted nothin' for a moonth yet ; they feed like nothin' I never seed o' my laife ! !'

" ' Ay ! ay !' replied the master, ' I'll warrant they'll soon fatten—I'se warrant they shall, Hodge—they be praime feeders—I'se warrant they shall ; and then, Hodge, we've bit the soft Hirishmun.'

" Hodge gave a knowing look at his master, and grinned at this observation.

" The next morning Hodge repaired to the sties to see how they were thriving ; when, to his utter astonishment, he found the feeding troughs clean as if they had been washed, but not a single Irish pig to be seen or heard about the premises ; but to what retreat their inmates could have betaken themselves, was completely beyond his comprehension. He scratched his head, and looked about him in much perplexity :

" ' Dang un !' he exclaimed, ' I never seed nought like this.'

" He would have proceeded in a strain of cogitation equally enlightened, had not a noise of shouting, alarm, and confusion in the neighbourhood, excited his attention. He looked about him, and to his utter astonishment saw that some extraordinary commotion prevailed, that the country was up, and the hills alive with people, who ran, and shouted, and wheeled at full flight in all possible directions. His first object was to join the crowds, which he did as soon as possible, and found that the pigs he had shut up the preceding night in sties, whose enclosures were at least four feet high, had cleared them like so many *chamois*, and were now closely pursued by the neighbours, who rose *en masse* to hunt down and secure such dreadful depredators.

" The waste and mischief they had committed in one night were absolutely astonishing. Bean and turnip fields, and vegetable enclosures of all descriptions, kitchen-gardens, corn-fields, and even flower-gardens, were rooted up and destroyed with an appearance of system which would have done credit to Terry Alt himself.

" Their speed was the theme of every tongue. Hedges were taken in their flight, and cleared in a style that occasioned the country people to turn up their eyes, and scratch their thick incomprehensive heads in wonder. Dogs of all degrees bit the dust, and were caught up dead in stupid amazement by their owners, who began to doubt whether or not these extraordinary animals were swine at all.— The depredators in the mean time had adopted the Horation style of battle. Whenever there was an ungenerous advantage taken in the pursuit, by slipping dogs across or before their path, they shot off at a tangent through the next crowd, many of whom they prostrated in their flight ; by this means they escaped the dogs until the latter were somewhat exhausted, when, on finding one in advance of the rest, they turned, and, with standing bristles and burning tusks, fatally checked their pursuer in his full career. To wheel and fly until another got in advance, was then the plan of fight ; but, in fact, the conflict was conducted on the part of the Irish pigs with a fertility of expediency that did credit to the country, and established

for those who displayed it, the possession of intellect far superior to that of their opponents. The pigs now began to direct their course towards the sties in which they had been so well fed the night before. This being their last flight, they radiated towards one common centre, with a fierceness and celerity that occasioned the women and children to take shelter within doors. On arriving at the sties, the ease with which they shot themselves over the four feet walls was incredible. The farmer had caught the alarm, and just came out in time to witness their return ; he stood with his hands driven down into the pockets of his red, capacious waistcoat, and uttered not a word. When the last of them came bounding into the sty, Hodge approached, quite breathless and exhausted :

" ' Oh, measter,' he exclaimed, ' these be not Hirish pigs at all, they be Hirish deevils : and yau mun ha' bought 'em fra a cunning mon !'

" ' Hodge,' replied his master, ' I'se be bit—I'se heard feather talk about un. That breed's *true* Hirish ; but I'se try and sell 'em to Squire Jolly to hunt wi' as beagles, for he wants a pack. They do say all the swoine that the deevils were put into ha' been drawned ; but for my peart, I'se sure that some on un must ha' escaped to Hireland.'

(To be continued.)

STAMMERING AND ITS CURE.

There is a paper on this subject in the *Medical Quarterly Review*, translated from a foreign Journal, which is, we presume, thought by our contemporary to be worth attention. This method of cure was, it appears, brought to Europe from America, by a Mrs. Leigh. She entered into partnership with Dr. Malbouche, at Brussels, from whom the secret was bought by the Belgian government ; the system has likewise met with approbation in Prussia. The whole art consists in the following rules :—The stammerer is to press the tip of his tongue, as hard as he can, against the upper row of teeth ; is to draw a deep breath every six minutes, and is to keep perfect silence for three days, during which, this pressing of the tongue and the deep inspirations are to be continued without intermission. During the night small rolls of linen are placed under the tongue in order to give it the required direction even during sleep. When the three days have expired, the patient is to read aloud slowly to his physician for an hour. During this exercise, care is to be taken that the stammerer is never in want of breath, and he must, therefore, be made to stop frequently, and inspire deeply. The patient is to be admonished to keep the tip of the tongue floating when he speaks, and never to allow it to sink into the anterior cavity of the lower jaw.—*Athenæum*.

NEW INVENTION FOR SAVING LIFE AND PROPERTY DURING FIRES.

M. Paulin, the Colonel of the Sapeurs Pompiers, at Paris, has invented an apparatus by means of which a man may go into a room on fire without injury ; or even into a cellar or place where the air is impure or very much heated. This apparatus envelopes the head and part of the body, but leaves the limbs at perfect freedom. It is so contrived, that fresh air is introduced to the mouth of the individual from the outside by means of leather pipes. An experiment was made with this apparatus, at Paris, a few days ago, and was found to be completely successful. Some combustibles in a cellar were ignited, and an individual descended in the midst of a thick flame ; he remained nineteen minutes, and said he could have stopped longer, although it was difficult to breathe even at the top of the stairs leading to the cellar, in consequence of the foul exhalations which emanated from it. The high temperature of the cellar may be judged of, from the fact that the pulse of the individual, when he came out, beat 130 times within the minute : the metallic portions of the apparatus were very hot. This apparatus may be employed very effectively in penetrating places where there is dangerous gas, or in wells, mines, &c.—*Ibid.*

Dublin : Printed and Published by P. D. HARDY, 3, Cecilia-street ; to whom all communications are to be addressed.
In London, by Richard Groombridge, 6, Panyer-alley, Paternoster-row ; in Liverpool, by Wilmer and Smith ; in Manchester, by Ambery ; in Birmingham, by Guest, 91, Steelhouse-lane ; in Glasgow, by John Macleod ; and in Edinburgh, by N. Bowack.

THE

DUBLIN PENNY JOURNAL

CONDUCTED BY P. DIXON HARDY, M.R.I.A.

| VOL. III. | MAY 23, 1835. | No. 151. |

HAROLD'S-CROSS.

RATHFARNHAM.

VILLAGES ROUND DUBLIN.

Although the villages surrounding our city have little in their appearance to attract particular attention, still as lying in the immediate vicinity of the metropolis, we may suppose them to have an interest, not only to the citizen strolling through them in his morning or evening rambles, but to the stranger who, coming from a distance, may be anxious to visit and view our immediate suburbs. The three villages represented in our present number lie to the south of the city.

HAROLD'S CROSS,

Scarcely one mile from the Castle, in the direction of the Grand Canal, is a pleasant village. The air in this neighbourhood has long been considered particularly favourable to invalids; and the village has, therefore, been much frequented by persons in a delicate state of health.

RATHFARNHAM

Lies about three miles south from the metropolis. The neat little church, with its handsome spire, gives it rather a pleasing appearance. But the Castle, which was at one time esteemed a magnificent building, with a fine collection of pictures, and having extensive gardens and pleasure-grounds, containing many foreign and scarce plants, is now converted into an extensive dairy!—*Sic transit gloria mundi.*

SIMPLE SCIENCE.

ON CALORIC.

By the term Caloric is meant that power, which existing in bodies in certain quantities, overcomes the cohesion of their constituent particles, and thus occasions their expansion;—it is it also that causes the sensation denominated heat in animals, as its abstraction does that of cold; hence it would appear, that with respect to caloric, the term cold, is a negative expression. It was the opinion of the ancient philosophers, that the cause of heat was an extremely subtile fluid, pervading all nature, which opinion, was universally adopted until the time of Bacon, when that eminent man observing that an increase of temperature always attends those circumstances, viz. mechanical friction and percussion, which tend to excite a vibratory motion in the particles of bodies, conjectured that all the phenomena of heat might be dependent on a mere condition or affection of matter, that is, a vibratory motion of its particles; this hypothesis was also supported by many other celebrated writers, particularly by Newton, yet notwithstanding the acquiescence with which every opinion of the last mentioned illustrious individual should be received, and the respect justly due to so great a name, the theory of the ancients was revived, and at this day all the phenomena of heat are believed to depend on the presence of an elastic and imponderable fluid. It would far exceed the limits of this article were we to follow those philosophers in their inquiries regarding the actual existence of a matter of heat, and it would be moreover nearly useless, for caloric, however unknown in its nature, is not so in its effects, and it is to attain a knowledge of these, that strict philosophy should aim.

As sensation varies in different individuals, and depends much on the relation between the temperature of the sentient organ and that of the body felt, it is evident that it cannot be an adequate measure of the absolute quantity of calpric in any body. Sensations are also much influenced by immediately preceding impressions; thus if one hand is immersed in a vessel containing pounded ice, while the other is plunged in one containing hot water, and both hands be subsequently placed in water at the ordinary temperature; this, to the hand which was immersed in the ice, will give the feeling of heat, while to the hand which was in the warm water, it will give the sensation of cold; now, if in this case we were to depend on our sensations, we should pronounce the water at the ordinary temperature, to be both hot and cold at the same time, which is manifestly absurd. It was circumstances of this kind that gave rise to the invention, and construction of the thermometer, an instrument by which the difficulties, and erroneous conclusions arising from sensation are obviated, and the absolute quantity of caloric existing in bodies, ascer-

tained with a degree of exactness hitherto unknown. The effects of the action of caloric on bodies, are enlargement of volume, fluidity, and vaporization; also when it acts with intensity on certain substances, another effect is produced, termed ignition. It would appear that during this last mentioned change the red rays only of the spectrum are at first given out; but gradually, and as the temperature is still more augmented, all those rays whose union produces white light are emitted, constituting what is called the stage of incandescence. With the nature of this phenomena we are entirely unacquainted; we are not able to perceive the connection between a certain degree of temperature, and the emission of one kind of light, rather than another. It is only solid bodies that suffer this change; gases do not appear susceptible of it. It takes place at about 800° of Fahrenheit's scale. When the temperature of a body is raised to a certain degree, its volume is enlarged in every direction, which is owing to the repulsive agency of caloric increasing the distance between its constituent particles; different bodies suffer this change at various temperatures, some (as among the metals lead and zinc) undergoing it at a comparatively low degree, while others (such as palladium and platina,) require an extremely high degree. The expansion of a solid body may be illustrated in the following manner. Let an iron bar be placed horizontally, having one of its ends immovably fixed, and the other connected with wheel work, which turns an index round a graduated circle, then on the application of heat, which may be effected by placing a train of lighted tapers underneath the bar, the longitudinal expansion of which will after a few moments be rendered evident by the motion of the index, and the number of degrees described by the index will be a true measure of the expansibility of the body, from a given temperature. It is upon this principle that we are enabled to explain the cracking of glass vessels containing hot fluids; thus when boiling water is poured into a glass vessel, the innermost layer or surface of the glass becomes heated and expands; this expansion is resisted by the outermost layer of the glass, which, still retaining its ordinary temperature and dimensions, does not yield sufficiently soon to the increasing volume of the innermost, and consequently cracks: hence, the thinner the glass is the less danger is there of this accident occurring; for in this case, both surfaces or layers, are heated in nearly the same time, and consequently expansion must proceed uniformly in both: thus Florence flasks and other vessels of thin glass, are little liable to crack under these circumstances. We have thus seen how an enlargement of volume accompanies an increase of temperature. If the temperature is raised still higher, the body is at last converted into the fluid form, and in this form will it remain as long as that certain temperature, its cause, is continued; thus ice, at ordinary temperatures, is converted into water, and the most refractory metals fused by a certain degree of heat. Quicksilver, which in Siberia, and other high latitudes, exists as a permanent solid, is in our comparatively warmer climates a permanent fluid. The change from mere expansion to fluidity, does not appear to depend on the greater increase of distance between the constituent particles of bodies; it seems rather to be owing to a new arrangement of these particles, with regard to each other—an arrangement in which they are allowed a greater freedom of motion. When the temperature is augmented beyond that point which is necessary to the existence of a body in the fluid form, the distance between its constituent particles is further increased, it becomes a gas or vapour, and is highly elastic; thus water at 212° becomes steam—quicksilver undergoes this change at 656°; and either at a few degrees above the ordinary temperature. We have now seen that the state of aggregation of bodies, viz. whether they shall exist as solids, fluids, or gases, is entirely dependent on the temperature to which they are exposed. The diffusion of caloric takes place in two different ways, by slow communication, and by radiation; the heat we feel on touching a heated body, is occasioned by slow communication, while that experienced from a similar body, not in immediate contact with us, is the result of radiation, in which case the calorific rays, darted from the surface of the heated body, produce the effect. When a body, at a high temperature is placed in contact with one at a lower, a portion of the redundant caloric in the one, is gradually imparted to the contiguous surface of the other; this surface becomes heated, and communicates a portion of its excess of caloric to the next layer, and this again to the next, and so on progressively, until both bodies arrive at an equal temperature. Though caloric has this tendency to pervade or diffuse itself through all bodies, until it has gained an equilibrium, yet it does not pervade all bodies with equal facility; thus if a rod of iron, and one of glass, are held in the hands, the extremities of each being placed in the fire, so rapidly will the heat be conducted by the iron, that the hand will soon be unable to retain it, while the glass may be held for any length of time; this faculty which bodies have of receiving caloric, and transmitting it, is called "their conducting power," and is, generally speaking, in proportion to their density; thus the metals, which are all very dense substances, conduct it with great rapidity; while porous bodies, such as clay, wood, &c. have scarce any conducting power whatever; this is owing to the interstices of these bodies containing much air, which is an exceedingly bad conductor of caloric. From some interesting experiments made by Count Rumford, with a view of ascertaining the relative warmth of several articles of clothing, we learn that linen has the greatest, and fur and woollen-cloth the least conducting power; hence linen is ill-adapted to maintain the warmth of the body, from the strong tendency it has to absorb its heat, and transmit it to the external air, while woollen articles, absorbing scarce any, are well adapted for this purpose. This difference in the conducting powers of bodies, occasions the difference in the sensation either of heat or cold which these various bodies may produce in us, notwithstanding the thermometer all the while indicates them to be at the same temperature; thus on a cold day, a piece of iron, from its rapidity of abstracting caloric from the sentient organ, feels very much colder than a piece of wood, which scarce abstracts any at all.

The other way in which caloric diffuses itself, is by radiation, during which this subtile fluid is darted in right lines, and with immense velocity from the surface of the heated body. This is termed *radiant* caloric, and is, like light, capable of being reflected; which may be illustrated by the following experiment. Let a red hot iron ball be placed in the focus of a concave metallic mirror, and opposite to this, and at the distance of eight or ten feet, another similar mirror be placed, having the bulb of a delicate air thermometer in its focus; the radiant caloric darted from the heated ball, will be thrown by the mirror in whose focus it is placed, upon the surface of the opposite one, in whose focus it will be again concentrated, as will appear by the rising of the thermometer, and if instead of the iron ball, a piece of burning charcoal is used, the heat radiated will be such as to set on fire an inflammable body. An experiment nearly similar to this, and attended with a similar result being capable of being performed in vacuo, almost demonstrates the materiality of caloric. Bodies differ much in their power of radiating caloric, the colour of their surfaces having great influence on them in this respect; thus boiling water will be cooled nearly twice as soon in a tin vessel whose sides are blackened, than it will be in one whose sides are clear and polished—the heat being more rapidly abstracted from the water and radiated by the coloured than by the uncoloured surface. It also appears that those bodies, whose tendency to radiate caloric is greatest, are also most disposed to absorb it when thrown on them. An experiment illustrative of this was made by the celebrated Franklin: on a clear winter day, he placed pieces of cloth of different colours, as black, blue, brown, and white, on the surface of the snow; after some time he found that the black had sunk the deepest, owing to its greater tendency to absorb the radiant heat of the sun, next the blue, next to this the brown, and the white had scarce sunk at all; hence, light-coloured clothes are best adapted to be worn in tropical climates, and during the summer season; hence if, in the experiment with the mirrors, their reflecting faces be blackened over, there will be no effect produced on the thermometer, for they will absorb all the heat that falls on them. The scources of caloric are, the solar rays, electricity and galvanism, percussion and friction, condensa-

tion and chemical action. By the mere exposure to the action of the solar rays, the thermometer is frequently raised to near 200°. But when these rays are concentrated by a lens, or in the focus of a powerful burning mirror, so intense is the heat produced, that most of the metals and earths have been melted. Electricity is also capable of exciting a powerful and sudden heat; but still more intense is the heat arising from galvanism. By the discharge from a galvanic battery, all the earths have been fused, and the most refractory metals melted, burned, and dissipated into vapour. Friction and percussion, as scources of heat, are well known; an instance of the former, is where two pieces of hard dry wood rubbed forcibly and rapidly against each other, become so much heated, as to take fire. Of heat produced by percussion, there are many instances; one is where an iron bar hammered repeatedly on an anvil, is at last raised to a red heat. The striking a flint with steel, and the increased temperature attending it, is also another and well-known example of percussion; in this case particles of steel are struck off in a state of ignition, which is probably owing to their suffering combustion with the air of the atmosphere, as they are not ignited when struck off in vacuo. By the condensation of bodies, particularly of the gases, a large quantity of the latent caloric which was necessary to maintain them in their expanded state, is evolved; thus a temperature capable of igniting a body is produced, when a gas is forcibly compressed by a piston in a condensing syringe. Chemical action is frequently productive of great heat. In chemical combination the capacity of the compound for caloric, is generally less than the mean capacity of its constituents, while its density becomes generally greater; consequently a great portion of the combined caloric contained by its constituents, is set free. Thus the capacity of sulphuric acid is 429, that of water being 1000; if equal parts of this acid and water are mixed, the temperature of the compound is not the mean between them, or 714 as it should be, but it is found to be only 605, which is much less than the mean; hence from this diminution of capacity a quantity of caloric is evolved, which is evident by the mixture becoming warm.

As connected with this subject, it should appear incumbent on us to make a few observations on the scources, and nature of the production of cold; but our limits (already too much transgressed) will not allow us to proceed farther.

G———Y.

ANECDOTE OF FAULKNER THE PRINTER.

Mr. Sheridan obtained an Irish act of Parliament, protecting him from arrests, on account of his debts in Dublin, amounting to sixteen hundred pounds; but having, the following season, saved eight hundred pounds, he gave notice that he was ready to pay his creditors ten shillings in the pound, and desired them to call on him for that purpose, with an account of their respective demands. Mr. Faulkner, the printer of one of the Dublin papers, was one of them: this gentleman told Mr. Sheridan, he would not trouble him with his demand till he dined with him: Mr. Sheridan accordingly called on Mr. Faulkner, who, after dinner, put a sealed paper into his hand, which he told him contained his demand, at the same time requesting Mr. Sheridan to examine it at his leisure at home. When he came home, he found, under seal, a bond for £200, due to Mr. Faulkner, cancelled, together with a receipt in full of a book debt, to the extent of £100. Whether is the conduct of the actor or printer the more generous and laudable?

ANECDOTE OF THE EARL OF DESMOND.

In the reign of Elizabeth, Gerald, earl of Desmond, was defeated, wounded, and taken prisoner, by his great rival, Butler, Earl of Ormond, with whom he was always at war. As the Ormondians were conveying him from the field, stretched upon a bier, his supporters, with a natural triumph, exclaimed, "Where is now the Earl of Desmond?" "Where," returned with energy the wounded chief—"Where, but in his proper place, on the necks of the Butlers."

THE DAUGHTER OF MEATH.

Turgesius, the chief of a turbulent band,
Came over from Norway and conquer'd the land ;
Rebellion had smoothed the invader's career,
The natives shrank from him, in hate, or in fear ;
While Erin's proud spirit seemed slumbering in peace,
In secret it panted for death—or release.

The tumult of battle was hushed for a while—
Turgesius was monarch of Erin's fair isle ;
The sword of the conqueror slept in its sheath,
His triumphs were honoured with trophy and wreath ;
The princes of Erin despaired of relief,
And knelt to the lawless Norwegian chief.

His heart knew the charm of a woman's sweet smile,
But ne'er till he came to this beautiful isle,
Did he know with what mild, yet resistless controul,
That sweet smile can conquer a conqueror's soul—
And, oh ! 'mid the sweet smiles most sure to enthrall,
He soon met with *one*—he thought sweetest of all.

The brave Prince of Meath had a daughter as fair
As the pearls from Loch Neagh which encircled her hair ;
The tyrant beheld her, and cried, "She shall come
To reign as the Queen of my gay mountain home ;
Ere sunset to-morrow hath crimson'd the sea,
Melachlin, send forth thy young daughter to me !"

Awhile paused the Prince—too indignant to speak,
There burned a reply in his glance—on his cheek ;
But quickly that hurried expression was gone,
And calm was his manner, and mild was his tone ;
He answer'd—"Ere sunset hath crimson'd the sea
To-morrow—I'll send my young daughter to thee !

"At sunset to-morrow your palace forsake,
With twenty young chiefs seek the Isle on yon lake ;
And there, in its coolest and pleasantest shades,
My child shall await you with twenty fair maids :
Yes—bright as my armour the damsels shall be,
I send with my daughter, Turgesius, to thee."

Turgesius returned to his palace ;—to him
The sports of that evening seemed languid and dim ;
And tediously long was the darkness of night,
And slowly the morning unfolded its light ;
The sun seemed to linger—as if it would be
An age ere his setting would crimson the sea.

At length came the moment—the king and his band
With rapture pushed off their light boat from the land ;
And bright shone the gems on their armour, and bright
Flashed their fast-moving oars in the setting sun's light ;
And long ere they landed, they saw through the trees,
The maidens' white garments that waved in the breeze.

More strong in the lake was the dash of each oar,
More swift the gay vessel flew on to the shore ;
Its keel touched the pebbles—but over the surf
The youths in a moment had leaped to the turf,
And rushed to a shady retreat in the wood,
Where many veiled forms mute and motionless stood.

"Say, which is Melachlin's fair daughter ?—away
With these veils," cried Turgesius, "no longer delay ;
Resistance is vain, we will quickly behold
Which robe hides the loveliest face in its fold ;
These clouds shall no longer o'ershadow our bliss,
Let each seize a veil—and *my* trophy be *this !*"

He seized a white veil, and before *him appeared*
No fearful, weak girl—but a foe *to be feared !*
A youth—who sprang forth from his female disguise,
Like lightning that flashes from calm summer skies ;
His hand grasped a weapon, and wild was the joy
That shone in the glance of the warrior-boy.

And under each white robe a youth was concealed,
Who met his opponent with sword, and with shield.
Turgesius was slain—and the maidens were blest,
Melachlin's fair daughter more blithe than the rest ;
And ere the last sunbeam had crimsoned the sea,
They hailed the boy-victors, and Erin was free !

MILLTOWN,

Situated little more than a mile from the Circular-road, and about two miles from the Castle, is the pass to the County Wicklow, through Dundrum, the Scalp, and Enniskerry. A few years since it was much frequented by the citizens, as a place of recreation and amusement ; but the scene of attraction is now changed to Kingstown. To the left of the bridge which crosses the Dodder, there was one of those raths or forts so common in this country, to which we have had occasion frequently to refer. So little of its original form now remains, however, that it would scarcely be noticed by the passing traveller.

PHIL PURCEL, THE PIG-DRIVER.

AN OUTLINE.

(Concluded from our last.)

" Phil, during the commotion excited by his knavery in Yorkshire, was traversing England, in order to dispose of his remaining pig; and the manner in which he effected his first sale of it was as follows :—

" A gentleman was one evening standing with some labourers by the wayside, when a tattered Irishman, equipped in a pair of white dusty brogues, stockings without feet, old patched breeches, a bag slung across his shoulder, his coarse shirt lying open about a neck tanned by the sun into a reddish yellow, a hat nearly the colour of the shoes, and a hay rope tied for comfort about his waist : in one hand he also held a straw rope, that depended from the hind leg of a pig, which he drove before him ; in the other was a cudgel, by the assistance of which he contrived to limp on after it, his two shoulder blades rising and falling alternately with a shrugging motion that indicated great fatigue.

" When he came opposite where the gentleman stood he checked the pig, which instinctively commenced regaling itself on the grass by the edge of the road.

" ' Och,' said he, wiping his brow with the cuff of his coat, ' *mavrone orth a amuck*,* but I'm kilt wit you.— Musha, Gad bless your haner, an' maybe ye'd buy a slip of a pig fwhrom me, that has my heart bruck, so she has, if ever any body's heart was bruck wit the likes of her ; an' sure so there was, no doubt, or I wouldn't be as I am wit her. I'll give her a dead bargain, Sir ; for it's only to get her aff av my hands I'm wantin', plase yer haner— *husht, amuck—husht, a veéhonee !*† Be asy, an' me in conversation wit his haner here !'

" ' You are an Irishman ?' the gentleman inquired.

"' I am, Sir, from Cannaught, yer haner, an' 'ill sell the crathur dag cheap, all out. Asy, you thief !'

" ' I don't want the pig, my good fellow,' replied the Englishman, without evincing curiosity enough to inquire how he came to have such a commodity for sale.

" ' She'd be the darlint in no time wit you, Sir ; the run o' your kitchen 'ud make her up a beauty, your haner, along wit no throuble to the sarwints about sweepin' it, or any thing. You'd only have to lay down the *scrahag* on the flure, or the mishthress, Gad bliss her, could do it, an' not lave a crumblin' behind her, besides sleepin', your haner, in the carner beyant, if she'd take the throuble.'

" The sluggish ¦phlegm of the Englishman was stirred up a little by the twisted, and somewhat incomprehensible nature of thes ⸺ ⸺uctions.

" ' How far ᴗ you intend to proceed to-night, Paddy ?' said he.

"' The sarra one o' myself knows, plaze yer haner : sure we've an ould sayin' of our own in Ireland beyant—that he's a wise man can tell how far he'll go, Sir, till he comes to his journey's ind. I'll give this crathur to you at more nor her value, yer haner.'

" ' More !—the man doesn't know what he's saying,' observed the gentleman : ' *less* you mean, I suppose, Paddy ?'

" ' More or less, Sir, you'll get her a bargain ; an' Gad bless you, Sir !'

" ' I don't want her, Paddy. I tell you I have pigs enough : try elsewhere.'

" ' She'd flog the counthry side, Sir ; an' if the misthress herself, Sir, 'ud shake the wishp o' sthraw fwor her in the kitchen, Sir, near the whoire. Yer haner could spake to her about it ; an' in no time put a knife in her whin you plased. In regard o' the other thing, Sir—she's like a Christyeen, yer haner, an' no throuble, Sir, if you'd be seein' company or any thing.'

" ' It's an extraordinary pig, Paddy.'

" ' It's no lie whor you, Sir ; she's as clane an' dacent

a crathur, Sir : och, if the same pig 'ud come into the care o' the misthress, Gad bliss her ! an' I'm sure if she has as much gudness in her face as the hanerable *dinnha ousiel*—the handsome gintleman she's marrid upon !— you'll have her thrivin' bravely, Sir, shortly, plase Gad, if you'll take courage. Will I dhrive her up the aveny whor you, Sir ? A good gintlewoman I'm sure is the same misl.— thriss ! Will I dhrive her up whor you, Sir ? *Shadh, amuck—shadh dherim ?'*

" ' Paddy, I have no further time to lose ; you may go forward.'

" ' Thank yer haner : is id whorid toarst the house above, Sir ? I wouldn't be standin' up, Sir, wit you about a thrifle ; an' you'll have her, Sir, whor any thing you plase beyant a pound, yer haner ; an' 'tis throwin' her away it is : but one can't be hard wit a rale gintleman, any way.'

" ' Paddy, I don't want the pig ; you only lose time ; I don't want to buy it.'

" ' Gad bliss you, Sir—Gad bliss you. Maybe, if I'd make up to the mishthress, yer haner, throth she wouldn't turn the crathur from the place, in regard that the tindherness ow the feelin' would come ower her—the rale gintlewoman, any way. 'Tis dog chape you have her at what I said, Sir ; an' Gad bliss you !'

" ' Paddy, do you want to compel me to purchase it whether I will or no ?'

" ' Throth, it's whor nixt to nothin' I'm givin' her to you, Sir ; but sure you can make your own price at any thing beyant a pound. *Hurrish a muck—stadh anish !*— be asy, you crathur ; sure you're gettin' into good quarthers, any how—goin' to the hanorable English gintleman's kitchen ; an' Gad knows it's a pleasure to dale with 'em. Och, the world's differ there is betuxt thim an' our own dirty Irish buckeens, that 'ud shkin a bad skilleen, an' pay their debts wit the remaindher. The gate-man 'ud let me in, yer haner, an' I'll meet you at the big-house abow.'

" ' Paddy,' said the gentleman, absolutely teased into compliance, ' you are forcing me to buy what I don't want.'

" ' Sure you will, Sir ; you'll want more nor that yit, plase Gad, if you be spared. Come, amuck—come, you crathur ; faix, you're in luck, so you are—gettin' so good a place wit his haner here, that you won't know yourself shortly, plase Gad.'

" He immediately commenced driving his pig towards the gentleman's residence with such an air of utter simplicity as would have imposed upon any man not guided by direct inspiration. Whilst he approached the house, its proprietor arrived there by another path a few minutes before him, and addressing his lady, said,

" ' My dear, will you come and look at a purchase which an Irishman has absolutely compelled me to make. He's a real one, I'm sure ; come and see him."

" The lady's curiosity was more easily excited than that of her husband. She not only came out, but brought some ladies of her acquaintance along with her, in order to hear the Irishman's *brogue*; and to amuse themselves at his expense. Of the pig, too, she was determined to know something.

" ' George, my love, is the pig also from Ireland ?'

" ' I don't know, my dear ; but I should think so from its fleshless appearance. I have never seen so spare an animal of that class in this country.'

" ' Juliana,' said one of the ladies to her companion, ' don't go too near him. Gracious ! look at the bludgeon, or beam, or something he carries in his hand, to fight and beat the people, I suppose : yet,' she added, putting up her glass, ' the man is actually not ill-looking ; and, though not so tall as the Irishman in Sheridan's Rivals, he is well made.'

" ' His eyes are good,' said her companion—' a bright grey and keen ; and were it not that his nose is rather short and turned up, he would be human.'

" ' George, my love,' exclaimed the lady of the mansion, ' he is like most Irishmen of his class that I have

---

seen; indeed, scarcely so intelligent, for he appears quite a simpleton, except, perhaps, a lurking kind of expression, which is a sign of their humour, I suppose. Don't you think so, my love?'

" 'No, my dear; I think him a bad specimen of the Irishman. Whether it is that he talks our language but imperfectly, or that he is a stupid creature, I can't say; but in selling the pig just now, he actually told me that he would let me have it for *more* than it was worth.'

" 'Oh, that was so laughable! We will speak to him, though.'

"The degree of estimation in which these civilized English held Phil was so low, that this conversation took place within a few yards of him, precisely as if he had been an animal of an inferior species, or one of the Aborigines of New Zealand.

" 'Pray what is your name?' inquired the matron.

" 'Phadhrumshagh Corfuffle, plase yer haner: my sadher carrid the same name upon him. We're av the Corfuffles av Leatherum Laghy, my lady; but my granmudher was a Dornyeen, an' my own mudher, plase yer haner, was o' the Shudhurthaghans o' Ballymadoghy, my ladyship.—*Stadh anish, a muck brudagh*—be asy, can't you, an' me in conwershtation wit the beauty o' the world that I'm spakin' to.'

" 'That's the Negu's language,' observed one of the young ladies, who was a wit and a blue-stocking; 'it's Irish and English mixed.'

" 'Thrath, an' but that the handsome young lady 's so purty,' observed Phil, 'I'd be sayin' myself that that's a quare remark upon a poor unlarned man; but, Gad bless her, she *is* so purty what can one say for lookin' an her!'

" 'The poor man, Adelaide, speaks as well as he can,' replied the lady, rather reprovingly: 'he is by no means so wild as one would have expected.'

" 'Candidly speaking, much *tamer* than *I* expected,' rejoined the wit. 'Really, I meant the poor Irishman no offence.'

" 'Where did you get the pig, friend? and how come you to have it for sale so far from home?'

" 'Fwhy it isn't whor sale, my lady,' replied Phil, evading the former question; 'the mashther here, Gad bless him an' spare him to you, ma'am—throth an' it's his four quarthers that knew how to pick out a wife, any how, whor beauty an' all hanorable whormations o' grandheur —so he did; an' well he desarves you, my lady; faix it's a fine houseful o' thim you'll have, plase Gad—an' fwhy not? whin it's all in the coorse o' Providence, bein' both so handsome;—he gev me a pound note whor her, my ladyship, an' his own plisure afthterwards; an' I'm now watin' to be ped.'

" 'What kind of a country is Ireland, as I understand you are an Irishman?'

" 'Thrath, my lady, it's like fwhat maybe you never seen—a fool's purse, ten guineas goin' out whor one that goes in.'

" 'Upon my word that's wit,' observed the young blue stocking.

" 'What think you of Irishwomen?' the lady continued; 'are they handsomer than the English ladies?'

" 'Murdher, my lady,' says Phil, raising his caubeen, and scratching his head in pretended perplexity with his finger and thumb, 'fwhat am I to say to that, ma'am, and all of yees to the fwhore? But the sarra one av me will give it agin the darling beyant.'

" 'But which do you think the handsomer?'

" 'Thrath I do, my lady; the Irish and English women would flog the world, an' sure it would be a burnin' shame to go to set them agin one another for beauty.'

" 'Whom did you mean by the "darlins beyant?"' inquired the blue stocking.

" 'Faix, Miss, who but the crathurs ower the wather, that kills us entirely, so they do.'

" 'I cannot comprehend him,' she added, to the lady of the mansion.

" 'Arrah, maybe I'd make bould to take up the manners from you fwhor a while, my lady, plase yer haner?' said Phil, addressing the latter.

" 'I do not properly understand you,' she replied, 'speak plainer.'

" 'Throth, that's fwhat they do, yer haner; they never go about the bush wit yees—the gintlemen, ma'am, of our counthry, fwhin they do 'be coortin' yees; an' I want to ax, ma'am, iv you plase, fwhat you think of them, that is, if ever any of them had the loock to come across you, my lady?'

" 'I have not been acquainted with many Irish gentlemen,' she replied; 'but I hear they are men of a remarkable character.'

" 'Faix, 'tis you may say that,' replied Phil; 'sowl, my lady, 'tis well for the masther here, plase yer haner, Sir, that none o' them met wit the mishthress before you war both marrid, or, wit reverence be it spoken, 'tis the sweet side o' the tongue they'd be layin' upon you, ma'am, an' the rough side to the masther himself, along wit a few scrapes of a pen on a slip of paper, jist to appoint the time and place, in regard of her ladyship's purty complexion—an' who can deny that, any way? Faix, ma'am, they've a way wit them, my counthrymin, that the ladies like well enough to thravel by. Asy, you deludher! an' me in conwersaytion wit the quality.'

" 'I am quite anxious to know how you came by the pig, Paddy?' said the wit.

" 'Arrah, Miss, sure 'tisa't pigs you're thinkin' on, an' us discoorsin' about the gintlemen from Ireland, that you're all so fond ow here; faix, Miss, they're the boys that can fwhoight for yees, an' 'ud rather be bringin' an *Englishman* to the *sod* fwhor your sakes, nor atin' bread an' butther. Fwhy now, Miss, if you were beyant wit us, the sarra ounce o' gunpowdher we'd have in no time for love or money.'

" 'Upon my word, I should like to *see* Ireland!' exclaimed the blue stocking; 'and why would the gunpowder get scarce, pray?'

" 'Faix, fightin' about you, Miss, an' all of yees sure, for myself sees no differ at all in your hanerable fwhormations of beauty an' grandeur, an' all highflown admirations.'

" 'But where did you get the pig, Paddy?' persisted the wit, struck naturally enough with the circumstance. 'Now how do you come to have an Irish pig so far from home?'

" 'Fwhy, thin, Miss, 'twas to a brodher's o' my own I was bringin' it, that was livin' down the counthry here, an' fwhin I came to fwhere he lived, the sarra one o' me knew the place, in regard o' havin' forgot the name of it entirely, an' there was I wit the poor crathur on my hands, till his haner here bought it fwhrom me—Gad bless you, Sir!'

" 'As I live, there's a fine Irish blunder,' observed the wit; 'I shall put it in my common-place book—it will be so genuine. I declare I'm quite delighted!'

" 'Well, Paddy,' said the Englishman, 'here's your money. There's a pound for you, and that's much more than the miserable animal is worth.'

" 'Thrath, Sir, you have the crathur at what we call in Ireland a bargain.* Maybe your haner 'ud spit upon the money fwhor luck, Sir. It's the way we do, Sir, beyant.'

" 'No, no, Paddy, take it as it is. Good heavens, what barbarous habits these Irish have in all their modes of life, and how far they are removed from any thing like civilization.'

" 'Thank yer haner. Faix, Sir, this'll come so handy for the landlord at home, in regard o' the rint for the bit o' phatie ground, so it will, if I can get home agin widout breakin' it. Arrah, maybe your haner 'ud give me the price o' my bed, an' a bit to ate, Sir, an' keep me from breakin' in upon this, Sir, Gad bless the money. I'm thinkin' o' the poor wife an' childhre, Sir—strivin' so I am to do fwhor the darlins.'

" 'Poor soul,' said the lady, 'he is affectionate in the midst of his wretchedness and ignorance.'

" 'Here—here,' replied the Englishman, anxious to get rid of him, 'there's a shilling, which I give because you appear to be attached to your family.'

" 'Och, och, fwhat can I say, Sir, only that long may you reign ower your family and the hanerable ladies to

---

* Ironically—a take in.

the fwhore, Sir. Gad fwhor ever bliss you, Sir, but you're the kind, noble gintleman, an' all belongin' to you, Sir.'

" Having received the shilling, he was in the act of departing, when, after turning it deliberately in his hand, shrugging his shoulders two or three times, and scratching his head, with a vacant face he approached the lady.

" 'Musha, ma'am, an' maybe ye'd have the tindherness in your heart, seein' that the gudness is in your honourable face any way, an' it would save the skillyeen that the masther gav'd me for payin' my passage, so it would, jist to bid the steward, my ladyship, to ardher me a bit to ate in the kitchen below. The hunger, ma'am, is hard upon me, my lady; an' fwhat I'm doin' sure is in regard o' the wife at home, an' the childhre, the crathurs, an' me far fwhrom them, in a sthrange counthry, Gad help me !'

" 'What a singular being, George ! and how beautifully is the economy of domestic affection exemplified, notwithstanding his half-savage state, in the little plans he devises for the benefit of his wife and children. Juliana, my love, desire Simmons to give him his dinner. Follow this young lady, good man, and she will order you refreshment.'

" 'Gad's blessin' upon your beauty an' gudness, my lady; an' a man might thravel far afore he'd meet the likes o' you for either o' them. Is it the other handsome young lady I'm to folly, ma'am ?'

" 'Yes,' replied the young wit, with an arch smile; 'come after me.'

" 'Throth, Miss, an' 'tis an easy task to do that, any way; wit a heart an' a half I go, acushla, an' I seen the day, Miss, that it's not much o' mate an' dhrink 'ud throuble me, if I jist got lave to be lookin' at you, wit nothin' but yourself to think on. But the wife an' childhre, Miss, make great changes in us entirely.'

" 'Why you are quite gallant, Paddy.'

" 'Thrath, I suppose I am now, Miss; but you see, my hanerable young lady, that's our fwhailin' at home—the counthry's poor, an' we can't help it whedher or not. We're fwhorced to it, Miss, whin we come ower here, by you, an' the likes o' you, mavourneen !'

" Phil then proceeded to the house, was sent to the kitchen by the young lady, and furnished through the steward with an abundant supply of cold meat, bread, and beer, of which he contrived to make a meal that somewhat astonished the servants. Having satisfied his hunger, he deliberately, but with the greatest simplicity of countenance, filled the wallet, which he carried slung across his back, with whatever he had left, observing as he did it :

" 'Fwhy, thin, 'tis sthrange it is that the same custom is wit us in Ireland beyant that is here; fwhor whinever a thraveller is axed in, he always brings fwhat he doesn't ate along wit him. An' sure enough it's the same here amongst yees,' he added, packing up the bread and beef as he spoke; 'but Gad bliss the custom, any how, fwhor it's a good one !'

" When he had secured the provender, and was ready to resume his journey, he began to yawn, and to exhibit the most unequivocal symptoms of fatigue;

" 'Arrah, Sir,' said he to the steward, 'you wouldn't have e'er an ould barn that I'd throw myself in for the night ? The sarra leg I have to put undher me, now that I've got stiff wit the sittin' so lang;† that, an' a wishp o' sthraw, Sir, to sleep an, an' Gad bliss you !'

" 'Paddy, I cannot say,' replied the steward; 'but I shall ask my master, and if he orders one, you shall have the comfort of a hard floor and clean straw, Paddy—that you shall.'

" 'Many thanks to you, Sir: it's in your face, in thrath, the same gudness an' ginerosity.'

" The gentleman, on hearing Phil's request to be permitted a sleeping place in the barn, was rather surprised at his wretched notion of comfort than at the request itself.

" 'Certainly, Simmons, let him sleep there,' he replied; 'give him sacks and straw enough. I dare say he will feel the privilege a luxury, poor fellow, after his fatigue

† This is pronounced as in the first syllable of " Langoles"— not like the Scotch " lang."

Give him his breakfast in the morning, Simmons. Good heavens,' he added, 'what a singular people! What an amazing progress civilization must make before these Irish can be brought at all near the commonest standard of humanity!'

" At this moment Phil, who was determined to back the steward's request, approached them.

" 'Paddy,' said the gentleman, 'I have ordered you sacks and straw in the barn, and your breakfast in the morning before you set out.'

" 'Thrath,' said Phil, 'if there's e'er a sthray blissin' goin', depind on it, Sir, you will get it, fwhor your hanerable ginerosity to the sthranger. But about the slip, Sir, if the misthress herself 'ud shake the wishp o' sthraw fwhor her in the far corner o' the kitchen below, an' see her gettin' her supper, the crathur, before she'd put her to bed, she'd be thrivin' like a salmon, Sir, in less than no time; an' to ardher the sarwints, Sir, if you plase, not to be defraudin' the crathur of the big piatees. Fwhor in regard it cannot spake fwhor itself, Sir, it frets as wise as a Christyeen, when it's not honestly thrated.'

" He then retired to the kitchen, where his assumed simplicity highly amused the servants, who, after an hour or two's fun with ' Paddy,' conducted him in a kind of contemptuous procession to the barn, where they left him to his repose.

" The next morning he failed to appear at the hour of breakfast, but his non-appearance was attributed to his fatigue, in consequence of which he was supposed to have overslept himself. On going, however, to call him from the barn, they discovered that he had decamped; and on looking after the ' slip,' it was found that both had taken French leave of the Englishman. Phil and the pig had actually travelled fifteen miles that morning before the hour on which he was missed—Phil going at a dog's trot, and the pig following at such a respectful distance as might not appear to identify them as fellow-travellers. In this manner Phil sold the pig to upwards of two dozen intelligent English gentlemen and farmers, and after winding up his bargains successfully, both arrived in Liverpool, highly delighted by their commercial trip through England.

" The passage from Liverpool to Dublin, in Phil's time, was far different from that which steam and British enterprize have since made it. A vessel was ready to sail for the latter place on the very day of Phil's arrival in town; and, as he felt rather anxious to get out of England as soon as he could, after selling his pig in good earnest, he came to the aforesaid vessel to ascertain if it were possible to get a deck passage. The year had then advanced to the latter part of autumn; so that it was the season when those inconceivable hordes of Irishmen who emigrate periodically for the purpose of lightening John Bull's labour, were in the act of returning to that country in which they find little to welcome them—but domestic affection and misery.

" When Phil arrived at the vessel, he found the captain in a state of peculiar difficulty. About twelve or fourteen gentlemen of rank and property, together with a score or upwards of highly respectable persons, but of less consideration, were in equal embarrassment. The fact was, that as no other vessel left Liverpool that day, about five hundred Irishmen, mostly reapers and mowers, had crowded upon deck, each determined to keep his place at all hazards. The captain, whose vessel was small, and none of the stoutest, flatly refused to put to sea with such a number. He told them it was madness to think of it; he could not risk the lives of the other passengers, not even their own, by sailing with five hundred on the deck of so small a vessel. If the one half of them would withdraw peaceably, he would carry the other half, which was as much as he could possibly accomplish. They were very willing to grant that what he said was true; but in the mean time, not a man of them would move, and to clear out two hundred and fifty fellows, who loved nothing better than fighting, armed, too, with sickles and scythes, was a task beyond either his ability or inclination to execute. He remonstrated with them, entreated, raged, swore, and threatened, but all to no purpose. His threats and entreaties were received with equal good humour. Gibes and jokes were broken on him without number, and as his passion increased, so did their mirth, until nothing could be seen but the captain in vehement gesticulation, and the Irishmen huzzaing him so vociferously, that his damns and curses, uttered against them, could not reach even his own ears.

" 'Gentlemen,' said he to his cabin passengers, 'for the love of heaven, tax your invention to discover some means whereby to get one-half of these men out of the vessel, otherwise it will be impossible that we can sail to-day. I have already proffered to take one half of them by lot, but they will not hear of it; and how to manage I am sure I don't know.'

" The matter, however, was beyond their depth; the thing seemed utterly impracticable, and the chances of their putting to sea were becoming fainter and fainter.

" ' Bl—t their eyes !' he at length exclaimed, 'the ragged, hungry devils! If they heard me with decency I could bear their obstinacy better : but no, they must turn me into ridicule, and break their jests, and turn their cursed barbarous grins upon me in my own vessel. I say, boys,' he added, proceeding to address them once more— ' I say, boys, I have just three observations to make. The first is'—

" ' Arrah, captain, avourneen, hadn't you betther get upon a stool,' said a voice, 'and put a text before it, divide it dacently into three halves, an' make a sarmon av it.'

" ' Captain, you war intinded for the church,' added another. ' You're the moral* of a Methodist preacher, if you war dhressed in black.'

" ' Let him alone,' said a third, ' he'd be a ginteel man enough in a wildherness, an' would make an illigant dancin'-masther to the bears.'

" ' He's as graceful as a shaved pig on his hind legs, dancin' the " Baltihorum Jig." '

" The captain's face was literally black with passion; he turned away with a curse, which produced another huzza, and swore that he would rather encounter the bay of Biscay in a storm, than have any thing to do with such an unmanageable mob.

" ' Captain,' said a little, shrewd-looking Connaughtman, 'what 'ud you be willin' to give any body, over an' abow his free passage, that 'ud tell you how to get one half o' them out ?'

" ' I'll give him a crown,' replied the captain, ' together with grog and rations to the eyes—I'll be hanged if I don't.'

" ' Thin I'll do it fwhor you, Sir, if you keep your word wit me.'

" ' Done,' said the captain, " it's a bargain, my good fellow, if you accomplish it: and what's more, I'll consider you a knowing one.'

" ' I'm a poor Cannaughtman, yer haner,' replied our friend Phil; 'but what's to prevint me thryin'. Tell them,' he continued, 'that you *must* go; purtind to be fwhor takin' thim wit you, Sir. Put Munsther agin Cannaught, one half an this side, an' the odher an that, to keep the crathur of a ship steady, your haner; an' fwhin you have them half an' half, wit a little room betuxt thim, " now," says your haner, " boys, you're divided into two halves; if one side kicks the other out o' the ship, I'll bring the conquerors.' "

" The captain said not a word in reply to Phil, but immediately ranged the Munster and Connaught men on each side of the deck—a matter which he found little difficulty in accomplishing, for each party, hoping that he intended to take themselves, readily declared his Province, and stood together. When they were properly separated, there still remained about fifty or sixty persons belonging to neither province; but, at Phil's suggestion, the captain paired them off to each division, man for man, until they were drawn up into two bodies.

" ' Now,' said he, ' there you stand: let one half of you drub the other out of the vessel, and the conquerors shall get their passage.'

" Instant, furious, and bitter was the struggle that ensued for the sake of securing a passage, and from the anxiety to save a shilling, by getting out of Liverpool on that day. The saving of the shilling is indeed a consideration with Paddy, which drives him to the various resources of begging, claiming kindred with his resident countrymen in England, pretended illness, coming to be passed from parish to parish, and all the other turnings and shiftings which his reluctance to part with the money renders necessary. Another night, therefore, and probably another day in Liverpool would have been attended with expense. This argument prevailed with all; with Munster as well as with Connaught, and they fought accordingly.

" When the attack first commenced, each party hoped to be able to expel the other without blows. This plan was soon abandoned. In a few minutes the sticks and fists were busy. Throttling, tugging, cuffing, and knocking down—shouting, hallooing, huzzaing, and yelling, gave evident proofs that the captain, in embracing Phil's proposal, had unwittingly applied the match to a mine, whose explosion was likely to be attended with disastrous consequences. As the fight became warm, and the struggle more desperate, the hooks and scythes were resorted to; blood began to flow, and men to fall, disabled and apparently dying. The immense crowd which had now assembled to witness the fight among the Irishmen, could not stand tamely by, and see so many lives likely to be lost without calling in the civil authorities. A number of constables in a few minutes attended; but these worthy officers of the civil authorities experienced very uncivil treatment from the fists, cudgels, and sickles of both parties. In fact, they were obliged to get from among the rioters with all possible celerity, and to suggest to the magistrates the necessity of calling in the military.

" In the mean time, the battle rose into a furious and bitter struggle for victory. The deck of the vessel was actually slippery with blood, and many were lying in an almost lifeless state. Several were pitched into the hold, and had their legs and arms broken by the fall; some were tossed over the sides of the vessel, and only saved from drowning by the activity of the sailors; and not a few of those who had been knocked down in the beginning of the fray, were trampled into insensibility.

" The Munster men at length gave way; and their opponents, following up their advantage, succeeded in driving them to a man out of the vessel, just as the military arrived. Fortunately their interference was unnecessary. The ruffianly captain's object was accomplished; and as no lives were lost, nor any injury more serious than broken bones and flesh-wounds sustained, he got the vessel in readiness, and put to sea.

" Who would not think that the Irish were a nation of misers, when our readers are informed, that all this bloodshed arose from their unwillingness to lose a shilling by remaining in Liverpool another night? Or, who could believe that these very men, on reaching home, and meeting their friends in a fair or market, or in a public-house after mass on a Sunday, would sit down and spend, recklessly and foolishly, that very money which in another country they part with as if it were their very heart's blood? Yet, so it is! Unfortunate Paddy is wiser any where than at home, where wisdom, sobriety, and industry are best calculated to promote his own interests.

" This slight sketch of Phil Purcel we have presented to our readers as a specimen of the low, cunning Connaughtman; and we have only to add, that neither the pig-selling scene, nor the battle on the deck of the vessel in Liverpool, is fictitious. On the contrary, we have purposely kept the tone of our description of the latter circumstance beneath the reality. Phil, however, is not drawn as a general portrait, but as one of that knavish class of men, called ' jobbers,' a description of swindlers certainly not more common in Ireland than in any other country. We have known Connaughtmen as honest and honourable as it was possible to be; yet there is a strong prejudice entertained against them in every other province of Ireland, as is evident by the old adage, ' Never *trust* a Connaughtman.' "

---

* Model.

Dublin : Printed and Published by P. D. Hardy, 3, Cecilia Street; to whom all communications are to be addressed.

THE
DUBLIN PENNY JOURNAL

CONDUCTED BY P. DIXON HARDY, M.R.I.A.

Vol. III.	MAY 30, 1835.	No. 152.

HOWTH CASTLE, COUNTY OF DUBLIN.

The castle of Howth stands to the right of the village or little town of Howth, on the northern shore of the Bay of Dublin. It is a long battlemented structure, flanked by square towers at each extremity, and approached by a large flight of steps. A spacious hall extends along the whole front of the building, ornamented within by the weapons and armour of ancient days, and among the rest is said to be the identical two-handed sword with which Sir Armoricus Tristram, its first English proprietor, defeated the Danes. The white battlements of this venerable mansion, present a pleasing appearance, as it emerges from the dark wood in which it is embosomed : the estate over which it appears constructed to reign, includes the whole peninsula of Howth, containing 1500 square acres, which, without increase or diminution, has continued for more than six centuries in his lordship's family, having been their residence since the arrival of the first adventurers from England. The name of the earliest of these, of this family, was Sir Armory Tristram, and the adventures recorded of his life, and received as authentic, are more extraordinary than those of any hero in romance. Happening to meet with Sir John de Courcy, who was married to his sister, in the church of St. Mary, at Rouen, he there made a compact with him, that whatever they should win in any realm, either by conquest or otherwise, should be divided between them. On the faith of this agreement, they sought adventures together through Normandy, France, and England, and finally proceeded to Ireland, where the first land they made was Howth. De Courcy was confined by illness to his ship, and the command devolved on Sir Armoricus, who having pushed to shore, was opposed by the Irish at the bridge of Evora, and a fierce encounter ensued, in which seven sons, nephews, and uncles of Sir Armoricus were slain. The Irish were finally defeated,

and the land and title of Howth were allotted to him as his share of the conquest. The bridge of Evora, where this battle is said to have been fought, crosses a mountain stream, which falls into the sea on the north side of Howth, nearly opposite the west end of Ireland's Eye. In clearing out the foundation for the new parish church, erected a few years ago near this spot, a quantity of bones were discovered scattered over an extensive space : and, in the neighbourhood, an antique anvil, with bridle bits and other parts of horse harness. It is conjectured, with some probability, that the armourers' forge was erected on this spot, where the knights were accoutred preparatory to the battle. Sir Armoricus, after a variety of other perilous and wild adventures in Ireland, was surrounded by a superior force in Connaught. His knights were inclined to avail themselves of their horses, and save themselves by flight, but their leader, dismounting, drew his sword, and kissing the cross of it, thrust it into his horse's side : his example was followed by all the knights except two, who were sent to a neighbouring hill, to be spectators of the approaching combat. The Normans were cut off, not a man escaping except the two who afterwards testified the circumstances of the heroic transaction. Some time after, the original family name of Tristram was changed to St. Lawrence, for the following reason :—One of them commanded an army near Clontarf, against the common invaders, the Danes. The battle was fought on St. Lawrence's day, and he made a vow to the Saint, common in those times, that if he were victorious he would assume his name, and entail it upon his posterity. The Danes were defeated, and his vow was religiously preserved. Another romantic circumstance is related of this family. The celebrated Grana Uile, or Grace O'Malley, was noted for her piratical depredations in the reign of Elizabeth. Returning on a certain time from England, where she had paid a visit to the queen, she landed at Howth, and proceeded to the castle. It was the hour of dinner, and the gates were shut. Shocked at an exclusion so repugnant to her notions of Irish hospitality, she immediately proceeded to the shore, where the young lord was at nurse, and seizing the child, embarked with him, and sailed to Connaught, where her own castle stood. After some time, however, she restored the child, with the express stipulation that the gates should be always thrown open when the family went to dinner, a practice which was observed to a very recent period.

In a chamber in the castle, is a painting said to represent the carrying off of the young lord. A female is mounted on a white horse, receiving a child from a peasant; above, the sky seems to open, and a figure is represented looking on the group below. The picture, however, is thought to allude to some other subject, though the tradition of the castle refers it to this. In the same room is a bed in which William III. slept, and which is said to be preserved exactly as it then was, in remembrance of that circumstance.

THE BLESSED TURF.

And flies the wild report—the baseless tale—
The vague concoction of some vaguer mind—
Sounding its many tongues o'er hill and dale,
The welcome herald of some woe or weal,
And swifter even than the winged wind.

It will be in the recollection of a great proportion of our readers, that about two years since an occurrence took place, strongly marking the peculiar features of the Irish character—superstitious fear, sudden impulse, and extraordinary excitement. I allude to what was, and now is, popularly denominated "The blessed turf;" when the entire population of a very extensive district of country, was aroused and excited to a degree exceeding belief in any other country than Ireland. It was, indeed, considered by many as a circumstance outrivalling in romantic interest many events in the history of our isle which have acquired much greater celebrity; and one which pourtrayed in vivid colours that restlessness of disposition, which is so singular a trait of the Irish character—that innate wildness and volatility of mind, which ever urges the people to acts of inconsiderate, fearful rashness. In no other country, but Ireland, would a sudden impulse fire almost to distraction half her population. The spring of excitement, once touched, knows not at what point to stand still, like Mynheer von Wodenblock's mysterious wooden-leg, whose wheels within wheels, and springs acting on springs, once set in motion, by its unlucky artifice carried him with the rapidity of an arrow, through towns and villages, the wilds and forests of Germany, and where still, as the story runs, it urges forward its course with whatever remains of the ingenious Dutchman's skeleton.

There were people who imagined that this sudden alarm was an expedient used by the disaffected, to ascertain in what space of time the whole nation could be aroused; others say it originated in some wag;—but certain it is, that whoever were the promulgators—whether it had its origin in chance or premeditation—the minds of the people were fearfully excited. All yielding to the sudden impulse, fled hither and thither, like a herd of stricken deer; and thus it has ever been with the Irish peasantry—their ardent, impetuous feelings rush like a mountain-torrent when confined within a narrow channel. Ever alive to a touch of novelty, and snatching at every stimulant to excitement, they are often carried along the tide of some chimerical fantasy; and not only are they carried, but they jump voluntarily and with delight into its gurgling vortex.

At the period referred to, there resided in Killeshin, about two miles from Carlow, one Rory O'Rourke, at whose house all that was strange, comical, extraordinary, new, or fanciful, was retailed—from the most ancient tradition, to the latest news from "Lineen;" the legend of other days was canvassed, as well as the speeches in parliament; superstitious stories of ghosts, sprites, banshees, leprahauns, fairies, and witches, were told by wholesale. Every thing that was awful and terrible in ancient lore, as well as the deaths, births, and marriages, within twenty miles round—the phantasies which swell the old tales of gossipers, and the newly fangled stories of modern events. Rory was an exhaustless fund of such "tales of the times of old;" and Rory Oge, or young Rory, spelled out the recent productions of the press.

As soon as night fell, the beaten path to Rory's house was footed by many a devourer of his ancient traditions. The way lay through a rough and wild mountainous country, along the bank of a small, but deep ravine, through which a gurgling stream forced its way on ledges of rocks. His house was, in fact, the rendezvous of all the story-tellers or news-mongers in the parish. Every evening, Molly, the wife, trimmed her fire, and cleaned down the hob for her cronies. The cabin consisted of a kitchen and one bed-room, with a kind of cock-loft over the latter, formed of hurdles plastered with clay. This was master Rory Oge's place of residence at night; but it contained more than the four bones of the houchal. It was, in fact, quite a curiosity: there were congregated, in vast profusion, bundles of scollops, spare heads and handles of rakes, pitch-forks, lumber of every description, pots and pans past use, old irons, broken chairs, tables, tea-pots, flax, heads of cabbage hung up for seed, nails, ropes—all the useless paraphernalia of husbandry, and Rory Oge.

The cabin was situated in a wild, romantic spot, having a still more wild and romantic people. A rivulet rushed over its pebbled course in the rear; and above frowned the barren, heath-covered brow of Knuc-na-raw mountain, with Carlow in the distance; and on the opposite side, towards the colliery, an extended sterile tract, terminated by a dimly blue mountain.

Rory was, of course, well versed in the local tradition and history of his native hills—could tell when Killeshin was "a mighty great place entirely"—of its courts, mansions, governors, &c.

The usual circle was nearly completed, when the latch was raised, and in stalked, shivering and shaking, Shemus Donohoe.

"Why the mischief run a-huntin' wid you, for a Shemus, is id now you're comin'? Did you see a ghost—or what's comin' over you at all?" said Molly.

"Yerrah, yerrah! but it's a murdherin' cowld night," said Shemus in reply—"it would skin a March hare. It's well for you, who needn't fear the cowld, an' your good selvige of fat linin' you. Have you e'er a drop o' the raal mountain stuff?—it's yerself hasn't yer heart in it."

"Arrah, to be sure I have;" for, reader, you must know, what it would not be fair to tell the gauger, the illicit mountain-dew was not only retailed, but manufactured at her house.

Shemus, seated on the hob, with the pipe in his mouth and the glass by his side, was soon in all his glory; the dudeen was so short—for an old seasoned one is always preferred—that the head alone could be seen protruding from his lips.

Molly laid down her own pipe, and said, "As sure as I'm a sinner, 'twas talkin' to his sweetheart he was."

"The sorra lie you tell there—I'll never deny it. Sure the boys an' the girls will be talkin' while there is a tack o' the world together. Tare-an'-ounty, sure it's not for the bit they eat we'd be athout 'em, the crathurs, the darlins o' the world."

"Will you, Rory avourneen, take a drop?" said Molly, holding over a glass to her mate.

"Musha, it was an angel spoke—who'd throw it over their shoulder—(takes a deep pull.) Oh, Molly dear, it's mighty good!—ha, ha!—it's the best run we had the year." Rory was softened of course by this deep libation from the cruiskeen lawn, and consequently love was the predominant feeling in his soul. Looking with swimming eyes over at Molly, who was sitting on her hunkers—"Well, Molly," said he, "I remember the time I was coortin' you," and he stroked back his aged locks, which were as fair as the white cliff that sheltered his door from the northern blast; "an' it's not that you're to the fore I say it, Molly asthore, but you war the purty girl, charmin' as the queen of May, the day I saw you first. I love you now as well as when, under the shade of the big spreading beech-tree at your father's house, I first pledged you my heart and soul, and devoted myself to your service for ever more."

The big tears chased each other down his cheeks, as the remembrance of his first and youthful love, shone in upon his aged faculties. Molly took the compliment as it was intended, but ascribed it to the all-powerful poteen. He wiped away the tears, the fond effusion of a loving soul, with the tail of his coat, and proceeded—

" There wasn't a droller boy then in the seven counties than I was—but no matther now, it's all past and gone. Did yees ever hear tell of Moran, the murdered pedlar, that haunts the road above?"

" Yes;" said all, " but we wish to hear it agin."

" My name is not Rory O'Rourke, if he didn't cross me more than once in my time. To make a long story short—he was murdered, an' robbed, an' kilt, and his ghost appears. I was coming from Carlow one night 'twixt twelve an' one, when the baste that carrid me stopped short, for brute bastes can see a ghost. Out of that she wouldn't stir a peg. I crossed myself, bekase I knew there was danger. I lit, and looked over her left shoulder, and there he was, a black man lying across the road. An' what does I do, well becomes me——But what's this ?— who thunders down the road as if the ould boy was at his heels ? Asy, we'll soon know."

The horseman stopped at the door, and flinging himself off, rapped with violence with his whip. Rory flew to open it.

" Did you git the blessed turf yit ?" asked the stranger, in a great fright.

" What blessed turf?"

" Oh, sure there's fire an' brimstone raining down on the Queen's County, an' the only protection you have is to keep this lightin'; and run and serve three houses before you stop."

" Oh, may the heaven save you that brought it, thin," said Molly.

" Arrah, thin, Molly darlint, you needn't thank me—it was to save myself I did it; and I have to go to two houses more yet—farewell !" and off he dashed.

All was now consternation in the house of Rory O'Rourke.

" Rory, avourneen," said Molly, " will you run to sarve the three houses. Oh ! but you're too late—that sthranger has gone to the neighbours, and they're off before this to all the other houses, and there won't be one left for us. Millia murdher, we're lost for ever !" She wept loudly, and wrung her hands in distraction. " Run, run, Rory acushla—run ! I'll go up the hill, an' do you go some other way."

" Ay, an' give me a scrusshin, too, to fetch home, and save my own little cabin," said Shemus.

Thus was the strange rumour spread. In all directions persons might be seen running for life or death, with terror in their countenance, panting and blowing—some barefooted, others half dressed—some with one shoe off, the other on—others with a breeches and shirt only, head and legs bare—and some again almost in a state of nudity—carrying in their hands a sod of turf, which they occasionally blew, lest the spark should become extinct. When miles sometimes intervened between each house, it would be impossible to picture all the disasters which befel them, thus skelping over ditches and hedges, bogs and swamps in the dead of night.

It was the only preservative, they imagined, against the destructive fire which they expected would descend every moment from heaven on their devoted heads. Even next morning, many an old man or woman, still searching for a house which had not as yet been blessed with the spark, might be observed wending their way up a mountain road, whose rugged acclivities, rocks, glens, and clumps of trees, woods, and bogs, would cause one to suppose that the original projectors of it had taken as their guide the tortuous windings of an eel.*

---

* The real cause of the abruptness and crookedness of old roads probably is—when first repaired, their projectors followed the beaten footpaths of their fathers through the woods, or perhaps the track of the red deer or wolves; land becoming valuable, these woods retained all their original intricacies, as the proprietors on each side were unwilling to have inroads made on their property.

But let us return to the little story-teller of the mountain. Shemus set out with fire in his eyes, and a sparkling sod of turf in his hand, across the field. As he darted forward on his moorless track, the darkness of night gloomed around, and seemed even more murky from the contrast of the light with which he had recently been surrounded. The rude scene through which he passed, the winding defiles, the undulated surface, the heights above crowned by furze, and bushes, and frowning rocks, from which the birds of night started in affright, screaming and crying with alarm, the mountain stream brawling in its deep, precipitous bed, the shrill gusts of wind which moaned amid the brushwood and over rock and glen, the heavy fall of rain—all, all scowled upon him, and rendered his way one of gloom and horror.

He endeavoured to steel his heart against the terrors which he was doomed to encounter—the world of ghosts which his fertile imagination conjured up, and with which he tenanted every rock and bush—it was the only fear that could affect his manly, adamantine breast. His heart quickly propelled its crimson current—his elastic step scarce touched the ground. He looked around, and in a tree with two immense arms, imagined he beheld the gigantic skeleton figure of a spirit, with uplifted arms stretching into the clouds, preparatory to seizing him within its mighty grasp, and hurling him he knew not where. He was convinced the ghost of old Moran the pedlar stood before him. Shemus inwardly muttered his prayers, and with eyes steadily fixed, hair erect, and glaring eye-balls starting from their sockets, approached the apparition, and, more dead than alive, gathered himself up to question it. In a voice raised by terror beyond its natural pitch, he used the following solemn invocation :—

" In the name of all the blessed saints in heaven, who or what are you ? Tell me, can I do any thing for you. Don't lay the point o' yer finger on me ! What brought you across me to-night ? Speak, why don't you ?"

To which hurried interrogation the spectre answered only by a doleful moan, as the wind whistled through its leafless branches. He was about to exorcise, and lay it on the Shores of the Red Sea, when a blast came sweeping from the mountains, which, coming in contact with the tree, bent it towards him. Shemus shrunk from what he imagined its intended embrace ; and as it yielded, he saw the withered arms of the woody monster, and was undeceived. But he had yet to pass the church-yard. This was the touchstone of his courage; but it must be passed.

As he came up to the burial-ground, his respiration became almost stifled. He feared to breathe, lest he should arouse the sleeping dead. He ascended a height which overlooked the burial-ground, and gazed about him. The moon brilliantly lit the graves, and shone on the cold tomb-tones. He reflected awhile, and thoughts to this effect shot across his mind :—Should the last trumpet sound, and the graves cast forth their dead—the world shake and totter on its basis—what a scene would meet his eye—the huddled and congregated dust and bones of ages and generations passed away, rumbling and mingling in the act of resurrection. His thoughts became absorbed in the notion—his imagination, aided by the silent stillness of the hour, became fired, his fancy worked up. At that moment, the long winding notes of a horn, re-echoed by a thousand tongues, fell with an alarming effect on his ear, almost snatching from him the remnant of his reason. It was an anxious and awful presage. His train of thought was favourable to the idea. The dread certainty flashed across his mind, that the last and awful day was come, when time would be no more. He was like one petrified—he stood aghast. He expected every moment to see the dead arise, and feel the earth quake. But his excited imagination soon raised from their clayey tombs the inmates of the church-yard, and peopled the ground with its skeleton occupants. He saw with the mental eye the indistinct mass assume a shape. Then he thought he heard a rustling of bones. He became quite certain that all nature was about to dissolve into its original nothing—its primitive chaos—that all, all, and his colleen Debby, with the rest, were about to be swallowed up in the gulf of eternity. Then he saw a sprite dart with unearthly swiftness over the mossy tombs, with bare legs, preternatural demeanour, dishevelled hair, bearing in his hands, and tossing high in air, a feathery like substance, whom Shemus, of course, set down as an inmate of the grave, loosed from his clay prison, and who was scattering to the winds his shroud. It was a curious coincidence; and all concurring—the trumpet, the spectre—he gave himself up for lost, and had nearly fallen senseless on the ground. Recovering, he fled with precipitation, still of opinion that the final demolition of all creation was about to be completed; and the vengeance of heaven coming in the form of "raining fire," confirmed him still more in that belief. But now his only, his last chance of safety rested in the little spark of fire which had fallen from his hand on the grass, and which the breeze of the hill had fanned into a flame. He eagerly snatched it up, and running with speed, deposited a portion of it in his own house "for loock;" and then, with the blessing of his old mother, given in the shape of an old shoe cast after him, he proceeded in search of the other three houses, and he had travelled six or seven miles before he could find the necessary number unsupplied. As he returned, he met an old man struggling on with the "blessed turf," and asked him if he had been successful.

"Oh, yeah aroune!" said the old man, "the life will start out of me afore I do that, I'm thinkin'. Did yerself?"

"An' shure enough, avourneen, it's myself that did? When was I lame or lazy when I should be on my limbs? But what do you think—is the ind of the world comin'?"

"Avick machree, I dunna."

"Faix, an' I'm not so. I know right well it is, for I saw a man risin' from the grave, an' I thought I hard the last trumpet."

"Tut, you omedhawn, it was the crackt man in the grave you saw, an' sorra one else."

This was the fact; and Shemus had heard the bugle blast, which so often resounded at night through the country, raised by the followers of Captain Rock from their telegraphs, as they sounded their gathering note, or tocsin of alarm. And it was a maniac who took up his abode among the tombs of the dead, that personified the spirit to Shemus's terrified eye. It was his ghost-like figure he had seen amid the ruins; and the badge he bore was a garland plucked from a recent grave, which was decked with wreathes of flowers, where a youth or maiden had been lately laid.

Molly set sail up the mountain, spreading her canvass to the breeze, and an ample resistance she offered to its wild career; for so swaddled was she in the complicated folds and twistings of flannels, bands, and stockings, that scarce a trace of the human face divine could be recognized. The only adventure Molly met with was one; but it was of a decided character. As she trudged along the ridge of the hill, her hands and arms muffled in her capacious cloak, she was tripped up by some briars, and sent reeling to the bottom, where her own house stopped her further progress. So her good genius thus saved her neck from being broken over some precipitous declivity, or being hurled headlong into some yawning river. When she re-assumed her upright position, the first thing she did was to ascertain whether her pipe had been broken, but, fortunately, it had not.

The poor old man did not succeed so well, for the anxiety he had for his soul's welfare prompted him to use every exertion to perform the stipulated requisites. After running a mile he came to a house, and knocking furiously at the door, demanded instant admittance. This was refused him. He then roared out from without—

"Have yees the blessed turf?"

"Yes, thank God, I am after gettin' it, and have served three houses."

"Murdher, an' thundher-an'-turf, what'll become of me? Do you know any one didn't get it?—the spark is jist out."

"Not one, avourneen—God help you!"

"What'll I do! What'll become of me! I'm done for ever if the sod goes out—not a mother's soul to help or assist me!" and tearing his hair in an agony of grief and despair, he skelped away again for another half

mile, and espied a cabin by the light peering through a chink in the wall. Out of breath, and gasping, he greeted them with, "God save all here."

"And you, too—what's amiss with you."

"Oh, enough, arone!—did you hear of the fire raining down from heaven?"

This produced a general panic and consternation.

"No, acushla! What fire?"

"Nor the blessed turf?"

"Not a taste of me."

"Well, praises be to heaven for that same, I have one house any way! Take that spark, and kindle a sod of turf wid it, and lave it in the grate, an' thin go an' do the same in three houses."

"What'ill I do if it goes out?"

"You'll be ruinated. I'll be off to two houses more—is there e'er a one near me."

"There is; but as I'm an ould man, lave that to me."

"Faix, I'll do no such thing, for I'm another."

He bolted again. The man inside came out, tied his garter round his horse's head, and set out in pursuit of Rory, in order to be at the house before him. He soon gained on the weary old man, and passed him; but Rory seized the horse's long flying tail, and kept up to him. The other did his best to shake him off in vain.

"For the tendher mercy of heaven let my ould beast go."

"Never till I die," responded Rory courageously.

However, he trembled, and let slip his hold. The man left him sprawling on the road, served the three houses, and was on his return, when he met Rory.

"Well now," said the latter, "as I was the manes of savin' you an' yours, will you lend me the loan of that baste to go to the next town, as I know there is little use to look for any houses nearer."

The man consented. Rory mounted, and flew away to Carlow. As he entered the town he shouted out—"The blessed turf—the blessed turf!" All was uproar in a few minutes—it spread through the town like wild fire. He served three houses, and then saw their owners depart to do the same, like incarcerated fiends let loose. Crowds soon filled the streets, running with a *scrumshin* of an ignited sod in the bottom of a saucepan or gallon, to save their houses from the desolating vengeance of enraged heaven.

H. K.

FORE ABBEY, COUNTY WESTMEATH.

The ruins of Fore Abbey (of which the above is a correct representation as they now appear) are situated in the parish and half barony of the same name, which before the Union returned two members to parliament. Fore was in the olden time a famous seat of monastic learning, called by the natives "Ballylichen"—i. e. "The Town of Books." It was a priory of canons regular, founded by St. Fechin, in A. D. 630, who died there of the plague in 665. His chapel is also here, remarkable for the ponderous masonry of its portal and window mullions; there is also a well, springing from a rock, and turning "the busy mill" of the village. Fore was at seven different periods destroyed by fire. But it is likely it did not assume the permanent character of an entire stone building until the time of its refoundation in 1218 by Walter de Lacy. Archdall, in his Monasticon Hibernicus, gives a list of the different abbots and their revenues up to 1505, when one William Nugent was the last prior. It contained at one time three thousand monks, who flocked from all nations to this retreat of learning. At the dissolution of the monasteries in the reign of Henry VIII. the Abbey of Fore, with its lands and appurtenances, was granted, on Sept. 30th, 1588, to Christopher Baron Delvin, traditionally named, "The Black Baron," at whose hands probably it met its fate. Fore is now a place scarcely deserving the title of village. Besides the ruins of the abbey itself, we find those of the walls and gates of the ancient town, which was probably chiefly constructed of oak-wood—these being built in Edward III.'s time, to protect the town from predatory incursions; and for defraying the expense of such walling, a tax was laid on all sorts of merchandize, coming for sale to the town, or going out of it. There is another well, near which grows an enormous ash-tree, apparently a sucker from a parent stem in the last stage of decay, and which was possibly cotemporary with the old abbey in all its glory. The ruins of some minor chapels are in and near the town, built for some orders of friars who were educating here. A stone cross, much broken and defaced, stands in the centre of the village. A square tower, built for defence in the time of Edward III. is used to this day as a burial vault by the Delvin family. There is a curious rath or dun about two hundred yards to the east of the monastery, from whence the natives affirm the "Black Baron" destroyed the abbey with his cannon. I believe artillery might have been used for its overthrow. There are some appearances about the walls to warrant the conjecture; but the potent element, fire, has evidently, by the fissures in various parts, done its share of the work of destruction. What fire and sword, however, spared, the pilfering bands of the building gentry of the neighbourhood completely removed. Not a door-frame, quoin, squared or ornamental stone, or window mullion or tracing, remains, except part of the eastern window of the chancel. The famous abbey is now, paradoxically speaking, a ruin of a ruin. The owner of the soil has lately taken steps to prevent the removal of any part of the building—but too late, like many plans which the head of an Irishman only could conceive. The ruin stands on a rock in the centre of a morass. The appearance of a double wall and fosse encircling it are visible, which could, as a mode of defence, at any moment be filled with water.

G. B.

RESIDENCE OF THE LATE LUNDY FOOT, ESQ.

Who was inhumanly murdered a short time since, in the open day, by one of his own tenantry.

The view is taken from that side of Mr. Foot's house which stands opposite the river at Rosbercon, near Ross. There is a melancholy interest attached to the place, from the circumstances connected with the death of its late owner. He was in excellent health and spirits on the morning of the day in which he met his death, walking as usual through his grounds. He was met in a retired situation by the assassin who perpetrated the deed, and shot dead upon the spot. The murderer had long entertained a deep rooted animosity against Mr. Foot, on account of his having had him ejected from a farm for non-payment of rent. He had sworn to be revenged. Although fondly thinking that no eye had witnessed the deed of blood, he was traced through various circumstances, tried, and condemned to die—a little girl being the principal evidence against him.

In the following narrative, which we are assured is true in every point, will be found an ample verification of the truth, that sooner or later the almighty vengeance will fall on the murderer, be he rich, or be he poor; and that however he may endeavour to conceal his crime, it will at length "find him out."

THE LAST OF THE M——ES OF C——Y.

A short time since, on a lovely morning in the pleasant month of June, I joined a friend on an excursion into one of the southern counties of England—a county beautifully diversified with hills and fertile valleys. At the time we started the sun had scarcely tinged the horizon with its faintest beams; yet we had not proceeded far till we met the cheerful haymakers, with their baskets suspended from their prongs, which they carried over their shoulders. It was one of those lovely mornings, when every thing tends to enliven the surrounding scene. As the morning advanced we proceeded. In some places the grass was just cut, and women and children were busily employed in turning it over for the sun to dry; while the men were as busily engaged carrying it to the farm-yard in waggons heavily laden. The greatest part of our way led us over a rough and mountainous country. Within a few miles of the town of M——t, the traveller might almost fancy that he was crossing the Alps, so lovely, extensive, and magnificent was the prospect which met the eye. The road wound in a serpentine form over the Downs; here you might see a number of cottages, with their neat gardens, and terraced walks, rising one above the other; further on a little way, above might be seen a cottage or two with a plot of grass in front, where they were busy making hay; while still higher up, the rugged rock frowned over the road with majestic grandeur. But the year before part of the rock had given way, and with it a quantity of earth rolled down, and partially filled the valley; but fortunately no one was near at the time, or their destruction must have been inevitable. At the foot of the Downs lies the town of M——t, and the beautiful ruins of C——y Castle, the subject of the following tale. M——t is a neat and cleanly town, delightfully situated in a deep and narrow valley; and though seated between two lofty ranges of hills, the views from the town and neighbourhood are far from being dull and uninteresting. We drove up to the Angel, a neat comfortable inn; and having finished our breakfast, we sallied forth to see the splendid ruins of C——y Castle. Yes! splendid in their ruined and desolate state. We opened the ancient and massive iron gates, and their rusty state, with the grass-grown carriage road, plainly told us that the stately pile was no longer inhabited. The ruin was not occasioned by the slow, though sure, hand of time, nor yet by the cruel and unrelenting hand of the conqueror; but by a consuming fire, occasioned by the carelessness of some workmen. The outside walls, as well as the inner walls of the rooms, are still standing entire—only the doors, floors, and roof are destroyed. The east tower is still perfect. This was the library, and it still contains a great quantity of papers, probates of wills, leases, old bills, &c.

When Edward the Second (I think) made a journey into Sussex, and into some of the adjoining counties, it was at this castle he and his train spent their Christmas, where they were entertained in a most princely style for several weeks. The principal room, called Bucks Hall, was a magnificent apartment. There is only one window to the room, which, I think, is the largest I ever saw. It is about sixty feet high by forty wide. In the chapel there are some beautiful pieces of sculpture projecting from the walls—they are mostly of the human form, with a few animals. The principal entrance hall is of stone, and also the roof, which is vaulted and beautifully carved in various devices. Over the door is placed the family arms, hewn out of stone, and in high relief. The walls of the rooms are ornamented in a singular way. They are covered with a kind of plaster, about four inches thick, and which is now as hard as stone, with various devices upon them—human figures, birds, flowers, and others of an imaginative character. In the rooms are now growing strawberries and flowers, with an abundant crop of nettles and thistles, where once used to be heard the voice of the gay, the beautiful, and the young. The once showy gardens are now overgrown with weeds, whilst the beautiful marble fountains, which used continually to throw out their cool and refreshing streams, are now prostrated to the earth. But enough of description—now for the tale, which unfortunately is but too much of a reality.

It is now about six and forty years since the last Lord M——e killed his butler in a fit of passion, whilst laying the cloth for dinner. The poor man having greatly displeased his lordship, in the heat of passion he took up a carving knife and stabbed him to the heart. The man fell down and instantly expired. His lordship being a person of great consequence, the affair was hushed up, and he for the moment escaped punishment; but justice must and will have its due, and though man will not give it, yet there is an eye that watches over human affairs, and will not allow the guilty to go unpunished, who will restore it two-fold to those who think that because they are rich and powerful, they may commit crimes with impunity. A few years after the murder, it was agreed, that before his

only son came of age he should travel two or three years on the Continent whilst the castle should undergo some requisite repairs and alterations. The young lord set out on his tour, accompanied by a faithful friend, and followed by an old and faithful valet, as Lord M——e was afraid to trust him by himself, being a wild and thoughtless youth. While spending a few days at a small town in Switzerland, near some of the falls on the Rhine, young M——e had several times expressed a wish of swimming down the falls; but his valet, knowing the hazard of the enterprise, expressly forbad him ever bathing unless he was with him. It was, I think, the day before they were to leave the place, that young M——e and his friend rose early, and left their valet in bed, determined to have a swim down the falls: and sure enough he did, for getting too near the edge of the falls before he was quite prepared, and not being strong enough to stem the torrent, he was washed down, and dashed to pieces against some rocks at the bottom. A messenger was dispatched to England with the sad intelligence. On the very same day the castle was burned to the ground, and a messenger was sent with all haste to the young nobleman, to inform him of the event. And what is singular is, that the messengers should meet on a bridge, though they did not know it till afterwards. The fire was occasioned through the negligence of some of the workmen. The repairs and alterations at the castle were nearly finished, when the carpenters one evening on leaving off work, left a few live embers, the remains of a fire over which they had been heating their glue-pots, and it is supposed a spark ignited some of the shavings in the room, and then communicated to the rest of the castle; and before assistance could be procured, the greatest part of the building was in flames. The family had quitted the castle whilst it was repairing, and had only left two or three servants to take care of it. Since the time alluded to, from what cause I have not been able to learn, there has been no exertion made to restore it to its former splendour. There it remains to this day, as it was six and forty years ago. Lord M——e had only one son and one daughter. The daughter married a gentleman in the neighbourhood, who is still living in a modern residence in the park, about half a mile from the ruins. His wife, Lord M——e's daughter died about a year and a half ago. Fourteen years after the fire, Mr. and Mrs. P——, with their two sons, were spending the summer at one of their seats on the sea-coast, and near the village of A——k, a few miles from C——r harbour. One fine and serene afternoon they went out on a sailing excursion of a few miles, with only the waterman and his son to manage the yacht. The sea was calm, and almost as smooth as the water of a pond; there was scarcely a breath of wind when they set sail, and hardly enough to make the sails of any use, and there were no indications, nor did it enter their minds, of there being a squall. Just before they left the town of S——n, to which they had gone, the clouds began to lour, and there was every indication of an approaching storm. But they made sail, in hopes of getting back before the storm began. However, they had hardly hoved off till the squall came on with extraordinary violence, and in a few minutes their boat was upset. Their two sons met with a watery grave; and it is a singular circumstance, that the rest of the party were all saved, though every thing was done that lay in their power to save the two young men. But it seemed as if it was ordained that there should never be another Lord M——e, as a punishment for the crimes of the grandfather. All the above circumstances happened before the old lord's death, and all of them on a Friday, which had such an effect on Mrs. P——, that she would never after allow her servants to do any more work than was necessary on a Friday, and kept it quite as strict as the Sabbath till her death.

The above is perfectly correct, as I have had it from some of the old domestics, and from some very respectable people in the town.

T. S.

. Our correspondent has furnished a list of the places and persons alluded to; we withhold them, however, as the circumstances might give pain to the relatives of the family who still survive.

SIMPLE SCIENCE.
LIGHT.

Light is transmitted to us from the sun in little more than eight minutes, which is a velocity of about 200,000 miles in a second of time; if, therefore, each of its particles weighed but the one-thousandth part of a grain, its force would be equal to that of a musket bullet; and even were it the millionth part of a grain, it would destroy every thing against which it struck. It is supposed by some of the most eminent philosophers, that the sun is not a huge ball of fire, but a habitable world, surrounded by a kind of phosphorescent atmosphere. Sir Isaac Newton describes light to be a substance consisting of small particles constantly separating from luminous bodies, moving in straight lines, and rendering bodies luminous by passing, or being reflected from them, and entering the eye. Some substances absorb the sun's rays, and appear luminous in the dark by emitting them for a longer or shorter period. There was an instance of a diamond which had been exposed to the sun's rays, and immediately covered with black wax; when the wax was removed some years afterward, it shone with great brilliancy in the dark. Light is composed of seven distinct rays of different colours. Some bodies absorb one coloured ray, others another, while they reflect or throw back the others; and this is the cause of colour in bodies. A red body, for instance, reflects the red rays, and absorbs the others. A white body reflects all the rays, making the paradoxical adage true, that every colour mixed makes white; and a black body absorbs all the rays, and reflecting none, makes a blank. It has been remarked, if a common artist made light, he would have made it of one colour, and every thing would have appeared of uniform colour; but we now have the infinite variety, which not only pleases, but enables us to distinguish accurately one object from another. Light and heat also are of great use to vegetables—thus, some of these shut themselves up when the sun retires. Many animals seem to have the power of absorbing light, and giving it out at pleasure. The glowworm is a singular instance of this. The female only emits light, which proceeds from the last three rings of its body. From the fact of the male being winged, and the female not, some contrivance was requisite to direct the rambler to his mate, from which necessity originated this hymeneal torch. Naturalists tell us of a sparrow in Hindostan that has instinct enough to light up its nest with glow-worms, which it collects for this purpose, and attaches to the nest by a kind of tenacious clay. M. Reron, in his voyage from Europe to the Isle of France, observed an animal called pyrosoma attanticum, which had the power of emitting light in a most extraordinary degree. The darkness, he says, was intense when it was first discovered—the wind blew violently, and the vessel was making rapid progress. All at once there appeared at some distance, as it were, a vast sheet of phosphorous floating on the waves, and occupying a large space before the vessel. Having passed through this inflamed part of the sea, the crew discovered that this prodigious light was occasioned by an immense number of small animals, which swam at different depths, and appeared to assume various shapes—those which were deepest looked like great red-hot cannon-balls, while those on the surface appeared like cylinders of red-hot iron. Some of them were soon caught, and varied in size from three to seven inches. All the exterior of the animals were bristled with tubercles which shone like diamonds, and seemed to be the seat of this peculiar property. The colour of the animal when in repose is an opal yellow; but the slightest movement which it makes, and which the observer can at pleasure cause by the least irritation, the animal inflames and becomes instantly like red-hot iron. Light was the first creature called into existence by the mandate of Deity. Without it the world would be no better than a chaotic mass, and its inhabitants would drag on an existence of the most wretched misery.

REMORSE.

We are not of those who have any faith in ghost stories as they are generally related: but we think it right to withhold an opinion which must be always speculative while the veil continues to spread forth between human reason and the secrets of another world. Innumerable and extraordinary have been the tales of individuals; some of which, although they leave us still credulous, make us pause and ponder, and ask ourselves—can such things be? It is certain that a belief in supernatural agency has never been confined to the vulgar. Many well known, and, as far as human testimony goes, well authenticated, anecdotes, are on record, which must, at least, stagger the faith of the most sceptical; and neither reason nor revelation justify us in altogether rejecting them as " cunningly devised fables." We know that all the plans of the Almighty are incomprehensible as himself; that we cannot, by searching, find them out; and that we must often believe and take for granted what, as creatures of clay, we cannot conceive. The circumstance we are about to relate is of recent date, and we are well informed of the authenticity of the fact. We shall simply state it, without further note or comment, and leave it to be added to the number of those mysterious occurrences which we shall never be able to understand until this " mortal hath put on immortality."

In the north of Ireland—delicacy forbids our mentioning the precise place—a few years ago, a young man gained the affections, and overcame the virtue, of a neighbour's daughter, who died in childbed. The seducer was in a state of the most pitiable remorse, from the hour of her death. It was whispered that the cause of it was one at which the soul sickens; and something more than even the pangs arising from a guilty deed, and its fatal consequences, appeared to prey on the mind of the young man. He shunned all society—of which he had been the life—seldom spoke except when alone, and then he would mutter as if he held converse with the air, or with some being which no other eye could distinguish. His pallid cheek and wasted frame told too forcibly his mind's disease, and his friends, who watched him with hope and affection, beheld the certain tokens that he was sinking into an early grave at the very moment when health and happiness seemed within his reach, and when there was nothing in his prospect of the future that did not promise joy. But the arrow rankled in his heart; and the wound, which with many would too soon have been cicatrised, with him festered more and more with every day that passed over the gloom of his existence. In a few months, he lay on his bed; and the physicians, having declared that *their* medicines could do nothing for him, had left him to the cares and attentions of his friends, as the only hope of prolonging a life which it would have appeared a mercy to terminate. But his malady gained ground, and his friends knew that he could have no comforter but death. On all subjects but the one, he remained sane and collected, but to the very last he continued to address the being he fancied stood before and listened to him. Remorse deeply preyed on his mind, and was consuming it:

" Remorse—she ne'er forsakes us;
A blood-hound staunch, she tracks our weary step;
   *   *   *   *   *
We hear her deep-mouthed bay, surmounting all
Of wrath and woe and punishment that bides us."

There was one friend to whom he would still listen with some degree of attention; and long and frequent were the endeavours of that friend to remove from his bosom the weight that was pressing him down into the grave. His exertions were vain—still the wretched young man persevered in declaring that all night a female figure, clad in a white shroud, with an infant in her arms, stood at his bed-side—that she waited for him, and he must go. As a last resource, his friend decided on an experiment, which he hoped might prove to the dying youth that he only fancied what he said he saw. He dressed himself in white, and carrying something in his arms to represent an infant, at midnight entered the young man's chamber. He lay, as usual, sleepless on his bed, muttering, in broken accents, on the subject of all his thoughts, and now and then breathing a prayer for mercy and pardon for his sin. The friend passed on, stood beside the bed where the youth lay, and drew aside the curtains. " Gracious God!" exclaimed the youth, as he started up, with looks of terror and despair —" Gracious God! there are *two*"—and died.—*Literary Observer.*

I HAVE A HOME.

Thou innocent and young in years,
   Thou hast not felt the thorn of pain
Press rudely on thy bosom's peace,
   Nor known the sun of gladness wane
Its beam of soft infantine joy,
Nor dimmed its wreath of pleasantries ;
And thou art gentle as yon dove,
   And fair as that pure lily's bloom,
And life's gay morn no sorrow brings,
      Within thy home !

Bright thing of hope! come tell to me
   The dreams thou cherishest within ;
The dawn, the spring-tide of thy day,
   Do whispering, floating breezes win,
With tone of angel watchfulness,
Thine heart, by promise of a ray
Of light divine, unfading still,
   Calm as the changeless blue skies' dome ?
Aye ! smile in hope, whilst joy is thine—
      Blest in a home !

I've gazed upon the winter clouds
   When surcharged with the sweeping blast,
When driving snows relentless wrapped
   Green Nature in a dreary waste—
And I have seen the full round tear
Flow from thy mellowed eye, when happed
The wanderer, halt, decrepid, blind,
   The hoary wretch of storm and gloom,
To pass. Then happy have we deemed
      Our humble home !

And I am young—yea, very young !—
   But not, like thine, my brow unclouded.
Oh ! even from my cradle, I
   Have felt my budding hopes enshrouded.
A tinting melancholy hung
Round e'en my baby bosom's sigh :
Yet whilst the flowers of youth expand,
   And birds of promise round me come,
My soul in sickness turns away—
      Earth is no home !

It is a scene of turmoiled strife,
   Its brightest hopes are rife with fears ;
Its flowers are fadeful !—pleasures brief—
   Its joys are born of guilt and tears !
And mischief lurks with meddling spleen,
And wreaking slander rends repose !
I've watched the ways of man, and wept
   His sunshine should be crossed with gloom ;
And wistfully I've prayed to gain
      The spirit's home !

But e'en when busy malice starts
   From its dark couch of short repose—
When some false friend, with falser heart,
   Around my name some slander throws—
E'en then, unconscious of its harming,
I feel a hope beyond the grave—
My harrowed mind with patience arming,
   I upward glance on heaven's fair dome,
And think, beyond its arching clouds
      I'll find a home !

This then, my gentle one, is hope !
   Still independent of the wrong
A vicious world will ever fling
   To mar the soul's seraphic song !
Thou fair in youth ! unversed in art !
Dost smile to hear life hath its sting.
And smile young bud ! I too will smile !
   For even on earth joys round me bloom :
Parents who love, and sisters fond,
    Are friends of home !

                   AMOLINA.

COMPARATIVE EXTENT OF THE PRODUCTIVE SOIL OF SCOTLAND AND IRELAND.

Scotland and Ireland are very nearly of the same extent, the area of the former, with its islands, being about 30,000, and that of Ireland about 31,000 square miles. Land is of value, however, only for what grows on it, or lies under it, and a large portion of Scotland is so destitute of mineral and vegetable wealth, that the real superiority of Ireland is very great. Sir John Sinclair estimates the productive soils of Scotland at 5,000,000 of acres out of 19,000,000, or very little more than one-fourth. In a Parliamentary Report the bogs and mountains of Ireland are estimated at 2,330,000 acres, and the arable land at 18,107,000. The productive soil of Ireland is, therefore, to that of Scotland as three and a half to one.

OLAN'S TOMB.

" Behold a monument of huge grey stone that marked a hero's tomb."

It is now many years since I took the above sketch. Having business to transact in the County of Cork, during my stay there I paid a visit to a place called Aghabullogue, East Muskerry, to view a famous stone, much reverenced by the peasantry about that neighbourhood, called " Olan's Tomb." It is not now in the same position as when the sketch was taken. The man who brought me there, and related its wonders, dug round its base, and raised it nearly upright. His so doing discovered an inscription, written in the Ogham, or old Irish, character. This inscription, and that on the upper part of the stone, I was unable to decypher. The stone stands about eight feet high, exclusive of the round stone resting on the top, which the guide called " Olan's cap." The inscriptions are written on two sides, the angle serving as the branch line on which the Ogham character was usually written. Olan's cap seems to be only part of a much larger one, a fracture being visible. It is an object of much veneration amongst the peasantry, who believe if it were removed, no matter to what distance, it would return to its former station of its own accord. Their practice, however, is very much against this belief of its miraculous powers, as they have supported it with small stones to prevent its falling. Both the stone and the cap are believed to possess many medicinal qualities. If a person carry the cap on his or her head round the chapel three times, saying Paternosters, they will be infallibly cured. The belief of this, however, I reserve to myself.

                   PHILO-HIBERNICA.

Dublin : Printed and Published by P. D. HARDY, 3, Cecilia-street ; to whom all communications are to be addressed.

Sold by all Booksellers in Ireland.

In London, by Richard Groombridge, 6, Panyer-alley, Paternoster-row ; in Liverpool, by Wilmer and Smith ; in Manchester, by Ambery ; in Birmingham, by Guest, 91, Steelhouse-lane ; in Glasgow, by John Macleod ; and in Edinburgh, by N. Bowack.

THE

DUBLIN PENNY JOURNAL

CONDUCTED BY P. DIXON HARDY, M.R.I.A.

| Vol. IIL | JUNE 6, 1835. | No. 153. |

PHŒNIX COLUMN, PHŒNIX PARK.

The above Pillar, erected in the Phœnix Park by the Earl of Chesterfield in the year 1745, stands in the centre of an area where four great avenues meet, and from which there are entrances to the Viceregal Lodge, and that of the Chief Secretary. The trees which shade the avenues form vistas through which the perspective views of the column assume rather a picturesque effect. It is of Portland stone, and of the Corinthian order, fluted, and highly ornamented. The base and pedestal five feet in height, the shaft and capital twenty, and the phœnix which surmounts the column five feet, so that the whole presents an object thirty feet high. On the north and south sides of the pedestal are the crest and arms of Stanhope in relief. On the east and west sides are the following inscriptions :—

Civivm Oblectamento
Campvm Rvdem et Incvltvm
Ornari Ivssit
Philippvs Stanhope,
Comes de Chesterfield
Prorex.

Impensis suis Posvit
Philippvs Stanhope, Comes
De Chesterfield, Prorex.

To protect the column from accidental violence it has

been enclosed by a circular iron railing; but it is to be regretted that, from the perishable nature of the stone, this ornament to the Park exhibits various symptoms of decay: while the railing keeps off the hand of man, it cannot keep off the hand of time, which is fast obliterating its ornaments.

BRITISH BOTANY.*

To those interested in the prosperity of Ireland, it must afford pleasure to observe the very superior manner in which books are now brought out by several of our Dublin publishers, when compared with those printed in the metropolis a few years since. Not only would the little work before us do credit to the first London house, as to the *manner* of its getting up, but to this it adds the much greater excellence of real value in the *matter* which it contains. Unlike many similar works published in London, which are mere bookselling speculations, *made up* by persons ignorant of the science of which they profess to treat, the work before us is evidently the production of a practical botanist. The flowers, of which there are twenty-eight plates in the volume, are very elegant, both as to the sketching and colouring, and have all the appearance of being accurately drawn from nature.

Although possessing these various recommendations, the author unassumingly informs us, that the work " is not intended for the study of those already learned in the science of Botany; but merely as an introduction for beginners, and has been compiled simply with that view. The writer has imagined that the easiest method of explaining any subject, is to represent it in a familiar dialogue, as being a less tedious manner of conveying information than a continued description, and has therefore been induced to offer the work in its present form."

The following extracts from the early chapters will sufficiently show the nature of the work:

" MISS HENLEY.—Since you are so impatient to begin, Sophia, I will endeavour to explain this rather difficult science to you, as well as I am able. Botany is that branch of science which treats of the structure and functions of vegetables: the systematical arrangement and denomination of their several kinds; and their peculiar properties and uses. Vegetables are organized, supported by air and food, endowed with life, and subject to death as well as animals.

" MARY.—Plants appear to be extremely numerous; has it ever been ascertained how many different species there are?

" MISS H.—The number of plants at present known is upwards of sixty thousand; not including those belonging to New Holland.

" SOPHIA.—How many are supposed to be natives of Great Britain?

" MISS H.—About two thousand: nearly one half of which are mosses and lichens, &c.

" SOPHIA.—How many principal parts does a flower consist of?

" MISS H——Seven; which are, the calyx, corolla, stamen, pistil, pericarp, or seed-vessel, seed and receptacle. The first four parts properly belong to the flower; the last three to the seed.

" MARY.—What parts of a plant ought we to be first acquainted with?

" MISS H.—The flower and fruit; these consist, as I have already told you, of seven parts, which are particularly requisite to be understood, as the classification of plants, according to the Linnæan system, is founded on them.

" But you will understand my explanation better by seeing all the different parts yourselves. Here is the convolvulus arvensis, (small bind-weed,) which will serve to show you the stamens and pistils, though if we could have procured a larger flower, it would have been better, certainly. However, as I do not perceive any other near me better adapted to my purpose, I will proceed to separate the different parts. This green part, which is situated immediately beneath the blossom, is called the calyx or flower-cup: its chief use is to enclose and protect the other parts of the flower: it sometimes consists of two or more leaves, as in the rose; and is sometimes tubular, as in the primrose.

" MARY.—Is there more than one kind of calyx?

" MISS H.—Yes, there are seven kinds of calyxes. The first, perianth or calyx, commonly so called, the most general, is that which is contiguous to, or actually makes a part of the flower, but is not always present: this is the kind I have already described as belonging to the rose, and also to the carnation. Hemlock, carrot, and other plants of the same character, have what is usually called a calyx, but what Dr. Smith considers floral leaves or bracteas, situated remote from the flower: this is called involucre. Daffodil, iris or flag, and crocus, before expanding, are shut up in a sheath-like covering, which bursts at the sides, called a sheath. Grasses are furnished with a peculiar chaff-like substance, or glume; a term also applied to the corolla of grasses. This calyx is denominated a glume. The minute, but curious tribes of mosses, have also their calyx, which, from being placed on the top of the flower, like a hood, is called calyptra.

" The calyx of the mushroom tribe, is called volva.

" MARY.—What part of the flower is the corolla?

" MISS H.—The corolla consists of those more delicate and dilated, generally more coloured leaves, which are always internal with respect to the calyx, and constitute the chief beauty of a flower. This pretty pink part of the convolvulus which I hold in my hand is the corolla. In the rose, the corolla is red and fragrant; in the violet, purple; and in the primrose, yellow. The leaves which compose the corolla, are called petals. In many plants, as, for example, this convolvulus, the corolla is formed of one single leaf or petal, and is then called one-petalled, or monopetalous; in the rose, which consists of more than one petal, the corolla is many-petalled, or polypetalous. The upper part of a monopetalous corolla, is termed the limb; the lower, or contracted portion, the tube. The base of each petal in a polypetalous corolla, is the claw; the expanded part is the border; but we will have another conversation about corollas to-morrow.

" SOPHIA.—Will you explain what the stamen is?

" MISS H.—The stamen is placed immediately within the corolla; at least, generally so; or, if there is no corolla, within the calyx. It is composed of two parts, a thread-like portion, or filament, which supports the upper part, or anther; this, when ripe, bursts and discharges a fine dust or pollen; on this essentially depends the fertilizing principle.

" MARY.—What is the pistil?

" MISS H.—The pistil is commonly in the centre of the flower, and consists of three parts, which are, the germen, the style, and the stigma. The germen is the pedestal or base of the pistil, generally of a roundish shape, though sometimes slender; its office is to contain the seeds which are not yet arrived at maturity; the style is the pillar, or thread-like part, which supports the stigma, which is the highest part of the pistil.

" SOPHIA.—Is not some part of the flower called the nectary?

" MISS H.—Yes, the nectary is sometimes a part of the pistil, sometimes separate from it; from being supposed to produce the honey or nectar, the term nectary is applied to it. Every singular appearance in a flower, which is not calyx, corolla, stamen, nor pistil, has the general name of nectary. I will take the larkspur as an example. This has no calyx; the corolla has five differently formed petals; the upper one ends in a spire-like projection; it has, also, another peculiarity, which is a somewhat divided petal-like portion, with a horn or spur, projecting and enclosing the spur of the petal; this is the nectary.

" MARY.—How may we distinguish the nectary in different flowers?

" MISS H.—In monopetalous flowers, as the dead nettle, the tube of the corolla contains, and probably secretes the honey, without any evident nectary. Sometimes it is a production or elongation of the corolla, as in the violet; sometimes also of the calyx, as in the garden nasturtium, whose calyx partakes frequently of the nature of the

* British Botany familiarly explained and described, in a Series of Dialogues, illustrated with Twenty-eight coloured Plates, drawn from Nature. Dublin; W. F. Wakeman.

petals. There are various kinds of nectaries, which you will be able to distinguish when you become better acquainted with the study of botany.

"MARY.—What is the pericarp, or seed-vessel?

"MISS H.—It is the case or covering of the seed, and is the external part of the germen, come to maturity. There are two different kinds of pericarps, which are of various shapes; globular, as in the poppy; long, as the pod of the pea; pulpy, with a stone in the middle, as in the plum; pulpy, containing seeds enclosed in a case, as in the pear; juicy, and containing seeds which have only an external case, as in the gooseberry. Filbert and hazel nuts have a kernel enclosed in a hard shell, called a nut. The fir-trees produce their seeds in a singular kind of fruit, called a cone; and there is another species of pericarp, not very common, which is a membranous seed-vessel, opening lengthwise on one side only, without an apparent suture, which is called a follicle.

"MARY.—What is the receptacle?

"MISS H.—The receptacle or base, is that part which supports and connects the whole. In some plants it is very conspicuous, particularly in the artichoke, and is that part of it which is eaten. In the cuckoo-pint, the receptacle is elongated into a club-shaped body or spadix, having the anthers and pistils set round it.

"MARY.—Will you explain some of the uses of the corolla?

"MISS H.—As a protection to the tender and important parts within, especially from wet; its use in many cases is obvious, but not in all. It probably fulfils some important office to the essential parts of the flower, with regard to air, and especially light. It not only presents itself in a remarkable manner to the sun-beams, frequently closing or drooping when they are withdrawn, but it is so peculiarly distinguished by beauty and brilliancy of colour, that we must suppose its functions somewhat different from those of the leaves, even with regard to light itself. Dr. Darwin calls the corolla the lungs of stamens and pistils, and with great probability, for they abound in air-vessels.

"You have, of course, often observed, Sophia, the variety there is in the roots of different plants.

"SOPHIA.—Yes; and I was going to ask you to describe some of them to us.

"MISS H.—That I shall have great pleasure in doing. The root consists of two parts—caudex, the body of the root, and radicula, the fibre. The letter only is essential, being the part which imbibes nourishment.

"MARY.—Of what use is the root?

"MISS H.—The use of the root, in general, is two-fold; to fix the plant in a commodious situation, and to derive nourishment for its support. This part is, therefore, commonly plunged deeply into the ground, having, indeed, a natural tendency to grow downwards. Roots are either of annual, biennial, or perennial duration.

"MARY.—Will you explain those terms to me?

"MISS H.—Annual roots belong to plants which live only one year, or rather one summer, as barley; biennial, to such as are produced one season, and, living through the ensuing winter, produce flowers and fruit the following summer, as fox-glove, and several species of mullein; and perennial, to those which live and blossom, through many successive seasons, to an indefinite period, as trees, and many herbaceous plants. The term biennial is applied to any plant that is produced one year and flowers another, provided it flowers but once.

"MARY.—Why is the autumn considered the best time of the year for transplanting? I wanted to take up a rose-tree out of my garden last summer, and the gardener said it would injure it.

"MISS H.—Because in the winter or torpid season of the year, the powers of the root lie dormant; and the autumn and winter is, therefore, the proper time for their transplantation. After they have begun to throw out new fibres, it is generally dangerous, or even fatal, to remove them. Very young annual plants, as they form new fibres with great facility, survive transplantation tolerably well, provided they receive abundant supplies of water by the leaves till the root has recovered itself.

"SOPHIA.—I think, Miss Henley, there appears to be much greater variety in the leaves of plants, than in either the corolla or the root; will you describe the different kinds, as I suppose each has some peculiar appellation?

"MISS H.—Folium, the leaf, is a very general, but not universal, organ of vegetables, of an expanded form, presenting a much greater surface to the atmosphere than all the other parts of the plant together.

"MARY.—The colour is always green—is it not?

"MISS H.—Almost universally so; and its internal substance pulpy and vascular, sometimes very succulent, and the upper and under surfaces generally differ in hue, as also in kind or degree of roughness.

"SOPHIA.—Leaves are very ornamental to plants, both from their colour and the beauty of their forms.

"MISS H.—They are of great importance to the plant which bears them, as they contribute to its health and increase."

In a similar way the author proceeds, and in the most familiar, pleasing, and instructive manner, describes every tree and plant at present known in the British islands, from the lordly pine to the modest primrose. It is altogether a work deserving of encouragement.

CANADA IN THE YEARS 1832, 1833, AND 1834.*

As a work published in Ireland, we notice the above; but being ourselves the publishers, we deem it unfair to say more for it than what we have already stated in an addenda to the author's preface:—

Advertisement by the Author—"The writer of the following pages has resided in Canada, chiefly in 'the Bush,' for the last two years; he has had some experience of the life of a Settler, and has seen something of the inducements and the advantages the country offers to such. Extrinsic circumstances have caused his return to Ireland, which he does not again intend to leave for America; and believing himself thereby free from any unfair bias, he has written a few of the most prominent remarks on the subject, his experience has suggested, which he now offers to the better classes of those who intend emigrating thither the ensuing Spring."

"Aware that the British public have, in many instances, been made the dupes of individuals interested in 'Emigration speculations,' by the publication of works calculated to mislead them; as the gentleman who is the author of the following pages does not wish his name to appear in the title, I feel called upon thus to authenticate the work, which may be relied on as written by the individual circumstanced as stated in the foregoing paragraph, and giving a fair and impartial statement of things as they are at the present moment in British America. I may, I trust, be allowed to add, without any charge of unfairness to others, that I have been induced to publish the little work, from the conviction that it contains much important practical information, and many hints for persons intending to emigrate, not to be met with in any other work yet published. "P. DIXON HARDY."

THE TROSACHS.
A SONNET BY WORDSWORTH.

There's not a nook within this solemn pass
But were an apt confessional for one
Taught by his summer spent, his autumn gone,
That life is but a tale of morning grass,
Withered at eve. From scenes of art that chase
That thought away, turn, and with watchful eyes
Feed it 'mid Nature's old felicities,
Rocks, rivers, and smooth lakes more clear than glass
Untouched, unbreathed upon. Thrice happy guest,
If from a golden perch of aspen spray,
(October's workmanship to rival May)
The pensive warbler of the ruddy breast
This moral sweeten by a heaven-taught lay,
Lulling the year, with all its cares, to rest.

* Canada in the years 1832, 1833, and 1834, containing important Information and Instructions to Persons intending to emigrate thither in 1836. By an Ex-Settler, who resided chiefly in "The Bush" for the last Two Years. Dublin: P. Dixon Hardy. Sold by all Booksellers.

THE PHŒNIX PARK, DUBLIN.

Who that has ever set foot on Irish soil, but has heard of the " *Phœnix Park*," with its *fifteen* acres of *fighting* ground,* level as a bowling-green, and skirted on every side with groves of hawthorn, beneath whose sheltering shadows so many *honourable men* have, from time to time, drawn the trigger, and, in the twinkling of an eye, sent into eternity, unblessed and unforgiven, so many of their fellow-creatures, without even a moment granted them to call for mercy—to ask forgiveness of that great Being into whose presence they were about to be hurried. Seriously, of all the fashionable follies that disgrace civilized society in the present day, the folly of *duelling* is the most monstrous. While we affect to condemn and deplore those evils which are the source of so much misery among the ignorant peasantry of the country—their faction fights and party quarrels—is it to be tolerated, that the higher orders shall, by their example, sanctioned by their " code of honour," falsely so called, furnish with an excuse for their conduct, those who are but too ready to imitate them in such inhuman proceedings? For, after all, is it not an inhuman thing, however it may be varnished with the name of honour, for an individual, what-

ever may be his rank in society, to take the life of his fellow-man, for some merely supposed injury, or want of etiquette in the common courtesies of life ? And yet that such has been the causes of many a fatal duel, the annals of duelling can but too well testify. Nay, farther, is it not inhuman, for an individual who may never have injured another, to expose not only his own life, but the welfare of a family, who may be altogether dependent upon him, in order to meet the absurd rules of a barbarous and unchristian code, merely because such may be sanctioned by the opinion of persons calling themselves *honourable men!* To say that it is an atonement for crime, or an apology for error, merely to take *an equal chance* of *shooting*, or being *shot at*, would, under any other circumstance, be counted absurd and ridiculous. It is only long continued custom that can at all hide the absurdity from the view of any. Duelling, then, we consider not merely a *folly*, but a *crime ;* and we trust that the day is not far distant, when such an unjust, unequal, and barbarous regulation, shall be for ever expunged from civilized society.

So much for the field of the fifteen acres, which, by an association of ideas, invariably brings with it thoughts of bloodshed and battery—of duelling and duellists.

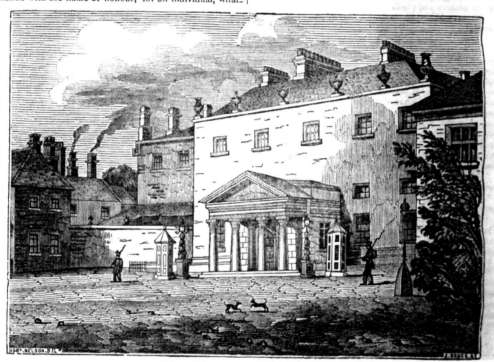

GRAND ENTRANCE TO THE VICEREGAL LODGE.

Of the various drives for recreation and amusement round the city, next to Kingstown, the preference appears

to be given to the Park. A distinguished writer* observes that " viewing all the particulars which should distinguish a place set apart for public recreation, the Phœnix Park, on the whole, would not suffer on comparison with any other in Europe. It is, like Hyde Park, most conveniently situated at one extremity of the town ; and, if the latter

* We have no doubt that our English readers must at times be disposed to question the reality of some of our sketches of Irish life—especially in those instances where descriptions of " fighting for fun" are introduced. The following simple statement of a transaction which took place some short time since in the Phœnix Park, must go a good length towards lessening their incredulity on the point referred to :—

" On Sunday evening, some thousands of countrymen assembled on the seven-acre field, opposite the Royal Infirmary in the Park. They consisted of two parties, from which champions were chosen to contend in wrestling, for the honour of their respective counties, Meath and Kildare. For some time the wrestlers were permitted to exhibit their skill in ' shinning and tripping,' and no tendency to a general conflict was evinced until about seven o'clock. At this juncture, a Meath man, who keeps a public-house in Smithfield, interrupted a 'match,' declaring that his countryman had not met with fair play from his antagonist. The publican was knocked down, and this became a signal for a general fight. Shillelaghs, which up to this period had

been concealed under friese coats, were now drawn forth, and a furious attack was commenced by one party against the other. For five or six minutes the belligerents fought, and broken heads were given and received, without any churlish disposition being evinced by either party of sneaking off without returning freely quite as much as they got. At length the Kildare boys took so their heels, and were pursued by the victors to the Park wall, where the fugitives crossed into the Conyngham-road. Great numbers were severely cut and bruised, and many left lying on the field of battle. But it is strange that not a single man came forward on Monday to the Police Office, to take criminal proceedings against another, though many knew perfectly well by whom they had been beaten."

* Dr. Walsh.

be laid out in a neater manner and more trimly dressed, with nicely gravelled walks better suited to pedestrians; if it even boast a finer piece of water, in what is miscalled the Serpentine River;—yet, in extent, in variety of grounds, and in grandeur of prospects, the other indisputably possesses a decided superiority.

"In 1776, the Phœnix Park was surveyed by Bernard Scale, when its extent and dimensions were found to be as follow:—From the Dublin gate by the Magazine and Hibernian School to Knockmaroon gate, two miles and sixty-six perches. From the Dublin gate by the Phœnix Column to Castleknock gate, two miles and thirty perches. From the Dublin gate by the rere of the Viceregal Lodge to Castleknock gate, two miles one quarter and twenty-seven perches; and from Castleknock gate to Knockmaroon gate, half a mile and fifty-four perches. Its contents were found to be 1086 acres, Irish plantation measure; or 1759 acres and twenty-two perches, English statute measure; contained in a circumference of five and a half Irish, or seven English miles.

"It may readily be conceived, that so extensive a demesne must comprise a variety of situations and scenery. In fact, the ground is very unequal, producing an undulating surface of hill and dale, agreeably diversified with wood and water. The exterior views from the Park are grand and beautiful. In the fore-ground the river Liffey

meanders through rich meadows, until it flows beneath the magnificent arch of Sarah's-bridge. The city itself terminates the horizon on the east. In front is a rich landscape highly embellished with country seats, through which the Grand Canal passes, marked in its course by fine rows of elms; and beyond all, the soft contour of the Wicklow mountains forms a suitable frame to the picture. Within the Park are several picturesque and romantic spots, forming very delightful and retired walks; some of these are skirted with groves of hawthorn of large and venerable growth; these trees clothe the sides of glens, which are intersected by paths that lead to 'alleys green, dingle, and bushy dell, in the wild wood,' strongly contrasted with the regularity of the other plantations. In spring, the beauty of these spots is much heightened by the rich blow of hawthorn blossoms which cover the trees, and load the air with their fragrance. Among these woods, there is but one open level space that can be properly termed a plain; this is called the *Fifteen Acres*, (already alluded to,) and here the troops in garrison are exercised. The Park is not destitute of water, though the magnitude of the space it occupies bears no proportion to the extent of the place. There were formerly three lakes, one of which has been some years ago drained, and its place occupied by an extensive plantation; the others still remain, forming fine objects in the approach to the Viceregal Lodge.

RERE ENTRANCE TO THE VICEREGAL LODGE.

The principal entrance to the Park, which is seven miles in circumference, is through a grand ornamental gate, situated a short distance from the King's-bridge on the Liffey, on the Dublin side.

On entering the Park in this direction, the objects which first attract the attention are, the Royal Military Hospital, standing a little off the main road on the right hand side, and the Wellington Testimonial, a little to the left. Of these we purpose giving a description and drawings in future numbers. A short way further on, are the Gardens of the Zoological Society, of which we gave some account in our last and preceding volumes, and to which we intend returning in an early number. A little distance from the Gardens stands the Viceregal Lodge—the rere facing the main road through the Park, and to the front of which the road immediately skirting the lake conducts. Of both front and rere a correct representation will be found in the engravings annexed.

The Viceregal Lodge was originally built by Mr. Cle-

ments, from whom it was purchased. It was a plain structure of brick. In 1802 Lord Hardwicke made the first important improvement, by adding the wings, in one of which is the great dining-hall. In 1808, the Duke of Richmond added the north portico, a structure of the Doric order, and the lodges by which the demesne is entered on the side of Dublin. But the most striking addition to the building is the north front, added by Lord Whitworth. This is ornamented with a pediment supported by four Ionic pillars of Portland stone, from a design of Johnson's. The whole façade has been made to correspond with this portico, and it now stands a fair architectural ornament in the Park.

"The Phœnix Park derives its name and origin from a manor-house, on whose site the present Powder Magazine was erected in 1738. The manor was called in the Irish vernacular tongue *Fionn-uisge*, pronounced *Finniské*, which signifies clear or fair water, and which, articulated in the brief English manner, exactly resembled the word *Phœnix;*

at length the Park became known, even at an early period, by no other appellative. The spring or well so called, still exists. It is situated in a glen, beside the lower lake, near the grand entrance into the Viceregal Lodge, and has been much frequented from time immemorial for the supposed salubrity of its waters. It is a strong chalybeate. It remained, however, in a rude and exposed state till the year 1800, when, in consequence of some supposed cures it had effected, it immediately acquired celebrity, and was much frequented. About five years after it was enclosed, and is now among the romantic objects of the Park. It is approached by a gradual descent through a planted avenue. The spa is covered by a small structure of Portland stone, on which sits a colossal eagle, as the emblem of longevity. This appropriate ornament was erected by Lord Whitworth. Behind the spring, under the brow of the hill, is a rustic dome, with seats round it for the accommodation of those who frequent the spa; in the back of which is an entablature with the following inscription :—

This seat,
Given by her Grace,
CHARLOTTE, DUCHESS OF RICHMOND,
For the Health and Comfort
Of the Inhabitants
Of Dublin. — August 19, 1813.

The Duke of Richmond and Lord Whitworth used this spa with much benefit, and their example has been followed by the citizens of Dublin.

The powder magazine was erected in 1738. It is a regular square fort, with demi-bastions at the angles, a dry ditch, and draw bridge; in the centre are the magazines for ammunition, well secured against accidental fire, and bomb proof, in evidence of which no casualty has happened since their construction. The fort occupies two acres and thirty-three perches of ground, and is fortified by ten twenty-four pounders; as a further security, and to contain barracks for troops, which before were drawn from Chapelizod, an additional triangular work was constructed in 1801.

At no great distance from the battery, stands the Hibernian School, a drawing of which we shall probably give in some future number with a particular description.

PAUL GUINAN; OR THE ASH POLE.

While putting over me one of those silent circuits which, it would appear, fate has ordained that all young barristers, be they good or bad, must perform, like a quarantine, before they can hope to set foot on that " terra grata," *practice*—I was deeply grieved when, sitting in the court of my native county, I heard the name of Paul Guinan called to the bar; and on his countenance, so well known to me in boyish days, appearing above that dreadful locality, listened to the arraignment, charging him with no less a crime than murder. The usual plea of not guilty—with which, from my former opinion of the man, I heartily concurred—being put in, the trial proceeded; and then circumstances were brought to light, so confirmatory of the charge, that even I could not entertain a reasonable doubt of the guilt of the prisoner—nor did the jury: and in a few moments every eye was turned on him—a being, living and moving, yet having no heritage in life, or link with living thing—within the confines of the certain grasp of death, and yet possessed of every healthful faculty that would seem to ensure to another a lengthened existence. He stood between the living and the dead—part of both, and all of neither. On my return home, in about three weeks after, with my curiosity and feelings on the subject still fresh, I made some inquiries regarding the steps by which a man of such unblemished and amiable character which Guinan at one time really possessed, could have reached such a height in crime; and was answered by details, serving well to illustrate the position, that most, if not all, of our temporal ills spring from some trifling aberration in the beginning, and that, perhaps, rather springing from carelessness and confidence, than actual depravity.

The father of Paul Guinan was a comfortable farmer, and had struggled long and well to live independent of his neighbours, and ultimately leave his only child, at least, not an outcast; but was called away before he could achieve that purpose, and while Paul was little better than a mere boy, leaving him and his widow with little more than a roof to cover them and an honest name. Paul, like the generality of our countrymen, was eminently possessed of a warm and sensitive heart; and when his dying father, after the last offices of religion, caught his hand, and endeavoured to say, " Paul, avick machree, don't be frettin', but whin I'm gone look to your poor mother, an' strive to keep the wind off her back. I'm lavin' ye poor, God help ye, an' look over ye; but, Paul avick, struggle honestly, an' ye'll have a blessin'," the heart of the poor boy rose to his throat in a convulsive sob; and he resolved within himself never to do any thing without first thinking, if his father was by, what would he think of it. With a pride, unjustifiable except by custom, a great portion of the scanty resources were lavished in the usual manner of paying an empty honour to the dead, at the expense of the already bereaved family; and poor Paul had, within the next year, many an opportunity of practising his promised reference to his dead father; but, according to the widow's account, " the great God, that took away the right hand, spared the left for her, an' made it a'most as strong; and shure, why should she fret, while she had such a bird as Paul in the nest, might heaven be his watch for ever an' ever;" and, indeed, if every body's word is to be believed, he in every respect deserved the encomium. As time passed on, however, the enthusiasm which had so long kept him uncontaminate began to yield to its influence, and ill-will at length found something to talk of even in Paul, on the score of company keeping, and that not of the most select description for a boy in his situation, it being, as the fool of the parish expressed it, " plaguey hard intirely, to dance all night, an' dhrink all day, an' make out a day's work afther."

The second winter after old Guinan's death, Paul was stretched along some stools by the fire-side nursing a fit of laziness, and occasionally breaking to pieces, with a stick he held in his hand, every piece of coal within his reach, until having scattered one farther than the rest, some of it fell among a heap of tow, which his mother was silently, and no doubt sorrowfully, carding opposite him; the exertion of quenching the inflammable material, and sweeping in the fire, roused both from their silence, which was first broken by the old woman observing,

" Why then, Paul, what's come over ye, and you havin' yer brogues to mend, an' twenty things to do ?"

" Augh, mother, I dunna—shure I can mend them to-morrow.'

" Tom Maher came home from the town to-day, an' he says the wheat got a rise of two or three shillings; maybe, if ye don't make haste an' thrash it, 'twill fall before you're ready."

" Well, mother, sorra a bit o' me, but I'll set about it to-morrow."

" But the *boulteen* of your flail is broken, so git up an' thry an' mend it."

" Och, ay, shure enough; but where 'ud I get a new one this time o' night. Well, mother, I'm blest, but if you give me six-pence, I'll go wid the day-dawn over to the wood an' buy an ash-pole, an' then I'll have the makins of all I want, the spade-handle, an' scythe-stick, an' boulteen; an' shure, any how, to-morrow 'ud be Saturday."

The six-pence was accordingly got, and the poor woman, rejoiced at having thus wakened him out of a lethargy with which she had been some time combating, recommended retirement for the night, which was at once acceded to by Paul.

Next morning the birds were scarce stirring before Paul; and with his mind full of good resolutions, he set forward on his journey, calculating, as he went on, how much he might spend next market-day on the strength of the rise in his wheat; and at length determining, as many do without being a whit the richer for it, that all should be laid by for the rainy day. The journey was soon over, but Paul had to rest himself; and sitting down on the ditch by the roadside, he began watching the woodcutters, until a voice from the road recalled him to his senses. It proceeded from a low, light, merry-looking man, dressed in a frieze *cotamore*, who, with an air of half recognition, bade him good-morrow.

" Good-morrow kindly," answered Paul. " I'm thinkin'

now that I ought to know you, though I can't tell where I saw you."

"Why, thin," said the stranger, "don't you recollect *Maurya* Brien's weddin', up in the glins beyant?"

"Avick machree, to be shure I do," replied Paul, bringing off the ditch, and grasping the stranger's hand with apparent delight; "an' is it yerself that's in it?— Think o' me not to know you; but sweepins to the step farther you'll go, until you take something to keep the chill of the mornin' off o' you;" and Paul, accordingly, with six-pence in his pocket, hurried him off to the adjacent shebeen. His companion was one of those waggish, idle, good humoured, young fellows, that we meet with in every walk of life, ever driven, by improvidence, to shifts not always the most honourable or honest. Paul had met him at a wedding, where he was the wit of the night, and almost divided with the bridegroom the honour of being the " *lion;*" and a recognition from such a character seemed to poor simple Paul, too desirable not to be improved.

Arrived at the whiskey house, Paul was not quite divested of anxiety with regard to his funds; but pride came to his aid, and he called for his half-pint with as great an air as if he had a pocket full of shillings.

"An' what brought you down this way, aviek?" asked Paul, after the first inquiries and conversation regarding the night they had spent together.

"'Deed thin, I come down on a visit to an uncle I have a couple o' miles from this. Maybe you know the Coghlans—a fine set o' boys they are. Sure you do, for I hard them talk of you. Bud, any how, we're to have great fun to-morrow, for half the country's to be out plunging the river that runs aby the bawn—it's alive with fish I'm tould—an' I kem down for my share, to be shure."

"Sorra bit, bud I b'lieve I'll go over, too," said Paul; "it's not far from our house."

"Why thin," replied the stranger, "it's mighty glad we'll be to see you: but finish your glass, man, there's more in the jug."

Poor Paul did as he was desired, and the half-pint was soon drank; and Paul, elated and confused, insisted on calling for another, which followed the fate of its predecessor in rapid time. Paul had never used so much whiskey at any time before, and his situation may easily be imagined, as, after paying his six-pence, he staggered with his worthless companion to the road, uttering and receiving many protestations of unalterable regard. The helpless condition in which the stranger found his entertainer after their sitting, seemed in some small degree to puzzle him; but at length, having with some difficulty got him again into the wood, and placed him at full length on a well shaded bank, he left him there, essaying to utter the tuneful breathings of some village minstrel in praise of " whiskey the jewel, mavrone," until sleep at length induced in his mind that utter chaos which drunkenness had but half effected.

The evening sun was glancing through the trees, and at times, intercepted by the waving of the branches, played wantonly on the face of the sleeper before he aroused himself. When he at length arrived at the consciousness of being awake, he stared around him, half-sober, half-stupid, and puzzled beyond all comprehension, began to soliloquize—

"Why thin, where am I—or what put me here? Jim! Jim Doyle!—the sorra a one at all near me. Och, maybe, thin, it's dhramin' I was. Murdher, shure I'm not dhrunk."

But the moment he rose from his couch, the sudden return of his body to its full length position, answered the question for him beyond the power of contradiction. Having made a second attempt, with less haste and self-confidence, he regained his erect stature with better success; and made his way by the branches, with many aberrations from the straight path, to where he heard the ripple of a shaded stream, the coolness of which promised some relief to his parched and scalded throat. After refreshing himself, and enjoying the sober effects of the water, he sat for some time on the bank, with his aching head leaning on both his hands, regretting his freak as bitterly as the confusion of his mind permitted him. According as his senses returned, however, the less imme-

diate consequences of his misconduct began to present themselves; and foremost among them was the reflection of how he had put it beyond his power to effect that for which he had lost his day, and pledged himself so firmly to his mother. He raised his head to consider what he should do in this emergency, preferable to appearing a culprit before her. Opposite the bank where he had fixed himself, was a portion of the wood where the workmen had been employed before the setting sun had warned them to their homes, and the quantities of cut timber which lay sorted before him, had not a single watch on them. He listened—there was not a sound in the whole wood but the hushing ripple of the river, and the cawing of the rooks settling themselves in their nests, and some, stripped of their homes, loudly complaining of the ruin which had been effected in their colony since morning; but his ear could not catch the slightest noise which he could assimilate to the stroke of the hatchet, or the voice of the woodman. His mind, giddy with drunkenness, grasped at the refuge that appeared to deliver him from the dilemma which awakened his remorse; and long before reason had weighed the impulse of volition, or balanced between theft and the blame which by theft he could avoid, he was trotting across the fields with such a pole as he wanted thrown across his shoulder. His first theft—his first real robbery—was committed. The rapidity with which he moved soon brought him to his own door; and having to pass the window of the kitchen, he looked in, and saw his mother sitting by the fireside in an attitude of uneasy expectation. The potatoes were keeping warm before the comfortable hearth, that blazed so as to illuminate with a deceitful brightness the farthest corner of the room. All was ready for him, and all seemed happy. Then, almost for the first time, it struck him that he was about bringing guilt, and perhaps infamy, to that quiet home—to plant a pain in that mother's bosom, which he knew years of contrition on his part could not remove. The thought staggered him: he stood irresolute at the door, fearful to enter, and yet unwilling to return and restore his stolen goods; until at length, vowing within himself that on the morrow, after mass, he would disclose all to the priest, and send the price of the pole by him to the owner, he was enabled to lift the latch, and meet his mother's eye with some complacency.

"Why thin, Paul," said she, on his entering, "isn't this quare thratement, now, I lave it to yourself, when you might be at home easily at twelve o'clock, an' it's dark night now."

"Och, mother," answered he, "I dunna what kept me—one thing or another; an' I met Jim Doyle, a man from the glins beyant, an'—an'——Arrah, mother, would you want a body to come an' go, jist as if 'twas a coal o' fire or the time o' day they wanted?"

"Well, sit down, any how, you unlucky omedhawn you, an' eat your supper. That's a good pole, avick, did you get it for the six-pence. Jim Doyle, an' Jim this, an' Jim that, is your excuse always when you stay beyant your time, an' that's often enough, I'm sure. God betune you an' harm, but I'm afeard they'll bring you into mischief yit."

The supper was soon set aside, for Paul was not in much humour for eating, though he had been fasting all the day, for his head was aching, and his heart heavy, in spite of the compromise he had made with his conscience; but pleading weariness, he was soon laid on his bed, and buried in sleep, but not the quiet sleep of his other days. It was, in fact, sufficiently restless to awake the fears of his anxious mother, as she bent over him in silent sadness before she sought her own rest, and sprinkled holy water on his pillow, consigning him to the guardianship of the " blessed Vargin."

The sun was not many minutes over the horizon in the morning, before he sent a few rays as messengers through the little window of the sleeping-room, to rouse Paul from his slumbers. First after he awoke came the sickening feel of something wrong; and then the full consciousness of guilt; and then the false, delusive feeling that he was about to make restitution, and win as much of Heaven's forgiveness and his own as he could. He lay for a long time, considering how he should open the matter to his reverence—so long, in fact, that he cooled on it. How could he lose the plunging party? He might make his peace any day; but meet such pleasure he might never again—or if he did, he would not have a pole so apropos. He wavered between pleasure and what he considered duty; and few who have ever done so, will feel any doubt as to which had the victory, or be surprised at the conversation which occurred between him and his mother that morning after their breakfast.

"Paul, avick, if ye see your aunt Judy at the chapel to-day, be sure to ax afther Thady, for I had mighty onaisy dhrames about them last night; an' 'deed, I think you might rub out a head or two ov the wheat, an' bring it for a sample, an' see what the jobbers 'ud be givin' you for it. You might have it ready afore Sathurday wid a little help. I have my misgivins but it'll fall again if we don't make haste. Stir, stir, avick, or you'll lose mass—your shirt is on the bed within."

"I b'lieve I'm not goin' to mass to-day, mother."

"Why then, why wouldn't you? or what laziness is come over you? Arrah, Paul aroon, maybe it's sick you are, you warn't aisy at all last night? so go an' lie down an the bed, an' I'll make a dhrop o' whey for you."

"Musha," said Paul, "I never was betther in my life: but it's what I said, I'd go look at a plungin' beyant at the big river to-day; an', mother, aroon, I never was at one afore, so you mustn't say agin me."

"Is it of a Sunday, an' to lose mass for it? Oh, Paul, Paul, it's a bad thing to be at sich work at all at all on sich a day—but worse an' worse if a body is to lose mass by id. But, Paul, you'll take your own way, so you will, in spite of me, an' I wash my hands out of it. So if you're goin', go, an' God pity you, you poor blind ome-dhawn!"

Paul was not without some compunctions as to the course he was about pursuing. Twice or three times he was on the point of obeying his mother's advice, and not going to the plunging; but pride stood between him and his better judgment, so shouldering his pole, and bidding a sulky good-bye to his mother, he proceeded to the rendezvous. Arrived there, whatever regrets or remorse had seized him during his walk, were soon dissipated by the exhilirating nature of the sports in which he soon became actively engaged. A large, long net was procured, and within the mouth, so as to keep it quite open, was fixed a bow of the necessary span; across this a large pole was fixed, like an arrow, fastened securely, and forked at the lower extremity, thus forming, as it were, a handle to the net, and admitting of being driven firm into the bed of the river. A fit spot was soon chosen, and the net fixed, with its arched mouth reaching from bank to bank, and intercepting within its meshes every thing borne down by the current. Sixty or eighty yards above this, the plungers, each armed with a long pole, having on the end a mallet-head or some such expedient, commenced their operations, by driving the extremities of their poles into all the recesses of the banks, and creating such a turmoil in the water, as to drive before them to the net whatever fish were at all in the interval; and immediately on their arriving at the net, it was at once drawn up, so that not one could escape. The net being then emptied of its prey, was borne down the river another space, and the same operation performed, until they reached the spot where they had determined to be contented. The number of accidents, none of them dangerous, and all enlivening to the spectators, precluded all thought; and the raising of the net, in itself an adventure as often as it was repeated, gave such an intoxicating interest to the scene, as none can imagine but those who have at some time joined in this illegal, but speedy, mode of emptying the richest river of its finny treasures. On their breaking up the sport, a division was made of the spoils, and Paul proceeded homeward with his share and his pole, each earned with an equal portion of remorse; for on his journey homewards, cold and weary, his naturally good heart began to tax him wildly for his errors of that day and the day before: and the stubborn heart was quite softened within him by the time he reached his own door. It is needless to dwell on this part of his story. The dissipation of one day, and the wet, chilly labours of another, in spite of all its excitement, did for him, as they have done for many a man. He did not rise the next day—nor the next—nor that week—nor the week after. A low fever was in his bones, and kept him on his bed senseless and helpless for many days; and his mother watched over him with the same care and fondness as if he had never erred, or she never warned him of his erring. Sickness is not the cheapest mode of life, and the poor widow, after having experienced that already, had now to feel it again under even less favourable circumstances. But all was well, in her mind, when she had him on her floor again, conscious of his errors, and desirous to amend them: but there still was a thunder-cloud to burst over her, for which she had been able to make no preparation. Arrears to a large amount had necessarily accrued on her little farm, and they were demanded by the agent at a most unfavourable time for her—the first day on which Paul was enabled to stir out. She pleaded her misfortunes, and asked a little time; but was answered by the remark, that she did not avail herself of time or high prices when she had both, and now that corn was down it was hardly to be supposed she would be wiser. A compromise was effected, and a few pounds given the desolate widow, on condition of her clearing out at once from her little homestead, and surrendering all, as it stood, to a new tenant, who became accountable for the arrear. Beggared as she was by the imprudence of her son, she still hesitated, perhaps weakly, to upbraid him with his old errors, to which the bitterness of despair was leading him back. His character had undergone a change, and a desperate one: and instead of making some exertion for the relief of his ruined mother, he was satisfied to sit brooding over his situation; particularly as it had been proved to him by some officious neighbour, that his successor in the farm had used underhand means to supplant him, so that his penury seemed to him less his fault than his misfortune. He thus became an easy prey to the designing Doyle, whose acquaintance had already been so ruinous to him. This man was foremost in some of the insurgent schemes which then agitated the country; and by the promise of revenge on his enemy, had little difficulty in alluring to his ranks the penniless and desperate Guinan. The ash-pole which, with other lumber, he had been permitted to remove to make a hut for his mother, was again called to work, in the character of a pike-handle. An early night was appointed by the others of the party to gratify the vengeance of their recruit; and with his own hand he fired the haggard which he had helped to raise. The proprietor rushed out to save his property, and paralyzed by fear, now stood motionless before Guinan. Doyle, the evil demon of the wretched young man, was beside him, as he gazed with a look of horrible, but undetermined, hate on him who beggared his poor mother.

"Now, your sowl you," whispered Doyle, "what's your pike for?" and in another moment it was buried to the wood in the bosom of the intruder.

Such a fiendish outrage could not by any possibility be overlooked by the executive; and, accordingly, every exertion was made by it to discover the perpetrators. Some clue or other procured Doyle's apprehension, and on his confession he was admitted king's evidence against his deluded victim. It is painful to dwell on such a story; but before I conclude, I shall state what may give some pleasure to my readers. The poor heartbroken widow was spared even the ignominy of her darling's trial. Long before that, the kindness of her neighbours had soothed the death-bed, to which, with all his kindness of heart and good resolutions, he had brought her, by an imprudence and giddy weakness, of which we are many of us as guilty as poor Paul Guinan.

MC.

Dublin: Printed and Published by P. D. HARDY, 3, Cecilia-street, to whom all communications are to be addressed.

Sold by all Booksellers in Ireland.

In London, by Richard Groombridge, 6, Panyer-alley, Paternoster-row; in Liverpool, by Wilmer and Smith; in Manchester, by Ambery; in Birmingham, by Guest, 91, Steelhouse-lane; in Glasgow, by John Macleod; and in Edinburgh, by N. Bowack,

THE

DUBLIN PENNY JOURNAL

CONDUCTED BY P. DIXON HARDY, M.R.I.A.

| Vol. III. | JUNE 13, 1835. | No. 154. |

DRAWN BY MISS NELSON.   ENGRAVED BY F. C. BRUCE.

THE WELLINGTON TESTIMONIAL.

This massive obelisk, designed to commemorate the achievements of the illustrious Irishman whose name it bears, stands on the highest ground in the Phœnix Park, on a site formerly occupied by the Salute Battery, where twelve pieces of cannon were mounted for discharge on days of public rejoicings. On the summit of an immense flight of steps stands a square pedestal, on the four sides of which are pannels, with figures in basso relievo, emblematic of the principal victories won by the noble Duke. From this rises the massive obelisk, truncated, and, as will be seen by the above drawing, of thick and heavy proportions. On the sides of the obelisk, from the top to the base, are inscribed the names of all the places in which victories were gained by the Duke, from his first career in India to the battle of Waterloo. Opposite to, and standing on the centre of, the principal point, is an insulated pedestal, on which it is intended to place an equestrian statue of the hero after his decease. The dimensions of this lofty, though not very elegant structure, may be estimated from the following measurements:—The lowest step, forming the base, 480 feet in circuit; perpendicular section of steps 20 feet; sub-plinth of pedestal, on top of steps, 60 feet square, by 10 feet high; pedestal, 56 feet square, by 24 feet high; obelisk, 28 feet square at base,

and 150 high, diminishing in the proportion of one inch to the foot. Total height of the Testimonial, 205 feet.

It is formed altogether of plain mountain granite; and cost £20,000, which was raised by public subscription, as a lasting testimony of a nation's gratitude to an individual, who had so well maintained the honour and valour of the country which gave him birth.

We feel that we cannot better follow up the preceding article, than by giving our readers a very brief outline of the history of the hero, to commemorate whose achievements the Testimonial was erected; as well as that of the very extraordinary individual from whose brow he snatched the laurel wreath, by a victory which, we have no doubt, will be looked upon in after ages as surpassing in splendour the very greatest of those achieved by the most renowned heroes of antiquity.

NAPOLEON BONAPARTE.

Napoleon Bonaparte, the most extraordinary character who has ever yet figured on the great theatre of the world, was born on the 15th August, 1769, at Ajaccio, in the island of Corsica. His family, although not noble, were respectable, and had been of some distinction during the middle ages, in Italy, whence his ancestors had emigrated during the bloody feuds of the Guelphs and Gibellines. At seven years of age, Napoleon was admitted into the military school of Brienne; in every study likely to serve the future soldier, he soon became pre-eminent. In his manners and temper he was reserved and proud, made no particular acquaintance, lived by himself, and absorbed entirely among his books and maps, cultivated that mighty mind, which in after days subjugated and governed Europe.

The following brief epitome of his victories and reverses, all that our space will permit us to give, will afford a tolerably correct idea of his extraordinary career through life :—He gained 41 victories; captured 6 strong towns that stood sieges; entered 12 capitals; subjugated the Continent of Europe; created 9 new sovereigns; made 3 retreats; raised 1 siege; suffered 28 defeats; married two wives, both alive at the same time; in 1814, abdicated the throne of France, and became Emperor of Elba; in 1815, returned from Elba; entered Paris after a triumphal progress; he'd his *Champ-de-Mai*; advanced to the Netherlands; captured Charleroi; obtained a victory at Ligney; was defeated at Quatre Bras and Waterloo; returned to Paris; abdicated the government; repaired to Rochfort; surrendered to an English man-of-war; arrived in a British port; and was transported to St. Helena, where he died in 1821.

THE DUKE OF WELLINGTON.

The Hon. Arthur Wellesley, Duke of Wellington, fourth son of the Earl of Mornington, was born May 1st, 1769, at Dangan Castle, County Meath, in Ireland. Having studied at Eton in England, and at Angers in France, in 1787, he was appointed ensign in the 41st regiment of foot : and after serving in the Netherlands, Cape of Good Hope, and India, where he gained several important victories, in 1806, took his seat in Parliament; was appointed colonel of the 33d regiment; and married Lady C. Pakenham, daughter of the Earl of Longford. In 1808, ne was appointed to command a force for the deliverance of Portugal ; and in 1809, after a succession of splendid victories, received the thanks of Parliament, and a grant of £100,000. In 1811, he was created Earl and Marquis of Wellington; elected a Knight of the Garter; received the thanks of Parliament, with a grant of £100,000; was appointed colonel of the Horse Guards, and created Duke of Ciudad Rodrigo and Vittoria. In 1813, he entered Spain the third time. In 1814, he was created Duke of Wellington and Marquis of Douro, and received a grant from Parliament of £300,000. In 1815, he obtained victories over Ney at Quatre Bras, and Napoleon at Waterloo ; advanced to Paris ; captured Cambray, Peronne, and Paris; was created Prince of Waterloo, and appointed generalissimo of the Army of Occupation; effected the definitive treaty of Paris; received the thanks of Parliament, with a grant of £200,000.

During his triumphant career, he gained 28 victories; captured 11 strong towns that stood sieges; entered 5 capitals; made 3 retreats; raised 2 sieges; and suffered no defeats. Delivered Spain and Portugal; conquered the conqueror, and was the chief instrument in giving peace to Europe. Obtained a Princedom, three Dukedoms, three Marquisates, two Earldoms, the dignities of a Viscount and Baron, the highest military rank, and the military orders of all the sovereigns of Europe.

ACCOUNT OF THE BATTLE OF WATERLOO.

The following account of the Battle of Waterloo, condensed from M'Gregor's History of the French Revolution, will at once afford an idea of the horrors of war, and give a proof, if proof were required, of the extraordinary powers of the commanders engaged on the occasion.

The night previous to the battle of Waterloo was a fit prelude to the fury and carnage of the coming day : the tempest raged and the thunder rolled unremittingly, with such sheets of lightning and deluges of rain as are seldom seen but in tropical climates. Both armies had to sustain the rage of the elements, without means either of shelter or refreshment. The British soldiers were up to their knees in mud, and many of the officers lay down on this comfortless bed in their ball dresses, which they had been unable to change. The men were employed during the intervals of rest in cleansing their arms, distributing ammunition, and making other necessary preparations for the approaching conflict, which they had cause to contemplate with feelings depressed below their ordinary tone. A toilsome advance and bloody action had been attended with no immediate result, but a retreat equally laborious. The defeat of the Prussians had left the enemy at liberty to assail them separately with superior forces, while more than half of their own army was composed of foreigners, on whose fidelity the British could not implicitly depend. To these gloomy reflections they had, indeed, to oppose the most enthusiastic reliance on the talents of their renowned leader, their own native undaunted courage, and a stern resolution to discharge their duty to their king and country, leaving the result to the all-wise Disposer of events. The French soldiers were animated by feelings of a very different kind, all among them was glow and triumph—"The Prussians were annihilated, the British defeated, and the great Lord astounded." They affected to fear that the English would not halt till they reached their vessels ; nothing was more certain than that the Belgian troops would join the Emperor in a mass; and not a doubt was entertained that Napoleon would enter Brussels on the following day. With such illusions the French soldiers amused themselves, and they appeared chiefly to regret the tempest, as it afforded to the despairing enemy the means of retiring unmolested.

The whole of the French troops had come up during the night, to join in the expected pursuit; but how great was their astonishment, when, at the dawn of day, they beheld the British army drawn up in order of battle on the opposite heights. Napoleon exclaimed, with apparent exultation, " *Ah, je les tiens donc, ces Anglois!*" (I have them at last, these English!) He instantly proceeded, with his usual quickness, to make the necessary arrangements for the approaching combat ; and having compelled a farmer named La Coste, who lived at the house called Belle Alliance, to act as his guide, he ascended an eminence, and acquainted himself with the various features of the surrounding country, every observation being carefully noted on a map which he carried in his hand. He then gave orders for the disposition of the troops, and before ten o'clock they were at their allotted stations. A courier had been previously dispatched to Marshal Grouchy, with orders to attack the Prussian position at Wavre with as much vivacity as possible, to cross the Dyle, and compel the main body of the Prussians to a general action. Though he must have been conscious that such an attempt would have terminated in the utter destruction of Grouchy's corps, yet he conceived any sacrifice necessary, which would afford him a considerable chance of obtaining a decisive victory over the Duke of Wellington, by giving full employment to Blucher's army.

The field upon which was now to be fought a battle, the most singular in its accompaniments, and the most momentous in its consequences, of any recorded in the history of Europe, fruitful as its pages are in deeds of heroism and of blood, was not far distant from the spot where Dumourier gained the first victory of Revolutionary France over the Austrians, under Duke Albert of Saxe Teschen, and thus opened the flood gates for that torrent of bloodshed, plunder, and devastation, which, impelled by republican frenzy, or the ambition of a despot, had, for nearly a quarter of a century, banished peace from the earth. Now, though the scourge of war had spared the fruitful fields of Belgium for more than twenty years, its return seemed permitted by Providence, to achieve at one blow, the utter destruction of that military tyranny, by which France had so long trampled on the rights and independence of the other Continental States. Here it was that the two greatest generals of the age, were to contend for the first time in mortal combat, one for the re-establishment of an usurped throne, and the other for the deliverance of Europe from the horrors of another protracted and sanguinary war, which would have been the too probable consequences of his adversary's success.

The road from Brussels runs through the forest of Soignies, a wood composed of beech trees, growing very close together, and upon issuing from the wood, reaches the village of Waterloo. Beyond this point, the wood assumes a more straggling appearance, and about a mile farther, at a ridge of heights called Mont Saint Jean, the trees almost disappear, and the country becomes quite open. This chain of heights extends for about a mile and a half, and corresponds with a similar, but somewhat higher chain, running parallel with it. The two lines are separated from each other by a valley which runs between them, varying in breadth from one half to three-quarters of a mile. The declivity on each side is, for the most part, a gentle slope, diversified by a number of undulating banks, which seem as if formed by the action of water, though the valley is at present destitute of any stream. The ground is traversed by two high roads or causeways, both leading to Brussels, the one from Charleroi through Genappe, and the other from Nivelles. On reaching the summit of the heights, these two roads unite at the hamlet of Mont Saint Jean, which is at some distance in the rear of the British position. The farm of Mont Saint Jean is closer to the rear, and another farm-house, called La Haye Sainte, is situated upon the Charleroi causeway, near the foot of its descent from the heights. In the centre of the valley, about half way between the two ridges, and considerably to the right of the English centre, stood the Chateau de Goumont, or Hougoumont, an old-fashioned Flemish villa, with a tower and species of battlement. It was bounded on one side by a large farm-yard, and on the other it opened to a garden, fenced by a brick wall, and an exterior hedge and ditch : the whole was encircled by an open grove of tall beech trees, covering a space of three or four acres.

The British army, which, deducting its losses at Quatre-Bras, did not exceed sixty-five thousand men, with one hundred and twenty pieces of artillery, was drawn up in two lines. The right wing, commanded by Lord Hill, consisted of the 2d and 4th English divisions, under Lieutenant-General Sir Henry Clinton, and Major-General Hinuber, the 3d and 6th Hanoverians, and the 1st Belgians : its extremity was stationed at Merke-Braine, where it was protected by an enclosed country and deep ravines. The chateau of Hougoumont, which stood in front of the centre of this wing, formed a very strong advanced post. The chateau and garden were occupied by the light companies of the Guards, under Lord Saltoun and Colonel Macdonnel ; and the wood or park, by the sharp-shooters of Nassau. At the commencement of the action the right wing presented the convex segment of a circle to the enemy ; but as the French gave ground, the extreme right came gradually round, and the curve being reversed, became concave, enfilading the field of battle, and the high road from Brussels to Charleroi, which intersects it. The centre, under the Prince of Orange, was stationed in front of Mont Saint Jean, it was composed of the Brunswick and Nassau troops, with the Guards under Major-General Cooke, and the 3d English division, commanded by Sir Charles Alten. The farm of La Haye Sainte served as a key to the centre : it was fortified as well as the time permitted, and strongly garrisoned with Hanoverians. The left wing consisted of the 5th and 6th divisions, under Sir Thomas Picton, with Generals Kempt, Lambert, and Pack. It extended to Ter La Haye, which it occupied, and the defiles of which protected its extremity, and prevented it from being turned : its extreme flank reached the hamlet of Smouhen, where it was sufficiently covered by buildings, inclosures, ravines, and thickets. From hence a road runs to Ohain, and the woody passes of St. Lambert, through which the Duke of Wellington kept up a communication with the Prussian army at Wavre. The front line was composed of the elite of the army—the second was placed behind the declivity of the heights in the rear —the cavalry were principally posted in the rear of the left of the centre, and the artillery on the heights in front. In case of disaster, the Wood of Soignies lay within two miles, and its verge might, by a few resolute troops, be defended against almost any force.

The amount of the French army on the heights of La Belle Alliance has been variously stated. We conceive that it could not have been less than ninety, nor more than one hundred thousand men ; and near three hundred pieces of cannon accompanied this powerful force. The 2d corps formed the left wing of the army, under the command of Prince Jerome, (the ex-king of Westphalia.) It leaned its right upon the road to Brussels, and its left upon a small wood within cannon-shot of the English army. The 1st corps was in the centre, under Counts Reille and D'Erlon, on the road to Brussels, and opposite the village of Mont Saint Jean. The 6th corps, under Count Lobau, with the cavalry of General D'Aumont, was kept in reserve, and destined to proceed in rear of the right, to oppose the Prussian corps as soon as they should make their appearance on the left of the British. The cavalry and the Guards were in reserve in the rear. The French line extended two miles, that of the English only a mile and a half. In such a confined theatre was this terrible battle to be fought ; and this may, in a great measure, account for its sanguinary consequences.

A short time before the conflict began, Napoleon again ascended an eminence, upon which an observatory had been lately erected by the King of the Netherlands, from whence he commanded the whole of both lines ; and he seemed forcibly struck with the fine appearance of some of the British corps : " How steadily," said he to his aides-de-camp, " these troops take their ground ! How beautifully those cavalry form ! Observe those grey horse ! (the Scotch Greys.) Are they not noble troops ! Yet in half an hour I shall cut them to pieces." All the combinations for the attack were now made under his own eye, with great skill and rapidity, being completely concealed from his antagonists by the nature of the ground.

The British army awaited with an anxiety unmixed with fear, the result of these mighty preparations. Their illustrious chief had taken a commanding station under a tree on the Brussels road, precisely in the centre of the British line, near the top of Mont Saint Jean, from which every movement made or threatened could, with the aid of an achromatic telescope, be distinctly seen, and every arrangement was adopted to meet the first onset of the foe, upon whatever point of the line it might be made. An officer at this moment, on viewing the formidable forces of the enemy, expressed a wish that the Prussians were arrived. " The roads are heavy," replied his Grace, " they cannot be here before two or three o'clock, and my brave fellows will keep double that force at bay until then."

About eleven o'clock the troops were busily engaged in cooking some provisions to recruit their strength, which was almost exhausted by long fasting and fatigue ; but before they could partake of this refreshment, the voice of the aides-de-camp was heard in every quarter giving the solemn note of warning, " Stand to your arms ! the French are moving !" A furious cannonade instantly began, which soon spread along the whole line, and an immense array of French cuirassiers was seen sweeping across the plain, to embarrass the British deployments. But this first essay was checked by a brilliant charge of the Life Guards and Oxford Blues, which in a moment put the enemy to flight. The 2d corps of the French army, in three divisions, now advanced towards the British right, it being the first object of Napoleon to get possession of the Chateau of Hougoumont, the occupation of which would have greatly facilitated his efforts to turn this wing. Prince Jerome advanced to the assault of this important post at the head of ten thousand men ; but after a vigorous contest with the Nassau troops for possession of the wood, he was compelled to retreat. The attack was almost instantly renewed by an equal force under General Foy, whose furious onset succeeded in driving the Nassau troops from the wood, and the chateau itself must have been carried, but for the desperate bravery of the light companies of the Guards, by whom it was defended. A French officer and a few of his men actually forced their way into the court-yard where Colonel Macdonnel fought hand to hand with the assailants ; and it was owing to an exertion of personal strength on the part of this gallant officer, that the gates of the chateau were closed against the enemy. Hougoumont now became completely invested, but its valiant defenders resolved to avail themselves to the utmost of the walls and deep ditches by which it was surrounded. The assailants made the most furious efforts to force the barriers, but every attempt was defeated by the rapid and well-directed fire of the British. At one time the French rushed dauntlessly through a hedge which they conceived to be the barrier of the garden; but this exterior boundary only masked a garden wall, which was loop-holed and scaffolded, and all who penetrated through this opening were instantly shot. A furious contest raged, at the same time, in the orchard, every avenue of which was strewed with the dead or wounded. Finding all other means to penetrate the chateau unavailing, the French brought up some howitzers, the shells from which soon set the houses on fire, together with a large hay-stack in the court-yard; and, horrible to contemplate! numbers of the wounded of both parties, who were laid indiscriminately in one of the out-houses, perished in the flames. Yet the intrepid defenders of Hougoumont, though surrounded by this assemblage of horrors, refused to yield; but, when they were driven by the flames into the garden, they maintained the combat through the remainder of the day, under Colonels Woodford and Macdonnel, and never permitted the enemy to advance beyond its precincts. The sanguinary nature of this dreadful combat may be appreciated from the fact, that more than two thousand dead and wounded lay around this post in a very short space of time.

The partial success of the enemy in getting possession of the wood, which in a great measure separated Hougoumont from the British line, favoured a desperate attack which was made by the remainder of Prince Jerome's corps on Lord Wellington's right wing. This movement was conducted in the most formidable style of French tactics, the preparations being carried on under cover o the clouds of smoke which were driven from the burning houses towards the British position. Artillery dexterously placed, and admirably served, with swarms of sharpshooters, endeavoured by their fire to thin the ranks, and distract the attention of the opposing battalions. Heavy bodies of cuirassiers and lancers advanced, supported by dense columns of infantry, marching with shouldered muskets to take advantage of the first impression made by the cavalry, to rush forward, and complete the destruction of the broken ranks of the British by musketry and the bayonet. The British chief was aware that Napoleon would resort to this his favourite mode of attack, and he was prepared to meet it. He had formed his battalions into separate squares, each side of which was four men deep, and the squares were arranged alternately, like the spots on a chess-board, so that each of those in the rear covered the interval between two of them in front. It was impossible that this formation could be broken by cavalry, if the men stood firm; for in the event of their venturing between the squares, they were necessarily exposed to an exterminating fire in front and on both flanks. The artillery was placed in the intervals of the line of squares, while light infantry, yagers, and sharp-shooters, detached in front, skirmished with the French tirailleurs, and preserved the battalions in a great measure from their desultory but destructive fire.

NAPOLEON BONAPARTE.*

This mode of formation presented such an apparent inequality of numbers to the eye, that a spectator unacquainted with military tactics, would not have supposed it possible that these small detached black masses could have resisted for a moment the furious torrent that seemed about to overwhelm them. The cuirassiers and lancers rushed on with a noise and clamour which seemed to unsettle the firm earth over which they galloped, and made a tremendous dash on the Guards and Brunswickers, but the steady appearance of these troops soon checked their ardour. Repulsed at the first onset by a destructive

* The Portraits in the present number are copied from a little work now publishing in monthly parts, entitled, "Portrait Gallery of the French Revolution;" each part, price 6d. containing three well-executed copper engravings, with a brief memoir.

volley fired at ten yards distance, the cuirassiers used every effort of the most determined valour to throw those immoveable phalanxes into disorder. As if reckless of life, they galloped up to the very bayonets, cut at the soldiers over their muskets, and fired their pistols at the officers. Others rode at random between the squares, and were mowed down by the crossing fires, or by repeated attacks of the British cavalry, who rushed at intervals from the rear, and carried havoc through the enemy's ranks ; while those squadrons which, less daring, stood at gaze, were swept off in hundreds by the British artillery, which was never in higher order, or more distinguished for excellent practice, than on this memorable day. Still undismayed, fresh squadrons of the enemy pressed on with desperate courage, or if the cavalry attacks were suspended for a moment, it was only to give place to the operations of their celebrated artillery, which, at one hundred yards distance, played on the British squares with the most destructive execution. The cuirassiers, meantime, waited like birds of prey, to dash at any point where the slaughter should make the slightest opening ; but their intrepid

opponents, closing their files with steady composure over the bodies of their dead and dying comrades, still presented to their view that compact array of battle, which rendered every new effort to disorder it abortive. During the interval of the cavalry attacks, the squares sought protection from the murderous effects of the French artillery, by deploying into a line four deep, and lying on the ground ; but in many instances they had scarcely time to perform this evolution, when they were again called upon to re-form square, to oppose fresh charges. The promptitude and coolness with which these manœuvres were executed, at length convinced the enemy of the rashness of their enterprise, and the battle slackened in this quarter to rage with greater fury on other points of the line. The right continued still exposed to a severe cannonade, but the interval of comparative tranquillity was seized to reinforce with six companies of the Guards, under Colonel Hepburn, the brave garrison of Hougoumont, which succeeded in driving back Foy's division, and regaining possession of the wood.

DUKE OF WELLINGTON.

Defeated in his object of turning the right wing, and establishing himself on the road to Nivelles, Napoleon now organized the whole of his forces for a combined attack, with all arms, on the centre and left of the British position, which, if successful, would cut it in two, separate the British army from that of the Prussians, and make him master of the road to Brussels. Preceded by the fire of their immense artillery and numerous sharp-shooters, vast columns of infantry and cavalry were seen moving across the plain to charge on different points at the same moment ; and while a strong body advanced to the attack of La Haye Sainte, the key of the British centre, which they speedily invested, another pressed on towards the heights of Mont St. Jean, and a third moved on Ter la Haye to the left of the position, where the 5th and 6th British divisions were posted, with some Belgians, and a brigade of heavy dragoons, under the command of Sir Thomas Picton. The mode of attack on this point was of the

most tremendous description, and was intended on the part of the French, to be a battle of cavalry and cannon. Headed by the iron-clad cuirassiers, on whose mail the musket-balls were heard to ring as they glanced off without injuring the wearers, the French infantry ascended the heights where the remnant of Pack's gallant brigade (the Royal Scots, 42d, 44th, and 92d regiments) were posted. Some Belgian troops were forced to give way before the rapid onset of the enemy ; but the Duke of Wellington, who happened to be in that part of the field, moved up the British brigade to a kind of natural embrazure, formed by a hedge and bank in front of the line, and from thence the brave Highlanders and their comrade regiments gave the enemy a reception similar to that which they had experienced from the Guards and Brunswickers on the right. Sir Thomas Picton now advanced to support this corps with Sir James Kempt's brigade, composed of the 28th, 32d, 79th, and 95th regiments. Vast masses of French infantry had arrived at this time behind the very hedge where the British were posted—their muskets were almost muzzle to muzzle, and a French mounted officer attempted to seize the colours of the 32d, when General Picton suddenly resolved on becoming the assailant, and promptly forming his division into squares, he rushed through the hedge, and attacked the advancing columns of infantry and cavalry with charged bayonets. Appalled by this almost unparalleled act of intrepidity, the enemy hesitated, fired a volley, and fled; but that volley proved fatal to one of the noblest commanders of whom the British army could boast. A musket-ball struck the right temple of the gallant Picton, which went through the brain, and in a moment numbered him with the dead. But notwithstanding this disastrous event, the division maintained its irresistible charge under the conduct of Sir James Kempt, till they repulsed the enemy from the crest of the hill, to which they had nearly attained.

Before the French had time to recover from the effects of this furious attack, a brigade of heavy British dragoons, commanded by Sir William Ponsonby, wheeled round the extremity of the cross-road, full on the flank of the foe. It was composed of the Royals, Greys, and Enniskillens—England, Scotland, and Ireland, in high rivalry, and irresistible union. The 92d Highlanders, (now reduced to two hundred men,) had at this moment pierced the centre of a column of French infantry of as many thousands, and the Greys dashing in at the opening, the two regiments cheered each other, shouting "Scotland for ever!" The cuirassiers and lancers now advanced to save their infantry, and the Greys being reinforced by the Royals and Enniskillen dragoons, one of the most dreadful cavalry engagements recorded in the history of modern warfare ensued. The far-famed cuirassiers maintained a long and murderous struggle against the British dragoons, in which some extraordinary feats of dexterity and courage were displayed. The impenetrable armour of the French, gave them a decided advantage over their antagonists, who could only strike at their necks or limbs. But after numbers of them were cut down, they were at length forced to yield to the determined valour and superior strength of the British men and horses. The cuirassiers and lancers fled in confusion, abandoning their artillery and infantry, while nearly three thousand prisoners, two eagles, and several pieces of cannon, rewarded the prowess of the victors.

The exultation which the success of this gallant brigade was calculated to inspire, received a severe check by the fall of their intrepid leader, Sir William Ponsonby.

Napoleon, from his commanding station near La Belle Alliance, viewed the progress of this mighty struggle, and the valorous but fruitless efforts which his devoted followers were making to secure the victory. The intrepid conduct of the British is said to have frequently called forth his eulogiums, and observing how the chasms were filled up the instant they were made by the French artillery, he exclaimed to Soult, his Lieutenant-General, "Qu'elles braves troupes! comme ils travaillent! tres-bien!"—"What brave troops! how they go through their work! admirable! admirable!" adding, "but they must give way!" "No, Sire!" replied Soult, "they prefer being cut to pieces." To the intelligence of every fresh repulse, his only reply was, "Avant! Avant!"—"Forward! Forward!" Acting on this principle, the defeat of his troops on the right and left, led him to adopt the most desperate efforts to break through the centre, in front of which La Haye Sainte was still vigorously defended by the Hanoverian light troops. At each end of the court-yard of this farm-house, stood a large door or gate, through which the besiegers and besieged fired at each other with dreadful effect. When the last cartridge of the Hanoverians was expended, they kept up an unequal contest with their swords and bayonets through the windows and embrasures, till the increasing numbers of the enemy enabled them to storm the farm-house; but the resistance of the gallant Germans did not cease till nearly their last man had ceased to breathe, and the whole building presented a scene of shattered ruin, which could not be looked upon without a degree of interest truly terrific.

The French had for some hours kept up a violent cannonade on the centre of the British line, but now having established a post on the causeway, Napoleon ordered his generals to direct their main force against that part of the British position which had become exposed. The troops posted in this direction resisted for hours the varied attacks of the enemy's cavalry and artillery, and a somewhat particular description of the kind of conflict sustained by a square composed of the 30th and 73d, commanded by Sir Colin Halket, may afford some idea of this extraordinary species of combat. To no square did the French artillery and cuirassiers pay more frequent visits, so that the soldiers began almost to recognize the faces of those messengers of death. Sometimes they galloped up to the very points of the bayonet; at other times, confiding in their armour, they fearlessly walked their horses round this bulwark of steel, that they should have more time to seek some chasm in the ranks at which they might rush in. General Halket, perceiving that the balls made little impression on those mail-clad men, ordered the soldiers to aim at the horses, as when the horse was brought down, the rider uniformly became a prisoner. By the imperturbable constancy of these two gallant corps, the cuirassiers were repeatedly driven off, and upon each of these occasions line was promptly formed to give the flying foe a more effective volley, or to render the enemy's artillery less destructive to themselves. When again the storm was seen gathering and rolling on, the command to re-form square, prepare to receive cavalry, was promptly and accurately obeyed. In a moment the whole were prostrate on their breasts, to let the iron shower fly over, and they were erect in an instant, when the cannon ceased and the cavalry charged. At one period of the combat, the commander of the cuirassiers attempted to throw this invincible phalanx off their guard by a ruse-de-guerre, by lowering his sword to Sir Colin Halket, and several of the officers cried out, "Sir, they surrender." But the British general, justly suspecting that a body of well-mounted cavalry would not surrender to a corps fixed to the spot in a defensive position, made no other reply than, "Be firm—fire;" and the volley put the colonel and his cuirassiers to flight, with a laugh of derision from the men he meant to cut in pieces. The Duke of Wellington paid frequent visits to this distinguished square. Upon one of these occasions he inquired, "How they were?" Their commander replied, that nearly two-thirds of their number had fallen, and the rest were so exhausted, that it might be attended with advantage if one of the foreign corps who had not suffered would take their station even for a short time. The reply of the Duke was, "It is impossible! the issue of the battle depends on the unflinching front of the British troops; you and I and every Englishman in the field must die on the spot we now occupy." "Enough, my Lord," said Sir Colin Halket, "we stand here till the last man falls." And, though himself severely wounded, this brave man would no doubt have kept his word, had not the British cavalry soon flown to his relief.[*]

The Duke of Wellington now felt that the critical situation of affairs called for all his energies, and they were exerted with decisive effect. Many of his short but encouraging phrases had a talismanic effect on the men. Riding up to the 95th, when in front of the line, awaiting a formidable charge of cavalry, he exclaimed "Stand fast, 95th—we must not be beat—what will they say in England?" To another regiment, when fiercely engaged, he said, "Hard pounding, this, gentlemen; let's see who will pound longest. Never mind, we'll win this battle yet."

---

[*] Mr. Simpson, in his "Visit to Flanders," relates the following instance of individual heroism:—"General Halket had a brother in the field, who was colonel of a Hanoverian corps. A trait of heroism is related of him, which has few examples in modern warfare, and is not excelled by the far-famed achievement of Robert Bruce, in his short combat with Sir Henry Bohun, in that memorable battle which stood foremost on history's brightest page, until Waterloo was fought. A French general was giving his orders with great confidence to a large body of troops, and had come to their front unattended. Colonel Halket made a dash at him at full gallop; and putting a pistol to his breast, seized his horse's reins, and brought him from the very beards of his wonder-struck soldiers."

The security of the British line became at this time extremely critical; several of the regiments having no longer a sufficient number of men left to form square, were obliged to receive the cavalry in line, in order to cover the necessary space of ground. A close column of French infantry now pressed forward to carry the village of Mont St. Jean in the rear of the British centre: some gallant charges from the British and German hussars and light dragoons, threw the advancing column into disorder. The hussars displayed their usual courage, but notwithstanding the heroic exertions of the Earl of Uxbridge, their light blood horses were forced to give way before the ponderous rush of the cuirassiers; and some of the light regiments suffered considerably on this occasion. At this critical moment, the household brigade, composed of the Life Guards, Oxford Blues, and 1st Dragoon Guards, led on by Sir John Elley, at his own request, made a charge on the French cavalry, which was productive of the most tremendous effects. The weight and armour of the cuirassiers proved ineffectual against the shock of this splendid and irresistible brigade—they were literally ridden down upon the field—hundreds were driven headlong into a quarry or gravel pit, where they rolled a confused and undistinguishable mass of men and horses, till the fire of the cavalry and artillery put a period to their sufferings. Those who for some time stood their ground proved also the superior strength of the British soldiers, with whom they fought hand to hand. A corporal of the Life Guards, named Shaw, well known as a pugilist, and equally formidable as a swordsman, slew or disabled ten of the cuirassiers with his own hand, before he was killed by a musket or pistol shot. The officers as well as the men of this heroic band, were closely engaged in individual combat with the enemy. Sir John Elley, who was remarkable for his strength, his horsemanship, and skill in the use of his sword, performed feats of valour that would have done honour to the days of chivalry, and being at one period of the combat surrounded by six or seven cuirassiers, he, though severely wounded, cut his way through them, leaving three or four of his assailants dead behind him, their wounds bearing striking indications of the unusual strength of the arm which inflicted them. Colonel Ferrier of the 1st Life Guards fell on this memorable occasion. He had led his regiment to the charge no less than eleven times; and most of the charges were not made till after his head had been laid open by the cut of a sabre, and his body was pierced with a lance. Major Pack, of the Royal Horse Guards, was also particularly distinguished. He had been among the first to dash into the ranks of the enemy, and he and his opponent having dismounted each other, he mounted on a troop-horse, and in the second charge led his squadron against a column of cuirassiers. He killed the officer commanding the column, but he himself was the next moment run through the body, and numbered with the slain. Colonel Fuller, and Major Bringhurst, of the 1st Dragoon Guards, met a similar fate. The results of this brilliant charge were most important—the enemy were driven in confusion from the heights, with the loss of 1200 prisoners, and great numbers killed; and the gallant victors followed up their success till the farm of La Haye Sainte was retaken, and the British again reestablished in the positions which they occupied before the attack. The Duke of Wellington could with difficulty restrain the impetuosity of his troops, who, after standing for so many hours exposed to the most furious charges, now eagerly demanded to be led against the enemy. "Not yet, not yet, my brave fellows!" was the Duke's reply: "be firm a little longer—you shall have at them by and by."

Indeed the patience of the illustrious chief, as well as that of his heroic followers, must have been put to the severest test. The combat had continued for six hours with unabated fury, and one-fourth of the allied troops were killed or wounded, while the remainder were worn out with fatigue, and destitute of the smallest refreshment. It would be impossible, under such circumstances, but that the spirits of the men must droop. In fact, during the intervals of the cavalry attacks, while the French artillery was spreading havock in the British ranks, an indifference to life seemed spreading fast among the soldiery, though on the near approach of the enemy, they became as alert

as ever. Yet Lord Wellington remained cool, and apparently cheerful, determined to maintain the contest while one regiment continued firm at its post. An aid-de-camp coming up with the intelligence that the 5th and 6th divisions, who were posted on the left, were nearly destroyed, and that it was utterly impossible that they could maintain their ground—"I cannot help it," said he, "they must keep their ground: would to God that Blucher or night were come!"

While the battle was thus raging in the centre, the 2d corps under Prince Jerome, had renewed their attacks upon the right wing. The post of Hougoumont, which had received repeated reinforcements from the division of Guards, had never ceased to be the object of the most desperate assaults; but its brave garrison maintained it to the last, and the loss of the French, in this attack alone, is estimated at 10,000 men. In the early part of the action, the extreme right, consisting of the 2d and 4th divisions, was protected by deep ravines from the charges of the enemy; but Sir Frederick Adam's brigade of the 2d, composed of the 52d, 71st, and a battalion of the 95th, who were close to the right of the centre, were for two hours exposed to a dreadful fire of artillery, without being able to discharge a musket at the enemy. This brigade had only joined the army the preceding evening, and were so exhausted after a fatiguing march of two days, that the continued roar of cannon and bursting of shells was not sufficient to prevent several of the men from falling asleep, in which state many fell victims to the cannon balls which flew thickly around them. At length the French lancers made a dash at some artillery in their rear. The brigade were instantly on their feet, formed square, and repelled the enemy. The latter returned again and again to the charge, but, aided by the 15th light dragoons, who came up to their assistance, under Colonel Boyce, the brigade finally succeeded in putting them to the route.

It was now five o'clock, and the British, though dreadfully weakened, still gallantly maintained their position at every point—but some movements on the enemy's right, now began to indicate that they were about to be supported in the unequal contest by their Prussian allies, whose arrival had been so long and so ardently expected. In fact, General Bulow, with two brigades of infantry and a corps of cavalry, was then defiling by Ohain, in the rear of the French army, after having encountered extraordinary difficulties in their passage through the woods of St. Lambert. But while Napoleon continued the main conflict against the British position, he opposed to this new enemy the 6th corps, under Count Lobau, and an engagement was immediately commenced in this quarter, but with little energy, as Bulow did not wish to undertake any thing serious till the arrival of Marshal Blucher.

It is thought, that Napoleon, as a prudent general, should at this moment have discontinued the action, the whole of the Imperial Guard being still in reserve, who, considering the exhausted state of the British, would have been more than sufficient to cover his retreat on the Dyle and Sambre. But his recollection of the day of Marengo, where his reiterated efforts, after the battle had been to all appearance lost, secured him the victory, led him to hope for a similar triumph on this occasion, as on it alone rested his hopes of uniting the French nation in support of his throne. After reflecting for some moments on his critical situation, he determined again to attack the weakest part of the British line in great force; hoping to carry it before the remainder of the Prussians could arrive. He accordingly brought forward the whole of the cavalry of his guard, and directed it, supported by fresh masses of infantry, on the centre of the position. Their first shock was irresistible; they ascended the heights, and thirty pieces of cannon fell into their power. But the presence of the Duke of Wellington quickly averted the dangers which now menaced the British army. Placing himself at the head of the three battalions of English, and three of Brunswickers, he addressed them in a few animating sentences, and then led them against the enemy, who were now proudly advancing to the very rear of his lines. In a moment victory was rescued from their grasp, they abandoned the artillery which they had taken, and fled with precipitation

During this conflict in the centre, Count Lobau had repulsed Bulow's advanced guard, and driven them again into the woods; and Napoleon expressed the strongest confidence that Grouchy was moving in the same line with the Prussians, and would shortly arrive to his assistance. He therefore resolved to persevere in his exertions to carry the British position, notwithstanding the immense sacrifice of lives which was the consequence of every fresh attack; and so certain was he of success, even at this advanced period of the battle, that he ordered his secretary to send an express to Paris, saying, that the victory was his. About seven o'clock it was announced to him, that powerful bodies of Prussians were opening from the woods near Frischermont on his right flank, and threatening his rear, but he treated the aid-de-camp who brought the intelligence with contempt. "Be off," said he, " you are frightened; ride up to the columns that are deploying, and you will find that they are Grouchy's." All who obeyed his command were killed or taken, and he was made sensible of his error, when the Prussians commenced an attack on his right wing. He still, however, believed that Grouchy must be as near to support, as this new enemy was to attack him, and he caused General Labedoyere to circulate this opinion amongst the troops, with whom he now resolved to make a last grand effort. Having detached the whole of the reserves of the 6th corps, and the Young Guard, with 100 pieces of cannon, against the Prussians, he brought forward fifteen thousand of the Imperial Guard, who remaining on the ridge of La Belle Alliance, or behind it, had scarcely yet drawn a trigger in the action. He placed himself at the head of these celebrated troops, descended the hill, and led them till he reached a ravine, half way between La Belle Alliance and La Haye Sainte, where he was protected from the fire of the British artillery. Here his veteran guards defiled before him for the last time. Led on by Marshal Ney, this noble column then pressed on with loud shouts, and the clang of warlike music, over ground covered with heaps of slain, and slippery with blood; rallying in their progress such of the broken cavalry and infantry of the line, as still maintained the combat. Such was the clamour, that the British believed that Napoleon himself would be the leader in this new attack; but they were not unprepared to meet it. The Duke of Wellington had not failed to improve the advantage which the repeated repulses of the enemy had given him. The extreme right of the line under Lord Hill, had gradually gained ground after each unsuccessful charge on the right of the centre, until the space between Hougoumont and Braine-la-Leude being completely cleared of the enemy, this wing, with its artillery and sharp-shooters, was brought round from a convex to a concave position, so that their guns raked the enemy as they debouched upon the causeway. The service of the British artillery upon this occasion was so accurate and destructive, that the heads of the French columns were enfiladed and almost annihilated before they could reach the high road, so that they seemed for a considerable time advancing from the hollow way, without gaining ground on the plain. The enthusiasm of the Imperial Guard, however, enabled them to overcome this obstacle, as well as a charge of the gallant Brunswickers, which they repelled with considerable slaughter. They rushed up the heights with great spirit, at a point where the British Guards lay prostrate in a hollow, to avoid the destructive fire of the French artillery, by which the assault was covered. The Duke of Wellington had placed himself on a ridge behind them, declaring that he would never quit it but in triumph; and as soon as the Imperial Guard had approached within one hundred yards, he suddenly exclaimed, "Up, Guards, and at them!" The French battalions appeared startled for a moment at the unexpected apparition of this fine body of men, who were drawn up in line four deep: but the French veterans soon recovering their composure, advanced at the charge step, their artillery filing off to the right and left, till they were within twenty yards of their opponents, and on the point of dashing at them with their bayonets, when a volley was poured upon them by the British, which literally drove them back with its shock: a second volley increased their confusion, and before they had time to deploy or manœuvre, the Bri-

tish cheered, and charged them with an effect that proved irresistible. The Duke himself at this crisis brought up General Adam's brigade, and completed the route of the enemy. A regiment of tirailleurs attempted to cover their retreat, and attack the pursuers, but they fled from the very cheers of the British. The Old Guard had still preserved their squares, but they were now charged by the British cavalry, forced, and almost entirely cut to pieces, and their leader, General Cambrone, was taken prisoner.

Napoleon beheld, from his station in the ravine, the rout of his chosen troops. He talked of rallying them to make another effort, still persisting that Grouchy was at hand; but from this he was dissuaded by Bertrand and Drouet, who represented to him how much the fate of France and of the army depended on his life. Hitherto he had shown the greatest coolness and indifference throughout this eventful day; but when he observed his celebrated guards recoil in disorder, the cavalry intermingled with the foot, and trampling them down, he said to his attendants. " Il sont mélés ensemble," (they are mixed together,) shook his head, and retired to his former station on the heights of Belle Alliance, and on the advance of the British line, he exclaimed, " A present c'est fini—sauvons nous." (It is over for the present—let us save ourselves.) He instantly left the field of battle, at about half past eight o'clock, accompanied by five or six of his officers, and galloped along the road to Genappe. No other course but flight now remained for him, in order to escape death or captivity.

The Duke of Wellington had hitherto suffered no prospect of advantage to withdraw him from his position; but now the decisive moment was come for bringing this dreadful conflict to a termination. The acuteness of his sight enabled him to perceive the advance of the Prussians in great force on the enemy's right flank, while the ruinous disorder in which the French fled before the British Guards declared them past the power of rallying. He therefore determined to become the assailant in his turn. He ordered his whole army to advance to the charge, the centre formed in line four deep, and the battalions on the flanks in squares for their security; the Duke himself, with his hat in his hand, leading the whole line, which was supported by the cavalry and artillery. This movement is represented as having been one of the finest military spectacles ever witnessed; and could it have been viewed apart from the scene of carnage which the field exhibited in every quarter, must have excited an indescribable glow of triumph in the bosoms of the gallant troops, who for so many hours had maintained with unwavering constancy the unequal contest. The setting sun, which through the sanguinary day had been veiled in clouds, now burst forth for a moment from its obscurity, and darted a cheering ray on the British columns as they rushed down the slopes, and crossed the plain which separated them from the French position. To ascend the heights of Belle Alliance was the work of a moment, though in presence of the fire of 150 pieces of cannon. Some resistance was still offered by the remnant of the Imperial Guard, which was rallied by Marshal Ney, but it was quickly overcome. The reserve of the Young Guard, which was posted in a hollow between Belle Alliance and Monplaisir, was totally routed by the 52d and 71st regiments, who, after they had put the enemy to flight, separated, and running on two sides of an oval for a considerable way, met again, and thus cut off a great number of prisoners. The first line of the French was now thrown back upon and mingled with the second, in inextricable confusion; pressed by the British in front, and by the Prussians on the right flank and in the rear, corps of every varied description were blended in one confused tide of flight, which no person attempted to guide or to restrain. Baggage waggons, dismounted guns, ammunition carts, and arms of every description, cumbered the open field as well as the causeway, and with them were intermingled in thick profusion the corpses of the slain, or the bodies of the wounded, who in vain shrieked and implored compassion as the fugitives and their pursuers drove headlong over them.

Dublin: Printed and Published by P. D. HARDY, 3, Cecilia Street, to whom all communications are to be addressed.

THE
DUBLIN PENNY JOURNAL

CONDUCTED BY P. DIXON HARDY, M.R.I.A.

| VoL. III. | JUNE 20, 1835. | No. 155. |

NELSON'S PILLAR.

This tribute of national gratitude to the memory of our great naval Hero, is situated in Sackville-street. It stands in the centre of four leading streets; and although rather an unmeaning kind of structure, adds considerably to the beauty of this part of the city. It consists of a pedestal, column, and capital of the Tuscan order, the whole being surmounted by a well executed statue of Lord Nelson, leaning against the capstan of a ship. The entire height of the column and statue is 134 feet 3 inches. There are within the pedestal and column 168 stone steps to ascend to the top, which is protected by a parapet and iron railing. Permission to ascend may be obtained for a trifle, and the trouble of the ascent is amply repaid by the delightful prospect from this elevated situation, of the City and Bay of Dublin, with the surrounding country. The names and dates of Lord Nelson's principal victories are inscribed on the four pannels of the pedestal, and a brass plate, covering a recess in the stone, filled with various coins, contains an inscription stating the object for which the pillar had been erected, and that the first stone had been laid on the 15th of February, 1808, by Charles Duke of Richmond, Lord Lieutenant of Ireland. The total expense of building amounted to £6,856 8s. 3d.

REMINISCENCES OF A TRANS-ATLANTIC TRAVELLER.*

This is rather a sketchy production. Several of the sketches are, however, tolerably well touched off; and will, we should think, be considered interesting by many about to make a trans-atlantic excursion. The following extracts, taken without any reference to connection, convey as favourable an impression of the work as it really merits :—

NEW YORK.

" New York is perhaps one of the gayest and most dissipated cities in the universe, and presents a thousand temptations to a foreigner, particularly a young one, to engage in expense and extravagance. Accordingly, I found that my remittances from Europe disappeared almost as fast as they arrived ; the theatre, balls, masquerades, and sleigh-riding, cigars, gin, sling, and mint julap, served in a very able manner to drain my purse. Of all the amusements of the Americans, sleigh-riding is the greatest favourite amongst the young citizens. So soon as the ground is sufficiently covered with snow, the roads are thronged with sleighs of every size and description, from the rude one-horse vehicle of the homely farmer to the splendid chariot of the wealthy trader drawn by four noble horses with splendid trappings and bells. Night is the favourite time for travelling when on an excursion of pleasure, and this is really delightful, when the moon is visible, shedding its pale silvery light over an immense tract of snow. When a sleigh excursion is determined on by any young citizens, they invite a number of pretty girls to accompany them, (which favour is rarely denied,) they then start off, late in the evening, and sometimes will make an excursion of forty or fifty miles before morning, stopping at every tavern on their route, in which they procure a supply of hot Irish whiskey punch, (a great favourite,) dance, and sometimes cut the most antic capers, not unfrequently arousing the inmates of the house, travellers, boarders, and every person they can lay hands on to join in the dance ; this is rarely complained of, as sleigh-riders are a privileged class, and the tavern keepers (finding them excellent customers) rarely thwart their humours. To guard against the severity of the frost, the parties are always well muffled with cloaks, coats, buffalo and bear skins ; the ladies having portable stoves, lit with charcoal, to keep their feet warm."

AMERICAN FEMALES.

" The American females rank high in the scale of beauty ; and next to my own fair countrywomen, I would certainly give them the preference ; there is a peculiar naivette about them which renders them extremely interesting, their figures are tall and elegant, their step light and graceful, and their countenances inclining more to the Asiatic than European caste, being very pale, faintly tinged with a roseate hue : their beauty, however, declines much sooner than that of Europeans, and they are very liable to consumption ; in the south it is quite common for females to become bald before thirty."

MEN IN THE SOUTHERN STATES.

" The southerns are haughty and vindictive, and form a great contrast to the cool calculating Yankee. Parties of half a dozen young men will sometimes fight with rifles ; and those meetings are generally fatal to most of the combatants.

" Gouging is a favourite system of warfare in the south, particularly in Kentucky. In tavern brawls, should any party quarrel, the first object is to attack the eyes, into the sockets of which they endeavour to get their thumbs, and gouge or pluck them out ; and it sometimes occurs, that some of these fellows carry off whole pockets full of eyes in triumph. The only punishment is, that if any of the party should be rendered wholly eyeless, and thereby deprived of the means of subsistence, the aggressor must make an allowance for his support."

* Reminiscences of a Trans-atlantic Traveller, being a Sketch of Fourteen Months' Residence in North America, in the years 1831-32. By W. T. M. Dublin : W. F. Wakeman.

FALLS OF NIAGARA.

" On the morning after my arrival at Queens-town, I proceeded to view the stupendous Cataract of Niagara, of which so much has been said and written. It is impossible for the imagination to conjure up a more magnificent scene. The spray is visible at a distance of five or six miles, ascending to the clouds in an immense body beautifully sparkling in the sunbeams. On approaching the Falls, the loud roar of the water in descending is deafening. The woods extend close to the banks of the river, and it is impossible to see the Falls until within a few yards of them. Emerging from the forest, the scene which suddenly strikes the beholder is truly grand. I advanced to a projecting cliff, and for some moments was lost in astonishment at the magnificent sight before me—

' A matchless cataract, horribly beautiful.'

" The Falls are divided in two curvetures, separated from each other by a large rock, called Goat Island, which is covered with trees. This rock might more truly be styled the ' Isle of tears,' or ' The Region of Mist,' for it is continually encircled with spray, the heavy fall of which soon forces the beholder to a hasty retreat. The curve on the American side is upwards of seventeen hundred, and that on the Canadian exceeding two thousand feet. The height of the Falls is one hundred and forty-nine ; and the breadth of the river eleven hundred. I heard the noise at Queenstown, seven miles distance, when the wind was light, and coming direct from them ; I have seen it stated in some publications, that they could be heard fourteen miles, and some go so far as forty ; but such is not the case, unless with the assistance of an ear trumpet of very considerable dimensions. I could not hear them a mile below Queenstown, and fancy that my organs of hearing are as acute as those of most persons.

" There are a number of fine farms in this neighbourhood, cleared land, averaging about twenty-five dollars per acre. And numbers of capitalists have lately settled here, invited by the beauty of the scenery, and the contiguity of the Falls. Within three miles of Niagara, is Lundy's Lane, where a battle was fought between the Americans and British ; and at Queenstown was fought the celebrated battle of Queenstown heights, where General Brock was killed, to whose memory a handsome monument has been erected. Queenstown is a very inconsiderable place. On the opposite bank of the river is a handsome American village called Lewistown."

RIVER ST. LAWRENCE.

" In three hours after leaving Niagara, I arrived at York, the capital of the province of Upper Canada. Making a stay of two or three hours here, I went on board a steamer bound for Prescot on the St. Lawrence. Lake Ontario presents an appearance similar to Erie, being about the same extent, and, like it, studded with numerous and beautiful islands. Kingston, at which we touched, is a considerable town, and has a very extensive navy yard. The Rideau canal runs between this and Montreal, to avoid the interruption in the navigation of that part of the immense chain of water communication which assumes the name of the St. Lawrence, by means of the Rapids. From Kingston I proceeded to Prescot, (seventy miles,) down the St. Lawrence. As this is one of the largest, so it is one of the most beautiful of the American rivers ; of immense width, it is covered with innumerable islands, each of which is separated by a broad and rapid stream, and each outvying the other in beauty and verdure. This portion of the river is very truly styled ' The thousand Isles,' each of which in itself would form a paradise. Touching at Brockville, a neat little village, we arrived at Prescot, a tolerable town, but far exceeded by Ogdensburg, on the American side of the river. Here I cannot avoid drawing a contrast between the towns of Canada and those of the United States ; the latter possessing all the bustle of enterprise and commerce, well and tastefully built, and elegant in their appearance, whilst the former present a heavy and dull appearance, are badly built, filthy in the extreme, and having little or no trade, except in the transmigration of poor emigrants. The St. Lawrence, from Montreal to its exit into the gulf, presents a noble appearance, being on an average three miles wide. The current is so great, that vessels have to be towed by steamers up to Montreal. I have frequently seen three vessels, of from three to four hundred tons, towed by one steamer."

THE RAPIDS.

"The Rapids commence about thirty miles below Prescot, and extend nearly to Montreal. The principal of them are the Galloos, near Prescot; the Long Saut, or Long Rapid, extending eight or nine miles, near Cornwall; the Coteau Lac, at the end of Lake St. Francis; the Cascades, and La Chine, near Montreal.

"The sensation felt coming down these Rapids is delightful; the light fanning breeze between each, assisted by the strong current, wafted us along at the rate of five miles an hour; occasionally the men took to their oars, to keep clear of any dangerous shoals; then arose the hoarse boat glee, in Canadian French, which, united to the half-savage appearance of the boatmen, and the wildness of the scenery around, had a most romantic effect; and when we entered a rapid, the batteo darted forward with the rapidity of lightning to its termination.

"A number of islands in the neighbourhood of the Rapids are inhabited by Indians, who receive very considerable sums of money for piloting the rafts or drams of timber which come from the head of Lake Ontario, during the spring and fall."

MONTREAL.

"Montreal is a good town, but there is nothing in it worthy of admiration. The houses of the respectable inhabitants are built of stone, and very much resemble prisons in appearance, having sheet iron doors and window-shutters. The tin roofing, however, gives the town a very imposing appearance at a distance. The dwellings of the poorer classes are of wood, and are tolerably neat. It contains a population of thirty thousand, principally French Canadians."

FRENCH CANADIAN PEASANTS.

"The banks of the St. Lawrence are thickly settled from Montreal to Quebec by French Canadians. At the distance of every nine miles, there is a handsome village and chapel; the inhabitants are poor, but remarkably neat; and their whitewashed cottages look extremely well. The French in Montreal, who are engaged in boating, rafting, &c. are a cunning, drunken, disorderly race of men, as are persons of the same class in every society. But the French Canadian peasant, or artizan, is frugal, sober, and harmless, and attached to his family. Their countenances are grave and thoughtful, and wholly free from that vivacity and animation for which the European French are so celebrated. They are a handsome race of people, having good features, dark olive complexions, and brilliant black eyes. The females wear a stuff petticoat, over which is a short cotton frock, barely reaching the knee, and a round straw hat. This I found to be their costume from the mouth of the Thames to Quebec."

QUEBEC.

"The approach to Quebec is through a number of beautiful coves; the land on each side is very high, particularly on the side of the town, where are the celebrated heights of Abraham, the scene of Wolfe's glory and death. Quebec is an irregular and inelegantly built town, containing a population of about twenty-seven thousand; it is remarkable for being one of the strongest fortifications in the world, and is built on a steep hill, round the base of which is a narrow, filthy street, upwards of three miles in length, inhabited by the poorest class of Irish. Here they have their Wexford and Wicklow taverns, their signs of St. Patrick, &c.

"Since Quebec fell into the hands of the British in 1759, it has been rendered almost impregnable from the river side, and the fortifications have been nearly all rebuilt. It commands a most imposing position on a curve of the St. Lawrence, and any approach from the sea is rendered almost impossible, whilst the immense height of the banks of the river, which are almost perpendicular, would render an attack descending the river fruitless, were the heights sufficiently guarded by redoubts. But there is

nothing to prevent an enemy's gaining the heights above the town, and with an army entrenched on the plains, the principal difficulty would be surmounted."

COMFORTS OF A VOYAGE.

"The chief who ruled the forecastle on board our vessel was an Irishman, as were most of the crew; he was a remarkable fine looking fellow, about six and twenty, of Herculean frame, possessed rather handsome features, was open-hearted and generous, but violently passionate, and jealous of his authority. There was a fiddler on board, and every fine evening the steerage passengers assembled on the quarter-deck to dance. Amongst these no one was more gay than O'Brien, or danced with better grace. He was admired and dreaded by all on board, and even the captain was obliged to conciliate him. The crew were divided into two gangs, called the starboard and larboard watches, one commanded by the first, the other by the second mate. These worked the vessel, alternately, every four hours.

"We had just cleared the foggy banks of Newfoundland, and the first and second mates having taken an observation of the sun, which had not been visible for several days, the latter retired to the forecastle, his watch being below; O'Brien was one of his party, and was giving vent to his passion, occasioned by some orders of the captain, which he considered infringing on the rights of his community. The mate justified the captain's conduct—an angry colloquy ensued, which ended in O'Brien's knocking the mate down. The forecastle became a scene of confusion, during which the mate made his escape on deck, but was quickly followed by O'Brien, foaming with rage. The captain was standing on the quarter-deck, and seeing the conflict between his mate and O'Brien, sprang forward, and seized the latter by the neck-cloth, which he twisted, and rendered O'Brien powerless—his face became black—his tongue hung out—and in a few minutes he would have been strangled, when one of the sailors cut his neck-cloth from behind. Freed from the deadly grasp, O'Brien knocked the captain down, and seizing a large oak stave, levelled it at his head. The crew remained passive spectators of the scene—another moment would have terminated the existence of the captain, when O'Reilly sprang forward, and pinioned O'Brien's arms behind. The stave fell from his hand—the captain retreated to the cabin, and O'Brien was conveyed by his messmates to the forecastle.

"A few hours afterwards, I was seated reading near the companion-way; the captain was leaning over the bulwarks of the quarter-deck. The evening being very fine, the crew and most of the passengers were collected in different groups on deck, and the vessel was proceeding steadily before a favourable breeze. O'Brien had remained below in sullen silence since the conflict, when reflection convinced him of the errors of his conduct, and his better feelings acquired the mastery of his passion. He came on deck; and all were surprised to see him approach the quarter-deck, with folded arms, and his countenance exhibiting evident symptoms of remorse. The quarter-deck being elevated about two feet above the main-deck, was ascended by a step-ladder. To the foot of this O'Brien approached, a tear starting in his eye, and his manly countenance struggling with remorse and pride. His shirt was open, and displayed his finely formed throat and chest, and his muscular arms, as they were folded across the latter, were bared nearly to his brawny shoulders.

"It was a noble sight to behold a man, who, but a few hours before, was like a raging lion, stand thus self-convicted. 'Captain H——,' he exclaimed—(the latter turned round, and O'Brien proceeded)—'Captain I have done wrong—I fear no man—no, hang me, if I do; but I feel that I have been guilty, and I ask your pardon.' This frank and manly appeal could not be resisted, and the captain extended him his hand. Tranquillity being restored, the remainder of the voyage was favourable; and on the 6th of October, I was safely landed on Kingstown pier, after a passage of twenty-eight days."

Having thus fairly introduced Mr. W. T. M. we now leave him to his fortunes, assured that if the volume does not make way with the public, it will not be in consequence of the extracts we have given.

ADMIRAL LORD NELSON.

Horatio Nelson, whose name must ever occupy one of the most honourable niches in the temple of Fame, was the son of the Rev. Edmond Nelson, rector of Burnham Thorpe, in the county of Norfolk, where he was born on the 29th September, 1758. His mother, whose maiden name was Suckling, was grandniece to Sir Robert Walpole, first Earl of Oxford, and he was named after his godfather, the first Lord Walpole. Upon his mother's death in 1767, her brother, Captain Maurice Suckling, a highly distinguished naval officer, promised to take care of one of her sons, and young Horatio having expressed a predilection for the sea, in the year 1770 repaired on board the Reasonable of 64 guns, then commanded by his uncle; and Captain Suckling being shortly afterwards removed to the Triumph of 74 guns, stationed as a guardship in the Thames, he accompanied him, and remained under his auspices (with the exception of a voyage to the West Indies on board a merchantman) until the following circumstances enabled him to embark on active service.

In the year 1773, the Honourable Captain Phipps, eldest son of Lord Mulgrave, was appointed to undertake a voyage to the north pole, to endeavour to ascertain the practicability of the north-west passage; and Nelson, although only in his fifteenth year, solicited to be employed. Captain Phipps took the command of the Race Horse, bomb vessel, and was accompanied by Captain Lutwidge in the Carcass; and in this last vessel young Nelson embarked as the captain's coxswain. They sailed from the Nore on the 4th June, and on the last day of the following July, they were suddenly surrounded in lat. 80° 21' by immense fields of ice, and remained in a situation truly perilous, until the 9th August, when a shift of wind caused the ice to separate, and they were carried into the open sea.

During this critical period, several circumstances occurred, which strongly marked the intrepid character of the future hero.

The object of the expedition being found unattainable, the ships returned to England, and Nelson was placed by his uncle on board the Seahorse of twenty guns, where he was soon rated as midshipman; and in this ship he traversed almost every part of the Indian Seas, from the head of the Persian Gulf, to the extremity of the Bay of Bengal: But after spending about eighteen months in India, the effects of the climate were such upon his constitution, as to deprive him for some time of the use of his limbs, and he was compelled to return to England.

His health being materially improved by the voyage home, he was soon after his return appointed acting lieutenant in the Worcester of 64 guns; and on the 8th April, 1777, passed examination for a lieutenancy; and on the following day, received his commission as second lieutenant of the Lowestoffe frigate, then fitting out for Jamaica, from which vessel he was removed to the Bristol of 50 guns. On the 8th December, 1778, he was appointed commander of the Badger brig; and on the 11th June, 1779, he was promoted to the rank of Post Captain, and received the command of the Hinchinbrooke of 28 guns, before he had attained his twenty-first year.

ADMIRAL LORD NELSON.

On the West India station Nelson distinguished himself on many occasions; and while here in 1787, in command of the Boreas frigate, he married Mrs. Nesbett, who, although a widow, was only in her eighteenth year, whose hand he received from our present gracious sovereign, then Prince William Henry, who commanded the Pegasus frigate. The course of service of his frigate being expired, Nelson returned in that vessel to England in June, 1787; and his health being still very precarious, he withdrew to the parsonage house of Burnham Thorpe, which his father gave up to him; where he continued in the enjoyment of domestic peace and rural occupations, until the commencement of hostilities with France, in 1793, again called for his services, and a field of enterprise was opened before him in some degree commensurate to his mighty genius.

It would be altogether impossible here to present even the most rapid recital of the numerous actions in which he bore a part from this date, till his death. Among the many bright names which illuminate this part of the naval history of England, his shines the brightest of all.—Wherever the cannon thundered on the deep, it might be said there was Nelson. When early in 1798 he presented his claim for a pension, in consequence of the loss of his right arm in an attack on Teneriffe, he stated in his memorial, that he had been engaged against the enemy upwards of one hundred and twenty times. On occasion of receiving that wound, which would have proved fatal but for the filial affection of his son-in-law, Lieutenant Nesbett, he came home to England : and Mr. Southey, who has related the story of his life with singular fascination, gives the following anecdote, in illustration of the popular feeling with which he was regarded by the public, alike honourable to all the parties concerned :—

"His sufferings from the lost limb were long and painful. He had scarcely any intermission of pain day or night for three months after his return to England. Lady Nelson, at his earnest request, attended the dressings of his arm, until she had acquired sufficient resolution and skill to dress it herself. One night, after a day of constant pain, Nelson retired early to bed, in hope of enjoying some respite by means of laudanum. He was at that time lodging in Bond-street, and the family was soon disturbed by a mob knocking loudly and violently at the door. The news of Duncan's victory had been made public, and the house was not illuminated. But when the mob were told that Admiral Nelson lay there in bed, badly wounded, the foremost of them made answer, ' You shall hear no more from us this night.' And, in fact, the feeling of respect and sympathy was communicated from one to the other with such effect, that, even under the confusion of such a night, the house was not molested again."

Nelson's greatest victories were those of the Nile, Copenhagen, and Trafalgar. The first was gained on the 1st of August, 1798, and effected the complete destruction of the enemy's force—all their ships, except two, being either captured or sunk. For this brilliant achievement he was elevated to the Peerage, by the title of Baron Nelson of the Nile.

At the battle of Copenhagen, fought on the 1st of April, 1801, although acting in a subordinate station, yet the glorious results must be mainly attributed to him. Here he gave an evidence of his personal coolness and intrepidity in the midst of danger, that strongly marked his character, and deserves to be recorded. About one o'clock, Sir Hyde Parker perceiving that the enemy's fire was not slackened, began to despair of success, and thinking it his duty to save what he could of the fleet, made the signal for retreat; but Lord Nelson, who was at that moment in the heat of action on the quarter-deck, paid no attention to it. When informed by Captain Foley that the signal was made to leave off action—"You know, Foley," replied the hero, "I have only one eye—I have a right to be blind sometimes :" and then putting the glass to his blind eye, he exclaimed, "I really do not see the signal. Keep mine for closer battle flying !—Nail it to the mast !" and continued the action.

The battle of Trafalgar was fought on the 21st of October, 1805; and there this renowned captain fell, amidst the blaze of the most splendid triumph ever gained upon the seas.

The intelligence of this great victory, (which entirely crushed the combined naval power of France and Spain,) was received in England with mingled feelings of admiration and sorrow. His Majesty, in particular, was so affected when informed of the death of Lord Nelson, that he is said to have exclaimed, "We have lost more than we have gained !" The same feeling was manifested by persons of every description. None of those enthusiastic emotions generally produced by our great naval victories were observable on this occasion; and the prevailing wish seemed to be, to manifest their gratitude to the deceased hero by conferring on his relatives those honours and rewards which the nation would with rapture have bestowed on himself, if he had lived to enjoy his triumph. The dignities of a Viscount and Earl were conferred on his brother, the Rev. Edward Nelson, by the titles of Viscount Merton and Earl Nelson of Trafalgar. A pension of £6 000 a year was settled upon him; and £120,000 was

granted for the purchase of an estate, to support the dignity of a title so nobly acquired. To the widow of Lord Nelson £2,000 a year was granted; and £10,000 to each of his sisters. A public funeral was decreed, and a monument was ordered to be erected in St. Paul's Church ; besides which, statues and other memorials of this illustrious man were voted by several of the principal cities in the British empire.

The funeral honours paid to Lord Nelson were at once calculated to gratify the eye and impress the heart. He was attended to the grave by the seven sons of his sovereign —the chief nobility and gentry of the empire—and a long train of heroes, many of them the companions of his danger and his glory. Never were honours more deserved. Never were the characters of the hero and the patriot more happily blended than in the person of Lord Nelson ; and never were great talents exercised with more brilliant success, or directed to the attainment of more useful ends. In reference to Nelson's character as an officer, Mr. Southey says, "Never was any commander more beloved. He governed men by their reason and their affections. They knew that he was incapable of caprice or tyranny ; and they obeyed him with alacrity and joy, because he possessed their confidence as well as their love. ' Our Nel,' they used to say, ' is as brave as a lion, and as gentle as a lamb.' Severe discipline he detested, though he had been bred in a severe school. He never inflicted corporal punishment if it were possible to avoid it; and when compelled to enforce it, he who was familiar with wounds and death suffered like a woman. In his whole life Nelson was never known to act unkindly towards an officer. If he was asked to prosecute one for ill-behaviour, he used to answer, ' That there was no occasion for him to ruin a poor devil, who was sufficiently his own enemy to ruin himself.' To his midshipmen he ever showed the most winning kindness—encouraging the diffident, tempering the hasty, counselling and befriending both." The same author adds—"He has left us, not indeed his mantle of inspiration, but a name and example which are at this hour inspiring hundreds of the youth of England : a name which is our pride, and an example which will continue to be our shield and our strength."

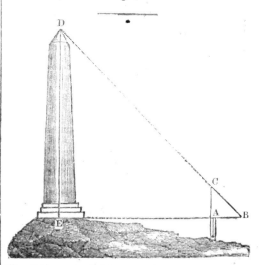

EASY METHOD OF MEASURING HEIGHTS.

The following very simple method which occurred to me for ascertaining the height of any (erect) inaccessible object, I have tried and found to answer very well; and should you deem it a fit subject for your very useful and widely circulated Journal, it is at your service.

Procure a piece of board of any convenient thickness, say half an inch, which make into a triangular form, as appears in the prefixed diagram, having the angle A a right angle, and each side subtending that angle equal, and from six to twelve inches in length ; then along the side A C, which is called the perpendicular, attach or continue a piece of wood to answer as a supporting leg, and in that leg hang a little plummet to show when the side A C is erect. Then by placing it near the object, and moving it either forward or backward, until the sight glanced along the side BC (which then forms an imaginary line as BCD) comes in contact with the top of the object. At the same time observe at what part of the base of the object the imaginary line continued along the side BA (as BAE) comes in contact, then the distance from B to E, or from where you stand to the base, is the exact height from that base to the top, as must appear obvious to any person possessing a slight knowledge of geometry.

N. B.—If it be a building, or any object of a conical or obelisk form, then the imaginary base line should be taken to the centre of one side. E. H.

REMINISCENCES OF A ROCKITE.
(Continued from page 12.*)
THE FACTION FIGHT.

The still-hunting party which had alarmed us so much at the poteen-house (which, by the bye, was utterly destroyed on the day after,) having called at my house for assistance in their progress, without finding me at home, suspicions as to my ways and haunts were whispered rather unfavourably among the neighbouring magistrates, and I was placed under a system of espionage, which only had the effect of compelling me to use greater secrecy and caution for the future. Thus the few meetings that took place under these circumstances, partook less and less of that drunken, reckless character which our former assemblies had exhibited; we met as desperadoes whose every act was watched, and the ferocity which at first only existed in the suspicions of our rulers, began gradually to find room in our breasts, from the consciousness of our being suspected. At the time of which I write, party spirit was just as high in Ireland as ever it was, and as ever it will be: and the little town in the neighbourhood of which I lived, was the focus of, perhaps, the fiercest and most ungovernable factions that existed then in our land of ire. A large fair was shortly to be held in it; and instinct, or a busy body, whichever you like. informed each party privately that they were to be attacked by the other, and murdered during the confusion and confidence of the occasion. This was not long reaching the local authorities, and every precaution which at the time was available was used to prevent bloodshed; but on the morning of the fair the quiet appearance of the peasantry, the circumstance so unusual of their coming without sticks, together with the immense quantity of women who accompanied them, (the very worst sign, if they knew but all,) lulled the magistracy into such security, that the measures at first taken were laid aside for the moment, and only not utterly abandoned from their negligence or indolence. In this state affairs stood until about noon, when they underwent a change as sudden to all parties, as it was fatal to me. About that time, a man of gigantic stature and make rushed yelling and bloody from one of the tents near which I was standing—his clothes, different in their colour, texture, and fashion, from those of the peasantry, as well as the general interest he excited among the towns-people, proclaimed him a mechanic of their body. It was not until some time after that I learned he was their champion, the redoubted Mosey M'Neil. He was a northern weaver, deeply imbued with northern notions, and with little, very little, of northern honesty, for he was known over the whole country as a sheep-stealer. However, his superior skill as a craftsman in a trade to which the lower order of Protestants in that district almost to a man belonged, as well as his immense strength, and high party spirit, gained for him the precedency in all matters of faction, or even of common life. No wonder, then, that the appearance of such a man, in such a state, was sufficient warning of an approaching combat, to all those versed in the signs and tokens of an Irish row. It seems he was drinking in a tent with a mixed party,

* Circumstances, which it is needless here to detail, prevented our before giving the continuation of this story. In our next number, we shall accompany the outlaw to the mountains, where we must leave him for the present.

and having become a little heated with liquor, upbraided some one with being a rebel; to which it was at once answered, that "Anyhow, it was dacinter to be a rebel nor a sheep-stealer." This allusion to his well known avocation not pleasing Mosey, he struck the man a blow, and in return got what is technically called a licking. Burning with rage, he hurried home for his arms, followed by his whole party; for the story had already spread through the town like wildfire, with, of course, some few additions to whet the appetite of those inclined to peace. Nor were the leaders of the other party so remiss in the necessary preparations as had been expected, or as appearances seemed to tell. On the preceding evening, large bundles of sticks had been deposited by trusty messenger in the areas and other secret places about town, alike for security and concealment; which, during the first moments of the disturbance, while the authorities were paralysed by their danger, the leaders took the opportunity of bringing to light, and dividing the concealed treasures among the eager expectants; while the few, who from the insufficiency of the supply, were left unarmed, flew to the girls, who, dear creatures, never saw a good fight yet spoiled for want of a stick or a stone, and had, accordingly, each brought with them under their cloaks, a good serviceable wattle, only for fear that Barny, or Micky, or Paddy, or any body, might want one. All stood now armed and ready for battle, to the amount of two or three hundred; to resist them, or attempt dispersing them, were mere madness, so that magistrates, constables, soldiers, and all who were not closely interested in the fray, flew from the dangerous arena to whatever house was open to them. Nor had they many choices, for at the moment of Mosey's sudden appearance every inhabitant of the town, well aware from habit of what was coming on, closed up shops, windows, doors; in fine, almost every access to the lower part of their houses, never opening them save for the admission of some near relative or peculiar favourite, and that only during the comparative quiet that existed before the actual collision of the conflicting parties; it but too often happening, that the fight raged even to the very garret of that house which might have been incautiously left open for the overpowered fugitive to seek as a refuge. From an idea of superior security, I was the last disinterested person that quitted the street, and was just about seeking an asylum at the little inn where my horse was stabled, when my old comrades, observing me sneak from among them, rushed forward, and pulled me into the very middle of the crowd, and with one universal shout of exultation, elected me their leader. My brain swam when I contemplated my dangerous eminence. I expostulated, I prayed; but the shouts made it useless—they did not understand my signs, and they could not hear my voice. Twenty or thirty offered me their sticks, each praising his own, and claiming for it the honour of my choice. The handiest wattle in the whole party was chosen for me, and placed in my unresisting hand amid the almost deafening whoops of my partizans, and to the surprise of those who viewed the scene from the windows above us. Scarce was the election completed when a dark mass and loud shouts at the other end of the town announced the approach of our adversaries, bristling with bayonets, pitchforks, and old swords, while not a few added to their imposing appearance by an old gun, rescued for the occasion from the dust and cobwebs in which it had lain perhaps for the last century. But the figure that moved in front arrested and claimed my whole attention. It was Mosey again—the marks of his recent discomfiture still crimsoning his upper person, and rendered more awful by the host of bad passions indicated on his brow, as well as the immense show of bone and muscle that appeared beneath his tattered shirt, for that bloodstained habiliment and his trowsers were the only covering that he retained. He strode some feet in front of his party, brandishing a rusty sword, which from its length and rude magnitude, appeared as if the genius of antiquity herself had preserved it for his special use, as the best and only image of her own darling giants. The scene altogether was almost new to me; need I say, the situation was utterly so. All combined, deprived me of sense or thought; I merely recollect a wild rushing of the combatants—the yells now of victory, now of defeat, deprived me of the little consciousness I possessed, nor did I recover it, until the jostling of the crowd threw me immediately before the terrible swordsman, and almost within the sweep of his weapon, whose deep red rust was already darkened by a deeper stain. He seemed to recognise me as the leader of his hated opponents, for with a wild yell of delight he sprung forward, singling me out as his victim. He raised his broad-sward high for a blow that would need no second. The whole of his immense strength was applied to it, and the only protection I had was the light stick that until now had hung useless in my hand. I threw it up as a guard, more from instinct than the slightest confidence in its efficacy; and the sneer with which he watched the movement, told me I had nothing to expect from mercy. The blow was descending, and with a desperate spring I shunned it; but ere it was more than begun, a stone from the rere, flung by some one enabled to take aim at his head so high above all others, struck him on the forehead. The immense weapon came sweeping harmless down, and with its impetus swung round the listless form of the giant, and hurled him senseless at the feet of those whose main stay he was until that fatal moment. The result needs not many words to tell. Bearing the carcase in safety from our re-invigorated attacks, they fled, or rather retreated, to their own houses. The authority with which I had been so unpleasantly invested, I now exerted with success in restraining my exulting followers. The show of resistance I made to him before whom all others fled, gained me a reputation so great, that when I directed them to return peacefully to the country, the retrograde movement was universal. I was borne away in triumph: and some of the party having secured my horse from the inn-stables, and decorated him with ribbons and other finery from the deserted standings, made even him share in the honours of the occasion. Luckily for me and the ringleaders of the disturbance, that night was spent in secret conclave, and the consideration of what measures we should take to resist or evade the expected hostility of the magistrates. This circumstance, in all probability, saved half a score of us from the gallows, as, long ere morning, an armed party scoured the whole country in search of us, but only succeeded in catching a few, who too securely remained at home, and whom, on account of the terrible confusion, and the comparatively subordinate parts which they filled in the day's work, they failed to identify. The failure of this attempt taught us all a precaution, which we were no way slow to practice. The same retreat which we had used then, served us as a nightly abode until the results were known, while the numerous videttes we had stationed in all quarters left surprise by day-time a measure which would have been as unavailing as it was unattempted. In addition to this, a constant communication was kept up between us and some friends in town who formed a watch on the motions of the opposite party. From these we learned, that the informations of our discomfited foes had been taken, and also received a list of the names sworn to as the aggressors. Mine was at the head of the list, sworn to by Mosey M'Neile as having inflicted his wound, and being the prime agitator of the whole disturbance! I must acknowledge I was but little anxious as to the result, from the consideration of the many disinterested witnesses who viewed my compulsory election, as well as the cause of Mosey's wounds being so generally known among my own party, not to mention the many frightful scars inflicted by the savage weapons they used against us, and which at least showed that we were but sharers in the list of misfortunes. In fact, we only waited Mosey's recovery to proceed in a body and demand a fair investigation, as until then matters were rather doubtful from the uncertainty of his life. The almost hourly accounts we received of his health were so fluctuating, as to leave it useless to depend on any one bulletin, if I may so call them. At length, towards the end of the week they became more steadily favourable. On the evening of the eighth day he actually plied his trade for some minutes, and sat until late with the crowds who came to congratulate him on his recovery. On the following day we determined to put our measures into execution. All was ready, and we were actually on our way, when the appalling news arrived of his sudden dissolution. It was the critical ninth day—and his dying words denounced me as his murderer. Terrified as I was at this announcement, my case still seemed far from desperate. At first I relied upon the inhabitants of the town, who were nearly all witnesses of the circumstances that occurred; but I soon learned that nothing was to be expected from that quarter—they all coincided in the death words of their favourite champion; and my last resource was to turn to my companions, as if they were not already overjoyed each at his own escape, and willing to shift on my shoulders the weight of that common danger, which they first compelled me to share, and then left me altogether to sustain alone. It was but too evident that my life was to pay the forfeit of my rashness, and their villainy; and if a doubt remained on my mind, it was removed, when, at the approach of a large body of military which had been sent for my capture, they fled to their homes or their hiding-places, according as each preferred to shun or brave the uncertain danger; but not one spoke to me, encouraged me, or even pointed out a mode of safety; and in less than a minute I stood abandoned even by my own. I still, however, had time to secrete myself, but where, was the question, since I feared lest, in the paroxysm of their cowardice, they should even betray my concealment. I heard the shouts of the military as they scattered to secure the cabins—they were coming nearer and nearer—and alone and unseen I at length succeeded in taking refuge in a large tract of scrub that was adjacent, in which were many hiding-places, unknown except to those in its immediate vicinity. In one of these I remained secure, while the wood was surrounded and searched; and often as I have braved the same danger since, never did my feelings reach the same pitch of intensity to which they were carried in that interval. It was the depth of the night before I ventured out of my bower, if I may so call it; and having reconnoitred the whole country as well as the darkness permitted, I stealthily sought the cabin of a man who, if any, would be true to me. Hunger and thirst had deprived me of the little strength that exertion and anxiety had left me, and it was with difficulty I crawled to the door and craved admittance. When it was opened, I fainted across the threshhold. On my revival I learned that I had not been wholly abandoned, for means had been found to communicate the circumstances to the captain, who, in return, directed that on the following night I should take the opportunity of joining him in the mountains, and appointed a place where I should meet the person under whose guidance I was to take this perilous and uncertain journey. Having partaken of food and sleep, and arranged to meet my guide, I set off at the dawn of day, with some cold potatoes in my pocket, to regain my hiding-place, it being a measure of too much danger to remain abroad while such a vigilant search was persevered in. Nor did I miscalculate the danger; for I was scarce couched in my lair, when the wood was again occupied, and searched with a determination almost vindictive, kept alive by the armed yeomanry, so many of whom swarmed about my concealment, and to whom the deceased was an old and dear comrade. Scarce a bush escaped from their vigorous search, and nothing would have saved me, but the circumstance of the scrub in which I was concealed being seated on a mass of loose limestone, in whose fissures it was possible for one young, active, and, moreover, reasonably fond of life, as I was, to insinuate himself. Foiled in their exertions, they next began to try the points of their weapons on every spot where a man could by any possibility fit, while others, less interested, skulked from the fruitless labour, and seated themselves wherever rest invited. The cozy little spot that I had selected could scarce escape having an inmate when this desire began to operate—nor did it. A fat serjeant of Highlanders came puffing to the place, and throwing himself on the treacherous branches that entwined so closely as to lead one to suppose them the actual soil, he tumbled through them, rustling and clattering, until he reached the bottom, where I had nestled myself among the rocks and grass, so that a man would want more senses than one to find me. Luckily for me, the sense of feeling, by far the most dangerous to me, was rendered so callous to the poor serjeant by the buffets he received in his fall, that when he alit seat-wise on my breast, the transition was too pleasing to require much investigation; and merely contenting himself with the observation, "Mon, mon, but the grass is vara soft!" he commenced picking the thorns out of those parts which his peculiarities of dress left most undefended; and now and then commenting on the chase, of which he had a splendid view through the bushes, in such a manner that even the imminent danger in which I was could scarce enable me to restrain my laughter.

"There they gang," said he—"there they gang, the doited carls, with their guns, and their spits, and their bayonets, and their swords. May they be protected from each other, for there'll be bloodshed among them, if they can't find the croppy to cool themselves on. Eh, sirs, there's corporal Campbell with his kilt in ribands, and his puir hurdies all bloody with the briars. Och, och! but the mon is a fule. Whisht, they have him. No, it's a puir crethur of a yeoman that tumbled through the brake, an' they're pullin' him out. Eh, but he's killed, I'm thinkin'. My certie, if they catch the croppy they'll mak' mince meat ov him. Dear, how that chiel Sawney blaws his trumpet, as if he wad never get out ov this place. Mon, mon! how will I get out mysel without breakin' my neck, an' they'll leave me here to the mercy of the croppies?"

The question, however, was quickly solved, for some of the yeomanry still prowling about, unwilling to abandon the pursuit, heard the rustle he made in the endeavour to rise, which was at once answered by a thrust of a bayonet in pike fashion, which wounding a part rather sensitive for such usage, helped the poor Highlander to clear all obstacles with a bound, screaming, "The croppy! the croppy!" at the pitch of his lungs, and at the same instant ten or a dozen yeomen plunged right through after him, to the imminent danger of their lower habiliments.

"Saul o' me," shouted the enraged Highlander, when he perceived his assailants, and foremost among them the weapon which achieved his dishonour, reeking with his blood—"Saul o' me! ye awkward loons, whilk o' ye did that?"

Roars of laughter succeeded his question, and not without cause—there stood the poor man, swelling with rage, and pressing his hand on the wound, from which a slight stream trickled down his thighs, already bracket with the consequences of his former mishap, and stamping and mouthing in a manner certainly not the most awe inspiring. The clamour excited by the incident drew together the retiring parties; and much to my satisfaction, cold iron and hot blood began to be displayed on both sides. At length the commanders and magistrates made their appearance, and after much exertions, and many attempts to appease the wounded serjeant, the tumult was at length got under. After a day spent in fruitless search, during which every cabin and hedge for miles around were examined, the party was at length drawn off, and a fine frosty moon, which soon after rose, aided me to trace them on their departure, until they were utterly beyond fear of returning; then cautiously gathering my cramped limbs from their several hiding-places, I emerged from the concealment, just in time to see the first blaze rise from my pleasant home, on which they now spent their baffled fury. Many regrets occupied me for a few bitter moments; but at length they subsided, at the reflection of how little it mattered to me now, for I had chosen the life of an outlaw.   M'C.

JONATHAN SIMPSON, THE HIGHWAYMAN.

He was possessed of about £5,000, but his expenses were so extravagant, that this large sum was soon exhausted. He then went to the highway, committed a robbery, was apprehended, and would certainly have been hung had not some of his rich relations procured a reprieve. The difficulty of obtaining it may be guessed from the fact, that it arrived at Tyburn just when the rope was about his neck. Such was his obduracy, that when returning to Newgate behind one of the sheriff's men, the latter asked him what he thought of a reprieve when he had come to the gallows. He replied—"No more than I thought of my dying day." When he came to the prison door, the turnkey refused to receive him, saying that he was sent to be executed, and that he was discharged of

him, and would not permit him to enter without a new warrant. Upon which Simpson exclaimed, "What an unhappy cast-off dog am I, that both Tyburn and Newgate should in one day refuse to entertain me! Well, I'll mend my ways for the future, and try whether I can't merit a reception at them both, next time I am brought thither." He immediately recommenced his operations, and one day robbed a gentleman of a purse full of counters, which he supposed were gold. He kept them in his pockets, always anxiously looking out for his benefactor. About four months after he met him on Bagshot Heath, riding in his coach. "Sir," said he, "I believe you made a mistake the last time I had the happiness of seeing you, in giving those pieces. I have been troubled ever since, lest you should have wanted them at cards, and am glad of this opportunity to return them; only, for my care, I require you to come at this moment out of your coach, and give me your breeches, that I may search them at leisure, and not trust any more to your generosity, lest you should mistake again." A pistol enforced his demand, and Simpson found a gold watch, a gold snuff box, and ninety-eight guineas, with five jacobuses. At another time he robbed Lord Delamore of three hundred and fifty guineas. He was almost unequalled in his depredations; in one day he robbed nineteen people, and took above two hundred pounds; and in the space of six weeks, committed forty robberies in the County of Middlesex. He even ventured to attack the Duke of Berwick, and took from him articles to a very great value. But wickedness has a boundary over which it cannot pass. Simpson attacked two captains of the Guards; a desperate struggle ensued, his horse was shot under him, and he was wounded in both arms and one of his legs before he was taken. He was sent to Newgate, and now found that he was not refused entrance; and he soon also discovered that Tyburn was equally ready to receive him. He was executed on the 8th of September, 1686.—*Whitehead's Lives of Highwaymen, &c.*

OH, CAN YOU LEAVE YOUR NATIVE LAND?

Oh, can you leave your native land,
   An exile's bride to be—
Your mother's home and cheerful hearth,
   To tempt the main with me—
Across the wide Atlantic
   To trace our foaming track,
And know the wave that heaves us on,
   Will never bear us back?

And can you in Canadian woods
   With me the harvest bind,
Nor feel one ling'ring sad regret
   For all you leave behind?
Can lily hands, unused to toil,
   The woodman's wants supply—
Nor shrink beneath the chilly blast,
   When wintry storms are nigh?

Amid the shade of forests dark,
   Thy loved isle will appear
An Eden, whose delicious bloom
   Will make the wild more drear.
And you in solitude may weep
   O'er scenes beloved in vain,
And pine away your soul to view,
   Once more your native plain.

Then pause, dear girl, ere those sweet lips
   Your wanderer's fate decide:
My spirit spurns the selfish wish—
   Thou shalt not be my bride!
But, oh! that smile—those tearful eyes
   My firmer purpose move;
Our hearts are one—and we will dare
   All perils, thus to love!

Dublin : Printed and Published by P. D. HARDY, 3, Cecilia-street; to whom all communications are to be addressed.
Sold by all Booksellers in Ireland.
In London, by Richard Groombridge, 6, Panyer-alley, Paternoster-row; in Liverpool, by Willmer and Smith; in Manchester, by Ambery, in Birmingham, by Guest, 91, Steelhouse-lane; in Glasgow, by John Macleod; and in Edinburgh, by N. Bowack.

THE
DUBLIN PENNY JOURNAL

CONDUCTED BY P. DIXON HARDY, M.R.I.A.

| Vol. III. | JUNE 27, 1835. | No. 156. |

BARRACK AND QUEEN'S BRIDGES.

Barrack Bridge (formerly Bloody Bridge) was originally built of wood in 1671, but afterwards constructed of stone. It consists of four plain semicircular arches. The erection, at the south end, of a grand gothic gateway leading to Kilmainham Hospital, and the scenery in the back ground, give to this bridge at present a very romantic appearance.

The Queen's Bridge, seen beneath the other, consists of three arches of hewn stone, and though small, being but 140 feet in length, is neat and well-proportioned. It was erected in 1768. On the site of the present structure Arran-bridge formerly stood, which was built in 1683, and swept away by a flood in 1763.

Relative to the original construction of the former Bridge, we have been favoured by a correspondent with the following:—

" Passing over the bridge that leads from Watling-street across the Liffey, I inquired its name, and found it was called Bloody Bridge, from a great battle that was fought there during the rebellion of 1641. I was told again, it derived its name from a number of apprentices who were hung on its battlements during "the affair of '98;" and some other causes are given for its sanguinary title. These contradictory reports induced me to consult history. Its origin is as follows:—A. D. 1408, the Duke of Lancaster made extraordinary preparations for subduing the Irish of Leinster, who, under the command of the King Art M'Murchad O'Cavanagh, were fearfully encroaching on the Pale. The consequence was, a most sanguinary conflict took place between the two armies at the western extremity of Dublin, where the Phœnix Park now stands. The English were defeated with dreadful slaughter, and hotly pursued to the gates of the city. Before they could enter the city, they had to cross the Liffey by a ford. Here the confusion became fearful—the Irish enemy were upon them, and before the half of the defeated army had crossed, the ford was completely choaked up with the dead and dying, and the water continued red for three days, whence it got the name of Ath Cro, i. e. the Bloody Ford, which name was communicated to a bridge afterwards built over the ford. Whether the present bridge is the original one or not, I cannot say. The Duke of Lancaster, who commanded the English, was wounded near the walls of Dublin, and soon after breathed his last.

"T. A. G—M—N."

MR. O'BRIEN'S ROUND TOWERS.

To apologize—or not to apologize—that is the question! Whether it be better to follow up the precedent of several of our "brethren of the grey goose quill," and at once offer an abject apology to Mr. Henry O'Brien, for having had the temerity to speak slightingly of his most learned lucubrations, on "The Mysteries of Freemasonry and Budism," or, in default of so doing, subject ourselves to the annoyance incident to defending a suit at law, as threatened by Mr. O'Brien and his solicitor—this is the question—and certainly a most important question—for us to consider. Know then, good reader, that forasmuch as we, being in the month of June, 1834, the editor and proprietor of the Dublin Penny Journal, and not having at that time the fear of the said Mr. Henry O'Brien before our eyes, did presume, on the 24th day of that month, in the 98th number of our Journal, to say of his very erudite work, that it was "an indecent, incongruous, and, in many instances, a blasphemous publication."* And inasmuch as our review of said publication hath "tended to injure the literary character of the said Mr. Henry O'Brien,"* and to retard the sale of said work, after various remonstrances and solicitations on the part of the learned author, in sundry long epistles addressed to us, we are now finally threatened with a legal prosecution, unless, amending the error of our ways, we make such honourable retribution, in the form of an ample apology, as he in his wisdom shall deem sufficient. So says Henry O'Brien, Esq. and thus the question stands between us at the present moment. In reference to the demand for an apology, we have only to say, that could we but bring ourselves to think, that we had in any way dealt unfairly with Mr. O'Brien, or the very erudite production of his genius, we would not hesitate an instant to make the most ample apology he could require. But feeling a conscientious conviction, that, with one little exception, which we shall presently explain, we have in no instance overstepped the bounds of fair, legitimate criticism—that in our observations on his book, we have "nothing extenuated, nor set down aught in malice"—that we intended nothing personal—we beg to tell the learned gentleman and his legal adviser, even at the risk of a suit at law, that we will not retract the opinion we have expressed on the subject. It is, indeed, preposterous to think, that because in the due and wholesome exercise of the power which the conducting of a literary periodical has placed in our hands, the sale of a work is injured, or the literary character of an author is lowered, that therefore we are to be forced to the dilemma of an apology, a duel, or a law suit. If our opinion were ill-founded, the voice of public opinion would be sufficient to counterbalance any evil effect which it might for a moment produce; but the very circumstance of that opinion having been responded to by the public, as he himself asserts, in the loss of literary character, and the diminished sale of the work, should be proof sufficient that we were not far astray in our decision, and might teach the author a lesson which he appears to have yet to learn, "not to think of himself or his productions more highly than he ought to think."

By a reference to the 98th number of our Journal, the reader will find the review which has excited Mr. O'Brien's bitter ire against us; and here we beg to say, that we do most readily apologize for having translated the A. B. affixed to his name, as Big Ass. Our publication had not gone through the press until we wished it expunged, for we felt it was bad taste on our part, and its point could not be seen by the generality of our readers, as it merely referred to Mr. O'Brien having appended the Esquire to his own name, and taken it from Mr. Petrie's, who was certainly at least as well entitled to it. We do, therefore, most unreservedly apologize to the gentleman for having called him a Big Ass, and most assuredly shall never be guilty of a like offence in future; but with this exception, we now affirm, on a re-perusal of the work itself, that the review is a fair, impartial, unbiassed judgment—nay more, that it is not as severe or pungent as the work demanded at our hands. Therefore, for having said of it, that it is an indecent, incongruous mass, and that it is in many instances blasphemous, we owe him no apology, and we shall make none; and if for so saying, he thinks proper to bring an action, we tell him we shall meet him in a Court of Law without any fear of the consequences; and to prevent any further correspondence, as soon as he gives security for the costs of the action, which we certainly will require him to do, he may proceed forthwith; nay more, to save him the trouble of gathering up our opinions from detached sentences, we now once again would record our judgment of the publication, that it is, from beginning to end, a heterogeneous compound of affected learning and illogical reasoning.— The preface itself is sufficient to show the man. It consists of no fewer than seven and thirty pages, altogether occupied with a silly dissertation to prove he had a right to "the fifty pound prize" offered by the Royal Irish Academy, for the best Essay on the Origin and Use of the Round Towers of Ireland, into which he has contrived to introduce several private conversations* held with members of the Royal Irish Academy—lengthy extracts from the Dublin Penny Journal, and from his own letters to the Council of the Academy, setting forth the various "manœuvres," plots and counterplots, practised, used, and devised by Dr. M'Donnell, F.T.C.D. Dr. Singer, F.T.C.D. the Rev. Cæsar Otway, and the Editor of the Dublin Penny Journal, to oust him of his fair claim to the fifty pounds. Then making a direct personal attack upon ourselves, which was certainly much more worthy of a suit than any thing we have said of him, he finishes his learned introduction by quoting from our pages, in one continuous sentence, the greater proportion of the address which we considered necessary to insert on taking the management of the Journal into our hands.†

So much for the preface. With regard to the body of the work, and the arguments brought forward, if arguments they can be called, we feel it would be but a waste of time and space again to notice the absurdities it contains. To show that we were fully justified in the character we gave it, we had marked several extracts for insertion; but feel the difficulty before stated, that the allusions they contain are too gross and indecent for the subscribers to the Penny Journal. Indeed the theory altogether is a disgusting one; and although our readers may have thought, that in alluding to Mr. O'Brien's "caves under ground, and pillars over ground," as representing parts of the human body to which decency forbids more particular allusion, we were only sporting with their fancies, we assure them, that it was an effort of ours, with as much delicacy as the subject would permit, to propound his theory in a way likely to be understood by those capable of understanding such matters.

On the whole, then, it is surely not to be tolerated, that Mr. O'Brien, after using what language he thought fit in reference to every author who had gone before him on the same subject—after abusing without mercy the Council of the Academy—after copying a very considerable portion of his work (the wood-cuts not excepted) from our Journal—and after here and there squirting the venom of his invective upon our pages, and doing us all the mischief a little mind could achieve—we say it is not to be tolerated that after all this, he should turn round upon ourselves, and continue to annoy us with threats of legal proceedings; because, forsooth, we dared to criticise his ill-digested theory, and to speak of his production in the terms it deserved. We trust such conduct will not be allowed to pass with impunity by those who have the charge of the public press, but that they may be induced to speak out their sentiments plainly on the subject. Ours is not the only Journal denounced by Mr. O'Brien—whoever has not joined him in his reveries is to be prose-

---

* The words for which the action is threatened by the Solicitor.

* He tells his readers—"I availed myself of a pretext for calling on Dr. M'Donnell, when the following conversation took place," which he relates at length.

† Surely common gratitude for having enabled him to fill so many pages of his volume, should prevent him bringing an action against us!

cuted; and although in no one instance can he recover damages, still it is a very great annoyance to be thus worried and tormented. Instead of making apologies, the editors and proprietors of literary works should set their faces as a flint against such a system; and by holding it up to public reprobation, preserve for the periodical press the liberty heretofore enjoyed of fairly discussing new-fangled theories and opinions, brought forward by authors of more zeal than judgment, and who carry more sail than ballast. We have always regarded fair discussion as the best friend of real merit, and the best means of detecting literary imposture, and checking literary impertinence. At all events, whatever may come relative to the present proceedings, we have the satisfaction of reflecting that we have done our duty; and shall prove to Mr. O'Brien in our review of his forthcoming work, "the Pyramids of Egypt," "the uses of which," in his advertisement, he presumptuously says "are for the first time revealed," that if he thinks by threatening us with a prosecution, to prevent our speaking of it as it may deserve, he is greatly mistaken. Please Providence, as soon as it comes to light, we shall do it justice—and faithfully award the praise or the censure the production may, in our opinion, fairly merit.

SIMPLE SCIENCE.

MAGNETISM.

As natural philosophy is a science in its own nature entertaining and delightful, and conducive in many instances to the ease and convenience of life, it is not to be wondered at that there have been men in all ages, who have laid themselves out for the improvement and cultivation of it. But it is a matter of no small surprise, to think how inconsiderable a progress the knowledge of nature had made in former ages, when compared with the vast improvements it has received from the numberless discoveries of latter times; insomuch, that some of the branches of natural philosophy, which at this day are almost complete in all their parts, were utterly unknown before the last century. If we look into the reason of this, we shall find it to be chiefly owing to the wrong measures that were taken by philosophers of former ages in their pursuits after natural knowledge; for they, disregarding experiments, (the only sure foundation whereon to build a rational philosophy,) busied themselves in framing hypotheses for the solution of natural appearances; which, as they were creatures of the brain, without any foundation in nature, were, generally speaking, so lame and defective, as, in many cases, not to answer those very phenomena for whose sakes they were contrived. Whereas the philosophers of later times, laying aside those false lights, as being of no other use than to misguide the understanding in its searches into nature, betook themselves to experiments and observations, and from them collected the general powers and laws of nature; which, with a proper application, and the assistance of mathematical learning, enabled them to account for most of the properties and operations of bodies, and to solve many difficulties in the natural appearances, which were utterly inexplicable on the foot of hypotheses, and much more will yet be discovered by the philosophers of the present day.

The phenomena of magnetism, like those of electricity, depend on a cause so little subject to the investigation of our senses, that any regular and well supported theory can as yet scarcely be expected. The subject is still more difficult than that of electricity; for in the latter, the fluid is made visible, and otherwise perceptible to our senses: but no experiment could ever render the cause of magnetism perceptible otherwise than by its effects. The idea of its being occasioned by a fluid entering in at one pole and passing out at another, has become pretty general; but the late discoveries in electricity have naturally suggested another theory—which is, that the magnetic phenomena may be occasioned by a fluid analogous to the electric, or perhaps the very same; and with a view to investigate this theory, the phenomena of magnetism and electricity have been accurately compared with each other, and the analogy between them carefully marked. This

analogy is found to consist principally in the following particulars:

1st.—Electricity is of two kinds, positive and negative, each of which repels its own kind and attracts the opposite. In magnetics, the north and south pole do the same—each being repulsive of its own kind, and attracting the opposite.

2d. In electricity, whenever a body in its natural state is brought near an electrified one, it becomes itself electrified, and possessed of the contrary electricity, after which an attraction takes place. In like manner, when a piece of iron or steel is brought within the influence of a magnet, it becomes itself possessed of a magnetism contrary to that which the magnet possesses, and is of course attracted.

3d.—One sort of electricity cannot be produced without the other: neither is it possible to produce one kind of magnetism without the other also.

4th.—The electric power may be retained by certain substances, as amber, glass, &c.; but easily pervades others, which are therefore called conductors. Magnetism has a similar conductor in soft iron; for by means of it, the virtue may be extended farther than can be done without it—at the same time that the iron itself loses all magnetic power the moment it is separated from the magnet. Hardened iron, cast iron, and steel, perform a part analogous to electrics.

5th.—The electric virtue exerts itself most powerfully on points, which are found to carry it off or receive it in vast quantities. In like manner, a magnet will hold a piece of iron more powerfully by a corner or blunt point than by a flat surface. On sharp points, indeed, the magnet has but little hold, by reason of the deficiency of surface.

6th.—From experiments, it appears possible to superinduce the negative and positive electricities upon one another; and in magnetics it is possible to do the same.

These are the most remarkable particulars in which magnetism and electricity are made to agree; but the differences between them are no less remarkable. The magnetic power affects none of our senses, and, most perceptible at least, attracts only iron; whilst electricity attracts and repels bodies of every kind indiscriminately. The electric virtue presides on the surface, but that of the magnet pervades the whole substance. A magnet loses nothing of its power by communicating its virtue to other bodies, but electricity always does. And, lastly, the magnetic virtue is permanent, whereas that of electricity is exceedingly perishable, and capable of being dissipated. Notwithstanding these disagreements, however, the analogies between magnetism and electricity are so great, that the hypothesis of a magnetic as well as of an electric fluid has now gained general credit.

ANIMAL MAGNETISM

Is a sympathy lately supposed by some persons to exist between the magnet and the human body, by means of which the former became capable of curing many diseases in an unknown way, something resembling the performances of the old magicians. It appears to have originated in 1774, from a German philosopher named Father Held, who greatly recommended the use of the magnet in medicine. M. Mesmer of the same country became the direct founder of the system. He went to Paris in the year 1778, where his patients increased so rapidly, that he was obliged to take in pupils to assist him. The new system now gained ground daily, and soon became so fashionable that the jealousy of the faculty was awakened, and an application concerning it was made to Government, in consequence of which a committee was appointed to inquire into the matter. This was a thunder-stroke to the supporters of the new doctrine. Mesmer himself refused to have any communication with the committee; but his most celebrated pupil, Deston, was less scrupulous, and explained the principles of this art in the following manner:

1st.—Animal magnetism is an universal fluid, constituting an actual plenum in nature, and the medium of all mutual influence between the celestial bodies, and between the earth and animal bodies.

2d.—It is the most subtile fluid in nature, capable of a flux and a reflux; and receiving, propagating, and continuing all kinds of motion.

3d.—The animal body is subjected to the influence of this fluid by means of the nerves, which are immediately affected by it.

4th.—The human body has poles, and other properties analogous to the magnet.

5th.—The action and virtue of animal magnetism may be communicated from one body to another, whether animate or inanimate.

6th.—It operates at a great distance without the intervention of any body.

7th.—It is increased and reflected by mirrors; communicated, propagated, and increased by sound; and may be accumulated, concentrated, and transported.

8th.—Notwithstanding the universality of this fluid, all animal bodies are not equally affected by it.

9th.—By means of this fluid, nervous diseases are cured immediately, and others mediately. And its virtues, in short, extend to the universal cure and preservation of mankind.

From this extraordinary theory Deston had fabricated a paper, in which he stated that there was in nature but one disease and one cure—and that this cure was animal magnetism. And he engaged, first, to prove to the commissioners that such a thing as animal magnetism existed, and the utility of it in the cure of diseases; after which he was to communicate to them all that he knew on the subject. The commissioners accordingly attended in the room, where the patients underwent the magnetical operations. The apparatus consisted of a platform raised from the ground; at the top of it were a number of holes, in which were iron rods, with moveable joints, for the purpose of applying them to any part of the body. The patients were placed in a circle, each touching an iron rod. They were joined together by a cord passing round their bodies, the design being to increase the effect by communication. Each of the patients held in his hand an iron rod ten or twelve feet long, which was to concentrate the magnetism. Sound is another conductor, and there was a piano-forte in the room to increase it. The effects of these operations on the patients were very different. Some felt nothing, nor was there any effect whatever upon them. Some spit, coughed, sweat, felt, or pretended to feel, extraordinary heats in different parts of the body. Some women had convulsions. The commissioners at last found that they could come to no conclusion from attending in this public way, and resolved to try the experiment themselves privately. For this purpose, they first tried it upon themselves, and felt nothing. Seven of Deston's patients were magnetised at the house of Dr. Franklin, who was the chief commissioner, four of whom felt nothing; the other three affected to feel something. Several persons in a higher sphere of life were magnetised, and felt nothing. The commissioners, however, were determined to discover what share imagination had in this business. They blindfolded several of the common people, and made them sometimes think that they were magnetised; at other times they magnetised them without telling them that they did so. The consequence was, that when they supposed themselves magnetised, they thought they felt something, and vice versa. Other instances were given, from which it was evident either that the patients were impostors, or in such a most wretched state of debility both of mind and body, that the most trifling effects of the former had the most powerful effects on the latter. The commissioners, therefore, entirely disapproved of the whole. It was observed that the operator sometimes pressed strongly and for a length of time upon different parts of the body, particularly the hypochondria and pit of the stomach; and it is well known, that a strong pressure on these parts will produce disagreeable sensations on those who enjoy perfect health.

It is needless to add more, than that Mesmer complained of the report of the commissioners—petitioned parliament—was by them commanded to discover the mysteries of his doctrine—and that it is now exploded by every man of sense.

The conclusion of the academicians concerning it was— That it is not entirely useless, even to philosophy, as it is one fact more to be consigned to the history of the errors and delusions of the human mind, and a signal instance of the power of the imagination.   H——N, T.C.D.

ROYAL MILITARY INFIRMARY.

This useful and ornamental edifice is finely situated in the south-east angle of the Phœnix Park. The front consists of a centre and two wings, built of Portland-stone, and extending 170 feet. The first stone was laid in 1786, by the Duke of Rutland, and the work completed in two years at the expense of £9,000. The interior contains apartments for the officers, and thirteen extensive and well ventilated wards, in which are 187 beds. At the rere is a fever hospital. A few acres of the Phœnix Park are walled off, in which the convalescents enjoy air and exercise, while on every side a scene of the most picturesque description is presented to the view. The accommodations and attendance in the hospital are of the very best kind, and the expense is nearly £9,000 a year, about one half of which is supplied by Parliamentary grants, and the remainder by deductions from the pay of the patients while in the Infirmary.

REMINISCENCES OF A ROCKITE.
(Continued from page 408.)

HEAD QUARTERS.

Having reached the place appointed as a rendezvous between me and my guide, I began to whistle (not at my loudest, however) the tune of Patrick's-day, which was the signal arranged for his appearance; but my teeth were chattering at such a rate, between cold and anxiety, that did not the fellow guess something by my appearance, he would never have been able to discover my identity by my musical endeavours. However, he showed himself from behind a clump within a few yards of me, and advancing to the spot whence my abortive attempts at whistling proceeded, announced his presence by the usual salutation, "God save you."

"God save you kindly," answered I; "I'm thinking we're looking for one another."

"'Deed, I'm thinkin' so, avick. An' what sort of a night is id, for we've two roads to choose—one for the darkness, an' one for the moonlight."

"Why, my good fellow," said I, "your eyes must be little use to you, if they haven't told you before this that we might pick pins where we're standing."

"'Deed, you're right, achra, you're right. 'Tis a good score o' years, come next Patrickmas, since my eyes wor the laste use to me—I'm blind, avourneen!"

"Blind!" shouted I—"why, what the deuce—oh, this is regular mockery!' 'How, in the name of wonder, can you lead me the length of my nose—and in the night too?"

"There's not a stone the road you're goin' that I don't know; an' thin, you know, night and day is all one to me—that's one advantage I have over yees that have eyes. But let us be goin'—down the boreen, avick, that's the road."

And so we proceeded; not, however, without a few curses escaping me at what I thought the wanton disposition of my new governor, in appointing me such a guide. I wronged him. The danger of despatching any of his outlawed and marked followers to fill such a service would, in the present distracted state of the country, most probably have been attended with the worst results; and he judged rightly, when he considered how few would suspect a blind piper of going on such an errand. The poor man himself was one little likely, even from his manners, to attract such a suspicion; and it was no small wonder to me, how a creature of such gentle habits and peaceable avocations, could have been connected with so lawless a gang. I expressed my surprise to him as soon as we reached the safe part of our road, and was answered by the following story, which I relate in his own words:

"It's more nor twinty years ago sence I was marrid to as purty a colleen as was in the seven counties—she's dead an' gone long afore the throuble kem on me that's weighin' me now. We wor coortin' for as good as three years afore we marrid, for we were poor, an' couldn't bring that about, ontill I by workin' hard on week-days, an' pipin' on Sundays an' holidays, an' she by spinnin' for the neighbours whin she could get it to do, scraped together a few pounds to pay the priest, an' buy a few sticks o' furniture; an' thin we got marrid—an', oh, it's I was the happy boy thin! I thought if I had only her, an' my spade, an' my pipes, the world might go where it liked for me. Well, I wint to live to her ould father, up jist where we're goin', an' brought my mother wid me; an' we wor goin' on, widout a pin's-worth to throuble us, ontil I raised the spite ov a big rascal ov the name ov Farrell—

the Farrells of Knocknamoe, your honour—by raison that I was takin' all the custom from him, for he was a musicianer too. An' what does he do, but goes to a magistrate, an' swears a robbery agin me, that a great reward intirely was offered for discoverin', an' that I'd no more to do wid than the child unborn. Jist about the same time, there was a terrible small-pox in this place, an' 'twas clearin' the people off by scores, and my poor Biddy cotch it—wirra, wirra! that was the sore sickness to me! ochone, ochone, my heart breaks whin I think ov it!—she cotch it, an' I ran off to the nearest town to get somethin' for her, an' 'twas there I hard the other throuble that was to come over me, by raison ov Jack Farrell: an' if my heart was heavy whin I set out, sure 'twas twice worse whin I was goin' back—the more especially since I found Biddy, the cushla, all as one as dyin'. Well, I tould the ould people what I hard, an' they wor for my lavin' the place intirely for a few days; but I'd as soon give myself up as do that: an' I cotch the poor sick crathur in my arms, an' said I'd never lave her, in spite of all their prayers. So, thin, the ould man ups an' he tells how, whin he was once workin' in the little piatee garden, he found a cave jist at the wall ov the cabin, an' he niver spoke to any one about it, so if I could get into id now, all would be safe. Well, avick, we groped about for id, an' found it, sure enough, an' what was lucky, found that by rootin' undher the bedstead we could make a way into id; an' so we did, an' I wint in, an' the place was covered up wid a big stone, so that sorra one could find me, barrin' they knew the saycret. I wasn't long in, whin I hard a great stampin' over head, for the sogers war come lookin' for me; an' through a little chink in the rock that looked outward, I saw as good as fifty horsemen all about the house, an' hard every word they war sayin'. To be sure, whin they found I was gone, they war angry enough; bud they had to go off with their fingers in their mouths. An' as soon as the war gone, my mother made off to him that's captain now, bud he was a farmin' gintleman thin—an', oh, Sir, did you hear how id kem about that he turned captain—dth, dth! wasn't id horrid? My mother, as I was sayin', wint off to him, for she was an ould retainer of his family, an' she tould him all how it was wid us; an', good loock be his portion, he gev his word that he would do his best to bring out the truth. They kem to me an' tould me the help I was to git, an' gev me somethin' to eat through the chink, an' tould me Biddy was better; bud they wouldn't let me out by no manner of manes, for they said the place was too well watched still. To make a long story short, Sir, I fell sick myself wid all I had to go through; an' thin a way was made for the ould woman to come in an' out to me, for I wasn't able to crawl the length of my shoe I was so sick: an' all I asked them was to carry me out, an' lave me by Biddy's side, an' let me live or die there as id 'ud plase God; bud that they wouldn't do, for they tould me the sogers war lookin' for me two or three times afther; an' I believed them, more especially as one night that I was half asleep an' awake, I thought I hard great rustling an' throuble about the place, an' guessed it was them. In a couple ov days news come that I was freed from the warrant. Mr.—the captain, I mane, took so much throuble to prove my innocence, that he wasn't long afore he showed them all the bottom of the schame, an' got Farrell thransported; an' thin I made my way out into the house to see my darlint, bud every thing seemed black night about me. I called her name, but there was no answer, an' my heart began to misgive me. I made over to the bed, for I knew the way, an' laid my hand softly on id, thinkin' she might be asleep. 'Twas empty, asthore—an' I flung myself on id, as if I was struck at once, an' began to cry as if the life was lavin' me. They all found me out, an' as soon as they saw I knew all, the grief that they kept down before, for fear I'd discover, bruck out, an' we all cried ourselves sick; an' if she wasn't keened at the funeral, she couldn't say bud we made up for id thin. Whin they carrid me half dead from the bed, they found I was blind; but 'twas little throuble to me whin I hadn't her to look at—more a relief than anything else, since I couldn't miss her sweet face—so what use would eyes be to a poor stripped crathur like me. The ould man died soon afther, between grief an' ould age; an', sure enough, whin I laid my hand on his cowld face, I cried salt tears that I wasn't in his place, huggin' the darlint that I knew was in his arms now in another world. It wasn't long ontil the captain's throuble kem, an' I bethought ov the cave, an' made it up for him; an' the place being lonely, an' one thing an' another that was said about it, he never was throubled in it by soger or any body else from that day to this. But, whisht —isn't that a voice? Down, down here—there's a scrub somewhere hereabouts—do you see it—now stoop, an' whoever it is, we're safe."

Crouching in the scrub, which I found no difficulty in reaching, we awaited in security the approach of the coming intruder, whom we first discovered by the snatches of singing borne to our ears by the slight night breeze. The voice was now near us, and I could discover the burthen of the song. Truly nothing could be more incongruous than the vociferous manner of the singer, and the words which he gave utterance to; and as he sung out, half drunken,

> "Past five o'clock on a fine frosty morning,
> I am asleep, an' don't waken me,"

I couldn't help laughing aloud, notwithstanding the imminent danger in which I lay. The piper seemed to recognise the voice, for, leaving the cover, he stood upright, and bade me do the same.

"It's only one ov the boys," said he, "comin', I suppose, to give you the welcome afore the others. He might hould his tongue, though. Half an hour ago, that noise 'ud put a halter about both yeer necks.'

We had just reached the path again when the deputation, if I may so call him, staggered up to us; and on recognising where he was, let a "Whoo!" out of him, that if there was a yeoman within a mile of us would have placed us in rather an awkward dilemma.

"Music, my darlint, is that you? Your honour, I'm mortial glad to see you. Och, an' it's I that's sorry for the accident that happened me there above—sore sorry, avick. You see, I was bringin' a bottle of the right sort, that niver got the blast of a gauger's eye, to welcome you to the mountains, an' to keep the cowld outside o' you; an' I wint jist to take a weeny taste of it to see if 'twas good, an', somehow or another, it all spilt. Och, sorra a word of lie in it. More betoken, there's the empty bottle."

Acknowledging how unanswerable this argument was in proof of the "accident," I expressed my thanks in appropriate terms for the honour done me, while he begged me to hould his arm, for the way was stony and rough to me who was not used to it. Of course, I accepted the proffered honour, more to get the drunken wretch on in haste, than in the light in which he intended it. The road, which until now had lain through bog and uninhabited wastes, began to assume a different aspect. We had now to wind, by a scarcely observable path, through rocks that opposed our passage at almost every step. More than once we were compelled to climb these obstacles by the aid of the scanty shrubs which chance had planted here and there through their crevices; and at length the path entered, by a sudden turn, into a dark ravine, overhung by sloe and arbutus that almost hid from our view the face of heaven. Just at this moment, a soldierly "Who goes there?" uttered from the depths of the ravine, caused me to start, as if I had been shot, and made my heart leap to my throat with agony and terror, as I conceived myself waylaid, and ruined at the very threshhold of safety. I was, however, quickly re-assured by my companions, who bade me never fear, that it was only "sodger Jim" (an old deserter, the drill-master of the corps) who was posted at the entrance of the forbidden locality in the light of a guard, and was a little addicted to old habits of discipline, and other little points that made him the butt of his less regular comrades. No answer having been returned to his challenge, he again repeated, in a more commanding tone, "Who goes there?"

"Friends, an' confound you, you ould lobster—what the mischief ud bring any one else to such a place as this?" growled he of the empty bottle.

"Stand, friend, and give the word," said the vigilant sentinel.

"Och, bad cess to you," muttered my companion, and proceeded to drag me onwards, while every limb in my body trembled lest a ball from the rigid martinet should arrest my further progress. I ventured to remonstrate with both parties, and at last induced the drunken vagabond to say something.

"Confound you, Jim," said he, "but you're the greatest botheration a quiet man ever met wid—an' it's to your face I say it."

"Stand, friends, an' give the word, or it'll be worse for you!" was the answer returned by the ci-devant red-coat; and then in his undress tone he proceeded—"Pat Mullen, can't you be regular, an' give the word—you'd be enough to raise a mutiny in a whole battalion. You won't? Well, then, here goes; an' you may pray for marcy."

"Whiskey, then! Whiskey! Whiskey! Whiskey! Monim an dhoul, have you enough of it yit?" shouted my enraged escort, "have you enough of it yit?" and at the same time seconded the question by a shower of stones, hurled in the direction of the speaker.

Good reader, will you be kind enough to imagine my situation, for positively I am utterly unable to describe it. I believe, however, I had the grace to utter a prayer, and had altogether given myself up as a lost man; when the same "on duty" voice, restored my hopes of life by uttering, as of old, "Pass, Whiskey!" and then in the undress tone, "Pat Mullen, my boy, I'll report you—nothing but three hours a day at the triangles will ever civilize you."

Giving some contemptuous answer to this threat, the denounced acolyte advanced, and hurling the sentinel out of his way, left him sprawling on his back. I flew to lift him, and got a cuff from the angry wretch that sent me staggering to the other side. When I recovered its effects they were struggling as if in mortal quarrel. Terrified at the probable consequences of the row, particularly as one party was armed, I rushed forward to seize the gun; but before I could achieve that purpose it had exploded, without hurting any of us, it is true, but attended with consequences little less fatal, to me at least. Both seemed pretty well sobered at the occurrence, and were indulging in loud recrimination as to whose was the fault, when five or six men, armed and aroused from their concealment by the noise, came hurriedly from the opposite direction to inquire the cause of the disturbance; and scarcely had this addition to our numbers been made, when the trampling of horses was distinctly heard advancing to us, and voices loudly hallooing told us but too clearly that we had been discovered by some patrolling party. A hurried council was held, and it was at once determined that we should show ourselves, and, if possible, lead our opponents from the scent so dangerous to the common safety, by appearing at some other point, from which we could, it necessary, retreat by a circuitous path to the house which we had so nearly discovered to them. The proposal was at once put in operation; and we were soon ensconced in some rocks a quarter of a mile distant from our former station, while the horsemen seemed rapidly approaching the spot from which the shot had issued. Before they could reach it, however, another shot allured them away to our present ground, and the echo of it scarce ceased to ring among the rocks, when they stood before us to the number of half a dozen, well-mounted, and far better armed than we were. A volley from the rocks, instead of checking their career, only seemed to give them additional incitement, and spurring onward, springing over every obstacle, they soon set us flying into a less accessible part within a few yards of us.

"After them—after them," shouted a loud voice among the horsemen, "don't you see M—— among them, in the shooting jacket. Now, boys, for the reward—a hundred pounds remember."

I was recognised, and, horrible to relate, I was the very rearmost man. Paralysed by terror, and nerveless with excess of energy, I was unable to keep up with my companions, and shouting for succour, fell almost senseless at the foot of the rock they were ascending. My call was answered, and the assailants kept at bay by a well-directed discharge; but there was too much to be won, and the prey was too near them. One bolder—perhaps poorer—

than the rest, spurred forward, in spite of all the missiles with which he was assailed, and grasping me by the collar, as I attempted to regain my feet, swung me with the force of a giant on the saddle before him. It was now neck or nothing with all parties; but though I could hear my friends spring forward to my rescue, all hope, in fact all energy, had left me. All was not lost, however, and before my captor could wheel round his horse, or his comrades come to his assistance, I was once more nearly dragged off the beast by the crowd now surrounding him. At the moment his life was more endangered than mine, nor did he appear ignorant of the circumstance; so prudently abandoning his prize, he burst back to his party, not, however, without venting his spite by inflicting on my shoulder a fearful gash of his sabre before I was quite out of his reach. A volley from the outlaws followed him, and was answered by another from the retreating horsemen, which passing harmlessly by the rest, lodged a brace of bullets in my side, as if fate herself was about to wreak her anger on me. I recollect nothing further, until animation began slowly to return in what appeared a closer atmosphere.

—" Any how, he's alive an' recoverin'," said a voice over me, which seemed to proceed from one tolerably far advanced in the stage of mortal existence.

" I sincerely pity him !" ejaculated another, in tones so soft and kind, as at once to dispel the fear, which seized me at the first moment of consciousness, that I was to open my eyes in a murderer's dungeon. Half my misery vanished at the bare idea that I was still free, and as looking around me, I caught merely a glimpse of the departing form of her whose words of pity had such a powerful effect on me. I saw enough, however, to know that I had never seen a lovelier face, or a lighter or more beautiful figure. I gazed for a moment on the place where she had vanished, and then turned my dim eye on her direct and perfect contrast, an old crone, who with bandage and fomentation in hand at once declared her office.

" 'Twas a bloody welcome, asthore, you got among us ; bud wid the Vargin's help it won't signify, if you lie quiet an' do what you're bid," said she, handing me a drink of some medicine.

" Am I safe ?" was my only reply, and uttered with the utmost difficulty and pain.

" Throth, you'll see that if you only look about you ; bud you musn't talk. You're here wid ourselves, avick ; an' that's the captain's daughter that was here jist now, an' that made the dhrink for you."

Exerting myself more than my weakened state could bear, I drank the potion, and sunk senseless on the bed on which I was laid.

In this distressing situation I must take my leave for the present, having some few matters to arrange before the short summer nights come on to disturb my operations, so that I hope my kind reader will have the goodness to excuse me, particularly as, when that idle season commences, it is my intention to present a few more sketches of as wild a life as ever was the portion of a luckless wight on this side the grave.

M'C.

RULES RECOMMENDED TO SERVANTS.

1. A good character is valuable to every one, but especially to servants, for it is their bread ; and without it they cannot be admitted into any creditable family ; and happy it is, that the best of characters is in every one's power to deserve.

2. Engage yourself cautiously, but stay long in your places ; for long service shows worth, as quitting a good place through passion is a folly, which is always repented of too late.

3. Never undertake any place you are not qualified for ; for pretending to do what you do not understand exposes yourself, and what is still worse, deceives them whom you serve.

4. Preserve your fidelity ; for a faithful servant is a jewel, for whom no encouragement can be too great.

5. Adhere to truth, for falsehood is detestable ; and he that tells one lie must tell more to conceal it.

6. Be strictly honest, for it is shameful to be thought unworthy of trust.

7. Be modest in your behaviour ; it becomes your situation, and is pleasing to your superiors.

8. Avoid pert answers ; for civil language is cheap, and impertinence provoking.

9. Be clean and neat in your person and business ; for nothing pleases more than cleanly habits ; besides, sluts and slovens are disrespectful servants, and never observe any order in their different employments ; without a proper method, every thing is in confusion ; with it, both time and labour are saved, and much credit gained.

10. Never tell the affairs of the family you belong to, for that is treachery, and often makes mischief ; but keep their secrets as carefully as you would your own.

11. Live friendly with your fellow-servants, for the contrary destroys the peace of the house ; yet if you discover dishonest practices, it is your duty, at once, to reveal them to your employer.

12. Above all things avoid drunkenness ; it is a sure inlet to vice, the ruin of your character, and the destruction of your constitution.

13. Prefer a peaceable life with moderate gains, to great advantages with irregularity.

14. Save your money, for that will be a friend to you in old age ; be not expensive in dress, nor marry too soon.

15. Be careful of your mistress's property ; for wastefulness is a sin.

16. Never swear, for that is a sin without a shadow of excuse, as there is no pleasure in it.

17. Be always ready to assist a fellow-servant ; for good-nature gains the love of every one.

18. Never stay when sent out on a message ; for waiting long is painful to a mistress, and quick return shows diligence ; besides, remember that your mistress pays you for your time, and if you rob her of it, you are as much guilty of fraud and dishonesty, as the tradesman who gives false weight or false measure.

19. Rise early ; for it is difficult to recover lost time, and this habit will give you much leisure during the day.

20. The servant that often changes place, works only to be poor ; for " the rolling stone gathers no moss."

21. Be not fond of increasing your acquaintance ; for visiting leads you out from your business, and puts you to an expense you cannot afford ; and, above all things, take care with whom you are acquainted, for persons are generally the better or the worse of the company they keep.

22. When out of place, be cautious where you lodge ; for living in a disreputable house puts you upon a footing with those that keep it, however innocent you are yourself.

23. Never go out on your own business without the knowledge of the family, lest in your absence you should be wanted ; for leave is light, and returning punctually at the time of your promise shows obedience, and is a proof of sobriety.

24. If you are dissatisfied in your place, mention your objections modestly to your master or mistress, and give a fair warning, and do not neglect your business or behave ill, in order to provoke them to turn you away, for this will be a blemish in your character, which you must always have from the place you served.

MATRIMONIAL DISPARITIES.

The following observations are made by a well known author on the disparities so frequently apparent in matrimonial connections :

Unions are often formed betwixt couples differing in complexion and stature, they take place still more frequently betwixt persons totally differing in feelings, in tastes, in pursuits, and in understanding ; and it would not be saying, perhaps, too much, to aver, that two-thirds of the marriages around us have been contracted betwixt persons, who, judging a priori, we should have thought had scarce any charms for each other. A moral and primary cause might be easily assigned for these anomalies, in the wise dispensations of Providence, that the general balance of wit, wisdom, and amiable qualities of all kinds, should be kept up through society at large ; for, what world would it be if the wise were to intermarry only with the wise, the learned with the learned, the amiable with the amiable, nay, even the handsome with the handsome; and is it not evident, that the degraded castes of the foolish, the ignorant, the brutal, and the deformed—including, by the way, far the greater part of mankind—must, when condemned to exclusive intercourse with each other, become gradually as much brutalized in person and disposition as so many ouran outangs? When, therefore, we see "the gentle joined to the rude," we may lament the fate of the suffering individual; but we must not the less admire the mysterious disposition of the wise Providence, who thus balances the moral good and evil of life, which secure for a family, unhappy in the dispositions of one parent, a share of better and sweeter blood transmitted from the other, and preserve to the offspring the affectionate care and protection of at least one of those from whom it is naturally due. Without the frequent occurrence of such alliances and unions, mis-sorted as they seem at first sight, the world could not be that for which eternal wisdom has designed it—a place of mixed good and evil; a place of trial at once and of suffering, where the worst ills are chequered with something that renders them tolerable to humble and patient minds, and where the best blessings carry with them a necessary alloy of embittering depreciation. When, indeed, we look a little closer on the causes of those unexpected and ill-suited attachments, we have occasion to acknowledge that the means by which they are produced do not infer that complete departure from, or inconsistency with, the character of the parties, which we might expect when the result alone is contemplated. The wise purposes which Providence appears to have had in view, by permitting such intermixture of dispositions, tempers, and understandings, in the married state, are not accomplished by any mysterious impulse by which, in contradiction to the ordinary laws of nature, men or women are urged to an union with those whom the world see to be unsuitable to them. The freedom of will is permitted to us in the occurrences of ordinary life, as in our moral conduct; and in the former as well as the latter case, is often the means of misguiding those who possess it. Thus it usually happens, more especially to the enthusiastic and imaginative, that having formed a picture of admiration in their own mind, they too often deceive themselves by some faint resemblance in some existing being, whom their fancy, as speedy as gratuitously, invests with all the attributes necessary to complete the *beau ideal* of mental perfection. No one, perhaps, even in the happiest marriage, with an object really beloved, ever found all the qualities he expected to possess; but, in far too many cases, he finds he has practised a much higher degree of mental deception, and has raised his airy castle of felicity upon some rainbow, which owed its very existence only to the peculiar state of the atmosphere of his mind.

THE TEAR.

Meek visitant that gives relief
When the sad heart's o'ercharged with grief—
Oh! gen'rous tear, ambrosial flow
When offered for another's wo—
Thy limpid current can the soul
'Mid passion's fiercest whelm control.
How dark the stream of sorrow's course
When Nature locks thy briny source!
Reliever of the fev'rish brain—
Mild antidote of hidden pain—
Thy humid pow'r, assuaging, bland,
None but the sternest can withstand;
Thy light to beauty gives new grace;
By it, we feeling's goal may trace.
Smiles may deceive—but, oh! a tear—
Gush of the soul—must be sincere.
Joy unexpected, powerful, e'er
Makes thee its herald, crystal tear!
But seldom in this world of wo
Thy gleam is seen to gladden so!
Precious, though transient gem, say why,
When mem'ry wafts the poignant sigh,

Art thou its handmaid? Is't to veil
Time's murky course—or yet conceal
The wreck of hope, long nurtur'd, dear—
You start to life thus, little tear?
Whate'er thy mission, sudden guest!
That sends emotion through the breast—
When thought awakes or smile or sigh—
I'd have thee glisten in mine eye.
For, oh! thou art the heart's o'erflow,
Whether it feasts on joy or wo;
While over mem'ry's bier you spread
A halo, though the soul be fled.

Kilkenny.   C. M. C.

TO A BUTTERFLY SEEN IN MID-WINTER.

Written in a Lady's Album, March, 1834.

Child of the summer! what dost thou here,
In the sorrow and gloom of the weeping year
When the roses have withered that bloom'd on thy birth
And the sunbeam that nurst thee has past from the earth
The flowers that fed thee are frozen and gone—
Thy kindred are perished, and thou art alone—
No one to welcome—no one to cheer—
Child of the summer! what dost thou here?

Yet 'tis sweet thy gossamer wing to view,
Revelling wild in the troubled blue—
Heeding nor rain, nor snow, nor storm—
Buffeting all with thy tiny form.
Even thus the hope of our summer days
In the heart's lone winter gaily plays—
Thou art the type of that hope so dear:
Child of the summer! thou'rt welcome here

Welcome, 'mid sorrow, and gloom, and showers,
Emblem of gladness that once was ours—
Emblem of gladness that yet will come,
When the sun-bright ether will be thy home,
And myriads of others, as bright as thou,
Will revel around us—all absent now:
Emblem of hope to the mourner dear,
Child of the summer! thou'rt welcome here.

M'C.

⁎ In closing our Third Volume, we have to express our grateful acknowledgments to our numerous correspondents for their continued support. But we must again claim the indulgence of those kind friends who may have sent us contributions which have not yet appeared. They may rest satisfied, however, that no article is overlooked, and that, generally speaking, when considered suitable for the Journal, it shall appear within three months from the period at which we may receive it. We are unable to reply to correspondents, from the circumstance of being obliged to have at all times four or five numbers in advance, in order to be worked off in time for the English and Scottish markets. Correspondents will therefore, we trust, excuse any apparent want of attention in this respect.

We this week publish a Supplement, price two-pence, which, besides a handsome vignette Title, Table of Contents, and List of Plates, contains Seven very handsome Engravings of Views in Dublin, viz.:

View of the Irish Parliament House, (now Bank of Ireland,) from an original painting taken in 1787.	The Lying-in Hospital and Rotunda.
Upper Castle Yard	East Front of the Bank of Ireland, from College-street.
Carlisle Bridge.	King's Bridge, Military Road. Aqueduct, Phibsborough.

Dublin: Printed and Published by P. D. Hardy, 3, Cecilia-street; to whom all communications are to be addressed. Sold by all Booksellers in Ireland.

£.
ur.

ÿ

E.

Gr
in
in
rxy s
of D
ssiccle
scitdes
by ce
uanable
of ho
then i
te Ei
l ther
saice :

o-graa
of Ca
salsom

thal a

ik of is
same
r kind
aph

——

cteas, I

Lightning Source UK Ltd.
Milton Keynes UK
UKOW02f2156301213

223797UK00010B/809/P